WORDSWORTH CLASSICS
OF WORLD LITERATURE

General Editor: Tom Griffith

CAPITAL

KARL MARX

Capital

A Critical Analysis
of Capitalist Production

*Volume 1 translated by Samuel Moore
and Edward Aveling*
Volume 2 translated by Ernest Untermann

*with an introduction by
Mark G. Spencer*

WORDSWORTH CLASSICS
OF WORLD LITERATURE

For my husband
ANTHONY JOHN RANSON
with love from your wife, the publisher
Eternally grateful for your
unconditional love

Readers who are interested in other titles from
Wordsworth Editions are invited to visit our
website at www.wordsworth-editions.com

This edition published 2013 by Wordsworth Editions Limited
8B East Street, Ware, Hertfordshire SG12 9HJ

ISBN 978 1 84022 699 7

This edition © Wordsworth Editions Limited 2013
Introduction © Mark G. Spencer 2013

Wordsworth® is a registered trademark of
Wordsworth Editions Limited

Wordsworth Editions is
the company founded in 1987 by
MICHAEL TRAYLER

Typeset in Great Britain by Roperford Editorial
Printed and bound by Clays Ltd, Elcograf S.p.A.

Contents

Volume 2. The Circulation of Capital

Notes

Introduction

for T. R. Sansom

Few writers have had a more notable impact on the modern world than has Karl Marx (1818–1883). And much of Marx's impact can be traced to *Das Kapital: Kritik der politischen Oekonomie*, or, as it is best known to its English readers, simply *Capital*. Marx's *Capital* and Darwin's *Origin of the Species* are often mentioned together as the two most influential books of the nineteenth century. Darwin's principal works are still in print and *Capital* can still be published in the twenty-first century in a prominent series celebrating classics of world literature. Both are still relevant, but initially neither was welcomed. When the first volume of *Capital* was finally published in 1867 (in German), the forty-nine-year-old Marx had labored over it for such a long time that he felt compelled to offer an apology in the opening line of his preface: 'The work, the first volume of which I now submit to the public,' wrote Marx, 'forms the continuation of my *Zur Kritik der Politischen Oekonomie* [*A Contribution to the Critique of Political Economy*] published in 1859. The long pause between the first part and the continuation is due to an illness of many years' duration that again and again interrupted my work.' What he did not say is that his ill health was largely rooted in what had become for Marx, and his family, a life in exile full of uncertainty, disappointment, and recurrent poverty. He also does not say, but could have, that *Capital* came out of a much wider historical and intellectual context or that it had a much longer gestation period than Marx there lets on. When he wrote in 1867, Marx did not know that *Capital's* immediate reception would be no more promising than its painstaking birth had been. Nor, of course, could he have known that his book would become one of the most acclaimed publications of the modern world.

Karl Heinrich Marx was himself born on 5 May 1818 in the ancient city of Trèves (or Trier) in the Mosel valley, a dependency of the Kingdom of Prussia (in a region that is a part of present-day Germany). His parents, Heinrich Marx (1777–1838) and Henrietta (*née* Pressburg, 1788–1863), provided him and his siblings (there were nine children in all) with a seemingly amicable middle-class upbringing which was in many respects not notable. One event that stands out from Marx's youth is noted by all of his biographers, some reading more into it than others. That is the conversion of Marx's father, a counselor-at-law to the High Court of Appeal, from Judaism to Protestantism in 1824 in order to help advance his career in the wake of anti-Jewish laws which were in effect. For some historians that event – and the unsettled station the young Marx, as a result of his Jewish background, may have felt – possibly explains some of Marx's later antipathy (called by some, 'self-hatred') towards Judaism in particular and religion ('the opiate of the masses') in general.

Marx's father left other imprints on his son. Heinrich was an avid reader; something that marked Karl from an early age. Along with reading from his father's collection of books, which included many works of the French rationalists of the eighteenth century, Marx also regularly pillaged the library of a close family friend, Ludwig von Westphalen (1770–1842). Westphalen became a senior reading companion of the young Marx. He introduced the boy to works ranging from the epic poems of the ancient Greek writer Homer, to the tragedies and comedies of Shakespeare (1564–1616), and the utopian schemes of Claude Henri de Saint-Simon (1760–1825), to name a few which, many years later, would surface in the pages of *Capital*. This home-schooling, and then attendance at the local High School from 1830 to 1835, prepared Marx to enter university at age seventeen.

In October 1835, Marx enrolled at Bonn University as a student in the Faculty of Law. In his first year there he also entered into club life at the university and dabbled with writing verse, but met with little scholarly success. On more than one occasion, he also managed to get himself into trouble with the school authorities for offences such as 'disturbing the peace of the night with drunken noise'. At the end of his first year, his father decided it was time for a change of location; in October 1836, Marx transferred to the University of Berlin. There, he continued to be interested in poetry and even more interested in writing verses for Jenny von Westphalen (1814–1881), Ludwig Westphalen's beautiful daughter, to whom Marx had become secretly engaged. His formal preparation for the law included quite wide reading in history and philosophy, studies which he would draw upon later in his wide-ranging writings. At Berlin, his studies also began to take on a more serious edge. Like any student then his reading encompassed many of the ancients (Aristotle was a favorite), but also the writers of the Enlightenment, with an emphasis on those from France, German, and Scotland – including Voltaire (1694–1778), Jean-Jacques Rousseau (1712–1778), Paul-Henri Thiry, Baron d'Holbach (1723–1789), Adam Smith (1723–1790), Immanuel Kant (1724–1804),

Johann Gottfried von Herder (1744–1803), Johann Wolfgang von Goethe (1749–1832), and Friedrich Schiller (1759–1805). Marx also read their critics. The most important of those was the recently deceased star of German intellectual life, the philosopher Georg Wilhelm Friedrich Hegel (1770–1831), who had held the Chair of Philosophy at Berlin. Hegel's conception of history as a process that progressed dialectically was to stay with Marx even as he came to question other aspects of Hegel's thought. And perhaps just as important for explaining the development of Marx's thought at this time was the company he kept.

At the University of Berlin, Marx, like many other German students of his generation, was introduced to the possibility of applying Hegel's theory of the dialectic to the real world, not only to understand the past but to achieve revolutionary change in the future. Marx's professors at the university included the conservative Friedrich Karl von Savigny (1779–1861) but, more importantly for the lesson mentioned above, Eduard Gans (1797–1838). Mixing with Gans and others who considered themselves to be the 'Young Hegelians', Marx became intimate with radical thought and its implications. Among his closest acquaintances at this time were Adolph Rutenberg (1808–1869) and the Bauer brothers – Bruno (1809–1882), Edgar (1820–1886), and Egbert – one of whom (Edgar) commented in verse on Marx's activities in the club:

But who advances here full of impetuosity?
It is a dark form from Trier, an unleashed monster,
With self-assured step he hammers the ground with his heels
And raises his arms in full fury to heaven
As though he wished to seize the celestial vault and lower it
to earth.
In rage he continually deals his redoubtable fist,
As if a thousand devils were gripping his hair.

However, Marx's letters home to his father during these years strike a far less self-assured tone and show him to have been searching for philosophical direction at the same time that he was finding himself as a young man. His father, like many fathers since, strongly preferred that his son drop his flighty pursuits of philosophy and history for something more practical that would lead directly to a well-paid government job. He asked pointedly in a letter sent before his death in 1838, 'And do you think that here in this workshop of senseless and aimless learning, you can ripen the fruits to bring you and your loved one happiness?' After his father's death, it did not take Marx long to give up any pretense of studying law. By January of 1839 he had begun work on his doctoral dissertation, 'The Difference between the

Philosophies of Nature in Democritus and Epicurus'. Had his father been alive to see it, he would not have been pleased. In April 1841, Marx submitted (by post) his thesis to the University of Jena and was awarded his degree *in absentia*.

Aspiring at first to a university appointment, Marx settled in the immediate term for work as a journalist. His first article was published in May 1843 in the *Rheinische Zeitung*, a newspaper published in Cologne and headed by Moses Hess (1812–1875), the so-called 'Communist Rabbi' who was the author of *The Sacred History of Mankind* (1817). From October 1842, Marx edited that paper. Only a few years older than Marx, Hess had quickly become infatuated with Marx's philosophical prowess. Hess wrote of the twenty-four-year-old Marx: 'He is the greatest, perhaps the one genuine philosopher now alive . . . Dr Marx . . . combines the deepest philosophical seriousness with the most biting wit. Imagine Rousseau, Voltaire, Holbach, Lessing, Heine and Hegel fused into one person – I say fused, not thrown together in a heap – and you have Dr Marx.' Under Marx's guidance the content of the *Rheinische Zeitung* took a decidedly radical turn and its circulation and reputation increased significantly. This notoriety probably ended any chance Marx had for a university position. Moreover, the Prussian government moved to shut down the newspaper in early 1843. Marx resigned his editorship in March.

Looking back at these years, Marx commented in his 'Preface' to *A Contribution to the Critique of Political Economy* (1859), that it was as editor of the *Rheinische Zeitung* that he 'experienced for the first time the embarrassment of having to take part in discussions on so-called material interests [which] . . . provided the first occasion for occupying myself with economic questions.' As Vladimir Ilyich Lenin (1870–1924) put it in his biographical sketch of Marx, 'Marx's journalistic activities convinced him that he was insufficiently acquainted with political economy, and he zealously set out to study it.' Applying his stock of knowledge to the close study of real-world questions of local concern may also have offered Marx the first glimpse of the power of intellectuals to bring about revolutionary change:

The system of profit and commerce, of property and human exploitation, leads much more quickly than an increase of population to a rift inside contemporary society that the old society is incapable of healing, because it never heals or creates, but only exists and enjoys. The existence of a suffering humanity which thinks and a thinking humanity which is oppressed must of necessity be disagreeable and unacceptable for the animal world of philistines who neither act nor think but merely enjoy.

For Marx, it was the self-assigned task of the intellectual to assure that 'the old world . . . [is] brought right out into the light of day and the new one given a positive form. The longer that events allow thinking humanity time to recollect itself and suffering humanity time to assemble itself the more perfect will be the birth of the product that the present carries in its womb.' Or, as he put it elsewhere:

> The weapon of criticism cannot, of course, replace criticism by weapons, material force must be overthrown by material force; but theory also becomes a material force as soon as it has gripped the masses. Theory is capable of gripping the masses as soon as it demonstrates *ad hominem*, and it demonstrates *ad hominem* as soon as it becomes radical.

The world of radical newspaper writers was always to be the place where Marx felt most at home.

The year 1843 was an important one for Marx. In the early spring of 1843, having resigned from the *Rheinische Zeitung*, Marx sought gainful employment in other ways. That became even more pressing when, in April, Marx and Jenny Westphalen were finally married after an exceedingly long engagement. Jenny would be his life-long companion; 'infinitely mercurial' in good times, and in bad. Together they would have six children, although only three would survive to adulthood. 1843 was also the year that Ludwig Feuerbach (1804–1872) published his *Preliminary Theses on the Reformation of Philosophy*, a book that Marx devoured with lasting effect. Isaiah Berlin (1909–1997), the historian of ideas, described Feuerbach's impact on Marx in this way: 'Feuerbach is one of those interesting authors, not infrequently met with in the history of thought, who, without being thinkers of the first order, nevertheless provide men of greater gifts with the sudden spark which sets on fire long-accumulated fuel.' But Feuerbach was not the only one whom Marx read in 1843. That year he began a period of intense study of political philosophy, reading Machiavelli's *The Prince* (1532), Montesquieu's *Spirit of the Laws* (1748), Rousseau's *Social Contract* (1762), and Adam Smith's *An Inquiry into the Nature and Causes of the Wealth of Nations* (1776). They were all read or re-read as Marx worked out a *Critique of Hegel's 'Philosophy of Right'* and took manuscript notes that would later inform parts of *Capital*. Finally, 1843 was also the year that Marx decided to leave Prussia for Paris, a city that was then the gathering point for Europe's radical intellectuals. In October 1843, as this eventful year drew to a close, Marx and his pregnant bride made their way to France where Marx helped Arnold Ruge (1802–1880), another political exile who had been one of the 'Young Hegelians', to edit the short-lived *Deutsche-französische Jahrbücher* [German-French Annals]. Working closely together, Marx and Ruge came to see they differed considerably in their understanding of socialist theories. With another contributor to the *Deutsche-französische Jahrbücher* Marx shared much more. This man would become Marx's most intimate of friends and most important of collaborators – Friedrich Engels (1820–1895).

Marx and Engels had met briefly in Prussia, in November of 1842, in the office of the *Rheinische Zeitung*. Looking back at their reunion in August 1844 in Paris at the Café de la Régence, Engels recorded that 'When I visited Marx in Paris in the summer of 1844, we found ourselves in complete agreement on questions of theory and our collaboration began at that time.' At the time, Engels was working on a project which aimed to describe and criticize the lives of the industrial poor in Manchester, England, and to suggest ways they might be improved. The expanding industrial world of nineteenth-century Europe was one that Engels knew well. He was an industrial insider since his wealthy family had business interests not only in Manchester but also in the Rhineland at Barmen (near Dusseldorf), a town that became known as the 'Little Manchester'. Engels's project, *The Condition of the Working Classes in England*, was first published in Leipzig in 1845.

The intellectual team of Marx and Engels has been considered by some to represent a merging of the theoretical mind of Marx with the empirical and practical mind of Engels. But that way of seeing things may not give sufficient weight to the empirical side of Marx which appears to have been with him from the beginning. When commenting on their collaboration, Engels always cast himself as the lesser of the two, later writing that

> Marx could very well have done without me. What Marx accomplished I would not have achieved. Marx stood higher, saw farther, and took a wider and quicker view than all the rest of us. Marx was genius; we others were at best talented. Without him the theory would not, by a long way, be what it is today. It therefore rightly bears his name.

In January 1845, as political tensions mounted throughout Europe and particularly in Paris, Marx was expelled from France. He made his way to Belgium which, like England was highly industrialized, and he and Jenny settled in Brussels. In 1846, Marx and Engels traveled to London together where they studied, talked, and wrote *The German Ideology*. That volume was not published until 1932, but it circulated as a manuscript in the nineteenth century and is a work that clearly articulated Marx's historical materialism:

In direct contrast to German philosophy which descends from heaven to earth, here we ascend from earth to heaven. That is to say, we do not set out from what men say, imagine, conceive, nor from men as narrated, thought of, imagined, conceived, in order to arrive at men in the flesh. We set out from real, active men, and on the basis of their real life-process we demonstrate the development of the ideological reflexes and echoes of this life-process.

In *The German Ideology*, 'communism' was 'an ideal to which reality will have to adjust itself . . . the real movement which abolishes the present state of things'. Marx had gradually drifted away from seeing philosophy – as the 'Young Hegelians' of his university years had, and continued to – as an intellectual endeavour. As Marx put it, 'The philosophers have only *interpreted* the world, in various ways; the point is to *change* it.'

Part of what needed to be righted, Marx and Engels argued, was the modern tendency towards a strict division of labor:

In communist society, where nobody has one exclusive sphere of activity but each can become accomplished in any branch he wishes, society regulates the general production and thus makes it possible for me to do one thing today and another tomorrow, to hunt in the morning, fish in the afternoon, rear cattle in the evening, criticize after dinner, just as I have a mind, without ever becoming hunter, fisherman, cowboy or critic.

At the same time, Marx was coming to see more clearly how the division of labor not only alienated the worker from his work, but also the worker from himself. Adam Ferguson's *An Essay on the History of Civil Society* (1767) and Adam Smith's *Wealth of Nations* (1776) were probably both in the background here. Smith was certainly not blind to the potentially negative moral consequences of market forces or the possibly devastating implications of the division of labor for individual labourers. As Smith had put it in the *Wealth of Nations*:

In the progress of the division of labour, the employment of the far greater part of those who live by labour, that is, of the great body of the people, comes to be confined to a few very simple operations; frequently to one or two. But the understandings of the greater part of men are necessarily formed by their ordinary employments. The man whose whole life is spent in performing a few simple operations, of which the effects too are, perhaps, always the same, or very nearly the same, has no occasion to exert his understanding, or to exercise his invention in finding out expedients for removing difficulties which never occur. He naturally loses, therefore the habit of such exertion, and generally becomes as stupid and ignorant as it is possible for a human creature to become.

Marx would come back to these themes in *Capital*, but that was still twenty years away.

In 1847, Marx published his *La Misère de la Philosophie*, an attack on Pierre-Joseph Proudhon (1809–1865), whose work Marx had once praised but now saw sorely lacking in historical content. What he kept was the idea that property was theft – of labour, time and life. Marx also set to work on his *Theses on Feuerbach*. He paid his bills and fed his family with donations from Engels. That would be a recurrent fact in their lives. It was also at this time that Marx's materialist conception of history came into sharper focus. For Marx, 'politics and its history have to be explained from the economic conditions and their evolution and not vice versa.' Again, Adam Smith and other Scots, such as David Hume (1711–1776), had been there first with their idea that consciousness was formed by work and that laws reflected economic conditions, as John Millar (1735–1801) had also argued.

Marx and Engels were becoming increasingly involved in revolutionary circles, even taking on organizational roles. That was the case in early 1847 when they were involved with the formation of a clandestine international political party that became known as the Communist League. In late 1847 and early 1848, encouraged by a group of German émigrés residing in London, Marx and Engels worked together to write for this party *The Communist Manifesto*, the most widely-read of all of Marx's literary productions. 'The history of all hitherto existing society,' Marx and Engels wrote, 'is the history of class struggle.' 'A spectre is haunting Europe – the spectre of communism.' By the middle of 1848, with revolution sweeping across Europe, Marx and his growing family moved to Cologne. Joined by Engels, the two men brought back to life a revamped *Rheinische Zeitung* as the *Neue Rheinische Zeitung*, the so-called 'Organ of Democracy'. The future must have looked potentially bright for Marx. But things were soon to change. Within a year, revolutionary regimes were failing around him and his newspaper was forced to close. Once again Marx was forced into exile; this time it involved travel by ship to England.

When he sailed to London in August 1849, Marx could not have known how bleak the next decade would be for him and his family. He would later refer to these years as his 'sleepless night of exile'. The 1850s began with some promise of success, personal and professional. Marx brought to the press *The Class Struggles in France* (1850) and *The Eighteenth Brumaire of Louis Bonaparte* (1851), a work in which Marx used Louis Bonaparte's dictatorship as Emperor Napoleon III to comment on the relationship between social classes, politics, and history. Even the failed 1848 revolutions Marx thought might be explained away as only a temporary setback which would, with time and changing social and political circumstances, give way to the inevitable march of history toward a revolution by the proletariat. The future, so to speak, looked bright and its realization was inevitable.

Historians are not agreed on the extent to which Marx and his family lived in poverty in the 1850s. However that is measured, life was not comfortable. Working as a free-lance journalist, as he was, provided some income, particularly when Marx was writing for the *New York Daily Tribune*. But there was not much security in that. Life in the Marx household in a cramped three-room Soho apartment on Dean Street was certainly very different from the bourgeois comforts of Marx's youth. Jenny, who had long fretted about financial security, had written soon after their marriage:

> Dear heart, I have too great an anxiety about our future, both in the long and the short term, and I think that I shall be punished for my present high spirits and exuberance. If you can, please calm my fears on this point. People talk far too much about a *steady* income. I then answer simply with my red cheeks, my white flesh, my velvet cloak, my feathered hat and my fine ribbons.

In the early 1850s, velvet cloaks and fine ribbons must indeed have seemed to Jenny only an extravagant memory of a distant past. Son Henry, born in 1849, had died in November 1850. A visitor to the household remarked: 'Marx lives in one of the worst, therefore one of the cheapest quarters in London . . . In the whole apartment there is not one clean and solid piece of furniture. Everything is broken, tattered and torn, with a half inch of dust over everything and the greatest disorder everywhere.' As David McLellan, one of Marx's twentieth-century biographers, put it, during the 1850s the 'pawn-shop was an indispensable institution for the Marx household'. In September 1852, Marx himself lamented:

> My wife is ill, little Jenny is ill, Lenchen has a sort of nervous fever, I cannot and could not call the doctor because I have no money for medicine. For 8–10 days I have fed the family on bread and potatoes of which it is still questionable whether I can rustle

up any today . . . I have tried everything, but in vain . . . How can
I get clear of all this hellish muck?

Born in early 1851, daughter Jenny (Franziska) had died by the
spring of 1853. On 6 April 1856 tragedy struck yet again; Edgar, their
only son, died, age 8. Four months later the loss was still palpable.
Marx wrote to a friend, 'The death of my child has deeply shaken
my heart and mind and I still feel the loss as freshly as on the first day.
My poor wife is also complete broken down.' Still, work on *Capital*
carried on, largely in the Reading Room of the British Library
(possibly a hiding place from debt collectors), sometimes standing
because of painful carbuncles, and always with a cigar close to hand.
Marx once lamented to a friend that '*Capital* will not even pay for the
cigars I smoked writing it.' During the same years that Marx was
working on what would be his masterpiece – in what we have seen to
have been far from ideal circumstances – he contributed some 500
separate pieces to the *New York Daily Tribune*. As always, Marx could
cast off pieces on daily affairs while working up timeless classics.

These were some of the various biographical, intellectual, and
political contexts in which *Capital* was envisioned, sketched, and
partly composed. In many ways *Capital* can be seen as an extension
of Marx's earlier collaborations with Engels and as a summary and
expansion of Marx's prior publications stretching all the way back to
the earliest of them. Indeed, many of those earlier publications are
referred to in *Capital* and even quoted or repeated verbatim. What
we now consider *Das Kapital* is a book of three Volumes: Volume 1,
The Process of Production of Capital; Volume 2, The Process of
Circulation of Capital; and Volume 3, The Process of Capitalist
Production as a Whole. Volume 1, first published on 14 September
1867, was the only volume that Marx saw through the press as it was
the only part of *Capital* published during his lifetime. Marx left
manuscript notes for Volume 2, but the volume was prepared by
Engels and not published until 1885. Volume 3, also prepared by
Engels, was not published until 1894.

Capital, taken as a whole, is a far-ranging book that is not easy to
summarize. Jon Elster's twentieth-century appraisal of Marx's writing
in general applies nicely to *Capital*: 'Even in his most carefully written
works, Marx's intellectual energy was not matched by a comparable
level of intellectual discipline. His intellectual profile is a complex
blend of relentless search for truth, wishful thinking, and polemical
intent.' At its core, *Capital* is concerned with the capitalist mode of
production, exchange, and distribution. Looking at the project as a
whole, Marx's aim was to pursue those themes, wherever they led,

through the various realms of political economy, European history, and sociology. Marx was critical of capitalism because as a system of political economy it was inefficient; historically it was, and promised to continue to be, exploitative; and perhaps most importantly of all, it alienated the workers without whom it would fail. For Marx, 'alienation' has a technical meaning. James Russell provides a useful definition in his *Marx-Engels Dictionary*:

> The separation of one or more humanly defining conditions for human beings. Marx specified two humanly defining conditions of human nature: humans are *social* beings, and they develop their societies and themselves through *creative* labour . . . The capitalist class owns and controls the means of production. Hence workers are separated (alienated) from control over how their work is planned, how the product is to be used, their interrelationships with other workers, and lastly themselves, since the capitalist directs them instead of allowing them to be creatively self-directed.

Volume 1 of *Capital* was intended 'to discover the economic law of motion of modern society'. The table of contents for that volume provides something of a roadmap to Marx's discussion of 'The Process of Production of Capital'. There are 8 parts in all: Part 1, 'Commodities and Money'; Part 2, 'The Transformation of Money into Capital'; Part 3, 'The Production of Absolute Surplus-Value'; Part 4, 'The Production of Relative Surplus-Value'; Part 5, 'The Production of Absolute and of Relative Surplus-Value'; Part 6, 'Wages'; Part 7, 'The Accumulation of Capital'; and Part 8, 'The So-Called Primitive Accumulation'. Even with this roadmap, readers have not always found the book easy to follow.

On reading it in the nineteenth century, William Morris (1834–1896) recorded in a memorable passage that he 'suffered agonies of confusion of the brain'. Jon Elster points out that while Marx wrote in part to motivate factory workers of the world, he frustratingly 'assumes that *his* readers know Greek, Latin, and the major European languages; that they are capable of recognizing remote allusions to literary and philosophical works, besides being thoroughly familiar with arcane matters of political economy.' Isaiah Berlin remarks quite simply with reference to Volume 1 of *Capital*, 'Marx is not the clearest of writers.' When modern students grapple with *Capital* they should take solace in the fact that they are not alone.

Few books have seen as many 'Reading Guides' published to help the lost, but persistent, navigate their way. For some, such as French philosopher Louis Althusser (1918–1990) for instance, part of the difficulty is that *Capital* is too much a work of theory. In Althusser's case, Part 1 is so theoretical that he recommends readers at first skip it entirely, and only come back to it when they are armed with a firm knowledge of the rest of the book. Marx himself wrote in the 'Preface' to the first edition that 'Beginnings are always difficult in all sciences. The understanding of the first chapter, especially the section that contains the analysis of commodities, will therefore present the greatest difficulty.' But are there other ways to approach the text that differ from what Althusser recommends?

What unites *Capital* is Marx's overarching sensitivity to the consequences of the science of political economy for the lives of real human beings. Despite the book's theoretical span and historical range, the frame of reference is always a human one. For instance, consider the very first page where Marx introduces 'commodities'. The book begins: 'The wealth of those societies in which the capitalist mode of production prevails, presents itself as an "immense accumulation of commodities"; its unit being a single commodity.' Theoretical, perhaps; but the opening paragraphs also explain that while a commodity is an 'object outside us' it is something that 'satisfies human wants of some sort or another'. Those wants might arise 'from the stomach or from fancy'; from which 'makes no difference'.

It is worth noting that this is an aspect of *Capital* that unites it with Marx's earlier writings. As Erich Fromm has argued in his volume on *Marx's Concept of Man*, 'Marx is primarily concerned with the emancipation of man as an individual.' When interviewed by his daughters in the Victorian parlour game known as 'Confessions', Mark answered the question, 'What is your Favourite Maxim?' with the simple answer: '*Nihil humani a me alienum puto.*' ['I regard nothing human as alien to me.'] This aspect of *Capital* is also something that unites it with the political economy of the Scottish Enlightenment from which Marx drew heavily. Many years ago the historian of economics Ronald L. Meek argued for the impact of what he referred to as the 'Scottish Historical School' on Marx. Meek had in mind Adam Smith, Adam Ferguson and James Millar, all mentioned above, but also William Robertson (1721–1793), Lord Kames (1696–1782), Gilbert Stuart (1742–1786), Lord Monboddo (1714–1799), Hugh Blair (1718–1800) and James Dunbar (1742–1798). For these Scots in the eighteenth century, as for Marx in the nineteenth, there are systems to be built when we attempt to understand economic and political man, but all of them focus on individuals in society. Meek claimed that 'Smith, like Marx, was a whole man, who tried to combine a theory of history, a theory of ethics, and a theory of political economy into one great general theoretical system.' When *Capital* is approached in this way – with a focus on the human dimension – some of its passage become easier. Illustrative of this possibility, recently Volume 1 has even been recast as a best-selling Japanese comic book! In *Capital in Manga!* we find the 'story of a cheese-maker turned capitalist and how greed, exploitation and its social consequences destroys lives and remakes workers into commodities.' As the Canadian publishers of the English translation put it on the back cover, 'As the gap between the rich and poor continues to widen, a new generation is once again reflecting on Karl Marx's revolutionary insights . . . It is hoped that this Manga may act as a bridge to Marx's original work . . . Marx not only stood against the global economic system but he also helped us understand it.'

It is worth remembering, as well, that for all of the commentary on *Capital* as a scientific work, Marx referred to it more than once as a 'work of art'. As Francis Wheen and others before him – such as S. S. Prawer – have pointed out, to overlook the literary aspects of Volume 1 is to overlook too much. It ought to be 'read as a work of the imagination: a Victorian melodrama, or a vast Gothic novel whose heroes enslaved and consumed the monster they created ("Capital which comes into the world soiled with mire from top to toe and oozing blood from every pore"); or perhaps a satirical utopia like Swift's land of the Houyhnhnms, where every prospect pleases and only man is vile.' Some of the most entertaining passages are found in Marx's caustic footnotes.

The initial muted reception of Volume 1 of *Capital* did not give Marx much cause for celebration, or hope. He wrote to Engels in October, 'The silence about my book makes me fidgety.' If possible, Jenny was even more frustrated than was her husband by the lack of public attention: 'There can be few books that have been written in more difficult circumstances, and I am sure I could write a secret history of it which would tell of many, extremely many unspoken troubles and anxieties and torments. If the workers had an inkling of the sacrifices that were necessary for this work, which was written only for them and for their sakes, to be completed they would perhaps show a little more interest.' Eventually reviews appeared – even some that had not been planted by Engels – but Marx's pamphlet of 1871, *The Civil War in France*, drew more attention than had the first volume of his masterpiece. In the wake of that uproar, Marx published a second edition of Volume 1 of *Capital* in the winter of 1872/3.

Marx continued to work on the manuscripts of Volumes 2 and 3, but progress was slow as the philosopher's rough life began to show in his aging body. Good health was in short supply; he was under doctor's orders to forgo his habit of working in the evenings, and serious scholarly pursuits increasingly gave way to more relaxed pastimes, such as playing with and reading to his growing number of grandchildren. Jenny, too, had not been well and sensed her end was near. She died on 2 December 1881. Marx's health was so poor at the time he was unable to attend her funeral or burial at London's Highgate Cemetery. In January 1883 Jenny Marx Longuet, the Marxs' eldest daughter, died, probably of bladder cancer. Marx's health went from bad to worse although he hung on to life until 14 March 1883, when he died at age 64. On 17 March, without much fanfare or even notice, he was buried alongside Jenny in Highgate Cemetery. His life–long friend, Engels, delivered a short eulogy which concluded: 'His name will endure through the ages, and so also will his work!' Fewer than a dozen were in attendance.

Engels inherited his friend's notes and manuscripts and from those completed Volume 2 of *Capital*, the first German edition of which was published in July 1885. Below, readers will find reprinted the complete text of Volume 2, The Process of Circulation of Capital. Engels explained in his Preface to that volume that, 'It was no easy task to prepare the second volume of *Capital* for the printer in such a way that it should make a connected and complete work and represent exclusively the ideas of its author, not of its publisher.' Volume 2 is divided into three parts: Part One, 'The Metamorphoses of Capital and their Cycles'; Part Two, 'The Turn–Over of Capital'; and Part Three, 'The Reproduction and Circulation of the Aggregate Social Capital'. The second volume is very different from the first. Gone, almost entirely, are the literary allusions and playful footnotes. Marx was a writer of genius, but from the manuscript he left of the second volume of *Capital* it was impossible for Engels to match the first volume. Despite its notable deficiencies, it is useful to include here to provide the reader with a fuller sense of what the project as a whole contained.

In 1887 the first English translation of Volume 1 of *Capital* appeared in London, published by Swan Sonnenschein, Lowrey & Co, on Paternoster Square. Edited by Engels, the translation was prepared by Samuel Moore and Edward Aveling (1849–1898), Eleanor Marx's partner. That is the text reprinted below. Volume 3 of *Capital*, also prepared by Engels, was first published in 1894. As Jon Elster noted, the modern consensus is that the economic theories espoused in Volume 3 are 'seriously flawed' and 'the non-specialist reader will not profit much from struggling with Marx's exposition of them.' Volume 3 is not reprinted below.

As with all authors of literary classics, Marx's reputation changes with the times. The reception of Marx and *Capital* has ebbed and flowed with the subsequent course of history. Little celebrated at the time of his death in 1883, by 1917 Marx was seen as the intellectual hero of the Russian Revolution. Since then, Marx's reputation has risen, and fallen, along with the fates of Marxist regimes around the world and with events like the Great Depression which made many Marxists in both America and Europe. In recent years, scholars such as John Cassidy have changed the focus, finding in Marx what Eric Hobsbawm artfully described as his 'predictions of an increasingly uncontrollable globalization of the capitalist economy.' After all, Marx had written at the mid-point of the nineteenth century lines which would not be out of place in a newspaper column of 2013:

> The need of a constantly expanding market for its products chases the bourgeoisie over the whole surface of the globe . . . The bourgeoisie has through its exploitation of the world-market given a cosmopolitan character to production and consumption in every country.

Explaining the emergence and subsequent impact of Marx's thought, then, is no easy task for historians. It is tempting to see his ideas and writings as being the product of a particular stage in the development of European thought and culture. Clearly *Capital* belongs to the general historical context in which it was written – that of the Utopian Socialists, the revolutionaries of 1848 and those who invented other forms of socialism and even communism. But there is also novelty and individual genius here as well. After all, it is not only Marx's ideas but Marx the individual who has become impressed on the modern mind. Some of that character, which this short essay has attempted to illuminate in a small way, comes through in the iconic image of Marx captured in John Mayall's (1813–1901) penetrating photograph of 1875 (shown on page xxvii).

Many years ago, Isaiah Berlin suggested that we separate the fate of Marxism from our assessment of Marx's thought. 'Even if all its specific conclusions were proved false,' Berlin wrote, 'its importance in creating a wholly new attitude to social and historical questions and so opening new avenues of human knowledge would be unimpaired.' David McLellan reminded us in a book about Marx's legacy, that even if one disagrees with Marx, there is no doubt that he 'has shaped our ideas about society. He built up a system which draws on philosophy, on history, on economics and on politics. And although the professional philosophers, the economists and the political scientists often do not accept his theories, they cannot ignore them.' Marx has 'become part of the mental scaffolding of the [twentieth] century with the result that a lot of our thinking about history and society is a dialogue with Marx's ghost.' In our century the Marxist historian Eric Hobsbawm (1917–2012) put it differently. In *How to Change the World: Marx and Marxism, 1840–2011*, one of his final publications, Hobsbawm confidently declared: 'Economic and political liberalism, singly or in combination, cannot provide the solution to the problems of the twenty-first century. Once again the time has come to take Marx seriously.' Regardless of how much or little truth there is in Hobsbawm's sentiments about liberalism's fate, there is no doubt of the continued relevance of Marx's masterpiece, *Capital*, to twenty-first-century readers of today and even, we can venture with some confidence, engaged readers of tomorrow.

Mark G. Spencer

St. Catharines, Ontario, Canada

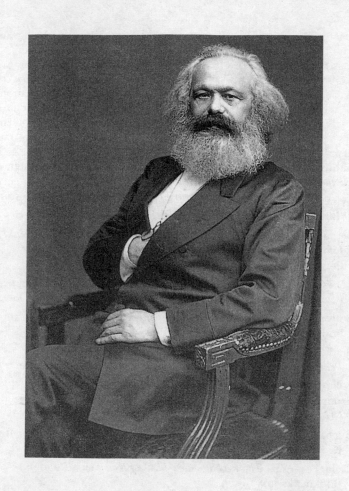

Further Reading

Althusser, Louis, and Étienne Balibar, translated by Ben Brewster. *Reading 'Capital'* (London: NLD, 1970).

Avineri, Shlomo. *The Social and Political Thought of Karl Marx* (London: Cambridge University Press, 1968).

Berlin, Isaiah, with a new forward by Alan Ryan. *Karl Marx, His Life and Environment*, 4th ed. (New York: Oxford University Press, 1996).

Bober, Mandell Morton. *Karl Marx's Interpretation of History*, 2nd ed. (Cambridge, MA: Harvard University Press, 1948).

Bottomore, Tom, et al., eds. *A Dictionary of Marxist Thought* (Cambridge, MA: Harvard University Press, 1983).

Bradley, Ian, and Michael Howard, eds. *Classical and Marxian Political Economy: Essays in Honor of Ronald L. Meek* (New York: St. Martin's Press, 1982).

Brudney, Daniel. *Marx's Attempt to Leave Philosophy* (Cambridge, MA: Harvard University Press, 1998).

Buchanan, Allen E. 'Marx, Morality, and History: An Assessment of Recent Analytical Work on Marx', *Ethics* 98 (1987): 104–36.

Callinicos, Alex. *The Revolutionary Ideas of Karl Marx* (London: Bookmarks, 1983).

Carver, Terrell. *A Marx Dictionary* (Cambridge and Oxford: Polity Press, 1987).

Carver, Terrell. *Marx's Social Theory* (New York: Oxford University Press, 1982).

Carver, Terrell, ed., *The Cambridge Companion to Marx* (Cambridge: Cambridge University Press, 1991).

Cassidy, John. 'The Return of Karl Marx', *New Yorker* 73, no. 32 (20–27 October 1997): 248–259.

Cohen, G.A. *Karl Marx's Theory of History: A Defense* (Princeton, NJ: Princeton University Press, 1978).

Cohen, Marshall, Thomas Nagel, and Thomas Scanlon, eds., *Marx, Justice, and History* (Princeton, NJ: Princeton University Press, 1980).

Cornu, Auguste. *The Origins of Marxian Thought* (Springfield, IL: Charles C. Thomas Publisher, 1957).

Elster, Jon. *Making Sense of Marx* (Cambridge: Cambridge University Press, 1985).

Elster, Jon. *An Introduction to Karl Marx* (New York: Cambridge University Press, 1986).

Gilbert, Alan. *Marx's Politics: Communists and Citizens* (New Brunswick, NJ: Rutgers University Press, 1981).

Fleischer, Helmut. *Marxism and History* translated by Eric Mosbacher (New York: Harper Torchbooks, 1973).

Fromm, Erich. *Marx's Concept of Man* (New York: Frederick Ungar Publishing, Co., 1961).

Harvey, David. *A Companion to Marx's 'Capital'* (London and New York: Verso, 2010).

Hobsbawm, Eric J., ed. *The History of Marxism. Volume One: Marxism in Marx's Day* (Bloomington, IN: Indiana University Press, 1982).

Hobsbawm, Eric J. *How to Change the World: Marx and Marxism, 1840–2011* (London: Little, Brown, 2011).

Hook, Sidney. *Towards the Understanding of Karl Marx: A Revolutionary Interpretation* (New York: John Day Co., 1933).

Hook, Sidney. *From Hegel to Marx: Studies in the Intellectual Development of Karl Marx* (New York: The Humanities Press, 1958).

Kolakowski, Leszek. *Main Currents of Marxism : its origins, growth, and dissolution*, 3 volumes, translated from the Polish by P. S. Falla (Oxford: Clarendon Press, 1978).

Laski, Harold J. *Karl Marx: An Essay* (London: The Fabian Society and Allen & Unwin limited, 1922).

Lenin, Vladimir Ilyich. *Karl Marx: A Brief Biographical Sketch with an Exposition of Marxism* (1918).

Levine, Andrew. *The General Will: Rousseau, Marx, Communism* (New York: Cambridge University Press, 1993).

Lichtheim, George. *The Origins of Socialism* (New York: Praeger, 1969).

Lindsay, A. D. *Karl Marx's Capital: An Introductory Essay* (London: Oxford University Press, 1925).

Little, Daniel. *The Scientific Marx* (Minneapolis, MN: University of Minnesota Press, 1986).

Marcuse, Herbert. *Soviet Marxism: A Critical Analysis* (New York: Columbia University Press, 1961).

Mazlish, Bruce. *The Meaning of Karl Marx* (New York: Oxford University Press, 1984).

McLellan, David. *Karl Marx: His Life and Thought* (New York: Harper & Row, 1973).

McLellan, David. *Karl Marx: The Legacy, from the BBC TV Series written and presented by Asa Briggs* (London: British Broadcasting Corporation, 1983).

McLellan, David, ed. *Marx: The First Hundred Years* (London: Fontana Books, 1983).

McLellan, David. *The Young Hegelians and Karl Marx* (London: MacMillan and Co., 1969).

McMurtry, John. *The Structure of Marx's World-View* (Princeton, NJ: Princeton University Press, 1978).

Meek, Ronald L. 'The Scottish Contribution to Marxist Sociology', in *Economics and Ideology and Other Essays* (London: Chapman and Hall, Ltd, 1967).

Meek, Ronald L. *Studies in the Labour Theory of Value* (London: Lawrence & Wishart, 1956).

Mehring, Franz. *Karl Marx: The Story of His Life*. Eng. trans. by Edward Fitzgerald, new introduction by Max Schachtman (Ann Arbor, MI: University of Michigan Press, 1962).

Miller, Richard W. *Analyzing Marx: Morality, Power and History* (Princeton, NJ: Princeton University Press, 1987).

Prawer, S. S. *Karl Marx and World Literature* (Oxford University Press, 1978).

Rader, Melvin. *Marx's Interpretation of History* (New York: Oxford University Press, 1979).

Rühle, Otto. *Karl Marx, His Life and Work*. Eng. trans. by Eden and Cedar Paul (New York: Garden City Press, 1936).

Russell, James. *Marx-Engels Dictionary* (Westport, CT: Greenwood Press, 1980).

Shipside, Steve. *Karl Marx's 'Das Kapital': A Modern-Day Interpretation of an Economic Classic* (Oxford: Infinite Ideas Limited, 2009).

Singer, Peter. *Marx* (Oxford: Oxford University Press, 1980).

Spencer, Mark G. 'Introduction: Adam Smith and the *Wealth of Nations*', in *Adam Smith: Wealth of Nations* (Ware, Hertfordshire: Wordsworth Editions, 2012).

Sperber, Jonathan. *Karl Marx: A Nineteenth-Century Life* (New York and London: Liverright Publishing Company, 2013).

Tucker, Robert C. *Philosophy and Myth in Karl Marx*, 3rd ed. (New Brunswick, NJ: Transaction Publishers, 2001).

Uchida, Hiroshi, ed. *Marx for the 21st Century* (London and New York: Routledge, 2006).

Walker, Angus. *Marx, His Theory and its Context: Politics as Economics, an introductory and critical essay on the political economy of Karl Marx* (London and New York: Longman, 1978).

Wendling, Amy E. *Karl Marx on Technology and Alienation* (New York: Palgrave Macmillan, 2009).

Wheen, Francis. *Karl Marx: A Life* (New York and London: W. W. Norton & Company, 2000).

Wheen, Francis. *Marx's 'Das Kapital': A Biography* (New York: Atlantic Monthly Press, 2006).

Wolff, Jonathan. *Why Read Marx Today?* (Oxford: Oxford University Press, 2002).

Wood, Allen W. *Karl Marx*, 2nd ed. (New York: Routledge, 2004).

Yasko, Guy. *Capital in Manga! Based on the Classic Text by Karl Marx* (Red Quill Books: Ottawa, 2012).

Zeitlin, Irving M. *Marxism: A Re-examination* (Princeton, NJ: Van Nostrand, 1967).

Typesetter's note

In Volume 1 Marx refers to the projected later parts of the work as Books 2, 3 and 4. However, when it comes to the projected second book, he refers to it as Volume 2, and to Book 1 sometimes as Book 1 and sometimes as Volume 1. I have not corrected this inconsistency.

Within Volume 1 (and to a lesser extent Volume 2) the longest chapters are divided into sections, subsections, sub-subsections and sub-sub-subsections. These are treated in the text as follows.

Section heading	*Section 1. Section Title*
Subsection heading	*A. Subsection Title*
Sub-subsection	*1. Sub-subsection Title*
Sub-sub-subsection	*(a) Sub-sub-subsection Title*

Volume 1
Capitalist Production

Editor's Preface

The publication of an English version of *Das Kapital* needs no apology. On the contrary, an explanation might be expected why this English version has been delayed until now, seeing that for some years past the theories advocated in this book have been constantly referred to, attacked and defended, interpreted and misinterpreted, in the periodical press and the current literature of both England and America.

When, soon after the author's death in 1883, it became evident that an English edition of the work was really required, Mr Samuel Moore, for many years a friend of Marx and of the present writer, and than whom, perhaps, no one is more conversant with the book itself, consented to undertake the translation which the literary executors of Marx were anxious to lay before the public. It was understood that I should compare the MS. with the original work, and suggest such alterations as I might deem advisable. When, by and by, it was found that Mr Moore's professional occupations prevented him from finishing the translation as quickly as we all desired, we gladly accepted Dr Aveling's offer to undertake a portion of the work; at the same time Mrs Aveling, Marx's youngest daughter, offered to check the quotations and to restore the original text of the numerous passages taken from English authors and Blue Books and translated by Marx into German. This has been done throughout, with but a few unavoidable exceptions.

The following portions of the book have been translated by Dr Aveling: (1) Chapters 10 (The Working-Day) and 11 (Rate and Mass of Surplus-Value); (2) Part 6 (Wages, comprising Chapters 19 to 22); (3) from Chapter 24, Section 4 (Circumstances that &c.) to the end of the book, comprising the latter part of Chapter 24, Chapter 25, and the whole of Part 8 (Chapters 26 to 33); (4) the two Author's Prefaces. All the rest of the book has been done by Mr Moore. While, thus, each of the translators is responsible for his share of the work only, I bear a joint responsibility for the whole.

The third German edition, which has been made the basis of our work throughout, was prepared by me, in 1883, with the assistance of notes left by the author, indicating the passages of the second edition to be replaced by designated passages, from the French text published in 1873.[1] The alterations thus effected in the text of the second edition generally coincided with changes prescribed by Marx in a set of MS. instructions for an English translation that was planned, about ten years ago, in America, but abandoned chiefly for want of a fit and proper translator. This MS. was placed at our disposal by our old friend Mr F. A. Sorge of Hoboken N. J. It designates some further interpolations from the French edition; but, being so many years older than the final instructions for the third edition, I did not consider myself at liberty to make use of it otherwise than sparingly, and chiefly in cases where it helped us over difficulties. In the same way, the French text has been referred to in most of the difficult passages, as an indicator of what the author himself was prepared to sacrifice wherever something of the full import of the original had to be sacrificed in the rendering.

There is, however, one difficulty we could not spare the reader: the use of certain terms in a sense different from what they have, not only in common life, but in ordinary Political Economy. But this was unavoidable. Every new aspect of a science involves a revolution in the technical terms of that science. This is best shown by chemistry, where the whole of the terminology is radically changed about once in twenty years, and where you will hardly find a single organic compound that has not gone through a whole series of different names. Political Economy has generally been content to take, just as they were, the terms of commercial and industrial life, and to operate with them, entirely failing to see that by so doing, it confined itself within the narrow circle of ideas expressed by those terms. Thus, though perfectly aware that both profits and rent are but sub-divisions, fragments of that unpaid part of the product which the labourer has to supply to his employer (its first appropriator, though not its ultimate exclusive owner), yet even classical Political Economy never went beyond the received notions of profits and rents, never examined this unpaid part of the product (called by Marx surplus-product) in its integrity as a whole, and therefore never arrived at a clear comprehension, either of its origin and nature, or of the laws that regulate the subsequent distribution of its value. Similarly all industry, not agricultural or handicraft, is indiscriminately comprised in the term of manufacture, and thereby the distinction is obliterated between two great and essentially different periods of economic history: the period of manufacture proper, based on the division of manual labour, and the period of modern industry based on machinery. It is, however, self-evident that a theory which views modern capitalist production as a mere passing stage in the economic history of mankind, must make use of terms different from those habitual to writers who look upon that form of production as imperishable and final.

A word respecting the author's method of quoting may not be out of place. In the majority of cases, the quotations serve, in the usual way, as documentary evidence in support of assertions made in the text. But in many instances, passages from economic writers are quoted in order to indicate when, where, and by whom a certain proposition was for the first time clearly enunciated. This is done in cases where the proposition quoted is of importance as being a more or less adequate expression of the conditions of social production and exchange prevalent at the time, and quite irrespective of Marx's recognition, or otherwise, of its general validity. These quotations, therefore, supplement the text by a running commentary taken from the history of the science.

Our translation comprises the first book of the work only. But this first book is in a great measure a whole in itself, and has for twenty years ranked as an independent work. The second book, edited in German by me, in 1885, is decidedly incomplete without the third, which cannot be published before the end of 1887. When Book 3 has been brought out in the original German, it will then be soon enough to think about preparing an English edition of both.

Das Kapital is often called, on the Continent, 'the Bible of the working-class'. That the conclusions arrived at in this work are daily more and more becoming the fundamental principles of the great working-class movement, not only in Germany and Switzerland, but in France, in Holland and Belgium, in America, and even in Italy and Spain, that everywhere the working-class more and more recognises, in these conclusions, the most adequate expression of its condition and of its aspirations, nobody acquainted with that movement will deny. And in England, too, the theories of Marx, even at this moment, exercise a powerful influence upon the socialist movement which is spreading in the ranks of 'cultured' people no less than in those of the working-class. But that is not all. The time is rapidly approaching when a thorough examination of England's economic position will impose itself as an irresistible national necessity. The working of the industrial system of this country, impossible without a constant and rapid extension of production, and therefore of markets, is coming to a dead stop.

Free-trade has exhausted its resources; even Manchester doubts this its quondam economic gospel.[2] Foreign industry, rapidly developing, stares English production in the face everywhere, not only in protected, but also in neutral markets, and even on this side of the Channel. While the productive power increases in a geometric, the extension of markets proceeds at best in an arithmetic ratio. The decennial cycle of stagnation, prosperity, over-production and crisis, ever recurrent from 1825 to 1867, seems indeed to have run its course; but only to land us in the slough of despond of a permanent and chronic depression. The sighed for period of prosperity will not come; as often as we seem to perceive its heralding symptoms, so often do they again vanish into air. Meanwhile, each succeeding winter brings up afresh the great question, 'what to do with the unemployed'; but while the number of the unemployed keeps swelling from year to year, there is nobody to answer that question; and we can almost calculate the moment when the unemployed losing patience will take their own fate into their own hands. Surely, at such a moment, the voice ought to be heard of a man whose whole theory is the result of a lifelong study of the economic history and condition of England, and whom that study led to the conclusion that, at least in Europe, England is the only country where the inevitable social revolution might be effected entirely by peaceful and legal means. He certainly never forgot to add that he hardly expected the English ruling classes to submit, without a 'pro-slavery rebellion', to this peaceful and legal revolution.

Frederick Engels
November 5, 1886

Author's Prefaces

1. To the First Edition.

The work, the first volume of which I now submit to the public, forms the continuation of my *Zur Kritik der Politischen Oekonomie* (*A Contribution to the Criticism of Political Economy*) published in 1859. The long pause between the first part and the continuation is due to an illness of many years' duration that again and again interrupted my work.

The substance of that earlier work is summarised in the first three chapters of this volume. This is done not merely for the sake of connection and completeness. The presentation of the subject-matter is improved. As far as circumstances in any way permit, many points only hinted at in the earlier book are here worked out more fully, whilst, conversely, points worked out fully there are only touched upon in this volume. The sections on the history of the theories of value and of money are now, of course, left out altogether. The reader of the earlier work will find, however, in the notes to the first chapter additional sources of reference relative to the history of those theories.

Every beginning is difficult, holds in all sciences. To understand the first chapter, especially the section that contains the analysis of commodities, will, therefore, present the greatest difficulty. That which concerns more especially the analysis of the substance of value and the magnitude of value, I have, as much as it was possible, popularised.[1] The value form, whose fully developed shape is the money form, is very elementary and simple. Nevertheless, the human mind has for more than 2,000 years sought in vain to get to the bottom of it all, whilst on the other hand, to the successful analysis of much more composite and complex forms, there has been at least an approximation. Why? Because the body, as an organic whole, is more easy of study than are the cells of that body. In the analysis of economic forms, moreover, neither microscopes nor chemical reagents are of use. The force of abstraction must replace both. But in bourgeois society, the commodity-form of the product of labour – or value form of the commodity – is the economic cell-form. To the superficial observer, the analysis of these forms seems to turn upon minutiae. It does in fact deal with minutiae, but they are of the same order as those dealt with in microscopic anatomy.

With the exception of the section of value form, therefore, this volume cannot stand accused on the score of difficulty. I presuppose, of course, a reader who is willing to learn something new and therefore to think for himself.

The physicist either observes physical phenomena where they occur in their most typical form and most free from disturbing influence, or, wherever possible, he makes experiments under conditions that assure the occurrence of the phenomenon in its normality. In this work I have to examine the capitalist mode of production, and the conditions of production and exchange corresponding to that mode. Up to the present time, their classic ground is England. That is the reason why England is used as the chief illustration in the development of my theoretical ideas. If, however, the German reader shrugs his shoulders at the condition of the English industrial and agricultural labourers, or in optimist fashion comforts himself with the thought that in Germany things are not nearly so bad; I must plainly tell him, 'De te fabula narratur!'

Intrinsically, it is not a question of the higher or lower degree of development of the social antagonisms that result from the natural laws of capitalist production. It is a question of these laws themselves, of these tendencies working with iron necessity towards inevitable results. The country that is more developed industrially only shows, to the less developed, the image of its own future.

But apart from this. Where capitalist production is fully naturalised among the Germans (for instance, in the factories proper) the condition of things is much worse than in England, because the counterpoise of the Factory Acts is wanting. In all other spheres, we, like all the rest of Continental Western Europe, suffer not only from the development of capitalist production, but also from the incompleteness of that development. Alongside the modern evils, a whole series of inherited evils oppress us, arising from the passive survival of antiquated modes of production, with their inevitable train of social and political anachronisms. We suffer not only from the living, but from the dead. *Le mort saisit le vif!*

The social statistics of Germany and the rest of Continental Western Europe are, in comparison with those of England, wretchedly compiled. But they raise the veil just enough to let us catch a glimpse of the Medusa head behind it. We should be appalled at the state of things at home, if, as in England, our governments and parliaments appointed periodically commissions of inquiry into economic conditions; if these commissions were armed with the same plenary powers to get at the truth; if it was possible to find for this purpose men as competent, as free from partisanship and respect of persons as are the English factory-inspectors, her medical reporters on public health, her commissioners of inquiry into the exploitation of women and children, into housing and food. Perseus wore a magic cap down over his eyes and ears as a make-believe that there are no monsters.

Let us not deceive ourselves on this. As in the 18th century, the American war of independence sounded the tocsin for the European middle-class, so in the 19th century, the American Civil War sounded it for the European working-class. In England the process of social disintegration is palpable. When it has reached a certain point, it must react on the Continent. There it will take a form more brutal or more humane, according to the degree of development of the working-class itself. Apart from higher motives, therefore, their own most important interests dictate to the classes that are for the nonce the ruling ones, the removal of all legally removable hindrances to the free development of the working-class. For this reason, as well as others, I have given so large a space in this volume to the history, the details, and the results of English factory legislation. One nation can and should learn from others. And even when a society has got upon the right track for the discovery of the natural laws of its movement – and it is the ultimate aim of this work, to lay bare the economic law of motion of modern society – it can neither clear by bold leaps, nor remove by legal enactments, the obstacles offered by the successive phases of its normal development. But it can shorten and lessen the birth-pangs.

To prevent possible misunderstand, a word. I paint the capitalist and the landlord in no sense *couleur de rose*. But here individuals are dealt with only in so far as they are the personifications of economic categories, embodiments of particular class-relations and class-interests. My standpoint, from which the evolution of the economic formation of society is viewed as a process of natural history, can less than any other make the individual responsible for relations whose creature he socially remains, however much he may subjectively raise himself above them.

In the domain of Political Economy, free scientific inquiry meets not merely the same enemies as in all other domains. The peculiar nature of the materials it deals with, summons as foes into the field of battle the most violent, mean and malignant passions of the human breast, the Furies of private interest. The English Established Church, e.g., will more readily pardon an attack on 38 of its 39 articles than on 1/39 of its income. Nowadays atheism is *culpa levis*, as compared with criticism of existing property relations. Nevertheless, there is an unmistakable advance. I refer, e.g., to the Blue Book published within the last few weeks: *Correspondence with Her Majesty's Missions Abroad, regarding Industrial Questions and Trades' Unions*. The representatives of the English Crown in foreign countries there declare in so many words that in Germany, in France, to be brief, in all the civilised states of the European Continent, radical change in the existing relations between capital and labour is as evident and inevitable as in England. At the same time, on the other side of the Atlantic Ocean, Mr Wade, vice-president of the United States, declared in public meetings that, after the abolition of slavery, a radical change of the relations of capital and of property in land is next upon the order of the day. These are signs of the times, not to be hidden by purple mantles or black cassocks. They do not signify that tomorrow a miracle will happen. They show that, within the ruling-classes themselves, a foreboding is dawning, that the present society is no solid crystal, but an organism capable of change, and is constantly changing.

The second volume of this book will treat of the process of the circulation of capital[2] (Book 2), and of the varied forms assumed by capital in the course of its development (Book 3), the third and last volume (Book 4), the history of the theory.

Every opinion based on scientific criticism I welcome. As to prejudices of so-called public opinion, to which I have never made concessions, now as aforetime the maxim of the great Florentine is mine: '*Segui il tuo corso, e lascia dir le genti.*'

Karl Marx
London, July 25, 1867

2. To The Second Edition.

To the present moment Political Economy, in Germany, is a foreign science. Gustav von Gülich in his *Historical Decription of Commerce, Industry, &c*[3] especially in the two first volumes published in 1830, has examined at length the historical circumstances that prevented, in Germany, the development of the capitalist mode of production, and consequently the development, in that country, of modern bourgeois society. Thus the soil whence Political Economy springs was wanting. This 'science' had to be imported from England and France as a ready-made article; its German professors remained schoolboys. The theoretical expression of a foreign reality was turned, in their hands, into a collection of dogmas, interpreted by them in terms of the petty trading world around them, and therefore misinterpreted. The feeling of scientific impotence, a feeling not wholly to be repressed, and the uneasy consciousness of having to touch a subject in reality foreign to them, was but imperfectly concealed, either under a parade of literary and historical erudition, or by an admixture of extraneous material, borrowed from the so-called 'Kameral' sciences, a medley of smatterings, through whose purgatory the hopeless candidate for the German bureaucracy has to pass.

Since 1848 capitalist production has developed rapidly in Germany, and at the preent time it is in the full bloom of speculation and swindling. But fate is still unpropitious to our professional economists. At the time when they were able to deal with Political Economy in a straightforward fashion, modern economic conditions did not actually exist in Germany. And as soon as these conditions did come into existence, they did so under circumstances that no longer allowed of their being really and impartially investigated within the bounds of the bourgeois horizon. in so far, i.e., as the capitalist régime is looked

upon as the absolutely final form of social production, instead of as a
passing historical phase of its evolution, Political economy can remain
a science only so long as the class struggle is latent or manifests itself
only in isolated and sporadic phenomena.

Let us take England. Its political economy belongs to the period
in which the class-struggle was as yet undeveloped. Its last great
representative, Ricardo, in the end, consciously makes the antagonism
of class-interests, of wages and profits, of profits and rent, the starting-
point of his investigations, naively taking this antagonism for a social
law of nature. But by this start the science of bourgeois economy had
reached the limits beyond which it could not pass. Already in the
lifetime of Ricardo, and in opposition to him, it was met by criticism,
in the person of Sismondi.[4].

The succeeding period, from 1820 to 1830, was notable in England
for scientific activity in the domain of Poltical Economy. It was the
time as well of the vulgarising and extending of Ricardo's theory, as of
the contest of that theory with the old school. Splendid tournaments
were held. What was done then, is little known to the Continent
generally, because the polemic is for the most part scattered through
articles in reviews, occasional literature and pamphlets. The unprejudiced character of this polemic – although the theory of Ricardo already
serves, in exceptional cases, as a weapon of attack upon bourgeois
economy – is explained by the circumstances of the time. On the one
hand, modern industry itself was only just emergning from the age of
childhood, as is shown by the fact that with the crisis of 1825 it for the
first time opens the periodic cycle of its modern life. On the other
hand, the class-struggle between capital and labour is forced into the
background, politically by the discord between the governments and
the feudal aristocracy gathered around the Holy Alliance on the one
hand, and the popular masses, led by the bourgeoisie on the other;
economically by the quarrel between industrial capital and aristocratic
landed property – a quarrel that in France was concealed by the
opposition between small and large landed property, and that in
England broke out openly after the Corn Laws. The literature of
Political Economy in England at this time calls to mind the stormy
forward movement in France after Dr Quesnay's death, but only as a
Saint Martin's summer reminds us of spring. With the year 1830 came
the decisive crisis

In France and in England the bourgeoisie had conquered political
power. Thenceforth, the class-struggle, practically as well as theoretically, took on more and more outspoken and threatening forms. I
sounded the knell of scientific bourgeois economy. It was thenceforth
no longer a question, whether this theorem or that was true, but

whether it was useful to capital or harmful, expedient or inexpedient, politically dangerous or not. In place of disinterested enquirers, there were hired prizefighters; in place of genuine scientific research, the bad conscience and the evil intent of apologetic. Still, even the obtrusive pamphlets with which the Anti-Corn Law League, led by the manufacturers Cobden and Bright, deluged the world, have a historic interest, if no scientific one, on account of their polemic against the landed aristocracy. But since then the Free Trade legislation, inaugurated by Sir Robert Peel, has deprived vulgar economy of this its last sting.

The Continental revolution of 1848–9 also had its reaction in England. Men who still claimed some scientific standing and aspired to be something more than mere sophists and sycophants of the ruling-classes, tried to harmonise the Political Economy of capital with the claims, no longer to be ignored, of the proletariat. Hence a shallow syncretism, of which John Stuart Mill is the best representative. It is a declaration of bankruptcy by bourgeois economy, an event on which the great Russian scholar and critic, N. Tschernyschevsky, has thrown the light of a master mind in his *Outlines of Political Economy according to Mill*.

In Germany, therefore, the capitalist mode of production came to a head, after its antagonistic character had already in France and England, shown itself in a fierce strife of classes. And meanwhile, moreover, the German proletariat had attained a much more clear class-consciousness than the German bourgeoisie. Thus, at the very moment when a bourgeois science of political economy seemed at last possible in Germany, it had in reality become impossible.

Under these circumstances its professors fell into two groups. The one set, prudent, practical business folk, flocked to the banner of Bastiat, the most superficial and therefore the most adequate representative of the apologetic of vulgar economy; the other, proud of the professorial dignity of their science, followed John Stuart Mill in his attempt to reconcile irreconciliables. Just as in the classical time of bourgeois economy, so also in the time of its decline, the Germans remained mere schoolboys, imitators and followers, petty retailers and hawkers in the service of the great foreign wholesale concern.

The peculiar historic development of German society therefore forbids, in that country, all the original work in bourgeois economy; but not the criticism of that economy. So far as such criticism represents a class, it can only represent the class whose vocation in history is the overthrow of the capitalist mode of production and the final abolition of all classes – the proletariat.

The learned and unlearned spokesmen of the German bourgeoisie tried at first to kill *Das Kapital* by silence, as they had managed to do with my earlier writings. As soon as they found that these tactics no longer fitted in the conditions of the time, they wrote, under pretence of criticising my book, prescriptions 'for the tranquillisation of the bourgeois mind'. But they found in the workers' press – see, e.g., Joseph Dietzgen's articles in the *Volksstaat* – antagonists stronger than themselves, to whom (down to this very day) they owe a reply.[5]

An excellent Russian translation of *Das Kapital* appeared in the spring of 1872. The edition of 3000 copies is already nearly exhausted. As early as 1871, A. Sieber, Professor of Political Economy in the University of Kiev, in his work *David Ricardo's Theory of Value and of Capital*, referred to my theory of value, of money and of capital, as in its fundamentals a necessary sequel to the teaching of Smith and Ricardo. That which astonishes the Western European in the reading of this excellent work, is the author's consistent and firm grasp of the purely theoretical position.

That the method employed in *Das Kapital* has been little understood, is shown by the various conceptions, contradictory one to another, that have been formed of it.

Thus the Paris *Revue Posiviste* reproaches me in that, on the one hand, I treat economics metaphysically, and on the other hand – imagine! – confine myself to the mere critical analysis of actual facts, instead of writing receipts (Comtist ones?) for the cook-shops of the future. In answer to the reproach *in re* metaphysics, Professor Sieber has it: 'In so far as it deals with actual theory, the method of Marx is the deductive method of the whole English school, a school whose failings and virtues are common to the best theoretic economists.' M. Block – *Les théoricians du socialisme en Allemagne, Extrait du Journal des Économistes, Juillet et Août 1872* – makes the discovery that my method is analytic and says: '*Par cet ouvrage M. Marx se classe parmi les esprits analytiques les plus éminents.*' German reviews, of course, shriek out at 'Hegelian sophistics.' The *European Messenger* of St Petersburg, in an article dealing exclusively with the method of Das Kapital (May number, 1872, pp. 427–436), finds my method of inquiry severely realistic, but my method of presentation, unfortunately, German-dialectical. It says: 'At first sight, if the judgement is based on the external form of the presentation of the subject, Marx is the most ideal of ideal philosophers, always in the German, i.e., the bad sense of the word. But in point of fact he is infinitely more realistic than all his fore-runners in the work of economic criticism. He can in no sense be called an idealist.' I cannot answer the writer better than by aid of a few extracts from his own criticism, which may interest some of my readers to whom the Russian original is inaccessible.

After a quotation from the preface to my *Criticism of Political Economy*, Berlin, 1859, pp. 4–7, where I discuss the materialistic basis of my method, the writer goes on: 'The one thing which is of moment to Marx, is to find the law of the phenomena with whose investigation he is concerned; and not only is that law of moment to him, which governs these phenomena, in so far as they have a definite form and mutual connection within a given historical period. Of still greater moment to him is the law of their variation, of their development, i.e., of their transition from one form into another, from one series of connections into a different one. This law once discovered, he investigates in detail the effects in which it manifests itself in social life. Consequently, Marx only troubles himself about one thing; to show, by rigid scientific investigation, the necessity of successive determinate orders of social conditions, and to establish, as impartially as possible, the facts that serve him for fundamental starting points. For this it is quite enough, if he proves, at the same time, both the necessity of another order into which the first must inevitably pass over; and this all the same, whether men believe or do not believe it, whether they are conscious or unconscious of it. Marx treats the social movement as a process of natural history, governed by laws not only independent of human will, consciousness and intelligence, but rather, on the contrary, determining that will, consciousness and intelligence . . . If in the history of civilisation the conscious element plays a part so subordinate, then it is self-evident that a critical inquiry whose subject matter is civilisation, can, less than anything else, have for its basis any form of, or any result of, consciousness. That is to say, that not the idea, but the material phenomenon alone can serve as its starting-point. Such an inquiry will confine itself to the confrontation and the comparison of a fact, not with ideas, but with another fact. For this inquiry, the one thing of moment is, that both facts be investigated as accurately as possible, and that they actually form, each with respect to the other, different momenta of an evolution; but most important of all is the rigid analysis of the series of successions, of the sequences and concatenations in which the different stages of such an evolution present themselves. But it will be said, the general laws of economic life are one and the same, no matter whether they are applied to the present or the past. This Marx directly dnies. According to him, such abstract laws do not exist. On the contrary, in his opinion every historical period has laws of its own . . . As soon as society has outlived a given period of development, and is passing over from one given stage to another, it begins to be subject also to other laws In a word, economic life offers us a phenomenon analogous to the history of evolution on other branches of biology. The old economists misunderstood the nature of economic laws when they likened them to the laws of physics and chemistry. A more thorough analysis of phenomena shows that social organisms differ among themselves as fundamentally as plants or animals. Nay, one and the same phenomenon falls under quite different laws in consequence of the different structure of those organisms as a whole, of the variations of their individual organs, of the different conditions in which those organs function, &c. Marx, e.g, denies that the law of population is the same at all times and in all places. He asserts, on the contrary, that every stage of development has its own law of population . . . With the varying degree of development of productive power, social conditions and the laws governing them vary too. Whilst Marx sets himself the task of following and explaining from this point of view the economic system established by the sway of capital, he is only formulating, in a strictly scientific manner, the aim that every accurate investigation into economic life must have. The scientific value of such an inquiry lies in the disclosing of the special laws that regulate the origin, existence, development, death of a given social organism and its replacement by another and higher one. And it is this value that, in point of fact, Marx's book has.'

Whilst the writer pictures what he takes to be actually my method, in this striking and (as far as concerns my own application of it) generous way, what else is he picturing but the dialiectic method?

Of course the method of presentation must differ in form from that of inquiry. The latter has to appropriate the material in detail, to analyse its different forms of development, to trace out their inner connection. Only after this work is done, can the actual movement be adequately described. If this is done successfully, if the life of the subject-matter is ideally reflected as in a mirror, then it may appear as if we had before us a mere *a priori* construction.

My dialectical method is not only different from the Hegelian, but is its direct opposite. To Hegel, the life-process of the human brain, i.e., the process of thinking, which, under the name of 'the Idea', he even transforms into an independent subject, is the demiurgos of the real world, and the real world is only the external, phenomenal form of 'the Idea'. With me, on the contrary, the ideal is nothing else than the material world reflected by the human mind, and translated into forms of thought.

The mystifying side of Hegelian dialectic I criticised nearly thirty years ago, at a time when it was still the fashion. But just as I was working at the first volume of *Das Kapital*, it was the good pleasure of the peevish, arrogant, mediocre *Epigonoi* who now talk large in cultured Germany, to treat Hegel in same way as the brave Moses Mendelssohn in Lessing's time treated Spinoza, i.e., as a 'dead dog'. I therefore openly avowed myself the pupil of that mighty thinker, and even here and there, in the chapter on the theory of value, coquetted with the modes of expression peculiar to him. The mystification which dialiectic suffers in Hegel's hands, by no means prevents him from being the first to present its general form of working in a comprehensive and conscious manner. With him it is standing on its head. It must be turned right side up again, if you would discover the rational kernel within the mystical shell.

In its mystified form, dialectic became the fashion in Germany, because it seemed to transfigure and to glorify the existing state of things. In its rational form it is a scandal and abomination to bourgeoisdom and its doctrinaire professors, because it includes in its comprehension and affirmative recognition of the existing state of things, at the same time also, the recognition of the negation of that state, of its inevitable breaking up; because it regards every historically devloped social form as in fluid movement, and therefore takes into account its transient nature not less than its momentary existence; because it lets nothing impose upon it, and is in its essence critical and revolutionary.

The contradictions inherent in the movement of capitalist society impress themselves upon the practical bourgeois most strikingly in the changes of the periodic cycle, though which modern industry runs, and whose crowning point is the universal crisis. That crisis is once again approaching, although as yet but in its preliminary stage; and by the unversality of its theatre and the intensity of its action it will drum dialectics even into the heads of the mushroom-upstarts of the new, holy Prusso-German empire.

Karl Marx
London, January 24, 1873

Part I
Commodities and Money

Chapter I
Commodities

Section 1. The Two Factors of a Commodity: Use-Value and Value (The Substance of Value and the Magnitude of Value).

The wealth of those societies in which the capitalist mode of production prevails, presents itself as 'an immense accumulation of commodities',[1] its unit being a single commodity. Our investigation must therefore begin with the analysis of a commodity.

A commodity is, in the first place, an object outside us, a thing that by its properties satisfies human wants of some sort or another. The nature of such wants, whether, for instance, they spring from the stomach or from fancy, makes no difference.[2] Neither are we here concerned to know how the object satisfies these wants, whether directly as means of subsistence, or indirectly as means of production.

Every useful thing, as iron, paper, &c., may be looked at from the two points of view of quality and quantity. It is an assemblage of many properties, and may therefore be of use in various ways. To discover the various uses of things is the work of history.[3] So also is the establishment of socially-recognised standards of measure for the quantities of these useful objects. The diversity of these measures has its origin partly in the diverse nature of the objects to be measured, partly in convention.

The utility of a thing makes it a use-value.[4] But this utility is not a thing of air. Being limited by the physical properties of the commodity, it has no existence apart from that commodity. A commodity, such as iron, corn, or a diamond, is therefore, so far as it is a material thing, a use-value, something useful. This property of a commodity is independent of the amount of labour required to appropriate its useful qualities. When treating of use-values, we always assume to be dealing with definite quantities, such as dozens of watches, yards of linen, or tons of iron. The use-values of commodities furnish the material for a special study, that of the commercial knowledge of commodities.[5] Use-values become a reality only by use or consumption: they also constitute the substance of all wealth, whatever may be the social form of that wealth. In the form of society we are about to consider, they are, in addition, the material depositories of exchange value.

Exchange value, at first sight, presents itself as a quantitative relation, as the proportion in which values in use of one sort are exchanged for those of another sort,[6] a relation constantly changing with time and place. Hence exchange value appears to be something accidental and purely relative, and consequently an intrinsic value, i.e., an exchange value that is inseparably connected with, inherent in commodities, seems a contradiction in terms.[7] Let us consider the matter a little more closely.

A given commodity, e.g., a quarter of wheat, is exchanged for x blacking, y silk, or z gold, &c. – in short, for other commodities in the most different proportions. Instead of one exchange value, the wheat has, therefore, a great many. But since x blacking, y silk, or z gold &c., each represents the exchange value of one quarter of wheat, x blacking, y silk, z gold, &c., must, as exchange values, be replaceable by each other, or equal to each other. Therefore, first: the valid exchange values of a given commodity express something equal; secondly, exchange value, generally, is only the mode of expression, the phenomenal form, of something contained in it, yet distinguishable from it.

Let us take two commodities, e.g., corn and iron. The proportions in which they are exchangeable, whatever those proportions may be, can always be represented by an equation in which a given quantity of corn is equated to some quantity of iron: e.g., 1 quarter corn = x cwt. iron. What does this equation tell us? It tells us that in two different things – in 1 quarter of corn and x cwt. of iron, there exists in equal quantities something common to both. The two things must therefore be equal to a third, which in itself is neither the one nor the other. Each of them, so far as it is exchange value, must therefore be reducible to this third.

A simple geometrical illustration will make this clear. In order to calculate and compare the areas of rectilinear figures, we decompose them into triangles. But the area of the triangle itself is expressed by something totally different from its visible figure, namely, by half the product of the base multiplied by the altitude. In the same way the exchange values of commodities must be capable of being expressed in terms of something common to them all, of which thing they represent a greater or less quantity.

This common 'something' cannot be either a geometrical, a chemical, or any other natural property of commodities. Such properties claim our attention only in so far as they affect the utility of those commodities, make them use-values. But the exchange of commodities is evidently an act characterised by a total abstraction from use-value. Then one use-value is just as good as another, provided only it be present in sufficient quantity. Or, as old Barbon says, 'one sort of wares are as good as another, if the values be equal. There is no difference or distinction in things of equal value . . . An hundred pounds' worth of lead or iron, is of as great value as one hundred pounds' worth of silver or gold.'[8] As use-values, commodities are, above all, of different qualities, but as exchange values they are merely different quantities, and consequently do not contain an atom of use-value.

If then we leave out of consideration the use-value of commodities, they have only one common property left, that of being products of labour. But even the product of labour itself has undergone a change in our hands. If we make abstraction from its use-value, we make abstraction at the same time from the material elements and shapes that make the product a use-value; we see in it no longer a table, a house, yarn, or any other useful thing. Its existence as a material thing is put out of sight. Neither can it any longer be regarded as the product of the labour of the joiner, the mason, the spinner, or of any other definite kind of productive labour. Along with the useful qualities of the products themselves, we put out of sight both the useful character of the various kinds of labour embodied in them, and the concrete forms of that labour; there is nothing left but what is common to them all; all are reduced to one and the same sort of labour, human labour in the abstract.

Let us now consider the residue of each of these products; it consists of the same unsubstantial reality in each, a mere congelation of homogeneous human labour, of labour power expended without regard to the mode of its expenditure. All that these things now tell us is, that human labour power has been expended in their production, that human labour is embodied in them. When looked at as crystals of this social substance, common to them all, they are – Values.

We have seen that when commodities are exchanged, their exchange value manifests itself as something totally independent of their use-value. But if we abstract from their use-value, there remains their Value as defined above. Therefore, the common substance that manifests itself in the exchange value of commodities, whenever they are exchanged, is their value. The progress of our investigation will show that exchange value is the only form in which the value of commodities can manifest itself or be expressed. For the present, however, we have to consider the nature of value independently of this, its form.

A use-value, or useful article, therefore, has value only because human labour in the abstract has been embodied or materialised in it. How, then, is the magnitude of this value to be measured? Plainly, by the quantity of the value-creating substance, the labour, contained in the article. The quantity of labour, however, is measured by its duration, and labour-time in its turn finds its standard in weeks, days, and hours.

Some people might think that if the value of a commodity is determined by the quantity of labour spent on it, the more idle and unskilful the labourer, the more valuable would his commodity be, because more time would be required in its production. The labour, however, that forms the substance of value, is homogeneous human labour, expenditure of one uniform labour power. The total labour power of society, which is embodied in the sum total of the values of all commodities produced by that society, counts here as one homogeneous mass of human labour power, composed though it be of innumerable individual units. Each of these units is the same as any other, so far as it has the character of the average labour power of society, and takes effect as such; that is, so far as it requires for producing a commodity, no more time than is needed on an average, no more than is socially necessary. The labour-time socially necessary is that required to produce an article under the normal conditions of production, and with the average degree of skill and intensity prevalent at the time. The introduction of power-looms into England probably reduced by one-half the labour required to weave a given quantity of yarn into cloth. The hand-loom weavers, as a matter of fact, continued to require the same time as before; but for all that, the product of one hour of their labour represented after the change only half an hour's social labour, and consequently fell to one-half its former value.

We see then that that which determines the magnitude of the value of any article is the amount of labour socially necessary, or the labour-time socially necessary for its production.[9] Each individual commodity, in this connection, is to be considered as an average sample of its class.[10] Commodities, therefore, in which equal quantities of labour are embodied, or which can be produced in the same time, have the same value. The value of one commodity is to the value of any other, as the labour-time necessary for the production of the one is to that necessary for the production of the other. 'As values, all commodities are only definite masses of congealed labour-time.'[11]

The value of a commodity would therefore remain constant, if the labour-time required for its production also remained constant. But the latter changes with every variation in the productiveness of labour. This productiveness is determined by various circumstances, amongst others, by the average amount of skill of the workmen, the state of science, and the degree of its practical application, the social organisation of production, the extent and capabilities of the means of production, and by physical conditions. For example, the same amount of labour in favourable seasons is embodied in 8 bushels of corn, and in unfavourable, only in four. The same labour extracts from rich mines more metal than from poor mines. Diamonds are of very rare occurrence on the earth's surface, and hence their discovery costs, on an average, a great deal of labour-time. Consequently much labour is represented in a small compass. Jacob doubts whether gold has ever been paid for at its full value. This applies still more to diamonds. According to Eschwege, the total produce of the Brazilian diamond mines for the eighty years, ending in 1823, had not realised the price of one and-a-half years' average produce of the sugar and coffee plantations of the same country, although the diamonds cost much more labour, and therefore represented more value. With richer mines, the same quantity of labour would embody itself in more diamonds, and their value would fall. If we could succeed at a small expenditure of labour, in converting carbon into diamonds, their value might fall below that of bricks. In general, the greater the productiveness of labour, the less is the labour-time required for the production of an article, the less is the amount of labour crystallised in that article, and the less is its value; and *vice versa*, the less the productiveness of labour, the greater is the labour-time required for the production of an article, and the greater is its value. The value of a commodity, therefore, varies directly as the quantity, and inversely as the productiveness, of the labour incorporated in it.

A thing can be a use-value, without having value. This is the case whenever its utility to man is not due to labour. Such are air, virgin soil, natural meadows, &c. A thing can be useful, and the product of human labour, without being a commodity. Whoever directly satisfies his wants with the produce of his own labour, creates, indeed, use-values, but not commodities. In order to produce the latter, he must not only produce use-values, but use-values for others, social use-values. Lastly, nothing can have value, without being an object of utility. If the thing is useless, so is the labour contained in it; the labour does not count as labour, and therefore creates no value.

Section 2. The TwoFold Character of the
Labour Embodied in Commodities.

At first sight a commodity presented itself to us as a complex of two things – use-value and exchange value. Later on, we saw also that labour, too, possesses the same two-fold nature; for, so far as it finds expression in value, it does not possess the same characteristics that belong to it as a creator of use-values. I was the first to point out and to examine critically this two-fold nature of the labour contained in commodities. As this point is the pivot on which a clear comprehension of Political Economy turns, we must go more into detail.

Let us take two commodities such as a coat and 10 yards of linen, and let the former be double the value of the latter, so that, if 10 yards of linen = W, the coat = 2W.

The coat is a use-value that satisfies a particular want. Its existence is the result of a special sort of productive activity, the nature of which is determined by its aim, mode of operation, subject, means, and result. The labour, whose utility is thus represented by the value in use of its product, or which manifests itself by making its product a use-value, we call useful labour. In this connection we consider only its useful effect.

As the coat and the linen are two qualitatively different use-values, so also are the two forms of labour that produce them, tailoring and weaving. Were these two objects not qualitatively different, not produced respectively by labour of different quality, they could not stand to each other in the relation of commodities. Coats are not exchanged for coats, one use-value is not exchanged for another of the same kind.

To all the different varieties of values in use there correspond as many different kinds of useful labour, classified according to the order, genus, species, and variety to which they belong in the social division of labour. This division of labour is a necessary condition for the production of commodities, but it does not follow, conversely, that the production of commodities is a necessary condition for the division of labour. In the primitive Indian community there is social division of labour, without production of commodities. Or, to take an example nearer home, in every factory the labour is divided according to a system, but this division is not brought about by the operatives mutually exchanging their individual products. Only such products can become commodities with regard to each other, as result from different kinds of labour, each kind being carried on independently and for the account of private individuals.

To resume, then: in the use-value of each commodity there is contained useful labour, i.e., productive activity of a definite kind and exercised with a definite aim. Use-values cannot confront each other as commodities, unless the useful labour embodied in them is qualitatively different in each of them.

In a community, the produce of which in general takes the form of commodities, i.e., in a community of commodity producers, this qualitative difference between the useful forms of labour that are carried on independently of individual producers, each on their own account, develops into a complex system, a social division of labour.

Anyhow, whether the coat be worn by the tailor or by his customer, in either case it operates as a use-value. Nor is the relation between the coat and the labour that produced it altered by the circumstance that tailoring may have become a special trade, an independent branch of the social division of labour. Wherever the want of clothing forced them to it, the human race made clothes for thousands of years, without a single man becoming a tailor. But coats and linen, like every other element of material wealth that is not the spontaneous produce of Nature, must invariably owe their existence to a special productive activity, exercised with a definite aim, an activity that appropriates particular nature-given materials to particular human wants. So far therefore as labour is a creator of use-value, is useful labour, it is a necessary condition, independent of all forms of society, for the existence of the human race; it is an eternal nature-imposed necessity, without which there can be no material exchanges between man and Nature, and therefore no life.

The use-values, coat, linen, &c., i.e., the bodies of commodities, are combinations of two elements – matter and labour. If we take away the useful labour expended upon them, a material substratum is always left, which is furnished by Nature without the help of man. The latter can work only as Nature does, that is by changing the form of matter.[12] Nay more, in this work of changing the form he is constantly helped by natural forces. We see, then, that labour is not the only source of material wealth, of use-values produced by labour. As William Petty puts it, labour is its father and the earth its mother.

Let us now pass from the commodity considered as a use-value to the value of commodities.

By our assumption, the coat is worth twice as much as the linen. But this is a mere quantitative difference, which for the present does not concern us. We bear in mind, however, that if the value of the coat is double that of 10 yds. of linen, 20 yds. of linen must have the same value as one coat. So far as they are values, the coat and the linen are things of a like substance, objective expressions of essentially identical labour. But tailoring and weaving are, qualitatively, different kinds of labour. There are, however, states of society in which one and the same man does tailoring and weaving alternately, in which case these two forms of labour are mere modifications of the labour of the same individual, and not special and fixed functions of different persons, just as the coat which our tailor makes one day, and the trousers which he makes another day, imply only a variation in the labour of one and the same individual. Moreover, we see at a glance that, in our capitalist society, a given portion of human labour is, in accordance with the varying demand, at one time supplied in the form of tailoring, at another in the form of weaving. This change may possibly not take place without friction, but take place it must.

Productive activity, if we leave out of sight its special form, viz., the useful character of the labour, is nothing but the expenditure of human labour power. Tailoring and weaving, though qualitatively different productive activities, are each a productive expenditure of human brains, nerves, and muscles, and in this sense are human labour. They are but two different modes of expending human labour power. Of course, this labour power, which remains the same under all its modifications, must have attained a certain pitch of development before it can be expended in a multiplicity of modes. But the value of a commodity represents human labour in the abstract, the expenditure of human labour in general. And just as in society, a general or a banker plays a great part, but mere man, on the other hand, a very shabby part,[13] so here with mere human labour. It is the expenditure of simple labour power, i.e., of the labour power which, on an average, apart from any special development, exists in the organism of every ordinary individual. Simple average labour, it is true, varies in character in different countries and at different times, but in a particular society it is given. Skilled labour counts only as simple labour intensified, or rather, as multiplied simple labour, a given quantity of skilled being considered equal to a greater quantity of simple labour. Experience shows that this reduction is constantly being made. A commodity may be the product of the most skilled labour, but its value, by equating it to the product of simple unskilled labour, represents a definite quantity of the latter labour alone.[14] The different proportions in which different sorts of labour are reduced to unskilled labour as their standard. are established by a social process that goes on behind the backs of the producers, and, consequently, appear to be fixed by custom. For simplicity's sake we shall henceforth account every kind of labour to be unskilled, simple labour; by this we do no more than save ourselves the trouble of making the reduction.

Just as, therefore, in viewing the coat and linen as values, we abstract from their different use-values, so it is with the labour represented by those values: we disregard the difference between its useful forms, weaving and tailoring. As the use-values, coat and linen, are combinations of special productive activities with cloth and yarn, while the values, coat and linen, are, on the other hand, mere homogeneous congelations of undifferentiated labour, so the labour embodied in these latter values does not count by virtue of its productive relation to cloth and yarn, but only as being expenditure of human labour power. Tailoring and weaving are necessary factors in the creation of the use-values, coat and linen, precisely because these two kinds of labour are of different qualities; but only in so far as abstraction is made from their special qualities, only in so far as both possess the same quality of being human labour, do tailoring and weaving form the substance of the values of the same articles.

Coats and linen, however, are not merely values, but values of definite magnitude, and according to our assumption, the coat is worth twice as much as the ten yards of linen. Whence this difference in their values? It is owing to the fact that the linen contains only half as much labour as the coat, and consequently, that in the production of the latter, labour power must have been expended during twice the time necessary for the production of the former.

While, therefore, with reference to use-value, the labour contained in a commodity counts only qualitatively, with reference to value it counts only quantitatively, and must first be reduced to human labour pure and simple. In the former case, it is a question of How and What, in the latter of How much? How long a time? Since the magnitude of the value of a commodity represents only the quantity of labour embodied in it, it follows that all commodities, when taken in certain proportions, must be equal in value.

If the productive power of all the different sorts of useful labour required for the production of a coat remains unchanged, the sum of the values of the coats produced increases with their number. If one coat represents x days' labour, two coats represent 2x days' labour, and so on. But assume that the duration of the labour necessary for he production of a coat becomes doubled or halved. In the first case one coat is worth as much as two coats were before; in the second case, two coats are only worth as much as one was before, although in both cases one coat renders the same service as before. and the useful labour embodied in it remains of the same quality. But the quantity of labour spent on its production has altered.

An increase in the quantity of use-values is an increase of material wealth. With two coats two men can be clothed, with one coat only one man. Nevertheless, an increased quantity of material wealth may correspond to a simultaneous fall in the magnitude of its value. This antagonistic movement has its origin in the two-fold character of labour. Productive power has reference, of course, only to labour of some useful concrete form, the efficacy of any special productive activity during a given time being dependent on its productiveness. Useful labour becomes, therefore, a more or less abundant source of products, in proportion to the rise or fall of its productiveness. On the other hand, no change in this productiveness affects the labour represented by value. Since productive power is an attribute of the concrete useful forms of labour, of course it can no longer have any bearing on that labour, so soon as we make abstraction from those concrete useful forms. However then productive power may vary, the same labour, exercised during equal periods of time, always yields equal amounts of value. But it will yield, during equal periods of time, different quantities of values in use; more, if the productive power rise, fewer, if it fall. The same change in productive power, which increases the fruitfulness of labour, and, in consequence, the quantity of use-values produced by that labour, will diminish the total value of this increased quantity of use-values, provided such change shorten the total labour-time necessary for their production; and *vice versa*.

On the one hand all labour is, speaking physiologically, an expenditure of human labour power, and in its character of identical abstract human labour, it creates and forms the value of commodities. On the other hand, all labour is the expenditure of human labour power in a special form and with a definite aim, and in this, its character of concrete useful labour, it produces use-values.[15]

Section 3. The Form of Value or Exchange Value.

Commodities come into the world in the shape of use-values, articles, or goods, such as iron, linen, corn, &c. This is their plain, homely, bodily form. They are, however, commodities, only because they are something two-fold, both objects of utility, and, at the same time, depositories of value. They manifest themselves therefore as commodities, or have the form of commodities, only in so far as they have two forms, a physical or natural form, and a value form.

The reality of the value of commodities differs in this respect from Dame Quickly, that we don't know 'where to have it'. The value of commodities is the very opposite of the coarse materiality of their substance, not an atom of matter enters into its composition. Turn and examine a single commodity, by itself, as we will, yet in so far as it remains an object of value, it seems impossible to grasp it. If, however we bear in mind that the value of commodities has a purely social reality, and that they acquire this reality only in so far as they are expressions or embodiments of one identical social substance, viz., human labour, it follows as a matter of course, that value can only manifest itself in the social relation of commodity to commodity. In fact we started from exchange value, or the exchange relation of commodities, in order to get at the value that lies hidden behind it. We must now return to this form under which value first appeared to us.

Every one knows, if he knows nothing else, that commodities have a value form common to them all, and presenting a marked contrast with the varied bodily forms of their use-values. I mean their money form. Here, however, a task is set us, the performance of which has never yet even been attempted by bourgeois economy, the task of tracing the genesis of this money form, of developing the expression of value implied in the value relation of commodities, from its simplest, almost imperceptible outline, to the dazzling money form. By doing this we shall, at the same time, solve the riddle presented by money.

The simplest value relation is evidently that of one commodity to some one other commodity of a different kind. Hence the relation between the values of two commodities supplies us with the simplest expression of the value of a single commodity.

A. Elementary or Accidental Form Of Value.

x commodity A = y commodity B, or
x commodity A is worth y commodity B.
20 yards of linen = 1 coat, or
20 yards of linen are worth 1 coat.

1. The two poles of the expression of value.
Relative form and Equivalent form.

The whole mystery of the form of value lies hidden in this elementary form. Its analysis, therefore, is our real difficulty.

Here two different kinds of commodities (in our example the linen and the coat), evidently play two different parts. The linen expresses its value in the coat; the coat serves as the material in which that value is expressed. The former plays an active, the latter a passive, part. The value of the linen is represented as relative value, or appears in relative form. The coat officiates as equivalent, or appears in equivalent form.

The relative form and the equivalent form are two intimately connected, mutually dependent and inseparable elements of the expression of value; but, at the same time, are mutually exclusive, antagonistic extremes – i.e., poles of the same expression. They are allotted respectively to the two different commodities brought into relation by that expression. It is not possible to express the value of linen in linen. 20 yards of linen = 20 yards of linen is no expression of value. On the contrary, such an equation merely says that 20 yards of linen are nothing else than 20 yards of linen, a definite quantity of the use-value linen. The value of the linen can therefore be expressed only relatively – i.e., in some other commodity. The relative form of the value of the linen presupposes, therefore, the presence of some other commodity – here the coat – under the form of an equivalent. On the other hand, the commodity that figures as the equivalent cannot at the same time assume the relative form. That second commodity is not the one whose value is expressed. Its function is merely to serve as the material in which the value of the first commodity is expressed.

No doubt, the expression 20 yards of linen = 1 coat, or 20 yards of linen are worth 1 coat, implies the opposite relation. 1 coat = 20 yards of linen, or 1 coat is worth 20 yards of linen. But, in that case, I must reverse the equation, in order to express the value of the coat relatively; and so soon as I do that, the linen becomes the equivalent instead of the coat. A single commodity cannot, therefore, simultaneously assume, in the same expression of value, both forms. The very polarity of these forms makes them mutually exclusive.

Whether, then, a commodity assumes the relative form, or the opposite equivalent form, depends entirely upon its accidental position in the expression of value – that is, upon whether it is the commodity whose value is being expressed or the commodity in which value is being expressed.

2. The Relative Form of Value:
(a) The Nature and Import of this Form.

In order to discover how the elementary expression of the value of a commodity lies hidden in the value relation of two commodities, we must, in the first place, consider the latter entirely apart from its quantitative aspect. The usual mode of procedure is generally the reverse, and in the value relation nothing is seen but the proportion between definite quantities of two different sorts of commodities that are considered equal to each other. It is apt to be forgotten that the magnitudes of different things can be compared quantitatively, only when those magnitudes are expressed in terms of the same unit. It is only as expressions of such a unit that they are of the same denomination, and therefore commensurable.[16]

Whether 20 yards of linen = 1 coat or = 20 coats or = x coats – that is, whether a given quantity of linen is worth few or many coats, every such statement implies that the linen and coats, as magnitudes of value, are expressions of the same unit, things of the same kind. Linen = coat is the basis of the equation.

But the two commodities whose identity of quality is thus assumed, do not play the same part. It is only the value of the linen that is expressed. And how? By its reference to the coat as its equivalent, as something that can be exchanged for it. In this relation the coat is the mode of existence of value, is value embodied, for only as such is it the same as the linen. On the other hand, the linen's own value comes to the front, receives independent expression, for it is only as being value that it is comparable with the coat as a thing of equal value, or exchangeable with the coat. To borrow an illustration from chemistry, butyric acid is a different substance from propyl formate. Yet both are made up of the same chemical substances, carbon (C), hydrogen (H), and oxygen (O), and that, too, in like proportions – namely, $C_4H_8O_2$. If now we equate butyric acid to propyl formate, then, in the first place, propyl formate would be, in this relation, merely a form of existence of $C_4H_8O_2$; and in the second place, we should be stating that butyric acid also consists of $C_4H_8O_2$. Therefore, by thus equating the two substances, expression would be given to their chemical composition, while their different physical forms would be neglected.

If we say that, as values, commodities are mere congelations of human labour, we reduce them by our analysis, it is true, to the abstraction, value; but we ascribe to this value no form apart from their bodily form. It is otherwise in the value relation of one commodity to another. Here, the one stands forth in its character of value by reason of its relation to the other.

By making the coat the equivalent of the linen, we equate the labour embodied in the former to that in the latter. Now, it is true that the tailoring, which makes the coat, is concrete labour of a different sort from the weaving which makes the linen. But the act of equating it to the weaving, reduces the tailoring to that which is really equal in the two kinds of labour, to their common character of human labour. In this roundabout way, then, the fact is expressed, that weaving also, in so far as it weaves value, has nothing to distinguish it from tailoring, and, consequently, is abstract human labour. It is the expression of equivalence between different sorts of commodities that alone brings into relief the specific character of value-creating labour, and this it does by actually reducing the different varieties of labour embodied in the different kinds of commodities to their common quality of human labour in the abstract.[17]

There is, however, something else required beyond the expression of the specific character of the labour of which the value of the linen consists. Human labour power in motion, or human labour, creates value, but is not itself value. It becomes value only in its congealed state, when embodied in the form of some object. In order to express the value of the linen as a congelation of human labour, that value must be expressed as having objective existence, as being a something materially different from the linen itself, and yet a something common to the linen and all other commodities. The problem is already solved.

When occupying the position of equivalent in the equation of value, the coat ranks qualitatively as the equal of the linen, as something of the same kind, because it is value. In this position it is a thing in which we see nothing but value, or whose palpable bodily form represents value. Yet the coat itself, the body of the commodity, coat, is a mere use-value. A coat as such no more tells us it is value, than does the first piece of linen we take hold of. This shows that when placed in value relation to the linen, the coat signifies more than when out of that relation, just as many a man strutting about in a gorgeous uniform counts for more than when in mufti.

In the production of the coat, human labour power, in the shape of tailoring, must have been actually expended. Human labour is therefore accumulated in it. In this aspect the coat is a depository of value, but though worn to a thread, it does not let this fact show through. And as equivalent of the linen in the value equation, it exists under this aspect alone, counts therefore as embodied value, as a body that is value. A, for instance, cannot be 'your majesty' to B, unless at the same time majesty in B's eyes assumes the bodily form of A, and, what is more, with every new father of the people, changes its features, hair, and many other things besides.

Hence, in the value equation, in which the coat is the equivalent of the linen, the coat officiates as the form of value. The value of the commodity linen is expressed by the bodily form of the commodity coat, the value of one by the use-value of the other. As a use-value, the linen is something palpably different from the coat; as value, it is the same as the coat, and now has the appearance of a coat. Thus the linen acquires a value form different from its physical form. The fact that it is value, is made manifest by its equality with the coat, just as the sheep's nature of a Christian is shown in his resemblance to the Lamb of God.

We see, then, all that our analysis of the value of commodities has already told us, is told us by the linen itself, so soon as it comes into communication with another commodity, the coat. Only it betrays its thoughts in that language with which alone it is familiar, the language of commodities. In order to tell us that its own value is created by labour in its abstract character of human labour, it says that the coat, in so far as it is worth as much as the linen, and therefore is value, consists of the same labour as the linen. In order to inform us that its sublime reality as value is not the same as its buckram body, it says that value has the appearance of a coat, and consequently that so far as the linen is value, it and the coat are as like as two peas. We may here remark, that the language of commodities has, besides Hebrew, many other more or less correct dialects. The German '*wertsein*', to be worth, for instance, expresses in a less striking manner than the Romance verbs '*valere*', '*valer*', '*valoir*', that the equating of commodity B to commodity A, is commodity A's own mode of expressing its value. *Paris vaut bien une messe.*

By means, therefore, of the value relation expressed in our equation, the bodily form of commodity B becomes the value form of commodity A, or the body of commodity B acts as a mirror to the value of commodity A.[18] By putting itself in relation with commodity B, as value in *propriâ personâ*, as the matter of which human labour is made up, the commodity A converts the value in use, B, into the substance in which to express its, A's, own value. The value of A, thus expressed in the use-value of B, has taken the form of relative value.

(b) Quantitative Determination of Relative Value.

Every commodity, whose value it is intended to express, is a useful object of given quantity, as 15 bushels of corn, or 100 lbs. of coffee. And a given quantity of any commodity contains a definite quantity of human labour. The value form must therefore not only express value generally, but also value in definite quantity. Therefore, in the value relation of commodity A to commodity B, of the linen to the coat, not only is the latter, as value in general, made the equal in quality of the linen, but a definite quantity of coat (1 coat) is made the equivalent of a definite quantity (20 yards) of linen.

The equation, 20 yards of linen = 1 coat, or 20 yards of linen are worth one coat, implies that the same quantity of value-substance (congealed labour) is embodied in both; that the two commodities have each cost the same amount of labour of the same quantity of labour-time. But the labour time necessary for the production of 20 yards of linen or 1 coat varies with every change in the productiveness of weaving or tailoring. We have now to consider the influence of such changes on the quantitative aspect of the relative expression of value.

I. Let the value of the linen vary,[19] that of the coat remaining constant. If, say in consequence of the exhaustion of flax-growing soil, the labour-time necessary for the production of the linen be doubled, the value of the linen will also be doubled. Instead of the equation, 20 yards of linen = 1 coat, we should have 20 yards of linen = 2 coats, since 1 coat would now contain only half the labour-time embodied in 20 yards of linen. If, on the other hand, in consequence, say, of improved looms, this labour-time be reduced by one-half, the value of the linen would fall by one-half. Consequently, we should have 20 yards of linen = 1/2 coat. The relative value of commodity A, i.e., its value expressed in commodity B, rises and falls directly as the value of A, the value of B being supposed constant.

II. Let the value of the linen remain constant, while the value of the coat varies. If, under these circumstances, in consequence, for instance, of a poor crop of wool, the labour-time necessary for the production of a coat becomes doubled, we have instead of 20 yards of linen = 1 coat, 20 yards of linen = 1/2 coat. If, on the other hand, the value of the coat sinks by one-half, then 20 yards of linen = 2 coats. Hence, if the value of commodity A remain constant, its relative value expressed in commodity B rises and falls inversely as the value of B.

If we compare the different cases in I and II, we see that the same change of magnitude in relative value may arise from totally opposite causes. Thus, the equation, 20 yards of linen = 1 coat, becomes 20 yards of linen = 2 coats, either, because the value of the linen has doubled, or because the value of the coat has fallen by one-half; and it becomes 20 yards of linen = 1/2 coat, either because the value of the linen has fallen by one-half, or because the value of the coat has doubled.

III. Let the quantities of labour-time respectively necessary for the production of the linen and the coat vary simultaneously in the same direction and in the same proportion. In this case 20 yards of linen continue equal to 1 coat, however much their values may have altered. Their change of value is seen as soon as they are compared with a third commodity, whose value has remained constant. If the values of all commodities rose or fell simultaneously, and in the same proportion, their relative values would remain unaltered. Their real change of value would appear from the diminished or increased quantity of commodities produced in a given time.

IV. The labour-time respectively necessary for the production of the linen and the coat, and therefore the value of these commodities, may simultaneously vary in the same direction, but at unequal rates or in opposite directions, or in other ways. The effect of all these possible different variations, on the relative value of a commodity, may be deduced from the results of I, II, and III.

Thus real changes in the magnitude of value are neither unequivocally nor exhaustively reflected in their relative expression, that is, in the equation expressing the magnitude of relative value. The relative value of a commodity may vary, although its value remains constant. Its relative value may remain constant, although its value varies; and finally, simultaneous variations in the magnitude of value and in that of its relative expression by no means necessarily correspond in amount.[20]

3. The Equivalent Form of Value.

We have seen that commodity A (the linen), by expressing its value in the use-value of a commodity differing in kind (the coat), at the same time impresses upon the latter a specific form of value, namely that of the equivalent. The commodity linen manifests its quality of having a value by the fact that the coat, without having assumed a value form different from its bodily form, is equated to the linen. The fact that the latter therefore has a value is expressed by saying that the coat is directly exchangeable with it. Therefore, when we say that a commodity is in the equivalent form, we express the fact that it is directly exchangeable with other commodities.

When one commodity, such as a coat, serves as the equivalent of another, such as linen, and coats consequently acquire the characteristic property of being directly exchangeable with linen, we are far from knowing in what proportion the two are exchangeable. The value of the linen being given in magnitude, that proportion depends on the value of the coat. Whether the coat serves as the equivalent and the linen as relative value, or the linen as the equivalent and the coat as relative value, the magnitude of the coat's value is determined, independently of its value form, by the labour time necessary for its production. But whenever the coat assumes in the equation of value, the position of equivalent, its value acquires no quantitative expression; on the contrary, the commodity coat now figures only as a definite quantity of some article.

For instance, 40 yards of linen are worth – what? 2 coats. Because the commodity coat here plays the part of equivalent, because the use-value coat, as opposed to the linen, figures as an embodiment of value, therefore a definite number of coats suffices to express the definite quantity of value in the linen. Two coats may therefore express the quantity of value of 40 yards of linen, but they can never express the quantity of their own value. A superficial observation of this fact, namely, that in the equation of value, the equivalent figures exclusively as a simple quantity of some article, of some use-value, has misled Bailey, as also many others, both before and after him, into seeing, in the expression of value, merely a quantitative relation. The truth being, that when a commodity acts as equivalent, no quantitative determination of its value is expressed.

The first peculiarity that strikes us, in considering the form of the equivalent, is this: use-value becomes the form of manifestation, the phenomenal form of its opposite, value.

The bodily form of the commodity becomes its value form. But, mark well, that this *quid pro quo* exists in the case of any commodity B, only when some other commodity A enters into a value relation with it, and then only within the limits of this relation. Since no commodity can stand in the relation of equivalent to itself, and thus turn its own bodily shape into the expression of its own value, every commodity is compelled to choose some other commodity for its equivalent, and to accept the use-value, that is to say, the bodily shape of that other commodity as the form of its own value.

One of the measures that we apply to commodities as material substances, as use-values, will serve to illustrate this point. A sugar-loaf being a body, is heavy, and therefore has weight: but we can neither see nor touch this weight. We then take various pieces of iron, whose weight has been determined beforehand. The iron, as iron, is no more the form of manifestation of weight, than is the sugar-loaf. Nevertheless, in order to express the sugar-loaf as so much weight, we put it into a weight-relation with the iron. In this relation, the iron officiates as a body representing nothing but weight. A certain quantity of iron therefore serves as the measure of the weight of the sugar, and represents, in relation to the sugar-loaf, weight embodied, the form of manifestation of weight. This part is played by the iron only within this relation, into which the sugar or any other body, whose weight has to be determined, enters with the iron. Were they not both heavy, they could not enter into this relation, and the one could therefore not serve as the expression of the weight of the other. When we throw both into the scales, we see in reality, that as weight they are both the same, and that, therefore, when taken in proper proportions, they have the same weight. Just as the substance iron, as a measure of weight, represents in relation to the sugar-loaf weight alone, so, in our expression of value, the material object, coat, in relation to the linen, represents value alone.

Here, however, the analogy ceases. The iron, in the expression of the weight of the sugar-loaf, represents a natural property common to both bodies, namely their weight; but the coat, in the expression of value of the linen, represents a non-natural property of both, something purely social, namely, their value.

Since the relative form of value of a commodity – the linen, for example – expresses the value of that commodity, as being something wholly different from its substance and properties, as being, for instance, coat-like, we see that this expression itself indicates that some social relation lies at the bottom of it. With the equivalent form it is just the contrary. The very essence of this form is that the material commodity itself – the coat – just as it is, expresses value, and is endowed with the form of value by Nature itself. Of course this holds good only so long as the value relation exists, in which the coat stands in the position of equivalent to the linen.[21] Since, however, the properties of a thing are not the result of its relations to other things, but only manifest themselves in such relations, the coat seems to be endowed with its equivalent form, its property of being directly exchangeable, just as much by Nature as it is endowed with the property of being heavy, or the capacity to keep us warm. Hence the enigmatical character of the equivalent form which escapes the notice of the bourgeois political economist, until this form, completely developed, confronts him in the shape of money. He then seeks to explain away the mystical character of gold and silver, by substituting for them less dazzling commodities, and by reciting, with ever renewed satisfaction, the catalogue of all possible commodities which at one time or another have played the part of equivalent. He has not the least suspicion that the most simple expression of value, such as 20 yds. of linen = 1 coat, already propounds the riddle of the equivalent form for our solution.

The body of the commodity that serves as the equivalent, figures as the materialisation of human labour in the abstract, and is at the same time the product of some specifically useful concrete labour. This concrete labour becomes, therefore, the medium for expressing abstract human labour. If on the one hand the coat ranks as nothing but the embodiment of abstract human labour, so, on the other hand, the tailoring which is actually embodied in it, counts as nothing but the form under which that abstract labour is realised. In the expression of value of the linen, the utility of the tailoring consists, not in making clothes, but in making an object, which we at once recognise to be Value, and therefore to be a congelation of labour, but of labour indistinguishable from that realised in the value of the linen. In order to act as such a mirror of value, the labour of tailoring must reflect nothing besides its own abstract quality of being human labour generally.

In tailoring, as well as in weaving, human labour power is expended. Both, therefore, possess the general property of being human labour, and may, therefore, in certain cases, such as in the production of value, have to be considered under this aspect alone. There is nothing mysterious in this. But in the expression of value there is a complete turn of the tables. For instance, how is the fact to be expressed that weaving creates the value of the linen, not by virtue of being weaving, as such, but by reason of its general property of being human labour? Simply by opposing to weaving that other particular form of concrete labour (in this instance tailoring), which produces the equivalent of the product of weaving. Just as the coat in its bodily form became a direct expression of value, so now does tailoring, a concrete form of labour, appear as the direct and palpable embodiment of human labour generally.

Hence, the second peculiarity of the equivalent form is, that concrete labour becomes the form under which its opposite, abstract human labour, manifests itself.

But because this concrete labour, tailoring in our case, ranks as, and is directly identified with, undifferentiated human labour, it also ranks as identical with any other sort of labour, and therefore with that embodied in the linen. Consequently, although, like all other commodity-producing labour, it is the labour of private individuals, yet, at the same time, it ranks as labour directly social in its character. This is the reason why it results in a product directly exchangeable with other commodities. We have then a third peculiarity of the equivalent form, namely, that the labour of private individuals takes the form of its opposite, labour directly social in its form.

The two latter peculiarities of the equivalent form will become more intelligible if we go back to the great thinker who was the first to analyse so many forms, whether of thought, society, or Nature, and amongst them also the form of value. I mean Aristotle.

In the first place, he clearly enunciates that the money form of commodities is only the further development of the simple form of value – i.e., of the expression of the value of one commodity in some other commodity taken at random; for he says –

> 5 beds = 1 house (*klinai pente anti oikias*) is not to be distinguished from
> 5 beds = so much money (*klinai pente anti . . . hosou hai pente klinai*)

He further sees that the value relation which gives rise to this expression makes it necessary that the house should qualitatively be made the equal of the bed, and that, without such an equalisation, these two clearly different things could not be compared with each other as commensurable quantities. 'Exchange,' he says, 'cannot take place without equality, and equality not without commensurability'. (*out' isotes me ouses summetrias*). Here, however, he comes to a stop, and gives up the further analysis of the form of value. 'It is, however, in reality, impossible (*tei men aletheiai adunaton*), that such unlike things can be commensurable' – i.e., qualitatively equal. Such an equalisation can only be something foreign to their real nature, consequently only 'a makeshift for practical purposes'.

Aristotle therefore, himself, tells us, what barred the way to his further analysis; it was the absence of any concept of value. What is that equal something, that common substance, which admits of the value of the beds being expressed by a house? Such a thing, in truth, cannot exist, says Aristotle. And why not? Compared with the beds, the house does represent something equal to them, in so far as it represents what is really equal, both in the beds and the house. And that is – human labour.

There was, however, an important fact which prevented Aristotle from seeing that to attribute value to commodities, is merely a mode of expressing all labour as equal human labour, and consequently as labour of equal quality. Greek society was founded upon slavery, and had, therefore, for its natural basis, the inequality of men and of their labour powers. The secret of the expression of value, namely, that all kinds of labour are equal and equivalent, because, and so far as, they are human labour in general, cannot be deciphered, until the notion of human equality has already acquired the fixity of a popular prejudice. This, however, is possible only in a society in which the great mass of the produce of labour takes the form of commodities, in which, consequently, the dominant relation between man and man, is that of owners of commodities. The brilliancy of Aristotle's genius is shown by this alone, that he discovered, in the expression of the value of commodities, a relation of equality. The peculiar conditions of the society in which he lived, alone prevented him from discovering what, 'in truth', was at the bottom of this equality.

4. The Elementary Form of Value considered as a whole.

The elementary form of value of a commodity is contained in the equation, expressing its value relation to another commodity of a different kind, or in its exchange-relation to the-same. The value of commodity A is qualitatively expressed by the fact that commodity B is directly exchangeable with it. Its value is quantitatively expressed by the fact, that a definite quantity of B is exchangeable with a definite quantity of A. In other words, the value of a commodity obtains independent and definite expression, by taking the form of exchange value. When, at the beginning of this chapter, we said, in common parlance, that a commodity is both a use-value and an exchange value, we were, accurately speaking, wrong. A commodity is a use-value or object of utility, and a value. It manifests itself as this two-fold thing, that it is, as soon as its value assumes an independent form – viz., the form of exchange value. It never assumes this form when isolated, but only when placed in a value or exchange relation with another commodity of a different kind. When once we know this, such a mode of expression does no harm; it simply serves as an abbreviation.

Our analysis has shown, that the form or expression of the value of a commodity originates in the nature of value, and not that value and its magnitude originate in the mode of their expression as exchange value. This, however, is the delusion as well of the mercantilists and their recent revivers, Ferrier, Ganilh,[22] and others, as also of their antipodes, the modern bagmen of Free-trade, such as Bastiat. The mercantilists lay special stress on the qualitative aspect of the expression of value, and consequently on the equivalent form of commodities, which attains its full perfection in money. The modern hawkers of Free-trade, who must get rid of their article at any price, on the other hand, lay most stress on the quantitative aspect of the relative form of value. For them there consequently exists neither value, nor magnitude of value, anywhere except in its expression by means of the exchange relation of commodities, that is, in the daily list of prices current. Macleod, who has taken upon himself to dress up the confused ideas of Lombard Street in the most learned finery, is a successful cross between the superstitious mercantilists, and the enlightened Free-trade bagmen.

A close scrutiny of the expression of the value of A in terms of B, contained in the equation expressing the value relation of A to B, has shown us that, within that relation, the bodily form of A figures only as a use-value, the bodily form of B only as the form or aspect of value. The opposition or contrast existing internally in each commodity between use-value and value, is, therefore, made evident externally by two commodities being placed in such relation to each other, that the commodity whose value it is sought to express, figures directly as a mere use-value, while the commodity in which that value is to be expressed, figures directly as mere exchange value. Hence the elementary form of value of a commodity is the elementary form in which the contrast contained in that commodity, between use-value and value, becomes apparent.

Every product of labour is, in all states of society, a use-value; but it is only at a definite historical epoch in a society's development that such a product becomes a commodity, viz., at the epoch when the labour spent on the production of a useful article becomes expressed as one of the objective qualities of that article, i.e., as its value. It therefore follows that the elementary value form is also the primitive form under which a product of labour appears historically as a commodity, and that the gradual transformation of such products into commodities, proceeds pari passu with the development of the value form.

We perceive, at first sight, the deficiencies of the elementary form of value: it is a mere germ, which must undergo a series of metamorphoses before it can ripen into the price-form.

The expression of the value of commodity A in terms of any other commodity B, merely distinguishes the value from the use-value of A, and therefore places A merely in a relation of exchange with a single different commodity, B; but it is still far from expressing A's qualitative equality, and quantitative proportionality, to all commodities. To the elementary relative value form of a commodity, there corresponds the single equivalent form of one other commodity. Thus, in the relative expression of value of the linen, the coat assumes the form of equivalent, or of being directly exchangeable, only in relation to a single commodity, the linen.

Nevertheless, the elementary form of value passes by an easy transition into a more complete form. It is true that by means of the elementary form, the value of a commodity A, becomes expressed in terms of one, and only one, other commodity. But that one may be a commodity of any kind, coat, iron, corn, or anything else. Therefore, according as A is placed in relation with one or the other, we get for one and the same commodity, different elementary expressions of value.[23] The number of such possible expressions is limited only by the number of the different kinds of commodities distinct from it. The isolated expression of A's value, is therefore convertible into a series, prolonged to any length, of the different elementary expressions of that value.

B. Total or Expanded Form of Value.

z Com. A = u Com. B or = v Com. C
or = w Com. D or = x Com. E or = &c.

(20 byards of linen=1 coat or=10 lb tea or=40 lb coffee or=1 quarter corn or=2 ounces gold or=1/2 ton iron or=&c.)

1. The Expanded Relative Form of Value.

The value of a single commodity, the linen, for example, is now expressed in terms of numberless other elements of the world of commodities. Every other commodity now becomes a mirror of the linen's value.[24] It is thus, that for the first time, this value shows itself in its true light as a congelation of undifferentiated human labour. For the labour that creates it, now stands expressly revealed, as labour that ranks equally with every other sort of human labour, no matter what its form, whether tailoring, ploughing, mining, &c., and no matter, therefore, whether it is realised in coats, corn, iron, or gold. The linen, by virtue of the form of its value, now stands in a social relation, no longer with only one other kind of commodity, but with the whole world of commodities. As a commodity, it is a citizen of that world. At the same time, the interminable series of value equations implies, that as regards the value of a commodity, it is a matter of indifference under what particular form, or kind, of use-value it appears.

In the first form, 20 yds. of linen = 1 coat, it might, for aught that otherwise appears, be pure accident, that these two commodities are exchangeable in definite quantities. In the second form, on the contrary, we perceive at once the background that determines, and is essentially different from, this accidental appearance. The value of the linen remains unaltered in magnitude, whether expressed in coats, coffee, or iron, or in numberless different commodities, the property of as many different owners. The accidental relation between two individual commodity-owners disappears. It becomes plain, that it is not the exchange of commodities which regulates the magnitude of their value; but, on the contrary, that it is the magnitude of their value which controls their exchange proportions.

2. The particular Equivalent Form.

Each commodity, such as, coat, tea, corn, iron, &c., figures in the expression of value of the linen, as an equivalent, and, consequently, as a thing that is value. The bodily form of each of these commodities figures now as a particular equivalent form, one out of many. In the same way the manifold concrete useful kinds of labour, embodied in these different commodities, rank now as so many different forms of the realisation, or manifestation, of undifferentiated human labour.

3. Defects of the Total or Expanded Form of Value.

In the first place, the relative expression of value is incomplete because the series representing it is interminable. The chain of which each equation of value is a link, is liable at any moment to be lengthened by each new kind of commodity that comes into existence and furnishes the material for a fresh expression of value. In the second place, it is a many-coloured mosaic of disparate and independent expressions of value. And lastly, if, as must be the case, the relative value of each commodity in turn, becomes expressed in this expanded form, we get for each of them a relative value form, different in every case, and consisting of an interminable series of expressions of value. The defects of the expanded relative value form are reflected in the corresponding equivalent form. Since the bodily form of each single commodity is one particular equivalent form amongst numberless others, we have, on the whole, nothing but fragmentary equivalent forms, each excluding the others. In the same way, also, the special, concrete, useful kind of labour embodied in each particular equivalent, is presented only as a particular kind of labour, and therefore not as an exhaustive representative of human labour generally. The latter, indeed, gains adequate manifestation in the totality of its manifold, particular, concrete forms. But, in that case, its expression in an infinite series is ever incomplete and deficient in unity.

The expanded relative value form is, however, nothing but the sum of the elementary relative expressions or equations of the first kind, such as:

20 yards of linen = 1 coat
20 yards of linen = 10 lbs. of tea, etc.

Each of these implies the corresponding inverted equation,

1 coat = 20 yards of linen
10 lbs. of tea = 20 yards of linen, etc.

In fact, when a person exchanges his linen for many other commodities, and thus expresses its value in a series of other commodities, it necessarily follows, that the various owners of the latter exchange them for the linen, and consequently express the value of their various commodities in one and the same third commodity, the linen. If then, we reverse the series, 20 yards of linen = 1 coat or = 10 lbs. of tea, etc., that is to say, if we give expression to the converse relation already implied in the series, we get,

C. The General Form of Value.

1 coat/10 lbs. of tea/40 lbs. of coffee/1 quarter of corn/2 ounces of gold/1/2 a ton of iron/x com. A., etc = 20 yards of linen

1. The altered character of the Form of Value.

All commodities now express their value (1) in an elementary form, because in a single commodity; (2) with unity, because in one and the same commodity. This form of value is elementary and the same for all, therefore general.

The forms A and B were fit only to express the value of a commodity as something distinct from its use-value or material form.

The first-form, A, furnishes such equations as the following: – 1 coat = 20 yards of linen, 10 lbs. of tea = 1/2 ton of iron. The value of the coat is equated to linen, that of the tea to iron. But to be equated to linen, and again to iron, is to be as different as are linen and iron.

This form, it is plain, occurs practically only in the first beginning, when the products of labour are converted into commodities by accidental and occasional exchanges.

The second form, B, distinguishes, in a more adequate manner than the first, the value of a commodity from its use-value, for the value of the coat is there placed in contrast under all possible shapes with the bodily form of the coat; it is equated to linen, to iron, to tea, in short, to everything else, only not to itself, the coat. On the other hand, any general expression of value common to all is directly excluded; for, in the equation of value of each commodity, all other commodities now appear only under the form of equivalents. The expanded form of value comes into actual existence for the first time so soon as a particular product of labour, such as cattle, is no longer exceptionally, but habitually, exchanged for various other commodities.

The third and lastly developed form expresses the values of the whole world of commodities in terms of a single commodity set apart for the purpose, namely, the linen, and thus represents to us their values by means of their equality with linen. The value of every commodity is now, by being equated to linen, not only differentiated from its own use-value, but from all other use-values generally, and is, by that very fact, expressed as that which is common to all commodities. By this form, commodities are, for the first time, effectively brought into relation with one another as values, or made to appear as exchange values.

The two earlier forms either express the value of each commodity in terms of a single commodity of a different kind, or in a series of many such commodities. In both cases, it is, so to say, the special business of each single commodity to find an expression for its value, and this it does without the help of the others. These others, with respect to the former, play the passive parts of equivalents. The general form of value, C, results from the joint action of the whole world of commodities, and from that alone. A commodity can acquire a general expression of its value only by all other commodities, simultaneously with it, expressing their values in the same equivalent; and every new commodity must follow suit. It thus becomes evident that since the existence of commodities as values is purely social, this social existence can be expressed by the totality of their social relations alone, and consequently that the form of their value must be a socially recognised form.

All commodities being equated to linen now appear not only as qualitatively equal as values generally, but also as values whose magnitudes are capable of comparison. By expressing the magnitudes of their values in one and the same material, the linen, those magnitudes are also compared with each other For instance, 10 Ibs. of tea = 20 yards of linen, and 40 lbs. of coffee = 20 yards of linen. Therefore, 10 Ibs of tea = 40 Ibs. of coffee. In other words, there is contained in 1 lb. of coffee only one-fourth as much substance of value – labour – as is contained in 1 lb. of tea.

The general form of relative value, embracing the whole world of commodities, converts the single commodity that is excluded from the rest, and made to play the part of equivalent – here the linen – into the universal equivalent. The bodily form of the linen is now the form assumed in common by the values of all commodities; it therefore becomes directly exchangeable with all and every one of them. The substance linen becomes the visible incarnation, the social chrysalis state of every kind of human labour. Weaving, which is the labour of certain private individuals producing a particular article, linen, acquires in consequence a social character, the character of equality with all other kinds of labour. The innumerable equations of which the general form of value is composed, equate in turn the labour embodied in the linen to that embodied in every other commodity, and they thus convert weaving into the general form of manifestation of undifferentiated human labour. In this manner the labour realised in the values of commodities is presented not only under its negative aspect, under which abstraction is made from every concrete form and useful property of actual work, but its own positive nature is made to reveal itself expressly. The general value form is the reduction of all kinds of actual labour to their common character of being human labour generally, of being the expenditure of human labour power.

The general value form, which represents all products of labour as mere congelations of undifferentiated human labour, shows by its very structure that it is the social *résumé* of the world of commodities. That form consequently makes it indisputably evident that in the world of commodities the character possessed by all labour of being human labour constitutes its specific social character.

2. The Interdependent Development of the Relative Form of Value, and of the Equivalent Form.

The degree of development of the relative form of value corresponds to that of the equivalent form. But we must bear in mind that the development of the latter is only the expression and result of the development of the former.

The primary or isolated relative form of value of one commodity converts some other commodity into an isolated equivalent. The expanded form of relative value, which is the expression of the value of one commodity in terms of all other commodities, endows those other commodities with the character of particular equivalents differing in kind. And lastly, a particular kind of commodity acquires the character of universal equivalent, because all other commodities make it the material in which they uniformly express their value.

The antagonism between the relative form of value and the equivalent form, the two poles of the value form, is developed concurrently with that form itself.

The first form, 20 yds. of linen = one coat, already contains this antagonism, without as yet fixing it. According as we read this equation forwards or backwards, the parts played by the linen and the coat are different. In the one case the relative value of the linen is expressed in the coat, in the other case the relative value of the coat is expressed in the linen. In this first form of value, therefore, it is difficult to grasp the polar contrast.

Form B shows that only one single commodity at a time can completely expand its relative value, and that it acquires this expanded form only because, and in so far as, all other commodities are, with respect to it, equivalents. Here we cannot reverse the equation, as we can the equation 20 yds. of linen = 1 coat, without altering its general character, and converting it from the expanded form of value into the general form of value.

Finally, the form C gives to the world of commodities a general social relative form of value, because, and in so far as, thereby all commodities, with the exception of one, are excluded from the equivalent form. A single commodity, the linen, appears therefore to have acquired the character of direct exchangeability with every other commodity because, and in so far as, this character is denied to every other commodity.[25]

The commodity that figures as universal equivalent, is, on the other hand, excluded from the relative value form. If the linen, or any other commodity serving as universal equivalent, were, at the same time, to share in the relative form of value, it would have to serve as its own equivalent. We should then have 20 yds. of linen = 20 yds. of linen; this tautology expresses neither value, nor magnitude of value. In order to express the relative value of the universal equivalent, we must rather reverse the form C. This equivalent has no relative form of value in common with other commodities, but its value is relatively expressed by a never ending series of other commodities. Thus, the expanded form of relative value, or form B, now shows itself as the specific form of relative value for the equivalent commodity.

3. Transition from the General Form of Value to the Money Form.

The universal equivalent form is a form of value in general. It can, therefore, be assumed by any commodity. On the other hand, if a commodity be found to have assumed the universal equivalent form (form C), this is only because and in so far as it has been excluded from the rest of all other commodities as their equivalent, and that by their own act. And from the moment that this exclusion becomes finally restricted to one particular commodity, from that moment only, the general form of relative value of the world of commodities obtains real consistence and general social validity.

The particular commodity, with whose bodily form the equivalent form is thus socially identified, now becomes the money-commodity, or serves as money. It becomes the special social function of that commodity, and consequently its social monopoly, to play within the world of commodities the part of the universal equivalent. Amongst the commodities which, in form B, figure as particular equivalents of the linen, and, in form C, express in common their relative values in linen, this foremost place has been attained by one in particular – namely, gold. If, then, in form C we replace the linen by gold, we get,

D. The Money Form.

20 yards of linen/1 coat/10 lb of tea/40 lb of coffee/1 qr. of corn/
1/2 a ton of iron/x commodity A = 2 ounces of gold

In passing from form A to form B, and from the latter to form C, the changes are fundamental. On the other hand, there is no difference between forms C and D, except that, in the latter, gold has assumed the equivalent form in the place of linen. Gold is in form D, what linen was in form C – the universal equivalent. The progress consists in this alone, that the character of direct and universal exchange-ability – in other words, that the universal equivalent form – has now, by social custom, become finally identified with the substance, gold.

Gold is now money with reference to all other commodities only because it was previously, with reference to them, a simple commodity. Like all other commodities, it was also capable of serving as an equivalent, either as simple equivalent in isolated exchanges, or as particular equivalent by the side of others. Gradually it began to serve, within varying limits, as universal equivalent. So soon as it monopolises this position in the expression of value for the world of commodities, it becomes the money commodity, and then, and not till then, does form D become distinct from form C, and the general form of value become changed into the money form.

The elementary expression of the relative value of a single commodity, such as linen, in terms of the commodity, such as gold, that plays the part of money, is the price-form of that commodity. The price-form of the linen is therefore

> 20 yards of linen = 2 ounces of gold, or, if 2 ounces of gold when coined are £2, 20 yards of linen = £2.

The difficulty in forming a concept of the money form, consists in clearly comprehending the universal equivalent form, and as a necessary corollary, the general form of value, form C. The latter is deducible from form B, the expanded form of value, the essential component element of which, we saw, is form A, 20 yards of linen = 1 coat or x commodity A = y commodity B. The simple commodity-form is therefore the germ of the money form.

Section 4. The Fetishism of Commodities and the Secret Thereof.

A commodity appears, at first sight, a very trivial thing, and easily understood. Its analysis shows that it is, in reality, a very queer thing, abounding in metaphysical subtleties and theological niceties. So far as it is a value in use, there is nothing mysterious about it, whether we consider it from the point of view that by its properties it is capable of satisfying human wants, or from the point that those properties are the product of human labour. It is as clear as noon-day, that man, by his industry, changes the forms of the materials furnished by Nature, in such a way as to make them useful to him. The form of wood, for instance, is altered, by making a table out of it. Yet, for all that, the table continues to be that common, every-day thing, wood. But, so soon as it steps forth as a commodity, it is changed into something transcendent. It not only stands with its feet on the ground, but, in relation to all other commodities, it stands on its head, and evolves out of its wooden brain grotesque ideas, far more wonderful than 'table-turning' ever was.

The mystical character of commodities does not originate, therefore, in their use-value. Just as little does it proceed from the nature of the determining factors of value. For, in the first place, however varied the useful kinds of labour, or productive activities, may be, it is a physiological fact, that they are functions of the human organism, and that each such function, whatever may be its nature or form, is essentially the expenditure of human brain, nerves, muscles, &c. Secondly, with regard to that which forms the ground-work for the quantitative determination of value, namely, the duration of that expenditure, or the quantity of labour, it is quite clear that there is a palpable difference between its quantity and quality. In all states of society, the labour-time that it costs to produce the means of subsistence, must necessarily be an object of interest to mankind, though not of equal interest in different stages of development. [26] And lastly, from the moment that men in any way work for one another, their labour assumes a social form.

Whence, then, arises the enigmatical character of the product of labour, so soon as it assumes the form of commodities? Clearly from this form itself. The equality of all sorts of human labour is expressed objectively by their products all being equally values; the measure of the expenditure of labour power by the duration of that expenditure, takes the form of the quantity of value of the products of labour; and finally the mutual relations of the producers, within which the social character of their labour affirms itself, take the form of a social relation between the products.

A commodity is therefore a mysterious thing, simply because in it the social character of men's labour appears to them as an objective character stamped upon the product of that labour; because the relation of the producers to the sum total of their own labour is presented to them as a social relation, existing not between themselves, but between the products of their labour. This is the reason why the products of labour become commodities, social things whose qualities are at the same time perceptible and imperceptible by the senses. In the same way the light from an object is perceived by us not as the subjective excitation of our optic nerve, but as the objective form of something outside the eye itself. But, in the act of seeing, there is at all events, an actual passage of light from one thing to another, from the external object to the eye. There is a physical relation between physical things. But it is different with commodities. There, the existence of the things *qua* commodities, and the value relation between the products of labour which stamps them as commodities, have absolutely no connection with their physical properties and with the material relations arising therefrom. There it is a definite social relation between men, that assumes, in their eyes, the fantastic form of a relation between things. In order, therefore, to find an analogy, we must have recourse to the mist-enveloped regions of the religious world. In that world the productions of the human brain appear as independent beings endowed with life, and entering into relation both with one another and the human race. So it is in the world of commodities with the products of men's hands. This I call the Fetishism which attaches itself to the products of labour, so soon as they are produced as commodities, and which is therefore inseparable from the production of commodities.

This Fetishism of commodities has its origin, as the foregoing analysis has already shown, in the peculiar social character of the labour that produces them.

As a general rule, articles of utility become commodities, only because they are products of the labour of private individuals or groups of individuals who carry on their work independently of each other. The sum total of the labour of all these private individuals forms the aggregate labour of society. Since the producers do not come into social contact with each other until they exchange their products, the specific social character of each producer's labour does not show itself except in the act of exchange. In other words, the labour of the individual asserts itself as a part of the labour of society, only by means of the relations which the act of exchange establishes directly between the products, and indirectly, through them, between the producers. To the latter, therefore, the relations connecting the labour of one individual with that of the rest appear, not as direct social relations between individuals at work, but as what they really are, material relations between persons and social relations between things. It is only by being exchanged that the products of labour acquire, as values, one uniform social status, distinct from their varied forms of existence as objects of utility. This division of a product into a useful thing and a value becomes practically important, only when exchange has acquired such an extension that useful articles are produced for the purpose of being exchanged, and their character as values has therefore to be taken into account, beforehand, during production. From this moment the labour of the individual producer acquires socially a two-fold character. On the one hand, it must, as a definite useful kind of labour, satisfy a definite social want, and thus hold its place as part and parcel of the collective labour of all, as a branch of a social division of labour that has sprung up spontaneously. On the other hand, it can satisfy the manifold wants of the individual producer himself, only in so far as the mutual exchangeability of all kinds of useful private labour is an established social fact, and therefore the private useful labour of each producer ranks on an equality with that of all others. The equalisation of the most different kinds of labour can be the result only of an abstraction from their inequalities, or of reducing them to their common denominator, viz. expenditure of human labour power or human labour in the abstract. The two-fold social character of the labour of the individual appears to him, when reflected in his brain, only under those forms which are impressed upon that labour in every-day practice by the exchange of products. In this way, the character that his own labour possesses of being socially useful takes the form of the condition, that the product must be not only useful, but useful for others, and the social character that his particular labour has of being the equal of all other particular kinds of labour, takes the form that all the physically different articles that are the products of labour, have one common quality, viz., that of having value.

Hence, when we bring the products of our labour into relation with each other as values, it is not because we see in these articles the material receptacles of homogeneous human labour. Quite the contrary: whenever, by an exchange, we equate as values our different products, by that very act, we also equate, as human labour, the different kinds of labour expended upon them. We are not aware of this, nevertheless we do it.[27] Value, therefore, does not stalk about with a label describing what it is. It is value, rather, that converts every product into a social hieroglyphic. Later on, we try to decipher the hieroglyphic, to get behind the secret of our own social products; for to stamp an object of utility as a value, is just as much a social product as language. The recent scientific discovery, that the products of labour, so far as they are values, are but material expressions of the human labour spent in their production, marks, indeed, an epoch in the history of the development of the human race, but by no means dissipates the mist through which the social character of labour appears to us to be an objective character of the products themselves. The fact, that in the particular form of production with which we are dealing, viz., the production of commodities, the specific social character of private labour carried on independently, consists in the equality of every kind of that labour, by virtue of its being human labour, which character, therefore, assumes in the product the form of value – this fact appears to the producers, notwithstanding the discovery above referred to, to be just as real and final, as the fact, that, after the discovery by science of the component gases of air, the atmosphere itself remained unaltered.

What, first of all, practically concerns producers when they make an exchange, is the question, how much of some other product they get for their own? in what proportions the products are exchangeable? When these proportions have, by custom, attained a certain stability, they appear to result from the nature of the products, so that, for instance, one ton of iron and two ounces of gold appear as naturally to be of equal value as a pound of gold and a pound of iron in spite of their different physical and chemical qualities appear to be of equal weight. The character of having value, when once impressed upon products, obtains fixity only by reason of their acting and re-acting upon each other as quantities of value. These quantities vary continually, independently of the will, foresight and action of the producers. To them, their own social action takes the form of the action of objects, which rule the producers instead of being ruled by them. It requires a fully developed production of commodities before, from accumulated experience alone, the scientific conviction springs up, that all the different kinds of private labour, which are carried on independently of each other, and yet as spontaneously developed branches of the social division of labour, are continually being reduced to the quantitative proportions in which society requires them. And why? Because, in the midst of all the accidental and ever fluctuating exchange-relations between the products, the labour-time socially necessary for their production forcibly asserts itself like an over-riding law of Nature. The law of gravity thus asserts itself when a house falls about our ears.[28] The determination of the magnitude of value by labour-time is therefore a secret, hidden under the apparent fluctuations in the relative values of commodities. Its discovery, while removing all appearance of mere accidentality from the determination of the magnitude of the values of products, yet in no way alters the mode in which that determination takes place.

Man's reflections on the forms of social life, and consequently, also, his scientific analysis of those forms, take a course directly opposite to that of their actual historical development. He begins, *post festum*, with the results of the process of development ready to hand before him. The characters that stamp products as commodities, and whose establishment is a necessary preliminary to the circulation of commodities, have already acquired the stability of natural, self-understood forms of social life, before man seeks to decipher, not their historical character, for in his eyes they are immutable, but their meaning. Consequently it was the analysis of the prices of commodities that alone led to the determination of the magnitude of value, and it was the common expression of all commodities in money that alone led to the establishment of their characters as values. It is, however, just this ultimate money form of the world of commodities that actually conceals, instead of disclosing, the social character of private labour, and the social relations between the individual producers. When I state that coats or boots stand in a relation to linen, because it is the universal incarnation of abstract human labour, the absurdity of the statement is self-evident. Nevertheless, when the producers of coats and boots compare those articles with linen, or, what is the same thing, with gold or silver, as the universal equivalent, they express the relation between their own private labour and the collective labour of society in the same absurd form.

The categories of bourgeois economy consist of such like forms. They are forms of thought expressing with social validity the conditions and relations of a definite, historically determined mode of production, viz., the production of commodities. The whole mystery of commodities, all the magic and necromancy that surrounds the products of labour as long as they take the form of commodities, vanishes therefore, so soon as we come to other forms of production.

Since Robinson Crusoe's experiences are a favourite theme with political economists,[29] let us take a look at him on his island. Moderate though he be, yet some few wants he has to satisfy, and must therefore do a little useful work of various sorts, such as making tools and furniture, taming goats, fishing and hunting. Of his prayers and the like we take no account, since they are a source of pleasure to him, and he looks upon them as so much recreation. In spite of the variety of his work, he knows that his labour, whatever its form, is but the activity of one and the same Robinson, and consequently, that it consists of nothing but different modes of human labour. Necessity itself compels him to apportion his time accurately between his different kinds of work. Whether one kind occupies a greater space in his general activity than another, depends on the difficulties, greater or less as the case may be, to be overcome in attaining the useful effect aimed at. This our friend Robinson soon learns by experience, and having rescued a watch, ledger, and pen and ink from the wreck, commences, like a true-born Briton, to keep a set of books. His stock-book contains a list of the objects of utility that belong to him, of the operations necessary for their production; and lastly, of the labour-time that definite quantities of those objects have, on an average, cost him. All the relations between Robinson and the objects that form this wealth of his own creation, are here so simple and clear as to be intelligible without exertion, even to Mr Sedley Taylor. And yet those relations contain all that is essential to the determination of value.

Let us now transport ourselves from Robinson's island bathed in light to the European middle ages shrouded in darkness. Here, instead of the independent man, we find everyone dependent, serfs and lords, vassals and suzerains, laymen and clergy. Personal dependence here characterises the social relations of production just as much as it does the other spheres of life organised on the basis of that production. But for the very reason that personal dependence forms the ground-work of society, there is no necessity for labour and its products to assume a fantastic form different from their reality. They take the shape, in the transactions of society, of services in kind and payments in kind. Here the particular and natural form of labour, and not, as in a society based on production of commodities, its general abstract form is the immediate social form of labour. Compulsory labour is just as properly measured by time, as commodity-producing labour; but every serf knows that what he expends in the service of his lord, is a definite quantity of his own personal labour power. The tithe to be rendered to the priest is more matter of fact than his blessing. No matter, then, what we may think of the parts played by the different classes of people themselves in this society, the social relations between individuals in the performance of their labour, appear at all events as their own mutual personal relations, and are not disguised under the shape of social relations between the products of labour.

For an example of labour in common or directly associated labour, we have no occasion to go back to that spontaneously developed form which we find on the threshold of the history of all civilised races.[30] We have one close at hand in the patriarchal industries of a peasant family, that produces corn, cattle, yarn, linen, and clothing for home use. These different articles are, as regards the family, so many products of its labour, but as between themselves, they are not commodities. The different kinds of labour, such as tillage, cattle tending, spinning, weaving and making clothes, which result in the various products, are in themselves, and such as they are, direct social functions, because functions of the family, which, just as much as a society based on the production of commodities, possesses a spontaneously developed system of division of labour. The distribution of the work within the family, and the regulation of the labour-time of the several members, depend as well upon differences of age and sex as upon natural conditions varying with the seasons. The labour power of each individual, by its very nature, operates in this case merely as a definite portion of the whole labour power of the family, and therefore, the measure of the expenditure of individual labour power by its duration, appears here by its very nature as a social character of their labour.

Let us now picture to ourselves, by way of change, a community of free individuals, carrying on their work with the means of production in common, in which the labour power of all the different individuals is consciously applied as the combined labour power of the community. All the characteristics of Robinson's labour are here repeated, but with this difference, that they are social, instead of individual. Everything produced by him was exclusively the result of his own personal labour, and therefore simply an object of use for himself. The total product of our community is a social product. One portion serves as fresh means of production and remains social. But another portion is consumed by the members as means of subsistence. A distribution of this portion amongst them is consequently necessary. The mode of this distribution will vary with the productive organisation of the community, and the degree of historical development attained by the producers. We will assume, but merely for the sake of a parallel with the production of commodities, that the share of each individual producer in the means of subsistence is determined by his labour-time. Labour-time would, in that case, play a double part. Its apportionment in accordance with a definite social plan maintains the proper proportion between the different kinds of work to be done and the various wants of the community. On the other hand, it also serves as a measure of the portion of the common labour borne by each individual, and of his share in the part of the total product destined for individual consumption. The social relations of the individual producers, with regard both to their labour and to its products, are in this case perfectly simple and intelligible, and that with regard not only to production but also to distribution.

The religious world is but the reflex of the real world. And for a society based upon the production of commodities, in which the producers in general enter into social relations with one another by treating their products as commodities and values, whereby they reduce their individual private labour to the standard of homogeneous human labour for such a society, Christianity with its *cultus* of abstract man, more especially in its bourgeois developments, Protestantism, Deism, &c., is the most fitting form of religion. In the ancient Asiatic and other ancient modes of production, we find that the conversion of products into commodities, and therefore the conversion of men into producers of commodities, holds a subordinate place, which, however, increases in importance as the primitive communities approach nearer and nearer to their dissolution. Trading nations, properly so called, exist in the ancient world only in its interstices, like the gods of Epicurus in the Intermundia, or like Jews in the pores of Polish society. Those ancient social organisms of production are, as compared with bourgeois society, extremely simple and transparent. But they are founded either on the immature development of man individually, who has not yet severed the umbilical cord that unites him with his fellow-men in a primitive tribal community, or upon direct relations of subjection. They can arise and exist only when the development of the productive power of labour has not risen beyond a low stage, and when, therefore, the social relations within the sphere of material life, between man and man, and between man and Nature, are correspondingly narrow. This narrowness is reflected in the ancient worship of Nature, and in the other elements of the popular religions. The religious reflex of the real world can, in any case, only then finally vanish, when the practical relations of every-day life offer to man none but perfectly intelligible and reasonable relations with regard to his fellow-men and to Nature.

The life-process of society, which is based on the process of material production, does not strip off its mystical veil until it is treated as production by freely associated men, and is consciously regulated by them in accordance with a settled plan. This, however, demands for society a certain material ground-work or set of conditions of existence which in their turn are the spontaneous product of a long and painful process of development.

Political Economy has indeed analysed, however incompletely,[31] value and its magnitude, and has discovered what lies beneath these forms. But it has never once asked the question why labour is represented by the value of its product and labour-time by the magnitude of that value.[32] These formulae, which bear it stamped upon them in unmistakable letters that they belong to a state of society, in which the process of production has the mastery over man, instead of being controlled by him, such formulae appear to the bourgeois intellect to be as much a self-evident necessity imposed by Nature as productive labour itself. Hence forms of social production that preceded the bourgeois form, are treated by the bourgeoisie in much the same way as the Fathers of the Church treated pre-Christian religions.[33]

To what extent some economists are misled by the Fetishism inherent in commodities, or by the objective appearance of the social characteristics of labour, is shown, amongst other ways, by the dull and tedious quarrel over the part played by Nature in the formation of exchange value. Since exchange value is a definite social manner of expressing the amount of labour bestowed upon an object, Nature has no more to do with it, than it has in fixing the course of exchange.

The mode of production in which the product takes the form of a commodity, or is produced directly for exchange, is the most general and most embryonic form of bourgeois production. It therefore makes its appearance at an early date in history, though not in the same predominating and characteristic manner as nowadays. Hence its Fetish character is comparatively easy to be seen through. But when we come to more concrete forms, even this appearance of simplicity vanishes. Whence arose the illusions of the monetary system? To it gold and silver, when serving as money, did not represent a social relation between producers, but were natural objects with strange social properties. And modern economy, which looks down with such disdain on the monetary system, does not its superstition come out as clear as noon-day, whenever it treats of capital? How long is it since economy discarded the physiocratic illusion, that rents grow out of the soil and not out of society?

But not to anticipate, we will content ourselves with yet another example relating to the commodity-form. Could commodities themselves speak, they would say: Our use-value may be a thing that interests men. It is no part of us as objects. What, however, does belong to us as objects, is our value. Our natural intercourse as commodities proves it. In the eyes of each other we are nothing but exchange values. Now listen how those commodities speak through the mouth of the economist. 'Value' – (i.e., exchange value) 'is a property of things, riches' – (i.e., use-value) 'of man. Value, in this sense, necessarily implies exchanges, riches do not.'[34] 'Riches' (use-value) 'are the attribute of men, value is the attribute of commodities. A man or a community is rich, a pearl or a diamond is valuable . . . A pearl or a diamond is valuable' as a pearl or a diamond.[35] So far no chemist has ever discovered exchange value either in a pearl or a diamond. The economic discoverers of this chemical element, who by-the-by lay special claim to critical acumen, find however that the use-value of objects belongs to them independently of their material properties, while their value, on the other hand, forms a part of them as objects. What confirms them in this view, is the peculiar circumstance that the use-value of objects is realised without exchange, by means of a direct relation between the objects and man, while, on the other hand, their value is realised only by exchange, that is, by means of a social process. Who fails here to call to mind our good friend, Dogberry, who informs neighbour Seacoal, that, 'To be a well-favoured man is the gift of fortune; but reading and writing comes by Nature.'[36]

Chapter 2
Exchange

It is plain that commodities cannot go to market and make exchanges of their own account. We must, therefore, have recourse to their guardians, who are also their owners. Commodities are things, and therefore without power of resistance against man. If they are wanting in docility he can use force; in other words, he can take possession of them.[1] In order that these objects may enter into relation with each other as commodities, their guardians must place themselves in relation to one another, as persons whose will resides in those objects, and must behave in such a way that each does not appropriate the commodity of the other, and part with his own, except by means of an act done by mutual consent. They must therefore, mutually recognise in each other the rights of private proprietors. This juridical relation, which thus expresses itself in a contract, whether such contract be part of a developed legal system or not, is a relation between two wills, and is but the reflex of the real economic relation between the two. It is this economic relation that determines the subject-matter comprised in each such juridical act.[2]

The persons exist for one another merely as representatives of, and therefore as owners of, commodities. In the course of our investigation we shall find, in general, that the characters who appear on the economic stage are but the personifications of the economic relations that exist between them.

What chiefly distinguishes a commodity from its owner is the fact, that it looks upon every other commodity as but the form of appearance of its own value. A born leveller and a cynic, it is always ready to exchange not only soul, but body, with any and every other commodity, be the same more repulsive than Maritornes herself. The owner makes up for this lack in the commodity of a sense of the concrete, by his own five and more senses. His commodity possesses for himself no immediate use-value. Otherwise, he would not bring it to the market. It has use-value for others; but for himself its only direct use-value is that of being a depository of exchange value, and, consequently, a means of exchange.[3] Therefore, he makes up his mind to part with it for commodities whose value in use is of service to him. All commodities are non-use-values for their owners, and use-values for their non-owners. Consequently, they must all change hands. But this change of hands is what constitutes their exchange, and the latter puts them in relation with each other as values, and realises them as values. Hence commodities must be realised as values before they can be realised as use-values.

On the other hand, they must show that they are use-values before they can be realised as values. For the labour spent upon them counts effectively, only in so far as it is spent in a form that is useful for others. Whether that labour is useful for others, and its product consequently capable of satisfying the wants of others, can be proved only by the act of exchange.

Every owner of a commodity wishes to part with it in exchange only for those commodities whose use-value satisfies some want of his. Looked at in this way, exchange is for him simply a private transaction. On the other hand, he desires to realise the value of his commodity, to convert it into any other suitable commodity of equal value, irrespective of whether his own commodity has or has not any use-value for the owner of the other. From this point of view, exchange is for him a social transaction of a general character. But one and the same set of transactions cannot be simultaneously for all owners of commodities both exclusively private and exclusively social and general.

Let us look at the matter a little closer. To the owner of a commodity, every other commodity is, in regard to his own, a particular equivalent, and consequently his own commodity is the universal equivalent for all the others. But since this applies to every owner, there is, in fact, no commodity acting as universal equivalent, and the relative value of commodities possesses no general form under which they can be equated as values and have the magnitude of their values compared. So far, therefore, they do not confront each other as commodities, but only as products or use-values. In their difficulties our commodity owners think like Faust: '*Im Anfang war die That.*' They therefore acted and transacted before they thought. Instinctively they conform to the laws imposed by the nature of commodities. They cannot bring their commodities into relation as values, and therefore as commodities, except by comparing them with some one other commodity as the universal equivalent. That we saw from the analysis of a commodity. But a particular commodity cannot become the universal equivalent except by a social act. The social action therefore of all other commodities, sets apart the particular commodity in which they all represent their values. Thereby the bodily form of this commodity becomes the form of the socially recognised universal equivalent. To be the universal equivalent becomes, by this social process, the specific function of the commodity thus excluded by the rest. Thus it becomes — money. '*Illi unum consilium habent et virtutem et potestatem suam bestiae tradunt. Et ne quis possit emere aut vendere, nisi qui habet characterem aut nomen bestiae, aut numerum nominis ejus.*' (*Apocalypse*)

Money is a crystal formed of necessity in the course of the exchanges, whereby different products of labour are practically equated to one another and thus by practice converted into commodities. The historical progress and extension of exchanges develops the contrast, latent in commodities, between use-value and value. The necessity for giving an external expression to this contrast for the purposes of commercial intercourse, urges on the establishment of an independent form of value, and finds no rest until it is once for all satisfied by the differentiation of commodities into commodities and money. At the same rate, then, as the conversion of products into commodities is being accomplished, so also is the conversion of one special commodity into money.[4]

The direct barter of products attains the elementary form of the relative expression of value in one respect, but not in another. That form is x Commodity A = y Commodity B. The form of direct barter is x use-value A = y use-value B.[5] The articles A and B in this case are not as yet commodities, but become so only by the act of barter. The first step made by an object of utility towards acquiring exchange value is when it forms a non-use-value for its owner, and that happens when it forms a superfluous portion of some article required for his immediate wants. Objects in themselves are external to man, and consequently alienable by him. In order that this alienation may be reciprocal, it is only necessary for men, by a tacit understanding, to treat each other as private owners of those alienable objects, and by implication as independent individuals. But such a state of reciprocal independence has no existence in a primitive society based on property in common, whether such a society takes the form of a patriarchal family, an ancient Indian community, or a Peruvian Inca State. The exchange of commodities, therefore, first begins on the boundaries of such communities, at their points of contact with other similar communities, or with members of the latter. So soon, however, as products once become commodities in the external relations of a community, they also, by reaction, become so in its internal intercourse. The proportions in which they are exchangeable are at first quite a matter of chance. What makes them exchangeable is the mutual desire of their owners to alienate them. Meantime the need for foreign objects of utility gradually establishes itself. The constant repetition of exchange makes it a normal social act. In the course of time, therefore, some portion at least of the products of labour must be produced with a special view to exchange. From that moment the distinction becomes firmly established between the utility of an object for the purposes of consumption, and its utility for the purposes of exchange. Its use-value becomes distinguished from its exchange value. On the other hand, the quantitative proportion in which the articles are exchangeable, becomes dependent on their production itself. Custom stamps them as values with definite magnitudes.

In the direct barter of products, each commodity is directly a means of exchange to its owner, and to all other persons an equivalent, but that only in so far as it has use-value for them. At this stage, therefore, the articles exchanged do not acquire a value form independent of their own use-value, or of the individual needs of the exchangers. The necessity for a value form grows with the increasing number and variety of the commodities exchanged. The problem and the means of solution arise simultaneously. Commodity-owners never equate their own commodities to those of others, and exchange them on a large scale, without different kinds of commodities belonging to different owners being exchangeable for, and equated as values to, one and the same special article. Such last-mentioned article, by becoming the equivalent of various other commodities, acquires at once, though within narrow limits, the character of a general social equivalent. This character comes and goes with the momentary social acts that called it into life. In turns and transiently it attaches itself first to this and then to that commodity. But with the development of exchange it fixes itself firmly and exclusively to particular sorts of commodities, and becomes crystallised by assuming the money form. The particular kind of commodity to which it sticks is at first a matter of accident. Nevertheless there are two circumstances whose influence is decisive. The money form attaches itself either to the most important articles of exchange from outside, and these in fact are primitive and natural forms in which the exchange value of home products finds expression; or else it attaches itself to the object of utility that forms, like cattle, the chief portion of indigenous alienable wealth. Nomad races are the first to develop the money form, because all their worldly goods consist of moveable objects and are therefore directly alienable; and because their mode of life, by continually bringing them into contact with foreign communities, solicits the exchange of products. Man has often made man himself, under the form of slaves, serve as the primitive material of money, but has never used land for that purpose. Such an idea could only spring up in a bourgeois society already well developed. It dates from the last third of the 17th century, and the first attempt to put it in practice on a national scale was made a century afterwards, during the French bourgeois revolution.

In proportion as exchange bursts its local bonds, and the value of commodities more and more expands into an embodiment of human labour in the abstract, in the same proportion the character of money attaches itself to commodities that are by nature fitted to perform the social function of a universal equivalent. Those commodities are the precious metals.

The truth of the proposition that, 'although gold and silver are not by Nature money, money is by nature gold and silver,'[6] is shown by the fitness of the physical properties of these metals for the functions of money.[7] Up to this point, however, we are acquainted only with one function of money, namely, to serve as the form of manifestation of the value of commodities, or as the material in which the magnitudes of their values are socially expressed. An adequate form of manifestation of value, a fit embodiment of abstract, undifferentiated, and therefore equal human labour, that material alone can be whose every sample exhibits the same uniform qualities. On the other hand, since the difference between the magnitudes of value is purely quantitative, the money commodity must be susceptible of merely quantitative differences, must therefore be divisible at will, and equally capable of being reunited. Gold and silver possess these properties by nature.

The use-value of the money-commodity becomes two-fold. In addition to its special use-value as a commodity (gold, for instance, serving to stop teeth, to form the raw material of articles of luxury, &c.), it acquires a formal use-value, originating in its specific social function.

Since all commodities are merely particular equivalents of money, the latter being their universal equivalent, they, with regard to the latter as the universal commodity, play the parts of particular commodities.[8]

We have seen that the money form is but the reflex, thrown upon one single commodity, of the value relations between all the rest. That money is a commodity[9] is therefore a new discovery only for those who, when they analyse it, start from its fully developed shape. The act of exchange gives to the commodity converted into money, not its value, but its specific value form. By confounding these two distinct things some writers have been led to hold that the value of gold and silver is imaginary.[10] The fact that money can, in certain functions, be replaced by mere symbols of itself, gave rise to that other mistaken notion, that it is itself a mere symbol. Nevertheless under this error lurked a presentiment that the money form of an object is not an inseparable part of that object, but is simply the form under which certain social relations manifest themselves. In this sense every commodity is a symbol, since, in so far as it is value, it is only the material envelope of the human labour spent upon it.[11] But if it be declared that the social characters assumed by objects, or the material forms assumed by the social qualities of labour under the régime of a definite mode of production, are mere symbols, it is in the same breath also declared that these characteristics are arbitrary fictions sanctioned by the so-called universal consent of mankind. This suited the mode of explanation in favour during the 18th century. Unable to account for the origin of the puzzling forms assumed by social relations between man and man, people sought to denude them of their strange appearance by ascribing to them a conventional origin.

It has already been remarked above that the equivalent form of a commodity does not imply the determination of the magnitude of its value. Therefore, although we may be aware that gold is money, and consequently directly exchangeable for all other commodities, yet that fact by no means tells how much 10 lbs., for instance, of gold is worth. Money, like every other commodity, cannot express the magnitude of its value except relatively in other commodities. This value is determined by the labour-time required for its production, and is expressed by the quantity of any other commodity that costs the same amount of labour-time.[12] Such quantitative determination of its relative value takes place at the source of its production by means of barter. When it steps into circulation as money, its value is already given. In the last decades of the 17th century it had already been shown that money is a commodity, but this step marks only the infancy of the analysis. The difficulty lies, not in comprehending that money is a commodity, but in discovering how, why, and by what means a commodity becomes money.[13]

We have already seen, from the most elementary expression of value, x commodity A = y commodity B, that the object in which the magnitude of the value of another object is represented, appears to have the equivalent form independently of this relation, as a social property given to it by Nature. We followed up this false appearance to its final establishment, which is complete so soon as the universal equivalent form becomes identified with the bodily form of a particular commodity, and thus crystallised into the money form. What appears to happen is, not that gold becomes money, in consequence of all other commodities expressing their values in it, but, on the contrary, that all other commodities universally express their values in gold, because it is money. The intermediate steps of the process vanish in the result and leave no trace behind. Commodities find their own value already completely represented, without any initiative on their part, in another commodity existing in company with them. These objects, gold and silver, just as they come out of the bowels of the earth, are forthwith the direct incarnation of all human labour. Hence the magic of money. In the form of society now under consideration, the behaviour of men in the social process of production is purely atomic. Hence their relations to each other in production assume a material character independent of their control and conscious individual action. These facts manifest themselves at first by products as a general rule taking the form of commodities. We have seen how the progressive development of a society of commodity-producers stamps one privileged commodity with the character of money. Hence the riddle presented by money is but the riddle presented by commodities; only it now strikes us in its most glaring form.

Chapter 3
Money, or the Circulation of Commodities

Section 1. *The Measure of Values.*

Throughout this work, I assume, for the sake of simplicity, gold as the money-commodity.

The first chief function of money is to supply commodities with the material for the expression of their values, or to represent their values as magnitudes of the same denomination, qualitatively equal, and quantitatively comparable. It thus serves as a *universal measure of value.* And only by virtue of this function does gold, the equivalent commodity *par excellence*, become money.

It is not money that renders commodities commensurable. Just the contrary. It is because all commodities, as values, are realised human labour, and therefore commensurable, that their values can be measured by one and the same special commodity, and the latter be converted into the common measure of their values, i.e., into money. Money as a measure of value, is the phenomenal form that must of necessity be assumed by that measure of value which is immanent in commodities, labour-time.[1]

The expression of the value of a commodity in gold — x commodity A = y money-commodity — is its money form or price. A single equation, such as 1 ton of iron = 2 ounces of gold, now suffices to express the value of the iron in a socially valid manner. There is no longer any need for this equation to figure as a link in the chain of equations that express the values of all other commodities, because the equivalent commodity, gold, now has the character of money. The general form of relative value has resumed its original shape of simple or isolated relative value. On the other hand, the expanded expression of relative value, the endless series of equations, has now become the form peculiar to the relative value of the money-commodity. The series itself, too, is now given, and has social recognition in the prices of actual commodities. We have only to read the quotations of a price-list backwards, to find the magnitude of the value of money expressed in all sorts of commodities. But money itself has no price. In order to put it on an equal footing with all other commodities in this respect, we should be obliged to equate it to itself as its own equivalent.

The price or money form of commodities is, like their form of value generally, a form quite distinct from their palpable bodily form; it is, therefore, a purely ideal or mental form. Although invisible, the value of iron, linen and corn has actual existence in these very articles: it is ideally made perceptible by their equality with gold, a relation that, so to say, exists only in their own heads. Their owner must, therefore, lend them his tongue, or hang a ticket on them, before their prices can be communicated to the outside world.[2] Since the expression of the value of commodities in gold is a merely ideal act, we may use for this purpose imaginary or ideal money. Every trader knows, that he is far from having turned his goods into money, when he has expressed their value in a price or in imaginary money, and that it does not require the least bit of real gold, to estimate in that metal millions of pounds' worth of goods. When, therefore, money serves as a measure of value, it is employed only as imaginary or ideal money. This circumstance has given rise to the wildest theories.[3] But, although the money that performs the functions of a measure of value is only ideal money, price depends entirely upon the actual substance that is money. The value, or in other words, the quantity of human labour contained in a ton of iron, is expressed in imagination by such a quantity of the money-commodity as contains the same amount of labour as the iron. According, therefore, as the measure of value is gold, silver, or copper, the value of the ton of iron will be expressed by very different prices, or will be represented by very different quantities of those metals respectively.

If, therefore, two different commodities, such as gold and silver, are simultaneously measures of value, all commodities have two prices – one a gold-price, the other a silver-price. These exist quietly side by side, so long as the ratio of the value of silver to that of gold remains unchanged, say, at 15:1. Every change in their ratio disturbs the ratio which exists between the gold-prices and the silver-prices of commodities, and thus proves, by facts, that a double standard of value is inconsistent with the functions of a standard.[4]

Commodities with definite prices present themselves under the form: a commodity A = x gold; b commodity B = z gold; c commodity C = y gold, &c., where a, b, c, represent definite quantities of the commodities A; B, C and x, z, y, definite quantities of gold. The values of these commodities are, therefore, changed in imagination into so many different quantities of gold. Hence, in spite of the confusing variety of the commodities themselves, their values become magnitudes of the same denomination, gold-magnitudes. They are now capable of being compared with each other and measured, and the want becomes technically felt of comparing them with some fixed quantity of gold as a unit measure. This unit, by subsequent division into aliquot parts, becomes itself the standard or scale. Before they become money, gold, silver, and copper already possess such standard measures in their standards of weight, so that, for example, a pound weight, while serving as the unit, is, on the one hand, divisible into ounces, and, on the other, may be combined to make up hundred-weights.[5] It is owing to this that, in all metallic currencies, the names given to the standards of money or of price were originally taken from the pre-existing names of the standards of weight.

As *measure of value*, and as *standard of price*, money has two entirely distinct functions to perform. It is the measure of value inasmuch as it is the socially recognised incarnation of human labour; it is the standard of price inasmuch as it is a fixed weight of metal. As the measure of value it serves to convert the values of all the manifold commodities into prices, into imaginary quantities of gold; as the standard of price it measures those quantities of gold. The measure of values measures commodities considered as values; the standard of price measures, on the contrary, quantities of gold by a unit quantity of gold, not the value of one quantity of gold by the weight of another. In order to make gold a standard of price, a certain weight must be fixed upon as the unit. In this case, as in all cases of measuring quantities of the same denomination, the establishment of an unvarying unit of measure is all-important. Hence, the less the unit is subject to variation, so much the better does the standard of price fulfil its office. But only in so far as it is itself a product of labour, and, therefore, potentially variable in value, can gold serve as a measure of value.[6]

It is, in the first place, quite clear that a change in the value of gold does not, in any way, affect its function as a standard of price. No matter how this value varies, the proportions between the values of different quantities of the metal remain constant. However great the fall in its value, 12 ounces of gold still have 12 times the value of 1 ounce; and in prices, the only thing considered is the relation between different quantities of gold. Since, on the other hand, no rise or fall in the value of an ounce of gold can alter its weight, no alteration can take place in the weight of its aliquot parts. Thus gold always renders the same service as an invariable standard of price, however much its value may vary.

In the second place, a change in the value of gold does not interfere with its functions as a measure of value. The change affects all commodities simultaneously, and, therefore, *ceteris paribus*, leaves their relative values inter se, unaltered, although those values are now expressed in higher or lower gold-prices.

Just as when we estimate the value of any commodity by a definite quantity of the use-value of some other commodity, so in estimating the value of the former in gold, we assume nothing more than that the production of a given quantity of gold costs, at the given period, a given amount of labour. As regards the fluctuations of prices generally, they are subject to the laws of elementary relative value investigated in a former chapter.

A general rise in the prices of commodities can result only, either from a rise in their values – the value of money remaining constant – or from a fall in the value of money, the values of commodities remaining constant. On the other hand, a general fall in prices can result only, either from a fall in the values of commodities – the value of money remaining constant – or from a rise in the value of money, the values of commodities remaining constant. It therefore by no means follows, that a rise in the value of money necessarily implies a proportional fall in the prices of commodities; or that a fall in the value of money implies a proportional rise in prices. Such change of price holds good only in the case of commodities whose value remains constant. With those, for example, whose value rises, simultaneously with, and proportionally to, that of money, there is no alteration in price. And if their value rise either slower or faster than that of money, the fall or rise in their prices will be determined by the difference between the change in their value and that of money; and so on.

Let us now go back to the consideration of the price-form.

By degrees there arises a discrepancy between the current money-names of the various weights of the precious metal figuring as money, and the actual weights which those names originally represented. This discrepancy is the result of historical causes, among which the chief are: (1) The importation of foreign money into an imperfectly developed community. This happened in Rome in its early days, where gold and silver coins circulated at first as foreign commodities. The names of these foreign coins never coincide with those of the indigenous weights. (2) As wealth increases, the less precious metal is thrust out by the more precious from its place as a measure of value, copper by silver, silver by gold, however much this order of sequence may be in contradiction with poetical chronology.[7] The word pound, for instance, was the money-name given to an actual pound weight of silver. When gold replaced silver as a measure of value, the same name was applied according to the ratio between the values of silver and gold, to perhaps 1/15th of a pound of gold. The word pound, as a money-name, thus becomes differentiated from the same word as a weight-name.[8] (3) The debasing of money carried on for centuries by kings and princes to such an extent that, of the original weights of the coins, nothing in fact remained but the names.[9]

These historical causes convert the separation of the money-name from the weight-name into an established habit with the community. Since the standard of money is on the one hand purely conventional, and must on the other hand find general acceptance, it is in the end regulated by law. A given weight of one of the precious metals, an ounce of gold, for instance, becomes officially divided into aliquot parts, with legally bestowed names, such as pound, dollar, &c. These aliquot parts, which thenceforth serve as units of money, are then subdivided into other aliquot parts with legal names, such as shilling, penny, &c.[10] But, both before and after these divisions are made, a definite weight of metal is the standard of metallic money. The sole alteration consists in the subdivision and denomination.

The prices, or quantities of gold, into which the values of commodities are ideally changed, are therefore now expressed in the names of coins, or in the legally valid names of the subdivisions of the gold standard. Hence, instead of saying: A quarter of wheat is worth an ounce of gold; we say, it is worth £3 17s. 10 1/2d. In this way commodities express by their prices how much they are worth, and money serves as *money of account* whenever it is a question of fixing the value of an article in its money form.[11]

The name of a thing is something distinct from the qualities of that thing. I know nothing of a man, by knowing that his name is Jacob. In the same way with regard to money, every trace of a value relation disappears in the names pound, dollar, franc, ducat, &c. The confusion caused by attributing a hidden meaning to these cabalistic signs is all the greater, because these money-names express both the values of commodities, and, at the same time, aliquot parts of the weight of the metal that is the standard of money.[12] On the other hand, it is absolutely necessary that value, in order that it may be distinguished from the varied bodily forms of commodities, should assume this material and unmeaning, but, at the same time, purely social form.[13]

Price is the money-name of the labour realised in a commodity. Hence the expression of the equivalence of a commodity with the sum of money constituting its price, is a tautology,[14] just as in general the expression of the relative value of a commodity is a statement of the equivalence of two commodities. But although price, being the exponent of the magnitude of a commodity's value, is the exponent of its exchange-ratio with money, it does not follow that the exponent of this exchange-ratio is necessarily the exponent of the magnitude of the commodity's value. Suppose two equal quantities of socially necessary labour to be respectively represented by 1 quarter of wheat and £2 (nearly 1/2 oz. of gold), £2 is the expression in money of the magnitude of the value of the quarter of wheat, or is its price. If now circumstances allow of this price being raised to £3, or compel it to be reduced to £1, then although £1 and £3 may be too small or too great properly to express the magnitude of the wheat's value, nevertheless they are its prices, for they are, in the first place, the form under which its value appears, i.e., money; and in the second place, the exponents of its exchange-ratio with money. If the conditions of production, in other words, if the productive power of labour remain constant, the same amount of social labour-time must, both before and after the change in price, be expended in the reproduction of a quarter of wheat. This circumstance depends, neither on the will of the wheat producer, nor on that of the owners of other commodities.

Magnitude of value expresses a relation of social production, it expresses the connection that necessarily exists between a certain article and the portion of the total labour-time of society required to produce it. As soon as magnitude of value is converted into price, the above necessary relation takes the shape of a more or less accidental exchange-ratio between a single commodity and another, the money-commodity. But this exchange-ratio may express either the real magnitude of that commodity's value, or the quantity of gold deviating from that value, for which, according to circumstances, it may be parted with. The possibility, therefore, of quantitative incongruity between price and magnitude of value, or the deviation of the former from the latter, is inherent in the price-form itself. This is no defect, but, on the contrary, admirably adapts the price-form to a mode of production whose inherent laws impose themselves only as the mean of apparently lawless irregularities that compensate one another.

The price-form, however, is not only compatible with the possibility of a quantitative incongruity between magnitude of value and price, i.e., between the former and its expression in money, but it may also conceal a qualitative inconsistency, so much so, that, although money is nothing but the value form of commodities, price ceases altogether to express value. Objects that in themselves are no commodities, such as conscience, honour, &c., are capable of being offered for sale by their holders, and of thus acquiring, through their price, the form of commodities. Hence an object may have a price without having value. The price in that case is imaginary, like certain quantities in mathematics. On the other hand, the imaginary price-form may sometimes conceal either a direct or indirect real value relation; for instance, the price of uncultivated land, which is without value, because no human labour has been incorporated in it.

Price, like relative value in general, expresses the value of a commodity (e.g., a ton of iron), by stating that a given quantity of the equivalent (e.g., an ounce of gold), is directly exchangeable for iron. But it by no means states the converse, that iron is directly exchangeable for gold. In order, therefore, that a commodity may in practice act effectively as exchange value, it must quit its bodily shape, must transform itself from mere imaginary into real gold, although to the commodity such transubstantiation may be more difficult than to the Hegelian 'Concept', the transition from 'necessity' to 'freedom', or to a lobster the casting of his shell, or to Saint Jerome the putting off of the old Adam.[15] Though a commodity may, side by side with its actual form (iron, for instance), take in our imagination the form of gold, yet it cannot at one and the same time actually be both iron and gold. To fix its price, it suffices to equate it to gold in imagination. But to enable it to render to its owner the service of a universal equivalent, it must be actually replaced by gold. If the owner of the iron were to go to the owner of some other commodity offered for exchange, and were to refer him to the price of the iron as proof that it was already money, he would get the same answer as St Peter gave in heaven to Dante, when the latter recited the creed –

> *Assai bene e trascorsa*
> *D'esta moneta già la lega e'l peso,*
> *Ma dimmi se tu l'hai nella tua borsa.*

A price therefore implies both that a commodity is exchangeable for money, and also that it must be so exchanged. On the other hand, gold serves as an ideal measure of value, only because it has already, in the process of exchange, established itself as the money-commodity. Under the ideal measure of values there lurks the hard cash.

Section 2. The Medium of Circulation.

A. The Metamorphosis of Commodities.

We saw in a former chapter that the exchange of commodities implies contradictory and mutually exclusive conditions. The differentiation of commodities into commodities and money does not sweep away these inconsistencies, but develops a *modus vivendi*, a form in which they can exist side by side. This is generally the way in which real contradictions are reconciled. For instance, it is a contradiction to depict one body as constantly falling towards another, and as, at the same time, constantly flying away from it. The ellipse is a form of motion which, while allowing this contradiction to go on, at the same time reconciles it.

In so far as exchange is a process, by which commodities are transferred from hands in which they are non-use-values, to hands in which they become use-values, it is a social circulation of matter. The product of one form of useful labour replaces that of another. When once a commodity has found a resting-place, where it can serve as a use-value, it falls out of the sphere of exchange into that of consumption. But the former sphere alone interests us at present. We have, therefore, now to consider exchange from a formal point of view; to investigate the change of form or metamorphosis of commodities which effectuates the social circulation of matter.

The comprehension of this change of form is, as a rule, very imperfect. The cause of this imperfection is, apart from indistinct notions of value itself, that every change of form in a commodity results from the exchange of two commodities, an ordinary one and the money-commodity. If we keep in view the material fact alone that a commodity has been exchanged for gold, we overlook the very thing that we ought to observe – namely, what has happened to the form of the commodity. We overlook the facts that gold, when a mere commodity, is not money, and that when other commodities express their prices in gold, this gold is but the money form of those commodities themselves.

Commodities, first of all, enter into the process of exchange just as they are. The process then differentiates them into commodities and money, and thus produces an external opposition corresponding to the internal opposition inherent in them, as being at once use-values and values. Commodities as use-values now stand opposed to money as exchange value. On the other hand, both opposing sides are commodities, unities of use-value and value. But this unity of differences manifests itself at two opposite poles, and at each pole in an opposite way. Being poles they are as necessarily opposite as they are connected. On the one side of the equation we have an ordinary commodity, which is in reality a use-value. Its value is expressed only ideally in its price, by which it is equated to its opponent, the gold, as to the real embodiment of its value. On the other hand, the gold, in its metallic reality, ranks as the embodiment of value, as money. Gold, as gold, is exchange value itself. As to its use-value, that has only an ideal existence, represented by the series of expressions of relative value in which it stands face to face with all other commodities, the sum of whose uses makes up the sum of the various uses of gold. These antagonistic forms of commodities are the real forms in which the process of their exchange moves and takes place.

Let us now accompany the owner of some commodity – say, our old friend the weaver of linen – to the scene of action, the market. His 20 yards of linen has a definite price, £2. He exchanges it for the £2, and then, like a man of the good old stamp that he is, he parts with the £2 for a family Bible of the same price. The linen, which in his eyes is a mere commodity, a depository of value, he alienates in exchange for gold, which is the linen's value form, and this form he again parts with for another commodity, the Bible, which is destined to enter his house as an object of utility and of edification to its inmates. The exchange becomes an accomplished fact by two metamorphoses of opposite yet supplementary character – the conversion of the commodity into money, and the re-conversion of the money into a commodity.[16] The two phases of this metamorphosis are both of them distinct transactions of the weaver – selling, or the exchange of the commodity for money; buying, or the exchange of the money for a commodity; and, the unity of the two acts, selling in order to buy.

The result of the whole transaction, as regards the weaver, is this, that instead of being in possession of the linen, he now has the Bible; instead of his original commodity, he now possesses another of the same value but of different utility. In like manner he procures his other means of subsistence and means of production. From his point of view, the whole process effectuates nothing more than the exchange of the product of his labour for the product of some one else's, nothing more than an exchange of products.

The exchange of commodities is therefore accompanied by the following changes in their form.

$$\text{Commodity—Money—Commodity.}$$
$$\text{C———M———C.}$$

The result of the whole process is, so far as concerns the objects themselves, C—C, the exchange of one commodity for another, the circulation of materialised social labour. When this result is attained, the process is at an end.

C—M. First metamorphosis, or sale.

The leap taken by value from the body of the commodity, into the body of the gold, is, as I have elsewhere called it, the *salto mortale* of the commodity. If it falls short, then, although the commodity itself is not harmed, its owner decidedly is. The social division of labour causes his labour to be as one-sided as his wants are many-sided. This is precisely the reason why the product of his labour serves him solely as exchange value. But it cannot acquire the properties of a socially recognised universal equivalent, except by being converted into money. That money, however, is in some one else's pocket. In order to entice the money out of that pocket, our friend's commodity must, above all things, be a use-value to the owner of the money. For this, it is necessary that the labour expended upon it, be of a kind that is socially useful, of a kind that constitutes a branch of the social division of labour. But division of labour is a system of production which has grown up spontaneously and continues to grow behind the backs of the producers. The commodity to be exchanged may possibly be the product of some new kind of labour, that pretends to satisfy

newly arisen requirements, or even to give rise itself to new requirements. A particular operation, though yesterday, perhaps, forming one
out of the many operations conducted by one producer in creating
a given commodity, may today separate itself from this connection,
may establish itself as an independent branch of labour and send its
incomplete product to market as an independent commodity. The
circumstances may or may not be ripe for such a separation. Today
the product satisfies a social want. Tomorrow the article may, either
altogether or partially, be superseded by some other appropriate product. Moreover, although our weaver's labour may be a recognised
branch of the social division of labour, yet that fact is by no means
sufficient to guarantee the utility of his 20 yards of linen. If the
community's want of linen, and such a want has a limit like every
other want, should already be saturated by the products of rival
weavers, our friend's product is superfluous, redundant, and consequently useless. Although people do not look a gift-horse in the
mouth, our friend does not frequent the market for the purpose of
making presents. But suppose his product turn out a real use-value,
and thereby attracts money? The question arises, how much will it
attract? No doubt the answer is already anticipated in the price of the
article, in the exponent of the magnitude of its value. We leave out
of consideration here any accidental miscalculation of value by our
friend, a mistake that is soon rectified in the market. We suppose him
to have spent on his product only that amount of labour-time that is
on an average socially necessary. The price then, is merely the money-
name of the quantity of social labour realised in his commodity. But
without the leave, and behind the back, of our weaver, the old-
fashioned mode of weaving undergoes a change. The labour-time that
yesterday was without doubt socially necessary to the production of a
yard of linen, ceases to be so today, a fact which the owner of the
money is only too eager to prove from the prices quoted by our
friend's competitors. Unluckily for him, weavers are not few and far
between. Lastly, suppose that every piece of linen in the market
contains no more labour-time than is socially necessary. In spite of
this, all these pieces taken as a whole, may have had superfluous
labour-time spent upon them. If the market cannot stomach the
whole quantity at the normal price of 2 shillings a yard, this proves
that too great a portion of the total labour of the community has been
expended in the form of weaving. The effect is the same as if each
individual weaver had expended more labour-time upon his particular
product than is socially necessary. Here we may say, with the German
proverb: caught together, hung together. All the linen in the market
counts but as one article of commerce, of which each piece is only an

aliquot part. And as a matter of fact, the value also of each single yard is but the materialised form of the same definite and socially fixed quantity of homogeneous human labour.

We see then, commodities are in love with money, but 'the course of true love never did run smooth.' The quantitative division of labour is brought about in exactly the same spontaneous and accidental manner as its qualitative division. The owners of commodities therefore find out, that the same division of labour that turns them into independent private producers, also frees the social process of production and the relations of the individual producers to each other within that process, from all dependence on the will of those producers, and that the seeming mutual independence of the individuals is supplemented by a system of general and mutual dependence through or by means of the products.

The division of labour converts the product of labour into a commodity, and thereby makes necessary its further conversion into money. At the same time it also makes the accomplishment of this transubstantiation quite accidental. Here, however, we are only concerned with the phenomenon in its integrity, and we therefore assume its progress to be normal. Moreover, if the conversion take place at all, that is, if the commodity be not absolutely unsaleable, its metamorphosis does take place although the price realised may be abnormally above or below the value.

The seller has his commodity replaced by gold, the buyer has his gold replaced by a commodity. The fact which here stares us in the face is, that a commodity and gold, 20 yards of linen and £2, have changed hands and places, in other words, that they have been exchanged. But for what is the commodity exchanged? For the shape assumed by its own value, for the universal equivalent. And for what is the gold exchanged? For a particular form of its own use-value. Why does gold take the form of money face to face with the linen? Because the linen's price of £2, its denomination in money, has already equated the linen to gold in its character of money. A commodity strips off its original commodity-form on being alienated, i.e., on the instant its use-value actually attracts the gold, that before existed only ideally in its price. The realisation of a commodity's price, or of its ideal value form, is therefore at the same time the realisation of the ideal use-value of money; the conversion of a commodity into money, is the simultaneous conversion of money into a commodity. The apparently single process is in reality a double one. From the pole of the commodity-owner it is a sale, from the opposite pole of the money-owner, it is a purchase. In other words, a sale is a purchase, C—M is also M—C.[17]

Up to this point we have considered men in only one economic capacity, that of owners of commodities, a capacity in which they appropriate the produce of the labour of others, by alienating that of their own labour. Hence, for one commodity-owner to meet with another who has money, it is necessary, either that the product of the labour of the latter person, the buyer, should be in itself money, should be gold, the material of which money consists, or that his product should already have changed its skin and have stripped off its original form of a useful object. In order that it may play the part of money, gold must of course enter the market at some point or other. This point is to be found at the source of production of the metal, at which place gold is bartered, as the immediate product of labour, for some other product of equal value. From that moment it always represents the realised price of some commodity.[18] Apart from its exchange for other commodities at the source of its production, gold, in whose-so-ever hands it may be, is the transformed shape of some commodity alienated by its owner; it is the product of a sale or of the first metamorphosis C—M.[19] Gold, as we saw, became ideal money, or a measure of values, in consequence of all commodities measuring their values by it, and thus contrasting it ideally with their natural shape as useful objects, and making it the shape of their value. It became real money, by the general alienation of commodities, by actually changing places with their natural forms as useful objects, and thus becoming in reality the embodiment of their values. When they assume this money-shape, commodities strip off every trace of their natural use-value, and of the particular kind of labour to which they owe their creation, in order to transform themselves into the uniform, socially recognised incarnation of homogeneous human labour. We cannot tell from the mere look of a piece of money, for what particular commodity it has been exchanged. Under their money form all commodities look alike. Hence, money may be dirt, although dirt is not money. We will assume that the two gold pieces, in consideration of which our weaver has parted with his linen, are the metamorphosed shape of a quarter of wheat. The sale of the linen, C—M, is at the same time its purchase, M—C. But the sale is the first act of a process that ends with a transaction of an opposite nature, namely, the purchase of a Bible; the purchase of the linen, on the other hand, ends a movement that began with a transaction of an opposite nature, namely, with the sale of the wheat. C—M (linen—money), which is the first phase of C—M—C (linen—money—Bible), is also M—C (money—linen), the last phase of another movement C—M—C (wheat—money—linen). The first metamorphosis of one commodity, its transformation from a commodity into money, is therefore also invariably the second metamorphosis of some other commodity, the retransformation of the latter from money into a commodity.[20]

M—C, or purchase.
The second and concluding metamorphosis of a commodity

Because money is the metamorphosed shape of all other commodities, the result of their general alienation, for this reason it is alienable itself without restriction or condition. It reads all prices backwards, and thus, so to say, depicts itself in the bodies of all other commodities, which offer to it the material for the realisation of its own use-value. At the same time the prices, wooing glances cast at money by commodities, define the limits of its convertibility, by pointing to its quantity. Since every commodity, on becoming money, disappears as a commodity, it is impossible to tell from the money itself, how it got into the hands of its possessor, or what article has been changed into it. *Non olet*, from whatever source it may come. Representing on the one hand a sold commodity, it represents on the other a commodity to be bought.[21]

M—C, a purchase, is, at the same time, C—M, a sale; the concluding metamorphosis of one commodity is the first metamorphosis of another. With regard to our weaver, the life of his commodity ends with the Bible, into which he has reconverted his £2. But suppose the seller of the Bible turns the £2 set free by the weaver into brandy. M—C, the concluding phase of C—M—C (linen—money—Bible), is also C—M, the first phase of C—M—C (Bible—money—brandy). The producer of a particular commodity has that one article alone to offer; this he sells very often in large quantities, but his many and various wants compel him to split up the price realised, the sum of money set free, into numerous purchases. Hence a sale leads to many purchases of various articles. The concluding metamorphosis of a commodity thus constitutes an aggregation of first metamorphoses of various other commodities.

If we now consider the completed metamorphosis of a commodity, as a whole, it appears in the first place, that it is made up of two opposite and complementary movements, C—M and M—C. These two antithetical transmutations of a commodity are brought about by two antithetical social acts on the part of the owner, and these acts in their turn stamp the character of the economic parts played by him. As the person who makes a sale, he is a seller; as the person who makes a purchase, he is a buyer. But just as, upon every such transmutation of a commodity, its two forms, commodity-form and money form, exist simultaneously but at opposite poles, so every seller has a buyer opposed to him, and every buyer a seller. While one particular commodity is going through its two transmutations in succession, from a commodity into money and from money into another commodity, the owner of the commodity changes in succession his part from that of seller to that of buyer. These characters of seller and buyer are therefore not permanent, but attach themselves in turns to the various persons engaged in the circulation of commodities.

The complete metamorphosis of a commodity, in its simplest form, implies four extremes, and three *dramatis personae*. First, a commodity comes face to face with money; the latter is the form taken by the value of the former, and exists in all its hard reality, in the pocket of the buyer. A commodity-owner is thus brought into contact with a possessor of money. So soon, now, as the commodity has been changed into money, the money becomes its transient equivalent-form, the use-value of which equivalent-form is to be found in the bodies of other commodities. Money, the final term of the first transmutation, is at the same time the starting-point for the second. The person who is a seller in the first transaction thus becomes a buyer in the second, in which a third commodity-owner appears on the scene as a seller.[22]

The two phases, each inverse to the other, that make up the metamorphosis of a commodity constitute together a circular movement, a circuit: commodity-form, stripping off of this form, and return to the commodity-form. No doubt, the commodity appears here under two different aspects. At the starting-point it is not a use-value to its owner; at the finishing point it is. So, too, the money appears in the first phase as a solid crystal of value, a crystal into which the commodity eagerly solidifies, and in the second, dissolves into the mere transient equivalent-form destined to be replaced by a use-value.

The two metamorphoses constituting the circuit are at the same time two inverse partial metamorphoses of two other commodities. One and the same commodity, the linen, opens the series of its own metamorphoses, and completes the metamorphosis of another (the wheat). In the first phase or sale, the linen plays these two parts in its own person. But, then, changed into gold, it completes its own second and final metamorphosis, and helps at the same time to accomplish the first metamorphosis of a third commodity. Hence the circuit made by one commodity in the course of its metamorphoses is inextricably mixed up with the circuits of other commodities. The total of all the different circuits constitutes *the circulation of commodities*.

The circulation of commodities differs from the direct exchange of products (barter), not only in form, but in substance. Only consider the course of events. The weaver has, as a matter of fact, exchanged his linen for a Bible, his own commodity for that of some one else. But this is true only so far as he himself is concerned. The seller of the Bible, who prefers something to warm his inside, no more thought of exchanging his Bible for linen than our weaver knew that wheat had been exchanged for his linen. B's commodity replaces that of A, but A and B do not mutually exchange those commodities. It may, of course, happen that A and B make simultaneous purchases, the one from the other; but such exceptional transactions are by no means the necessary result of the general conditions of the circulation of commodities. We see here, on the one hand, how the exchange of commodities breaks through all local and personal bounds inseparable from direct barter, and develops the circulation of the products of social labour; and on the other hand, how it develops a whole network of social relations spontaneous in their growth and entirely beyond the control of the actors. It is only because the farmer has sold his wheat that the weaver is enabled to sell his linen, only because the weaver has sold his linen that our Hotspur is enabled to sell his Bible, and only because the latter has sold the water of everlasting life that the distiller is enabled to sell his *eau-de-vie*, and so on.

The process of circulation, therefore, does not, like direct barter of products, become extinguished upon the use-values changing places and hands. The money does not vanish on dropping out of the circuit of the metamorphosis of a given commodity. It is constantly being precipitated into new places in the arena of circulation vacated by other commodities. In the complete metamorphosis of the linen, for example, linen—money—Bible, the linen first falls out of circulation, and money steps into its place. Then the Bible falls out of circulation, and again money takes its place. When one commodity replaces another, the money-commodity always sticks to the hands of some third person.[23] Circulation sweats money from every pore.

Nothing can be more childish than the dogma, that because every sale is a purchase, and every purchase a sale, therefore the circulation of commodities necessarily implies an equilibrium of sales and purchases. If this means that the number of actual sales is equal to the number of purchases, it is mere tautology. But its real purport is to prove that every seller brings his buyer to market with him. Nothing of the kind. The sale and the purchase constitute one identical act, an exchange between a commodity-owner and an owner of money, between two persons as opposed to each other as the two poles of a magnet. They form two distinct acts, of polar and opposite characters, when performed by one single person. Hence the identity of sale and purchase implies that the commodity is useless, if, on being thrown into the alchemistical retort of circulation, it does not come out again in the shape of money; if, in other words, it cannot be sold by its owner, and therefore be bought by the owner of the money. That identity further implies that the exchange, if it do take place, constitutes a period of rest, an interval, long or short, in the life of the commodity. Since the first metamorphosis of a commodity is at once a sale and a purchase, it is also an independent process in itself. The purchaser has the commodity, the seller has the money, i.e., a commodity ready to go into circulation at any time. No one can sell unless some one else purchases. But no one is forthwith bound to purchase, because he has just sold. Circulation bursts through all restrictions as to time, place, and individuals, imposed by direct barter, and this it effects by splitting up, into the antithesis of a sale and a purchase, the direct identity that in barter does exist between the alienation of one's own and the acquisition of some other man's product. To say that these two independent and antithetical acts have an intrinsic unity, are essentially one, is the same as to say that this intrinsic oneness expresses itself in an external antithesis. If the interval in time between the two complementary phases of the complete metamorphosis of a commodity become too great, if the split between the sale and the purchase become too pronounced, the intimate connection between them, their oneness, asserts itself by producing – a crisis. The antithesis, use-value and value; the contradictions that private labour is bound to manifest itself as direct social labour, that a particularised concrete kind of labour has to pass for abstract human labour; the contradiction between the personification of objects and the representation of persons by things; all these antitheses and contradictions, which are immanent in commodities, assert themselves, and develop their modes of motion, in the antithetical phases of the metamorphosis of a commodity. These modes therefore imply the possibility, and no more than the possibility, of crises. The conversion of this mere possibility into a reality is the result of a long series of relations, that, from our present standpoint of simple circulation, have as yet no existence.[24]

B. The currency [25] of money.

The change of form, C—M—C, by which the circulation of the material products of labour is brought about, requires that a given value in the shape of a commodity shall begin the process, and shall, also in the shape of a commodity, end it. The movement of the commodity is therefore a circuit. On the other hand, the form of this movement precludes a circuit from being made by the money. The result is not the return of the money, but its continued removal further and further away from its starting-point. So long as the seller sticks fast to his money, which is the transformed shape of his commodity, that commodity is still in the first phase of its metamorphosis, and has completed only half its course. But so soon as he completes the process, so soon as he supplements his sale by a purchase, the money again leaves the hands of its possessor. It is true that if the weaver, after buying the Bible, sell more linen, money comes back into his hands. But this return is not owing to the circulation of the first 20 yards of linen; that circulation resulted in the money getting into the hands of the seller of the Bible. The return of money into the hands of the weaver is brought about only by the renewal or repetition of the process of circulation with a fresh commodity, which renewed process ends with the same result as its predecessor did. Hence the movement directly imparted to money by the circulation of commodities takes the form of a constant motion away from its starting-point, of a course from the hands of one commodity-owner into those of another. This course constitutes its currency (*cours de la monnaie*).

The currency of money is the constant and monotonous repetition of the same process. The commodity is always in the hands of the seller; the money, as a means of purchase, always in the hands of the buyer. And money serves as a means of purchase by realising the price of the commodity. This realisation transfers the commodity from the seller to the buyer and removes the money from the hands of the buyer into those of the seller, where it again goes through the same process with another commodity. That this one-sided character of the money's motion arises out of the two-sided character of the commodity's motion, is a circumstance that is veiled over. The very nature of the circulation of commodities begets the opposite appearance. The first metamorphosis of a commodity is visibly, not only the money's movement, but also that of the commodity itself; in the second metamorphosis, on the contrary, the movement appears to us as the movement of the money alone. In the first phase of its circulation the commodity changes place with the money. Thereupon the commodity, under its aspect of a useful object, falls out of circulation into consumption.[26] In its stead we have its value-shape – the money. It then goes through the second phase of its circulation, not under its own natural shape, but under the shape of money. The continuity of the movement is therefore kept up by the money alone, and the same movement that as regards the commodity consists of two processes of an antithetical character, is, when considered as the movement of the money, always one and the same process, a continued change of places with ever fresh commodities. Hence the result brought about by the circulation of commodities, namely, the replacing of one commodity by another, takes the appearance of having been effected not by means of the change of form of the commodities but rather by the money acting as a medium of circulation, by an action that circulates commodities, to all appearance motionless in themselves, and transfers them from hands in which they are non-use-values, to hands in which they are use-values; and that in a direction constantly opposed to the direction of the money. The latter is continually withdrawing commodities from circulation and stepping into their places, and in this way continually moving further and further from its starting-point Hence although the movement of the money is merely the expression of the circulation of commodities, yet the contrary appears to be the actual fact, and the circulation of commodities seems to be the result of the movement of the money.[27]

Again, money functions as a means of circulation, only because in it the values of commodities have independent reality. Hence its movement, as the medium of circulation, is, in fact, merely the movement of commodities while changing their forms. This fact must therefore make itself plainly visible in the currency of money. The twofold change of form in a commodity is reflected in the twice repeated change of place of the same piece of money during the complete metamorphosis of a commodity, and in its constantly repeated change of place, as metamorphosis follows metamorphosis, and each becomes interlaced with the others.

The linen, for instance, first of all exchanges its commodity-form into its money-form. The last term of its first metamorphosis (C—M), or the money form, is the first term of its final metamorphosis (M—C), of its re-conversion into a useful commodity, the Bible. But each of these two changes of form is accomplished by an exchange between commodity and money, by their reciprocal displacement. The same pieces of coin, in the first act, changed places with the linen, in the second, with the Bible. They are displaced twice. The first metamorphosis puts them into the weaver's pocket, the second draws them out of it. The two inverse changes undergone by the same commodity are reflected in the displacement, twice repeated, but in opposite directions, of the same pieces of coin.

If, on the contrary, only one phase of the metamorphosis is gone through, if there are only sales or only purchases, then a given piece of money changes its place only once. Its second change of place always expresses the second metamorphosis of the commodity, its re-conversion from money. The frequent repetition of the displacement of the same coins reflects not only the series of metamorphoses that a single commodity has gone through, but also the intertwining of the innumerable metamorphoses in the world of commodities in general. It is a matter of course, that all this is applicable to the simple circulation of commodities alone, the only form that we are now considering.

Every commodity, when it first steps into circulation, and undergoes its first change of form, does so only to fall out of circulation again and to be replaced by other commodities. Money, on the contrary, as the medium of circulation, keeps continually within the sphere of circulation, and moves about in it. The question therefore arises, how much money this sphere constantly absorbs?

In a given country there take place every day at the same time, but in different localities, numerous one-sided metamorphoses of commodities, or, in other words, numerous sales and numerous purchases. The commodities are equated beforehand in imagination, by their prices, to definite quantities of money. And since, in the form of circulation now under consideration, money and commodities always come bodily face to face, one at the positive pole of purchase, the other at the negative pole of sale, it is clear that the amount of the means of circulation required, is determined beforehand by the sum of the prices of all these commodities. As a matter of fact, the money in reality represents the quantity or sum of gold ideally expressed beforehand by the sum of the prices of the commodities. The equality of these two sums is therefore self-evident. We know, however, that, the values of commodities remaining constant, their prices vary with the value of gold (the material of money), rising in proportion as it falls, and falling in proportion as it rises. Now if, in consequence of such a rise or fall in the value of gold, the sum of the prices of commodities fall or rise, the quantity of money in currency must fall or rise to the same extent. The change in the quantity of the circulating medium is, in this case, it is true, caused by the money itself, yet not in virtue of its function as a medium of circulation, but of its function as a measure of value. First, the price of the commodities varies inversely as the value of the money, and then the quantity of the medium of circulation varies directly as the price of the commodities. Exactly the same thing would happen if, for instance, instead of the value of gold falling, gold were replaced by silver as the measure of value, or if, instead of the value of silver rising, gold were to thrust silver out from being the measure of value. In the one case, more silver would be current than gold was before; in the other case, less gold would be current than silver was before. In each case the value of the material of money, i. e., the value of the commodity that serves as the measure of value, would have undergone a change, and therefore so, too, would the prices of commodities which express their values in money, and so, too, would the quantity of money current whose function it is to realise those prices. We have already seen, that the sphere of circulation has an opening through which gold (or the material of money generally) enters into it as a commodity with a given value. Hence, when money enters on its functions as a measure of value, when it expresses prices, its value is already determined. If now its value fall, this fact is first evidenced by a change in the prices of those commodities that are directly bartered for the precious metals at the sources of their production. The greater part of all other commodities, especially in the imperfectly developed stages of civil society, will continue for a long time to be estimated by the former antiquated and illusory value of the measure of value. Nevertheless, one commodity infects another through their common value relation, so that their prices, expressed in gold or in silver, gradually settle down into the proportions determined by their comparative values, until finally the values of all commodities are estimated in terms of the new value of the metal that constitutes money. This process is accompanied by the continued increase in the quantity of the precious metals, an increase caused by their streaming in to replace the articles directly bartered for them at their sources of production. In proportion therefore as commodities in general acquire their true prices, in proportion as their values become estimated according to the fallen value of the precious metal, in the same proportion the quantity of that metal necessary for realising those new prices is provided beforehand. A one-sided observation of the results that followed upon the discovery of fresh supplies of gold and silver, led some economists in the 17th, and particularly in the 18th century, to the false conclusion, that the prices of commodities had gone up in consequence of the increased quantity of gold and silver serving as means of circulation. Henceforth we shall consider the value of gold to be givem, as, in fact, it is momentarily whenever we estimate the price of a commodity.

On this supposition then, the quantity of the medium of circulation is determined by the sum of the prices that have to be realised. If now we further suppose the price of each commodity to be given, the sum of the prices clearly depends on the mass of commodities in circulation. It requires but little racking of brains to comprehend that if one quarter of wheat costs £2, 100 quarters will cost £200, 200 quarters £400, and so on, that consequently the quantity of money that changes place with the wheat, when sold, must increase with the quantity of that wheat.

If the mass of commodities remain constant, the quantity of circulating money varies with the fluctuations in the prices of those commodities. It increases and diminishes because the sum of the prices increases or diminishes in consequence of the change of price. To produce this effect, it is by no means requisite that the prices of all commodities should rise or fall simultaneously. A rise or a fall in the prices of a number of leading articles, is sufficient in the one case to increase, in the other to diminish, the sum of the prices of all commodities, and, therefore, to put more or less money in circulation. Whether the change in the price correspond to an actual change of value in the commodities, or whether it be the result of mere fluctuations in market-prices, the effect on the quantity of the medium of circulation remains the same. Suppose the following articles to be sold or partially metamorphosed simultaneously in different localities: say, one quarter of wheat, 20 yards of linen, one Bible, and 4 gallons of brandy. If the price of each article be £2, and the sum of the prices to be realised be consequently £8, it follows that £8 in money must go into circulation. If, on the other hand, these same articles are links in the following chain of metamorphoses: 1 quarter of wheat—£2—20 yards of linen—£2—1 Bible—£2—4 gallons of brandy—£2, a chain that is already well known to us, in that case the £2 cause the different commodities to circulate one after the other, and after realising their prices successively, and therefore the sum of those prices, £8, they come to rest at last in the pocket of the distiller. The £2 thus make four moves. This repeated change of place of the same pieces of money corresponds to the double change in form of the commodities, to their motion in opposite directions through two stages of circulation. and to the interlacing of the metamorphoses of different commodities.[28] These antithetic and complementary phases, of which the process of metamorphosis consists, are gone through, not simultaneously, but successively. Time is therefore required for the completion of the series. Hence the velocity of the currency of money is measured by the number of moves made by a given piece of money in a given time. Suppose the circulation of the 4 articles takes a day. The sum of the prices to be realised in the day is £8, the number of moves of the two pieces of money is four, and the quantity of money circulating is £2. Hence, for a given interval of time during the process of circulation, we have the following relation: the quantity of money functioning as the circulating medium is equal to the sum of the prices of the commodities divided by the number of moves made by coins of the same denomination. This law holds generally.

The total circulation of commodities in a given country during a given period is made up on the one hand of numerous isolated and simultaneous partial metamorphoses, sales which are at the same time purchases, in which each coin changes its place only once, or makes only one move; on the other hand, of numerous distinct series of metamorphoses partly running side by side, and partly coalescing with each other, in each of which series each coin makes a number of moves, the number being greater or less according to circumstances. The total number of moves made by all the circulating coins of one denomination being given, we can arrive at the average number of moves made by a single coin of that denomination, or at the average velocity of the currency of money. The quantity of money thrown into the circulation at the beginning of each day is of course determined by the sum of the prices of all the commodities circulating simultaneously side by side. But once in circulation, coins are, so to say, made responsible for one another. If the one increase its velocity, the other either retards its own, or altogether falls out of circulation; for the circulation can absorb only such a quantity of gold as when multiplied by the mean number of moves made by one single coin or element, is equal to the sum of the prices to be realised. Hence if the number of moves made by the separate pieces increase, the total number of those pieces in circulation diminishes. If the number of the moves diminish, the total number of pieces increases. Since the quantity of money capable of being absorbed by the circulation is given for a given mean velocity of currency, all that is necessary in order to abstract a given number of sovereigns from the circulation is to throw the same number of one-pound notes into it, a trick well known to all bankers.

Just as the currency of money, generally considered, is but a reflex of the circulation of commodities, or of the antithetical metamorphoses they undergo, so, too, the velocity of that currency reflects the rapidity with which commodities change their forms, the continued inter-lacing of one series of metamorphoses with another, the hurried social interchange of matter, the rapid disappearance of commodities from the sphere of circulation, and the equally rapid substitution of fresh ones in their places. Hence, in the velocity of the currency we have the fluent unity of the antithetical and complementary phases, the unity of the conversion of the useful aspect of commodities into their value-aspect, and their re-conversion from the latter aspect to the former, or the unity of the two processes of sale and purchase. On the other hand, the retardation of the currency reflects the separation of these two processes into isolated antithetical phases, reflects the stagnation in the change of form, and therefore, in the social inter-change of matter. The circulation itself, of course, gives no clue to the origin of this stagnation; it merely puts in evidence the phenomenon itself. The general public, who, simultaneously with the retardation of the currency, see money appear and disappear less frequently at the periphery of circulation, naturally attribute this retardation to a quantitative deficiency in the circulating medium.[29]

The total quantity of money functioning during a given period as the circulating medium, is determined, on the one hand, by the sum of the prices of the circulating commodities, and on the other hand, by the rapidity with which the antithetical phases of the metamorphoses follow one another. On this rapidity depends what proportion of the sum of the prices can, on the average, be realised by each single coin. But the sum of the prices of the circulating commodities depends on the quantity, as well as on the prices, of the commodities. These three factors, however, state of prices, quantity of circulating commodities, and velocity of money-currency, are all variable. Hence, the sum of the prices to be realised, and consequently the quantity of the circulating medium depending on that sum, will vary with the numerous variations of these three factors in combination. Of these variations we shall consider those alone that have been the most important in the history of prices.

While prices remain constant, the quantity of the circulating medium may increase owing to the number of circulating commodities increasing, or to the velocity of currency decreasing, or to a combination of the two. On the other hand the quantity of the circulating medium may decrease with a decreasing number of commodities, or with an increasing rapidity of their circulation.

With a general rise in the prices of commodities, the quantity of the circulating medium will remain constant, provided the number of commodities in circulation decrease proportionally to the increase in their prices, or provided the velocity of currency increase at the same rate as prices rise, the number of commodities in circulation remaining constant. The quantity of the circulating medium may decrease, owing to the number of commodities decreasing more rapidly, or to the velocity of currency increasing more rapidly, than prices rise.

With a general fall in the prices of commodities, the quantity of the circulating medium will remain constant, provided the number of commodities increase proportionally to their fall in price, or provided the velocity of currency decrease in the same proportion. The quantity of the circulating medium will increase, provided the number of commodities increase quicker, or the rapidity of circulation decrease quicker, than the prices fall.

The variations of the different factors may mutually compensate each other, so that notwithstanding their continued instability, the sum of the prices to be realised and the quantity of money in circulation remain constant; consequently, we find, especially if we take long periods into consideration, that the deviations from the average level, of the quantity of money current in any country, are much smaller than we should at first sight expect, apart of course from excessive perturbations periodically arising from industrial and commercial crises, or less frequently, from fluctuations in the value of money.

The law, that the quantity of the circulating medium is determined by the sum of the prices of the commodities circulating, and the average velocity of currency[30] may also be stated as follows: given the sum of the values of commodities, and the average rapidity of their metamorphoses, the quantity of precious metal current as money depends on the value of that precious metal. The erroneous opinion that it is, on the contrary, prices that are determined by the quantity of the circulating medium, and that the latter depends on the quantity of the precious metals in a country;[31] this opinion was based by those who first held it, on the absurd hypothesis that commodities are without a price, and money without a value, when they first enter into circulation, and that, once in the circulation, an aliquot part of the medley of commodities is exchanged for an aliquot part of the heap of precious metals.[32]

C. Coin and symbols of value.

That money takes the shape of coin, springs from its function as the circulating medium. The weight of gold represented in imagination by the prices or money-names of commodities, must confront those commodities, within the circulation, in the shape of coins or pieces of gold of a given denomination. Coining, like the establishment of a standard of prices, is the business of the State. The different national uniforms worn at home by gold and silver as coins, and doffed again in the market of the world, indicate the separation between the internal or national spheres of the circulation of commodities, and their universal sphere.

The only difference, therefore, between coin and bullion, is one of shape, and gold can at any time pass from one form to the other.[33] But no sooner does coin leave the mint, than it immediately finds itself on the high-road to the melting pot. During their currency, coins wear away, some more, others less. Name and substance, nominal weight and real weight, begin their process of separation. Coins of the same denomination become different in value, because they are different in weight. The weight of gold fixed upon as the standard of prices, deviates from the weight that serves as the circulating medium, and the latter thereby ceases any longer to be a real equivalent of the commodities whose prices it realises. The history of coinage during the middle ages and down into the 18th century, records the ever renewed confusion arising from this cause. The natural tendency of circulation to convert coins into a mere semblance of what they profess to be, into a symbol of the weight of metal they are officially supposed to contain, is recognised by modern legislation, which fixes the loss of weight sufficient to demonetise a gold coin, or to make it no longer legal tender.

The fact that the currency of coins itself effects a separation between their nominal and their real weight, creating a distinction between them as mere pieces of metal on the one hand, and as coins with a definite function on the other – this fact implies the latent possibility of replacing metallic coins by tokens of some other material, by symbols serving the same purposes as coins. The practical difficulties in the way of coining extremely minute quantities of gold or silver, and the circumstance that at first the less precious metal is used as a measure of value instead of the more precious, copper instead of silver, silver instead of gold, and that the less precious circulates as money until dethroned by the more precious – all these facts explain the parts historically played by silver and copper tokens as substitutes for gold coins. Silver and copper tokens take the place of gold in those regions of the circulation where coins pass from hand to hand most rapidly, and are subject to the maximum amount of wear and tear. This occurs where sales and purchases on a very small scale are continually happening. In order to prevent these satellites from establishing themselves permanently in the place of gold, positive enactments determine the extent to which they must be compulsorily received as payment instead of gold. The particular tracks pursued by the different species of coin in currency, run naturally into each other. The tokens keep company with gold, to pay fractional parts of the smallest gold coin; gold is, on the one hand, constantly pouring into retail circulation, and on the other hand is as constantly being thrown out again by being changed into tokens.[34]

The weight of metal in the silver and copper tokens is arbitrarily fixed by law. When in currency, they wear away even more rapidly than gold coins. Hence their functions are totally independent of their weight, and consequently of all value. The function of gold as coin becomes completely independent of the metallic value of that gold. Therefore things that are relatively without value, such as paper notes, can serve as coins in its place. This purely symbolic character is to a certain extent masked in metal tokens. In paper money it stands out plainly. In fact, *ce n'est que le premier pas qui coûte.*

We allude here only to inconvertible paper money issued by the State and having compulsory circulation. It has its immediate origin in the metallic currency. Money based upon credit implies on the other hand conditions, which, from our standpoint of the simple circulation of commodities, are as yet totally unknown to us. But we may affirm this much, that just as true paper money takes its rise in the function of money as the circulating medium, so money based upon credit takes root spontaneously in the function of money as the means of payment.[35]

The State puts in circulation bits of paper on which their various denominations, say £1, £5, &c., are printed. In so far as they actually take the place of gold to the same amount, their movement is subject to the laws that regulate the currency of money itself. A law peculiar to the circulation of paper money can spring up only from the proportion in which that paper money represents gold. Such a law exists; stated simply, it is as follows: the issue of paper money must not exceed in amount the gold (or silver as the case may be) which would actually circulate if not replaced by symbols. Now the quantity of gold which the circulation can absorb, constantly fluctuates about a given level. Still, the mass of the circulating medium in a given country never sinks below a certain minimum easily ascertained by actual experience. The fact that this minimum mass continually undergoes changes in its constituent parts, or that the pieces of gold of which it consists are being constantly replaced by fresh ones, causes of course no change either in its amount or in the continuity of its circulation. It can therefore be replaced by paper symbols. If, on the other hand, all the conduits of circulation were today filled with paper money to the full extent of their capacity for absorbing money, they might tomorrow be overflowing in consequence of a fluctuation in the circulation of commodities. There would no longer be any standard. If the paper money exceed its proper limit, which is the amount in gold coins of the like denomination that can actually be current, it would, apart from the danger of falling into general disrepute, represent only that quantity of gold, which, in accordance with the laws of the circulation of commodities, is required, and is alone capable of being represented by paper. If the quantity of paper money issued be double what it ought to be, then, as a matter of fact, £1 would be the money-name not of 1/4 of an ounce, but of 1/8 of an ounce of gold. The effect would be the same as if an alteration had taken place in the function of gold as a standard of prices. Those values that were previously expressed by the price of £1 would now be expressed by the price of £2.

Paper money is a token representing gold or money. The relation between it and the values of commodities is this, that the latter are ideally expressed in the same quantities of gold that are symbolically represented by the paper. Only in so far as paper money represents gold, which like all other commodities has value, is it a symbol of value.[36]

Finally, some one may ask why gold is capable of being replaced by tokens that have no value? But, as we have already seen, it is capable of being so replaced only in so far as it functions exclusively as coin, or as the circulating medium, and as nothing else. Now, money has other functions besides this one, and the isolated function of serving as the mere circulating medium is not necessarily the only one attached to gold coin, although this is the case with those abraded coins that continue to circulate. Each piece of money is a mere coin, or means of circulation, only so long as it actually circulates. But this is just the case with that minimum mass of gold, which is capable of being replaced by paper money. That mass remains constantly within the sphere of circulation, continually functions as a circulating medium, and exists exclusively for that purpose. Its movement therefore represents nothing but the continued alternation of the inverse phases of the metamorphosis C—M—C, phases in which commodities confront their value forms, only to disappear again immediately. The independent existence of the exchange value of a commodity is here a transient apparition, by means of which the commodity is immediately replaced by another commodity. Hence, in this process which continually makes money pass from hand to hand, the mere symbolical existence of money suffices. Its functional existence absorbs, so to say, its material existence. Being a transient and objective reflex of the prices of commodities, it serves only as a symbol of itself, and is therefore capable of being replaced by a token.[37] One thing is, however, requisite; this token must have an objective social validity of its own, and this the paper symbol acquires by its forced currency. This compulsory action of the State can take effect only within that inner sphere of circulation which is coterminous with the territories of the community, but it is also only within that sphere that money completely responds to its function of being the circulating medium, or becomes coin.

Section 3. Money

The commodity that functions as a measure of value, and, either in its own person or by a representative, as the medium of circulation, is money. Gold (or silver) is therefore money. It functions as money, on the one hand, when it has to be present in its own golden person. It is then the money-commodity, neither merely ideal, as in its function of a measure of value, nor capable of being represented, as in its function of circulating medium. On the other hand, it also functions as money, when by virtue of its function, whether that function be performed in person or by representative, it congeals into the sole form of value, the only adequate form of existence of exchange value, in opposition to use-value, represented by all other commodities.

A. Hoarding

The continual movement in circuits of the two antithetical meta-morphoses of commodities, or the never ceasing alternation of sale and purchase, is reflected in the restless currency of money, or in the function that money performs of a *perpetuum mobile* of circulation. But so soon as the series of metamorphoses is interrupted, so soon as sales are not supplemented by subsequent purchases, money ceases to be mobilised; it is transformed, as Boisguillebert says, from '*meuble*' into '*immeuble*', from movable into immovable, from coin into money.

With the very earliest development of the circulation of com-modities, there is also developed the necessity, and the passionate desire, to hold fast the product of the first metamorphosis. This product is the transformed shape of the commodity, or its gold-chrysalis.[38] Commodities are thus sold not for the purpose of buying others, but in order to replace their commodity-form by their money form. From being the mere means of effecting the circulation of commodities, this change of form becomes the end and aim. The changed form of the commodity is thus prevented from functioning as its unconditionally alienable form, or as its merely transient money form. The money becomes petrified into a hoard, and the seller becomes a hoarder of money.

In the early stages of the circulation of commodities, it is the surplus use-values alone that are converted into money. Gold and silver thus become of themselves social expressions for superfluity or wealth. This naive form of hoarding becomes perpetuated in those com-munities in which the traditional mode of production is carried on for the supply of a fixed and limited circle of home wants. It is thus with the people of Asia, and particularly of the East Indies. Vanderlint, who fancies that the prices of commodities in a country are determined by the quantity of gold and silver to be found in it, asks himself why Indian commodities are so cheap. Answer: Because the Hindus bury their money. From 1602 to 1734, he remarks, they buried 150 millions of pounds sterling of silver, which originally came from America to Europe.[39] In the 10 years from 1856 to 1866, England exported to India and China £120,000,000 in silver, which had been received in exchange for Australian gold. Most of the silver exported to China makes its way to India.

As the production of commodities further develops, every producer of commodities is compelled to make sure of the *nexus rerum* or the social pledge.[40] His wants are constantly making themselves felt, and necessitate the continual purchase of other people's commodities, while the production and sale of his own goods require time, and depend upon circumstances. In order then to be able to buy without selling, he must have sold previously without buying. This operation, conducted on a general scale, appears to imply a contradiction. But the precious metals at the sources of their production are directly exchanged for other commodities. And here we have sales (by the owners of commodities) without purchases (by the owners of gold or silver).[41] And subsequent sales, by other producers, unfollowed by purchases, merely bring about the distribution of the newly produced precious metals among all the owners of commodities. In this way, all along the line of exchange, hoards of gold and silver of varied extent are accumulated. With the possibility of holding and storing up exchange value in the shape of a particular commodity, arises also the greed for gold. Along with the extension of circulation, increases the power of money, that absolutely social form of wealth ever ready for use. 'Gold is a wonderful thing! Whoever possesses it is lord of all he wants. By means of gold one can even get souls into Paradise.' (Columbus in his letter from Jamaica, 1503.) Since gold does not disclose what has been transformed into it, everything, commodity or not, is convertible into gold. Everything becomes saleable and buyable. The circulation becomes the great social retort into which everything is thrown, to come out again as a gold-crystal. Not even are the bones of saints, and still less are more delicate *res sacrosanctae extra commercium hominum* able to withstand this alchemy.[42] Just as every qualitative difference between commodities is extinguished in money, so money, on its side, like the radical leveller that it is, does away with all distinctions.[43] But money itself is a commodity, an external object, capable of becoming the private property of any individual. Thus social power becomes the private power of private persons. The ancients therefore denounced money as subversive of the economic and moral order of things.[44] Modern society, which, soon after its birth, pulled Plutus by the hair of his head from the bowels of the earth,[45] greets gold as its Holy Grail, as the glittering incarnation of the very principle of its own life.

A commodity, in its capacity of a use-value, satisfies a particular want, and is a particular element of material wealth. But the value of a commodity measures the degree of its attraction for all other elements of material wealth, and therefore measures the social wealth of its owner. To a barbarian owner of commodities, and even to a West-European peasant, value is the same as value form, and therefore, to him the increase in his hoard of gold and silver is an increase in value. It is true that the value of money varies, at one time in consequence of a variation in its own value, at another, in consequence of a change in the values of commodities. But this, on the one hand, does not prevent 200 ounces of gold from still containing more value than 100 ounces, nor, on the other hand, does it hinder the actual metallic form of this article from continuing to be the universal equivalent form of all other commodities, and the immediate social incarnation of all human labour. The desire after hoarding is in its very nature unsatiable. In its qualitative aspect, or formally considered, money has no bounds to its efficacy, i.e., it is the universal representative of material wealth, because it is directly convertible into any other commodity. But, at the same time, every actual sum of money is limited in amount, and, therefore, as a means of purchasing, has only a limited efficacy. This antagonism between the quantitative limits of money and its qualitative boundlessness, continually acts as a spur to the hoarder in his Sisyphus-like labour of accumulating. It is with him as it is with a conqueror who sees in every new country annexed, only a new boundary.

In order that gold may be held as money, and made to form a hoard, it must be prevented from circulating, or from transforming itself into a means of enjoyment. The hoarder, therefore, makes a sacrifice of the lusts of the flesh to his gold fetish. He acts in earnest up to the Gospel of abstention. On the other hand, he can withdraw from circulation no more than what he has thrown into it in the shape of commodities. The more he produces, the more he is able to sell. Hard work, saving, and avarice are, therefore, his three cardinal virtues, and to sell much and buy little the sum of his political economy.[46]

By the side of the gross form of a hoard, we find also its aesthetic form in the possession of gold and silver articles. This grows with the wealth of civil society. '*Soyons riches ou paraissons riches.*' (Diderot) In this way there is created, on the one hand, a constantly extending market for gold and silver, unconnected with their functions as money, and, on the other hand, a latent source of supply, to which recourse is had principally in times of crisis and social disturbance.

Hoarding serves various purposes in the economy of the metallic circulation. Its first function arises out of the conditions to which the currency of gold and silver coins is subject. We have seen how, along with the continual fluctuations in the extent and rapidity of the circulation of commodities and in their prices, the quantity of money current unceasingly ebbs and flows. This mass must, therefore, be capable of expansion and contraction. At one time money must be attracted in order to act as circulating coin, at another, circulating coin must be repelled in order to act again as more or less stagnant money. In order that the mass of money, actually current, may constantly saturate the absorbing power of the circulation, it is necessary that the quantity of gold and silver in a country be greater than the quantity required to function as coin. This condition is fulfilled by money taking the form of hoards. These reserves serve as conduits for the supply or withdrawal of money to or from the circulation, which in this way never overflows its banks.47

B. Means of Payment.

In the simple form of the circulation of commodities hitherto considered, we found a given value always presented to us in a double shape, as a commodity at one pole, as money at the opposite pole. The owners of commodities came therefore into contact as the respective representatives of what were already equivalents. But with the development of circulation, conditions arise under which the alienation of commodities becomes separated, by an interval of time, from the realisation of their prices. It will be sufficient to indicate the most simple of these conditions. One sort of article requires a longer, another a shorter time for its production. Again, the production of different commodities depends on different seasons of the year. One sort of commodity may be born on its own market place, another has to make a long journey to market. Commodity-owner No. 1 may therefore be ready to sell, before No. 2 is ready to buy. When the same transactions are continually repeated between the same persons, the conditions of sale are regulated in accordance with the conditions of production. On the other hand, the use of a given commodity, of a house, for instance, is sold (in common parlance, let) for a definite period. Here, it is only at the end of the term that the buyer has actually received the use-value of the commodity. He therefore buys it before he pays for it. The vendor sells an existing commodity, the purchaser buys as the mere representative of money, or rather of future money. The vendor becomes a creditor, the purchaser becomes a debtor. Since the metamorphosis of commodities, or the development of their value form, appears here under a new aspect, money also acquires a fresh function; it becomes the means of payment.

The character of creditor, or of debtor, results here from the simple circulation. The change in the form of that circulation stamps buyer and seller with this new die. At first, therefore, these new parts are just as transient and alternating as those of seller and buyer, and are in turns played by the same actors. But the opposition is not nearly so pleasant, and is far more capable of crystallisation.48 The same characters can, however, be assumed independently of the circulation of commodities. The class-struggles of the ancient world took the form chiefly of a contest between debtors and creditors, which in Rome ended in the ruin of the plebeian debtors. They were displaced by slaves. In the middle ages the contest ended with the ruin of the feudal debtors, who lost their political power together with the economic basis on which it was established. Nevertheless, the money relation of debtor and creditor that existed at these two periods reflected only the deeper-lying antagonism between the general economic conditions of existence of the classes in question.

Let us return to the circulation of commodities. The appearance of the two equivalents, commodities and money, at the two poles of the process of sale, has ceased to be simultaneous. The money functions now, first as a measure of value in the determination of the price of the commodity sold; the price fixed by the contract measures the obligation of the debtor, or the sum of money that he has to pay at a fixed date. Secondly, it serves as an ideal means of purchase. Although existing only in the promise of the buyer to pay, it causes the commodity to change hands. It is not before the day fixed for payment that the means of payment actually steps into circulation, leaves the hand of the buyer for that of the seller. The circulating medium was transformed into a hoard, because the process stopped short after the first phase, because the converted shape of the commodity, viz., the money, was withdrawn from circulation. The means of payment enters the circulation, but only after the commodity has left it. The money is no longer the means that brings about the process. It only brings it to a close, by stepping in as the absolute form of existence of exchange value, or as the universal commodity. The seller turned his commodity into money, in order thereby to satisfy some want, the hoarder did the same in order to keep his commodity in its money-shape, and the debtor in order to be able to pay; if he do not pay, his goods will be sold by the sheriff. The value form of commodities, money, is therefore now the end and aim of a sale, and that owing to a social necessity springing out of the process of circulation itself.

The buyer converts money back into commodities before he has turned commodities into money: in other words, he achieves the second metamorphosis of commodities before the first. The seller's commodity circulates, and realises its price, but only in the shape of a legal claim upon money. It is converted into a use-value before it has been converted into money. The completion of its first metamorphosis follows only at a later period.[49]

The obligations falling due within a given period, represent the sum of the prices of the commodities, the sale of which gave rise to those obligations. The quantity of gold necessary to realise this sum, depends, in the first instance, on the rapidity of currency of the means of payment. That quantity is conditioned by two circumstances: first the relations between debtors and creditors form a sort of chain, in such a way that A, when he receives money from his debtor B, straightway hands it over to C his creditor, and so on; the second circumstance is the length of the intervals between the different due-days of the obligations. The continuous chain of payments, or retarded first metamorphoses, is essentially different from that interlacing of the series of metamorphoses which we considered on a former page. By the currency of the circulating medium, the connection between buyers and sellers, is not merely expressed. This connection is originated by, and exists in, the circulation alone. Contrariwise, the movement of the means of payment expresses a social relation that was in existence long before.

The fact that a number of sales take place simultaneously, and side by side, limits the extent to which coin can be replaced by the rapidity of currency. On the other hand, this fact is a new lever in economising the means of payment. In proportion as payments are concentrated at one spot, special institutions and methods are developed for their liquidation. Such in the middle ages were the *virements* at Lyons. The debts due to A from B, to B from C, to C from A, and so on, have only to be confronted with each other, in order to annul each other to a certain extent like positive and negative quantities. There thus remains only a single balance to pay. The greater the amount of the payments concentrated, the less is this balance relatively to that amount, and the less is the mass of the means of payment in circulation.

The function of money as the means of payment implies a contradiction without a *terminus medius*. In so far as the payments balance one another, money functions only ideally as money of account, as a measure of value. In so far as actual payments have to be made, money does not serve as a circulating medium, as a mere transient agent in the interchange of products, but as the individual incarnation of social labour, as the independent form of existence of exchange value, as the universal commodity. This contradiction comes to a head in those phases of industrial and commercial crises which are known as monetary crises.[50] Such a crisis occurs only where the ever-lengthening chain of payments, and an artificial system of settling them, has been fully developed. Whenever there is a general and extensive disturbance of this mechanism, no matter what its cause, money becomes suddenly and immediately transformed, from its merely ideal shape of money of account, into hard cash. Profane commodities can no longer replace it. The use-value of commodities becomes valueless, and their value vanishes in the presence of its own independent form. On the eve of the crisis, the bourgeois, with the self-sufficiency that springs from intoxicating prosperity, declares money to be a vain imagination. Commodities alone are money. But now the cry is everywhere:

money alone is a commodity! As the hart pants after fresh water, so pants his soul after money, the only wealth.[51] In a crisis, the antithesis between commodities and their value form, money, becomes heightened into an absolute contradiction. Hence, in such events, the form under which money appears is of no importance. The money famine continues, whether payments have to be made in gold or in credit money such as bank-notes.[52]

If we now consider the sum total of the money current during a given period, we shall find that, given the rapidity of currency of the circulating medium and of the means of payment, it is equal to the sum of the prices to be realised, plus the sum of the payments falling due, minus the payments that balance each other, minus finally the number of circuits in which the same piece of coin serves in turn as means of circulation and of payment. Hence, even when prices, rapidity of currency, and the extent of the economy in payments, are given, the quantity of money current and the mass of commodities circulating during a given period, such as a day, no longer correspond. Money that represents commodities long withdrawn from circulation, continues to be current. Commodities circulate, whose equivalent in money will not appear on the scene till some future day. Moreover, the debts contracted each day, and the payments falling due on the same day, are quite incommensurable quantities.[53]

Credit-money springs directly out of the function of money as a means of payment. Certificates of the debts owing for the purchased commodities circulate for the purpose of transferring those debts to others. On the other hand, to the same extent as the system of credit is extended, so is the function of money as a means of payment. In that character it takes various forms peculiar to itself under which it makes itself at home in the sphere of great commercial transactions. Gold and silver coin, on the other hand, are mostly relegated to the sphere of retail trade.[54]

When the production of commodities has sufficiently extended itself, money begins to serve as the means of payment beyond the sphere of the circulation of commodities. It becomes the commodity that is the universal subject-matter of all contracts.[55] Rents, taxes, and such like payments are transformed from payments in kind into money payments. To what extent this transformation depends upon the general conditions of production, is shown, to take one example, by the fact that the Roman Empire twice failed in its attempt to levy all contributions in money. The unspeakable misery of the French agricultural population under Louis XIV, a misery so eloquently denounced by Boisguillebert, Marshal, Vauban, and others, was due not only to the weight of the taxes, but also to the conversion of taxes in kind into money taxes.[56] In Asia, on the other hand, the fact that state taxes are chiefly composed of rents payable in kind, depends on conditions of production that are reproduced with the regularity of natural phenomena. And this mode of payment tends in its turn to maintain the ancient form of production. It is one of the secrets of the conservation of the Ottoman Empire. If the foreign trade, forced upon Japan by Europeans, should lead to the substitution of money rents for rents in kind, it will be all up with the exemplary agriculture of that country. The narrow economic conditions under which that agriculture is carried on, will be swept away.

In every country, certain days of the year become by habit recognised settling days for various large and recurrent payments. These dates depend, apart from other revolutions in the wheel of reproduction, on conditions closely connected with the seasons. They also regulate the dates for payments that have no direct connection with the circulation of commodities such as taxes, rents, and so on. The quantity of money requisite to make the payments, falling due on those dates all over the country, causes periodical, though merely superficial, perturbations in the economy of the medium of payment.[57]

From the law of the rapidity of currency of the means of payment, it follows that the quantity of the means of payment required for all periodical payments, whatever their source, is in inverse[58] proportion to the length of their periods.

The development of money into a medium of payment makes it necessary to accumulate money against the dates fixed for the payment of the sums owing. While hoarding, as a distinct mode of acquiring riches, vanishes with the progress of civil society, the formation of reserves of the means of payment grows with that progress.

C. Universal Money

When money leaves the home sphere of circulation, it strips off the local garbs which it there assumes, of a standard of prices, of coin, of tokens, and of a symbol of value, and returns to its original form of bullion. In the trade between the markets of the world, the value of commodities is expressed so as to be universally recognised. Hence their independent value form also, in these cases, confronts them under the shape of universal money. It is only in the markets of the world that money acquires to the full extent the character of the commodity whose bodily form is also the immediate social incarnation of human labour in the abstract. Its real mode of existence in this sphere adequately corresponds to its ideal concept.

Within the sphere of home circulation, there can be but one commodity which, by serving as a measure of value, becomes money.

In the markets of the world a double measure of value holds sway, gold and silver.[59]

Money of the world serves as the universal medium of payment, as the universal means of purchasing, and as the universally recognised embodiment of all wealth. Its function as a means of payment in the settling of international balances is its chief one. Hence the watchword of the mercantilists, balance of trade.[60] Gold and silver serve as international means of purchasing chiefly and necessarily in those periods when the customary equilibrium in the interchange of products between different nations is suddenly disturbed. And lastly, it serves as the universally recognised embodiment of social wealth, whenever the question is not of buying or paying, but of transferring wealth from one country to another, and whenever this transference in the form of commodities is rendered impossible, either by special conjunctures in the markets or by the purpose itself that is intended.[61]

Just as every country needs a reserve of money for its home circulation so, too, it requires one for external circulation in the markets of the world. The functions of hoards, therefore, arise in part out of the function of money, as the medium of the home circulation and home payments, and in part out of its function of money of the world.[62] For this latter function, the genuine money-commodity, actual gold and silver, is necessary. On that account, Sir James Steuart, in order to distinguish them from their purely local substitutes, calls gold and silver 'money of the world'.

The current of the stream of gold and silver is a double one. On the one hand, it spreads itself from its sources over all the markets of the world, in order to become absorbed, to various extents, into the different national spheres of circulation, to fill the conduits of currency, to replace abraded gold and silver coins, to supply the material of articles of luxury, and to petrify into hoards.[63] This first current is started by the countries that exchange their labour, realised in commodities, for the labour embodied in the precious metals by gold and silver-producing countries. On the other hand, there is a continual flowing backwards and forwards of gold and silver between the different national spheres of circulation, a current whose motion depends on the ceaseless fluctuations in the course of exchange.[64]

Countries in which the bourgeois form of production is developed to a certain extent, limit the hoards concentrated in the strong rooms of the banks to the minimum required for the proper performance of their peculiar functions.[65] Whenever these hoards are strikingly above their average level, it is, with some exceptions, an indication of stagnation in the circulation of commodities, of an interruption in the even flow of their metamorphoses.[66]

Part 2. *The Transformation of Money into Capital*

Chapter 4
The General Formula for Capital.

The circulation of commodities is the starting-point of capital. The production of commodities, their circulation, and that more developed form of their circulation called commerce, these form the historical ground-work from which it rises. The modern history of capital dates from the creation in the 16th century of a world-embracing commerce and a world-embracing market.

If we abstract from the material substance of the circulation of commodities, that is, from the exchange of the various use-values, and consider only the economic forms produced by this process of circulation, we find its final result to be money: this final product of the circulation of commodities is the first form in which capital appears.

As a matter of history, capital, as opposed to landed property, invariably takes the form at first of money; it appears as moneyed wealth, as the capital of the merchant and of the usurer.[1] But we have no need to refer to the origin of capital in order to discover that the first form of appearance of capital is money. We can see it daily under our very eyes. All new capital, to commence with, comes on the stage, that is, on the market, whether of commodities, labour, or money, even in our days, in the shape of money that by a definite process has to be transformed into capital.

The first distinction we notice between money that is money only, and money that is capital, is nothing more than a difference in their form of circulation.

The simplest form of the circulation of commodities is C—M—C, the transformation of commodities into money, and the change of the money back again into commodities; or selling in order to buy. But alongside of this form we find another specifically different form: M—C—M, the transformation of money into commodities, and the change of commodities back again into money; or buying in order to sell. Money that circulates in the latter manner is thereby transformed into, becomes capital, and is already potentially capital.

Now let us examine the circuit M—C—M a little closer. It consists, like the other, of two antithetical phases. In the first phase, M—C, or the purchase, the money is changed into a commodity. In the second phase, C—M, or the sale, the commodity is changed back again into money. The combination of these two phases constitutes the single movement whereby money is exchanged for a commodity, and the same commodity is again exchanged for money; whereby a commodity is bought in order to be sold, or, neglecting the distinction in form between buying and selling, whereby a commodity is bought with money, and then money is bought with a commodity.[2] The result, in which the phases of the process vanish, is the exchange of money for money, M—M. If I purchase 2,000 lbs. of cotton for £100, and resell the 2,000 lbs. of cotton for £110, I have, in fact, exchanged £100 for £110, money for money.

Now it is evident that the circuit M—C—M would be absurd and without meaning if the intention were to exchange by this means two equal sums of money, £100 for £100. The miser's plan would be far simpler and surer; he sticks to his £100 instead of exposing it to the dangers of circulation. And yet, whether the merchant who has paid £100 for his cotton sells it for £110, or lets it go for £100, or even £50, his money has, at all events, gone through a characteristic and original movement, quite different in kind from that which it goes through in the hands of the peasant who sells corn, and with the money thus set free buys clothes. We have therefore to examine first the distinguishing characteristics of the forms of the circuits M—C—M and C—M—C, and in doing this the real difference that underlies the mere difference of form will reveal itself.

Let us see, in the first place, what the two forms have in common.

Both circuits are resolvable into the same two antithetical phases, C—M, a sale, and M—C, a purchase. In each of these phases the same material elements – a commodity, and money – and the same economic *dramatis personae* – a buyer and a seller – confront one another. Each circuit is the unity of the same two antithetical phases, and in each case this unity is brought about by the intervention of three contracting parties, of whom one only sells, another only buys, while the third both buys and sells.

What, however, first and foremost distinguishes the circuit C—M—C from the circuit M—C—M, is the inverted order of succession of the two phases. The simple circulation of commodities begins with a sale and ends with a purchase, while the circulation of money as capital begins with a purchase and ends with a sale. In the one case both the starting-point and the goal are commodities, in the other they are money. In the first form the movement is brought about by the intervention of money, in the second by that of a commodity.

In the circulation C—M—C, the money is in the end converted into a commodity, that serves as a use-value; it is spent once for all. In the inverted form, M—C—M, on the contrary, the buyer lays out money in order that, as a seller, he may recover money. By the purchase of his commodity he throws money into circulation, in order to withdraw it again by the sale of the same commodity. He lets the money go, but only with the sly intention of getting it back again. The money, therefore, is not spent, it is merely advanced.[3]

In the circuit C—M—C, the same piece of money changes its place twice. The seller gets it from the buyer and pays it away to another seller. The complete circulation, which begins with the receipt, concludes with the payment, of money for commodities. It is the very contrary in the circuit M—C—M. Here it is not the piece of money that changes its place twice, but the commodity. The buyer takes it from the hands of the seller and passes it into the hands of another buyer. Just as in the simple circulation of commodities the double change of place of the same piece of money effects its passage from one hand into another, so here the double change of place of the same commodity brings about the reflux of the money to its point of departure.

Such reflux is not dependent on the commodity being sold for more than was paid for it. This circumstance influences only the amount of the money that comes back. The reflux itself takes place, so soon as the purchased commodity is resold, in other words, so soon as the circuit M—C—M is completed. We have here, therefore, a palpable difference between the circulation of money as capital, and its circulation as mere money.

The circuit C—M—C comes completely to an end, so soon as the money brought in by the sale of one commodity is abstracted again by the purchase of another.

If, nevertheless, there follows a reflux of money to its starting-point, this can only happen through a renewal or repetition of the operation. If I sell a quarter of corn for £3, and with this £3 buy clothes, the money, so far as I am concerned, is spent and done with. It belongs to the clothes merchant. If I now sell a second quarter of corn, money indeed flows back to me, not however as a sequel to the first transaction, but in consequence of its repetition. The money again leaves me, so soon as I complete this second transaction by a fresh purchase. Therefore, in the circuit C—M—C, the expenditure of money has nothing to do with its reflux. On the other hand, in M—C—M, the reflux of the money is conditioned by the very mode of its expenditure. Without this reflux, the operation fails, or the process is interrupted and incomplete, owing to the absence of its complementary and final phase, the sale.

The circuit C—M—C starts with one commodity, and finishes with another, which falls out of circulation and into consumption. Consumption, the satisfaction of wants, in one word, use-value, is its end and aim. The circuit M—C—M, on the contrary, commences with money and ends with money. Its leading motive, and the goal that attracts it, is therefore mere exchange value.

In the simple circulation of commodities, the two extremes of the circuit have the same economic form. They are both commodities, and commodities of equal value. But they are also use-values differing in their qualities, as, for example, corn and clothes. The exchange of products, of the different materials in which the labour of society is embodied, forms here the basis of the movement. It is otherwise in the circulation C—M, which at first sight appears purposeless, because tautological. Both extremes have the same economic form. They are both money, and therefore are not qualitatively different use-values; for money is but the converted form of commodities, in which their particular use-values vanish. To exchange £100 for cotton, and then this same cotton again for £100, is merely a roundabout way of exchanging money for money, the same for the same, and appears to be an operation just as purposeless as it is absurd.[4] One sum of money is distinguishable from another only by its amount. The character and tendency of the process M—C—M, is therefore not due to any qualitative difference between its extremes, both being money, but solely to their quantitative difference. More money is withdrawn from circulation at the finish than was thrown into it at the start. The cotton that was bought for £100 is perhaps resold for £100 + £10 or £110. The exact form of this process is therefore M—C—M', where $M' = M + \text{delta } M =$ the original sum advanced, plus an increment. This increment or excess over the original value I call 'surplus-value'. The value originally advanced, therefore, not only remains intact while in circulation, but adds to itself a surplus-value or expands itself. It is this movement that converts it into capital.

Of course, it is also possible, that in C—M—C, the two extremes C-C, say corn and clothes, may represent different quantities of value. The farmer may sell his corn above its value, or may buy the clothes at less than their value. He may, on the other hand, 'be done' by the clothes merchant. Yet, in the form of circulation now under consideration, such differences in value are purely accidental. The fact that the corn and the clothes are equivalents, does not deprive the process of all meaning, as it does in M—C—M. The equivalence of their values is rather a necessary condition to its normal course.

The repetition or renewal of the act of selling in order to buy, is kept within bounds by the very object it aims at, namely, consumption or the satisfaction of definite wants, an aim that lies altogether outside the sphere of circulation. But when we buy in order to sell, we, on the contrary, begin and end with the same thing, money, exchange value; and thereby the movement becomes interminable. No doubt, M becomes M + delta m, £100 become £110. But when viewed in their qualitative aspect alone, £110 are the same as £100, namely money; and considered quantitatively, £110 is, like £100, a sum of definite and limited value. If now, the £110 be spent as money, they cease to play their part. They are no longer capital. Withdrawn from circulation, they become petrified into a hoard, and though they remained in that state till doomsday, not a single farthing would accrue to them. If, then, the expansion of value is once aimed at, there is just the same inducement to augment the value of the £110 as that of the £100; for both are but limited expressions for exchange value, and therefore both have the same vocation to approach, by quantitative increase, as near as possible to absolute wealth. Momentarily, indeed, the value originally advanced, the £100, is distinguishable from the surplus-value of £10 that is annexed to it during circulation; but the distinction vanishes immediately. At the end of the process, we do not receive with one hand the original £100, and with the other, the surplus-value of £10. We simply get a value of £110, which is in exactly the same condition and fitness for commencing the expanding process, as the original £100 was. Money ends the movement only to begin it again.[5] Therefore, the final result of every separate circuit, in which a purchase and consequent sale are completed, forms of itself the starting-point of a new circuit. The simple circulation of commodities — selling in order to buy — is a means of carrying out a purpose unconnected with circulation, namely, the appropriation of use-values, the satisfaction of wants. The circulation of money as capital is, on the contrary, an end in itself, for the expansion of value takes place only within this constantly renewed movement. The circulation of capital has therefore no limits.[6]

As the conscious representative of this movement, the possessor of money becomes a capitalist. His person, or rather his pocket, is the point from which the money starts and to which it returns. The expansion of value, which is the objective basis or main-spring of the circulation M—C—M, becomes his subjective aim, and it is only in so far as the appropriation of ever more and more wealth in the abstract becomes the sole motive of his operations, that he functions as a capitalist, that is, as capital personified and endowed with consciousness and a will. Use-values must therefore never be looked upon as the real aim of the capitalist;[7] neither must the profit on any single transaction. The restless never-ending process of profit-making alone is what he aims at.[8] This boundless greed after riches, this passionate chase after exchange value[9], is common to the capitalist and the miser; but while the miser is merely a capitalist gone mad, the capitalist is a rational miser. The never-ending augmentation of exchange value, which the miser strives after, by seeking to save[10] his money from circulation, is attained by the more acute capitalist, by constantly throwing it afresh into circulation.[11]

The independent form, i.e., the money form, which the value of commodities assumes in the case of simple circulation, serves only one purpose, namely, their exchange, and vanishes in the final result of the movement. On the other hand, in the circulation M—C—M, both the money and the commodity represent only different modes of existence of value itself, the money its general mode, and the commodity its particular, or, so to say, disguised mode.[12] It is constantly changing from one form to the other without thereby becoming lost, and thus assumes an automatically active character. If now we take in turn each of the two different forms which self-expanding value successively assumes in the course of its life, we then arrive at these two propositions: Capital is money: Capital is commodities.[13] In truth, however, value is here the active factor in a process, in which, while constantly assuming the form in turn of money and commodities, it at the same time changes in magnitude, differentiates itself by throwing off surplus-value from itself; the original value, in other words, expands spontaneously. For the movement, in the course of which it adds surplus-value, is its own movement, its expansion, therefore, is automatic expansion. Because it is value, it has acquired the occult quality of being able to add value to itself. It brings forth living offspring, or, at the least, lays golden eggs.

Value, therefore, being the active factor in such a process, and assuming at one time the form of money, at another that of commodities, but through all these changes preserving itself and expanding, it requires some independent form, by means of which its identity may at any time be established. And this form it possesses only in the shape of money. It is under the form of money that value begins and ends, and begins again, every act of its own spontaneous generation. It began by being £100, it is now £110, and so on. But the money itself is only one of the two forms of value. Unless it takes the form of some commodity, it does not become capital. There is here no antagonism, as in the case of hoarding, between the money and commodities. The capitalist knows that all commodities, however scurvy they may look, or however badly they may smell, are in faith and in truth money, inwardly circumcised Jews, and what is more, a wonderful means whereby out of money to make more money.

In simple circulation, C—M—C, the value of commodities attained at the most a form independent of their use-values, i.e., the form of money; but that same value now in the circulation M—C—M, or the circulation of capital, suddenly presents itself as an independent substance, endowed with a motion of its own, passing through a life-process of its own, in which money and commodities are mere forms which it assumes and casts off in turn. Nay, more: instead of simply representing the relations of commodities, it enters now, so to say, into private relations with itself. It differentiates itself as original value from itself as surplus-value; as the father differentiates himself from himself *quâ* the son, yet both are one and of one age: for only by the surplus-value of £10 does the £100 originally advanced become capital, and so soon as this takes place, so soon as the son, and by the son, the father, is begotten, so soon does their difference vanish, and they again become one, £110.

Value therefore now becomes value in process, money in process, and, as such, capital. It comes out of circulation, enters into it again, preserves and multiplies itself within its circuit, comes back out of it with expanded bulk, and begins the same round ever afresh.[14] M—M', money which begets money, such is the description of Capital from the mouths of its first interpreters, the Mercantilists.

Buying in order to sell, or, more accurately, buying in order to sell dearer, M—C—M', appears certainly to be a form peculiar to one kind of capital alone, namely, merchants' capital. But industrial capital too is money, that is changed into commodities, and by the sale of these commodities, is re-converted into more money. The events that take place outside the sphere of circulation, in the interval between the buying and selling, do not affect the form of this movement. Lastly, in the case of interest-bearing capital, the circulation M—C—M' appears abridged. We have its result without the intermediate stage, in the form M—M', '*en style lapidaire*' so to say, money that is worth more money, value that is greater than itself.

M—C—M' is therefore in reality the general formula of capital as it appears *prima facie* within the sphere of circulation.

Chapter 5
Contradictions in the General Formula of Capital

The form which circulation takes when money becomes capital, is opposed to all the laws we have hitherto investigated bearing on the nature of commodities, value and money, and even of circulation itself. What distinguishes this form from that of the simple circulation of commodities, is the inverted order of succession of the two antithetical processes, sale and purchase. How can this purely formal distinction between these processes change their character as it were by magic?

But that is not all. This inversion has no existence for two out of the three persons who transact business together. As capitalist, I buy commodities from A and sell them again to B, but as a simple owner of commodities, I sell them to B and then purchase fresh ones from A. A and B see no difference between the two sets of transactions. They are merely buyers or sellers. And I on each occasion meet them as a mere owner of either money or commodities, as a buyer or a seller, and, what is more, in both sets of transactions, I am opposed to A only as a buyer and to B only as a seller, to the one only as money, to the other only as commodities, and to neither of them as capital or a capitalist, or as representative of anything that is more than money or commodities, or that can produce any effect beyond what money and commodities can. For me the purchase from A and the sale to B are part of a series. But the connection between the two acts exists for me alone. A does not trouble himself about my transaction with B, nor does B about my business with A. And if I offered to explain to them the meritorious nature of my action in inverting the order of succession, they would probably point out to me that I was mistaken as to that order of succession, and that the whole transaction, instead of beginning with a purchase and ending with a sale, began, on the contrary, with a sale and was concluded with a purchase. In truth, my first act, the purchase, was from the standpoint of A, a sale, and my second act, the sale, was from the standpoint of B, a purchase. Not content with that, A and B would declare that the whole series was superfluous and nothing but Hokus Pokus; that for the future A would buy direct from B, and B sell direct to A. Thus the whole transaction would be reduced to a single act forming an isolated, non-complemented phase in the ordinary circulation of commodities, a mere sale from A's point of view, and from B's, a mere purchase. The inversion, therefore, of the order of succession, does not take us outside the sphere of the simple circulation of commodities, and we must rather look, whether there is in this simple circulation anything permitting an expansion of the value that enters into circulation, and, consequently, a creation of surplus-value.

Let us take the process of circulation in a form under which it presents itself as a simple and direct exchange of commodities. This is always the case when two owners of commodities buy from each other, and on the settling day the amounts mutually owing are equal and cancel each other. The money in this case is money of account and serves to express the value of the commodities by their prices, but is not, itself, in the shape of hard cash, confronted with them. So far as regards use-values, it is clear that both parties may gain some advantage. Both part with goods that, as use-values, are of no service to them, and receive others that they can make use of. And there may also be a further gain. A, who sells wine and buys corn, possibly produces more wine, with given labour-time, than farmer B could, and B on the other hand, more corn than wine-grower A could. A, therefore, may get, for the same exchange value, more corn, and B more wine, than each would respectively get without any exchange by producing his own corn and wine. With reference, therefore, to use-value, there is good ground for saying that 'exchange is a transaction by which both sides gain.'[1] It is otherwise with exchange value. 'A man who has plenty of wine and no corn treats with a man who has plenty of corn and no wine; an exchange takes place between them of corn to the value of 50, for wine of the same value. This act produces no increase of exchange value either for the one or the other; for each of them already possessed, before the exchange, a value equal to that which he acquired by means of that operation.'[2] The result is not altered by introducing money, as a medium of circulation, between the commodities, and making the sale and the purchase two distinct acts.[3] The value of a commodity is expressed in its price before it goes into circulation, and is therefore a precedent condition of circulation, not its result.[4]

Abstractedly considered, that is, apart from circumstances not immediately flowing from the laws of the simple circulation of commodities, there is in an exchange nothing (if we except the replacing of one use-value by another) but a metamorphosis, a mere change in the form of the commodity. The same exchange value, i.e., the same quantity of incorporated social labour, remains throughout in the hands of the owner of the commodity, first in the shape of his own commodity, then in the form of the money for which he exchanged it, and lastly, in the shape of the commodity he buys with that money. This change of form does not imply a change in the magnitude of the value. But the change, which the value of the commodity undergoes in this process, is limited to a change in its money form. This form exists first as the price of the commodity offered for sale, then as an actual sum of money, which, however, was already expressed in the price, and lastly, as the price of an equivalent commodity. This change of form no more implies, taken alone, a change in the quantity of value, than does the change of a £5 note into sovereigns, half sovereigns and shillings. So far therefore as the circulation of commodities effects a change in the form alone of their values, and is free from disturbing influences, it must be the exchange of equivalents. Little as Vulgar-Economy knows about the nature of value, yet whenever it wishes to consider the phenomena of circulation in their purity, it assumes that supply and demand are equal, which amounts to this, that their effect is nil. If therefore, as regards the use-values exchanged, both buyer and seller may possibly gain something, this is not the case as regards the exchange values. Here we must rather say, 'Where equality exists there can be no gain.'[5] It is true, commodities may be sold at prices deviating from their values, but these deviations are to be considered as infractions of the laws of the exchange of commodities,[6] which in its normal state is an exchange of equivalents, consequently, no method for increasing value.[7]

Hence, we see that behind all attempts to represent the circulation of commodities as a source of surplus-value, there lurks a *quid pro quo*, a mixing up of use-value and exchange value. For instance, Condillac says: 'It is not true that on an exchange of commodities we give value for value. On the contrary, each of the two contracting parties in every case, gives a less for a greater value . . . If we really exchanged equal values, neither party could make a profit. And yet, they both gain, or ought to gain. Why? The value of a thing consists solely in its relation to our wants. What is more to the one is less to the other, and *vice versa* . . . It is not to be assumed that we offer for sale articles required for our own consumption . . . We wish to part with a useless thing, in order to get one that we need; we want to give less for more . . . It was natural to think that, in an exchange, value was given for value, whenever each of the articles exchanged was of equal value with the same quantity of gold . . . But there is another point to be considered in our calculation. The question is, whether we both exchange something superfluous for something necessary.'[8] We see in this passage, how Condillac not only confuses use-value with exchange value, but in a really childish manner assumes, that in a society, in which the production of commodities is well developed, each producer produces his own means of subsistence, and throws into circulation only the excess over his own requirements.[9] Still, Condillac's argument is frequently used by modern economists, more especially when the point is to show, that the exchange of commodities in its developed form, commerce, is productive of surplus-value. For instance, 'Commerce . . . adds value to products, for the same products in the hands of consumers, are worth more than in the hands of producers, and it may strictly be considered an act of production.'[10] But commodities are not paid for twice over, once on account of their use-value, and again on account of their value. And though the use-value of a commodity is more serviceable to the buyer than to the seller, its money form is more serviceable to the seller. Would he otherwise sell it? We might therefore just as well say that the buyer performs 'strictly an act of production', by converting stockings, for example, into money.

If commodities, or commodities and money, of equal exchange value, and consequently equivalents, are exchanged, it is plain that no one abstracts more value from, than he throws into, circulation. There is no creation of surplus-value. And, in its normal form, the circulation of commodities demands the exchange of equivalents. But in actual practice, the process does not retain its normal form. Let us, therefore, assume an exchange of non-equivalents.

In any case the market for commodities is only frequented by owners of commodities, and the power which these persons exercise over each other, is no other than the power of their commodities. The material variety of these commodities is the material incentive to the act of exchange, and makes buyers and sellers mutually dependent, because none of them possesses the object of his own wants, and each holds in his hand the object of another's wants. Besides these material differences of their use-values, there is only one other difference between commodities, namely, that between their bodily form and the form into which they are converted by sale, the difference between commodities and money. And consequently the owners of commodities are distinguishable only as sellers, those who own commodities, and buyers, those who own money.

Suppose then, that by some inexplicable privilege, the seller is enabled to sell his commodities above their value, what is worth 100 for 110, in which case the price is nominally raised 10%. The seller therefore pockets a surplus-value of 10. But after he has sold he becomes a buyer. A third owner of commodities comes to him now as seller, who in this capacity also enjoys the privilege of selling his commodities 10% too dear. Our friend gained 10 as a seller only to lose it again as a buyer.[11] The net result is, that all owners of commodities sell their goods to one another at 10% above their value, which comes precisely to the same as if they sold them at their true value. Such a general and nominal rise of prices has the same effect as if the values had been expressed in weight of silver instead of in weight of gold. The nominal prices of commodities would rise, but the real relation between their values would remain unchanged.

Let us make the opposite assumption, that the buyer has the privilege of purchasing commodities under their value. In this case it is no longer necessary to bear in mind that he in his turn will become a seller. He was so before he became buyer; he had already lost 10% in selling before he gained 10% as buyer.[12] Everything is just as it was.

The creation of surplus-value, and therefore the conversion of money into capital, can consequently be explained neither on the assumption that commodities are sold above their value, nor that they are bought below their value.[13]

The problem is in no way simplified by introducing irrelevant matters after the manner of Col. Torrens: 'Effectual demand consists in the power and inclination (!), on the part of consumers, to give for commodities, either by immediate or circuitous barter, some greater portion of . . . capital than their production costs.'[14] In relation to circulation, producers and consumers meet only as buyers and sellers. To assert that the surplus-value acquired by the producer has its origin in the fact that consumers pay for commodities more than their value, is only to say in other words: The owner of commodities possesses, as a seller, the privilege of selling too dear. The seller has himself produced the commodities or represents their producer, but the buyer has to no less extent produced the commodities represented by his money, or represents their producer. The distinction between them is, that one buys and the other sells. The fact that the owner of the commodities, under the designation of producer, sells them over their value, and under the designation of consumer, pays too much for them, does not carry us a single step further.[15]

To be consistent therefore, the upholders of the delusion that surplus-value has its origin in a nominal rise of prices or in the privilege which the seller has of selling too dear, must assume the existence of a class that only buys and does not sell, i.e., only consumes and does not produce. The existence of such a class is inexplicable from the standpoint we have so far reached, viz., that of simple circulation. But let us anticipate. The money with which such a class is constantly making purchases, must constantly flow into their pockets, without any exchange, gratis, by might or right, from the pockets of the commodity-owners themselves. To sell commodities above their value to such a class, is only to crib back again a part of the money previously given to it.[16] The towns of Asia Minor thus paid a yearly money tribute to ancient Rome. With this money Rome purchased from them commodities, and purchased them too dear. The provincials cheated the Romans, and thus got back from their conquerors, in the course of trade, a portion of the tribute. Yet, for all that, the conquered were the really cheated. Their goods were still paid for with their own money. That is not the way to get rich or to create surplus-value.

Let us therefore keep within the bounds of exchange where sellers are also buyers, and buyers, sellers. Our difficulty may perhaps have arisen from treating the actors as personifications instead of as individuals.

A may be clever enough to get the advantage of B or C without their being able to retaliate. A sells wine worth £40 to B, and obtains from him in exchange corn to the value of £50. A has converted his £40 into £50, has made more money out of less, and has converted his commodities into capital. Let us examine this a little more closely. Before the exchange we had £40 worth of wine in the hands of A, and £50 worth of corn in those of B, a total value of £90. After the exchange we have still the same total value of £90. The value in circulation has not increased by one iota, it is only distributed differently between A and B. What is a loss of value to B is surplus-value to A; what is 'minus' to one is 'plus' to the other. The same change would have taken place, if A, without the formality of an exchange, had directly stolen the £10 from B. The sum of the values in circulation can clearly not be augmented by any change in their distribution, any more than the quantity of the precious metals in a country by a Jew selling a Queen Anne's farthing for a guinea. The capitalist class, as a whole, in any country, cannot over-reach themselves.[17]

Turn and twist then as we may, the fact remains unaltered. If equivalents are exchanged, no surplus-value results, and if non-equivalents are exchanged, still no surplus-value.[18] Circulation, or the exchange of commodities, begets no value.[19]

The reason is now therefore plain why, in analysing the standard form of capital, the form under which it determines the economic organisation of modern society, we entirely left out of consideration its most popular, and, so to say, antediluvian forms, merchants' capital and money-lenders' capital.

The circuit M—C—M', buying in order to sell dearer, is seen most clearly in genuine merchants' capital. But the movement takes place entirely within the sphere of circulation. Since, however, it is impossible, by circulation alone, to account for the conversion of money into capital, for the formation of surplus-value, it would appear, that merchants' capital is an impossibility, so long as equivalents are exchanged;[20] that, therefore, it can only have its origin in the two-fold advantage gained, over both the selling and the buying producers, by the merchant who parasitically shoves himself in between them. It is in this sense that Franklin says, 'war is robbery, commerce is generally cheating.'[21] If the transformation of merchants' money into capital is to be explained otherwise than by the producers being simply cheated, a long series of intermediate steps would be necessary, which, at present, when the simple circulation of commodities forms our only assumption, are entirely wanting.

What we have said with reference to merchants' capital, applies still more to money-lenders' capital. In merchants' capital, the two extremes, the money that is thrown upon the market, and the augmented money that is withdrawn from the market, are at least connected by a purchase and a sale, in other words by the movement of the circulation. In money-lenders' capital the form M—C—M' is reduced to the two extremes without a mean, M—M', money exchanged for more money, a form that is incompatible with the nature of money, and therefore remains inexplicable from the standpoint of the circulation of commodities. Hence Aristotle: 'since chrematistic is a double science, one part belonging to commerce, the other to economic, the latter being necessary and praiseworthy, the former based on circulation and with justice disapproved (for it is not based on nature, but on mutual cheating), therefore the usurer is most rightly hated, because money itself is the source of his gain, and is not used for the purposes for which it was invented. For it originated for the exchange of commodities, but interest makes out of money, more money. Hence its name (*tokos*: interest and offspring). For the begotten are like those who beget them. But interest is money of money, so that of all modes of making a living, this is the most contrary to nature.'[22]

In the course of our investigation, we shall find that both merchants' capital and interest-bearing capital are derivative forms, and at the same time it will become clear, why these two forms appear in the course of history before the modern standard form of capital.

We have shown that surplus-value cannot be created by circulation, and, therefore, that in its formation, something must take place in the background, which is not apparent in the circulation itself.[23] But can surplus-value possibly originate anywhere else than in circulation, which is the sum total of all the mutual relations of commodity-owners, as far as they are determined by their commodities? Apart from circulation, the commodity-owner is in relation only with his own commodity. So far as regards value, that relation is limited to this, that the commodity contains a quantity of his own labour, that quantity being measured by a definite social standard. This quantity is expressed by the value of the commodity, and since the value is reckoned in money of account, this quantity is also expressed by the price, which we will suppose to be £10. But his labour is not represented both by the value of the commodity, and by a surplus over that value, not by a price of 10 that is also a price of 11, not by a value that is greater than itself. The commodity owner can, by his labour, create value, but not self-expanding value. He can increase the value of his commodity, by adding fresh labour, and therefore more value to the value in hand, by making, for instance, leather into boots. The same material has now more value, because it contains a greater quantity of labour. The boots have therefore more value than the leather, but the value of the leather remains what it was; it has not expanded itself, has not, during the making of the boots, annexed surplus-value. It is therefore impossible that outside the sphere of circulation, a producer of commodities can, without coming into contact with other commodity-owners, expand value, and consequently convert money or commodities into capital.

It is therefore impossible for capital to be produced by circulation, and it is equally impossible for it to originate apart from circulation. It must have its origin both in circulation and yet not in circulation.

We have, therefore, got a double result.

The conversion of money into capital has to be explained on the basis of the laws that regulate the exchange of commodities, in such a way that the starting-point is the exchange of equivalents.[24] Our friend, Moneybags, who as yet is only an embryo capitalist, must buy his commodities at their value, must sell them at their value, and yet at the end of the process must withdraw more value from circulation than he threw into it at starting. His development into a full-grown capitalist must take place, both within the sphere of circulation and without it. These are the conditions of the problem. *Hic Rhodus, hic salta!*

Chapter 6
The Buying and Selling of Labour Power

The change of value that occurs in the case of money intended to be converted into capital, cannot take place in the money itself, since in its function of means of purchase and of payment, it does no more than realise the price of the commodity it buys or pays for; and, as hard cash, it is value petrified, never varying.[1] Just as little can it originate in the second act of circulation, the re-sale of the commodity, which does no more than transform the article from its bodily form back again into its money form. The change must, therefore, take place in the commodity bought by the first act, M—C, but not in its value, for equivalents are exchanged, and the commodity is paid for at its full value. We are, therefore, forced to the conclusion that the change originates in the use-value, as such, of the commodity, i.e., in its consumption. In order to be able to extract value from the consumption of a commodity, our friend, Moneybags, must be so lucky as to find, within the sphere of circulation, in the market, a commodity, whose use-value possesses the peculiar property of being a source of value, whose actual consumption, therefore, is itself an embodiment of labour, and, consequently, a creation of value. The possessor of money does find on the market such a special commodity in capacity for labour or labour power.

By labour power or capacity for labour is to be understood the aggregate of those mental and physical capabilities existing in a human being, which he exercises whenever he produces a use-value of any description.

But in order that our owner of money may be able to find labour power offered for sale as a commodity, various conditions must first be fulfilled. The exchange of commodities of itself implies no other relations of dependence than those which result from its own nature. On this assumption, labour power can appear upon the market as a commodity, only if, and so far as, its possessor, the individual whose labour power it is, offers it for sale, or sells it, as a commodity. In order that he may be able to do this, he must have it at his disposal, must be the untrammelled owner of his capacity for labour, i.e., of his person.[2] He and the owner of money meet in the market, and deal with each other as on the basis of equal rights, with this difference alone, that one is buyer, the other seller; both, therefore, equal in the eyes of the law. The continuance of this relation demands that the owner of the labour power should sell it only for a definite period, for if he were to sell it rump and stump, once for all, he would be selling himself, converting himself from a free man into a slave, from an owner of a commodity into a commodity. He must constantly look upon his labour power as his own property, his own commodity, and this he can only do by placing it at the disposal of the buyer temporarily, for a definite period of time. By this means alone can he avoid renouncing his rights of ownership over it.[3]

The second essential condition to the owner of money finding labour power in the market as a commodity is this – that the labourer instead of being in the position to sell commodities in which his labour is incorporated, must be obliged to offer for sale as a commodity that very labour power, which exists only in his living self.

In order that a man may be able to sell commodities other than labour power, he must of course have the means of production, as raw material, implements, &c. No boots can be made without leather. He requires also the means of subsistence. Nobody – not even 'a musician of the future' – can live upon future products, or upon use-values in an unfinished state; and ever since the first moment of his appearance on the world's stage, man always has been, and must still be a consumer, both before and while he is producing. In a society where all products assume the form of commodities, these commodities must be sold after they have been produced; it is only after their sale that they can serve in satisfying the requirements of their producer. The time necessary for their sale is superadded to that necessary for their production.

For the conversion of his money into capital, therefore, the owner of money must meet in the market with the free labourer, free in the double sense, that as a free man he can dispose of his labour power as his own commodity, and that on the other hand he has no other commodity for sale, is short of everything necessary for the realisation of his labour power.

The question why this free labourer confronts him in the market, has no interest for the owner of money, who regards the labour-market as a branch of the general market for commodities. And for the present it interests us just as little. We cling to the fact theoretically, as he does practically. One thing, however, is clear – Nature does not produce on the one side owners of money or commodities, and on the other men possessing nothing but their own labour power. This relation has no natural basis, neither is its social basis one that is common to all historical periods. It is clearly the result of a past historical development, the product of many economic revolutions, of the extinction of a whole series of older forms of social production.

So, too, the economic categories, already discussed by us, bear the stamp of history. Definite historical conditions are necessary that a product may become a commodity. It must not be produced as the immediate means of subsistence of the producer himself. Had we gone further, and inquired under what circumstances all, or even the majority of products take the form of commodities, we should have found that this can only happen with production of a very specific kind, capitalist production. Such an inquiry, however, would have been foreign to the analysis of commodities. Production and circulation of commodities can take place, although the great mass of the objects produced are intended for the immediate requirements of their producers, are not turned into commodities, and consequently social production is not yet by a long way dominated in its length and breadth by exchange value. The appearance of products as commodities presupposes such a development of the social division of labour, that the separation of use-value from exchange value, a separation which first begins with barter, must already have been completed. But such a degree of development is common to many forms of society, which in other respects present the most varying historical features. On the other hand, if we consider money, its existence implies a definite stage in the exchange of commodities. The particular functions of money which it performs, either as the mere equivalent of commodities, or as means of circulation, or means of payment, as hoard or as universal money, point, according to the extent and relative preponderance of the one function or the other, to very different stages in the process of social production. Yet we know by experience that a circulation of commodities relatively primitive, suffices for the production of all these forms. Otherwise with capital. The historical conditions of its existence are by no means given with the mere circulation of money and commodities. It can spring into life, only when the owner of the means of production and subsistence meets in the market with the free labourer selling his labour power. And this one historical condition comprises a world's history. Capital, therefore, announces from its first appearance a new epoch in the process of social production.[4]

We must now examine more closely this peculiar commodity, labour power.[5] How is that value determined?

The value of labour power is determined, as in the case of every other commodity, by the labour-time necessary for the production, and consequently also the reproduction, of this special article. So far as it has value, it represents no more than a definite quantity of the average labour of society incorporated in it. Labour power exists only as a capacity, or power of the living individual. Its production consequently presupposes his existence. Given the individual, the production of labour power consists in his reproduction of himself or his maintenance. For his maintenance he requires a given quantity of the means of subsistence. Therefore the labour-time requisite for the production of labour power reduces itself to that necessary for the production of those means of subsistence; in other words, the value of labour power is the value of the means of subsistence necessary for the maintenance of the labourer. Labour power, however, becomes a reality only by its exercise; it sets itself in action only by working. But thereby a definite quantity of human muscle, nerve, brain, &c., is wasted, and these require to be restored. This increased expenditure demands a larger income.[6] If the owner of labour power works today, tomorrow he must again be able to repeat the same process in the same conditions as regards health and strength. His means of subsistence must therefore be sufficient to maintain him in his normal state as a labouring individual. His natural wants, such as food, clothing, fuel, and housing, vary according to the climatic and other physical conditions of his country. On the other hand, the number and extent of his so-called necessary wants, as also the modes of satisfying them, are themselves the product of historical development, and depend therefore to a great extent on the degree of civilisation of a country, more particularly on the conditions under which, and consequently on the habits and degree of comfort in which, the class of free labourers has been formed.[7] In contradistinction therefore to the case of other commodities, there enters into the determination of the value of labour power a historical and moral element. Nevertheless, in a given country, at a given period, the average quantity of the means of subsistence necessary for the labourer is practically known.

The owner of labour power is mortal. If then his appearance in the market is to be continuous, and the continuous conversion of money into capital assumes this, the seller of labour power must perpetuate himself, 'in the way that every living individual perpetuates himself, by procreation.'[8] The labour power withdrawn from the market by wear and tear and death, must be continually replaced by, at the very least, an equal amount of fresh labour power. Hence the sum of the means of subsistence necessary for the production of labour power must include the means necessary for the labourer's substitutes, i.e., his children, in order that this race of peculiar commodity-owners may perpetuate its appearance in the market.[9]

In order to modify the human organism, so that it may acquire skill and handiness in a given branch of industry, and become labour power of a special kind, a special education or training is requisite, and this, on its part, costs an equivalent in commodities of a greater or less amount. This amount varies according to the more or less complicated character of the labour power. The expenses of this education (excessively small in the case of ordinary labour power), enter *pro tanto* into the total value spent in its production.

The value of labour power resolves itself into the value of a definite quantity of the means of subsistence. It therefore varies with the value of these means or with the quantity of labour requisite for their production.

Some of the means of subsistence, such as food and fuel, are consumed daily, and a fresh supply must be provided daily. Others such as clothes and furniture last for longer periods and require to be replaced only at longer intervals. One article must be bought or paid for daily, another weekly, another quarterly, and so on. But in whatever way the sum total of these outlays may be spread over the year, they must be covered by the average income, taking one day with another. If the total of the commodities required daily for the production of labour power = A, and those required weekly = B, and those required quarterly = C, and so on, the daily average of these commodities = 365A + 52B + 4C + &c/365. Suppose that in this mass of commodities requisite for the average day there are embodied 6 hours of social labour, then there is incorporated daily in labour power half a day's average social labour, in other words, half a day's labour is requisite for the daily production of labour power. This quantity of labour forms the value of a day's labour power or the value of the labour power daily reproduced. If half a day's average social labour is incorporated in three shillings, then three shillings is the price corresponding to the value of a day's labour power. If its owner therefore offers it for sale at three shillings a day, its selling price is equal to its value, and according to our supposition, our friend Moneybags, who is intent upon converting his three shillings into capital, pays this value.

The minimum limit of the value of labour power is determined by the value of the commodities, without the daily supply of which the labourer cannot renew his vital energy, consequently by the value of those means of subsistence that are physically indispensable. If the price of labour power fall to this minimum, it falls below its value, since under such circumstances it can be maintained and developed only in a crippled state. But the value of every commodity is determined by the labour-time requisite to turn it out so as to be of normal quality.

It is a very cheap sort of sentimentality which declares this method of determining the value of labour power, a method prescribed by the very nature of the case, to be a brutal method, and which wails with Rossi that, 'To comprehend capacity for labour (puissance de travail) at the same time that we make abstraction from the means of subsistence of the labourers during the process of production, is to comprehend a phantom (être de raison). When we speak of labour, or capacity for labour, we speak at the same time of the labourer and his means of subsistence, of labourer and wages.'[10] When we speak of capacity for labour, we do not speak of labour, any more than when we speak of capacity for digestion, we speak of digestion. The latter process requires something more than a good stomach. When we speak of capacity for labour, we do not abstract from the necessary means of subsistence. On the contrary, their value is expressed in its value. If his capacity for labour remains unsold, the labourer derives no benefit from it, but rather he will feel it to be a cruel nature-imposed necessity that this capacity has cost for its production a definite amount of the means of subsistence and that it will continue to do so for its reproduction. He will then agree with Sismondi: 'that capacity for labour . . . is nothing unless it is sold.'[11]

One consequence of the peculiar nature of labour power as a commodity is, that its use-value does not, on the conclusion of the contract between the buyer and seller, immediately pass into the hands of the former. Its value, like that of every other commodity, is already fixed before it goes into circulation, since a definite quantity of social labour has been spent upon it; but its use-value consists in the subsequent exercise of its force. The alienation of labour power and its actual appropriation by the buyer, its employment as a use-value, are separated by an interval of time. But in those cases in which the formal alienation by sale of the use-value of a commodity, is not simultaneous with its actual delivery to the buyer, the money of the latter usually functions as means of payment.[12] In every country in which the capitalist mode of production reigns, it is the custom not to pay for labour power before it has been exercised for the period fixed by the contract, as for example, the end of each week. In all cases, therefore, the use-value of the labour power is advanced to the capitalist: the labourer allows the buyer to consume it before he receives payment of the price; he everywhere gives credit to the capitalist. That this credit is no mere fiction, is shown not only by the occasional loss of wages on the bankruptcy of the capitalist,[13] but also by a series of more enduring consequences.[14] Nevertheless, whether money serves as a means of purchase or as a means of payment, this makes no alteration in the nature of the exchange of commodities. The price of the labour power is fixed by the contract, although it is not realised till later, like the rent of a house. The labour power is sold, although it is only paid for at a later period. It will, therefore, be useful, for a clear comprehension of the relation of the parties, to assume provisionally, that the possessor of labour power, on the occasion of each sale, immediately receives the price stipulated to be paid for it.

We now know how the value paid by the purchaser to the possessor of this peculiar commodity, labour power, is determined. The use-value which the former gets in exchange, manifests itself only in the actual usufruct, in the consumption of the labour power. The money-owner buys everything necessary for this purpose, such as raw material, in the market, and pays for it at its full value. The consumption of labour power is at one and the same time the production of commodities and of surplus-value. The consumption of labour power is completed, as in the case of every other commodity, outside the limits of the market or of the sphere of circulation. Accompanied by Mr Moneybags and by the possessor of labour power, we therefore take leave for a time of this noisy sphere, where everything takes place on the surface and in view of all men, and follow them both into the hidden abode of production, on whose threshold there stares us in the face 'No admittance except on business.' Here we shall see, not only how capital produces, but how capital is produced. We shall at last force the secret of profit making.

This sphere that we are deserting, within whose boundaries the sale and purchase of labour power goes on, is in fact a very Eden of the innate rights of man. There alone rule Freedom, Equality, Property and Bentham. Freedom, because both buyer and seller of a commodity, say of labour power, are constrained only by their own free will. They contract as free agents, and the agreement they come to, is but the form in which they give legal expression to their common will. Equality, because each enters into relation with the other, as with a simple owner of commodities, and they exchange equivalent for equivalent. Property, because each disposes only of what is his own. And Bentham, because each looks only to himself. The only force that brings them together and puts them in relation with each other, is the selfishness, the gain and the private interests of each. Each looks to himself only, and no one troubles himself about the rest, and just because they do so, do they all, in accordance with the pre-established harmony of things, or under the auspices of an all-shrewd providence, work together to their mutual advantage, for the common weal and in the interest of all.

On leaving this sphere of simple circulation or of exchange of commodities, which furnishes the 'Free-trader Vulgaris' with his views and ideas, and with the standard by which he judges a society based on capital and wages, we think we can perceive a change in the physiognomy of our *dramatis personae*. He, who before was the money-owner, now strides in front as capitalist; the possessor of labour power follows as his labourer. The one with an air of importance, smirking, intent on business; the other, timid and holding back, like one who is bringing his own hide to market and has nothing to expect but – a hiding.

Part 3
The Production of Absolute Surplus-Value

Chapter 7
The Labour-Process and the Process of Producing Surplus-Value

Section 1. The Labour-Process or the Production of Use-Values.

The capitalist buys labour power in order to use it; and labour power in use is labour itself. The purchaser of labour power consumes it by setting the seller of it to work. By working, the latter becomes actually, what before he only was potentially, labour power in action, a labourer. In order that his labour may re-appear in a commodity, he must, before all things, expend it on something useful, on something capable of satisfying a want of some sort. Hence, what the capitalist sets the labourer to produce, is a particular use-value, a specified article. The fact that the production of use-values, or goods, is carried on under the control of a capitalist and on his behalf, does not alter the general character of that production. We shall, therefore, in the first place, have to consider the labour-process independently of the particular form it assumes under given social conditions.

Labour is, in the first place, a process in which both man and Nature participate, and in which man of his own accord starts, regulates, and controls the material re-actions between himself and Nature. He opposes himself to Nature as one of her own forces, setting in motion arms and legs, head and hands, the natural forces of his body, in order to appropriate Nature's productions in a form adapted to his own wants. By thus acting on the external world and changing it, he at the same time changes his own nature. He develops his slumbering powers and compels them to act in obedience to his sway. We are not now dealing with those primitive instinctive forms of labour that remind us of the mere animal. An immeasurable interval of time separates the state of things in which a man brings his labour power to market for sale as a commodity, from that state in which human labour was still in its first instinctive stage. We presuppose labour in a form that stamps it as exclusively human. A spider conducts operations that resemble those of a weaver, and a bee puts to shame many an architect in the construction of her cells. But what distinguishes the worst architect from the best of bees is this, that the architect raises his structure in imagination before he erects it in reality. At the end of every labour-process, we get a result that already existed in the imagination of the labourer at its commencement. He not only effects a change of form in the material on which he works, but he also realises a purpose of his own that gives the law to his modus operandi, and to which he must subordinate his will. And this subordination is no mere momentary act. Besides the exertion of the bodily organs, the process demands that, during the whole operation, the workman's will be steadily in consonance with his purpose. This means close attention. The less he is attracted by the nature of the work, and the mode in which it is carried on, and the less, therefore, he enjoys it as something which gives play to his bodily and mental powers, the more close his attention is forced to be.

The elementary factors of the labour-process are 1, the personal activity of man, i.e., work itself, 2, the subject of that work, and 3, its instruments.

The soil (and this, economically speaking, includes water) in the virgin state in which it supplies[1] man with necessaries or the means of subsistence ready to hand, exists independently of him, and is the universal subject of human labour. All those things which labour merely separates from immediate connection with their environment, are subjects of labour spontaneously provided by Nature. Such are fish which we catch and take from their element, water, timber which we fell in the virgin forest, and ores which we extract from their veins. If, on the other hand, the subject of labour has, so to say, been filtered through previous labour, we call it raw material; such is ore already extracted and ready for washing. All raw material is the subject of labour, but not every subject of labour is raw material: it can only become so, after it has undergone some alteration by means of labour.

An instrument of labour is a thing, or a complex of things, which the labourer interposes between himself and the subject of his labour, and which serves as the conductor of his activity. He makes use of the mechanical, physical, and chemical properties of some substances in order to make other substances subservient to his aims.[2] Leaving out of consideration such ready-made means of subsistence as fruits, in gathering which a man's own limbs serve as the instruments of his labour, the first thing of which the labourer possesses himself is not the subject of labour but its instrument. Thus Nature becomes one of the organs of his activity, one that he annexes to his own bodily organs, adding stature to himself in spite of the Bible. As the earth is his original larder, so too it is his original tool house. It supplies him, for instance, with stones for throwing, grinding, pressing, cutting, &c. The earth itself is an instrument of labour, but when used as such in agriculture implies a whole series of other instruments and a comparatively high development of labour.[3] No sooner does labour undergo the least development, than it requires specially prepared instruments. Thus in the oldest caves we find stone implements and weapons. In the earliest period of human history domesticated animals, i.e., animals which have been bred for the purpose, and have undergone modifications by means of labour, play the chief part as instruments of labour along with specially prepared stones, wood, bones, and shells.[4] The use and fabrication of instruments of labour, although existing in the germ among certain species of animals, is specifically characteristic of the human labour-process, and Franklin therefore defines man as a tool-making animal. Relics of bygone instruments of labour possess the same importance for the investigation of extinct economic forms of society, as do fossil bones for the determination of extinct species of animals. It is not the articles made, but how they are made, and by what instruments, that enables us to distinguish different economic epochs.[5] Instruments of labour not only supply a standard of the degree of development to which human labour has attained, but they are also indicators of the social conditions under which that labour is carried on. Among the instruments of labour, those of a mechanical nature, which, taken as a whole, we may call the bone and muscles of production, offer much more decided characteristics of a given epoch of production, than those which, like pipes, tubs, baskets, jars, &c., serve only to hold the materials for labour, which latter class, we may in a general way, call the vascular system of production. The latter first begins to play an important part in the chemical industries.

In a wider sense we may include among the instruments of labour, in addition to those things that are used for directly transferring labour to its subject, and which therefore, in one way or another, serve as conductors of activity, all such objects as are necessary for carrying on the labour-process. These do not enter directly into the process, but without them it is either impossible for it to take place at all, or possible only to a partial extent. Once more we find the earth to be a universal instrument of this sort, for it furnishes a *locus standi* to the labourer and a field of employment for his activity. Among instruments that are the result of previous labour and also belong to this class, we find workshops, canals, roads, and so forth.

In the labour-process, therefore, man's activity, with the help of the instruments of labour, effects an alteration, designed from the commencement, in the material worked upon. The process disappears in the product, the latter is a use-value, Nature's material adapted by a change of form to the wants of man. Labour has incorporated itself with its subject: the former is materialised, the latter transformed. That which in the labourer appeared as movement, now appears in the product as a fixed quality without motion. The blacksmith forges and the product is a forging.

If we examine the whole process from the point of view of its result, the product, it is plain that both the instruments and the subject of labour, are means of production,[6] and that the labour itself is productive labour.[7]

Though a use-value, in the form of a product, issues from the labour-process, yet other use-values, products of previous labour, enter into it as means of production. The same use-value is both the product of a previous process, and a means of production in a later process. Products are therefore not only results, but also essential conditions of labour.

With the exception of the extractive industries, in which the material for labour is provided immediately by Nature, such as mining, hunting, fishing, and agriculture (so far as the latter is confined to breaking up virgin soil), all branches of industry manipulate raw material, objects already filtered through labour, already products of labour. Such is seed in agriculture. Animals and plants, which we are accustomed to consider as products of Nature, are in their present form, not only products of, say last year's labour, but the result of a gradual transformation, continued through many generations, under man's superintendence, and by means of his labour. But in the great majority of cases, instruments of labour show even to the most superficial observer, traces of the labour of past ages.

Raw material may either form the principal substance of a product, or it may enter into its formation only as an accessory. An accessory may be consumed by the instruments of labour, as coal under a boiler, oil by a wheel, hay by draft-horses, or it may be mixed with the raw material in order to produce some modification thereof, as chlorine into unbleached linen, coal with iron, dye-stuff with wool, or again, it may help to carry on the work itself, as in the case of the materials used for heating and lighting workshops. The distinction between principal substance and accessory vanishes in the true chemical industries, because there none of the raw material re-appears, in its original composition, in the substance of the product.[8]

Every object possesses various properties, and is thus capable of being applied to different uses. One and the same product may therefore serve as raw material in very different processes. Corn, for example, is a raw material for millers, starch-manufacturers, distillers, and cattlebreeders. It also enters as raw material into its own production in the shape of seed; coal, too, is at the same time the product of, and a means of production in, coal-mining.

Again, a particular product may be used in one and the same process, both as an instrument of labour and as raw material. Take, for instance, the fattening of cattle, where the animal is the raw material, and at the same time an instrument for the production of manure.

A product, though ready for immediate consumption, may yet serve as raw material for a further product, as grapes when they become the raw material for wine. On the other hand, labour may give us its product in such a form, that we can use it only as raw material, as is the case with cotton, thread, and yarn. Such a raw material, though itself a product, may have to go through a whole series of different processes: in each of these in turn, it serves, with constantly varying form, as raw material, until the last process of the series leaves it a perfect product, ready for individual consumption, or for use as an instrument of labour.

Hence we see, that whether a use-value is to be regarded as raw material, as instrument of labour, or as product, this is determined entirely by its function in the labour-process, by the position it there occupies: as this varies, so does its character.

Whenever therefore a product enters as a means of production into a new labour-process, it thereby loses its character of product, and becomes a mere factor in the process. A spinner treats spindles only as implements for spinning, and flax only as the material that he spins. Of course it is impossible to spin without material and spindles; and therefore the existence of these things as products, at the commencement of the spinning operation, must be presumed: but in the process itself, the fact that they are products of previous labour, is a matter of utter indifference; just as in the digestive process, it is of no importance whatever, that bread is the produce of the previous labour of the farmer, the miller, and the baker. On the contrary, it is generally by their imperfections as products, that the means of production in any process assert themselves in their character of products. A blunt knife or weak thread forcibly remind us of Mr A, the cutler, or Mr B, the spinner. In the finished product the labour by means of which it has acquired its useful qualities is not palpable, has apparently vanished.

A machine which does not serve the purposes of labour, is useless. In addition, it falls a prey to the destructive influence of natural forces. Iron rusts and wood rots. Yarn with which we neither weave nor knit, is cotton wasted. Living labour must seize upon these things and rouse them from their death-sleep, change them from mere possible use-values into real and effective ones. Bathed in the fire of labour, appropriated as part and parcel of labour's organism, and, as it were, made alive for the performance of their functions in the process, they are in truth consumed, but consumed with a purpose, as elementary constituents of new use-values, of new products, ever ready as means of subsistence for individual consumption, or as means of production for some new labour-process.

If then, on the one hand, finished products are not only results, but also necessary conditions, of the labour-process, on the other hand, their assumption into that process, their contact with living labour, is the sole means by which they can be made to retain their character of use-values, and be utilised.

Labour uses up its material factors, its subject and its instruments, consumes them, and is therefore a process of consumption. Such productive consumption is distinguished from individual consumption by this, that the latter uses up products, as means of subsistence for the living individual; the former, as means whereby alone, labour, the labour power of the living individual, is enabled to act. The product, therefore, of individual consumption, is the consumer himself; the result of productive consumption, is a product distinct from the consumer.

In so far then, as its instruments and subjects are themselves products, labour consumes products in order to create products, or in other words, consumes one set of products by turning them into means of production for another set. But, just as in the beginning, the only participators in the labour-process were man and the earth, which latter exists independently of man, so even now we still employ in the process many means of production, provided directly by Nature, that do not represent any combination of natural substances with human labour.

The labour-process, resolved as above into its simple elementary factors, is human action with a view to the production of use-values, appropriation of natural substances to human requirements; it is the necessary condition for effecting exchange of matter between man and Nature; it is the everlasting Nature-imposed condition of human existence, and therefore is independent of every social phase of that existence, or rather, is common to every such phase. It was, therefore, not necessary to represent our labourer in connection with other labourers; man and his labour on one side, Nature and its materials on the other, sufficed. As the taste of the porridge does not tell you who grew the oats, no more does this simple process tell you of itself what are the social conditions under which it is taking place, whether under the slave-owner's brutal lash, or the anxious eye of the capitalist, whether Cincinnatus carries it on in tilling his modest farm or a savage in killing wild animals with stones. 9

Let us now return to our would-be capitalist. We left him just after he had purchased, in the open market, all the necessary factors of the labour-process – its objective factors, the means of production, as well as its subjective factor, labour power. With the keen eye of an expert, he has selected the means of production and the kind of labour power best adapted to his particular trade, be it spinning, bootmaking, or any other kind. He then proceeds to consume the commodity, the labour power that he has just bought, by causing the labourer, the impersonation of that labour power, to consume the means of production by his labour. The general character of the labour-process is evidently not changed by the fact, that the labourer works for the capitalist instead of for himself; moreover, the particular methods and operations employed in bootmaking or spinning are not immediately changed by the intervention of the capitalist. He must begin by taking the labour power as he finds it in the market, and consequently be satisfied with labour of such a kind as would be found in the period immediately preceding the rise of capitalists. Changes in the methods of production by the subordination of labour to capital, can take place only at a later period, and therefore will have to be treated of in a later chapter.

The labour-process, turned into the process by which the capitalist consumes labour power, exhibits two characteristic phenomena. First, the labourer works under the control of the capitalist to whom his labour belongs; the capitalist taking good care that the work is done in a proper manner, and that the means of production are used with intelligence, so that there is no unnecessary waste of raw material, and no wear and tear of the implements beyond what is necessarily caused by the work.

Secondly, the product is the property of the capitalist and not that of the labourer, its immediate producer. Suppose that a capitalist pays for a day's labour power at its value; then the right to use that power for a day belongs to him, just as much as the right to use any other commodity, such as a horse that he has hired for the day. To the purchaser of a commodity belongs its use, and the seller of labour power, by giving his labour, does no more, in reality, than part with the use-value that he has sold. From the instant he steps into the workshop, the use-value of his labour power, and therefore also its use, which is labour, belongs to the capitalist. By the purchase of labour power, the capitalist incorporates labour, as a living ferment, with the lifeless constituents of the product. From his point of view, the labour-process is nothing more than the consumption of the commodity purchased, i.e., of labour power; but this consumption cannot be effected except by supplying the labour power with the means of production. The labour-process is a process between things that the capitalist has purchased, things that have become his property. The product of this process belongs, therefore, to him, just as much as does the wine which is the product of a process of fermentation completed in his cellar.[10]

Section 2. The Production of Surplus-Value.

The product appropriated by the capitalist is a use-value, as yarn, for example, or boots. But, although boots are, in one sense, the basis of all social progress, and our capitalist is a decided 'progressist', yet he does not manufacture boots for their own sake. Use-value is, by no means, the thing '*qu'on aime pour lui-même*' in the production of commodities. Use-values are only produced by capitalists, because, and in so far as, they are the material substratum, the depositories of exchange value. Our capitalist has two objects in view: in the first place, he wants to produce a use-value that has a value in exchange, that is to say, an article destined to be sold, a commodity; and secondly, he desires to produce a commodity whose value shall be greater than the sum of the values of the commodities used in its production, that is, of the means of production and the labour power, that he purchased with his good money in the open market. His aim is to produce not only a use-value, but a commodity also; not only use-value, but value; not only value, but at the same time surplus-value.

It must be borne in mind, that we are now dealing with the production of commodities, and that, up to this point, we have only considered one aspect of the process. Just as commodities are, at the same time, use-values and values, so the process of producing them must be a labour-process, and at the same time, a process of creating value.[11]

Let us now examine production as a creation of value.

We know that the value of each commodity is determined by the quantity of labour expended on and materialised in it, by the working-time necessary, under given social conditions, for its production. This rule also holds good in the case of the product that accrued to our capitalist, as the result of the labour-process carried on for him. Assuming this product to be 10 lbs. of yarn, our first step is to calculate the quantity of labour realised in it.

For spinning the yarn, raw material is required; suppose in this case 10 lbs. of cotton. We have no need at present to investigate the value of this cotton, for our capitalist has, we will assume, bought it at its full value, say of ten shillings. In this price the labour required for the production of the cotton is already expressed in terms of the average labour of society. We will further assume that the wear and tear of the spindle, which, for our present purpose, may represent all other instruments of labour employed, amounts to the value of 2s. If, then, twenty-four hours' labour, or two working-days, are required to produce the quantity of gold represented by twelve shillings, we have here, to begin with, two days' labour already incorporated in the yarn.

We must not let ourselves be misled by the circumstance that the cotton has taken a new shape while the substance of the spindle has to a certain extent been used up. By the general law of value, if the value of 40 lbs. of yarn = the value of 40 lbs. of cotton + the value of a whole spindle, i. e., if the same working-time is required to produce the commodities on either side of this equation, then 10 lbs. of yarn are an equivalent for 10 lbs. of cotton, together with one-fourth of a spindle. In the case we are considering the same working-time is materialised in the 10 lbs. of yarn on the one hand, and in the 10 lbs. of cotton and the fraction of a spindle on the other. Therefore, whether value appears in cotton, in a spindle, or in yarn, makes no difference in the amount of that value. The spindle and cotton, instead of resting quietly side by side, join together in the process, their forms are altered, and they are turned into yarn; but their value is no more affected by this fact than it would be if they had been simply exchanged for their equivalent in yarn.

The labour required for the production of the cotton, the raw material of the yarn, is part of the labour necessary to produce the yarn, and is therefore contained in the yarn. The same applies to the labour embodied in the spindle, without whose wear and tear the cotton could not be spun.

Hence, in determining the value of the yarn, or the labour-time required for its production, all the special processes carried on at various times and in different places, which were necessary, first to produce the cotton and the wasted portion of the spindle, and then with the cotton and spindle to spin the yarn, may together be looked on as different and successive phases of one and the same process. The whole of the labour in the yarn is past labour; and it is a matter of no importance that the operations necessary for the production of its constituent elements were carried on at times which, referred to the present, are more remote than the final operation of spinning. If a definite quantity of labour, say thirty days, is requisite to build a house, the total amount of labour incorporated in it is not altered by the fact that the work of the last day is done twenty-nine days later than that of the first. Therefore the labour contained in the raw material and the instruments of labour can be treated just as if it were labour expended in an earlier stage of the spinning process, before the labour of actual spinning commenced.

The values of the means of production, i. e., the cotton and the spindle, which values are expressed in the price of twelve shillings, are therefore constituent parts of the value of the yarn, or, in other words, of the value of the product.

Two conditions must nevertheless be fulfilled. First, the cotton and spindle must concur in the production of a use-value; they must in the present case become yarn. Value is independent of the particular use-value by which it is borne, but it must be embodied in a use-value of some kind. Secondly, the time occupied in the labour of production must not exceed the time really necessary under the given social conditions of the case. Therefore, if no more than 1 lb. of cotton be requisite to spin 11 lbs. of yarn, care must be taken that no more than this weight of cotton is consumed in the production of 11 lbs. of yarn; and similarly with regard to the spindle. Though the capitalist have a hobby, and use a gold instead of a steel spindle, yet the only labour that counts for anything in the value of the yarn is that which would be required to produce a steel spindle, because no more is necessary under the given social conditions.

We now know what portion of the value of the yarn is owing to the cotton and the spindle. It amounts to twelve shillings or the value of two days' work. The next point for our consideration is, what portion of the value of the yarn is added to the cotton by the labour of the spinner.

We have now to consider this labour under a very different aspect from that which it had during the labour-process; there, we viewed it solely as that particular kind of human activity which changes cotton into yarn; there, the more the labour was suited to the work, the better the yarn, other circumstances remaining the same. The labour of the spinner was then viewed as specifically different from other kinds of productive labour, different on the one hand in its special aim, viz., spinning, different, on the other hand, in the special character of its operations, in the special nature of its means of production and in the special use-value of its product. For the operation of spinning, cotton and spindles are a necessity, but for making rifled cannon they would be of no use whatever. Here, on the contrary, where we consider the labour of the spinner only so far as it is value-creating, i.e., a source of value, his labour differs in no respect from the labour of the man who bores cannon, or (what here more nearly concerns us), from the labour of the cotton-planter and spindle-maker incorporated in the means of production. It is solely by reason of this identity, that cotton planting, spindle making and spinning, are capable of forming the component parts differing only quantitatively from each other, of one whole, namely, the value of the yarn. Here, we have nothing more to do with the quality, the nature and the specific character of the labour, but merely with its quantity. And this simply requires to be calculated. We proceed upon the assumption that spinning is simple, unskilled labour, the average labour of a given state of society. Hereafter we shall see that the contrary assumption would make no difference.

While the labourer is at work, his labour constantly undergoes a transformation: from being motion, it becomes an object without motion; from being the labourer working, it becomes the thing produced. At the end of one hour's spinning, that act is represented by a definite quantity of yarn; in other words, a definite quantity of labour, namely that of one hour, has become embodied in the cotton. We say labour, i.e., the expenditure of his vital force by the spinner, and not spinning labour, because the special work of spinning counts here, only so far as it is the expenditure of labour power in general, and not in so far as it is the specific work of the spinner.

In the process we are now considering it is of extreme importance, that no more time be consumed in the work of transforming the cotton into yarn than is necessary under the given social conditions. If under normal, i.e. average, social conditions of production, a pounds of cotton ought to be made into b pounds of yarn by one hour's labour, then a day's labour does not count as 12 hours' labour unless 12a pounds of cotton have been made into 12b pounds of yarn; for in the creation of value, the time that is socially necessary alone counts.

Not only the labour, but also the raw material and the product now appear in quite a new light, very different from that in which we viewed them in the labour-process pure and simple. The raw material serves now merely as an absorbent of a definite quantity of labour. By this absorption it is in fact changed into yarn, because it is spun, because labour power in the form of spinning is added to it; but the product, the yarn, is now nothing more than a measure of the labour absorbed by the cotton. If in one hour 1 2/3 lbs. of cotton can be spun into 1 2/3 lbs. of yarn, then 10 lbs. of yarn indicate the absorption of 6 hours' labour. Definite quantities of product, these quantities being determined by experience, now represent nothing but definite quantities of labour, definite masses of crystallised labour-time. They are nothing more than the materialisation of so many hours or so many days of social labour.

We are here no more concerned about the facts, that the labour is the specific work of spinning, that its subject is cotton and its product yarn, than we are about the fact that the subject itself is already a product and therefore raw material. If the spinner, instead of spinning, were working in a coal mine, the subject of his labour, the coal, would be supplied by Nature; nevertheless, a definite quantity of extracted coal, a hundredweight for example, would represent a definite quantity of absorbed labour.

We assumed, on the occasion of its sale, that the value of a day's labour power is three shillings, and that six hours' labour is incorporated in that sum; and consequently that this amount of labour is requisite to produce the necessaries of life daily required on an average by the labourer. If now our spinner by working for one hour, can convert 1 2/3 lbs. of cotton into 1 2/3 lbs. of yarn,[12] it follows that in six hours he will convert 10 lbs. of cotton into 10 lbs. of yarn. Hence, during the spinning process, the cotton absorbs six hours' labour. The same quantity of labour is also embodied in a piece of gold of the value of three shillings. Consequently by the mere labour of spinning, a value of three shillings is added to the cotton.

Let us now consider the total value of the product, the 10 lbs. of yarn. Two and a half days' labour has been embodied in it, of which two days were contained in the cotton and in the substance of the spindle worn away, and half a day was absorbed during the process of spinning. This two and a half days' labour is also represented by a piece of gold of the value of fifteen shillings. Hence, fifteen shillings is an adequate price for the 10 lbs. of yarn, or the price of one pound is eighteenpence.

Our capitalist stares in astonishment. The value of the product is exactly equal to the value of the capital advanced. The value so advanced has not expanded, no surplus-value has been created, and consequently money has not been converted into capital. The price of the yarn is fifteen shillings, and fifteen shillings were spent in the open market upon the constituent elements of the product, or, what amounts to the same thing, upon the factors of the labour-process; ten shillings were paid for the cotton, two shillings for the substance of the spindle worn away, and three shillings for the labour power. The swollen value of the yarn is of no avail, for it is merely the sum of the values formerly existing in the cotton, the spindle, and the labour power: out of such a simple addition of existing values, no surplus-value can possibly arise.[13] These separate values are now all concentrated in one thing; but so they were also in the sum of fifteen shillings, before it was split up into three parts, by the purchase of the commodities.

There is in reality nothing very strange in this result. The value of one pound of yarn being eighteenpence, if our capitalist buys 10 lbs.

of yarn in the market, he must pay fifteen shillings for them. It is clear that, whether a man buys his house ready built, or gets it built for him, in neither case will the mode of acquisition increase the amount of money laid out on the house.

Our capitalist, who is at home in his vulgar economy, exclaims: 'Oh! but I advanced my money for the express purpose of making more money.' The way to Hell is paved with good intentions, and he might just as easily have intended to make money, without producing at all.[14] He threatens all sorts of things. He won't be caught napping again. In future he will buy the commodities in the market, instead of manufacturing them himself. But if all his brother capitalists were to do the same, where would he find his commodities in the market? And his money he cannot eat. He tries persuasion. 'Consider my abstinence; I might have played ducks and drakes with the 15 shillings; but instead of that I consumed it productively, and made yarn with it.' Very well, and by way of reward he is now in possession of good yarn instead of a bad conscience; and as for playing the part of a miser, it would never do for him to relapse into such bad ways as that; we have seen before to what results such asceticism leads. Besides, where nothing is, the king has lost his rights; whatever may be the merit of his abstinence, there is nothing wherewith specially to remunerate it, because the value of the product is merely the sum of the values of the commodities that were thrown into the process of production. Let him therefore console himself with the reflection that virtue is its own reward, But no, he becomes importunate. He says: 'The yarn is of no use to me: I produced it for sale.' In that case let him sell it, or, still better, let him for the future produce only things for satisfying his personal wants, a remedy that his physician MacCulloch has already prescribed as infallible against an epidemic of over-production. He now gets obstinate. 'Can the labourer,' he asks, 'merely with his arms and legs, produce commodities out of nothing? Did I not supply him with the materials, by means of which, and in which alone, his labour could be embodied? And as the greater part of society consists of such ne'er-do-wells, have I not rendered society incalculable service by my instruments of production, my cotton and my spindle, and not only society, but the labourer also, whom in addition I have provided with the necessaries of life? And am I to be allowed nothing in return for all this service?' Well, but has not the labourer rendered him the equivalent service of changing his cotton and spindle into yarn? Moreover, there is here no question of service.[15] A service is nothing more than the useful effect of a use-value, be it of a commodity, or be it of labour.[16] But here we are dealing with exchange value. The capitalist paid to the labourer a value of 3 shillings, and the labourer gave him back an exact equivalent in the value of 3 shillings, added by him to the cotton: he gave him value for value. Our friend, up to this time so purse-proud, suddenly assumes the modest demeanour of his own workman, and exclaims: 'Have I myself not worked? Have I not performed the labour of superintendence and of overlooking the spinner? And does not this labour, too, create value?' His overlooker and his manager try to hide their smiles. Meanwhile, after a hearty laugh, he re-assumes his usual mien. Though he chanted to us the whole creed of the economists, in reality, he says, he would not give a brass farthing for it. He leaves this and all such like subterfuges and juggling tricks to the professors of Political Economy, who are paid for it. He himself is a practical man; and though he does not always consider what he says outside his business, yet in his business he knows what he is about.

Let us examine the matter more closely. The value of a day's labour power amounts to 3 shillings, because on our assumption half a day's labour is embodied in that quantity of labour power, i.e., because the means of subsistence that are daily required for the production of labour power, cost half a day's labour. But the past labour that is embodied in the labour power, and the living labour that it can call into action; the daily cost of maintaining it, and its daily expenditure in work, are two totally different things. The former determines the exchange value of the labour power, the latter is its use-value. The fact that half a day's labour is necessary to keep the labourer alive during 24 hours, does not in any way prevent him from working a whole day. Therefore, the value of labour power, and the value which that labour power creates in the labour-process, are two entirely different magnitudes; and this difference of the two values was what the capitalist had in view, when he was purchasing the labour power. The useful qualities that labour power possesses, and by virtue of which it makes yarn or boots, were to him nothing more than a *conditio sine qua non*; for in order to create value, labour must be expended in a useful manner. What really influenced him was the specific use-value which this commodity possesses, of being *a source not only of value, but of more value than it has itself.* This is the special service that the capitalist expects from labour power, and in this transaction he acts in accordance with the 'eternal laws' of the exchange of commodities. The seller of labour power, like the seller of any other commodity, realises its exchange value, and parts with its use-value. He cannot take the one without giving the other. The use-value of labour power, or in other words, labour, belongs just as little to its seller, as the use-value of oil after it has been sold belongs to the dealer who has sold it. The owner of the money has paid the value of a day's labour power; his, therefore, is the use of it for a day; a day's labour belongs to him. The circumstance, that on the one hand the daily sustenance of labour power costs only half a day's labour, while on the other hand the very same labour power can work during a whole day, that consequently the value which its use during one day creates, is double what he pays for that use, this circumstance is, without doubt, a piece of good luck for the buyer, but by no means an injury to the seller.

Our capitalist foresaw this state of things, and that was the cause of his laughter. The labourer therefore finds, in the workshop, the means of production necessary for working, not only during six, but during twelve hours. Just as during the six hours' process our 10 lbs. of cotton absorbed six hours' labour, and became 10 lbs. of yarn, so now, 20 lbs. of cotton will absorb 12 hours' labour and be changed into 20 lbs. of yarn. Let us now examine the product of this prolonged process. There is now materialised in this 20 lbs. of yarn the labour of five days, of which four days are due to the cotton and the lost steel of the spindle, the remaining day having been absorbed by the cotton during the spinning process. Expressed in gold, the labour of five days is thirty shillings. This is therefore the price of the 20 lbs. of yarn, giving, as before, eighteenpence as the price of a pound. But the sum of the values of the commodities that entered into the process amounts to 27 shillings. The value of the yarn is 30 shillings. Therefore the value of the product is 1/9 greater than the value advanced for its production; 27 shillings have been transformed into 30 shillings; a surplus-value of 3 shillings has been created. The trick has at last succeeded; money has been converted into capital.

Every condition of the problem is satisfied, while the laws that regulate the exchange of commodities, have been in no way violated. Equivalent has been exchanged for equivalent. For the capitalist as buyer paid for each commodity, for the cotton, the spindle and the labour power, its full value. He then did what is done by every purchaser of commodities; he consumed their use-value. The consumption of the labour power, which was also the process of producing commodities, resulted in 20 lbs. of yarn, having a value of 30 shillings. The capitalist, formerly a buyer, now returns to market as a seller, of commodities. He sells his yarn at eighteenpence a pound, which is its exact value. Yet for all that he withdraws 3 shillings more from circulation than he originally threw into it. This metamorphosis, this conversion of money into capital, takes place both within the sphere of circulation and also outside it; within the circulation, because conditioned by the purchase of the labour power in the market; outside the circulation, because what is done within it is only a stepping-stone to the production of surplus-value, a process which is entirely confined to the sphere of production. Thus 'tout est pour le mieux dans le meilleur des mondes possibles.'

By turning his money into commodities that serve as the material elements of a new product, and as factors in the labour-process, by incorporating living labour with their dead substance, the capitalist at the same time converts value, i.e., past, materialised, and dead labour into capital, into value big with value, a live monster that is fruitful and multiplies.

If we now compare the two processes of producing value and of creating surplus-value, we see that the latter is nothing but the continuation of the former beyond a definite point. If on the one hand the process be not carried beyond the point, where the value paid by the capitalist for the labour power is replaced by an exact equivalent, it is simply a process of producing value; if, on the other hand, it be continued beyond that point, it becomes a process of creating surplus-value.

If we proceed further, and compare the process of producing value with the labour-process, pure and simple, we find that the latter consists of the useful labour, the work, that produces use-values. Here we contemplate the labour as producing a particular article; we view it under its qualitative aspect alone, with regard to its end and aim. But viewed as a value-creating process, the same labour-process presents itself under its quantitative aspect alone. Here it is a question merely of the time occupied by the labourer in doing the work; of the period during which the labour power is usefully expended. Here, the commodities that take part in the process, do not count any longer as necessary adjuncts of labour power in the production of a definite, useful object. They count merely as depositories of so much absorbed or materialised labour; that labour, whether previously embodied in the means of production, or incorporated in them for the first time during the process by the action of labour power, counts in either case only according to its duration; it amounts to so many hours or days as the case may be.

Moreover, only so much of the time spent in the production of any article is counted, as, under the given social conditions, is necessary. The consequences of this are various. In the first place, it becomes necessary that the labour should be carried on under normal conditions. If a self-acting mule is the implement in general use for spinning, it would be absurd to supply the spinner with a distaff and spinning wheel. The cotton too must not be such rubbish as to cause extra waste in being worked, but must be of suitable quality. Otherwise the spinner would be found to spend more time in producing a pound of yarn than is socially necessary, in which case the excess of time would create neither value nor money. But whether the material factors of the process are of normal quality or not, depends not upon the labourer, but entirely upon the capitalist. Then again, the labour power itself must be of average efficacy. In the trade in which it is being employed, it must possess the average skill, handiness and quickness prevalent in that trade, and our capitalist took good care to buy labour power of such normal goodness. This power must be applied with the average amount of exertion and with the usual degree of intensity; and the capitalist is as careful to see that this is done, as that his workmen are not idle for a single moment. He has bought the use of the labour power for a definite period, and he insists upon his rights. He has no intention of being robbed. Lastly, and for this purpose our friend has a penal code of his own, all wasteful consumption of raw material or instruments of labour is strictly forbidden, because what is so wasted, represents labour super-fluously expended, labour that does not count in the product or enter into its value.[17]

We now see, that the difference between labour, considered on the one hand as producing utilities, and on the other hand, as creating value, a difference which we discovered by our analysis of a com-modity, resolves itself into a distinction between two aspects of the process of production.

The process of production, considered on the one hand as the unity of the labour-process and the process of creating value, is production of commodities; considered on the other hand as the unity of the labour-process and the process of producing surplus-value, it is the capitalist process of production, or capitalist produc-tion of commodities.

We stated, on a previous page, that in the creation of surplus-value it does not in the least matter, whether the labour appropriated by the capitalist be simple unskilled labour of average quality or more complicated skilled labour. All labour of a higher or more complicated character than average labour is expenditure of labour power of a more costly kind, labour power whose production has cost more time and labour, and which therefore has a higher value, than unskilled or simple labour power. This power being higher-value, its consumption is labour of a higher class, labour that creates in equal times proportionally higher values than unskilled labour does. Whatever difference in skill there may be between the labour of a spinner and that of a jeweller, the portion of his labour by which the jeweller merely replaces the value of his own labour power, does not in any way differ in quality from the additional portion by which he creates surplus-value. In the making of jewellery, just as in spinning, the surplus-value results only from a quantitative excess of labour, from a lengthening-out of one and the same labour-process, in the one case, of the process of making jewels, in the other of the process of making yarn.[18]

But on the other hand, in every process of creating value, the reduction of skilled labour to average social labour, e.g., one day of skilled to six days of unskilled labour, is unavoidable.[19] We therefore save ourselves a superfluous operation, and simplify our analysis, by the assumption, that the labour of the workman employed by the capitalist is unskilled average labour.

Chapter 8
Constant Capital and Variable Capital

The various factors of the labour-process play different parts in forming the value of the product.

The labourer adds fresh value to the subject of his labour by expending upon it a given amount of additional labour, no matter what the specific character and utility of that labour may be. On the other hand, the values of the means of production used up in the process are preserved, and present themselves afresh as constituent parts of the value of the product; the values of the cotton and the spindle, for instance, re-appear again in the value of the yarn. The value of the means of production is therefore preserved, by being transferred to the product. This transfer takes place during the conversion of those means into a product, or in other words, during the labour-process. It is brought about by labour; but how?

The labourer does not perform two operations at once, one in order to add value to the cotton, the other in order to preserve the value of the means of production, or, what amounts to the same thing, to transfer to the yarn, to the product, the value of the cotton on which he works, and part of the value of the spindle with which he works. But, by the very act of adding new value, he preserves their former values. Since, however, the addition of new value to the subject of his labour, and the preservation of its former value, are two entirely distinct results, produced simultaneously by the labourer, during one operation, it is plain that this two-fold nature of the result can be explained only by the two-fold nature of his labour; at one and the same time, it must in one character create value, and in another character preserve or transfer value.

Now, in what manner does every labourer add new labour and consequently new value? Evidently, only by labouring productively in a particular way; the spinner by spinning, the weaver by weaving, the smith by forging. But, while thus incorporating labour generally, that is value, it is by the particular form alone of the labour, by the spinning, the weaving and the forging respectively, that the means of production, the cotton and spindle, the yarn and loom, and the iron and anvil become constituent elements of the product, of a new use-value.[1] Each use-value disappears, but only to re-appear under a new form in a new use-value. Now, we saw, when we were considering the process of creating value, that, if a use-value be effectively consumed in the production of a new use-value, the quantity of labour expended in the production of the consumed article, forms a portion of the quantity of labour necessary to produce the new use-value; this portion is therefore labour transferred from the means of production to the new product. Hence, the labourer preserves the values of the consumed means of production, or transfers them as portions of its value to the product, not by virtue of his additional labour, abstractedly considered, but by virtue of the particular useful character of that labour, by virtue of its special productive form. In so far then as labour is such specific productive activity, in so far as it is spinning, weaving, or forging, it raises, by mere contact, the means of production from the dead, makes them living factors of the labour-process, and combines with them to form the new products.

If the special productive labour of the workman were not spinning, he could not convert the cotton into yarn, and therefore could not transfer the values of the cotton and spindle to the yarn. Suppose the same workman were to change his occupation to that of a joiner, he would still by a day's labour add value to the material he works upon. Consequently, we see, first, that the addition of new value takes place not by virtue of his labour being spinning in particular, or joinering in particular, but because it is labour in the abstract, a portion of the total labour of society; and we see next, that the value added is of a given definite amount, not because his labour has a special utility, but because it is exerted for a definite time. On the one hand, then, it is by virtue of its general character, as being expenditure of human labour power in the abstract, that spinning adds new value to the values of the cotton and the spindle; and on the other hand, it is by virtue of its special character, as being a concrete, useful process, that the same labour of spinning both transfers the values of the means of production to the product, and preserves them in the product. Hence at one and the same time there is produced a two-fold result.

By the simple addition of a certain quantity of labour, new value is added, and by the quality of this added labour, the original values of the means of production are preserved in the product. This two-fold effect, resulting from the two-fold character of labour, may be traced in various phenomena.

Let us assume, that some invention enables the spinner to spin as much cotton in 6 hours as he was able to spin before in 36 hours. His labour is now six times as effective as it was, for the purposes of useful production. The product of 6 hours' work has increased six-fold, from 6 lbs. to 36 lbs. But now the 36 lbs. of cotton absorb only the same amount of labour as formerly did the 6 lbs. One-sixth as much new labour is absorbed by each pound of cotton, and consequently, the value added by the labour to each pound is only one-sixth of what it formerly was. On the other hand, in the product, in the 36 lbs. of yarn, the value transferred from the cotton is six times as great as before. By the 6 hours' spinning, the value of the raw material preserved and transferred to the product is six times as great as before, although the new value added by the labour of the spinner to each pound of the very same raw material is one-sixth what it was formerly. This shows that the two properties of labour, by virtue of which it is enabled in one case to preserve value, and in the other to create value, are essentially different. On the one hand, the longer the time necessary to spin a given weight of cotton into yarn, the greater is the new value added to the material; on the other hand, the greater the weight of the cotton spun in a given time, the greater is the value preserved, by being transferred from it to the product.

Let us now assume, that the productiveness of the spinner's labour, instead of varying, remains constant, that he therefore requires the same time as he formerly did, to convert one pound of cotton into yarn, but that the exchange value of the cotton varies, either by rising to six times its former value or falling to one-sixth of that value. In both these cases, the spinner puts the same quantity of labour into a pound of cotton, and therefore adds as much value, as he did before the change in the value: he also produces a given weight of yarn in the same time as he did before. Nevertheless, the value that he transfers from the cotton to the yarn is either one-sixth of what it was before the variation, or, as the case may be, six times as much as before. The same result occurs when the value of the instruments of labour rises or falls, while their useful efficacy in the process remains unaltered.

Again, if the technical conditions of the spinning process remain unchanged, and no change of value takes place in the means of production, the spinner continues to consume in equal working-times equal quantities of raw material, and equal quantities of machinery of unvarying value. The value that he preserves in the product is directly proportional to the new value that he adds to the product. In two weeks he incorporates twice as much labour, and therefore twice as much value, as in one week, and during the same time he consumes twice as much material, and wears out twice as much machinery, of double the value in each case: he therefore preserves, in the product of two weeks, twice as much value as in the product of one week. So long as the conditions of production remain the same, the more value the labourer adds by fresh labour, the more value he transfers and preserves; but he does so merely because this addition of new value takes place under conditions that have not varied and are independent of his own labour. Of course, it may be said in one sense, that the labourer preserves old value always in proportion to the quantity of new value that he adds. Whether the value of cotton rise from one shilling to two shillings, or fall to sixpence, the workman invariably preserves in the product of one hour only one half as much value as he preserves in two hours. In like manner, if the productiveness of his own labour varies by rising or falling, he will in one hour spin either more or less cotton, as the case may be, than he did before, and will consequently preserve in the product of one hour, more or less value of cotton; but, all the same, he will preserve by two hours' labour twice as much value as he will by one.

Value exists only in articles of utility, in objects: we leave out of consideration its purely symbolical representation by tokens. (Man himself, viewed as the impersonation of labour power, is a natural object, a thing, although a living conscious thing, and labour is the manifestation of this power residing in him.) If therefore an article loses its utility, it also loses its value. The reason why means of production do not lose their value, at the same time that they lose their use-value, is this: they lose in the labour-process the original form of their use-value, only to assume in the product the form of a new use-value. But, however important it may be to value, that it should have some object of utility to embody itself in, yet it is a matter of complete indifference what particular object serves this purpose; this we saw when treating of the metamorphosis of commodities. Hence it follows that in the labour-process the means of production transfer their value to the product only so far as along with their use-value they lose also their exchange value. They give up to the product that value alone which they themselves lose as means of production. But in this respect the material factors of the labour-process do not all behave alike.

The coal burnt under the boiler vanishes without leaving a trace; so, too, the tallow with which the axles of wheels are greased. Dye stuffs and other auxiliary substances also vanish but re-appear as properties of the product. Raw material forms the substance of the product, but only after it has changed its form. Hence raw material and auxiliary substances lose the characteristic form with which they are clothed on entering the labour-process. It is otherwise with the instruments of labour. Tools, machines, workshops, and vessels, are of use in the labour-process, only so long as they retain their original shape, and are ready each morning to renew the process with their shape unchanged. And just as during their lifetime, that is to say, during the continued labour-process in which they serve, they retain their shape independent of the product, so, too, they do after their death. The corpses of machines, tools, workshops, &c., are always separate and distinct from the product they helped to turn out. If we now consider the case of any instrument of labour during the whole period of its service, from the day of its entry into the workshop, till the day of its banishment into the lumber room, we find that during this period its use-value has been completely consumed, and therefore its exchange value completely transferred to the product. For instance, if a spinning machine lasts for 10 years, it is plain that during that working period its total value is gradually transferred to the product of the 10 years. The lifetime of an instrument of labour, therefore, is spent in the repetition of a greater or less number of similar operations. Its life may be compared with that of a human being. Every day brings a man 24 hours nearer to his grave: but how many days he has still to travel on that road, no man can tell accurately by merely looking at him. This difficulty, however, does not prevent life insurance offices from drawing, by means of the theory of averages, very accurate, and at the same time very profitable conclusions. So it is with the instruments of labour. It is known by experience how long on the average a machine of a particular kind will last. Suppose its use-value in the labour-process to last only six days. Then, on the average, it loses each day one-sixth of its use-value, and therefore parts with one-sixth of its value to the daily product. The wear and tear of all instruments, their daily loss of use-value, and the corresponding quantity of value they part with to the product, are accordingly calculated upon this basis.

It is thus strikingly clear, that means of production never transfer more value to the product than they themselves lose during the labour-process by the destruction of their own use-value. If such an instrument has no value to lose, if, in other words, it is not the product of human labour, it transfers no value to the product. It helps to create use-value without contributing to the formation of exchange value. In this class are included all means of production supplied by Nature without human assistance, such as land, wind, water, metals *in situ*, and timber in virgin forests.

Yet another interesting phenomenon here presents itself. Suppose a machine to be worth £1,000, and to wear out in 1,000 days. Then one thousandth part of the value of the machine is daily transferred to the day's product. At the same time, though with diminishing vitality, the machine as a whole continues to take part in the labour-process. Thus it appears, that one factor of the labour-process, a means of production, continually enters as a whole into that process, while it enters into the process of the formation of value by fractions only. The difference between the two processes is here reflected in their material factors, by the same instrument of production taking part as a whole in the labour-process, while at the same time as an element in the formation of value, it enters only by fractions.[2]

On the other hand, a means of production may take part as a whole in the formation of value, while into the labour-process it enters only bit by bit. Suppose that in spinning cotton, the waste for every 115 lbs. used amounts to 15 lbs., which is converted, not into yarn, but into 'devil's dust'. Now, although this 15 lbs. of cotton never becomes a constituent element of the yarn, yet assuming this amount of waste to be normal and inevitable under average conditions of spinning, its value is just as surely transferred to the value of the yarn, as is the value of the 100 lbs. that form the substance of the yarn. The use-value of 15 lbs. of cotton must vanish into dust, before 100 lbs. of yarn can be made. The destruction of this cotton is therefore a necessary condition in the production of the yarn. And because it is a necessary condition, and for no other reason, the value of that cotton is transferred to the product. The same holds good for every kind of refuse resulting from a labour-process, so far at least as such refuse cannot be further employed as a means in the production of new and independent use-values. Such an employment of refuse may be seen in the large machine works at Manchester, where mountains of iron turnings are carted away to the foundry in the evening, in order the next morning to re-appear in the workshops as solid masses of iron.

We have seen that the means of production transfer value to the new product, so far only as during the labour-process they lose value in the shape of their old use-value. The maximum loss of value that they can suffer in the process, is plainly limited by the amount of the original value with which they came into the process, or in other words, by the labour-time necessary for their production. Therefore, the means of production can never add more value to the product than they themselves possess independently of the process in which they assist. However useful a given kind of raw material, or a machine, or other means of production may be, though it may cost £150, or, say, 500 days' labour, yet it cannot, under any circumstances, add to the value of the product more than £150. Its value is determined not by the labour-process into which it enters as a means of production, but by that out of which it has issued as a product. In the labour-process it only serves as a mere use-value, a thing with useful properties, and could not, therefore, transfer any value to the product, unless it possessed such value previously.[3]

While productive labour is changing the means of production into constituent elements of a new product, their value undergoes a metempsychosis. It deserts the consumed body, to occupy the newly created one. But this transmigration takes place, as it were, behind the back of the labourer. He is unable to add new labour, to create new value, without at the same time preserving old values, and this, because the labour he adds must be of a specific useful kind; and he cannot do work of a useful kind, without employing products as the means of production of a new product, and thereby transferring their value to the new product. The property therefore which labour power in action, living labour, possesses of preserving value, at the same time that it adds it, is a gift of Nature which costs the labourer nothing, but which is very advantageous to the capitalist inasmuch as it preserves the existing value of his capital.[4] So long as trade is good, the capitalist is too much absorbed in money-grubbing to take notice of this gratuitous gift of labour. A violent interruption of the labour-process by a crisis, makes him sensitively aware of it.[5]

As regards the means of production, what is really consumed is their use-value, and the consumption of this use-value by labour results in the product. There is no consumption of their value,[6] and it would therefore be inaccurate to say that it is reproduced. It is rather preserved; not by reason of any operation it undergoes itself in the process; but because the article in which it originally exists, vanishes, it is true, but vanishes into some other article. Hence, in the value of the product, there is a reappearance of the value of the means of production, but there is, strictly speaking, no reproduction of that value. That which is produced is a new use-value in which the old exchange value reappears.[7]

It is otherwise with the subjective factor of the labour-process, with labour power in action. While the labourer, by virtue of his labour being of a specialised kind that has a special object, preserves and transfers to the product the value of the means of production, he at the same time, by the mere act of working, creates each instant an additional or new value. Suppose the process of production to be stopped just when the workman has produced an equivalent for the value of his own labour power, when, for example, by six hours' labour, he has added a value of three shillings. This value is the surplus, of the total value of the product, over the portion of its value that is due to the means of production. It is the only original bit of value formed during this process, the only portion of the value of the product created by this process. Of course, we do not forget that this new value only replaces the money advanced by the capitalist in the purchase of the labour power, and spent by the labourer on the necessaries of life. With regard to the money spent, the new value is merely a reproduction; but, nevertheless, it is an actual, and not, as in the case of the value of the means of production, only an apparent, reproduction. The substitution of one value for another, is here effected by the creation of new value.

We know, however, from what has gone before, that the labour-process may continue beyond the time necessary to reproduce and incorporate in the product a mere equivalent for the value of the labour power. Instead of the six hours that are sufficient for the latter purpose, the process may continue for twelve hours. The action of labour power, therefore, not only reproduces its own value, but produces value over and above it. This surplus-value is the difference between the value of the product and the value of the elements consumed in the formation of that product, in other words, of the means of production and the labour power.

By our explanation of the different parts played by the various factors of the labour-process in the formation of the product's value, we have, in fact, disclosed the characters of the different functions allotted to the different elements of capital in the process of expanding its own value. The surplus of the total value of the product, over the sum of the values of its constituent factors, is the surplus of the expanded capital over the capital originally advanced. The means of production on the one hand, labour power on the other, are merely the different modes of existence which the value of the original capital assumed when from being money it was transformed into the various factors of the labour-process. That part of capital then, which is represented by the means of production, by the raw material, auxiliary material and the instruments of labour does not, in the process of production, undergo any quantitative alteration of value. I therefore call it the constant part of capital, or, more shortly, *constant capital*.

On the other hand, that part of capital, represented by labour power, does, in the process of production, undergo an alteration of value. It both reproduces the equivalent of its own value, and also produces an excess, a surplus-value, which may itself vary, may be more or less according to circumstances. This part of capital is continually being transformed from a constant into a variable magnitude. I therefore call it the variable part of capital, or, shortly, *variable capital*. The same elements of capital which, from the point of view of the labour-process, present themselves respectively as the objective and subjective factors, as means of production and labour power, present themselves, from the point of view of the process of creating surplus-value, as constant and variable capital.

The definition of constant capital given above by no means excludes the possibility of a change of value in its elements. Suppose the price of cotton to be one day sixpence a pound, and the next day, in consequence of a failure of the cotton crop, a shilling a pound. Each pound of the cotton bought at sixpence, and worked up after the rise in value, transfers to the product a value of one shilling; and the cotton already spun before the rise, and perhaps circulating in the market as yarn, likewise transfers to the product twice its original value. It is plain, however, that these changes of value are independent of the increment or surplus-value added to the value of the cotton by the spinning itself. If the old cotton had never been spun, it could, after the rise, be resold at a shilling a pound instead of at sixpence. Further, the fewer the processes the cotton has gone through, the more certain is this result. We therefore find that speculators make it a rule when such sudden changes in value occur, to speculate in that material on which the least possible quantity of labour has been spent: to speculate, therefore, in yarn rather than in cloth, in cotton itself, rather than in yarn. The change of value in the case we have been considering, originates, not in the process in which the cotton plays the part of a means of production, and in which it therefore functions as constant capital, but in the process in which the cotton itself is produced. The value of a commodity, it is true, is determined by the quantity of labour contained in it, but this quantity is itself limited by social conditions. If the time socially necessary for the production of any commodity alters – and a given weight of cotton represents, after a bad harvest, more labour than after a good one – all previously existing commodities of the same class are affected, because they are, as it were, only individuals of the species,[8] and their value at any given time is measured by the labour socially necessary, i.e., by the labour necessary for their production under the then existing social conditions.

As the value of the raw material may change, so, too, may that of the instruments of labour, of the machinery, &c., employed in the process; and consequently that portion of the value of the product transferred to it from them, may also change. If in consequence of a new invention, machinery of a particular kind can be produced by a diminished expenditure of labour, the old machinery becomes depreciated more or less, and consequently transfers so much less value to the product. But here again, the change in value originates outside the process in which the machine is acting as a means of production. Once engaged in this process, the machine cannot transfer more value than it possesses apart from the process.

Just as a change in the value of the means of production, even after they have commenced to take a part in the labour-process, does not alter their character as constant capital, so, too, a change in the proportion of constant to variable capital does not affect the respective functions of these two kinds of capital. The technical conditions of the labour-process may be revolutionised to such an extent, that where formerly ten men using ten implements of small value worked up a relatively small quantity of raw material, one man may now, with the aid of one expensive machine, work up one hundred times as much raw material. In the latter case we have an enormous increase in the constant capital, that is represented by the total value of the means of production used, and at the same time a great reduction in the variable capital, invested in labour power. Such a revolution, however, alters only the quantitative relation between the constant and the variable capital, or the proportions in which the total capital is split up into its constant and variable constituents; it has not in the least degree affected the essential difference between the two.

Chapter 9
The Rate of Surplus-Value

Section 1. The Degree of Exploitation of Labour Power.

The surplus-value generated in the process of production by C, the capital advanced, or in other words, the self-expansion of the value of the capital C, presents itself for our consideration, in the first place, as a surplus, as the amount by which the value of the product exceeds the value of its constituent elements.

The capital C is made up of two components, one, the sum of money c laid out upon the means of production, and the other, the sum of money v expended upon the labour power; c represents the portion that has become constant capital, and v the portion that has become variable capital. At first then, C = c + v: for example, if £500 is the capital advanced, its components may be such that the £500 = £410 const. + £90 var. When the process of production is finished, we get a commodity whose value = (c + v) + s, where s is the surplus-value; or taking our former figures, the value of this commodity may be (£410 const. + £90 var.) + £90 surpl. The original capital has now changed from C to C', from £500 to £590. The difference is s or a surplus-value of £90, Since the value of the constituent elements of the product is equal to the value of the advanced capital, it is mere tautology to say, that the excess of the value of the product over the value of its constituent elements, is equal to the expansion of the capital advanced or to the surplus-value produced.

Nevertheless, we must examine this tautology a little more closely. The two things compared are, the value of the product and the value of its constituents consumed in the process of production. Now we have seen how that portion of the constant capital which consists of the instruments of labour, transfers to the production only a fraction of its value, while the remainder of that value continues to reside in those instruments. Since this remainder plays no part in the formation of value, we may at present leave it on one side. To introduce it into the calculation would make no difference. For instance, taking our former example, c = £410: suppose this sum to consist of £312 value of raw material, £44 value of auxiliary material, and £54 value of the machinery worn away in the process; and suppose that the total value of the machinery employed is £1,054. Out of this latter sum, then, we reckon as advanced for the purpose of turning out the product, the sum of £54 alone, which the machinery loses by wear and tear in the process; for this is all it parts with to the product. Now if we also reckon the remaining £1,000, which still continues in the machinery, as transferred to the product, we ought also to reckon it as part of the value advanced, and thus make it appear on both sides of our calculation.[1] We should, in this way, get £1,500 on one side and £1,590 on the other. The difference of these two sums, or the surplus-value, would still be £90. Throughout this Book therefore, by constant capital advanced for the production of value, we always mean, unless the context is repugnant thereto, the value of the means of production actually consumed in the process, and that value alone.

This being so, let us return to the formula C = c + v, which we saw was transformed into C' = (c + v) + s, C becoming C'. We know that the value of the constant capital is transferred to, and merely re-appears in the product. The new value actually created in the process, the value produced, or value-product, is therefore not the same as the value of the product; it is not, as it would at first sight appear, (c + v) +

s or £410 const. + £90 var. + £90 surpl.; but v + s or £90 var. + £90 surpl., not £590 but £180. If c = o, or in other words, if there were branches of industry in which the capitalist could dispense with all means of production made by previous labour, whether they be raw material, auxiliary material, or instruments of labour, employing only labour power and materials supplied by Nature, in that case, there would be no constant capital to transfer to the product. This component of the value of the product, i.e., the £410 in our example, would be eliminated, but the sum of £180, the amount of new value created, or the value produced, which contains £90 of surplus-value, would remain just as great as if c represented the highest value imaginable. We should have C = (o + v) = v or C' the expanded capital = v + s and therefore C'-C = s as before. On the other hand, if s = o, or in other words, if the labour power, whose value is advanced in the form of variable capital, were to produce only its equivalent, we should have C = c + v or C' the value of the product − (c + v) + o or C = C'. The capital advanced would, in this case, not have expanded its value.

From what has gone before, we know that surplus-value is purely the result of a variation in the value of v, of that portion of the capital which is transformed into labour power; consequently, v + s = v + v', or v plus an increment of v. But the fact that it is v alone that varies, and the conditions of that variation, are obscured by the circumstance that in consequence of the increase in the variable component of the capital, there is also an increase in the sum total of the advanced capital. It was originally £500 and becomes £590. Therefore in order that our investigation may lead to accurate results, we must make abstraction from that portion of the value of the product, in which constant capital alone appears, and consequently must equate the constant capital to zero or make c = o. This is merely an application of a mathematical rule, employed whenever we operate with constant and variable magnitudes, related to each other by the symbols of addition and subtraction only.

A further difficulty is caused by the original form of the variable capital. In our example, C' = £410 const. + £90 var. + £90 surpl.; but £90 is a given and therefore a constant quantity; hence it appears absurd to treat it as variable. But in fact, the term £90 var. is here merely a symbol to show that this value undergoes a process. The portion of the capital invested in the purchase of labour power is a definite quantity of materialised labour, a constant value like the value of the labour power purchased. But in the process of production the place of the £90 is taken by the labour power in action, dead labour is replaced by living labour, something stagnant by something flowing, a constant by a variable. The result is the reproduction of v plus an increment of v. From the point of view then of capitalist production, the whole process appears as the spontaneous variation of the originally constant value, which is transformed into labour power. Both the process and its result, appear to be owing to this value. If, therefore, such expressions as '£90 variable capital', or 'so much self-expanding value', appear contradictory, this is only because they bring to the surface a contradiction immanent in capitalist production.

At first sight it appears a strange proceeding, to equate the constant capital to zero. Yet it is what we do every day. If, for example, we wish to calculate the amount of England's profits from the cotton industry, we first of all deduct the sums paid for cotton to the United States, India, Egypt and other countries; in other words, the value of the capital that merely re-appears in the value of the product, is put = 0.

Of course the ratio of surplus-value not only to that portion of the capital from which it immediately springs, and whose change of value it represents, but also to the sum total of the capital advanced, is economically of very great importance. We shall, therefore, in the third book, treat of this ratio exhaustively. In order to enable one portion of a capital to expand its value by being converted into labour power, it is necessary that another portion be converted into means of production. In order that variable capital may perform its function, constant capital must be advanced in proper proportion, a proportion given by the special technical conditions of each labour-process. The circumstance, however, that retorts and other vessels, are necessary to a chemical process, does not compel the chemist to notice them in the result of his analysis. If we look at the means of production, in their relation to the creation of value, and to the variation in the quantity of value, apart from anything else, they appear simply as the material in which labour power, the value-creator, incorporates itself. Neither the nature, nor the value of this material is of any importance. The only requisite is that there be a sufficient supply to absorb the labour expended in the process of production. That supply once given, the material may rise or fall in value, or even be, as land and the sea, without any value in itself; but this will have no influence on the creation of value or on the variation in the quantity of value.[2]

In the first place then we equate the constant capital to zero. The capital advanced is consequently reduced from c + v to v, and instead of the value of the product (c + v) + s we have now the value produced (v + s). Given the new value produced = £180, which sum consequently represents the whole labour expended during the process, then subtracting from it £90 the value of the variable capital, we have remaining £90, the amount of the surplus-value. This sum of

£90 or s expresses the absolute quantity of surplus-value produced. The relative quantity produced, or the increase per cent of the variable capital, is determined, it is plain, by the ratio of the surplus-value to the variable capital, or is expressed by s/v. In our example this ratio is 90/90, which gives an increase of 100%. This relative increase in the value of the variable capital, or the relative magnitude of the surplus-value, I call, 'the rate of surplus-value'.[3]

We have seen that the labourer, during one portion of the labour-process, produces only the value of his labour power, that is, the value of his means of subsistence. Now since his work forms part of a system, based on the social division of labour, he does not directly produce the actual necessaries which he himself consumes; he produces instead a particular commodity, yarn for example, whose value is equal to the value of those necessaries or of the money with which they can be bought. The portion of his day's labour devoted to this purpose, will be greater or less, in proportion to the value of the necessaries that he daily requires on an average, or, what amounts to the same thing, in proportion to the labour-time required on an average to produce them. If the value of those necessaries represent on an average the expenditure of six hours' labour, the workman must on an average work for six hours to produce that value. If instead of working for the capitalist, he worked independently on his own account, he would, other things being equal, still be obliged to labour for the same number of hours, in order to produce the value of his labour power, and thereby to gain the means of subsistence necessary for his conservation or continued reproduction. But as we have seen, during that portion of his day's labour in which he produces the value of his labour power, say three shillings, he produces only an equivalent for the value of his labour power already advanced[4] by the capitalist; the new value created only replaces the variable capital advanced. It is owing to this fact, that the production of the new value of three shillings takes the semblance of a mere reproduction. That portion of the working-day, then, during which this reproduction takes place, I call 'necessary' labour-time, and the labour expended during that time I call 'necessary' labour.[5] Necessary, as regards the labourer, because independent of the particular social form of his labour; necessary, as regards capital, and the world of capitalists, because on the continued existence of the labourer depends their existence also.

During the second period of the labour-process, that in which his labour is no longer necessary labour, the workman, it is true, labours, expends labour power; but his labour, being no longer necessary labour, he creates no value for himself. He creates surplus-value which, for the capitalist, has all the charms of a creation out of nothing. This portion of the working-day, I name surplus labour-time, and to the labour expended during that time, I give the name of surplus-labour. It is every bit as important, for a correct understanding of surplus-value, to conceive it as a mere congelation of surplus labour-time, as nothing but materialised surplus-labour, as it is, for a proper comprehension of value, to conceive it as a mere congelation of so many hours of labour, as nothing but materialised labour. The essential difference between the various economic forms of society, between, for instance, a society based on slave-labour, and one based on wage-labour, lies only in the mode in which this surplus-labour is in each case extracted from the actual producer, the labourer.[6]

Since, on the one hand, the values of the variable capital and of the labour power purchased by that capital are equal, and the value of this labour power determines the necessary portion of the working-day; and since, on the other hand, the surplus-value is determined by the surplus portion of the working-day, it follows that surplus-value bears the same ratio to variable capital, that surplus-labour does to necessary labour, or in other words, the rate of surplus-value s/v = surplus-labour/necessary labour. Both ratios, s/v and surplus-labour/necessary-labour, express the same thing in different ways; in the one case by reference to materialised, incorporated labour, in the other by reference to living, fluent labour.

The rate of surplus-value is therefore an exact expression for the degree of exploitation of labour power by capital, or of the labourer by the capitalist.[7]

We assumed in our example, that the value of the product = £410 const. + £90 var. + £90 surpl., and that the capital advanced = £500. Since the surplus-value = £90, and the advanced capital = £500, we should, according to the usual way of reckoning, get as the rate of surplus-value (generally confounded with rate of profits) 18%, a rate so low as possibly to cause a pleasant surprise to Mr Carey and other harmonisers. But in truth, the rate of surplus-value is not equal to s/c or $s/(c + v)$: thus it is not 90/500 but 90/90 or 100%, which is more than five times the apparent degree of exploitation. Although, in the case we have supposed, we are ignorant of the actual length of the working-day, and of the duration in days or weeks of the labour-process, as also of the number of labourers employed, yet the rate of surplus-value s/v accurately discloses to us, by means of its equivalent expression, surplus-labour/necessary labour, the relation between the two parts of the working-day. This relation is here one of equality, the rate being 100%. Hence, it is plain, the labourer, in our example, works one half of the day for himself, the other half for the capitalist.

The method of calculating the rate of surplus-value is therefore, shortly, as follows. We take the total value of the product and put the constant capital which merely re-appears in it, equal to zero. What remains, is the only value that has, in the process of producing the commodity, been actually created. If the amount of surplus-value be given, we have only to deduct it from this remainder, to find the variable capital. And *vice versa*, if the latter be given, and we require to find the surplus-value. If both be given, we have only to perform the concluding operation, viz., to calculate s/v, the ratio of the surplus-value to the variable capital.

Though the method is so simple, yet it may not be amiss, by means of a few examples, to exercise the reader in the application of the novel principles underlying it.

First we will take the case of a spinning mill containing 10,000 mule spindles, spinning No. 32 yarn from American cotton, and producing 1 lb. of yarn weekly per spindle. We assume the waste to be 6%: under these circumstances 10,600 lbs. of cotton are consumed weekly, of which 600 lbs. go to waste. The price of the cotton in April, 1871, was 7 3/4d. per lb.; the raw material therefore costs in round numbers £342. The 10,000 spindles, including preparation-machinery, and motive power, cost, we will assume, £1 per spindle, amounting to a total of £10,000. The wear and tear we put at 10%, or £1,000 yearly = £20 weekly. The rent of the building we suppose to be £300 a year, or £6 a week. Coal consumed (for 100 horse-power indicated, at 4 lbs. of coal per horse-power per hour during 60 hours, and inclusive of that consumed in heating the mill), 11 tons a week at 8s. 6d. a ton, amounts to about £4 1/2 a week: gas, £1 a week: oil, &c., £4 1/2 a week. Total cost of the above auxiliary materials, £10 weekly. Therefore the constant portion of the value of the week's product is £378. Wages amount to £52 a week. The price of the yarn is 12 1/4d. per. lb. which gives for the value of 10,000 lbs. the sum of £510. The surplus-value is therefore in this case £510-£430 = £80. We put the constant part of the value of the product = 0, as it plays no part in the creation of value. There remains £132 as the weekly value created, which = £52 var. + £80 surpl. The rate of surplus-value is therefore 80/52 = 153 11/13%. In a working-day of 10 hours with average labour the result is: necessary labour = 3 31/33 hours, and surplus-labour = 6 2/33.[8]

One more example. Jacob gives the following calculation for the year 1815. Owing to the previous adjustment of several items it is very imperfect; nevertheless for our purpose it is sufficient. In it he assumes the price of wheat to be 8s. a quarter, and the average yield per acre to be 22 bushels.

Value Produced Per Acre

Seed	£1 9 0	Tithes, Rates, Taxes	£1 1 0
Manure	2 10 0	Rent	1 8 0
Wages	3 10 0	Farmer's profit and Interest	1 2 0
Total	£7 9 0	Total	£3 11 0

Assuming that the price of the product is the same as its value, we here find the surplus-value distributed under the various heads of profit, interest, rent, &c. We have nothing to do with these in detail; we simply add them together, and the sum is a surplus-value of £3 11s. 0d. The sum of £3 19s. 0d., paid for seed and manure, is constant capital, and we put it equal to zero. There is left the sum of £3 10s. 0d., which is the variable capital advanced: and we see that a new value of £3 10s. 0d + £3 11s. 0d. has been produced in its place. Therefore s/v = £3 11s. 0d./£3 10s. 0d., giving a rate of surplus-value of more than 100%. The labourer employs more than one half of his working-day in producing the surplus-value, which different persons, under different pretexts, share amongst themselves.[9]

Section 2. The Representation of the Components of the Value of the Product by Corresponding Proportional Parts of the Product Itself.

Let us now return to the example by which we were shown how the capitalist converts money into capital.

The product of a working-day of 12 hours is 20 lbs. of yarn, having a value of 30s. No less than 8/10ths of this value, or 24s., is due to mere re-appearance in it, of the value of the means of production (20 lbs. of cotton, value 20s., and spindle worn away, 4s.): it is therefore constant capital. The remaining 2/10ths or 6s. is the new value created during the spinning process: of this one half replaces the value of the day's labour power, or the variable capital, the remaining half constitutes a surplus-value of 3s. The total value then of the 20 lbs. of yarn is made up as follows: 30s. value of yarn = 24s. const. + 3s. var. + 3s. surpl.

Since the whole of this value is contained in the 20 lbs. of yarn produced, it follows that the various component parts of this value, can be represented as being contained respectively in corresponding parts of the product.

If the value of 30s. is contained in 20 lbs. of yarn, then 8/10ths of this value, or the 24s. that form its constant part, is contained in 8/10ths of the product or in 16 lbs. of yarn. Of the latter 13 1/3 lbs. represent the value of the raw material, the 20s. worth of cotton spun, and 2 2/3 lbs. represent the 4s. worth of spindle, &c., worn away in the process.

Hence the whole of the cotton used up in spinning the 20 lbs. of yarn, is represented by 13 1/3 lbs. of yarn. This latter weight of yarn contains, it is true, by weight, no more than 13 1/3 lbs. of cotton, worth 13 1/3 shillings; but the 6 2/3 shillings additional value contained in it, are the equivalent for the cotton consumed in spinning the remaining 6 2/3 lbs. of yarn. The effect is the same as if these 6 2/3 lbs. of yarn contained no cotton at all, and the whole 20 lbs. of cotton were concentrated in the 13 1/3 lbs. of yarn. The latter weight, on the other hand, does not contain an atom either of the value of the auxiliary materials and implements, or of the value newly created in the process.

In the same way, the 2 2/3 lbs. of yarn, in which the 4s., the remainder of the constant capital, is embodied, represents nothing but the value of the auxiliary materials and instruments of labour consumed in producing the 20 lbs. of yarn.

We have, therefore, arrived at this result: although eight-tenths of the product, or 16 lbs. of yarn, is, in its character of an article of utility, just as much the fabric of the spinner's labour, as the remainder of the same product, yet when viewed in this connection, it does not contain, and has not absorbed any labour expended during the process of spinning. It is just as if the cotton had converted itself into yarn, without help; as if the shape it had assumed was mere trickery and deceit: for so soon as our capitalist sells it for 24s., and with the money replaces his means of production, it becomes evident that this 16 lbs. of yarn is nothing more than so much cotton and spindle-waste in disguise.

On the other hand, the remaining 2/10ths of the product, or 4 lbs. of yarn, represent nothing but the new value of 6s., created during the 12 hours' spinning process. All the value transferred to those 4 lbs., from the raw material and instruments of labour consumed, was, so to say, intercepted in order to be incorporated in the 16 lbs. first spun. In this case, it is as if the spinner had spun 4 lbs. of yarn out of air, or as if he had spun them with the aid of cotton and spindles, that, being the spontaneous gift of Nature, transferred no value to the product.

Of this 4 lbs. of yarn, in which the whole of the value newly created during the process, is condensed, one half represents the equivalent for the value of the labour consumed, or the 3s. variable capital, the other half represents the 3s. surplus-value.

Since 12 working-hours of the spinner are embodied in 6s., it follows that in yarn of the value of 30s., there must be embodied 60 working-hours. And this quantity of labour-time does in fact exist in the 20 lbs. of yarn; for in 8/10ths or 16 lbs. there are materialised the 48 hours of labour expended, before the commencement of the spinning process, on the means of production; and in the remaining 2/10ths or 4 lbs. there are materialised the 12 hours' work done during the process itself.

On a former page we saw that the value of the yarn is equal to the sum of the new value created during the production of that yarn plus the value previously existing in the means of production.

It has now been shown how the various component parts of the value of the product, parts that differ functionally from each other, may be represented by corresponding proportional parts of the product itself.

To split up in this manner the product into different parts, of which one represents only the labour previously spent on the means of production, or the constant capital, another, only the necessary labour spent during the process of production, or the variable capital, and another and last part, only the surplus-labour expended during the same process, or the surplus-value; to do this is, as will be seen later on from its application to complicated and hitherto unsolved problems, no less important than it is simple.

In the preceding investigation we have treated the total product as the final result, ready for use, of a working-day of 12 hours. We can however follow this total product through all the stages of its production; and in this way we shall arrive at the same result as before, if we represent the partial products, given off at the different stages, as functionally different parts of the final or total product.

The spinner produces in 12 hours 20 lbs. of yarn, or in 1 hour 1 2/3 lbs; consequently he produces in 8 hours 13 2/3 lbs., or a partial product equal in value to all the cotton that is spun in a whole day. In like manner the partial product of the next period of 1 hour and 36 minutes, is 2 2/3 lbs. of yarn: this represents the value of the instruments of labour that are consumed in 12 hours. In the following hour and 12 minutes, the spinner produces 2 lbs. of yarn worth 3 shillings, a value equal to the whole value he creates in his 6 hours' necessary labour. Finally, in the last hour and 12 minutes he produces another 2 lbs. of yarn, whose value is equal to the surplus-value, created by his surplus-labour during half a day. This method of calculation serves the English manufacturer for everyday use; it shows, he will say, that in the first 8 hours, or 2/3 of the working-day, he gets back the value of his cotton; and so on for the remaining hours. It is also a perfectly correct method: being in fact the first method given above with this difference, that instead of being applied to space, in which the different parts of the completed product lie side by side, it deals with time, in which those parts are successively produced. But it can also be accompanied by very barbarian notions, more especially in the heads of those who are as much interested, practically, in the process of making value beget value, as they are in misunderstanding that process theoretically. Such people may get the notion into their heads, that our spinner, for example, produces or replaces in the first 8 hours of his working-day the value of the cotton; in the following hour and 36 minutes the value of the instruments of labour worn away; in the next hour and 12 minutes the value of the wages; and that he devotes to the production of surplus-value for the manufacturer, only that well known 'last hour'. In this way the poor spinner is made to perform the two-fold miracle not only of producing cotton, spindles, steam-engine, coal, oil, &c., at the same time that he spins with them, but also of turning one working-day into five; for, in the example we are considering, the production of the raw material and instruments of labour demands four working-days of twelve hours each, and their conversion into yarn requires another such day. That the love of lucre induces an easy belief in such miracles, and that sycophant doctrinaires are never wanting to prove them, is vouched for by the following incident of historical celebrity.

Section 3. Senior's 'Last Hour'.

One fine morning, in the year 1836, Nassau W. Senior, who may be called the *bel-esprit* of English economists, well known, alike for his economic 'science', and for his beautiful style, was summoned from Oxford to Manchester, to learn in the latter place, the Political Economy that he taught in the former. The manufacturers elected him as their champion, not only against the newly passed Factory Act, but against the still more menacing Ten-hours' agitation. With their usual practical acuteness, they had found out that the learned Professor 'wanted a good deal of finishing'; it was this discovery that caused them to write for him. On his side the Professor has embodied the lecture he received from the Manchester manufacturers, in a pamphlet, entitled: *Letters on the Factory Act, as it affects the cotton manufacture*. London, 1837. Here we find, amongst others, the following edifying passage: 'Under the present law, no mill in which persons under 18 years of age are employed, . . . can be worked more than 11 1/2 hours a day, that is 12 hours for 5 days in the week, and nine on Saturday.

'Now the following analysis (!) will show that in a mill so worked, the whole net profit is derived from the last hour. I will suppose a manufacturer to invest £100,000: − £80,000 in his mill and machinery, and £20,000 in raw material and wages. The annual return of that mill, supposing the capital to be turned once a year, and gross profits to be 15 per cent., ought to be goods worth £15,000 . . . Of this £115,000, each of the twenty-three half-hours of work produces 5/115ths or one twenty-third. Of these 23/23rds (constituting the whole £115,000) twenty, that is to say £100,000 out of the £115,000, simply replace the capital; – one twenty-third (or £5,000 out of the £115,000) makes up for the deterioration of the mill and machinery. The remaining 2/23rds, that is, the last two of the twenty-three half-hours of every day, produce the net profit of 10 per cent. If, therefore (prices remaining the same), the factory could be kept at work thirteen hours instead of eleven and a half, with an addition of about £2,600 to the circulating capital, the net profit would be more than doubled. On the other hand, if the hours of working were reduced by one hour per day (prices remaining the same), the net profit would be destroyed – if they were reduced by one hour and a half, even the gross profit would be destroyed.'[10]

And the Professor calls this an 'analysis'! If, giving credence to the outcries of the manufacturers, he believed that the workmen spend the best part of the day in the production, i.e., the reproduction or replacement of the value of the buildings, machinery, cotton, coal, &c., then his analysis was superfluous. His answer would simply have been: – Gentlemen! if you work your mills for 10 hours instead of 11 1/2, then, other things being equal, the daily consumption of cotton, machinery, &c., will decrease in proportion. You gain just as much as you lose. Your work-people will in future spend one hour and a half less time in reproducing or replacing the capital that has been advanced. – If, on the other hand, he did not believe them without further inquiry, but, as being an expert in such matters, deemed an analysis necessary, then he ought, in a question that is concerned exclusively with the relations of net profit to the length of the working-day, before all things to have asked the manufacturers, to be careful not to lump together machinery, workshops, raw material, and labour, but to be good enough to place the constant capital, invested in buildings, machinery, raw material, &c., on one side of the account, and the capital advanced in wages on the other side. If the Professor then found, that in accordance with the calculation of the manufacturers, the workman reproduced or replaced his wages in 2 half-hours, in that case, he should have continued his analysis thus:

'According to your figures, the workman in the last hour but one produces his wages, and in the last hour your surplus-value or net profit. Now, since in equal periods he produces equal values, the produce of the last hour but one, must have the same value as that of the last hour. Further, it is only while he labours that he produces any value at all, and the amount of his labour is measured by his labour-time. This you say, amounts to 11 1/2 hours a day. He employs one portion of these 11 1/2 hours, in producing or replacing his wages, and the remaining portion in producing your net profit. Beyond this he does absolutely nothing. But since, on your assumption, his wages, and the surplus-value he yields, are of equal value, it is clear that he produces his wages in 5 3/4 hours, and your net profit in the other 5 3/4 hours. Again, since the value of the yarn produced in 2 hours, is equal to the sum of the values of his wages and of your net profit, the measure of the value of this yarn must be 11 1/2 working-hours, of which 5 3/4 hours measure the value of the yarn produced in the last hour but one, and 5 3/4, the value of the yarn produced in the last hour. We now come to a ticklish point; therefore, attention! The last working-hour but one is, like the first, an ordinary working-hour, neither more nor less. How then can the spinner produce in one hour, in the shape of yarn, a value that embodies 5 3/4 hours' labour? The truth is that he performs no such miracle. The use-value produced by him in one hour, is a definite quantity of yarn. The value of this yarn is measured by 5 3/4 working-hours, of which 4 3/4 were, without any assistance from him, previously embodied in the means of production, in the cotton, the machinery, and so on; the remaining one hour alone is added by him. Therefore since his wages are produced in 5 3/4 hours, and the yarn produced in one hour also contains 5 3/4 hours' work, there is no witchcraft in the result, that the value created by his 5 3/4 hours' spinning, is equal to the value of the product spun in one hour. You are altogether on the wrong track, if you think that he loses a single moment of his working-day, in reproducing or replacing the values of the cotton, the machinery, and so on. On the contrary, it is because his labour converts the cotton and spindles into yarn, because he spins, that the values of the cotton and spindles go over to the yarn of their own accord. This result is owing to the quality of his labour, not to its quantity. It is true, he will in one hour transfer to the yarn more value, in the shape of cotton, than he will in half an hour; but that is only because in one hour he spins up more cotton than in half an hour. You see then, your assertion, that the workman produces, in the last hour but one, the value of his wages, and in the last hour your net profit, amounts to no more than this, that in the yarn produced by him in 2 working-hours, whether they are the 2 first or the 2 last hours of the working-day, in that yarn, there are incorporated 11 1/2 working-hours, or just a whole day's work, i.e., two hours of his own work and 9 1/2 hours of other people's. And my assertion that, in the first 5 3/4 hours, he produces his wages, and in the last 5 3/4 hours your net profit, amounts only to this, that you pay him for the former, but not for the latter. In speaking of payment of labour, instead of payment of labour power, I only talk your own slang. Now, gentlemen, if you compare the working-time you pay for, with that which you do not pay for, you will find that they are to one another, as half a day is to half a day; this gives a rate of 100%, and a very pretty percentage it is. Further, there is not the least doubt, that if you make your 'hands' toil for 13 hours, instead of 11 1/2, and, as may be expected from you, treat the work done in that extra one hour and a half, as pure surplus-labour, then the latter will be increased from 5 3/4 hours' labour to 7 1/4 hours' labour, and the rate of surplus-value from 100% to 126 2/23%. So that you are altogether too sanguine, in expecting that by such an addition of 1 1/2 hours to the working-day, the rate will rise from 100% to 200% and more, in other words that it will be 'more than doubled'. On the other hand – man's heart is a wonderful thing, especially when carried in the purse – you take too pessimist a view, when you fear, that with a reduction of the hours of labour from 11 1/2 to 10, the whole of your net profit will go to the dogs. Not at all. All other conditions remaining the same, the surplus-labour will fall from 5 3/4 hours to 4 3/4 hours, a period that still gives a very profitable rate of surplus-value, namely 82 14/23%. But this dreadful "last hour", about which you have invented more stories than have the millennarians about the day of judgment, is "all bosh". If it goes, it will cost neither you, your net profit, nor the boys and girls whom you employ, their "purity of mind".[11] Whenever your "last hour" strikes in earnest, think of the Oxford Professor. And now, gentlemen, "farewell, and may we meet again in yonder better world, but not before." '

Senior invented the battle cry of the 'last hour' in 1836.[12] In the *London Economist* of the 15th April, 1848, the same cry was again raised by James Wilson, an economic mandarin of high standing: this time in opposition to the 10 hours' bill.

Section 4. Surplus-Produce.

The portion of the product that represents the surplus-value, (one tenth of the 20 lbs., or 2 lbs. of yarn, in the example given in Sec. 2) we call 'surplus-produce'. Just as the rate of surplus-value is determined by its relation, not to the sum total of the capital, but to its variable part; in like manner, the relative quantity of surplus-produce is determined by the ratio that this produce bears, not to the remaining part of the total product, but to that part of it in which is incorporated the necessary labour. Since the production of surplus-value is the chief end and aim of capitalist production, it is clear, that the greatness of a man's or a nation's wealth should be measured, not by the absolute quantity produced, but by the relative magnitude of the surplus-produce.[13]

The sum of the necessary labour and the surplus-labour, i.e., of the periods of time during which the workman replaces the value of his labour power, and produces the surplus-value, this sum constitutes the actual time during which he works, i.e., the working-day.

Chapter 10
The Working-Day

Section 1. The Limits of the Working-Day.

We started with the supposition that labour power is bought and sold at its value. Its value, like that of all other commodities, is determined by the working-time necessary to its production. If the production of the average daily means of subsistence of the labourer takes up 6 hours, he must work, on the average, 6 hours every day, to produce his daily labour power, or to reproduce the value received as the result of its sale. The necessary part of his working-day amounts to 6 hours, and is, therefore, *ceteris paribus*, a given quantity. But with this, the extent of the working-day itself is not yet given.

Let us assume that the line A—B represents the length of the necessary working-time, say 6 hours. If the labour be prolonged 1, 3, or 6 hours beyond A B, we have 3 other lines:

Working day 1   Working day 2   Working day 3
A———B—C   A———B—C   A———B———C

representing 3 different working-days of 7, 9, and 12 hours. The extension BC of the line A—B represents the length of the surplus-labour. As the working-day is AB + BC or AC, it varies with the variable quantity BC. Since AB is constant, the ratio of BC to AB can always be calculated. In working-day 1, it is 1/6, in working-day 2, 3/6, in working day 3, 6/6 of AB. Since, further, the ratio surplus working-time/necessary working-time, determines the rate of the surplus-value, the latter is given by the ratio of BC to AB. It amounts in the 3 different working-days respectively to 16 2/3, 50 and 100 per cent. On the other hand, the rate of surplus-value alone would not give us the extent of the working-day. If this rate, e.g., were 100 per cent., the working-day might be of 8, 10, 12, or more hours. It would indicate that the 2 constituent parts of the working-day, necessary-labour and surplus-labour time, were equal in extent, but not how long each of these two constituent parts was.

The working-day is thus not a constant, but a variable quantity. One of its parts, certainly, is determined by the working-time required for the reproduction of the labour power of the labourer himself. But its total amount varies with the duration of the surplus-labour. The working-day is, therefore, determinable, but is, *per se*, indeterminate.[1]

Although the working-day is not a fixed, but a fluent quantity, it can, on the other hand, only vary within certain limits. The minimum limit is, however, not determinable; of course, if we make the extension line BC or the surplus-labour = 0, we have a minimum limit, i.e., the part of the day which the labourer must necessarily work for his own maintenance. On the basis of capitalist production, however, this necessary labour can form a part only of the working-day; the working-day itself can never be reduced to this minimum. On the other hand, the working-day has a maximum limit. It cannot be prolonged beyond a certain point. This maximum limit is conditioned by two things. First, by the physical bounds of labour power. Within the 24 hours of the natural day a man can expend only a definite quantity of his vital force. A horse, in like manner, can only work from day to day, 8 hours. During part of the day this force must rest, sleep; during another part the man has to satisfy other physical needs, to feed, wash, and clothe himself. Besides these purely physical limitations, the extension of the working-day encounters moral ones. The labourer needs time for satisfying his intellectual and social wants, the extent and number of which are conditioned by the general state of social advancement. The variation of the working-day fluctuates, therefore, within physical and social bounds. But both these limiting conditions are of a very elastic nature, and allow the greatest latitude. So we find working-days of 8, 10, 12, 14, 16, 18 hours, i.e., of the most different lengths.

The capitalist has bought the labour power at its day-rate. To him its use-value belongs during one working-day. He has thus acquired the right to make the labourer work for him during one day. But, what is a working-day?[2]

At all events, less than a natural day. By how much? The capitalist has his own views of this *ultima Thule*, the necessary limit of the working-day. As capitalist, he is only capital personified. His soul is the soul of capital. But capital has one single life impulse, the tendency to create value and surplus-value, to make its constant factor, the means of production, absorb the greatest possible amount of surplus-labour.[3]

Capital is dead labour, that, vampire-like, only lives by sucking living labour, and lives the more, the more labour it sucks. The time during which the labourer works, is the time during which the capitalist consumes the labour power he has purchased of him.[4]

If the labourer consumes his disposable time for himself, he robs the capitalist.[5]

The capitalist then takes his stand on the law of the exchange of commodities. He, like all other buyers, seeks to get the greatest possible benefit out of the use-value of his commodity. Suddenly the voice of the labourer, which had been stifled in the storm and stress of the process of production, rises:

The commodity that I have sold to you differs from the crowd of other commodities, in that its use creates value, and a value greater than its own. That is why you bought it. That which on your side appears a spontaneous expansion of capital, is on mine extra expenditure of labour power. You and I know on the market only one law, that of the exchange of commodities. And the consumption of the commodity belongs not to the seller who parts with it, but to the buyer, who acquires it. To you, therefore, belongs the use of my daily labour power. But by means of the price that you pay for it each day, I must be able to reproduce it daily, and to sell it again. Apart from natural exhaustion through age, &c., I must be able on the morrow to work with the same normal amount of force, health and freshness as today. You preach to me constantly the gospel of 'saving' and 'abstinence'. Good! I will, like a sensible saving owner, husband my sole wealth, labour power, and abstain from all foolish waste of it. I will each day spend, set in motion, put into action only as much of it as is compatible with its normal duration, and healthy development. By an unlimited extension of the working-day, you may in one day use up a quantity of labour power greater than I can restore in three. What you gain in labour I lose in substance. The use of my labour power and the spoliation of it are quite different things. If the average time that (doing a reasonable amount of work) an average labourer can live, is 30 years, the value of my labour power, which you pay me from day to day is $1/365 \times 30$ or $1/10950$ of its total value. But if you consume it in 10 years, you pay me daily $1/10950$ instead of $1/3650$ of its total value, i.e., only $1/3$ of its daily value, and you rob me, therefore, every day of $2/3$ of the value of my commodity. You pay me for one day's labour power, whilst you use that of 3 days. That is against our contract and the law of exchanges. I demand, therefore, a working-day of normal length, and I demand it without any appeal to your heart, for in money matters sentiment is out of place. You may be a model citizen, perhaps a member of the Society for the Prevention of Cruelty to Animals, and in the odour of sanctity to boot; but the thing that you represent face to face with me has no heart in its breast. That which seems to throb there is my own heart-beating. I demand the normal working-day because I, like every other seller, demand the value of my commodity.[6]

We see then, that, apart from extremely elastic bounds, the nature of the exchange of commodities itself imposes no limit to the working-day, no limit to surplus-labour. The capitalist maintains his rights as a purchaser when he tries to make the working-day as long as possible, and to make, whenever possible, two working-days out of one. On the other hand, the peculiar nature of the commodity sold implies a limit to its consumption by the purchaser, and the labourer maintains his right as seller when he wishes to reduce the working-day to one of definite normal duration. There is here, therefore, an antinomy, right against right, both equally bearing the seal of the law of exchanges. Between equal rights force decides. Hence is it that in the history of capitalist production, the determination of what is a working-day, presents itself as the result of a struggle, a struggle between collective capital, i.e., the class of capitalists, and collective labour, i.e., the working-class.

Section 2. The Greed for Surplus-Labour. Manufacturer and Boyard.

Capital has not invented surplus-labour. Wherever a part of society possesses the monopoly of the means of production, the labourer, free or not free, must add to the working-time necessary for his own maintenance an extra working-time in order to produce the means of subsistence for the owners of the means of production,[7] whether this proprietor be the Athenian *kalos kagathos*, Etruscan theocrat, *civis Romanus*, Norman baron, American slave-owner, Wallachian Boyard, modern landlord or capitalist.[8] It is, however, clear that in any given economic formation of society, where not the exchange value but the use-value of the product predominates, surplus-labour will be limited by a given set of wants which may be greater or less, and that here no boundless thirst for surplus-labour arises from the nature of the production itself. Hence in antiquity over-work becomes horrible only when the object is to obtain exchange value in its specific independent money form; in the production of gold and silver. Compulsory working to death is here the recognised form of over-work. Only read

Diodorus Siculus.[9] Still these are exceptions in antiquity. But as soon as people, whose production still moves within the lower forms of slave-labour, *corvée*-labour, &c., are drawn into the whirlpool of an international market dominated by the capitalistic mode of production, the sale of their products for export becoming their principal interest, the civilised horrors of over-work are grafted on the barbaric horrors of slavery, serfdom, &c. Hence the negro labour in the Southern States of the American Union preserved something of a patriarchal character, so long as production was chiefly directed to immediate local consumption. But in proportion, as the export of cotton became of vital interest to these states, the over-working of the negro and sometimes the using up of his life in 7 years of labour became a factor in a calculated and calculating system. It was no longer a question of obtaining from him a certain quantity of useful products. It was now a question of production of surplus-labour itself: so was it also with the *corvée*, e.g., in the Danubian Principalities (now Roumania).

The comparison of the greed for surplus-labour in the Danubian Principalities with the same greed in English factories has a special interest, because surplus-labour in the *corvée* has an independent and palpable form.

Suppose the working-day consists of 6 hours of necessary labour, and 6 hours of surplus-labour. Then the free labourer gives the capitalist every week 6 x 6 or 36 hours of surplus-labour. It is the same as if he worked 3 days in the week for himself, and 3 days in the week gratis for the capitalist. But this is not evident on the surface. Surplus-labour and necessary labour glide one into the other. I can, therefore, express the same relationship by saying, e.g., that the labourer in every minute works 30 seconds for himself, and 30 for the capitalist, etc. It is otherwise with the *corvée*. The necessary labour which the Wallachian peasant does for his own maintenance is distinctly marked off from his surplus-labour on behalf of the Boyard. The one he does on his own field, the other on the seignorial estate. Both parts of the labour-time exist, therefore, independently, side by side one with the other. In the *corvée* the surplus-labour is accurately marked off from the necessary labour. This, however, can make no difference with regard to the quantitative relation of surplus-labour to necessary labour. Three days' surplus-labour in the week remain three days that yield no equivalent to the labourer himself, whether it be called *corvée* or wage-labour. But in the capitalist the greed for surplus-labour appears in the straining after an unlimited extension of the working-day, in the Boyard more simply in a direct hunting after days of *corvée*.[10]

In the Danubian Principalities the *corvée* was mixed up with rents in kind and other appurtenances of bondage, but it formed the most important tribute paid to the ruling class. Where this was the case, the *corvée* rarely arose from serfdom; serfdom much more frequently on the other hand took origin from the *corvée*.[11] This is what took place in the Roumanian provinces. Their original mode of production was based on community of the soil, but not in the Slavonic or Indian form. Part of the land was cultivated in severalty as freehold by the members of the community, another part – *ager publicus* – was cultivated by them in common. The products of this common labour served partly as a reserve fund against bad harvests and other accidents, partly as a public store for providing the costs of war, religion, and other common expenses. In course of time military and clerical dignitaries usurped, along with the common land, the labour spent upon it. The labour of the free peasants on their common land was transformed into *corvée* for the thieves of the common land. This *corvée* soon developed into a servile relationship existing in point of fact, not in point of law, until Russia, the liberator of the world, made it legal under presence of abolishing serfdom. The code of the *corvée*, which the Russian General Kisseleff proclaimed in 1831, was of course dictated by the Boyards themselves. Thus Russia conquered with one blow the magnates of the Danubian provinces, and the applause of liberal *crétins* throughout Europe.

According to the *Règlement organique*, as this code of the *corvée* is called, every Wallachian peasant owes to the so-called landlord, besides a mass of detailed payments in kind: (1), 12 days of general labour; (2), one day of field labour; (3), one day of wood carrying. In all, 14 days in the year. With deep insight into Political Economy, however, the working-day is not taken in its ordinary sense, but as the working-day necessary to the production of an average daily product; and that average daily product is determined in so crafty a way that no Cyclops would be done with it in 24 hours. In dry words, the *Règlement* itself declares with true Russian irony that by 12 working-days one must understand the product of the manual labour of 36 days, by 1 day of field labour 3 days, and by 1 day of wood carrying in like manner three times as much. In all, 42 *corvée* days. To this had to be added the so-called *jobagie*, service due to the lord for extraordinary occasions. In proportion to the size of its population, every village has to furnish annually a definite contingent to the *jobagie*. This additional *corvée* is estimated at 14 days for each Wallachian peasant. Thus the prescribed *corvée* amounts to 56 working-days yearly. But the agricultural year in Wallachia numbers in consequence of the severe climate only 210 days, of which 40 for Sundays and holidays, 30 on an average for bad weather, together 70 days, do not count. 140 working-days remain. The ratio of the *corvée* to the necessary labour – 56/84 or 66 2/3 % – gives a much smaller rate of surplus-value than that which regulates the labour of the English agricultural or factory labourer. This is, however, only the legally prescribed *corvée*. And in a spirit yet more 'liberal' than the English Factory Acts, the '*Règlement organique*' has known how to facilitate its own evasion. After it has made 56 days out of 12, the nominal day's work of each of the 56 *corvée* days is again so arranged that a portion of it must fall on the ensuing day. In one day, e.g., must be weeded an extent of land, which, for this work, especially in maize plantations, needs twice as much time. The legal day's work for some kinds of agricultural labour is interpretable in such a way that the day begins in May and ends in October. In Moldavia conditions are still harder. 'The 12 *corvée* days of the *Règlement organique*, cried a Boyard drunk with victory, amount to 365 days in the year.'[12]

If the *Règlement organique* of the Danubian provinces was a positive expression of the greed for surplus-labour which every paragraph legalised, the English Factory Acts are the negative expression of the same greed. These acts curb the passion of capital for a limitless draining of labour power, by forcibly limiting the working-day by state regulations, made by a state that is ruled by capitalist and land-lord. Apart from the working-class movement that daily grew more threatening, the limiting of factory labour was dictated by the same necessity which spread guano over the English fields. The same blind eagerness for plunder that in the one case exhausted the soil, had, in the other, torn up by the roots the living force of the nation. Periodical epidemics speak on this point as clearly as the diminishing military standard in Germany and France.[13]

The Factory Act of 1850 now in force (1867) allows for the average working-day 10 hours, i.e., for the first 5 days 12 hours from 6 a.m. to 6 p.m., including 1/2 an hour for breakfast and an hour for dinner, and thus leaving 10 1/2 working-hours, and 8 hours for Saturday, from 6 a.m. to 2 p.m., of which 1/2 an hour is subtracted for breakfast. 60 working-hours are left, 10 1/2 for each of the first 5 days, 7 1/2 for the last.[14] Certain guardians of these laws are appointed, Factory Inspectors, directly under the Home Secretary, whose reports are published half-yearly, by order of Parliament. They give regular and official statistics of the capitalistic greed for surplus-labour.

Let us listen, for a moment, to the Factory Inspectors.[15] 'The fraudulent mill-owner begins work a quarter of an hour (sometimes more, sometimes less) before 6 a.m., and leaves off a quarter of an hour (sometimes more, sometimes less) after 6 p.m. He takes 5 minutes from the beginning and from the end of the half hour

nominally allowed for breakfast, and 10 minutes at the beginning and
end of the hour nominally allowed for dinner. He works for a quarter
of an hour (sometimes more, sometimes less) after 2 p.m. on Saturday.
Thus his gain is –

Before 6 a.m	15 minutes
After 6 p.m	15 minutes
At breakfast time	10 minutes
At dinner time	20 minutes
	60 minutes
Five days – 300 minutes	
On Saturday before 6 a.m	15 minutes
At breakfast time	10 minutes
After 2 p.m.	15 minutes
	40 minutes
Total weekly	340 minutes

or 5 hours and 40 minutes weekly, which multiplied by 50 working
weeks in the year (allowing two for holidays and occasional stoppages)
is equal to 27 working-days.'[16]

'Five minutes a day's increased work, multiplied by weeks, are equal
to two and a half days of produce in the year.'[17]

'An additional hour a day gained by small instalments before 6 a.m.,
after 6 p.m., and at the beginning and end of the times nominally fixed
for meals, is nearly equivalent to working 13 months in the year.'[18]

Crises during which production is interrupted and the factories
work 'short time', i.e., for only a part of the week, naturally do not
affect the tendency to extend the working-day. The less business there
is, the more profit has to be made on the business done. The less time
spent in work, the more of that time has to be turned into surplus
labour-time.

Thus the Factory Inspector's report on the period of the crisis from
1857 to 1858:

'It may seem inconsistent that there should be any overworking
at a time when trade is so bad; but that very badness leads to the
transgression by unscrupulous men, they get the extra profit of it . . .
In the last half year,' says Leonard Horner, '122 mills in my district
have been given up; 143 were found standing,' yet, over-work is
continued beyond the legal hours.[19]

'For a great part of the time,' says Mr Howell, 'owing to
the depression of trade, many factories were altogether closed, and a
still greater number were working short time. I continue, however, to receive about the usual number of complaints that half, or
three-quarters of an hour in the day, are snatched from the workers
by encroaching upon the times professedly allowed for rest and

refreshment.'[20] The same phenomenon was reproduced on a smaller scale during the frightful cotton-crises from 1861 to 1865.[21] 'It is sometimes advanced by way of excuse, when persons are found at work in a factory, either at a meal hour, or at some illegal time, that they will not leave the mill at the appointed hour, and that compulsion is necessary to force them to cease work [cleaning their machinery, &c.], especially on Saturday afternoons. But, if the hands remain in a factory after the machinery has ceased to revolve . . . they would not have been so employed if sufficient time had been set apart specially for cleaning, &c., either before 6 a.m. [sic!] or before 2 p.m. on Saturday afternoons.'[22]

'The profit to be gained by it (over-working in violation of the Act) appears to be, to many, a greater temptation than they can resist; they calculate upon the chance of not being found out; and when they see the small amount of penalty and costs, which those who have been convicted have had to pay, they find that if they should be detected there will still be a considerable balance of gain . . . [23] In cases where the additional time is gained by a multiplication of small thefts in the course of the day, there are insuperable difficulties to the inspectors making out a case.'[24]

These 'small thefts' of capital from the labourer's meal and recreation time, the factory inspectors also designate as 'petty pilferings of minutes',[25] 'snatching a few minutes'.[26] or, as the labourers technically called them, 'nibbling and cribbling at meal-times'.[27]

It is evident that in this atmosphere the formation of surplus-value by surplus-labour, is no secret. 'If you allow me,' said a highly respectable master to me, 'to work only ten minutes in the day overtime, you put one thousand a year in my pocket.'[28] 'Moments are the elements of profit.'[29]

Nothing is from this point of view more characteristic than the designation of the workers who work full time as 'full-timers', and the children under 13 who are only allowed to work 6 hours as 'half-timers'. The worker is here nothing more than personified labour-time. All individual distinctions are merged in those of 'full-timers' and 'half-timers'.[30]

Section 3. Branches of English Industry without Legal Limits to Exploitation.

We have hitherto considered the tendency to the extension of the working-day, the were-wolf's hunger for surplus-labour in a department where the monstrous exactions, not surpassed, says an English bourgeois economist, by the cruelties of the Spaniards to the American red-skins,[31] caused capital at last to be bound by the chains of legal regulations. Now, let us cast a glance at certain branches of production in which the exploitation of labour is either free from fetters to this day, or was so yesterday.

Mr Broughton Charlton, county magistrate, declared, as chairman of a meeting held at the Assembly Rooms, Nottingham, on the 14th January, 1860, 'that there was an amount of privation and suffering among that portion of the population connected with the lace trade, unknown in other parts of the kingdom, indeed, in the civilised world . . . Children of nine or ten years are dragged from their squalid beds at two, three, or four o'clock in the morning and compelled to work for a bare subsistence until ten, eleven, or twelve at night, their limbs wearing away, their frames dwindling, their faces whitening, and their humanity absolutely sinking into a stone-like torpor, utterly horrible to contemplate . . . We are not surprised that Mr Mallett, or any other manufacturer, should stand forward and protest against discussion . . . The system, as the Rev. Montagu Valpy describes it, is one of unmitigated slavery, socially, physically, morally, and spirit-ually . . . What can be thought of a town which holds a public meeting to petition that the period of labour for men shall be dimin-ished to eighteen hours a day? . . . We declaim against the Virginian and Carolinian cotton-planters. Is their black-market, their lash, and their barter of human flesh more detestable than this slow sacrifice of humanity which takes place in order that veils and collars may be fabricated for the benefit of capitalists?'[32]

The potteries of Staffordshire have, during the last 22 years, been the subject of three parliamentary inquiries. The result is embodied in Mr Scriven's Report of 1841 to the Children's Employment Commissioners, in the report of Dr Greenhow of 1860 published by order of the medical officer of the Privy Council (Public Health, 3rd Report, 112–113), lastly, in the report of Mr Longe of 1862 in the *First Report of the Children's Employment Commission, of the 13th June, 1863*. For my purpose it is enough to take, from the reports of 1860 and 1863, some depositions of the exploited children them-selves. From the children we may form an opinion as to the adults, especially the girls and women, and that in a branch of industry by the side of which cotton-spinning appears an agreeable and healthful occupation.[33]

William Wood, 9 years old, was 7 years and 10 months when he began to work. He 'ran moulds' (carried ready-moulded articles into the drying-room, afterwards bringing back the empty mould) from the beginning. He came to work every day in the week at 6 a.m., and left off about 9 p.m. 'I work till 9 o'clock at night six days in the week.

I have done so seven or eight weeks.' Fifteen hours of labour for a child 7 years old! J. Murray, 12 years of age, says: 'I turn jigger, and run moulds. I come at 6. Sometimes I come at 4. I worked all night last night, till 6 o'clock this morning. I have not been in bed since the night before last. There were eight or nine other boys working last night. All but one have come this morning. I get 3 shillings and sixpence. I do not get any more for working at night. I worked two nights last week.' Fernyhough, a boy of ten: 'I have not always an hour (for dinner). I have only half an hour sometimes; on Thursday, Friday, and Saturday.[34]

Dr Greenhow states that the average duration of life in the pottery districts of Stoke-on-Trent, and Wolstanton is extraordinarily short. Although in the district of Stoke, only 36.6% and in Wolstanton only 30.4% of the adult male population above 20 are employed in the potteries, among the men of that age in the first district more than half, in the second, nearly 2/5 of the whole deaths are the result of pulmonary diseases among the potters. Dr Boothroyd, a medical practitioner at Hanley, says: 'Each successive generation of potters is more dwarfed and less robust than the preceding one.' In like manner another doctor, Mr M'Bean: 'Since he began to practise among the potters 25 years ago, he had observed a marked degeneration especially shown in diminution of stature and breadth.' These statements are taken from the report of Dr Greenhow in 1860.[35]

From the report of the Commissioners in 1863, the following. Dr J. T. Arledge, senior physician of the North Staffordshire Infirmary, says: 'The potters as a class, both men and women, represent a degenerated population, both physically and morally. They are, as a rule, stunted in growth, ill-shaped, and frequently ill-formed in the chest; they become prematurely old, and are certainly short-lived; they are phlegmatic and bloodless, and exhibit their debility of constitution by obstinate attacks of dyspepsia, and disorders of the liver and kidneys, and by rheumatism. But of all diseases they are especially prone to chest-disease, to pneumonia, phthisis, bronchitis, and asthma. One form would appear peculiar to them, and is known as potter's asthma, or potter's consumption. Scrofula attacking the glands, or bones, or other parts of the body, is a disease of two-thirds or more of the potters . . . That the "degenerescence" of the population of this district is not even greater than it is, is due to the constant recruiting from the adjacent country, and intermarriages with more healthy races.'[36]

Mr Charles Parsons, late house surgeon of the same institution, writes in a letter to Commissioner Longe, amongst other things: 'I can only speak from personal observation and not from statistical data, but I do not hesitate to assert that my indignation has been aroused again and again at the sight of poor children whose health has been sacrificed to gratify the avarice of either parents or employers.' He enumerates the causes of the diseases of the potters, and sums them up in the phrase, 'long hours'. The report of the Commission trusts that 'a manufacture which has assumed so prominent a place in the whole world, will not long be subject to the remark that its great success is accompanied with the physical deterioration, widespread bodily suffering, and early death of the workpeople . . . by whose labour and skill such great results have been achieved.'[37] And all that holds of the potteries in England is true of those in Scotland.[38]

The manufacture of lucifer matches dates from 1833, from the discovery of the method of applying phosphorus to the match itself. Since 1845 this manufacture has rapidly developed in England, and has extended especially amongst the thickly populated parts of London as well as in Manchester, Birmingham, Liverpool, Bristol, Norwich, Newcastle and Glasgow. With it has spread the form of lockjaw, which a Vienna physician in 1845 discovered to be a disease peculiar to lucifer-matchmakers. Half the workers are children under thirteen, and young persons under eighteen. The manufacture is on account of its unhealthiness and unpleasantness in such bad odour that only the most miserable part of the labouring class, half-starved widows and so forth, deliver up their children to it, 'the ragged, half-starved, untaught children'.[39]

Of the witnesses that Commissioner White examined (1863), 270 were under 18, 50 under 10, 10 only 8, and 5 only 6 years old. A range of the working-day from 12 to 14 or 15 hours, night-labour, irregular meal-times, meals for the most part taken in the very workrooms that are pestilent with phosphorus. Dante would have found the worst horrors of his *Inferno* surpassed in this manufacture.

In the manufacture of paper-hangings the coarser sorts are printed by machine; the finer by hand (block-printing). The most active business months are from the beginning of October to the end of April. During this time the work goes on fast and furious without intermission from 6 a.m. to 10 p.m. or further into the night.

J. Leach deposes: 'Last winter six out of nineteen girls were away from ill-health at one time from over-work. I have to bawl at them to keep them awake.' W. Duffy: 'I have seen when the children could none of them keep their eyes open for the work; indeed, none of us could.' J. Lightbourne: 'Am 13 . . . We worked last winter till 9 (evening), and the winter before till 10. I used to cry with sore feet every night last winter.' G. Apsden: 'That boy of mine . . . when he was 7 years old I used to carry him on my back to and fro through the snow, and he used to have 16 hours a day . . . I have often knelt down to feed him as he stood by the machine, for he could not leave it or stop.' Smith, the managing partner of a Manchester factory: 'We (he means his 'hands' who work for 'us') work on with no stoppage for meals, so that the day's work of 10 1/2 hours is finished by 4.30 p.m., and all after that is over-time.'[40] (Does this Mr Smith take no meals himself during 10 1/2 hours?) 'We (this same Smith) seldom leave off working before 6 p.m. (he means leave off the consumption of 'our' labour power machines), so that we (*iterum Crispinus*) are really work-ing over-time the whole year round. For all these, children and adults alike (152 children and young persons and 140 adults), the average work for the last 18 months has been at the very least 7 days, 5 hours, or 78 1/2 hours a week. For the six weeks ending May 2nd this year (1862), the average was higher – 8 days or 84 hours a week.' Still this same Mr Smith, who is so extremely devoted to the *pluralis majestatis*, adds with a smile, 'Machine-work is not great.' So the employers in the block-printing say: 'Hand labour is more healthy than mach-ine work.' On the whole, manufacturers declare with indignation against the proposal 'to stop the machines at least during meal-times'. A clause, says Mr Otley, manager of a wall-paper factory in the Borough, 'which allowed work between, say 6 a.m. and 9 p.m. would suit us (!) very well, but the factory hours, 6 a.m. to 6 p.m., are not suitable. Our machine is always stopped for dinner. (What gener-osity!) There is no waste of paper and colour to speak of. But,' he adds sympathetically, 'I can understand the loss of time not being liked.' The report of the Commission opines with naïveté that the fear of some 'leading firms' of losing time, i.e., the time for appropriating the labour of others, and thence losing profit is not a sufficient reason for allowing children under 13, and young persons under 18, working 12 to 16 hours per day, to lose their dinner, nor for giving it to them as coal and water are supplied to the steam-engine, soap to wool, oil to the wheel – as merely auxiliary material to the instruments of labour, during the process of production itself.[41]

No branch of industry in England (we do not take into account the making of bread by machinery recently introduced) has preserved up to the present day a method of production so archaic, so – as we see from the poets of the Roman Empire – pre-christian, as baking. But capital, as was said earlier, is at first indifferent as to the technical character of the labour-process; it begins by taking it just as it finds it.

The incredible adulteration of bread, especially in London, was first revealed by the House of Commons Committee 'on the adulteration of articles of food' (1855–56), and Dr Hassall's work, *Adulterations detected*.[42] The consequence of these revelations was the Act of August 6th, 1860, 'for preventing the adulteration of articles of food and drink', an inoperative law, as it naturally shows the tenderest consideration for every Free-trader who determines by the buying or selling of adulterated commodities 'to turn an honest penny'.[43] The Committee itself formulated more or less naïvely its conviction that Free-trade meant essentially trade with adulterated, or as the English ingeniously put it, 'sophisticated' goods. In fact this kind of sophistry knows better than Protagoras how to make white black, and black white, and better than the Eleatics how to demonstrate *ad oculos* that everything is only appearance.[44]

At all events the Committee had directed the attention of the public to its 'daily bread', and therefore to the baking trade. At the same time in public meetings and in petitions to Parliament rose the cry of the London journeymen bakers against their over-work, &c. The cry was so urgent that Mr H. S. Tremenheere, also a member of the Commission of 1863 several times mentioned, was appointed Royal Commissioner of Inquiry. His report,[45] together with the evidence given, roused not the heart of the public, but its stomach. Englishmen, always well up in the Bible, knew well enough that man, unless by elective grace a capitalist, or landlord, or sinecurist, is commanded to eat his bread in the sweat of his brow, but they did not know that he had to eat daily in his bread a certain quantity of human perspiration mixed with the discharge of abscesses, cobwebs, dead black-beetles, and putrid German yeast, without counting alum, sand, and other agreeable mineral ingredients. Without any regard to his holiness, Free trade, the free baking-trade was therefore placed under the supervision of the State inspectors (Close of the Parliamentary session of 1863), and by the same Act of Parliament, work from 9 in the evening to 5 in the morning was forbidden for journeymen bakers under 18. The last clause speaks volumes as to the over-work in this old-fashioned, homely line of business.

'The work of a London journeyman baker begins, as a rule, at about eleven at night. At that hour he "makes the dough" – a laborious process, which lasts from half an hour to three quarters of an hour, according to the size of the batch or the labour bestowed upon it. He then lies down upon the kneading-board, which is also the covering of the trough in which the dough is "made"; and with a sack under him, and another rolled up as a pillow, he sleeps for about a couple of hours. He is then engaged in a rapid and continuous labour for about five hours – throwing out the dough, "scaling it off", moulding it, putting it into the oven, preparing and baking rolls and fancy bread, taking the batch bread out of the oven, and up into the shop, &c., &c. The temperature of a bakehouse ranges from about 75 to upwards of 90 degrees, and in the smaller bakehouses approximates usually to the higher rather than to the lower degree of heat. When the business of making the bread, rolls, &c., is over, that of its distribution begins, and a considerable proportion of the journeymen in the trade, after working hard in the manner described during the night, are upon their legs for many hours during the day, carrying baskets, or wheeling hand-carts, and sometimes again in the bakehouse, leaving off work at various hours between 1 and 6 p.m. according to the season of the year, or the amount and nature of their master's business; while others are again engaged in the bakehouse in "bringing out" more batches until late in the afternoon.[46] . . . During what is called "the London season" the operatives belonging to the "full-priced" bakers at the West End of the town, generally begin work at 11 p.m., and are engaged in making the bread, with one or two short (sometimes very short) intervals of rest, up to 8 o'clock the next morning. They are then engaged all day long, up to 4, 5, 6, and as late as 7 o'clock in the evening carrying out bread, or sometimes in the afternoon in the bakehouse again, assisting in the biscuit-baking. They may have, after they have done their work, sometimes five or six, sometimes only four or five hours' sleep before they begin again. On Fridays they always begin sooner, some about ten o'clock, and continue in some cases, at work, either in making or delivering the bread up to 8 p.m. on Saturday night, but more generally up to 4 or 5 o'clock, Sunday morning. On Sundays the men must attend twice or three times during the day for an hour or two to make preparations for the next day's bread . . . The men employed by the underselling masters (who sell their bread under the "full price", and who, as already pointed out, comprise three-fourths of the London bakers) have not only to work on the average longer hours, but their work is almost entirely confined to the bakehouse. The underselling masters generally sell their bread . . . in the shop. If they send it out, which is not common, except as supplying chandlers' shops, they usually employ other hands for that purpose. It is not their practice to deliver bread from house to house. Towards the end of the week . . . the men begin on Thursday night at 10 o'clock, and continue on with only slight intermission until late on Saturday evening.'[47]

Even the bourgeois intellect understands the position of the 'under-selling' masters. 'The unpaid labour of the men was made the source whereby the competition was carried on.'[48] And the 'full-priced' baker denounces his underselling competitors to the Commission of Inquiry as thieves of foreign labour and adulterators. 'They only exist now by first defrauding the public, and next getting 18 hours' work out of their men for 12 hours' wages.'[49]

The adulteration of bread and the formation of a class of bakers that sells the bread below the full price, date from the beginning of the 18th century, from the time when the corporate character of the trade was lost, and the capitalist in the form of the miller or flour-factor, rises behind the nominal master baker.[50] Thus was laid the foundation of capitalistic production in this trade, of the unlimited extension of the working-day and of night-labour, although the latter only since 1824 gained a serious footing, even in London.[51]

After what has just been said, it will be understood that the Report of the Commission classes journeymen bakers among the short-lived labourers, who, having by good luck escaped the normal decimation of the children of the working-class, rarely reach the age of 42. Nevertheless, the baking trade is always overwhelmed with applicants. The sources of the supply of these labour powers to London are Scotland, the western agricultural districts of England, and Germany.

In the years 1858–60, the journeymen bakers in Ireland organised at their own expense great meetings to agitate against night and Sunday work. The public – e.g., at the Dublin meeting in May, 1860 – took their part with Irish warmth. As a result of this movement, day-labour alone was successfully established in Wexford, Kilkenny, Clonmel, Waterford, &c. 'In Limerick, where the grievances of the journeymen are demonstrated to be excessive, the movement has been defeated by the opposition of the master bakers, the miller bakers being the greatest opponents. The example of Limerick led to a retrogression in Ennis and Tipperary. In Cork, where the strongest possible demonstration of feeling took place, the masters, by exercising their power of turning the men out of employment, have defeated the movement. In Dublin, the master bakers have offered the most determined opposition to the movement, and by discountenancing as much as possible the journeymen promoting it, have succeeded in leading the men into acquiescence in Sunday work and night-work, contrary to the convictions of the men.'[52]

The Committee of the English Government, which Government, in Ireland, is armed to the teeth, and generally knows how to show it, remonstrates in mild, though funereal, tones with the implacable master bakers of Dublin, Limerick, Cork, &c.: 'The Committee believe that the hours of labour are limited by natural laws, which cannot be violated with impunity. That for master bakers to induce their workmen, by the fear of losing employment, to violate their religious convictions and their better feelings, to disobey the laws of the land, and to disregard public opinion (this all refers to Sunday labour), is calculated to provoke ill-feeling between workmen and masters . . . and affords an example dangerous to religion, morality, and social order . . . The Committee believe that any constant work beyond 12 hours a day encroaches on the domestic and private life of the working man, and so leads to disastrous moral results, interfering with each man's home, and the discharge of his family duties as a son, a brother, a husband, a father. That work beyond 12 hours has a tendency to undermine the health of the workingman, and so leads to premature old age and death, to the great injury of families of working-men, thus deprived of the care and support of the head of the family when most required.'[53]

So far, we have dealt with Ireland. On the other side of the channel, in Scotland, the agricultural labourer, the ploughman, protests against his 13–14 hours' work in the most inclement climate, with 4 hours' additional work on Sunday (in this land of Sabbatarians!),[54] whilst, at the same time, three railway men are standing before a London coroner's jury – a guard, an engine-driver, a signalman. A tremendous railway accident has hurried hundreds of passengers into another world. The negligence of the employee is the cause of the misfortune. They declare with one voice before the jury that ten or twelve years before, their labour only lasted eight hours a day. During the last five or six years it had been screwed up to 14, 18, and 20 hours, and under a specially severe pressure of holiday-makers, at times of excursion trains, it often lasted for 40 or 50 hours without a break. They were ordinary men, not Cyclops. At a certain point their labour power failed. Torpor seized them. Their brain ceased to think, their eyes to see. The thoroughly 'respectable' British jurymen answered by a verdict that sent them to the next assizes on a charge of manslaughter, and, in a gentle 'rider' to their verdict, expressed the pious hope that the capitalistic magnates of the railways would, in future, be more extravagant in the purchase of a sufficient quantity of labour power, and more 'abstemious', more 'self-denying', more 'thrifty', in the draining of paid labour power.[55]

From the motley crowd of labourers of all callings, ages, sexes, that press on us more busily than the souls of the slain on Ulysses, on whom – without referring to the Blue Books under their arms – we see at a glance the mark of over-work, let us take two more figures whose striking contrast proves that before capital all men are alike – a milliner and a blacksmith.

In the last week of June, 1863, all the London daily papers published a paragraph with the 'sensational' heading, 'Death from simple over-work'. It dealt with the death of the milliner, Mary Anne Walkley, 20 years of age, employed in a highly-respectable dressmaking establishment, exploited by a lady with the pleasant name of Elise. The old, often-told story[56] was once more recounted. This girl worked, on an average, 16 1/2 hours, during the season often 30 hours, without a break, whilst her failing labour power was revived by occasional supplies of sherry, port, or coffee. It was just now the height of the season. It was necessary to conjure up in the twinkling of an eye the gorgeous dresses for the noble ladies bidden to the ball in honour of the newly-imported Princess of Wales. Mary Anne Walkley had worked without intermission for 26 1/2 hours, with 60 other girls, 30 in one room, that only afforded 3 of the cubic feet of air required for them. At night, they slept in pairs in one of the stifling holes into which the bedroom was divided by partitions of board.[57] And this was one of the best millinery establishments in London. Mary Anne Walkley fell ill on the Friday, died on Sunday, without, to the astonishment of Madame Elise, having previously completed the work in hand. The doctor, Dr Keys, called too late to the death-bed, duly bore witness before the coroner's jury that 'Mary Anne Walkley had died from long hours of work in an over-crowded work-room, and a too small and badly ventilated bedroom.' In order to give the doctor a lesson in good manners, the coroner's jury thereupon brought in a verdict that 'the deceased had died of apoplexy, but there was reason to fear that her death had been accelerated by over-work in an over-crowded workroom, &c.' 'Our white slaves,' cried the *Morning Star*, the organ of the Free-traders, Cobden and Bright, 'our white slaves, who are toiled into the grave, for the most part silently pine and die.'[58]

'It is not in dressmakers' rooms that working to death is the order of the day, but in a thousand other places; in every place I had almost said, where "a thriving business" has to be done . . . We will take the blacksmith as a type. If the poets were true, there is no man so hearty, so merry, as the blacksmith; he rises early and strikes his sparks before the sun; he eats and drinks and sleeps as no other man. Working in moderation, he is, in fact, in one of the best of human positions, physically speaking. But we follow him into the city or town, and we see the stress of work on that strong man, and what then is his position in the death-rate of his country. In Marylebone, blacksmiths die at the rate of 31 per thousand per annum, or 11 above the mean of the male adults of the country in its entirety. The occupation, instinctive almost as a portion of human art, unobjectionable as a branch of human industry, is made by mere excess of work, the destroyer of the man. He can strike so many blows per day, walk so many steps, breathe so many breaths, produce so much work, and live an average, say of fifty years; he is made to strike so many more blows, to walk so many more steps, to breathe so many more breaths per day, and to increase altogether a fourth of his life. He meets the effort; the result is, that producing for a limited time a fourth more work, he dies at 37 for 50.'[59]

Section 4. Day and Night Work. The Relay System.

Constant capital, the means of production, considered from the standpoint of the creation of surplus-value, only exist to absorb labour, and with every drop of labour a proportional quantity of surplus-labour. While they fail to do this, their mere existence causes a relative loss to the capitalist, for they represent during the time they lie fallow, a useless advance of capital. And this loss becomes positive and absolute as soon as the intermission of their employment necessitates additional outlay at the recommencement of work. The prolongation of the working-day beyond the limits of the natural day, into the night, only acts as a palliative. It quenches only in a slight degree the vampire thirst for the living blood of labour. To appropriate labour during all the 24 hours of the day is, therefore, the inherent tendency of capitalist production. But as it is physically impossible to exploit the same individual labour power constantly during the night as well as the day, to overcome this physical hindrance, an alternation becomes necessary between the workpeople whose powers are exhausted by day, and those who are used up by night. This alternation may be effected in various ways; e.g., it may be so arranged that part of the workers are one week employed on day-work, the next week on night-work. It is well known that this relay system, this alternation of two sets of workers, held full sway in the full-blooded youth-time of the English cotton manufacture, and that at the present time it still flourishes, among others, in the cotton spinning of the Moscow district. This 24 hours' process of production exists today as a system in many of the branches of industry of Great Britain that are still 'free', in the blast-furnaces, forges, plate-rolling mills, and other metallurgical establishments in England, Wales, and Scotland. The working-time here includes, besides the 24 hours of the 6 working-days, a great part also of the 24 hours of Sunday. The workers consist of men and women, adults and children of both sexes. The ages of the children and young persons run through all intermediate grades, from 8 (in some cases from 6) to 18.[60]

In some branches of industry, the girls and women work through the night together with the males.[61]

Placing on one side the generally injurious influence of night-labour,[62] the duration of the process of production, unbroken during the 24 hours, offers very welcome opportunities of exceeding the limits of the normal working-day, e.g., in the branches of industry already mentioned, which are of an exceedingly fatiguing nature; the official working-day means for each worker usually 12 hours by night or day. But the over-work beyond this amount is in many cases, to use the words of the English official report, 'truly fearful.'[63]

'It is impossible,' the report continues, 'for any mind to realise the amount of work described in the following passages as being performed by boys of from 9 to 12 years of age . . . without coming irresistibly to the conclusion that such abuses of the power of parents and of employers can no longer be allowed to exist.'[64]

The practice of boys working at all by day and night turns either in the usual course of things, or at pressing times, seems inevitably to open the door to their not unfrequently working unduly long hours. These hours are, indeed, in some cases, not only cruelly but even incredibly long for children. Amongst a number of boys it will, of course, not unfrequently happen that one or more are from some cause absent. When this happens, their place is made up by one or more boys, who work in the other turn. That this is a well understood system is plain . . . from the answer of the manager of some large rolling-mills, who, when I asked him how the place of the boys absent from their turn was made up, "I dare say, sir, you know that as well as I do," and admitted the fact.'[65]

'At a rolling-mill where the proper hours were from 6 a.m. to 5 1/2 p.m., a boy worked about four nights every week till 8 1/2 p.m. at least . . . and this for six months. Another, at 9 years old, sometimes made three 12-hour shifts running, and, when 10, has made two days and two nights running.' A third, 'now 10 . . . worked from 6 a.m. till 12 p.m. three nights, and till 9 p.m. the other nights.' 'Another, now 13, . . . worked from 6 p.m. till 12 noon next day, for a week together, and sometimes for three shifts together, e.g., from Monday morning till Tuesday night.' 'Another, now 12, has worked in an iron foundry at Stavely from 6 a.m. till 12 p.m. for a fortnight on end; could not do it any more.' 'George Allinsworth, age 9, came here as cellar-boy last Friday; next morning we had to begin at 3, so I stopped here all night. Live five miles off. Slept on the floor of the furnace, over head, with an apron under me, and a bit of a jacket over me. The two other days I have been here at 6 a.m. Aye! it is hot in here. Before I came here I was nearly a year at the same work at some works in the country. Began there, too, at 3 on Saturday morning – always did, but was very gain [near] home, and could sleep at home. Other days I began at 6 in the morning, and gi'en over at 6 or 7 in the evening,'[66]

Let us now hear how capital itself regards this 24 hours' system. The extreme forms of the system, its abuse in the 'cruel and incredible' extension of the working-day are naturally passed over in silence. Capital only speaks of the system in its 'normal' form.

Messrs Naylor & Vickers, steel manufacturers, who employ between 600 and 700 persons, among whom only 10 per cent are under 18, and of those, only 20 boys under 18 work in night sets, thus express themselves: 'The boys do not suffer from the heat. The temperature is probably from 86° to 90° . . . At the forges and in the rolling mills the hands work night and day, in relays, but all the other parts of the work are day-work, i.e., from 6 a.m. to 6 p.m. In the forge the hours are from 12 to 12. Some of the hands always work in the night, without any alternation of day and night work . . . We do not find any difference in the health of those who work regularly by night and those who work by day, and probably people can sleep better if they have the same period of rest than if it is changed . . . About 20 of the boys under the age of 18 work in the night sets . . . We could not well do without lads under 18 working by night. The objection would be the increase in the cost of production . . . Skilled hands and the heads in every department are difficult to get, but of lads we could get any number . . . But from the small proportion of boys that we employ, the subject (i.e., of restrictions on night-work) is of little importance or interest to us.'[67]

Mr J. Ellis, one of the firm of Messrs John Brown & Co., steel and iron works, employing about 3,000 men and boys, part of whose operations, namely, iron and heavier steel work, goes on night and day by relays, states 'that in the heavier steel work one or two boys are employed to a score or two men.' Their concern employs upwards of 500 boys under 18, of whom about 1/3 or 170 are under the age of 13. With reference to the proposed alteration of the law, Mr Ellis says: 'I do not think it would be very objectionable to require that no person under the age of 18 should work more than 12 hours in the 24. But we do not think that any line could be drawn over the age of 12, at which boys could be dispensed with for night-work. But we would sooner be prevented from employing boys under the age of 13, or even so high as 14, at all, than not be allowed to employ boys that we do have at night. Those boys who work in the day sets must take their turn in the night sets also, because the men could not work in the night sets only; it would ruin their health . . . We think, however, that night-work in alternate weeks is no harm. (Messrs Naylor & Vickers, on the other hand, in conformity with the interest of their business, considered that periodically changed night-labour might possibly do more harm than continual night-labour.) 'We find the men who do it, as

well as the others who do other work only by day . . . Our objections
to not allowing boys under 18 to work at night, would be on account
of the increase of expense, but this is the only reason. (What cynical
naïveté!) We think that the increase would be more than the trade,
with due regard to its being successfully carried out, could fairly bear.
(What mealy-mouthed phraseology!) Labour is scarce here, and might
fall short if there were such a regulation.' (i.e., Ellis Brown & Co.
might fall into the fatal perplexity of being obliged to pay labour
power its full value.)[68]

The 'Cyclops Steel and Iron Works', of Messrs Cammell & Co., are
concocted on the same large scale as those of the above-mentioned
John Brown & Co. The managing director had handed in his evidence
to the Government Commissioner, Mr White, in writing. Later he
found it convenient to suppress the MS. when it had been returned to
him for revision. Mr White, however, has a good memory. He
remembered quite clearly that for the Messrs Cyclops the forbidding
of the night-labour of children and young persons 'would be impossible, it would be tantamount to stopping their works,' and yet their
business employs little more than 6% of boys under 18, and less than
1% under 13.[69]

On the same subject Mr E. F. Sanderson, of the firm of Sanderson,
Bros., & Co., steel rolling-mills and forges, Attercliffe, says: 'Great
difficulty would be caused by preventing boys under 18 from working at night. The chief would be the increase of cost from employing
men instead of boys. I cannot say what this would be, but probably it
would not be enough to enable the manufacturers to raise the price
of steel, and consequently it would fall on them, as of course the men
(what queer-headed folk!) would refuse to pay it.' Mr Sanderson
does not know how much he pays the children, but 'perhaps the
younger boys get from 4s. to 5s. a week . . . The boys' work is of a
kind for which the strength of the boys is generally ("generally", of
course not always) quite sufficient, and consequently there would be
no gain in the greater strength of the men to counterbalance the loss,
or it would be only in the few cases in which the metal is heavy. The
men would not like so well not to have boys under them, as men
would be less obedient. Besides, boys must begin young to learn the
trade. Leaving day-work alone open to boys would not answer this
purpose.' And why not? Why could not boys learn their handicraft
in the day-time? Your reason? 'Owing to the men working days and
nights in alternate weeks, the men would be separated half the time
from their boys, and would lose half the profit which they make
from them. The training which they give to an apprentice is considered as part of the return for the boys' labour, and thus enables the

man to get it at a cheaper rate. Each man would want half of this profit.' In other words, Messrs Sanderson would have to pay part of the wages of the adult men out of their own pockets instead of by the night-work of the boys. Messrs Sanderson's profit would thus fall to some extent, and this is the good Sandersonian reason why boys cannot learn their handicraft in the day.[70] In addition to this, it would throw night-labour on those who worked instead of the boys, which they would not be able to stand. The difficulties in fact would be so great that they would very likely lead to the giving up of night-work altogether, and 'as far as the work itself is concerned,' says E. F. Sanderson, 'this would suit as well, but – ' But Messrs Sanderson have something else to make besides steel. Steel-making is simply a pretext for surplus-value making. The smelting furnaces, rolling-mills, &c., the buildings, machinery, iron, coal, &c., have something more to do than transform themselves into steel. They are there to absorb surplus-labour, and naturally absorb more in 24 hours than in 12. In fact they give, by grace of God and law, the Sandersons a cheque on the working-time of a certain number of hands for all the 24 hours of the day, and they lose their character as capital, are therefore a pure loss for the Sandersons, as soon as their function of absorbing labour is interrupted. 'But then there would be the loss from so much expensive machinery, lying idle half the time, and to get through the amount of work which we are able to do on the present system, we should have to double our premises and plant, which would double the outlay.' But why should these Sandersons pretend to a privilege not enjoyed by the other capitalists who only work during the day, and whose buildings, machinery, raw material, therefore lie 'idle' during the night? E. F. Sanderson answers in the name of all the Sandersons: 'It is true that there is this loss from machinery lying idle in those manufactories in which work only goes on by day. But the use of furnaces would involve a further loss in our case. If they were kept up there would be a waste of fuel (instead of, as now, a waste of the living substance of the workers), and if they were not, there would be loss of time in laying the fires and getting the heat up (whilst the loss of sleeping time, even to children of 8 is a gain of working-time for the Sanderson tribe), and the furnaces themselves would suffer from the changes of temperature.' (Whilst those same furnaces suffer nothing from the day and night change of labour.)[71]

Section 5. *The Struggle for a Normal Working-Day. Compulsory Laws for the Extension of the Working-Day from the Middle of the 14th to the End of the 17th Century.*

'What is a working-day? What is the length of time during which capital may consume the labour power whose daily value it buys? How far may the working-day be extended beyond the working-time necessary for the reproduction of labour power itself?' It has been seen that to these questions capital replies: the working-day contains the full 24 hours, with the deduction of the few hours of repose without which labour power absolutely refuses its services again. Hence it is self-evident that the labourer is nothing else, his whole life through, than labour power, that therefore all his disposable time is by nature and law labour-time, to be devoted to the self-expansion of capital. Time for education, for intellectual development, for the fulfilling of social functions and for social intercourse, for the free play of his bodily and mental activity, even the rest time of Sunday (and that in a country of Sabbatarians!)[72] – moonshine! But in its blind unrestrainable passion, its were-wolf hunger for surplus-labour, capital oversteps not only the moral, but even the merely physical maximum bounds of the working-day. It usurps the time for growth, development, and healthy maintenance of the body. It steals the time required for the consumption of fresh air and sunlight. It higgles over a meal-time, incorporating it where possible with the process of production itself, so that food is given to the labourer as to a mere means of production, as coal is supplied to the boiler, grease and oil to the machinery. It reduces the sound sleep needed for the restoration, reparation, refreshment of the bodily powers to just so many hours of torpor as the revival of an organism, absolutely exhausted, renders essential. It is not the normal maintenance of the labour power which is to determine the limits of the working-day; it is the greatest possible daily expenditure of labour power, no matter how diseased, compulsory, and painful it may be, which is to determine the limits of the labourers' period of repose. Capital cares nothing for the length of life of labour power. All that concerns it is simply and solely the maximum of labour power, that can be rendered fluent in a working-day. It attains this end by shortening the extent of the labourer's life, as a greedy farmer snatches increased produce from the soil by robbing it of its fertility.

The capitalistic mode of production (essentially the production of surplus-value, the absorption of surplus-labour), produces thus, with the extension of the working-day, not only the deterioration of human labour power by robbing it of its normal, moral and physical, conditions of development and function. It produces also the premature exhaustion and death of this labour power itself.[73] It extends the labourer's time of production during a given period by shortening his actual life-time.

But the value of the labour power includes the value of the commodities necessary for the reproduction of the worker, or for the keeping up of the working-class. If then the unnatural extension of the working-day, that capital necessarily strives after in its unmeasured passion for self-expansion, shortens the length of life of the individual labourer, and therefore the duration of his labour power, the forces used up have to be replaced at a more rapid rate and the sum of the expenses for the reproduction of labour power will be greater; just as in a machine the part of its value to be reproduced every day is greater the more rapidly the machine is worn out. It would seem therefore that the interest capital itself points in the direction of a normal working-day.

The slave-owner buys his labourer as he buys his horse. If he loses his slave, he loses capital that can only be restored by new outlay in the slave-mart. But 'the rice-grounds of Georgia, or the swamps of the Mississippi may be fatally injurious to the human constitution; but the waste of human life which the cultivation of these districts necessitates, is not so great that it cannot be repaired from the teeming preserves of Virginia and Kentucky. Considerations of economy, moreover, which, under a natural system, afford some security for humane treatment by identifying the master's interest with the slave's preservation, when once trading in slaves is practiced, become reasons for racking to the uttermost the toil of the slave; for, when his place can at once be supplied from foreign preserves, the duration of his life becomes a matter of less moment than its productiveness while it lasts. It is accordingly a maxim of slave management, in slave-importing countries, that the most effective economy is that which takes out of the human chattel in the shortest space of time the utmost amount of exertion it is capable of putting forth. It is in tropical culture, where annual profits often equal the whole capital of plantations, that negro life is most recklessly sacrificed. It is the agriculture of the West Indies, which has been for centuries prolific of fabulous wealth, that has engulfed millions of the African race. It is in Cuba, at this day, whose revenues are reckoned by millions, and whose planters are princes, that we see in the servile class, the coarsest fare, the most exhausting and unremitting toil, and even the absolute destruction of a portion of its numbers every year.'[74]

Mutato nomine de te fabula narratur. For slave-trade read labour-market; for Kentucky and Virginia, Ireland and the agricultural districts of England, Scotland, and Wales; for Africa, Germany. We heard how over-work thinned the ranks of the bakers in London. Nevertheless, the London labour-market is always over-stocked with German and other candidates for death in the bakeries. Pottery, as we saw, is one of the shortest-lived industries. Is there any want therefore of potters? Josiah Wedgwood, the inventor of modern pottery, himself originally a common workman, said in 1785 before the House of Commons that the whole trade employed from 15,000 to 20,000 people.[75] In the year 1861 the population alone of the town centres of this industry in Great Britain numbered 101,302. 'The cotton trade has existed for ninety years . . . It has existed for three generations of the English race, and I believe I may safely say that during that period it has destroyed nine generations of factory operatives.'[76]

No doubt in certain epochs of feverish activity the labour-market shows significant gaps. In 1834, e.g. But then the manufacturers proposed to the Poor Law Commissioners that they should send the 'surplus-population' of the agricultural districts to the north, with the explanation 'that the manufacturers would absorb and use it up.' [77] Agents were appointed with the consent of the Poor Law Commissioners . . . An office was set up in Manchester, to which lists were sent of those workpeople in the agricultural districts wanting employment, and their names were registered in books. The manufacturers attended at these offices, and selected such persons as they chose; when they had selected such persons as their "wants required", they gave instructions to have them forwarded to Manchester, and they were sent, ticketed like bales of goods, by canals, or with carriers, others tramping on the road, and many of them were found on the way lost and half-starved. This system had grown up unto a regular trade. This House will hardly believe it, but I tell them, that this traffic in human flesh was as well kept up, they were in effect as regularly sold to these [Manchester] manufacturers as slaves are sold to the cotton-grower in the United States . . . In 1860, "the cotton trade was at its zenith." . . . The manufacturers again found that they were short of hands . . . They applied to the "flesh agents", as they are called. Those agents sent to the southern downs of England, to the pastures of Dorsetshire, to the glades of Devonshire, to the people tending kine in Wiltshire, but they sought in vain. The surplus-population was "absorbed".' The *Bury Guardian* said, on the completion of the French treaty, that '10,000 additional hands could be absorbed by Lancashire, and that 30,000 or 40,000 will be needed.' After the 'flesh agents and sub-agents' had in vain sought through the agricultural districts, 'a deputation came up to London, and waited on the right hon. gentleman [Mr Villiers, President of the Poor Law Board] with a view of obtaining poor children from certain union houses for the mills of Lancashire.'[78]

What experience shows to the capitalist generally is a constant excess of population, i.e., an excess in relation to the momentary requirements of surplus-labour-absorbing capital, although this excess is made up of generations of human beings stunted, short-lived, swiftly replacing each other, plucked, so to say, before maturity.[79] And, indeed, experience shows to the intelligent observer with what swiftness and grip the capitalist mode of production, dating, historically speaking, only from yesterday, has seized the vital power of the people by the very root – shows how the degeneration of the industrial population is only retarded by the constant absorption of primitive and physically uncorrupted elements from the country – shows how even the country labourers, in spite of fresh air and the principle of natural selection, that works so powerfully amongst them, and only permits the survival of the strongest, are already beginning to die off.[80] Capital that has such good reasons for denying the sufferings of the legions of workers that surround it, is in practice moved as much and as little by the sight of the coming degradation and final depopulation of the human race, as by the probable fall of the earth into the sun. In every stockjobbing swindle every one knows that some time or other the crash must come, but every one hopes that it may fall on the head of his neighbour, after he himself has caught the shower of gold and placed it in safety. *Après moi le déluge!* is the watchword of every capitalist and of every capitalist nation. Hence Capital is reckless of the health or length of life of the labourer, unless under compulsion from society.[81] To the out-cry as to the physical and mental degradation, the premature death, the torture of over-work, it answers: Ought these to trouble us since they increase our profits? But looking at things as a whole, all this does not, indeed, depend on the good or ill will of the individual capitalist. Free competition brings out the inherent laws of capitalist production, in the shape of external coercive laws having power over every individual capitalist.[82]

The establishment of a normal working-day is the result of centuries of struggle between capitalist and labourer. The history of this struggle shows two opposed tendencies. Compare, e.g., the English factory legislation of our time with the English Labour Statutes from the 14th century to well into the middle of the 18th.[83] Whilst the modern Factory Acts compulsorily shortened the working-day, the earlier statutes tried to lengthen it by compulsion. Of course the pretensions of capital in embryo – when, beginning to grow, it secures the right of absorbing a *quantum sufficit* of surplus-labour, not merely by the force of economic relations, but by the help of the State – appear very modest when put face to face with the concessions that, growling and struggling, it has to make in its adult condition. It takes centuries ere the 'free' labourer, thanks to the development of capital- istic production, agrees, i.e., is compelled by social conditions, to sell the whole of his active life, his very capacity for work, for the price of the necessaries of life, his birth-right for a mess of pottage. Hence it is natural that the lengthening of the working-day, which capital, from the middle of the 14th to the end of the 17th century, tries to impose by State-measures on adult labourers, approximately coincides with the shortening of the working-day which, in the second half of the 19th century, has here and there been effected by the State to prevent the coining of children's blood into capital. That which today, e.g., in the State of Massachusetts, until recently the freest State of the North- American Republic, has been proclaimed as the statutory limit of the labour of children under 12, was in England, even in the middle of the 17th century, the normal working-day of able-bodied artisans, robust labourers, athletic blacksmiths.[84]

The first 'Statute of Labourers' (23 Edward III, 1349) found its immediate pretext (not its cause, for legislation of this kind lasts centuries after the pretext for it has disappeared) in the great plague that decimated the people, so that, as a Tory writer says, 'The difficulty of getting men to work on reasonable terms (i.e., at a price that left their employers a reasonable quantity of surplus-labour) grew to such a height as to be quite intolerable.'[85] Reasonable wages were, therefore, fixed by law as well as the limits of the working-day. The latter point, the only one that here interests us, is repeated in the Statute of 1496 (Henry VII). The working-day for all artificers and field labourers from March to September ought, according to this statute (which, however, could not be enforced), to last from 5 in the morning to between 7 and 8 in the evening. But the meal-times consist of 1 hour for breakfast, 1 1/2 hours for dinner, and 1/2 an hour for 'noon-meate', i.e., exactly twice as much as under the factory acts now in force.[86] In winter, work was to last from 5 in the morning until dark, with the same intervals. A statute of Elizabeth of 1562 leaves the length of the working-day for all labourers 'hired for daily or weekly wage' untouched, but aims at limiting the intervals to 2 1/2 hours in the summer, or to 2 in the winter. Dinner is only to last 1 hour, and the 'afternoon-sleep of half an hour' is only allowed between the middle of May and the middle of August. For every hour of absence 1d. is to be subtracted from the wage. In practice, however, the conditions were much more favourable to the labourers than in the statute-book. William Petty, the father of Political Economy, and to some extent the founder of Statistics, says in a work that he published in the last third of the 17th century: 'Labouring-men (then meaning field-labourers) work 10 hours per diem, and make 20 meals per week, viz., 3 a day for working-days, and 2 on Sundays; whereby it is plain, that if they could fast on Friday nights, and dine in one hour and an half, whereas they take two, from eleven to one; thereby thus working 1/20 more, and spending 1/20 less, the above-mentioned (tax) might be raised.'[87] Was not Dr Andrew Ure right in crying down the 12 hours' bill of 1833 as a retrogression to the times of the dark ages? It is true these regulations contained in the statute mentioned by Petty, apply also to apprentices. But the condition of child-labour, even at the end of the 17th century, is seen from the following complaint: ''Tis not their practice (in Germany) as with us in this kingdom, to bind an apprentice for seven years; three or four is their common standard: and the reason is, because they are educated from their cradle to something of employment, which renders them the more apt and docile, and consequently the more capable of attaining to a ripeness and quicker proficiency in business. Whereas our youth, here in England, being bred to nothing before they come to be apprentices, make a very slow progress and require much longer time wherein to reach the perfection of accomplished artists.'[88]

Still, during the greater part of the 18th century, up to the epoch of Modern Industry and machinism, capital in England had not succeeded in seizing for itself, by the payment of the weekly value of labour power, the whole week of the labourer, with the exception, however, of the agricultural labourers. The fact that they could live for a whole week on the wage of four days, did not appear to the labourers a sufficient reason that they should work the other two days for the capitalist. One party of English economists, in the interest of capital, denounces this obstinacy in the most violent manner, another party defends the labourers. Let us listen, e.g., to the contest between Postlethwayt, whose *Dictionary of Trade* then had the same reputation as the kindred works of MacCulloch and MacGregor today, and the author (already quoted) of the *Essay on Trade and Commerce*.[89]

Postlethwayt says among other things: 'We cannot put an end to those few observations, without noticing that trite remark in the mouth of too many; that if the industrious poor can obtain enough to maintain themselves in five days, they will not work the whole six. Whence they infer the necessity of even the necessaries of life being made dear by taxes, or any other means, to compel the working artisan and manufacturer to labour the whole six days in the week, without ceasing. I must beg leave to differ in sentiment from those great politicians, who contend for the perpetual slavery of the working people of this kingdom; they forget the vulgar adage, all work and no play. Have not the English boasted of the ingenuity and dexterity of her working artists and manufacturers which have heretofore given credit and reputation to British wares in general? What has this been owing to? To nothing more probably than the relaxation of the working people in their own way. Were they obliged to toil the year round, the whole six days in the week, in a repetition of the same work, might it not blunt their ingenuity, and render them stupid instead of alert and dexterous; and might not our workmen lose their reputation instead of maintaining it by such eternal slavery? . . . And what sort of workmanship could we expect from such hard-driven animals? . . . Many of them will execute as much work in four days as a Frenchman will in five or six. But if Englishmen are to be eternal drudges, 'tis to be feared they will degenerate below the Frenchmen. As our people are famed for bravery in war, do we not say that it is owing to good English roast beef and pudding in their bellies, as well as their constitutional spirit of liberty? And why may not the superior ingenuity and dexterity of our artists and manufacturers, be owing to that freedom and liberty to direct themselves in their own way, and I hope we shall never have them deprived of such privileges and that good living from whence their ingenuity no less than their courage may proceed.'[90] Thereupon the author of the *Essay on Trade and Commerce* replies: 'If the making of every seventh day an holiday is supposed to be of divine institution, as it implies the appropriating the other six days to labour' (he means capital as we shall soon see) 'surely it will not be thought cruel to enforce it . . . That mankind in general, are naturally inclined to ease and indolence, we fatally experience to be true, from the conduct of our manufacturing populace, who do not labour, upon an average, above four days in a week, unless provisions happen to be very dear . . . Put all the necessaries of the poor under one denomination; for instance, call them all wheat, or suppose that . . . the bushel of wheat shall cost five shillings and that he (a manufacturer) earns a shilling by his labour, he then would be obliged to work five days only in a week. If the bushel of wheat should cost but four shillings, he would be obliged to work but four days; but as wages in this kingdom are much higher in proportion to the price of necessaries . . . the manufacturer, who labours four days, has a surplus of money to live idle with the rest of the week . . . I hope I have said enough to make it appear that the moderate labour of six days in a week is no slavery. Our labouring people do this, and to all appearance are the happiest of all our labouring poor,[91] but the Dutch do this in manufactures, and appear to be a very happy people. The French do so, when holidays do not intervene.[92] But our populace have adopted a notion, that as Englishmen they enjoy a birthright privilege of being more free and independent than in any country in Europe. Now this idea, as far as it may affect the bravery of our troops, may be of some use; but the less the manufacturing poor have of it, certainly the better for themselves and for the State. The labouring people should never think themselves independent of their superiors . . . It is extremely dangerous to encourage mobs in a commercial state like ours, where, perhaps, seven parts out of eight of the whole, are people with little or no property. The cure will not be perfect, till our manufacturing poor are contented to labour six days for the same sum which they now earn in four days.'[93] To this end, and for 'extirpating idleness debauchery and excess', promoting a spirit of industry, 'lowering the price of labour in our manufactories, and easing the lands of the heavy burden of poor's rates', our 'faithful Eckart' of capital proposes this approved device: to shut up such labourers as become dependent on public support, in a word, paupers, in 'an ideal workhouse'. Such ideal workhouse must be made a 'House of Terror', and not an asylum for the poor, 'where they are to be plentifully fed, warmly and decently clothed, and where they do but little work.'[94] In this 'House of Terror', this 'ideal workhouse, the poor shall work 14 hours in a day, allowing proper time for meals, in such manner that there shall remain 12 hours of neat-labour.'[95]

Twelve working-hours daily in the Ideal Workhouse, in the 'House of Terror' of 1770! 63 years later, in 1833, when the English Parliament reduced the working-day for children of 13 to 18, in four branches of industry to 12 full hours, the judgment day of English Industry had dawned! In 1852, when Louis Bonaparte sought to secure his position with the bourgeoisie by tampering with the legal working-day, the French working people cried out with one voice 'the law that limits the working-day to 12 hours is the one good that has remained to us of the legislation of the Republic!'[96] At Zürich the work of children over 10, is limited to 12 hours; in Aargau in 1862, the work of children between 13 and 16, was reduced from 12 1/2 to 12 hours; in Austria in 1860, for children between 14 and 16, the same reduction was made.[97] 'What a progress,' since 1770! Macaulay would shout with exultation!

The 'House of Terror' for paupers of which the capitalistic soul of 1770 only dreamed, was realised a few years later in the shape of a gigantic 'Workhouse' for the industrial worker himself. It is called the Factory. And the ideal this time fades before the reality.

Section 6. The Struggle for the Normal Working-Day. Compulsory Limitation by Law of the Working-Time. The English Factory Acts, 1833 to 1864.

After capital had taken centuries in extending the working-day to its normal maximum limit, and then beyond this to the limit of the natural day of 12 hours,[98] there followed on the birth of machinism and modern industry in the last third of the 18th century, a violent encroachment like that of an avalanche in its intensity and extent. All bounds of morals and nature, age and sex, day and night, were broken down. Even the ideas of day and night, of rustic simplicity in the old statutes, became so confused that an English judge, as late as 1860, needed a quite Talmudic sagacity to explain 'judicially' what was day and what was night.[99] Capital celebrated its orgies.

As soon as the working-class, stunned at first by the noise and turmoil of the new system of production, recovered, in some measure, its senses, its resistance began, and first in the native land of machinism, in England. For 30 years, however, the concessions conquered by the workpeople were purely nominal. Parliament passed 5 Labour Laws between 1802 and 1833, but was shrewd enough not to vote a penny for their carrying out, for the requisite officials.[100]

They remained a dead letter. 'The fact is, that prior to the Act of 1833, young persons and children were worked all night, all day, or both *ad libitum*.'[101]

A normal working-day for modern industry only dates from the Factory Act of 1833, which included cotton, wool, flax, and silk factories. Nothing is more characteristic of the spirit of capital than the history of the English Factory Acts from 1833 to 1864.

The Act of 1833 declares the ordinary factory working-day to be from half-past five in the morning to half-past eight in the evening and within these limits, a period of 15 hours, it is lawful to employ young persons (i.e., persons between 13 and 18 years of age), at any time of the day, provided no one individual young person should work more than 12 hours in any one day, except in certain cases especially provided for. The 6th section of the Act provided, 'That there shall be allowed in the course of every day not less than one and a half hours for meals to every such person restricted as hereinbefore provided.' The employment of children under 9, with exceptions mentioned later was forbidden; the work of children between 9 and 13 was limited to 8 hours a day; night-work, i.e., according to this Act, work between 8:30 p.m. and 5:30 a.m., was forbidden for all persons between 9 and 18.

The law-makers were so far from wishing to trench on the freedom of capital to exploit adult labour power, or, as they called it, 'the freedom of labour', that they created a special system in order to prevent the Factory Acts from having a consequence so outrageous.

'The great evil of the factory system as at present conducted,' says the first report of the Central Board of the Commission of June 28th 1833, 'has appeared to us to be that it entails the necessity of continuing the labour of children to the utmost length of that of the adults. The only remedy for this evil, short of the limitation of the labour of adults which would, in our opinion, create an evil greater than that which is sought to be remedied, appears to be the plan of working double sets of children.' . . . Under the name of System of Relays, this 'plan' was therefore carried out, so that, e.g., from 5.30 a.m. until 1.30 in the afternoon, one set of children between 9 and 13, and from 1.30 p.m. to 8.30 in the evening another set were 'put to', &c.

In order to reward the manufacturers for having, in the most barefaced way, ignored all the Acts as to children's labour passed during the last twenty-two years, the pill was yet further gilded for them. Parliament decreed that after March 1st, 1834, no child under 11, after March 1st 1835, no child under 12, and after March 1st, 1836, no child under 13 was to work more than eight hours in a factory. This 'liberalism', so full of consideration for 'capital', was the more noteworthy as Dr Farre, Sir A. Carlisle, Sir B. Brodie, Sir C. Bell, Mr Guthrie, &c., in a word, the most distinguished physicians and surgeons in London, had declared in their evidence before the House of Commons, that there was danger in delay. Dr Farre expressed himself still more coarsely. 'Legislation is necessary for the prevention of death, in any form in which it can be prematurely inflicted, and certainly this (i.e., the factory method) must be viewed as a most cruel mode of inflicting it.'

That same 'reformed' Parliament, which in its delicate consideration for the manufacturers, condemned children under 13, for years to come, to 72 hours of work per week in the Factory Hell, on the other hand, in the Emancipation Act, which also administered freedom drop by drop, forbade the planters, from the outset, to work any negro slave more than 45 hours a week.

But in no wise conciliated, capital now began a noisy agitation that went on for several years. It turned chiefly on the age of those who, under the name of children, were limited to 8 hours' work, and were subject to a certain amount of compulsory education. According to capitalistic anthropology, the age of childhood ended at 10, or at the outside, at 11. The more nearly the time approached for the coming into full force of the Factory Act, the fatal year 1836, the more wildly raged the mob of manufacturers. They managed, in fact, to intimidate the government to such an extent that in 1835 it proposed to lower the limit of the age of childhood from 13 to 12. In the meantime the pressure from without grew more threatening. Courage failed the House of Commons. It refused to throw children of 13 under the Juggernaut Car of capital for more than 8 hours a day, and the Act of 1833 came into full operation. It remained unaltered until June, 1844.

In the ten years during which it regulated factory work, first in part, and then entirely, the official reports of the factory inspectors teem with complaints as to the impossibility of putting the Act into force. As the law of 1833 left it optional with the lords of capital during the 15 hours, from 5.30 a.m. to 8.30 p.m., to make every 'young person', and 'every child' begin, break off, resume, or end his 12 or 8 hours at any moment they liked, and also permitted them to assign to different persons, different times for meals, these gentlemen soon discovered a new 'system of relays', by which the labour-horses were not changed at fixed stations, but were constantly re-harnessed at changing stations. We do not pause longer on the beauty of this system, as we shall have to return to it later. But this much is clear at the first glance: that this system annulled the whole Factory Act, not only in the spirit, but in the letter. How could factory inspectors, with this complex book-keeping in respect to each individual child or young person, enforce the legally determined work-time and the granting of the legal meal-times? In a great many of the factories, the old brutalities soon blossomed out again unpunished. In an interview with the Home Secretary (1844), the factory inspectors demonstrated the impossibility of any control under the newly invented relay system.[102] In the meantime, however, circumstances had greatly changed. The factory hands, especially since 1838, had made the Ten Hours' Bill their economic, as they had made the Charter their political, election-cry. Some of the manufacturers, even, who had managed their factories in conformity with the Act of 1833, overwhelmed Parliament with memorials on the immoral competition of their false brethren whom greater impudence, or more fortunate local circumstances, enabled to break the law. Moreover, however much the individual manufacturer might give the rein to his old lust for gain, the spokesmen and political leaders of the manufacturing class ordered a change of front and of speech towards the workpeople. They had entered upon the contest for the repeal of the Corn Laws, and needed the workers to help them to victory. They promised therefore, not only a double-sized loaf of bread, but the enactment of the Ten Hours' Bill in the Free-trade millennium.[103] Thus they still less dared to oppose a measure intended only to make the law of 1833 a reality. Threatened in their holiest interest, the rent of land, the Tories thundered with philanthropic indignation against the 'nefarious practices'[104] of their foes.

This was the origin of the additional Factory Act of June 7th, 1844. It came into effect on September 10th, 1844. It places under protection a new category of workers, viz., the women over 18. They were placed in every respect on the same footing as the young persons, their worktime limited to twelve hours, their night-labour forbidden, &c. For the first time, legislation saw itself compelled to control directly and officially the labour of adults. In the Factory Report of 1844–1845, it is said with irony: 'No instances have come to my knowledge of adult women having expressed any regret at their rights being thus far interfered with.'[105] The working-time of children under 13 was reduced to 6 1/2, and in certain circumstances to 7 hours a day.[106]

To get rid of the abuses of the 'spurious relay system', the law established besides others the following important regulations: – 'That the hours of work of children and young persons shall be reckoned from the time when any child or young person shall begin to work in the morning.' So that if A, e.g., begins work at 8 in the morning, and B at 10, B's work-day must nevertheless end at the same hour as A's. 'The time shall be regulated by a public clock,' for example, the nearest railway clock, by which the factory clock is to be set. The occupier is to hang up a 'legible' printed notice stating the hours for the beginning and ending of work and the times allowed for the several meals. Children beginning work before 12 noon may not be again employed after 1 p.m. The afternoon shift must therefore consist of other children than those employed in the morning. Of the hour and a half for meal-times, 'one hour thereof at the least shall be given before three of the clock in the afternoon . . . and at the same period of the day. No child or young person shall be employed more than five hours before 1 p.m. without an interval for meal-time of at least 30 minutes. No child or young person [or female] shall be employed or allowed to remain in any room in which any manufacturing process is then [i.e., at mealtimes] carried on,' &c.

It has been seen that these minutiae, which, with military uniformity, regulate by stroke of the clock the times, limits, pauses of the work were not at all the products of Parliamentary fancy. They developed gradually out of circumstances as natural laws of the modern mode of production. Their formulation, official recognition, and proclamation by the State, were the result of a long struggle of classes. One of their first consequences was that in practice the working-day of the adult males in factories became subject to the same limitations, since in most processes of production the co-operation of the children. young persons, and women is indispensable. On the whole, therefore, during the period from 1844 to 1847, the 12 hours' working-day became general and uniform in all branches of industry under the Factory Act.

The manufacturers, however, did not allow this 'progress' without a compensating 'retrogression'. At their instigation the House of Commons reduced the minimum age for exploitable children from 9 to 8, in order to assure that additional supply of factory children which is due to capitalists, according to divine and human law.[107]

The years 1846–47 are epoch-making in the economic history of England. The Repeal of the Corn Laws, and of the duties on cotton and other raw material; Free-trade proclaimed as the guiding star of legislation; in a word, the arrival of the millennium. On the other hand, in the same years, the Chartist movement and the 10 hours' agitation reached their highest point. They found allies in the Tories panting for revenge. Despite the fanatical opposition of the army of perjured Free-traders, with Bright and Cobden at their head, the Ten Hours' Bill, struggled for so long, went through Parliament.

The new Factory Act of June 8th, 1847, enacted that on July 1st, 1847, there should be a preliminary shortening of the working-day for 'young persons' (from 13 to 18), and all females to 11 hours, but that on May 1st, 1848, there should be a definite limitation of the working-day to 10 hours. In other respects, the Act only amended and completed the Acts of 1833 and 1844.

Capital now entered upon a preliminary campaign in order to hinder the Act from coming into full force on May 1st, 1848. And the workers themselves, under the pretence that they had been taught by experience, were to help in the destruction of their own work. The moment was cleverly chosen. 'It must be remembered, too, that there has been more than two years of great suffering (in consequence of the terrible crisis of 1846–47) among the factory operatives, from many mills having worked short time, and many being altogether closed. A considerable number of the operatives must therefore be in very narrow circumstances; many, it is to be feared, in debt; so that it might fairly have been presumed that at the present time they would prefer working the longer time, in order to make up for past losses, perhaps to pay off debts, or get their furniture out of pawn, or replace that sold, or to get a new supply of clothes for themselves and their families.'[108]

The manufacturers tried to aggravate the natural effect of these circumstances by a general reduction of wages by 10%. This was done, so to say, to celebrate the inauguration of the new Free-trade era. Then followed a further reduction of 8 1/3 % as soon as the working-day was shortened to 11, and a reduction of double that amount as soon as it was finally shortened to 10 hours. Wherever, therefore, circumstances allowed it, a reduction of wages of at least 25% took place.[109] Under such favourably prepared conditions the agitation among the factory workers for the repeal of the Act of 1847 was begun. Neither lies, bribery, nor threats were spared in this attempt. But all was in vain. Concerning the half-dozen petitions in which workpeople were made to complain of 'their oppression by the Act', the petitioners themselves declared under oral examination, that their signatures had been extorted from them. 'They felt themselves oppressed, but not exactly by the Factory Act.'[110] But if the manufacturers did not succeed in making the workpeople speak as they wished, they themselves shrieked all the louder in press and Parliament in the name of the workpeople. They denounced the Factory Inspectors as a kind of revolutionary commissioners like those of the French National Convention, ruthlessly sacrificing the unhappy factory workers to their humanitarian crotchet. This manoeuvre also failed. Factory Inspector Leonard Horner conducted in his own person, and through his sub-inspectors, many examinations of witnesses in the factories of Lancashire. About 70% of the workpeople examined declared in favour of 10 hours, a much smaller percentage in favour of 11, and an altogether insignificant minority for the old 12 hours.[111]

Another 'friendly' dodge was to make the adult males work 12 to 15 hours, and then to blazon abroad this fact as the best proof of what the proletariat desired in its heart of hearts. But the 'ruthless' Factory Inspector Leonard Horner was again to the fore. The majority of the 'over-times' declared: 'They would much prefer working ten hours for less wages, but that they had no choice; that so many were out of employment (so many spinners getting very low wages by having to work as piecers, being unable to do better), that if they refused to work the longer time, others would immediately get their places, so that it was a question with them of agreeing to work the longer time, or of being thrown out of employment altogether.'[112]

The preliminary campaign of capital thus came to grief, and the Ten Hours' Act came into force May 1st, 1848. But meanwhile the fiasco of the Chartist party whose leaders were imprisoned, and whose organisation was dismembered, had shaken the confidence of the English working-class in its own strength. Soon after this the June insurrection in Paris and its bloody suppression united, in England as on the Continent, all fractions of the ruling classes, landlords and capitalists, stock-exchange wolves and shop-keepers, Protectionists and Freetraders, government and opposition, priests and freethinkers, young whores and old nuns, under the common cry for the salvation of Property, Religion, the Family and Society. The working-class was everywhere proclaimed, placed under a ban, under a virtual law of suspects. The manufacturers had no need any longer to restrain themselves. They broke out in open revolt not only against the Ten Hours' Act, but against the whole of the legislation that since 1833 had aimed at restricting in some measure the 'free' exploitation of labour power. It was a pro-slavery rebellion in miniature, carried on for over two years with a cynical recklessness, a terrorist energy all the cheaper because the rebel capitalist risked nothing except the skin of his 'hands'.

To understand that which follows we must remember that the Factory Acts of 1833, 1844, and 1847 were all three in force so far as the one did not amend the other: that not one of these limited the working-day of the male worker over 18, and that since 1833 the 15 hours from 5.30 a.m. to 8.30 p.m. had remained the legal 'day', within the limits of which at first the 12, and later the 10 hours' labour of young persons and women had to be performed under the prescribed conditions.

The manufacturers began by here and there discharging a part of, in many cases half of the young persons and women employed by them, and then, for the adult males, restoring the almost obsolete night-work. The Ten Hours' Act, they cried, leaves no other alternative.[113]

Their second step dealt with the legal pauses for meals. Let us hear the Factory Inspectors. 'Since the restriction of the hours of work to ten, the factory occupiers maintain, although they have not yet practically gone the whole length, that supposing the hours of work to be from 9 a.m. to 7 p.m. they fulfil the provisions of the statutes by allowing an hour before 9 a.m. and half an hour after 7 p.m. [for meals]. In some cases they now allow an hour, or half an hour for dinner, insisting at the same time, that they are not bound to allow any part of the hour and a half in the course of the factory working-day.'[114] The manufacturers maintained therefore that the scrupulously strict provisions of the Act of 1844 with regard to meal-times only gave the operatives permission to eat and drink before coming into, and after leaving the factory – i.e., at home. And why should not the workpeople eat their dinner before 9 in the morning? The crown lawyers, however, decided that the prescribed meal-times 'must be in the interval during the working-hours, and that it will not be lawful to work for 10 hours continuously, from 9 a.m. to 7 p.m., without any interval.'[115]

After these pleasant demonstrations, Capital preluded its revolt by a step which agreed with the letter of the law of 1844, and was therefore legal.

The Act of 1844 certainly prohibited the employment after 1 p.m. of such children, from 8 to 13, as had been employed before noon. But it did not regulate in any way the 6 1/2 hours' work of the children whose work-time began at 12 midday or later. Children of 8 might, if they began work at noon, be employed from 12 to 1, 1 hour; from 2 to 4 in the afternoon, 2 hours; from 5 to 8.30 in the evening, 3 1/2 hours; in all, the legal 6 1/2 hours. Or better still. In order to make their work coincide with that of the adult male labourers up to 8.30 p.m., the manufacturers only had to give them no work till 2 in the afternoon, they could then keep them in the factory without intermission till 8.30 in the evening. 'And it is now expressly admitted that the practice exists in England from the desire of mill-owners to have their machinery at work for more than 10 hours a day, to keep the children at work with male adults after all the young persons and women have left, and until 8.30 p.m. if the factory-owners choose."[116] Workmen and factory inspectors protested on hygienic and moral grounds, but Capital answered:

> My deeds upon my head! I crave the law,
> The penalty and forfeit of my bond.'

In fact, according to statistics laid before the House of Commons on July 26th, 1850, in spite of all protests, on July 15th, 1850, 3,742 children were subjected to this 'practice' in 257 factories.[117]

Still, this was not enough. The Lynx eye of Capital discovered that the Act of 1844 did not allow 5 hours' work before mid-day without a pause of at least 30 minutes for refreshment, but prescribed nothing of the kind for work after mid-day. Therefore, it claimed and obtained the enjoyment not only of making children of 8 drudge without intermission from 2 to 8.30 p.m., but also of making them hunger during that time.

> Ay, his heart.

So says the bond.

This Shylock-clinging[118] to the letter of the law of 1844, so far as it regulated children's labour, was but to lead up to an open revolt against the same law, so far as it regulated the labour of 'young persons and women'. It will be remembered that the abolition of the 'false relay system' was the chief aim and object of that law. The masters began their revolt with the simple declaration that the sections of the Act of 1844 which prohibited the *ad libitum* use of young persons and women in such short fractions of the day of 15 hours as the employer chose, were 'comparatively harmless' so long as the work-time was fixed at 12 hours. But under the Ten Hours' Act they were a 'grievous hardship'.[119] They informed the inspectors in the coolest manner that they should place themselves above the letter of the law, and re-introduce the old system on their own account.[120] They were acting in the interests of the ill-advised operatives themselves, 'in order to be able to pay them higher wages'. 'This was the only possible plan by which to maintain, under the Ten Hours' Act, the industrial supremacy of Great Britain.' 'Perhaps it may be a little difficult to detect irregularities under the relay system; but what of that? Is the great manufacturing interest of this country to be treated as a secondary matter in order to save some little trouble to Inspectors and Sub-Inspectors of Factories?'[121]

All these shifts naturally were of no avail. The Factory Inspectors appealed to the Law Courts. But soon such a cloud of dust in the way of petitions from the masters overwhelmed the Home Secretary, Sir George Grey, that in a circular of August 5th, 1848, he recommends the inspectors not 'to lay informations against mill-owners for a breach of the letter of the Act, or for employment of young persons by relays in cases in which there is no reason to believe that such young persons have been actually employed for a longer period than that sanctioned by law.' Hereupon, Factory Inspector J. Stuart allowed the so-called relay system during the 15 hours of the factory day throughout Scotland, where it soon flourished again as of old. The English Factory Inspectors, on the other hand, declared that the Home Secretary had no power dictatorially to suspend the law, and continued their legal proceedings against the pro-slavery rebellion.

But what was the good of summoning the capitalists when the Courts in this case the country magistrates – Cobbett's 'Great Un-paid' – acquitted them? In these tribunals, the masters sat in judgment on themselves. An example. One Eskrigge, cotton-spinner, of the firm of Kershaw, Leese, & Co., had laid before the Factory Inspector of his district the scheme of a relay system intended for his mill. Receiving a refusal, he at first kept quiet. A few months later, an individual named Robinson, also a cotton-spinner, and if not his Man Friday, at all events related to Eskrigge, appeared before the borough magistrates of Stock-port on a charge of introducing the identical plan of relays invented by Eskrigge. Four Justices sat, among them three cotton-spinners, at their head this same inevitable Eskrigge. Eskrigge acquitted Robinson, and now was of opinion that what was right for Robinson was fair for Eskrigge. Supported by his own legal decision, he introduced the system at once into his own factory.[122] Of course, the composition of this tribunal was in itself a violation of the law.[123] These judicial farces, exclaims Inspector Howell, 'urgently call for a remedy – either that the law should be so altered as to be made to conform to these decisions, or that it should be administered by a less fallible tribunal, whose decisions would conform to the law . . . when these cases are brought forward. I long for a stipendiary magistrate.'[124]

The crown lawyers declared the masters' interpretation of the Act of 1848 absurd. But the Saviours of Society would not allow themselves to be turned from their purpose. Leonard Horner reports, 'Having endeavoured to enforce the Act . . . by ten prosecutions in seven magisterial divisions, and having been supported by the magistrates in one case only . . . I considered it useless to prosecute more for this evasion of the law. That part of the Act of 1848 which was framed for securing uniformity in the hours of work, . . . is thus no longer in force in my district (Lancashire). Neither have the sub-inspectors or myself any means of satisfying ourselves, when we inspect a mill working by shifts, that the young persons and women are not working more than 10 hours a day . . . In a return of the 30th April . . . of millowners working by shifts, the number amounts to 114, and has been for some time rapidly increasing. In general, the time of working the mill is extended to 13 1/2 hours from 6 a.m. to 7 1/2 p.m., . . . in some instances it amounts to 15 hours, from 5 1/2 a.m. to 8 1/2 p.m.'[125] Already, in December, 1848, Leonard Horner had a list of 65 manufacturers and 29 overlookers who unanimously declared that no system of supervision could, under this relay system, prevent enormous overwork.[126] Now, the same children and young persons were shifted from the spinning-room to the weaving-room, now, during 15 hours, from one factory to another.[127] How was it possible to control a system which, 'under the guise of relays, is some one of the many plans for shuffling "the hands" about in endless variety, and shifting the hours of work and of rest for different individuals throughout the day, so that you may never have one complete set of hands working together in the same room at the same time.'[128]

But altogether independently of actual over-work, this so-called relay system was an offspring of capitalistic fantasy, such as Fourier, in his humorous sketches of *Courses Séances*, has never surpassed, except that the 'attraction of labour' was changed into the attraction of capital. Look, for example, at those schemes of the masters which the 'respectable' press praised as models of 'what a reasonable degree of care and method can accomplish.' The *personnel* of the workpeople was sometimes divided into from 12 to 14 categories, which themselves constantly changed and rechanged their constituent parts. During the 15 hours of the factory day, capital dragged in the labourer now for 30 minutes, now for an hour, and then pushed him out again, to drag him into the factory and to thrust him out afresh, hounding him hither and thither, in scattered shreds of time, without ever losing hold of him until the full 10 hours' work was done. As on the stage, the same persons had to appear in turns in the different scenes of the different acts. But as an actor during the whole course of the play belongs to the stage, so the operatives, during 15 hours, belonged to the factory, without reckoning the time for going and coming. Thus the hours of rest were turned into hours of enforced idleness, which drove the youths to the pot-house, and the girls to the brothel. At every new trick that the capitalist, from day to day, hit upon for keeping his machinery going 12 or 15 hours without increasing the number of his hands, the worker had to swallow his meals now in this fragment of time, now in that. At the time of the 10 hours' agitation, the masters cried out that the working mob petitioned in the hope of obtaining 12 hours' wages for 10 hours' work. Now they reversed the medal. They paid 10 hours' wages for 12 or 15 hours' lordship over labour power.[129] This was the gist of the matter, this the masters' interpretation of the 10 hours' law! These were the same unctuous Free-traders, perspiring with the love of humanity, who for full 10 years, during the Anti-Corn Law agitation, had preached to the operatives, by a reckoning of pounds, shillings, and pence, that with free importation of corn, and with the means possessed by English industry, 10 hours' labour would be quite enough to enrich the capitalists.[130] This revolt of capital, after two years was at last crowned with victory by a decision of one of the four highest Courts of Justice in England, the Court of Exchequer, which in a case brought before it on February 8th, 1850, decided that the manufacturers were certainly acting against the sense of the Act of 1844, but that this Act itself contained certain words that rendered it meaningless. 'By this decision, the Ten Hours' Act was abolished.'[131] A crowd of masters, who until then had been afraid of using the relay system for young persons and women, now took it up heart and soul.[132]

But on this apparently decisive victory of capital, followed at once a revulsion. The workpeople had hitherto offered a passive, although inflexible and unremitting resistance. They now protested in Lancashire and Yorkshire in threatening meetings. The pretended Ten Hours' Act was thus simple humbug, parliamentary cheating, had never existed! The Factory Inspectors urgently warned the Government that the antagonism of classes had arrived at an incredible tension. Some of the masters themselves murmured: 'On account of the contradictory decisions of the magistrates, a condition of things altogether abnormal and anarchical obtains. One law holds in Yorkshire, another in Lancashire; one law in one parish of Lancashire, another in its immediate neighbourhood. The manufacturer in large towns could evade the law, the manufacturer in country districts could not find the people necessary for the relay system, still less for the shifting of hands from one factory to another,' &c. And the first birthright of capital is equal exploitation of labour power by all capitalists.

Under these circumstances a compromise between masters and men was effected that received the seal of Parliament in the additional Factory Act of August 5th, 1850. The working-day for 'young persons and women', was raised from 10 to 10 1/2 hours for the first five days of the week, and shortened to 7 1/2 on the Saturday. The work was to go on between 6 a.m. and 6 p.m.,[133] with pauses of not less than 1 1/2 hours for meal-times, these meal-times to be allowed at one and the same time for all, and conformably to the conditions of 1844. By this an end was put to the relay system once for all.[134] For children's labour, the Act of 1844 remained in force.

One set of masters, this time as before, secured to itself special seigneurial rights over the children of the proletariat. These were the silk manufacturers. In 1833 they had howled out in threatening fashion, 'if the liberty of working children of any age for 10 hours a day were taken away, it would stop their works.'[135] It would be impossible for them to buy a sufficient number of children over 13. They extorted the privilege they desired. The pretext was shown on subsequent investigation to be a deliberate lie.[136] It did not, however, prevent them, during 10 years, from spinning silk 10 hours a day out of the blood of little children who had to be placed upon stools for the performance of their work.[137] The Act of 1844 certainly 'robbed' them of the 'liberty' of employing children under 11 longer than 6 1/2 hours a day. But it secured to them, on the other hand, the privilege of working children between 11 and 13, 10 hours a day, and of annulling in their case the education made compulsory for all other factory children. This time the pretext was 'the delicate texture of the fabric in which they were employed, requiring a lightness of touch, only to be acquired by their early introduction to these factories'.[138] The children were slaughtered out-and-out for the sake of their delicate fingers, as in Southern Russia the horned cattle for the sake of their hide and tallow. At length, in 1850, the privilege granted in 1844, was limited to the departments of silk-twisting and silk-winding. But here, to make amends to capital bereft of its 'freedom', the work-time for children from 11 to 13 was raised from 10 to 10 1/2 hours. Pretext: 'Labour in silk mills was lighter than in mills for other fabrics, and less likely in other respects also to be prejudicial to health.'[139] Official medical inquiries proved afterwards that, on the contrary, 'the average death-rate is exceedingly high in the silk districts and amongst the female part of the population is higher even than it is in the cotton districts of Lancashire.'[140] Despite the protests of the Factory Inspector, renewed every 6 months, the mischief continues to this hour.[141]

The Act of 1850 changed the 15 hours' time from 6 a.m. to 8.30 p.m., into the 12 hours from 6 a.m. to 6 p.m. for 'young persons and women' only. It did not, therefore, affect children who could always be employed for half an hour before and 2 1/2 hours after this period, provided the whole of their labour did not exceed 6 1/2 hours. Whilst the bill was under discussion, the Factory Inspectors laid before Parliament statistics of the infamous abuses due to this anomaly. To no purpose. In the background lurked the intention of screwing up, during prosperous years, the working-day of adult males to 15 hours by the aid of the children. The experience of the three following years showed that such an attempt must come to grief against the resistance of the adult male operatives. The Act of 1850 was therefore finally completed in 1853 by forbidding the 'employment of children in the morning before and in the evening after young persons and women'. Henceforth with a few exceptions the Factory Act of 1850 regulated the working-day of all workers in the branches of industry that come under it.[142] Since the passing of the first Factory Act half a century had elapsed.[143]

Factory legislation for the first time went beyond its original sphere in the 'Printworks Act of 1845'. The displeasure with which capital received this new 'extravagance' speaks through every line of the Act. It limits the working-day for children from 8 to 13, and for women to 16 hours, between 6 a.m. and 10 p.m., without any legal pause for meal-times. It allows males over 13 to be worked at will day and night.[144] It is a Parliamentary abortion.[145]

However, the principle had triumphed with its victory in those great branches of industry which form the most characteristic creation of the modern mode of production. Their wonderful development from 1853 to 1860, hand-in-hand with the physical and moral regeneration of the factory workers, struck the most purblind. The masters from whom the legal limitation and regulation had been wrung step by step after a civil war of half a century, themselves referred ostentatiously to the contrast with the branches of exploitation still 'free'.[146] The Pharisees of 'Political Economy' now proclaimed the discernment of the necessity of a legally fixed working-day as a characteristic new discovery of their 'science'.[147] It will be easily understood that after the factory magnates had resigned themselves and become reconciled to the inevitable, the power of resistance of capital gradually weakened, whilst at the same time the power of attack of the working-class grew with the number of its allies in the classes of society not immediately interested in the question. Hence the comparatively rapid advance since 1860.

The dye-works and bleach-works all came under the Factory Act of 1850 in 1860;[148] lace and stocking manufactures in 1861.

In consequence of the first report of the Commission on the employment of children (1863), the same fate was shared by the manufacturers of all earthenwares (not merely pottery), Lucifer-matches, percussion caps, cartridges, carpets, fustian-cutting, and many processes included under the name of 'finishing'. In the year 1863 bleaching in the open air[149] and baking were placed under special Acts, by which, in the former, the labour of young persons and women during the night-time (from 8 in the evening to 6 in the morning), and in the latter, the employment of journeymen bakers under 18, between 9 in the evening and 5 in the morning were forbidden. We shall return to the later proposals of the same Commission, which threatened to deprive of their 'freedom' all the important branches of English Industry, with the exception of agriculture, mines, and the means of transport.[150]

Section 7. The Struggle for the Normal Working-Day. Reaction of the English Factory Acts on Other Countries.

The reader will bear in mind that the production of surplus-value, or the extraction of surplus-labour, is the specific end and aim, the sum and substance, of capitalist production, quite apart from any changes in the mode of production, which may arise from the subordination of labour to capital. He will remember that as far as we have at present gone, only the independent labourer, and therefore only the labourer legally qualified to act for himself, enters as a vendor of a commodity into a contract with the capitalist. If, therefore, in our historical sketch, on the one hand, modern industry, on the other, the labour of those who are physically and legally minors, play important parts, the former was to us only a special department, and the latter only a specially striking example of labour exploitation. Without, however, anticipating the subsequent development of our inquiry, from the mere connection of the historic facts before us it follows:

First. The passion of capital for an unlimited and reckless extension of the working-day, is first gratified in the industries earliest revolutionised by water-power, steam, and machinery, in those first creations of the modern mode of production, cotton, wool, flax and silk spinning, and weaving. The changes in the material mode of production, and the corresponding changes in the social relations of the producers[151] gave rise first to an extravagance beyond all bounds, and then in opposition to this, called forth a control on the part of Society which legally limits, regulates, and makes uniform the working-day and its pauses. This control appears, therefore, during the first half of the nineteenth century simply as exceptional legislation.[152] As soon as this primitive dominion of the new mode of production was conquered, it was found that, in the meantime, not only had many other branches of production been made to adopt the same factory system, but that manufactures with more or less obsolete methods, such as potteries, glass-making, &c., that old-fashioned handicrafts, like baking, and, finally, even that the so-called domestic industries, such as nail-making,[153] had long since fallen as completely under capitalist exploitation as the factories themselves. Legislation was, therefore, compelled to gradually get rid of its exceptional character, or where, as in England, it proceeds after the manner of the Roman Casuists, to declare any house in which work was done to be a factory.[154]

Second. The history of the regulation of the working-day in certain branches of production, and the struggle still going on in others in regard to this regulation, prove conclusively that the isolated labourer, the labourer as 'free' vendor of his labour power, when capitalist production has once attained a certain stage, succumbs without any power of resistance. The creation of a normal working-day is, therefore, the product of a protracted civil war, more or less dissembled, between the capitalist class and the working-class. As the contest takes place in the arena of modern industry, it first breaks out in the home of that industry – England.[155] The English factory workers were the champions, not only of the English, but of the modern working-class generally, as their theorists were the first to throw down the gauntlet to the theory of capital.[156] Hence, the philosopher of the Factory, Ure, denounces as an ineffable disgrace to the English working-class that they inscribed 'the slavery of the Factory Acts' on the banner which they bore against capital, manfully striving for 'perfect freedom of labour'.[157]

France limps slowly behind England. The February revolution was necessary to bring into the world the 12 hours' law,[158] which is much more deficient than its English original. For all that, the French revolutionary method has its special advantages. It once for all commands the same limit to the working-day in all shops and factories without distinction, whilst English legislation reluctantly yields to the pressure of circumstances, now on this point, now on that, and is getting lost in a hopelessly bewildering tangle of contradictory enactments.[159] On the other hand, the French law proclaims as a principle that which in England was only won in the name of children, minors, and women, and has been only recently for the first time claimed as a general right.[160]

In the United States of North America, every independent movement of the workers was paralysed so long as slavery disfigured a part of the Republic. Labour cannot emancipate itself in the white skin where in the black it is branded. But out of the death of slavery a new life at once arose. The first fruit of the Civil War was the eight hours' agitation, that ran with the seven-leagued boots of the locomotive from the Atlantic to the Pacific, from New England to California. The General Congress of Labour at Baltimore (August 16th, 1866) declared: 'The first and great necessity of the present, to free the labour of this country from capitalistic slavery, is the passing of a law by which eight hours shall be the normal working-day in all States of the American Union. We are resolved to put forth all our strength until this glorious result is attained.'[161] At the same time, the Congress of the International Working Men's Association at Geneva, on the proposition of the London General Council, resolved that 'the limitation of the working-day is a preliminary condition without which all further attempts at improvement and emancipation must prove abortive . . . the Congress proposes eight hours as the legal limit of the working-day.'

Thus the movement of the working-class on both sides of the Atlantic, that had grown instinctively out of the conditions of production themselves, endorsed the words of the English Factory Inspector, R. J. Saunders 'Further steps towards a reformation of society can never be carried out with any hope of success, unless the hours of labour be limited, and the prescribed limit strictly enforced.'[162]

It must be acknowledged that our labourer comes out of the process of production other than he entered. In the market he stood as owner of the commodity 'labour power' face to face with other owners of commodities, dealer against dealer. The contract by which he sold to the capitalist his labour power proved, so to say, in black and white that he disposed of himself freely. The bargain concluded, it is discovered that he was no 'free agent', that the time for which he is free to sell his labour power is the time for which he is forced to sell it,[163] that in fact the vampire will not loose its hold on him 'so long as there is a muscle, a nerve, a drop of blood to be exploited.'[164] For 'protection' against 'the serpent of their agonies', the labourers must put their heads together, and, as a class, compel the passing of a law, an all-powerful social barrier that shall prevent the very workers from selling, by voluntary contract with capital, themselves and their families into slavery and death.[165] In place of the pompous catalogue of the 'inalienable rights of man' comes the modest Magna Charta of a legally limited working-day, which shall make clear 'when the time which the worker sells is ended, and when his own begins.'[166] *Quantum mutatus ab illo!*

Chapter 11
Rate and Mass of Surplus-Value

In this chapter, as hitherto, the value of labour power, and therefore the part of the working-day necessary for the reproduction or maintenance of that labour power, are supposed to be given, constant magnitudes.

This premised, with the rate, the mass is at the same time given of the surplus-value that the individual labourer furnishes to the capitalist in a definite period of time. If, e.g., the necessary labour amounts to 6 hours daily, expressed in a quantum of gold = 3 shillings, then 3s. is the daily value of one labour power or the value of the capital advanced in the buying of one labour power. If, further, the rate of surplus-value be = 100%, this variable capital of 3s. produces a mass of surplus-value of 3s., or the labourer supplies daily a mass of surplus-labour equal to 6 hours.

But the variable capital of a capitalist is the expression in money of the total value of all the labour powers that he employs simultaneously. Its value is, therefore, equal to the average value of one labour power, multiplied by the number of labour powers employed. With a given value of labour power, therefore, the magnitude of the variable capital varies directly as the number of labourers employed simultaneously. If the daily value of one labour power = 3s., then a capital of 300s. must be advanced in order to exploit daily 100 labour powers, of n times 3s., in order to exploit daily n labour powers.

In the same way, if a variable capital of 3s., being the daily value of one labour power, produce a daily surplus-value of 3s., a variable capital of 300s. will produce a daily surplus-value of 300s., and one of n times 3s. a daily surplus-value of n x 3s. The mass of the surplus-value produced is therefore equal to the surplus-value which the working-day of one labourer supplies multiplied by the number of labourers employed. But as further the mass of surplus-value which a single labourer produces, the value of labour power being given, is determined by the rate of the surplus-value, this law follows: the mass of the surplus-value produced is equal to the amount of the variable capital advanced, multiplied by the rate of surplus-value; in other words: it is determined by the compound ratio between the number of labour powers exploited simultaneously by the same capitalist and the degree of exploitation of each individual labour power.

Let the mass of the surplus-value be S; the surplus-value supplied by the individual labourer in the average day s; the variable capital daily advanced in the purchase of one individual labour power v; the sum total of the variable capital V; the value of an average labour power P; its degree of exploitation a'/a (surplus-labour/necessary-labour); and the number of labourers employed n; we have:

$$S = s/v \times V = P \times a'/a \times n$$

It is always supposed, not only that the value of an average labour power is constant, but that the labourers employed by a capitalist are reduced to average labourers. There are exceptional cases in which the surplus-value produced does not increase in proportion to the number of labourers exploited, but then the value of the labour power does not remain constant.

In the production of a definite mass of surplus-value, therefore, the decrease of one factor may be compensated by the increase of the other. If the variable capital diminishes, and at the same time the rate of surplus-value increases in the same ratio, the mass of surplus-value produced remains unaltered. If on our earlier assumption the capitalist must advance 300s., in order to exploit 100 labourers a day, and if the rate of surplus-value amounts to 50%, this variable capital of 300s. yields a surplus-value of 150s. or of 100 x 3 working hours. If the rate of surplus-value doubles, or the working-day, instead of being extended from 6 to 9, is extended from 6 to 12 hours and at the same time variable capital is lessened by half, and reduced to 150s., it yields also a surplus-value of 150s. or 50 x 6 working hours. Diminution of the variable capital may therefore be compensated by a proportionate rise in the degree of exploitation of labour power, or the decrease in the number of the labourers employed by a proportionate extension of the working-day. Within certain limits therefore the supply of labour exploitable by capital is independent of the supply of labourers.[1] On the contrary, a fall in the rate of surplus-value leaves unaltered the mass of the surplus-value produced, if the amount of the variable capital, or number of the labourers employed, increases in the same proportion.

Nevertheless, the compensation of a decrease in the number of labourers employed, or of the amount of variable capital advanced by a rise in the rate of surplus-value. or by the lengthening of the working-day, has impassable limits. Whatever the value of labour power may be, whether the working time necessary for the maintenance of the labourer is 2 or 10 hours, the total value that a labourer can produce, day in, day out, is always less than the value in which 24 hours of labour are embodied, less than 12s., if 12s. is the money expression for 24 hours of realised labour. In our former assumption, according to which 6 working hours are daily necessary in order to reproduce the labour power itself or to replace the value of the capital advanced in its purchase, a variable capital of 1,500s., that employs 500 labourers at a rate of surplus-value of 100% with a 12 hours' working-day, produces daily a surplus-value of 1,500s. or of 6 x 500 working hours. A capital of 300s. that employs 100 labourers a day with a rate of surplus-value of 200% or with a working-day of 18 hours, produces only a mass of surplus-value of 600s. or 12 x 100 working hours; and its total value-product, the equivalent of the variable capital advanced plus the surplus-value, can, day in, day out, never reach the sum of 1,200s. or 24 x 100 working hours. The absolute limit of the average working day – this being by nature always less than 24 hours – sets an absolute limit to the compensation of a reduction of variable capital by a higher rate of surplus-value, or of the decrease of the number of labourers exploited by a higher degree of exploitation of labour power. This palpable law is of importance for the clearing up of many phenomena, arising from a tendency (to be worked out later on) of capital to reduce as much as possible the number of labourers employed by it, or its variable constituent transformed into labour power, in contradiction to its other tendency to produce the greatest possible mass of surplus-value. On the other hand, if the mass of labour power employed, or the amount of variable capital, increases, but not in proportion to the fall in the rate of surplus-value, the mass of the surplus-value produced, falls.

A third law results from the determination, of the mass of the surplus-value produced, by the two factors: rate of surplus-value and amount of variable capital advanced. The rate of surplus-value, or the degree of exploitation of labour power, and the value of labour power, or the amount of necessary working time being given, it is self-evident that the greater the variable capital, the greater would be the mass of the value produced and of the surplus value. If the limit of the working-day is given, and also the limit of its necessary constituent, the mass of value and surplus-value that an individual capitalist produces, is clearly exclusively dependent on the mass of labour that he sets in motion. But this, under the conditions supposed above, depends on the mass of labour power, or the number of labourers whom he exploits, and this number in its turn is determined by the amount of the variable capital advanced. With a given rate of surplus-value, and a given value of labour power, therefore, the masses of surplus-value produced vary directly as the amounts of the variable capitals advanced. Now we know that the capitalist divides his capital into two parts. One part he lays out in means of production. This is the constant part of his capital. The other part he lays out in living labour power. This part forms his variable capital. On the basis of the same mode of social production, the division of capital into constant and variable differs in different branches of production, and within the same branch of production, too, this relation changes with changes in the technical conditions and in the social combinations of the processes of production. But in whatever proportion a given capital breaks up into a constant and a variable part, whether the latter is to the former as 1:2 or 1:10 or 1:x, the law just laid down is not affected by this. For, according to our previous analysis, the value of the constant capital reappears in the value of the product, but does not enter into the newly produced value, the newly created value-product. To employ 1,000 spinners, more raw material, spindles, &c., are, of course, required, than to employ 100. The value of these additional means of production however may rise, fall, remain un-altered, be large or small; it has no influence on the process of creation of surplus-value by means of the labour powers that put them in motion. The law demonstrated above now, therefore, takes this form: the masses of value and of surplus-value produced by different capitals – the value of labour power being given and its degree of exploitation being equal – vary directly as the amounts of the variable constituents of these capitals, i.e., as their constituents transformed into living labour power.

This law clearly contradicts all experience based on appearance. Everyone knows that a cotton spinner, who, reckoning the percent-age on the whole of his applied capital, employs much constant and little variable capital, does not, on account of this, pocket less profit or surplus-value than a baker, who relatively sets in motion much variable and little constant capital. For the solution of this apparent contradiction, many intermediate terms are as yet wanted, as from the standpoint of elementary algebra many intermediate terms are wanted to understand that 0/0 may represent an actual magnitude. Classical economy, although not formulating the law, holds instinct-ively to it, because it is a necessary consequence of the general law of value. It tries to rescue the law from collision with contradictory phenomena by a violent abstraction. It will be seen later[2] how the school of Ricardo has come to grief over this stumbling-block. Vulgar economy which, indeed, 'has really learnt nothing', here as everywhere sticks to appearances in opposition to the law which regulates and explains them. In opposition to Spinoza, it believes that 'ignorance is a sufficient reason.'

The labour which is set in motion by the total capital of a society, day in, day out, may be regarded as a single collective working-day. If, e.g., the number of labourers is a million, and the average working-day of a labourer is 10 hours, the social working-day consists of ten million hours. With a given length of this working-day, whether its limits are fixed physically or socially, the mass of surplus-value can only be increased by increasing the number of labourers, i.e., of the labouring population. The growth of population here forms the mathematical limit to the production of surplus-value by the total social capital. On the contrary, with a given amount of population, this limit is formed by the possible lengthening of the working-day.[3] It will, however, be seen in the following chapter that this law only holds for the form of surplus-value dealt with up to the present.

From the treatment of the production of surplus-value, so far, it follows that not every sum of money, or of value, is at pleasure transformable into capital. To effect this transformation, in fact, a certain minimum of money or of exchange-value must be presupposed in the hands of the individual possessor of money or commodities. The minimum of variable capital is the cost price of a single labour power, employed the whole year through, day in, day out, for the production of surplus-value. If this labourer were in possession of his own means of production, and were satisfied to live as a labourer, he need not work beyond the time necessary for the reproduction of his means of subsistence, say 8 hours a day. He would, besides, only require the means of production sufficient for 8 working hours. The capitalist, on the other hand, who makes him do, besides these 8 hours, say 4 hours' surplus-labour, requires an additional sum of money for furnishing the additional means of production. On our supposition, however, he would have to employ two labourers in order to live, on the surplus-value appropriated daily, as well as, and no better than a labourer, i.e., to be able to satisfy his necessary wants. In this case the mere maintenance of life would be the end of his production, not the increase of wealth; but this latter is implied in capitalist production. That he may live only twice as well as an ordinary labourer, and besides turn half of the surplus-value produced into capital, he would have to raise, with the number of labourers, the minimum of the capital advanced 8 times. Of course he can, like his labourer, take to work himself, participate directly in the process of production, but he is then only a hybrid between capitalist and labourer, a 'small master'. A certain stage of capitalist production necessitates that the capitalist be able to devote the whole of the time during which he functions as a capitalist, i.e., as personified capital, to the appropriation and therefore control of the labour of others, and to the selling of the products of this labour.[4] The guilds of the middle ages therefore tried to prevent by force the transformation of the master of a trade into a capitalist, by limiting the number of labourers that could be employed by one master within a very small maximum. The possessor of money or commodities actually turns into a capitalist in such cases only where the minimum sum advanced for production greatly exceeds the maximum of the middle ages. Here, as in natural science, is shown the correctness of the law discovered by Hegel (in his *Logic*), that merely quantitative differences beyond a certain point pass into qualitative changes.[5]

The minimum of the sum of value that the individual possessor of money or commodities must command, in order to metamorphose himself into a capitalist, changes with the different stages of development of capitalist production, and is at given stages different in different spheres of production, according to their special and technical conditions. Certain spheres of production demand, even at the very outset of capitalist production, a minimum of capital that is not as yet found in the hands of single individuals. This gives rise partly to state subsidies to private persons, as in France in the time of Colbert, and as in many German states up to our own epoch, partly to the formation of societies with legal monopoly for the exploitation of certain branches of industry and commerce, the forerunners of our modern joint-stock companies.[6]

Within the process of production, as we have seen, capital acquired the command over labour, i.e., over functioning labour power or the labourer himself. Personified capital, the capitalist, takes care that the labourer does his work regularly and with the proper degree of intensity.

Capital further developed into a coercive relation, which compels the working-class to do more work than the narrow round of its own life-wants prescribes. As a producer of the activity of others, as a pumper-out of surplus-labour and exploiter of labour power, it surpasses in energy, disregard of bounds, recklessness and efficiency, all earlier systems of production based on directly compulsory labour.

At first, capital subordinates labour on the basis of the technical conditions in which it historically finds it. It does not, therefore, change immediately the mode of production. The production of surplus-value – in the form hitherto considered by us – by means of simple extension of the working-day, proved, therefore, to be independent of any change in the mode of production itself. It was not less active in the old-fashioned bakeries than in the modern cotton factories.

If we consider the process of production from the point of view of the simple labour-process, the labourer stands in relation to the means of production, not in their quality as capital, but as the mere means and material of his own intelligent productive activity. In tanning, e.g., he deals with the skins as his simple object of labour. It is not the capitalist whose skin he tans. But it is different as soon as we deal with the process of production from the point of view of the process of creation of surplus-value. The means of production are at once changed into means for the absorption of the labour of others. It is now no longer the labourer that employs the means of production, but the means of production that employ the labourer. Instead of being consumed by him as material elements of his productive activity, they consume him as the ferment necessary to their own life-process, and the life-process of capital consists only in its movement as value constantly expanding, constantly multiplying itself. Furnaces and workshops that stand idle by night, and absorb no living labour, are 'a mere loss' to the capitalist. Hence, furnaces and workshops constitute lawful claims upon the night-labour of the workpeople. The simple transformation of money into the material factors of the process of production, into means of production, transforms the latter into a title and a right to the labour and surplus-labour of others. An example will show, in conclusion, how this sophistication, peculiar to and characteristic of capitalist production, this complete inversion of the relation between dead and living labour, between value and the force that creates value, mirrors itself in the consciousness of capitalists. During the revolt of the English factory lords between 1848 and 1850, 'the head of one of the oldest and most respectable houses in the West of Scotland, Messrs Carlile Sons & Co., of the linen and cotton thread factory at Paisley, a company which has now existed for about a century, which was in operation in 1752, and four generations of the same family have conducted it' . . . this 'very intelligent gentleman' then wrote a letter[7] in the *Glasgow Daily Mail* of April 25th, 1849, with the title, 'The relay system', in which among other things the following grotesquely naïve passage occurs: 'Let us now . . . see what evils will attend the limiting to 10 hours the working of the factory . . . They amount to the most serious damage to the mill-owner's prospects and property. If he (i.e., his 'hands') worked 12 hours before, and is limited to 10, then every 12 machines or spindles in his establishment shrink to 10, and should the works be disposed of, they will be valued only as 10, so that a sixth part would thus be deducted from the value of every factory in the country.'[8]

To this West of Scotland bourgeois brain, inheriting the accumulated capitalistic qualities of 'four generations', the value of the means of production, spindles, &c., is so inseparably mixed up with their property, as capital, to expand their own value, and to swallow up daily a definite quantity of the unpaid labour of others, that the head of the firm of Carlile & Co. actually imagines that if he sells his factory, not only will the value of the spindles be paid to him, but, in addition, their power of annexing surplus-value, not only the labour which is embodied in them, and is necessary to the production of spindles of this kind, but also the surplus-labour which they help to pump out daily from the brave Scots of Paisley, and for that very reason he thinks that with the shortening of the working-day by 2 hours, the selling price of 12 spinning machines dwindles to that of 10!

Part 4
The Production of Relative Surplus-Value

Chapter 12
The Concept of Relative Surplus-Value.

That portion of the working-day which merely produces an equivalent for the value paid by the capitalist for his labour power, has, up to this point, been treated by us as a constant magnitude, and such in fact it is, under given conditions of production and at a given stage in the economic development of society. Beyond this, his necessary labour-time, the labourer, we saw, could continue to work for 2, 3, 4, 6, &c., hours. The rate of surplus–value and the length of the working-day depended on the magnitude of this prolongation. Though the necessary labour-time was constant, we saw, on the other hand, that the total working-day was variable. Now suppose we have a working-day whose length, and whose apportionment between necessary labour and surplus-labour, are given. Let the whole line ac, a————b—c represent, for example, a working-day of 12 hours; the portion of ab 10 hours of necessary labour, and the portion bc 2 hours of surplus-labour. How now can the production of surplus-value be increased, i.e., how can the surplus-labour be prolonged, without, or independently of, any prolongation of ac?

Although the length of ac is given, bc appears to be capable of prolongation, if not by extension beyond its end c, which is also the end of the working-day ac, yet, at all events, by pushing back its starting-point b in the direction of a. Assume that b'—b in the line ab'bc is equal to half of bc

$$a\text{————}b'\text{—}b\text{————}c$$

or to one hour's labour-time. If now, in ac, the working-day of 12 hours, we move the point b to b', bc becomes b'c; the surplus-labour increases by one half, from 2 hours to 3 hours, although the working-day remains as before at 12 hours. This extension of the surplus labour-time from bc to b'c, from 2 hours to 3 hours, is, however, evidently impossible, without a simultaneous contraction of the necessary labour-time from ab into ab', from 10 hours to 9 hours. The prolongation of the surplus-labour would correspond to a shortening of the necessary labour; or a portion of the labour-time previously consumed, in reality, for the labourer's own benefit, would be converted into labour-time for the benefit of the capitalist. There would be an alteration, not in the length of the working-day, but in its division into necessary labour-time and surplus labour-time.

On the other hand, it is evident that the duration of the surplus-labour is given, when the length of the working-day, and the value of labour power, are given. The value of labour power, i.e., the labour-time requisite to produce labour power, determines the labour-time necessary for the reproduction of that value. If one working-hour be embodied in sixpence, and the value of a day's labour power be five shillings, the labourer must work 10 hours a day, in order to replace the value paid by capital for his labour power, or to produce an equivalent for the value of his daily necessary means of subsistence. Given the value of these means of subsistence, the value of his labour power is given;[1] and given the value of his labour power, the duration of his necessary labour-time is given. The duration of the surplus-labour, however, is arrived at, by subtracting the necessary labour-time from the total working-day. Ten hours subtracted from twelve, leave two, and it is not easy to see how, under the given conditions, the surplus-labour can possibly be prolonged beyond two hours. No doubt, the capitalist can, instead of five shillings, pay the labourer four shillings and sixpence or even less. For the reproduction of this value of four shillings and sixpence, nine hours' labour-time would suffice; and consequently three hours of surplus-labour, instead of two, would accrue to the capitalist, and the surplus-value would rise from one shilling to eighteen-pence. This result, however, would be obtained only by lowering the wages of the labourer below the value of his labour power. With the four shillings and sixpence which he produces in nine hours, he commands one-tenth less of the necessaries of life than before, and consequently the proper reproduction of his labour power is crippled. The surplus-labour would in this case be prolonged only by an overstepping of its normal limits; its domain would be extended only by a usurpation of part of the domain of necessary labour-time. Despite the important part which this method plays in actual practice, we are excluded from considering it in this place, by our assumption, that all commodities, including labour power, are bought and sold at their full value. Granted this, it follows that the labour-time necessary for the production of labour power, or for the reproduction of its value, cannot be lessened by a fall in the labourer's wages below the value of his labour power, but only by a fall in this value itself. Given the length of the working-day, the prolongation of the surplus-labour must of necessity originate in the curtailment of the necessary labour-time; the latter cannot arise from the former. In the example we have taken, it is necessary that the value of labour power should actually fall by one-tenth, in order that the necessary labour-time may be diminished by one-tenth, i.e., from ten hours to nine, and in order that the surplus labour may consequently be prolonged from two hours to three.

Such a fall in the value of labour power implies, however, that the same necessaries of life which were formerly produced in ten hours, can now be produced in nine hours. But this is impossible without an increase in the productiveness of labour. For example, suppose a shoe-maker, with given tools, makes in one working-day of twelve hours, one pair of boots. If he must make two pairs in the same time, the productiveness of his labour must be doubled; and this cannot be done, except by an alteration in his tools or in his mode of working, or in both. Hence, the conditions of production, i.e., his mode of production, and the labour-process itself, must be revolutionised. By increase in the productiveness of labour, we mean, generally, an alteration in the labour-process, of such a kind as to shorten the labour-time socially necessary for the production of a commodity, and to endow a given quantity of labour with the power of producing a greater quantity of use-value.[2] Hitherto in treating of surplus-value, arising from a simple prolongation of the working-day, we have assumed the mode of production to be given and invariable. But when surplus-value has to be produced by the conversion of necessary labour into surplus-labour, it by no means suffices for capital to take over the labour-process in the form under which it has been historically handed down, and then simply to prolong the duration of that process. The technical and social conditions of the process, and consequently the very mode of production must be revolutionised, before the product-iveness of labour can be increased. By that means alone can the value of labour power be made to sink, and the portion of the working-day necessary for the reproduction of that value, be shortened.

The surplus-value produced by prolongation of the working-day, I call *absolute surplus-value*. On the other hand, the surplus-value arising from the curtailment of the necessary labour-time, and from the corresponding alteration in the respective lengths of the two compon-ents of the working-day, I call *relative surplus-value*.

In order to effect a fall in the value of labour power, the increase in the productiveness of labour must seize upon those branches of industry whose products determine the value of labour power, and consequently either belong to the class of customary means of subsistence, or are capable of supplying the place of those means. But the value of a commodity is determined, not only by the quantity of labour which the labourer directly bestows upon that commodity, but also by the labour contained in the means of production. For instance, the value of a pair of boots depends not only on the cobbler's labour, but also on the value of the leather, wax, thread, &c. Hence, a fall in the value of labour power is also brought about by an increase in the productiveness of labour, and by a corresponding cheapening of commodities in those industries which supply the instruments of labour and the raw material, that form the material elements of the constant capital required for producing the necessaries of life. But an increase in the productiveness of labour in those branches of industry which supply neither the necessaries of life, nor the means of production for such necessaries, leaves the value of labour power undisturbed.

The cheapened commodity, of course, causes only a *pro tanto* fall in the value of labour power, a fall proportional to the extent of that commodity's employment in the reproduction of labour power. Shirts, for instance, are a necessary means of subsistence, but are only one out of many. The totality of the necessaries of life consists, however, of various commodities, each the product of a distinct industry; and the value of each of those commodities enters as a component part into the value of labour power. This latter value decreases with the decrease of the labour-time necessary for its reproduction; the total decrease being the sum of all the different curtailments of labour-time effected in those various and distinct industries. This general result is treated, here, as if it were the immediate result directly aimed at in each individual case. Whenever an individual capitalist cheapens shirts, for instance by increasing the productiveness of labour, he by no means necessarily aims at reducing the value of labour power and shortening, *pro tanto*, the necessary labour-time. But it is only in so far as he ultimately contributes to this result, that he assists in raising the general rate of surplus-value.[3] The general and necessary tendencies of capital must be distinguished from their forms of manifestation.

It is not our intention to consider, here, the way in which the laws, immanent in capitalist production, manifest themselves in the movements of individual masses of capital, where they assert themselves as coercive laws of competition, and are brought home to the mind and consciousness of the individual capitalist as the directing motives of his operations. But this much is clear; a scientific analysis of competition is not possible, before we have a conception of the inner nature of capital, just as the apparent motions of the heavenly bodies are not intelligible to any but him, who is acquainted with their real motions, motions which are not directly perceptible by the senses. Nevertheless, for the better comprehension of the production of relative surplus-value, we may add the following remarks, in which we assume nothing more than the results we have already obtained.

If one hour's labour is embodied in sixpence, a value of six shillings will be produced in a working-day of 12 hours. Suppose, that with the prevailing productiveness of labour, 12 articles are produced in these 12 hours. Let the value of the means of production used up in each article be sixpence. Under these circumstances, each article costs one shilling: sixpence for the value of the means of production, and sixpence for the value newly added in working with those means. Now let some one capitalist contrive to double the productiveness of labour, and to produce in the working-day of 12 hours, 24 instead of 12 such articles. The value of the means of production remaining the same, the value of each article will fall to ninepence, made up of sixpence for the value of the means of production and threepence for the value newly added by the labour. Despite the doubled productiveness of labour, the day's labour creates, as before, a new value of six shillings and no more, which, however, is now spread over twice as many articles. Of this value each article now has embodied in it 1/24th, instead of 1/12th, threepence instead of sixpence; or, what amounts to the same thing, only half an hour's instead of a whole hour's labour-time, is now added to the means of production while they are being transformed into each article. The individual value of these articles is now below their social value; in other words, they have cost less labour-time than the great bulk of the same article produced under the average social conditions. Each article costs, on an average, one shilling, and represents 2 hours of social labour; but under the altered mode of production it costs only ninepence, or contains only 1 1/2 hours' labour. The real value of a commodity is, however, not its individual value, but its social value; that is to say, the real value is not measured by the labour-time that the article in each individual case costs the producer, but by the labour-time socially required for its production. If therefore, the capitalist who applies the new method, sells his commodity at its social value of one shilling, he sells it for threepence above its individual value, and thus realises an extra surplus-value of threepence. On the other hand, the working-day of 12 hours is, as regards him, now represented by 24 articles instead of 12. Hence, in order to get rid of the product of one working-day, the demand must be double what it was, i.e., the market must become twice as extensive. Other things being equal, his commodities can command a more extended market only by a diminution of their prices. He will therefore sell them above their individual but under their social value, say at tenpence each. By this means he still squeezes an extra surplus-value of one penny out of each. This augmentation of surplus-value is pocketed by him, whether his commodities belong or not to the class of necessary means of subsistence that participate in determining the general value of labour power. Hence, independently of this latter circumstance, there is a motive for each individual capitalist to cheapen his commodities, by increasing the productiveness of labour.

Nevertheless, even in this case, the increased production of surplus-value arises from the curtailment of the necessary labour-time, and from the corresponding prolongation of the surplus-labour.[4] Let the necessary labour-time amount to 10 hours, the value of a day's labour power to five shillings, the surplus labour-time to 2 hours, and the daily surplus-value to one shilling. But the capitalist now produces 24 articles, which he sells at tenpence a-piece, making twenty shillings in all. Since the value of the means of production is twelve shillings, 14 2/5 of these articles merely replace the constant capital advanced. The labour of the 12 hours' working-day is represented by the remaining 9 3/5 articles. Since the price of the labour power is five shillings, 6 articles represent the necessary labour-time, and 3 3/5 articles the surplus-labour. The ratio of the necessary labour to the surplus-labour, which under average social conditions was 5:1, is now only 5:3. The same result may be arrived at in the following way. The value of the product of the working-day of 12 hours is twenty shillings. Of this sum, twelve shillings belong to the value of the means of production, a value that merely re-appears. There remain eight shillings, which are the expression in money, of the value newly created during the working-day. This sum is greater than the sum in which average social labour of the same kind is expressed: twelve hours of the latter labour are expressed by six shillings only. The exceptionally productive labour operates as intensified labour; it creates in equal periods of time greater values than average social labour of the same kind. (See Ch. 1. Sect 1.) But our capitalist still continues to pay as before only five shillings as the value of a day's labour power. Hence, instead of 10 hours, the labourer need now work only 7 1/5 hours, in order to reproduce this value. His surplus-labour is, therefore, increased by 2 4/5 hours, and the surplus-value he produces grows from one, into three shillings. Hence, the capitalist who applies the improved method of production, appropriates to surplus-labour a greater portion of the working-day, than the other capitalists in the same trade. He does individually, what the whole body of capitalists engaged in producing relative surplus-value, do collectively. On the other hand, however, this extra surplus-value vanishes, so soon as the new method of production has become general, and has consequently caused the difference between the individual value of the cheapened commodity and its social value to vanish. The law of the determination of value by labour-time, a law which brings under its sway the individual capitalist who applies the new method of production, by compelling him to sell his goods under their social value, this same law, acting as a coercive law of competition, forces his competitors to adopt the new method.[5] The general rate of surplus-value is, therefore, ultimately affected by the whole process, only when the increase in the productiveness of labour, has seized upon those branches of production that are connected with, and has cheapened those commodities that form part of, the necessary means of subsistence, and are therefore elements of the value of labour power.

The value of commodities is in inverse ratio to the productiveness of labour. And so, too, is the value of labour power, because it depends on the values of commodities. Relative surplus-value is, on the contrary, directly proportional to that productiveness. It rises with rising and falls with falling productiveness. The value of money being assumed to be constant, an average social working-day of 12 hours always produces the same new value, six shillings, no matter how this sum may be apportioned between surplus-value and wages. But if, in consequence of increased productiveness, the value of the necessaries of life fall, and the value of a day's labour power be thereby reduced from five shillings to three, the surplus-value increases from one shilling to three. Ten hours were necessary for the reproduction of the value of the labour power; now only six are required. Four hours have been set free, and can be annexed to the domain of surplus-labour. Hence there is immanent in capital an inclination and constant tendency, to heighten the productiveness of labour, in order to cheapen commodities, and by such cheapening to cheapen the labourer himself.[6]

The value of a commodity is, in itself, of no interest to the capitalist. What alone interests him, is the surplus-value that dwells in it, and is realisable by sale. Realisation of the surplus-value necess-arily carries with it the refunding of the value that was advanced. Now, since relative surplus-value increases in direct proportion to the development of the productiveness of labour, while, on the other hand, the value of commodities diminishes in the same pro-portion; since one and the same process cheapens commodities, and augments the surplus-value contained in them; we have here the solution of the riddle: why does the capitalist, whose sole concern is the production of exchange value, continually strive to depress the exchange value of commodities? A riddle with which Quesnay, one of the founders of Political Economy, tormented his opponents, and to which they could give him no answer. 'You acknowledge,' he says, 'that the more expenses and the cost of labour can, in the manufacture of industrial products, be reduced without injury to production, the more advantageous is such reduction, because it diminishes the price of the finished article. And yet, you believe that the production of wealth, which arises from the labour of the workpeople, consists in the augmentation of the exchange value of their products.'[7]

The shortening of the working-day is, therefore, by no means what is aimed at, in capitalist production, when labour is economised by increasing its productiveness.[8] It is only the shortening of the labour-time, necessary for the production of a definite quantity of commodities, that is aimed at. The fact that the workman, when the productiveness of his labour has been increased, produces, say 10 times as many commodities as before, and thus spends one-tenth as much labour-time on each, by no means prevents him from continuing to work 12 hours as before, nor from producing in those 12 hours 1,200 articles instead of 120. Nay, more, his working-day may be prolonged at the same time, so as to make him produce, say 1,400 articles in 14 hours. In the treatises, therefore, of economists of the stamp of MacCulloch, Ure, Senior, and *tutti quanti*, we may read upon one page, that the labourer owes a debt of gratitude to capital for developing his productiveness, because the necessary labour-time is thereby shortened, and on the next page, that he must prove his gratitude by working in future for 15 hours instead of 10. The object of all development of the productiveness of labour, within the limits of capitalist production, is to shorten that part of the working-day, during which the workman must labour for his own benefit, and by that very shortening, to lengthen the other part of the day, during which he is at liberty to work gratis for the capitalist. How far this result is also attainable, without cheapening commodities, will appear from an examination of the particular modes of producing relative surplus-value, to which examination we now proceed.

Chapter 13: Co-Operation

Capitalist production only then really begins, as we have already seen, when each individual capital employs simultaneously a comparatively large number of labourers; when consequently the labour-process is carried on on an extensive scale and yields, relatively, large quantities of products. A greater number of labourers working together, at the same time, in one place (or, if you will, in the same field of labour), in order to produce the same sort of commodity under the mastership of one capitalist, constitutes, both historically and logically, the starting-point of capitalist production. With regard to the mode of production itself, manufacture, in its strict meaning, is hardly to be distinguished, in its earliest stages, from the handicraft trades of the guilds, otherwise than by the greater number of workmen simultaneously employed by one and the same individual capital. The workshop of the medieval master handicraftsman is simply enlarged.

At first, therefore, the difference is purely quantitative. We have shown that the surplus-value produced by a given capital is equal to the surplus-value produced by each workman multiplied by the number of workmen simultaneously employed. The number of workmen in itself does nor affect, either the rate of surplus-value, or the degree of exploitation of labour power. If a working-day of 12 hours be embodied in six shillings, 1,200 such days will be embodied in 1,200 times 6 shillings. In one case 12 x 1,200 working-hours, and in the other 12 such hours are incorporated in the product. In the production of value a number of workmen rank merely as so many individual workmen; and it therefore makes no difference in the value produced whether the 1,200 men work separately, or united under the control of one capitalist.

Nevertheless, within certain limits, a modification takes place. The labour realised in value, is labour of an average social quality; is consequently the expenditure of average labour power. Any average magnitude, however, is merely the average of a number of separate magnitudes all of one kind, but differing as to quantity. In every industry, each individual labourer, be he Peter or Paul, differs from the average labourer. These individual differences, or 'errors' as they are called in mathematics, compensate one another, and vanish, whenever a certain minimum number of workmen are employed together. The celebrated sophist and sycophant, Edmund Burke, goes so far as to make the following assertion, based on his practical observations as a farmer; viz., that 'in so small a platoon' as that of five farm labourers, all individual differences in the labour vanish, and that consequently any given five adult farm labourers taken together, will in the same time do as much work as any other five.[1] But, however that may be, it is clear, that the collective working-day of a large number of workmen simultaneously employed, divided by the number of these workmen, gives one day of average social labour. For example, let the working-day of each individual be 12 hours. Then the collective working-day of 12 men simultaneously employed, consists of 144 hours; and although the labour of each of the dozen men may deviate more or less from average social labour, each of them requiring a different time for the same operation, yet since the working-day of each is one-twelfth of the collective working-day of 144 hours, it possesses the qualities of an average social working-day. From the point of view, however, of the capitalist who employs these 12 men, the working-day is that of the whole dozen. Each individual man's day is an aliquot part of the collective working-day, no matter whether the 12 men assist one another in their work, or whether the connection between their operations consists merely in the fact, that the men are all working for the same capitalist. But if the 12 men are employed in six pairs, by as many different small masters, it will be quite a matter of chance, whether each of these masters produces the same value, and consequently whether he realises the general rate of surplus-value. Deviations would occur in individual cases. If one workman required considerably more time for the production of a commodity than is socially necessary, the duration of the necessary labour-time would, in his case, sensibly deviate from the labour-time socially necessary on an average; and consequently his labour would not count as average labour, nor his labour power as average labour power. It would either be not saleable at all, or only at something below the average value of labour power. A fixed minimum of efficiency in all labour is therefore assumed, and we shall see, later on, that capitalist production provides the means of fixing this minimum. Nevertheless, this minimum deviates from the average, although on the other hand the capitalist has to pay the average value of labour power. Of the six small masters, one would therefore squeeze out more than the average rate of surplus-value, another less. The inequalities would be compensated for the society at large, but not for the individual masters. Thus the laws of the production of value are only fully realised for the individual producer, when he produces as a capitalist, and employs a number of workmen together, whose labour, by its collective nature, is at once stamped as average social labour.[2]

Even without an alteration in the system of working, the simultaneous employment of a large number of labourers effects a revolution in the material conditions of the labour-process. The buildings in which they work, the store-houses for the raw material, the implements and utensils used simultaneously or in turns by the workmen; in short, a portion of the means of production, are now consumed in common. On the one hand, the exchange value of these means of production is not increased; for the exchange value of a commodity is not raised by its use-value being consumed more thoroughly and to greater advantage. On the other hand, they are used in common, and therefore on a larger scale than before. A room where twenty weavers work at twenty looms must be larger than the room of a single weaver with two assistants. But it costs less labour to build one workshop for twenty persons than to build ten to accommodate two weavers each; thus the value of the means of production that are concentrated for use in common on a large scale does not increase in direct proportion to the expansion and to the increased useful effect of those means. When consumed in common, they give up a smaller part of their value to each single product; partly because the total value they part with is spread over a greater quantity of products, and partly because their value, though absolutely greater, is, having regard to their sphere of action in the process, relatively less than the value of isolated means of production. Owing to this, the value of a part of the constant capital falls, and in proportion to the magnitude of the fall, the total value of the commodity also falls. The effect is the same as if the means of production had cost less. The economy in their application is entirely owing to their being consumed in common by a large number of workmen. Moreover, this character of being necessary conditions of social labour, a character that distinguishes them from the dispersed and relatively more costly means of production of isolated, independent labourers, or small masters, is acquired even when the numerous workmen assembled together do not assist one another, but merely work side by side. A portion of the instruments of labour acquires this social character before the labour-process itself does so.

Economy in the use of the means of production has to be considered under two aspects. First, as cheapening commodities, and thereby bringing about a fall in the value of labour power. Secondly, as altering the ratio of the surplus-value to the total capital advanced, i.e., to the sum of the values of the constant and variable capital. The latter aspect will not be considered until we come to the third book, to which, with the object of treating them in their proper connection, we also relegate many other points that relate to the present question. The march of our analysis compels this splitting up of the subject-matter, a splitting up that is quite in keeping with the spirit of capitalist production. For since, in this mode of production, the workman finds the instruments of labour existing independently of him as another man's property, economy in their use appears, with regard to him, to be a distinct operation, one that does not concern him, and which, therefore, has no connection with the methods by which his own personal productiveness is increased.

When numerous labourers work together side by side, whether in one and the same process, or in different but connected processes, they are said to co-operate, or to work in co-operation.[3]

Just as the offensive power of a squadron of cavalry, or the defensive power of a regiment of infantry is essentially different from the sum of the offensive or defensive powers of the individual cavalry or infantry soldiers taken separately, so the sum total of the mechanical forces exerted by isolated workmen differs from the social force that is developed, when many hands take part simultaneously in one and the same undivided operation, such as raising a heavy weight, turning a winch, or removing an obstacle.[4] In such cases the effect of the combined labour could either not be produced at all by isolated individual labour, or it could only be produced by a great expenditure of time, or on a very dwarfed scale. Not only have we here an increase in the productive power of the individual, by means of co-operation, but the creation of a new power, namely, the collective power of masses.[5]

Apart from the new power that arises from the fusion of many forces into one single force, mere social contact begets in most industries an emulation and a stimulation of the animal spirits that heighten the efficiency of each individual workman. Hence it is that a dozen persons working together will, in their collective working-day of 144 hours, produce far more than twelve isolated men each working 12 hours, or than one man who works twelve days in succession.[6] The reason of this is that man is, if not as Aristotle contends, a political,[7] at all events a social animal.

Although a number of men may be occupied together at the same time on the same, or the same kind of work, yet the labour of each, as a part of the collective labour, may correspond to a distinct phase of the labour-process, through all whose phases, in consequence of co-operation, the subject of their labour passes with greater speed. For instance, if a dozen masons place themselves in a row, so as to pass stones from the foot of a ladder to its summit, each of them does the same thing; nevertheless, their separate acts form connected parts of one total operation; they are particular phases, which must be gone through by each stone; and the stones are thus carried up quicker by the 24 hands of the row of men than they could be if each man went separately up and down the ladder with his burden.[8] The object is carried over the same distance in a shorter time. Again, a combination of labour occurs whenever a building, for instance, is taken in hand on different sides simultaneously; although here also the co-operating masons are doing the same, or the same kind of work. The 12 masons, in their collective working-day of 144 hours, make much more progress with the building than one mason could make working for 12 days, or 144 hours. The reason is, that a body of men working in concert has hands and eyes both before and behind, and is, to a certain degree, omnipresent. The various parts of the work progress simultaneously.

In the above instances we have laid stress upon the point that the men do the same, or the same kind of work, because this, the most simple form of labour in common, plays a great part in co-operation, even in its most fully developed stage. If the work be complicated, then the mere number of the men who co-operate allows of the various operations being apportioned to different hands, and, con-sequently, of being carried on simultaneously. The time necessary for the completion of the whole work is thereby shortened.[9]

In many industries, there are critical periods, determined by the nature of the process, during which certain definite results must be obtained. For instance, if a flock of sheep has to be shorn, or a field of wheat to be cut and harvested, the quantity and quality of the product depends on the work being begun and ended within a certain time. In these cases, the time that ought to be taken by the process is pre-scribed, just as it is in herring fishing. A single person cannot carve a working-day of more than, say 12 hours, out of the natural day, but 100 men co-operating extend the working-day to 1,200 hours. The shortness of the time allowed for the work is compensated for by the large mass of labour thrown upon the field of production at the decisive moment. The completion of the task within the proper time depends on the simultaneous application of numerous combined working-days; the amount of useful effect depends on the number of labourers; this number, however, is always smaller than the number of isolated labourers required to do the same amount of work in the same period.[10] It is owing to the absence of this kind of co-operation that, in the western part of the United States, quantities of corn, and in those parts of East India where English rule has destroyed the old communities, quantities of cotton, are yearly wasted.[11]

On the one hand, co-operation allows of the work being carried on over an extended space; it is consequently imperatively called for in certain undertakings, such as draining, constructing dykes, irrig-ation works, and the making of canals, roads and railways. On the other hand, while extending the scale of production, it renders possible a relative contraction of the arena. This contraction of arena simultaneous with, and arising from, extension of scale, whereby a number of useless expenses are cut down, is owing to the conglomeration of labourers, to the aggregation of various processes, and to the concentration of the means of production.[12]

The combined working-day produces, relatively to an equal sum of isolated working-days, a greater quantity of use-values, and, consequently, diminishes the labour-time necessary for the production of a given useful effect. Whether the combined working-day, in a given case, acquires this increased productive power, because it heightens the mechanical force of labour, or extends its sphere of action over a greater space, or contracts the field of production relatively to the scale of production, or at the critical moment sets large masses of labour to work, or excites emulation between individuals and raises their animal spirits, or impresses on the similar operations carried on by a number of men the stamp of continuity and many-sidedness, or performs simultaneously different operations, or economises the means of production by use in common, or lends to individual labour the character of average social labour – whichever of these be the cause of the increase, the special productive power of the combined working-day is, under all circumstances, the social productive power of labour, or the productive power of social labour. This power is due to co-operation itself. When the labourer co-operates systematically with others, he strips off the fetters of his individuality, and develops the capabilities of his species.[13]

As a general rule, labourers cannot co-operate without being brought together: their assemblage in one place is a necessary condition of their co-operation. Hence wage-labourers cannot co-operate, unless they are employed simultaneously by the same capital, the same capitalist, and unless therefore their labour powers are bought simultaneously by him. The total value of these labour powers, or the amount of the wages of these labourers for a day, or a week, as the case may be, must be ready in the pocket of the capitalist, before the workmen are assembled for the process of production. The payment of 300 workmen at once, though only for one day, requires a greater outlay of capital, than does the payment of a smaller number of men, week by week, during a whole year. Hence the number of the labourers that co-operate, or the scale of co-operation, depends, in the first instance, on the amount of capital that the individual capitalist can spare for the purchase of labour power; in other words, on the extent to which a single capitalist has command over the means of subsistence of a number of labourers.

And as with the variable, so it is with the constant capital. For example, the outlay on raw material is 30 times as great, for the capitalist who employs 300 men, as it is for each of the 30 capitalists who employ 10 men. The value and quantity of the instruments of labour used in common do not, it is true, increase at the same rate as the number of workmen, but they do increase very considerably. Hence, concentration of large masses of the means of production in the hands of individual capitalists, is a material condition for the co-operation of wage-labourers, and the extent of the co-operation or the scale of production, depends on the extent of this concentration.

We saw in a former chapter, that a certain minimum amount of capital was necessary, in order that the number of labourers simultaneously employed, and, consequently, the amount of surplus-value produced, might suffice to liberate the employer himself from manual labour, to convert him from a small master into a capitalist, and thus formally to establish capitalist production. We now see that a certain minimum amount is a necessary condition for the conversion of numerous isolated and independent processes into one combined social process.

We also saw that at first, the subjection of labour to capital was only a formal result of the fact, that the labourer, instead of working for himself, works for and consequently under the capitalist. By the co-operation of numerous wage-labourers, the sway of capital develops into a requisite for carrying on the labour-process itself, into a real requisite of production. That a capitalist should command on the field of production, is now as indispensable as that a general should command on the field of battle.

All combined labour on a large scale requires, more or less, a directing authority, in order to secure the harmonious working of the individual activities, and to perform the general functions that have their origin in the action of the combined organism, as distinguished from the action of its separate organs. A single violin player is his own conductor; an orchestra requires a separate one. The work of directing, superintending, and adjusting, becomes one of the functions of capital, from the moment that the labour under the control of capital, becomes co-operative. Once a function of capital, it acquires special characteristics.

The directing motive, the end and aim of capitalist production, is to extract the greatest possible amount of surplus-value,[14] and consequently to exploit labour power to the greatest possible extent. As the number of the co-operating labourers increases, so too does their resistance to the domination of capital, and with it, the necessity for capital to overcome this resistance by counterpressure. The control exercised by the capitalist is not only a special function, due to the nature of the social labour-process, and peculiar to that process, but it is, at the same time, a function of the exploitation of a social labour-process, and is consequently rooted in the unavoidable antagonism between the exploiter and the living and labouring raw material he exploits.

Again, in proportion to the increasing mass of the means of production, now no longer the property of the labourer, but of the capitalist, the necessity increases for some effective control over the proper application of those means.[15] Moreover, the co-operation of wage-labourers is entirely brought about by the capital that employs them. Their union into one single productive body and the establishment of a connection between their individual functions, are matters foreign and external to them, are not their own act, but the act of the capital that brings and keeps them together. Hence the connection existing between their various labours appears to them, ideally, in the shape of a preconceived plan of the capitalist, and practically in the shape of the authority of the same capitalist, in the shape of the powerful will of another, who subjects their activity to his aims. If, then, the control of the capitalist is in substance two-fold by reason of the two-fold nature of the process of production itself – which, on the one hand, is a social process for producing use-values, on the other, a process for creating surplus-value – in form that control is despotic. As co-operation extends its scale, this despotism takes forms peculiar to itself. Just as at first the capitalist is relieved from actual labour so soon as his capital has reached that minimum amount with which capitalist production, as such, begins, so now, he hands over the work of direct and constant supervision of the individual workmen, and groups of workmen, to a special kind of wage-labourer. An industrial army of workmen, under the command of a capitalist, requires, like a real army, officers (managers), and sergeants (foremen, overlookers), who, while the work is being done, command in the name of the capitalist. The work of supervision becomes their established and exclusive function. When comparing the mode of production of isolated peasants and artisans with production by slave-labour, the political economist counts this labour of superintendence among the *faux frais* of production.[16] But, when considering the capitalist mode of production, he, on the contrary, treats the work of control made necessary by the co-operative character of the labour-process as identical with the different work of control, necessitated by the capitalist character of that process and the antagonism of interests between capitalist and labourer.[17] It is not because he is a leader of industry that a man is a capitalist; on the contrary, he is a leader of industry because he is a capitalist. The leadership of industry is an attribute of capital, just as in feudal times the functions of general and judge, were attributes of landed property.[18]

The labourer is the owner of his labour power until he has done bargaining for its sale with the capitalist; and he can sell no more than what he has i.e., his individual, isolated labour power. This state of things is in no way altered by the fact that the capitalist, instead of buying the labour power of one man, buys that of 100, and enters into separate contracts with 100 unconnected men instead of with one. He is at liberty to set the 100 men to work, without letting them co-operate. He pays them the value of 100 independent labour powers, but he does not pay for the combined labour power of the hundred. Being independent of each other, the labourers are isolated persons, who enter into relations with the capitalist, but not with one another. This co-operation begins only with the labour-process, but they have then ceased to belong to themselves. On entering that process, they become incorporated with capital. As co-operators, as members of a working organism, they are but special modes of existence of capital. Hence, the productive power developed by the labourer when working in co-operation, is the productive power of capital. This power is developed gratuitously, whenever the workmen are placed under given conditions, and it is capital that places them under such conditions. Because this power costs capital nothing, and because, on the other hand, the labourer himself does not develop it before his labour belongs to capital, it appears as a power with which capital is endowed by Nature – a productive power that is immanent in capital.

The colossal effects of simple co-operation are to be seen in the gigantic structures of the ancient Asiatics, Egyptians, Etruscans, &c. 'It has happened in times past that these Oriental States, after supplying the expenses of their civil and military establishments, have found themselves in possession of a surplus which they could apply to works of magnificence or utility, and in the construction of these their command over the hands and arms of almost the entire non-agricultural population has produced stupendous monuments which still indicate their power. The teeming valley of the Nile . . . produced food for a swarming non-agricultural population, and this food, belonging to the monarch and the priesthood, afforded the means of erecting the mighty monuments which filled the land . . . In moving the colossal statues and vast masses of which the transport creates wonder, human labour almost alone, was prodigally used . . . The number of the labourers and the concentration of their efforts sufficed. We see mighty coral reefs rising from the depths of the ocean into islands and firm land, yet each individual depositor is puny, weak, and contemptible. The non-agricultural labourers of an

Asiatic monarchy have little but their individual bodily exertions to bring to the task, but their number is their strength, and the power of directing these masses gave rise to the palaces and temples, the pyramids, and the armies of gigantic statues of which the remains astonish and perplex us. It is that confinement of the revenues which feed them, to one or a few hands, which makes such undertakings possible.'[19] This power of Asiatic and Egyptian kings, Etruscan theocrats, &c., has in modern society been transferred to the capitalist, whether he be an isolated, or as in joint-stock companies, a collective capitalist.

Co-operation, such as we find it at the dawn of human development, among races who live by the chase,[20] or, say, in the agriculture of Indian communities, is based, on the one hand, on ownership in common of the means of production, and on the other hand, on the fact, that in those cases, each individual has no more torn himself off from the navel-string of his tribe or community, than each bee has freed itself from connection with the hive. Such co-operation is distinguished from capitalistic co-operation by both of the above characteristics. The sporadic application of co-operation on a large scale in ancient times, in the middle ages, and in modern colonies, reposes on relations of dominion and servitude, principally on slavery. The capitalistic form, on the contrary, presupposes from first to last, the free wage-labourer, who sells his labour power to capital. Historically, however, this form is developed in opposition to peasant agriculture and to the carrying on of independent handicrafts whether in guilds or not.[21] From the standpoint of these, capitalistic co-operation does not manifest itself as a particular historical form of co-operation, but co-operation itself appears to be a historical form peculiar to, and specifically distinguishing, the capitalist process of production.

Just as the social productive power of labour that is developed by co-operation, appears to be the productive power of capital, so co-operation itself, contrasted with the process of production carried on by isolated independent labourers, or even by small employers, appears to be a specific form of the capitalist process of production. It is the first change experienced by the actual labour-process, when subjected to capital. This change takes place spontaneously. The simultaneous employment of a large number of wage-labourers, in one and the same process, which is a necessary condition of this change, also forms the starting-point of capitalist production. This point coincides with the birth of capital itself. If then, on the one hand, the capitalist mode of production presents itself to us historically, as a necessary condition to the transformation of the labour-process into a social process, so, on the other hand, this social form of the labour-process presents itself, as a method employed by capital for the more profitable exploitation of labour, by increasing that labour's productiveness.

In the elementary form, under which we have hitherto viewed it, co-operation is a necessary concomitant of all production on a large scale, but it does not, in itself, represent a fixed form characteristic of a particular epoch in the development of the capitalist mode of production. At the most it appears to do so, and that only approximately, in the handicraft-like beginnings of manufacture,[22] and in that kind of agriculture on a large scale, which corresponds to the epoch of manufacture, and is distinguished from peasant agriculture, mainly by the number of the labourers simultaneously employed, and by the mass of the means of production concentrated for their use. Simple co-operation is always the prevailing form, in those branches of production in which capital operates on a large scale, and division of labour and machinery play but a subordinate part.

Co-operation ever constitutes the fundamental form of the capitalist mode of production, nevertheless the elementary form of co-operation continues to subsist as a particular form of capitalist production side by side with the more developed forms of that mode of production.

Chapter 14
Division of Labour and Manufacture

Section 1. Two-Fold Origin of Manufacture.

That co-operation which is based on division of labour, assumes its typical form in manufacture, and is the prevalent characteristic form of the capitalist process of production throughout the manufacturing period properly so called. That period, roughly speaking, extends from the middle of the 16th to the last third of the 18th century.

Manufacture takes its rise in two ways:

(1.) By the assemblage, in one workshop under the control of a single capitalist, of labourers belonging to various independent handicrafts, but through whose hands a given article must pass on its way to completion. A carriage, for example, was formerly the product of the labour of a great number of independent artificers, such as wheelwrights, harness-makers, tailors, locksmiths, upholsterers, turners, fringe-makers, glaziers, painters, polishers, gilders, &c. In the manufacture of carriages, however, all these different artificers are assembled in one building where they work into one another's hands. It is true that a carriage cannot be gilt before it has been made. But if a number of carriages are being made simultaneously, some may be in the hands of the gilders while others are going through an earlier process. So far, we are still in the domain of simple co-operation, which finds its materials ready to hand in the shape of men and things. But very soon an important change takes place. The tailor, the locksmith, and the other artificers, being now exclusively occupied in carriage-making, each gradually loses, through want of practice, the ability to carry on, to its full extent, his old handicraft. But, on the other hand, his activity now confined in one groove, assumes the form best adapted to the narrowed sphere of action. At first, carriage manufacture is a combination of various independent handicrafts. By degrees, it becomes the splitting up of carriage-making into its various detail processes, each of which crystallises into the exclusive function of a particular workman, the manufacture, as a whole, being carried on by the men in conjunction. In the same way, cloth manufacture, as also a whole series of other manufactures, arose by combining different handicrafts together under the control of a single capitalist.[1]

(2.) Manufacture also arises in a way exactly the reverse of this — namely, by one capitalist employing simultaneously in one workshop a number of artificers, who all do the same, or the same kind of work, such as making paper, type, or needles. This is co-operation in its most elementary form. Each of these artificers (with the help, perhaps, of one or two apprentices), makes the entire commodity, and he consequently performs in succession all the operations necessary for its production. He still works in his old handicraft-like way. But very soon external circumstances cause a different use to be made of the concentration of the workmen on one spot, and of the simultaneousness of their work. An increased quantity of the article has perhaps to be delivered within a given time. The work is therefore redistributed. Instead of each man being allowed to perform all the various operations in succession, these operations are changed into disconnected, isolated ones, carried on side by side; each is assigned to a different artificer, and the whole of them together are performed simultaneously by the co-operating workmen. This accidental repartition gets repeated, develops advantages of its own, and gradually ossifies into a systematic division of labour. The commodity, from being the individual product of an independent artificer, becomes the social product of a union of artificers, each of whom performs one, and only one, of the constituent partial operations. The same operations which, in the case of a papermaker belonging to a German Guild, merged one into the other as the successive acts of one artificer, became in the Dutch paper manufacture so many partial operations carried on side by side by numerous co-operating labourers. The needlemaker of the Nuremberg Guild was the cornerstone on which the English needle manufacture was raised. But while in Nuremberg that single artificer performed a series of perhaps 20 operations one after another, in England it was not long before there were 20 needlemakers side by side, each performing one alone of those 20 operations, and in consequence of further experience, each of those 20 operations was again split up, isolated, and made the exclusive function of a separate workman.

The mode in which manufacture arises, its growth out of handicrafts, is therefore two-fold. On the one hand, it arises from the union of various independent handicrafts, which become stripped of their independence and specialised to such an extent as to be reduced to mere supplementary partial processes in the production of one particular commodity. On the other hand, it arises from the co-operation of artificers of one handicraft; it splits up that particular handicraft into its various detail operations, isolating, and making these operations independent of one another up to the point where each becomes the exclusive function of a particular labourer. On the one hand, therefore, manufacture either introduces diversion of labour into a process of production, or further develops that division; on the other hand, it unites together handicrafts that were formerly separate. But whatever may have been its particular starting-point, its final form is invariably the same – a productive mechanism whose parts are human beings.

For a proper understanding of the division of labour in manufacture, it is essential that the following points be firmly grasped. First, the decomposition of a process of production into its various successive steps coincides, here, strictly with the resolution of a handicraft into its successive manual operations. Whether complex or simple, each operation has to be done by hand, retains the character of a handicraft, and is therefore dependent on the strength, skill, quickness, and sureness, of the individual workman in handling his tools. The handicraft continues to be the basis. This narrow technical basis excludes a really scientific analysis of any definite process of industrial production, since it is still a condition that each detail process gone through by the product must be capable of being done by hand and of forming, in its way, a separate handicraft. It is just because handicraft skill continues, in this way, to be the foundation of the process of production, that each workman becomes exclusively assigned to a partial function, and that for the rest of his life, his labour power is turned into the organ of this detail function.

Secondly, this division of labour is a particular sort of co-operation, and many of its disadvantages spring from the general character of co-operation, and not from this particular form of it.

Section 2. The Detail Labourer and his Implements.

If we now go more into detail, it is, in the first place, clear that a labourer who all his life performs one and the same simple operation, converts his whole body into the automatic, specialised implement of that operation. Consequently, he takes less time in doing it, than the artificer who performs a whole series of operations in succession. But the collective labourer, who constitutes the living mechanism of manufacture, is made up solely of such specialised detail labourers. Hence, in comparison with the independent handicraft, more is produced in a given time, or the productive power of labour is increased.[2] Moreover, when once this fractional work is established as the exclusive function of one person, the methods it employs become perfected. The workman's continued repetition of the same simple act, and the concentration of his attention on it, teach him by experience how to attain the desired effect with the minimum of exertion. But since there are always several generations of labourers living at one time, and working together at the manufacture of a given article, the technical skill, the tricks of the trade thus acquired, become established, and are accumulated and handed down.[3]

Manufacture, in fact, produces the skill of the detail labourer, by reproducing, and systematically driving to an extreme within the workshop, the naturally developed differentiation of trades which it found ready to hand in society at large. On the other hand, the conversion of fractional work into the life-calling of one man, corresponds to the tendency shown by earlier societies, to make trades hereditary; either to petrify them into castes, or whenever definite historical conditions beget in the individual a tendency to vary in a manner incompatible with the nature of castes, to ossify them into guilds. Castes and guilds arise from the action of the same natural law, that regulates the differentiation of plants and animals into species and varieties, except that, when a certain degree of development has been reached, the heredity of castes and the exclusiveness of guilds are ordained as a law of society.[4]

'The muslins of Dakka in fineness, the calicoes and other piece goods of Coromandel in brilliant and durable colours, have never been surpassed. Yet they are produced without capital, machinery, division of labour, or any of those means which give such facilities to the manufacturing interest of Europe. The weaver is merely a detached individual, working a web when ordered of a customer, and with a loom of the rudest construction, consisting sometimes of a few branches or bars of wood, put roughly together. There is even no expedient for rolling up the warp; the loom must therefore be kept stretched to its full length, and becomes so inconveniently large, that it cannot be contained within the hut of the manufacturer, who is therefore compelled to ply his trade in the open air, where it is interrupted by every vicissitude of the weather.'⁵ It is only the special skill accumulated from generation to generation, and transmitted from father to son, that gives to the Hindu, as it does to the spider, this proficiency. And yet the work of such a Hindu weaver is very complicated, compared with that of a manufacturing labourer.

An artificer, who performs one after another the various fractional operations in the production of a finished article, must at one time change his place, at another his tools. The transition from one operation to another interrupts the flow of his labour, and creates, so to say, gaps in his working-day. These gaps close up so soon as he is tied to one and the same operation all day long; they vanish in proportion as the changes in his work diminish. The resulting increased productive power is owing either to an increased expenditure of labour power in a given time – i.e., to increased intensity of labour – or to a decrease in the amount of labour power unproductively consumed. The extra expenditure of power, demanded by every transition from rest to motion, is made up for by prolonging the duration of the normal velocity when once acquired. On the other hand, constant labour of one uniform kind disturbs the intensity and flow of a man's animal spirits, which find recreation and delight in mere change of activity.

The productiveness of labour depends not only on the proficiency of the workman, but on the perfection of his tools. Tools of the same kind, such as knives, drills, gimlets. hammers, &c., may be employed in different processes; and the same tool may serve various purposes in a single process. But so soon as the different operations of a labour-process are disconnected the one from the other, and each fractional operation acquires in the hands of the detail labourer a suitable and peculiar form, alterations become necessary in the implements that previously served more than one purpose. The direction taken by this change is determined by the difficulties experienced in consequence of the unchanged form of the implement. Manufacture is characterised by the differentiation of the instruments of labour – a differentiation whereby implements of a given sort acquire fixed shapes, adapted to each particular application, and by the specialisation of those instruments, giving to each special implement its full play only in the hands of a specific detail labourer. In Birmingham alone 500 varieties of hammers are produced, and not only is each adapted to one particular process, but several varieties often serve exclusively for the different operations in one and the same process. The manufacturing period simplifies, improves, and multiplies the implements of labour, by adapting them to the exclusively special functions of each detail labourer.[6] It thus creates at the same time one of the material conditions for the existence of machinery, which consists of a combination of simple instruments.

The detail labourer and his implements are the simplest elements of manufacture. Let us now turn to its aspect as a whole.

Section 3. The Two Fundamental Forms of Manufacture: Heterogeneous Manufacture, Serial Manufacture.

The organisation of manufacture has two fundamental forms which, in spite of occasional blending, are essentially different in kind, and, moreover, play very distinct parts in the subsequent transformation of manufacture into modern industry carried on by machinery. This double character arises from the nature of the article produced. This article either results from the mere mechanical fitting together of partial products made independently, or owes its completed shape to a series of connected processes and manipulations.

A locomotive, for instance, consists of more than 5,000 independent parts. It cannot, however, serve as an example of the first kind of genuine manufacture, for it is a structure produced by modern mechanical industry. But a watch can; and William Petty used it to illustrate the division of labour in manufacture. Formerly the individual work of a Nuremberg artificer, the watch has been transformed into the social product of an immense number of detail labourers, such as mainspring makers, dial makers, spiral spring makers, jewelled hole makers, ruby lever makers, hand makers, case makers, screw makers, gilders, with numerous subdivisions, such as wheel makers (brass and steel separate), pin makers, movement makers, *acheveur de pignon* (fixes the wheels on the axles, polishes the facets, &c.), pivot makers, *planteur de finissage* (puts the wheels and springs in the works), *finisseur de barillet* (cuts teeth in the wheels, makes the holes of the right size, &c.), escapement makers, cylinder makers for cylinder escapements, escapement wheel makers, balance wheel makers, *raquette* makers (apparatus for regulating the watch), the *planteur d'échappement* (escapement maker proper); then the *repasseur de barillet* (finishes the box for the spring, &c.), steel polishers, wheel polishers, screw polishers, figure painters, dial enamellers (melt the enamel on the copper), *fabricant de pendants* (makes the ring by which the case is hung), *finisseur de charnière* (puts the brass hinge in the cover, &c.), *faiseur de secret* (puts in the springs that open the case), *graveur, ciseleur, polisseur de boîte*, &c., &c., and last of all the *repasseur*, who fits together the whole watch and hands it over in a going state. Only a few parts of the watch pass through several hands; and all these *membra disjecta* come together for the first time in the hand that binds them into one mechanical whole. This external relation between the finished product and its various and diverse elements makes it, as well in this case as in the case of all similar finished articles, a matter of chance whether the detail labourers are brought together in one workshop or not. The detail operations may further be carried on like so many independent handicrafts, as they are in the Cantons of Vaud and Neufchâtel; while in Geneva there exist large watch manufactories where the detail labourers directly co-operate under the control of a single capitalist. And even in the latter case the dial, the springs, and the case, are seldom made in the factory itself. To carry on the trade as a manufacture, with concentration of workmen, is, in the watch trade, profitable only under exceptional conditions, because competition is greater between the labourers who desire to work at home, and because the splitting up of the work into a number of heterogeneous processes, permits but little use of the instruments of labour in common, and the capitalist, by scattering the work, saves the outlay on workshops, &c.[7] Nevertheless the position of this detail labourer who, though he works at home, does so for a capitalist (manufacturer, *établisseur*), is very different from that of the independent artificer, who works for his own customers.[8]

The second kind of manufacture, its perfected form, produces articles that go through connected phases of development, through a series of processes step by step, like the wire in the manufacture of needles, which passes through the hands of 72 and sometimes even 92 different detail workmen.

In so far as such a manufacture, when first started, combines scattered handicrafts, it lessens the space by which the various phases of production are separated from each other. The time taken in passing from one stage to another is shortened, so is the labour that effectuates this passage.[9] In comparison with a handicraft, productive power is gained, and this gain is owing to the general co-operative character of manufacture. On the other hand, division of labour, which is the distinguishing principle of manufacture, requires the isolation of the various stages of production and their independence of each other. The establishment and maintenance of a connection between the isolated functions necessitates the incessant transport of the article from one hand to another, and from one process to another. From the standpoint of modern mechanical industry, this necessity stands forth as a characteristic and costly disadvantage, and one that is immanent in the principle of manufacture.[10]

If we confine our attention to some particular lot of raw materials, of rags, for instance, in paper manufacture, or of wire in needle manufacture, we perceive that it passes in succession through a series of stages in the hands of the various detail workmen until completion. On the other hand, if we look at the workshop as a whole, we see the raw material in all the stages of its production at the same time. The collective labourer, with one set of his many hands armed with one kind of tools, draws the wire, with another set, armed with different tools, he at the same time straightens it, with another he cuts it, with another points it, and so on. The different detail processes, which were successive in time, have become simultaneous, go on side by side in space. Hence, production of a greater quantum of finished commodities in a given time.[11] This simultaneity, it is true, is due to the general co-operative form of the process as a whole; but Manufacture not only finds the conditions for co-operation ready to hand, it also, to some extent, creates them by the sub-division of handicraft labour. On the other hand, it accomplishes this social organisation of the labour-process only by riveting each labourer to a single fractional detail.

Since the fractional product of each detail labourer is, at the same time, only a particular stage in the development of one and the same finished article, each labourer, or each group of labourers, prepares the raw material for another labourer or group. The result of the labour of the one is the starting-point for the labour of the other. The one workman therefore gives occupation directly to the other. The labour-time necessary in each partial process, for attaining the desired effect, is learnt by experience; and the mechanism of Manufacture, as a whole, is based on the assumption that a given result will be obtained in a given time. It is only on this assumption that the various supplementary labour-processes can proceed uninterruptedly, simultaneously, and side by side. It is clear that this direct dependence of the operations, and therefore of the labourers, on each other, compels each one of them to spend on his work no more than the necessary time, and thus a continuity, uniformity, regularity, order,[12] and even intensity of labour, of quite a different kind, is begotten than is to be found in an independent handicraft or even in simple co-operation. The rule, that the labour-time expended on a commodity should not exceed that which is socially necessary for its production, appears, in the production of commodities generally, to be established by the mere effect of competition; since, to express ourselves superficially, each single producer is obliged to sell his commodity at its market-price. In Manufacture, on the contrary, the turning out of a given quantum of product in a given time is a technical law of the process of production itself.[13]

Different operations take, however, unequal periods, and yield therefore, in equal times unequal quantities of fractional products. If, therefore, the same labourer has, day after day, to perform the same operation, there must be a different number of labourers for each operation; for instance, in type manufacture, there are four founders and two breakers to one rubber: the founder casts 2,000 type an hour, the breaker breaks up 4,000, and the rubber polishes 8,000. Here we have again the principle of co-operation in its simplest form, the simultaneous employment of many doing the same thing; only now, this principle is the expression of an organic relation. The division of labour, as carried out in Manufacture, not only simplifies and multiplies the qualitatively different parts of the social collective labourer, but also creates a fixed mathematical relation or ratio which regulates the quantitative extent of those parts – i.e., the relative number of labourers, or the relative size of the group of labourers, for each detail operation. It develops, along with the qualitative sub-division of the social labour-process, a quantitative rule and proportionality for that process.

When once the most fitting proportion has been experimentally established for the numbers of the detail labourers in the various groups when producing on a given scale, that scale can be extended only by employing a multiple of each particular group.[14] There is this to boot, that the same individual can do certain kinds of work just as well on a large as on a small scale; for instance, the labour of superintendence, the carriage of the fractional product from one stage to the next, &c. The isolation of such functions, their allotment to a particular labourer, does not become advantageous till after an increase in the number of labourers employed; but this increase must affect every group proportionally.

The isolated group of labourers to whom any particular detail function is assigned, is made up of homogeneous elements, and is one of the constituent parts of the total mechanism. In many manufactures, however, the group itself is an organised body of labour, the total mechanism being a repetition or multiplication of these elementary organisms. Take, for instance, the manufacture of glass bottles. It may be resolved into three essentially different stages. First, the preliminary stage, consisting of the preparation of the components of the glass, mixing the sand and lime, &c., and melting them into a fluid mass of glass.[15] Various detail labourers are employed in this first stage, as also in the final one of removing the bottles from the drying furnace, sorting and packing them, &c. In the middle, between these two stages, comes the glass melting proper, the manipulation of the fluid mass. At each mouth of the furnace, there works a group, called 'the hole', consisting of one bottlemaker or finisher, one blower, one gatherer, one putter-up or whetter-off, and one taker-in. These five detail workers are so many special organs of a single working organism that acts only as a whole, and therefore can operate only by the direct co-operation of the whole five. The whole body is paralysed if but one of its members be wanting. But a glass furnace has several openings (in England from 4 to 6), each of which contains an earthenware melting-pot full of molten glass, and employs a similar five-membered group of workers. The organisation of each group is based on division of labour, but the bond between the different groups is simple co-operation, which, by using in common one of the means of production, the furnace, causes it to be more economically consumed. Such a furnace, with its 4–6 groups, constitutes a glass house; and a glass manufactory comprises a number of such glass houses, together with the apparatus and workmen requisite for the preparatory and final stages.

Finally, just as Manufacture arises in part from the combination of various handicrafts, so, too, it develops into a combination of various manufactures. The larger English glass manufacturers, for instance, make their own earthenware melting-pots, because on the quality of these depends, to a great extent, the success or failure of the process. The manufacture of one of the means of production is here united with that of the product. On the other hand, the manufacture of the product may be united with other manufactures, of which that product is the raw material, or with the products of which it is itself subsequently mixed. Thus, we find the manufacture of flint glass combined with that of glass cutting and brass founding; the latter for the metal settings of various articles of glass. The various manufactures so combined form more or less separate departments of a larger manufacture, but are at the same time independent processes, each with its own division of labour. In spite of the many advantages offered by this combination of manufactures, it never grows into a complete technical system on its own foundation. That happens only on its transformation into an industry carried on by machinery.

Early in the manufacturing period, the principle of lessening the necessary labour-time in the production of commodities,[16] was accepted and formulated: and the use of machines, especially for certain simple first processes that have to be conducted on a very large scale, and with the application of great force, sprang up here and there.

Thus, at an early period in paper manufacture, the tearing up of the rags was done by paper-mills; and in metal works, the pounding of the ores was effected by stamping mills.[17] The Roman Empire had handed down the elementary form of all machinery in the water-wheel.[18]

The handicraft period bequeathed to us the great inventions of the compass, of gunpowder, of type-printing, and of the automatic clock. But, on the whole, machinery played that subordinate part which Adam Smith assigns to it in comparison with division of labour.[19] The sporadic use of machinery in the 17th century was of the greatest importance, because it supplied the great mathematicians of that time with a practical basis and stimulant to the creation of the science of mechanics.

The collective labourer, formed by the combination of a number of detail labourers, is the machinery specially characteristic of the manufacturing period. The various operations that are performed in turns by the producer of a commodity, and coalesce one with another during the progress of production, lay claim to him in various ways. In one operation he must exert more strength, in another more skill, in another more attention; and the same individual does not possess all these qualities in an equal degree. After Manufacture has once separated, made independent, and isolated the various operations, the labourers are divided, classified, and grouped according to their predominating qualities. If their natural endowments are, on the one hand, the foundation on which the division of labour is built up, on the other hand, Manufacture, once introduced, develops in them new powers that are by nature fitted only for limited and special functions. The collective labourer now possesses, in an equal degree of excellence, all the qualities requisite for production, and expends them in the most economical manner, by exclusively employing all his organs, consisting of particular labourers, or groups of labourers, in performing their special functions.[20] The one-sidedness and the deficiencies of the detail labourer become perfections when he is a part of the collective labourer.[21] The habit of doing only one thing converts him into a never-failing instrument, while his connection with the whole mechanism compels him to work with the regularity of the parts of a machine.[22]

Since the collective labourer has functions, both simple and complex, both high and low, his members, the individual labour powers, require different degrees of training, and must therefore have different values. Manufacture, therefore, develops a hierarchy of labour powers, to which there corresponds a scale of wages. If, on the one hand, the individual labourers are appropriated and annexed for life by a limited function; on the other hand, the various operations of the hierarchy are parcelled out among the labourers according to both their natural and their acquired capabilities.[23] Every process of production, however, requires certain simple manipulations, which every man is capable of doing. They too are now severed from their connection with the more pregnant moments of activity, and ossified into exclusive functions of specially appointed labourers. Hence, Manufacture begets, in every handicraft that it seizes upon, a class of so-called unskilled labourers, a class which handicraft industry strictly excluded. If it develops a one-sided speciality into a perfection, at the expense of the whole of a man's working capacity, it also begins to make a speciality of the absence of all development. Alongside of the hierarchic gradation there steps the simple separation of the labourers into skilled and unskilled. For the latter, the cost of apprenticeship vanishes; for the former, it diminishes, compared with that of artificers, in consequence of the functions being simplified. In both cases the value of labour power falls.[24] An exception to this law holds good whenever the decomposition of the labour-process begets new and comprehensive functions, that either had no place at all, or only a very modest one, in handicrafts. The fall in the value of labour power, caused by the disappearance or diminution of the expenses of apprenticeship, implies a direct increase of surplus-value for the benefit of capital; for everything that shortens the necessary labour-time required for the reproduction of labour power, extends the domain of surplus-labour.

Section 4. Division of Labour in Manufacture, and Division of Labour in Society.

We first considered the origin of Manufacture, then its simple elements, then the detail labourer and his implements, and finally, the totality of the mechanism. We shall now lightly touch upon the relation between the division of labour in manufacture, and the social division of labour, which forms the foundation of all production of commodities.

If we keep labour alone in view, we may designate the separation of social production into its main divisions or genera – viz., agriculture, industries, &c., as division of labour in general, and the splitting up of these families into species and sub-species, as division of labour in particular, and the division of labour within the workshop as division of labour in singular or in detail.[25]

Division of labour in a society, and the corresponding tying down of individuals to a particular calling, develops itself, just as does the division of labour in manufacture, from opposite starting-points.

Within a family,[26] and after further development within a tribe, there springs up naturally a division of labour, caused by differences of sex and age, a division that is consequently based on a purely physiological foundation, which division enlarges its materials by the expansion of the community, by the increase of population, and more especially, by the conflicts between different tribes, and the subjugation of one tribe by another. On the other hand, as I have before remarked, the exchange of products springs up at the points where different families, tribes, communities, come in contact; for, in the beginning of civilisation, it is not private individuals but families, tribes, &c., that meet on an independent footing. Different communities find different means of production, and different means of subsistence in their natural environment. Hence, their modes of production, and of living, and their products are different. It is this spontaneously developed difference which, when different communities come in contact, calls forth the mutual exchange of products, and the consequent gradual conversion of those products into commodities. Exchange does not create the differences between the spheres of production, but brings what are already different into relation, and thus converts them into more or less inter-dependent branches of the collective production of an enlarged society. In the latter case, the social division of labour arises from the exchange between spheres of production, that are originally distinct and independent of one another. In the former, where the physiological division of labour is the starting-point, the particular organs of a compact whole grow loose, and break off, principally owing to the exchange of commodities with foreign communities, and then isolate themselves so far, that the sole bond, still connecting the various kinds of work, is the exchange of the products as commodities. In the one case, it is the making dependent what was before independent; in the other case, the making independent what was before dependent.

The foundation of every division of labour that is well developed, and brought about by the exchange of commodities, is the separation between town and country.[27] It may be said, that the whole economic history of society is summed up in the movement of this antithesis. We pass it over, however, for the present.

Just as a certain number of simultaneously employed labourers are the material pre-requisites for division of labour in manufacture, so are the number and density of the population, which here correspond to the agglomeration in one workshop, a necessary condition for the division of labour in society.[28] Nevertheless, this density is more or less relative. A relatively thinly populated country, with well-developed means of communication, has a denser population than a more numerously populated country, with badly-developed means of communication; and in this sense the Northern States of the American Union, for instance, are more thickly populated than India.[29]

Since the production and the circulation of commodities are the general pre-requisites of the capitalist mode of production, division of labour in manufacture demands, that division of labour in society at large should previously have attained a certain degree of development. Inversely, the former division reacts upon and develops and multiplies the latter. Simultaneously, with the differentiation of the instruments of labour, the industries that produce these instruments, become more and more differentiated.[30] If the manufacturing system seize upon an industry, which, previously, was carried on in connection with others, either as a chief or as a subordinate industry, and by one producer, these industries immediately separate their connection, and become independent. If it seize upon a particular stage in the production of a commodity, the other stages of its production become converted into so many independent industries. It has already been stated, that where the finished article consists merely of a number of parts fitted together, the detail operations may re-establish themselves as genuine and separate handicrafts. In order to carry out more perfectly the division of labour in manufacture, a single branch of production is, according to the varieties of its raw material, or the various forms that one and the same raw material may assume, split up into numerous, and to some extent, entirely new manufactures. Accordingly, in France alone, in the first half of the 18th century, over 100 different kinds of silk stuffs were woven, and, in Avignon, it was law, that 'every apprentice should devote himself to only one sort of fabrication, and should not learn the preparation of several kinds of stuff at once.' The territorial division of labour, which confines special branches of production to special districts of a country, acquires fresh stimulus from the manufacturing system, which exploits every special advantage.[31] The Colonial system and the opening out of the markets of the world, both of which are included in the general conditions of existence of the manufacturing period, furnish rich material for developing the division of labour in society. It is not the place, here, to go on to show how division of labour seizes upon, not only the economic, but every other sphere of society, and everywhere lays the foundation of that all-engrossing system of specialising and sorting men, that development in a man of one single faculty at the expense of all other faculties, which caused A. Ferguson, the master of Adam Smith, to exclaim: 'We make a nation of Helots, and have no free citizens.'[32]

But, in spite of the numerous analogies and links connecting them, division of labour in the interior of a society, and that in the interior of a workshop, differ not only in degree, but also in kind. The analogy appears most indisputable where there is an invisible bond uniting the various branches of trade. For instance the cattle-breeder produces hides, the tanner makes the hides into leather, and the shoemaker, the leather into boots. Here the thing produced by each of them is but a step towards the final form, which is the product of all their labours combined. There are, besides, all the various industries that supply the cattle-breeder, the tanner, and the shoemaker with the means of production. Now it is quite possible to imagine, with Adam Smith, that the difference between the above social division of labour, and the division in manufacture, is merely subjective, exists merely for the observer, who, in a manufacture, can see with one glance, all the numerous operations being performed on one spot, while in the instance given above, the spreading out of the work over great areas, and the great number of people employed in each branch of labour, obscure the connection.[33] But what is it that forms the bond between the independent labours of the cattle-breeder, the tanner, and the shoemaker? It is the fact that their respective products are commodities. What, on the other hand, characterises division of labour in manufactures? The fact that the detail labourer produces no commodities.[34] It is only the common product of all the detail labourers that becomes a commodity.[35] Division of labour in society is brought about by the purchase and sale of the products of different branches of industry, while the connection between the detail operations in a workshop, is due to the sale of the labour power of several workmen to one capitalist, who applies it as combined labour power. The division of labour in the workshop implies concentration of the means of production in the hands of one capitalist; the division of labour in society implies their dispersion among many independent producers of commodities. While within the workshop, the iron law of proportionality subjects definite numbers of workmen to definite functions, in the society outside the workshop, chance and caprice have full play in distributing the producers and their means of production among the various branches of industry. The different spheres of production, it is true, constantly tend to an equilibrium: for, on the one hand, while each producer of a commodity is bound to produce a use-value, to satisfy a particular social want, and while the extent of these wants differs quantitatively, still there exists an inner relation which settles their proportions into a regular system, and that system one of spontaneous growth; and, on the other hand, the law of the value of commodities ultimately determines how much of its disposable working-time society can expend on each particular class of commodities. But this constant tendency to equilibrium, of the various spheres of production, is exercised, only in the shape of a reaction against the constant upsetting of this equilibrium. The *a priori* system on which the division of labour, within the workshop, is regularly carried out, becomes in the division of labour within the society, an *a posteriori*, nature-imposed necessity, controlling the lawless caprice of the producers, and perceptible in the barometrical fluctuations of the market-prices. Division of labour within the workshop implies the undisputed authority of the capitalist over men, that are but parts of a mechanism that belongs to him. The division of labour within the society brings into contact independent commodity-producers, who acknowledge no other authority but that of competition, of the coercion exerted by the pressure of their mutual interests; just as in the animal kingdom, the *bellum omnium contra omnes* more or less preserves the conditions of existence of every species. The same bourgeois mind which praises division of labour in the workshop, life-long annexation of the labourer to a partial operation, and his complete subjection to capital, as being an organisation of labour that increases its productiveness – that same bourgeois mind denounces with equal vigour every conscious attempt to socially control and regulate the process of production, as an inroad upon such sacred things as the rights of property, freedom and unrestricted play for the bent of the individual capitalist. It is very characteristic that the enthusiastic apologists of the factory system have nothing more damning to urge against a general organisation of the labour of society, than that it would turn all society into one immense factory.

If, in a society with capitalist production, anarchy in the social division of labour and despotism in that of the workshop are mutual conditions the one of the other, we find, on the contrary, in those earlier forms of society in which the separation of trades has been spontaneously developed, then crystallised, and finally made permanent by law, on the one hand, a specimen of the organisation of the labour of society, in accordance with an approved and authoritative plan, and on the other, the entire exclusion of division of labour in the workshop, or at all events a mere dwarflike or sporadic and accidental development of the same.[36]

Those small and extremely ancient Indian communities, some of which have continued down to this day, are based on possession in common of the land, on the blending of agriculture and handicrafts, and on an unalterable division of labour, which serves, whenever a new community is started, as a plan and scheme ready cut and dried. Occupying areas of from 100 up to several thousand acres, each forms a compact whole producing all it requires. The chief part of the products is destined for direct use by the community itself, and does not take the form of a commodity. Hence, production here is independent of that division of labour brought about, in Indian society as a whole, by means of the exchange of commodities. It is the surplus alone that becomes a commodity, and a portion of even that, not until it has reached the hands of the State, into whose hands from time immemorial a certain quantity of these products has found its way in the shape of rent in kind. The constitution of these communities varies in different parts of India. In those of the simplest form, the land is tilled in common, and the produce divided among the members. At the same time, spinning and weaving are carried on in each family as subsidiary industries. Side by side with the masses thus occupied with one and the same work, we find the 'chief inhabitant,' who is judge, police, and tax-gatherer in one; the book-keeper, who keeps the accounts of the tillage and registers everything relating thereto; another official, who prosecutes criminals, protects strangers travelling through and escorts them to the next village; the boundary man, who guards the boundaries against neighbouring communities; the water-overseer, who distributes the water from the common tanks for irrigation; the Brahmin, who conducts the religious services; the schoolmaster, who on the sand teaches the children reading and writing; the calendar-Brahmin, or astrologer, who makes known the lucky or unlucky days for seed-time and harvest, and for every other kind of agricultural work; a smith and a carpenter, who make and repair all the agricultural implements; the potter, who makes all the pottery of the village; the barber, the washerman, who washes clothes, the silversmith, here and there the poet, who in some communities replaces the silversmith, in others the schoolmaster. This dozen of individuals is maintained at the expense of the whole community. If the population increases, a new community is founded, on the pattern of the old one, on unoccupied land. The whole mechanism discloses a systematic division of labour; but a division like that in manufactures is impossible, since the smith and the carpenter, &c., find an unchanging market, and at the most there occur, according to the sizes of the villages, two or three of each, instead of one.[37] The law that regulates the division of labour in the community acts with the irresistible authority of a law of Nature, at the same time that each individual artificer, the smith, the carpenter, and so on, conducts in his workshop all the operations of his handicraft in the traditional way, but independently, and without recognising any authority over him. The simplicity of the organisation for production in these self-sufficing communities that constantly reproduce themselves in the same form, and when accidentally destroyed, spring up again on the spot and with the same name[38] – this simplicity supplies the key to the secret of the unchangeableness of Asiatic societies, an unchangeableness in such striking contrast with the constant dissolution and refounding of Asiatic States, and the never-ceasing changes of dynasty. The structure of the economic elements of society remains untouched by the storm-clouds of the political sky.

The rules of the guilds, as I have said before, by limiting most strictly the number of apprentices and journeymen that a single master could employ, prevented him from becoming a capitalist. Moreover, he could not employ his journeymen in many other handicrafts than the one in which he was a master. The guilds zealously repelled every encroachment by the capital of merchants, the only form of free capital with which they came in contact. A merchant could buy every kind of commodity, but labour as a commodity he could not buy. He existed only on sufferance, as a dealer in the products of the handicrafts. If circumstances called for a further division of labour, the existing guilds split themselves up into varieties, or founded new guilds by the side of the old ones; all this, however, without concentrating various handicrafts in a single workshop. Hence, the guild organisation, however much it may have contributed by separating, isolating, and perfecting the handicrafts, to create the material conditions for the existence of manufacture, excluded division of labour in the workshop. On the whole, the labourer and his means of production remained closely united, like the snail with its shell, and thus there was wanting the principal basis of manufacture, the separation of the labourer from his means of production, and the conversion of these means into capital.

While division of labour in society at large, whether such division be brought about or not by exchange of commodities, is common to economic formations of society the most diverse, division of labour in the workshop, as practised by manufacture, is a special creation of the capitalist mode of production alone.

Section 5. The Capitalistic Character of Manufacture.

An increased number of labourers under the control of one capitalist is the natural starting-point, as well of co-operation generally, as of manufacture in particular. But the division of labour in manufacture makes this increase in the number of workmen a technical necessity. The minimum number that any given capitalist is bound to employ is here prescribed by the previously established division of labour. On the other hand, the advantages of further division are obtainable only by adding to the number of workmen, and this can be done only by adding multiples of the various detail groups. But an increase in the variable component of the capital employed necessitates an increase in its constant component, too, in the workshops, implements, &c., and, in particular, in the raw material, the call for which grows quicker than the number of workmen. The quantity of it consumed in a given time, by a given amount of labour, increases in the same ratio as does the productive power of that labour in consequence of its division. Hence, it is a law, based on the very nature of manufacture, that the minimum amount of capital, which is bound to be in the hands of each capitalist, must keep increasing; in other words, that the transformation into capital of the social means of production and subsistence must keep extending.[39]

In manufacture, as well as in simple co-operation, the collective working organism is a form of existence of capital. The mechanism that is made up of numerous individual detail labourers belongs to the capitalist. Hence, the productive power resulting from a combination of labours appears to be the productive power of capital. Manufacture proper not only subjects the previously independent workman to the discipline and command of capital, but, in addition, creates a hierarchic gradation of the workmen themselves. While simple co-operation leaves the mode of working by the individual for the most part un-changed, manufacture thoroughly revolutionises it, and seizes labour power by its very roots. It converts the labourer into a crippled monstrosity, by forcing his detail dexterity at the expense of a world of productive capabilities and instincts; just as in the States of La Plata they butcher a whole beast for the sake of his hide or his tallow. Not only is the detail work distributed to the different individuals, but the individual himself is made the automatic motor of a fractional oper-ation,[40] and the absurd fable of Menenius Agrippa, which makes man a mere fragment of his own body, becomes realised.'[41] If, at first, the workman sells his labour power to capital, because the material means of producing a commodity fail him, now his very labour power refuses its services unless it has been sold to capital. Its functions can be exercised only in an environment that exists in the workshop of the capitalist after the sale. By nature unfitted to make anything indepen-dently, the manufacturing labourer develops productive activity as a mere appendage of the capitalist's workshop.[42] As the chosen people bore in their features the sign manual of Jehovah, so division of labour brands the manufacturing workman as the property of capital.

The knowledge, the judgement, and the will, which, though in ever so small a degree, are practised by the independent peasant or handi-craftsman, in the same way as the savage makes the whole art of war consist in the exercise of his personal cunning – these faculties are now required only for the workshop as a whole. Intelligence in production expands in one direction, because it vanishes in many others. What is lost by the detail labourers, is concentrated in the capital that employs them.[43] It is a result of the division of labour in manufactures, that the labourer is brought face to face with the intellectual potencies of the material process of production, as the property of another, and as a ruling power. This separation begins in simple co-operation, where the capitalist represents to the single workman, the oneness and the will of the associated labour. It is developed in manufacture which cuts down the labourer into a detail labourer. It is completed in modern industry, which makes science a productive force distinct from labour and presses it into the service of capital.[44]

In manufacture, in order to make the collective labourer, and through him capital, rich in social productive power, each labourer must be made poor in individual productive powers. 'Ignorance is the mother of industry as well as of superstition. Reflection and fancy are subject to err; but a habit of moving the hand or the foot is independent of either. Manufactures, accordingly, prosper most where the mind is least consulted, and where the workshop may . . . be considered as an engine, the parts of which are men.'[45] As a matter of fact, some few manufacturers in the middle of the 18th century preferred, for certain operations that were trade secrets, to employ half-idiotic persons.[46]

'The understandings of the greater part of men,' says Adam Smith, 'are necessarily formed by their ordinary employments. The man whose whole life is spent in performing a few simple operations . . . has no occasion to exert his understanding . . . He generally becomes as stupid and ignorant as it is possible for a human creature to become.' After describing the stupidity of the detail labourer he goes on: 'The uniformity of his stationary life naturally corrupts the courage of his mind . . . It corrupts even the activity of his body and renders him incapable of exerting his strength with vigour and perseverance in any other employments than that to which he has been bred. His dexterity at his own particular trade seems in this manner to be acquired at the expense of his intellectual, social, and martial virtues. But in every improved and civilised society, this is the state into which the labouring poor, that is, the great body of the people, must necessarily fall.'[47] For preventing the complete deterioration of the great mass of the people by division of labour, A. Smith recommends education of the people by the State, but prudently, and in homeopathic doses. G. Garnier, his French translator and commentator, who, under the first French Empire, quite naturally developed into a senator, quite as naturally opposes him on this point. Education of the masses, he urges, violates the first law of the division of labour, and with it 'our whole social system would be proscribed.' 'Like all other divisions of labour,' he says, 'that between hand labour and head labour[48] is more pronounced and decided in proportion as society (he rightly uses this word, for capital, landed property and their State) becomes richer. This division of labour, like every other, is an effect of past, and a cause of future progress . . . ought the government then to work in opposition to this division of labour, and to hinder its natural course? Ought it to expend a part of the public money in the attempt to confound and blend together two classes of labour, which are striving after division and separation?'[49]

Some crippling of body and mind is inseparable even from division of labour in society as a whole. Since, however, manufacture carries this social separation of branches of labour much further, and also, by its peculiar division, attacks the individual at the very roots of his life, it is the first to afford the materials for, and to give a start to, industrial pathology.[50]

'To subdivide a man is to execute him, if he deserves the sentence, to assassinate him if he does not . . . The subdivision of labour is the assassination of a people.'[51]

Co-operation based on division of labour, in other words, manufacture, commences as a spontaneous formation. So soon as it attains some consistence and extension, it becomes the recognised methodical and systematic form of capitalist production. History shows how the division of labour peculiar to manufacture, strictly so called, acquires the best adapted form at first by experience, as it were behind the backs of the actors, and then, like the guild handicrafts, strives to hold fast that form when once found, and here and there succeeds in keeping it for centuries. Any alteration in this form, except in trivial matters, is solely owing to a revolution in the instruments of labour. Modern manufacture wherever it arises – I do not here allude to modern industry based on machinery – either finds the *disjecta membra poetae* ready to hand, and only waiting to be collected together, as is the case in the manufacture of clothes in large towns, or it can easily apply the principle of division, simply by exclusively assigning the various operations of a handicraft (such as book-binding) to particular men. In such cases, a week's experience is enough to determine the proportion between the numbers of the hands necessary for the various functions.[52]

By decomposition of handicrafts, by specialisation of the instruments of labour, by the formation of detail labourers, and by grouping and combining the latter into a single mechanism, division of labour in manufacture creates a qualitative gradation, and a quantitative proportion in the social process of production; it consequently creates a definite organisation of the labour of society, and thereby develops at the same time new productive forces in the society. In its specific capitalist form – and under the given conditions, it could take no other form than a capitalistic one – manufacture is but a particular method of begetting relative surplus-value, or of augmenting at the expense of the labourer the self-expansion of capital usually called social wealth, 'Wealth of Nations', &c. It increases the social productive power of labour, not only for the benefit of the capitalist instead of for that of the labourer, but it does this by crippling the individual labourers. It creates new conditions for the lordship of capital over labour. If, therefore, on the one hand, it presents itself historically as a progress and as a necessary phase in the economic development of society, on the other hand, it is a refined and civilised method of exploitation.

Political Economy, which as an independent science, first sprang into being during the period of manufacture, views the social division of labour only from the standpoint of manufacture,[53] and sees in it only the means of producing more commodities with a given quantity of labour, and, consequently, of cheapening commodities and hurrying on the accumulation of capital. In most striking contrast with this accentuation of quantity and exchange value, is the attitude of the writers of classical antiquity, who hold exclusively by quality and use-value.[54] In consequence of the separation of the social branches of production, commodities are better made, the various bents and talents of men select a suitable field,[55] and without some restraint no important results can be obtained anywhere.[56] Hence both product and producer are improved by division of labour. If the growth of the quantity produced is occasionally mentioned, this is only done with reference to the greater abundance of use-values. There is not a word alluding to exchange value or to the cheapening of commodities. This aspect, from the standpoint of use-value alone, is taken as well by Plato,[57] who treats division of labour as the foundation on which the division of society into classes is based, as by Xenophon,[58] who with characteristic bourgeois instinct, approaches more nearly to division of labour within the workshop. Plato's *Republic*, in so far as division of labour is treated in it, as the formative principle of the State, is merely the Athenian idealisation of the Egyptian system of castes, Egypt having served as the model of an industrial country to many of his contemporaries also, amongst others to Isocrates,[59] and it continued to have this importance to the Greeks of the Roman Empire.[60]

During the manufacturing period proper, i.e., the period during which manufacture is the predominant form taken by capitalist production, many obstacles are opposed to the full development of the peculiar tendencies of manufacture. Although manufacture creates, as we have already seen, a simple separation of the labourers into skilled and unskilled, simultaneously with their hierarchic arrangement in classes, yet the number of the unskilled labourers, owing to the preponderating influence of the skilled, remains very limited. Although it adapts the detail operations to the various degrees of maturity, strength, and development of the living instruments of labour, thus conducing to exploitation of women and children, yet this tendency as a whole is wrecked on the habits and the resistance of the male labourers. Although the splitting up of handicrafts lowers the cost of forming the workman, and thereby lowers his value, yet for the more difficult detail work, a longer apprenticeship is necessary, and, even where it would be superfluous, is jealously insisted upon by the workmen. In England, for instance, we find the laws of apprenticeship, with their seven years' probation, in full force down to the end of the manufacturing period; and they are not thrown on one side till the advent of Modern Industry. Since handicraft skill is the foundation of manufacture, and since the mechanism of manufacture as a whole possesses no framework, apart from the labourers themselves, capital is constantly compelled to wrestle with the insubordination of the workmen. 'By the infirmity of human nature,' says friend Ure, 'it happens that the more skilful the workman, the more self-willed and intractable he is apt to become, and of course the less fit a component of a mechanical system in which . . . he may do great damage to the whole.'[61] Hence throughout the whole manufacturing period there runs the complaint of want of discipline among the workmen.[62] And had we not the testimony of contemporary writers, the simple facts, that during the period between the 16th century and the epoch of Modern Industry, capital failed to become the master of the whole disposable working-time of the manufacturing labourers, that manufactures are short-lived, and change their locality from one country to another with the emigrating or immigrating workmen, these facts would speak volumes. 'Order must in one way or another be established,' exclaims in 1770 the oft-cited author of the *Essay on Trade and Commerce*. 'Order,' re-echoes Dr Andrew Ure 66 years later, 'Order' was wanting in manufacture based on 'the scholastic dogma of division of labour', and 'Arkwright created order.'

At the same time manufacture was unable, either to seize upon the production of society to its full extent, or to revolutionise that production to its very core. It towered up as an economic work of art, on the broad foundation of the town handicrafts, and of the rural domestic industries. At a given stage in its development, the narrow technical basis on which manufacture rested, came into conflict with requirements of production that were created by manufacture itself.

One of its most finished creations was the workshop for the production of the instruments of labour themselves, including especially the complicated mechanical apparatus then already employed. A machine-factory, says Ure, 'displayed the division of labour in manifold gradations – the file, the drill, the lathe, having each its different workman in the order of skill.' (p.21.) This workshop, the product of the division of labour in manufacture, produced in its turn – machines. It is they that sweep away the handicraftsman's work as the regulating principle of social production. Thus, on the one hand, the technical reason for the life-long annexation of the workman to a detail function is removed. On the other hand, the fetters that this same principle laid on the dominion of capital, fall away.

Chapter 15
Machinery and Modern Industry

Section 1. The Development of Machinery.

John Stuart Mill says in his *Principles of Political Economy*: 'It is questionable if all the mechanical inventions yet made have lightened the day's toil of any human being.'[1] That is, however, by no means the aim of the capitalistic application of machinery. Like every other increase in the productiveness of labour, machinery is intended to cheapen commodities, and, by shortening that portion of the working-day, in which the labourer works for himself, to lengthen the other portion that he gives, without an equivalent, to the capitalist. In short, it is a means for producing surplus-value.

In manufacture, the revolution in the mode of production begins with the labour power, in modern industry it begins with the instruments of labour. Our first inquiry then is, how the instruments of labour are converted from tools into machines, or what is the difference between a machine and the implements of a handicraft? We are only concerned here with striking and general characteristics; for epochs in the history of society are no more separated from each other by hard and fast lines of demarcation, than are geological epochs.

Mathematicians and mechanicians, and in this they are followed by a few English economists, call a tool a simple machine, and a machine a complex tool. They see no essential difference between them, and even give the name of machine to the simple mechanical powers, the lever, the inclined plane, the screw, the wedge, &c.[2] As a matter of fact, every machine is a combination of those simple powers, no matter how they may be disguised. From the economic standpoint this explanation is worth nothing, because the historical element is wanting. Another explanation of the difference between tool and machine is that in the case of a tool, man is the motive power, while the motive power of a machine is something different from man, as, for instance, an animal, water, wind, and so on.[3] According to this, a plough drawn by oxen, which is a contrivance common to the most different epochs, would be a machine, while Claussen's circular loom, which, worked by a single labourer, weaves 96,000 picks per minute, would be a mere tool. Nay, this very loom, though a tool when worked by hand, would, if worked by steam, be a machine. And since the application of animal power is one of man's earliest inventions, production by machinery would have preceded production by handicrafts. When in 1735, John Wyatt brought out his spinning machine, and began the industrial revolution of the 18th century, not a word did he say about an ass driving it instead of a man, and yet this part fell to the ass. He described it as a machine 'to spin without fingers'.[4]

All fully developed machinery consists of three essentially different parts, the motor mechanism, the transmitting mechanism, and finally the tool or working machine. The motor mechanism is that which puts the whole in motion. It either generates its own motive power, like the steam-engine, the caloric engine, the electromagnetic machine, &c., or it receives its impulse from some already existing natural force, like the water-wheel from a head of water, the wind-mill from wind, &c. The transmitting mechanism, composed of fly-wheels, shafting, toothed wheels, pullies, straps, ropes, bands, pinions, and gearing of the most varied kinds, regulates the motion, changes its form where necessary, as for instance, from linear to circular, and divides and distributes it among the working machines. These two first parts of the whole mechanism are there, solely for putting the working machines in motion, by means of which motion the subject of labour is seized upon and modified as desired. The tool or working machine is that part of the machinery with which the industrial revolution of the 18th century started. And to this day it constantly serves as such a starting-point, whenever a handicraft, or a manufacture, is turned into an industry carried on by machinery.

On a closer examination of the working machine proper, we find in it, as a general rule, though often, no doubt, under very altered forms, the apparatus and tools used by the handicraftsman or manufacturing workman; with this difference, that instead of being human implements, they are the implements of a mechanism, or mechanical implements. Either the entire machine is only a more or less altered mechanical edition of the old handicraft tool, as, for instance, the power-loom,[5] or the working parts fitted in the frame of the machine are old acquaintances, as spindles are in a mule, needles in a stocking-loom, saws in a sawing-machine, and knives in a chopping machine. The distinction between these tools and the body proper of the machine, exists from their very birth; for they continue for the most part to be produced by handicraft, or by manufacture, and are afterwards fitted into the body of the machine, which is the product of machinery.[6] The machine proper is therefore a mechanism that, after being set in motion, performs with its tools the same operations that were formerly done by the workman with similar tools. Whether the motive power is derived from man, or from some other machine, makes no difference in this respect. From the moment that the tool proper is taken from man, and fitted into a mechanism, a machine takes the place of a mere implement. The difference strikes one at once, even in those cases where man himself continues to be the prime mover. The number of implements that he himself can use simultaneously, is limited by the number of his own natural instruments of production, by the number of his bodily organs. In Germany, they tried at first to make one spinner work two spinning-wheels, that is, to work simultaneously with both hands and both feet. This was too difficult. Later, a treddle spinning-wheel with two spindles was invented, but adepts in spinning, who could spin two threads at once, were almost as scarce as two-headed men. The Jenny, on the other hand, even at its very birth, spun with 12–18 spindles, and the stocking-loom knits with many thousand needles at once. The number of tools that a machine can bring into play simultaneously, is from the very first emancipated from the organic limits that hedge in the tools of a handicraftsman.

In many manual implements the distinction between man as mere motive power, and man as the workman or operator properly so called, is brought into striking contrast. For instance, the foot is merely the prime mover of the spinning-wheel, while the hand, working with the spindle, and drawing and twisting, performs the real operation of spinning. It is this last part of the handicraftsman's implement that is first seized upon by the industrial revolution, leaving to the workman, in addition to his new labour of watching the machine with his eyes and correcting its mistakes with his hands, the merely mechanical part of being the moving power. On the other hand, implements, in regard to which man has always acted as a simple motive power, as, for instance, by turning the crank of a mill,[7] by pumping, by moving up and down the arm of a bellows, by pounding with a mortar, &c., such implements soon call for the application of animals, water[8] and wind as motive powers. Here and there, long before the period of manufacture, and also, to some extent, during that period, these implements pass over into machines, but without creating any revolution in the mode of production. It becomes evident, in the period of Modern Industry, that these implements, even under their form of manual tools, are already machines. For instance, the pumps with which the Dutch, in 1836–7, emptied the Lake of Harlem, were constructed on the principle of ordinary pumps; the only difference being, that their pistons were driven by cyclopean steam-engines, instead of by men. The common and very imperfect bellows of the blacksmith is, in England, occasionally converted into a blowing-engine, by connecting its arm with a steam-engine. The steam-engine itself, such as it was at its invention, during the manufacturing period at the close of the 17th century, and such as it continued to be down to 1780,[9] did not give rise to any industrial revolution. It was, on the contrary, the invention of machines that made a revolution in the form of steam-engines necessary. As soon as man, instead of working with an implement on the subject of his labour, becomes merely the motive power of an implement-machine, it is a mere accident that motive power takes the disguise of human muscle; and it may equally well take the form of wind, water or steam. Of course, this does not prevent such a change of form from producing great technical alterations in the mechanism that was originally constructed to be driven by man alone. Nowadays, all machines that have their way to make, such as sewing-machines, bread-making machines, &c., are, unless from their very nature their use on a small scale is excluded, constructed to be driven both by human and by purely mechanical motive power.

The machine, which is the starting-point of the industrial revolution, supersedes the workman, who handles a single tool, by a mechanism operating with a number of similar tools, and set in motion by a single motive power, whatever the form of that power may be.[10] Here we have the machine, but only as an elementary factor of production by machinery.

Increase in the size of the machine, and in the number of its working tools, calls for a more massive mechanism to drive it; and this mechanism requires, in order to overcome its resistance, a mightier moving power than that of man, apart from the fact that man is a very imperfect instrument for producing uniform continued motion. But assuming that he is acting simply as a motor, that a machine has taken the place of his tool, it is evident that he can be replaced by natural forces. Of all the great motors handed down from the manufacturing period, horse-power is the worst, partly because a horse has a head of his own, partly because he is costly, and the extent to which he is applicable in factories is very restricted.[11] Nevertheless the horse was extensively used during the infancy of Modern Industry. This is proved, as well by the complaints of contemporary agriculturists, as by the term 'horse-power', which has survived to this day as an expression for mechanical force.

Wind was too inconstant and uncontrollable, and besides, in England, the birthplace of Modern Industry, the use of water-power preponderated even during the manufacturing period. In the 17th century attempts had already been made to turn two pairs of millstones with a single water-wheel. But the increased size of the gearing was too much for the water-power, which had now become insufficient, and this was one of the circumstances that led to a more accurate investigation of the laws of friction. In the same way the irregularity caused by the motive power in mills that were put in motion by pushing and pulling a lever, led to the theory, and the application, of the fly-wheel, which afterwards plays so important a part in Modern Industry.[12] In this way, during the manufacturing period, were developed the first scientific and technical elements of Modern Mechanical Industry. Arkwright's throstle-spinning mill was from the very first turned by water. But for all that, the use of water, as the predominant motive power, was beset with difficulties. It could not be increased at will, it failed at certain seasons of the year, and, above all, it was essentially local.[13] Not till the invention of Watt's second and so-called double-acting steam-engine, was a prime mover found, that begot its own force by the consumption of coal and water, whose power was entirely under man's control, that was mobile and a means of locomotion, that was urban and not, like the water-wheel, rural, that permitted production to be concentrated in towns instead of, like the water-wheels, being scattered up and down the country,[14] that was of universal technical application, and, relatively speaking, little affected in its choice of residence by local circumstances. The greatness of Watt's genius showed itself in the specification of the patent that he took out in April, 1784. In that specification his steam-engine is described, not as an invention for a specific purpose, but as an agent universally applicable in Mechanical Industry. In it he points out applications, many of which, as for instance, the steam-hammer, were not introduced till half a century later. Nevertheless he doubted the use of steam-engines in navigation. His successors, Boulton and Watt, sent to the exhibition of 1851 steam-engines of colossal size for ocean steamers.

As soon as tools had been converted from being manual implements of man into implements of a mechanical apparatus, of a machine, the motive mechanism also acquired an independent form, entirely emancipated from the restraints of human strength. Thereupon the individual machine, that we have hitherto been considering, sinks into a mere factor in production by machinery. One motive mechanism was now able to drive many machines at once. The motive mechanism grows with the number of the machines that are turned simultaneously, and the transmitting mechanism becomes a wide-spreading apparatus.

We now proceed to distinguish the co-operation of a number of machines of one kind from a complex system of machinery.

In the one case, the product is entirely made by a single machine, which performs all the various operations previously done by one handicraftsman with his tool; as, for instance, by a weaver with his loom; or by several handicraftsman successively, either separately or as members of a system of Manufacture.[15] For example, in the manufacture of envelopes, one man folded the paper with the folder, another laid on the gum, a third turned the flap over, on which the device is impressed, a fourth embossed the device, and so on; and for each of these operations the envelope had to change hands. One single envelope machine now performs all these operations at once, and makes more than 3,000 envelopes in an hour. In the London exhibition of 1862, there was an American machine for making paper cornets. It cut the paper, pasted, folded, and finished 300 in a minute. Here, the whole process, which, when carried on as Manufacture, was split up into, and carried out by, a series of operations, is completed by a single machine, working a combination of various tools. Now, whether such a machine be merely a reproduction of a complicated manual implement, or a combination of various simple implements specialised by Manufacture, in either case, in the factory, i.e., in the workshop in which machinery alone is used, we meet again with simple co-operation; and, leaving the workman out of consideration for the moment, this co-operation presents itself to us, in the first instance, as the conglomeration in one place of similar and simultaneously acting machines. Thus, a weaving factory is constituted of a number of power-looms, working side by side, and a sewing factory of a number of sewing-machines all in the same building. But there is here a technical oneness in the whole system, owing to all the machines receiving their impulse simultaneously, and in an equal degree, from the pulsations of the common prime mover, by the intermediary of the transmitting mechanism; and this mechanism, to a certain extent, is also common to them all, since only particular ramifications of it branch off to each machine. Just as a number of tools, then, form the organs of a machine, so a number of machines of one kind constitute the organs of the motive mechanism.

A real machinery system, however, does not take the place of these independent machines, until the subject of labour goes through a connected series of detail processes, that are carried out by a chain of machines of various kinds, the one supplementing the other. Here we have again the co-operation by division of labour that characterises Manufacture; only now, it is a combination of detail machines. The special tools of the various detail workmen, such as those of the beaters, combers, spinners, &c., in the woollen manufacture, are now transformed into the tools of specialised machines, each machine constituting a special organ, with a special function, in the system. In those branches of industry in which the machinery system is first introduced, Manufacture itself furnishes, in a general way, the natural basis for the division, and consequent organisation, of the process of production.[16] Nevertheless an essential difference at once manifests itself. In Manufacture it is the workmen who, with their manual implements, must, either singly or in groups, carry on each particular detail process. If, on the one hand, the workman becomes adapted to the process, on the other, the process was previously made suitable to the workman. This subjective principle of the division of labour no longer exists in production by machinery. Here, the process as a whole is examined objectively, in itself, that is to say, without regard to the question of its execution by human hands, it is analysed into its constituent phases; and the problem, how to execute each detail process, and bind them all into a whole, is solved by the aid of machines, chemistry, &c.[17] But, of course, in this case also, theory must be perfected by accumulated experience on a large scale. Each detail machine supplies raw material to the machine next in order; and since they are all working at the same time, the product is always going through the various stages of its fabrication, and is also constantly in a state of transition, from one phase to another. Just as in Manufacture, the direct co-operation of the detail labourers establishes a numerical proportion between the special groups, so in an organised system of machinery, where one detail machine is constantly kept employed by another, a fixed relation is established between their numbers, their size, and their speed. The collective machine, now an organised system of various kinds of single machines, and of groups of single machines, becomes more and more perfect, the more the process as a whole becomes a continuous one, i.e., the less the raw material is interrupted in its passage from its first phase to its last; in other words, the more its passage from one phase to another is effected, not by the hand of man, but by the machinery itself. In Manufacture the isolation of each detail process is a condition imposed by the nature of division of labour, but in the fully developed factory the continuity of those processes is, on the contrary, imperative.

A system of machinery, whether it reposes on the mere co-operation of similar machines, as in weaving, or on a combination of different machines, as in spinning, constitutes in itself a huge automaton, whenever it is driven by a self-acting prime mover. But although the factory as a whole be driven by its steam-engine, yet either some of the individual machines may require the aid of the workman for some of their movements (such aid was necessary for the running in of the mule carriage, before the invention of the self-acting mule, and is still necessary in fine-spinning mills); or, to enable a machine to do its work, certain parts of it may require to be handled by the workman like a manual tool; this was the case in machine-makers' workshops, before the conversion of the slide rest into a self-actor. As soon as a machine executes, without man's help, all the movements requisite to elaborate the raw material, needing only attendance from him, we have an automatic system of machinery, and one that is susceptible of constant improvement in its details. Such improvements as the apparatus that stops a drawing frame, whenever a sliver breaks, and the self-acting stop, that stops the power-loom so soon as the shuttle bobbin is emptied of weft, are quite modern inventions. As an example, both of continuity of production, and of the carrying out of the automatic principle, we may take a modern paper mill. In the paper industry generally, we may advantageously study in detail not only the distinctions between modes of production based on different means of production, but also the connection of the social conditions of production with those modes: for the old German paper-making furnishes us with a sample of handicraft production; that of Holland in the 17th and of France in the 18th century with a sample of manufacturing in the strict sense; and that of modern England with a sample of automatic fabrication of this article. Besides these, there still exist, in India and China, two distinct antique Asiatic forms of the same industry.

An organised system of machines, to which motion is communicated by the transmitting mechanism from a central automaton, is the most developed form of production by machinery. Here we have, in the place of the isolated machine, a mechanical monster whose body fills whole factories, and whose demon power, at first veiled under the slow and measured motions of his giant limbs, at length breaks out into the fast and furious whirl of his countless working organs.

There were mules and steam-engines before there were any labourers, whose exclusive occupation it was to make mules and steam-
engines; just as men wore clothes before there were such people as
tailors. The inventions of Vaucanson, Arkwright, Watt, and others,
were, however, practicable, only because those inventors found,
ready to hand, a considerable number of skilled mechanical workmen, placed at their disposal by the manufacturing period. Some of
these workmen were independent handicraftsman of various trades,
others were grouped together in manufactures, in which, as before-
mentioned, division of labour was strictly carried out. As inventions
increased in number, and the demand for the newly discovered
machines grew larger, the machine-making industry split up, more
and more, into numerous independent branches, and division of
labour in these manufactures was more and more developed. Here,
then, we see in Manufacture the immediate technical foundation of
Modern Industry. Manufacture produced the machinery, by means of
which Modern Industry abolished the handicraft and manufacturing
systems in those spheres of production that it first seized upon. The
factory system was therefore raised, in the natural course of things, on
an inadequate foundation. When the system attained to a certain
degree of development, it had to root up this ready-made foundation,
which in the meantime had been elaborated on the old lines, and to
build up for itself a basis that should correspond to its methods of
production. Just as the individual machine retains a dwarfish character,
so long as it is worked by the power of man alone, and just as no
system of machinery could be properly developed before the steam-
engine took the place of the earlier motive powers, animals, wind, and
even water; so, too, Modern Industry was crippled in its complete
development, so long as its characteristic instrument of production,
the machine, owed its existence to personal strength and personal
skill, and depended on the muscular development, the keenness of
sight, and the cunning of hand, with which the detail workmen in
manufactures, and the manual labourers in handicrafts, wielded their
dwarfish implements' Thus, apart from the dearness of the machines
made in this way, a circumstance that is ever present to the mind of
the capitalist, the expansion of industries carried on by means of
machinery, and the invasion by machinery of fresh branches of
production, were dependent on the growth of a class of workmen,
who, owing to the almost artistic nature of their employment, could
increase their numbers only gradually, and not by leaps and bounds.
But besides this, at a certain stage of its development, Modern
Industry became technologically incompatible with the basis furnished for it by handicraft and Manufacture. The increasing size of

the prime movers, of the transmitting mechanism, and of the machines proper, the greater complication, multiformity and regularity of the details of these machines, as they more and more departed from the model of those originally made by manual labour, and acquired a form, untrammelled except by the conditions under which they worked, [18] the perfecting of the automatic system, and the use, every day more unavoidable, of a more refractory material, such as iron instead of wood – the solution of all these problems, which sprang up by the force of circumstances, everywhere met with a stumbling-block in the personal restrictions, which even the collective labourer of Manufacture could not break through, except to a limited extent. Such machines as the modern hydraulic press, the modern power-loom, and the modern carding engine, could never have been furnished by Manufacture.

A radical change in the mode of production in one sphere of industry involves a similar change in other spheres. This happens at first in such branches of industry as are connected together by being separate phases of a process, and yet are isolated by the social division of labour, in such a way, that each of them produces an independent commodity. Thus spinning by machinery made weaving by machinery a necessity, and both together made the mechanical and chemical revolution that took place in bleaching, printing, and dyeing, imperative. So too, on the other hand, the revolution in cotton-spinning called forth the invention of the gin, for separating the seeds from the cotton fibre; it was only by means of this invention, that the production of cotton became possible on the enormous scale at present required.[19] But more especially, the revolution in the modes of production of industry and agriculture made necessary a revolution in the general conditions of the social process of production, i.e., in the means of communication and of transport. In a society whose pivot, to use an expression of Fourier, was agriculture on a small scale, with its subsidiary domestic industries, and the urban handicrafts, the means of communication and transport were so utterly inadequate to the productive requirements of the manufacturing period, with its extended division of social labour, its concentration of the instruments of labour, and of the workmen, and its colonial markets, that they became in fact revolutionised. In the same way the means of communication and transport handed down from the manufacturing period soon became unbearable trammels on Modern Industry, with its feverish haste of production, its enormous extent, its constant flinging of capital and labour from one sphere of production into another, and its newly-created connections with the markets of the whole world. Hence, apart from the radical changes introduced in the construction of sailing vessels, the means of communication and transport became gradually adapted to the modes of production of mechanical industry, by the creation of a system of river steamers, railways, ocean steamers, and telegraphs. But the huge masses of iron that had now to be forged, to be welded, to be cut, to be bored, and to be shaped, demanded, on their part, cyclopean machines, for the construction of which the methods of the manufacturing period were utterly inadequate.

Modern Industry had therefore itself to take in hand the machine, its characteristic instrument of production, and to construct machines by machines. It was not till it did this, that it built up for itself a fitting technical foundation, and stood on its own feet. Machinery, simultaneously with the increasing use of it, in the first decades of this century, appropriated, by degrees, the fabrication of machines proper. But it was only during the decade preceding 1866, that the construction of railways and ocean steamers on a stupendous scale called into existence the cyclopean machines now employed in the construction of prime movers.

The most essential condition to the production of machines by machines was a prime mover capable of exerting any amount of force, and yet under perfect control. Such a condition was already supplied by the steam-engine. But at the same time it was necessary to produce the geometrically accurate straight lines, planes, circles, cylinders, cones, and spheres, required in the detail parts of the machines. This problem Henry Maudsley solved in the first decade of this century by the invention of the slide rest, a tool that was soon made automatic, and in a modified form was applied to other constructive machines besides the lathe, for which it was originally intended. This mechanical appliance replaces, not some particular tool, but the hand itself, which produces a given form by holding and guiding the cutting tool along the iron or other material operated upon. Thus it became possible to produce the forms of the individual parts of machinery 'with a degree of ease, accuracy, and speed, that no accumulated experience of the hand of the most skilled workman could give.'[20]

If we now fix our attention on that portion of the machinery employed in the construction of machines, which constitutes the operating tool, we find the manual implements re-appearing, but on a cyclopean scale. The operating part of the boring machine is an immense drill driven by a steam-engine; without this machine, on the other hand, the cylinders of large steam-engines and of hydraulic presses could not be made. The mechanical lathe is only a cyclopean reproduction of the ordinary foot-lathe; the planing machine, an iron carpenter, that works on iron with the same tools that the human carpenter employs on wood; the instrument that, on the London wharves, cuts the veneers, is a gigantic razor; the tool of the shearing machine, which shears iron as easily as a tailor's scissors cut cloth, is a monster pair of scissors; and the steam-hammer works with an ordinary hammer head, but of such a weight that not Thor himself could wield it.[21] These steam-hammers are an invention of Nasmyth, and there is one that weighs over 6 tons and strikes with a vertical fall of 7 feet, on an anvil weighing 36 tons. It is mere child's-play for it to crush a block of granite into powder, yet it is no less capable of driving, with a succession of light taps, a nail into a piece of soft wood.[22]

The implements of labour, in the form of machinery, necessitate the substitution of natural forces for human force, and the conscious application of science, instead of rule of thumb. In Manufacture, the organisation of the social labour-process is purely subjective; it is a combination of detail labourers; in its machinery system, Modern Industry has a productive organism that is purely objective, in which the labourer becomes a mere appendage to an already existing material condition of production. In simple co-operation, and even in that founded on division of labour, the suppression of the isolated, by the collective, workman still appears to be more or less accidental. Machinery, with a few exceptions to be mentioned later, operates only by means of associated labour, or labour in common. Hence the co-operative character of the labour-process is, in the latter case, a technical necessity dictated by the instrument of labour itself.

Section 2. The Value Transferred by Machinery to the Product.

We saw that the productive forces resulting from co-operation and division of labour cost capital nothing. They are natural forces of social labour. So also physical forces, like steam, water, &c., when appropriated to productive processes, cost nothing. But just as a man requires lungs to breathe with, so he requires something that is work of man's hand, in order to consume physical forces productively. A water-wheel is necessary to exploit the force of water, and a steam-engine to exploit the elasticity of steam. Once discovered, the law of the deviation of the magnetic needle in the field of an electric current, or the law of the magnetisation of iron, around which an electric current circulates, cost never a penny.[23] But the exploitation of these laws for the purposes of telegraphy, &c., necessitates a costly and extensive apparatus. The tool, as we have seen, is not exterminated by the machine. From being a dwarf implement of the human organism, it expands and multiplies into the implement of a mechanism created by man. Capital now sets the labourer to work, not with a manual tool, but with a machine which itself handles the tools. Although, therefore, it is clear at the first glance that, by incorporating both stupendous physical forces, and the natural sciences, with the process of production, Modern Industry raises the productiveness of labour to an extraordinary degree, it is by no means equally clear, that this increased productive force is not, on the other hand, purchased by an increased expenditure of labour. Machinery, like every other component of constant capital, creates no new value, but yields up its own value to the product that it serves to beget. In so far as the machine has value, and, in consequence, parts with value to the product, it forms an element in the value of that product. Instead of being cheapened, the product is made dearer in proportion to the value of the machine. And it is clear as noon-day, that machines and systems of machinery, the characteristic instruments of labour of Modern Industry, are incomparably more loaded with value than the implements used in handicrafts and manufactures.

In the first place, it must be observed that the machinery, while always entering as a whole into the labour-process, enters into the value-begetting process only by bits. It never adds more value than it loses, on an average, by wear and tear. Hence there is a great difference between the value of a machine, and the value transferred in a given time by that machine to the product. The longer the life of the machine in the labour-process, the greater is that difference. It is true, no doubt, as we have already seen, that every instrument of labour enters as a whole into the labour-process, and only piece-meal, proportionally to its average daily loss by wear and tear, into the value-begetting process. But this difference between the instrument as a whole and its daily wear and tear, is much greater in a machine than in a tool, because the machine, being made from more durable material, has a longer life; because its employment, being regulated by strictly scientific laws, allows of greater economy in the wear and tear of its parts, and in the materials it consumes; and lastly, because its field of production is incomparably larger than that of a tool. After making allowance, both in the case of the machine and of the tool, for their average daily cost, that is for the value they transmit to the product by their average daily wear and tear, and for their consumption of auxiliary substance, such as oil, coal, and so on, they each do their work gratuitously, just like the forces furnished by Nature without the help of man. The greater the productive power of the machinery compared with that of the tool, the greater is the extent of its gratuitous service compared with that of the tool. In Modern Industry man succeeded for the first time in making the product of his past labour work on a large scale gratuitously, like the forces of Nature.[24]

In treating of Co-operation and Manufacture, it was shown that certain general factors of production, such as buildings, are, in comparison with the scattered means of production of the isolated workman, economised by being consumed in common, and that they therefore make the product cheaper. In a system of machinery, not only is the framework of the machine consumed in common by its numerous operating implements, but the prime mover, together with a part of the transmitting mechanism, is consumed in common by the numerous operative machines.

Given the difference between the value of the machinery, and the value transferred by it in a day to the product, the extent to which this latter value makes the product dearer, depends in the first instance, upon the size of the product; so to say, upon its area. Mr Baynes, of Blackburn, in a lecture published in 1858, estimates that 'each real mechanical horse-power'[25] will drive 450 self-acting mule spindles, with preparation, or 200 throstle spindles, or 15 looms for 40-inch cloth with the appliances for warping, sizing, &c.' In the first case, it is the day's produce of 450 mule spindles, in the second, of 200 throstle spindles, in the third, of 15 power-looms, over which the daily cost of one horse-power, and the wear and tear of the machinery set in motion by that power, are spread; so that only a very minute value is transferred by such wear and tear to a pound of yarn or a yard of cloth. The same is the case with the steam-hammer mentioned above. Since its daily wear and tear, its coal-consumption, &c., are spread over the stupendous masses of iron hammered by it in a day, only a small value is added to a hundred weight of iron; but that value would be very great, if the cyclopean instrument were employed in driving in nails.

Given a machine's capacity for work, that is, the number of its operating tools, or, where it is a question of force, their mass, the amount of its product will depend on the velocity of its working parts, on the speed, for instance, of the spindles, or on the number of blows given by the hammer in a minute. Many of these colossal hammers strike seventy times in a minute, and Ryder's patent machine for forging spindles with small hammers gives as many as 700 strokes per minute.

Given the rate at which machinery transfers its value to the product, the amount of value so transferred depends on the total value of the machinery.[26] The less labour it contains, the less value it imparts to the product. The less value it gives up, so much the more productive it is, and so much the more its services approximate to those of natural forces. But the production of machinery by machinery lessens its value relatively to its extension and efficacy.

An analysis and comparison of the prices of commodities produced by handicrafts or manufactures, and of the prices of the same commodities produced by machinery, shows generally that, in the product of machinery, the value due to the instruments of labour increases relatively, but decreases absolutely. In other words, its absolute amount decreases, but its amount, relatively to the total value of the product, of a pound of yarn, for instance, increases.[27]

It is evident that whenever it costs as much labour to produce a machine as is saved by the employment of that machine, there is nothing but a transposition of labour; consequently the total labour required to produce a commodity is not lessened or the productiveness of labour is not increased. It is clear, however, that the difference between the labour a machine costs, and the labour it saves, in other words, that the degree of its productiveness does not depend on the difference between its own value and the value of the implement it replaces. As long as the labour spent on a machine, and consequently the portion of its value added to the product, remains smaller than the value added by the workman to the product with his tool, there is always a difference of labour saved in favour of the machine. The productiveness of a machine is therefore measured by the human labour power it replaces. According to Mr Baynes, 2 operatives are required for the 450 mule spindles, inclusive of preparation machinery,[28] that are driven by one-horse power; each self-acting mule spindle, working ten hours, produces 13 ounces of yarn (average number of thickness); consequently 2 1/2 operatives spin weekly 365 5/8 lbs. of yarn. Hence, leaving waste on one side, 366 lbs. of cotton absorb, during their conversion into yarn, only 150 hours' labour, or fifteen days' labour of ten hours each. But with a spinning-wheel, supposing the hand-spinner to produce thirteen ounces of yarn in sixty hours, the same weight of cotton would absorb 2,700 days' labour of ten hours each, or 27,000 hours' labour.[29] Where block-printing, the old method of printing calico by hand, has been superseded by machine printing, a single machine prints, with the aid of one man or boy, as much calico of four colours in one hour, as it formerly took 200 men to do.[30] Before Eli Whitney invented the cotton gin in 1793, the separation of the seed from a pound of cotton cost an average day's labour. By means of his invention one negress was enabled to clean 100 lbs. daily; and since then, the efficacy of the gin has been considerably increased. A pound of cotton wool, previously costing 50 cents to produce, included after that invention more unpaid labour, and was consequently sold with greater profit, at 10 cents. In India they employ for separating the wool from the seed, an instrument, half machine, half tool, called a churka; with this one man and a woman can clean 28 lbs. daily. With the churka invented some years ago by Dr Forbes, one man and a boy produce 250 lbs. daily. If oxen, steam, or water, be used for driving it, only a few boys and girls as feeders are required. Sixteen of these machines driven by oxen do as much work in a day as formerly 750 people did on an average.[31]

As already stated, a steam-plough does as much work in one hour at a cost of three-pence, as 66 men at a cost of 15 shillings. I return to this example in order to clear up an erroneous notion. The 15 shillings are by no means the expression in money of all the labour expended in one hour by the 66 men. If the ratio of surplus-labour to necessary labour were 100%, these 66 men would produce in one hour a value of 30 shillings, although their wages, 15 shillings, represent only their labour for half an hour. Suppose, then, a machine cost as much as the wages for a year of the 150 men it displaces, say £3,000; this £3,000 is by no means the expression in money of the labour added to the object produced by these 150 men before the introduction of the machine, but only of that portion of their year's labour which was expended for themselves and represented by their wages. On the other hand, the £3,000, the money-value of the machine, expresses all the labour expended on its production, no matter in what proportion this labour constitutes wages for the workman, and surplus-value for the capitalist. Therefore, though a machine cost as much as the labour power displaced by it costs, yet the labour materialised in it is even then much less than the living labour it replaces.[32]

The use of machinery for the exclusive purpose of cheapening the product, is limited in this way, that less labour must be expended in producing the machinery than is displaced by the employment of that machinery, For the capitalist, however, this use is still more limited. Instead of paying for the labour, he only pays the value of the labour power employed; therefore, the limit to his using a machine is fixed by the difference between the value of the machine and the value of the labour power replaced by it. Since the division of the day's work into necessary and surplus-labour differs in different countries, and even in the same country at different periods, or in different branches of industry; and further, since the actual wage of the labourer at one time sinks below the value of his labour power, at another rises above it, it is possible for the difference between the price of the machinery and the price of the labour power replaced by that machinery to vary very much, although the difference between the quantity of labour requisite to produce the machine and the total quantity replaced by it, remain constant.[33] But it is the former difference alone that determines the cost, to the capitalist, of producing a commodity, and, through the pressure of competition, influences his action. Hence the invention nowadays of machines in England that are employed only in North America; just as in the sixteenth and seventeenth centuries, machines were invented in Germany to be used only in Holland, and just as many a French invention of the eighteenth century was exploited in England alone. In the older countries, machinery, when employed in some branches of industry, creates such a redundancy of labour in other branches that in these latter the fall of wages below the value of labour power impedes the use of machinery, and, from the standpoint of the capitalist, whose profit comes, not from a diminution of the labour employed, but of the labour paid for, renders that use superfluous and often impossible. In some branches of the woollen manufacture in England the employment of children has during recent years been considerably diminished, and in some cases has been entirely abolished. Why? Because the Factory Acts made two sets of children necessary, one working six hours, the other four, or each working five hours. But the parents refused to sell the 'half-timers' cheaper than the 'full-timers'. Hence the substitution of machinery for the 'half-timers'.[34] Before the labour of women and of children under 10 years of age was forbidden in mines, capitalists considered the employment of naked women and girls, often in company with men, so far sanctioned by their moral code, and especially by their ledgers, that it was only after the passing of the Act that they had recourse to machinery. The Yankees have invented a stone-breaking machine. The English do not make use of it, because the 'wretch'[35] who does this work gets paid for such a small portion of his labour, that machinery would increase the cost of production to the capitalist.[36] In England women are still occasionally used instead of horses for hauling canal boats,[37] because the labour required to produce horses and machines is an accurately known quantity, while that required to maintain the women of the surplus-population is below all calculation. Hence nowhere do we find a more shameful squandering of human labour power for the most despicable purposes than in England, the land of machinery.

Section 3. The Proximate Effects of Machinery on the Workman.

The starting-point of Modern Industry is, as we have shown, the revolution in the instruments of labour, and this revolution attains its most highly developed form in the organised system of machinery in a factory. Before we inquire how human material is incorporated with this objective organism, let us consider some general effects of this revolution on the labourer himself.

A. Appropriation of Supplementary Labour power by Capital. The Employment of Women and Children.

In so far as machinery dispenses with muscular power, it becomes a means of employing labourers of slight muscular strength, and those whose bodily development is incomplete, but whose limbs are all the more supple. The labour of women and children was, therefore, the first thing sought for by capitalists who used machinery. That mighty substitute for labour and labourers was forthwith changed into a means for increasing the number of wage-labourers by enrolling, under the direct sway of capital, every member of the workman's family, without distinction of age or sex. Compulsory work for the capitalist usurped the place, not only of the children's play, but also of free labour at home within moderate limits for the support of the family.[38]

The value of labour power was determined, not only by the labour-time necessary to maintain the individual adult labourer, but also by that necessary to maintain his family. Machinery, by throwing every member of that family on to the labour-market, spreads the value of the man's labour power over his whole family. It thus depreciates his labour power. To purchase the labour power of a family of four workers may, perhaps, cost more than it formerly did to purchase the labour power of the head of the family, but, in return, four days' labour takes the place of one, and their price falls in proportion to the excess of the surplus-labour of four over the surplus-labour of one. In order that the family may live, four people must now, not only labour, but expend surplus-labour for the capitalist. Thus we see, that machinery, while augmenting the human material that forms the principal object of capital's exploiting power,[39] at the same time raises the degree of exploitation.

Machinery also revolutionises out and out the contract between the labourer and the capitalist, which formally fixes their mutual relations. Taking the exchange of commodities as our basis, our first assumption was that capitalist and labourer met as free persons, as independent owners of commodities; the one possessing money and means of production, the other labour power. But now the capitalist buys children and young persons under age. Previously, the workman sold his own labour power, which he disposed of nominally as a free agent. Now he sells wife and child. He has become a slave-dealer.[40] The demand for children's labour often resembles in form the inquiries for negro slaves, such as were formerly to be read among the advertisements in American journals. 'My attention,' says an English factory inspector, 'was drawn to an advertisement in the local paper of one of the most important manufacturing towns of my district, of which the following is a copy: Wanted, 12 to 20 young persons, not younger than what can pass for 13 years. Wages, 4 shillings a week. Apply &c.'⁴¹ The phrase 'what can pass for 13 years', has reference to the fact, that by the Factory Act, children under 13 years may work only 6 hours. A surgeon officially appointed must certify their age. The manufacturer, therefore, asks for children who look as if they were already 13 years old. The decrease, often by leaps and bounds, in the number of children under 13 years employed in factories, a decrease that is shown in an astonishing manner by the English statistics of the last 20 years, was for the most part, according to the evidence of the factory inspectors themselves, the work of the certifying surgeons, who over-stated the age of the children, agreeably to the capitalist's greed for exploitation, and the sordid trafficking needs of the parents. In the notorious district of Bethnal Green, a public market is held every Monday and Tuesday morning, where children of both sexes from 9 years of age upwards, hire themselves out to the silk manufacturers. 'The usual terms are 1s. 8d. a week (this belongs to the parents) and "2d. for myself and tea". The contract is binding only for the week. The scene and language while this market is going on are quite disgraceful.'⁴² It has also occurred in England, that women have taken 'children from the workhouse and let any one have them out for 2s. 6d. a week.'⁴³ In spite of legislation, the number of boys sold in Great Britain by their parents to act as live chimney-sweeping machines (although there exist plenty of machines to replace them) exceeds 2,000.⁴⁴ The revolution effected by machinery in the juridical relations between the buyer and the seller of labour-power, causing the transaction as a whole to lose the appearance of a contract between free persons, afforded the English Parliament an excuse, founded on juridical principles, for the interference of the state with factories. Whenever the law limits the labour of children to 6 hours in industries not before interfered with, the complaints of the manufacturers are always renewed. They allege that numbers of the parents withdraw their children from the industry brought under the Act, in order to sell them where 'freedom of labour' still rules, i.e., where children under 13 years are compelled to work like grown-up people, and therefore can be got rid of at a higher price. But since capital is by nature a leveller, since it exacts in every sphere of production equality in the conditions of the exploitation of labour, the limitation by law of children's labour, in one branch of industry, becomes the cause of its limitation in others.

We have already alluded to the physical deterioration as well of the children and young persons as of the women, whom machinery, first directly in the factories that shoot up on its basis, and then indirectly in all the remaining branches of industry, subjects to the exploitation of capital. In this place, therefore, we dwell only on one point, the enormous mortality, during the first few years of their life, of the children of the operatives. In sixteen of the registration districts into which England is divided, there are, for every 100,000 children alive under the age of one year, only 9,000 deaths in a year on an average (in one district only 7,047); in 24 districts the deaths are over 10,000, but under 11,000; in 39 districts, over 11,000, but under 12,000; in 48 districts over 12,000, but under 13,000; in 22 districts over 20,000; in 25 districts over 21,000; in 17 over 22,000; in 11 over 23,000; in Hoo, Wolverhampton, Ashton-under-Lyne, and Preston, over 24,000; in Nottingham, Stockport, and Bradford, over 25,000; in Wisbeach, 26,000; and in Manchester, 26,125.[45] As was shown by an official medical inquiry in the year 1861, the high death-rates are, apart from local causes, principally due to the employment of the mothers away from their homes, and to the neglect and maltreatment, consequent on her absence, such as, amongst others, insufficient nourishment, unsuitable food, and dosing with opiates; besides this, there arises an unnatural estrangement between mother and child, and as a consequence intentional starving and poisoning of the children.[46] In those agricultural districts, 'where a minimum in the employment of women exists, the death-rate is on the other hand very low.'[47] The Inquiry Commission of 1861 led, however, to the unexpected result, that in some purely agricultural districts bordering on the North Sea, the death-rate of children under one year old almost equalled that of the worst factory districts. Dr Julian Hunter was therefore commissioned to investigate this phenomenon on the spot. His report is incorporated with the *Sixth Report on Public Health*.[48] Up to that time it was supposed, that the children were decimated by malaria, and other diseases peculiar to low-lying and marshy districts. But the inquiry showed the very opposite, namely, that the same cause which drove away malaria, the conversion of the land, from a morass in winter and a scanty pasture in summer, into fruitful corn land, created the exceptional death-rate of the infants.[49] The 70 medical men, whom Dr Hunter examined in that district, were 'wonderfully in accord' on this point. In fact, the revolution in the mode of cultivation had led to the introduction of the industrial system. Married women, who work in gangs along with boys and girls, are, for a stipulated sum of money, placed at the disposal of the farmer, by a man called the 'undertaker', who contracts for the whole gang. 'These gangs will sometimes travel many miles from their own village; they are to be met morning and evening on the roads, dressed in short petticoats, with suitable coats and boots, and sometimes trousers, looking wonderfully strong and healthy, but tainted with a customary immorality and heedless of the fatal results which their love of this busy and independent life is bringing on their unfortunate offspring who are pining at home.'[50] Every phenomenon of the factory districts is here reproduced, including, but to a greater extent, ill-disguised infanticide, and dosing children with opiates.[51] 'My knowledge of such evils,' says Dr Simon, the medical officer of the Privy Council and editor in chief of the Reports on Public Health, 'may excuse the profound misgiving with which I regard any large industrial employment of adult women.'[52] 'Happy indeed,' exclaims Mr Baker, the factory inspector, in his official report, 'happy indeed will it be for the manufacturing districts of England, when every married woman having a family is prohibited from working in any textile works at all.'[53]

The moral degradation caused by the capitalistic exploitation of women and children has been so exhaustively depicted by F. Engels in his *Lage der Arbeitenden Klasse Englands*, and other writers, that I need only mention the subject in this place. But the intellectual desolation artificially produced by converting immature human beings into mere machines for the fabrication of surplus-value, a state of mind clearly distinguishable from that natural ignorance which keeps the mind fallow without destroying its capacity for development, its natural fertility, this desolation finally compelled even the English Parliament to make elementary education a compulsory condition to the 'productive' employment of children under 14 years, in every industry subject to the Factory Acts. The spirit of capitalist production stands out clearly in the ludicrous wording of the so-called education clauses in the Factory Acts, in the absence of an administrative machinery, an absence that again makes the compulsion illusory, in the opposition of the manufacturers themselves to these education clauses, and in the tricks and dodges they put in practice for evading them. 'For this the legislature is alone to blame, by having passed a delusive law, which, while it would seem to provide that the children employed in factories shall be educated, contains no enactment by which that professed end can be secured. It provides nothing more than that the children shall on certain days of the week, and for a certain number of hours (three) in each day, be inclosed within the four walls of a place called a school, and that the employer of the child shall receive weekly a certificate to that effect signed by a person designated by the subscriber as a schoolmaster or schoolmistress.'[54] Previous to the passing of the amended Factory Act, 1844, it happened, not unfrequently, that the certificates of attendance at school were signed by the schoolmaster or schoolmistress with a cross, as they themselves were unable to write. 'On one occasion, on visiting a place called a school, from which certificates of school attendance, had issued, I was so struck with the ignorance of the master, that I said to him: "Pray, sir, can you read?" His reply was: "Aye, summat!" and as a justification of his right to grant certificates, he added: "At any rate, I am before my scholars." The inspectors, when the Bill of 1844 was in preparation, did not fail to represent the disgraceful state of the places called schools, certificates from which they were obliged to admit as a compliance with the laws, but they were successful only in obtaining thus much, that since the passing of the Act of 1844, the figures in the school certificate must be filled up in the handwriting of the schoolmaster, who must also sign his Christian and surname in full.'[55] Sir John Kincaid, factory inspector for Scotland, relates experiences of the same kind. 'The first school we visited was kept by a Mrs Ann Killin. Upon asking her to spell her name, she straightway made a mistake, by beginning with the letter C, but correcting herself immediately, she said her name began with a K. On looking at her signature, however, in the school certificate books, I noticed that she spelt it in various ways, while her handwriting left no doubt as to her unfitness to teach. She herself also acknowledged that she could not keep the register . . . In a second school I found the schoolroom 15 feet long, and 10 feet wide, and counted in this space 75 children, who were gobbling something unintelligible[56] But it is not only in the miserable places above referred to that the children obtain certificates of school attendance without having received instruction of any value, for in many schools where there is a competent teacher, his efforts are of little avail from the distracting crowd of children of all ages, from infants of 3 years old and upwards; his livelihood, miserable at the best, depending on the pence received from the greatest number of children whom it is possible to cram into the space. To this is to be added scanty school furniture, deficiency of books, and other materials for teaching, and the depressing effect upon the poor children themselves of a close, noisome atmosphere. I have been in many such schools, where I have seen rows of children doing absolutely nothing; and this is certified as school attendance, and, in statistical returns, such children are set down as being educated.'[57] In Scotland the manufacturers try all they can to do without the children that are obliged to attend school. 'It requires no further argument to prove that the educational clauses of the Factory Act, being held in such disfavour among mill-owners, tend in a great measure to exclude that class of children alike from the employment and the benefit of education contemplated by this Act.'[58] Horribly grotesque does this appear in print works, which are regulated by a special Act. By that Act, 'every child, before being employed in a print work must have attended school for at least 30 days, and not less than 150 hours, during the six months immediately preceding such first day of employment, and during the continuance of its employment in the print works, it must attend for a like period of 30 days, and 150 hours during every successive period of six months . . . The attendance at school must be between 8 a.m. and 6 p.m. No attendance of less than 2 1/2 hours, nor more than 5 hours on any one day, shall be reckoned as part of the 150 hours. Under ordinary circumstances the children attend school morning and afternoon for 30 days, for at least 5 hours each day, and upon the expiration of the 30 days, the statutory total of 150 hours having been attained, having, in their language, made up their book, they return to the print work, where they continue until the six months have expired, when another instalment of school attendance becomes due, and they again seek the school until the book is again made up . . . Many boys having attended school for the required number of hours, when they return to school after the expiration of their six months' work in the print work, are in the same condition as when they first attended school as print-work boys, that they have lost all they gained by their previous school attendance . . . In other print works the children's attendance at school is made to depend altogether upon the exigencies of the work in the establishment. The requisite number of hours is made up each six months, by instalments consisting of from 3 to 5 hours at a time, spreading over, perhaps, the whole six months . . . For instance, the attendance on one day might be from 8 to 11 a.m., on another day from 1 p.m. to 4 p.m., and the child might not appear at school again for several days, when it would attend from 3 p.m. to 6 p.m.; then it might attend for 3 or 4 days consecutively, or for a week, then it would not appear in school for 3 weeks or a month, after that upon some odd days at some odd hours when the operative who employed it chose to spare it; and thus the child was, as it were, buffeted from school to work, from work to school, until the tale of 150 hours was told.'[59]

By the excessive addition of women and children to the ranks of the workers, machinery at last breaks down the resistance which the male operatives in the manufacturing period continued to oppose to the despotism of capital.[60]

B. Prolongation of the Working-Day.

If machinery be the most powerful means for increasing the productiveness of labour – i.e., for shortening the working-time required in the production of a commodity, it becomes in the hands of capital the most powerful means, in those industries first invaded by it, for lengthening the working-day beyond all bounds set by human nature. It creates, on the one hand, new conditions by which capital is enabled to give free scope to this its constant tendency, and on the other hand, new motives with which to whet capital's appetite for the labour of others.

In the first place, in the form of machinery, the implements of labour become automatic, things moving and working independent of the workman. They are thenceforth an industrial *perpetuum mobile*, that would go on producing forever, did it not meet with certain natural obstructions in the weak bodies and the strong wills of its human attendants. The automaton, as capital, and because it is capital, is endowed, in the person of the capitalist, with intelligence and will; it is therefore animated by the longing to reduce to a minimum the resistance offered by that repellent yet elastic natural barrier.[61] This resistance is moreover lessened by the apparent lightness of machine work, and by the more pliant and docile character of the women and children employed on it.[62]

The productiveness of machinery is, as we saw, inversely proportional to the value transferred by it to the product. The longer the life of the machine, the greater is the mass of the products over which the value transmitted by the machine is spread, and the less is the portion of that value added to each single commodity. The active lifetime of a machine is, however, clearly dependent on the length of the working-day, or on the duration of the daily labour-process multiplied by the number of days for which the process is carried on.

The wear and tear of a machine is not exactly proportional to its working-time. And even if it were so, a machine working 16 hours daily for 7 1/2 years, covers as long a working period as, and transmits to the total product no more value than, the same machine would if it worked only 8 hours daily for 15 years. But in the first case the value of the machine would be reproduced twice as quickly as in the latter, and the capitalist would, by this use of the machine, absorb in 7 1/2 years as much surplus-value as in the second case he would in 15.

The material wear and tear of a machine is of two kinds. The one arises from use, as coins wear away by circulating, the other from non-use, as a sword rusts when left in its scabbard. The latter kind is due to the elements. The former is more or less directly proportional, the latter to a certain extent inversely proportional, to the use of the machine.[63]

But in addition to the material wear and tear, a machine also undergoes, what we may call a moral depreciation. It loses exchange-value, either by machines of the same sort being produced cheaper than it, or by better machines entering into competition with it.[64] In both cases, be the machine ever so young and full of life, its value is no longer determined by the labour actually materialised in it, but by the labour-time requisite to reproduce either it or the better machine. It has, therefore, lost value more or less. The shorter the period taken to reproduce its total value, the less is the danger of moral depreciation; and the longer the working-day, the shorter is that period. When machinery is first introduced into an industry, new methods of reproducing it more cheaply follow blow upon blow,[65] and so do improvements, that not only affect individual parts and details of the machine, but its entire build. It is, therefore, in the early days of the life of machinery that this special incentive to the prolongation of the working-day makes itself felt most acutely.[66]

Given the length of the working-day, all other circumstances remaining the same, the exploitation of double the number of workmen demands, not only a doubling of that part of constant capital which is invested in machinery and buildings, but also of that part which is laid out in raw material and auxiliary substances. The lengthening of the working-day, on the other hand, allows of production on an extended scale without any alteration in the amount of capital laid out on machinery and buildings.[67] Not only is there, therefore, an increase of surplus-value, but the outlay necessary to obtain it diminishes. It is true that this takes place, more or less, with every lengthening of the working-day; but in the case under consideration, the change is more marked, because the capital converted into the instruments of labour preponderates to a greater degree.[68] The development of the factory system fixes a constantly increasing portion of the capital in a form, in which, on the one hand, its value is capable of continual self-expansion, and in which, on the other hand, it loses both use-value and exchange-value whenever it loses contact with living labour. 'When a labourer,' said Mr Ashworth, a cotton magnate, to Professor Nassau W. Senior, 'lays down his spade, he renders useless, for that period, a capital worth eighteen-pence. When one of our people leaves the mill, he renders useless a capital that has cost £100,000.'[69] Only fancy! making 'useless' for a single moment, a capital that has cost £100,000! It is, in truth, monstrous, that a single one of our people should ever leave the factory! The increased use of machinery, as Senior after the instruction he received from Ashworth clearly perceives, makes a constantly increasing lengthening of the working-day 'desirable'. [70]

Machinery produces relative surplus-value; not only by directly depreciating the value of labour power, and by indirectly cheapening the same through cheapening the commodities that enter into its reproduction, but also, when it is first introduced sporadically into an industry, by converting the labour employed by the owner of that machinery, into labour of a higher degree and greater efficacy, by raising the social value of the article produced above its individual value, and thus enabling the capitalist to replace the value of a day's labour power by a smaller portion of the value of a day's product. During this transition period, when the use of machinery is a sort of monopoly, the profits are therefore exceptional, and the capitalist endeavours to exploit thoroughly 'the sunny time of this his first love', by prolonging the working-day as much as possible. The magnitude of the profit whets his appetite for more profit.

As the use of machinery becomes more general in a particular industry, the social value of the product sinks down to its individual value, and the law that surplus-value does not arise from the labour power that has been replaced by the machinery, but from the labour power actually employed in working with the machinery, asserts itself. Surplus-value arises from variable capital alone, and we saw that the amount of surplus-value depends on two factors, viz., the rate of surplus-value and the number of the workmen simultaneously employed. Given the length of the working-day, the rate of surplus-value is determined by the relative duration of the necessary labour and of the surplus-labour in a day. The number of the labourers simultaneously employed depends, on its side, on the ratio of the variable to the constant capital. Now, however much the use of machinery may increase the surplus-labour at the expense of the necessary labour by heightening the productiveness of labour, it is clear that it attains this result, only by diminishing the number of workmen employed by a given amount of capital. It converts what was formerly variable capital, invested in labour power, into machinery which, being constant capital, does not produce surplus-value. It is impossible, for instance, to squeeze as much surplus-value out of 2 as out of 24 labourers. If each of these 24 men gives only one hour of surplus-labour in 12, the 24 men give together 24 hours of surplus-labour, while 24 hours is the total labour of the two men. Hence, the application of machinery to the production of surplus-value implies a contradiction which is immanent in it, since of the two factors of the surplus-value created by a given amount of capital, one, the rate of surplus-value, cannot be increased, except by diminishing the other, the number of workmen. This contradiction comes to light, as soon as by the general employment of machinery in a given industry, the value of the machine-produced commodity regulates the value of all commodities of the same sort; and it is this contradiction, that in its turn, drives the capitalist, without his being conscious of the fact,[71] to excessive lengthening of the working-day, in order that he may compensate the decrease in the relative number of labourers exploited, by an increase not only of the relative, but of the absolute surplus-labour.

If, then, the capitalistic employment of machinery, on the one hand, supplies new and powerful motives to an excessive lengthening of the working-day, and radically changes, as well the methods of labour, as also the character of the social working organism, in such a manner as to break down all opposition to this tendency, on the other hand it produces, partly by opening out to the capitalist new strata of the working-class, previously inaccessible to him, partly by setting free the labourers it supplants, a surplus working population,[72] which is compelled to submit to the dictation of capital. Hence that remarkable phenomenon in the history of Modern Industry, that machinery sweeps away every moral and natural restriction on the length of the working-day. Hence, too, the economic paradox, that the most powerful instrument for shortening labour-time, becomes the most unfailing means for placing every moment of the labourer's time and that of his family, at the disposal of the capitalist for the purpose of expanding the value of his capital. 'If,' dreamed Aristotle, the greatest thinker of antiquity, 'if every tool, when summoned, or even of its own accord, could do the work that befits it, just as the creations of Daedalus moved of themselves, or the tripods of Hephaestos went of their own accord to their sacred work, if the weavers' shuttles were to weave of themselves, then there would be no need either of apprentices for the master workers, or of slaves for the lords.'[73] And Antipatros, a Greek poet of the time of Cicero, hailed the invention of the water-wheel for grinding corn, an invention that is the elementary form of all machinery, as the giver of freedom to female slaves, and the bringer back of the golden age.[74] Oh! those heathens! They understood, as the learned Bastiat, and before him the still wiser MacCulloch have discovered, nothing of Political Economy and Christianity. They did not, for example, comprehend that machinery is the surest means of lengthening the working-day. They perhaps excused the slavery of one on the ground that it was a means to the full development of another. But to preach slavery of the masses, in order that a few crude and half-educated *parvenus*, might become 'eminent spinners', 'extensive sausage-makers', and 'influential shoe-black dealers', to do this, they lacked the bump of Christianity.

C. Intensification of Labour.

The immoderate lengthening of the working-day, produced by machinery in the hands of capital, leads to a reaction on the part of society, the very sources of whose life are menaced; and, thence, to a normal working-day whose length is fixed by law. Thenceforth a phenomenon that we have already met with, namely, the intensification of labour, develops into great importance. Our analysis of absolute surplus-value had reference primarily to the extension or duration of the labour, its intensity being assumed as given. We now proceed to consider the substitution of a more intensified labour for labour of more extensive duration, and the degree of the former.

It is self-evident, that in proportion as the use of machinery spreads, and the experience of a special class of workmen habituated to machinery accumulates, the rapidity and intensity of labour increase as a natural consequence. Thus in England, during half a century, lengthening of the working-day went hand in hand with increasing intensity of factory labour. Nevertheless the reader will clearly see, that where we have labour, not carried on by fits and starts, but repeated day after day with unvarying uniformity, a point must inevitably be reached, where extension of the working-day and intensity of the labour mutually exclude one another, in such a way that lengthening of the working-day becomes compatible only with a lower degree of intensity, and a higher degree of intensity, only with a shortening of the working-day. So soon as the gradually surging revolt of the working-class compelled Parliament to shorten compulsorily the hours of labour, and to begin by imposing a normal working-day on factories proper, so soon consequently as an increased production of surplus-value by the prolongation of the working-day was once for all put a stop to, from that moment capital threw itself with all its might into the production of relative surplus-value, by hastening on the further improvement of machinery. At the same time a change took place in the nature of relative surplus-value. Generally speaking, the mode of producing relative surplus-value consists in raising the productive power of the workman, so as to enable him to produce more in a given time with the same expenditure of labour. Labour-time continues to transmit as before the same value to the total product, but this unchanged amount of exchange-value is spread over more use-value; hence the value of each single commodity sinks. Otherwise, however, so soon as the compulsory shortening of the hours of labour takes place, the immense impetus it gives the development of productive power, and to economy in the means of production, imposes on the workman increased expenditure of labour in a given time, heightened tension of labour power, and closer filling up of the pores of the working-day, or condensation of labour to a degree that is attainable only within the limits of the shortened working-day. This condensation of a greater mass of labour into a given period thenceforward counts for what it really is, a greater quantity of labour. In addition to a measure of its extension, i.e., duration, labour now acquires a measure of its intensity or of the degree of its condensation or density.[75] The denser hour of the ten hours' working-day contains more labour, i.e., expended labour power. than the more porous hour of the twelve hours' working-day. The product therefore of one of the former hours has as much or more value than has the product of 1 1/5 of the latter hours. Apart from the increased yield of relative surplus-value through the heightened productiveness of labour, the same mass of value is now produced for the capitalist say by 3 1/3 hours of surplus-labour, and 6 2/3 hours of necessary labour, as was previously produced by four hours of surplus-labour and eight hours of necessary labour.

We now come to the question: How is the labour intensified?

The first effect of shortening the working-day results from the self-evident law, that the efficiency of labour power is in an inverse ratio to the duration of its expenditure. Hence, within certain limits what is lost by shortening the duration is gained by the increasing tension of labour power. That the workman moreover really does expend more labour power, is ensured by the mode in which the capitalist pays him.[76] In those industries, such as potteries, where machinery plays little or no part, the introduction of the Factory Acts has strikingly shown that the mere shortening of the working-day increases to a wonderful degree the regularity, uniformity, order, continuity, and energy of the labour.[77] It seemed, however, doubtful whether this effect was produced in the factory proper, where the dependence of the workman on the continuous and uniform motion of the machinery had already created the strictest discipline. Hence, when in 1844 the reduction of the working-day to less than twelve hours was being debated, the masters almost unanimously declared 'that their overlookers in the different rooms took good care that the hands lost no time,' that 'the extent of vigilance and attention on the part of the workmen was hardly capable of being increased,' and, therefore, that the speed of the machinery and other conditions remaining unaltered, 'to expect in a well-managed factory any important result from increased attention of the workmen was an absurdity.'[78] This assertion was contradicted by experiments. Mr Robert Gardner reduced the hours of labour in his two large factories at Preston, on and after the 20th April, 1844, from twelve to eleven hours a day. The result of about a year's working was that 'the same amount of product for the same cost was received, and the workpeople as a whole earned in eleven hours as much wages as they did before in twelve.'[79] I pass over the experiments made in the spinning and carding rooms, because they were accompanied by an increase of 2% in the speed of the machines. But in the weaving department, where, moreover, many sorts of figured fancy articles were woven, there was not the slightest alteration in the conditions of the work. The result was: 'From 6th January to 20th April, 1844, with a twelve hours' day, average weekly wages of each hand 10s. 1 1/2d.; from 20th April to 29th June, 1844, with day of eleven hours, average weekly wages 10s. 3 1/2d.'[80] Here we have more produced in eleven hours than previously in twelve, and entirely in consequence of more steady application and economy of time by the workpeople. While they got the same wages and gained one hour of spare time, the capitalist got the same amount produced and saved the cost of coal, gas, and other such items, for one hour. Similar experiments, and with the like success, were carried out in the mills of Messrs Horrocks and Jacson.[81]

The shortening of the hours of labour creates, to begin with, the subjective conditions for the condensation of labour, by enabling the workman to exert more strength in a given time. So soon as that shortening becomes compulsory, machinery becomes in the hands of capital the objective means, systematically employed for squeezing out more labour in a given time. This is effected in two ways: by increasing the speed of the machinery, and by giving the workman more machinery to tent. Improved construction of the machinery is necessary, partly because without it greater pressure cannot be put on the workman, and partly because the shortened hours of labour force the capitalist to exercise the strictest watch over the cost of production. The improvements in the steam-engine have increased the piston speed, and at the same time have made it possible, by means of a greater economy of power, to drive with the same or even a smaller consumption of coal more machinery with the same engine. The improvements in the transmitting mechanism have lessened friction, and, what so strikingly distinguishes modern from the older machinery, have reduced the diameter and weight of the shafting to a constantly decreasing minimum. Finally, the improvements in the operative machines have, while reducing their size, increased their speed and efficiency, as in the modern power-loom; or, while increasing the size of their framework, have also increased the extent and number of their working parts, as in spinning-mules, or have added to the speed of these working parts by imperceptible alterations of detail, such as those which ten years ago increased the speed of the spindles in self-acting mules by one-fifth.

The reduction of the working-day to 12 hours dates in England from 1832. In 1836 a manufacturer stated: 'The labour now undergone in the factories is much greater than it used to be . . . compared with thirty or forty years ago . . . owing to the greater attention and activity required by the greatly increased speed which is given to the machinery.'[82] In the year 1844, Lord Ashley, now Lord Shaftesbury, made in the House of Commons the following statements, supported by documentary evidence:

'The labour performed by those engaged in the processes of manufacture, is three times as great as in the beginning of such operations. Machinery has executed, no doubt, the work that would demand the sinews of millions of men; but it has also prodigiously multiplied the labour of those who are governed by its fearful movements . . . In 1815, the labour of following a pair of mules spinning cotton of No. 40 – reckoning 12 hours to the working-day – involved a necessity of walking 8 miles. In 1832, the distance travelled in following a pair of mules, spinning cotton yarn of the same number, was 20 miles, and frequently more. In 1835' (query – 1815 or 1825?) 'the spinner put up daily, on each of these mules, 820 stretches, making a total of 1,640 stretches in the course of the day. In 1832, the spinner put up on each mule 2,200 stretches, making a total of 4,400. In 1844, 2,400 stretches, making a total of 4,800; and in some cases the amount of labour required is even still greater . . . I have another document sent to me in 1842, stating that the labour is progressively increasing – increasing not only because the distance to be travelled is greater, but because the quantity of goods produced is multiplied, while the hands are fewer in proportion than before; and, moreover, because an inferior species of cotton is now often spun, which it is more difficult to work . . . In the carding-room there has also been a great increase of labour. One person there does the work formerly divided between two. In the weaving-room, where a vast number of persons are employed, and principally females . . . the labour has increased within the last few years fully 10 per cent., owing to the increased speed of the machinery in spinning. In 1838, the number of hanks spun per week was 18,000, in 1843 it amounted to 21,000. In 1819, the number of picks in power-loom-weaving per minute was 60 – in 1842 it was 140, showing a vast increase of labour.'[83]

In the face of this remarkable intensity of labour which had already been reached in 1844 under the Twelve Hours' Act, there appeared to be a justification for the assertion made at that time by the English manufacturers, that any further progress in that direction was impossible, and therefore that every further reduction of the hours of labour meant a lessened production. The apparent correctness of their reasons will be best shown by the following contemporary statement by Leonard Horner, the factory inspector, their ever watchful censor.

'Now, as the quantity produced must, in the main, be regulated by the speed of the machinery, it must be the interest of the mill-owner to drive it at the utmost rate of speed consistent with these following conditions, viz., the preservation of the machinery from too rapid deterioration; the preservation of the quality of the article manufactured; and the capability of the workman to follow the motion without a greater exertion than he can sustain for a constancy. One of the most important problems, therefore, which the owner of a factory has to solve is to find out the maximum speed at which he can run, with a due regard to the above conditions. It frequently happens that he finds he has gone too fast, that breakages and bad work more than counterbalance the increased speed, and that he is obliged to slacken his pace. I therefore concluded, that as an active and intelligent mill-owner would find out the safe maximum, it would not be possible to produce as much in eleven hours as in twelve. I further assumed that the operative paid by piecework, would exert himself to the utmost consistent with the power of continuing at the same rate.' [84] Horner, therefore, came to the conclusion that a reduction of the working-hours below twelve would necessarily diminish production? [85] He himself, ten years later, cites his opinion of 1845 in proof of how much he under-estimated in that year the elasticity of machinery, and of man's labour power, both of which are simultaneously stretched to an extreme by the compulsory shortening of the working-day.

We now come to the period that follows the introduction of the Ten Hours' Act in 1847 into the English cotton, woollen, silk, and flax mills.

'The speed of the spindles has increased upon throstles 500, and upon mules 1,000 revolutions a minute, i.e., the speed of the throstle spindle, which in 1839 was 4,500 times a minute, is now (1862) 5,000; and of the mule spindle, that was 5,000, is now 6,000 times a minute, amounting in the former case to one-tenth, and in the second case to one-fifth additional increase.' [86] James Nasmyth, the eminent civil engineer of Patricroft, near Manchester, explained in a letter to Leonard Horner, written in 1852, the nature of the improvements in the steam-engine that had been made between the years 1848 and 1852. After remarking that the horse-power of steam-engines, being always estimated in the official returns according to the power of similar engines in 1828,[87] is only nominal, and can serve only as an index of their real power, he goes on to say: 'I am confident that from the same weight of steam-engine machinery, we are now obtaining at least 50 per cent. more duty or work performed on the average, and that in many cases the identical steam-engines which in the days of the restricted speed of 220 feet per minute, yielded 50 horsepower, are now yielding upwards of 100 . . . ' 'The modern steam-engine of 100 horse-power is capable of being driven at a much greater force than formerly, arising from improvements in its construction, the capacity and construction of the boilers, &c . . . ' 'Although the same number of hands are employed in proportion to the horse-power as at former periods, there are fewer hands employed in proportion to the machinery.'[88] 'In the year 1850, the factories of the United Kingdom employed 134,217 nominal horse-power to give motion to 25,638,716 spindles and 301,445 looms. The number of spindles and looms in 1856 was respectively 33,503,580 of the former, and 369,205 of the latter, which, reckoning the force of the nominal horse-power required to be the same as in 1850, would require a force equal to 175,000 horses, but the actual power given in the return for 1856 is 161,435, less by above 10,000 horses than, calculating upon the basis of the return of 1850, the factories ought to have required in 1856.'[89] 'The facts thus brought out by the Return (of 1856) appear to be that the factory system is increasing rapidly; that although the same number of hands are employed in proportion to the horse-power as at former periods, there are fewer hands employed in proportion to the machinery; that the steam-engine is enabled to drive an increased weight of machinery by economy of force and other methods, and that an increased quantity of work can be turned off by improvements in machinery, and in methods of manufacture, by increase of speed of the machinery, and by a variety of other causes.' [90]

'The great improvements made in machines of every kind have raised their productive power very much. Without any doubt, the shortening of the hours of labour . . . gave the impulse to these improvements. The latter, combined with the more intense strain on the workman, have had the effect, that at least as much is produced in the shortened (by two hours or one-sixth) working-day as was previously produced during the longer one.'[91]

One fact is sufficient to show how greatly the wealth of the manufacturers increased along with the more intense exploitation of labour power. From 1838 to 1850, the average proportional increase in English cotton and other factories was 32%, while from 1850 to 1856 it amounted to 86%.

But however great the progress of English industry had been during the 8 years from 1848 to 1856 under the influence of a working-day of 10 hours, it was far surpassed during the next period of 6 years from 1856 to 1862. In silk factories, for instance, there were in 1856, spindles 1,093,799; in 1862, 1,388,544; in 1856, looms 9,260; in 1862, 10,709. But the number of operatives was, in 1856, 56,131; in 1862, 52,429. The increase in the spindles was therefore 26.9% and in the looms 15.6%, while the number of the operatives decreased 7%. In the year 1850 there were employed in worsted mills 875,830 spindles;

in 1856, 1,324,549 (increase 51.2%), and in 1862, 1,289,172 (decrease 2.7%). But if we deduct the doubling spindles that figure in the numbers for 1856, but not in those for 1862, it will be found that after 1856 the number of spindles remained nearly stationary. On the other hand, after 1850, the speed of the spindles and looms was in many cases doubled. The number of power-looms in worsted mills was, in 1850, 32,617; in 1856, 38,956; in 1862, 43,048. The number of the operatives was, in 1850, 79,737; in 1856, 87,794; in 1862, 86,063; included in these, however, the children under 14 years of age were; in 1850, 9,956; in 1856, 11,228; in 1862, 13,178. In spite, therefore, of the greatly increased number of looms in 1862, compared with 1856, the total number of the workpeople employed decreased, and that of the children exploited increased.[92]

On the 27th April, 1863, Mr Ferrand said in the House of Commons: 'I have been informed by delegates from 16 districts of Lancashire and Cheshire, in whose behalf I speak, that the work in the factories is, in consequence of the improvements in machinery, constantly on the increase. Instead of as formerly one person with two helps tenting two looms, one person now tents three looms without help, and it is no uncommon thing for one person to tent four. Twelve hours' work, as is evident from the facts adduced, is now compressed into less than 10 hours. It is therefore self-evident, to what an enormous extent the toil of the factory operative has increased during the last 10 years.'[93]

Although, therefore, the Factory Inspectors unceasingly and with justice, commend the results of the Acts of 1844 and 1850, yet they admit that the shortening of the hours of labour has already called forth such an intensification of the labour as is injurious to the health of the workman and to his capacity for work. 'In most of the cotton, worsted, and silk mills, an exhausting state of excitement necessary to enable the workers satisfactorily to mind the machinery, the motion of which has been greatly accelerated within the last few years, seems to me not unlikely to be one of the causes of that excess of mortality from lung disease, which Dr Greenhow has pointed out in his recent report on this subject.'[94] There cannot be the slightest doubt that the tendency that urges capital, so soon as a prolongation of the hours of labour is once for all forbidden, to compensate itself, by a systematic heightening of the intensity of labour, and to convert every improvement in machinery into a more perfect means of exhausting the workman, must soon lead to a state of things in which a reduction of the hours of labour will again be inevitable.[95] On the other hand, the rapid advance of English industry between 1848 and the present time, under the influence of a day of 10 hours, surpasses the advance made between 1833 and 1847, when the day was 12 hours long, by far more than the latter surpasses the advance made during the half century after the first introduction of the factory system, when the working-day was without limits.[96]

Section 4. The Factory.

At the commencement of this chapter we considered that which we may call the body of the factory, i.e., machinery organised into a system. We there saw how machinery, by annexing the labour of women and children, augments the number of human beings who form the material for capitalistic exploitation, how it confiscates the whole of the workman's disposable time, by immoderate extension of the hours of labour, and how finally its progress, which allows of enormous increase of production in shorter and shorter periods, serves as a means of systematically getting more work done in a shorter time, or of exploiting labour power more intensely. We now turn to the factory as a whole, and that in its most perfect form.

Dr Ure, the Pindar of the automatic factory, describes it, on the one hand, as 'Combined co-operation of many orders of workpeople, adult and young, in tending with assiduous skill, a system of productive machines, continuously impelled by a central power' (the prime mover); on the other hand, as 'a vast automaton, composed of various mechanical and intellectual organs, acting in uninterrupted concert for the production of a common object, all of them being subordinate to a self-regulated moving force.' These two descriptions are far from being identical. In one, the collective labourer, or social body of labour, appears as the dominant subject, and the mechanical automaton as the object; in the other, the automaton itself is the subject, and the workmen are merely conscious organs, co-ordinate with the unconscious organs of the automaton, and together with them, subordinated to the central moving-power. The first description is applicable to every possible employment of machinery on a large scale, the second is characteristic of its use by capital, and therefore of the modern factory system. Ure prefers therefore, to describe the central machine, from which the motion comes, not only as an automaton, but as an autocrat. 'In these spacious halls the benignant power of steam summons around him his myriads of willing menials.'[97]

Along with the tool, the skill of the workman in handling it passes over to the machine. The capabilities of the tool are emancipated from the restraints that are inseparable from human labour power. Thereby the technical foundation on which is based the division of labour in Manufacture, is swept away. Hence, in the place of the hierarchy of specialised workmen that characterises manufacture, there steps, in the automatic factory, a tendency to equalise and reduce to one and the same level every kind of work that has to be done by the minders of the machines;[98] in the place of the artificially produced differentiations of the detail workmen, step the natural differences of age and sex.

So far as division of labour re-appears in the factory, it is primarily a distribution of the workmen among the specialised machines; and of masses of workmen, not however organised into groups, among the various departments of the factory, in each of which they work at a number of similar machines placed together; their co-operation, therefore, is only simple. The organised group, peculiar to manufacture, is replaced by the connection between the head workman and his few assistants. The essential division is, into workmen who are actually employed on the machines (among whom are included a few who look after the engine), and into mere attendants (almost exclusively children) of these workmen. Among the attendants are reckoned more or less all 'Feeders' who supply the machines with the material to be worked. In addition to these two principal classes, there is a numerically unimportant class of persons, whose occupation it is to look after the whole of the machinery and repair it from time to time; such as engineers, mechanics, joiners, &c. This is a superior class of workmen, some of them scientifically educated, others brought up to a trade; it is distinct from the factory operative class, and merely aggregated to it.[99] This division of labour is purely technical.

To work at a machine, the workman should be taught from childhood, in order that he may learn to adapt his own movements to the uniform and unceasing motion of an automaton. When the machinery, as a whole, forms a system of manifold machines, working simultaneously and in concert, the co-operation based upon it, requires the distribution of various groups of workmen among the different kinds of machines. But the employment of machinery does away with the necessity of crystallising this distribution after the manner of Manufacture, by the constant annexation of a particular man to a particular function.[100] Since the motion of the whole system does not proceed from the workman, but from the machinery, a change of persons can take place at any time without an interruption of the work. The most striking proof of this is afforded by the relays system, put into operation by the manufacturers during their revolt from 1848–1850. Lastly, the quickness with which machine work is learnt by young people, does away with the necessity of bringing up for exclusive employment by machinery, a special class of operatives.[101] With regard to the work of the mere attendants, it can, to some extent, be replaced in the mill by machines,[102] and owing to its extreme simplicity, it allows of a rapid and constant change of the individuals burdened with this drudgery.

Although then, technically speaking, the old system of division of labour is thrown overboard by machinery, it hangs on in the factory, as a traditional habit handed down from Manufacture, and is afterwards systematically re-moulded and established in a more hideous form by capital, as a means of exploiting labour power. The life-long speciality of handling one and the same tool, now becomes the life-long speciality of serving one and the same machine. Machinery is put to a wrong use, with the object of transforming the workman, from his very childhood, into a part of a detail-machine.[103] In this way, not only are the expenses of his reproduction considerably lessened, but at the same time his helpless dependence upon the factory as a whole, and therefore upon the capitalist, is rendered complete. Here as everywhere else, we must distinguish between the increased productiveness due to the development of the social process of production, and that due to the capitalist exploitation of that process. In handicrafts and manufacture, the workman makes use of a tool, in the factory, the machine makes use of him. There the movements of the instrument of labour proceed from him, here it is the movements of the machine that he must follow. In manufacture the workmen are parts of a living mechanism. In the factory we have a lifeless mechanism independent of the workman, who becomes its mere living appendage. 'The miserable routine of endless drudgery and toil in which the same mechanical process is gone through over and over again, is like the labour of Sisyphus. The burden of labour, like the rock, keeps ever falling back on the worn-out labourer.'[104] At the same time that factory work exhausts the nervous system to the uttermost, it does away with the many-sided play of the muscles, and confiscates every atom of freedom, both in bodily and intellectual activity.[105] The lightening of the labour, even, becomes a sort of torture, since the machine does not free the labourer from work, but deprives the work of all interest. Every kind of capitalist production, in so far as it is not only a labour-process, but also a process of creating surplus-value, has this in common, that it is not the workman that employs the instruments of labour, but the instruments of labour that employ the workman. But it is only in the factory system that this inversion for the first time acquires technical and palpable reality. By means of its conversion into an automaton, the instrument of labour confronts the labourer, during the labour-process, in the shape of capital, of dead labour, that dominates, and pumps dry, living labour power. The separation of the intellectual powers of production from the manual labour, and the conversion of those powers into the might of capital over labour, is, as we have already shown. finally completed by modern industry erected on the foundation of machinery. The special skill of each individual insignificant factory operative vanishes as an infinitesimal quantity before the science, the gigantic physical forces, and the mass of labour that are embodied in the factory mechanism and, together with that mechanism, constitute the power of the 'master'. This 'master', therefore, in whose brain the machinery and his monopoly of it are inseparably united, whenever he falls out with his 'hands', contemptuously tells them: 'The factory operatives should keep in wholesome remembrance the fact that theirs is really a low species of skilled labour; and that there is none which is more easily acquired, or of its quality more amply remunerated, or which by a short training of the least expert can be more quickly, as well as abundantly, acquired . . . The master's machinery really plays a far more important part in the business of production than the labour and the skill of the operative, which six months' education can teach, and a common labourer can learn.'[106] The technical subordination of the workman to the uniform motion of the instruments of labour, and the peculiar composition of the body of workpeople, consisting as it does of individuals of both sexes and of all ages, give rise to a barrack discipline, which is elaborated into a complete system in the factory, and which fully develops the before-mentioned labour of overlooking, thereby dividing the workpeople into operatives and overlookers, into private soldiers and sergeants of an industrial army. 'The main difficulty [in the automatic factory] . . . lay . . . above all in training human beings to renounce their desultory habits of work, and to identify themselves with the unvarying regularity of the complex automaton. To devise and administer a successful code of factory discipline, suited to the necessities of factory diligence, was the Herculean enterprise, the noble achievement of Arkwright! Even at the present day, when the system is perfectly organised and its labour lightened to the utmost, it is found nearly impossible to convert persons past the age of puberty, into useful factory hands.'[107] The factory code in which capital formulates, like a private legislator, and at his own good will, his autocracy over his workpeople, unaccompanied by that division of responsibility, in other matters so much approved of by the bourgeoisie, and unaccompanied by the still more approved representative system, this code is but the capitalistic caricature of that social regulation of the labour-process which becomes requisite in co-operation on a great scale, and in the employment in common, of instruments of labour and especially of machinery. The place of the slave-driver's lash is taken by the overlooker's book of penalties. All punishments naturally resolve themselves into fines and deductions from wages, and the law-giving talent of the factory Lycurgus so arranges matters, that a violation of his laws is, if possible, more profitable to him than the keeping of them.[108] We shall here merely allude to the material conditions under which factory labour is carried on. Every organ of sense is injured in an equal degree by artificial elevation of the temperature, by the dust-laden atmosphere, by the deafening noise, not to mention danger to life and limb among the thickly crowded machinery, which, with the regularity of the seasons, issues its list of the killed and wounded in the industrial battle.[109] Economy of the social means of production, matured and forced as in a hothouse by the factory system, is turned, in the hands of capital, into systematic robbery of what is necessary for the life of the workman while he is at work, robbery of space, light, air, and of protection to his person against the dangerous and unwholesome accompaniments of the productive process, not to mention the robbery of appliances for the comfort of the workman.[110] Is Fourier wrong when he calls factories 'tempered *bagnos*'?[111]

Section 5. The Strife Between Workman and Machine.

The contest between the capitalist and the wage-labourer dates back to the very origin of capital. It raged on throughout the whole manufacturing period.[112] But only since the introduction of machinery has the workman fought against the instrument of labour itself, the material embodiment of capital. He revolts against this particular form of the means of production, as being the material basis of the capitalist mode of production.

In the 17th century nearly all Europe experienced revolts of the workpeople against the ribbon-loom, a machine for weaving ribbons and trimmings, called in Germany *Bandmühle*, *Schnurmühle*, and *Mühlenstuhl*. These machines were invented in Germany. Abbé Lancellotti, in a work that appeared in Venice in 1636, but which was written in 1579, says as follows: 'Anthony Müller of Danzig saw about 50 years ago in that town, a very ingenious machine, which weaves 4 to 6 pieces at once. But the Mayor being apprehensive that this invention might throw a large number of workmen on the streets, caused the inventor to be secretly strangled or drowned.' In Leyden, this machine was not used till 1629; there the riots of the ribbon-weavers at length compelled the Town Council to prohibit it. '*In hac urbe,*' says Boxhorn (*Inst. Pol.*, 1663), referring to the introduction of this machine into Leyden, '*ante hos viginti circiter annos instrumentum quidam invenerunt textorium, quo solus plus panni et facilius conficere poterat, quan plures aequali tempore. Hinc turbae ortae et querulae textorum, tandemque usus hujus instrumenti a magistratu prohibitus est.*' After making various decrees more or less prohibitive against this loom in 1632, 1639, &c., the States General of Holland at length permitted it to be used, under certain conditions, by the decree of the 15th December, 1661. It was also prohibited in Cologne in 1676, at the same time that its introduction into England was causing disturbances among the workpeople. By an Imperial Edict of 19th Feb., 1685, its use was forbidden throughout all Germany. In Hamburg it was burnt in public by order of the Senate. The Emperor Charles VI, on 9th Feb., 1719, renewed the edict of 1685, and not till 1765 was its use openly allowed in the Electorate of Saxony. This machine, which shook Europe to its foundations, was in fact the precursor of the mule and the power-loom, and of the industrial revolution of the 18th century. It enabled a totally inexperienced boy, to set the whole loom with all its shuttles in motion, by simply moving a rod backwards and forwards, and in its improved form produced from 40 to 50 pieces at once.

About 1630, a wind-sawmill, erected near London by a Dutchman, succumbed to the excesses of the populace. Even as late as the beginning of the 18th century, sawmills driven by water overcame the opposition of the people, supported as it was by Parliament, only with great difficulty. No sooner had Everet in 1758 erected the first wool-shearing machine that was driven by water-power, than it was set on fire by 100,000 people who had been thrown out of work. Fifty thousand workpeople, who had previously lived by carding wool, petitioned Parliament against Arkwright's scribbling mills and carding engines. The enormous destruction of machinery that occurred in the English manufacturing districts during the first 15 years of this century, chiefly caused by the employment of the power-loom, and known as the Luddite movement, gave the anti-Jacobin governments of a Sidmouth, a Castlereagh, and the like, a pretext for the most reactionary and forcible measures. It took both time and experience before the workpeople learnt to distinguish between machinery and its employment by capital, and to direct their attacks, not against the material instruments of production, but against the mode in which they are used.[113]

The contests about wages in Manufacture, presuppose manufacture, and are in no sense directed against its existence. The opposition against the establishment of new manufactures, proceeds from the guilds and privileged towns, not from the workpeople. Hence the writers of the manufacturing period treat the division of labour chiefly as a means of virtually supplying a deficiency of labourers, and not as a means of actually displacing those in work. This distinction is self-evident. If it be said that 100 millions of people would be required in

England to spin with the old spinning-wheel the cotton that is now spun with mules by 500,000 people, this does not mean that the mules took the place of those millions who never existed. It means only this, that many millions of workpeople would be required to replace the spinning machinery. If, on the other hand, we say, that in England the power-loom threw 800,000 weavers on the streets, we do not refer to existing machinery, that would have to be replaced by a definite number of workpeople, but to a number of weavers in existence who were actually replaced or displaced by the looms. During the manufacturing period, handicraft labour, altered though it was by division of labour, was yet the basis. The demands of the new colonial markets could not be satisfied owing to the relatively small number of town operatives handed down from the middle ages, and the manufactures proper opened out new fields of production to the rural population, driven from the land by the dissolution of the feudal system. At that time, therefore, division of labour and co-operation in the workshops, were viewed more from the positive aspect, that they made the workpeople more productive.[114] Long before the period of Modern Industry, co-operation and the concentration of the instruments of labour in the hands of a few, gave rise, in numerous countries where these methods were applied in agriculture, to great, sudden and forcible revolutions in the modes of production, and consequentially, in the conditions of existence, and the means of employment of the rural populations. But this contest at first takes place more between the large and the small landed proprietors, than between capital and wage-labour; on the other hand, when the labourers are displaced by the instruments of labour, by sheep, horses, &c., in this case force is directly resorted to in the first instance as the prelude to the industrial revolution. The labourers are first driven from the land, and then come the sheep. Land grabbing on a great scale, such as was perpetrated in England, is the first step in creating a field for the establishment of agriculture on a great scale. Hence this subversion of agriculture puts on, at first, more the appearance of a political revolution.

The instrument of labour, when it takes the form of a machine, immediately becomes a competitor of the workman himself.[115] The self-expansion of capital by means of machinery is thenceforward directly proportional to the number of the workpeople, whose means of livelihood have been destroyed by that machinery. The whole system of capitalist production is based on the fact that the workman sells his labour power as a commodity. Division of labour specialises this labour power, by reducing it to skill in handling a particular tool. So soon as the handling of this tool becomes the work of a machine, then, with the use-value, the exchange-value too, of the workman's labour power vanishes; the workman becomes unsaleable, like paper money thrown out of currency by legal enactment. That portion of the working-class, thus by machinery rendered superfluous, i.e., no longer immediately necessary for the self-expansion of capital, either goes to the wall in the unequal contest of the old handicrafts and manufactures with machinery, or else floods all the more easily accessible branches of industry, swamps the labour-market, and sinks the price of labour power below its value. It is impressed upon the workpeople, as a great consolation, first, that their sufferings are only temporary ('a temporary inconvenience'), secondly, that machinery acquires the mastery over the whole of a given field of production, only by degrees, so that the extent and intensity of its destructive effect is diminished. The first consolation neutralises the second. When machinery seizes on an industry by degrees, it produces chronic misery among the operatives who compete with it. Where the transition is rapid, the effect is acute and felt by great masses. History discloses no tragedy more horrible than the gradual extinction of the English hand-loom weavers, an extinction that was spread over several decades, and finally sealed in 1838. Many of them died of starvation, many with families vegetated for a long time on 2 1/2 d. a day.[116] On the other hand, the English cotton machinery produced an acute effect in India. The Governor General reported 1834–35: 'The misery hardly finds a parallel in the history of commerce. The bones of the cotton-weavers are bleaching the plains of India.' No doubt, in turning them out of this 'temporal' world, the machinery caused them no more than 'a temporary inconvenience'. For the rest, since machinery is continually seizing upon new fields of production, its temporary effect is really permanent. Hence, the character of independence and estrangement which the capitalist mode of production as a whole gives to the instruments of labour and to the product, as against the workman, is developed by means of machinery into a thorough antagonism.[117] Therefore, it is with the advent of machinery, that the workman for the first time brutally revolts against the instruments of labour.

The instrument of labour strikes down the labourer. This direct antagonism between the two comes out most strongly, whenever newly introduced machinery competes with handicrafts or manufactures, handed down from former times. But even in Modern Industry the continual improvement of machinery, and the development of the automatic system, has an analogous effect. 'The object of improved machinery is to diminish manual labour, to provide for the performance of a process or the completion of a link in a manufacture by the aid of an iron instead of the human apparatus.'[118] 'The adaptation of power to machinery heretofore moved by hand, is almost of daily occurrence . . . the minor improvements in machinery having for their object economy of power, the production of better work, the turning off more work in the same time, or in supplying the place of a child, a female, or a man, are constant, and although sometimes apparently of no great moment, have somewhat important results.'[119] 'Whenever a process requires peculiar dexterity and steadiness of hand, it is withdrawn, as soon as possible, from the cunning workman, who is prone to irregularities of many kinds, and it is t)laced in charge of a peculiar mechanism, so self-regulating that a child can super-intend it.'[120] 'On the automatic plan skilled labour gets progressively superseded.'[121] 'The effect of improvements in machinery, not merely in superseding the necessity for the employment of the same quantity of adult labour as before, in order to produce a given result, but in substituting one description of human labour for another, the less skilled for the more skilled, juvenile for adult, female for male, causes a fresh disturbance in the rate of wages.'[122] 'The effect of substituting the self-acting mule for the common mule, is to discharge the greater part of the men spinners, and to retain adolescents and children.'[123] The extraordinary power of expansion of the factory system owing to accumulated practical experience, to the mechanical means at hand, and to constant technical progress, was proved to us by the giant strides of that system under the pressure of a shortened working-day. But who, in 1860, the Zenith year of the English cotton industry, would have dreamt of the galloping improvements in machinery, and the corresponding displacement of working people, called into being during the following 3 years, under the stimulus of the American Civil War? A couple of examples from the Reports of the Inspectors of Factories will suffice on this point. A Manchester manufacturer states: 'We formerly had 75 carding engines, now we have 12, doing the same quantity of work . . . We are doing with fewer hands by 14, at a saving in wages of £10 a-week. Our estimated saving in waste is about 10% in the quantity of cotton consumed.' 'In another fine-spinning mill in Manchester, I was informed that through increased speed and the adoption of some self-acting processes, a reduction had been made, in number, of a fourth in one department, and of above half in another, and that the introduction of the combing machine in place of the second carding, had considerably reduced the number of hands formerly employed in the carding-room.' Another spinning-mill is estimated to effect a saving of labour of 10%. The Messrs Gilmour, spinners at Manchester, state: 'In our blowing-room department we consider our expense with new machinery is fully one-third less in wages and hands . . . in the jack-frame and drawing-frame room, about one-third less in expense, and likewise one-third less in hands; in the spinning-room about one-third less in expenses. But this is not all; when our yarn goes to the manufacturers, it is so much better by the application of our new machinery, that they will produce a greater quantity of cloth, and cheaper than from the yarn produced by old machinery.'[124] Mr Redgrave further remarks in the same Report: 'The reduction of hands against increased production is, in fact, constantly taking place, in woollen mills the reduction commenced some time since, and is continuing; a few days since, the master of a school in the neighbourhood of Rochdale said to me, that the great falling off in the girls' school is not only caused by the distress, but by the changes of machinery in the woollen mills, in consequence of which a reduction of 70 short-timers had taken place.'[125]

The following table shows the total result of the mechanical improvements in the English cotton industry due to the American Civil War.

Number of Factories

	1858	1861	1868
England and Wales	2046	2715	2405
Scotland	152	163	131
Ireland	12	9	13
United Kingdom	2210	2887	2549

Number of Power-looms

	1858	1861	1868
England and Wales	275,590	368,125	344,719
Scotland	21,624	30,110	31,864
Ireland	1,633	1,757	2,746
United Kingdom	298,847	399,992	379,329

Number of Spindles

	1858	1861	1868
England and Wales	25,818,576	28,352,152	30,478,228
Scotland	2,041,129	1,915,398	1,397,546
Ireland	150,512	119,944	124,240
United Kingdom	28,010,217	30,387,494	32,000,014

Number of Persons Employed

	1858	1861	1868
England and Wales	341,170	407,598	357,052
Scotland	34,698	41,237	39,809
Ireland	3,345	2,734	4,203
United Kingdom	379,213	451,569	401,064

Hence, between 1861 and 1868, 338 cotton factories disappeared, in other words more productive machinery on a larger scale was concentrated in the hands of a smaller number of capitalists. The number of power-looms decreased by 20,663; but since their product increased in the same period, an improved loom must have yielded more than an old one. Lastly the number of spindles increased by 1,612,541, while the number of operatives decreased by 50,505. The 'temporary' misery inflicted on the workpeople by the cotton-crisis, was heightened, and from being temporary made permanent, by the rapid and persistent progress of machinery.

But machinery not only acts as a competitor who gets the better of the workman, and is constantly on the point of making him superfluous. It is also a power inimical to him, and as such capital proclaims it from the roof tops and as such makes use of it. It is the most powerful weapon for repressing strikes, those periodical revolts of the working-class against the autocracy of capital.[126] According to Gaskell, the steam-engine was from the very first an antagonist of human power, an antagonist that enabled the capitalist to tread under foot the growing claims of the workmen, who threatened the newly born factory system with a crisis.[127] It would be possible to write quite a history of the inventions, made since 1830, for the sole purpose of supplying capital with weapons against the revolts of the working-class. At the head of these in importance, stands the self-acting mule, because it opened up a new epoch in the automatic system.[128]

Nasmyth, the inventor of the steam-hammer, gives the following evidence before the Trades' Union Commission, with regard to the improvements made by him in machinery and introduced in consequence of the wide-spread and long strikes of the engineers in 1851. 'The characteristic feature of our modern mechanical improvements, is the introduction of self-acting tool machinery. What every mechanical workman has now to do, and what every boy can do, is not to work himself but to superintend the beautiful labour of the machine. The whole class of workmen that depend exclusively on their skill, is now done away with. Formerly, I employed four boys to every mechanic. Thanks to these new mechanical combinations, I have reduced the number of grown-up men from 1,500 to 750. The result was a considerable increase in my profits.'

Ure says of a machine used in calico printing: 'At length capitalists sought deliverance from this intolerable bondage' [namely the, in their eyes, burdensome terms of their contracts with the workmen] 'in the resources of science, and were speedily re-instated in their legitimate rule, that of the head over the inferior members.' Speaking of an invention for dressing warps: 'Then the combined malcontents, who fancied themselves impregnably entrenched behind the old lines of division of labour, found their flanks turned and their defences rendered useless by the new mechanical tactics, and were obliged to surrender at discretion.' With regard to the invention of the self-acting mule, he says: 'A creation destined to restore order among the industrious classes . . . This invention confirms the great doctrine already propounded, that when capital enlists science into her service, the refractory hand of labour will always be taught docility.'[129] Although Ure's work appeared 30 years ago, at a time when the factory system was comparatively but little developed, it still perfectly expresses the spirit of the factory, not only by its undisguised cynicism, but also by the nalveté with which it blurts out the stupid contradictions of the capitalist brain. For instance, after propounding the 'doctrine' stated above, that capital, with the aid of science taken into its pay, always reduces the refractory hand of labour to docility, he grows indignant because 'it (physico-mechanical science) has been accused of lending itself to the rich capitalist as an instrument for harassing the poor.' After preaching a long sermon to show how advantageous the rapid development of machinery is to the working-classes, he warns them, that by their obstinacy and their strikes they hasten that development. 'Violent revulsions of this nature,' he says, 'display short-sighted man in the contemptible character of a self-tormentor.' A few pages before he states the contrary. 'Had it not been for the violent collisions and interruptions resulting from erroneous views among the factory operatives, the factory system would have been developed still more rapidly and beneficially for all concerned.' Then he exclaims again: 'Fortunately for the state of society in the cotton districts of Great Britain, the improvements in machinery are gradual.' 'It' (improvement in machinery) 'is said to lower the rate of earnings of adults by displacing a portion of them, and thus rendering their number superabundant as compared with the demand for their labour. It certainly augments the demand for the labour of children and increases the rate of their wages.' On the other hand, this same dispenser of consolation defends the lowness of the children's wages on the ground that it prevents parents from sending their children at too early an age into the factory. The whole of his book is a vindication of a working-day of unrestricted length; that Parliament should forbid children of 13 years to be exhausted by working 12 hours a day, reminds his liberal soul of the darkest days of the middle ages. This does not prevent him from calling upon the factory operatives to thank Providence, who by means of machinery has given them the leisure to think of their 'immortal interests'.[130]

Section 6. The Theory of Compensation as Regards the Workpeople Displaced by Machinery.

James Mill, MacCulloch, Torrens, Senior, John Stuart Mill, and a whole series besides, of bourgeois political economists, insist that all machinery that displaces workmen, simultaneously and necessarily sets free an amount of capital adequate to employ the same identical workmen.[131]

Suppose a capitalist to employ 100 workmen, at £30 a year each, in a carpet factory. The variable capital annually laid out amounts, therefore, to £3,000. Suppose, also, that he discharges 50 of his workmen, and employs the remaining 50 with machinery that costs him £1,500. To simplify matters, we take no account of buildings, coal, &c. Further suppose that the raw material annually consumed costs £3,000, both before and after the change.[132] Is any capital set free by this metamorphosis? Before the change, the total sum of £6,000 consisted half of constant, and half of variable capital. After the change it consists of £4,500 constant (£3,000 raw material and £1,500 machinery), and £1,500 variable capital. The variable capital, instead of being one half, is only one quarter, of the total capital. Instead of being set free, a part of the capital is here locked up in such a way as to cease to be exchanged against labour power: variable has been changed into constant capital. Other things remaining unchanged, the capital of £6,000, can, in future, employ no more than 50 men. With each improvement in the machinery, it will employ fewer. If the newly introduced machinery had cost less than did the labour power and implements displaced by it, if, for instance, instead of costing £1,500, it had cost only £1,000, a variable capital of £1,000 would have been converted into constant capital, and locked up; and a capital of £500 would have been set free. The latter sum, supposing wages unchanged, would form a fund sufficient to employ about 16 out of the 50 men discharged; nay, less than 16, for, in order to be employed as capital, a part of this £500 must now become constant capital, thus leaving only the remainder to be laid out in labour power.

But, suppose, besides, that the making of the new machinery affords employment to a greater number of mechanics, can that be called compensation to the carpet-makers, thrown on the streets? At the best, its construction employs fewer men than its employment displaces. The sum of £1,500 that formerly represented the wages of the discharged carpet-makers, now represents in the shape of machinery: (1) the value of the means of production used in the construction of that machinery, (2) the wages of the mechanics employed in its construction, and (3) the surplus-value falling to the share of their 'master'. Further, the machinery need not be renewed till it is worn out. Hence, in order to keep the increased number of mechanics in constant employment, one carpet manufacturer after another must displace workmen by machines.

As a matter of fact the apologists do not mean this sort of setting free. They have in their minds the means of subsistence of the liberated work-people. It cannot be denied, in the above instance, that the machinery not only liberates 50 men, thus placing them at others' disposal, but, at the same time, it withdraws from their consumption, and sets free, means of subsistence to the value of £1,500. The simple fact, by no means a new one, that machinery cuts off the workmen from their means of subsistence is, therefore, in economic parlance tantamount to this, that machinery liberates means of subsistence for the workman, or converts those means into capital for his employment. The mode of expression, you see, is everything. *Nominibus mollire licet mala.*

This theory implies that the £1,500 worth of means of subsistence was capital that was being expanded by the labour of the 50 men discharged. That, consequently, this capital falls out of employment so soon as they commence their forced holidays, and never rests till it has found a fresh investment, where it can again be productively consumed by these same 50 men. That sooner or later, therefore, the capital and the workmen must come together again, and that, then, the compensation is complete. That the sufferings of the workmen displaced by machinery are therefore as transient as are the riches of this world.

In relation to the discharged workmen, the £1,500 worth of means of subsistence never was capital. What really confronted them as capital, was the sum of £1,500, afterwards laid out in machinery. On looking closer it will be seen that this sum represented part of the carpets produced in a year by the 50 discharged men, which part they received as wages from their employer in money instead of in kind. With the carpets in the form of money, they bought means of subsistence to the value of £1,500. These means, therefore, were to them, not capital, but commodities, and they, as regards these commodities, were not wage-labourers, but buyers. The circumstance that they were 'freed' by the machinery, from the means of purchase, changed them from buyers into non-buyers. Hence a lessened demand for those commodities – *voilà tout.* If this diminution be not compensated by an increase from some other quarter, the market price of the commodities falls. If this state of things lasts for some time, and extends, there follows a discharge of workmen employed in the production of these commodities. Some of the capital that was previously devoted to production of necessary means of subsistence, has to become reproduced in another form. While prices fall, and capital is being displaced, the labourers employed in the production of necessary means of subsistence are in their turn 'freed' from a part of their wages. Instead, therefore, of proving that, when machinery frees the workman from his means of subsistence, it simultaneously converts those means into capital for his further employment, our apologists, with their cut-and-dried law of supply and demand, prove, on the contrary, that machinery throws workmen on the streets, not only in that branch of production in which it is introduced, but also in those branches in which it is not introduced.

The real facts, which are travestied by the optimism of economists, are as follows: the labourers, when driven out of the workshop by the machinery, are thrown upon the labour-market, and there add to the number of workmen at the disposal of the capitalists. In Part 7 of this book it will be seen that this effect of machinery, which, as we have seen, is represented to be a compensation to the working-class, is on the contrary a most frightful scourge. For the present I will only say this: the labourers that are thrown out of work in any branch of industry, can no doubt seek for employment in some other branch. If they find it, and thus renew the bond between them and the means of subsistence, this takes place only by the intermediary of a new and additional capital that is seeking investment; not at all by the intermediary of the capital that formerly employed them and was afterwards converted into machinery. And even should they find employment, what a poor look-out is theirs! Crippled as they are by division of labour, these poor devils are worth so little outside their old trade, that they cannot find admission into any industries, except a few of inferior kind, that are over-supplied with underpaid workmen.[133] Further, every branch of industry attracts each year a new stream of men, who furnish a contingent from which to fill up vacancies, and to draw a supply for expansion. So soon as machinery sets free a part of the workmen employed in a given branch of industry, the reserve men are also diverted into new channels of employment, and become absorbed in other branches; meanwhile the original victims, during the period of transition, for the most part starve and perish.

It is an undoubted fact that machinery, as such, is not responsible for 'setting free' the workman from the means of subsistence. It cheapens and increases production in that branch which it seizes on, and at first makes no change in the mass of the means of subsistence produced in other branches. Hence, after its introduction, the society possesses as much, if not more, of the necessaries of life than before, for the labourers thrown out of work; and that quite apart from the enormous share of the annual produce wasted by the non-workers. And this is the point relied on by our apologists! The contradictions and antagonisms inseparable from the capitalist employment of machinery, do not exist, they say, since they do not arise out of machinery, as such, but out of its capitalist employment! Since therefore machinery, considered alone, shortens the hours of labour, but, when in the service of capital, lengthens them; since in itself it lightens labour, but when employed by capital, heightens the intensity of labour; since in itself it is a victory of man over the forces of Nature, but in the hands of capital, makes man the slave of those forces; since in itself it increases the wealth of the producers, but in the hands of capital, makes them paupers – for all these reasons and others besides, says the bourgeois economist without more ado, it is clear as noon-day that all these contradictions are a mere semblance of the reality, and that, as a matter of fact, they have neither an actual nor a theoretical existence. Thus he saves himself from all further puzzling of the brain, and what is more, implicitly declares his opponent to be stupid enough to contend against, not the capitalistic employment of machinery, but machinery itself.

No doubt he is far from denying that temporary inconvenience may result from the capitalist use of machinery. But where is the medal without its reverse! Any employment of machinery, except by capital, is to him an impossibility. Exploitation of the workman by the machine is therefore, with him, identical with exploitation of the machine by the workman. Whoever, therefore, exposes the real state of things in the capitalistic employment of machinery, is against its employment in any way, and is an enemy of social progress![134] Exactly the reasoning of the celebrated Bill Sykes. 'Gentlemen of the jury, no doubt the throat of this commercial traveller has been cut. But that is not my fault, it is the fault of the knife. Must we, for such a temporary inconvenience, abolish the use of the knife? Only consider! where would agriculture and trade be without the knife? Is it not as salutary in surgery, as it is knowing in anatomy? And in addition a willing help at the festive board? If you abolish the knife – you hurl us back into the depths of barbarism.'[135]

Although machinery necessarily throws men out of work in those industries into which it is introduced, yet it may, notwithstanding this, bring about an increase of employment in other industries. This effect, however, has nothing in common with the so-called theory of compensation. Since every article produced by a machine is cheaper than a similar article produced by hand, we deduce the following infallible law: if the total quantity of the article produced by machinery, be equal to the total quantity of the article previously produced by a handicraft or by manufacture, and now made by machinery, then the total labour expended is diminished. The new labour spent on the instruments of labour, on the machinery, on the coal, and so on, must necessarily be less than the labour displaced by the use of the machinery; otherwise the product of the machine would be as dear, or dearer, than the product of the manual labour. But, as a matter of fact, the total quantity of the article produced by machinery with a diminished number of workmen, instead of remaining equal to, by far exceeds the total quantity of the hand-made article that has been displaced. Suppose that 400,000 yards of cloth have been produced on power-looms by fewer weavers than could weave 100,000 yards by hand. In the quadrupled product there lies four times as much raw material. Hence the production of raw material must be quadrupled. But as regards the instruments of labour, such as buildings, coal, machinery, and so on, it is different; the limit up to which the additional labour required for their production can increase, varies with the difference between the quantity of the machine-made article, and the quantity of the same article that the same number of workmen could make by hand.

Hence, as the use of machinery extends in a given industry, the immediate effect is to increase production in the other industries that furnish the first with means of production. How far employment is thereby found for an increased number of men, depends, given the length of the working-day and the intensity of labour, on the composition of the capital employed, i.e., on the ratio of its constant to its variable component. This ratio, in its turn, varies considerably with the extent to which machinery has already seized on, or is then seizing on, those trades. The number of the men condemned to work in coal and metal mines increased enormously owing to the progress of the English factory system; but during the last few decades this increase of number has been less rapid, owing to the use of new machinery in mining.[136] A new type of workman springs into life along with the machine, namely, its maker. We have already learnt that machinery has possessed itself even of this branch of production on a scale that grows greater every day.[137] As to raw material,[138] there is not the least doubt that the rapid strides of cotton spinning, not only pushed on with tropical luxuriance the growth of cotton in the United States, and with it the African slave trade, but also made the breeding of slaves the chief business of the border slave-states. When, in 1790, the first census of slaves was taken in the United States, their number was 697,000; in 1861 it had nearly reached four millions. On the other hand, it is no less certain that the rise of the English woollen factories, together with the gradual conversion of arable land into sheep pasture, brought about the superfluity of agricultural labourers that led to their being driven in masses into the towns. Ireland, having during the last twenty years reduced its population by nearly one half, is at this moment undergoing the process of still further reducing the number of its inhabitants, so as exactly to suit the requirements of its landlords and of the English woollen manufacturers.

When machinery is applied to any of the preliminary or intermediate stages through which the subject of labour has to pass on its way to completion, there is an increased yield of material in those stages, and simultaneously an increased demand for labour in the handicrafts or manufactures supplied by the produce of the machines. Spinning by machinery, for example, supplied yarn so cheaply and so abundantly that the hand-loom weavers were, at first, able to work full time without increased outlay. Their earnings accordingly rose.[139] Hence a flow of people into the cotton-weaving trade, till at length the 800,000 weavers, called into existence by the Jenny, the throstle and the mule, were overwhelmed by the power-loom. So also, owing to the abundance of clothing materials produced by machinery, the number of tailors, seamstresses and needlewomen, went on increasing until the appearance of the sewing-machine.

In proportion as machinery, with the aid of a relatively small number of workpeople, increases the mass of raw materials, intermediate products, instruments of labour, &c., the working-up of these raw materials and intermediate products becomes split up into numberless branches; social production increases in diversity. The factory system carries the social division of labour immeasurably further than does manufacture, for it increases the productiveness of the industries it seizes upon, in a far higher degree.

The immediate result of machinery is to augment surplus-value and the mass of products in which surplus-value is embodied. And, as the substances consumed by the capitalists and their dependents become more plentiful, so too do these orders of society. Their growing wealth, and the relatively diminished number of workmen required to produce the necessaries of life beget, simultaneously with the rise of new and luxurious wants, the means of satisfying those wants. A larger portion of the produce of society is changed into surplus-produce, and a larger part of the surplus-produce is supplied for consumption in a multiplicity of refined shapes. In other words, the production of luxuries increases.[140] The refined and varied forms of the products are also due to new relations with the markets of the world, relations that are created by Modern Industry. Not only are greater quantities of foreign articles of luxury exchanged for home products, but a greater mass of foreign raw materials, ingredients, and intermediate products, are used as means of production in the home industries. Owing to these relations with the markets of the world, the demand for labour increases in the carrying trades, which split up into numerous varieties.[141]

The increase of the means of production and subsistence, accompanied by a relative diminution in the number of labourers, causes an increased demand for labour in making canals, docks, tunnels, bridges, and so on, works that can only bear fruit in the far future. Entirely new branches of production, creating new fields of labour, are also formed, as the direct result either of machinery or of the general industrial changes brought about by it. But the place occupied by these branches in the general production is, even in the most developed countries, far from important. The number of labourers that find employment in them is directly proportional to the demand, created by those industries, for the crudest form of manual labour. The chief industries of this kind are, at present, gas-works, telegraphs, photography, steam navigation, and railways. According to the census of 1861 for England and Wales, we find in the gas industry (gas-works, production of mechanical apparatus, servants of the gas companies, &c), 15,211 persons; in telegraphy, 2,399; in photography, 2,366; steam navigation, 3,570; and in railways, 70,599, of whom the unskilled 'navvies', more or less permanently employed, and the whole administrative and commercial staff, make up about 28,000. The total number of persons, therefore, employed in these five new industries amounts to 94,145.

Lastly, the extraordinary productiveness of modern industry, accompanied as it is by both a more extensive and a more intense exploitation of labour power in all other spheres of production, allows of the unproductive employment of a larger and larger part of the working-class, and the consequent reproduction, on a constantly extending scale, of the ancient domestic slaves under the name of a servant class, including men-servants, women-servants, lackeys, &c. According to the census of 1861, the population of England and Wales was 20,066,244; of these, 9,776,259 males, and 10,289,965 females. If we deduct from this population all who are too old or too young for work, all unproductive women, young persons and children, the 'ideological' classes, such as government officials, priests, lawyers, soldiers, &c.; further, all who have no occupation but to consume the labour of others in the form of rent, interest, &c.; and, lastly, paupers, vagabonds, and criminals, there remain in round numbers eight millions of the two sexes of every age, including in that number every capitalist who is in any way engaged in industry, commerce, or finance. Among these 8 millions are:

Agricultural labourers (including shepherds, farm servants, and maidservants living in the houses of farmers	1,098,261
All who are employed in cotton, woollen, worsted, flax, hemp, silk, and jute factories, in stocking making and lace making by machinery	642,607[142]
All who are employed in coal mines and metal mines	565,835
All who are employed in metal works (blast-furnaces, rolling mills, &c.), and metal manufactures of every kind	396,998[143]
The servant class	1,208,648[144]

All the persons employed in textile factories and in mines, taken together, number 1,208,442; those employed in textile factories and metal industries, taken together, number 1,039,605; in both cases less than the number of modern domestic slaves. What a splendid result of the capitalist exploitation of machinery!

Section 7. Repulsion and Attraction of Workpeople by the Factory System. Crises in the Cotton Trade.

All political economists of any standing admit that the introduction of new machinery has a baneful effect on the workmen in the old handicrafts and manufactures with which this machinery at first competes. Almost all of them bemoan the slavery of the factory operative. And what is the great trump-card that they play? That machinery, after the horrors of the period of introduction and development have subsided, instead of diminishing, in the long run increases the number of the slaves of labour! Yes, Political Economy revels in the hideous theory, hideous to every 'philanthropist' who believes in the eternal Nature-ordained necessity for capitalist production, that after a period of growth and transition, even its crowning success, the factory system based on machinery, grinds down more workpeople than on its first introduction it throws on the streets.[145]

It is true that in some cases, as we saw from instances of English worsted and silk factories, an extraordinary extension of the factory system may, at a certain stage of its development, be accompanied not only by a relative, but by an absolute decrease in the number of operatives employed. In the year 1860, when a special census of all the factories in the United Kingdom was taken by order of Parliament, the factories in those parts of Lancashire, Cheshire, and Yorkshire, included in the district of Mr Baker, the factory inspector, numbered 652; 570 of these contained 85,622 power-looms, 6,819,146 spindles (exclusive of doubling spindles) employed 27,439 horse-power (steam), and 1,390 (water), and 94,119 persons. In the year 1865, the same factories contained, looms 95,163, spindles 7,025,031, had a steam-power of 28,925 horses, and a water-power of 1,445 horses, and employed 88,913 persons. Between 1860 and 1865, therefore, the increase in looms was 11%, in spindles 3%, and in engine-power 3%, while the number of persons employed decreased.[146] Between 1852 and 1862, considerable extension of the English woollen manufacture took place, while the number of hands employed in it remained almost stationary, showing how greatly the introduction of new machines had superseded the labour of preceding periods.[147] In certain cases, the increase in the number of hands employed is only apparent;

that is, it is not due to the extension of the factories already established, but to the gradual annexation of connected trades; for instance, the increase in power-looms, and in the hands employed by them between 1838 and 1856, was, in the cotton trade, simply owing to the extension of this branch of industry; but in the other trades to the application of steam-power to the carpet-loom, to the ribbon-loom, and to the linen-loom, which previously had been worked by the power of men.[148] Hence the increase of the hands in these latter trades was merely a symptom of a diminution in the total number employed. Finally, we have considered this question entirely apart from the fact, that everywhere, except in the metal industries, young persons (under 18), and women and children form the preponderating element in the class of factory hands.

Nevertheless, in spite of the mass of hands actually displaced and virtually replaced by machinery, we can understand how the factory operatives, through the building of more mills and the extension of old ones in a given industry, may become more numerous than the manufacturing workmen and handicraftsman that have been displaced. Suppose, for example, that in the old mode of production, a capital of £500 is employed weekly, two-fifths being constant and three-fifths variable capital, i.e., £200 being laid out in means of production, and £300, say £1 per man, in labour power. On the introduction of machinery the composition of this capital becomes altered. We will suppose it to consist of four-fifths constant and one-fifth variable, which means that only £100 is now laid out in labour power. Consequently, two-thirds of the workmen are discharged. If now the business extends, and the total capital employed grows to £1,500 under unchanged conditions, the number of operatives employed will increase to 300, just as many as before the introduction of the machinery. If the capital further grows to £2,000, 400 men will be employed, or one-third more than under the old system. Their numbers have, in point of fact, increased by 100, but relatively, i.e., in proportion to the total capital advanced, they have diminished by 800, for the £2,000 capital would, in the old state of things, have employed 1,200 instead of 400 men. Hence, a relative decrease in the number of hands is consistent with an actual increase. We assumed above that while the total capital increases, its composition remains the same, because the conditions of production remain constant. But we have already seen that, with every advance in the use of machinery, the constant component of capital, that part which consists of machinery, raw material, &c., increases, while the variable component, the part laid out in labour power, decreases. We also know that in no other system of production is improvement so continuous, and the composition of the capital employed so constantly changing as in the factory system. These changes are, however, continually interrupted by periods of rest, during which there is a mere quantitative extension of the factories on the existing technical basis. During such periods the operatives increase in number. Thus, in 1835, the total number of operatives in the cotton, woollen, worsted, flax, and silk factories of the United Kingdom was only 354,684; while in 1861 the number of the power-loom weavers alone (of both sexes and of all ages, from eight years upwards), amounted to 230,654. Certainly, this growth appears less important when we consider that in 1838 the hand-loom weavers with their families still numbered 800,000,[149] not to mention those thrown out of work in Asia, and on the Continent of Europe.

In the few remarks I have still to make on this point, I shall refer to some actually existing relations, the existence of which our theoretical investigation has not yet disclosed.

So long as, in a given branch of industry, the factory system extends itself at the expense of the old handicrafts or of manufacture, the result is as sure as is the result of an encounter between an army furnished with breach-loaders, and one armed with bows and arrows. This first period, during which machinery conquers its field of action, is of decisive importance owing to the extraordinary profits that it helps to produce. These profits not only form a source of accelerated accumulation, but also attract into the favoured sphere of production a large part of the additional social capital that is being constantly created, and is ever on the look-out for new investments. The special advantages of this first period of fast and furious activity are felt in every branch of production that machinery invades. So soon, however, as the factory system has gained a certain breadth of footing and a definite degree of maturity, and, especially, so soon as its technical basis, machinery, is itself produced by machinery; so soon as coal mining and iron mining, the metal industries, and the means of transport have been revolutionised; so soon, in short, as the general conditions requisite for production by the modern industrial system have been established, this mode of production acquires an elasticity, a capacity for sudden extension by leaps and bounds that finds no hindrance except in the supply of raw material and in the disposal of the produce. On the one hand, the immediate effect of machinery is to increase the supply of raw material in the same way, for example, as the cotton gin augmented the production of cotton.[150] On the other hand, the cheapness of the articles produced by machinery, and the improved means of transport and communication furnish the weapons for conquering foreign markets. By ruining handicraft production in other countries, machinery forcibly converts them into fields for the supply

of its raw material. In this way East India was compelled to produce
cotton, wool, hemp, jute, and indigo for Great Britain.[151] By constantly making a part of the hands 'supernumerary', modern industry,
in all countries where it has taken root, gives a spur to emigration and
to the colonisation of foreign lands, which are thereby converted into
settlements for growing the raw material of the mother country; just
as Australia, for example, was converted into a colony for growing
wool.[152] A new and international division of labour, a division suited
to the requirements of the chief centres of modern industry, springs
up, and converts one part of the globe into a chiefly agricultural field
of production, for supplying the other part which remains a chiefly
industrial field. This revolution hangs together with radical changes in
agriculture which we need not here further inquire into.[153]

On the motion of Mr Gladstone, the House of Commons ordered,
on the 17th February, 1867, a return of the total quantities of grain,
corn, and flour, of all sorts, imported into, and exported from, the
United Kingdom, between the years 1831 and 1866. I give below a
summary of the result. The flour is given in quarters of corn.

Quinquennial Periods and the Year 1866

Annual Average	1831–1835	1836–1840	1841–1845	1846–1850
Import (Qrs.)	1,096,373	2,389,729	2,843,865	8,776,552
Export (Qrs.)	225,363	251,770	139,056	155,461
Excess of Import over export	871,110	2,137,959	2,704,809	8,621,091
Population Yearly average in each period	24,621,107	25,929,507	27,262,5569	27,797,598
Average quantity of corn, &c., in Qrs., consumed annually per head over and above the home produce consumed	0·036	0·082	0·099	0·310

Quinquennial Periods &c. (continued)

Annual Average	1851–1855	1856–1860	1861–1865	1866–1870
Import (Qrs.)	8,345,237	10,912,612	15,009,871	16,457,340
Export (Qrs.)	307,491	341,150	302,754	216,218
Excess of Import over export	8,037,746	10,572,462	14,707,117	16,241,122
Population Yearly average in each period	25,572,923	28,391,544	29,381,460	29,935,404
Average quantity of corn, &c., in Qrs., consumed annually per head over and above the home produce consumed	0·291	0·372	0·543	0·543

The enormous power, inherent in the factory system, of expanding
by jumps, and the dependence of that system on the markets of the
world, necessarily beget feverish production, followed by over-filling

of the markets, whereupon contraction of the markets brings on crippling of production. The life of modern industry becomes a series of periods of moderate activity, prosperity, over-production, crisis and stagnation. The uncertainty and instability to which machinery subjects the employment, and consequently the conditions of existence, of the operatives become normal, owing to these periodic changes of the industrial cycle. Except in the periods of prosperity, there rages between the capitalists the most furious combat for the share of each in the markets. This share is directly proportional to the cheapness of the product. Besides the rivalry that this struggle begets in the application of improved machinery for replacing labour power, and of new methods of production, there also comes a time in every industrial cycle, when a forcible reduction of wages beneath the value of labour power, is attempted for the purpose of cheapening commodities.[154]

A necessary condition, therefore, to the growth of the number of factory hands, is a proportionally much more rapid growth of the amount of capital invested in mills. This growth, however, is conditioned by the ebb and flow of the industrial cycle. It is, besides, constantly interrupted by the technical progress that at one time virtually supplies the place of new workmen, at another, actually displaces old ones. This qualitative change in mechanical industry continually discharges hands from the factory, or shuts its doors against the fresh stream of recruits, while the purely quantitative extension of the factories absorbs not only the men thrown out of work, but also fresh contingents. The workpeople are thus continually both repelled and attracted, hustled from pillar to post, while, at the same time, constant changes take place in the sex, age, and skill of the levies.

The lot of the factory operatives will be best depicted by taking a rapid survey of the course of the English cotton industry.

From 1770 to 1815 this trade was depressed or stagnant for 5 years only. During this period of 45 years the English manufacturers had a monopoly of machinery and of the markets of the world. From 1815 to 1821 depression; 1822 and 1823 prosperity; 1824 abolition of the laws against Trades' Unions, great extension of factories everywhere; 1825 crisis; 1826 great misery and riots among the factory operatives; 1827 slight improvement; 1828 great increase in power-looms, and in exports; 1829 exports, especially to India, surpass all former years; 1830 glutted markets, great distress; 1831 to 1833 continued depression, the monopoly of the trade with India and China withdrawn from the East India Company; 1834 great increase of factories and machinery, shortness of hands. The new poor law furthers the migration of agricultural labourers into the factory districts. The country districts swept of children. White slave trade; 1835 great prosperity, contemporaneous starvation of the hand-loom weavers; 1836 great prosperity; 1837 and 1838 depression and crisis; 1839 revival; 1840 great depression, riots, calling out of the military; 1841 and 1842 frightful suffering among the factory operatives; 1842 the manufacturers lock the hands out of the factories in order to enforce the repeal of the Corn Laws. The operatives stream in thousands into the towns of Lancashire and Yorkshire, are driven back by the military, and their leaders brought to trial at Lancaster; 1843 great misery; 1844 revival; 1845 great prosperity; 1846 continued improvement at first, then reaction. Repeal of the Corn Laws; 1847 crisis, general reduction of wages by 10 and more per cent. in honour of the 'big loaf'; 1848 continued depression; Manchester under military protection; 1849 revival; 1850 prosperity; 1851 falling prices, low wages, frequent strikes; 1852 improvement begins, strikes continue, the manufacturers threaten to import foreign hands; 1853 increasing exports. Strike for 8 months, and great misery at Preston; 1854 prosperity, glutted markets; 1855 news of failures stream in from the United States, Canada, and the Eastern markets; 1856 great prosperity; 1857 crisis; 1858 improvement; 1859 great prosperity, increase in factories; 1860 Zenith of the English cotton trade, the Indian, Australian, and other markets so glutted with goods that even in 1863 they had not absorbed the whole lot; the French Treaty of Commerce, enormous growth of factories and machinery; 1861 prosperity continues for a time, reaction, the American Civil War, cotton famine: 1862 to 1863 complete collapse.

The history of the cotton famine is too characteristic to dispense with dwelling upon it for a moment. From the indications as to the condition of the markets of the world in 1860 and 1861, we see that the cotton famine came in the nick of time for the manufacturers, and was to some extent advantageous to them, a fact that was acknowledged in the reports of the Manchester Chamber of Commerce, proclaimed in Parliament by Palmerston and Derby, and confirmed by events.[155] No doubt, among the 2,887 cotton mills in the United Kingdom in 1861, there were many of small size. According to the report of Mr A. Redgrave, out of the 2,109 mills included in his district, 392, or 19% employed less than ten horse-power each; 345, or 16% employed 10 H. P., and less than 20 H. P.; while 1,372 employed upwards of 20 H. P.[156] The majority of the small mills were weaving sheds, built during the period of prosperity after 1858, for the most part by speculators, of whom one supplied the yarn, another the machinery, a third the buildings, and were worked by men who had been overlookers, or by other persons of small means. These small manufacturers mostly went to the wall. The same fate would have overtaken them in the commercial crisis that was staved off only by the cotton famine. Although they formed one-third of the total number of manufacturers, yet their mills absorbed a much smaller part of the capital invested in the cotton trade. As to the extent of the stoppage, it appears from authentic estimates, that in October 1862, 60.3% of the spindles, and 58% of the looms were standing. This refers to the cotton trade as a whole, and, of course, requires considerable modification for individual districts. Only very few mills worked full time (60 hours a week), the remainder worked at intervals. Even in those few cases where full time was worked, and at the customary rate of piece-wage, the weekly wages of the operatives necessarily shrank, owing to good cotton being replaced by bad, Sea Island by Egyptian (in fine spinning mills), American and Egyptian by Surat, and pure cotton by mixings of waste and Surat. The shorter fibre of the Surat cotton and its dirty condition, the greater fragility of the thread, the substitution of all sorts of heavy ingredients for flour in sizing the warps, all these lessened the speed of the machinery, or the number of the looms that could be superintended by one weaver, increased the labour caused by defects in the machinery, and reduced the piece-wage by reducing the mass of the product turned off. Where Surat cotton was used, the loss to the operatives when on full time, amounted to 20, 30, and more per cent. But besides this, the majority of the manufacturers reduced the rate of piece-wage by 5, 7 1/2, and 10 per cent. We can therefore conceive the situation of those hands who were employed for only 3, 3 1/2 or 4 days a week, or for only 6 hours a day. Even in 1863, after a comparative improvement had set in, the weekly wages of spinners and of weavers were 3s. 4d., 3s. 10d., 4s. 6d. and 5s. 1d.[157] Even in this miserable state of things, however, the inventive spirit of the master never stood still, but was exercised in making deductions from wages. These were to some extent inflicted as a penalty for defects in the finished article that were really due to his bad cotton and to his unsuitable machinery. Moreover, where the manufacturer owned the cottages of the workpeople, he paid himself his rents by deducting the amount from these miserable wages. Mr Redgrave tells us of self-acting minders (operatives who manage a pair of self-acting mules) 'earning at the end of a fortnight's full work 8s. 11d., and that from this sum was deducted the rent of the house, the manufacturer, however, returning half the rent as a gift. The minders took away the sum of 6s. 11d. In many places the self-acting minders ranged from 5s. to 9s. per week, and the weavers from 2s. to 6s. per week, during the latter part of 1862.'[158] Even when working short time the rent was frequently deducted from the wages of the operatives.[159] No wonder that in some parts of Lancashire a kind of famine fever broke out. But more characteristic than all this, was, the revolution that took place in the process of production at the expense of the workpeople. *Experimenta in corpore vili*, like those of anatomists on frogs, were formally made. 'Although,' says Mr Redgrave, 'I have given the actual earnings of the operatives in the several mills, it does not follow that they earn the same amount week by week. The operatives are subject to great fluctuation from the constant experimentalising of the manufacturers . . . the earnings of the operatives rise and fall with the quality of the cotton mixings; sometimes they have been within 15 per cent. of former earnings, and then, in a week or two, they have fallen off from 50 to 60 per cent.'[160] These experiments were not made solely at the expense of the workman's means of subsistence. His five senses also had to pay the penalty. 'The people who are employed in making up Surat cotton complain very much. They inform me, on opening the bales of cotton there is an intolerable smell, which causes sickness . . . In the mixing, scribbling and carding rooms, the dust and dirt which are disengaged, irritate the air passages, and give rise to cough and difficulty of breathing. A disease of the skin, no doubt from the irritation of the dirt contained in the Surat cotton, also prevails . . . The fibre being so short, a great amount of size, both animal and vegetable, is used . . . Bronchitis is more prevalent owing to the dust. Inflammatory sore throat is common, from the same cause. Sickness and dyspepsia are produced by the frequent breaking of the weft, when the weaver sucks the weft through the eye of the shuttle.' On the other hand, the substitutes for flour were a Fortunatus' purse to the manufacturers, by increasing the weight of the yarn. They caused '15 lbs. of raw material to weigh 26 lbs. after it was woven.'[161] In the Report of Inspectors of Factories for 30th April, 1864, we read as follows: 'The trade is availing itself of this resource at present to an extent which is even discreditable. I have heard on good authority of a cloth weighing 8 lbs. which was made of 5 1/4 lbs. cotton and 2 3/4 lbs. size; and of another cloth weighing 5 1/4 lbs., of which 2 lbs. was size. These were ordinary export shirtings. In cloths of other descriptions, as much as 50 per cent. size is sometimes added; so that a manufacturer may, and does truly boast, that he is getting rich by selling cloth for less money per pound than he paid for the mere yarn of which they are composed.'[162] But the workpeople had to suffer, not only from the experiments of the manufacturers inside the mills, and of the municipalities outside, not only from reduced wages and absence of work, from want and from charity, and from the eulogistic speeches of lords and commons. 'Unfortunate females who, in consequence of the cotton famine, were at its commencement thrown out of employment, and have thereby become outcasts of society; and now, though trade has revived, and work is plentiful, continue members of that unfortunate class, and are likely to continue so. There are also in the borough more youthful prostitutes than I have known for the last 25 years.'[163]

We find then, in the first 45 years of the English cotton trade, from 1770 to 1815, only 5 years of crisis and stagnation; but this was the period of monopoly. The second period from 1815 to 1863 counts, during its 48 years, only 20 years of revival and prosperity against 28 of depression and stagnation. Between 1815 and 1830 the competition with the continent of Europe and with the United States sets in. After 1833, the extension of the Asiatic markets is enforced by 'destruction of the human race' (the wholesale extinction of Indian hand-loom weavers). After the repeal of the Corn Laws, from 1846 to 1863, there are 8 years of moderate activity and prosperity against 9 years of depression and stagnation. The condition of the adult male operatives, even during the years of prosperity, may be judged from the note subjoined.[164]

Section 8. Revolution Effected in Manufacture, Handicrafts, and Domestic Industry by Modern Industry.

A. Overthrow of Co-operation Based on Handicraft, and on the Division of Labour.

We have seen how machinery does away with co-operation based on handicrafts, and with manufacture based on the division of handicraft labour. An example of the first sort is the mowing-machine; it replaces co-operation between mowers. A striking example of the second kind, is the needle-making machine. According to Adam Smith, 10 men, in his day, made in co-operation, over 48,000 needles a day. On the other hand, a single needle-machine makes 145,000 in a working-day of 11 hours. One woman or one girl superintends four such machines, and so produces near upon 600,000 needles in a day, and upwards of 3,000,000 in a week.[165] A single machine, when it takes the place of co-operation or of manufacture, may itself serve as the basis of an industry of a handicraft character. Still, such a return to handicrafts is but a transition to the factory system, which, as a rule, makes its appearance so soon as the human muscles are replaced, for the purpose of driving the machines, by a mechanical motive power, such as steam or water. Here and there, but in any case only for a time, an industry may be carried on, on a small scale, by means of mechanical power. This is effected by hiring steam-power, as is done in some of the Birmingham trades, or by the use of small caloric-engines, as in some branches of weaving.[166] In the Coventry silk weaving industry the experiment of 'cottage factories' was tried. In the centre of a square surrounded by rows of cottages, an engine-house was built and the engine connected by shafts with the looms in the cottages. In all cases the power was hired at so much per loom. The rent was payable weekly, whether the looms worked or not. Each cottage held from 2 to 6 looms; some belonged to the weaver, some were bought on credit, some were hired. The struggle between these cottage factories and the factory proper, lasted over 12 years. It ended with the complete ruin of the 300 cottage factories.[167] Wherever the nature of the process did not involve production on a large scale, the new industries that have sprung up in the last few decades, such as envelope making, steel-pen making, &c., have, as a general rule, first passed through the handicraft stage, and then the manufacturing stage, as short phases of transition to the factory stage. The transition is very difficult in those cases where the production of the article by manufacture consists, not of a series of graduated processes, but of a great number of disconnected ones. This circum-stance formed a great hindrance to the establishment of steel-pen factories. Nevertheless, about 15 years ago, a machine was invented that automatically performed 6 separate operations at once. The first steel-pens were supplied by the handicraft system, in the year 1820, at £7 4s. the gross; in 1830 they-were supplied by manufacture at 8s., and today the factory system supplies them to the trade at from 2s. to 6d. the gross.[168]

B. Reaction of the Factory System on Manufacture and Domestic Industries.

Along with the development of the factory system and of the revolution in agriculture that accompanies it, production in all the other branches of industry not only extends, but alters its character. The principle, carried out in the factory system, of analysing the process of production into its constituent phases, and of solving the problems thus proposed by the application of mechanics, of chemistry, and of the whole range of the natural sciences, becomes the determining principle everywhere. Hence, machinery squeezes itself into the manufacturing industries first for one detail process, then for another. Thus the solid crystal of their organisation, based on the old division of labour, becomes dissolved, and makes way for constant changes. Independently of this, a radical change takes place in the composition of the collective labourer, a change of the persons working in combination. In contrast with the manufacturing period, the division of labour is thenceforth based, wherever possible, on the employment of women, of children of all ages, and of unskilled labourers, in one word, on cheap labour, as it is characteristically called in England. This is the case not only with all production on a large scale, whether employing machinery or not, but also with the so-called domestic industry, whether carried on in the houses of the workpeople or in small workshops. This modern so-called domestic industry has nothing, except the name, in common with the old-fashioned domestic industry, the existence of which presupposes independent urban handicrafts, independent peasant farming, and above all, a dwelling-house for the labourer and his family. That old-fashioned industry has now been converted into an outside department of the factory, the manufactory, or the warehouse. Besides the factory operatives, the manufacturing workmen and the handicraftsman, whom it concentrates in large masses at one spot, and directly commands, capital also sets in motion, by means of invisible threads, another army; that of the workers in the domestic industries, who dwell in the large towns and are also scattered over the face of the country. An example: the shirt factory of Messrs Tillie at Londonderry, which employs 1,000 operatives in the factory itself, and 9,000 people spread up and down the country and working in their own houses.[169]

The exploitation of cheap and immature labour power is carried out in a more shameless manner in modern Manufacture than in the factory proper. This is because the technical foundation of the factory system, namely, the substitution of machines for muscular power, and the light character of the labour, is almost entirely absent in Manufacture, and at the same time women and over-young children are subjected, in a most unconscionable way, to the influence of poisonous or injurious substances. This exploitation is more shameless in the so-called domestic industry than in manufactures, and that because the power of resistance in the labourers decreases with their dissemination; because a whole series of plundering parasites insinuate themselves between the employer and the workman; because a domestic industry has always to compete either with the factory system, or with manufacturing in the same branch of production; because poverty robs the workman of the conditions most essential to his labour, of space, light and ventilation; because employment becomes more and more irregular; and, finally, because in these the last resorts of the masses made 'redundant' by Modern Industry and Agriculture, competition for work attains its maximum. Economy in the means of production, first systematically carried out in the factory system, and there, from the very beginning, coincident with the most reckless squandering of labour power, and robbery of the conditions normally requisite for labour – this economy now shows its antagonistic and murderous side more and more in a given branch of industry, the less the social productive power of labour and the technical basis for a combination of processes are developed in that branch.

C. Modern Manufacture.

I now proceed, by a few examples, to illustrate the principles laid down above. As a matter of fact, the reader is already familiar with numerous instances given in the chapter on the working-day. In the hardware manufactures of Birmingham and the neighbourhood, there are employed, mostly in very heavy work, 30,000 children and young persons, besides 10,000 women. There they are to be seen in the unwholesome brass-foundries, button factories, enamelling, galvanising, and lackering works.[170] Owing to the excessive labour of their workpeople, both adult and non-adult, certain London houses where newspapers and books are printed, have got the ill-omened name of 'slaughterhouses'.[171] Similar excesses are practised in book-binding, where the victims are chiefly women, girls, and children; young persons have to do heavy work in rope-walks and night-work in salt mines, candle manufactories, and chemical works; young people are worked to death at turning the looms in silk weaving, when it is not carried on by machinery.[172] One of the most shameful, the most dirty, and the worst paid kinds of labour, and one on which women and young girls are by preference employed, is the sorting of rags. It is well known that Great Britain, apart from its own immense store of rags, is the emporium for the rag trade of the whole world. They flow in from Japan, from the most remote States of South America, and from the Canary Islands. But the chief sources of their supply are Germany, France, Russia, Italy, Egypt, Turkey, Belgium, and Holland. They are used for manure, for making bedflocks, for shoddy, and they serve as the raw material of paper. The rag-sorters are the medium for the spread of small-pox and other infectious diseases, and they themselves are the first victims.[173] A classical example of over-work, of hard and inappropriate labour, and of its brutalising effects on the workman from his childhood upwards, is afforded not only by coal-mining and miners generally, but also by tile and brick making, in which industry the recently invented machinery is, in England, used only here and there. Between May and September the work lasts from 5 in the morning till 8 in the evening, and where the drying is done in the open air, it often lasts from 4 in the morning till 9 in the evening. Work from 5 in the morning till 7 in the evening is considered 'reduced' and 'moderate'. Both boys and girls of 6 and even of 4 years of age are employed. They work for the same number of hours, often longer, than the adults. The work is hard and the summer heat increases the exhaustion. In a certain tile-field at Mosley, e.g., a young woman, 24 years of age, was in the habit of making 2,000 tiles a day, with the assistance of 2 little girls, who carried the clay for her, and stacked the tiles. These girls carried daily 10 tons up the slippery sides of the clay pits, from a depth of 30 feet, and then for a distance of 210 feet. 'It is impossible for a child to pass through the purgatory of a tile-field without great moral degradation . . . the low language, which they are accustomed to hear from their tenderest years, the filthy, indecent, and shameless habits, amidst which, unknowing, and half wild, they grow up, make them in after-life lawless, abandoned, dissolute . . . A frightful source of demoralisation is the mode of living. Each moulder, who is always a skilled labourer, and the chief of a group, supplies his 7 subordinates with board and lodging in his cottages Whether members of his family or not, the men, boys, and girls all sleep in the cottage, which contains generally two, exceptionally 3 rooms, all on the ground floor, and badly ventilated. These people are so exhausted after the day's hard work, that neither the rules of health, of cleanliness, nor of decency are in the least observed. Many of these cottages are models of untidiness, dirt, and dust . . . The greatest evil of the system that employs young girls on this sort of work, consists in this, that, as a rule, it chains them fast from childhood for the whole of their after-life to the most abandoned rabble. They become rough, foul-mouthed boys, before Nature has taught them that they are women. Clothed in a few dirty rags, the legs naked far above the knees, hair and face besmeared with dirt, they learn to treat all feelings of decency and of shame with contempt. During meal–times they lie at full length in the fields, or watch the boys bathing in a neighbouring canal. Their heavy day's work at length completed, they put on better clothes, and accompany the men to the public houses.' That excessive insobriety is prevalent from childhood upwards among the whole of this class, is only natural. 'The worst is that the brickmakers despair of themselves. You might as well, said one of the better kind to a chaplain of Southallfield, try to raise and improve the devil as a brickie, sir!'[174]

As to the manner, in which capital effects an economy in the requisites of labour, in modern Manufacture (in which I include all workshops of larger size, except factories proper), official and most ample material bearing on it is to be found in the *Public Health Reports IV (1863)* and *VI (1864)*. The description of the workshops, more especially those of the London printers and tailors, surpasses the most loathsome phantasies of our romance writers. The effect on the health of the workpeople is self-evident. Dr Simon, the chief medical officer of the Privy Council and the official editor of the Public Health Reports, says: 'In my fourth Report (1863) I showed, how it is practically impossible for the workpeople to insist upon that which is their first sanitary right, viz., the right that, no matter what the work for which their employer brings them together, the labour, so far as it depends upon him, should be freed from all avoidably unwholesome conditions. I pointed out, that while the workpeople are practically incapable of doing themselves this sanitary justice, they are unable to obtain any effective support from the paid administrations of the sanitary police . . . The life of myriads of workmen and workwomen is now uselessly tortured and shortened by the never-ending physical suffering that their mere occupation begets.'[175] In illustration of the way in which the workrooms influence the state of health Dr Simon gives the following table of mortality.[176]

(a) Number of persons of all ages employed in the respective industries
(b) Industries compared as regards health
(c) Death rate per 100,00 men in the respective industries between the stated ages

		(a) 25–35	(b) 35–45	(c) 45–55
958, 265	Agriculture in England and Wales	743	805	1,145
22,301	London tailors (men)	958	1,262	2,093
12,379	London tailors (women)			
13,803	London printers	894	1,747	2,367

D. Modern Domestic Industry.

I now come to the so-called domestic industry. In order to get an idea of the horrors of this sphere, in which capital conducts its exploitation in the background of modern mechanical industry, one must go to the apparently quite idyllic trade of nail-making,[177] carried on in a few remote villages of England. In this place, however, it will be enough to give a few examples from those branches of the lace-making and straw-plaiting industries that are not yet carried on by the aid of machinery, and that as yet do not compete with branches carried on in factories or in manufactories.

Of the 150,000 persons employed in England in the production of lace, about 10,000 fall under the authority of the Factory Act, 1861. Almost the whole of the remaining 140,000 are women, young persons, and children of both sexes, the male sex, however, being weakly represented. The state of health of this cheap material for exploitation will be seen from the following table, computed by Dr Trueman, physician to the Nottingham General Dispensary. Out of 686 female patients who were lace-makers, most of them between the ages of 17 and 24, the number of consumptive ones were:

1852	1 in 45	1853	1 in 28
1854	1 in 17	1855	1 in 18
1856	1 in 15	1857	1 in 13
1861	1 in 8[178]	1858	1 in 15
1859	1 in 9	1860	1 in 8

This progress in the rate of consumption ought to suffice for the most optimist of progressists, and for the biggest hawker of lies among the Free-trade bagmen of Germany.

The Factory Act of 1861 regulates the actual making of the lace, so far as it is done by machinery, and this is the rule in England. The branches that we are now about to examine, solely with regard to those of the workpeople who work at home, and not those who work in manufactories or warehouses, fall into two divisions, viz. (1), finishing; (2), mending. The former gives the finishing touches to the machine-made lace, and includes numerous sub-divisions.

The lace finishing is done either in what are called 'mistresses' houses', or by women in their own houses, with or without the help of their children. The women who keep the 'mistresses' houses' are themselves poor. The workroom is in a private house. The mistresses take orders from manufacturers, or from warehousemen, and employ as many women, girls, and young children as the size of their rooms and the fluctuating demand of the business will allow. The number of the workwomen employed in these workrooms varies from 20 to 40 in some, and from 10 to 20 in others. The average age at which the children commence work is six years, but in many cases it is below five. The usual working-hours are from 8 in the morning till eight in the evening, with 1 1/2 hours for meals, which are taken at irregular intervals, and often in the foul workrooms. When business is brisk, the labour frequently lasts from 8 or even 6 o'clock in the morning till 10, 11, or 12 o'clock at night. In English barracks the regulation space allotted to each soldier is 500–600 cubic feet, and in the military hospitals 1,200 cubic feet. But in those finishing sties there are but 67 to 100 cubic feet to each person. At the same time the oxygen of the air is consumed by gas-lights. In order to keep the lace clean, and although the floor is tiled or flagged, the children are often compelled, even in winter, to pull off their shoes. 'It is not at all uncommon in Nottingham to find 14 to 20 children huddled together in a small room, of, perhaps, not more than 12 feet square, and employed for 15 hours out of the 24, at work that of itself is exhausting, from its weariness and monotony, and is besides carried on under every possible unwholesome condition . . . Even the very youngest children work with a strained attention and a rapidity that is astonishing, hardly ever giving their fingers rest or slowering their motion. If a question be asked them, they never raise their eyes from their work from fear of losing a single moment.' The 'long stick' is used by the mistresses as a stimulant more and more as the working hours are prolonged. 'The children gradually tire and become as restless as birds towards the end of their long detention at an occupation that is monotonous, eye-straining, and exhausting from the uniformity in the posture of the body. Their work is like slavery.' [179] When women and their children work at home, which nowadays means in a hired room, often in a garret, the state of things is, if possible, still worse. This sort of work is given out within a circle of 80 miles radius from Nottingham. On leaving the warehouses at 9 or 10 o'clock at night, the children are often given a bundle of lace to take home with them and finish. The Pharisee of a capitalist represented by one of his servants, accompanies this action, of course, with the unctuous phrase: 'That's for mother', yet he knows well enough that the poor children must sit up and help. [180]

Pillow lace-making is chiefly carried on in England in two agricultural districts; one, the Honiton lace district, extending from 20 to 30 miles along the south coast of Devonshire, and including a few places in North Devon; the other comprising a great part of the counties of Buckingham, Bedford, and Northampton, and also the adjoining portions of Oxfordshire and Huntingdonshire. The cottages of the agricultural labourers are the places where the work is usually carried on. Many manufacturers employ upwards of 3,000 of these lace-makers, who are chiefly children and young persons of the female sex exclusively. The state of things described as incidental to lace finishing is here repeated, save that instead of the 'mistresses' houses', we find what are called 'lace-schools', kept by poor women in their cottages. From their fifth year and often earlier, until their twelfth or fifteenth year, the children work in these schools; during the first year the very young ones work from four to eight hours, and later on, from six in the morning till eight and ten o'clock at night. 'The rooms are generally the ordinary living rooms of small cottages, the chimney stopped up to keep out draughts, the inmates kept warm by their own animal heat alone, and this frequently in winter. In other cases, these so-called school-rooms are like small store-rooms without fire-places . . . The over-crowding in these dens and the consequent vitiation of the air are often extreme. Added to this is the injurious effect of drains, privies, decomposing substances, and other filth usual in the purlieus of the smaller cottages.' With regard to space: 'In one lace-school 18 girls and a mistress, 35 cubic feet to each person; in another, where the smell was unbearable, 18 persons and 24 1/2 cubic feet per head. In this industry are to be found employed children of 2 and 2 1/2 years.'[181]

Where lace-making ends in the counties of Buckingham and Bed-ford, straw-plaiting begins, and extends over a large part of Hertford-shire and the westerly and northerly parts of Essex. In 1861, there were 40,043 persons employed in straw-plaiting and straw-hat making; of these 3,815 were males of all ages, the rest females, of whom 14,913, including about 7,000 children, were under 20 years of age. In the place of the lace-schools we find here the 'straw-plait schools'. The children commence their instruction in straw-plaiting generally in their 4th, often between their 3rd and 4th year. Educ-ation, of course, they get none. The children themselves call the elementary schools, 'natural schools', to distinguish them from these blood-sucking institutions, in which they are kept at work simply to get through the task, generally 30 yards daily, prescribed by their half-starved mothers. These same mothers often make them work at home, after school is over, till 10, 11, and 12 o'clock at night. The straw cuts their mouths, with which they constantly moisten it, and their fingers. Dr Ballard gives it as the general opinion of the whole body of medical officers in London, that 300 cubic feet is the minimum space proper for each person in a bedroom or workroom. But in the straw-plait schools space is more sparingly allotted than in the lace-schools, '12 2/3, 17, 18 1/2 and below 22 cubic feet for each person.' The smaller of these numbers, says one of the com-missioners, Mr White, represents less space than the half of what a child would occupy if packed in a box measuring 3 feet in each direction. Thus do the children enjoy life till the age of 12 or 14. The wretched half-starved parents think of nothing but getting as much as possible out of their children. The latter, as soon as they are grown up, do not care a farthing, and naturally so, for their parents, and leave them. 'It is no wonder that ignorance and vice abound in a population so brought up . . . Their morality is at the lowest ebb, . . . a great number of the women have illegitimate children, and that at such an immature age that even those most conversant with criminal statistics are astounded.'[182] And the native land of these model families is the pattern Christian country for Europe; so says at least Count Montalembert, certainly a competent authority on Christianity!

Wages in the above industries, miserable as they are (the max-imum wages of a child in the straw-plait schools rising in rare cases to 3 shillings), are reduced far below their nominal amount by the prevalence of the truck system everywhere, but especially in the lace districts.[183]

E. Passage of Modern Manufacture, and Domestic Industry into Modern Mechanical Industry. The Hastening of This Revolution by the Application of the Factory Acts to those Industries.

The cheapening of labour power, by sheer abuse of the labour of women and children, by sheer robbery of every normal condition requisite for working and living, and by the sheer brutality of over-work and night-work, meets at last with natural obstacles that cannot be overstepped. So also, when based on these methods, do the cheapening of commodities and capitalist exploitation in general. So soon as this point is at last reached – and it takes many years – the hour has struck for the introduction of machinery, and for the thenceforth rapid conversion of the scattered domestic industries and also of manufactures into factory industries.

An example, on the most colossal scale, of this movement is afforded by the production of wearing apparel. This industry, according to the classification of the Children's Employment Commission, comprises straw-hat makers, ladies'-hat makers, cap-makers, tailors, milliners and dressmakers, shirt-makers, corset-makers, glove-makers, shoemakers, besides many minor branches, such as the making of neck-ties, collars, &c. In 1861, the number of females employed in these industries, in England and Wales, amounted to 586,299, of these 115,242 at the least were under 20, and 16,650. under 15 years of age. The number of these workwomen in the United Kingdom in 1861, was 750,334. The number of males employed in England and Wales, in hat-making, shoemaking, glove-making and tailoring was 437,969; of these 14,964 under 15 years, 89,285 between 15 and 20, and 333,117 over 20 years. Many of the smaller branches are not included in these figures. But take the figures as they stand; we then have for England and Wales alone, according to the census of 1861, a total of 1,024,277 persons, about as many as are absorbed by agriculture and cattle breeding. We begin to understand what becomes of the immense quantities of goods conjured up by the magic of machinery, and of the enormous masses of workpeople, which that machinery sets free.

The production of wearing apparel is carried on partly in manu-factories in whose workrooms there is but a reproduction of that division of labour, the *membra disjecta* of which were found ready to hand; partly by small master-handicraftsmen; these, however, do not, as formerly, work for individual consumers, but for manufactories and warehouses, and to such an extent that often whole towns and stretches of country carry on certain branches, such as shoemaking, as a speciality; finally, on a very great scale by the so-called domestic workers, who form an external department of the manufactories, warehouses, and even of the workshops of the smaller masters.[184]

The raw material, &c., is supplied by mechanical industry, the mass of cheap human material (*taillable à merci et miséricorde*) is composed of the individuals 'liberated' by mechanical industry and improved agriculture. The manufactures of this class owed their origin chiefly to the capitalist's need of having at hand an army ready equipped to meet any increase of demand.[185] These manufactures, nevertheless, allowed the scattered handicrafts and domestic industries to continue to exist as a broad foundation. The great production of surplus-value in these branches of labour, and the progressive cheapening of their articles, were and are chiefly due to the minimum wages paid, no more than requisite for a miserable vegetation, and to the extension of working-time up to the maximum endurable by the human organism. It was in fact by the cheapness of the human sweat and the human blood, which were converted into commodities, that the markets were constantly being extended, and continue daily to be extended; more especially was this the case with England's colonial markets, where, besides, English tastes and habits prevail. At last the critical point was reached. The basis of the old method, sheer brutality in the exploitation of the workpeople, accompanied more or less by a systematic division of labour, no longer sufficed for the extending markets and for the still more rapidly extending competition of the capitalists. The hour struck for the advent of machinery. The decisively revolutionary machine, the machine which attacks in an equal degree the whole of the numberless branches of this sphere of production, dressmaking, tailoring, shoemaking, sewing, hat-making, and many others, is the sewing-machine.

Its immediate effect on the workpeople is like that of all machinery, which, since the rise of modern industry, has seized upon new branches of trade. Children of too tender an age are sent adrift. The wage of the machine hands rises compared with that of the house-workers, many of whom belong to the poorest of the poor. That of the better situated handicraftsman, with whom the machine competes, sinks. The new machine hands are exclusively girls and young women. With the help of mechanical force, they destroy the monopoly that male labour had of the heavier work, and they drive off from the lighter work numbers of old women and very young children. The overpowering competition crushes the weakest of the manual labourers. The fearful increase in death from starvation during the last 10 years in London runs parallel with the extension of machine sewing.[186] The new workwomen turn the machines by hand and foot, or by hand alone, sometimes sitting, sometimes standing, according to the weight, size, and special make of the machine, and expend a great deal of labour power. Their occupation is unwholesome, owing to the long hours, although in most cases they are not so long as under the old system. Wherever the sewing-machine locates itself in narrow and already over-crowded workrooms, it adds to the unwholesome influences. 'The effect,' says Mr Lord, 'on entering low-ceiled workrooms in which 30 to 40 machine hands are working is unbearable . . . The heat, partly due to the gas stoves used for warming the irons, is horrible . . . Even when moderate hours of work, i.e., from 8 in the morning till 6 in the evening, prevail in such places, yet 3 or 4 persons fall into a swoon regularly every day.'[187]

The revolution in the industrial methods which is the necessary result of the revolution in the instruments of production, is effected by a medley of transition forms. These forms vary according to the extent to which the sewing-machine has become prevalent in one branch of industry or the other, to the time during which it has been in operation, to the previous condition of the workpeople, to the preponderance of manufacture, of handicrafts or of domestic industry, to the rent of the workrooms,[188] &c. In dressmaking, for instance, where the labour for the most part was already organised, chiefly by simple co-operation, the sewing-machine at first formed merely a new factor in that manufacturing industry. In tailoring, shirtmaking, shoemaking, &c., all the forms are intermingled. Here the factory system proper. There middlemen receive the raw material from the capitalist *en chef*, and group around their sewing-machines, in 'chambers' and 'garrets', from 10 to 50 or more workwomen. Finally, as is always the case with machinery when not organised into a system, and when it can also be used in dwarfish proportions, handicraftsman and domestic workers, along with their families, or with a little extra labour from without, make use of their own sewing-machines.[189] The system actually prevalent in England is, that the capitalist concentrates a large number of machines on his premises, and then distributes the produce of those machines for further manipulation amongst the domestic workers.[190] The variety of the transition forms, however, does not conceal the tendency to conversion into the factory system proper. This tendency is nurtured by the very nature of the sewing-machine, the manifold uses of which push on the concentration, under one roof, and one management, of previously separated branches of a trade. It is also favoured by the circumstance that preparatory needlework, and certain other operations, are most conveniently done on the premises where the machine is at work; as well as by the inevitable expropriation of the hand sewers, and of the domestic workers who work with their own machines. This fate has already in part overtaken them. The constantly increasing amount of capital invested in sewing-machines,[191] gives the spur to the production of, and gluts the markets with, machine-made articles, thereby giving the signal to the domestic workers for the sale of their machines. The overproduction of sewing-machines themselves, causes their producers, in bad want of a sale, to let them out for so much a week, thus crushing by their deadly competition the small owners of machines.[192] Constant changes in the construction of the machines, and their ever-increasing cheapness, depreciate day by day the older makes, and allow of their being sold in great numbers, at absurd prices, to large capitalists, who alone can thus employ them at a profit. Finally, the substitution of the steam-engine for man gives in this, as in all similar revolutions, the finishing blow. At first, the use of steam power meets with mere technical difficulties, such as unsteadiness in the machines, difficulty in controlling their speed, rapid wear and tear of the lighter machines, &c., all of which are soon overcome by experience.[193] If, on the one hand, the concentration of many machines in large manufactories leads to the use of steam power, on the other hand, the competition of steam with human muscles hastens on the concentration of work-people and machines in large factories. Thus England is at present experiencing, not only in the colossal industry of making wearing apparel, but in most of the other trades mentioned above, the conversion of manufacture, of handicrafts, and of domestic work into the factory system, after each of those forms of production, totally changed and disorganised under the influence of modern industry, has long ago reproduced, and even overdone, all the horrors of the factory system, without participating in any of the elements of social progress it contains.[194]

This industrial revolution which takes place spontaneously, is artificially helped on by the extension of the Factory Acts to all industries in which women, young persons and children are employed. The compulsory regulation of the working-day as regards its length, pauses, beginning and end, the system of relays of children, the exclusion of all children under a certain age, &c., necessitate on the one hand more machinery[195] and the substitution of steam as a motive power in the place of muscles.[196] On the other hand, in order to make up for the loss of time, an expansion occurs of the means of production used in common, of the furnaces, buildings, &c., in one word, greater concentration of the means of production and a correspondingly greater concourse of workpeople. The chief objection, repeatedly and passionately urged on behalf of each manufacture threatened with the Factory Act, is in fact this, that in order to continue the business on the old scale a greater outlay of capital will be necessary. But as regards labour in the so-called domestic industries and the intermediate forms between them and anufacture, so soon as limits are

put to the working-day and to the employment of children, those
industries go to the wall. Unlimited exploitation of cheap labour
power is the sole foundation of their power to compete.

One of the essential conditions for the existence of the factory
system, especially when the length of the working-day is fixed, is
certainty in the result, i.e., the production in a given time of a given
quantity of commodities, or of a given useful effect. The statutory
pauses in the working-day, moreover, imply the assumption that
periodical and sudden cessation of the work does no harm to the
article undergoing the process of production. This certainty in the
result, and this possibility of interrupting the work are, of course,
easier to be attained in the purely mechanical industries than in those
in which chemical and physical processes play a part; as, for instance,
in the earthenware trade, in bleaching, dyeing, baking, and in most
of the metal industries. Wherever there is a working day without
restriction as to length, wherever there is night-work and unrestricted
waste of human life, there the slightest obstacle presented by the
nature of the work to a change for the better is soon looked upon as
an everlasting barrier erected by Nature. No poison kills vermin with
more certainty than the Factory Act removes such everlasting barriers.
No one made a greater outcry over 'impossibilities' than our friends
the earthenware manufacturers. In 1864, however, they were brought
under the Act, and within sixteen months every 'impossibility' had
vanished. 'The improved method', called forth by the Act, 'of making
slip by pressure instead of by evaporation, the newly-constructed
stoves for drying the ware in its green state, &c., are each events of
great importance in the pottery art, and mark an advance which the
preceding century could not rival . . . It has even considerably reduced
the temperature of the stoves themselves with a considerable saving of
fuel, and with a readier effect on the ware.'[197] In spite of every
prophecy, the cost-price of earthenware did not rise, but the quantity
produced did, and to such an extent that the export for the twelve
months ending December, 1865, exceeded in value by £138,628 the
average of the preceding three years. In the manufacture of matches it
was thought to be an indispensable requirement, that boys, even while
bolting their dinner, should go on dipping the matches in melted
phosphorus, the poisonous vapour from which rose into their faces.
The Factory Act (1864) made the saving of time a necessity, and so
forced into existence a dipping machine, the vapour from which
could not come in contact with the workers.[198] So, at the present
time, in those branches of the lace manufacture not yet subject to the
Factory Act, it is maintained that the meal-times cannot be regular
owing to the different periods required by the various kinds of lace for

drying, which periods vary from three minutes up to an hour and more. To this the Children's Employment Commissioners answer: 'The circumstances of this case are precisely analogous to that of the paper-stainers, dealt with in our first report. Some of the principal manufacturers in the trade urged that in consequence of the nature of the materials used, and their various processes, they would be unable, without serious loss, to stop for meal-times at any given moment. But it was seen from the evidence that, by due care and previous arrangement, the apprehended difficulty would be got over; and accordingly, by clause 6 of section 6 of the Factory Acts Extension Act, passed during this Session of Parliament, an interval of eighteen months is given to them from the passing of the Act before they are required to conform to the meal hours, specified by the Factory Acts.'[199] Hardly had the Act been passed when our friends the manufacturers found out: 'The inconveniences we expected to arise from the introduction of the Factory Acts into our branch of manufacture, I am happy to say, have not arisen. We do not find the production at all interfered with; in short, we produce more in the same time.'[200] It is evident that the English legislature, which certainly no one will venture to reproach with being overdosed with genius, has been led by experience to the conclusion that a simple compulsory law is sufficient to enact away all the so-called impediments, opposed by the nature of the process, to the restriction and regulation of the working-day. Hence, on the introduction of the Factory Act into a given industry, a period varying from six to eighteen months is fixed within which it is incumbent on the manufacturers to remove all technical impediments to the working of the Act. Mirabeau's '*Impossible! ne me dites jamais ce bête de mot!*' is particularly applicable to modern technology. But though the Factory Acts thus artificially ripen the material elements necessary for the conversion of the manufacturing system into the factory system, yet at the same time, owing to the necessity they impose for greater outlay of capital, they hasten on the decline of the small masters, and the concentration of capital.[201]

Besides the purely technical impediments that are removable by technical means, the irregular habits of the workpeople themselves obstruct the regulation of the hours of labour. This is especially the case where piece-wage predominates, and where loss of time in one part of the day or week can be made good by subsequent over-time, or by night-work, a process which brutalises the adult workman, and ruins his wife and children.[202] Although this absence of regularity in the expenditure of labour power is a natural and rude reaction against the tedium of monotonous drudgery, it originates, also, to a much greater degree from anarchy in production, anarchy that in its turn presupposes unbridled exploitation of labour power by the capitalist. Besides the general periodic changes of the industrial cycle, and the special fluctuations in the markets to which each industry is subject, we may also reckon what is called 'the season', dependent either on the periodicity of favourable seasons of the year for navigation; or on fashion, and the sudden placing of large orders that have to be executed in the shortest possible time. The habit of giving such orders becomes more frequent with the extension of railways and telegraphs. 'The extension of the railway system throughout the country has tended very much to encourage giving short notice. Purchasers now come up from Glasgow, Manchester, and Edinburgh once every fortnight or so to the wholesale city warehouses which we supply, and give small orders requiring immediate execution, instead of buying from stock as they used to do. Years ago we were always able to work in the slack times, so as to meet demand of the next season, but now no one can say beforehand what will be the demand then.'[203]

In those factories and manufactories that are not yet subject to the Factory Acts, the most fearful over-work prevails periodically during what is called the season, in consequence of sudden orders. In the outside department of the factory, of the manufactory, and of the warehouse, the so-called domestic workers, whose employment is at the best irregular, are entirely dependent for their raw material and their orders on the caprice of the capitalist, who, in this industry, is not hampered by any regard for depreciation of his buildings and machinery, and risks nothing by a stoppage of work, but the skin of the worker himself. Here then he sets himself systematically to work to form an industrial reserve force that shall be ready at a moment's notice; during one part of the year he decimates this force by the most inhuman toil, during the other part, he lets it starve for want of work. 'The employers avail themselves of the habitual irregularity in the homework, when any extra work is wanted at a push, so that the work goes on till 11, and 12 p.m. or 2 a.m., or as the usual phrase is, 'all hours', and that in localities where 'the stench is enough to knock you down, you go to the door, perhaps, and open it, but shudder to go further.'[204] 'They are curious men,' said one of the witnesses, a shoemaker, speaking of the masters, 'they think it does a boy no harm to work too hard for half the year, if he is nearly idle for the other half.'[205]

In the same way as technical impediments, so, too, those 'usages which have grown with the growth of trade' were and still are proclaimed by interested capitalists as obstacles due to the nature of the work. This was a favourite cry of the cotton lords at the time they were first threatened with the Factory Acts. Although their industry more than any other depends on navigation, yet experience has given them the lie. Since then, every pretended obstruction to business has been treated by the Factory Inspectors as a mere sham.[206] The thoroughly conscientious investigations of the Children's Employment Commission prove that the effect of the regulation of the hours of work, in some industries, was to spread the mass of labour previously employed more evenly over the whole year;[207] that this regulation was the first rational bridle on the murderous, meaningless caprices of fashion,[208] caprices that consort so badly with the system of modern industry; that the development of ocean navigation and of the means of communication generally, has swept away the technical basis on which season-work was really supported,[209] and that all other so-called unconquerable difficulties vanish before larger buildings, additional machinery, increase in the number of workpeople employed,[210] and the alterations caused by all these in the mode of conducting the wholesale trade.[211] But for all that, capital never becomes reconciled to such changes – and this is admitted over and over again by its own representatives – except 'under the pressure of a General Act of Parliament'[212] for the compulsory regulation of the hours of labour.

Section 9. The Factory Acts. Sanitary and Educational Clauses of the Same. Their General Extension in England.

Factory legislation, that first conscious and methodical reaction of society against the spontaneously developed form of the process of production, is, as we have seen, just as much the necessary product of modern industry as cotton yarn, self-actors, and the electric telegraph. Before passing to the consideration of the extension of that legislation in England, we shall shortly notice certain clauses contained in the Factory Acts, and not relating to the hours of work.

Apart from their wording, which makes it easy for the capitalist to evade them, the sanitary clauses are extremely meagre, and, in fact, limited to provisions for whitewashing the walls, for insuring cleanliness in some other matters, for ventilation, and for protection against dangerous machinery. In the third book we shall return again to the fanatical opposition of the masters to those clauses which imposed upon them a slight expenditure on appliances for protecting the limbs of their workpeople, an opposition that throws a fresh and glaring light on the Free-trade dogma, according to which, in a society with conflicting interests, each individual necessarily furthers the common weal by seeking nothing but his own personal advantage! One example is enough. The reader knows that during the last 20 years, the flax industry has very much extended, and that, with that extension, the number of scutching mills in Ireland has increased. In 1864 there were in that country 1,800 of these mills. Regularly in autumn and winter women and 'young persons', the wives, sons, and daughters of the neighbouring small farmers, a class of people totally unaccustomed to machinery, are taken from field labour to feed the rollers of the scotching mills with flax. The accidents, both as regards number and kind, are wholly unexampled in the history of machinery. In one scotching mill, at Kildinan, near Cork, there occurred between 1852 and 1856, six fatal accidents and sixty mutilations; every one of which might have been prevented by the simplest appliances, at the cost of a few shillings. Dr W. White, the certifying surgeon for factories at Downpatrick, states in his official report, dated the 15th December, 1865: 'The serious accidents at the scutching mills are of the most fearful nature. In many cases a quarter of the body is torn from the trunk, and either involves death, or a future of wretched incapacity and suffering. The increase of mills in the country will, of course, extend these dreadful results, and it will be a great boon if they are brought under the legislature. I am convinced that by proper supervision of scutching mills a vast sacrifice of life and limb would be averted.'[213]

What could possibly show better the character of the capitalist mode of production, than the necessity that exists for forcing upon it, by Acts of Parliament, the simplest appliances for maintaining cleanliness and health? In the potteries the Factory Act of 1864 'has whitewashed and cleansed upwards of 200 workshops, after a period of abstinence from any such cleaning, in many cases of 20 years, and in some, entirely,' (this is the 'abstinence' of the capitalist!) 'in which were employed 27,800 artisans, hitherto breathing through protracted days and often nights of labour, a mephitic atmosphere, and which rendered an otherwise comparatively innocuous occupation, pregnant with disease and death. The Act has improved the ventilation very much.'[214] At the same time, this portion of the Act strikingly shows that the capitalist mode of production, owing to its very nature, excludes all rational improvement beyond a certain point. It has been stated over and over again that the English doctors are unanimous in declaring that where the work is continuous, 500 cubic feet is the very least space that should be allowed for each person. Now, if the Factory Acts, owing to their compulsory provisions, indirectly hasten on the conversion of small workshops into factories, thus indirectly attacking the proprietary rights of the smaller capitalists, and assuring a monopoly to the great ones, so, if it were made obligatory to provide the proper space for each workman in every workshop, thousands of small employers would, at one full swoop, be expropriated directly! The very root of the capitalist mode of production, i.e., the self-expansion of all capital, large or small, by means of the 'free' purchase and consumption of labour power, would be attacked. Factory legislation is therefore brought to a deadlock before these 500 cubic feet of breathing space. The sanitary officers, the industrial inquiry commissioners, the factory inspectors, all harp, over and over again, upon the necessity for those 500 cubic feet, and upon the impossibility of wringing them out of capital. They thus, in fact, declare that consumption and other lung diseases among the workpeople are necessary conditions to the existence of capital.[215]

Paltry as the education clauses of the Act appear on the whole, yet they proclaim elementary education to be an indispensable condition to the employment of children.[216] The success of those clauses proved for the first time the possibility of combining education and gymnastics[217] with manual labour, and, consequently, of combining manual labour with education and gymnastics. The factory inspectors soon found out by questioning the schoolmasters, that the factory children, although receiving only one half the education of the regular day scholars, yet learnt quite as much and often more. 'This can be accounted for by the simple fact that, with only being at school for one half of the day, they are always fresh, and nearly always ready and willing to receive instruction. The system on which they work, half manual labour, and half school, renders each employment a rest and a relief to the other; consequently, both are far more congenial to the child, than would be the case were he kept constantly at one. It is quite clear that a boy who has been at school all the morning, cannot (in hot weather particularly) cope with one who comes fresh and bright from his work.'[218] Further information on this point will be found in Senior's speech at the Social Science Congress at Edinburgh in 1863. He there shows, amongst other things, how the monotonous and uselessly long school hours of the children of the upper and middle classes, uselessly add to the labour of the teacher, 'while he not only fruitlessly but absolutely injuriously, wastes the time, health, and energy of the children.' [219] From the Factory system budded, as Robert Owen has shown us in detail, the germ of the education of the future, an education that will, in the case of every child over a given age, combine productive labour with instruction and gymnastics, not only as one of the methods of adding to the efficiency of production, but as the only method of producing fully developed human beings.

Modern Industry, as we have seen, sweeps away by technical means the manufacturing division of labour, under which each man is bound hand and foot for life to a single detail-operation. At the same time, the capitalistic form of that industry reproduces this same division of labour in a still more monstrous shape; in the factory proper, by converting the workman into a living appendage of the machine; and everywhere outside the factory, partly by the sporadic use of machinery and machine workers,[220] partly by re-establishing the division of labour on a fresh basis by the general introduction of the labour of women and children, and of cheap unskilled labour.

The antagonism between the manufacturing division of labour and the methods of Modern Industry makes itself forcibly felt. It manifests itself, amongst other ways, in the frightful fact that a great part of the children employed in modern factories and manufactures, are from their earliest years riveted to the most simple manipulations, and exploited for years, without being taught a single sort of work that would afterwards make them of use, even in the same manufactory or factory. In the English letter-press printing trade, for example, there existed formerly a system, corresponding to that in the old manufactures and handicrafts, of advancing the apprentices from easy to more and more difficult work. They went through a course of teaching till they were finished printers. To be able to read and write was for every one of them a requirement of their trade. All this was changed by the printing machine. It employs two sorts of labourers, one grown up, renters, the other, boys mostly from 11 to 17 years of age whose sole business is either to spread the sheets of paper under the machine, or to take from it the printed sheets. They perform this weary task, in London especially, for 14, 15, and 16 hours at a stretch, during several days in the week, and frequently for 36 hours, with only 2 hours' rest for meals and sleep.[221] A great part of them cannot read, and they are, as a rule, utter savages and very extraordinary creatures. 'To qualify them for the work which they have to do, they require no intellectual training; there is little room in it for skill, and less for judgment; their wages, though rather high for boys, do not increase proportionately as they grow up, and the majority of them cannot look for advancement to the better paid and more responsible post of machine minder, because while each machine has but one minder, it has at least two, and often four boys attached to it.'[222] As soon as they get too old for such child's work, that is about 17 at the latest, they are discharged from the printing establishments. They become recruits of crime. Several attempts to procure them employment elsewhere, were rendered of no avail by their ignorance and brutality, and by their mental and bodily degradation.

As with the division of labour in the interior of the manufacturing workshops, so it is with the division of labour in the interior of

society. So long as handicraft and manufacture form the general
groundwork of social production, the subjection of the producer to
one branch exclusively, the breaking up of the multifariousness of
his employment,[223] is a necessary step in the development. On that
groundwork each separate branch of production acquires empirically
the form that is technically suited to it, slowly perfects it, and, so soon
as a given degree of maturity has been reached, rapidly crystallises that
form. The only thing, that here and there causes a change, besides
new raw material supplied by commerce, is the gradual alteration of
the instruments of labour. But their form, too, once definitely settled
by experience, petrifies, as is proved by their being in many cases
handed down in the same form by one generation to another during
thousands of years. A characteristic feature is, that, even down into
the eighteenth century, the different trades were called 'mysteries'
(*mystères*);[224] into their secrets none but those duly initiated could
penetrate. Modern Industry rent the veil that concealed from men
their own social process of production, and that turned the various,
spontaneously divided branches of production into so many riddles,
not only to outsiders, but even to the. initiated. The principle which it
pursued, of resolving each process into its constituent movements,
without any regard to their possible execution by the hand of man,
created the new modern science of technology. The varied, apparently
unconnected, and petrified forms of the industrial processes now
resolved themselves into so many conscious and systematic applications of natural science to the attainment of given useful effects.
Technology also discovered the few main fundamental forms of
motion, which, despite the diversity of the instruments used, are
necessarily taken by every productive action of the human body; just as
the science of mechanics sees in the most complicated machinery
nothing but the continual repetition of the simple mechanical powers.

Modern Industry never looks upon and treats the existing form of a
process as final. The technical basis of that industry is therefore
revolutionary, while all earlier modes of production were essentially
conservative.[225] By means of machinery, chemical processes and
other methods, it is continually causing changes not only in the
technical basis of production, but also in the functions of the labourer, and in the social combinations of the labour-process. At the
same time, it thereby also revolutionises the division of labour within
the society, and incessantly launches masses of capital and of workpeople from one branch of production to another. But if Modern
Industry, by its very nature, therefore necessitates variation of labour,
fluency of function, universal mobility of the labourer, on the other
hand, in its capitalistic form, it reproduces the old division of labour

with its ossified particularisations. We have seen how this absolute contradiction between the technical necessities of Modern Industry, and the social character inherent in its capitalistic form, dispels all fixity and security in the situation of the labourer; how it constantly threatens, by taking away the instruments of labour, to snatch from his hands his means of subsistence,[226] and, by suppressing his detail-function, to make him superfluous, We have seen, too, how this antagonism vents its rage in the creation of that monstrosity, an industrial reserve army, kept in misery in order to be always at the disposal of capital; in the incessant human sacrifices from among the working-class, in the most reckless squandering of labour power and in the devastation caused by a social anarchy which turns every economic progress into a social calamity. This is the negative side. But if, on the one hand, variation of work at present imposes itself after the manner of an overpowering natural law, and with the blindly destructive action of a natural law that meets with resistance[227] at all points, Modern Industry, on the other hand, through its catastrophes imposes the necessity of recognising, as a fundamental law of production, variation of work, consequently fitness of the labourer for varied work, consequently the greatest possible development of his varied aptitudes. It becomes a question of life and death for society to adapt the mode of production to the normal functioning of this law. Modern Industry, indeed, compels society, under penalty of death, to replace the detail-worker of today, grappled by life-long repetition of one and the same trivial operation, and thus reduced to the mere fragment of a man, by the fully developed individual, fit for a variety of labours, ready to face any change of production, and to whom the different social functions he performs, are but so many modes of giving free scope to his own natural and acquired powers.

One step already spontaneously taken towards effecting this revolution is the establishment of technical and agricultural schools, and of 'écoles d'enseignement professionnel', in which the children of the working-men receive some little instruction in technology and in the practical handling of the various implements of labour. Though the Factory Act, that first and meagre concession wrung from capital, is limited to combining elementary education with work in the factory, there can be no doubt that when the working-class comes into power, as inevitably it must, technical instruction, both theoretical and practical, will take its proper place in the working-class schools. There is also no doubt that such revolutionary ferments, the final result of which is the abolition of the old division of labour, are diametrically opposed to the capitalistic form of production, and to the economic status of the labourer corresponding to that form. But the historical development of the antagonisms, immanent in a given form of production, is the only way in which that form of production can be dissolved and a new form established. '*Ne sutor ultra crepidam*' – this *ne plus ultra* of handicraft wisdom became sheer nonsense, from the moment the watchmaker Watt invented the steam-engine, the barber Arkwright, the throstle, and the working-jeweller, Fulton, the steamship.[228]

So long as Factory legislation is confined to regulating the labour in factories, manufactories, &c., it is regarded as a mere interference with the exploiting rights of capital. But when it comes to regulating the so-called 'home-labour',[229] it is immediately viewed as a direct attack on the *patria potestas*, on parental authority. The tender-hearted English Parliament long affected to shrink from taking this step. The force of facts, however, compelled it at last to acknowledge that modern industry, in overturning the economic foundation on which was based the traditional family, and the family labour corresponding to it, had also unloosened all traditional family ties. The rights of the children had to be proclaimed. The final report of the Ch. Empl. Comm. of 1866, states: 'It is unhappily, to a painful degree, apparent throughout the whole of the evidence, that against no persons do the children of both sexes so much require protection as against their parents.' The system of unlimited exploitation of children's labour in general and the so-called home-labour in particular is 'maintained only because the parents are able, without check or control, to exercise this arbitrary and mischievous power over their young and tender offspring . . . Parents must not possess the absolute power of making their children mere machines to earn so much weekly wage . . . ' The children and young persons, therefore, in all such cases may justifiably claim from the legislature, as a natural right, that an exemption should be secured to them, from what destroys prematurely their physical strength, and lowers them in the scale of intellectual and moral beings.'[230] It was not, however, the misuse of parental authority that created the capitalistic exploitation, whether direct or indirect, of children's labour; but, on the contrary, it was the capitalistic mode of exploitation which, by sweeping away the economic basis of parental authority, made its exercise degenerate into a mischievous misuse of power. However terrible and disgusting the dissolution, under the capitalist system, of the old family ties may appear, nevertheless, modern industry, by assigning as it does an important part in the process of production, outside the domestic sphere, to women, to young persons, and to children of both sexes, creates a new economic foundation for a higher form of the family and of the relations between the sexes. It is, of course, just as absurd to hold the Teutonic-Christian form of the family to be absolute and final as it would be to apply that character to the ancient Roman, the ancient Greek, or the Eastern forms which, moreover, taken together form a series in historical development. Moreover, it is obvious that the fact of the collective working group being composed of individuals of both sexes and all ages, must necessarily, under suitable conditions, become a source of humane development; although in its spontaneously developed, brutal, capitalistic form, where the labourer exists for the process of production, and not the process of production for the labourer, that fact is a pestiferous source of corruption and slavery.[231]

The necessity for a generalisation of the Factory Acts, for transforming them from an exceptional law relating to mechanical spinning and weaving – those first creations of machinery – into a law affecting social production as a whole, arose, as we have seen, from the mode in which Modern Industry was historically developed. In the rear of that industry, the traditional form of manufacture, of handicraft, and of domestic industry, is entirely revolutionised; manufactures are constantly passing into the factory system, and handicrafts into manufactures; and lastly, the spheres of handicraft and of the domestic industries become, in a, comparatively speaking, wonderfully short time, dens of misery in which capitalistic exploitation obtains free play for the wildest excesses. There are two circumstances that finally turn the scale: first, the constantly recurring experience that capital, so soon as it finds itself subject to legal control at one point, compensates itself all the more recklessly at other points;[232] secondly, the cry of the capitalists for equality in the conditions of competition, i.e., for equal restraint on all exploitation of labour.[233] On this point let us listen to two heart-broken cries. Messrs Cooksley of Bristol, nail and chain, &c., manufacturers, spontaneously introduced the regulations of the Factory Act into their business. 'As the old irregular system prevails in neighbouring works, the Messrs Cooksley are subject to the disadvantage of having their boys enticed to continue their labour elsewhere after 6 p.m. "This," they naturally say, "is an unjustice and loss to us, as it exhausts a portion of the boy's strength, of which we ought to have the full benefit." '[234] Mr J. Simpson (paper box and bagmaker, London) states before the commissioners of the Ch. Empl. Comm.: 'He would sign any petition for it' (legislative interference) . . . 'As it was, he always felt restless at night, when he had closed his place, lest others should be working later than him and getting away his orders.'[235] Summarising, the Ch. Empl. Comm. says: 'It would be unjust to the larger employers that their factories should be placed under regulation, while the hours of labour in the smaller places in their own branch of business were under no legislative restriction. And to the injustice arising from the unfair conditions of competition, in regard to hours, that would be created if the smaller places of work were exempt, would be added the disadvantage to the larger manufacturers, of finding their supply of juvenile and female labour drawn off to the places of work exempt from legislation. Further, a stimulus would be given to the multi-plication of the smaller places of work, which are almost invariably the least favourable to the health, comfort, education, and general improvement of the people.'[236]

In its final report the Commission proposes to subject to the Factory Act more than 1,400,000 children, young persons, and women, of which number about one half are exploited in small industries and by the so-called home-work.[237] It says, 'But if it should seem fit to Parliament to place the whole of that large number of children, young persons and females under the protective legislation above adverted to . . . it cannot be doubted that such legislation would have a most beneficent effect, not only upon the young and the feeble, who are its more immediate objects, but upon the still larger body of adult workers, who would in all these employments, both directly and indirectly, come immediately under its influence. It would enforce upon them regular and moderate hours; it would lead to their places of work being kept in a healthy and cleanly state; it would therefore husband and improve that store of physical strength on which their own well-being and that of the country so much depends; it would save the rising generation from that over-exertion at an early age which undermines their constitutions and leads to premature decay; finally, it would ensure them – at least up to the age of 13 – the opportunity of receiving the elements of education, and would put an end to that utter ignorance . . . so faithfully exhibited in the Reports of our Assistant Commissioners, and which cannot be regarded without the deepest pain, and a profound sense of national degradation.[238]

Twenty-four years before, another Commission of Inquiry on the labour of children had already, as Senior remarks, disclosed 'the most frightful picture of avarice, selfishness and cruelty on the part of masters and of parents, and of juvenile and infantile misery, degrad-ation and destruction ever presented . . . It may be supposed that it describes the horrors of a past age. But there is unhappily evidence that those horrors continue as intense as they were. A pamphlet published by Hardwicke about 2 years ago states that the abuses complained of in 1842, are in full bloom at the present day. It is a strange proof of the general neglect of the morals and health of the children of the working-class, that this report lay unnoticed for 20 years, during which the children, "bred up without the remotest sign of comprehension as to what is meant by the term morals, who had neither knowledge, nor religion, nor natural affection", were allowed to become the parents of the present generation.'[241]

The social conditions having undergone a change, Parliament could not venture to shelve the demands of the Commission of 1862, as it had done those of the Commission of 1840. Hence in 1864, when the Commission had not yet published more than a part of its reports, the earthenware industries (including the potteries), makers of paper-hangings, matches, cartridges, and caps, and fustian cutters were made subject to the Acts in force in the textile industries. In the Speech from the Throne, on 5th February, 1867, the Tory Cabinet of the day announced the introduction of Bills, founded on the final recommendations of the Commission, which had completed its labours in 1866.

On the 15th August, 1867, the Factory Acts Extension Act, and on the 21st August, the Workshops' Regulation Act received the Royal Assent; the former Act having reference to large industries, the latter to small.

The former applies to blast-furnaces, iron and copper mills, foundries, machine shops, metal manufactories, gutta-percha works, paper mills, glass-works, tobacco manufactories, letter-press printing (including newspapers), book-binding, in short to all industrial establishments of the above kind, in which 50 individuals or more are occupied simultaneously, and for not less than 100 days during the year.

To give an idea of the extent of the sphere embraced by the Workshops' Regulation Act in its application, we cite from its interpretation clause, the following passages:

'*Handicraft* shall mean any manual labour exercised by way of trade, or for purposes of gain in, or incidental to, the making any article or part of an article, or in, or incidental to, the altering, repairing, ornamenting, finishing, or otherwise adapting for sale any article.'

'*Workshop* shall mean any room or place whatever in the open air or under cover, in which any handicraft is carried on by any child, young person, or woman, and to which and over which the person by whom such child, young person, or woman is employed, has the right of access and control.'

'*Employed* shall mean occupied in any handicraft, whether for wages or not, under a master or under a parent as herein defined.'

'*Parent* shall mean parent, guardian, or person, having the custody of, or control over, any . . . child or young person.'

Clause 7, which imposes a penalty for employment of children, young persons, and women, contrary to the provisions of the Act, subjects to fines, not only the occupier of the workshop, whether parent or not, but even 'the parent of, or the person deriving any direct benefit from the labour of, or having the control over, the child, young person or woman.'

The Factory Acts Extension Act, which affects the large establishments, derogates from the Factory Act by a crowd of vicious exceptions and cowardly compromises with the masters.

The Workshops' Regulation Act, wretched in all its details, remained a dead letter in the hands of the municipal and local authorities who were charged with its execution. When, in 1871, Parliament withdrew from them this power, in order to confer it on the Factory Inspectors, to whose province it thus added by a single stroke more than one hundred thousand workshops, and three hundred brickworks, care was taken at the same time not to add more than eight assistants to their already undermanned staff.[242]

What strikes us, then, in the English legislation of 1867, is, on the one hand, the necessity imposed on the parliament of the ruling classes, of adopting in principle measures so extraordinary, and on so great a scale, against the excesses of capitalistic exploitation; and on the other hand, the hesitation, the repugnance, and the bad faith, with which it lent itself to the task of carrying those measures into practice.

The Inquiry Commission of 1862 also proposed a new regulation of the mining industry, an industry distinguished from others by the exceptional characteristic that the interests of landlord and capitalist there join hands. The antagonism of these two interests had been favourable to Factory legislation, while on the other hand the absence of that antagonism is sufficient to explain the delays and chicanery of the legislation on mines.

The Inquiry Commission of 1840 had made revelations so terrible, so shocking, and creating such a scandal all over Europe, that to salve its conscience Parliament passed the Mining Act of 1842, in which it limited itself to forbidding the employment underground in mines of children under 10 years of age and females.

Then another Act, The Mines' Inspecting Act of 1860, provides that mines shall be inspected by public officers nominated specially for that purpose, and that boys between the ages of 10 and 12 years shall not be employed, unless they have a school certificate, or go to school for a certain number of hours. This Act was a complete dead letter owing to the ridiculously small number of inspectors, the meagreness of their powers, and other causes that will become apparent as we proceed.

One of the most recent Blue Books on mines is the *Report from the Select Committee on Mines, together with &c. Evidence, 23rd July, 1866.* This Report is the work of a Parliamentary Committee selected from members of the House of Commons, and authorised to summon and examine witnesses. It is a thick folio volume in which the Report itself occupies only five lines to this effect; that the committee has nothing to say, and that more witnesses must be examined!

The mode of examining the witnesses reminds one of the cross-examination of witnesses in English courts of justice, where the advocate tries, by means of impudent, unexpected, equivocal and involved questions, put without connection, to intimidate, surprise, and confound the witness, and to give a forced meaning to the answers extorted from him. In this inquiry the members of the committee themselves are the cross-examiners, and among them are to be found both mine-owners and mine exploiters; the witnesses are mostly working coal miners. The whole farce is too characteristic of the spirit of capital, not to call for a few extracts from this Report. For the sake of conciseness I have classified them. I may also add that every question and its answer are numbered in the English Blue Books.

I. *Employment in mines of boys of 10 years and upwards.* – In the mines the work, inclusive of going and returning, usually lasts 14 or 15 hours, sometimes even from 3, 4 and 5 o'clock a.m., till 5 and 6 o'clock p.m. (n. 6, 452, 83). The adults work in two shifts, of eight hours each; but there is no alternation with the boys, on account of the expense (n. 80, 203, 204). The younger boys are chiefly employed in opening and shutting the ventilating doors in the various parts of the mine; the older ones are employed on heavier work, in carrying coal, &c. (n. 122, 739, 1747). They work these long hours underground until their 18th or 22nd year, when they are put to miner's work proper (n. 161). Children and young persons are at present worse treated, and harder worked than at any previous period (n. 1663–1667). The miners demand almost unanimously an act of Parliament prohibiting the employment in mines of children under 14. And now Hussey Vivian (himself an exploiter of mines) asks: 'Would not the opinion of the workman depend upon the poverty of the workman's family?' Mr Bruce: 'Do you not think it would be a very hard case, where a parent had been injured, or where he was sickly, or where a father was dead, and there was only a mother, to prevent a child between 12 and 14 earning 1s. 7d. a day for the good of the family? . . . You must lay down a general rule . . . Are you prepared to recommend legislation which would prevent the employment of children under 12 and 14, whatever the state of their parents might be?' 'Yes.' (ns. 107–110). Vivian: 'Supposing that an enactment were passed preventing the employment of children under the age of 14, would it not be probable that . . . the parents of children would seek employment for their children in other directions, for instance, in manufacture?' 'Not generally I think' (n. 174). Kinnaird: 'Some of the boys are keepers of doors?' 'Yes.' 'Is there not generally a very great draught every time you open a door or close it?' 'Yes, generally there is.' 'It sounds a very easy thing, but it is in fact rather a painful one?' 'He is imprisoned there just the same as if he was in a cell of a gaol.' Bourgeois Vivian: 'Whenever a boy is furnished with a lamp cannot he read?' 'Yes, he can read, if he finds himself in candles . . . I suppose he would be found fault with if he were discovered reading; he is there to mind his business, he has a duty to perform, and he has to attend to it in the first place, and I do not think it would be allowed down the pit.' (ns. 139, 141, 143, 158, 160).

II. *Education*. – The working miners want a law for the compulsory education of their children, as in factories. They declare the clauses of the Act of 1860, which require a school certificate to be obtained before employing boys of 10 and 12 years of age, to be quite illusory. The examination of the witnesses on this subject is truly droll. 'Is it (the Act) required more against the masters or against the parents?' 'It is required against both I think.' 'You cannot say whether it is required against one more than against the other?' 'No; I can hardly answer that question.' (ns. 115, 116). 'Does there appear to be any desire on the part of the employers that the boys should have such hours as to enable them to go to school?' 'No; the hours are never shortened for that purpose.' (n. 137) Mr Kinnaird: 'Should you say that the colliers generally improve their education; have you any instances of men who have, since they began to work, greatly improved their education, or do they not rather go back, and lose any advantage that they may have gained?' 'They generally become worse: they do not improve; they acquire bad habits; they get on to drinking and gambling and such like, and they go completely to wreck.' (n. 211.) 'Do they make any attempt of the kind (for providing instruction) by having schools at night?' 'There are few collieries where night schools are held, and perhaps at those collieries a few boys do go to those schools; but they are so physically exhausted that it is to no purpose that they go there.' (n. 454.) 'You are then,' concludes the bourgeois, 'against education?' 'Most certainly not; but,' &c. (n. 443.) 'But are they (the employers) not compelled to demand them (school certificates)?' 'By law they are; but I am not aware that they are demanded by the employers.' 'Then it is your opinion, that this provision of the Act as to requiring certificates, is not generally carried out in the collieries?' 'It is not carried out.' (ns. 443, 444.) 'Do the men take a great interest in this question (of education)?' 'The majority of them do.' (n. 717.) 'Are they very anxious to see the law enforced?' 'The majority are.' (n. 718.) 'Do you think that in this country any law that you pass . . . can really be effectual unless the population themselves assist in putting it into operation?' 'Many a man might wish to object to employing a boy, but he would perhaps become marked by it.' (n. 720.) 'Marked by whom?' 'By his employers.' (n. 721.) 'Do you think that the employers would find any fault with a man who obeyed the law . . . ?' 'I believe they would.' (n. 722.) 'Have you ever heard of any workman objecting to employ a boy between 10 and 12, who could not write or read?' 'It is not left to men's option.' (n. 123.) 'Would you call for the interference of Parliament?' 'I think that if anything effectual is to be done in the education of the colliers' children, it will have to be made compulsory by Act of Parliament.' (n. 1634.) 'Would you lay that obligation upon the colliers only, or all the workpeople of Great Britain?' 'I came to speak for the colliers.' (n. 1636.) 'Why should you distinguish them (colliery boys) from other boys?' 'Because I think they are an exception to the rule.' (n. 1638.) 'In what respect?' 'In a physical respect.' (n. 1639.) 'Why should education be more valuable to them than to other classes of lads?' 'I do not know that it is more valuable; but through the over-exertion in mines there is less chance for the boys that are employed there to get education, either at Sunday schools, or at day schools.' (n. 1640.) 'It is impossible to look at a question of this sort absolutely by itself?' (n. 1644.) 'Is there a sufficiency of schools?' – 'No' . . . (n. 1646). 'If the State were to require that every child should be sent to school, would there be schools for the children to go to?' 'No; but I think if the circumstances were to spring up, the schools would be forthcoming.' (n. 1647.) 'Some of them (the boys) cannot read and write at all, I suppose?' 'The majority cannot. The majority of the men themselves cannot.' (ns. 705, 725.)

III. *Employment of women.* – Since 1842 women are no more employed underground, but are occupied on the surface in loading the coal, &c., in drawing the tubs to the canals and railway waggons, in sorting, &c. Their numbers have considerably increased during the last three or four years. (n. 1727.) They are mostly the wives, daughters, and widows of the working miners, and their ages range from 12 to

50 or 60 years. (ns. 645, 1779.) 'What is the feeling among the working miners as to the employment of women?' 'I think they generally condemn it.' (n. 648.) 'What objection do you see to it?' 'I think it is degrading to the sex.' (n. 649.) 'There is a peculiarity of dress?' 'Yes . . . it is rather a man's dress, and I believe in some cases, it drowns all sense of decency.' 'Do the women smoke?' 'Some do.' 'And I suppose it is very dirty work?' 'Very dirty.' 'They get black and grimy?' 'As black as those who are down the mines . . . I believe that a woman having children (and there are plenty on the banks that have) cannot do her duty to her children.' (ns. 650–654, 701.) 'Do you think that those widows could get employment anywhere else, which would bring them in as much wages as that (from 8s. to 10s. a week)?' 'I cannot speak to that.' (n. 709.) 'You would still be prepared, would you,' (flint-hearted fellow!) 'to prevent their obtaining a livelihood by these means?' 'I would.' (n. 710.) 'What is the general feeling in the district . . . as to the employment of women?' 'The feeling is that it is degrading; and we wish as miners to have more respect to the fair sex than to see them placed on the pit bank . . . Some part of the work is very hard; some of these girls have raised as much as 10 tons of stuff a day.' (ns. 1715,1717.) 'Do you think that the women employed about the collieries are less moral than the women employed in the factories?' '. ..the percentage of bad ones may be a little more . . . than with the girls in the factories.' (n. 1237.) 'But you are not quite satisfied with the state of morality in the factories?' 'No.' (n. 1733.) 'Would you prohibit the employment of women in factories also?' 'No, I would not.' (n. 1734.) 'Why not?' 'I think it a more honourable occupation for them in the mills.' (n. 1735.) 'Still it is injurious to their morality, you think?' 'Not so much as working on the pit bank; but it is more on the social position I take it; I do not take it on its moral ground alone. The degradation, in its social bearing on the girls, is deplorable in the extreme. When these 400 or 500 girls become colliers' wives, the men suffer greatly from this degradation, and it causes them to leave their homes and drink.' (n. 1736.) 'You would be obliged to stop the employment of women in the ironworks as well, would you not, if you stopped it in the collieries?' 'I cannot speak for any other trade.' (n. 1737.) 'Can you see any difference in the circumstances of women employed in ironworks, and the circumstances of women employed above ground in collieries?' 'I have not ascertained anything as to that.' (n. 1740.) 'Can you see anything that makes a distinction between one class and the other?' 'I have not ascertained that, but I know from house to house visitation, that it is a deplorable state of things in our district . . . ' (n. 1741.) 'Would you interfere in every case with the employment of women where

that employment was degrading?' 'It would become injurious, I think, in this way: the best feelings of Englishmen have been gained from the instruction of a mother. . . (n. 1750.) 'That equally applies to agricultural employments, does it not?' 'Yes, but that is only for two seasons, and we have work all the four seasons.' (n. 1751.) 'They often work day and night, wet through to the skin, their constitution undermined and their health ruined.' 'You have not inquired into that subject perhaps?' 'I have certainly taken note of it as I have gone along, and certainly I have seen nothing parallel to the effects of the employment of women on the pit bank . . . It is the work of a man . . . a strong man.' (ns. 1753, 1793, 1794.) 'Your feeling upon the whole subject is that the better class of colliers who desire to raise themselves and humanise themselves, instead of deriving help from the women, are pulled down by them?' 'Yes.' (n. 1808.) After some further crooked questions from these bourgeois, the secret of their 'sympathy' for widows, poor families, &c., comes out at last. 'The coal proprietor appoints certain gentlemen to take the oversight of the workings, and it is their policy, in order to receive approbation, to place things on the most economical basis they can, and these girls are employed at from 1s. up to 1s. 6d. a day, where a man at the rate of 2s. 6d. a day would have to be employed.' (n. 1816.)

IV. *Coroner's inquests*. – 'With regard to coroner's inquests in your district, have the workmen confidence in the proceedings at those inquests when accidents occur?' 'No; they have not.' (n. 360.) 'Why not?' 'Chiefly because the men who are generally chosen, are men who know nothing about mines and such like.' 'Are not workmen summoned at all upon the juries?' 'Never but as witnesses to my knowledge.' 'Who are the people who are generally summoned upon these juries?' 'Generally tradesmen in the neighbourhood . . . from their circumstances they are sometimes liable to be influenced by their employers . . . the owners of the works. They are generally men who have no knowledge, and can scarcely understand the witnesses who are called before them, and the terms which are used and such like.' 'Would you have the jury composed of persons who had been employed in mining?' 'Yes, partly . . . they (the workmen) think that the verdict is not in accordance with the evidence given generally.' (ns. 361, 364, 366, 368, 371, 375.) 'One great object in summoning a jury is to have an impartial one, is it not?' 'Yes, I should think so.' 'Do you think that the juries would be impartial if they were composed to a considerable extent of workmen?' 'I cannot see any motive which the workmen would have to act partially . . . they necessarily have a better knowledge of the operations in connection with the mine.'

'You do not think there would be a tendency on the part of the workmen to return unfairly severe verdicts?' 'No, I think not.' (ns. 378, 379, 380.)

V. *False weights and measures.* – The workmen demand to be paid weekly instead of fortnightly, and by weight instead of by cubical contents of the tubs; they also demand protection against the use of false weights, &c. (n. 1071.) 'If the tubs were fraudulently increased, a man could discontinue working by giving 14 days' notice?' 'But if he goes to another place, there is the same thing going on there.' (n. 1071.) 'But he can leave that place where the wrong has been committed?' 'It is general; wherever he goes, he has to submit to it.' (n. 1072.) 'Could a man leave by giving 14 days' notice?' 'Yes.' (n. 1073.) And yet they are not satisfied!

VI. *Inspection of mines.* – Casualties from explosions are not the only things the workmen suffer from. (n. 234, sqq.) 'Our men complained very much of the bad ventilation of the collieries . . . the ventilation is so bad in general that the men can scarcely breathe; they are quite unfit for employment of any kind after they have been for a length of time in connection with their work; indeed, just at the part of the mine where I am working, men have been obliged to leave their employment and come home in consequence of that . . . some of them have been out of work for weeks just in consequence of the bad state of the ventilation where there is not explosive gas . . . there is plenty of air generally in the main courses, yet pains are not taken to get air into the workings where men are working.' 'Why do you not apply to the inspector?' 'To tell the truth there are many men who are timid on that point; there have been cases of men being sacrificed and losing their employment in consequence of applying to the inspector.' 'Why; is he a marked man for having complained?' 'Yes . . . And he finds it difficult to get employment in another mine?' 'Yes.' 'Do you think the mines in your neighbourhood are sufficiently inspected to insure a compliance with the provisions of the Act?' 'No; they are not inspected at all . . . the inspector has been down just once in the pit, and it has been going seven years . . . In the district to which I belong there are not a sufficient number of inspectors. We have one old man more than 70 years of age to inspect more than 130 collieries.' 'You wish to have a class of sub-inspectors?' 'Yes.' (ns. 234, 241, 251, 254, 274, 275, 554, 276, 293.) 'But do you think it would be possible for Government to maintain such an army of inspectors as would be necessary to do all that you want them to do, without information from the men?' 'No, I should think it would be next to impossible . . .'

'It would be desirable the inspectors should come oftener?' 'Yes, and without being sent for.' (n. 280, 277.) 'Do you not think that the effect of having these inspectors examining the collieries so frequently would be to shift the responsibility (!) of supplying proper ventilation from the owners of the collieries to the Government officials?' 'No, I do not think that, I think that they should make it their business to enforce the Acts which are already in existence.' (n. 285.) 'When you speak of sub-inspectors, do you mean men at a less salary, and of an inferior stamp to the present inspectors?' 'I would not have them inferior, if you could get them otherwise.' (n. 294.) 'Do you merely want more inspectors, or do you want a lower class of men as an inspector?' 'A man who would knock about, and see that things are kept right; a man who would not be afraid of himself.' (n. 295.) 'If you obtained your wish in getting an inferior class of inspectors appointed, do you think that there would be no danger from want of skill, &c?' 'I think not, I think that the Government would see after that, and have proper men in that position.' (n. 297.) This kind of examination becomes at last too much even for the chairman of the committee, and he interrupts with the observation: 'You want a class of men who would look into all the details of the mine, and would go into all the holes and corners, and go into the real facts . . . they would report to the chief inspector, who would then bring his scientific knowledge to bear on the facts they have stated?' (ns. 298, 299.) 'Would it not entail very great expense if all these old workings were kept ventilated?' 'Yes, expense might be incurred, but life would be at the same time protected.' (n. 53 1.) A working miner objects to the 17th section of the Act of 1860; he says, 'At the present time, if the inspector of mines finds a part of the mine unfit to work in, he has to report it to the mine-owner and the Home Secretary. After doing that, there is given to the owner 20 days to look over the matter; at the end of 20 days he has the power to refuse making any alteration in the mine; but, when he refuses, the mine-owner writes to the Home Secretary, at the same time nominating five engineers, and from those five engineers named by the mine-owner himself, the Home Secretary appoints one, I think, as arbitrator, or appoints arbitrators from them; now we think in that case the mine-owner virtually appoints his own arbitrator.' (n. 581.) Bourgeois examiner, himself a mine-owner: 'But . . . is this a merely speculative objection?' (n. 586.) 'Then you have a very poor opinion of the integrity of mining engineers?' 'It is most certainly unjust and inequitable.' (n. 588.) 'Do not mining engineers possess a sort of public character, and do not you think that they are above making such a partial decision as you apprehend?' 'I do not wish to answer such a question as that with respect to the personal character of those men. I believe that in many cases they would act very partially indeed, and that it ought not to be in their hands to do so, where men's lives are at stake.' (n. 589.) This same bourgeois is not ashamed to put this question: 'Do you not think that the mine-owner also suffers loss from an explosion?' Finally, 'Are not you workmen in Lancashire able to take care of your own interests without calling in the Government to help you?' 'No.' (n. 1042.)

In the year 1865 there were 3,217 coal mines in Great Britain, and 12 inspectors. A Yorkshire mine-owner himself calculates (*Times*, 26th January, 1867), that putting on one side their office work, which absorbs all their time, each mine can be visited but once in ten years by an inspector. No wonder that explosions have increased progressively, both in number and extent (sometimes with a loss of 200–300 men), during the last ten years.

The very defective Act, passed in 1872, is the first that regulates the hours of labour of the children employed in mines, and makes exploiters and owners, to a certain extent, responsible for so-called accidents.

The Royal Commission appointed in 1867, to inquire into the employment in agriculture of children, young persons, and women, has published some very important reports. Several attempts to apply the principles of the Factory Acts, but in a modified form, to agriculture have been made, but have so far resulted in complete failure. All that I wish to draw attention to here is the existence of an irresistible tendency towards the general application of those principles.

If the general extension of factory legislation to all trades for the purpose of protecting the working-class both in mind and body has become inevitable, on the other hand, as we have already pointed out, that extension hastens on the general conversion of numerous isolated small industries into a few combined industries carried on upon a large scale; it therefore accelerates the concentration of capital and the exclusive predominance of the factory system. It destroys both the ancient and the transitional forms, behind which the dominion of capital is still in part concealed, and replaces them by the direct and open sway of capital; but thereby it also generalises the direct opposition to this sway. While in each individual workshop it enforces uniformity, regularity, order, and economy, it increases by the immense spur which the limitation and regulation of the working-day give to technical improvement, the anarchy and the catastrophes of capitalist production as a whole, the intensity of labour, and the competition of machinery with the labourer. By the destruction of petty and domestic industries it destroys the last resort of the 'redundant population', and with it the sole remaining safety-valve of the whole social mechanism.

By maturing the material conditions, and the combination on a social scale of the processes of production, it matures the contradictions and antagonisms of the capitalist form of production, and thereby provides, along with the elements for the formation of a new society, the forces for exploding the old one.[243]

Section 10. Modern Industry and Agriculture.

The revolution called forth by modern industry in agriculture, and in the social relations of agricultural producers, will be investigated later on. In this place, we shall merely indicate a few results by way of anticipation. If the use of machinery in agriculture is for the most part free from the injurious physical effect it has on the factory operative, its action in superseding the labourers is more intense, and finds less resistance, as we shall see later in detail. In the counties of Cambridge and Suffolk, for example, the area of cultivated land has extended very much within the last 20 years (up to 1868), while in the same period the rural population has diminished, not only relatively, but absolutely. In the United States it is as yet only virtually that agricultural machines replace labourers; in other words, they allow of the cultivation by the farmer of a larger surface, but do not actually expel the labourers employed. In 1861 the number of persons occupied in England and Wales in the manufacture of agricultural machines was 1,034, whilst the number of agricultural labourers employed in the use of agricultural machines and steam-engines did not exceed 1,205.

In the sphere of agriculture, modern industry has a more revolutionary effect than elsewhere, for this reason, that it annihilates the peasant, that bulwark of the old society, and replaces him by the wage-labourer. Thus the desire for social changes, and the class antagonisms are brought to the same level in the country as in the towns. The irrational, old-fashioned methods of agriculture are replaced by scientific ones. Capitalist production completely tears asunder the old bond of union which held together agriculture and manufacture in their infancy. But at the same time it creates the material conditions for a higher synthesis in the future, viz., the union of agriculture and industry on the basis of the more perfected forms they have each acquired during their temporary separation. Capitalist production, by collecting the population in great centres, and causing an ever-increasing preponderance of town population, on the one hand concentrates the historical motive power of society; on the other hand, it disturbs the circulation of matter between man and the soil, i.e., prevents the return to the soil of its elements consumed by man in the form of food and clothing; it therefore violates the conditions necessary to lasting fertility of the soil. By this action it destroys at the same time the health of the town labourer and the intellectual life of the rural labourer.[244] But while upsetting the naturally grown conditions for the maintenance of that circulation of matter, it imperiously calls for its restoration as a system, as a regulating law of social production, and under a form appropriate to the full development of the human race. In agriculture as in manufacture, the transformation of production under the sway of capital means, at the same time, the martyrdom of the producer; the instrument of labour becomes the means of enslaving, exploiting, and impoverishing the labourer; the social combination and organisation of labour-processes is turned into an organised mode of crushing out the workman's individual vitality, freedom, and independence. The dispersion of the rural labourers over larger areas breaks their power of resistance while concentration increases that of the town operatives. In modern agriculture, as in the urban industries, the increased productiveness and quantity of the labour set in motion are bought at the cost of laying waste and consuming by disease labour power itself. Moreover, all progress in capitalistic agriculture is a progress in the art, not only of robbing the labourer, but of robbing the soil; all progress in increasing the fertility of the soil for a given time, is a progress towards ruining the lasting sources of that fertility. The more a country starts its development on the foundation of modern industry, like the United States, for example, the more rapid is this process of destruction.[245] Capitalist production, therefore, develops technology, and the combining together of various processes into a social whole, only by sapping the original sources of all wealth — the soil and the labourer.

Chapter 16
Absolute and Relative Surplus-Value

In considering the labour-process, we began (see Chapter 5) by treating it in the abstract, apart from its historical forms, as a process between man and Nature. We there stated, 'If we examine the whole labour-process, from the point of view of its result, it is plain that both the instruments and the subject of labour are means of production, and that the labour itself is productive labour.' And in Note 2, same page, we further added: 'This method of determining, from the standpoint of the labour-process alone, what is productive labour, is by no means directly applicable to the case of the capitalist process of production.' We now proceed to the further development of this subject.

So far as the labour-process is purely individual, one and the same labourer unites in himself all the functions, that later on become separated. When an individual appropriates natural objects for his livelihood, no one controls him but himself. Afterwards he is controlled by others. A single man cannot operate upon Nature without calling his own muscles into play under the control of his own brain. As in the natural body head and hand wait upon each other, so the labour-process unites the labour of the hand with that of the head. Later on they part company and even become deadly foes. The product ceases to be the direct product of the individual, and becomes a social product, produced in common by a collective labourer, i.e., by a combination of workmen, each of whom takes only a part, greater or less, in the manipulation of the subject of their labour. As the co-operative character of the labour-process becomes more and more marked, so, as a necessary consequence, does our notion of productive labour, and of its agent the productive labourer, become extended. In order to labour productively, it is no longer necessary for you to do manual work yourself; enough, if you are an organ of the collective labourer, and perform one of its subordinate functions. The first definition given above of productive labour, a definition deduced from the very nature of the production of material objects, still remains correct for the collective labourer, considered as a whole. But it no longer holds good for each member taken individually.

On the other hand, however, our notion of productive labour becomes narrowed. Capitalist production is not merely the production of commodities, it is essentially the production of surplus-value. The labourer produces, not for himself, but for capital. It no longer suffices, therefore, that he should simply produce. He must produce surplus-value. That labourer alone is productive, who produces surplus-value for the capitalist, and thus works for the self-expansion of capital. If we may take an example from outside the sphere of production of material objects, a schoolmaster is a productive labourer when, in addition to belabouring the heads of his scholars, he works like a horse to enrich the school proprietor. That the latter has laid out his capital in a teaching factory, instead of in a sausage factory, does not altr the relation. Hence the notion of a productive labourer implies not merely a relation between work and useful effect, between labourer and product of labour, but also a specific, social relation of production, a relation that has sprung up historically and stamps the labourer and product of labour, but also a specific, social relation of production, a relation that has sprung up historically and stamps the labourer as the direct means of creating surplus-value. To be a productive labourr is, therefore not a piece of luck, but a misfortune. In Book 4, which treats of the history of the theory, it will be more clearly seen, that the production of surplus-value has at all times been made, by classical political economists, the distinguishing characteristic of the productive labourer. Hence their definition of a productive labourer changes with their comprehension of the nature of surplus-value. Thus the Physiocrats insist that only agricultural labour is productive, since that alone, they say, yields a surplus-value. And they say so because, with them, surplus-value has no existence except in the form of rent.

The prolongation of the working day beyond the point at which the labourer would have produced just an equivalent for the value of his labour power, and the appropriation of that surplus-labour by capital, this is production of absolute surplus-value. It forms the general groundwork of the capitalist system, and the starting point for the production of relative surplus-value. The latter presupposes that the working day is already divided into two parts, necessary labour, and surplus-labour. In order to prolong the surplus-labour, the necessary labour is shortened by methods whereby the equivalent for the wages is produced in less time. The production of absolute surplus-value turns exclusively upon the length of the working day; the production of relative surplus-value, revolutionises out and out the technical processes of labour, and the composition of society. It therefore presupposes a specific mode, the capitalistic mode of production, a mode which, along with its methods, means, and conditions, arises and developes itself spontaneously on the foundation afforded by the formal subjection of labour to capital. In the course of this development, the formal subjection is replaced by the real subjection of labour to capital.

It will suffice merely to refer to certain intermediate forms in which surplus-labour is not extorted by direct compulsion from the producer, nor the producer himself yet formally subjected to capital. In such forms capital has not yet acquired the direct control of the labour process. By the side of independent producers who carry on their handicrafts and agriculture in the traditional old-fashioned way, there stands the usurer or the merchant, with his usurer's capital or merchant's capital, feeding on them like a parasite. The predominance, in a society, of this form of exploitation excludes the capitalist mode of production; to which mode, however, this form may serve as a tradition, as it did towards the close of the Middle Ages. Finally, as is shown by modern 'domestic industry', some intermediate forms are here and there reproduced in the background of Modern Industry, though their physiognomy is totally changed.

If, on the one hand, the mere formal subjection of labour to capital suffices for the production of absolute surplus-value, if, e.g., it is sufficient that handicraftsmen who previously worked on their own account, or as apprentices of a master, should become wage labourers under the direct control of a capitalist; so, on the other hand, we have seen, how the methods of producing relative surplus-value are, at the same time, methods of producing absolute surplus-value. Nay, more, the excessive prolongation of the working day turned out to be the peculiar product of Modern Industry. Generally speaking, the specifically capitalist mode of production ceases to be a mere means of producing relative surplus-value, so soon as that mode has conquered an entire branch of production; and still more so, so soon as it has conquered all the important branches. It then becomes the general, socially predominant form of production. As a special method of producing relative surplus-value, it remains effective only, first, in so far as it seizes upon industries that previously were only formally subject to capital, that is, so far as it is propagandist; secondly, in so far as the industies that have been taken over by it, continue to be revolutionised by changes in the methods of production.

From one standpoint, any distinction between absolute and relative surplus-value appears illusory. Relative surplus-value is absolute, since it compels the absolute prolongation of the working day beyond the labour-time necessary to the existence of the labourer himself. Absolute surplus-value is relative, since it makes necessary such development of the productiveness of labour, as will allow of the necessary labour-time being confined to a portion of the working day. But if we keep in mind the behaviour of surplus value, this appearance of identity vanishes. Once the capitalist mode of production is established and becone general, the difference between absolute and relative surplus-value makes itself felt, whenever there is a question of raising the rate of surplus-value. Assuming that labour power is paid for at its value, we are confronted by this alternative: given the productiveness of labour and its normal intensity, the rate of surplus-value can be raised only by the actual prolongation of the working day; on the other hand, given the length of the working day, that rise can be effected only by a change in the relative magnitudes of the components of the working day, viz., necessary labour and surplus-labour; a change which, if the wages are not to fall below the value of labour power, presupposes a change either in the productiveness or in the intensity of the labour.

If the labourer wants all his time to produce the necessary means of subsistence for himself and his race, he has no time left in which to work gratis for others. Without a certain degree of productiveness in his labour, he has no such superfluous time at his disposal; without such superfluous time, no surplus-labour, and therefore no capitalists, no slave-owners, no feudal lords, in one word, no class of large proprietors.[1] Thus we may say that surplus-value rests on a natural basis; but this is permissible only in the very general sense, that there is no natural obstacle absolutely preventing one man from disburdening himself of the labour requisite for his own existence, and burdening another with it, any more, for instance, than unconquerable natural obstacles prevent one man from eating the flesh of another.[2] No mystical ideas must in any way be connected, as sometimes happens, with this historically developed productiveness of labour. It is only after men have raised themselves above the rank of animals, when therefore their labour has been to some extent socialised, that a state of things arises in which the surplus-labour of the one becomes a condition of existence for the other. At the dawn of civilisation the productiveness acquired by labour is small, but so too are the wants which develop with and by the means of satisfying them. Further, at that early period, the portion of society that lives on the labour of others is infinitely small compared with the mass of direct producers. Along with the progress in the productiveness of labour, that small portion of society increases both absolutely and relatively.[3] Besides, capital with its accompanying relations springs up from an economic soil that is the product of a long process of development. The productiveness of labour that serves as its foundation and starting point, is a gift, not of nature, but of a history embracing thousands of centuries.

Apart from the degree of development, greater or less, in the form of social production, the productiveness of labour is fettered by physical conditions. These are all referable to the constitution of man himself (race, &c.), and to surrounding nature. The external physical conditions fall into two great economical classes, (1) natural wealth in means of subsistence, i.e., a fruitful soil, waters teeming with fish, &c., and (2), natural wealth in the instruments of labour, such as waterfalls, navigable rivers, wood, metal, coal, &c. At the dawn of civilisation, it is the first class that turns the scale; at a higher stage of development, it is the second. Compare, for example, England with India, or in ancient times, Athens and Corinth with the shores of the Black Sea.

The fewer the number of natural wants imperatively calling for satisfaction, and the greater the natural fertility of the soil and the favourableness of the climate, so much less is the labour-time necessary for the maintenance and reproduction of the producer. So much greater therefore can be the excess of his labour for others over his labour for himself. Diodorus long ago remarked this in relation to the ancient Egyptians. 'It is altogether incredible how little trouble and expense the bringing up of their children causes them. They cook for them the first simple food at band; they also give them the lower part of the papyrus stem to eat, so far as it can he roasted in the fire, and the roots and stalks of marsh plants, some raw, some boiled and roasted. Most of the children go without shoes and unclothed, for the air is so mild. Hence a child, until he is grown up, costs his parents not more, on the whole, than twenty drachmas. It is this, chiefly, which explains why the population of Egypt is so numerous, and, therefore, why so many great works can be undertaken.'[4] Nevertheless the grand structures of ancient Egypt are less due to the extent of its population than to the large proportion of it that was freely disposable. Just as the individual labourer can do more surplus-labour in proportion as his necessary labour-time is less, so with regard to the working population. The smaller the part of it which is required for the production of the necessary means of subsistence, so much the greater is the part that can be set to do other work.

Capitalist production once assumed, then, all other circumstances remaining the saine, and given the length of the working day, the quantity of surplus-labour will vary with the physical conditions of labour, especially with the fertility of the soil. But it by no means follows from this that the most fruitful soil is the most fitted for the growth of the capitalist mode of production. This mode is based on the dominion of man over nature. Where nature is too lavish, she 'keeps him in hand, like a child in leading-strings.' She does not impose upon him any necessity to develop himself.[5] It is not the tropics with their luxuriant vegetation, but the temperate zone, that is the mother country of capital. It is not the mere fertility of the soil, but the differentiation of the soil, the variety of its natural products, the changes of the seasons which form the physical basis for the social division of labour, and which, by changes in the natural surroundings, spur man on to the multiplication of his wants, his capabilities, his means and modes of labour. It is the necessity of bringing a natural force under the control of society, of economising, of appropriating or subduing it on a large scale by the work of man's hand, that first plays the decisive part in the history of industry. Examples are, the irrigation works in Egypt,[6] Lombardy, Holland, or in India and Persia where irrigation by means of artificial canals, not only supplies the soil with the water indispensable to it, but also carries down to it, in the shape of sediment from the hills, mineral fertilisers. The secret of the flourishing state of industry in Spain and Sicily under the dominion of the Arabs lay in their irrigation works.[7]

Favourable natural conditions alone, give us only the possibility, never the reality, of surplus-labour, nor, consequently, of surplus-value and a surplus-product. The result of difference in the natural conditions of labour is this, that the same quantity of labour satisfies, in different countries, a different mass of requirements,[8] consequently, that under circumstances in other respects analogous, the necessary labour-time is different. These conditions affect surplus-labour only as natural limits, i.e., by fixing the points at which labour for others can begin. In proportion as industry advances, these natural limits recede. In the midst of our West European society, where the labourer purchases the right to work for his own livelihood only by paying for it in surplus-labour, the idea easily takes root that it is an inherent quality of human labour to furnish a surplus-product.[9] But consider, for example, an inhabitant of the eastern islands of the Asiatic Archipelago, where sago grows wild in the forests. 'When the inhabitants have convinced themselves, by boring a hole in the tree, that the pith is ripe, the trunk is cut down and divided into several pieces, the pith is extracted, mixed with water and filtered: it is then quite fit for use as sago. One tree commonly yields 300 lbs., and occasionally 500 to 600 lbs. There, then, people go into the forests, and cut bread for themselves, just as with us they cut fire-wood.'[10] Suppose now such an

eastem bread-cutter requires 12 working hours a week for the satisfaction of all his wants. Nature's direct gift to him is plenty of leisure
time. Before he can apply this leisure time productively for himself, a
whole series of historical events is required; before he spends it in
surplus-labour for strangers, compulsion is necessary. If capitalist production were introduced, the honest fellow would perhaps have to
work six days a week, in order to appropriate to himself the product
of one working day. The bounty of Nature does not explain why he
would then have to work 6 days a week, or why he must furnish 5
days of surplus-labour. It explains only why his necessary labour-time
would be limited to one day a week. But in no case would his surplus-
product arise from some occult quality inherent in human labour.

Thus, not only does the historically developed social productiveness
of labour, but also its natural productiveness, appear to be productiveness of the capital with which that labour is incorporated.

Ricardo never concerns himself about the origin of surplus-value.
He treats it as a thing inherent in the capitalist mode of production,
which mode, in his eyes, is the natural form of social production.
Whenever he discusses the productiveness of labour, he seeks in it,
not the cause of surplus-value, but the cause that determines the
magnitude of that value. On the other hand, his school has openly
proclaimed the productiveness of labour to be the originating cause of
profit (read: Surplus-value). This at all events is a progress as against
the mercantilists who, on their side, derived the excess of the price
over the cost of production of the product, from the act of exchange,
from the product being sold above its value. Nevertheless, Ricardo's
school simply shirked the problem, they did not solve it. In fact these
bourgeois economists instinctively saw, and rightly so, that it is very
dangerous to stir too deeply the burning question of the origin of
surplus-value. But what are we to think of John Stuart Mill, who, half
a century after Ricardo, solemnly claims superiority over the mercantilists, by clumsily repeating the wretched evasions of Ricardo's earliest
vulgarisers?

Mill says: 'The cause of profit is that labour produces more than is
required for its support.' So far, nothing but the old story; but Mill
wishing to add something of his own, proceeds: 'To vary the form of
the theorem; the reason why capital yields a profit, is because food,
clothing, materials and tools, last longer than the time which was
required to produce them.' He here confounds the duration of labour-
time with the duration of its products. According to this view, a baker
whose product lasts only a day, could never extract from his workpeople the same profit, as a machine maker whose products endure for
20 years and more. Of course it is very true, that if a bird's nest did not

last longer than the time it takes in building, birds would have to do without nests.

This fundamental truth once established, Mill establishes his own superiority over the mercantilists. 'We thus see,' he proceeds, 'that profit arises, not from the incident of exchange, but from the productive power of labour; and the general profit of the country is always what the productive power of labour makes it, whether any exchange takes place or not. If there were no division of employments, there would be no buying or selling, but there would still be profit.' For Mill then, exchange, buying and selling, those general conditions of capitalist production, are but an incident, and there would always be profits even without the purchase and sale of labour power!

'If,' he continues, 'the labourers of the country collectively produce twenty per cent more than their wages, profits will be twenty per cent, whatever prices may or may not be.' This is, on the one hand, a rare bit of tautology; for if labourers produce a surplus-value of 20% for the capitalist, his profit will be to the total wages of the labourers as 20:100. On the other hand, it is absolutely false to say that 'profits will be 20%.' They will always be less, because they are calculated upon the sum total of the capital advanced. If, for example, the capitalist have advanced £500, of which £400 is laid out in means of production and £100 in wages, and if the rate of surplus-value be 20%, the rate of profit will be 20:500, i.e., 4% and not 20%.

Then follows a splendid example of Mill's method of handling the different historical forms of social production. 'I assume, throughout, the state of things which, where the labourers and capitalists are separate classes, prevails, with few exceptions, universally; namely, that the capitalist advances the whole expenses, including the entire remuneration of the labourer.' Strange optical illusion to see everywhere a state of things which as yet exists only exceptionally on our earth. But let us finish – Mill is willing to concede, 'that he should do so is not a matter of inherent necessity.' On the contrary: 'the labourer might wait, until the production is complete, for all that part of his wages which exceeds mere necessaries: and even for the whole, if he has funds in hand sufficient for his temporary support. But in the latter case, the labourer is to that extent really a capitalist in the concern, by supplying a portion of the funds necessary for carrying it on.' Mill might have gone further and have added, that the labourer who advances to himself not only the necessaries of life but also the means of production, is in reality nothing but his own wage-labourer. He might also have said that the American peasant proprietor is but a serf who does enforced labour for himself instead of for his lord.

After thus proving clearly, that even if capitalist production had no existence, still it would always exist, Mill is consistent enough to show, on the contrary, that it has no existence, even when it does exist. 'And even in the former case' (when the workman is a wage labourer to whom the capitalist advances all the necessaries of life, he the labourer), 'may be looked upon in the same light,' (i.e., as a capitalist), 'since, contributing his labour at less than the market-price, (!) he may be regarded as lending the difference (?) to his employer and receiving it back with interest, &c.'[11] In reality, the labourer advances his labour gratuitously to the capitalist during, say one week, in order to receive the market price at the end of the week, &c., and it is this which, according to Mill, transforms him into a capitalist. On the level plain, simple mounds look like hills; and the imbecile flatness of the present bourgeoisie is to be measured by the altitude of its great intellects.

Chapter 17

Changes of Magnitude in the Price of Labour Power and in Surplus-Value

The value of labour power is determined by the value of the necessaries of life habitually required by the average labourer. The quantity of these necessaries is known at any given epoch of a given society, and can therefore be treated as a constant magnitude. What changes, is the value of this quantity. There are, besides, two other factors that enter into the determination of the value of labour power. One, the expenses of developing that power, which expenses vary with the mode of production; the other, its natural diversity, the difference between the labour power of men and women, of children and adults. The employment of these different sorts of labour power, an employment which is, in its turn, made necessary by the mode of production, makes a great difference in the cost of maintaining the family of the labourer, and in the value of the labour power of the adult male. Both these factors, however, are excluded in the following investigation.[1]

I assume (1) that commodities are sold at their value; (2) that the price of labour power rises occasionally above its value, but never sinks below it.

On this assumption we have seen that the relative magnitudes of surplus-value and of price of labour power are determined by three circumstances; (1) the length of the working-day, or the extensive magnitude of labour; (2) the normal intensity of labour, its intensive magnitude, whereby a given quantity of labour is expended in a given time; (3) the productiveness of labour,whereby the same quantum of labour yields, in a given time, a greater or less quantum of product, dependent on the degree of development in the conditions of production. Very different combinations are clearly possible, according as one of the three factors is constant and two variable, or two constant and one variable, or lastly, all three simultaneously variable. And the number of these combinations is augmented by the fact that, when these factors simultaneously vary, the amount and direction of their respective variations may differ. In what follows the chief combinations alone are considered.

Section 1. Length of the Working-Day and Intensity of Labour Constant. Productiveness of Labour Variable.

On these assumptions the value of labour power, and the magnitude of surplus-value, are determined by three laws.

(1.) A working day of given length always creates the same amount of value, no matter how the productiveness of labour, and, with it, the mass of the product, and the price of each single commodity produced, may vary.

If the value created by a working-day of 12 hours be, say, six shillings, then, although the mass of the articles produced varies with the productiveness of labour, the only result is that the value represented by six shillings is spread over a greater or less number of articles.

(2.) Surplus-value and the value of labour power vary in opposite directions. A variation in the productiveness of labour, its increase or diminution, causes a variation in the opposite direction in the value of labour power, and in the same direction in surplus-value.

The value created by a working day of 12 hours is a constant quantity, say six shillings. This constant quantity is the sum of the surplus-value plus the value of the labour power, which latter value the labourer replaces by an equivalent. It is self-evident, that if a constant quantity consists of two parts, neither of them can increase without the other diminishing. Let the two parts at starting be equal; 3 shillings value of labour power, 3 shillings surplus-value. Then the value of the labour power cannot rise from three shillings to four, without the surplus-value falling from three shillings to two; and the surplus-value cannot rise from three shillings to four, without the value of labour power falling from three shillings to two. Under these circumstances, therefore, no change can take place in the absolute magnitude, either of the surplus-value, or of the value of labour-power, without a simultaneous change in their relative magnitudes, i.e., relatively to each other. It is impossible for them to rise or fall simultaneously.

Further, the value of labour power cannot fall, and consequently surplus-value cannot rise, without a rise in the productiveness of labour. For instance, in the above case, the value of the labour power cannot sink from three shillings to two, unless an increase in the productiveness of labour makes it possible to produce in 4 hours the same quantity of necessaries as previously required 6 hours to produce. On the other hand, the value of the labour power cannot rise from three shillings to four, without a decrease in the productiveness of labour, whereby eight hours become requisite to produce the same quantity of necessaries, for the production of which six hours previously sufficed. It follows from this, that an increase in the productiveness of labour causes a fall in the value of labour power and a consequent rise in surplus-value, while, on the other hand, a decrease in such productiveness causes a rise in the value of labour power, and a fall in surplus-value.

In formulating this law, Ricardo overlooked one circumstance; although a change in the magnitude of the surplus-value or surplus-labour causes a change in the opposite direction in the magnitude of the value of labour power, or in the quantity of necessary labour, it by no means follows that they vary in the same proportion. They do increase or diminish by the same quantity. But their proportional increase or diminution depends on their original magnitudes before the change in the productiveness of labour took place. If the value of the labour power be 4 shillings, or the necessary labour-time 8 hours, and the surplus-value be 2 shillings, or the surplus-labour 4 hours, and if, in consequence of an increase in the productiveness of labour, the value of the labour power fall to 3 shillings, or the necessary labour to 6 hours, the surplus-value will rise to 3 shillings, or the surplus-labour to 6 hours. The same quantity, 1 shilling or 2 hours, is added in one case and subtracted in the other. But the proportional change of magnitude is different in each case. While the value of the labour power falls from 4 shillings to 3, i.e., by 1/4 or 25%, the surplus-value rises from 2 shillings to 3, i.e., by 1/2 or 50%. It therefore follows that the proportional increase or diminution in surplus-value, consequent on a given change in the productiveness of labour, depends on the original magnitude of that portion of the working day which embodies itself in surplus-value; the smaller that portion, the greater is the proportional change; the greater that portion, the less is the proportional change.

(3.) Increase or diminution in surplus-value is always consequent on, and never the cause of, the corresponding diminution or increase in the value of labour power.[2]

Since the working-day is constant in magnitude, and is represented by a value of constant magnitude, since, to every variation in the magnitude of surplus-value, there corresponds an inverse variation in the value of labour power, and since the value of labour power cannot change, except in consequence of a change in the productiveness of labour, it clearly follows, under these conditions, that every change of magnitude in surplus-value arises from an inverse change of magnitude in the value of labour power. If, then, as we have already seen, there can be no change of absolute magnitude in the value of labour power, and in surplus-value, unaccompanied by a change in their relative magnitudes, so now it follows that no change in their relative magnitudes is possible, without a previous change in the absolute magnitude of the value of labour power.

According to the third law, a change in the magnitude of surplus-value, presupposes a movement in the value of labour power, which movement is brought about by a variation in the productiveness of labour. The limit of this change is given by the altered value of labour power. Nevertheless, even when circumstances allow the law to operate, subsidiary movements may occur. For example: if in consequence of the increased productiveness of labour, the value of labour power falls from 4 shillings to 3, or the necessary labour-time from 8 hours to 6, the price of labour power may possibly not fall below 3s. 8d., 3s. 6d., or 3s. 2d., and the surplus-value consequently not rise above 3s. 4d., 3s. 6d., or 3s. 10d. The amount of this fall, the lowest limit of which is 3 shillings (the new value of labour power), depends on the relative weight, which the pressure of capital on the one side, and the resistance of the labourer on the other, throws into the scale.

The value of labour power is determined by the value of a given quantity of necessaries. It is the value and not the mass of these necessaries that varies with the productiveness of labour. It is, however, possible that, owing to an increase of productiveness, both the labourer and the capitalist may simultaneously be able to appropriate a greater quantity of these necessaries, without any change in the price of labour power or in surplus-value. If the value of labour power be 3 shillings, and the necessary labour-time amount to 6 hours, if the surplus-value likewise be 3 shillings, and the surplus-labour 6 hours, then if the productiveness of labour were doubled without altering the ratio of necessary labour to surplus-labour, there would be no change of magnitude in surplus-value and price of labour power. The only result would be that each of them would represent twice as many use-values as before; these use-values being twice as cheap as before. Although labour power would be unchanged in price, it would be above its value. If, however, the price of labour power had fallen, not to 1s. 6d., the lowest possible point consistent with its new value, but to 2s. 10d. or 2s. 6d., still this lower price would represent an increased mass of necessaries. In this way it is possible with an increasing productiveness of labour, for the price of labour power to keep on falling, and yet this fall to be accompanied by a constant growth in the mass of the labourer's means of subsistence. But even in such case, the fall in the value of labour power would cause a corresponding rise of surplus-value, and thus the abyss between the labourer's position and that of the capitalist would keep widening.[3]

Ricardo was the first who accurately formulated the three laws we have above stated. But he falls into the following errors: (1) he looks upon the special conditions under which these laws hold good as the general and sole conditions of capitalist production. He knows no change, either in the length of the working-day, or in the intensity of labour; consequently with him there can be only one variable factor, viz., the productiveness of labour; (2), and this error vitiates his analysis much more than (1), he has not, any more than have the other economists, investigated surplus-value as such, i.e., independently of its particular forms, such as profit, rent, &c. He therefore confounds together the laws of the rate of surplus-value and the laws of the rate of profit. The rate of profit is, as we have already said, the ratio of the surplus-value to the total capital advanced; the rate of surplus-value is the ratio of the surplus-value to the variable part of that capital. Assume that a capital C of £500 is made up of raw material, instruments of labour, &c. (c) to the amount of £400; and of wages (v) to the amount of £100; and further, that the surplus-value (s) = £100. Then we have rate of surplus-value $s/v = £100/£100 = 100\%$. But the rate of profit $s/c = £100/£500 = 20\%$. It is, besides, obvious that the rate of profit may depend on circumstances that in no way affect the rate of surplus-value. I shall show in Book 3 that, with a given rate of surplus-value, we may have any number of rates of profit, and that various rates of surplus-value may, under given conditions, express themselves in a single rate of profit.

Section 2. Working-Day Constant. Productiveness of Labour Constant. Intensity of Labour Variable.

Increased intensity of labour means increased expenditure of labour in a given time. Hence a working-day of more intense labour is embodied in more products than is one of less intense labour, the length of each day being the same. Increased productiveness of labour also, it is true, will supply more products in a given working-day. But in this latter case, the value of each single product falls, for it costs less labour than before; in the former case, that value remains unchanged, for each article costs the same labour as before. Here we have an increase in the number of products, unaccompanied by a fall in their individual prices: as their number increases, so does the sum of their prices. But in the case of increased productiveness, a given value is spread over a greater mass of products. Hence the length of the working-day being constant, a day's labour of increased intensity will be incorporated in an increased value, and, the value of money remaining unchanged, in more money. The value created varies with the extent to which the intensity of labour deviates from its normal intensity in the society. A given working-day, therefore, no longer creates a constant, but a variable value; in a day of 12 hours of ordinary intensity, the value created is, say 6 shillings, but with increased intensity, the value created may be 7, 8, or more shillings. It is clear that, if the value created by a day's labour increases from, say, 6 to 8 shillings then the two parts into which this value is divided, viz., price of labour power and surplus-value, may both of them increase simultaneously, and either equally or unequally. They may both simultaneously increase from 3 shillings to 4. Here, the rise in the price of labour power does not necessarily imply that the price has risen above the value of labour power. On the contrary, the rise in price may be accompanied by a fall in value. This occurs whenever the rise in the price of labour power does not compensate for its increased wear and tear.

We know that, with transitory exceptions, a change in the productiveness of labour does not cause any change in the value of labour power, nor consequently in the magnitude of surplus-value, unless the products of the industries affected are articles habitually consumed by the labourers. In the present case this condition no longer applies. For when the variation is either in the duration or in the intensity of labour, there is always a corresponding change in the magnitude of the value created, independently of the nature of the article in which that value is embodied.

If the intensity of labour were to increase simultaneously and equally in every branch of industry, then the new and higher degree of intensity would become the normal degree for the society, and would therefore cease to be taken account of. But still, even then, the intensity of labour would be different in different countries, and would modify the international application of the law of value. The more intense working-day of one nation would be represented by a greater sum of money than would the less intense day of another nation.[4]

Section 3. Productiveness and Intensity of Labour Constant. Length of the Working-Day Variable.

The working-day may vary in two ways. It may be made either longer or shorter. From our present data, and within the limits of the assumptions made on at the beginning of this chapter we obtain the following laws:

(1.) The working-day creates a greater or less amount of value in proportion to its length – thus, a variable and not a constant quantity of value.

(2.) Every change in the relation between the magnitudes of surplus value and of the value of labour power arises from a change in the absolute magnitude of the surplus-labour, and consequently of the surplus-value.

(3.) The absolute value of labour power can change only in consequence of the reaction exercised by the prolongation of surplus-labour upon the wear and tear of labour power. Every change in this absolute value is therefore the effect, but never the cause, of a change in the magnitude of surplus-value.

We begin with the case in which the working-day is shortened.

(1.) A shortening of the working-day under the conditions given above, leaves the value of labour power, and with it, the necessary labour-time, unaltered. It reduces the surplus-labour and surplus-value. Along with the absolute magnitude of the latter, its relative magnitude also falls, i.e., its magnitude relatively to the value of labour power whose magnitude remains unaltered. Only by lowering the price of labour power below its value could the capitalist save himself harmless.

All the usual arguments against the shortening of the working-day, assume that it takes place under the conditions we have here supposed to exist; but in reality the very contrary is the case: a change in the productiveness and intensity of labour either precedes, or immediately follows, a shortening of the working-day.[5]

(2.) Lengthening of the working-day. Let the necessary labour-time be 6 hours, or the value of labour power 3 shillings; also let the surplus-labour be 6 hours or the surplus-value 3 shillings. The whole working-day then amounts to 12 hours and is embodied in a value of 6 shillings. If, now, the working-day be lengthened by 2 hours and the price of labour power remain unaltered, the surplus-value increases both absolutely and relatively. Although there is no absolute change in the value of labour power, it suffers a relative fall. Under the conditions assumed in 1. there could not be a change of relative magnitude in the value of labour power without a change in its absolute magnitude. Here, on the contrary, the change of relative magnitude in the value of labour power is the result of the change of absolute magnitude in surplus-value.

Since the value in which a day's labour is embodied, increases with the length of that day, it is evident that the surplus-value and the price of labour power may simultaneously increase, either by equal or unequal quantities. This simultaneous increase is therefore possible in two cases, one, the actual lengthening of the working-day, the other, an increase in the intensity of labour unaccompanied by such lengthening.

When the working-day is prolonged, the price of labour power may fall below its value, although that price be nominally unchanged or even rise. The value of a day's labour power is, as will be remembered, estimated from its normal average duration, or from the normal duration of life among the labourers, and from corresponding normal transformations of organised bodily matter into motion,[6] in conformity with the nature of man. Up to a certain point, the increased wear and tear of labour power, inseparable from a lengthened working-day, may be compensated by higher wages. But beyond this point the wear and tear increases in geometrical progression, and every condition suitable for the normal reproduction and functioning of labour power is suppressed. The price of labour power and the degree of its exploitation cease to be commensurable quantities.

Section 4. Simultaneous Variaions in the Duration, Productiveness, and Intensity of Labour.

It is obvious that a large number of combinations are here possible. Any two of the factors may vary and the third remain constant, or all three may vary at once. They may vary either in the same or in different degrees, in the same or in opposite directions, with the result that the variations counteract one another, either wholly or in part. Nevertheless the analysis of every possible case is easy in view of the results given in 1, 2, and 3. The effect of every possible combination may be found by treating each factor in turn as variable, and the other two constant for the time being. We shall, therefore, notice, and that briefly, but two important cases.

A. Diminishing productiveness of labour with a simultaneous lengthening of the working-day.

In speaking of diminishing productiveness of labour, we here refer to diminution in those industries whose products determine the value of labour power; such a diminution, for example, as results from decreasing fertility of the soil, and from the corresponding dearness of its products. Take the working-day at 12 hours and the value created by it at 6 shillings, of which one half replaces the value of the labour power, the other forms the surplus-value. Suppose, in consequence of the increased dearness of the products of the soil, that the value of labour power rises from 3 shillings to 4, and therefore the necessary labour-time from 6 hours to 8. If there be no change in the length of the working-day, the surplus-labour would fall from 6 hours to 4, the surplus-value from 3 shillings to 2. If the day be lengthened by 2 hours, i.e., from 12 hours to 14, the surplus-labour remains at 6 hours, the surplus-value at 6 shillings, but the surplus-value decreases compared with the value of labour power, as measured by the necessary labour-time. If the day be lengthened by 4 hours, viz., from 12 hours to 16, the proportional magnitudes of surplus-value and value of labour power, of surplus-labour and necessary labour, continue unchanged, but the absolute magnitude of surplus-value rises from 3 shillings to 4, that of the surplus-labour from 6 hours to 8, an increment of 33 1/3 %. Therefore, with diminishing productiveness of labour and a simultaneous lengthening of the working-day, the absolute magnitude of surplus-value may continue unaltered, at the same time that its relative magnitude diminishes; its relative magnitude may continue unchanged, at the same time that its absolute magnitude increases; and, provided the lengthening of the day be sufficient, both may increase.

In the period between 1799 and 1815 the increasing price of provisions led in England to a nominal rise in wages, although the real wages, expressed in the necessaries of life, fell. From this fact West and Ricardo drew the conclusion, that the diminution in the productiveness of agricultural labour had brought about a fall in the rate of surplus-value, and they made this assumption of a fact that existed only in their imaginations, the starting-point of important investigations into the relative magnitudes of wages, profits, and rent. But, as a matter of fact, surplus-value had at that time, thanks to the increased intensity of labour, and to the prolongation of the working-day, increased both in absolute and relative magnitude. This was the period in which the right to prolong the hours of labour to an outrageous extent was established;[7] the period that was especially characterised by an accelerated accumulation of capital here, by pauperism there.[8]

B. Increasing intensity and productiveness of labour with simultaneous shortening of the working-day.

Increased productiveness and greater intensity of labour, both have a like effect. They both augment the mass of articles produced in a given time. Both, therefore, shorten that portion of the working-day which the labourer needs to produce his means of subsistence or their equivalent. The minimum length of the working-day is fixed by this necessary but contractile portion of it. If the whole working-day were to shrink to the length of this portion, surplus-labour would vanish, a consummation utterly impossible under the régime of capital. Only by suppressing the capitalist form of production could the length of the working-day be reduced to the necessary labour-time. But, even in that case, the latter would extend its limits. On the one hand, because the notion of 'means of subsistence' would considerably expand, and the labourer would lay claim to an altogether different standard of life. On the other hand, because a part of what is now surplus-labour, would then count as necessary labour; I mean the labour of forming a fund for reserve and accumulation.

The more the productiveness of labour increases, the more can the working-day be shortened; and the more the working-day is shortened, the more can the intensity of labour increase. From a social point of view, the productiveness increases in the same ratio as the economy of labour, which, in its turn, includes not only economy of the means of production, but also the avoidance of all useless labour. The capitalist mode of production, while on the one hand, enforcing economy in each individual business, on the other hand, begets, by its anarchical system of competition, the most outrageous squandering of labour power and of the social means of production, not to mention the creation of a vast number of employments, at present indispensable, but in themselves superfluous.

The intensity and productiveness of labour being given, the time which society is bound to devote to material production is shorter, and as a consequence, the time at its disposal for the free development, intellectual and social, of the individual is greater, in proportion as the work is more and more evenly divided among all the able-bodied members of society, and as a particular class is more and more deprived of the power to shift the natural burden of labour from its own shoulders to those of another layer of society. In this direction, the shortening of the working-day finds at last a limit in the generalisation of labour. In capitalist society spare time is acquired for one class by converting the whole life-time of the masses into labour-time.

Chapter 18
Various Formulae for the Rate of Surplus-Value

We have seen that the rate of surplus-value is represented by the following formulae:

I. Surplus-value/Variable Capital (s/v)
   = Surplus-value/value of labour power
   = Surplus-labour/Necessary labour

The two first of these formulae represent, as a ratio of values, that which, in the third, is represented as a ratio of the times during which those values are produced. These formulae, supplementary the one to the other, are rigorously definite and correct. We therefore find them substantially, but not consciously, worked out in classical Political Economy. There we meet with the following derivative formulae.

II. Surplus-labour/Working-day
    = Surplus-value/Value of the Product
    = Surplus-product/Total Product

One and the same ratio is here expressed as a ratio of labour-times, of the values in which those labour-times are embodied, and of the products in which those values exist. It is of course understood that, by 'Value of the Product', is meant only the value newly created in a working-day, the constant part of the value of the product being excluded.

In all of these formulae (II), the actual degree of exploitation of labour, or the rate of surplus-value, is falsely expressed. Let the working-day be 12 hours. Then, making the same assumptions as in former instances, the real degree of exploitation of labour will be represented in the following proportions.

6 hours surplus-labour/6 hours necessary labour
    = Surplus-value of 3 sh./Variable Capital of 3sh.   = 100%

From formulae II we get very differently,

6 hours surplus-labour/Working-day of 12 hours
    = Surplus-value of 3 sh./Value created of 6 sh. = 50%

These derivative formulae express, in reality, only the proportion in which the working-day, or the value produced by it, is divided between capitalist and labourer. If they are to be treated as direct expressions of the degree of self-expansion of capital, the following erroneous law would hold good: Surplus-labour or surplus-value can never reach 100%.[1] Since the surplus-labour is only an aliquot part of the working-day, or since surplus-value is only an aliquot part of the value created, the surplus-labour must necessarily be always less than the working-day, or the surplus-value always less than the total value created. In order, however, to attain the ratio of 100:100 they must be equal. In order that the surplus-labour may absorb the whole day (i.e., an average day of any week or year), the necessary labour must sink to zero. But if the necessary labour vanish, so too does the surplus-labour, since it is only a function of the former. The ratio (Surplus-labour/Working day) or (Surplus-value/Value created) can therefore never reach the limit 100/100, still less rise to (100 + x)/100. But not so the rate of surplus-value, the real degree of exploitation of labour. Take, *e.g.*, the estimate of L. de Lavergne, according to which the English agricultural labourer gets only 1/4, the capitalist (farmer) on the other hand 3/4 of the product[2] or of its value, apart from the question of how the booty is subsequently divided between the capitalist, the landlord, and others. According to this, this surplus-labour of the English agricultural labourer is to his necessary labour as 3:1, which gives a rate of exploitation of 300%.

The favourite method of treating the working-day as constant in magnitude became, through the use of formulae II, a fixed usage, because in them surplus-labour is always compared with a working-day of given length. The same holds good when the repartition of the value produced is exclusively kept in sight. The working-day that has already been realised in a given value, must necessarily be a day of given length.

The habit of representing surplus-value and value of labour power as fractions of the value created – a habit that originates in the capitalist mode of production itself, and whose import will hereafter be disclosed – conceals the very transaction that characterises capital, namely the exchange of variable capital for living labour power, and the consequent exclusion of the labourer from the product. Instead of the real fact, we have the false semblance of an association, in which labourer and capitalist divide the product in proportion to the different elements which they respectively contribute towards its formation.[3]

Moreover, the formulae II. can at any time be reconverted into formulae I. If, for instance, we have (Surplus-labour of 6 hours/Working-day of 12 hours) then the necessary labour-time being 12 hours less the surplus-labour of 6 hours, we get the following result,

Surplus-labour of 6 hours/Necessary labour of 6 hours = 100/100

There is a third formula which I have occasionally already anticipated; it is

III. Surplus–value/Value of labour power
       = Surplus–labour/Necessary labour
       = Unpaid labour/Paid labour

After the investigations we have given above, it is no longer possible to be misled, by the formula (Unpaid labour/Paid labour) into concluding, that the capitalist pays for labour and not for labour power. This formula is only a popular expression for (Surplus–labour/Necessary labour). The capitalist pays the value, so far as price coincides with value, of the labour power, and receives in exchange the disposal of the living labour power itself. His usufruct is spread over two periods. During one the labourer produces a value that is only equal to the value of his labour power; he produces its equivalent. This the capitalist receives in return for his advance of the price of the labour power, a product ready made in the market. During the other period, the period of surplus–labour, the usufruct of the labour power creates a value for the capitalist, that costs him no equivalent.[4] This expenditure of labour power comes to him gratis. In this sense it is that surplus–labour can be called unpaid labour.

Capital, therefore, it not only, as Adam Smith says, the command over labour. It is essentially the command over unpaid labour. All surplus–value, whatever particular form (profit, interest, or rent), it may subsequently crystallise into, is in substance the materialisation of unpaid labour. The secret of the self-expansion of capital resolves itself into having the disposal of a definite quantity of other people's unpaid labour.

Part 6
Wages

Chapter 19
The Transformation of the Value (and Respectively the Price) of Labour Power into Wages

On the surface of bourgeois society the wage of the labourer appears as the price of labour, a certain quantity of money that is paid for a certain quantity of labour. Thus people speak of the value of labour and call its expression in money its necessary or natural price. On the other hand they speak of the market-prices of labour, i.e., prices oscillating above or below its natural price.

But what is the value of a commodity? The objective form of the social labour expended in its production. And how do we measure the quantity of this value? By the quantity of the labour contained in it. How then is the value, e.g., of a 12 hour working-day to be determined? By the 12 working-hours contained in a working-day of 12 hours, which is an absurd tautology.[1]

In order to be sold as a commodity in the market, labour must at all events exist before it is sold. But, could the labourer give it an independent objective existence, he would sell a commodity and not labour.[2]

Apart from these contradictions, a direct exchange of money, i.e., of realised labour, with living labour would either do away with the law of value which only begins to develop itself freely on the basis of capitalist production, or do away with capitalist production itself, which rests directly on wage-labour. The working-day of 12 hours embodies itself, e.g., in a money-value of 6s. Either equivalents are exchanged, and then the labourer receives 6s. for 12 hours' labour; the price of his labour would be equal to the price of his product. In this case he produces no surplus-value for the buyer of his labour, the 6s. are not transformed into capital, the basis of capitalist production vanishes. But it is on this very basis that he sells his labour and that his labour is wage-labour. Or else he receives for 12 hours' labour less than 6s., i.e., less than 12 hours' labour. Twelve hours' labour are exchanged against 10, 6, &c., hours' labour. This equalisation of unequal quantities not merely does away with the determination of value. Such a self-destructive contradiction cannot be in any way even enunciated or formulated as a law.[3]

It is of no avail to deduce the exchange of more labour against less, from their difference of form, the one being realised, the other living.[4] This is the more absurd as the value of a commodity is determined not by the quantity of labour actually realised in it, but by the quantity of living labour necessary for its production. A commodity represents, say, 6 working-hours. If an invention is made by which it can be produced in 3 hours, the value, even of the commodity already produced, falls by half. It represents now 3 hours of social labour instead of the 6 formerly necessary. It is the quantity of labour required for its production, not the realised form of that labour, by which the amount of the value of a commodity is determined.

That which comes directly face to face with the possessor of money on the market, is in fact not labour, but the labourer. What the latter sells is his labour power. As soon as his labour actually begins, it has already ceased to belong to him; it can therefore no longer be sold by him. Labour is the substance, and the immanent measure of value, but has itself no value.[5]

In the expression 'value of labour', the idea of value is not only completely obliterated, but actually reversed. It is an expression as imaginary as the value of the earth. These imaginary expressions, arise, however, from the relations of production themselves. They are categories for the phenomenal forms of essential relations. That in their appearance things often represent themselves in inverted form is pretty well known in every science except Political Economy.[6]

Classical Political Economy borrowed from every-day life the category 'price of labour' without further criticism, and then simply asked the question, how is this price determined? It soon recognised that the change in the relations of demand and supply explained in regard to the price of labour, as of all other commodities, nothing except its changes, i.e., the oscillations of the market-price above or below a certain mean. If demand and supply balance, the oscillation of prices ceases, all other conditions remaining the same. But then demand and supply also cease to explain anything. The price of labour, at the moment when demand and supply are in equilibrium, is its natural price, determined independently of the relation of demand and supply. And how this price is determined is just the question. Or a larger period of oscillations in the market-price is taken, e.g., a year, and they are found to cancel one the other, leaving a mean average quantity, a relatively constant magnitude. This had naturally to be determined otherwise than by its own compensating variations. This price which always finally predominates over the accidental market-prices of labour and regulates them, this 'necessary price' (Physiocrats) or 'natural price' of labour (Adam Smith) can, as with all other commodities, be nothing else than its value expressed in money. In this way Political Economy expected to penetrate athwart the accidental prices of labour, to the value of labour. As with other commodities, this value was determined by the cost of production. But what is the cost of production – of the labourer, i.e., the cost of producing or reproducing the labourer himself? This question unconsciously substituted itself in Political Economy for the original one; for the search after the cost of production of labour as such turned in a circle and never left the spot. What economists therefore call value of labour, is in fact the value of labour power, as it exists in the personality of the labourer, which is as different from its function, labour, as a machine is from the work it performs. Occupied with the difference between the market-price of labour and its so-called value, with the relation of this value to the rate of profit, and to the values of the commodities produced by means of labour, &c., they never discovered that the course of the analysis had led not only from the market-prices of labour to its presumed value, but had led to the resolution of this value of labour itself into the value of labour power. Classical economy never arrived at a consciousness of the results of its own analysis; it accepted uncritically the categories 'value of labour', 'natural price of labour', &c., as final and as adequate expressions for the value relation under consideration, and was thus led, as will be seen later, into inextricable confusion and contradiction, while it offered to the vulgar economists a secure basis of operations for their shallowness, which on principle worships appearances only.

Let us next see how value (and price) of labour power, present themselves in this transformed condition as wages.

We know that the daily value of labour power is calculated upon a certain length of the labourer's life, to which, again, corresponds a certain length of working-day. Assume the habitual working-day as 12 hours, the daily value of labour power as 3s., the expression in money of a value that embodies 6 hours of labour. If the labourer receives 3s., then he receives the value of his labour power functioning through 12 hours. If, now, this value of a day's labour power is expressed as the value of a day's labour itself, we have the formula: Twelve hours' labour has a value of 3s. The value of labour power thus determines the value of labour, or, expressed in money, its necessary price. If, on the other hand, the price of labour power differs from its value, in like manner the price of labour differs from its so-called value.

As the value of labour is only an irrational expression for the value of labour power, it follows, of course, that the value of labour must always be less than the value it produces, for the capitalist always makes labour power work longer than is necessary for the repro-duction of its own value. In the above example, the value of the labour power that functions through 12 hours is 3s., a value for the reproduction of which 6 hours are required. The value which the labour power produces is, on the other hand, 6s., because it, in fact, functions during 12 hours, and the value it produces depends, not on its own value, but on the length of time it is in action. Thus, we have a result – absurd at first sight – that labour which creates a value of 6s. possesses a value of 3s.[7]

We see, further: The value of 3s. by which a part only of the working-day – i.e., 6 hours' labour – is paid for, appears as the value or price of the whole working-day of 12 hours, which thus includes 6 hours unpaid for. The wage-form thus extinguishes every trace of the division of the working-day into necessary labour and surplus-labour, into paid and unpaid labour. All labour appears as paid labour. In the *corvée*, the labour of the worker for himself, and his compulsory labour for his lord, differ in space and time in the clearest possible way. In slave labour, even that part of the working-day in which the slave is only replacing the value of his own means of existence, in which, therefore, in fact, he works for himself alone, appears as labour for his master. All the slave's labour appears as unpaid labour.[8] In wage labour, on the contrary, even surplus-labour, or unpaid labour, appears as paid. There the property-relation conceals the labour of the slave for himself; here the money-relation conceals the unrequited labour of the wage labourer.

Hence, we may understand the decisive importance of the trans-formation of value and price of labour power into the form of wages, or into the value and price of labour itself. This phenomenal form, which makes the actual relation invisible, and, indeed, shows the direct opposite of that relation, forms the basis of all the juridical notions of both labourer and capitalist, of all the mystifications of the capitalistic mode of production, of all its illusions as to liberty, of all the apologetic shifts of the vulgar economists.

If history took a long time to get at the bottom of the mystery of wages, nothing, on the other hand, is more easy to understand than the necessity, the *raison d' être*, of this phenomenon.

The exchange between capital and labour at first presents itself to the mind in the same guise as the buying and selling of all other commodities. The buyer gives a certain sum of money, the seller an article of a nature different from money. The jurist's consciousness recognises in this, at most, a material difference, expressed in the juridically equivalent formula: '*Do ut des, do ut facias, facio ut des, facio ut facias.*'⁹

Furthermore, exchange-value and use-value, being intrinsically incommensurable magnitudes, the expressions 'value of labour,' 'price of labour', do not seem more irrational than the expressions 'value of cotton', 'price of cotton'. Moreover, the labourer is paid after he has given his labour. In its function of means of payment, money realises subsequently the value or price of the article supplied – i.e., in this particular case, the value or price of the labour supplied. Finally, the use-value supplied by the labourer to the capitalist is not, in fact, his labour power, but its function, some definite useful labour, the work of tailoring, shoemaking, spinning, &c. That this same labour is, on the other hand, the universal value-creating element, and thus possesses a property by which it differs from all other commodities, is beyond the cognisance of the ordinary mind.

Let us put ourselves in the place of the labourer who receives for 12 hours' labour, say the value produced by 6 hours' labour, say 3s. For him, in fact, his 12 hours' labour is the means of buying the 3s. The value of his labour power may vary, with the value of his usual means of subsistence, from 3 to 4 shillings, or from 3 to 2 shillings; or, if the value of his labour power remains constant, its price may, in consequence of changing relations of demand and supply, rise to 4s. or fall to 2s. He always gives 12 hours of labour. Every change in the amount of the equivalent that he receives appears to him, therefore, necessarily as a change in the value or price of his 12 hours' work. This circumstance misled Adam Smith, who treated the working-day as a constant quantity,¹⁰ to the assertion that the value of labour is constant, although the value of the means of subsistence may vary, and the same working-day, therefore, may represent itself in more or less money for the labourer.

Let us consider, on the other hand, the capitalist. He wishes to receive as much labour as possible for as little money as possible. Practically, therefore, the only thing that interests him is the difference between the price of labour power and the value which its function creates. But, then, he tries to buy all commodities as cheaply as possible, and always accounts for his profit by simple cheating, by buying under, and selling over the value. Hence, he never comes to see that, if such a thing as the value of labour really existed, and he really paid this value, no capital would exist, his money would not be turned into capital.

Moreover, the actual movement of wages presents phenomena which seem to prove that not the value of labour power is paid, but the value of its function, of labour itself. We may reduce these phenomena to two great classes: 1.) Change of wages with the changing length of the working-day. One might as well conclude that not the value of a machine is paid, but that of its working, because it costs more to hire a machine for a week than for a day. 2.) The individual difference in the wages of different labourers who do the same kind of work. We find this individual difference, but are not deceived by it, in the system of slavery, where, frankly and openly, without any circumlocution, labour power itself is sold. Only, in the slave system, the advantage of a labour power above the average, and the disadvantage of a labour power below the average, affects the slave-owner; in the wage-labour system, it affects the labourer himself, because his labour power is, in the one case, sold by himself, in the other, by a third person.

For the rest, in respect to the phenomenal form, 'value and price of labour', or 'wages', as contrasted with the essential relation manifested therein, viz., the value and price of labour power, the same difference holds that holds in respect to all phenomena and their hidden substratum. The former appear directly and spontaneously as current modes of thought; the latter must first be discovered by science. Classical Political Economy nearly touches the true relation of things, without, however, consciously formulating it. This it cannot, so long as it sticks in its bourgeois skin.

Chapter 20
Time-Wages

Wages themselves again take many forms, a fact not recognizable in the ordinary economic treatises which, exclusively interested in the material side of the question, neglect every difference of form. An exposition of all these forms however, belongs to the special study of wage labour, not therefore to this work. Still the two fundamental forms must be briefly worked out here.

The sale of labour power, as will be remembered, takes place for a definite period of time. The converted form under which the daily, weekly, &c., value of labour power presents itself, is hence that of time wages, therefore day-wages, &c.

Next it is to be noted that the laws set forth, in the 17th chapter, on the changes in the relative magnitudes of price of labour power and surplus-value, pass by a simple transformation of form, into laws of wages. Similarly the distinction between the exchange-value of labour power, and the sum of the necessaries of life into which this value is converted, now reappears as the distinction between nominal and real wages. It would be useless to repeat here, with regard to the phenomenal form, what has been already worked out in the substantial form. We limit ourselves therefore to a few points characteristic of time-wages.

The sum of money[1] which the labourer receives for his daily or weekly labour, forms the amount of his nominal wages, or of his wages estimated in value. But it is clear that according to the length of the working-day, that is, according to the amount of actual labour daily supplied, the same daily or weekly wage may represent very different prices of labour, i.e., very different sums of money for the same quantity of labour.[2] We must, therefore, in considering time-wages, again distinguish between the sum-total of the daily or weekly wages, &c., and the price of labour. How then, to find this price, i.e., the money-value of a given quantity of labour? The average price of labour is found, when the average daily value of the labour power is divided by the average number of hours in the working-day. If, e.g., the daily value of labour power is 3 shillings, the value of the product of 6 working-hours, and if the working-day is 12 hours, the price of 1 working hour is 3/12 shillings = 3d. The price of the working-hour thus found serves as the unit measure for the price of labour.

It follows, therefore, that the daily and weekly wages, &c., may remain the same, although the price of labour falls constantly. If, e.g., the habitual working-day is 10 hours and the daily value of the labour power 3s., the price of the working-hour is 3 3/5d. It falls to 3d. as soon as the working-day rises to 12 hours, to 2 2/5d as soon as it rises to 15 hours. Daily or weekly wages remain, despite all this, unchanged. On the contrary, the daily or weekly wages may rise, although the price of labour remains constant or even falls. If, e.g., the working-day is 10 hours, and the daily value of labour power 3 shillings, the price of one working-hour is 3 3/5d. If the labourer, in consequence of increase of trade, works 12 hours, the price of labour remaining the same, his daily wage now rises to 3 shillings 7 1/5d. without any variation in the price of labour. The same result might follow if, instead of the extensive amount of labour, its intensive amount increased.[3] The rise of the nominal daily or weekly wages may therefore be accompanied by a price of labour that remains stationary or falls. The same holds as to the income of the labourer's family, as soon as the quantity of labour expended by the head of the family is increased by the labour of the members of his family. There are, therefore, methods of lowering the price of labour independent of the reduction of the nominal daily or weekly wages.[4]

As a general law it follows that, given the amount of daily or weekly labour, &c., the daily or weekly wages depend on the price of labour which itself varies either with the value of labour power, or with the difference between its price and its value. Given, on the other hand, the price of labour, the daily or weekly wages depend on the quantity of the daily or weekly labour.

The unit-measure for time-wages, the price of the working-hour, is the quotient of the value of a day's labour power, divided by the number of hours of the average working-day. Let the latter be 12 hours, and the daily value of labour power 3 shillings, the value of the product of 6 hours of labour. Under these circumstances the price of a working hour is 3d.; the value produced in it is 6d. If the labourer is now employed less than 12 hours (or less than 6 days in the week), e.g., only 6 or 8 hours, he receives, with this price of labour, only 2s. or 1s. 6d. a day. [5] As on our hypothesis he must work on the average 6 hours daily, in order to produce a day's wage corresponding merely to the value of his labour power, as according to the same hypothesis he works only half of every hour for himself, and half for the capitalist, it is clear that he cannot obtain for himself the value of the product of 6 hours if he is employed less than 12 hours. In previous chapters we saw the destructive consequences of over-work; here we find the sources of the sufferings that result to the labourer from his insufficient employment.

If the hour's wage is fixed so that the capitalist does not bind himself to pay a day's or a week's wage, but only to pay wages for the hours during which he chooses to employ the labourer, he can employ him for a shorter time than that which is originally the basis of the calculation of the hour-wage, or the unit-measure of the price of labour. Since this unit is determined by the ratio (daily value of labour power)/(working-day of a given number of hours) it, of course, loses all meaning as soon as the working-day ceases to contain a definite number of hours. The connection between the paid and the unpaid labour is destroyed. The capitalist can now wring from the labour a certain quantity of surplus-labour without allowing him the labour-time necessary for his own subsistence. He can annihilate all regularity of employment, and according to his own convenience, caprice, and the interest of the moment, make the most enormous over-work alternate with relative or absolute cessation of work. He can, under the pretence of paying 'the normal price of labour', abnormally lengthen the working-day without any corresponding compensation to the labourer. Hence the perfectly rational revolt in 1860 of the London labourers, employed in the building trades, against the attempt of the capitalists to impose on them this sort of wage by the hour. The legal limitation of the working-day puts an end to such mischief, although not, of course, to the diminution of employment caused by the competition of machinery, by changes in the quality of the labourers employed, and by crises partial or general.

With an increasing daily or weekly wage the price of labour may remain nominally constant, and yet may fall below its normal level. This occurs every time that, the price of labour (reckoned per working-hour) remaining constant, the working-day is prolonged beyond its customary length. If in the fraction (daily value of labour power)/(working-day) the denominator increases, the numerator increases yet more rapidly. The value of labour power, as dependent on its wear and tear, increases with the duration of its functioning, and in more rapid proportion than the increase of that duration. In many branches of industry where time-wage is the general rule without legal limits to the working-time, the habit has, therefore, spontaneously grown up of regarding the working day as normal only up to a certain point, e.g., up to the expiration of the tenth hour ('normal working-day', 'the day's work', 'the regular hours of work'). Beyond this limit the working-time is over-time, and is, taking the hour as unit-measure, paid better ('extra pay'), although often in a proportion ridiculously small.[6] The normal working-day exists here as a fraction of the actual working-day, and the latter, often during the whole year, lasts longer than the former.[7] The increase in the price of labour with the extension of the working-day beyond a certain normal limit, takes such a shape in various British industries that the low price of labour during the so-called normal time compels the labourer to work during the better paid over-time, if he wishes to obtain a sufficient wage at all.[8] Legal limitation of the working-day puts an end to these amenities.[9]

It is a fact generally known that, the longer the working-days, in any branch of industry, the lower are the wages.[10] A. Redgrave, factory inspector, illustrates this by a comparative review of the 20 years from 1839–1859, according to which wages rose in the factories under the 10 Hours Law, whilst they fell in the factories in which the work lasted 14 to 15 hours daily.[11]

From the law, 'the price of labour being given, the daily or weekly wage depends on the quantity of labour expended,' it follows, first of all, that the lower the price of labour, the greater must be the quantity of labour, or the longer must be the working-day for the labourer to secure even a miserable average wage. The lowness of the price of labour acts here as a stimulus to the extension of the labour-time.[12]

On the other hand, the extension of the working-time produces, in its turn, a fall in the price of labour, and with this a fall in the day's or week's wages.

The determination of the price of labour by (daily value of labour power)/(working day of a given number of hours) shows that a mere prolongation of the working-day lowers the price of labour, if no compensation steps in. But the same circumstances which allow the capitalist in the long run to prolong the working-day, also allow him first, and compel him finally, to nominally lower the price of labour until the total price of the increased number of hours is lowered, and, therefore, the daily or weekly wage. Reference to two circumstances is sufficient here. If one man does the work of 1 1/2 or 2 men, the supply of labour increases, although the supply of labour power on the market remains constant. The competition thus created between the labourers allows the capitalist to beat down the price of labour, whilst the falling price of labour allows him, on the other hand, to screw up still further the working-time.[13] Soon, however, this command over abnormal quantities of unpaid labour, i.e., quantities in excess of the average social amount, becomes a source of competition amongst the capitalists themselves. A part of the price of the commodity consists of the price of labour. The unpaid part of the labour-price need not be reckoned in the price of the commodity. It may be presented to the buyer. This is the first step to which competition leads. The second step to which it drives is to exclude also from the selling price of the commodity at least a part of the abnormal surplus-value created by the extension of the working-day. In this way, an abnormally low selling price of the commodity arises, at first sporadically, and becomes fixed by degrees; a lower selling price which henceforward becomes the constant basis of a miserable wage for an excessive working-time, as originally it was the product of these very circumstances. This movement is simply indicated here, as the analysis of competition does not belong to this part of our subject. Nevertheless, the capitalist may, for a moment, speak for himself. 'In Birmingham there is so much competition of masters one against another that many are obliged to do things as employers that they would otherwise be ashamed of; and yet no more money is made, but only the public gets the benefit.'[14] The reader will remember the two sorts of London bakers, of whom one sold the bread at its full price (the 'full-priced' bakers), the other below its normal price ('the under-priced,' 'the undersellers'). The 'full-priced' denounced their rivals before the Parliamentary Committee of Inquiry: 'They only exist now by first defrauding the public, and next getting 18 hours' work out of their men for 12 hours' wages . . . The unpaid labour of the men was made . . . the source whereby the competition was carried on, and continues so to this day . . . The competition among the master bakers is the cause of the difficulty in getting rid of night-work. An underseller, who sells his bread below the cost-price according to the price of flour, must make it up by getting more out of the labour of the men . . . If I got only 12 hours' work out of my men, and my neighbor got 18 or 20, he must beat me in the selling price. If the men could insist on payment for over-work, this would be set right . . . A large number of those employed by the undersellers are foreigners and youths, who are obliged to accept almost any wages they can obtain.'[15]

This jeremiad is also interesting because it shows how the appearance only of the relations of production mirrors itself in the brain of the capitalist. The capitalist does not know that the normal price of labour also includes a definite quantity of unpaid labour, and that this very unpaid labour is the normal source of his gain. The category of surplus labour-time does not exist at all for him, since it is included in the normal working-day, which he thinks he has paid for in the day's wages. But over-time does exist for him, the prolongation of the working-day beyond the limits corresponding with the usual price of labour. Face to face with his underselling competitor, he even insists upon extra pay for this over-time. He again does not know that this extra pay includes unpaid labour, just as well as does the price of the customary hour of labour. For example, the price of one hour of the 12 hours' working-day is 3d., say the value-product of half a working-hour, whilst the price of the over-time working-hour is 4d., or the value-product of 2/3 of a working hour. In the first case the capitalist appropriates to himself one-half, in the second, one-third of the working-hour without paying for it.

Chapter 21
Piece-Wages

Wages by the piece are nothing else than a converted form of wages by time, just as wages by time are a converted form of the value or price of labour power.

In piece-wages it seems at first sight as if the use-value bought from the labourer was, not the function of his labour power, living labour, but labour already realised in the product, and as if the price of this labour was determined, not as with time-wages, by the fraction (daily value of labour power)/(the working day of a given number of hours) but by the capacity for work of the producer.[1]

The confidence that trusts in this appearance ought to receive a first severe shock from the fact that both forms of wages exist side by side, simultaneously, in the same branches of industry; e.g., 'the compositors of London, as a general rule, work by the piece, time-work being the exception, while those in the country work by the day, the exception being work by the piece. The shipwrights of the port of London work by the job or piece, while those of all other parts work by the day.'[2]

In the same saddlery shops of London, often for the same work, piece-wages are paid to the French, time-wages to the English. In the regular factories in which throughout piece-wages predominate, particular kinds of work are unsuitable to this form of wage, and are therefore paid by time.[3] But it is, moreover, self-evident that the difference of form in the payment of wages alters in no way their essential nature, although the one form may be more favourable to the development of capitalist production than the other.

Let the ordinary working-day contain 12 hours of which 6 are paid, 6 unpaid. Let its value-product be 6 shillings, that of one hour's labour therefore 6d. Let us suppose that, as the result of experience, a labourer who works with the average amount of intensity and skill, who, therefore, gives in fact only the time socially necessary to the production of an article, supplies in 12 hours 24 pieces, either distinct products or measurable parts of a continuous whole. Then the value of these 24 pieces, after. subtraction of the portion of constant capital contained in them, is 6 shillings, and the value of a single piece 3d. The labourer receives 1 1/2d. per piece, and thus earns in 12 hours 3 shillings. Just as, with time-wages, it does not matter whether we assume that the labourer works 6 hours for himself and 6 hours for the capitalist, or half of every hour for himself, and the other half for the capitalist, so here it does not matter whether we say that each individual piece is half paid, and half unpaid for, or that the price of 12 pieces is the equivalent only of the value of the labour power, whilst in the other 12 pieces surplus-value is incorporated.

The form of piece-wages is just as irrational as that of time-wages. Whilst in our example two pieces of a commodity, after subtraction of the value of the means of production consumed in them, are worth 6d. as being the product of one hour, the labourer receives for them a price of 3d. Piece-wages do not, in fact, distinctly express any relation of value. It is not, therefore, a question of measuring the value of the piece by the working-time incorporated in it, but on the contrary, of measuring the working-time the labourer has expended by the number of pieces he has produced. In time-wages, the labour is measured by its immediate duration; in piece-wages, by the quantity of products in which the labour has embodied itself during a given time.[4] The price of labour time itself is finally determined by the equation: (value of a day's labour) = (daily value of labour power). Piece-wage is, therefore, only a modified form of time-wage.

Let us now consider a little more closely the characteristic peculiarities of piece-wages.

The quality of the labour is here controlled by the work itself, which must be of average perfection if the piece-price is to be paid in full. Piece-wages become, from this point of view, the most fruitful source of reductions of wages and capitalistic cheating.

They furnish to the capitalist an exact measure for the intensity of labour. Only the working-time which is embodied in a quantum of commodities determined beforehand, and experimentally fixed, counts as socially necessary working-time, and is paid as such. In the larger workshops of the London tailors, therefore, a certain piece of work, a waistcoat, e.g., is called an hour, or half an hour, the hour at 6d. By practice it is known how much is the average product of one hour. With new fashions, repairs, &c., a contest arises between master and labourer as to whether a particular piece of work is one hour, and so on, until here also experience decides. Similarly in the London furniture workshops, &c. If the labourer does not possess the average capacity, if he cannot in consequence supply a certain minimum of work per day, he is dismissed.[5]

Since the quality and intensity of the work are here controlled by the form of wage itself, superintendence of labour becomes in great part superfluous. Piece-wages therefore lay the foundation of the modern 'domestic labour', described above, as well as of a hierarchically organised system of exploitation and oppression. The latter has two fundamental forms. On the one hand, piece-wages facilitate the interposition of parasites between the capitalist and the wage-labourer, the 'sub-letting of labour'. The gain of these middlemen comes entirely from the difference between the labour-price which the capitalist pays, and the part of that price which they actually allow to reach the labourer.[6] In England this system is characteristically called the 'sweating system'. On the other hand, piece-wage allows the capitalist to make a contract for so much per piece with the head labourer – in manufactures with the chief of some group, in mines with the extractor of the coal, in the factory with the actual machine-worker – at a price for which the head labourer himself undertakes the enlisting and payment of his assistant work people. The exploitation of the labourer by capital is here effected through the exploitation of the labourer by the labourer.[7]

Given piece-wage, it is naturally the personal interest of the labourer to strain his labour power as intensely as possible; this enables the capitalist to raise more easily the normal degree of intensity of labour. [8] It is moreover now the personal interest of the labourer to lengthen the working-day, since with it his daily or weekly wages rise.[9] This gradually brings on a reaction like that already described in time-wages, without reckoning that the prolongation of the working-day, even if the piece wage remains constant, includes of necessity a fall in the price of the labour.

In time-wages, with few exceptions, the same wage holds for the same kind of work, whilst in piece-wages, though the price of the working time is measured by a certain quantity of product, the day's or week's wage will vary with the individual differences of the labourers, of whom one supplies in a given time the minimum of product only, another the average, a third more than the average. With regard to actual receipts there is, therefore, great variety according to the different skill, strength, energy, staying-power, &c., of the individual labourers.[10] Of course this does not alter the general relations between capital and wage-labour. First, the individual differences balance one another in the workshop as a whole, which thus supplies in a given working-time the average product, and the total wages paid will be the average wages of that particular branch of industry. Second, the proportion between wages and surplus-value remains unaltered, since the mass of surplus labour supplied by each particular labourer corresponds with the wage received by him. But the wider scope that piece-wage gives to individuality tends to develop on the one hand that individuality, and with it the sense of liberty, independence, and self-control of the labourers, and on the other, their competition one with another. Piece-work has, therefore, a tendency, while raising individual wages above the average, to lower this average itself. But where a particular rate of piece-wage has for a long time been fixed by tradition, and its lowering, therefore, presented especial difficulties, the masters, in such exceptional cases, sometimes had recourse to its compulsory transformation into time-wages. Hence, e.g., in 1860 a great strike among the ribbon-weavers of Coventry.[11] Piece-wage is finally one of the chief supports of the hour-system described in the preceding chapter.[12]

From what has been shown so far, it follows that piece-wage is the form of wages most in harmony with the capitalist mode of production. Although by no means new – it figures side by side with time-wages officially in the French and English labour statutes of the 14th century – it only conquers a larger field for action during the period of manufacture, properly so-called. In the stormy youth of modern industry, especially from 1797 to 1815, it served as a lever for the lengthening of the working-day, and the lowering of wages. Very important materials for the fluctuation of wages during that period are to be found in the Blue Books: *Report and Evidence from the Select Committee on Petitions respecting the Corn Laws* (Parliamentary Session of 1813–14), and *Report from the Lords' Committee, on the State of the Growth, Commerce, and Consumption of Grain, and all Laws relating thereto* (Session of 1814–15). Here we find documentary evidence of the constant lowering of the price of labour from the beginning of the anti-Jacobin War. In the weaving industry, e.g., piece-wages had fallen so low that, in spite of the very great lengthening of the working-day, the daily wages were then lower than before. 'The real earnings of the cotton weaver are now far less than they were; his superiority over the common labourer, which at first was very great, has now almost entirely ceased. Indeed . . . the difference in the wages of skilful and common labour is far less now than at any former period.'[13] How little the increased intensity and extension of labour through piece-wages benefited the agricultural proletariat, the following passage borrowed from a work on the side of the landlords and farmers shows: 'By far the greater part of agricultural operations is done by people who are hired for the day or on piece-work. Their weekly wages are about 12s., and although it may be assumed that a man earns on piece-work under the greater stimulus to labour, 1s. or perhaps 2s. more than on weekly wages, yet it is found, on calculating his total income, that his loss of employment, during the year, outweighs this gain . . . Further, it will generally be found that the wages of these men bear a certain proportion to the price of the necessary means of subsistence, so that a man with two children is able to bring up his family without recourse to parish relief.'[14] Malthus at that time remarked with reference to the facts published by Parliament: 'I confess that I see, with misgiving, the great extension of the practice of piece-wage. Really hard work during 12 or 14 hours of the day, or for any longer time, is too much for any human being.[15]

In the workshops under the Factory Acts, piece-wages become the general rule, because capital can there only increase the efficacy of the working-day by intensifying labour.[16]

With the changing productiveness of labour the same quantum of product represents a varying working-time. Therefore, piece-wage also varies, for it is the money expression of a determined working-time. In our example above, 24 pieces were produced in 12 hours, whilst the value of the product of the 12 hours was 6s., the daily value of the labour power 3s., the price of the labour-hour 3d., and the wage for one piece 1/2d. In one piece half-an-hour's labour was absorbed. If the same working-day now supplies, in consequence of the doubled productiveness of labour, 48 pieces instead of 24, and all other circumstances remain unchanged, then the piece-wage falls from 1 1/2d. to 3/4d., as every piece now only represents 1/4, instead of 1/2 of a working-hour. 24 by 1 1/2d. = 3s., and in like manner 48 by 3/4d. = 3s. In other words, piece-wage is lowered in the same proportion as the number of the pieces produced in the same time rises,[17] and, therefore, as the working time spent on the same piece falls. This change in piece-wage, so far purely nominal, leads to constant battles between capitalist and labour. Either because the capitalist uses it as a pretext for actually lowering the price of labour, or because increased productive power of labour is accompanied by an increased intensity of the same. Or because the labourer takes seriously the appearance of piece-wages (viz., that his product is paid for, and not his labour power) and therefore revolts against a lowering of wages, unaccompanied by a lowering in the selling price of the commodity. 'The operatives . . . carefully watch the price of the raw material and the price of manufactured goods, and are thus enabled to form an accurate estimate of their master's profits.'[18]

The capitalist rightly knocks on the head such pretensions as gross errors as to the nature of wage-labour.[19] He cries out against this usurping attempt to lay taxes on the advance of industry, and declares roundly that the productiveness of labour does not concern the labourer at all.[20]

Chapter 22
National Differences of Wages

In the 17th chapter we were occupied with the manifold combinations which may bring about a change in magnitude of the value of labour power – this magnitude being considered either absolutely or relatively, i.e., as compared with surplus-value; whilst on the other hand, the quantum of the means of subsistence in which the price of labour is realised might again undergo fluctuations independent of, or different from, the changes of this price.[1] As has been already said, the simple translation of the value, or respectively of the price, of labour power into the exoteric form of wages transforms all these laws into laws of the fluctuations of wages. That which appears in these fluctuations of wages within a single country as a series of varying combinations, may appear in different countries as contemporaneous difference of national wages. In the comparison of the wages in different nations, we must therefore take into account all the factors that determine changes in the amount of the value of labour power; the price and the extent of the prime necessaries of life as naturally and historically developed, the cost of training the labourers, the part played by the labour of women and children, the productiveness of labour, its extensive and intensive magnitude. Even the most superficial comparison requires the reduction first of the average day-wage for the same trades, in different countries, to a uniform working-day. After this reduction to the same terms of the day-wages, time-wage must again be translated into piece-wage, as the latter only can be a measure both of the productivity and the intensity of labour.

In every country there is a certain average intensity of labour below which the labour for the production of a commodity requires more than the socially necessary time, and therefore does not reckon as labour of normal quality. Only a degree of intensity above the national average affects, in a given country, the measure of value by the mere duration of the working-time. This is not the case on the universal market, whose integral parts are the individual countries. The average intensity of labour changes from country to country; here it is greater, there less. These national averages form a scale, whose unit of measure is the average unit of universal labour. The more intense national labour, therefore, as compared with the less intense, produces in the same time more value, which expresses itself in more money.

But the law of value in its international application is yet more modified by the fact that on the world-market the more productive national labour reckons also as the more intense, so long as the more productive nation is not compelled by competition to lower the selling price of its commodities to the level of their value.

In proportion as capitalist production is developed in a country, in the same proportion do the national intensity and productivity of labour there rise above the international level.[2] The different quantities of commodities of the same kind, produced in different countries in the same working-time, have, therefore, unequal international values, which are expressed in different prices, i.e., in sums of money varying according to international values. The relative value of money will, therefore, be less in the nation with more developed capitalist mode of production than in the nation with less developed. It follows, then, that the nominal wages, the equivalent of labour power expressed in money, will also be higher in the first nation than in the second; which does not at all prove that this holds also for the real wages, i.e., for the means of subsistence placed at the disposal of the labourer.

But even apart from these relative differences of the value of money in different countries, it will be found, frequently, that the daily or weekly, &c., wage in the first nation is higher than in the second, whilst the relative price of labour, i.e., the price of labour as compared both with surplus-value and with the value of the product, stands higher in the second than in the first.[3]

J. W. Cowell, member of the Factory Commission of 1833, after careful investigation of the spinning trade, came to the conclusion that 'in England wages are virtually lower to the capitalist, though higher to the operative than on the Continent of Europe.'[4] The English Factory Inspector, Alexander Redgrave, in his report of Oct. 31st, 1866, proves by comparative statistics with continental states, that in spite of lower wages and much longer working-time, continental labour is, in proportion to the product, dearer than English. An English manager of a cotton factory in Oldenburg declares that the working time there lasted from 5:30 a.m. to 8 p.m., Saturdays included, and that the workpeople there, when under English over-lookers, did not supply during this time quite so much product as the English in 10 hours, but under German overlookers much less. Wages are much lower than in England, in many cases 50%, but the number of hands in proportion to the machinery was much greater, in certain departments in the proportion of 5:3. – Mr Redgrave gives very full details as to the Russian cotton factories. The data were given him by an English manager until recently employed there. On this Russian soil, so fruitful of all infamies, the old horrors of the early days of English factories are in full swing. The managers are, of course, English, as the native Russian capitalist is of no use in factory business. Despite all over-work, continued day and night, despite the most shameful under-payment of the workpeople, Russian manufacture manages to vegetate only by prohibition of foreign competition.

I give, in conclusion, a comparative table of Mr Redgrave's, on the average number of spindles per factory and per spinner in the different countries of Europe. He himself remarks that he had collected these figures a few years ago, and that since that time the size of the factories and the number of spindles per labourer in England has increased. He supposes, however, an approximately equal progress in the contin-ental countries mentioned, so that the numbers given would still have their value for purposes of comparison.

Average Number of Spindles Per Factory

England	average of spindles per factory	12,600
France	average of spindles per factory	1,500
Prussia	average of spindles per factory	1,500
Belgium	average of spindles per factory	4,000
Saxony	average of spindles per factory	4,500
Austria	average of spindles per factory	7,000
Switzerland	average of spindles per factory	8,000

Average Number of Persons Employed to Spindles

France	one person to	14 spindles
Russia	one person to	28 spindles
Prussia	one person to	37 spindles
Bavaria	one person to	46 spindles
Austria	one person to	49 spindles
Belgium	one person to	50 spindles
Saxony	one person to	50 spindles
Switzerland	one person to	55 spindles
Smaller States of Germany	one person to	55 spindles
Great Britain	one person to	74 spindles

'This comparison,' says Mr Redgrave, 'is yet more unfavourable to Great Britain, inasmuch as there is so large a number of factories in which weaving by power is carried on in conjunction with spinning' (whilst in the table the weavers are not deducted), 'and the factories abroad are chiefly spinning factories; if it were possible to compare like with like, strictly, I could find many cotton spinning factories in my district in which mules containing 2,200 spindles are minded by one man (the minder) and two assistants only, turning off daily 220 lbs. of yarn, measuring 400 miles in length.'[5]

It is well known that in Eastern Europe, as well as in Asia, English companies have undertaken the construction of railways, and have, in making them, employed side by side with the native labourers, a certain number of English working-men. Compelled by practical necessity, they thus have had to take into account the national difference in the intensity of labour, but this has brought them no loss. Their experience shows that even if the height of wages corresponds more or less with the average intensity of labour, the relative price of labour varies generally in the inverse direction.

In an *Essay on the Rate of Wages*,[6] one of his first economic writings, H. Carey tries to prove that the wages of the different nations are directly proportional to the degree of productiveness of the national working-days, in order to draw from this international relation the conclusion that wages everywhere rise and fall in proportion to the productiveness of labour. The whole of our analysis of the production of surplus-value shows the absurdity of this conclusion, even if Carey himself had proved his premises instead of, after his usual uncritical and superficial fashion, shuffling to and fro a confused mass of statistical materials. The best of it is that he does not assert that things actually are as they ought to be according to his theory. For State intervention has falsified the natural economic relations. The different national wages must be reckoned, therefore, as if that part of each that goes to the State in the form of taxes, came to the labourer himself. Ought not Mr Carey to consider further whether those 'State expenses' are not the 'natural' fruits of capitalistic development? The reasoning is quite worthy of the man who first declared the relations of capitalist production to be eternal laws of nature and reason, whose free, harmonious working is only disturbed by the intervention of the State, in order afterwards to discover that the diabolical influence of England on the world-market (an influence which, it appears, does not spring from the natural laws of capitalist production) necessitates State intervention, i.e., the protection of those laws of nature and reason by the State, alias the System of Protection. He discovered further that the theorems of Ricardo and others, in which existing social antagonisms and contradictions are formulated, are not the ideal product of the real economic movement, but on the contrary, that the real antagonisms of capitalist production in England and elsewhere are the result of the theories of Ricardo and others! Finally he discovered that it is, in the last resort, commerce that destroys the inborn beauties and harmonies of the capitalist mode of production. A step further and he will, perhaps, discover that the one evil in capitalist production is capital itself. Only a man with such atrocious want of the critical faculty and such spurious erudition deserved, in spite of his Protectionist heresy, to become the secret source of the harmonious wisdom of a Bastiat, and of all the other Free-trade optimists of today.

Part 7

The Accumulation of Capital

The conversion of a sum of money into means of production and labour power, is the first step taken by the quantum of value that is going to function as capital. This conversion takes place in the market, within the sphere of circulation. The second step, the process of production, is complete so soon as the means of production have been converted into commodities whose value exceeds that of their component parts, and, therefore, contains the capital originally advanced, plus a surplus-value. These commodities must then be thrown into circulation. They must be sold, their value realised in money, this money afresh converted into capital, and so over and over again. This circular movement, in which the same phases are continually gone through in succession, forms the circulation of capital.

The first condition of accumulation is that the capitalist must have contrived to sell his commodities, and to reconvert into capital the greater part of the money so received. In the following pages we shall assume that capital circulates in its normal way. The detailed analysis of the process will be found in Book 2.

The capitalist who produces surplus-value – i.e., who extracts unpaid labour directly from the labourers, and fixes it in commodities, is, indeed, the first appropriator, but by no means the ultimate owner, of this surplus-value. He has to share it with capitalists, with land-owners, &c., who fulfil other functions in the complex of social production. Surplus-value, therefore, splits up into various parts. Its fragments fall to various categories of persons, and take various forms, independent the one of the other, such as profit, interest, merchants' profit, rent, &c. It is only in Book 3 that we can take in hand these modified forms of surplus-value.

On the one hand, then, we assume that the capitalist sells at their value the commodities he has produced, without concerning our-selves either about the new forms that capital assumes while in the sphere of circulation, or about the concrete conditions of repro-duction hidden under these forms. On the other hand, we treat the capitalist producer as owner of the entire surplus-value, or, better perhaps, as the representative of all the sharers with him in the booty. We, therefore, first of all consider accumulation from an abstract point of view – i.e., as a mere phase in the actual process of production.

So far as accumulation takes place, the capitalist must have succeeded in selling his commodities, and in reconverting the sale-money into capital. Moreover, the breaking-up of surplus-value into fragments neither alters its nature nor the conditions under which it becomes an element of accumulation. Whatever be the proportion of surplus-value which the industrial capitalist retains for himself, or yields up to others, he is the one who, in the first instance, appropriates it. We, therefore, assume no more than what actually takes place. On the other hand, the simple fundamental form of the process of accumulation is obscured by the incident of the circulation which brings it about, and by the splitting up of surplus-value. An exact analysis of the process, therefore, demands that we should, for a time, disregard all phenomena that hide the pity of its inner mechanism.

Chapter 23
Simple Reproduction

Whatever the form of the process of production in a society, it must be a continuous process, must continue to go periodically through the same phases. A society can no more cease to produce than it can cease to consume. When viewed, therefore, as a connected whole, and as flowing on with incessant renewal, every social process of production is, at the same time, a process of reproduction.

The conditions of production are also those of reproduction. No society can go on producing, in other words, no society can reproduce, unless it constantly reconverts a part of its products into means of production, or elements of fresh products. All other circumstances remaining the same, the only mode by which it can reproduce its wealth, and maintain it at one level, is by replacing the means of production – i.e., the instruments of labour, the raw material, and the auxiliary substances consumed in the course of the year – by an equal quantity of the same kind of articles; these must be separated from the mass of the yearly products, and thrown afresh into the process of production. Hence, a definite portion of each year's product belongs to the domain of production. Destined for productive consumption from the very first, this portion exists, for the most part, in the shape of articles totally unfitted for individual consumption.

If production be capitalistic in form, so, too, will be reproduction. Just as in the former the labour-process figures but as a means towards the self-expansion of capital, so in the latter it figures but as a means of reproducing as capital – i.e., as self-expanding value – the value advanced. It is only because his money constantly functions as capital that the economic guise of a capitalist attaches to a man. If, for instance, a sum of £100 has this year been converted into capital, and produced a surplus-value of £20, it must continue during next year, and subsequent years, to repeat the same operation. As a periodic increment of the capital advanced, or periodic fruit of capital in process, surplus-value acquires the form of a revenue flowing out of capital.[1]

If this revenue serve the capitalist only as a fund to provide for his consumption, and be spent as periodically as it is gained, then, *ceteris paribus*, simple reproduction will take place. And although this reproduction is a mere repetition of the process of production on the old scale, yet this mere repetition, or continuity, gives a new character to the process, or, rather, causes the disappearance of some apparent characteristics which it possessed as an isolated discontinuous process.

The purchase of labour power for a fixed period is the prelude to the process of production; and this prelude is constantly repeated when the stipulated term comes to an end, when a definite period of production, such as a week or a month, has elapsed. But the labourer is not paid until after he has expended his labour power, and realised in commodities not only its value, but surplus-value. He has, therefore, produced not only surplus-value, which we for the present regard as a fund to meet the private consumption of the capitalist, but he has also produced, before it flows back to him in the shape of wages, the fund out of which he himself is paid, the variable capital; and his employment lasts only so long as he continues to reproduce this fund. Hence, that formula of the economists, referred to in Chapter 18, which represents wages as a share in the product itself.[2] What flows back to the labourer in the shape of wages is a portion of the product that is continuously reproduced by him. The capitalist, it is true, pays him in money, but this money is merely the transmuted form of the product of his labour. While he is converting a portion of the means of production into products, a portion of his former product is being turned into money. It is his labour of last week, or of last year, that pays for his labour power this week or this year. The illusion begotten by the intervention of money vanishes immediately, if, instead of taking a single capitalist and a single labourer, we take the class of capitalists and the class of labourers as a whole. The capitalist class is constantly giving to the labouring class order-notes, in the form of money, on a portion of the commodities produced by the latter and appropriated by the former. The labourers give these order-notes back just as constantly to the capitalist class, and in this way get their share of their own product. The transaction is veiled by the commodity-form of the product and the money form of the commodity.

Variable capital is therefore only a particular historical form of appearance of the fund for providing the necessaries of life, or the labour-fund which the labourer requires for the maintenance of himself and family, and which, whatever be the system of social production, he must himself produce and reproduce. If the labour-fund constantly flows to him in the form of money that pays for his labour, it is because the product he has created moves constantly away from him in the form of capital. But all this does not alter the fact, that it is the labourer's own labour, realised in a product, which is advanced to him by the capitalist.[3] Let us take a peasant liable to do compulsory service for his lord. He works on his own land, with his own means of production, for, say, 3 days a week. The 3 other days he does forced work on the lord's domain. He constantly reproduces his own labour-fund, which never, in his case, takes the form of a money payment for his labour, advanced by another person. But in return, his unpaid forced labour for the lord, on its side, never acquires the character of voluntary paid labour. If one fine morning the lord appropriates to himself the land, the cattle, the seed, in a word, the means of production of this peasant, the latter will thenceforth be obliged to sell his labour power to the lord. He will, *ceteris paribus*, labour 6 days a week as before, 3 for himself, 3 for his lord, who thenceforth becomes a wages-paying capitalist. As before, he will use up the means of production as means of production, and transfer their value to the product. As before, a definite portion of the product will be devoted to reproduction. But from the moment that the forced labour is changed into wage-labour, from that moment the labour-fund, which the peasant himself continues as before to produce and reproduce, takes the form of a capital advanced in the form of wages by the lord. The bourgeois economist whose narrow mind is unable to separate the form of appearance from the thing that appears, shuts his eyes to the fact, that it is but here and there on the face of the earth, that even nowadays the labour-fund crops up in the form of capital.[4]

Variable capital, it is true, only then loses its character of a value advanced out of the capitalist's funds,[5] when we view the process of capitalist production in the flow of its constant renewal. But that process must have had a beginning of some kind. From our present standpoint it therefore seems likely that the capitalist, once upon a time, became possessed of money, by some accumulation that took place independently of the unpaid labour of others, and that this was, therefore, how he was enabled to frequent the market as a buyer of labour power. However this may be, the mere continuity of the process, the simple reproduction, brings about some other wonderful changes, which affect not only the variable, but the total capital.

If a capital of £1,000 beget yearly a surplus-value of £200, and if this surplus-value be consumed every year, it is clear that at the end of 5 years the surplus-value consumed will amount to 5 x £200 or the £1,000 originally advanced. If only a part, say one half, were consumed, the same result would follow at the end of 10 years, since 10 x £100= £1,000. General Rule: The value of the capital advanced divided by the surplus-value annually consumed, gives the number of years, or reproduction periods, at the expiration of which the capital originally advanced has been consumed by the capitalist and has disappeared. The capitalist thinks, that he is consuming the produce of the unpaid labour of others, i.e., the surplus-value, and is keeping intact his original capital; but what he thinks cannot alter facts. After the lapse of a certain number of years, the capital value he then possesses is equal to the sum total of the surplus-value appropriated by him during those years, and the total value he has consumed is equal to that of his original capital. It is true, he has in hand a capital whose amount has not changed, and of which a part, viz., the buildings, machinery, &c., were already there when the work of his business began. But what we have to do with here, is not the material elements, but the value, of that capital. When a person gets through all his property, by taking upon himself debts equal to the value of that property, it is clear that his property represents nothing but the sum total of his debts. And so it is with the capitalist; when he has consumed the equivalent of his original capital, the value of his present capital represents nothing but the total amount of the surplus-value appropriated by him without payment. Not a single atom of the value of his old capital continues to exist.

Apart then from all accumulation, the mere continuity of the process of production, in other words simple reproduction, sooner or later, and of necessity, converts every capital into accumulated capital, or capitalised surplus-value. Even if that capital was originally acquired by the personal labour of its employer, it sooner or later becomes value appropriated without an equivalent, the unpaid labour of others materialised either in money or in some other object. We saw in Chapt. 4-6 that in order to convert money into capital something more is required than the production and circulation of commodities. We saw that on the one side the possessor of value or money, on the other, the possessor of the value-creating substance; on the one side, the possessor of the means of production and subsistence, on the other, the possessor of nothing but labour power, must confront one another as buyer and seller. The separation of labour from its product, of subjective labour power from the objective conditions of labour, was therefore the real foundation in fact, and the starting-point of capitalist production.

But that which at first was but a starting-point, becomes, by the mere continuity of the process, by simple reproduction, the peculiar result, constantly renewed and perpetuated, of capitalist production. On the one hand, the process of production incessantly converts material wealth into capital, into means of creating more wealth and means of enjoyment for the capitalist. On the other hand, the labourer, on quitting the process, is what he was on entering it, a source of wealth, but devoid of all means of making that wealth his own. Since, before entering on the process, his own labour has already been alienated from himself by the sale of his labour power, has been appropriated by the capitalist and incorporated with capital, it must, during the process, be realised in a product that does not belong to him. Since the process of production is also the process by which the capitalist consumes labour power, the product of the labourer is incessantly converted, not only into commodities, but into capital, into value that sucks up the value-creating power, into means of subsistence that buy the person of the labourer, into means of production that command the producers.[6] The labourer therefore constantly produces material, objective wealth, but in the form of capital, of an alien power that dominates and exploits him: and the capitalist as constantly produces labour power, but in the form of a subjective source of wealth, separated from the objects in and by which it can alone be realised; in short he produces the labourer, but as a wage-labourer.[7] This incessant reproduction, this perpetuation of the labourer, is the *sine quâ non* of capitalist production.

The labourer consumes in a two-told way. While producing he consumes by his labour the means of production, and converts them into products with a higher value than that of the capital advanced. This is his productive consumption. It is at the same time consumption of his labour power by the capitalist who bought it. On the other hand, the labourer turns the money paid to him for his labour power, into means of subsistence: this is his individual consumption. The labourer's productive consumption, and his individual consumption, are therefore totally distinct. In the former, he acts as the motive power of capital, and belongs to the capitalist. In the latter, he belongs to himself, and performs his necessary vital functions outside the process of production. The result of the one is, that the capitalist lives; of the other, that the labourer lives.

When treating of the working-day, we saw that the labourer is often compelled to make his individual consumption a mere incident of production. In such a case, he supplies himself with necessaries in order to maintain his labour power, just as coal and water are supplied to the steam-engine and oil to the wheel. His means of consumption, in that case, are the mere means of consumption required by a means of production; his individual consumption is directly productive consumption. This, however, appears to be an abuse not essentially appertaining to capitalist production.[8]

The matter takes quite another aspect, when we contemplate, not the single capitalist, and the single labourer, but the capitalist class and the labouring class, not an isolated process of production, but capitalist production in full swing, and on its actual social scale. By converting part of his capital into labour power, the capitalist augments the value of his entire capital. He kills two birds with one stone. He profits, not only by what he receives from but by what be gives to, the labourer. The capital given in exchange for labour power is converted into necessaries, by the consumption of which the muscles, nerves, bones, and brains of existing labourers are reproduced, and new labourers are begotten. Within the limits of what is strictly necessary, the individual consumption of the working-class is, therefore, the reconversion of the means of subsistence given by capital in exchange for labour power, into fresh labour power at the disposal of capital for exploitation. It is the production and reproduction of that means of production so indispensable to the capitalist: the labourer himself. The individual consumption of the labourer, whether it proceed within the workshop or outside it, whether it be part of the process of production or not, forms therefore a factor of the production and reproduction of capital; just as cleaning machinery does, whether it be done while the machinery is working or while it is standing. The fact that the labourer consumes his means of subsistence for his own purposes, and not to please the capitalist, has no bearing on the matter. The consumption of food by a beast of burden is none the less a necessary factor in the process of production, because the beast enjoys what it eats. The maintenance and reproduction of the working-class is, and must ever be, a necessary condition to the reproduction of capital. But the capitalist may safely leave its fulfilment to the labourer's instincts of self-preservation and of propagation. All the capitalist cares for, is to reduce the labourer's individual consumption as far as possible to what is strictly necessary, and he is far away from imitating those brutal South Americans, who force their labourers to take the more substantial, rather than the less substantial, kind of food.[9]

Hence both the capitalist and his ideological representative, the political economist, consider that part alone of the labourer's individual consumption to be productive, which is requisite for the perpetuation of the class, and which therefore must take place in order that the capitalist may have labour power to consume; what the labourer consumes for his own pleasure beyond that part, is unproductive consumption.[10] If the accumulation of capital were to cause a rise of wages and an increase in the labourer's consumption, unaccompanied by increase in the consumption of labour power by capital, the additional capital would be consumed unproductively.[11] In reality, the individual consumption of the labourer is unproductive as regards himself, for it reproduces nothing but the needy individual; it is productive to the capitalist and to the State, since it is the production of the power that creates their wealth.[12]

From a social point of view, therefore, the working-class, even when not directly engaged in the labour-process, is just as much an appendage of capital as the ordinary instruments of labour. Even its individual consumption is, within certain limits, a mere factor in the process of production. That process, however, takes good care to prevent these self-conscious instruments from leaving it in the lurch, for it removes their product, as fast as it is made, from their pole to the opposite pole of capital. Individual consumption provides, on the one hand, the means for their maintenance and reproduction: on the other hand, it secures by the annihilation of the necessaries of life, the continued re-appearance of the workman in the labour-market. The Roman slave was held by fetters: the wage-labourer is bound to his owner by invisible threads. The appearance of independence is kept up by means of a constant change of employers, and by the *fictio juris* of a contract.

In former times, capital resorted to legislation, whenever necessary, to enforce its proprietary rights over the free labourer. For instance, down to 1815, the emigration of mechanics employed in machine making was, in England, forbidden, under grievous pains and penalties.

The reproduction of the working-class carries with it the accumulation of skill, that is handed down from one generation to another.[13] To what extent the capitalist reckons the existence of such a skilled class among the factors of production that belong to him by right, and to what extent he actually regards it as the reality of his variable capital, is seen so soon as a crisis threatens him with its loss. In consequence of the civil war in the United States and of the accompanying cotton famine, the majority of the cotton operatives in

Lancashire were, as is well known, thrown out of work. Both from the working-class itself, and from other ranks of society, there arose a cry for State aid, or for voluntary national subscriptions, in order to enable the 'superfluous' hands to emigrate to the colonies or to the United States. Thereupon, *The Times* published on the 24th March, 1863, a letter from Edmund Potter, a former president of the Manchester Chamber of Commerce. This letter was rightly called in the House of Commons, the manufacturers' manifesto.[14] We cull here a few characteristic passages, in which the proprietary rights of capital over labour power are unblushingly asserted.

'He' (the man out of work) 'may be told the supply of cotton-workers is too large . . . and . . . must . . . in fact be reduced by a third, perhaps, and that then there will be a healthy demand for the remaining two-thirds . . . Public opinion . . . urges emigration . . . The master cannot willingly see his labour supply being removed; he may think, and perhaps justly, that it is both wrong and unsound . . . But if the public funds are to be devoted to assist emigration, he bas a right to be heard, and perhaps to protest.' Mr Potter then shows how useful the cotton trade is, how the 'trade has undoubtedly drawn the surplus-population from Ireland and from the agricultural districts,' how immense is its extent, how in the year 1860 it yielded $5/13$ ths of the total English exports, how, after a few years, it will again expand by the extension of the market, particularly of the Indian market, and by calling forth a plentiful supply of cotton at 6d. per lb. He then continues: 'Some time . . . one, two, or three years, it may be, will produce the quantity . . . The question I would put then is this – Is the trade worth retaining? Is it worth while to keep the machinery (he means the living labour machines) in order, and is it not the greatest folly to think of parting with that? I think it is. I allow that the workers are not a property, not the property of Lancashire and the masters; but they are the strength of both; they are the mental and trained power which cannot be replaced for a generation; the mere machinery which they work might much of it be beneficially replaced, nay improved, in a twelvemonth.'[15] Encourage or allow (!) the working-power to emigrate, and what of the capitalist? . . . Take away the cream of the workers, and fixed capital will depreciate in a great degree, and the floating will not subject itself to a struggle with the short supply of inferior labour . . . We are told the workers wish it' (emigration). 'Very natural it is that they should do so . . . Reduce, compress the cotton trade by taking away its working power and reducing their wages expenditure, say one-fifth, or five millions, and what then would happen to the class above, the small shopkeepers; and what of the rents, the cottage rents . . . Trace out the effects upwards to the small farmer, the better householder, and . . . the landowner, and say if there could be any suggestion more suicidal to all classes of the country than by enfeebling a nation by exporting the best of its manufacturing population, and destroying the value of some of its most productive capital and enrichment . . . I advise a loan (of five or six millions sterling), . . . extending it may be over two or three years, administered by special commissioners added to the Boards of Guardians in the cotton districts, under special legislative regulations, enforcing some occupation or labour, as a means of keeping up at least the moral standard of the recipients of the loan . . . can anything be worse for landowners or masters than parting with the best of the workers, and demoralising and disappointing the rest by an extended depletive emigration, a depletion of capital and value in an entire province?'

Potter, the chosen mouthpiece of the manufacturers, distinguishes two sorts of 'machinery', each of which belongs to the capitalist, and of which one stands in his factory, the other at night-time and on Sundays is housed outside the factory, in cottages. The one is inanimate, the other living. The inanimate machinery not only wears out and depreciates from day to day, but a great part of it becomes so quickly superannuated, by constant technical progress, that it can be replaced with advantage by new machinery after a few months. The living machinery, on the contrary gets better the longer it lasts, and in proportion as the skill, handed from one generation to another, accumulates. *The Times* answered the cotton lord as follows:

Mr Edmund Potter is so impressed with the exceptional and supreme importance of the cotton masters that, in order to pre-serve this class and perpetuate their profession, he would keep half a million of the labouring class confined in a great moral workhouse against their will. 'Is the trade worth retaining?' asks Mr Potter. 'Certainly by all honest means it is,' we answer. 'Is it worth while keeping the machinery in order?' again asks Mr Potter. Here we hesitate. By the 'machinery' Mr Potter means the human machinery, for he goes on to protest that he does not mean to use them as an absolute property. We must confess that we do not think it 'worth while', or even possible, to keep the human machinery in order – that is, to shut it up and keep it oiled till it is wanted. Human machinery will rust under inaction, oil and rub it as you may. Moreover, the human machinery will, as we have just seen, get the steam up of its own accord, and burst or run amuck in our great towns. It might, as Mr Potter says, require some time to reproduce the workers, but, having machinists and capitalists at hand, we could always find thrifty, hard, industrious men

wherewith to improvise more master-manufacturers than we can
ever want. Mr Potter talks of the trade reviving 'in one, two, or
three years', and he asks us not 'to encourage or allow (!) the
working power to emigrate.'[16] He says that it is very natural the
workers should wish to emigrate; but he thinks that in spite of
their desire, the nation ought to keep this half million of workers
with their 700,000 dependents, shut up in the cotton districts; and
as a necessary consequence, he must of course think that the
nation ought to keep down their discontent by force, and sustain
them by alms – and upon the chance that the cotton masters may
some day want them . . . The time is come when the great public
opinion of these islands must operate to save this 'working power'
from those who would deal with it as they would deal with iron,
and coal, and cotton.

The Times's article was only a *jeu d'esprit*. The 'great public opinion'
was, in fact, of Mr Potter's opinion, that the factory operatives are part
of the movable fittings of a factory. Their emigration was prevented.
They were locked up in that 'moral workhouse', the cotton districts,
and they form, as before, 'the strength' of the cotton manufacturers of
Lancashire.

Capitalist production, therefore, of itself reproduces the separation
between labour power and the means of labour. It thereby reproduces
and perpetuates the condition for exploiting the labourer. It incessantly forces him to sell his labour power in order to live, and enables
the capitalist to purchase labour power in order that he may enrich
himself.[17] It is no longer a mere accident, that capitalist and labourer
confront each other in the market as buyer and seller. It is the process
itself that incessantly hurls back the labourer on to the market as a
vendor of his labour power, and that incessantly converts his own
product into a means by which another man can purchase him. In
reality, the labourer belongs to capital before he has sold himself to
capital. His economic bondage[18] is both brought about and concealed
by the periodic sale of himself, by his change of masters, and by the
oscillations in the market-price of labour power.[19]

Capitalist production, therefore, under its aspect of a continuous
connected process, of a process of reproduction, produces not only
commodities, not only surplus-value, but it also produces and reproduces the capitalist relation; on the one side the capitalist, on the other
the wage-labourer.[20]

Chapter 24
Conversion of Surplus-Value into Capital

Section 1. Capitalist Production on a Progressively Increasing Scale. Transition of the Laws of Property that Characterise Production of Commodities into Laws of Capitalist Appropriation.

Hitherto we have investigated how surplus-value emanates from capital; we have now to see how capital arises from surplus-value. Employing surplus-value as capital, reconverting it into capital, is called accumulation of capital.[1]

First let us consider this transaction from the standpoint of the individual capitalist. Suppose a spinner to have advanced a capital of £10,000, of which four-fifths (£8,000) are laid out in cotton, machinery, &c., and one-fifth (£2,000) in wages. Let him produce 240,000 lbs. of yarn annually, having a value of £2,000. The rate of surplus-value being 100%, the surplus-value lies in the surplus or net product of 40,000 lbs. of yarn, one-sixth of the gross product, with a value of £2,000 which will be realised by a sale. £2,000 is £2,000. We can neither see nor smell in this sum of money a trace of surplus-value. When we know that a given value is surplus-value, we know how its owner came by it; but that does not alter the nature either of value or of money.

In order to convert this additional sum of £2,000 into capital, the master-spinner will, all circumstances remaining as before, advance four-fifths of it (£1,600) in the purchase of cotton, &c., and one-fifth (£400) in the purchase of additional spinners, who will find in the market the necessaries of life whose value the master has advanced to them.

Then the new capital of £2,000 functions in the spinning-mill, and brings in, in its turn, a surplus-value of £400.

The capital-value was originally advanced in the money form. The surplus-value on the contrary is, originally, the value of a definite portion of the gross product. If this gross product be sold, converted into money, the capital-value regains its original form. From this moment the capital-value and the surplus-value are both of them sums of money, and their reconversion into capital takes place in precisely the same way. The one, as well as the other, is laid out by the capitalist in the purchase of commodities that place him in a position to begin afresh the fabrication of his goods, and this time, on an extended scale. But in order to be able to buy those commodities, he must find them ready in the market.

His own yams circulate, only because he brings his annual product to market, as all other capitalists likewise do with their commodities. But these commodities, before coming to market, were part of the general annual product, part of the total mass of objects of every kind, into which the sum of the individual capitals, i.e., the total capital of society, had been converted in the course of the year, and of which each capitalist had in hand only an aliquot part. The transactions in the market effectuate only the interchange of the individual components of this annual product, transfer them from one hand to another, but can neither augment the total annual production, nor alter the nature of the objects produced. Hence the use that can be made of the total annual product, depends entirely upon its own composition, but in no way upon circulation.

The annual production, must in the first place furnish all those objects (use-values) from which the material components of capital, used up in the course of the year, have to be replaced. Deducting these there remains the net or surplus-product, in which the surplus-value lies. And of what does this surplus-product consist? Only of things destined to satisfy the wants and desires of the capitalist class, things which, consequently, enter into the consumption-fund of the capitalists? Were that the case, the cup of surplus-value would be drained to the very dregs, and nothing but simple reproduction would ever take place.

To accumulate it is necessary to convert a portion of the surplus-product into capital. But we cannot, except by a miracle, convert into capital anything but such articles as can be employed in the labour-process (i.e., means of production), and such further articles as are suitable for the sustenance of the labourer (i.e., means of subsistence). Consequently, a part of the annual surplus-labour must have been applied to the production of additional means of production and subsistence, over and above the quantity of these things required to replace the capital advanced. In one word, surplus-value is convertible into capital solely because the surplus-product, whose value it is, already comprises the material elements of new capital.[2]

Now in order to allow of these elements actually functioning as capital, the capitalist class requires additional labour. If the exploitation of the labourers already employed do not increase, either extensively or intensively, then additional labour power must be found. For this the mechanism of capitalist production provides beforehand, by converting the working-class into a class dependent on wages, a class whose ordinary wages suffice, not only for its maintenance, but for its increase. It is only necessary for capital to incorporate this additional labour power, annually supplied by the working-class in the shape of labourers of all ages, with the surplus means of production comprised in the annual produce, and the conversion of surplus-value into capital is complete. From a concrete point of view, accumulation resolves itself into the reproduction of capital on a progressively increasing scale. The circle in which simple reproduction moves, alters its form, and, to use Sismondi's expression, changes into a spiral.'³

Let us now return to our illustration. It is the old story: Abraham begat Isaac, Isaac begat Jacob, and so on. The original capital of £10,000 brings in a surplus-value of £2,000, which is capitalised. The new capital of £2,000 brings in a surplus-value of £400, and this, too, is capitalised, converted into a second additional capital, which, in its turn, produces a further surplus-value of £80. And so the ball rolls on.

We here leave out of consideration the portion of the surplus-value consumed by the capitalist. Just as little does it concern us, for the moment, whether the additional capital is joined on to the original capital, or is separated from it to function independently; whether the same capitalist, who accumulated it, employs it, or whether he hands it over to another. This only we must not forget, that by the side of the newly-formed capital, the original capital continues to reproduce itself, and to produce surplus-value, and that this is also true of all accumulated capital, and the additional capital engendered by it.

The original capital was formed by the advance of £10,000. How did the owner become possessed of it? 'By his own labour and that of his forefathers,' answer unanimously the spokesmen of Political Economy.⁴ And, in fact, their supposition appears the only one consonant with the laws of the production of commodities.

But it is quite otherwise with regard to the additional capital of £2,000. How that originated we know perfectly well. There is not one single atom of its value that does not owe its existence to unpaid labour. The means of production, with which the additional labour power is incorporated, as well as the necessaries with which the labourers are sustained, are nothing but component parts of the surplus-product, of the tribute annually exacted from the working-class by the capitalist class. Though the latter with a portion of that tribute purchases the additional labour power even at its full price, so that equivalent is exchanged for equivalent, yet the transaction is for all that only the old dodge of every conqueror who buys commodities from the conquered with the money he has robbed them of.

If the additional capital employs the person who produced it, this producer must not only continue to augment the value of the original capital, but must buy back the fruits of his previous labour with more labour than they cost. When viewed as a transaction between the capitalist class and the working-class, it makes no difference that additional labourers are employed by means of the unpaid labour of the previously employed labourers. The capitalist may even convert the additional capital into a machine that throws the producers of that capital out of work, and that replaces them by a few children. In every case the working-class creates by the surplus-labour of one year the capital destined to employ additional labour in the following year.[5] And this is what is called: creating capital out of capital.

The accumulation of the first additional capital of £2,000 pre-supposes a value of £10,000 belonging to the capitalist by virtue of his 'primitive labour', and advanced by him. The second additional capital of £400 presupposes, on the contrary, only the previous accumulation of the £2,000, of which the £400 is the surplus-value capitalised. The ownership of past unpaid labour is thenceforth the sole condition for the appropriation of living unpaid labour on a constantly increasing scale. The more the capitalist has accumulated, the more is he able to accumulate.

In so far as the surplus-value, of which the additional capital, No. 1, consists, is the result of the purchase of labour power with part of the original capital, a purchase that conformed to the laws of the exchange of commodities, and that, from a legal standpoint, pre-supposes nothing beyond the free disposal, on the part of the labourer, of his own capacities, and on the part of the owner of money or commodities, of the values that belong to him; in so far as the additional capital, No. 2, &c., is the mere result of No. 1, and, therefore, a consequence of the above conditions; in so far as each single transaction invariably conforms to the laws of the exchange of commodities, the capitalist buying labour power, the labourer selling it, and we will assume at its real value; in so far as all this is true, it is evident that the laws of appropriation or of private property, laws that are based on the production and circulation of commodities, become by their own inner and inexorable dialectic changed into their very opposite.[6] The exchange of equivalents, the original operation with which we started, has now become turned round in such a way that there is only an apparent exchange. This is owing to the fact, first, that the capital which is exchanged for labour power is itself but a portion of the product of others' labour appropriated without an equivalent; and, secondly, that this capital must not only be replaced by its producer, but replaced together with an added surplus. The relation of exchange subsisting between capitalist and labourer becomes a mere semblance appertaining to the process of circulation, a mere form, foreign to the real nature of the transaction, and only mystifying it. The ever repeated purchase and sale of labour power is now the mere form; what really takes place is this – the capitalist again and again appropriates, without equivalent, a portion of the previously materialised labour of others, and exchanges it for a greater quantity of living labour. At first the rights of property seemed to us to be based on a man's own labour. At least, some such assumption was necessary since only commodity-owners with equal rights confronted each other, and the sole means by which a man could become possessed of the commodities of others, was by alienating his own commodities; and these could be replaced by labour alone. Now, however, property turns out to be the right, on the part of the capitalist, to appropriate the unpaid labour of others or its product, and to be the impossibility, on the part of the labourer, of appropriating his own product. The separation of property from labour has become the necessary consequence of a law that apparently originated in their identity.[7]

We have seen that even in the case of simple reproduction, all capital, whatever its original source, becomes converted into accumulated capital, capitalised surplus-value. But in the flood of production all the capital originally advanced becomes a vanishing quantity (*magnitudo evanescens*, in the mathematical sense), compared with the directly accumulated capital, i.e., with the surplus-value or surplus-product that is reconverted into capital, whether it functions in the hands of its accumulator, or in those of others. Hence, Political Economy describes capital in general as 'accumulated wealth' (converted surplus-value or revenue), 'that is employed over again in the production of surplus-value,'[8] and the capitalist as 'the owner of surplus-value'.[9] It is merely another way of expressing the same thing to say that all existing capital is accumulated or capitalised interest, for interest is a mere fragment of surplus-value.[10]

Section 2. Erroneous Conception, by Political Economy, of Reproduction on a Progressively Increasing Scale.

Before we further investigate accumulation or the reconversion of surplus-value into capital, we must brush on one side an ambiguity introduced by the classical economists.

Just as little as the commodities that the capitalist buys with a part of the surplus-value for his own consumption, serve the purpose of production and of creation of value, so little is the labour that he buys for the satisfaction of his natural and social requirements, productive labour. Instead of converting surplus-value into capital, he, on the contrary, by the purchase of those commodities and that labour, consumes or expends it as revenue. In the face of the habitual mode of life of the old feudal nobility, which, as Hegel rightly says, 'consists in consuming what is in hand', and more especially displays itself in the luxury of personal retainers, it was extremely important for bourgeois economy to promulgate the doctrine that accumulation of capital is the first duty of every citizen, and to preach without ceasing, that a man cannot accumulate, if he eats up all his revenue, instead of spending a good part of it in the acquisition of additional productive labourers, who bring in more than they cost. On the other hand the economists had to contend against the popular prejudice, that confuses capitalist production with hoarding,[11] and fancies that accumulated wealth is either wealth that is rescued from being destroyed in its existing form, i.e., from being consumed, or wealth that is withdrawn from circulation. Exclusion of money from circulation would also exclude absolutely its self-expansion as capital, while accumulation of a hoard in the shape of commodities would be sheer tomfoolery.[12] The accumulation of commodities in great masses is the result either of over-production or of a stoppage of circulation.[13] It is true that the popular mind is impressed by the sight, on the one hand, of the mass of goods that are stored up for gradual consumption by the rich,[14] and on the other hand, by the formation of reserve stocks; the latter, a phenomenon that is common to all modes of production, and on which we shall dwell for a moment, when we come to analyse circulation. Classical economy is therefore quite right, when it maintains that the consumption of surplus-products by productive, instead of by unproductive labourers, is a characteristic feature of the process of accumulation. But at this point the mistakes also begin. Adam Smith has made it the fashion, to represent accumulation as nothing more than consumption of surplus-products by productive labourers, which amounts to saying, that the capitalising of surplus-value consists in merely turning surplus-value into labour power. Let us see what Ricardo, e.g., says: 'It must be understood that all the productions of a country are consumed; but it makes the greatest difference imaginable whether they are consumed by those who reproduce, or by those who do not reproduce another value. When we say that revenue is saved, and added to capital, what we mean is, that the portion of revenue, so said to be added to capital, is consumed by productive instead of unproductive labourers. There can be no greater error than in supposing that capital is increased by non-consumption.'[15] There can be no greater error than that which Ricardo and all subsequent economists repeat after A. Smith, viz., that 'the part of revenue, of which it is said, it has been added to capital, is consumed by productive labourers.' According to this, all surplus-value that is changed into capital becomes variable capital. So far from this being the case, the surplus-value, like the original capital, divides itself into constant capital and variable capital, into means of production and labour power. Labour power is the form under which variable capital exists during the process of production. In this process the labour power is itself consumed by the capitalist while the means of production are consumed by the labour power in the exercise of its function, labour. At the same time, the money paid for the purchase of the labour power, is converted into necessaries, that are consumed, not by 'productive labour', but by the 'productive labourer'. Adam Smith, by a fundamentally perverted analysis, arrives at the absurd conclusion, that even though each individual capital is divided into a constant and a variable part, the capital of society resolves itself only into variable capital, i.e, is laid out exclusively in payment of wages. For instance, suppose a cloth manufacturer converts £2,000 into capital. One portion he lays out in buying weavers, the other in woollen yam, machinery, &c. But the people, from whom he buys the yarn and the machinery, pay for labour with a part of the purchase money, and so on until the whole £2,000 are spent in the payment of wages, i.e, until the entire product represented by the £2,000 has been consumed by productive labourers. It is evident that the whole gist of this argument lies in the words 'and so on', which send us from pillar to post. In truth, Adam Smith breaks his investigation off, just where its difficulties begin.[16]

The annual process of reproduction is easily understood, so long as we keep in view merely the sum total of the year's production. But every single component of this product must be brought into the market as a commodity, and there the difficulty begins. The movements of the individual capitals, and of the personal revenues, cross and intermingle and are lost in the general change of places, in the circulation of the wealth of society; this dazes the sight, and propounds very complicated problems for solution. In the third part of Book 2 I shall give the analysis of the real bearings of the facts. It is one of the great merits of the Physiocrats, that in their *Tableau économique* they were the first to attempt to depict the annual production in the shape in which it is presented to us after passing through the process of circulation.[17]

For the rest, it is a matter of course, that Political Economy, acting in the interests of the capitalist class, has not failed to exploit the doctrine of Adam. Smith, viz., that the whole of that part of the surplus-product which is converted into capital, is consumed by the working-class.

Section 3. Separation of Surplus-Value into Capital and Revenue. The Abstinence Theory.

In the last preceding chapter, we treated surplus-value (or the surplus-product) solely as a fund for supplying the individual consumption of the capitalist. In this chapter we have, so far, treated it solely as a fund for accumulation. It is, however, neither the one nor the other, but is both together. One portion is consumed by the capitalist as revenue,[18] the other is employed as capital, is accumulated.

Given the mass of surplus-value, then, the larger the one of these parts, the smaller is the other. *Ceteris paribus*, the ratio of these parts determines the magnitude of the accumulation. But it is by the owner of the surplus-value, by the capitalist alone, that the division is made. It is his deliberate act. That part of the tribute exacted by him which he accumulates, is said to be saved by him, because he does not eat it, i.e, because he performs the function of a capitalist, and enriches himself.

Except as personified capital, the capitalist has no historical value, and no right to that historical existence, which, to use an expression of the witty Lichnowsky, 'hasn't got no date.' And so far only is the necessity for his own transitory existence implied in the transitory necessity for the capitalist mode of production. But, so far as he is personified capital, it is not values in use and the enjoyment of them, but exchange-value and its augmentation, that spur him into action. Fanatically bent on making value expand itself, he ruthlessly forces the human race to produce for production's sake; he thus forces the development of the productive powers of society, and creates those material conditions, which alone can form the real basis of a higher form of society, a society in which the full and free development of every individual forms the ruling principle. Only as personified capital is the capitalist respectable. As such, he shares with the miser the passion for wealth as wealth. But that which in the miser is a mere idiosyncrasy, is, in the capitalist, the effect of the social mechanism, of which he is but one of the wheels. Moreover, the development of capitalist production makes it constantly necessary to keep increasing the amount of the capital laid out in a given industrial undertaking, and competition makes the immanent laws of capitalist production to be felt by each individual capitalist, as external coercive laws. It compels him to keep constantly extending his capital, in order to preserve it, but extend it he cannot, except by means of progressive accumulation.

So far, therefore, as his actions are a mere function of capital – endowed as capital is, in his person, with consciousness and a will – his own private consumption is a robbery perpetrated on accumulation, just as in book-keeping by double entry, the private expenditure of the capitalist is placed on the debtor side of his account against his capital. To accumulate, is to conquer the world of social wealth, to increase the mass of human beings exploited by him, and thus to extend both the direct and the indirect sway of the capitalist.[19]

But original sin is at work everywhere. As capitalist production, accumulation, and wealth, become developed, the capitalist ceases to be the mere incarnation of capital. He has a fellow-feeling for his own Adam, and his education gradually enables him to smile at the rage for asceticism, as a mere prejudice of the old-fashioned miser. While the capitalist of the classical type brands individual consumption as a sin against his function, and as 'abstinence' from accumulating, the modernised capitalist is capable of looking upon accumulation as 'abstinence' from pleasure.

> Two souls, alas, do dwell with in his breast;
> The one is ever parting from the other.[20]

At the historical dawn of capitalist production, – and every capitalist upstart has personally to go through this historical stage – avarice, and desire to get rich, are the ruling passions. But the progress of capitalist production not only creates a world of delights; it lays open, in speculation and the credit system, a thousand sources of sudden enrichment. When a certain stage of development has been reached, a conventional degree of prodigality, which is also an exhibition of wealth, and consequently a source of credit, becomes a business necessity to the 'unfortunate' capitalist. Luxury enters into capital's expenses of representation. Moreover, the capitalist gets rich, not like the miser, in proportion to his personal labour and restricted consumption, but at the same rate as he squeezes out the labour power of others, and enforces on the labourer abstinence from all life's enjoyments. Although, therefore, the prodigality of the capitalist never possesses the *bonâ-fide* character of the open-handed feudal lord's prodigality, but, on the contrary, has always lurking behind it the most sordid avarice and the most anxious calculation, yet his expenditure grows with his accumulation, without the one necessarily restricting the other. But along with this growth, there is at the same time developed in his breast, a Faustian conflict between the passion for accumulation, and the desire for enjoyment.

Dr Aikin says in a work published in 1795: 'The trade of Manchester may be divided into four periods. First, when manufacturers were obliged to work hard for their livelihood.' They enriched themselves chiefly by robbing the parents, whose children were bound as apprentices to them; the parents paid a high premium, while the apprentices were starved. On the other hand, the average profits were low, and to accumulate, extreme parsimony was requisite. They lived like misers and were far from consuming even the interest on their capital. 'The second period, when they had begun to acquire little fortunes, but worked as hard as before,' – for direct exploitation of labour costs labour, as every slave-driver knows – 'and lived in as plain a manner as before . . . The third, when luxury began, and the trade was pushed by sending out riders for orders into every market town in the Kingdom . . . It is probable that few or no capitals of £3,000 to £4,000 acquired by trade existed here before 1690. However, about that time, or a little later, the traders had got money beforehand, and began to build modem brick houses, instead of those of wood and plaster.' Even in the early part of the 18th century, a Manchester manufacturer, who placed a pint of foreign wine before his guests, exposed himself to the remarks and headshakings of all his neighbours. Before the rise of machinery, a manufacturer's evening expenditure at the public house where they all met, never exceeded sixpence for a glass of punch, and a penny for a screw of tobacco. It was not till 1758, and this marks an epoch, that a person actually engaged in business was seen with an equipage of his own. 'The fourth period,' the last 30 years of the 18th century, 'is that in which expense and luxury have made great progress, and was supported by a trade extended by means of riders and factors through every part of Europe.'[21] What would the good Dr Aikin say if he could rise from his grave and see the Manchester of today?

Accumulate, accumulate! That is Moses and the prophets! 'Industry furnishes the material which saving accumulates.'[22] Therefore, save, save, i.e, reconvert the greatest possible portion of surplus-value, or surplus-product into capital! Accumulation for accumulation's sake, production for production's sake: by this formula classical economy expressed the historical mission of the bourgeoisie, and did not for a single instant deceive itself over the birth-throes of wealth.'[23] But what avails lamentation in the face of historical necessity? If to classical economy, the proletarian is but a machine for the production of surplus-value; on the other hand, the capitalist is in its eyes only a machine for the conversion of this surplus-value into additional capital. Political Economy takes the historical function of the capitalist in bitter earnest. In order to charm out of his bosom the awful conflict between the desire for enjoyment and the chase after riches, Malthus, about the year 1820, advocated a division of labour, which assigns to the capitalist actually engaged in production, the business of accumulating, and to the other sharers in surplus-value, to the landlords, the place-men, the beneficed clergy, &c., the business of spending. It is of the highest importance, he says, 'to keep separate the passion for expenditure and the passion for accumulation.'[24] The capitalists having long been good livers and men of the world, uttered loud cries. What, exclaimed one of their spokesmen, a disciple of Ricardo, Mr Malthus preaches high rents, heavy taxes, &c., so that the pressure of the spur may constantly be kept on the industrious by unproductive consumers! By all means, production, production on a constantly increasing scale, runs the shibboleth; but 'production will, by such a process, be far more curbed in than spurred on. Nor is it quite fair thus to maintain in idleness a number of persons, only to pinch others, who are likely, from their characters, if you can force them to work, to work with success.'[25] Unfair as he finds it to spur on the industrial capitalist, by depriving his bread of its butter, yet he thinks it necessary to reduce the labourer's wages to a minimum 'to keep him industrious'. Nor does he for a moment conceal the fact, that the appropriation of unpaid labour is the secret of surplus-value. 'Increased demand on the part of the labourers means nothing more than their willingness to take less of their own product for themselves, and leave a greater part of it to their employers; and if it be said, that this begets glut, by lessening consumption' (on the part of the labourers), 'I can only reply that glut is synonymous with large profits.'[26]

The learned disputation, how the booty pumped out of the labourer may be divided, with most advantage to accumulation, between the industrial capitalist and the rich idler, was hushed in face of the revolution of July. Shortly afterwards, the town proletariat at Lyons sounded the tocsin of revolution, and the country proletariat in England began to set fire to farm-yards and corn-stacks. On this side of the Channel Owenism began to spread; on the other side, St Simonism and Fourierism. The hour of vulgar economy had struck. Exactly a year before Nassau W. Senior discovered at Manchester, that the profit (including interest) of capital is the product of the last hour of the twelve, he had announced to the world another discovery. 'I substitute,' he proudly says, 'for the word capital, considered as an instrument of production, the word "abstinence".' An unparalleled sample this, of the discoveries of vulgar economy! It substitutes for an economic category, a sycophantic phrase – voilà tout. 'When the savage,' says Senior, 'makes bows, he exercises an industry, but he does not practise abstinence.'[27] This explains how and why, in the earlier states of society, the implements of labour were fabricated without abstinence on the part of the capitalist. 'The more society progresses, the more abstinence is demanded,'[28] namely, from those who ply the industry of appropriating the fruits of others' industry.

All the conditions for carrying on the labour-process are suddenly converted into so many acts of abstinence on the part of the capitalist. If the corn is not all eaten, but part of it also sown – abstinence of the capitalist. If the wine gets time to mature – abstinence of the capitalist.[29] The capitalist robs his own self, whenever he 'lends (!) the instruments of production to the labourer,' that is, whenever by incorporating labour power with them, he uses them to extract surplus-value out of that labour-power, instead of eating them up, steam-engines, cotton, railways, manure, horses, and all; or as the vulgar economist childishly puts it, instead of dissipating 'their value' in luxuries and other articles of consumption.[30] How the capitalists as a class are to perform that feat, is a secret that vulgar economy has hitherto obstinately refused to divulge. Enough, that the world still jogs on, solely through the self-chastisement of this modern penitent of Vishnu, the capitalist. Not only accumulation, but the simple 'conservation of a capital requires a constant effort to resist the temptation of consuming it.'[31] The simple dictates of humanity therefore plainly enjoin the release of the capitalist from this martyrdom and temptation, in the same way that the Georgian slave-owner was lately delivered, by the abolition of slavery, from the painful dilemma, whether to squander the surplus-product, lashed out of his niggers, entirely in champagne, or whether to reconvert a part of it into more niggers and more land.

In economic forms of society of the most different kinds, there occurs, not only simple reproduction, but, in varying degrees, reproduction on a progressively increasing scale. By degrees more is produced and more consumed, and consequently more products have to be converted into means of production. This process, however, does not present itself as accumulation of capital, nor as the function of a capitalist, so long as the labourer's means of production, and with them, his product and means of subsistence, do not confront him in the shape of capital.[32] Richard Jones, who died a few years ago, and was the successor of Malthus in the chair of Political Economy at Haileybury College, discusses this point well in the light of two important facts. Since the great mass of the Hindu population are peasants cultivating their land themselves, their products, their instruments of labour and means of subsistence never take 'the shape of a fund saved from revenue, which fund has, therefore, gone through a previous process of accumulation.'[33] On the other hand, the non-agricultural labourers in those provinces where the English rule has least disturbed the old system, are directly employed by the magnates, to whom a portion of the agricultural surplus-product is rendered in the shape of tribute or rent. One portion of this product is consumed

by the magnates in kind, another is converted, for their use, by the
labourers, into articles of luxury and such like things, while the rest
forms the wages of the labourers, who own their implements of
labour. Here, production and reproduction on a progressively increasing scale, go on their way without any intervention from that queer
saint, that knight of the woeful countenance, the capitalist 'abstainer'.

Section 4. Circumstances that, Independently of the Proportional Division of Surplus-Value into Capital and Revenue, Determine the Amount of Accumulation. Degree of Exploitation of Labour power. Productivity of Labour. Growing Difference in Amount Between Capital Employed and Capital Consumed. Magnitude of Capital Advanced.

The proportion in which surplus-value breaks up into capital and
revenue being given, the magnitude of the capital accumulated clearly
depends on the absolute magnitude of the surplus-value. Suppose that
80 per cent. were capitalised and 20 per cent. eaten up, the accumulated capital will be £2,400 or £200, according as the total surplus-
value has amounted to £3,000 or £1,500. Hence all the circumstances
that determine the mass of surplus-value, operate to determine the
magnitude of the accumulation. We sum them up once again, but only
in so far as they afford new points of view in regard to accumulation.

It will be remembered that the rate of surplus-value depends, in the
first place, on the degree of exploitation of labour power. Political
Economy values this fact so highly, that it occasionally identifies the
acceleration of accumulation due to increased productiveness of
labour, with its acceleration due to increased exploitation of the
labourer.[34] In the chapters on the production of surplus-value it was
constantly pre-supposed that wages are at least equal to the value of
labour power. Forcible reduction of wages below this value plays,
however, in practice too important a part, for us not to pause upon
it for a moment. It, in fact, transforms, within certain limits, the
labourer's necessary consumption-fund into a fund for the accumulation of capital.

'Wages,' says John Stuart Mill, 'have no productive power; they are
the price of a productive power. Wages do not contribute, along with
labour, to the production of commodities, no more than the price of
tools contributes along with the tools themselves. If labour could be
had without purchase, wages might be dispensed with.'[35] But if the
labourers could live on air they could not be bought at any price. The
zero of their cost is therefore a limit in a mathematical sense, always
beyond reach, although we can always approximate more and more

nearly to it. The constant tendency of capital is to force the cost of labour back towards this zero. A writer of the 18th century, often quoted already, the author of the *Essay on Trade and Commerce*, only betrays the innermost secret soul of English capitalism, when he declares the historic mission of England to be the forcing down of English wages to the level of the French and the Dutch.[36] With other things he says naively: 'But if our poor' (technical term for labourers) 'will live luxuriously . . . then labour must, of course, be dear . . . when it is considered what luxuries the manufacturing populace consume, such as brandy, gin, tea, sugar, foreign fruit, strong beer, printed linens, snuff, tobacco, &c.'[37] He quotes the work of a Northamptonshire manufacturer, who, with eyes squinting heavenward moans: 'Labour is one-third cheaper in France than in England; for their poor work hard, and fare hard, as to their food and clothing. Their chief diet is bread, fruit, herbs, roots, and dried fish; for they very seldom eat flesh; and when wheat is dear, they eat very little bread.'[38] 'To which may be added,' our essayist goes on, 'that their drink is either water or other small liquors, so that they spend very little money . . . These things are very difficult to be brought about; but they are not impracticable, since they have been effected both in France and in Holland.'[39] Twenty years later, an American humbug, the baronised Yankee, Benjamin Thompson (alias Count Rumford) followed the same line of philanthropy to the great satisfaction of God and man. His *Essays* are a cookery book with receipts of all kinds for replacing by some *succedaneum* the ordinary dear food of the labourer. The following is a particularly successful receipt of this wonderful philosopher: '5 lbs. of barleymeal, 7 1/2 d.; 5 lbs. of Indian corn, 6 1/4 d.; 3d. worth of red herring, 1d. salt, 1d. vinegar, 2d. pepper and sweet herbs, in all 20 3/4.; make a soup for 64 men, and at the medium price of barley and of Indian corn . . . this soup may be provided at 1/4 d., the portion of 20 ounces.'[40] With the advance of capitalistic production, the adulteration of food rendered Thompson's ideal superfluous.[41] At the end of the 18th and during the first ten years of the 19th century, the English farmers and landlords enforced the absolute minimum of wage, by paying the agricultural labourers less than the minimum in the form of wages, and the remainder in the shape of parochial relief. An example of the waggish way in which the English Dogberries acted in their 'legal' fixing of a wages tariff: 'The squires of Norfolk had dined, says Mr Burke, when they fixed the rate of wages; the squires of Berks evidently thought the labourers ought not to do so, when they fixed the rate of wages at Speenhamland, 1795 . . . There they decide that "income (weekly) should be 3s. for a man," when the gallon or half-peck loaf of 8 lbs. 11 oz. is at 1s., and increase regularly till bread is 1s. 5d.; when it is above that sum decrease regularly till it be at 2s., and then his food should be 1/5th less.'⁴² Before the Committee of Inquiry of the House of Lords, 1814, a certain A. Bennett, a large farmer, magistrate, poor-law guardian, and wage-regulator, was asked: 'Has any proportion of the value of daily labour been made up to the labourers out of the poors' rate?' Answer: 'Yes, it has; the weekly income of every family is made up to the gallon loaf (8 lbs. 11 oz.), and 3d. per head! . . . The gallon loaf per week is what we suppose sufficient for the maintenance of every person in the family for the week; and the 3d. is for clothes, and if the parish think proper to find clothes, the 3d. is deducted. This practice goes through all the western part of Wiltshire, and, I believe, through-out the country.'⁴³ 'For years,' exclaims a bourgeois author of that time, 'they (the farmers) have degraded a respectable class of their countrymen, by forcing them to have recourse to the workhouse . . . the farmer, while increasing his own gains, has prevented any accum-ulation on the part of his labouring dependants.'⁴⁴ The part played in our days by the direct robbery from the labourer's necessary consumption-fund in the formation of surplus-value, and, therefore, of the accumulation-fund of capital, the so-called domestic industry has served to show. (Ch.15., Sect.8, c.) Further facts on this subject will be given later.

Although in all branches of industry that part of the constant capital consisting of instruments of labour must be sufficient for a certain number of labourers (determined by the magnitude of the under-taking), it by no means always necessarily increases in the same proportion as the quantity of labour employed. In a factory, suppose that 100 labourers working 8 hours a day yield 800 working-hours. If the capitalist wishes to raise this sum by one half, he can employ 50 more workers; but then he must also advance more capital, not merely for wages, but for instruments of labour. But he might also let the 100 labourers work 12 hours instead of 8, and then the instruments of labour already to hand would be enough. These would then simply be more rapidly consumed. Thus additional labour, begotten of the greater tension of labour power, can augment surplus-product and surplus-value (i.e., the subject-matter of accumulation), without corresponding augmentation in the constant part of capital.

In the extractive industries, mines, &c., the raw materials form no part of the capital advanced. The subject of labour is in this case not a product of previous labour, but is furnished by Nature gratis, as in the case of metals, minerals, coal, stone, &c. In these cases the constant capital consists almost exclusively of instruments of labour, which can very well absorb an increased quantity of labour (day and night shifts of labourers, e.g.). All other things being equal, the mass and value of the product will rise in direct proportion to the labour expended. As on the first day of production,. the original produce-formers, now turned into the creators of the material elements of capital – man and Nature – still work together. Thanks to the elasticity of labour power, the domain of accumulation has extended without any previous enlargement of constant capital.

In agriculture the land under cultivation cannot be increased without the advance of more seed and manure. But this advance once made, the purely mechanical working of the soil itself produces a marvellous effect on the amount of the product. A greater quantity of labour, done by the same number of labourers as before, thus increases the fertility, without requiring any new advance in the instruments of labour. It is once again the direct action of man on Nature which becomes an immediate source of greater accumulation, without the intervention of any new capital.

Finally, in what is called manufacturing industry, every additional expenditure of labour presupposes a corresponding additional expenditure of raw materials, but not necessarily of instruments of labour. And as extractive industry and agriculture supply manufacturing industry with its raw materials and those of its instruments of labour, the additional product the former have created without additional advance of capital, tells also in favour of the latter.

General result: by incorporating with itself the two primary creators of wealth, labour power and the land, capital acquires a power of expansion that permits it to augment the elements of its accumulation beyond the limits apparently fixed by its own magnitude, or by the value and the mass of the means of production, already produced, in which it has its being.

Another important factor in the accumulation of capital is the degree of productivity of social labour.

With the productive power of labour increases the mass of the products, in which a certain value, and, therefore, a surplus-value of a given magnitude, is embodied. The rate of surplus-value remaining the same or even falling, so long as it only falls more slowly, than the productive power of labour rises, the mass of the surplus-product increases. The division of this product into revenue and additional capital remaining the same, the consumption of the capitalist may, therefore, increase without any decrease in the fund of accumulation. The relative magnitude of the accumulation-fund may even increase at the expense of the consumption-fund, whilst the cheapening of commodities places at the disposal of the capitalist as many means of enjoyment as formerly, or even more than formerly. But hand-in-hand with the increasing productivity of labour, goes, as we have seen, the cheapening of the labourer, therefore a higher rate of surplus-value, even when the real wages are rising. The latter never rise proportionally to the productive power of labour. The same value in variable capital therefore sets in movement more labour power, and, therefore, more labour. The same value in constant capital is embodied in more means of production, i.e., in more instruments of labour, materials of labour and auxiliary materials; it therefore also supplies more elements for the production both of use-value and of value, and with these more absorbers of labour. The value of the additional capital, therefore, remaining the same or even diminishing, accelerated accumulation still takes place. Not only does the scale of reproduction materially extend, but the production of surplus-value increases more rapidly than the value of the additional capital.

The development of the productive power of labour reacts also on the original capital already engaged in the process of production. A part of the functioning constant capital consists of instruments of labour, such as machinery, &c., which are not consumed, and therefore not reproduced, or replaced by new ones of the same kind, until after long periods of time. But every year a part of these instruments of labour perishes or reaches the limit of its productive function. It reaches, therefore, in that year, the time for its periodical reproduction, for its replacement by new ones of the same kind. If the productiveness of labour has, during the using up of these instruments of labour, increased (and it develops continually with the uninterrupted advance of science and technology), more efficient and (considering their increased efficiency) cheaper machines, tools, apparatus, &c., replace the old. The old capital is reproduced in a more productive form, apart from the constant detail improvements in the instruments of labour already in use. The other part of the constant capital, raw material and auxiliary substances, is constantly reproduced in less than a year; those produced by agriculture, for the most part annually. Every introduction of improved methods, therefore, works almost simultaneously on the new capital and on that already in action. Every advance in Chemistry not only multiplies the number of useful materials and the useful applications of those already known, thus extending with the growth of capital its sphere of investment. It teaches at the same time how to throw the excrements of the processes of production and consumption back again into the circle of the process of reproduction, and thus, without any previous outlay of capital, creates new matter for capital. Like the increased exploitation of natural wealth by the mere increase in the tension of labour power, science and technology give capital a power of expansion independent of the given magnitude of the capital actually functioning. They react at the same time on that part of the original capital which has entered upon its stage of renewal. This, in passing into its new shape, incorporates gratis the social advance made while its old shape was being used up. Of course, this development of productive power is accompanied by a partial depreciation of functioning capital. So far as this depreciation makes itself acutely felt in competition, the burden falls on the labourer, in the increased exploitation of whom the capitalist looks for his indemnification.

Labour transmits to its product the value of the means of production consumed by it. On the other hand, the value and mass of the means of production set in motion by a given quantity of labour increase as the labour becomes more productive. Though the same quantity of labour adds always to its products only the same sum of new value, still the old capital-value, transmitted by the labour to the products, increases with the growing productivity of labour.

An English and a Chinese spinner, e.g., may work the same number of hours with the same intensity; then they will both in a week create equal values. But in spite of this equality, an immense difference will obtain between the value of the week's product of the Englishman, who works with a mighty automaton, and that of the Chinaman, who has but a spinning-wheel. In the same time as the Chinaman spins one pound of cotton, the Englishman spins several hundreds of pounds. A sum, many hundred times as great, of old values swells the value of his product, in which those re-appear in a new, useful form, and can thus function anew as capital. 'In 1782,' as Frederick Engels teaches us, 'all the wool crop in England of the three preceding years, lay untouched for want of labourers, and so it must have lain, if newly invented machinery had not come to its aid and spun it.'[45] Labour embodied in the form of machinery of course did not directly force into life a single man, but it made it possible for a smaller number of labourers, with the addition of relatively less living labour, not only to consume the wool productively, and put into it new value, but to preserve in the form of yarn, &c., its old value. At the same time, it caused and stimulated increased reproduction of wool. It is the natural property of living labour, to transmit old value, whilst it creates new. Hence, with the increase in efficacy, extent and value of its means of production, consequently with the accumulation that accompanies the development of its productive power, labour keeps up and eternises an always increasing capital-value in a form ever new.'[46] This natural power of labour takes the appearance of an intrinsic property of capital, in which it is incorporated, just as the productive forces of social labour take the appearance of inherent properties of capital, and as the constant appropriation of surplus-labour by the capitalists, takes that of a constant self-expansion of capital.

With the increase of capital, the difference between the capital employed and the capital consumed increases. In other words, there is increase in the value and the material mass of the instruments of labour, such as buildings, machinery, drain-pipes, working-cattle, apparatus of every kind that function for a longer or shorter time in processes of production constantly repeated, or that serve for the attainment of particular useful effects, whilst they themselves only gradually wear out, therefore only lose their value piecemeal, therefore transfer that value to the product only bit by bit. In the same proportion as these instruments of labour serve as product-formers without adding value to the product, i.e., in the same proportion as they are wholly employed but only partly consumed, they perform, as we saw earlier, the same gratuitous service as the natural forces, water, steam, air, electricity, etc. This gratuitous service of past labour, when seized and filled with a soul by living labour, increases with the advancing stages of accumulation.

Since past labour always disguises itself as capital, i.e, since the passive of the labour of A, B, C, etc., takes the form of the active of the non-labourer X, bourgeois and political economists are full of praises of the services of dead and gone labour, which, according to the Scotch genius MacCulloch, ought to receive a special remuneration in the shape of interest, profit, etc.[47] The powerful and ever-increasing assistance given by past labour to the living labour-process under the form of means of production is, therefore, attributed to that form of past labour in which it is alienated, as unpaid labour, from the worker himself, i.e, to its capitalistic form. The practical agents of capitalistic production and their pettifogging ideologists are as unable to think of the means of production as separate from the antagonistic social mask they wear today, as a slave-owner to think of the worker himself as distinct from his character as a slave.

With a given degree of exploitation of labour power, the mass of the surplus-value produced is determined by the number of workers simultaneously exploited; and this corresponds, although in varying proportions, with the magnitude of the capital. The more, therefore, capital increases by means of successive accumulations, the more does the sum of the value increase that is divided into consumption-fund and accumulation-fund. The capitalist can, therefore, live a more jolly life, and at the same time show more 'abstinence'. And, finally, all the springs of production act with greater elasticity, the more its scale extends with the mass of the capital advanced.

Section 5. The So-Called Labour-Fund.

It has been shown in the course of this inquiry that capital is not a fixed magnitude, but is a part of social wealth, elastic and constantly fluctuating with the division of fresh surplus-value into revenue and additional capital. It has been seen further that, even with a given magnitude of functioning capital, the labour power, the science, and the land (by which are to be understood, economically, all conditions of labour furnished by Nature independently of man), embodied in it, form elastic powers of capital, allowing it, within certain limits, a field of action independent of its own magnitude. In this inquiry we have neglected all effects of the process of circulation, effects which may produce very different degrees of efficiency in the same mass of capital. And as we pre-supposed the limits set by capitalist production, that is to say, pre-supposed the process of social production in a form developed by purely spontaneous growth, we neglected any more rational combination, directly and systematically practicable with the means of production, and the mass of labour power at present disposable. Classical economy always loved to conceive social capital as a fixed magnitude of a fixed degree of efficiency. But this prejudice was first established as a dogma by the arch-Philistine, Jeremy Bentham, that insipid, pedantic, leather-tongued oracle of the ordinary bourgeois intelligence of the 19th century.[48] Bentham is among philosophers what Martin Tupper is among poets. Both could only have been manufactured in England.[49] In the light of his dogma the commonest phenomena of the process of production, as, e.g., its sudden expansions and contractions, nay, even accumulation itself, become perfectly inconceivable.[50] The dogma was used by Bentham himself, as well as by Malthus, James Mill, MacCulloch, etc., for an apologetic purpose, and especially in order to represent one part of capital, namely, variable capital, or that part convertible into labour power, as a fixed magnitude. The material of variable capital, i.e, the mass of the means of subsistence it represents for the labourer, or the so-called labour-fund, was fabled as a separate part of social wealth, fixed by natural laws and unchangeable. To set in motion the part of social wealth which is to function as constant capital, or, to express it in a material form, as means of production, a definite mass of living labour is required. This mass is given technologically. But neither is the number of labourers required to render fluid this mass of labour power given (it changes with the degree of exploitation of the individual labour power), nor is the price of this labour power given, but only its minimum limit, which is moreover very variable. The facts that lie at the bottom of this dogma are these: on the one hand, the labourer has no right to interfere in the division of social wealth into means of enjoyment for the non-labourer and means of production.[51] On the other hand, only in favourable and exceptional cases, has he the power to enlarge the so-called labour-fund at the expense of the 'revenue' of the wealthy.

What silly tautology results from the attempt to represent the capitalistic limits of the labour-fund as its natural and social limits may be seen, e.g., in Professor Fawcett.[52] 'The circulating capital of a country,' he says, 'is its wage-fund. Hence, if we desire to calculate the average money wages received by each labourer, we have simply to divide the amount of this capital by the number of the labouring population.'[53] That is to say, we first add together the individual wages actually paid, and then we affirm that the sum thus obtained, forms the total value of the 'labour-fund' determined and vouchsafed to us by God and Nature. Lastly, we divide the sum thus obtained by the number of labourers to find out again how much may come to each on the average. An uncommonly knowing dodge this. It did not prevent Mr Fawcett saying in the same breath: 'The aggregate wealth which is annually saved in England, is divided into two portions; one portion is employed as capital to maintain our industry, and the other portion is exported to foreign countries . . . Only a portion, and perhaps, not a large portion of the wealth which is annually saved in this country, is invested in our own industry.[54]

The greater part of the yearly accruing surplus-product, embezzled, because abstracted without return of an equivalent, from the English labourer, is thus used as capital, not in England, but in foreign countries. But with the additional capital thus exported, a part of the 'labour-fund' invented by God and Bentham is also exported.[55]

Chapter 25
The General Law of Capitalist Accumulation

Section 1. The Increased Demand for Labour Power that Accompanies Accumulation, the Composition of Capital Remaining the Same.

In this chapter we consider the influence of the growth of capital on the lot of the labouring class. The most important factor in this inquiry is the composition of capital and the changes it undergoes in the course of the process of accumulation.

The composition of capital is to be understood in a two-fold sense. On the side of value, it is determined by the proportion in which it is divided into constant capital or value of the means of production, and variable capital or value of labour power, the sum total of wages. On the side of material, as it functions in the process of production, all capital is divided into means of production and living labour power. This latter composition is determined by the relation between the mass of the means of production employed, on the one hand, and the mass of labour necessary for their employment on the other. I call the former the *value-composition*, the latter the *technical composition* of capital. Between the two there is a strict correlation. To express this, I call the value-composition of capital, in so far as it is determined by its tech-nical composition and mirrors the changes of the latter, the *organic com-position* of capital. Wherever I refer to the composition of capital, without further qualification, its organic composition is always understood.

The many individual capitals invested in a particular branch of production have, one with another, more or less different compositions. The average of their individual compositions gives us the composition of the total capital in this branch of production. Lastly, the average of these averages, in all branches of production, gives us the composition of the total social capital of a country, and with this alone are we, in the last resort, concerned in the following investigation.

Growth of capital involves growth of its variable constituent or of the part invested in labour power. A part of the surplus-value turned into additional capital must always be re-transformed into variable capital, or additional labour-fund. If we suppose that, all other circumstances remaining the same, the composition of capital also remains constant (i.e., that a definite mass of means of production constantly needs the same mass of labour power to set it in motion), then the demand for labour and the subsistence-fund of the labourers clearly increase in the same proportion as the capital, and the more rapidly, the more rapidly the capital increases. Since the capital produces yearly a surplus-value, of which one part is yearly added to the original capital; since this increment itself grows yearly along with the augmentation of the capital already functioning; since lastly, under special stimulus to enrichment, such as the opening of new markets, or of new spheres for the outlay of capital in consequence of newly developed social wants, &c., the scale of accumulation may be suddenly extended, merely by a change in the division of the surplus-value or surplus-product into capital and revenue, the requirements of accumulating capital may exceed the increase of labour power or of the number of labourers; the demand for labourers may exceed the supply, and, therefore, wages may rise. This must, indeed, ultimately be the case if the conditions supposed above continue. For since in each year more labourers are employed than in its predecessor, sooner or later a point must be reached, at which the requirements of accumulation begin to surpass the customary supply of labour, and, therefore, a rise of wages takes place. A lamentation on this score was heard in England during the whole of the fifteenth, and the first half of the eighteenth centuries. The more or less favourable circumstances in which the wage-working class supports and multiplies itself, in no way alter the fundamental character of capitalist production. As simple reproduction constantly reproduces the capital-relation itself, i.e., the relation of capitalists on the one hand, and wage-workers on the other, so reproduction on a progressive scale, i.e., accumulation, reproduces the capital-relation on a progressive scale, more capitalists or larger capitalists at this pole, more wage-workers at that. The reproduction of a mass of labour power, which must incessantly re-incorporate itself with capital for that capital's self-expansion; which cannot get free from capital, and whose enslavement to capital is only concealed by the variety of individual capitalists to whom it sells itself, this reproduction of labour power forms, in fact, an essential of the reproduction of capital itself. Accumulation of capital is, therefore, increase of the proletariat.[1]

Classical economy grasped this fact so thoroughly that Adam Smith, Ricardo, &c., as mentioned earlier, inaccurately identified accumulation with the consumption, by the productive labourers, of all the capitalised part of the surplus-product, or with its transformation into additional wage-labourers. As early as 1696 John Bellers says: 'For if one had a hundred thousand acres of land and as many pounds in money, and as many cattle, without a labourer, what would the rich man be, but a labourer? And as the labourers make men rich, so the more labourers there will be, the more rich men . . . the labour of the poor being the mines of the rich.'[2] So also Bernard de Mandeville at the beginning of the eighteenth century: 'It would be easier, where property is well secured, to live without money than without poor; for who would do the work? . . . As they [the poor] ought to be kept from starving, so they should receive nothing worth saving. If here and there one of the lowest class by uncommon industry, and pinching his belly, lifts himself above the condition he was brought up in, nobody ought to hinder him; nay, it is undeniably the wisest course for every person in the society, and for every private family to be frugal; but it is the interest of all rich nations, that the greatest part of the poor should almost never be idle, and yet continually spend what they get . . . Those that get their living by their daily labour . . . have nothing to stir them up to be serviceable but their wants which it is prudence to relieve, but folly to cure. The only thing then that can render the labouring man industrious, is a moderate quantity of money, for as too little will, according as his temper is, either dispirit or make him desperate, so too much will make him insolent and lazy . . . From what has been said, it is manifest, that, in a free nation, where slaves are not allowed of, the surest wealth consists in a multitude of laborious poor; for besides, that they are the never-failing nursery of fleets and armies, without them there could be no enjoyment, and no product of any country could be valuable. 'To make the society' [which of course consists of non-workers] 'happy and people easier under the meanest circumstances, it is requisite that great numbers of them should be ignorant as well as poor; knowledge both enlarges and multiplies our desires, and the fewer things a man wishes for, the more easily his necessities may be supplied.'[3] What Mandeville, an honest, clear-headed man, had not yet seen, is that the mechanism of the process of accumulation itself increases, along with the capital, the mass of 'labouring poor', i.e., the wage-labourers, who turn their labour power into an increasing power of self-expansion of the growing capital, and even by doing so must eternise their dependent relation on their own product, as personified in the capitalists. In reference to this relation of dependence, Sir F. M. Eden in his *The State of the Poor, an History of the Labouring Classes in England*, says, 'the natural produce of our soil is certainly not fully adequate to our subsistence; we can neither be clothed, lodged nor fed but in consequence of some previous labour. A portion at least of the society must be indefatigably employed . . . There are others who, though they "neither toil nor spin", can yet command the produce of industry, but who owe their exemption from labour solely to civilisation and order . . . They are peculiarly the creatures of civil institutions,[4] which have recognised that individuals may acquire property by various other means besides the exertion of labour . . . Persons of independent fortune . . . owe their superior advantages by no means to any superior abilities of their own, but almost entirely . . . to the industry of others. It is not the possession of land, or of money, but the command of labour which distinguishes the opulent from the labouring part of the community . . . This [scheme approved by Eden] would give the people of property sufficient (but by no means too much) influence and authority over those who . . . work for them; and it would place such labourers, not in an abject or servile condition, but in such a state of easy and liberal dependence as all who know human nature, and its history, will allow to be necessary for their own comfort.'[5] Sir F. M. Eden, it may be remarked in passing, is the only disciple of Adam Smith during the eighteenth century that produced any work of importance.[6]

Under the conditions of accumulation supposed thus far, which conditions are those most favourable to the labourers, their relation of dependence upon capital takes on a form endurable or, as Eden says: 'easy and liberal'. Instead of becoming more intensive with the growth of capital, this relation of dependence only becomes more extensive, i.e., the sphere of capital's exploitation and rule merely extends with its own dimensions and the number of its subjects. A larger part of their own surplus-product, always increasing and continually transformed into additional capital, comes back to them in the shape of means of payment, so that they can extend the circle of their enjoyments; can make some additions to their consumption-fund of clothes, furniture, &c., and can lay by small reserve-funds of money. But just as little as better clothing, food, and treatment, and a larger *peculium*, do away with the exploitation of the slave, so little do they set aside that of the wage-worker. A rise in the price of labour, as a consequence of accumulation of capital, only means, in fact, that the length and weight of the golden chain the wage-worker has already forged for himself, allow of a relaxation of the tension of it. In the controversies on this subject the chief fact has generally been overlooked, viz., the *differentia specifica* of capitalistic production. Labour power is sold today, not with a view of satisfying, by its service or by its product, the personal needs of the buyer. His aim is augmentation of his capital, production of commodities containing more labour than he pays for, containing therefore a portion of value that costs him nothing, and that is nevertheless realised when the commodities are sold. Production of surplus-value is the absolute law of this mode of production. Labour power is only saleable so far as it preserves the means of production in their capacity of capital, reproduces its own value as capital, and yields in unpaid labour a source of additional capital.[7] The conditions of its sale, whether more or less favourable to the labourer, include therefore the necessity of its constant re-selling, and the constantly extended reproduction of all wealth in the shape of capital. Wages, as we have seen, by their very nature, always imply the performance of a certain quantity of unpaid labour on the part of the labourer. Altogether, irrespective of the case of a rise of wages with a falling price of labour, &c., such an increase only means at best a quantitative diminution of the unpaid labour that the worker has to supply. This diminution can never reach the point at which it would threaten the system itself. Apart from violent conflicts as to the rate of wages (and Adam Smith has already shown that in such a conflict, taken on the whole, the master is always master), a rise in the price of labour resulting from accumulation of capital implies the following alternative:

Either the price of labour keeps on rising, because its rise does not interfere with the progress of accumulation. In this there is nothing wonderful, for, says Adam Smith, 'after these (profits) are diminished, stock may not only continue to increase, but to increase much faster than before . . . A great stock, though with small profits, generally increases faster than a small stock with great profits.' (l.c., ii, p.189.) In this case it is evident that a diminution in the unpaid labour in no way interferes with the extension of the domain of capital. – Or, on the other hand, accumulation slackens in consequence of the rise in the price of labour, because the stimulus of gain is blunted. The rate of accumulation lessens; but with its lessening, the primary cause of that lessening vanishes, i.e., the disproportion between capital and exploitable labour power. The mechanism of the process of capitalist production removes the very obstacles that it temporarily creates. The price of labour falls again to a level corresponding with the needs of the self-expansion of capital, whether the level be below, the same as, or above the one which was normal before the rise of wages took place. We see thus: In the first case, it is not the diminished rate either of the absolute, or of the proportional, increase in labour power, or labouring population, which causes capital to be in excess, but conversely the excess of capital that makes exploitable labour power insufficient. In the second case, it is not the increased rate either of the absolute, or of the proportional, increase in labour power, or labouring population, that makes capital insufficient; but, conversely, the relative diminution of capital that causes the exploitable labour power, or rather its price, to be in excess. It is these absolute movements of the accumulation of capital which are reflected as relative movements of the mass of exploitable labour power, and therefore seem produced by the latter's own independent movement. To put it mathematically: the rate of accumulation is the independent, not the dependent, variable; the rate of wages, the dependent, not the independent, variable. Thus, when the industrial cycle is in the phase of crisis, a general fall in the price of commodities is expressed as a rise in the value of money, and, in the phase of prosperity, a general rise in the price of commodities, as a fall in the value of money. The so-called currency school concludes from this that with high prices too much, with low prices too little money is in circulation. Their ignorance and complete misunderstanding of facts [8] are worthily paralleled by the economists, who interpret the above phenomena of accumulation by saying that there are now too few, now too many wage-labourers.

The law of capitalist production, that is at the bottom of the pretended 'natural law of population', reduces itself simply to this: The correlation between accumulation of capital and rate of wages is nothing else than the correlation between the unpaid labour transformed into capital, and the additional paid labour necessary for the setting in motion of this additional capital. It is therefore in no way a relation between two magnitudes, independent one of the other: on the one hand, the magnitude of the capital; on the other, the number of the labouring population; it is rather, at bottom, only the relation between the unpaid and the paid labour of the same labouring population. If the quantity of unpaid labour supplied by the working-class, and accumulated by the capitalist class, increases so rapidly that its conversion into capital requires an extraordinary addition of paid labour, then wages rise, and, all other circumstances remaining equal, the unpaid labour diminishes in proportion. But, as soon as this diminution touches the point at which the surplus-labour that nourishes capital is no longer supplied in normal quantity, a reaction sets in: a smaller part of revenue is capitalised, accumulation lags, and the movement of rise in wages receives a check. The rise of wages therefore is confined within limits that not only leave intact the foundations of the capitalistic system, but also secure its reproduction on a progressive scale. The law of capitalistic accumulation, metamorphosed by economists into a pretended law of nature, in reality merely states that the very nature of accumulation excludes every diminution in the degree of exploitation of labour, and every rise in the price of labour, which could seriously imperil the continual reproduction, on an ever-enlarging scale, of the capitalistic relation. It cannot be otherwise in a mode of production in which the labourer exists to satisfy the needs of self-expansion of existing values, instead of, on the contrary, material wealth existing to satisfy the needs of development on the part of the labourer. As, in religion, man is governed by the products of his own brain, so in capitalistic production, he is governed by the products of his own hand.[9]

Section 2. Relative Diminution of the Variable Part of Capital Simultaneously with the Progress of Accumulation and of the Concentration that Accompanies it.

According to the economists themselves, it is neither the actual extent of social wealth, nor the magnitude of the capital already functioning, that lead to a rise of wages, but only the constant growth of accumulation and the degree of rapidity of that growth. (Adam Smith, Book I, chapter 8.) So far, we have only considered one special phase of this process, that in which the increase of capital occurs along with a constant technical composition of capital. But the process goes beyond this phase.

Once given the general basis of the capitalistic system, then, in the course of accumulation, a point is reached at which the development of the productivity of social labour becomes the most powerful lever of accumulation. 'The same cause,' says Adam Smith, 'which raises the wages of labour, the increase of stock, tends to increase its productive powers, and to make a smaller quantity of labour produce a greater quantity of work.'

Apart from natural conditions, such as fertility of the soil, &c., and from the skill of independent and isolated producers (shown rather qualitatively in the goodness than quantitatively in the mass of their products), the degree of productivity of labour, in a given society, is expressed in the relative extent of the means of production that one labourer, during a given time, with the same tension of labour power, turns into products. The mass of the means of production which he thus transforms, increases with the productiveness of his labour. But those means of production play a double part. The increase of some is a consequence, that of the others a condition of the increasing productivity of labour. e.g., with the division of labour in manufacture, and with the use of machinery, more raw material is worked up in the same time, and, therefore, a greater mass of raw material and auxiliary substances enter into the labour-process. That is the consequence of the increasing productivity of labour. On the other hand, the mass of machinery, beasts of burden, mineral manures, drain-pipes, &c., is a condition of the increasing productivity of labour. So also is it with the means of production concentrated in buildings, furnaces, means of transport, &c. But whether condition or consequence, the growing extent of the means of production, as compared with the labour power incorporated with them, is an expression of the growing productiveness of labour. The increase of the latter appears, therefore, in the diminution of the mass of labour in proportion to the mass of means of production moved by it, or in the diminution of the subjective factor of the labour-process as compared with the objective factor.

This change in the technical composition of capital, this growth in the mass of means of production, as compared with the mass of the labour power that vivifies them, is reflected again in its value-composition, by the increase of the constant constituent of capital at the expense of its variable constituent. There may be, e.g., originally 50 per cent. of a capital laid out in means of production, and 50 per cent. in labour power; later on, with the development of the productivity of labour, 80 per cent. in means of production, 20 per cent. in labour power, and so on. This law of the progressive increase in constant capital, in proportion to the variable, is confirmed at every step (as already shown) by the comparative analysis of the prices of commodities, whether we compare different economic epochs or different nations in the same epoch. The relative magnitude of the element of price, which represents the value of the means of production only, or the constant part of capital consumed, is in direct, the relative magnitude of the other element of price that pays labour (the variable part of capital) is in inverse proportion to the advance of accumulation.

This diminution in the variable part of capital as compared with the constant, or the altered value-composition of the capital, however, only shows approximately the change in the composition of its material constituents. If, e.g., the capital-value employed today in spinning is 7/8 constant and 1/8 variable, whilst at the beginning of the 18th century it was 1/2 constant and 1/2 variable, on the other hand, the mass of raw material, instruments of labour, &c., that a certain quantity of spinning labour consumes productively today, is many hundred times greater than at the beginning of the 18th century. The reason is simply that, with the increasing productivity of labour, not only does the mass of the means of production consumed by it increase, but their value compared with their mass diminishes. Their value therefore rises absolutely, but not in proportion to their mass. The increase of the difference between constant and variable capital is, therefore, much less than that of the difference between the mass of the means of production into which the constant, and the mass of the labour power into which the variable, capital is converted. The former difference increases with the latter, but in a smaller degree.

But, if the progress of accumulation lessens the relative magnitude of the variable part of capital, it by no means, in doing this, excludes the possibility of a rise in its absolute magnitude. Suppose that a capital-value at first is divided into 50 per cent. of constant and 50 per cent. of variable capital; later into 80 per cent. of constant and 20 per cent. of variable. If in the meantime the original capital, say £6,000, has increased to £18,000, its variable constituent has also increased. It was £3,000, it is now £3,600. But whereas formerly an increase of capital by 20 per cent. would have sufficed to raise the demand for labour 20 per cent., now this latter rise requires a tripling of the original capital.

In Part 4 it was shown, how the development of the productiveness of social labour presupposes co-operation on a large scale; how it is only upon this supposition that division and combination of labour can be organised, and the means of production economised by concentration on a vast scale; how instruments of labour which, from their very nature, are only fit for use in common, such as a system of machinery, can be called into being; how huge natural forces can be pressed into the service of production; and how the transformation can be effected of the process of production into a technological application of science. On the basis of the production of commodities, where the means of production are the property of private persons, and where the artisan therefore either produces commodities, isolated from and independent of others, or sells his labour power as a commodity, because he lacks the means for independent industry, co-operation on a large scale can realise itself only in the increase of individual capitals, only in proportion as the means of social production and the means of subsistence are transformed into the private property of capitalists. The basis of the production of commodities can admit of production on a large scale in the capitalistic form alone. A certain accumulation of capital, in the hands of individual producers of commodities, forms therefore the necessary preliminary of the specifically capitalistic mode of production. We had, therefore, to assume that this occurs during the transition from handicraft to capitalistic industry. It may be called primitive accumulation, because it is the historic basis, instead of the historic result of specifically capitalist production. How it itself originates, we need not here inquire as yet. It is enough that it forms the starting-point. But all methods for raising the social productive power of labour that are developed on this basis, are at the same time methods for the increased production of surplus-value or surplus-product, which in its turn is the formative element of accumulation. They are, therefore, at the same time methods of the production of capital by capital, or methods of its accelerated accumulation. The continual re-transformation of surplus-value into capital now appears in the shape of the increasing magnitude of the capital that enters into the process of production. This in turn is the basis of an extended scale of production, of the methods for raising the productive power of labour that accompany it, and of accelerated production of surplus-value. If, therefore, a certain degree of accumulation of capital appears as a condition of the specifically capitalist mode of production, the latter causes conversely an accelerated accumulation of capital. With the accumulation of capital, therefore, the specifically capitalistic mode of production develops, and with the capitalist mode of production the accumulation of capital. Both these economic factors bring about, in the compound ratio of the impulses they reciprocally give one another, that change in the technical composition of capital by which the variable constituent becomes always smaller and smaller as compared with the constant.

Every individual capital is a larger or smaller concentration of means of production, with a corresponding command over a larger or smaller labour-army. Every accumulation becomes the means of new accumulation. With the increasing mass of wealth which functions as capital, accumulation increases the concentration of that wealth in the hands of individual capitalists, and thereby widens the basis of production on a large scale and of the specific methods of capitalist production. The growth of social capital is effected by the growth of many individual capitals. All other circumstances remaining the same, individual capitals, and with them the concentration of the means of production, increase in such proportion as they form aliquot parts of the total social capital. At the same time portions of the original capitals disengage themselves and function as new independent capitals. Besides other causes, the division of property, within capitalist families, plays a great part in this. With the accumulation of capital, therefore, the number of capitalists grows to a greater or less extent. Two points characterise this kind of concentration which grows directly out of, or rather is identical with, accumulation. First: the increasing concentration of the social means of production in the hands of individual capitalists is, other things remaining equal, limited by the degree of increase of social wealth. Second: the part of social capital domiciled in each particular sphere of production is divided among many capitalists who face one another as independent commodity-producers competing with each other. Accumulation and the concentration accompanying it are, therefore, not only scattered over many points, but the increase of each functioning capital is thwarted by the formation of new and the sub-division of old capitals. Accumulation, therefore, presents itself on the one hand as increasing concentration of the means of production, and of the command over labour; on the other, as repulsion of many individual capitals one from another.

This splitting-up of the total social capital into many individual capitals or the repulsion of its fractions one from another, is counteracted by their attraction. This last does not mean that simple concentration of the means of production and of the command over labour, which is identical with accumulation. It is concentration of capitals already formed, destruction of their individual independence, expropriation of capitalist by capitalist, transformation of many small into few large capitals. This process differs from the former in this, that it only presupposes a change in the distribution of capital already to hand, and functioning; its field of action is therefore not limited by the absolute growth of social wealth, by the absolute limits of accumulation. Capital grows in one place to a huge mass in a single hand, because it has in another place been lost by many. This is centralisation proper, as distinct from accumulation and concentration.

The laws of this centralisation of capitals, or of the attraction of capital by capital, cannot be developed here. A brief hint at a few facts must suffice. The battle of competition is fought by cheapening of commodities. The cheapness of commodities depends, *ceteris paribus*, on the productiveness of labour, and this again on the scale of production. Therefore, the larger capitals beat the smaller. It will further be remembered that, with the development of the capitalist mode of production, there is an increase in the minimum amount of individual capital necessary to carry on a business under its normal conditions. The smaller capitals, therefore, crowd into spheres of production which Modern Industry has only sporadically or incompletely got hold of. Here competition rages in direct proportion to the number, and in inverse proportion to the magnitudes, of the antagonistic capitals. It always ends in the ruin of many small capitalists, whose capitals partly pass into the hands of their conquerors, partly vanish. Apart from this, with capitalist production an altogether new force comes into play – the credit system. Not only is this itself a new and mighty weapon in the battle of competition. By unseen threads it, moreover, draws the disposable money, scattered in larger or smaller masses over the surface of society, into the hands of individual or associated capitalists. It is the specific machine for the centralisation of capitals.

The centralisation of capitals or the process of of their attraction becomes more intense, in proportion as the specifically capitalist mode of production develops along with accumulation. In its turn, centralisation becomes one of the greatest levers of this development. It shortens and quickens the transformation of separate processes of production into processes socially combined and carried out on a large scale.

The increasing bulk of individual masses of capital becomes the material basis of an uninterrupted revolution in the mode of production itself. Continually the capitalist mode of production conquers branches of industry not yet wholly, or only sporadically, or only formally, subjugated by it. At the same time there grow up on its soil new branches of industry, such as could not exist without it. Finally, in the branches of industry already carried on upon the capitalist basis, the productiveness of labour is made to ripen, as in a hothouse. In all these cases, the number of labourers falls in proportion to the mass of the means of production worked up by them. An ever increasing part of the capital is turned into means of production, an ever decreasing one into labour-power. With the extent, the concentration and the technical efficiency of the means of production, the degree lessens progressively, in which the latter are means of employment for labourers. A steam plough is an incomparably more efficient means of production than an ordinary plough, but the capital-value laid out in it is an incomparably smaller means for employing men than if it were laid out in ordinary ploughs. At first, it is the mere adding of new capital to old, which allows of the expansion and technical revolution of the material conditions of the process of production. But soon the change of composition and the technical transformation get more or less completely hold of all old capital that has reached the term of its reproduction, and therefore has to be replaced. This metamorphosis of old capital is independent, to a certain extent, of the absolute growth of social capital, in the same way as its centralisation. But this centralisation which only redistributes the social capital already to hand, and melts into one a number of old capitals, works in its turn as a powerful agent in this metamorphosis of old capital.

On the one hand, therefore, the additional capital formed in the course of accumulation attracts fewer and fewer labourers in proportion to its magnitude. On the other hand, the old capital periodically reproduced with change of composition, repels more and more of the labourers formerly employed by it.

Section 3. Progressive Production of a Relative Surplus-Population or Industrial Reserve Army.

The accumulation of capital, though originally appearing as its quantitative extension only, is effected, as we have seen, under a progressive qualitative change in its composition, under a constant increase of its constant, at the expense of its variable constituent.[10]

The specifically capitalist mode of production, the development of the productive power of labour corresponding to it, and the change thence resulting in the organic composition of capital, do not merely keep pace with the advance of accumulation, or with the growth of social wealth. They develop at a much quicker rate, because mere accumulation, the absolute increase of the total social capital, is accompanied by the centralisation of the individual capitals of which that total is made up; and because the change in the technological composition of the additional capital goes hand in hand with a similar change in the technological composition of the original capital. With the advance of accumulation, therefore, the proportion of constant to variable capital changes. If it was originally say 1:1, it now becomes successively 2:1, 3:1, 4:1, 5:1, 7:1, &c., so that, as the capital increases, instead of 1/2 of its total value, only 1/3, 1/4, 1/5, 1/6, 1/8, &c., is transformed into labour power, and, on the other hand, 2/3, 3/4, 4/5, 5/6, 7/8 into means of production. Since the demand for labour is determined not by the amount of capital as a whole, but by its variable constituent alone, that demand falls progressively with the increase of the total capital, instead of, as previously assumed, rising in proportion to it. It falls relatively to the magnitude of the total capital, and at an accelerated rate, as this magnitude increases. With the growth of the total capital, its variable constituent or the labour incorporated in it, also does increase, but in a constantly diminishing proportion. The intermediate pauses are shortened, in which accumulation works as simple extension of production, on a given technical basis. It is not merely that an accelerated accumulation of total capital, accelerated in a constantly growing progression, is needed to absorb an additional number of labourers, or even, on account of the constant metamorphosis of old capital, to keep employed those already functioning. In its turn, this increasing accumulation and centralisation becomes a source of new changes in the composition of capital, of a more accelerated diminution of its variable, as compared with its constant constituent. This accelerated relative diminution of the variable constituent, that goes along with the accelerated increase of the total capital, and moves more rapidly than this increase, takes the inverse form, at the other pole, of an apparently absolute increase of the labouring population, an increase always moving more rapidly than that of the variable capital or the means of employment. But in fact, it is capitalistic accumulation itself that constantly produces, and produces in the direct ratio of its own energy and extent, a relatively redundant population of labourers, i.e., a population of greater extent than suffices for the average needs of the self-expansion of capital, and therefore a surplus-population.

Considering the social capital in its totality, the movement of its accumulation now causes periodical changes, affecting it more or less as a whole, now distributes its various phases simultaneously over the different spheres of production. In some spheres a change in the composition of capital occurs without increase of its absolute magnitude, as a consequence of simple centralisation; in others the absolute growth of capital is connected with absolute diminution of its variable constituent, or of the labour power absorbed by it; in others again, capital continues growing for a time on its given technical basis, and attracts additional labour power in proportion to its increase, while at other times it undergoes organic change, and lessens its variable constituent; in all spheres, the increase of the variable part of capital, and therefore of the number of labourers employed by it, is always connected with violent fluctuations and transitory production of surplus-population, whether this takes the more striking form of the repulsion of labourers already employed, or the less evident but not less real form of the more difficult absorption of the additional labouring population through the usual channels.[11] With the magnitude of social capital already functioning, and the degree of its increase, with the extension of the scale of production, and the mass of the labourers set in motion, with the development of the productiveness of their labour, with the greater breadth and fulness of all sources of wealth, there is also an extension of the scale on which greater attraction of labourers by capital is accompanied by their greater repulsion; the rapidity of the change in the organic composition of capital, and in its technical form increases, and an increasing number of spheres of production becomes involved in this change, now simultaneously, now alternately. The labouring population therefore produces, along with the accumulation of capital produced by it, the means by which it itself is made relatively superfluous, is turned into a relative surplus-population; and it does this to an always increasing extent.[12] This is a law of population peculiar to the capitalist mode of production; and in fact every special historic mode of production has its own special laws of population, historically valid within its limits and only in so far as man has not interfered with them.

But if a surplus labouring population is a necessary product of accumulation or of the development of wealth on a capitalist basis, this surplus-population becomes, conversely, the lever of capitalistic accumulation, nay, a condition of existence of the capitalist mode of production. It forms a disposable industrial reserve army, that belongs to capital quite as absolutely as if the latter had bred it at its own cost. Independently of the limits of the actual increase of population, it creates, for the changing needs of the self-expansion of capital, a mass of human material always ready for exploitation. With accumulation, and the development of the productiveness of labour that accompanies it, the power of sudden expansion of capital grows also; it grows, not merely because the elasticity of the capital already functioning increases, not merely because the absolute wealth of society expands, of which capital only forms an elastic part, not merely because credit, under every special stimulus, at once places an unusual part of this wealth at the disposal of production in the form of additional capital; it grows, also, because the technical conditions of the process of production themselves – machinery, means of transport, &c. – now admit of the rapidest transformation of masses of surplus-product into additional means of production. The mass of social wealth, overflowing with the advance of accumulation, and transformable into additional capital, thrusts itself frantically into old branches of production, whose market suddenly expands, or into newly formed branches, such as railways, &c., the need for which grows out of the development of the old ones. In all such cases, there must be the possibility of throwing great masses of men suddenly on the decisive points without injury to the scale of production in other spheres. Overpopulation supplies these masses. The course characteristic of modern industry, viz., a decennial cycle (interrupted by smaller oscillations), of periods of average activity, production at high pressure, crisis and stagnation, depends on the constant formation, the greater or less absorption, and the re-formation of the industrial reserve army or surplus-population. In their turn, the varying phases of the industrial cycle recruit the surplus-population, and become one of the most energetic agents of its reproduction. This peculiar course of modern industry, which occurs in no earlier period of human history, was also impossible in the childhood of capitalist production. The composition of capital changed but very slowly. With its accumulation, therefore, there kept pace, on the whole, a corresponding growth in the demand for labour. Slow as was the advance of accumulation compared with that of more modern times, it found a check in the natural limits of the exploitable labouring population, limits which could only be got rid of by forcible means to be mentioned later. The expansion by fits and starts of the scale of production is the preliminary to its equally sudden contraction; the latter again evokes the former, but the former is impossible without disposable human material, without an increase in the number of labourers independently of the absolute growth of the population. This increase is effected by the simple process that constantly 'sets free' a part of the labourers; by methods which lessen the number of labourers employed in proportion to the increased production. The whole form of the movement of modern industry depends, therefore, upon the constant transformation of a part of the labouring population into unemployed or half-employed hands. The superficiality of Political Economy shows itself in the fact that it looks upon the expansion and contraction of credit, which is a mere symptom of the periodic changes of the industrial cycle, as their cause. As the heavenly bodies, once thrown into a certain definite motion, always repeat this, so is it with social production as soon as it is once thrown into this movement of alternate expansion and contraction. Effects, in their turn, become causes, and the varying accidents of the whole process, which always reproduces its own conditions, take on the form of periodicity. When this periodicity is once consolidated, even Political Economy then sees that the production of a relative surplus-population – i.e., surplus with regard to the average needs of the self-expansion of capital – is a necessary condition of modern industry.

'Suppose,' says H. Merivale, formerly Professor of Political Economy at Oxford, subsequently employed in the English Colonial Office, 'suppose that, on the occasion of some of these crises, the nation were to rouse itself to the effort of getting rid by emigration of some hundreds of thousands of superfluous arms, what would be the consequence? That, at the first returning demand for labour, there would be a deficiency. However rapid reproduction may be, it takes, at all events, the space of a generation to replace the loss of adult labour. Now, the profits of our manufacturers depend mainly on the power of making use of the prosperous moment when demand is brisk, and thus compensating themselves for the interval during which it is slack. This power is secured to them only by the command of machinery and of manual labour. They must have hands ready by them, they must be able to increase the activity of their operations when required, and to slacken it again, according to the state of the market, or they cannot possibly maintain that pre-eminence in the race of competition on which the wealth of the country is founded.'[13] Even Malthus recognises overpopulation as a necessity of modem industry, though, after his narrow fashion, he explains it by the absolute over-growth of the labouring population, not by their becoming relatively supernumerary. He says: 'Prudential habits with regard to marriage, carried to a considerable extent among the labouring class of a country mainly depending upon manufactures and commerce, might injure it . . . From the nature of a population, an increase of labourers cannot be brought into market in consequence of a particular demand till after the lapse of 16 or 18 years, and the conversion of revenue into capital, by saving, may take place much more rapidly: a country is always liable to an increase in the quantity of the funds for the maintenance of labour faster than the increase of population.'[14] After Political Economy has thus demonstrated the constant production of a relative surplus-population of labourers to be a necessity of capitalistic accumulation, she very aptly, in the guise of an old maid, puts in the mouth of her 'beau ideal' of a capitalist the following words addressed to those supernumeraries thrown on the streets by their own creation of additional capital: – 'We manufacturers do what we can for you, whilst we are increasing that capital on which you must subsist, and you must do the rest by accommodating your numbers to the means of subsistence.'[15]

Capitalist production can by no means content itself with the quantity of disposable labour power which the natural increase of population yields. It requires for its free play an industrial reserve army independent of these natural limits.

Up to this point it has been assumed that the increase or diminution of the variable capital corresponds rigidly with the increase or diminution of the number of labourers employed.

The number of labourers commanded by capital may remain the same, or even fall, while the variable capital increases. This is the case if the individual labourer yields more labour, and therefore his wages increase, and this although the price of labour remains the same or even falls, only more slowly than the mass of labour rises. Increase of variable capital, in this case, becomes an index of more labour, but not of more labourers employed. It is the absolute interest of every capitalist to press a given quantity of labour out of a smaller, rather than a greater number of labourers, if the cost is about the same. In the latter case, the outlay of constant capital increases in proportion to the mass of labour set in action; in the former that increase is much smaller. The more extended the scale of production, the stronger this motive. Its force increases with the accumulation of capital.

We have seen that the development of the capitalist mode of production and of the productive power of labour – at once the cause and effect of accumulation – enables the capitalist, with the same outlay of variable capital, to set in action more labour by greater exploitation (extensive or intensive) of each individual labour power. We have further seen that the capitalist buys with the same capital a greater mass of labour power, as he progressively replaces skilled labourers by less skilled, mature labour power by immature, male by female, that of adults by that of young persons or children.

On the one hand, therefore, with the progress of accumulation, a larger variable capital sets more labour in action without enlisting more labourers; on the other, a variable capital of the same magnitude sets in action more labour with the same mass of labour power; and, finally, a greater number of inferior labour powers by displacement of higher.

The production of a relative surplus-population, or the setting free of labourers, goes on therefore yet more rapidly than the technical revolution of the process of production that accompanies, and is accelerated by, the advance of accumulation; and more rapidly than the corresponding diminution of the variable part of capital as compared with the constant. If the means of production, as they increase in extent and effective power, become to a less extent means of employment of labourers, this state of things is again modified by the fact that in proportion as the productiveness of labour increases, capital increases its supply of labour more quickly than its demand for labourers. The over-work of the employed part of the working-class swells the ranks of the reserve, whilst conversely the greater pressure that the latter by its competition exerts on the former, forces these to submit to overwork and to subjugation under the dictates of capital. The condemnation of one part of the working-class to enforced idleness by the overwork of the other part, and the converse, becomes a means of enriching the individual capitalists,[16] and accelerates at the same time the production of the industrial reserve army on a scale corresponding with the advance of social accumulation. How important is this element in the formation of the relative surplus-population, is shown by the example of England. Her technical means for saving labour are colossal. Nevertheless, if tomorrow morning labour generally were reduced to a rational amount, and proportioned to the different sections of the working-class according to age and sex, the working population to hand would be absolutely insufficient for the carrying on of national production on its present scale. The great majority of the labourers now 'unproductive' would have to be turned into 'productive' ones.

Taking them as a whole, the general movements of wages are exclusively regulated by the expansion and contraction of the industrial reserve army, and these again correspond to the periodic changes of the industrial cycle. They are, therefore, not determined by the variations of the absolute number of the working population, but by the varying proportions in which the working-class is divided into active and reserve army, by the increase or diminution in the relative amount of the surplus-population, by the extent to which it is now absorbed, now set free. For Modern Industry with its decennial cycles and periodic phases, which, moreover, as accumulation advances, are complicated by irregular oscillations following each other more and more quickly, that would indeed be a beautiful law, which pretends to make the action of capital dependent on the absolute variation of the population, instead of regulating the demand and supply of labour by the alternate expansion and contraction of capital, the labour-market now appearing relatively under-full, because capital is expanding, now again over-full, because it is contracting. Yet this is the dogma of the economists. According to them, wages rise in consequence of accumulation of capital. The higher wages stimulate the working population to more rapid multiplication, and this goes on until the labour-market becomes too full, and therefore capital, relatively to the supply of labour, becomes insufficient. Wages fall, and now we have the reverse of the medal. The working population is little by little decimated as the result of the fall in wages, so that capital is again in excess relatively to them, or, as others explain it, falling wages and the corresponding increase in the exploitation of the labourer again accelerates accumulation, whilst, at the same time, the lower wages hold the increase of the working-class in check. Then comes again the time, when the supply of labour is less than the demand, wages rise, and so on. A beautiful mode of motion this for developed capitalist production! Before, in consequence of the rise of wages, any positive increase of the population really fit for work could occur, the time would have been passed again and again, during which the industrial campaign must have been carried through, the battle fought and won.

Between 1849 and 1859, a rise of wages practically insignificant, though accompanied by falling prices of corn, took place in the English agricultural districts. In Wiltshire, e.g., the weekly wages rose from 7s. to 8s.; in Dorsetshire from 7s. or 8s., to 9s., &c. This was the result of an unusual exodus of the agricultural surplus-population caused by the demands of war, the vast extension of railroads, factories, mines, &c. The lower the wages, the higher is the proportion in which ever so insignificant a rise of them expresses itself. If the weekly wage, e.g., is 20s. and it rises to 22s., that is a rise of 10 per cent.; but if it is only 7s. and it rises to 9s., that is a rise of 28 4/7 per cent., which sounds very fine. Everywhere the farmers were howling, and the London Economist, with reference to these starvation-wages, prattled quite seriously of 'a general and substantial advance'.[17] What did the farmers do now? Did they wait until, in consequence of this brilliant remuneration, the agricultural labourers had so increased and multiplied that their wages must fall again, as prescribed by the dogmatic economic brain? They introduced more machinery, and in a moment the labourers were redundant again in a proportion satisfactory even to the farmers. There was now 'more capital' laid out in agriculture than before, and in a more productive form. With this the demand for labour fell, not only relatively, but absolutely.

The above economic fiction confuses the laws that regulate the general movement of wages, or the ratio between the working-class – i.e., the total labour power – and the total social capital, with the laws that distribute the working population over the different spheres of production. If, e.g., in consequence of favourable circumstances, accumulation in a particular sphere of production becomes especially active, and profits in it, being greater than the average profits, attract additional capital, of course the demand for labour rises and wages also rise. The higher wages draw a larger part of the working population into the more favoured sphere, until it is glutted with labour power, and wages at length fall again to their average level or below it, if the pressure is too great. Then, not only does the immigration of labourers into the branch of industry in question cease; it gives place to their emigration. Here the political economist thinks he sees the why and wherefore of an absolute increase of workers accompanying an increase of wages, and of a diminution of wages accompanying an absolute increase of labourers. But he sees really only the local oscillation of the labour-market in a particular sphere of production – he sees only the phenomena accompanying the distribution of the working population into the different spheres of outlay of capital, according to its varying needs.

The industrial reserve army, during the periods of stagnation and average prosperity, weighs down the active labour-army; during the periods of over-production and paroxysm, it holds its pretensions in check. Relative surplus-population is therefore the pivot upon which the law of demand and supply of labour works. It confines the field of action of this law within the limits absolutely convenient to the activity of exploitation and to the domination of capital.

This is the place to return to one of the grand exploits of economic apologetics. It will be remembered that if through the introduction of new, or the extension of old, machinery, a portion of variable capital is transformed into constant, the economic apologist interprets this operation which 'fixes' capital and by that very act sets labourers 'free,' in exactly the opposite way, pretending that it sets free capital for the labourers. Only now can one fully understand the effrontery of these apologists. What are set free are not only the labourers immediately turned out by the machines, but also their future substitutes in the rising generation, and the additional contingent, that with the usual extension of trade on the old basis would be regularly absorbed. They are now all 'set free', and every new bit of capital looking out for employment can dispose of them. Whether it attracts them or others, the effect on the general labour demand will be nil, if this capital is just sufficient to take out of the market as many labourers as the machines threw upon it. If it employs a smaller number, that of the super-numeraries increases; if it employs a greater, the general demand for labour only increases to the extent of the excess of the employed over those 'set free'. The impulse that additional capital, seeking an outlet, would otherwise have given to the general demand for labour, is therefore in every case neutralised to the extent of the labourers thrown out of employment by the machine. That is to say, the mechanism of capitalistic production so manages matters that the absolute increase of capital is accompanied by no corresponding rise in the general demand for labour. And this the apologist calls a compensation for the misery, the sufferings, the possible death of the displaced labourers during the transition period that banishes them into the industrial reserve army! The demand for labour is not identical with increase of capital, nor supply of labour with increase of the working-class. It is not a case of two independent forces working on one another. *Les dés sont pipés.* Capital works on both sides at the same time. If its accumulation, on the one hand, increases the demand for labour, it increases on the other the supply of labourers by the 'setting free' of them, whilst at the same time the pressure of the unemployed compels those that are employed to furnish more labour, and therefore makes the supply of labour, to a certain extent, independent of the supply of labourers. The action of the law of supply and demand of labour on this basis completes the despotism of capital. As soon, therefore, as the labourers learn the secret, how it comes to pass that in the same measure as they work more, as they produce more wealth for others, and as the productive power of their labour increases, so in the same measure even their function as a means of the self-expansion of capital becomes more and more precarious for them; as soon as they discover that the degree of intensity of the competition among themselves depends wholly on the pressure of the relative surplus-population; as soon as, by Trades' Unions, &c., they try to organise a regular co-operation between employed and unemployed in order to destroy or to weaken the ruinous effects of this natural law of capitalistic production on their class, so soon capital and its sycophant, Political Economy, cry out at the infringement of the 'eternal' and so to say 'sacred' law of supply and demand. Every combination of employed and unemployed disturbs the 'harmonious' action of this law. But, on the other hand, as soon as (in the colonies, e.g.) adverse circumstances prevent the creation of an industrial reserve army and, with it, the absolute dependence of the working-class upon the capitalist class, capital, along with its commonplace Sancho Panza, rebels against the 'sacred' law of supply and demand, and tries to check its inconvenient action by forcible means and State interference.

Section 4. Different Forms of the Relative Surplus-Population. The General Law of Capitalistic Accumulation.

The relative surplus-population exists in every possible form. Every labourer belongs to it during the time when he is only partially employed or wholly unemployed. Not taking into account the great periodically recurring forms that the changing phases of the industrial cycle impress on it, now an acute form during the crisis, then again a chronic form during dull times – it has always three forms, the floating, the latent, the stagnant.

In the centres of modern industry – factories, manufactures, iron-works, mines, &c. – the labourers are sometimes repelled, sometimes attracted again in greater masses, the number of those employed increasing on the whole, although in a constantly decreasing proportion to the scale of production. Here the surplus-population exists in the floating form.

In the automatic factories, as in all the great workshops, where machinery enters as a factor, or where only the modern division of labour is carried out, large numbers of boys are employed up to the age of maturity. When this term is once reached, only a very small number continue to find employment in the same branches of industry, whilst the majority are regularly discharged. This majority forms an element of the floating surplus-population, growing with the extension of those branches of industry. Part of them emigrates, following in fact capital that has emigrated. One consequence is that the female population grows more rapidly than the male, *teste* England. That the natural increase of the number of labourers does not satisfy the requirements of the accumulation of capital, and yet all the time is in excess of them, is a contradiction inherent to the movement of capital itself. It wants larger numbers of youthful labourers, a smaller number of adults. The contradiction is not more glaring than that other one that there is a complaint of the want of hands, while at the same time many thousands are out of work, because the division of labour chains them to a particular branch of industry.[18]

The consumption of labour power by capital is, besides, so rapid that the labourer, half-way through his life, has already more or less completely lived himself out. He falls into the ranks of the super-numeraries, or is thrust down from a higher to a lower step in the scale. It is precisely among the work-people of modern industry that we meet with the shortest duration of life. Dr Lee, Medical Officer of Health for Manchester, stated 'that the average age at death of the Manchester . . . upper middle class was 38 years, while the average age at death of the labouring class was 17; while at Liverpool those figures were represented as 35 against 15. It thus appeared that the well-to-do classes had a lease of life which was more than double the value of that which fell to the lot of the less favoured citizens.'[19] In order to conform to these circumstances, the absolute increase of this section of the proletariat must take place under conditions that shall swell their numbers, although the individual elements are used up rapidly. Hence, rapid renewal of the generations of labourers (this law does not hold for the other classes of the population). This social need is met by early marriages, a necessary consequence of the conditions in which the labourers of modern industry live, and by the premium that the exploitation of children sets on their production.

As soon as capitalist production takes possession of agriculture, and in proportion to the extent to which it does so, the demand for an agricultural labouring population falls absolutely, while the accumulation of the capital employed in agriculture advances, without this repulsion being, as in non-agricultural industries, compensated by a greater attraction. Part of the agricultural population is therefore constantly on the point of passing over into an urban or manufacturing proletariat. and on the look-out for circumstances favourable to this transformation. (Manufacture is used here in the sense of all non-agricultural industries.)[20] This source of relative surplus-population is thus constantly flowing. But the constant flow towards the towns presupposes, in the country itself, a constant latent surplus-population, the extent of which becomes evident only when its channels of outlet open to exceptional width. The agricultural labourer is therefore reduced to the minimum of wages, and always stands with one foot already in the swamp of pauperism.

The third category of the relative surplus-population, the stagnant, forms a part of the active labour army, but with extremely irregular employment. Hence it furnishes to capital an inexhaustible reservoir of disposable labour power. Its conditions of life sink below the average normal level of the working-class; this makes it at once the broad basis of special branches of capitalist exploitation. It is characterised by maximum of working-time, and minimum of wages. We have learnt to know its chief form under the rubric of 'domestic industry'. It recruits itself constantly from the supernumerary forces of modern industry and agriculture, and specially from those decaying branches of industry where handicraft is yielding to manufacture, manufacture to machinery. Its extent grows, as with the extent and energy of accumulation, the creation of a surplus-population advances. But it forms at the same time a self-reproducing and self-perpetuating element of the working-class, taking a proportionally greater part in the general increase of that class than the other elements. In fact, not only the number of births and deaths, but the absolute size of the families stand in inverse proportion to the height of wages, and therefore to the amount of means of subsistence of which the different categories of labourers dispose. This law of capitalistic society would sound absurd to savages, or even civilised colonists. It calls to mind the boundless reproduction of animals individually weak and constantly hunted down.[21]

The lowest sediment of the relative surplus-population finally dwells in the sphere of pauperism. Exclusive of vagabonds, criminals, prostitutes, in a word, the 'dangerous' classes, this layer of society consists of three categories. First, those able to work. One need only glance superficially at the statistics of English pauperism to find that the quantity of paupers increases with every crisis, and diminishes with every revival of trade. Second, orphans and pauper children. These are candidates for the industrial reserve army, and are, in times of great prosperity, as 1860, e.g., speedily and in large numbers enrolled in the active army of labourers. Third, the demoralised and ragged, and those unable to work, chiefly people who succumb to their incapacity for adaptation, due to the division of labour; people who have passed the normal age of the labourer; the victims of industry, whose number increases with the increase of dangerous machinery, of mines, chemical works, &c., the mutilated, the sickly, the widows, &c. Pauperism is the hospital of the active labour-army and the dead weight of the industrial reserve army. Its production is included in that of the relative surplus-population, its necessity in theirs; along with the surplus-population, pauperism forms a condition of capitalist production, and of the capitalist development of wealth. It enters into the *faux frais* of capitalist production; but capital knows how to throw these, for the most part, from its own shoulders on to those of the working-class and the lower middle class.

The greater the social wealth, the functioning capital, the extent and energy of its growth, and, therefore, also the absolute mass of the proletariat and the productiveness of its labour, the greater is the industrial reserve army. The same causes which develop the expansive power of capital, develop also the labour power at its disposal. The relative mass of the industrial reserve army increases therefore with the potential energy of wealth. But the greater this reserve army in proportion to the active labour-army, the greater is the mass of a consolidated surplus-population, whose misery is in inverse ratio to its torment of labour. The more extensive, finally, the lazarus-layers of the working-class, and the industrial reserve army, the greater is official pauperism. *This is the absolute general law of capitalist accumulation.* Like all other laws it is modified in its working by many circumstances, the analysis of which does not concern us here.

The folly is now patent of the economic wisdom that preaches to the labourers the accommodation of their number to the requirements of capital. The mechanism of capitalist production and accumulation constantly effects this adjustment. The first word of this adaptation is the creation of a relative surplus-population, or industrial reserve army. Its last word is the misery of constantly extending strata of the active army of labour, and the dead weight of pauperism.

The law by which a constantly increasing quantity of means of production, thanks to the advance in the productiveness of social labour, may be set in movement by a progressively diminishing expenditure of human power, this law, in a capitalist society – where the labourer does not employ the means of production, but the means of production employ the labourer – undergoes a complete inversion and is expressed thus: the higher the productiveness of labour, the greater is the pressure of the labourers on the means of employment, the more precarious, therefore, becomes their condition of existence, viz., the sale of their own labour power for the increasing of another's wealth, or for the self-expansion of capital. The fact that the means of production, and the productiveness of labour, increase more rapidly than the productive population, expresses itself, therefore, capitalistic-ally in the inverse form that the labouring population always increases more rapidly than the conditions under which capital can employ this increase for its own self-expansion.

We saw in Part 4, when analysing the production of relative surplus-value: within the capitalist system all methods for raising the social productiveness of labour are brought about at the cost of the individual labourer; all means for the development of production transform themselves into means of domination over, and exploitation of, the producers; they mutilate the labourer into a fragment of a man, degrade him to the level of an appendage of a machine, destroy every remnant of charm in his work and turn it into a hated toil; they estrange from him the intellectual potentialities of the labour-process in the same proportion as science is incorporated in it as an independent power; they distort the conditions under which he works, subject him during the labour-process to a despotism the more hateful for its meanness; they transform his life-time into working-time, and drag his wife and child beneath the wheels of the Juggernaut of capital. But all methods for the production of surplus-value are at the same time methods of accumulation; and every extension of accumulation becomes again a means for the development of those methods. It follows therefore that in proportion as capital accum-ulates, the lot of the labourer, be his payment high or low, must grow worse. The law, finally, that always equilibrates the relative surplus-population, or industrial reserve army, to the extent and energy of accumulation, this law rivets the labourer to capital more firmly than the wedges of Vulcan did Prometheus to the rock. It establishes an accumulation of misery, corresponding with accumulation of capital. Accumulation of wealth at one pole is, therefore, at the same time accumulation of misery, agony of toil, slavery, ignorance, brutality, mental degradation, at the opposite pole, i.e., on the side of the class that produces its own product in the form of capital.[22] This antagonistic character of capitalistic accumulation is enunciated in various forms by political economists, although by them it is confounded with phenomena, certainly to some extent analogous, but nevertheless essentially distinct, and belonging to pre-capitalistic modes of production.

The Venetian monk Ortes, one of the great economic writers of the 18th century, regards the antagonism of capitalist production as a general natural law of social wealth. 'In the economy of a nation, advantages and evils always balance one another (*il bene ed il male economico in una nazione sempre all' istessa misura*): the abundance of wealth with some people, is always equal to the want of it with others (*la copia dei beni in alcuni sempre eguale alla mancanza di essi in altri*): the great riches of a small number are always accompanied by the absolute privation of the first necessaries of life for many others. The wealth of a nation corresponds with its population, and its misery corresponds with its wealth. Diligence in some compels idleness in others. The poor and idle are a necessary consequence of the rich and active.'[23] In a thoroughly brutal way about 10 years after Ortes, the Church of England parson, Townsend, glorified misery as a necessary condition of wealth. 'Legal constraint (to labour) is attended with too much trouble, violence, and noise, whereas hunger is not only a peaceable, silent, unremitted pressure, but as the most natural motive to industry and labour, it calls forth the most powerful exertions.' Everything therefore depends upon making hunger permanent among the working-class, and for this, according to Townsend, the principle of population, especially active among the poor, provides. 'It seems to be a law of Nature that the poor should be to a certain degree improvident' [i.e., so improvident as to be born without a silver spoon in the mouth], 'that there may always be some to fulfil the most servile, the most sordid, and the most ignoble offices in the community. The stock of human happiness is thereby much increased, whilst the more delicate are not only relieved from drudgery . . . but are left at liberty without interruption to pursue those callings which are suited to their various dispositions . . . it [the Poor Law] tends to destroy the harmony and beauty, the symmetry and order of that system which God and Nature have established in the world.'[24] If the Venetian monk found in the fatal destiny that makes misery eternal, the *raison d'être* of Christian charity, celibacy, monasteries and holy houses, the Protestant prebendary finds in it a pretext for condemning the laws in virtue of which the poor possessed a right to a miserable public relief.

'The progress of social wealth,' says Storch, 'begets this useful class of society . . . which performs the most wearisome, the vilest, the most disgusting functions, which takes, in a word, on its shoulders all that is disagreeable and servile in life, and procures thus for other classes leisure, serenity of mind and conventional [*c'est bon!*] dignity of character.'[25] Storch asks himself in what then really consists the progress of this capitalistic civilisation with its misery and its degradation of the masses, as compared with barbarism. He finds but one answer: security!

'Thanks to the advance of industry and science,' says Sismondi, 'every labourer can produce every day much more than his consumption requires. But at the same time, whilst his labour produces wealth, that wealth would, were he called on to consume it himself, make him less fit for labour.' According to him, 'men' [i.e., non-workers] 'would probably prefer to do without all artistic perfection, and all the enjoyments that manufacturers procure for us, if it were necessary that all should buy them by constant toil like that of the labourer . . . Exertion today is separated from its recompense; it is not the same man that first works, and then reposes; but it is because the one works that the other rests . . . The indefinite multiplication of the productive powers of labour can then only have for result the increase of luxury and enjoyment of the idle rich.'[26]

Finally Destutt de Tracy, the fish-blooded bourgeois doctrinaire, blurts out brutally: 'In poor nations the people are comfortable, in rich nations they are generally poor.'[27]

Section 5. Illustrations of the General Law of Capitalist Accumulation.

A. England from 1846–1866.

No period of modern society is so favourable for the study of capitalist accumulation as the period of the last 20 years. It is as if this period had found Fortunatus' purse. But of all countries England again furnishes the classical example, because it holds the foremost place in the world-market, because capitalist production is here alone completely developed, and lastly, because the introduction of the Free-trade millennium since 1846 has cut off the last retreat of vulgar economy. The titanic advance of production – the latter half of the 20 years' period again far surpassing the former – has been already pointed out sufficiently in Part 4.

Although the absolute increase of the English population in the last half century was very great, the relative increase or rate of growth fell constantly, as the following table borrowed from the census shows.

Annual increase per cent. of the population of England and Wales in decimal numbers:

1811–1821	1.533 per cent
1821–1831	1.446 per cent
1831–1841	1.326 per cent
1841–1851	1.216 per cent
1851–1861	1.141 per cent

Let us now, on the other hand, consider the increase of wealth. Here the movement of profit, rent of land, &c., that come under the income tax, furnishes the surest basis. The increase of profits liable to income tax (farmers and some other categories not included) in Great Britain from 1853 to 1864 amounted to 50.47% or 4.58% as the annual average,[28] that of the population during the same period to about 12%. The augmentation of the rent of land subject to taxation (including houses, railways, mines, fisheries, &c.), amounted for 1853 to 1864 to 38% or 3 5/12% annually. Under this head the following categories show the greatest increase:

Excess of annual income of 1864 over that of 1853		Increase per year
Houses	38.60%	3.50%
Quarries	84.76%	7.70%
Mines	68.85%	6.26%
Iron-works	39.92%	3.63%
Fisheries	57.37%	5.21%
Gasworks	126.02%	11.45%
Railways	83.29%	7.57%

If we compare the years from 1853 to 1864 in three sets of four consecutive years each, the rate of augmentation of the income increases constantly. [29] It is, e.g., for that arising from profits between 1853 to 1857, 1.73% yearly; 1857–1861, 2.74%, and for 1861–64, 9.30% yearly. The sum of the incomes of the United Kingdom that come under the income tax was in 1856, £307,068,898; in 1859, £328,127,416; in 1862. £351,745,241; in 1863, £359,142,897; in 1864, £362,462,279; in 1865, £385,530,020.[30]

The accumulation of capital was attended at the same time by its concentration and centralisation. Although no official statistics of agriculture existed for England (they did for Ireland), they were voluntarily given in 10 counties. These statistics gave the result that from 1851 to 1861 the number of farms of less than 100 acres had fallen from 31,583 to 26,597, so that 5,016 had been thrown together into larger farms.[31] From 1815 to 1825 no personal estate of more than

£1,000,000 came under the succession duty; from 1825 to 1855, however, 8 did; and 4 from 1856 to June, 1859, i.e., in 4 1/2 years.[32] The centralisation will, however, be best seen from a short analysis of the Income Tax Schedule D (profits, exclusive of farms, &c.), in the years 1864 and 1865. I note beforehand that incomes from this source pay income tax on everything over £60. These incomes liable to taxation in England, Wales and Scotland, amounted in 1864 to £95,844,222, in 1865 to £105,435,579.[33] The number of persons taxed were in 1864, 308,416, out of a population of 23,891,009; in 1865, 332,431 out of a population of 24,127,003. The following table shows the distribution of these incomes in the two years:

| Year Ending April 5th, 1864 | | Year Ending April 5th, 1865 | |
Income from Profits	Persons	Income from Profits	Persons
Total Income £95,844,222	308,416	Total Income £105,435,738	332,431
of these 57,028,289	23,334	of these 64,554,297	24,265
of these 36,415,225	3,619	of these 42,535,576	4,021
of these 22,809,781	832	of these 27,555,313	973
of these 8,744,762	91	of these 11,077,238	107

In 1855 there were produced in the United Kingdom 61,453,079 tons of coal, of value £16,113,167; in 1864, 92,787,873 tons, of value £23,197,968; in 1855, 3,218,154 tons of pig-iron, of value £8,045,385; 1864, 4,767,951 tons, of value £11,919,877. In 1854 the length of the railroads worked in the United Kingdom was 8,054 miles, with a paid-up capital of £286,068,794; in 1864 the length was 12,789 miles, with capital paid up of £425,719,613. In 1854 the total sum of the exports and imports of the United Kingdom was £268,210,145; in 1865, £489,923,285. The following table shows the movement of the exports:

1846	£58,842,377
1849	63,596,052
1856	115,826,948
1860	135,842,817
1865	165,862,402
1866	188,917,563[34]

After these few examples one understands the cry of triumph of the Registrar-General of the British people: 'Rapidly as the population has increased, it has not kept pace with the progress of industry and wealth.'[35]

Let us turn now to the direct agents of this industry, or the producers of this wealth, to the working-class. 'It is one of the most melancholy features in the social state of this country,' says Gladstone, 'that while there was a decrease in the consuming powers of the people, and while there was an increase in the privations and distress of the labouring class and operatives, there was at the same time a constant accumulation of wealth in the upper classes, and a constant increase of capital.'[36] Thus spake this unctuous minister in the House of Commons on February 13th, 1843. On April 16th, 1863, 20 years later, in the speech in which he introduced his Budget: 'From 1842 to 1852 the taxable income of the country increased by 6 per cent . . . In the 8 years from 1853 to 1861 it had increased from the basis taken in 1853 by 20 per cent.! The fact is so astonishing as to be almost incredible . . . this intoxicating augmentation of wealth and power . . . entirely confined to classes of property . . . must be of indirect benefit to the labouring population, because it cheapens the commodities of general consumption. While the rich have been growing richer, the poor have been growing less poor. At any rate, whether the extremes of poverty are less, I do not presume to say.'[37] How lame an anticlimax! If the working-class has remained 'poor', only 'less poor' in proportion as it produces for the wealthy class 'an intoxicating augmentation of wealth and power', then it has remained relatively just as poor. If the extremes of poverty have not lessened, they have increased, because the extremes of wealth have. As to the cheapening of the means of subsistence, the official statistics, e.g., the accounts of the London Orphan Asylum, show an increase in price of 20% for the average of the three years 1860–1862, compared with 1851–1853. In the following three years, 1863–1865, there was a progressive rise in the price of meat, butter, milk, sugar, salt, coals, and a number of other necessary means of subsistence.[38] Gladstone's next Budget speech of April 7th, 1864, is a Pindaric dithyrambus on the advance of surplus-value-making and the happiness of the people 'tempered by poverty'. He speaks of masses 'on the border' of pauperism, of branches of trade in which 'wages have not increased', and finally sums up the happiness of the working-class in the words: 'human life is but, in nine cases out of ten, a struggle for existence.'[39] Professor Fawcett, not bound like Gladstone by official considerations, declares roundly: 'I do not, of course, deny that money wages have been augmented by this increase of capital (in the last ten years), but this apparent advantage is to a great extent lost, because many of the necessaries of life are becoming dearer' (he believes because of the fall in value of the precious metals) . . . 'the rich grow rapidly richer, whilst there is no perceptible advance in the comfort enjoyed by the industrial classes . . . They (the labourers) become almost the slaves of the tradesman, to whom they owe money.'[40]

In the chapters on the 'working-day' and 'machinery', the reader has seen under what circumstances the British working-class created an 'intoxicating augmentation of wealth and power' for the propertied classes. There we were chiefly concerned with the social functioning of the labourer. But for a full elucidation of the law of accumulation, his condition outside the workshop must also be looked at, his condition as to food and dwelling. The limits of this book compel us to concern ourselves chiefly with the worst paid part of the industrial proletariat, and with the agricultural labourers, who together form the majority of the working-class.

But first, one word on official pauperism, or on that part of the working-class which has forfeited its condition of existence (the sale of labour power), and vegetates upon public alms. The official list of paupers numbered in England[41] in 1885 851,369 persons; in 1856, 877,767; in 1865, 971,433. In consequence of the cotton famine, it grew in the years 1863 and 1864 to 1,079,382 and 1,014,978. The crisis of 1866, which fell most heavily on London, created in this centre of the world-market, more populous than the kingdom of Scotland, an increase of pauperism for the year 1866 of 19.5% compared with 1865, and of 24.4% compared with 1864, and a still greater increase for the first months of 1867 as compared with 1866. From the analysis of the statistics of pauperism, two points are to be taken. On the one hand, the fluctuation up and down of the number of paupers, reflects the periodic changes of the industrial cycle. On the other, the official statistics become more and more misleading as to the actual extent of pauperism in proportion as, with the accumulation of capital, the class-struggle, and, therefore, the class-consciousness of the working-men, develop. e.g., the barbarity in the treatment of the paupers, at which the English Press (*The Times*, *Pall Mall Gazette*, etc.) have cried out so loudly during the last two years, is of ancient date. F. Engels showed in 1844 exactly the same horrors, exactly the same transient canting outcries of 'sensational literature'. But frightful increase of 'deaths by starvation' in London during the last ten years proves beyond doubt the growing horror in which the working-people hold the slavery of the workhouse, that place of punishment for misery.[42]

B. The Badly Paid Strata of the British Industrial Class.

During the cotton famine of 1862, Dr Smith was charged by the Privy Council with an inquiry into the conditions of nourishment of the distressed operatives in Lancashire and Cheshire. His observations during many preceding years had led him to the conclusion that 'to avert starvation diseases', the daily food of an average woman ought to contain at least 3,900 grains of carbon with 180 grains of nitrogen; the daily food of an average man, at least 4,300 grains of carbon with

200 grains of nitrogen; for women, about the same quantity of nutritive elements as are contained in 2 lbs. of good wheaten bread, for men 1/9 more; for the weekly average of adult men and women, at least 28,600 grains of carbon and 1,330 grains of nitrogen. His calculation was practically confirmed in a surprising manner by its agreement with the miserable quantity of nourishment to which want had forced down the consumption of the cotton operatives. This was, in December, 1862, 29,211 grains of carbon, and 1,295 grains of nitrogen weekly.

In the year 1863, the Privy Council ordered an inquiry into the state of distress of the worst-nourished part of the English working-class. Dr Simon, medical officer to the Privy Council, chose for this work the above-mentioned Dr Smith. His inquiry ranges on the one hand over the agricultural labourers, on the other, over silk-weavers, needlewomen, kid-glovers, stocking-weavers, glove-weavers, and shoemakers. The latter categories are, with the exception of the stocking-weavers, exclusively town-dwellers. It was made a rule in the inquiry to select in each category the most healthy families, and those comparatively in the best circumstances.

As a general result it was found that 'in only one of the examined classes of in-door operatives did the average nitrogen-supply just exceed, while in another it nearly reached, the estimated standard of bare sufficiency [i.e., sufficient to avert starvation diseases], and that in two classes there was defect – in one, a very large defect – of both nitrogen and carbon. Moreover, as regards the examined families of the agricultural population, it appeared that more than a fifth were with less than the estimated sufficiency of carbonaceous food, that more than one-third were with less than the estimated sufficiency of nitrogenous food, and that in three counties (Berkshire, Oxfordshire, and Somersetshire), insufficiency of nitrogenous food was the average local diet.'[43] Among the agricultural labourers, those of England, the wealthiest part of the United Kingdom, were the worst fed.[44] The insufficiency of food among the agricultural labourers, fell, as a rule, chiefly on the women and children, for 'the man must eat to do his work.' Still greater penury ravaged the town-workers examined. 'They are so ill fed that assuredly among them there must be many cases of severe and injurious privation.'[45] ('Privation' of the capitalist all this! i.e., 'abstinence' from paying for the means of subsistence absolutely necessary for the mere vegetation of his 'hands'.)

The following table shows the conditions of nourishment of the above-named categories of purely town-dwelling work-people, as compared with the minimum assumed by Dr Smith, and with the food-allowance of the cotton operatives during the time of their greatest distress:

Both Sexes	Average Weekly Carbon	Average Weekly Nitrogen
Five in-door occupations . . .	28,876 grains	1,192 grains
Unemployed Lancashire Operatives	28,211 grains	1,295 grains
Minimum quantity to be allowed to the Lancashire Operatives, equal number of males and females	28,600	1,330 grains[46]

One half, or 60/125, of the industrial labour categories investigated, had absolutely no beer, 28% no milk. The weekly average of the liquid means of nourishment in the families varied from seven ounces in the needle-women to 24 3/4 ounces in the stocking-makers. The majority of those who did not obtain milk were needle-women in London. The quantity of bread-stuffs consumed weekly varied from 7 3/4 lbs. for the needle-women to 11 1/2 lbs. for the shoemakers, and gave a total average of 9.9 lbs. per adult weekly. Sugar (treacle, etc.) varied from 4 ounces weekly for the kid-glovers to 11 ounces for the stocking-makers; and the total average per week for all categories was 8 ounces per adult weekly. Total weekly average of butter (fat, etc.) 5 ounces per adult. The weekly average of meat (bacon, etc.) varied from 7 1/4 ounces for the silk-weavers, to 18 1/4 ounces for the kid-glovers; total average for the different categories 13.6 ounces. The weekly cost of food per adult, gave the following average figures: silk-weavers 2s. 2 1/2d., needle-women 2s. 7d., kid-glovers 2s. 9 1/2d., shoemakers 2s 7 3/4d., stocking-weavers 2s. 6 1/4d. For the silk-weavers of Macclesfield the average was only 1s. 8 1/2d. The worst categories were the needle-women, silk-weavers and kid-glovers.[47] Of these facts, Dr Simon in his General Health Report says: 'That cases are innumerable in which defective diet is the cause or the aggravator of disease, can be affirmed by any one who is conversant with poor law medical practice, or with the wards and out-patient rooms of hospitals . . . Yet in this point of view, there is, in my opinion, a very important sanitary context to be added. It must be remembered that privation of food is very reluctantly borne, and that as a rule great poorness of diet will only come when other privations have preceded it. Long before insufficiency of diet is a matter of hygienic concern, long before the physiologist would think of counting the grains of nitrogen and carbon which intervene between life and starvation, the household will have been utterly destitute of material comfort; clothing and fuel will have been even scantier than food – against inclemencies of weather there will have been no adequate protection – dwelling space will have been stinted to the degree in which over-crowding produces or increases disease; of household utensils and furniture there will have been scarcely any – even cleanliness will have been found costly or difficult, and if there still be self-respectful endeavours to maintain it, every such endeavour will represent additional pangs of hunger. The home, too, will be where shelter can be cheapest bought; in quarters where commonly there is least fruit of sanitary supervision, least drainage, least scavenging, least suppression of public nuisances, least or worst water supply, and, if in town, least light and air. Such are the sanitary dangers to which poverty is almost certainly exposed, when it is poverty enough to imply scantiness of food. And while the sum of them is of terrible magnitude against life, the mere scantiness of food is in itself of very serious moment . . . These are painful reflections, especially when it is remembered that the poverty to which they advert is not the deserved poverty of idleness. In all cases it is the poverty of working populations. Indeed, as regards the in-door operatives, the work which obtains the scanty pittance of food, is for the most part excessively prolonged. Yet evidently it is only in a qualified sense that the work can be deemed self-supporting . . . And on a very large scale the nominal self-support can be only a circuit, longer or shorter, to pauperism.'[48]

The intimate connection between the pangs of hunger of the most industrious layers of the working-class, and the extravagant consumption, coarse or refined, of the rich, for which capitalist accumulation is the basis, reveals itself only when the economic laws are known. It is otherwise with the 'housing of the poor'. Every unprejudiced observer sees that the greater the centralisation of the means of production, the greater is the corresponding heaping together of the labourers, within a given space; that therefore the swifter capitalistic accumulation, the more miserable are the dwellings of the working-people. 'Improvements' of towns, accompanying the increase of wealth, by the demolition of badly built quarters, the erection of palaces for banks, warehouses, &c., the widening of streets for business traffic, for the carriages of luxury, and for the introduction of tramways, &c., drive away the poor into even worse and more crowded hiding places. On the other hand, every one knows that the dearness of dwellings is in inverse ratio to their excellence, and that the mines of misery are exploited by house speculators with more profit or less cost than ever were the mines of Potosi. The antagonistic character of capitalist accumulation, and therefore of the capitalistic relations of property generally,[49] is here so evident, that even the official English reports on this subject teem with heterodox onslaughts on 'property and its rights'. With the development of industry, with the accumulation of capital, with the growth and 'improvement' of towns, the evil makes such progress that the mere fear of contagious diseases which do not spare even 'respectability', brought into existence from 1847 to 1864 no less than 10 Acts of Parliament on sanitation, and that the frightened bourgeois in some towns, as Liverpool, Glasgow, &c., took strenuous measures through their municipalities. Nevertheless Dr Simon, in his report of 1865, says: 'Speaking generally, it may be said that the evils are uncontrolled in England.' By order of the Privy Council, in 1864, an inquiry was made into the conditions of the housing of the agricultural labourers, in 1865 of the poorer classes in the towns. The results of the admirable work of Dr Julian Hunter are to be found in the seventh (1865) and eighth (1866) reports on 'Public Health'. To the agricultural labourers, I shall come later. On the condition of town dwellings, I quote, as preliminary, a general remark of Dr Simon. 'Although my official point of view,' he says, 'is one exclusively physical, common humanity requires that the other aspect of this evil should not be ignored . . . In its higher degrees it [i.e., overcrowding] almost necessarily involves such negation of all delicacy, such unclean confusion of bodies and bodily functions, such exposure of animal and sexual nakedness, as is rather bestial than human. To be subject to these influences is a degradation which must become deeper and deeper for those on whom it continues to work. To children who are born under its curse, it must often be a very baptism into infamy. And beyond all measure hopeless is the wish that persons thus circumstanced should ever in other respects aspire to that atmosphere of civilisation which has its essence in physical and moral cleanliness.'[50]

London takes the first place in over-crowded habitations, absolutely unfit for human beings. 'He feels clear,' says Dr Hunter, 'on two points; first, that there are about 20 large colonies in London, of about 10,000 persons each, whose miserable condition exceeds almost anything he has seen elsewhere in England, and is almost entirely the result of their bad house accommodation; and second, that the crowded and dilapidated condition of the houses of these colonies is much worse than was the case 20 years ago.'[51] 'It is not too much to say that life in parts of London and Newcastle is infernal.'[52]

Further, the better-off part of the working-class, together with the small shopkeepers and other elements of the lower middle class, falls in London more and more under the curse of these vile conditions of dwelling, in proportion as 'improvements', and with them the demolition of old streets and houses, advance, as factories and the afflux of human beings grow in the metropolis, and finally as house rents rise with the ground-rents. 'Rents have become so heavy that few labouring men can afford more than one room.'[53] There is almost no house-property in London that is not overburdened with a number of middlemen. For the price of land in London is always very high in comparison with its yearly revenue, and therefore every buyer speculates on getting rid of it again at a jury price (the expropriation valuation fixed by jurymen), or on pocketing an extraordinary increase of value arising from the neighbourhood of some large establishment. As a consequence of this there is a regular trade in the purchase of 'fag-ends of leases'. 'Gentlemen in this business may be fairly expected to do as they do – get all they can from the tenants while they have them, and leave as little as they can for their successors.'[54]

The rents are weekly, and these gentlemen run no risk. In consequence of the making of railroads in the City, 'the spectacle has lately been seen in the East of London of a number of families wandering about some Saturday night with their scanty worldly goods on their backs, without any resting place but the workhouse.'[55] The workhouses are already over-crowded. and the 'improvements' already sanctioned by Parliament are only just begun. If labourers are driven away by the demolition of their old houses, they do not leave their old parish, or at most they settle down on its borders, as near as they can get to it. 'They try, of course, to remain as near as possible to their workshops. The inhabitants do not go beyond the same or the next parish, parting their two-room tenements into single rooms, and crowding even those . . . Even at an advanced rent, the people who are displaced will hardly be able to get an accommodation so good as the meagre one they have left . . . Half the workmen . . . of the Strand . . . walked two miles to their work.'[56] This same Strand, a main thoroughfare which gives strangers an imposing idea of the wealth of London, may serve as an example of the packing together of human beings in that town. In one of its parishes, the Officer of Health reckoned 581 persons per acre, although half the width of the Thames was reckoned in. It will be self-understood that every sanitary measure, which, as has been the case hitherto in London, hunts the labourers from one quarter, by demolishing uninhabitable houses, serves only to crowd them together yet more closely in another. 'Either,' says Dr Hunter, 'the whole proceeding will of necessity stop as an absurdity, or the public compassion (!) be effectually aroused to the obligation which may now be without exaggeration called national, of supplying cover to those who by reason of their having no capital, cannot provide it for themselves, though they can by periodical payments reward those who will provide it for them.'[57] Admire this capitalistic justice! The owner, of land, of houses, the businessman, when expropriated by 'improvements' such as railroads, the building of new streets, &c., not only receives full indemnity. He must, according to law, human and divine, be comforted for his enforced 'abstinence' over and above this by a thumping profit. The labourer, with his wife and child and chattels, is thrown out into the street, and – if he crowds in too large numbers towards quarters of the town where the vestries insist on decency, he is prosecuted in the name of sanitation!

Except London, there was at the beginning of the 19th century no single town in England of 100,000 inhabitants. Only five had more than 50,000. Now there are 28 towns with more than 50,000 inhabitants. 'The result of this change is not only that the class of town people is enormously increased, but the old close-packed little towns are now centres, built round on every side, open nowhere to air, and being no longer agreeable to the rich are abandoned by them for the pleasanter outskirts. The successors of these rich are occupying the larger houses at the rate of a family to each room [. . . and find accommodation for two or three lodgers . . .] and a population, for which the houses were not intended and quite unfit, has been created, whose surroundings are truly degrading to the adults and ruinous to the children.'[58] The more rapidly capital accumulates in an industrial or commercial town, the more rapidly flows the stream of exploitable human material, the more miserable are the improvised dwellings of the labourers.

Newcastle-on-Tyne, as the centre of a coal and iron district of growing productiveness, takes the next place after London in the housing inferno. Not less than 34,000 persons live there in single rooms. Because of their absolute danger to the community, houses in great numbers have lately been destroyed by the authorities in Newcastle and Gateshead. The building of new houses progresses very slowly, business very quickly. The town was, therefore, in 1865, more full than ever. Scarcely a room was to let. Dr Embleton, of the Newcastle Fever Hospital, says: 'There can be little doubt that the great cause of the continuance and spread of the typhus has been the over-crowding of human beings, and the uncleanliness of their dwellings. The rooms, in which labourers in many cases live, are situated in confined and unwholesome yards or courts, and for space, light, air, and cleanliness, are models of insufficiency and insalubrity, and a disgrace to any civilised community; in them men, women, and children lie at night huddled together: and as regards the men, the night-shift succeed the day-shift, and the day-shift the night-shift in unbroken series for some time together, the beds having scarcely time to cool; the whole house badly supplied with water and worse with privies; dirty, unventilated, and pestiferous.'[59] The price per week of such lodgings ranges from 8d. to 3s. 'The town of Newcastle-on-Tyne,' says Dr Hunter, 'contains a sample of the finest tribe of our countrymen, often sunk by external circumstances of house and street into an almost savage degradation.'[60]

As a result of the ebbing and flowing of capital and labour, the state of the dwellings of an industrial town may today be bearable, tomorrow hideous. Or the aedileship of the town may have pulled itself together for the removal of the most shocking abuses. Tomorrow, like a swarm of locusts, come crowding in masses of ragged Irishmen or decayed English agricultural labourers. They are stowed away in cellars and lofts, or the hitherto respectable labourer's dwelling is transformed into a lodging-house whose personnel changes as quickly as the billets in the 30 years' war. Example: Bradford (Yorkshire). There the municipal philistine was just busied with urban improvements. Besides, there were still in Bradford, in 1861, 1,751 uninhabited houses. But now comes that revival of trade which the mildly liberal Mr Forster, the negro's friend, recently crowed over with so much grace. With the revival of trade came of course an overflow from the waves of the ever fluctuating 'reserve army' or 'relative surplus-population'. The frightful cellar habitations and rooms registered in the list,[61] which Dr Hunter obtained from the agent of an Insurance Company, were for the most part inhabited by well-paid labourers. They declared that they would willingly pay for better dwellings if they were to be had. Meanwhile, they become degraded, they fall ill, one and all, whilst the mildly liberal Forster, M. P., sheds tears over the blessings of Free-trade, and the profits of the eminent men of Bradford who deal in worsted. In the Report of September, 1865, Dr Bell, one of the Poor Law doctors of Bradford, ascribes the frightful mortality of fever-patients in his district to the nature of their dwellings. 'In one small cellar measuring 1,500 cubic feet . . . there are ten persons . . . Vincent Street, Green Aire Place, and the Leys include 223 houses having 1,450 inhabitants, 435 beds, and 36 privies . . . The beds – and in that term I include any roll of dirty old rags, or an armful of shavings – have an average of 3.3 persons to each, many have 5 and 6 persons to each, and some people, I am told, are absolutely without beds; they sleep in their ordinary clothes, on the bare boards – young men and women, married and unmarried, all together. I need scarcely add that many of these dwellings are dark, damp, dirty, stinking holes, utterly unfit for human habitations; they are the centres from which disease and death are distributed amongst those in better circumstances, who have allowed them thus to fester in our midst.'[62]

Bristol takes the third place after London in the misery of its dwellings. 'Bristol, where the blankest poverty and domestic misery abound in the wealthiest town of Europe.'[63]

C. The Nomad Population.

We turn now to a class of people whose origin is agricultural, but whose occupation is in great part industrial. They are the light infantry of capital, thrown by it, according to its needs, now to this point, now to that. When they are not on the march, they 'camp'. Nomad labour is used for various operations of building and draining, brick-making, lime-burning, railway-making, &c. A flying column of pestilence, it carries into the places in whose neighbourhood it pitches its camp, small-pox, typhus, cholera, scarlet fever, &c.[64] In undertakings that involve much capital outlay, such as railways, &c., the contractor himself generally provides his army with wooden huts and the like, thus improvising villages without any sanitary provisions, outside the control of the local boards, very profitable to the contractor, who exploits the labourers in two-fold fashion – as soldiers of industry and as tenants. According as the wooden hut contains 1, 2, or 3 holes, its inhabitant, navvy, or whatever he may be, has to pay 1, 3, or 4 shillings weekly.[65] One example will suffice. In September, 1864, Dr Simon reports that the Chairman of the Nuisances Removal Committee of the parish of Sevenoaks sent the following denunciation to Sir George Grey, Home Secretary: – 'Small-pox cases were rarely heard of in this parish until about twelve months ago. Shortly before that time, the works for a railway from Lewisham to Tunbridge were commenced here, and, in addition to the principal works being in the immediate neighbourhood of this town, here was also established the depôt for the whole of the works, so that a large number of persons was of necessity employed here. As cottage accommodation could not be obtained for them all, huts were built in several places along the line of the works by the contractor, Mr Jay, for their especial occupation. These huts possessed no ventilation nor drainage, and, besides, were necessarily over-crowded, because each occupant had to accommodate lodgers, whatever the number in his own family might be, although there were only two rooms to each tenement. The consequences were, according to the medical report we received, that in the night-time these poor people were compelled to endure all the horror of suffocation to avoid the pestiferous smells arising from the filthy, stagnant water, and the privies close under their windows. Complaints were at length made to the Nuisances Removal Committee by a medical gentleman who had occasion to visit these huts, and he spoke of their condition as dwellings in the most severe terms, and he expressed his fears that some very serious consequences might ensue, unless some sanitary measures were adopted. About a year ago, Mr Jay promised to appropriate a hut, to which persons in his employ, who were suffering from contagious diseases, might at once be removed. He repeated that promise on the 23rd July last, but although since the date of the last promise there have been several cases of small-pox in his huts, and two deaths from the same disease, yet he has taken no steps whatever to carry out his promise. On the 9th September instant, Mr Kelson, surgeon, reported to me further cases of small-pox in the same huts, and he described their condition as most disgraceful. I should add, for your (the Home Secretary's) information that an isolated house, called the Pest-house, which is set apart for parishioners who might be suffering from infectious diseases, has been continually occupied by such patients for many months past, and is also now occupied; that in one family five children died from small-pox and fever; that from the 1st April to the 1st September this year, a period of five months, there have been no fewer than ten deaths from small-pox in the parish, four of them being in the huts already referred to; that it is impossible to ascertain the exact number of persons who have suffered from that disease, although they are known to be many, from the fact of the families keeping it as private as possible.'[66]

The labourers in coal and other mines belong to the best-paid categories of the British proletariat. The price at which they buy their wages was shown on an earlier page.[67] Here I merely cast a hurried glance over the conditions of their dwellings. As a rule, the exploiter of a mine, whether its owner or his tenant, builds a number of cottages for his hands. They receive cottages and coal for firing 'for nothing' – i.e., these form part of their wages, paid in kind. Those who are not lodged in this way receive in compensation £4 per annum. The mining districts attract with rapidity a large population, made up of the miners themselves, and the artisans, shopkeepers, &c., that group themselves around them. The ground-rents are high, as they are generally where population is dense. The master tries, therefore, to run up, within the smallest space possible at the mouth of the pit, just so many cottages as are necessary to pack together his hands and their families. If new mines are opened in the neighborhood, or old ones are again set working, the pressure increases. In the construction of the cottages, only one point of view is of moment, the 'abstinence' of the capitalist from all expenditure that is not absolutely unavoidable. 'The lodging which is obtained by the pitman and other labourers connected with the collieries of Northumberland and Durham,' says Dr Julian Hunter, 'is perhaps, on the whole, the worst and the dearest of which any large specimens can be found in England, the similar parishes of Monmouthshire excepted . . . The extreme badness is in the high number of men found in one room, in the smallness of the ground-plot on which a great number of houses are thrust, the want of water, the absence of privies, and the frequent placing of one house on the top of another, or distribution into flats, . . . the lessee acts as if the whole colony were encamped, not resident.'[68]

'In pursuance of my instructions,' says Dr Stevens, 'I visited most of the large colliery villages in the Durham Union . . . With very few exceptions, the general statement that no means are taken to secure the health of the inhabitants would be true of all of them . . . All colliers are bound' ['bound', an expression which, like bondage, dates from the age of serfdom] 'to the colliery lessee or owner for twelve months . . . If the colliers express discontent, or in any way annoy the "viewer", a mark of memorandum is made against their names, and, at the annual "binding", such men are turned off . . . It appears to me that no part of the "truck system" could be worse than what obtains in these densely-populated districts. The collier is bound to take as part of his hiring a house surrounded with pestiferous influences; he cannot help himself, and it appears doubtful whether anyone else can help him except his proprietor (he is, to all intents and purposes, a serf), and his proprietor first consults his balance-sheet, and the result is tolerably certain. The collier is also often supplied with water by the proprietor, which, whether it be good or bad, he has to pay for, or rather he suffers a deduction for from his wages.'[69]

In conflict with 'public opinion', or even with the Officers of Health, capital makes no difficulty about 'justifying' the conditions, partly dangerous, partly degrading, to which it confines the working and domestic life of the labourer, on the ground that they are necessary for profit. It is the same thing when capital 'abstains' from protective measures against dangerous machinery in the factory, from appliances for ventilation and for safety in mines, &c. It is the same here with the housing of the miners. Dr Simon, medical officer of the Privy Council, in his official Report says: 'In apology for the wretched household accommodation . . . it is alleged that mines are commonly worked on lease; that the duration of the lessee's interest (which in collieries is commonly for 21 years), is not so long that he should deem it worth his while to create good accommodation for his labourers, and for the tradespeople and others whom the work attracts; that even if he were disposed to act liberally in the matter, this disposition would commonly be defeated by his landlord's tendency to fix on him, as ground-rent, an exorbitant additional charge for the privilege of having on the surface of the ground the decent and comfortable village which the labourers of the subterranean property ought to inhabit, and that prohibitory price (if not actual prohibition) equally excludes others who might desire to build. It would be foreign to the purpose of this report to enter upon any discussion of the merits of the above apology. Nor here is it even needful to consider where it would be that, if decent accommodation were provided, the cost . . . would eventually fall – whether on landlord, or lessee, or labourer, or public. But in presence of such shameful facts as are vouched for in the annexed reports [those of Dr Hunter, Dr Stevens, &c.] a remedy may well be claimed . . . Claims of landlordship are being so used as to do great public wrong. The landlord in his capacity of mine-owner invites an industrial colony to labour on his estate, and then in his capacity of surface-owner makes it impossible that the labourers whom he collects, should find proper lodging where they must live. The lessee [the capitalist exploiter] meanwhile has no pecuniary motive for resisting that division of the bargain; well knowing that if its latter conditions be exorbitant, the consequences fall, not on him, that his labourers on whom they fall have not education enough to know the value of their sanitary rights, that neither obscenest lodging nor foulest drinking water will be appreciable inducements towards a "strike".'[70]

D. Effect of Crises on the Best-Paid Part of the Working-Class.

Before I turn to the regular agricultural labourers, I may be allowed to show, by one example, how industrial revulsions affect even the best-paid, the aristocracy, of the working-class. It will be remembered that the year 1857 brought one of the great crises with which the industrial cycle periodically ends. The next termination of the cycle was due in 1866. Already discounted in the regular factory districts by the cotton famine, which threw much capital from its wonted sphere into the great centres of the money-market, the crisis assumed, at this time, an especially financial character. Its outbreak in 1866 was signalised by the failure of a gigantic London Bank, immediately followed by the collapse of countless swidling companies. One of the great London branches of industry involved in the catastrophe was iron shipbuilding. The magnates of this trade had not only over-produced beyond all measure during the overtrading time, but they had, besides, engaged in enormous contracts on the speculation that credit would be forthcoming to an equivalent extent. Now, a terrible reaction set in, that even at this hour (the end of March, 1867) continues in this and other London industries.[71] To show the condition of the labourers, I quote the following from the circumstantial report of a correspondent of the *Morning Star*, who, at the end of 1866, and beginning of 1867, visited the chief centres of distress: 'In the East End districts of Poplar, Millwall, Greenwich, Deptford, Limehouse and Canning Town, at least 15,000 workmen and their families were in a state of utter destitution, and 3,000 skilled mechanics were breaking stones in the workhouse yard (after distress of over half a year's duration) . . . I had great difficulty in reaching the workhouse door, for a hungry crowd besieged it . . . They were waiting for their tickets, but the time had not yet arrived for the distribution. The yard was a great square place with an open shed running all round it, and several large heaps of snow covered the paving-stones in the middle. In the middle, also, were little wicker-fenced spaces, like sheep pens, where in finer weather the men worked; but on the day of my visit the pens were so snowed up that nobody could sit in them. Men were busy, however, in the open shed breaking paving-stones into macadam. Each man had a big paving-stone for a seat, and he chipped away at the rime-covered granite with a big hammer until he had broken up, and think! five bushels of it, and then he had done his day's work, and got his day's pay – threepence and an allowance of food. In another part of the yard was a rickety little wooden house, and when we opened the door of it, we found it filled with men who were huddled together shoulder to shoulder for the warmth of one another's bodies and breath. They were picking oakum and disputing the while as to which could work the longest on a given quantity of food – for endurance was the point of honour. Seven thousand . . . in this one workhouse . . . were recipients of relief . . . many hundreds of them . . . it appeared, were, six or eight months ago, earning the highest wages paid to artisans . . . Their number would be more than doubled by the count of those who, having exhausted all their savings, still refuse to apply to the parish, because they have a little left to pawn. Leaving the workhouse, I took a walk through the streets, mostly of little one-storey houses, that abound in the neighbourhood of Poplar. My guide was a member of the Committee of the Unemployed . . . My first call was on an ironworker who had been seven and twenty weeks out of employment. I found the man with his family sitting in a little back room. The room was not bare of furniture, and there was a fire in it. This was necessary to keep the naked feet of the young children from getting frost bitten, for it was a bitterly cold day. On a tray in front of the fire lay a quantity of oakum, which the wife and children were picking in return for their allowance from the parish. The man worked in the stone yard of the workhouse for a certain ration of food, and threepence per day. He had now come home to dinner quite hungry, as he told us with a melancholy smile, and his dinner consisted of a couple of slices of bread and dripping, and a cup of milkless tea . . . The next door at which we knocked was opened by a middle-aged woman, who, without saying a word, led us into a little back parlour, in which sat all her family, silent and fixedly staring at a rapidly dying fire. Such desolation, such hopelessness was about these people and their little room, as I should not care to witness again. "Nothing have they done, sir," said the woman, pointing to her boys, "for six and twenty weeks; and all our money gone – all the twenty pounds that me and father saved when times were better, thinking it would yield a little to keep us when we got past work. Look at it," she said, almost fiercely, bringing out a bank-book with all its well-kept entries of money paid in, and money taken out, so that we could see how the little fortune had begun with the first five shilling deposit, and had grown by little and little to be twenty pounds, and how it had melted down again till the sum in hand got from pounds to shillings, and the last entry made the book as worthless as a blank sheet. This family received relief from the workhouse, and it furnished them with just one scanty meal per day . . . Our next visit was to an iron labourer's wife, whose husband had worked in the yards. We found her ill from want of food, lying on a mattress in her clothes, and just covered with a strip of carpet, for all the bedding had been pawned. Two wretched children were tending her, themselves looking as much in need of nursing as their mother. Nineteen weeks of enforced idleness had brought them to this pass, and while the mother told the history of that bitter past, she moaned as if all her faith in a future that should atone for it were dead . . . On getting outside a young fellow came running after us, and asked us to step inside his house and see if anything could be done for him. A young wife, two pretty children, a cluster of pawn-tickets, and a bare room were all he had to show.'

On the after-pains of the crisis of 1866, the following extract from a Tory newspaper. It must not be forgotten that the East-end of London, which is here dealt with, is not only the seat of the iron ship-building mentioned above,. but also of a so-called 'home-industry' always underpaid. 'A frightful spectacle was to be seen yesterday in one part of the metropolis. Although the unemployed thousands of the East-end did not parade with their black flags *en masse*, the human torrent was imposing enough. Let us remember what these people suffer. They are dying of hunger. That is the simple and terrible fact. There are 40,000 of them . . . In our presence, in one quarter of this wonderful metropolis, are packed – next door to the most enormous accumulation of wealth the world ever saw – cheek by jowl with this are 40,000 helpless, starving people. These thousands are now breaking in upon the other quarters; always half-starving, they cry their misery in our ears, they cry to Heaven, they tell us from their miserable dwellings, that it is impossible for them to find work, and useless for them to beg. The local ratepayers themselves are driven by the parochial charges to the verge of pauperism.' – (*Standard*, 5th April, 1867.)

As it is the fashion amongst English capitalists to quote Belgium as the Paradise of the labourer because 'freedom of labour', or what is the same thing, 'freedom of capital', is there limited neither by the despotism of Trades' Unions, nor by Factory Acts, a word or two on the 'happiness' of the Belgian labourer. Assuredly no one was more thoroughly initiated in the mysteries of this happiness than the late M. Ducpétiaux, inspector-general of Belgian prisons and charitable institutions, and member of the central commission of Belgian statistics. Let us take his work: *Budgets économiques des classes ouvrières de la Belgique*, Bruxelles, 1855. Here we find among other matters, a normal Belgian labourer's family, whose yearly income and expenditure he calculates on very exact data, and whose conditions of nourishment are then compared with those of the soldier, sailor, and prisoner. The family 'consists of father, mother, and four children.' Of these 6 persons 'four may be usefully employed the whole year through.' It is assumed that 'there is no sick person nor one incapable of work, among them,' nor are there 'expenses for religious, moral, and intellectual purposes, except a very small sum for church sittings', nor 'contributions to savings banks or benefit societies', nor 'expenses due to luxury or the result of improvidence'. The father and eldest son, however, allow themselves 'the use of tobacco', and on Sundays 'go to the cabaret', for which a whole 86 centimes a week are reckoned. 'From a general compilation of wages allowed to the labourers in different trades, it follows that the highest average of daily wage is 1 franc 56c. for men, 89 centimes for women, 56 centimes for boys, and 55 centimes for girls. Calculated at this rate, the resources of the family would amount, at the maximum, to 1,068 francs a year . . . In the family . . . taken as typical we have calculated all possible resources. But in ascribing wages to the mother of the family we raise the question of the direction of the household. How will its internal economy be cared for? Who will look after the young children? Who will get ready the meals, do the washing and mending? This is the dilemma incessantly presented to the labourers.'

According to this the budget of the family is:

The father 300 working days at	fr. 1.56	fr. 468
The mother 300 working days at	fr. 89	fr. 267
The boy 300 working days at fr.	fr.56	fr. 168
The girl 300 working days at fr.	fr.55	fr. 165
Total		fr. 1,068

The annual expenditure of the family would cause a deficit upon the hypothesis that the labourer has the food of:

The man of war's man	fr. 1828	Deficit	fr. 760
The soldier	fr. 1473	Deficit	fr. 405
The prisoner	fr. 1112	Deficit	fr. 44

'We see that few labouring families can reach, we will not say the average of the sailor or soldier, but even that of the prisoner. The general average (of the cost of each prisoner in the different prisons during the period 1847–1849), has been 63 centimes for all prisons. This figure, compared with that of the daily maintenance of the labourer, shows a difference of 13 centimes. It must be remarked further, that if in the prisons it is necessary to set down in the account the expenses of administration and surveillance, on the other hand, the prisoners have not to pay for their lodging; that the purchases they make at the canteens are not included in the expenses of maintenance, and that these expenses are greatly lowered in consequence of the large number of persons that make up the establishments, and of contracting for or buying wholesale, the food and other things that enter into their consumption . . . How comes it, however, that a great number, we might say, a great majority, of labourers, live in a more economical way? It is . . . by adopting expedients, the secret of which only the labourer knows;, by reducing his daily rations; by substituting rye-bread for wheat; by eating less meat, or even none at all, and the same with butter and condiments; by contenting themselves with one or two rooms where the family is crammed together, where boys and girls sleep side by side, often on the same pallet; by economy of clothing, washing, decency: by giving up the Sunday diversions; by, in short, resigning themselves to the most painful privations. Once arrived at this extreme limit, the least rise in the price of food, stoppage of work, illness, increases the labourer's distress and determines his complete ruin; debts accumulate, credit fails, the most necessary clothes and furniture are pawned, and finally, the family asks to be enrolled on the list of paupers.' (Ducpétiaux, l.c., pp.151, 154, 155.) In fact, in this 'Paradise of capitalists' there follows, on the smallest change in the price of the most essential means of subsistence, a change in the number of deaths and crimes! (See *Manifesto of the Maatschappij: De Vlamingen Vooruit*, Brussels, 1860, pp.15, 16.) In all Belgium are 930,000 families, of whom, according to the official statistics, 90,000 are wealthy and on the list of voters = 450,000 persons; 390,000 families of the lower middle-class in towns and villages, the greater part of them constantly sinking into the proletariat, = 1,950,000 persons, Finally, 450,000 working-class families = 2,250,000 persons, of whom the model ones enjoy the happiness depicted by Ducpétiaux. Of the 450,000 working-class families, over 200,000 are on the pauper list.

E. The British Agricultural Proletariat.

Nowhere does the antagonistic character of capitalistic product and accumulation assert itself more brutally than in the progress of English agriculture (including cattle-breeding) and the retrogression of the English agricultural labourer. Before I turn to his present situation, a rapid retrospect. Modern agriculture dates in England from the middle of the 18th century, although the revolution in landed property, from which the changed mode of production starts as a basis, has a much earlier date.

If we take the statements of Arthur Young, a careful observer, though a superficial thinker, as to the agricultural labourer of 1771, the latter plays a very pitiable part compared with his predecessor of the end of the 14th century, 'when the labourer . . . could live in plenty, and accumulate wealth,'[72] not to speak of the 15th century, 'the golden age of the English labourer in town and country'. We need not, however, go back so far. In a very instructive work of the year 1777 we read: 'The great farmer is nearly mounted to a level with him [the gentleman]; while the poor labourer is depressed almost to the earth. His unfortunate situation will fully appear, by taking a comparative view of it, only forty years ago, and at present . . . Landlord and tenant . . . have both gone hand in hand in keeping the labourer down.'[73] It is then proved in detail that the real agricultural wages between 1737 and 1777 fell nearly 1/4 or 25 per cent. 'Modern policy,' says Dr Richard Price also, 'is, indeed, more favourable to the higher classes of people; and the consequences may in time prove that the whole kingdom will consist of only gentry and beggars, or of grandees and slaves.'[74]

Nevertheless, the position of the English agricultural labourer from 1770 to 1780, with regard to his food and dwelling, as well as to his self-respect, amusements, &c., is an ideal never attained again since that time. His average wage expressed in pints of wheat was from 1770 to 1771, 90 pints, in Eden's time (1797) only 65, in 1808 but 60.[75]

The state of the agricultural labourer at the end of the Anti-Jacobin War, during which landed proprietors, farmers, manufacturers, merchants, bankers, stockbrokers, army-contractors, &c., enriched themselves so extraordinarily, has been already indicated above. The nominal wages rose in consequence partly of the bank-note depreciation, partly of a rise in the price of the primary means of subsistence independent of this depreciation. But the actual wage-variation can be evidenced in a very simple way, without entering into details that are here unnecessary. The Poor Law and its administration were in 1795 and 1814 the same. It will be remembered how this law was carried out in the country districts: in the form of alms the parish made up the nominal wage to the nominal sum required for the simple vegetation of the labourer. The ratio between the wages paid by the farmer, and the wage-deficit made good by the parish, shows us two things. First, the falling of wages below their minimum; second, the degree in which the agricultural labourer was a compound of wage-labourer and pauper, or the degree in which he had been turned into a serf of his parish. Let us take one county that represents the average condition of things in all counties. In Northamptonshire, in 1795, the average weekly wage was 7s. 6d.; the total yearly expenditure of a family of 6 persons, £36 12s. 5d.; their total income, £29 18s.; deficit made good by the parish, £6 14s. 5d. In 1814, in the same county, the weekly wage was 12s. 2d.; the total yearly expenditure of a family of 5 persons, £54 18s. 4d.; their total income, £36, 2s.; deficit made good by the parish, £18 6s. 4d.[76] In 1795 the deficit was less than 1/4 the wage, in 1814, more than half. It is self-evident that, under these circumstances, the meagre comforts that Eden still found in the cottage of the agricultural labourer, had vanished by 1814.[77] Of all the animals kept by the farmer, the labourer, the *instrumentum vocale*, was, thenceforth, the most oppressed, the worst nourished, the most brutally treated.

The same state of things went on quietly until 'the Swing riots, in 1830, revealed to us (i.e., the ruling classes) by the light of blazing corn-stacks, that misery and black mutinous discontent smouldered quite as fiercely under the surface of agricultural as of manufacturing England.'[78] At this time, Sadler, in the House of Commons, christened the agricultural labourers 'white slaves', and a Bishop echoed the epithet in the Upper House. The most notable political economist of that period – E. G. Wakefield – says: 'The peasant of the South of England . . . is not a freeman, nor is he a slave; he is a pauper.'[79]

The time just before the repeal of the Corn Laws threw new light on the condition of the agricultural labourers. On the one hand, it was to the interest of the middle-class agitators to prove how little the Corn Laws protected the actual producers of the corn. On the other hand, the industrial bourgeoisie foamed with sullen rage at the denunciations of the factory system by the landed aristocracy, at the pretended sympathy with the woes of the factory operatives, of those utterly corrupt, heartless, and genteel loafers, and at their 'diplomatic zeal' for factory legislation. It is an old English proverb that 'when thieves fall out, honest men come by their own,' and, in fact, the noisy, passionate quarrel between the two fractions of the ruling class about the question, which of the two exploited the labourers the more shamefully, was on each hand the midwife of the truth. Earl Shaftesbury, then Lord Ashley, was commander-in-chief in the aristocratic, philanthropic, anti-factory campaign. He was, therefore, in 1845, a favourite subject in the revelations of the *Morning Chronicle* on the condition of the agricultural labourers. This journal, then the most important Liberal organ, sent special commissioners into the agricultural districts, who did not content themselves with mere general descriptions and statistics, but published the names both of the labouring families examined and of their landlords. The following list gives the wages paid in three villages in the neighbourhood of Blandford, Wimbourne, and Poole. The villages are the property of Mr G. Bankes and of the Earl of Shaftesbury. It will be noted that, just like Bankes, this 'low church pope', this head of English pietists, pockets a great part of the miserable wages of the labourers under the pretext of house-rent: –

First Village

(a) Children; (b) Number of Members in Family; (c) Weekly Wage of the Men; (d) Weekly Wage of the Children; (e) Weekly Income of the whole Family; (f) Weekly Rent; (g) Total weekly wage after deduction of Rent; (h) Weekly Income per head

(a)	(b)	(c)	(d)	(e)	(f)	(g)	(h)
		s. d.	s. d.	s. d.	s. d.	s. d.	s. d.
2	4	8 0	–	8 0	2 0	6 0	1 6
3	5	8 0	–	8 0	1 6	6 6	1 3 1/2
2	4	8 0	–	8 0	1 0	7 0	1 9
2	4	8 0	–	8 0	1 0	7 0	1 9
6	8	7 0	1/-, 1/6	10 6	2 0	8 6	1 0
3	5	7 0	1/-, 2/-	7 0	1 4	5 8	1 1

Second Village

(a)	(b)	(c)	(d)	(e)	(f)	(g)	(h)
			s. d.	s. d.	s. d.	s. d.	s. d.
6	8	7 0	1/-, 1/6	10 0	1 6	8 6	1 0
6	8	7 0	1/-, 1/6	7 0	1 3		
8	10	7 0	–	1 3	5 81/2	0 7	
4	6	7 0	–	7 0	1 61/2	5 51/2	0 11
3	5	7 0	–	7 0	1 61/2	5 51/2	1 1

Third Village

(a)	(b)	(c)	(d)	(e)	(f)	(g)	(h)
4	6	7 0	–	7 0	1 0	6 0	1 0
3	5	7 0	1/-, 2/-	11 6	0 10	10 8	2 1 1/2
0	2	5 0	1/-, 2/6	5 0	1 0	4 0	2 0[80]

The repeal of the Corn Laws gave a marvellous impulse to English agriculture.[81] Drainage on the most extensive scale, new methods of

stall-feeding, and of the artificial cultivation of green crops, introduction of mechanical manuring apparatus, new treatment of clay
soils, increased use of numeral manures, employment of the steam-
engine, and of all kinds of new machinery, more intensive cultivation
generally, characterised this epoch. Mr Pusey, Chairman of the
Royal Agricultural Society, declares that the (relative) expenses of
farming have been reduced nearly one half by the introduction of
new machinery. On the other hand, the actual return of the soil rose
rapidly. Greater outlay of capital per acre, and, as a consequence, more
rapid concentration of farms, were essential conditions of the new
method.[82] At the same time, the area under cultivation increased,
from 1846 to 1856, by 464,119 acres, without reckoning the great area
in the Eastern Counties which was transformed from rabbit warrens
and poor pastures into magnificent corn-fields. It has already been
seen that, at the same time, the total number of persons employed in
agriculture fell. As far as the actual agricultural labourers of both sexes
and of all ages are concerned, their number fell from 1,241,396, in
1851, to 1,163, 217 in 1861.[83] If the English Registrar-General, therefore, rightly remarks: 'The increase of farmers and farm-labourers,
since 1801, bears no kind of proportion . . . to the increase of
agricultural produce,'[84] this disproportion obtains much more for the
last period, when a positive decrease of the agricultural population
went hand in hand with increase of the area under cultivation, with
more intensive cultivation, unheard-of accumulation of the capital
incorporated with the soil, and devoted to its working, an augmentation in the products of the soil without parallel in the history of
English agriculture, plethoric rent-rolls of landlords, and growing
wealth of the capitalist farmers. If we take this, together with the swift,
unbroken extension of the markets, viz., the towns, and the reign of
Free-trade, then the agricultural labourer was at last, *post tot discrimina
rerum*, placed in circumstances that ought, *secundum ariem*, to have
made him drunk with happiness.

But Professor Rogers comes to the conclusion that the lot of the
English agricultural labourer of today, not to speak of his predecessor
in the last half of the 14th and in the 15th century, but only compared
with his predecessor from 1770 to 1780, has changed for the worse to
an extraordinary extent, that 'the peasant has again become a serf,' and
a serf worse fed and worse clothed.[85] Dr Julian Hunter, in his epoch-
making report on the dwellings of the agricultural labourers, says:
'The cost of the hind' (a name for the agricultural labourer, inherited
from the time of serfdom) 'is fixed at the lowest possible amount on
which he can live . . . the supplies of wages and shelter are not
calculated on the profit to be derived from him. He is a zero in

farming calculations . . . [86] The means [of subsistence] being always supposed to be a fixed quantity.[87] As to any further reduction of his income, he may say, *nihil habeo nihil curo.* He has no fears for the future, because he has now only the spare supply necessary to keep him. He has reached the zero from which are dated the calculations of the farmer. Come what will, he has no share either in prosperity or adversity.'[88]

In the year 1863, an official inquiry took place into the conditions of nourishment and labour of the criminals condemned to transportation and penal servitude. The results are recorded in two voluminous Blue Books. Among other things it is said: 'From an elaborate comparison between the diet of convicts in the convict prisons in England, and that of paupers in workhouses and of free labourers in the same country . . . it certainly appears that the former are much better fed than either of the two other classes,'[89] whilst 'the amount of labour required from an ordinary convict under penal servitude is about one half of what would be done by an ordinary day-labourer.'[90] A few characteristic depositions of witnesses: John Smith, governor of the Edinburgh prison, deposes: No. 5056. 'The diet of the English prisons [is] superior to that of ordinary labourers in England.' No 50. 'It is the fact . . . that the ordinary agricultural labourers in Scotland very seldom get any meat at all.' Answer No. 3047. 'Is there anything that you are aware of to account for the necessity of feeding them very much better than ordinary labourers? – Certainly not.' No. 3048. 'Do you think that further experiments ought to be made in order to ascertain whether a dietary might not be hit upon for prisoners employed on public works nearly approaching to the dietary of free labourers? . . . '[91] 'He [the agricultural labourer] might say: "I work hard, and have not enough to eat, and when in prison I did not work harder where I had plenty to eat, and therefore it is better for me to be in prison again than here." '[92] From the tables appended to the first volume of the Report I have compiled the annexed comparative summary.

Weekly Amount of Nutriment

(a) Quantity of Nitrogenous Ingredients
(b) Quantity of Non-nitrogenous Ingredients
(c) Quantity of Mineral Matter

	(a)	(b)	(c)	Total
	Ounces	Ounces	Ounces	Ounces
Portland (convict)	28.95	150.06	4.68	183.69
Sailor in the Navy	29.63	152.91	4.52	187.06
Soldier	25.55	114.56	3.94	14.98
Working Coachmaker	24.53	162.06	4.23	190.82
Compositor	21.24	100.83	3.29	139.08[93]

The general result of the inquiry by the medical commission of 1863 on the food of the lowest fed classes, is already known to the reader. He will remember that the diet of a great part of the agricultural labourers' families is below the minimum necessary 'to arrest starvation diseases'. This is especially the case in all the purely rural districts of Cornwall, Devon, Somerset, Wilts, Stafford, Oxford, Berks, and Herts. 'The nourishment obtained by the labourer himself,' says Dr E. Smith, 'is larger than the average quantity indicates, since he eats a larger share . . . necessary to enable him to perform his labour . . . of food than the other members of the family, including in the poorer districts nearly all the meat and bacon . . . The quantity of food obtained by the wife and also by the children at the period of rapid growth, is in many cases, in almost every county, deficient, and particularly in nitrogen.'[94] The male and female servants living with the farmers themselves are sufficiently nourished. Their number fell from 288,277 in 1851, to 204,962 in 1861. 'The labour of women in the fields,' says Dr Smith, 'whatever may be its disadvantages, . . . is under present circumstances of great advantage to the family, since it adds that amount of income which . . . provides shoes and clothing and pays the rent, and thus enables the family to be better fed.'[95] One of the most remarkable results of the inquiry was that the agricultural labourer of England, as compared with other parts of the United Kingdom, 'is considerably the worst fed', as the appended table shows:

Quantities of Carbon and Nitrogen weekly consumed by an average agricultural adult:

	Carbon, grains	Nitrogen, grains
England	46.673	1.594
Wales	48.354	2.031
Scotland	48.980	2.348
Ireland	43.366	2.434[96]

'To the insufficient quantity and miserable quality of the house accommodation generally had,' says Dr Simon, in his official Health Report, 'by our agricultural labourers, almost every page of Dr Hunter's report bears testimony. And gradually, for many years past, the state of the labourer in these respects has been deteriorating, house-room being now greatly more difficult for him to find, and, when found, greatly less suitable to his needs than, perhaps, for centuries had been the case. Especially within the last twenty or thirty years, the evil has been in very rapid increase, and the household circumstances of the labourer are now in the highest degree deplorable. Except in so far as they whom his labour enriches, see fit to treat him with a kind of pitiful indulgence, he is quite peculiarly helpless in the matter. Whether he shall find house-room on the land which he contributes to till, whether the house-room which he gets shall be human or swinish, whether he shall have the little space of garden that so vastly lessens the pressure of his poverty – all this does not depend on his willingness and ability to pay reasonable rent for the decent accommodation he requires, but depends on the use which others may see fit to make of their "right to do as they will with their own". However large may be a farm, there. is no law that a certain proportion of labourers' dwellings (much less of decent dwellings) shall be upon it; nor does any law reserve for the labourer ever so little right in that soil to which his industry is as needful as sun and rain . . . An extraneous element weighs the balance heavily against him . . . the influence of the Poor Law in its provisions concerning settlement and chargeability.[97] Under this influence, each parish has a pecuniary interest in reducing to a minimum the number of its resident labourers: – for, unhappily, agricultural labour instead of implying a safe and permanent independence for the hardworking labourer and his family, implies for the most part only a longer or shorter circuit to eventual pauperism – a pauperism which, during the whole circuit, is so near, that any illness or temporary failure of occupation necessitates immediate recourse to parochial relief – and thus all residence of agricultural population in a parish is glaringly an addition to its poor-rates . . . Large proprietors[98] . . . have but to resolve that there shall be no labourers' dwellings on their estates, and their estates will thenceforth be virtually free from half their responsibility for the poor. How far it has been intended, in the English constitution and law, that this kind of unconditional property in land should be acquirable, and that a landlord "doing as he wills with his own", should be able to treat the cultivators of the soil as aliens, whom he may expel from his territory, is a question which I do not pretend to discuss . . . For that (power) of eviction . . . does not exist only in theory. On a very large scale it prevails in practice – prevails . . . as a main governing condition in the house-hold circumstances of agricultural labour . . . As regards the extent of the evil, it may suffice to refer to the evidence which Dr Hunter has compiled from the last census, that destruction of houses, notwith-standing increased local demands for them, had, during the last ten years, been in progress in 821 separate parishes or townships of England, so that irrespectively of persons who had been forced to become non-resident (that is in the parishes in which they work), these parishes and townships were receiving in 1861, as compared with 1851, a population 5 1/3 per cent. greater, into houseroom 4 1/2 per cent. less . . . When the process of depopulation has completed itself, the result, says Dr Hunter, is a show-village where the cottages have been reduced to a few, and where none but persons who are needed as shepherds, gardeners, or game-keepers, are allowed to live; regular servants who receive the good treatment usual to their class.[99] But the land requires cultivation, and it will be found that the labourers employed upon it are not the tenants of the owner, but that they come from a neighbouring open village, perhaps three miles off, where a numerous small proprietary had received them when their cottages were destroyed in the close villages around. Where things are tending to the above result, often the cottages which stand, testify, in their unrepaired and wretched condition, to the extinction to which they are doomed. They are seen standing in the various stages of natural decay. While the shelter holds together, the labourer is permitted to rent it, and glad enough he will often be to do so, even at the price of decent lodging. But no repair, no improvement shall it receive, except such as its penniless occupants can supply. And when at last it becomes quite uninhabitable – uninhabitable even to the humblest standard of serfdom – it will be but one more destroyed cottage, and future poor-rates will be somewhat lightened. While great owners are thus escaping from poor-rates through the depopulation of lands over which they have control, the nearest town or open village receive the evicted labourers: the nearest, I say, but this 'nearest' may mean three or four miles distant from the farm where the labourer has his daily toil. To that daily toil there will then have to be added, as though it were nothing, the daily need of walking six or eight miles for power of earning his bread. And whatever farmwork is done by his wife and children, is done at the same disadvantage. Nor is this nearly all the toil which the distance occasions him. In the open village, cottage-speculators buy scraps of land, which they throng as densely as they can with the cheapest of all possible hovels. And into those wretched habitations (which, even if they adjoin the open country, have some of the worst features of the worst town residences) crowd the agricultural labourers of England.[100] . . . Nor on the other hand must it be supposed that even when the labourer is housed upon the lands which he cultivates, his household circumstances are generally such as his life of productive industry would seem to deserve. Even on princely estates . . . his cottage . . . may be of the meanest description. There are landlords who deem any stye good enough for their labourer and his family, and who yet do not disdain to drive with him the hardest possible bargain for rent.[101] It may be but a ruinous one-bedroomed hut, having no fire-grate, no privy, no opening window, no water supply but the ditch, no garden – but the labourer is helpless against the wrong . . . And the Nuisances

Removal Acts . . . are . . . a mere dead letter . . . in great part dependent for their working on such cottage-owners as the one from whom his (the labourer's) hovel is rented . . . From brighter, but exceptional scenes, it is requisite in the interests of justice, that attention should again be drawn to the overwhelming preponderance of facts which are a reproach to the civilisation of England. Lamentable indeed, must be the case, when, notwithstanding all that is evident with regard to the quality of the present accommodation, it is the common conclusion of competent observers that even the general badness of dwellings is an evil infinitely less urgent than their mere numerical insufficiency. For years the over-crowding of rural labourers' dwellings has been a matter of deep concern, not only to persons who care for sanitary good, but to persons who care for decent and moral life. For, again and again in phrases so uniform that they seem stereotyped, reporters on the spread of epidemic disease in rural districts, have insisted en the extreme importance of that over-crowding, as an influence which renders it a quite hopeless task, to attempt the limiting of any infection which is introduced. And again and again it has been pointed out that, notwithstanding the many salubrious influences which there are in country life, the crowding which so favours the extension of contagious disease, also favours the origination of disease which is not contagious. And those who have denounced the over-crowded state of our rural population have not been silent as to a further mischief. Even where their primary concern has been only with the injury to health, often almost perforce they have referred to other relations on the subject. In showing how frequently it happens that adult persons of both sexes, married and unmarried, are huddled together in single small sleeping rooms, their reports have carried the conviction that, under the circumstances they describe, decency must always be outraged, and morality almost of necessity must suffer.[102] Thus, for instance, in the appendix of my last annual report, Dr Ord, reporting on an outbreak of fever at Wing, in Buckinghamshire, mentions how a young man who had come thither from Wingrave with fever, 'in the first days of his illness slept in a room with nine other persons. Within a fortnight several of these persons were attacked, and in the course of a few weeks five out of the nine had fever, and one died . . . ' From Dr Harvey, of St George's Hospital, who, on private professional business, visited Wing during the time of the epidemic, I received information exactly in the sense of the above report . . . 'A young woman having fever, lay at night in a room occupied by her father and mother, her bastard child, two young men (her brothers), and her two sisters, each with a bastard child – 10 persons in all. A few weeks ago 13 persons slept in it.'[103]

Dr Hunter investigated 5,375 cottages of agricultural labourers, not only in the purely agricultural districts, but in all counties of England. Of these, 2,195 had only one bedroom (often at the same time used as living-room), 2,930 only two, and 250, more than two. I will give a few specimens culled from a dozen counties.

(1) Bedfordshire

Wrestlingworth. Bedrooms about 12 feet long and 10 broad, although many are smaller than this. The small, one-storeyed cots are often divided by partitions into two bedrooms, one bed frequently in a kitchen, 5 feet 6 inches in height. Rent, £3 a year. The tenants have to make their own privies, the landlord only supplies a hole. As soon as one has made a privy, it is made use of by the whole neighbourhood. One house, belonging to a family called Richardson, was of quite unapproachable beauty. 'Its plaster walls bulged very like a lady's dress in a curtsey. One gable end was convex, the other concave, and on this last, unfortunately, stood the chimney, a curved tube of clay and wood like an elephant's trunk. A long stick served as prop to prevent the chimney from falling. The doorway and window were rhomboidal.' Of 17 houses visited, only 4 had more than one bedroom, and those four over-crowded. The cots with one bedroom sheltered 3 adults and 3 children, a married couple with 6 children, &c.

Dunton. High rents, from £4 to £5; weekly wages of the man, 10s. They hope to pay the rent by the straw-plaiting of the family. The higher the rent, the greater the number that must work together to pay it. Six adults, living with 4 children in one sleeping apartment, pay £3 10s. for it. The cheapest house in Dunton, 15 feet long externally, 10 broad, let for £3. Only one of the houses investigated had 2 bedrooms. A little outside the village, a house whose 'tenants dunged against the house-side,' the lower 9 inches of the door eaten away through sheer rottenness; the doorway, a single opening closed at night by a few bricks, ingeniously pushed up after shutting and covered with some matting. Half a window, with glass and frame, had gone the way of all flesh. Here, without furniture, huddled together were 3 adults and 5 children. Dunton is not worse than the rest of Biggleswade Union.

(2) Berkshire

Beenham. In June, 1864, a man, his wife and 4 children lived in a cot (one-storeyed cottage). A daughter came home from service with scarlet fever. She died. One child sickened and died. The mother and one child were down with typhus when Dr Hunter was called in. The father and one child slept outside, but the difficulty of securing isolation was seen here, for in the crowded market of the miserable village lay the linen of the fever-stricken household, waiting for the wash. The rent of H.'s house, 1s. a-week; one bedroom for man, wife, and 6 children. One house let for 8d. a week, 14 feet 6 inches long, 7 feet broad, kitchen, 6 feet high; the bedroom without window, fireplace, door, or opening, except into the lobby; no garden. A man lived here for a little while, with two grown-up daughters and one grown-up son; father and son slept on the bed, the girls in the passage. Each of the latter had a child while the family was living here, but one went to the workhouse for her confinement and then came home.

(3) Buckinghamshire

30 cottages – on 1,000 acres of land – contained here about 130–140 persons. The parish of *Bradenham* comprises 1,000 acres; it numbered, in 1851, 36 houses and a population of 84 males and 54 females. This inequality of the sexes was partly remedied in 1861, when they numbered 98 males and 87 females; increase in 10 years of 14 men and 33 women. Meanwhile, the number of houses was one less.

Winslow. Great part of this newly built in good style; demand for houses appears very marked, since very miserable cots let at 1s. to 1s. 3d. per week.

Water Eaton. Here the landlords, in view of the increasing population, have destroyed about 20 per cent. of the existing houses. A poor labourer, who had to go about 4 miles to his work, answered the question, whether he could not find a cot nearer: 'No; they know better than to take a man in with my large family.'

Tinker's End, near Winslow. A bedroom in which were 4 adults and 4 children; 11 feet long, 9 feet broad, 6 feet 5 inches high at its highest part; another 11 feet 3 inches by 9 feet, 5 feet 10 inches high, sheltered 6 persons. Each of these families had less space than is considered necessary for a convict. No house had more than one bedroom, not one of them a back-door; water very scarce; weekly rent from 1s. 4d. to 2s. In 16 of the houses visited, only 1 man that earned 10s. a week. The quantity of air for each person under the circumstances just described corresponds to that which he would have if he were shut up in a box of 4 feet measuring each way, the whole night. But then, the ancient dens afforded a certain amount of unintentional ventilation.

(4) Cambridgeshire

Gamblingay belongs to several landlords. It contains the wretchedest cots to be found anywhere. Much straw-plaiting. 'A deadly lassitude, a hopeless surrendering up to filth,' reigns in Gamblingay. The neglect in its centre, becomes mortification at its extremities, north and south, where the houses are rotting to pieces. The absentee landlords bleed this poor rookery too freely. The rents are very high; 8 or 9 persons packed in one sleeping apartment, in 2 cases 6 adults, each with 1 or 2 children in one small bedroom.

(5) Essex

In this county, diminutions in the number of persons and of cottages go, in many parishes, hand in hand. In not less than 22 parishes, however, the destruction of houses has not prevented increase of population, or has not brought about that expulsion which, under the name 'migration to towns', generally occurs. In Fingringhoe, a parish of 3,443 acres, were in 1851, 145 houses; in 1861, only 110. But the people did not wish to go away, and managed even to increase under these circumstances. In 1851, 252 persons inhabited 61 houses, but in 1861, 262 persons were squeezed into 49 houses. In Basilden, in 1851, 157 persons lived on 1,827 acres, in 35 houses; at the end of ten years, 180 persons in 27 houses. In the parishes of Fingringhoe, South Fambridge, Widford, Basilden, and Ramsden Crags, in 1851, 1,392 persons were living on 8,449 acres in 316 houses; in 1861, on the same area, 1,473 persons in 249 houses.

(6) Herefordshire

This little county has suffered more from the 'eviction-spirit' than any other in England. At Nadby, over-crowded cottages generally, with only 2 bedrooms, belonging for the most part to the farmers. They easily let them for £3 or £4 a year, and paid a weekly wage of 9s.

(7) Huntingdon

Hartford had, in 1851, 87 houses; shortly after this, 19 cottages were destroyed in this small parish of 1,720 acres; population in 1831, 452; in 1852, 832; and in 1861, 341. 14 cottages, each with 1 bedroom, were visited. In one, a married couple, 3 grown-up sons, 1 grown-up daughter, 4 children – in all 10; in another, 3 adults, 6 children. One of these rooms, in which 8 people slept, was 12 feet 10 inches long, 12 feet 2 inches broad, 6 feet 9 inches high: the average, without making any deduction for projections into the apartment, gave about 130 cubic feet per head. In the 14 sleeping rooms, 34 adults and 33 children. These cottages are seldom provided with gardens, but many of the inmates are able to farm small allotments at 10s. or 12s. per rood. These allotments are at a distance from the houses, which are without privies. The family 'must either go to the allotment to deposit their ordures,' or, as happens in this place, saving your presence, 'use a closet with a trough set like a drawer in a chest of drawers, and drawn out weekly and conveyed to the allotment to be emptied where its contents were wanted.' In Japan, the circle of life-conditions moves more decently than this.

(8) Lincolnshire

Langtoft. A man lives here, in Wright's house, with his wife, her mother, and 5 children; the house has a front kitchen, scullery, bedroom over the front kitchen; front kitchen and bedroom, 12 feet 2 inches by 9 feet 5 inches; the whole ground floor, 21 feet 2 inches by 9 feet 5 inches. The bedroom is a garret: the walls run together into the roof like a sugar-loaf, a dormer-window opening in front. 'Why did he live here? On account of the garden? No; it is very small. Rent? High, 1s. 3d. per week. Near his work? No; 6 miles away, so that he walks daily, to and fro, 12 miles. He lived there, because it was a tenantable cot,' and because he wanted to have a cot for himself alone, anywhere, at any price, and in any conditions. The following are the statistics of 12 houses in Langtoft, with 12 bedrooms, 38 adults, and 36 children.

Twelve Houses in Langtoft

House	Bedroom	Adults	Children	Number of Persons
No. 1	1	3	5	8
No. 2	1	4	3	7
No. 3	1	4	4	8
No. 4	1	5	4	9
No. 5	1	2	2	4
No. 6	1	5	3	8
No. 7	1	3	3	6
No. 8	1	3	2	5
No. 9	1	2	0	2
No. 10	1	2	3	5
No. 11	1	3	3	6
No. 12	1	2	4	6

(9) Kent

Kennington, very seriously over-populated in 1859, when diphtheria appeared, and the parish doctor instituted a medical inquiry into the condition of the poorer classes. He found that in this locality, where much labour is employed, various cots had been destroyed and no new ones built. In one district stood four houses, named birdcages; each had 4 rooms of the following dimensions in feet and inches:

Kitchen:	9 ft. 5 by 8 ft. 11 by 6 ft. 6
Scullery:	8 ft. 6 by 4 ft. 6 by 6 ft 6
Bedroom:	8 ft. 5 by 5 ft. 10 by 6 ft. 3
Bedroom:	8 ft. 3 by 8 ft. 4 by 6 ft. 3

(10) Northamptonshire

Brinworth, Pickford and *Floore*: in these villages in the winter 20-30 men were lounging about the streets from want of work. The farmers do not always till sufficiently the corn and turnip lands, and the landlord has found it best to throw all his farms together into 2 or 3. Hence want of employment. Whilst on one side of the wall, the land calls for labour, on the other side the defrauded labourers are casting at it longing glances. Feverishly over-worked in summer, and half-starved in winter, it is no wonder if they say in their peculiar dialect, 'the parson and gentlefolk seem frit to death at them.'

At Floore, instances, in one bedroom of the smallest size, of couples with 4, 5, 6 children; 3 adults with 5 children; a couple with grandfather and 6 children down with scarlet fever, &c.; in two houses with two bedrooms, two families of 8 and 9 adults respectively.

(11) Wiltshire

Stratton. 31 houses visited, 8 with only one bedroom. Pentill, in the same parish: a cot let at 1s. 3d. weekly with 4 adults and 4 children, had nothing good about it, except the walls, from the floor of rough-hewn pieces of stones to the roof of worn-out thatch.

(12) Worcestershire

House-destruction here not quite so excessive; yet from 1851 to 1861, the number of inhabitants to each house on the average, has risen from 4.2 to 4.6.

Badsey. Many cots and little gardens here. Some of the farmers declare that the cots are 'a great nuisance here, because they bring the poor.' On the statement of one gentleman: 'The poor are none the better for them; if you build 500 they will let fast enough, in fact, the more you build, the more they want' (according to him the houses give birth to the inhabitants, who then by a law of Nature press on 'the means of housing'). Dr Hunter remarks: 'Now these poor must come from somewhere, and as there is no particular attraction, such as doles, at Badsey, it must be repulsion from some other unfit place, which will send them here. If each could find an allotment near his work, he would not prefer Badsey, where he pays for his scrap of ground twice as much as the farmer pays for his.'

The continual emigration to the towns, the continual formation of surplus-population in the country through the concentration of farms, conversion of arable land into pasture, machinery, &c., and the continual eviction of the agricultural population by the destruction of their cottages, go hand in hand. The more empty the district is of men, the greater is its 'relative surplus-population', the greater is their pressure on the means of employment, the greater is the absolute excess of the agricultural population over the means for housing it, the greater, therefore, in the villages is the local surplus-population and the most pestilential packing together of human beings. The packing together of knots of men in scattered little villages and small country towns corresponds to the forcible draining of men from the surface of the land. The continuous superseding of the agricultural labourers, in spite of their diminishing number and the increasing mass of their products, gives birth to their pauperism. Their pauperism is ultimately a motive to their eviction and the chief source of their miserable housing which breaks down their last power of resistance. and makes them mere slaves of the landed proprietors and the farmers.[104] Thus the minimum of wages becomes a law of Nature to them. On the other hand, the land, in spite of its constant 'relative surplus-population', is at the same time under-populated. This is seen, not only locally at the points where the efflux of men to towns, mines, railroad-making, &c., is most marked. It is to be seen everywhere, in harvest-time as well as in spring and summer, at those frequently recurring times when English agriculture, so careful and intensive, wants extra hands. There are always too many agricultural labourers for the ordinary, and always too few for the exceptional or temporary needs of the cultivation of the soil.[105] Hence we find in the official documents contradictory complaints from the same places of deficiency and excess of labour simultaneously. The temporary or local want of labour brings about no rise in wages, but a forcing of the women and children into the fields, and exploitation at an age constantly lowered. As soon as the exploitation of the women and children takes place on a larger scale, it becomes in turn a new means of making a surplus-population of the male agricultural labourer and of keeping down his wage. In the east of England thrives a beautiful fruit of this vicious circle – the so-called gang-system, to which I must briefly return here.[106]

The gang-system obtains almost exclusively in the counties of Lincoln, Huntingdon, Cambridge, Norfolk, Suffolk, and Nottingham, here and there in the neighbouring counties of Northampton, Bedford, and Rutland. Lincolnshire will serve us as an example. A large part of this county is new land, marsh formerly, or even, as in others of the eastern counties just named, won lately from the sea. The steam-engine has worked wonders in the way of drainage. What were once fens and sandbanks, bear now a luxuriant sea of corn and the highest of rents. The same thing holds of the alluvial lands won by human endeavour, as in the island of Axholme and other parishes on the banks of the Trent. In proportion as the new farms arose, not only were no new cottages built: old ones were demolished, and the supply of labour had to come from open villages, miles away, by long roads that wound along the sides of the hills. There alone had the population formerly found shelter from the incessant floods of the wintertime. The labourers that dwell on the farms of 400–1,000 acres (they are called 'confined labourers') are solely employed on such kinds of agricultural work as is permanent, difficult, and carried on by aid of horses. For every 100 acres there is, on an average, scarcely one cottage. A fen farmer, e.g., gave evidence before the Commission of Inquiry: 'I farm 320 acres, all arable land. I have not one cottage on my farm. I have only one labourer on my farm now. I have four horsemen lodging about. We get light work done by gangs.'[107] The soil requires much light field labour, such as weeding, hoeing, certain processes of manuring, removing of stones, &c. This is done by the gangs, or organised bands that dwell in the open villages.

The gang consists of 10 to 40 or 50 persons, women, young persons of both sexes (13–18 years of age, although the boys are for the most part eliminated at the age of 13), and children of both sexes (6–13 years of age). At the head is the gang-master, always an ordinary agricultural labourer, generally what is called a bad lot, a scapegrace, unsteady, drunken, but with a dash of enterprise and *savoir-faire*. He is the recruiting-sergeant for the gang, which works under him, not under the farmer. He generally arranges with the latter for piece-work, and his income, which on the average is not very much above that of an ordinary agricultural labourer,[108] depends almost entirely upon the dexterity with which he manages to extract within the shortest time the greatest possible amount of labour from his gang. The farmers have discovered that women work steadily only under the direction of men, but that women and children, once set going, impetuously spend their life-force – as Fourier knew – while the adult male labourer is shrewd enough to economise his as much as he can. The gang-master goes from one farm to another, and thus employs his gang from 6 to 8 months in the year. Employment by him is, therefore, much more lucrative and more certain for the labouring families, than employment by the individual farmer, who only employs children occasionally. This circumstance so completely rivets his influence in the open villages that children are generally only to be hired through his instrumentality. The lending out of these individually, independently of the gang, is his second trade.

The 'drawbacks' of the system are the over-work of the children and young persons, the enormous marches that they make daily to and from the farms, 5, 6, and sometimes 7 miles distant; finally, the demoralisation of the gang. Although the gang-master, who, in some districts is called 'the driver', is armed with a long stick, he uses it but seldom, and complaints of brutal treatment are exceptional. He is a democratic emperor, or a kind of Pied Piper of Hamelin. He must therefore be popular with his subjects, and he binds them to himself by the charms of the gipsy life under his direction. Coarse freedom, a noisy jollity, and obscenest impudence give attractions to the gang. Generally the gangmaster pays up in a public house; then he returns home at the head of the procession reeling drunk, propped up right and left by a stalwart virago, while children and young persons bring up the rear, boisterous, and singing chaffing and bawdy songs. On the return journey what Fourier calls '*phanéro-gamie*', is the order of the day. The getting with child of girls of 13 and 14 by their male companions of the same age, is common. The open villages which supply the contingent of the gang, become Sodoms and Gomorrahs,[109] and have twice as high a rate of illegitimate births as the rest of the kingdom. The moral character of girls bred in these schools, when married women, was shown above. Their children, when opium does not give them the finishing stroke, are born recruits of the gang.

The gang in its classical form just described, is called the public, common, or tramping gang. For there are also private gangs. These are made up in the same way as the common gang, but count fewer members, and work, not under a gang-master, but under some old farm servant, whom the farmer does not know how to employ in any better way. The gipsy fun has vanished here, but according to all witnesses, the payment and treatment of the children is worse.

The gang-system, which during the last years has steadily increased,[110] clearly does not exist for the sake of the gang-master. it exists for the enrichment of the large farmers,[111] and indirectly of the landlords.[112] For the farmer there is no more ingenious method of keeping his labourers well below the normal level, and yet of always having an extra hand ready for extra work, of extracting the greatest possible amount of labour with the least possible amount of money[113] and of making adult male labour 'redundant'. From the exposition already made, it will be understood why, on the one hand, a greater or less lack of employment for the agricultural labourer is admitted, while on the other, the gang-system is at the same time declared 'necessary' on account of the want of adult male labour and its migration to the towns.[114] The cleanly weeded land, and the uncleanly human weeds, of Lincolnshire, are pole and counterpole of capitalistic production.[115]

F. Ireland.

In concluding this section, we must travel for a moment to Ireland. First, the main facts of the case.

The population of Ireland had, in 1841, reached 8,222,664; in 1851, it had dwindled to 6,623,985; in 1861, to 5,850,309; in 1866, to 5 1/2 millions, nearly to its level in 1801. The diminution began with the famine year, 1846, so that Ireland, in less than twenty years, lost more than 5/16 ths of its people.[116] Its total emigration from May, 1851, to July, 1865, numbered 1,591,487: the emigration during the years 1861–1865 was more than half a million. The number of inhabited houses fell, from 1851–1861, by 52,990. From 1851–1861, the number of holdings of 15 to 30 acres increased 61,000, that of holdings over 30 acres, 109,000, whilst the total number of all farms fell 120,000, a fall, therefore, solely due to the suppression of farms under 15 acres – i.e., to their centralisation.

Table A Live Stock

Year	Horses Total Number	Horses Decrease	Cattle Total Number	Cattle Decrease	Cattle Increase
1860	619,811	3,606,374			
1861	614,232	5,993	3,471,688	138,316	
1862	602,894	11,338	3,254,890	216,798	
1863	579,978	22,916	3,144,231	110,695	
1864	562,158	17,820	3,262,294		118,063
1865	14,291	14,291	3,493,414		231,120

Year	Sheep Total	Sheep Decrease	Sheep Increase	Pigs Total	Pigs Decrease	Pigs Increase
1860	3,542,080			1,271,072		
1861	3,556,050		13,970	1,102,042	169,030	
1862	3,456,132	99,918		1,154,324		52,282
1863	3,308,204	147,982		1,067,458	86,866	
1864	3,366,941		58,737	1,058,480	8,978	
1865	3,688,742		321,801	1,299,893		241,413

The decrease of the population was naturally accompanied by a decrease in the mass of products. For our purpose, it suffices to consider the 5 years from 1861–1865 during which over half a million emigrated, and the absolute number of people sank by more than 1/3 of a million. From the above table it results: –

Horses Absolute Decrease	Cattle Absolute Decrease	Sheep Absolute Increase	Pigs Absolute Increase
72,358	116,626	146,608	28,819[117]

Let us now turn to agriculture, which yields the means of subsistence for cattle and for men. In the following table is calculated the decrease or increase for each separate year, as compared with its immediate predecessor. The Cereal Crops include wheat, oats, barley, rye, beans, and peas; the Green Crops, potatoes, turnips, marigolds, beet-root, cabbages, carrots, parsnips, vetches. &c.

Table B. *Increase or Decrease in the Area Under Crops and Grass in Acreage*

[Dec. = Decrease   Inc. = Increase]

Year	Cereal Crops Dec. Acres	Green Crops Dec. Acres	Inc. Acres	Grass and Clover Dec. Acres	Inc. Acres	Flax Dec. Acres	Inc. Acres	Total Cultivated Land Dec. Acres	Inc. Acres
1861	15,701	36,974			47,969		19,271	81,873	
1862	72,734	74,785		6,623			2,055	138,841	
1863	144,719	19,358		7,724			63,922	92,431	
1864	122,437	2,317		47,486			87,761		10,493
1865	72,450		25,241	68,970	50,159			28,218	
'61–65	428,041	107,984		82,834			122,850	330,860	

In the year 1865, 127,470 additional acres came under the heading 'grass land', chiefly because the area under the heading of 'bog and waste unoccupied', decreased by 101,543 acres. If we compare 1865 with 1864, there is a decrease in cereals of 246,667 qrs., of which 48,999 were wheat, 166,605 oats, 29,892 barley, &c.: the decrease in potatoes was 446,398 tons, although the area of their cultivation increased in 1865.

Table C. *The Increase or Decrease in the Area Under Cultivation, Product Per Acre, and Total Product of 1865 Compared with 1864*[118]

Product	Cultivated Land (acres) 1864	1865	1865 +	1865 −	Product per Acre 1864	1865
Wheat	276,483	266,989		9,494	cwt. 13.3	13.0 −0.3
Oats	1,814,886	1,745,228		69,658	cwt. 12.1	12.3 +0.2
Barley	172,700	177,102	4,402		cwt. 15.9	14.9 −1.0
Bere, Rye	8,894	10,091	1,197		bere cwt. 16.4	14.8 −1.6
					rye cwt. 8.5	10.4 +1.9
Potatoes	1,039,724	1,066,260	26,536		tons 4.1	3.6 −0.5
Turnips	337,355	334,212		3,143	tons 10.3	9.9 −0.4
Mangold-wurzel	14,673	14,839	316		tons 10.5	13.3 +2.8
Cabbages	31,821	33,622	1,801		tons 9.3	10.4 +1.1
Flax	301,693	251,433		50,260	st (14lb) 34.2	25.2 −9.0
Hay	1,609,569	1,678,493	68,924		tons 1.6	1.8 +0.2

Product	Total Product 1864	1865	1865 +	1865 −
Wheat, qrs	875,782	826,783		48,999
Oats, qrs	7,826,332	7,659,727		166,605
Barley, qrs	761,909	732,017		29,892
Bere, qrs	15,160	13,989		1,171
Rye, qrs	12,680	18,364	5,684	
Potatoes, tons	4,312,388	3,865,990		446,398
Turnips, tons	3,467,659	3,301,683		165,976
Mangold-wurzel, tons	147,284	191,937	44,653	
Cabbages, tons	297,375	350,252	52,877	
Flax, st (14lb)	64,506	39,561		24,945
Hay, tons	2,607,153	3,068,707	461,554	

From the movement of population and the agricultural produce of Ireland, we pass to the movement in the purse of its landlords, larger farmers, and industrial capitalists. It is reflected in the rise and fall of the Income-tax. It may be remembered that Schedule D (profits with the exception of those of farmers), includes also the so-called, 'professional' profits-*i.e.* the incomes of lawyers, doctors, &c.; and the Schedule C. and E., in which no special details are given, include the incomes of employes, officers, State sinecurists, State fundholders, &c.

Table D.   The Income-Tax on the Subjoined Incomes in Pounds Sterling[119]

(A) = Schedule A, Rent of Land   (B) = Schedule B, Farmers' Profits
(D) = Schedule D, Industrial, &c.Profits   Total = Total Schedules A to K

	1860	1861	1862	1863	1864	1865
(A)	13,893,829	13,003,554	13,398,938	13,494,091	13,470,700	13,801,616
(B)	2,765,387	2,773,644	2,937,899	2,938,823	2,930,874	2,946,072
(D)	4,89,652	4,836,203	4,858,800	4,846,497	4,546,147	4,850,199
Total	22,962,885	22,998,394	23,597,574	23,658,631	23,236,298	23,930,340

Under Schedule D., the average annual increase of income from 1853–1864 was only 0.93; whilst, in the same period, in Great Britain, it was 4.58. The following table shows the distribution of the profits (with the exception of those of farmers) for the years 1864 and 1865: –

Table E   Schedule D. Income from Profits (over £60) in Ireland.[120]

Total yearly income of:
    1864   £4,368,610 divided among 17,467 persons.
    1865   £4,669,979 divided among 18,081 persons.
Yearly income over £60 and under £100:
    1864   £238,626 divided among 5,015 persons
    1865   £222,575 divided among 4,703 persons
Of the yearly total income:
    1864   £1,979,066 divided among 11,321 persons
    1865   £2,028,471 divided among 12,184 people
Remainder of the total yearly income:
    1864   £2,150,818 divided among 1,131 persons
    1865   £2,418,933 divided among 1,194 persons
Of these:
    1864   £1,083,906 divided among 910 persons
          £1,066,912 divided among 121 persons
          £430,535 divided among 105 persons
          £646,377 divided among 26 persons
          £262,610 divided among 3 persons
    1865   £1,097,937 divided among 1,044 persons
          £1,320,996 divided among 186 persons
          £584,458 divided among 122 persons
          £736,448 divided among 28 persons
          £264,528 divided among 3 persons

England, a country with fully developed capitalist production, and pre-eminently industrial, would have bled to death with such a drain of population as Ireland has suffered. But Ireland is at present only an agricultural district of England, marked off by a wide channel from the country to which it yields corn, wool, cattle, industrial and military recruits.

The depopulation of Ireland has thrown much of the land out of cultivation, has greatly diminished the produce of the soil,[121] and, in spite of the greater area devoted to cattle breeding, has brought about, in some of its branches, an absolute diminution, in others, an advance scarcely worthy of mention, and constantly interrupted by retrogressions. Nevertheless, with the fall in numbers of the population, rents and farmers' profits rose, although the latter not as steadily as the former. The reason of this is easily comprehensible. On the one hand, with the throwing of small holdings into large ones, and the change of arable into pasture land, a larger part of the whole produce was transformed into surplus-produce. The surplus-produce increased, although the total produce, of which it formed a fraction, decreased. On the other hand, the money-value of this surplus-produce increased yet more rapidly than its mass, in consequence of the rise in the English market-price of meat, wool, &c., during the last 20, and especially during the last 10, years.

The scattered means of production that serve the producers themselves as means of employment and of subsistence, without expanding their own value by the incorporation of the labour of others, are no more capital than a product consumed by its own producer is a commodity. If, with the mass of the population, that of the means of production employed in agriculture also diminished, the mass of the capital employed in agriculture increased, because a part of the means of production that were formerly scattered, was concentrated and turned into capital.

The total capital of Ireland outside agriculture, employed in industry and trade, accumulated during the last two decades slowly, and with great and constantly recurring fluctuations; so much the more rapidly did the concentration of its individual constituents develop. And, however small its absolute increase, in proportion to the dwindling population it had increased largely.

Here, then, under our own eyes and on a large scale, a process is revealed, than which nothing more excellent could be wished for by orthodox economy for the support of its dogma: that misery springs from absolute surplus-population, and that equilibrium is re-established by depopulation. This is a far more important experiment than was the plague in the middle of the 14th century so belauded of Malthusians. Note further: if only the naïveté of the schoolmaster could apply, to the conditions of production and population of the nineteenth century, the standard of the 14th, this naïveté, into the bargain, overlooked the fact that whilst, after the plague and the decimation that accompanied it, followed on this side of the Channel, in England, enfranchisement and enrichment of the agricultural population, on that side, in France, followed greater servitude and more misery.[122]

The Irish famine of 1846 killed more than 1,000,000 people, but it killed poor devils only. To the wealth of the country it did not the slightest damage. The exodus of the next 20 years, an exodus still constantly increasing, did not, as, e.g., the Thirty Years' War, decimate, along with the human beings, their means of production. Irish genius discovered an altogether new way of spiriting a poor people thousands of miles away from the scene of its misery. The exiles transplanted to the United States, send home sums of money every year as travelling expenses for those left behind. Every troop that emigrates one year, draws another after it the next. Thus, instead of costing Ireland anything, emigration forms one of the most lucrative branches of its export trade. Finally, it is a systematic process, which does not simply make a passing gap in the population, but sucks out of it every year more people than are replaced by the births, so that the absolute level of the population falls year by year.[123]

What were the consequences for the Irish labourers left behind and freed from the surplus-population? That the relative surplus-population is today as great as before 1846; that wages are just as low, that the oppression of the labourers has increased, that misery is forcing the country towards a new crisis. The facts are simple. The revolution in agriculture has kept pace with emigration. The production of relative surplus-population has more than kept pace with the absolute depopulation. A glance at Table C shows that the change of arable to pasture land must work yet more acutely in Ireland than in England. In England the cultivation of green crops increases with the breeding of cattle; in Ireland, it decreases. Whilst a large number of acres, that were formerly tilled, lie idle or are turned permanently into grass-land, a great part of the waste land and peat bogs that were unused formerly, become of service for the extension of cattle-breeding. The smaller and medium farmers – I reckon among these all who do not cultivate more than 100 acres – still make up about 8/10ths of the whole number.[124] They are one after the other, and with a degree of force unknown before, crushed by the competition of an agriculture managed by capital, and therefore they continually furnish new recruits to the class of wage-labourers. The one great industry of Ireland, linen-manufacture, requires relatively few adult men and only employs altogether, in spite of its expansion since the price of cotton rose in 1861–1866, a comparatively insignificant part of the population. Like all other great modern industries, it constantly produces, by incessant fluctuations, a relative surplus-population within its own sphere, even with an absolute increase in the mass of human beings absorbed by it. The misery of the agricultural population forms the pedestal for gigantic shirt-factories, whose armies of labourers are, for the most part, scattered over the country. Here, we encounter again the system described above of domestic industry, which in underpayment and over-work, possesses its own systematic means for creating supernumerary labourers. Finally, although the depopulation has not such destructive consequences as would result in a country with fully developed capitalistic production, it does not go on without constant reaction upon the home-market. The gap which emigration causes here, limits not only the local demand for labour, but also the incomes of small shopkeepers, artisans, tradespeople generally. Hence the diminution in incomes between £60 and £100 in Table E.

A clear statement of the condition of the agricultural labourers in Ireland is to be found in the Reports of the Irish Poor Law Inspectors (1870).[125] Officials of a government which is maintained only by bayonets and by a state of siege, now open, now disguised, they have to observe all the precautions of language that their colleagues in England disdain. In spite of this, however, they do not let their government cradle itself in illusions. According to them the rate of wages in the country, still very low, has within the last 20 years risen 50—60 per cent., and stands now, on the average, at 6s. to 9s. per week. But behind this apparent rise, is hidden an actual fall in wages, for it does not correspond at all to the rise in price of the necessary means of subsistence that has taken place in the meantime. For proof, the following extract from the official accounts of an Irish workhouse.

Average Weekly Cost per Head

Year ended	Provisions and Necessaries	Clothing	Total
29th Sept., 1849.	1s. 3d.	3d.	1s. 6d.
29th Sept., 1869.	2s. 7d.	6d.	3s. 1d.

The price of the necessary means of subsistence is therefore fully twice, and that of clothing exactly twice, as much as they were 20 years before.

Even apart from this disproportion, the mere comparison of the rate of wages expressed in gold would give a result far from accurate. Before the famine, the great mass of agricultural wages were paid in kind, only the smallest part in money; today, payment in money is the rule. From this it follows that, whatever the amount of the real wage, its money rate must rise. 'Previous to the famine, the labourer enjoyed his cabin . . . with a rood, or half-acre or acre of land, and facilities for . . . a crop of potatoes. He was able to rear his pig and keep fowl . . . But they now have to buy bread, and they have no refuse upon which they can feed a pig or fowl, and they have consequently no benefit from the sale of a pig, fowl, or eggs.'[126] In fact, formerly, the agricultural labourers were but the smallest of the small farmers, and formed for the most part a kind of rear-guard of the medium and large farms on which they found employment. Only since the catastrophe of 1846 have they begun to form a fraction of the class of purely wage-labourers, a special class, connected with its wage-masters only by monetary relations.

We know what were the conditions of their dwellings in 1846. Since then they have grown yet worse. A part of the agricultural labourers, which, however, grows less day by day, dwells still on the holdings of the farmers in over-crowded huts, whose hideousness far surpasses the worst that the English agricultural labourers offered us in this way. And this holds generally with the exception of certain tracts of Ulster; in the south, in the counties of Cork, Limerick, Kilkenny, &c.; in the east, in Wicklow, Wexford, &c.; in the centre of Ireland, in King's and Queen's County, Dublin, &c.; in the west, in Sligo, Roscommon, Mayo, Galway, &c. 'The agricultural labourers' huts,' an inspector cries out, 'are a disgrace to the Christianity and to the civilisation of this country.'[127] In order to increase the attractions of these holes for the labourers, the pieces of land belonging thereto from time immemorial, are systematically confiscated. 'The mere sense that they exist subject to this species of ban, on the part of the landlords and their agents, has . . . given birth in the minds of the labourers to corresponding sentiments of antagonism and dissatisfaction towards those by whom they are thus led to regard themselves as being treated as . . . a proscribed race.'[128]

The first act of the agricultural revolution was to sweep away the huts situated on the field of labour. This was done on the largest scale, and as if in obedience to a command from on high. Thus many labourers were compelled to seek shelter in villages and towns. There they were thrown like refuse into garrets, holes, cellars and corners, in the worst back slums. Thousands of Irish families, who according to the testimony of the English, eaten up as these are with national prejudice, are notable for their rare attachment to the domestic hearth, for their gaiety and the purity of their home-life, found themselves suddenly transplanted into hotbeds of vice. The men are now obliged to seek work of the neighbouring farmers and are only hired by the day, and therefore under the most precarious form of wage. Hence 'they sometimes have long distances to go to and from work, often get wet, and suffer much hardship, not unfrequently ending in sickness, disease and want.'[129]

'The towns have had to receive from year to year what was deemed to be the surplus-labour of the rural division;'[130] and then people still wonder 'there is still a surplus of labour in the towns and villages, and either a scarcity or a threatened scarcity in some of the country divisions.'[131] The truth is that this want only becomes perceptible 'in harvest-time, or during spring, or at such times as agricultural operations are carried on with activity; at other periods of the year many hands are idle;'[132] that 'from the digging out of the main crop of potatoes in October until the early spring following . . . there is no employment for them;'[133] and further, that during the active times they 'are subject to broken days and to all kinds of interruptions.'[134]

These results of the agricultural revolution – i.e., the change of arable into pasture land, the use of machinery, the most rigorous economy of labour, &c., are still further aggravated by the model landlords, who, instead of spending their rents in other countries, condescend to live in Ireland on their demesnes. In order that the law of supply and demand may not be broken, these gentlemen draw their 'labour-supply . . . chiefly from their small tenants, who are obliged to attend when required to do the landlord's work, at rates of wages, in many instances, considerably under the current rates paid to ordinary labourers, and without regard to the inconvenience or loss to the tenant of being obliged to neglect his own business at critical periods of sowing or reaping.'[135]

The uncertainty and irregularity of employment, the constant return and long duration of gluts of labour, all these symptoms of a relative surplus-population, figure therefore in the reports of the Poor Law administration, as so many hardships of the agricultural proletariat. It will be remembered that we met, in the English agricultural proletariat, with a similar spectacle. But the difference is that in England, an industrial country, the industrial reserve recruits itself from the country districts, whilst in Ireland, an agricultural country, the agricultural reserve recruits itself from the towns, the cities of refuge of the expelled agricultural labourers. In the former, the supernumeraries of agriculture are transformed into factory operatives; in the latter, those forced into the towns, whilst at the same time they press on the wages in towns, remain agricultural labourers, and are constantly sent back to the country districts in search of work.

The official inspectors sum up the material condition of the agricultural labourer as follows: 'Though living with the strictest frugality, his own wages are barely sufficient to provide food for an ordinary family and pay his rent, and he depends upon other sources for the means of clothing himself, his wife, and children . . . The atmosphere of these cabins, combined with the other privations they are subjected to, has made this class particularly susceptible to low fever and pulmonary consumption.'[136] After this, it is no wonder that, according to the unanimous testimony of the inspectors, a sombre discontent runs through the ranks of this class, that they long for the return of the past, loathe the present, despair of the future, give themselves up 'to the evil influence of agitators', and have only one fixed idea, to emigrate to America. This is the land of Cockaigne, into which the great Malthusian panacea, depopulation, has transformed green Erin.

What a happy life the Irish factory operative leads one example will show: 'On my recent visit to the North of Ireland,' says the English Factory Inspector, Robert Baker, 'I met with the following evidence of effort in an Irish skilled workman to afford education to his children; and I give his evidence *verbatim*, as I took it from his mouth. That he was a skilled factory hand, may be understood when I say that he was employed on goods for the Manchester market. "Johnson. – I am a beetler and work from 6 in the morning till 11 at night, from Monday to Friday. Saturday we leave off at 6 p.m., and get three hours of it (for meals and rest). I have five children in all. For this work I get 10s. 6d. a week,; my wife works here also, and gets 5s. a week. The oldest girl who is 12, minds the house. She is also cook, and all the servant we have. She gets the young ones ready for school. A girl going past the house wakes me at half past five in the morning. My wife gets up and goes along with me. We get nothing (to eat) before we come to work. The child of 12 takes care of the little children all the day, and we get nothing till breakfast at eight. At eight we go home. We get tea once a week; at other times we get stirabout, sometimes of oat-meal, sometimes of Indian meal, as we are able to get it. In the winter we get a little sugar and water to our Indian meal. In the summer we get a few potatoes, planting a small patch ourselves; and when they are done we get back to stirabout. Sometimes we get a little milk as it may be. So we go on from day to day, Sunday and week day, always the same the year round. I am always very much tired when I have done at night. We may see a bit of flesh meat sometimes, but very seldom. Three of our children attend school, for whom we pay 1d. a week a head. Our rent is 9d. a week. Peat for firing costs 1s. 6d. a fortnight at the very lowest." '[137] Such are Irish wages, such is Irish life!

In fact the misery of Ireland is again the topic of the day in England. At the end of 1866 and the beginning of 1867, one of the Irish land magnates, Lord Dufferin, set about its solution in *The Times*. '*Wie menschlich von solch grossem Herrn!*'

From Table E. we saw that, during 1864, of £4,368,610 of total profits, three surplus-value makers pocketed only £262,819; that in

1865, however, out of £4,669,979 total profits, the same three virtuosi of 'abstinence' pocketed £274,528; in 1864, 26 surplus-value makers reached to £646,377; in 1865, 28 surplus-value makers reached to £736,448; in 1864, 121 surplus-value makers, £1,066,912; in 1865, 150 surplus-value makers, £1,320,906; in 1864, 1,131 surplus-value makers £2,150,818, nearly half of the total annual profit; in 1865, 1,194 surplus-value makers, £2,418,833, more than half of the total annual profit. But the lion's share, which an inconceivably small number of land magnates in England, Scotland and Ireland swallow up of the yearly national rental, is so monstrous that the wisdom of the English State does not think fit to afford the same statistical materials about the distribution of rents as about the distribution of profits. Lord Dufferin is one of those land magnates. That rent-rolls and profits can ever be 'excessive', or that their plethora is in any way connected with plethora of the people's misery is, of course, an idea as 'disreputable' as 'unsound'. He keeps to facts. The fact is that, as the Irish population diminishes, the Irish rent-rolls swell; that depopulation benefits the landlords, therefore also benefits the soil, and, therefore, the people, that mere accessory of the soil. He declares, therefore, that Ireland is still over-populated, and the stream of emigration still flows too lazily. To be perfectly happy, Ireland must get rid of at least one-third of a million of labouring men. Let no man imagine that this lord, poetic into the bargain, is a physician of the school of Sangrado, who as often as he did not find his patient better, ordered phlebotomy and again phlebotomy, until the patient lost his sickness at the same time as his blood. Lord Dufferin demands a new blood-letting of one-third of a million only, instead of about two millions; in fact, without the getting rid of these, the millennium in Erin is not to be. The proof is easily given.

Number and Extent of Farms in Ireland in 1864[138]

	Number	Acres
(1) Farms not over 1 acre:	48,653	25,394
(2) Farms over 1, not over 5 acres	82,037	288,916
(3) Farms over 5, not over 15 acres	176,368	1,836,310
(4) Farms over 15, not over over 30 acres	136,578	3,051,343
(5) Farms over 30, not over 50 acres	71,961	2,906,274
(6) Farms over 50, not over 100 acres	54,247	3,983,880
(7) Farms over 100 acres	31,927	8,227,807
(8) Total area		26,319,924

Centralisation has from 1851 to 1861 destroyed principally farms of the first three categories, under 1 and not over 15 acres. These above all must disappear. This gives 307,058 'supernumerary' farmers, and reckoning the families the low average of 4 persons, 1,228,232 persons. On the extravagant supposition that, after the agricultural revolution is complete one-fourth of these are again absorbable, there remain for emigration 921,174 persons. Categories 4, 5, 6, of over 15 and not over 100 acres, are, as was known long since in England, too small for capitalistic cultivation of corn, and for sheep-breeding are almost vanishing quantities. On the same supposition as before, therefore, there are further 788,761 persons to emigrate; total, 1,709,532. And as *l'appétit vient en mangeant*, Rentroll's eyes will soon discover that Ireland, with 3 1/2 millions, is still always miserable, and miserable because she is over-populated. Therefore her depopulation must go yet further, that thus she may fulfil her true destiny, that of an English sheep-walk and cattle-pasture.'[139]

Like all good things in this bad world, this profitable method has its drawbacks. With the accumulation of rents in Ireland, the accumulation of the Irish in America keeps pace. The Irishman, banished by sheep and ox, re-appears on the other side of the ocean as a Fenian, and face to face with the old queen of the seas rises, threatening and more threatening, the young giant Republic:

> *Acerba fata Romanos agunt*
> *Scelusque fraternae necis.*

Part 8
The So-Called Primitive Accumulation

Chapter 26
The Secret of Primitive Accumulation

We have seen how money is changed into capital; how through capital surplus-value is made, and from surplus-value more capital. But the accumulation of capital presupposes surplus-value; surplus-value presupposes capitalistic production; capitalistic production presupposes the pre-existence of considerable masses of capital and of labour power in the hands of producers of commodities. The whole movement, therefore, seems to turn in a vicious circle, out of which we can only get by supposing a primitive accumulation (previous accumulation of Adam Smith) preceding capitalistic accumulation; an accumulation not the result of the capitalistic mode of production, but its starting point.

This primitive accumulation plays in Political Economy about the same part as original sin in theology. Adam bit the apple, and thereupon sin fell on the human race. Its origin is supposed to be explained when it is told as an anecdote of the past. In times long gone by there were two sorts of people; one, the diligent, intelligent, and, above all, frugal élite; the other, lazy rascals, spending their substance, and more, in riotous living. The legend of theological original sin tells us certainly how man came to be condemned to eat his bread in the sweat of his brow; but the history of economic original sin reveals to us that there are people to whom this is by no means essential. Never mind! Thus it came to pass that the former sort accumulated wealth, and the latter sort had at last nothing to sell except their own skins. And from this original sin dates the poverty of the great majority that, despite all its labour, has up to now nothing to sell but itself, and the wealth of the few that increases constantly although they have long ceased to work. Such insipid childishness is every day preached to us in the defence of property. M. Thiers, e.g., had the assurance to repeat it with all the solemnity of a statesman to the French people, once so *spirituel.* But as soon as the question of property crops up, it becomes a sacred duty to proclaim the intellectual food of the infant as the one thing fit for all ages and for all stages of development. In actual history it is notorious that conquest, enslavement, robbery, murder – briefly force – play the great part. In the tender annals of Political Economy, the idyllic reigns from time immemorial. Right and 'labour' were from all time the sole means of enrichment, the present year of course always excepted. As a matter of fact, the methods of primitive accumulation are anything but idyllic.

In themselves money and commodities are no more capital than are the means of production and of subsistence. They want transforming into capital. But this transformation itself can only take place under certain circumstances that centre in this, viz., that two very different kinds of commodity-possessors must come face to face and into contact, on the one hand, the owners of money, means of production, means of subsistence, who are eager to increase the sum of values they possess, by buying other people's labour power; on the other hand, free labourers, the sellers of their own labour power, and therefore the sellers of labour. Free labourers, in the double sense that neither they themselves form part and parcel of the means of production, as in the case of slaves, bondsmen, &c., nor do the means of production belong to them, as in the case of peasant-proprietors; they are, therefore, free from, unencumbered by, any means of production of their own. With this polarisation of the market for commodities, the fundamental conditions of capitalist production are given. The capitalist system presupposes the complete separation of the labourers from all property in the means by which they can realise their labour. As soon as capitalist production is once on its own legs, it not only maintains this separation, but reproduces it on a continually extending scale. The process, therefore, that clears the way for the capitalist system, can be none other than the process which takes away from the labourer the possession of his means of production; a process that transforms, on the one hand, the social means of subsistence and of production into capital, on the other, the immediate producers into wage-labourers. The so-called primitive accumulation, therefore, is nothing else than the historical process of divorcing the producer from the means of production. It appears as primitive, because it forms the pre-historic stage of capital and of the mode of production corresponding with it.

The economic structure of capitalist society has grown out of the economic structure of feudal society. The dissolution of the latter set free the elements of the former.

The immediate producer, the labourer, could only dispose of his own person after he had ceased to be attached to the soil and ceased to be the slaver, serf, or bondsman of another. To become a free seller of labour power, who carries his commodity wherever he finds a market, he must further have escaped from the regime of the guilds, their rules for apprentices and journeymen, and the impediments of their labour regulations. Hence, the historical movement which changes the producers into wage-workers, appears, on the one hand, as their emancipation from serfdom and from the fetters of the guilds, and this side alone exists for our bourgeois historians. But, on the other hand, these new freedmen became sellers of themselves only after they had been robbed of all their own means of production, and of all the guarantees of existence afforded by the old feudal arrangements. And the history of this, their expropriation, is written in the annals of mankind in letters of blood and fire.

The industrial capitalists, these new potentates, had on their part not only to disgrace the guild maters of handicrafts, but also the feudal lords, the possessors of the sources of wealth. In this respect, their conquest of social power appears as the fruit of a victorious struggle both against feudal lordship and its revolting prerogatives, and against the guilds and the fetters they laid on the free development of production and the free exploitation of man by man. The *chevaliers d'industrie*, however, only succeeded in supplanting the *chevaliers* of the sword by making use of events of which they themselves were wholly innocent. They have risen by means as vile as those by which the Roman freedman once on a time made himself the master of his *patronus*.

The starting-point of the development that gave rise to the wage-labourer as well as to the capitalist, was the servitude of the labourer. The advance consisted in a change of form of this servitude, in the transformation of feudal exploitation into capitalist exploitation. To understand its march, we need not go back very far. Although we come across the first beginnings of capitalist production as early as the 14th or 15th century, sporadically, in certain towns of the Mediterranean, the capitalistic era dates from the 16th century. Wherever it appears, the abolition of serfdom has been long effected, and the highest development of the middle ages, the existence of sovereign towns, has been long on the wane.

In the history of primitive accumulation, all revolutions are epoch-making that act as levers for the capital class in course of formation; but, above all, those moments when great masses of men are suddenly and forcibly torn from their means of subsistence, and hurled as free and 'unattached' proletarians on the labour market. The expropriation of the agricultural producer, of the peasant, from the soil, is the basis of the whole process. The history of this expropriation, in different countries, assumes different aspects, and runs through its various phases in different orders of succession, and at different periods. In England alone, which we take as our example, has it the classic form.[1]

Chapter 27
Expropriation of the Agricultural Population from the Land

In England, serfdom had practically disappeared in the last part of the 14th century. The immense majority of the population[1] consisted then, and to a still larger extent, in the 15th century, of free peasant proprietors, whatever was the feudal title under which their right of property was hidden. In the larger seignorial domains, the old bailiff, himself a serf, was displaced by the free farmer. The wage-labourers of agriculture consisted partly of peasants, who utilised their leisure time by working on the large estates, partly of an independent special class of wage-labourers, relatively and absolutely few in numbers. The latter also were practically at the same time peasant farmers, since, besides their wages, they had allotted to them arable land to the extent of 4 or more acres, together with their cottages, Besides they, with the rest of the peasants, enjoyed the usufruct of the common land, which gave pasture to their cattle, furnished them with timber, fire-wood, turf, &c.[2] In all countries of Europe, feudal production is characterised by division of the soil amongst the greatest possible number of sub-feudatories. The might of the feudal lord, like that of the sovereign, depended not on the length of his rent-roll, but on the number of his subjects, and the latter depended on the number of peasant proprietors.[3] Although, therefore, the English land, after the Norman Conquest, was distributed in gigantic baronies, one of which often included some 900 of the old Anglo-Saxon lordships, it was bestrewn with small peasant properties, only here and there inter-spersed with great seignorial domains. Such conditions, together with the prosperity of the towns so characteristic of the 15th century, allowed of that wealth of the people which Chancellor Fortescue so eloquently paints in his *Laudes legum Angliae*; but it excluded the possibility of capitalistic wealth.

The prelude of the revolution that laid the foundation of the capitalist mode of production, was played in the last third of the 15th, and the first decade of the 16th century. A mass of free proletarians was hurled on the labour-market by the breaking-up of the bands of feudal retainers, who, as Sir James Steuart well says, 'everywhere uselessly filled house and castle'. Although the royal power, itself a product of bourgeois development, in its strife after absolute sovereignty forcibly hastened on the dissolution of these bands of retainers, it was by no means the sole cause of it. In insolent conflict with king and parliament, the great feudal lords created an incomparably larger proletariat by the forcible driving of the peasantry from the land, to which the latter had the same feudal right as the lord himself, and by the usurpation of the common lands. The rapid rise of the Flemish wool manufactures, and the corresponding rise in the price of wool in England, gave the direct impulse to these evictions. The old nobility had been devoured by the great feudal wars. The new nobility was the child of its time, for which money was the power of all powers. Transformation of arable land into sheep-walks was, therefore, its cry. Harrison, in his *Description of England, prefixed to Holinshed's Chronicles*, describes how the expropriation of small peasants is ruining the country. 'What care our great encroachers?' The dwellings of the peasants and the cottages of the labourers were razed to the ground or doomed to decay. 'If,' says Harrison, 'the old records of euerie manour be sought it will soon appear that in some manour seventeene, eighteene, or twentie houses are shrunk . . . that England was neuer less furnished with people than at the present . . . Of cities and townes either utterly decaied or more than a quarter or half diminished, though some one be a little increased here or there; of townes pulled downe for sheepe-walks, and no more but the lordships now standing in them . . . I could saie somewhat.' The complaints of these old chroniclers are always exaggerated, but they reflect faithfully the impression made on contemporaries by the revolution in the conditions of production. A comparison of the writings of Chancellor Fortescue and Thomas More reveals the gulf between the 15th and 16th century. As Thornton rightly has it, the English working-class was precipitated without any transition from its golden into its iron age.

Legislation was terrified at this revolution. It did not yet stand on that height of civilisation where the 'wealth of the nation' (i.e., the formation of capital, and the reckless exploitation and impoverishing of the mass of the people) figure as the *ultima Thule* of all state-craft. In his history of Henry VII, Bacon says: 'Inclosures at that time (1489) began to be more frequent, whereby arable land (which could not be manured without people and families) was turned into pasture, which was easily rid by a few herdsmen; and tenancies for years, lives, and at will (whereupon much of the yeomanry lived) were turned into demesnes. This bred a decay of people, and (by consequence) a decay of towns, churches, tithes, and the like . . . In remedying of this inconvenience the king's wisdom was admirable, and the parliament's at that time . . . they took a course to take away depopulating enclosures, and depopulating pasturage.' An Act of Henry VII, 1489, cap. 19, forbad the destruction of all 'houses of husbandry' to which at least 20 acres of land belonged. By an Act, 25 Henry VIII, the same law was renewed. It recites, among other things, that many farms and large flocks of cattle, especially of sheep, are concentrated in the hands of a few men, whereby the rent of land has much risen and tillage has fallen off, churches and houses have been pulled down, and marvellous numbers of people have been deprived of the means wherewith to maintain themselves and their families. The Act, therefore, ordains the rebuilding of the decayed farmsteads, and fixes a proportion between corn land and pasture land, &c. An Act of 1533 recites that some owners possess 24,000 sheep, and limits the number to be owned to 2,000.[4] The cry of the people and the legislation directed, for 150 years after Henry VII, against the expropriation of the small farmers and peasants, were alike fruitless. The secret of their inefficiency Bacon, without knowing it, reveals to us. 'The device of King Henry VII,' says Bacon, in his *Essays, Civil and Moral*, Essay 29, 'was profound and admirable, in making farms and houses of husbandry of a standard; that is, maintained with such a proportion of land unto them as may breed a subject to live in convenient plenty, and no servile condition, and to keep the plough in the hands of the owners and not mere hirelings.'[5] What the capitalist system demanded was, on the other hand, a degraded and almost servile condition of the mass of the people. the transformation of them into mercenaries. and of their means of labour into capital. During this transformation period, legislation also strove to retain the 4 acres of land by the cottage of the agricultural wage-labourer, and forbad him to take lodgers into his cottage. In the reign of James I, 1627, Roger Crocker of Front Mill, was condemned for having built a cottage on the manor of Front Mill without 4 acres of land attached to the same in perpetuity. As late as Charles I's reign, 1638, a royal commission was appointed to enforce the carrying out of the old laws, especially that referring to the 4 acres of land. Even in Cromwell's time, the building of a house within 4 miles of London was forbidden unless it was endowed with 4 acres of land. As late as the first half of the 18th century complaint is made if the cottage of the agricultural labourer has not an adjunct of one or two acres of laud. Nowadays he is lucky if it is furnished with a little garden, or if he may rent, far away from his cottage, a few roods. 'Landlords and farmers,' says Dr Hunter, 'work here hand in hand. A few acres to the cottage would make the labourers too independent.'[6]

The process of forcible expropriation of the people received in the 16th century a new and frightful impulse from the Reformation, and from the consequent colossal spoliation of the church property. The Catholic church was, at the time of the Reformation, feudal proprietor of a great part of the English land. The suppression of the monasteries, &c., hurled their inmates into the proletariat. The estates of the church were to a large extent given away to rapacious royal favourites, or sold at a nominal price to speculating farmers and citizens, who drove out, *en masse*, the hereditary sub-tenants and threw their holdings into one. The legally guaranteed property of the poorer folk in a part of the church's tithes was tacitly confiscated.'[7] '*Pauper ubique jacet*,' cried Queen Elizabeth, after a journey through England. In the 43rd year of her reign the nation was obliged to recognise pauperism officially by the introduction of a poor-rate. 'The authors of this law seem to have been ashamed to state the grounds of it, for [contrary to traditional usage] it has no preamble whatever.'[8] By the 16th of Charles I, ch. 4, it was declared perpetual, and in fact only in 1834 did it take a new and harsher form.[9] These immediate results of the Reformation were not its most lasting ones. The property of the church formed the religious bulwark of the traditional conditions of landed property. With its fall these were no longer tenable.[10]

Even in the last decade of the 17th century, the yeomanry, the class of independent peasants, were more numerous than the class of farmers. They had formed the backbone of Cromwell's strength, and, even according to the confession of Macaulay, stood in favourable contrast to the drunken squires and to their servants, the country clergy, who had to marry their masters' cast-off mistresses. About 1750, the yeomanry had disappeared,[11] and so had, in the last decade of the 18th century, the last trace of the common land of the agricultural labourer. We leave on one side here the purely economic causes of the agricultural revolution. We deal only with the forcible means employed.

After the restoration of the Stuarts, the landed proprietors carried, by legal means, an act of usurpation, effected everywhere on the Continent without any legal formality. They abolished the feudal tenure of land, i.e., they got rid of all its obligations to the State, 'indemnified' the State by taxes on the peasantry and the rest of the mass of the people, vindicated for themselves the rights of modern private property in estates to which they had only a feudal title, and, finally, passed those laws of settlement, which, *mutatis mutandis*, had the same effect on the English agricultural labourer, as the edict of the Tartar Boris Godunof on the Russian peasantry.

The 'glorious Revolution' brought into power, along with William of Orange, the landlord and capitalist appropriators of surplus-value.[12] They inaugurated the new era by practising on a colossal scale thefts of state lands, thefts that had been hitherto managed more modestly. These estates were given away, sold at a ridiculous figure, or even annexed to private estates by direct seizure.[13] All this happened without the slightest observation of legal etiquette. The Crown lands thus fraudulently appropriated, together with the robbery of the Church estates, as far as these had not been lost again during the republican revolution, form the basis of the today princely domains of the English oligarchy.[14] The bourgeois capitalists favoured the operation with the view, among others, to promoting free trade in land, to extending the domain of modern agriculture on the large farm-system, and to increasing their supply of the free agricultural proletarians ready to hand. Besides, the new landed aristocracy was the natural ally of the new bankocracy, of the newly-hatched *haute finance*, and of the large manufacturers, then depending on protective duties. The English bourgeoisie acted for its own interest quite as wisely as did the Swedish bourgeoisie who, reversing the process, hand in hand with their economic allies, the peasantry, helped the kings in the forcible resumption of the Crown lands from the oligarchy. This happened since 1604 under Charles X and Charles XI.

Communal property – always distinct from the State property just dealt with – was an old Teutonic institution which lived on under cover of feudalism. We have seen how the forcible usurpation of this, generally accompanied by the turning of arable into pasture land, begins at the end of the 15th and extends into the 16th century. But, at that time, the process was carried on by means of individual acts of violence against which legislation, for a hundred and fifty years, fought in vain. The advance made by the 18th century shows itself in this, that the law itself becomes now the instrument of the theft of the people's land, although the large farmers make use of their little independent methods as well.[15] The parliamentary form of the robbery is that of Acts for enclosures of Commons, in other words, decrees by which the landlords grant themselves the people's land as private property, decrees of expropriation of the people. Sir F. M. Eden refutes his own crafty special pleading, in which he tries to represent communal property as the private property of the great landlords who have taken the place of the feudal lords, when he, himself, demands a 'general Act of Parliament for the enclosure of Commons' (admitting thereby that a parliamentary *coup d'état* is necessary for its transformation into private property), and moreover calls on the legislature for the indemnification for the expropriated poor.[16]

Whilst the place of the independent yeoman was taken by tenants at will, small farmers on yearly leases, a servile rabble dependent on the pleasure of the landlords, the systematic robbery of the Communal lands helped especially, next to the theft of the State domains, to swell those large farms, that were called in the 18th century capital farms[17] or merchant farms,[18] and to 'set free' the agricultural population as proletarians for manufacturing industry.

The 18th century, however, did not yet recognise as fully as the 19th, the identity between national wealth and the poverty of the people. Hence the most vigorous polemic, in the economic literature of that time, on the 'enclosure of commons'. From the mass of materials that lie before me, I give a few extracts that will throw a strong light on the circumstances of the time. 'In several parishes of Hertfordshire,' writes one indignant person, '24 farms, numbering on the average 50–150 acres, have been melted up into three farms.'[19] 'In Northamptonshire and Leicestershire the enclosure of common lands has taken place on a very large scale, and most of the new lordships, resulting from the enclosure, have been turned into pasturage, in consequence of which many lordships have not now 50 acres ploughed yearly, in which 1,500 were ploughed formerly. The ruins of former dwelling-houses, barns, stables, &c.,' are the sole traces of the former inhabitants. 'An hundred houses and families have in some open-field villages dwindled to eight or ten . . . The landholders in most parishes that have been enclosed only 15 or 20 years, are very few in comparison of the numbers who occupied them in their open-field state. It is no uncommon thing for 4 or 5 wealthy graziers to engross a large enclosed lordship which was before in the hands of 20 or 30 farmers, and as many smaller tenants and proprietors. All these are hereby thrown out of their livings with their families and many other families who were chiefly employed and supported by them.'[20] It was not only the land that lay waste, but often land cultivated either in common or held under a definite rent paid to the community, that was annexed by the neighbouring landlords under pretext of enclosure. 'I have here in view enclosures of open fields and lands already improved. It is acknowledged by even the writers in defence of enclosures that these diminished villages increase the monopolies of farms, raise the prices of provisions, and produce depopulation . . . and even the enclosure of waste lands (as now carried on) bears hard on the poor, by depriving them of a part of their subsistence, and only goes towards increasing farms already too large.'[21] 'When,' says Dr Price, 'this land gets into the hands of a few great farmers, the consequence must be that the little farmers' (earlier designated by him 'a multitude of little proprietors and tenants, who maintain themselves and families by the produce of the ground they occupy, by sheep kept on a common, by poultry, hogs, &c., and who therefore have little occasion to purchase any of the means of subsistence') 'will be converted into a body of men who earn their subsistence by working for others, and who will be under a necessity of going to market for all they want . . . There will, perhaps, be more labour, because there will be more compulsion to it . . . Towns and manufactures will increase, because more will be driven to them in quest of places and employ-ment. This is the way in which the engrossing of farms naturally operates. And this is the way in which, for many years, it has been actually operating in this kingdom.'[22] He sums up the effect of the enclosures thus: 'Upon the whole, the circumstances of the lower ranks of men are altered in almost every respect for the worse. From little occupiers of land, they are reduced to the state of day-labourers and hirelings; and, at the same time, their subsistence in that state has become more difficult.'[23] In fact, usurpation of the common lands and the revolution in agriculture accompanying this, told so acutely on the agricultural labourers that, even according to Eden, between 1765 and 1780, their wages began to fall below the minimum, and to be supplemented by official poor-law relief. Their wages, he says, 'were not more than enough for the absolute necessaries of life.'

Let us hear for a moment a defender of enclosures and an opponent of Dr Price. 'Not is it a consequence that there must be depopulation, because men are not seen wasting their labour in the open field . . . If, by converting the little farmers into a body of men who must work for others, more labour is produced, it is an advantage which the nation' (to which, of course, the 'converted' ones do not belong) 'should wish for . . . the produce being greater when their joint labours are employed on one farm, there will be a surplus for manufactures, and by this means manufactures, one of the mines of the nation, will increase, in proportion to the quantity of corn produced.'[24]

The stoical peace of mind with which the political economist regards the most shameless violation of the 'sacred rights of property' and the grossest acts of violence to persons, as soon as they are necessary to lay the foundations of the capitalistic mode of pro-duction, is shown by Sir F. M. Eden, philanthropist and tory, to boot. The whole series of thefts, outrages, and popular misery, that accompanied the forcible expropriation of the people, from the last third of the 15th to the end of the 18th century, lead him merely to the comfortable conclusion: 'The due proportion between arable land and pasture had to be established. During the whole of the 14th and the greater part of the 15th century, there was one acre of pasture to 2, 3, and even 4 of arable land. About the middle of the 16th century the proportion was changed of 2 acres of pasture to 2, later on, of 2 acres of pasture to one of arable, until at last the just proportion of 3 acres of pasture to one of arable land was attained.'

In the 19th century, the very memory of the connection between the agricultural labourer and the communal property had, of course, vanished. To say nothing of more recent times, have the agricultural population received a farthing of compensation for the 3,511,770 acres of common land which between 1801 and 1831 were stolen from them and by parliamentary devices presented to the landlords by the landlords?

The last process of wholesale expropriation of the agricultural population from the soil is, finally, the so-called clearing of estates, i.e., the sweeping men off them. All the English methods hitherto considered culminated in 'clearing'. As we saw in the picture of modern conditions given in a former chapter, where there are no more independent peasants to get rid of, the 'clearing' of cottages begins; so that the agricultural labourers do not find on the soil cultivated by them even the spot necessary for their own housing. But what 'clearing of estates' really and properly signifies, we learn only in the promised land of modern romance, the Highlands of Scotland. There the process is distinguished by its systematic character, by the magnitude of the scale on which it is carried out at one blow (in Ireland landlords have gone to the length of sweeping away several villages at once; in Scotland areas as large as German principalities are dealt with), finally by the peculiar form of property, under which the embezzled lands were held.

The Highland Celts were organised in clans, each of which was the owner of the land on which it was settled. The representative of the clan, its chief or 'great man', was only the titular owner of this property, just as the Queen of England is the titular owner of all the national soil. When the English government succeeded in suppressing the intestine wars of these 'great men', and their constant incursions into the Lowland plains, the chiefs of the clans by no means gave up their time-honoured trade as robbers; they only changed its form. On their own authority they transformed their nominal right into a right of private property, and as this brought them into collision with their clansmen, resolved to drive them out by open force. 'A king of England might as well claim to drive his subjects into the sea,' says Professor Newman.[25] This revolution, which began in Scotland after the last rising of the followers of the Pretender, can be followed through its first phases in the writings of Sir James Steuart[26] and James

Anderson.[27] In the 18th century the hunted-out Gaels were forbidden to emigrate from the country, with a view to driving them by force to Glasgow and other manufacturing towns.[28] As an example of the method[29] obtaining in the 19th century, the 'clearing' made by the Duchess of Sutherland will suffice here. This person, well instructed in economy, resolved, on entering upon her government, to effect a radical cure, and to turn the whole country, whose population had already been, by earlier processes of the like kind, reduced to 15,000, into a sheep-walk. From 1814 to 1820 these 15,000 inhabitants, about 3,000 families, were systematically hunted and rooted out. All their villages were destroyed and burnt, all their fields turned into pasturage. British soldiers enforced this eviction, and came to blows with the inhabitants. One old woman was burnt to death in the flames of the hut, which she refused to leave. Thus this fine lady appropriated 794,000 acres of land that had from time immemorial belonged to the clan. She assigned to the expelled inhabitants about 6,000 acres on the sea-shore – 2 acres per family. The 6,000 acres had until this time lain waste, and brought in no income to their owners. The Duchess, in the nobility of her heart, actually went so far as to let these at an average rent of 2s. 6d. per acre to the clansmen, who for centuries had shed their blood for her family. The whole of the stolen clanland she divided into 29 great sheep farms, each inhabited by a single family, for the most part imported English farm-servants. In the year 1835 the 15,000 Gaels were already replaced by 131,000 sheep. The remnant of the aborigines flung on the sea-shore tried to live by catching fish. They became amphibious and lived, as an English author says, half on land and half on water, and withal only half on both.[30]

But the brave Gaels must expiate yet more bitterly their idolatry, romantic and of the mountains, for the 'great men' of the clan. The smell of their fish rose to the noses of the great men. They scented some profit in it, and let the sea-shore to the great fishmongers of London. For the second time the Gaels were hunted out.[31]

But, finally, part of the sheep-walks are turned into deer preserves. Every one knows that there are no real forests in England. The deer in the parks of the great are demurely domestic cattle, fat as London aldermen. Scotland is therefore the last refuge of the 'noble passion'. 'In the Highlands,' says Somers in 1848, 'new forests are springing up like mushrooms. Here, on one side of Gaick, you have the new forest of Glenfeshie; and there on the other you have the new forest of Ardverikie. In the same line you have the Black Mount, an immense waste also recently erected. From east to west – from the neighbourhood of Aberdeen to the crags of Oban – you have now a continuous line of forests; while in other parts of the Highlands there are the new forests of Loch Archaig, Glengarry, Glenmoriston, &c. Sheep were introduced into glens which had been the seats of communities of small farmers; and the latter were driven to seek subsistence on coarser and more sterile tracks of soil. Now deer are supplanting sheep; and these are once more dispossessing the small tenants, who will necessarily be driven down upon still coarser land and to more grinding penury. Deer-forests [32] and the people cannot co-exist. One or other of the two must yield. Let the forests be increased in number and extent during the next quarter of a century, as they have been in the last, and the Gaels will perish from their native soil . . . This movement among the Highland proprietors is with some a matter of ambition . . . with some love of sport . . . while others, of a more practical cast, follow the trade in deer with an eye solely to profit. For it is a fact, that a mountain range laid out in forest is, in many cases, more profitable to the proprietor than when let as a sheep-walk . . . The huntsman who wants a deer-forest limits his offers by no other calculation than the extent of his purse . . . Sufferings have been inflicted in the Highlands scarcely less severe than those occasioned by the policy of the Norman kings. Deer have received extended ranges, while men have been hunted within a narrower and still narrower circle . . . One after one the liberties of the people have been cloven down . . . And the oppressions are daily on the increase . . . The clearance and dispersion of the people is pursued by the proprietors as a settled principle, as an agricultural necessity, just as trees and brushwood are cleared from the wastes of America or Australia; and the operation goes on in a quiet, businesslike way, &c.'[33]

The spoliation of the church's property, the fraudulent alienation of the State domains, the robbery of the common lands, the usurpation of feudal and clan property, and its transformation into modern private property under circumstances of reckless terrorism, were just so many idyllic methods of primitive accumulation. They conquered the field for capitalistic agriculture, made the soil part and parcel of capital, and created for the town industries the necessary supply of a 'free' and outlawed proletariat.

Chapter 28

Bloody Legislation against the Expropriated, from the End of the 15th Century. Forcing Down of Wages by Acts of Parliament.

The proletariat created by the breaking up of the bands of feudal retainers and by the forcible expropriation of the people from the soil, this 'free' proletariat could not possibly be absorbed by the nascent manufactures as fast as it was thrown upon the world. On the other hand, these men, suddenly dragged from their wonted mode of life, could not as suddenly adapt themselves to the discipline of their new condition. They were turned *en masse* into beggars, robbers, vagabonds, partly from inclination, in most cases from stress of circumstances. Hence at the end of the 15th and during the whole of the 16th century, throughout Western Europe a bloody legislation against vagabondage. The fathers of the present working-class were chastised for their enforced transformation into vagabonds and paupers. Legislation treated them as 'voluntary' criminals, and assumed that it depended on their own good will to go on working under the old conditions that no longer existed.

In England this legislation began under Henry VII.

Henry VIII. 1530: Beggars old and unable to work receive a beggar's licence. On the other hand, whipping and imprisonment for sturdy vagabonds. They are to be tied to the cart-tail and whipped until the blood streams from their bodies, then to swear an oath to go back to their birthplace or to where they have lived the last three years and to 'put themselves to labour'. What grim irony! In 27 Henry VIII the former statute is repeated, but strengthened with new clauses. For the second arrest for vagabondage the whipping is to be repeated and half the ear sliced off; but for the third relapse the offender is to be executed as a hardened criminal and enemy of the common weal.

Edward VI: A statute of the first year of his reign, 1547, ordains that if anyone refuses to work, he shall be condemned as a slave to the person who has denounced him as an idler. The master shall feed his slave on bread and water, weak broth and such refuse meat as he thinks fit. He has the right to force him to do any work, no matter how disgusting, with whip and chains. If the slave is absent a fortnight, he is condemned to slavery for life and is to be branded on forehead or

back with the letter S; if he runs away thrice, he is to be executed as a
felon. The master can sell him, bequeath him, let him out on hire as a
slave, just as any other personal chattel or cattle. If the slaves attempt
anything against the masters, they are also to be executed. Justices of
the peace, on information, are to hunt the rascals down. If it happens
that a vagabond has been idling about for three days, he is to be taken
to his birthplace, branded with a red-hot iron with the letter V on the
breast and be set to work, in chains, in the streets or at some other
labour. If the vagabond gives a false birthplace, he is then to become
the slave for life of this place, of its inhabitants, or its corporation, and
to be branded with an S. All persons have the right to take away the
children of the vagabonds and to keep them as apprentices, the young
men until the 24th year, the girls until the 20th. If they run away, they
are to become up to this age the slaves of their masters, who can put
them in irons, whip them, &c., if they like. Every master may put an
iron ring round the neck, arms or legs of his slave, by which to know
him more easily and to be more certain of him.[1] The last part of this
statute provides, that certain poor people may be employed by a place
or by persons, who are willing to give them food and drink and to find
them work. This kind of parish-slaves was kept up in England until far
into the 19th century under the name of 'roundsmen'.

Elizabeth, 1572: Unlicensed beggars above 14 years of age are to be
severely flogged and branded on the left ear unless some one will take
them into service for two years; in case of a repetition of the offence, if
they are over 18, they are to be executed, unless some one will take
them into service for two years; but for the third offence they are to
be executed without mercy as felons. Similar statutes: 18 Elizabeth, c.
13, and another of 1597.[2]

James I: Any one wandering about and begging is declared a rogue
and a vagabond. Justices of the peace in petty sessions are authorised to
have them publicly whipped and for the first offence to imprison them
for 6 months, for the second for 2 years. Whilst in prison they are
to be whipped as much and as often as the justices of the peace think
fit . . . Incorrigible and dangerous rogues are to be branded with an R
on the left shoulder and set to hard labour, and if they are caught
begging again, to be executed without mercy. These statutes, legally
binding until the beginning of the 18th century, were only repealed
by 12 Anne, c. 23.

Similar laws in France, where by the middle of the 17th century a
kingdom of vagabonds (*truands*) was established in Paris. Even at the
beginning of Louis XVI's reign (Ordinance of July 13th, 1777) every
man in good health from 16 to 60 years of age, if without means of
subsistence and not practising a trade, is to be sent to the galleys. Of

the same nature are the statute of Charles V for the Netherlands (October, 1537), the first edict of the States and Towns of Holland (March 10, 1614), the '*Plakaat*' of the United Provinces (June 26, 1649), &c.

Thus were the agricultural people, first forcibly expropriated from the soil, driven from their homes, turned into vagabonds, and then whipped, branded, tortured by laws grotesquely terrible, into the discipline necessary for the wage system

It is not enough that the conditions of labour are concentrated in a mass, in the shape of capital, at the one pole of society, while at the other are grouped masses of men, who have nothing to sell but their labour power. Neither is it enough that they are compelled to sell it voluntarily. The advance of capitalist production develops a working-class, which by education, tradition, habit, looks upon the conditions of that mode of production as self-evident laws of Nature. The organisation of the capitalist process of production, once fully developed, breaks down all resistance. The constant generation of a relative surplus-population keeps the law of supply and demand of labour, and therefore keeps wages, in a rut that corresponds with the wants of capital. The dull compulsion of economic relations completes the subjection of the labourer to the capitalist. Direct force, outside economic conditions, is of course still used, but only exceptionally. In the ordinary run of things, the labourer can be left to the 'natural laws of production', i.e., to his dependence on capital, a dependence springing from, and guaranteed in perpetuity by, the conditions of production themselves. It is otherwise during the historic genesis of capitalist production. The bourgeoisie, at its rise, wants and uses the power of the state to 'regulate' wages, i.e., to force them within the limits suitable for surplus-value making, to lengthen the working-day and to keep the labourer himself in the normal degree of dependence. This is an essential element of the so-called primitive accumulation.

The class of wage-labourers, which arose in the latter half of the 14th century, formed then and in the following century only a very small part of the population, well protected in its position by the independent peasant proprietary in the country and the guild-organisation in the town. In country and town master and workmen stood close together socially. The subordination of labour to capital was only formal – i.e., the mode of production itself had as yet no specific capitalistic character. Variable capital preponderated greatly over constant. The demand for wage-labour grew, therefore, rapidly with every accumulation of capital, whilst the supply of wage-labour followed but slowly. A large part of the national product, changed later into a fund of capitalist accumulation, then still entered into the consumption-fund of the labourer.

Legislation on wage-labour (from the first, aimed at the exploitation of the labourer and, as it advanced, always equally hostile to him),[3] is started in England by the Statute of Labourers, of Edward III, 1349. The ordinance of 1350 in France, issued in the name of King John, corresponds with it. English and French legislation run parallel and are identical in purport. So far as the labour-statutes aim at compulsory extension of the working-day, I do not return to them, as this point was treated earlier (Chap. 10,Section 5).

The Statute of Labourers was passed at the urgent instance of the House of Commons. A Tory says naively: 'Formerly the poor demanded such high wages as to threaten industry and wealth. Next, their wages are so low as to threaten industry and wealth equally and perhaps more, but in another way.'[4] A tariff of wages was fixed by law for town and country, for piece-work and day-work. The agricultural labourers were to hire themselves out by the year, the town ones 'in open market'. It was forbidden, under pain of imprisonment, to pay higher wages than those fixed by the statute, but the taking of higher wages was more severely punished than the giving them. [So also in Sections 18 and 19 of the Statute of Apprentices of Elizabeth, ten days' imprisonment is decreed for him that pays the higher wages, but twenty-one days for him that receives them.] A statute of 1360 increased the penalties and authorised the masters to extort labour at the legal rate of wages by corporal punishment. All combinations, contracts, oaths, &c.. by which masons and carpenters reciprocally bound themselves, were declared null and void. Coalition of the labourers is treated as a heinous crime from the 14th century to 1825, the year of the repeal of the laws against Trades' Unions. The spirit of the Statute of Labourers of 1349 and of its offshoots, comes out clearly in the fact, that indeed a maximum of wages is dictated by the State, but on no account a minimum.

In the 16th century, the condition of the labourers had, as we know, become much worse. The money wage rose, but not in proportion to the depreciation of money and the corresponding rise in the prices of commodities. Wages, therefore, in reality fell. Nevertheless, the laws for keeping them down remained in force, together with the ear-clipping and branding of those 'whom no one was willing to take into service'. By the Statute of Apprentices 5 Elizabeth, c. 3, the justices of the peace were empowered to fix certain wages and to modify them according to the time of the year and the price of commodities. James I extended these regulations of labour also to weavers, spinners, and all possible categories of workers.[5] George II extended the laws against coalitions of labourers to manufacturers. In the manufacturing period *par excellence*, the capitalist mode of production had become sufficiently strong to render legal regulation of wages as impracticable as it was unnecessary; but the ruling classes were unwilling in case of necessity to be without the weapons of the old arsenal. Still, 8 George II forbade a higher day's wage than 2s. 7 1/2d. for journeymen tailors in and around London, except in cases of general mourning; still, 13 George III, c. 68, gave the regulation of the wages of silk-weavers to the justices of the peace; still, in 1706, it required two judgments of the higher courts to decide, whether the mandates of justices of the peace as to wages held good also for non-agricultural labourers; still, in 1799, an act of Parliament ordered that the wages of the Scotch miners should continue to be regulated by a statute of Elizabeth and two Scotch acts of 1661 and 1671. How completely in the meantime circumstances had changed, is proved by an occurrence unheard-of before in the English Lower House. In that place, where for more than 400 years laws had been made for the maximum, beyond which wages absolutely must not rise, Whitbread in 1796 proposed a legal minimum wage for agricultural labourers. Pitt opposed this, but confessed that the 'condition of the poor was cruel.' Finally, in 1813, the laws for the regulation of wages were repealed. They were an absurd anomaly, since the capitalist regulated his factory by his private legislation, and could by the poor-rates make up the wage of the agricultural labourer to the indispensable minimum. The provisions of the labour statutes as to contracts between master and workman, as to giving notice and the like, which only allow of a civil action against the contract-breaking master, but on the contrary permit a criminal action against the contract-breaking workman, are to this hour (1873) in full force. The barbarous laws against Trades' Unions fell in 1825 before the threatening bearing of the proletariat. Despite this, they fell only in part. Certain beautiful fragments of the old statute vanished only in 1859. Finally, the act of Parliament of June 29, 1871, made a pretence of removing the last traces of this class of legislation by legal recognition of Trades' Unions. But an act of Parliament of the same date (an act to amend the criminal law relating to violence, threats, and molestation), re-established, in point of fact, the former state of things in a new shape. By this Parliamentary *escamotage* the means which the labourers could use in a strike or lock-out were withdrawn from the laws common to all citizens, and placed under exceptional penal legislation, the interpretation of which fell to the masters themselves in their capacity as justices of the peace. Two years earlier, the same House of Commons and the same Mr Gladstone in the well-known straightforward fashion brought in a bill for the abolition of all exceptional penal legislation against the working-class. But this was never allowed to go beyond the second reading, and the matter was thus protracted until at last the 'great Liberal party', by an alliance with the Tories, found courage to turn against the very proletariat that had carried it into power. Not content with this treachery, the 'great Liberal party' allowed the English judges, ever complaisant in the service of the ruling classes, to dig up again the earlier laws against 'conspiracy', and to apply them to coalitions of labourers. We see that only against its will and under the pressure of the masses did the English Parliament give up the laws against Strikes and Trades' Unions, after it had itself, for 500 years, held, with shameless egoism, the position of a permanent Trades' Union of the capitalists against the labourers.

During the very first storms of the revolution, the French bourgeoisie dared to take away from the workers the right of association but just acquired. By a decree of June 14, 1791, they declared all coalition of the workers as 'an attempt against liberty and the declaration of the rights of man', punishable by a fine of 500 livres, together with deprivation of the rights of an active citizen for one year.[6] This law which, by means of State compulsion, confined the struggle between capital and labour within limits comfortable for capital, has outlived revolutions and changes of dynasties. Even the Reign of Terror left it untouched. It was but quite recently struck out of the Penal Code. Nothing is more characteristic than the pretext for this bourgeois *coup d'état*. 'Granting,' says Chapelier, the reporter of the Select Committee on this law, 'that wages ought to be a little higher than they are, . . . that they ought to be high enough for him that receives them, to be free from that state of absolute dependence due to the want of the necessaries of life, and which is almost that of slavery,' yet the workers must not be allowed to come to any understanding about their own interests, nor to act in common and thereby lessen their 'absolute dependence, which is almost that of slavery'; because, forsooth, in doing this they injure 'the freedom of their *ci-devant* masters, the present entrepreneurs,' and because a coalition against the despotism of the quondam masters of the corporations is − guess what! − is a restoration of the corporations abolished by the French constitution.[7]

Chapter 29
Genesis of the Capitalist Farmer

Now that we have considered the forcible creation of a class of outlawed proletarians, the bloody discipline that turned them into wage-labourers, the disgraceful action of the State which employed the police to accelerate the accumulation of capital by increasing the degree of exploitation of labour, the question remains: whence came the capitalists originally? For the expropriation of the agricultural population creates, directly, none but the greatest landed proprietors. As far, however, as concerns the genesis of the farmer, we can, so to say, put our hand on it, because it is a slow process evolving through many centuries. The serfs, as well as the free small proprietors, held land under very different tenures, and were therefore emancipated under very different economic conditions. In England the first form of the farmer is the bailiff, himself a serf. His position is similar to that of the old Roman *villicus*, only in a more limited sphere of action. During the second half of the 14th century he is replaced by a farmer, whom the landlord provided with seed, cattle and implements. His condition is not very different from that of the peasant. Only he exploits more wage-labour. Soon he becomes a *metayer*, a half-farmer. He advances one part of the agricultural stock, the landlord the other. The two divide the total product in proportions determined by contract. This form quickly disappears in England, to give the place to the farmer proper, who makes his own capital breed by employing wage-labourers, and pays a part of the surplus-product, in money or in kind, to the landlord as rent. So long, during the 15th century, as the independent peasant and the farm-labourer working for himself as well as for wages, enriched themselves by their own labour, the circumstances of the farmer, and his field of production, were equally mediocre. The agricultural revolution which commenced in the last third of the 15th century, and continued during almost the whole of the 16th (excepting, however, its last decade), enriched him just as speedily as it impoverished the mass of the agricultural people.[1]

The usurpation of the common lands allowed him to augment greatly his stock of cattle, almost without cost, whilst they yielded him a richer supply of manure for the tillage of the soil. To this was added in the 16th century a very important element. At that time the contracts for farms ran for a long time, often for 99 years. The progressive fall in the value of the precious metals, and therefore of money, brought the farmers golden fruit. Apart from all the other circumstances discussed above, it lowered wages. A portion of the latter was now added to the profits of the farm. The continuous rise in the price of corn, wool, meat, in a word of all agricultural produce, swelled the money capital of the farm without any action on his part, whilst the rent he paid (being calculated on the old value of money) diminished in reality.[2] Thus they grew rich at the expense both of their labourers and their landlords. No wonder, therefore, that England, at the end of the 16th century, had a class of capitalist farmers, rich, considering the circumstances of the time.[3]

Chapter 30

Reaction of the Agricultural Revolution on Industry. Creation of the Home-Market for Industrial Capital

The expropriation and expulsion of the agricultural population, intermittent but renewed again and again, supplied, as we saw, the town industries with a mass of proletarians entirely unconnected with the corporate guilds and unfettered by them; a fortunate circumstance that makes old A. Anderson (not to be confounded with James Anderson), in his *History of Commerce*, believe in the direct intervention of Providence. We must still pause a moment on this element of primitive accumulation. The thinning-out of the independent, self-supporting peasants not only brought about the crowding together of the industrial proletariat, in the way that Geoffroy Saint Hilaire explained the condensation of cosmical matter at one place, by its rarefaction at another.[1] In spite of the smaller number of its cultivators, the soil brought forth as much or more produce, after as before, because the revolution in the conditions of landed property was accompanied by improved methods of culture, greater co-operation, concentration of the means of production, &c., and because not only were the agricultural wage-labourers put on the strain more intensely,[2] but the field of production on which they worked for themselves became more and more contracted. With the setting free of a part of the agricultural population, therefore, their former means of nourishment were also set free. They were now transformed into material elements of variable capital. The peasant, expropriated and cast adrift, must buy their value in the form of wages, from his new master, the industrial capitalist. That which holds good of the means of subsistence holds with the raw materials of industry dependent upon home agriculture. They were transformed into an element of constant capital. Suppose, e.g., a part of the Westphalian peasants, who, at the time of Frederick II, all span flax, forcibly expropriated and hunted from the soil; and the other part that remained, turned into day-labourers of large farmers. At the same time arise large establishments for flax-spinning and weaving, in which the men 'set free' now work for wages. The flax looks exactly as before. Not a fibre of it is changed, but a new social soul has popped into its body. It forms now a part of the constant capital of the master manufacturer. Formerly divided among a number of small producers, who cultivated it themselves and with their families spun it in retail fashion, it is now concentrated in the hand of one capitalist, who sets others to spin and weave it for him. The extra labour expended in flax-spinning realised itself formerly in extra income to numerous peasant families, or maybe, in Frederick II's time, in *taxes pour le roi de Prusse*. It realises itself now in profit for a few capitalists. The spindles and looms, formerly scattered over the face of the country, are now crowded together in a few great labour-barracks, together with the labourers and the raw material. And spindles, looms, raw material, are now transformed from means of independent existence for the spinners and weavers, into means for commanding them and sucking out of them unpaid labour.[3] One does not perceive, when looking at the large manufactories and the large farms, that they have originated from the throwing into one of many small centres of production, and have been built up by the expropriation of many small independent producers. Nevertheless, the popular intuition was not at fault. In the time of Mirabeau, the lion of the Revolution, the great manufactories were still called *manufactures réunies*, workshops thrown into one, as we speak of fields thrown into one. Says Mirabeau: 'We are only paying attention to the grand manufactories, in which hundreds of men work under a director and which are commonly called *manufactures réunies*. Those where a very large number of labourers work, each separately and on his own account, are hardly considered; they are placed at an infinite distance from the others. This is a great error, as the latter alone make a really important object of national prosperity . . . The large workshop (*manufacture réunie*) will enrich prodigiously one or two entrepreneurs, but the labourers will only be journeymen, paid more or less, and will not have any share in the success of the undertaking. In the discrete workshop (*manufacture séparée*), on the contrary, no one will become rich, but many labourers will be comfortable; the saving and the industrious will be able to amass a little capital, to put by a little for a birth of a child, for an illness, for themselves or their belongings. The number of saving and industrious labourers will increase, because they will see in good conduct, in activity, a means of essentially bettering their condition, and not of obtaining a small rise in wages that can never be of any importance for the future, and whose sole result is to place men in the position to live a little better, but only from day to day . . . The large workshops, undertakings of certain private persons who pay labourers from day to day to work for their gain, may be able to put these private individuals at their ease, but they will never be an object worth the attention of governments. Discrete workshops, for the most part combined with cultivation of small holdings, are the only free ones.'[4] The expropriation and eviction of a part of the agricultural population not only set free for industrial capital, the labourers, their means of subsistence, and material for labour; it also created the home-market.

In fact, the events that transformed the small peasants into wage-labourers, and their means of subsistence and of labour into material elements of capital, created, at the same time, a home-market for the latter. Formerly, the peasant family produced the means of subsistence and the raw materials, which they themselves, for the most part, consumed. These raw materials and means of subsistence have now become commodities; the large farmer sells them, he finds his market in manufactures. Yarn, linen, coarse woollen stuffs – things whose raw materials had been within the reach of every peasant family, had been spun and woven by it for its own use – were now transformed into articles of manufacture, to which the country districts at once served for markets. The many scattered customers, whom stray artisans until now had found in the numerous small producers working on their own account, concentrate themselves now into one great market provided for by industrial capital.[5] Thus, hand in hand with the expropriation of the self-supporting peasants, with their separation from their means of production, goes the destruction of rural domestic industry, the process of separation between manufacture and agriculture. And only the destruction of rural domestic industry can give the internal market of a country that extension and consistence which the capitalist mode of production requires. Still the manufacturing period, properly so called, does not succeed in carrying out this transformation radically and completely. It will be remembered that manufacture, properly so called, conquers but partially the domain of national production, and always rests on the handicrafts of the town and the domestic industry of the rural districts as its ultimate basis. If it destroys these in one form, in particular branches, at certain points, it calls them up again elsewhere, because it needs them for the preparation of raw material up to a certain point. It produces, therefore, a new class of small villagers who, while following the cultivation of the soil as an accessory calling, find their chief occupation in industrial labour, the products of which they sell to the manufacturers directly, or through the medium of merchants. This is one, though not the chief, cause of a phenomenon which, at first, puzzles the student of English history. From the last third of the 15th century he finds continually complaints, only interrupted at certain intervals, about the encroachment of capitalist farming in the country districts, and the progressive destruction of the peasantry. On the other hand, he always finds this peasantry turning up again, although in diminished number, and always under worse conditions. The chief reason is: England is at one time chiefly a cultivator of corn, at another chiefly a breeder of cattle, in alternate periods, and with these the extent of peasant cultivation fluctuates. Modern Industry alone, and finally, supplies, in machinery, the lasting basis of capitalistic agriculture, expropriates radically the enormous majority of the agricultural population, and completes the separation between agriculture and rural domestic industry, whose roots – spinning and weaving – it tears up.[6] It therefore also, for the first time, conquers for industrial capital the entire home-market.[7]

Chapter 31
Genesis of the Industrial Capitalist

The genesis of the industrial[1] capitalist did not proceed in such a gradual way as that of the farmer. Doubtless many small guild-masters, and yet more independent small artisans, or even wage-labourers, transformed themselves into small capitalists, and (by gradually extending exploitation of wage-labour and corresponding accumulation) into full-blown capitalists. In the infancy of capitalist production, things often happened as in the infancy of medieval towns, where the question, which of the escaped serfs should be master and which servant, was in great part decided by the earlier or later date of their flight. The snail's pace of this method corresponded in no wise with the commercial requirements of the new world-market that the great discoveries of the end of the 15th century created. But the middle ages had handed down two distinct forms of capital, which mature in the most different economic social formations, and which before the era of the capitalist mode of production, are considered as capital *quand même* – usurer's capital and merchant's capital.

'At present, all the wealth of society goes first into the possession of the capitalist . . . he pays the landowner his rent, the labourer his wages, the tax and tithe gatherer their claims, and keeps a large, indeed the largest, and a continually augmenting share, of the annual produce of labour for himself. The capitalist may now be said to be the first owner of all the wealth of the community, though no law has conferred on him the right to this property . . . this change has been effected by the taking of interest on capital . . . and it is not a little curious that all the law-givers of Europe endeavoured to prevent this by statutes, viz., statutes against usury . . . The power of the capitalist over all the wealth of the country is a complete change in the right of property, and by what law, or series of laws, was it effected?'[2] The author should have remembered that revolutions are not made by laws.

The money capital formed by means of usury and commerce was prevented from turning into industrial capital, in the country by the feudal constitution, in the towns by the guild organisation.[3] These fetters vanished with the dissolution of feudal society, with the expropriation and partial eviction of the country population. The new manufactures were established at sea-ports, or at inland points beyond the control of the old municipalities and their guilds. Hence in England an embittered struggle of the corporate towns against these new industrial nurseries.

The discovery of gold and silver in America, the extirpation, enslavement and entombment in mines of the aboriginal population, the beginning of the conquest and looting of the East Indies, the turning of Africa into a warren for the commercial hunting of black-skins, signalised the rosy dawn of the era of capitalist production. These idyllic proceedings are the chief momenta of primitive accumulation. On their heels treads the commercial war of the European nations, with the globe for a theatre. It begins with the revolt of the Netherlands from Spain, assumes giant dimensions in England's Anti-Jacobin War, and is still going on in the opium wars against China, &c.

The different momenta of primitive accumulation distribute themselves now, more or less in chronological order, particularly over Spain, Portugal, Holland, France, and England. In England at the end of the 17th century, they arrive at a systematical combination, embracing the colonies, the national debt, the modern mode of taxation, and the protectionist system. These methods depend in part on brute force, e.g., the colonial system. But, they all employ the power of the State, the concentrated and organised force of society, to hasten, hot-house fashion, the process of transformation of the feudal mode of production into the capitalist mode, and to shorten the transition. Force is the midwife of every old society pregnant with a new one. It is itself an economic power.

Of the Christian colonial system, W. Howitt, a man who makes a speciality of Christianity, says: 'The barbarities and desperate outrages of the so-called Christian race, throughout every region of the world, and upon every people they have been able to subdue, are not to be paralleled by those of any other race, however fierce, however untaught, and however reckless of mercy and of shame, in any age of the earth.'4 The history of the colonial administration of Holland – and Holland was the head capitalistic nation of the 17th century – 'is one of the most extraordinary relations of treachery, bribery, massacre, and meanness.'5 Nothing is more characteristic than their system of stealing men, to get slaves for Java. The men stealers were trained for this purpose. The thief, the interpreter, and the seller, were the chief agents in this trade, native princes the chief sellers. The young people stolen, were thrown into the secret dungeons of Celebes, until they were ready for sending to the slave-ships. An official report says: 'This one town of Macassar, e.g., is full of secret prisons, one more horrible than the other, crammed with unfortunates, victims of greed and tyranny fettered in chains, forcibly torn from their families.' To secure Malacca, the Dutch corrupted the Portuguese governor. He let them into the town in 1641. They hurried at once to his house and assassinated him, to 'abstain' from the payment of £21,875, the price of his treason. Wherever they set foot, devastation and depopulation followed. Banjuwangi, a province of Java, in 1750 numbered over 80,000 inhabitants, in 1811 only 18,000. Sweet commerce!

The English East India Company, as is well known, obtained, besides the political rule in India, the exclusive monopoly of the tea-trade, as well as of the Chinese trade in general, and of the transport of goods to and from Europe. But the coasting trade of India and between the islands, as well as the internal trade of India, were the monopoly of the higher employés of the company. The monopolies of salt, opium, betel and other commodities, were inexhaustible mines of wealth. The employés themselves fixed the price and plundered at will the unhappy Hindus. The Governor-General took part in this private traffic. His favourites received contracts under conditions whereby they, cleverer than the alchemists, made gold out of nothing. Great fortunes sprang up like mushrooms in a day; primitive accumulation went on without the advance of a shilling. The trial of Warren Hastings swarms with such cases. Here is an instance. A contract for opium was given to a certain Sullivan at the moment of his departure on an official mission to a part of India far removed from the opium district. Sullivan sold his contract to one Binn for £40,000; Binn sold it the same day for £60,000, and the ultimate purchaser who carried out the contract declared that after all he realised an enormous gain. According to one of the lists laid before Parliament, the Company and its employés from 1757–1766 got £6,000,000 from the Indians as gifts. Between 1769 and 1770, the English manufactured a famine by buying up all the rice and refusing to sell it again, except at fabulous prices. [6]

The treatment of the aborigines was, naturally, most frightful in plantation-colonies destined for export trade only, such as the West Indies, and in rich and well-populated countries, such as Mexico and India, that were given over to plunder. But even in the colonies properly so called, the Christian character of primitive accumulation did not belie itself. Those sober virtuosi of Protestantism, the Puritans of New England, in 1703, by decrees of their assembly set a premium of £40 on every Indian scalp and every captured red-skin: in 1720 a premium of £100 on every scalp; in 1744, after Massachusetts-Bay had proclaimed a certain tribe as rebels, the following prices: for a male scalp of 12 years and upwards £100 (new currency), for a male prisoner £105, for women and children prisoners £50, for scalps of women and children £50. Some decades later, the colonial system took its revenge on the descendants of the pious pilgrim fathers, who had grown seditious in the meantime. At English instigation and for English pay they were tomahawked by red-skins. The British Parliament proclaimed bloodhounds and scalping as 'means that God and Nature had given into its hand'.

The colonial system ripened, like a hot-house, trade and navigation. The 'societies Monopolia' of Luther were powerful levers for concentration of capital. The colonies secured a market for the budding manufactures, and, through the monopoly of the market, an increased accumulation. The treasures captured outside Europe by undisguised looting, enslavement, and murder, floated back to the mother-country and were there turned into capital. Holland, which first fully developed the colonial system, in 1648 stood already in the acme of its commercial greatness. It was 'in almost exclusive possession of the East Indian trade and the commerce between the south-east and north-west of Europe. Its fisheries, marine, manufactures, surpassed those of any other country. The total capital of the Republic was probably more important than that of all the rest of Europe put together.' Gülich forgets to add that by 1648, the people of Holland were more over-worked, poorer and more brutally oppressed than those of all the rest of Europe put together.

Today industrial supremacy implies commercial supremacy. In the period of manufacture properly so called, it is, on the other hand, the commercial supremacy that gives industrial predominance. Hence the preponderant rôle that the colonial system plays at that time. It was 'the strange God' who perched himself on the altar cheek by jowl with the old Gods of Europe, and one fine day with a shove and a kick chucked them all of a heap. It proclaimed surplus-value making as the sole end and aim of humanity.

The system of public credit, i.e., of national debts, whose origin we discover in Genoa and Venice as early as the middle ages, took possession of Europe generally during the manufacturing period. The colonial system with its maritime trade and commercial wars served as a forcing-house for it. Thus it first took root in Holland. National debts, i.e., the alienation of the state – whether despotic, constitutional or republican – marked with its stamp the capitalistic era. The only part of the so-called national wealth that actually enters into the collective possessions of modern peoples is their national debt.[7] Hence, as a necessary consequence, the modern doctrine that a nation becomes the richer the more deeply it is in debt. Public credit becomes the credo of capital. And with the rise of national debt-making, want of faith in the national debt takes the place of the blasphemy against the Holy Ghost, which may not be forgiven.

The public debt becomes one of the most powerful levers of primitive accumulation. As with the stroke of an enchanter's wand, it endows barren money with the power of breeding and thus turns it into capital, without the necessity of its exposing itself to the troubles and risks inseparable from its employment in industry or even in usury. The state-creditors actually give nothing away, for the sum lent is transformed into public bonds, easily negotiable, which go on functioning in their hands just as so much hard cash would. But further, apart from the class of lazy annuitants thus created, and from the improvised wealth of the financiers, middlemen between the government and the nation – as also apart from the tax-farmers, merchants, private manufacturers, to whom a good part of every national loan renders the service of a capital fallen from heaven – the national debt has given rise to joint-stock companies, to dealings in negotiable effects of all kinds, and to *agiotage*, in a word to stock-exchange gambling and the modern bankocracy.

At their birth the great banks, decorated with national titles, were only associations of private speculators, who placed themselves by the side of governments, and, thanks to the privileges they received, were in a position to advance money to the State. Hence the accumulation of the national debt has no more infallible measure than the successive rise in the stock of these banks, whose full development dates from the founding of the Bank of England in 1694. The Bank of England began with lending its money to the Government at 8%; at the same time it was empowered by Parliament to coin money out of the same capital, by lending it again to the public in the form of banknotes. It was allowed to use these notes for discounting bills, making advances on commodities, and for buying the precious metals. It was not long ere this credit-money, made by the bank itself, became the coin in which the Bank of England made its loans to the State, and paid, on account of the State, the interest on the public debt. It was not enough that the bank gave with one hand and took back more with the other; it remained, even whilst receiving, the eternal creditor of the nation down to the last shilling advanced. Gradually it became inevitably the receptacle of the metallic hoard of the country, and the centre of gravity of all commercial credit. What effect was produced on their contemporaries by the sudden uprising of this brood of bankocrats, financiers, rentiers, brokers, stock-jobbers, &c., is proved by the writings of that time, e.g., by Bolingbroke's.[8]

With the national debt arose an international credit system, which often conceals one of the sources of primitive accumulation in this or that people. Thus the villainies of the Venetian thieving system formed one of the secret bases of the capital-wealth of Holland to whom Venice in her decadence lent large sums of money. So also was it with Holland and England. By the beginning of the 18th century the Dutch manufactures were far outstripped. Holland had ceased to be the nation preponderant in commerce and industry. One of its main lines of business, therefore, from 1701–1776, is the lending out of enormous amounts of capital, especially to its great rival England. The same thing is going on today between England and the United States. A great deal of capital, which appears today in the United States without any certificate of birth, was yesterday, in England, the capitalised blood of children.

As the national debt finds its support in the public revenue, which must cover the yearly payments for interest, &c., the modern system of taxation was the necessary complement of the system of national loans. The loans enable the government to meet extraordinary expenses, without the tax-payers feeling it immediately, but they necessitate, as a consequence, increased taxes. On the other hand, the raising of taxation caused by the accumulation of debts contracted one after another, compels the government always to have recourse to new loans for new extraordinary expenses. Modern fiscality, whose pivot is formed by taxes on the most necessary means of subsistence (thereby increasing their price), thus contains within itself the germ of automatic progression. Over-taxation is not an incident, but rather a principle. In Holland, therefore, where this system was first inaugurated, the great patriot, DeWitt, has in his *Maxims* extolled it as the best system for making the wage-labourer submissive, frugal, industrious, and overburdened with labour. The destructive influence that it exercises on the condition of the wage-labourer concerns us less however, here, than the forcible expropriation, resulting from it, of peasants, artisans, and in a word, all elements of the lower middle-class. On this there are not two opinions, even among the bourgeois economists. Its expropriating efficacy is still further heightened by the system of protection, which forms one of its integral parts.

The great part that the public debt, and the fiscal system corresponding with it, has played in the capitalisation of wealth and the expropriation of the masses, has led many writers, like Cobbett, Doubleday and others, to seek in this, incorrectly, the fundamental cause of the misery of the modern peoples.

The system of protection was an artificial means of manufacturing manufacturers, of expropriating independent labourers, of capitalising the national means of production and subsistence, of forcibly abbreviating the transition from the medieval to the modern mode of production. The European states tore one another to pieces about the patent of this invention, and, once entered into the service of the surplus-value makers, did not merely lay under contribution in the pursuit of this purpose their own people, indirectly through protective duties, directly through export premiums. They also forcibly rooted out, in their dependent countries, all industry, as, e.g., England did with the Irish woollen manufacture. On the continent of Europe, after Colbert's example, the process was much simplified. The primitive industrial capital, here, came in part directly out of the state treasury. 'Why,' cries Mirabeau, 'why go so far to seek the cause of the manufacturing glory of Saxony before the war? 180,000,000 of debts contracted by the sovereigns!'9

Colonial system, public debts, heavy taxes, protection, commercial wars, &c., these children of the true manufacturing period, increase gigantically during the infancy of Modem Industry. The birth of the latter is heralded by a great slaughter of the innocents. Like the royal navy, the factories were recruited by means of the press-gang. Blasé as Sir F. M. Eden is as to the horrors of the expropriation of the agricultural population from the soil, from the last third of the 15th century to his own time; with all the self-satisfaction with which he rejoices in this process, 'essential' for establishing capitalistic agriculture and 'the due proportion between arable and pasture land' –

he does not show, however, the same economic insight in respect to the necessity of child-stealing and child-slavery for the transformation of manufacturing exploitation into factory exploitation, and the establishment of the 'true relation' between capital and labour power. He says: 'It may, perhaps, be worthy the attention of the public to consider, whether any manufacture, which, in order to be carried on successfully, requires that cottages and workhouses should be ransacked for poor children; that they should be employed by turns during the greater part of the night and robbed of that rest which, though indispensable to all, is most required by the young; and that numbers of both sexes, of different ages and dispositions, should be collected together in such a manner that the contagion of example cannot but lead to profligacy and debauchery; will add to the sum of individual or national felicity?'[10]

'In the counties of Derbyshire, Nottinghamshire, and more particularly in Lancashire,' says Fielden, 'the newly-invented machinery was used in large factories built on the sides of streams capable of turning the water-wheel. Thousands of hands were suddenly required in these places, remote from towns; and Lancashire, in particular, being, till then, comparatively thinly populated and barren, a population was all that she now wanted. The small and nimble fingers of little children being by very far the most in request, the custom instantly sprang up of procuring apprentices from the different parish workhouses of London, Birmingham, and elsewhere. Many, many thousands of these little, hapless creatures were sent down into the north, being from the age of 7 to the age of 13 or 14 years old. The custom was for the master to clothe his apprentices and to feed and lodge them in an 'apprentice house' near the factory; overseers were appointed to see to the works, whose interest it was to work the children to the utmost, because their pay was in proportion to the quantity of work that they could exact. Cruelty was, of course, the consequence . . . In many of the manufacturing districts, but particularly, I am afraid, in the guilty county to which I belong [Lancashire], cruelties the most heart-rending were practised upon the unoffending and friendless creatures who were thus consigned to the charge of master-manufacturers; they were harassed to the brink of death by excess of labour . . . were flogged, fettered and tortured in the most exquisite refinement of cruelty; . . . they were in many cases starved to the bone while flogged to their work and . . . even in some instances . . . were driven to commit suicide . . . The beautiful and romantic valleys of Derbyshire, Nottinghamshire and Lancashire, secluded from the public eye, became the dismal solitudes of torture, and of many a murder. The profits of manufacturers were enormous;

but this only whetted the appetite that it should have satisfied, and therefore the manufacturers had recourse to an expedient that seemed to secure to them those profits without any possibility of limit; they began the practice of what is termed 'night-working', that is, having tired one set of hands, by working them throughout the day, they had another set ready to go on working throughout the night; the day-set getting into the beds that the night-set had just quitted, and in their turn again, the night-set getting into the beds that the day-set quitted in the morning. It is a common tradition in Lancashire, that the beds *never get cold.*'11

With the development of capitalist production during the manufacturing period, the public opinion of Europe had lost the last remnant of shame and conscience. The nations bragged cynically of every infamy that served them as a means to capitalistic accumulation. Read, e.g., the naïve *Annals of Commerce* of the worthy A. Anderson. Here it is trumpeted forth as a triumph of English statecraft that at the Peace of Utrecht, England extorted from the Spaniards by the Asiento Treaty the privilege of being allowed to ply the negro-trade, until then only carried on between Africa and the English West Indies, between Africa and Spanish America as well. England thereby acquired the right of supplying Spanish America until 1743 with 4,800 negroes yearly. This threw, at the same time, an official cloak over British smuggling. Liverpool waxed fat on the slave-trade. This was its method of primitive accumulation. And, even to the present day, Liverpool 'respectability' is the Pindar of the slave-trade which – compare the work of Aikin [1795] already quoted – 'has coincided with that spirit of bold adventure which has characterised the trade of Liverpool and rapidly carried it to its present state of prosperity; has occasioned vast employment for shipping and sailors, and greatly augmented the demand for the manufactures of the country.' (p. 339) Liverpool employed in the slave-trade, in 1730, 15 ships; in 1751, 53; in 1760, 74; in 1770, 96; and in 1792, 132.

Whilst the cotton industry introduced child-slavery in England, it gave in the United States a stimulus to the transformation of the earlier, more or less patriarchal slavery, into a system of commercial exploitation. In fact, the veiled slavery of the wage-workers in Europe needed, for its pedestal, slavery pure and simple in the new world.'12

Tantae molis erat, to establish the 'eternal laws of Nature' of the capitalist mode of production, to complete the process of separation between labourers and conditions of labour, to transform, at one pole, the social means of production and subsistence into capital, at the opposite pole, the mass of the population into wage-labourers, into 'free labouring poor', that artificial product of modern society.[13] If money, according to Augier,[14] 'comes into the world with a congenital blood-stain on one cheek,' capital comes dripping from head to foot, from every pore, with blood and dirt.[15]

Chapter 32
Historical Tendency of Capitalist Accumulation

What does the primitive accumulation of capital, i.e., its historical genesis, resolve itself into? In so far as it is not immediate transformation of slaves and serfs into wage-labourers, and therefore a mere change of form, it only means the expropriation of the immediate producers, i.e., the dissolution of private property based on the labour of its owner. Private property, as the antithesis to social, collective property, exists only where the means of labour and the external conditions of labour belong to private individuals. But according as these private individuals are labourers or not labourers, private property has a different character. The numberless shades, that it at first sight presents, correspond to the intermediate stages lying between these two extremes. The private property of the labourer in his means of production is the foundation of petty industry, whether agricultural, manufacturing, or both; petty industry, again, is an essential condition for the development of social production and of the free individuality of the labourer himself. Of course, this petty mode of production exists also under slavery, serfdom, and other states of dependence. But it flourishes, it lets loose its whole energy, it attains its adequate classical form, only where the labourer is the private owner of his own means of labour set in action by himself: the peasant of the land which he cultivates, the artisan of the tool which he handles as a virtuoso. This mode of production presupposes parcelling of the soil and scattering of the other means of production. As it excludes the concentration of these means of production, so also it excludes co-operation, division of labour within each separate process of production, the control over, and the productive application of the forces of Nature by society, and the free development of the social productive powers. It is compatible only with a system of production, and a society, moving within narrow and more or less primitive bounds. To perpetuate it would be, as Pecqueur rightly says, 'to decree universal mediocrity'. At a certain stage of development, it brings forth the material agencies for its own dissolution. From that moment new forces and new passions spring up in the bosom of society; but the old social organisation fetters them and keeps them down. It must be annihilated; it is annihilated. Its annihilation, the transformation of the individualised and scattered means of production into socially concentrated ones, of the pigmy property of the many into the huge property of the few, the expropriation of the great mass of the people from the soil, from the means of subsistence, and from the means of labour, this fearful and painful expropriation of the mass of the people forms the prelude to the history of capital. It comprises a series of forcible methods, of which we have passed in review only those that have been epoch-making as methods of the primitive accumulation of capital. The expropriation of the immediate producers was accomplished with merciless vandalism, and under the stimulus of passions the most infamous, the most sordid, the pettiest, the most meanly odious. Self-earned private property, that is based, so to say, on the fusing together of the isolated, independent labouring-individual with the conditions of his labour, is supplanted by capitalistic private property, which rests on exploitation of the nominally free labour of others, i.e., on wage-labour.[1]

As soon as this process of transformation has sufficiently decomposed the old society from top to bottom, as soon as the labourers are turned into proletarians, their means of labour into capital, as soon as the capitalist mode of production stands on its own feet, then the further socialisation of labour and further transformation of the land and other means of production into socially exploited and, therefore, common means of production, as well as the further expropriation of private proprietors, takes a new form. That which is now to be expropriated is no longer the labourer working for himself, but the capitalist exploiting many labourers. This expropriation is accomplished by the action of the immanent laws of capitalistic production itself, by the centralisation of capital. One capitalist always kills many. Hand in hand with this centralisation, or this expropriation of many capitalists by few, develop, on an ever-extending scale, the co-operative form of the labour-process, the conscious technical application of science, the methodical cultivation of the soil, the transformation of the instruments of labour into instruments of labour only usable in common, the economising of all means of production by their use as means of production of combined, socialised labour, the entanglement of all peoples in the net of the world-market, and with this, the international character of the capitalistic regime. Along with the constantly diminishing number of the magnates of capital, who usurp and monopolise all advantages of this process of transformation, grows the mass of misery, oppression, slavery, degradation, exploitation; but with this too grows the revolt of the working-class, a class always increasing in numbers, and disciplined, united, organised by the very mechanism of the process of capitalist production itself. The monopoly of capital becomes a fetter upon the mode of production, which has sprung up and flourished along with, and under it. Centralisation of the means of production and socialisation of labour at last reach a point where they become incompatible with their capitalist integument. This integument is burst asunder. The knell of capitalist private property sounds. The expropriators are expropriated.

The capitalist mode of appropriation, the result of the capitalist mode of production, produces capitalist private property. This is the first negation of individual private property, as founded on the labour of the proprietor. But capitalist production begets, with the inexorability of a law of Nature, its own negation. It is the negation of negation. This does not re-establish private property for the producer, but gives him individual property based on the acquisition of the capitalist era: i.e., on co-operation and the possession in common of the land and of the means of production.

The transformation of scattered private property, arising from individual labour, into capitalist private property is, naturally, a process, incomparably more protracted, violent, and difficult, than the transformation of capitalistic private property, already practically resting on socialised production, into socialised property. In the former case, we had the expropriation of the mass of the people by a few usurpers; in the latter, we have the expropriation of a few usurpers by the mass of the people.[2]

Chapter 33
The Modern Theory of Colonisation[1]

Political economy confuses on principle two very different kinds of private property, of which one rests on the producers' own labour, the other on the employment of the labour of others. It forgets that the latter not only is the direct antithesis of the former, but absolutely grows on its tomb only. In Western Europe, the home of Political Economy, the process of primitive accumulation is more of less accomplished. Here the capitalist regime has either directly conquered the whole domain of national production, or, where economic conditions are less developed, it, at least, indirectly controls those strata of society which, though belonging to the antiquated mode of production, continue to exist side by side with it in gradual decay. To this ready-made world of capital, the political economist applies the notions of law and of property inherited from a pre-capitalistic world with all the more anxious zeal and all the greater unction, the more loudly the facts cry out in the face of his ideology. It is otherwise in the colonies. There the capitalist régime everywhere comes into collision with the resistance of the producer, who, as owner of his own conditions of labour, employs that labour to enrich himself, instead of the capitalist. The contradiction of these two diametrically opposed economic systems, manifests itself here practically in a struggle between them. Where the capitalist has at his back the power of the mother-country, he tries to clear out of his way by force the modes of production and appropriation based on the independent labour of the producer. The same interest, which compels the sycophant of capital, the political economist, in the mother-country, to proclaim the theoretical identity of the capitalist mode of production with its contrary, that same interest compels him in the colonies to make a clean breast of it, and to proclaim aloud the antagonism of the two modes of production. To this end, he proves how the development of the social productive power of labour, co-operation, division of labour, use of machinery on a large scale, &c., are impossible without the expropriation of the labourers, and the corresponding transformation of their means of production into capital. In the interest of the so-called national wealth, he seeks for artificial means to ensure the poverty of the people. Here his apologetic armour crumbles off, bit by bit, like rotten touchwood. It is the great merit of E. G. Wakefield to have discovered, not anything new about the Colonies[2], but to have discovered in the Colonies the truth as to the conditions of capitalist production in the mother country. As the system of protection at its origin[3] attempted to manufacture capitalists artificially in the mother-country, so Wakefield's colonisation theory, which England tried for a time to enforce by Acts of Parliament, attempted to effect the manufacture of wage-workers in the Colonies. This he calls 'systematic colonisation'.

First of all, Wakefield discovered that in the Colonies, property in money, means of subsistence, machines, and other means of production, does not as yet stamp a man as a capitalist if there be wanting the correlative – the wage-worker, the other man who is compelled to sell himself of his own free-will. He discovered that capital is not a thing, but a social relation between persons, established by the instrumentality of things.[4] Mr Peel, he moans, took with him from England to Swan River, West Australia, means of subsistence and of production to the amount of £50,000. Mr Peel had the foresight to bring with him, besides, 3,000 persons of the working-class, men, women, and children. Once arrived at his destination, 'Mr Peel was left without a servant to make his bed or fetch him water from the river.'⁵ Unhappy Mr Peel who provided for everything except the export of English modes of production to Swan River!

For the understanding of the following discoveries of Wakefield, two preliminary remarks: we know that the means of production and subsistence, while they remain the property of the immediate producer, are not capital. They become capital only under circumstances in which they serve at the same time as means of exploitation and subjection of the labourer. But this capitalist soul of theirs is so intimately wedded, in the head of the political economist, to their material substance, that he christens them capital under all circumstances, even when they are its exact opposite. Thus is it with Wakefield. Further: the splitting up of the means of production into the individual property of many independent labourers, working on their own account, he calls equal division of capital. It is with the political economist as with the feudal jurist. The latter stuck on to pure monetary relations the labels supplied by feudal law.

'If,' says Wakefield, 'all members of the society are supposed to possess equal portions of capital . . . no man would have a motive for accumulating more capital than he could use with his own hands. This is to some extent the case in new American settlements, where a passion for owning land prevents the existence of a class of labourers for hire.'⁶ So long, therefore, as the labourer can accumulate for himself – and this he can do so long as he remains possessor of his means of production – capitalist accumulation and the capitalistic mode of production are impossible. The class of wage-labourers, essential to these, is wanting. How, then, in old Europe, was the expropriation of the labourer from his conditions of labour, i.e., the co-existence of capital and wage-labour, brought about? By a social contract of a quite original kind. 'Mankind have adopted a . . . simple contrivance for promoting the accumulation of capital,' which, of course, since the time of Adam, floated in their imagination as the sole and final end of their existence: 'they have divided themselves into owners of capital and owners of labour . . . The division was the result of concert and combination.'⁷ In one word: the mass of mankind expropriated itself in honour of the 'accumulation of capital'. Now, one would think that this instinct of self-denying fanaticism would give itself full fling especially in the Colonies, where alone exist the men and conditions that could turn a social contract from a dream to a reality. But why, then, should 'systematic colonisation' be called in to replace its opposite, spontaneous, unregulated colonisation? But – but – 'In the Northern States of the American Union, it may be doubted whether so many as a tenth of the people would fall under the description of hired labourers . . . In England . . . the labouring class compose the bulk of the people.'[8] Nay, the impulse to self-expropriation on the part of labouring humanity for the glory of capital, exists so little that slavery, according to Wakefield himself, is the sole natural basis of Colonial wealth. His systematic colonisation is a mere *pis aller*, since he unfortunately has to do with free men, not with slaves. 'The first Spanish settlers in Saint Domingo did not obtain labourers from Spain. But, without labourers, their capital must have perished, or at least, must soon have been diminished to that small amount which each individual could employ with his own hands. This has actually occurred in the last Colony founded by England – the Swan River Settlement – where a great mass of capital, of seeds, implements, and cattle, has perished for want of labourers to use it, and where no settler has preserved much more capital than he can employ with his own hands.'[9]

We have seen that the expropriation of the mass of the people from the soil forms the basis of the capitalist mode of production. The essence of a free colony, on the contrary, consists in this – that the bulk of the soil is still public property, and every settler on it therefore can turn part of it into his private property and individual means of production, without hindering the later settlers in the same operation.[10] This is the secret both of the prosperity of the colonies and of their inveterate vice – opposition to the establishment of capital. 'Where land is very cheap and all men are free, where every one who so pleases can easily obtain a piece of land for himself, not only is labour very dear, as respects the labourer's share of the produce, but the difficulty is to obtain combined labour at any price.'[11]

As in the colonies the separation of the labourer from the conditions of labour and their root, the soil, does not exist, or only sporadically, or on too limited a scale, so neither does the separation of agriculture from industry exist, nor the destruction of the household industry of the peasantry. Whence then is to come the internal market for capital? 'No part of the population of America is exclusively agricultural, excepting slaves and their employers who combine capital and labour in particular works. Free Americans, who cultivate the soil, follow many other occupations. Some portion of the furniture and tools which they use is commonly made by themselves. They frequently build their own houses, and carry to market, at whatever distance, the produce of their own industry. They are spinners and weavers; they make soap and candles, as well as, in many cases, shoes and clothes for their own use. In America the cultivation of land is often the secondary pursuit of a blacksmith, a miller or a shopkeeper.'[12]

With such queer people as these, where is the 'field of abstinence' for the capitalists?

The great beauty of capitalist production consists in this – that it not only constantly reproduces the wage-worker as wage-worker, but produces always, in production to the accumulation of capital, a relative surplus-population of wage-workers. Thus the law of supply and demand of labour is kept in the right rut, the oscillation of wages is penned within limits satisfactory to capitalist exploitation, and lastly, the social dependence of the labourer on the capitalist, that indispensable requisite, is secured; an unmistakable relation of dependence, which the smug political economist, at home in the mother-country, can transmogrify into one of free contract between buyer and seller, between equally independent owners of commodities, the owner of the commodity capital and the owner of the commodity labour. But in the colonies, this pretty fancy is torn asunder. The absolute population here increases much more quickly than in the mother-country, because many labourers enter this world as ready-made adults, and yet the labour-market is always understocked. The law of supply and demand of labour falls to pieces. On the one hand, the old world constantly throws in capital, thirsting after exploitation and 'abstinence'; on the other, the regular reproduction of the wage-labourer as wage-labourer comes into collision with impediments the most impertinent and in part invincible. What becomes of the production of wage-labourers into independent producers, who work for themselves instead of for capital, and enrich themselves instead of the capitalist gentry, reacts in its turn very perversely on the conditions of the labour-market. Not only does the degree of exploitation of the wage-labourer remain indecently low. The wage-labourer loses into the bargain, along with the relation of dependence, also the sentiment of dependence on the abstemious capitalist. Hence all the inconveniences that our E. G. Wakefield pictures so doughtily, so eloquently, so pathetically. The supply of wage-labour, he complains, is neither constant, nor regular, nor sufficient. 'The supply of labour is always not only small but uncertain.'[13] 'Though the produce divided between the capitalist and the labourer be large, the labourer takes so great a share that he soon becomes a capitalist . . . Few, even those whose lives are unusually long, can accumulate great masses of wealth.'[14] The labourers most distinctly decline to allow the capitalist to abstain from the payment of the greater part of their labour. It avails him nothing, is he is so cunning as to import from Europe, with his own capital, his own wage-workers. They soon 'cease . . . to be labourers for hire; they . . . become independent landowners, if not competitors with their former masters in the labour-market.'[15]

Think of the horror! The excellent capitalist has imported bodily from Europe, with his own good money, his own competitors! The end of the world has come! No wonder Wakefield laments the absence of all dependence and of all sentiment of dependence on the part of the wage-workers in the colonies. On account of the high wages, says his disciple, Merivale, there is in the colonies 'the urgent desire for cheaper and more subservient labourers – for a class to whom the capitalist might dictate terms, instead of being dictated to by them . . . In ancient civilised countries the labourer, though free, is by a law of Nature dependent on capitalists; in colonies this dependence must be created by artificial means.'[16]

What is now, according to Wakefield, the consequence of this unfortunate state of things in the colonies? A 'barbarising tendency of dispersion' of producers and national wealth.[17] The parcelling-out of the means of production among innumerable owners, working on their own account, annihilates, along with the centralisation of capital, all the foundation of combined labour. Every long-winded undertaking, extending over several years and demanding outlay of fixed capital, is prevented from being carried out. In Europe, capital invests without hesitating a moment, for the working-class constitutes its living appurtenance, always in excess, always at disposal. But in the colonies! Wakefield tells an extremely doleful anecdote. He was talking with some capitalists of Canada and the state of New York, where the immigrant wave often becomes stagnant and deposits a sediment of 'supernumerary' labourers. 'Our capital,' says one of the characters in the melodrama, 'was ready for many operations which require a considerable period of time for their completion; but we could not begin such operations with labour which, we knew, would soon leave us. If we had been sure of retaining the labour of such emigrants, we should have been glad to have engaged it at once, and for a high price: and we should have engaged it, even though we had been sure it would leave us, provided we had been sure of a fresh supply whenever we might need it.'[18]

After Wakefield has contrasted the English capitalist agriculture and its 'combined' labour with the scattered cultivation of American peasants, he unwittingly gives us a glimpse at the reverse of the medal. He depicts the mass of the American people as well-to-do, independent, enterprising, and comparatively cultured, whilst 'the English agricultural labourer is a miserable wretch, a pauper . . . In what country, except North America and some new colonies, do the wages of free labour employed in agriculture much exceed a bare subsistence for the labourer? . . . Undoubtedly, farm-horses in England, being a valuable property, are better fed than English peasants.'[19] But, never mind, national wealth is, once again, by its very nature, identical with misery of the people.

How, then, to heal the anti-capitalistic cancer of the colonies? If men were willing, at a blow, to turn all the soil from public into private property, they would destroy certainly the root of the evil, but also – the colonies. The trick is how to kill two birds with one stone. Let the Government put upon the virgin soil an artificial price, independent of the law of supply and demand, a price that compels the immigrant to work a long time for wages before he can earn enough money to buy land, and turn himself into an independent peasant.[20] The fund resulting from the sale of land at a price relatively prohibitory for the wage-workers, this fund of money extorted from the wages of labour by violation of the sacred law of supply and demand, the Government is to employ, on the other hand, in proportion as it grows; to import have-nothings from Europe into the colonies, and thus keep the wage-labour market full for the capitalists. Under these circumstances, *tout sera pour le mieux dans le meilleur des mondes possibles*. This is the great secret of 'systematic colonisation'. By this plan, Wakefield cries in triumph, 'the supply of labour *must* be constant and regular, because, first, as no labourer would be able to procure land until he had worked for money, all immigrant labourers, working for a time for wages and in combination, would produce capital for the employment of more labourers; secondly, because every labourer who left off working for wages and became a land-owner would, by purchasing land, provide a fund for bringing fresh labour to the colony.'[21] The price of the soil imposed by the State must, of course, be a 'sufficient price' – i.e., so high 'as to prevent the labourers from becoming independent landowners until others had followed to take their place.'[22] This 'sufficient price for the land' is nothing but a euphemistic circumlocution for the ransom which the labourer pays to the capitalist for leave to retire from the wage-labour market to the land. First, he must create for the capitalist 'capital', with which the latter may be able to exploit more labourers; then he must place, at his own expense, a *locum tenens* on the labour-market, whom the Government forwards across the sea for the benefit of his old master, the capitalist.

It is very characteristic that the English Government for years practised this method of 'primitive accumulation' prescribed by Mr Wakefield expressly for the use of the colonies. The fiasco was, of course, as complete as that of Sir Robert Peel's Bank Act. The stream of emigration was only diverted from the English colonies to the United States. Meanwhile, the advance of capitalistic production in Europe, accompanied by increasing Government pressure, has rendered Wakefield's recipe superfluous. On the one hand, the enormous and ceaseless stream of men, year after year driven upon America, leaves behind a stationary sediment in the east of the United States, the wave of immigration from Europe throwing men on the labour-market there more rapidly than the wave of emigration westwards can wash them away. On the other hand, the American Civil War brought in its train a colossal national debt, and, with it, pressure of taxes, the rise of the vilest financial aristocracy, the squandering of a huge part of the public land on speculative companies for the exploitation of railways, mines, &c., in brief, the most rapid centralisation of capital. The great republic has, therefore, ceased to be the promised land for emigrant labourers. Capitalistic production advances there with giant strides, even though the lowering of wages and the dependence of the wage-worker are yet far from being brought down to the normal European level. The shameless lavishing of uncultivated colonial land on aristocrats and capitalists by the Government, so loudly denounced even by Wakefield, has produced, especially in Australia,[23] in conjunction with the stream of men that the gold-diggings attract, and with the competition that the importation of English commodities causes even to the smallest artisan, an ample 'relative surplus labouring population', so that almost every mail brings the Job's news of a 'glut of the Australia labour-market', and the prostitution in some places flourishes as wantonly as in the London Haymarket.

However, we are not concerned here with the conditions of the colonies. The only thing that interests us is the secret discovered in the new world by the Political Economy of the old world, and proclaimed on the housetops: that the capitalist mode of production and accumulation, and therefore capitalist private property, have for their fundamental condition the annihilation of self-earned private property; in other words, the expropriation of the labourer.

Volume 2

The Circulation of Capital

Preface

It was no easy task to prepare the second volume of *Capital* for the printer in such a way that it should make a connected and complete work and represent exclusively the ideas of its author, not of its publisher. The great number of available manuscripts, and their fragmentary character, added to the difficulties of this task. At best one single manuscript (No. 4) had been revised throughout and made ready for the printer. And while it treated its subject-matter fully, the greater part had become obsolete through subsequent revision. The bulk of the material was not polished as to language, even if the subject-matter was for the greater part fully worked out. The language was that in which Marx used to make his outlines, that is to say his style was careless, full of colloquial, often rough and humorous, expressions and phrases, interspersed with English and French technical terms, or with whole sentences or pages of English. The thoughts were jotted down as they developed in the brain of the author. Some parts of the argument would be fully treated, others of equal importance only indicated. The material to be used for the illustration of facts would be collected, but barely arranged, much less worked out. At the conclusion of the chapters there would be only a few incoherent sentences as milestones of the incomplete deductions, showing the haste of the author in passing on to the next chapter. And finally, there was the well-known handwriting which Marx himself was sometimes unable to decipher.

I have been content to interpret these manuscripts as literally as possible, changing the style only in places where Marx would have changed it himself and interpolating explanatory sentences or connecting statements only where this was indispensable, and where the meaning was so clear that there could be no doubt of the correctness of my interpretation. Sentences which seemed in the least ambiguous were preferably reprinted literally. The passages which I have remodelled or interpolated cover barely ten pages in print, and concern mainly matters of form.

The mere enumeration of the manuscripts left by Marx as a basis for Volume 2 proves the unparalleled conscientiousness and strict self-criticism which he practised in his endeavour to fully elaborate his great economic discoveries before he published them. This self-criticism rarely permitted him to adapt his presentation of the subject, in content as well as in form, to his ever-widening horizon, which he enlarged by incessant study.

The material for this second volume consists of the following parts: First, a manuscript entitled *A Contribution to the Critique of Political Economy*, containing 1472 quarto pages in 23 divisions, written in the time from August, 1861, to June, 1863. It is a continuation of the work of the same title, the first volume of which appeared in Berlin, in 1859. It treats on pages 1–220, and again pages 1159–1472, of the subject analysed in Volume 1 of *Capital*, beginning with the transformation of money into capital and continuing to the end of the volume, and is the first draft for this subject. Pages 973–1158 deal with capital and profit, rate of profit, merchant's capital and money capital, that is to say with subjects which have been farther developed in the manuscript for Volume 3. The questions belonging to Volume 2 and many of those which are part of Volume 3 are not arranged by themselves in this manuscript. They are merely treated in passing, especially in the section which makes up the main body of the manuscript, viz. pages 220–972, entitled *Theories of Surplus Value*. This section contains an exhaustive critical history of the main point of political economy, the theory of surplus value, and develops at the same time, in polemic remarks against the position of the predecessors of Marx, most of the points which he has later on discussed individually and in their logical connection in Volume 2 and 3. I reserve for myself the privilege of publishing the critical part of this manuscript, after the elimination of the numerous parts covered by Volumes 2 and 3, in the form of Volume 4. This manuscript, valuable though it is, could not be used in the present edition of Volume 2.

The manuscript next following in the order of time is that of Volume 3. It was written for the greater part in 1864 and 1865. After this manuscript had been completed in its essential parts, Marx undertook the elaboration of Volume 1, which was published in 1867. I am now preparing this manuscript of Volume 3 for the printer.

The period after the publication of Volume 1, which is next in order, is represented by a collection of four manuscripts for Volume 2, marked 1–4 by Marx himself. Manuscript 1 (150 pages), presumably written in 1865 or 1867, is the first independent, but more or less fragmentary, elaboration of the questions now contained in Volume 2. This manuscript is likewise unsuited for this edition. Manuscript 2 is partly a compilation of quotations and references to the manuscripts

containing Marx's extracts and comments, most of them relating to
the first section of Volume 2, partly an elaboration of special points,
particularly a critique of Adam Smith's statements as to fixed and
circulating capital and the source of profits; furthermore, a discussion
of the relation of the rate of surplus value to the rate of profit, which
belongs in Volume 3. The references furnished little that was new,
while the elaborations for Volumes 2 and 3 were rendered valueless
through subsequent revisions and had to be ruled out for the greater
part. Manuscript 4 is an elaboration, ready for printing, of the first
section and the first chapters of the second section of Volume 2,
and has been used in its proper place. Although it was found that
this manuscript had been written earlier than Manuscript 2, yet it
was far more finished in form and could be used with advantage
for the corresponding part of this volume. I had to add only a
few supplementary parts of Manuscript 2. This last manuscript is
the only fairly complete elaboration of Volume 2 and dates from the
year 1870. The notes for the final revision, which I shall mention
immediately, say explicitly: 'The second elaboration must be used
as a basis.'

There is another interruption after 1870, due mainly to ill health.
Marx employed this time in his customary way, that is to say he
studied agronomics, agricultural conditions in America and especially
Russia, the money market and banking institutions, and finally natural
sciences, such as geology and physiology. Independent mathematical
studies also form a large part of the numerous manuscripts of this
period. In the beginning of 1877, Marx had recovered sufficiently to
resume once more his chosen life's work. The beginning of 1877 is
marked by references and notes from the above-named four manuscripts intended for a new elaboration of Volume 2, the beginning of
which is represented by Manuscript 5 (56 pages in folio). It comprises
the first four chapters and is not very fully worked out. Essential points
are treated in footnotes. The material is rather collected than sifted,
but it is the last complete presentation of this most important first
section. A preliminary attempt to prepare this part for the printer was
made in Manuscript 6 (after October, 1877, and before July, 1878),
embracing 17 quarto pages, the greater part of the first chapter. A
second and last attempt was made in Manuscript 7, dated July 2, 1878,
and consisting of 7 pages in folio.

About this time Marx seems to have realised that he would never be
able to complete the second and third volume in a manner satisfactory
to himself, unless a complete revolution in his health took place.
Manuscripts 5–8 show traces of hard struggles against depressing physical conditions far too frequently to be ignored. The most difficult

part of the first section had been worked over in Manuscript 5. The remainder of the first, and the entire second section, with the exception of Chapter 17, presented no great theoretical difficulties. But the third section, dealing with the reproduction and circulation of social capital, seemed to be very much in need of revision. Manuscript 2, it must be pointed out, had first treated of this reproduction without regard to the circulation which is instrumental in effecting it, and then taken up the same question with regard to circulation. It was the intention of Marx to eliminate this section and to reconstruct it in such a way that it would conform to his wider grasp of the subject. This gave rise to Manuscript 8, containing only 70 pages in quarto. A comparison with section 3, as printed after deducting the paragraphs inserted out of Manuscript 2, shows the amount of matter compressed by Marx into this space.

Manuscript 8 is likewise merely a preliminary presentation of the subject, and its main object was to ascertain and develop the new points of view not set forth in Manuscript 2, while those points were ignored about which there was nothing new to say. An essential part of Chapter 17, Section 2, which is more or less relevant to Section 3, was at the same time drawn into this discussion and expanded. The logical sequence was frequently interrupted, the treatment of the subject was incomplete in various places, and especially the conclusion was very fragmentary. But Marx expressed as nearly as possible what he intended to say on the subject.

This is the material for Volume 2, out of which I was supposed 'to make something', as Marx said to his daughter Eleanor shortly before his death. I have interpreted this request in its most literal meaning. So far as this was possible, I have confined my work to a mere selection of the various revised parts. And I always based my work on the last revised manuscript and compared this with the preceding ones. Only the first and third section offered any real difficulties, of more than a technical nature, and these were indeed considerable. I have endeavoured to solve them exclusively in the spirit of the author of this work.

For Volume 3, the following manuscripts were available, apart from the corresponding sections of the above-named manuscript, entitled 'A Contribution to the Critique of Political Economy', from the sections in Manuscript 3 likewise mentioned above, and from a few occasional notes scattered through various extracts: The folio manuscript of 1864–65, referred to previously, which is about as fully elaborated as Manuscript 2 of Volume 2; furthermore, a manuscript dated 1875 and entitled 'The Relation of the Rate of Surplus Value to the Rate of Profit', which treats the subject in mathematical equations. The preparation of Volume 3 for the printer is proceeding rapidly. So far as I am enabled to judge at present, it will present mainly technical difficulties, with the exception of a few very important sections.

I avail myself of this opportunity to refute a certain charge which has been raised against Marx, first indistinctly and at various intervals, but more recently, after the death of Marx, as a statement of fact by the German state and university socialists. It is claimed that Marx plagiarised the work of Rodbertus. I have already expressed myself on the main issue in my preface to the German edition of Marx's *Poverty of Philosophy* (1885),[1] but I will now produce the most convincing testimony for the refutation of this charge.

To my knowledge this charge is made for the first time in R. Meyer's *Emancipationskampf des Vierten Standes* (*Struggles for the Emancipation of the Fourth Estate*), page 43: 'It can be demonstrated that Marx has gathered the greater part of his critique from these publications' – meaning the works of Rodbertus dating back to the last half of the thirties of this century. I may well assume, until such time as will produce further proof, that the 'demonstration' of this assertion rests on a statement made by Rodbertus to Mr Meyer. Furthermore, Rodbertus himself appears on the stage in 1879 and writes to J. Zeller (*Zeitschrift für die Gesammte Staatswissenschaft*, Tübingen, 1879, page 219), with reference to his work *Zur Erkenntniss Unserer Staatswirthschaftlichen Zustände* (*A Contribution to the Understanding of our Political and Economic Conditions*), 1842, as follows: 'You will find that this line of thought has been very nicely used . . . by Marx, without, however, giving me credit for it.' The publisher of Rodbertus' posthumous works, Th. Kozak, repeats his insinuation without further ceremony. (*Das Kapital von Rodbertus*. Berlin, 1884. Introduction, page 15.) Finally in the *Briefe und Sozialpolitische Aufsatze von Dr Rodbertus-Jagetzow*', (*Letters and Essays on Political Economy by Dr Rodbertus-Jagetzow*), published by R. Meyer in 1881, Rodbertus says directly: 'Today I find that I am robbed by Schäffle and Marx without having my name mentioned.' (Letter No. 60, page 134.) And in another place, the claim of Rodbertus assumes a more definite form: 'In my third letter on political economy, I have shown practically in the same way as Marx, only more briefly and clearly, the source of the surplus value of the capitalists.' (Letter No. 48, page 111.)

Marx never heard anything definite about any of these charges of plagiarism. In his copy of the *Emancipationskampf* only that part had been opened with a knife which related to the International. The remaining pages were not opened until I cut them myself after his death. The *Zeitschrift* of Tübingen was never read by him. The *Letters, etc.*, to R. Meyer likewise remained unknown to him, and I did not learn of the passage referring to the 'robbery' of which Rodbertus was supposed to be the victim until Mr Meyer himself called my attention to it. However, Marx was familiar with letter No. 48. Mr Meyer had been kind enough to present the original to the youngest daughter of Marx. Some of the mysterious whispering about the secret source of his critique and his connection with Rodbertus having reached the ear of Marx, he showed me this letter with the remark that he had at last discovered authentic information as to what Rodbertus claimed for himself; if that was all Rodbertus wanted, he Marx, had no objection, and he could well afford to let Rodbertus enjoy the pleasure of considering his own version the briefer and clearer one. In fact, Marx considered the matter settled by this letter of Rodbertus.

He could so much the more afford this, as I know positively that he was not in the least acquainted with the literary activity of Rodbertus until about 1859, when his own critique of political economy had been completed, not only in its fundamental outlines, but also in its more important details. Marx began his economic studies in Paris, in 1843, starting with the prominent Englishmen and Frenchmen. Of German economists he knew only Rau and List, and he did not want any more of them. Neither Marx nor I heard a word of Rodbertus' existence, until we had to criticise, in the *Neue Rheinische Zeitung*, 1848, the speeches he made as the representative of Berlin and as Minister of Commerce. We were both of us so ignorant that we had to ask the Rhenish representatives who this Rodbertus was that had become a Minister so suddenly. But these representatives could not tell us anything about the economic writings of Rodbertus. On the other hand, Marx showed that he knew even then, without the help of Rodbertus, whence came 'the surplus value of the capitalists', and he showed furthermore how it was produced, as may be seen in his *Poverty of Philosophy*, 1847, and in his lectures on wage labour and capital, delivered in Brussels in 1847, and published in Nos. 264–69 of the *Neue Rheinische Zeitung*, 1849. Marx did not learn that an economist Rodbertus existed, until Lassalle called his attention to the fact in 1859, and thereupon Marx looked up the *Third Letter on Political Economy* in the British Museum.

This is the actual condition of things. And now let us see what there is to the content of Rodbertus which Marx is charged with appropriating by 'robbery'. Says Rodbertus: 'In my third letter on political economy, I have shown practically in the same way as Marx, only more briefly and clearly, the source of the surplus-value of the capitalists.' This, then, is the disputed point: the theory of surplus value. And indeed, it would be difficult to say what else there is in Rodbertus which Marx might have found worth appropriating. Rodbertus here claims to be the real originator of the theory of surplus-value of which Marx is supposed to have robbed him.

And what has this third letter on political economy to say in regard to the origin of surplus-value? Simply this: that the 'rent', as he terms the sum of ground rent and profit, does not consist of an 'addition to the value' of a commodity, but is obtained 'by means of a deduction of value from the wages of labour, in other words, the wages represent only a part of the value of a certain product', and provided that labour is sufficiently productive, wages need not be 'equal to the natural exchange value of the product of labour in order to leave enough of it for the replacing of capital and for rent'. We are not informed, however, what sort of a 'natural exchange value' of a product it is that leaves nothing for the 'replacing' of capital, or in other words, I suppose, for the replacing of raw material and the wear and tear of tools.

I am happy to say that we are enabled to ascertain what impression was produced on Marx by this stupendous discovery of Rodbertus. In the manuscript entitled 'A Contribution to the Critique of Political Economy', Section 10, pages 445 and following, we find, 'A deviation. Mr Rodbertus. A new theory of ground rent.' This is the only point of view from which Marx there looks upon the third letter on political economy. The Rodbertian theory of surplus value is dismissed with the ironical remark: 'Mr Rodbertus first analyses what happens in a country where property in land and property in capital are not separated, and then he arrives at the important discovery that rent – meaning the entire surplus-value – is only equal to the unpaid labour or to the quantity of products in which it is embodied.'

Now it is a fact, that capitalist humanity has been producing surplus-value for several hundred years, and has in the course of this time also arrived at the point where people began to ponder over the origin of surplus-value. The first explanation for this phenomenon grew out of the practice of commerce and was to the effect that surplus-value arose by raising the value of the product. This idea was current among the mercantilists. But James Steuart already saw that in that case the one would lose what the other would gain. Nevertheless, this idea persists for a long time after him, especially in the heads of the 'socialists'. But it is crowded out of classical science by Adam Smith.

He says in *Wealth of Nations*, Vol. 1, Ch. 6: 'As soon as stock has accumulated in the hands of particular persons, some of them will naturally employ it in setting to work industrious people, whom they will supply with materials and subsistence, in order to make a profit by the sale of their work, or, by what their labour adds to the value of the materials . . . The value which the workmen add to the materials, therefore, resolves itself in this case into two parts, of which the one pays their wages, the other the profits of their employer upon the whole stock of materials and wages which he advanced.' And a little farther on he says: 'As soon as the land of any country has all become private property, the landlords, like all other men, love to reap where they never sowed, and demand a rent even for its natural produce . . . The labourer . . . must give up to the landlord a portion of what his labour either collects or produces. This portion, or what comes to the same thing, the price of this portion, constitutes the rent of land.'

Marx comments on this passage in the above-named manuscript, entitled, 'A Contribution, etc.', page 253: 'Adam Smith, then, regards surplus-value, that is to say the surplus labour, the surplus of labour performed and embodied in its product over and above the paid labour, over and above that labour which has received its equivalent in wages, as the general category, and profit and ground rent merely as its ramifications.'

Adam Smith says, furthermore, Vol. 1, Chap. 8: 'As soon as land becomes private property, the landlord demands a share of almost all the produce which the labourer can either raise or collect from it. His rent makes the first deduction from the produce of labour which is employed upon land. It seldom happens that the person who tills the ground has wherewithal to maintain himself till he reaps the harvest. His maintenance is generally advanced to him from the stock of a master, the farmer who employs him, and who would have no interest to employ him, unless he was to share in the produce of his labour, or unless his stock was to be replaced by him with a profit. This profit makes a second deduction from the produce of the labour which is employed upon land. The produce of almost all other labour is liable to the like deduction of profit. In all arts and manufactures the greater part of the workmen stand in need of a master to advance them the materials for their work, and their wages and maintenance till it be completed. He shares in the produce of their labour, or in the value which it adds to the materials upon which it is bestowed; and in this share consists his profit.'

The comment of Marx on this passage (on page 256 of his manuscript) is as follows: 'Here Adam Smith declares in so many words that ground rent and profit of capital are simply deductions from the product of the labourer, or from the value of his product, and equal to the additional labour expended on the raw material. But this deduction, as Adam Smith himself has previously explained, can consist only of that part of labour which the labourer expends over and above the quantity of work which pays for his wages and furnishes the equivalent of wages; in other words, this deduction consists of the surplus labour, the unpaid part of his labour.'

It is therefore evident that even Adam Smith knew 'the source of the surplus-value of the capitalists', and furthermore also that of the surplus-value of the landlords. Marx acknowledged this as early as 1861, while Rodbertus and the swarming mass of his admirers, who grew like mushrooms under the warm summer showers of state socialism, seem to have forgotten all about that.

'Nevertheless', continues Marx, 'Smith did not separate surplus-value proper as a separate category from the special form which it assumes in profit and ground rent. Hence there is much error and incompleteness in his investigation, and still more in that of Ricardo.' This statement literally fits Rodbertus. His 'rent' is simply the sum of ground rent plus profit. He builds up an entirely erroneous theory of ground rent, and he takes surplus-value without any critical reservation just as his predecessors hand it over to him. On the other hand, Marx's surplus-value represents the general form of the sum of values appropriated without any equivalent return by the owners of the means of production, and this form is then seen to transform itself into profit and ground rent by very particular laws which Marx was the first to discover. These laws are traced in Volume 3. We shall see there how many intermediate links are required for the passage from an understanding of surplus-value in general to that of its transformation into profits and ground rent; in other words, for the understanding of the laws of the distribution of surplus-value within the capitalist class.

Ricardo goes considerably farther than Adam Smith. He bases his conception of surplus-value on a new theory of value which is contained in the germ in Adam Smith, but which is generally forgotten when it comes to applying it. This theory of value became the starting point of all subsequent economic science. Ricardo starts out with the determination of the value of commodities by the quantity of labour embodied in them, and from this premise he derives his theory of the distribution, between labourers and capitalists, of the quantity of value added by labour to the raw materials, this value being divided into wages and profit (meaning surplus-value). He shows that the value of the commodities remains the same, no matter what may be the proportion of these two parts, and he claims that this law has only a few exceptions. He even formulates a few fundamental laws relative to the mutual relations of wages and surplus-value (the latter considered by him as profit), although his statements are too general (see Marx, *Capital*, Vol. 1, Chap. 17, 1), and he shows that ground rent is a quantity realised under certain conditions over and above profit. Rodbertus did not improve on Ricardo in any of these respects. He either remained unfamiliar with the internal contradictions which caused the downfall of the Ricardian theory and school, or they misled him into utopian demands instead of enabling him to solve economic problems (see his *Zur Erkenntniss, etc.*, page 130).

But the Ricardian theory of value and surplus-value did not have to wait for Rodbertus' *Zur Erkenntniss* in order to be utilised for socialist purposes. On page 609 of the second edition of the German original of *Capital*, Vol. 1, we find the following quotation: 'The possessors of surplus produce or capital.' This quotation is taken from a pamphlet entitled *The Source and Remedy of the National Difficulties. A Letter to Lord John Russell. London, 1821.* In this pamphlet, the importance of which should have been recognised on account of the terms surplus produce or capital, and which Marx saved from being forgotten, we read the following statements:

'Whatever may be due to the capitalist,' (from the capitalist standpoint) 'he can never appropriate more than the surplus labour of the labourer, for the labourer must live.' (page 23.) As for the way in which the labourer lives and for the quantity of the surplus value appropriated by the capitalist, these are very relative things. – 'If capital does not decrease in value in proportion as it increases in volume, the capitalist will squeeze out of the labourer the product of every hour of labour above the minimum on which the labourer can live . . . the capitalist can ultimately say to the labourer: You shall not eat bread, for you can live on beets and potatoes; and this is what we have to come to.' (page 24.) 'If the labourer can be reduced to living on potatoes, instead of bread, it is undoubtedly true that more can be gotten out of his labour; that is to say, if, in order to live on bread, he was compelled, for his own subsistence and that of his family, to keep for himself the labour of Monday and Tuesday, he will, when living on potatoes, keep only half of Monday's labour for himself; and the other half of Monday, and all of Tuesday, are set free, either for the benefit of the state or for the capitalist.' (page 26.) 'It is admitted that the sums of interest paid to the capitalist, either in the form of rent, money-interest, or commercial profit, are paid from the labour of others.' (page 23.) Here we have the same idea of 'rent' which Rodbertus has, only the writer says 'interest' instead of rent.

Marx makes the following comment (manuscript of *A Contribution, etc.*, page 852): 'The little known pamphlet – published at a time when the "incredible cobbler" MacCulloch began to be talked about – represents an essential advance over Ricardo. It directly designates surplus-value or "profit" in the language of Ricardo (sometimes surplus produce), or interest, as the author of this pamphlet calls it, as surplus labour, which the labourer performs gratuitously, which he performs in excess of that quantity of labour required for the reproduction of his labour-power, the equivalent of his wages. It was no more important to reduce value down to labour than it is to reduce surplus-value, represented by surplus-produce, to surplus-labour. This had already been stated by Adam Smith, and forms a main factor in the analysis of Ricardo. But neither of them said so anywhere clearly and frankly in such a way that it could not be misunderstood.' We read furthermore, on page 859 of this manuscript: 'Moreover, the author is limited by the economic theories which he finds at hand and which he accepts. Just as the confounding of surplus-value and profit misleads Ricardo into irreconcilable contradictions, so this author fares by baptising surplus-value with the name of "interest of capital". It is true, he advances beyond Ricardo by reducing all surplus-value to surplus-labour. And furthermore, in calling surplus-value "interest of capital", he emphasises that he is referring by this term to the general form of surplus-labour as distinguished from its special forms, rent, money interest, and commercial profit. But yet he chooses the name of one of these special forms, interest, at the same time for the general form. And this causes his relapse into the economic slang.'

This last passage fits Rodbertus just as if it were made to order for him. He, too, is limited by the economic categories which he finds at hand. He, too, applies the name of one of the minor categories to surplus-value, and he makes it quite indefinite at that by calling it 'rent'. The result of these two mistakes is that he relapses into the economic slang, that he makes no attempt to follow up his advance over Ricardo by a critical analysis, and that he is misled into using his imperfect theory, even before it has gotten rid of its egg-shells, as a basis for a utopia which is in every respect too late. The above-named pamphlet appeared in 1821 and anticipated completely Rodbertus' 'rent' of 1842.

This pamphlet is but the farthest outpost of an entire literature which the Ricardian theories of value and surplus-value directed against capitalist production in the interest of the proletariat, fighting the bourgeoisie with its own weapons. The entire communism of Owen, so far as it plays a role in economics and politics, is based on Ricardo. Apart from him, there are still numerous other writers, some of whom Marx quoted as early as 1847 in his *Poverty of Philosophy* against Proudhon, such as Edmonds, Thompson, Hodgskin, etc., etc., 'and four more pages of et cetera'. I select from among this large number of writings the following by a random choice: *An Inquiry into the Principles of the Distribution of Wealth, Most Conducive to Human Happiness,* by William Thompson; a new edition. London, 1850. This work, written in 1822, first appeared in 1827. It likewise regards the wealth appropriated by the non-producing classes as a deduction from the product of the labourer, and uses pretty strong terms in referring to it. The author says that the ceaseless endeavour of that which we call society consisted in inducing, by fraud or persuasion, by intimidation or compulsion, the productive labourer to perform his labours in return for the minimum of his own product. He asks why the labourer should not be entitled to the full product of his labour. He declares that the compensations, which the capitalists filch from the productive labourer under the name of ground rent or profit, are claimed in return for the use of land or other things. According to him, all physical substances, by means of which the propertiless productive labourer who has no other means of existence but the capacity of producing things, can make use of his faculties, are in the possession of others with opposite material interests; the consent of these is required in order that the labourer may find work; under these circumstances, he says, it depends on the good will of the capitalists how much of the fruit of his own labour the labourer shall receive. And he speaks of 'these defalcations' and of their relation to the unpaid product, whether this is called taxes, profit, or theft, etc.

I must admit that I do not write these lines without a certain mortification. I will not make so much of the fact that the anti-capitalist literature of England of the 20's and 30's is so little known in Germany, in spite of the fact that Marx referred to it even in his *Poverty of Philosophy,* and quoted from it, as for instance that pamphlet of 1821, or Ravenstone, Hodgskin, etc., in Volume 1 of *Capital.* But it is a proof of the degradation into which official political economy has fallen, that not only the vulgar economist, who clings desperately to the coat tails of Rodbertus and really has not learned anything, but also the duly installed professor, who boasts of his wisdom, have forgotten their classical economy to such an extent that they seriously charge Marx with having robbed Rodbertus of things which may be found even in Adam Smith and Ricardo.

But what is there that is new about Marx's statements on surplus-value? How is it that Marx's theory of surplus-value struck home like a thunderbolt out of a clear sky, in all modern countries, while the theories of all his socialist predecessors, including Rodbertus, remained ineffective?

The history of chemistry offers an illustration which explains this.

Until late in the 18th century, the phlogistic theory was accepted. It assumed that in the process of burning, a certain hypothetical substance, an absolute combustible, named phlogiston, separated from the burning bodies. This theory sufficed for the explanation of most of the chemical phenomena then known, although it had to be considerably twisted in some cases. But in 1774, Priestley discovered a certain kind of air which was so pure, or so free from phlogiston, that common air seemed adulterated in comparison to it. He called it 'dephlogisticised air'. Shortly after him, Scheele obtained the same kind of air in Sweden, and demonstrated its existence in the atmosphere. He also found that this air disappeared, whenever some body was burned in it or in the open air, and therefore he called it 'fire-air'. 'From these facts he drew the conclusion that the combination arising from the union of phlogiston with one of the elements of the atmosphere' (that is to say by combustion) 'was nothing but fire or heat which escaped through the glass.'[2]

Priestley and Scheele had produced oxygen, without knowing what they had discovered. They remained 'limited by the phlogistic categories which they found at hand'. The element, which was destined to abolish all phlogistic ideas and to revolutionise chemistry, remained barren in their hands. But Priestley had immediately communicated his discovery to Lavoisier in Paris, and Lavoisier, by means of this discovery, now analysed the entire phlogistic chemistry and came to the conclusion that this new air was a new chemical element, that it was not the mysterious phlogiston which departed from a burning body, but that this new element combined with the burning body. Thus he placed chemistry, which had so long stood on its head, squarely on its feet. And although he did not obtain the oxygen simultaneously and independently of the other two scientists, as he claimed later on, he nevertheless is the real discoverer of oxygen as compared to the others who had produced it without knowing what they had found.

Marx stands in the same relation to his predecessors in the theory of surplus-value that Lavoisier maintains to Priestley and Scheele. The existence of those parts of the value of products, which we now call surplus-value, had been ascertained long before Marx. It had also been stated with more or less precision that it consisted of that part of the labourer's product for which its appropriator does not give any equivalent. But there the economists halted. Some of them, for instance the classical bourgeois economists, investigated, perhaps, the proportion in which the product of labour was divided among the labourer and the owner of the means of production. Others, the socialists, declared that this division was unjust and looked for utopian means of abolishing this injustice. They remained limited by the economic categories which they found at hand.

Now Marx appeared. And he took an entirely opposite view from all his predecessors. What they had regarded as a solution, he considered a problem. He saw that he had to deal neither with dephlogisticised air, nor with fire-air, but with oxygen. He understood that it was not simply a matter of stating an economic fact, or of pointing out the conflict of this fact with 'eternal justice and true morals', but of explaining a fact which was destined to revolutionise the entire political economy, and which offered a key for the understanding of the entire capitalist production, provided you knew how to use it. With this fact for a starting point Marx analysed all the economic categories which he found at hand, just as Lavoisier had analysed the categories of the phlogistic chemistry which he found at hand. In order to understand what surplus-value is, Marx had to find out what value is. Therefore he had above all to analyse critically the Ricardian theory of value. Marx also analysed labour as to its capacity for producing value, and he was the first to ascertain what kind of labour it was that produced value, and why it did so, and by what means it accomplished this. He found that value was nothing but crystallised labour of this kind, and this is a point which Rodbertus never grasped to his dying day. Marx then analysed the relation of commodities to money and demonstrated how, and why, thanks to the immanent character of value, commodities and the exchange of commodities must produce the opposition of money and commodities. His theory of money, founded on this basis, is the first exhaustive treatment of this subject, and it is tacitly accepted everywhere. He analysed the transformation of money into capital and demonstrated that this transformation is based on the purchase and sale of labour-power. By substituting labour-power, as a value-producing quality, for labour he solved with one stroke one of the difficulties which caused the downfall of the Ricardian school, viz. the impossibility of harmonising the mutual exchange of capital and labour with the Ricardian law of determining value by labour. By ascertaining the distinction between constant and variable capital, he was enabled to trace the process of the formation of surplus-value in its details and thus to explain it, a feat which none of his predecessors had accomplished. In other words, he found a distinction inside of capital itself with which neither Rodbertus nor the capitalist economists know what to do, but which nevertheless furnished a key for the solution of the most complicated economic problems, as is proved by this Volume 2 and will be proved still more by Volume 3. He furthermore analysed surplus-value and found its two forms, absolute and relative surplus-value. And he showed that both of them had played a different, and each time a decisive role, in the historical development of capitalist production. On the basis of this surplus-value he developed the first rational theory of wages which we have, and drew for the first time an outline of the history of capitalist accumulation and a sketch of its historical tendencies.

And Rodbertus? After he has read all that, he regards it as 'an assault on society', and finds that he has said much more briefly and clearly by what means surplus-value is originated, and finally declares that all this does indeed apply to 'the present form of capital', that is to say to capital as it exists historically, but not to the 'conception of capital', that is to say, not to the utoptan idea which Rodbertus has of capital. He is just like old Priestley, who stood by phlogiston to the end and refused to have anything to do with oxygen. There is only this difference: Priestley had actually produced oxygen, while Rodbertus had merely rediscovered a commonplace in his surplus-value, or rather his 'rent;' and Marx declined to act like Lavoisier and to claim that he was the first to discover the fact of the existence of surplus-value.

The other economic feats of Rodbertus were performed on about the same plane. His elaboration of surplus-value into a utopia has already been inadvertently criticised by Marx in his *Poverty of Philosophy*. What may be said about this point in other respects, I have said in my preface to the German edition of that work. Rodbertus' explanation of commercial crises out of the underconsumption of the working class has been stated before him by Sismondi in his *Nouveaux Principes de l'Économie Politique*', liv.4, ch.4.[3] However, Sismondi always had the world-market in mind, while the horizon of Rodbertus does not extend beyond Prussia. His speculations as to whether wages are derived from capital or from income belong to the domain of scholasticism and are definitely settled by the third part of this second volume of *Capital*. His theory of rent has remained his exclusive property and may rest in peace, until the manuscript of Marx criticising it will be published. Finally his suggestions for the emancipation of the old Prussian landlords from the oppression of capital are entirely utopian; for they avoid the only practical question, which has to be solved, viz. how can the old Prussian landlord have a yearly income of, say, 20,000 marks and a yearly expense of, say, 30,000 marks, without running into debt?

The Ricardian school failed about the year 1830, being unable to solve the riddle of surplus-value. And what was impossible for this school, remained still more insoluble for its successor, vulgar economy. The two points which caused its failure were these.

1. Labour is the measure of value. However, actual labour in its exchange with capital has a lower value than labour embodied in the commodities for which actual labour is exchanged. Wages, the value of a definite quantity of actual labour, are always lower than the value of the commodity produced by this same quantity of labour and in which it is embodied. The question is indeed insoluble, if put in this form. It has been correctly formulated by Marx and then answered. It is not labour which has any value. As an activity which creates values it can no more have any special value in itself than gravity can have any special weight, heat any special temperature, electricity any special strength of current. It is not labour which is bought and sold as a commodity, but labour-power. As soon as labour-power becomes a commodity, its value is determined by the labour embodied in this commodity as a social product. This value is equal to the social labour required for the production and reproduction of this commodity. Hence the purchase and sale of labour-power on the basis of this value does not contradict the economic law of value.

2. According to the Ricardian law of value, two capitals employing the same and equally paid labour, all other conditions being equal, produce the same value and surplus-value, or profit, in the same time. But if they employ unequal quantities of actual labour, they cannot produce equal surplus-values, or, as the Ricardians say, equal profits. Now in reality, the exact opposite takes place. As a matter of fact, equal capitals, regardless of the quantity of actual labour employed by them, produce equal average profits in equal times. Here we have, therefore, a clash with the law of value, which had been noticed by Ricardo himself, but which his school was unable to reconcile. Rodbertus likewise could not but note this contradiction. But instead of solving it, he made it a starting point of his utopia (*Zur Erkenntniss, etc.*). Marx had solved this contradiction even in his manuscript for his *Critique of Political Economy*. According to the plan of *Capital*, this solution will be made public in Volume 3. Several months will pass before this can be published. Hence those economists, who claim to have discovered that Rodbertus is the secret source and the superior predecessor of Marx, have now an opportunity to demonstrate what the economics of Rodbertus can accomplish. If they can show in which way an equal average rate of profit can and must come about, not only without a violation of the law of value, but by means of it, I am willing to discuss the matter further with them. In the meantime, they had better make haste. The brilliant analyses of this Volume 2 and its entirely new conclusions on an almost untilled ground are but the initial statements preparing the way for the contents of Volume 3, which

develops the final conclusions of Marx's analysis of the social process of reproduction on a capitalist basis. When this Volume 3 will appear, little mention will be made of a certain economist called Rodbertus.

The second and third volumes of *Capital* were to be dedicated, as Marx stated repeatedly, to his wife.

Friedrich Engels
London, on Marx's birthday, May 5, 1885

The present second edition is, in the main, a faithful reprint of the first. Typographical errors have been corrected, a few inconsistencies of style eliminated, and a few short passages containing repetitions struck out.

The third volume, which presented quite unforeseen difficulties, is likewise almost ready for the printer. If my health holds out, it will be ready for the press this fall.

Friedrich Engels
London, July 15, 1893

Translator's Note

The conditions and the location of the place in which I translated Volumes 2 and 3 of this work made it impossible for me to get access to the original works of the authors quoted by Marx. I was compelled, under these circumstances, to retranslate many quotations from English authors from the German translation, without an opportunity to compare my retranslated version with the English original. But whatever may be the difference in the wording of the originals and of my retranslation from the German, it does not affect the substance of the quotations in the least. The meaning of the originals will be found to be the same as that of my retranslation. The interpretation given by Marx to the various quotations from other authors, and the conclusions drawn by him from them, are not altered in the least by any deviation, which my translation may show from the original texts. If any one should be inclined to turn these statements of mine to any controversial advantage, he should remember that he cannot use them against Marx, but only against me.

Ernest Untermann

Part 1: *The Metamorphoses of Capital and Their Cycles*

Chapter 1
The Circulation of Money-Capital

The circulation process[1] of capital takes place in three stages, which, according to the presentation of the matter in Volume 1, form the following series:

First stage: The capitalist appears as a buyer on the commodity and labour market; his money is transformed into commodities, or it goes through the circulation process M—C.

Second stage: Productive consumption of the purchased commodities by the capitalist. He acts in the capacity of a capitalist producer of commodities; his capital passes through the process of production. The result is a commodity of more value than that of the elements composing it.

Third stage: The capitalist returns to the market as a seller; his commodities are exchanged for money, or they pass through the circulation process C—M.

Hence the formula for the circulation process of money capital is: M—C...P...C'—M', the dots indicating the points where the process of circulation was interrupted, and C' and M' designating C and M increased by surplus value.

The first and third stages were discussed in Volume 1 only in so far as it was required for an understanding of the second stage, the process of production of capital. For this reason, the various forms which capital assumes in its different stages, and which it either retains or discards in the repetition of the circulation process, were not considered. These forms are now the first objects of our study.

In order to conceive of these forms in their purest state, we must first of all abstract from all factors which have nothing to do directly with the discarding or adopting of any of these forms. It is therefore taken for granted at this point that the commodities are sold at their value and that this takes place under the same conditions throughout. Abstraction is likewise made of any changes of value which might occur during the process of circulation.

Section 1. First Stage. M—C.[2]

M—C represents the exchange of a sum of money for a sum of commodities; the purchaser exchanges his money for commodities, the sellers exchange their commodities for money. It is not so much the form of this act of exchange which renders it simultaneously a part of the general circulation of commodities and a definite organic section in the independent circulation of some individual capital, as its substance, that is to say the specific use-values of the commodities which are exchanged for money. These commodities represent on the one hand means of production, on the other labour-power, and these objective and personal factors in the production of commodities must naturally correspond in their peculiarities to the special kind of articles to be manufactured. If we call labour-power L, and the means of production Pm, the sum of commodities to be purchased is $C = L + Pm$, or more briefly $C\{L/Pm\}$. M—C, considered as to its substance, is therefore represented by $M—C\{L/Pm\}$, that is to say M—C is composed of M—L and M—Pm. The sum of money M is separated into two parts, one of which buys labour-power, the other means of production. These two series of purchases belong to entirely different markets, the one to the commodity-market proper, the other to the labour-market.

Aside from this qualitative division of the sum of commodities into which M is transformed, the formula $M—C\{L/Pm\}$ also represents a very characteristic quantitative relation.

We know that the value, or price, of labour-power is paid to its owner, who offers it for sale as a commodity, in the form of wages, that is to say it is the price of a sum of labour containing surplus-value. For instance, if the daily value of labour-power is equal to the product of five hours' labour valued at three shillings, this sum figures in the contract between the buyer and seller of labour-power as the price, or wages, for say, ten hours of labour time. If such a contract is made, for instance, with 50 labourers, they are supposed to work 500 hours per day for their purchaser, and one-half of this time, or 250 hours equal to 25 days of labour of 10 hours each, represent nothing but surplus-value. The quantity and the volume of the commodities to be purchased must be sufficient for the utilisation of this labour-power.

$M—C\{L/Pm\}$, then, does not merely express the qualitative relation represented by the exchange of a certain sum of money, say 422 pounds sterling, for a corresponding sum of means of production and labour-power, but also a quantitative relation between certain parts of that same money spent for the labour-power L and the means of production Pm. This relation is determined at the outset by the quantity of surplus-labour to be expended by a certain number of labourers.

If, for instance, a certain manufacturer pays a weekly wage of 50 pounds sterling to 50 labourers, he must spend 372 pounds sterling for means of production, if this is the value of the means of production which a weekly labour of 3,000 hours, 1,500 of which are surplus-labour, transforms into factory products.

It is immaterial for the point under discussion, how much additional value in the form of means of production is required in the various lines of industry by the utilisation of surplus-labour. We merely emphasise the fact that the amount of money M spent for means of production in the exchange M—Pm must buy a proportional quantity of them. The quantity of means of production must suffice for the absorption of the amount of labour which is to transform them into products. If the means of production were insufficient, the surplus-labour available for the purchaser would not be utilised, and he could not dispose of it. On the other hand, if there were more means of production than available labour, they would not be saturated with labour and would not be transformed into products.

As soon as the process M—C{L/Pm} has been completed, the purchaser has more than simply the means of production and labour-power required for the manufacture of some useful article. He has also at his disposal a greater supply of labour-power, or a greater quantity of labour, than is necessary for the reproduction of the value of this labour-power, and he has at the same time the means of production required for the materialisation of this quantity of labour. In other words, he has at his disposal the elements required for the production of articles of a greater value than these elements, he has a mass of commodities containing surplus-value. The value advanced by him in the form of money has then assumed a natural form in which it can be incarnated as a value generating more value. In brief, value exists then in the form of productive capital which has the faculty of creating value and surplus-value. Let us call capital in this form P.

Now the value of P is equal to that of L + Pm, it is equal to M exchanged for L and Pm. M is the same capital-value as P, only it has a different form of existence, it is capital value in the form of money – money-capital.

M—C{L/Pm}, or the more general formula M—C, a sum of purchases of commodities, a process within the general circulation of commodities, is therefore at the same time, seeing that it is a stage in the independent circulation of capital, a process of transforming capital-value from its money form into its productive form. It is the transformation of money-capital into productive capital. In the diagram of the circulation which we are here discussing, money appears as the first bearer of capital-value, and money-capital therefore represents the form in which capital is advanced.

Money in the form of money-capital finds itself employed in the functions of a medium of exchange; in the present case it performs the service of a general purchasing medium and general paying medium. The last-named service is required inasmuch as labour-power, though first bought is not paid until it has been utilised. If the means of production are not found ready on the market, but have to be ordered, money in the process M—Pm likewise serves as a paying medium. These functions are not due to the fact that money-capital is capital, but that it is money.

On the other hand, money-capital, or capital-value in the form of money, cannot perform any other service but that of money. This service appears as a function of capital simply because it plays a certain role in the movements of capital. The stage in which this function is performed is interrelated with other stages of the circulation of money-capital. Take, for instance, the case with which we are here dealing. Money is here exchanged for commodities which represent the natural form of productive capital, and this form contains in the germ the phenomena of the process of capitalist production.

A part of the money performing the function of money-capital in the process M—C{L/Pm} assumes, in the course of this circulation, a function in which it loses its capital character but preserves its money character. The circulation of money-capital M is divided into the stages M—Pm and M—L, into the purchase of means of production and of labour-power.

Let us consider the last-named stage by itself. M—L is the purchase of labour-power by the capitalist. It is also the sale of labour-power, or we may say of labour, since we have assumed the existence of wages, by the labourer who owns it. What is M—C, or in this case M—L, from the standpoint of the buyer, is here, as in every other transaction of this kind, C—M from the standpoint of the seller, L—M from the standpoint of the labourer. It is the sale of labour-power by the labourer. This is the first stage of circulation, or the first metamorphosis, of commodities (Vol. 1, Chap. 3, Sect. 2a). It is for the seller of labour-power a transformation of his commodity into the money-form. The labourer spends the money so obtained gradually for a number of commodities required for the satisfaction of his needs, for articles of consumption. The complete circulation of his commodity therefore appears as L—M—C, that is to say first as L—M, or C—M, second as M—C, which is the general form of the simple circulation of commodities, C—M—C. Money is in this case merely a passing circulation-medium, a mere mediator in the exchange of one commodity for another.

M—L is the typical stage of the transformation of money-capital into productive capital. It is the essential condition for the transformation of value advanced in the form of money into capital, that is to say into a value producing surplus-value. M—Pm is necessary only for the purpose of realising the quantity of labour bought in the process M—L. This process was discussed from this point of view in Vol. I, Part 2, under the head of 'Transformation of Money into Capital'. But at this point, we shall have to consider it also from another side, relating especially to money-capital as a form of capital.

M—L is regarded as a general characteristic of the capitalist mode of production. But in this case we are doing so, not so much because the purchase of labour-power represents a contract which stipulates the delivery of a certain quantity of labour-power for the reproduction of the price of labour-power, or of wages, not so much for the reason that it means the delivery of surplus-labour which is the fundamental condition for the capitalisation of the value advanced, or for the production of surplus-value; but we do so rather on account of its money form, because wages in the form of money buy labour-power, and this is the characteristic mark of the money system.

Nor is it the irrational feature of the money form which we shall note as the characteristic part. We shall overlook the irrationalities. The irrationality consists in the fact that labour itself as a value-creating element cannot have any value which could be expressed in its price, and that, therefore, a certain quantity of labour cannot have any equivalent in a certain quantity of money. But we know that wages are but a disguised form in which, for instance, the price of one day's labour-power is seen to be the price of the quantity of labour materialised by this labour-power in one day. The value produced by this labour-power in six hours of labour is then expressed as the value of twelve hours of its labour.

M—L is regarded as the characteristic signature of the so-called money system, because labour there appears as the commodity of its owner, and money as the buyer. In other words, it is the money relation in the sale and purchase of human activity which is considered. It is a fact, however, that money appears at an early stage as a buyer of so-called services, without the transformation of M into money-capital, and without any change in the general character of the economic system.

It makes no difference to money into what sort of commodities it is transformed. It is the general equivalent of all commodities, which show by their prices that they represent in an abstract way a certain sum of money and anticipate their exchange for money. They do not assume the form in which they may be translated into use-values for their owners, until they change places with money. Once labour-power has come into the market as the commodity of its owner, to be sold for wages in return for labour, its sale and purchase is no more startling than the sale and purchase of any other commodity. The peculiar characteristic is not that the commodity labour-power is saleable, but that labour-power appears in the shape of a commodity.

By means of M—C{L/Pm}, that is to say by the transformation of money-capital into productive capital, the capitalist accomplishes the combination of the objective and personal factors of production so far as they consist of commodities. If money is transformed into productive capital for the first time, or if it performs for the first time the function of money-capital for its owner, he must begin by buying means of production, such as buildings, machinery, etc., before he buys any labour-power. For as soon as labour-power passes into his control, he must have means of production for it, in order to utilise it.

This is the capitalist's point of view.

The labourer, on the other hand, looks at this question in the following light: the productive application of his labour-power is not possible, until he has sold it and brought it into contact with means of production. Before its sale, it exists in a state of separation from the means of production which it requires for its materialisation. So long as it remains in this state, it cannot be used either for the production of use-values for its owner, or for the production of commodities, by the sale of which he might live. But from the moment that it is brought into touch with means of production, it forms part of the productive capital of its purchaser, the same as the means of production.

It is true, that in the act M—L the owner of money and the owner of labour-power enter into the relation of buyer and seller, of money-owner and commodity-owner. To this extent they enter into a money relation. But at the same time the buyer also appears in the role of an owner of means of production, which are the material conditions for the productive expenditure of labour-power on the part of its owner. The means of production, then, meet the owner of labour-power in the form of the property of another. On the other hand, the seller of labour meets its buyer in the form of the labour-power of another and it must pass into the buyer's possession, it must become a part of his capital, in order that it may become productive capital. The class relation between the capitalist and the wage labourer is therefore established from the moment that they meet in the act M—L, which signifies L—M from the standpoint of the labourer. It is indeed a sale and a purchase, a money relation, but it is a sale and a purchase in which the buyer is a capitalist and the seller a wage-labourer. And this relation arises out of the fact that the conditions required for the materialisation of labour-power, viz. means of subsistence and means of production, are separated from the owner of labour-power and are the property of another.

We are not here concerned in the origin of this separation. It is a fact, as soon as the act M—L can be performed. The thing which interests us here is that M—L does not become a function of money-capital for the sole reason that it is a means of paying for a useful human activity or service. The function of money as a paying medium is not the main object of our attention. Money can be expended in this form only because labour-power finds itself separated from its means of production, including the means of subsistence required for its reproduction; because this separation can be overcome only by the sale of the labour-power to the owner of the means of production; because the materialisation of labour-power, which is by no means limited to the quantity of labour required for the reproduction of its own price, is likewise in the control of its buyer. The capital relation during the process of production arises only because it is inherent in the process of circulation based on the different economic conditions, the class distinctions between the buyer and the seller of labour-power. It is not money which by its nature creates this relation; it is rather the existence of this relation which permits of the transformation of a mere money-function into a capital-function.

In the conception of money-capital, so far as it relates to the special function which we are discussing, two errors run parallel to one another or cross each other. In the first place, the functions performed by capital-value in its capacity of money-capital, which are due to its money form, are erroneously derived from its character as capital. But they are due only to the money form of capital-value. In the second and reverse case, the specific nature of the money-function, which renders it simultaneously a capital-function, is attributed to its money nature. Money is here confounded with capital, while the specific nature of the money-function is conditioned on social relations such as are indicated by the act M—L, and these conditions do not exist in the mere circulation of commodities and money.

The sale and purchase of slaves is formally also a sale and purchase of commodities. But money cannot perform this function without the existence of slavery. If slavery exists, then money can be invested in the purchase of slaves. On the other hand, the mere possession of money cannot make slavery possible.

In order that the sale of his labour-power by the labourer, in the form of the sale of labour for wages, may take place as a result of social conditions which make it the basis of the production of commodities, in order that it may not be an isolated instance, so that money-capital may perform, on a social scale, the function in the process M—C{L/Pm}, definite historical processes are required, by which the original connection of the means of production with labour-power is dissolved. These processes must have resulted in opposing the mass of the people, the labourers, as propertiless to the idle owners of the means of production. It makes no difference in this case, whether the connection between the labour-power and the means of production before its dissolution was such that the labourer belonged to the means of production and was a part of them, or whether he was their owner.

The fact which lies back of the process M—C{L/Pm} is distribution; not distribution in the ordinary meaning of a distribution of articles of consumption, but the distribution of the elements of production themselves. These consist of the objective things which are concentrated on one side, and labour-power which is isolated on the other.

The means of production, the objective things of productive capital, must therefore stand opposed to the labourer as capital, before the process M—L can become a universal, social one.

We have seen on previous occasions that capitalist production, once it is established, does not only reproduce in its further development this separation, but extends its scope more and more, until it becomes the prevailing social condition. However, there is still another side to this question. In order that capital may be able to arise and take control of production, a definite stage in the development of commerce must precede. This includes the circulation of commodities, and therefore also the production of commodities; for no articles can enter circulation in the form of commodities, unless they are manufactured for sale, and intended for commerce. But the production of commodities does not become the normal mode of production, until it finds as its basis the capitalist system of production.

The Russian landowners, who are compelled to carry on agriculture by the help of wage-labourers instead of serfs, since the so-called emancipation of the serfs, complain about two things. They wail in the first place about the lack of money-capital. They say, for instance, that large sums must be paid to wage-labourers, before the crops can be sold, and there is a dearth of ready cash. Capital in the form of money must always be available for the payment of wages, before production on a capitalist scale can be carried on. But the landowners may take hope. In due time the industrial capitalist will have at his disposal, not alone his own money, but also that of others.

The second complaint is more characteristic. It is to the effect that even if money is available, there are not enough labourers at hand at any time. The reason is that the Russian farm labourer, owing to the communal property in land, has not been fully separated from his means of production, and hence is not yet a 'free wage-worker' in the full capitalist meaning of the word. But the existence of 'free' wage-workers is the indispensable condition for the realisation of the act M—C, the exchange of money for commodities, the transformation of money-capital into productive capital.

As a matter of course, the formula M—C...P...C'—M' does not represent the normal form of the circulation of money-capital, until capitalist production is fully developed, because it is conditioned on the existence of a social class of wage-labourers. We have seen that capitalist production does not only create commodities and surplus-values, but also gives rise to an ever growing class of wage-labourers, either by propagation or by the transformation of independent producers into proletarians.

Since the first condition for the realisation of the act M—C...P... C'—M' is the permanent existence of a class of wage-workers, capital in the form of productive capital and the circulation of productive capital must precede it.

Section 2. Second Stage. Functions of Productive Capital.

The circulation of capital which we have here considered begins with the act of circulation represented by the formula M—C, the transformation of money into commodities, or purchase. Circulation must therefore be supplemented by the reverse metamorphosis C—M, the transformation of commodities into money, or sale. But the immediate result of M—C{L/Pm} is the interruption of the circulation of the capital advanced in the form of money. By the transformation of money-capital into productive capital the value of capital has assumed a natural form in which it cannot continue to circulate, but must enter into consumption, more accurately into productive consumption.

The application of labour-power, labour, can not be carried into effect anywhere but in the labour process. The capitalist cannot sell the labourer along with the commodities, because the wage-worker is not a chattel slave and the capitalist does not buy anything from the labourer but the privilege of utilising the labour-power purchased in the person of the labourer for a certain time. On the other hand, the capitalist cannot use this labour-power in any other way than by using it up in transforming, by its help, means of production into commodities. The result of the first stage of the circulation of money-capital is therefore its entrance into the second stage, that of productive capital.

This movement is represented by the formula M—C{L/Pm}...P, in which the dots indicate the place where the circulation of capital is interrupted, while its rotation continues, since it passes from the sphere of the circulation of commodities into that of production. The first stage, the transformation of money-capital into productive capital, is therefore merely the harbinger of the second, the productive stage of capital.

The act M{L/Pm} presupposes that the person performing it not only has at his or her disposal values of some useful form, but also that he or she has them in the form of money. And the act consists precisely in giving away money. A man can, therefore, remain the owner of money only on the condition, that the giving away of money at the same time implies a return of money. But money can return only through the sale of commodities. Hence the above formula assumes the owner of money to be a producer of commodities.

Now let us look at the formula M—L. The wage worker lives only by the sale of his labour-power. The preservation of this power, equivalent to the self-preservation of the labourer, requires a daily consumption. Hence the payment of wages must be continually repeated at short intervals, in order that the wage labourer may be able to repeat acts L—M or C—M—C, by means of which he is enabled to purchase the articles required for his self-preservation. For this reason the capitalist must stand opposed to the wage worker in the capacity of a money-capitalist, and his capital must be money-capital. On the other hand, if the wage labourers, the mass of direct producers, are to perform the act L—M—C, the means of subsistence required for it must be present in the form of purchasable commodities. This state of affairs necessitates a high degree of development of the circulation of products in the form of commodities, and this again must be preceded by a corresponding extension of the production of commodities. As soon as production by means of wage labour has become universal, the production of commodities must be the typical form of production. If this mode of production is general, it carries in its wake an ever-increasing division of labour, that is to say an ever-growing differentiation in the special nature of the products which are manufactured in the form of commodities by the various capitalists, an ever-greater division of supplementary processes of production into independent specialties. To the extent that M—L develops, M—Pm also develops, that is to say the production of means of production to that extent differentiates from the production of commodities with those means. The means of production then stand opposed as commodities to every producer of commodities, and he must buy those means in order to be able to carry on his special line of commodity production. They are derived from branches of production which are entirely divorced from his own and enter into his own branch as commodities which he must buy. The objective materials of commodity production assume more and more the character of products of other commodity manufacturers which he must purchase. And to the same extent the capitalist must become a money-capitalist, in the same ratio his capital must assume the functions of money-capital.

On the other hand, the same conditions which are the cause of the fundamental constitution of capitalist production, especially the existence of a class of wage labourers, also demand the transition of all commodity production into the capitalist mode of commodity production. In proportion as the capitalist mode of production develops, it has a disintegrating effect on all older forms of production, which were mainly adjusted to the individual needs and transformed only the surplus over and above those needs into commodities. Capitalist production makes the sale of products the main incentive, without at first apparently affecting the mode of production itself. Such was, for instance, the first effect of capitalist world commerce on such nations as the Chinese, Indians, Arabs, etc. But wherever it takes root, there it destroys all forms of commodity production which are either based on the self-employment of the producers, or merely on the sale of the surplus product. The production of commodities is first made general and then transformed by degrees into the capitalist mode of commodity production.[3]

Whatever may be the social form of production, labourers and means of production always remain its main elements. But either of these factors can become effective only when they unite. The special manner in which this union is accomplished distinguishes the different economic epochs from one another. In the present case, the separation of the so-called free labourer from his means of production is the starting point, and we have observed the way and the conditions in which these two elements are united in the hands of the capitalist, as the productive mode of existence of his capital. The actual process which combines the personal and objective materials of commodity production under these conditions, the process of production thus becomes in its turn a function of capital, a capitalist process of production, the nature of which has been fully analysed in the first volume of this work. Every process of commodity production at the same time becomes a process of exploiting labour-power. But it is not until the capitalist production of commodities is established that this mode of exploitation becomes universal and typical, and revolutionises in the course of its historical development, through the organisation of the labour process and the enormous improvement of technique, the entire economic structure of society, in a manner eclipsing all former epochs.

The means of production and labour-power, in so far as they are forms of existence of advanced capital values, are distinguished by the different roles assumed by them in the production of value, hence also of surplus-value, and known under the names of constant and variable capital. As different parts of productive capital they are furthermore distinguished by the fact that the means of production in the possession of the capitalist remain his capital even outside of the process of production, while labour-power exists in the form of individual capital only within this process. While labour-power is a commodity only in the hands of its seller, the wage worker, it becomes capital only in the hands of its buyer, the capitalist who uses it temporarily. And the means of production do not become objective parts of productive capital, until labour-power, the personal form of productive capital, is embodied in them. Human labour-power is originally no more capital than are the means of production. They assume this specific social character only under definite historically developed conditions, and the same character is impregnated upon precious metals, and still more upon money, by the same circumstances.

Productive capital, in performing its functions, consumes its own component parts for the purpose of transforming them into a mass of products of a higher value. Seeing that labour-power acts likewise merely as an organ of productive capital, the surplus-value produced by its surplus-labour over and above the value of its component elements is also gathered by capital. The surplus-labour of labour-power is the inexpensive labour of capital and thus forms surplus-value for the capitalist, a value which costs him no equivalent return. The product is, therefore, not only a commodity, but a commodity pregnant with surplus-value. Its value is equal to P + S, that is to say equal to the value of the productive capital consumed in its manufacture plus the surplus-value S created by it. Assuming that this product were represented by 10,000 pounds of yarn, let us say that means of production valued at 372 pounds sterling and labour-power valued at 50 pounds sterling were consumed in the production of this quantity of yarn. During the process of spinning, the spinners transferred the value of the means of production to the amount of

372 pounds sterling to the yarn, and at the same time they created, by means of their labour-power, new values to the amount of 128 pounds sterling. The 10,000 pounds of yarn therefore represent a value of 500 pounds sterling.

Section 3. Third Stage. C'—M'.

Commodities become commodity-capital by springing into existence as a direct result of commodity-production, embodying in a new form the capital values already utilised. If the production of commodities were carried on as capitalist production in all spheres of society, all commodities would be elements of commodity-capital from the outset, whether they would be composed of crude iron, Brussels laces, sulphuric acid, or cigars. The problem as to what class of commodities is destined by its nature to rank as capital and what class to serve as general commodities, is one of the self-prepared ills of the scholastic economists.

In the form of commodities, capital has to perform the functions of commodities. The articles of which commodity capital is composed are produced for sale and must be exchanged for money, must go through the process C—M.

The commodities of the capitalist may consist of 10,000 pounds of yarn. If 372 pounds sterling represent the value of the means of production consumed in the spinning process, and new values to the amount of 128 pounds sterling have been created, the yarn has a value of 500 pounds sterling, which is expressed in its price of the same amount. This price is realised by the sale C—M. What is it that makes of this simple process of all commodity circulation at the same time a capital function? It is not any change that takes place inside of it. Neither the use-value of the product has been changed, for it passes into the hands of the buyer as an object of use, nor has anything been altered in its exchange-value, for this value has not experienced any change of magnitude, but only of form. It first existed as yarn, while now it exists as money. Thus a plain distinction is evident between the first stage C—M, and the last stage C'—M'. There the advanced money serves as money-capital, because it is transformed, by means of the circulation of commodities, into articles of a specific use-value. Here, on the other hand, the commodities can only serve as capital, since they brought this character with them from the process of production before their circulation began. During the spinning process, the spinners created new values to the amount of 128 pounds sterling in the shape of yarn. Of this sum, say 50 pounds sterling are regarded by the capitalist merely as an equivalent for wages advanced for labour-power, while 78 pounds sterling – representing an exploitation of 156 per cent – are his surplus-value.

The value of the 10,000 pounds of yarn therefore embodies first the value of the consumed productive capital P, which consists of a constant capital of 372 pounds sterling and a variable capital of 50 pounds sterling, their sum being 422 pounds sterling, equal to 8,440 pounds of yarn. Now the value of the productive capital P is equal to C, the value of the elements constituting it which the capitalist found to be in the hands of their sellers in the stage M—C. In the second place, the value of the yarn embodies a surplus-value of 78 pounds sterling, equal to 1,560 pounds of yarn. C as an expression of the value of 10,000 pounds of yarn is therefore equal to C plus surplus C, or C plus an increment of C worth 78 pounds sterling, which we shall call c, since it exists in the same commodity form as that now assumed by the original value C. The value of the 10,000 pounds of yarn, equal to 500 pounds sterling, is therefore represented by the formula $C + c = C'$. What changes C, the value of the 10,000 pounds of yarn, into C' is not its absolute value of 500 pounds sterling, for it is determined, the same as C standing for the expression of the value of any other sum of commodities, by the quantity of labour embodied in it. It is rather its relative value, its value as compared to that of the productive capital P consumed in its production, which is the essential thing. This value is contained in it plus the surplus-value created through the productive capital. Its value exceeds that of the capital by the surplus-value c. The 10,000 pounds of yarn are the bearers of the consumed capital value increased by this surplus-value, and they are so by virtue of the capitalist process of production. C' expresses the relation of the value of the commodities to that of the capital advanced in its production, in other words the composition of the value of the commodities, of capital value and surplus-value. The 10,000 pounds of yarn represent a commodity-capital C' only because they are an altered form of the productive capital P, and this relation exists originally by virtue of the circulation of this individual capital; it applies primarily to the capitalist who produced the yarn by the help of his capital. It is, so to say, an internal, not an external relation which makes a commodity capital of the 10,000 pounds of yarn in their capacity of representatives of value. They are bearing the imprint of capital not in the absolute magnitude of their value, but in its relative magnitude, in the proportion of their value to that of productive capital embodied in them before they became commodities. If, then, these 10,000 pounds of yarn are sold at their value of 500 pounds sterling, this act of circulation, considered by itself, is identical with C—M, a mere transformation of the same value from the form of a commodity into that of money. But as a special stage in the circulation of a certain individual capital, the same act is also a realisation of the capital value, embodied in the commodity, to the amount of 422 pounds sterling plus the surplus-value, likewise embodied in it, of 78 pounds sterling. That is to say, it also represents C'—M', the transformation of the commodity-capital from its commodity form into that of money.[4]

The function of C' is now that of all commodities, viz. to transform itself into money, to be sold, to go through the circulation stage C—M. So long as the capital utilised so far remains in the form of commodity-capital and stays on the market, the process of production rests. The commodity-capital serves then neither as a creator of value nor of products. In proportion to the degree of speed with which capital throws off the commodity-form and assumes that of money, in other words, in proportion to the rapidity of the sale, the same capital-value will serve in widely different degrees as a creator of products or of values, and the scale of reproduction will be extended or abridged. It has been shown in Volume 1 that the effectiveness of any given capital is conditioned on factors in the productive process which are to a certain extent independent of the magnitude of its own value. Here we see that the process of circulation sets in motion new factors which are independent of the value of the capital, its effectiveness, its expansion or contraction.

The mass of commodities C', being the embodiment of the consumed capital, must furthermore pass in its entire volume through the metamorphosis C'—M'. The quantity sold is here the main determinant. The individual commodity figures only as an integral part of the total mass. The 500 pounds sterling are embodied in 10,000 pounds of yarn. If the capitalist succeeds in selling only 7,440 pounds of yarn at their value of 372 pounds sterling, he has recovered only the value of his constant capital, the value expended by him for means of production. If he sells 8,440 pounds of yarn, he recovers only the value of his total capital. He must sell more, in order to obtain some surplus-value, and he must sell the entire 10,000 pounds in order to get the entire surplus-value of 78 pounds sterling (1,560 pounds of yarn). In 500 pounds sterling he receives merely an equivalent for the commodity sold. His transaction within the process of circulation is simply C—M. If he had paid his labourers 64 pounds sterling instead of 50 pounds sterling, his surplus-value would be only 64 pounds sterling instead of 78, and the degree of exploitation would have been only 100 per cent instead of 150. But the value of the yarn would remain the same; only the relation of its component parts would be changed. The circulation-act C—M would still represent the sale of 10,000 pounds of yarn for 500 pounds sterling, which is their value.

C' is equal to C + c (or 422 plus 78 pounds st.). C equals the value of P, the productive capital, and this equals the value of M, the money advanced in the act M—C, the purchase of the elements of production, amounting to 422 pounds sterling in our example. If the mass of commodities is sold at its value, then C equals 422 pounds sterling, and c, the value of the surplus product of 1,560 pounds of yarn, equals 78 pounds sterling. If we call c, expressed in money, m, then C'—M' = (C + c) − (M + m), and the cycle M—C...P...C'—M', in its expanded form, is represented by M—C{L/Pm}...P...(C + c) − (M + m).

In the first stage, the capitalist takes articles of use out of the commodity-market proper and the labour-market. And in the third stage he throws commodities back, but only into one market, the commodity-market proper. But the fact that he extracts from the market, by means of his commodities, a greater value than he threw upon it originally, is due only to the circumstance that he throws more commodity-values back upon it than he first drew out of it. He threw the value M into it and drew out of it the equivalent C; he throws the value C + c back into it, and draws out of it the equivalent M.

M was in our example equal to the value of 8,440 pounds of yarn. But he throws 10,000 pounds of yarn into the market, he returns a greater value than he drew out of it. On the other hand, he threw this increased value into it only by virtue of the fact that he obtained a surplus-value through the exploitation of labour-power (this value being expressed by an aliquot part of the product). The mass of commodities becomes a commodity-capital only by virtue of this process, it is the impersonation of the used-up capital value only through it. By the act C'—M' the advanced capital-value is recovered as well as the surplus-value. The realisation of both coincides with that series of sales, or with that one sale, of the entire mass of commodities, which is expressed by C'—M'. But this same act of circulation is different for capital-value and surplus-value, because it expresses for each one of these two values a different stage of their circulation, a different section of the series of metamorphoses through which each of them passes in its circulation. The surplus-value c did not come into the world until the process of production began. It appeared for the first time on the commodity-market in the form of commodities. This is its first form of circulation, hence the act c—m is its first circulation act, or its first metamorphosis, which remains to be supplemented by the reverse circulation, or the opposite metamorphosis, m—c.[5]

It is different with the circulation which the capital-value C performs in the same circulation act C'—M', and which constitutes for it the circulation act C—M, in which C is equal to P, the M originally advanced. It opened its circulation in the form of M, money-capital, and returns through the act C—M to the same form. In other words, it has now passed through the two opposite stages of the circulation, first M—C, second C—M, and finds itself once more in the form in which it can begin its cycle anew. What constitutes for surplus-value the first transformation of the commodity-form into that of money, constitutes for capital-value its return, or retransformation, into its original money-form.

By means of M—C{L/Pm}, money-capital is transformed into an equivalent mass of commodities, L and Pm. These commodities no longer perform the function of commodities, of articles of sale. Their value now exists in the hands of the capitalist who bought them, they represent the value of his productive capital P. And in the function P, productive consumption, they are transformed into commodities substantially different from the means of production, into yarn, in which their value is not only preserved but increased, rising from 422 pounds sterling to 500 pounds sterling. By means of this metamorphosis, the commodities taken from the market in the first stage, M—C, are replaced by commodities of a different substance and value, which now perform the function of commodities, being exchanged for money and sold. The process of production, therefore, appears to us as an interruption of the process of circulation of capital-value, since up to production it has passed only through the phase M—C. It passes through the second and concluding phase, C—M, after C has been altered in substance and value. But so far as capital-value, considered by itself, is concerned, it has merely gone through a transformation of its use-form in the process of production. It existed in the form of 422 pounds sterling's worth of L and Pm, while now it exists in the form of 8,440 pounds of yarn valued at 422 pounds sterling. If we consider merely the two circulation phases of capital-value, apart from its surplus-value, we find that it passes through the stages M—C and C—M, in which the second C represents a different use-value, but the same exchange-value as the first C. And the process M—C—M is, therefore, a cycle which requires the return of the value advanced in money to its money-form, because the commodity here changes places twice and in the opposite direction, the first change being from the money to the commodity-form, the second from the commodity to the money-form. Capital-value is retransformed into money.

The same circulation act C'—M', which constituted the second and concluding metamorphosis, a return to the money-form, for capital-value, represents for the surplus-value simultaneously embodied in the commodity-capital, and realised by its exchange for money, its first metamorphosis, its transformation from the commodity to the money-form, C—M, its first circulation phase.

We have, then, two observations to make. First, the final return of capital-value to its original money-form is a function of commodity-capital. Second, this function includes the first transformation of surplus-value from its original commodity-form to that of money. The money-form, then, plays a double role here. On the one hand, it is a return of a value, originally advanced in money, to its old form, a return to that form of value which opened the process. On the other hand, it is the first metamorphosis of a value which originally enters the circulation in the form of a commodity. If the commodities composing the commodity-capital are sold at their value, as we assume, then C plus c is transformed into M plus m, its equivalent. The sold commodity-capital now exists in the hands of the capitalist in the form of M plus m (422 pounds sterling plus 78 pounds sterling, equal to 500 pounds sterling). Capital-value and surplus-value are now present in the form of money, the form of the general equivalent.

At the conclusion of the process, capital-value has resumed the form in which it entered, and can now open a new cycle of the same kind, in the form of money-capital, and go through it. Just because the opening and concluding form of this process is that of money-capital, M, we call this form of the circulation process the circulation of money-capital. It is not the form, but merely the magnitude of the advanced value which is changed in the end.

M plus m is a sum of money of a definite magnitude, in this case 500 pounds sterling. As a result of the circulation of capital, of the sale of commodity-capital, this sum of money contains the capital-value and the surplus-value. And these values are now no longer organically connected, as they were in the yarn, they are now arranged side by side. Their sale has given both of them an independent money form; 211/250ths of this money represent the capital value of 422 pounds sterling, and 39/250ths constitute the surplus-value of 78 pounds sterling. This separation of capital-value and surplus-value, which results from the sale of the commodity-capital, has not only the formal meaning to which we shall refer presently. It becomes important in the process of the reproduction of capital, according to whether m is entirely, or partially, or not at all, lumped together with M, that is to say according to whether or not it continues to perform the functions of capital-value. Both m and M may also pass through widely different cycles of circulation.

In M', capital has returned to its original form M, to its money-form. But it then has a form, in which it is materialised capital.

There is in the first place a difference of quantity. It was M, 422 pounds sterling. It is now M', 500 pounds sterling, and this difference is expressed by the quantitatively different points M...M' of the cycle, the movement of which is indicated by the dots. M' is greater than M, and M' − M is equal to the surplus-value s. But as a result of this cycle M...M' it is only M' which exists now; it is the product which marks the close of the process of formation of money-capital. M' now exists independently of the movement which it started. This movement is completed, and M' exists in its place.

But M', being M plus m, or in this case 500 pounds sterling, composed of 422 pounds sterling advanced capital plus an increment of 78 pounds sterling, represents at the same time a qualitative relation. It is true that this qualitative relation does not exist outside of the quantitative relation of the parts of one and the same sum. M, the advanced capital, which is now once more present in its original form (422 pounds sterling), exists as the realisation of capital. It has not only preserved itself, but also realised its own capital-form, distinguished from m (78 pounds sterling), to which it stands in the relation of creator, m being its fruit, an increment born by it. It has realised its capital-form, because it is a value which has created more value. M' exists as a capital relation. M no longer appears as mere money, but it is explicitly used as money-capital, as a value which has utilised itself by creating a higher value than itself. M acts as capital by virtue of its relation to another part of M', which it has created. Thus M' appears as a sum of values expressing the capital relation, being differentiated into functionally different parts.

But this expresses only a result, without showing the intermediate process which caused it.

Parts of value as such are not qualitatively different from one another, except in so far as they are values of different articles, of concrete things, embodied in different use-values. They are values of different commodities, and this difference is not due to their character as exchange-values. In money, all differences of commodities are extinguished, because it is an equivalent form common to all of them. A sum of money of 500 pounds sterling consists of equal elements of one pound sterling each. Since the intermediate links of descent are extinguished in the simple form of this sum of money, and all traces of the specific differences of the individual parts of capital in the productive process have disappeared, there exists only the mental distinction between the main sum of 422 pounds sterling, which was the capital advanced, and a surplus sum of 78 pounds sterling.

Or, again, let M' be equal to 110 pounds sterling, of which 100 may be equal to the main sum M and 10 equal to the surplus-value s. There is an absolute homogeneity, an absence of distinctions, between the two constituent parts of the sum of 110 pounds sterling. Any 10 pounds of this sum always constitute 1/11th of the sum of 110 pounds regardless of the fact that they are also 1/10th of the advanced main sum of 100 pounds, or the excess of 10 pounds above it. Main sum and surplus sum (capital and surplus-value), may simply be expressed as fractional parts of the total sum. In our illustration, 10/11ths form the main sum, and 1/11th the surplus sum. Materialised capital, at the end of its cycle, therefore appears as an undifferentiated expression, the money expression, of the capital relation.

True, this applies also to C' (C plus c). But there is this difference, that C', of which C and c are also proportional parts of the same homogeneous mass of commodities, indicates its origin P, the immediate product of which it is, while in M', a form derived immediately from circulation, the direct relation to P is obliterated.

The undifferentiated distinction between the main sum and the surplus sum, which are contained in M', so far as this expresses the result of the movement M...M', disappears as soon as it performs its active function of money-capital and is not preserved as a fixed expression of materialised industrial capital. The circulation of money-capital can never begin with M' (although M' now performs the function of M). It can begin only with M, that is to say, it can never begin as an expression of the capital relation, but only as an advance of capital-value. As soon as the 500 pounds sterling are once more advanced as capital, in order to be again utilised, they constitute a point of departure, not one of conclusion. Instead of a capital of 422 pounds sterling, a capital of 500 pounds sterling is now advanced. It is more money than before, more capital-value, but the relation between its two constituent parts has disappeared. In fact, a sum of 500 pounds sterling might have served instead of the 422 pounds sterling as the original capital.

It is not an active function of money-capital to materialise in the form of M'; this is rather a function of C'. Even in the simple circulation of commodities, first in C—M, then in M—C₂, money M does not figure actively until in the second movement, M—C₂. Its embodiment in the form of M is the result of the first act, by virtue of which it becomes a transformation of C₁. The capital relation contained in M', the relation of its constituent parts in the form of capital-value and surplus-value, assumes a functional importance only in so far as the repeated cycle M...M' splits M' into two circulations, one of them a circulation of capital, the other of surplus-value. In this case these two parts perform not only quantitatively, but also qualitatively different functions, M rather than m. But considered by itself, M...M' does not include the consumption of the capitalist, but emphatically only the self-utilisation and accumulation of money-capital, the latter function expressing itself at the outset as a periodical augmentation of ever renewed advances of money-capital.

Although M' (M plus m) is the undifferentiated form of capital, it is at the same time a materialisation of money-capital, it is money which has generated more money. But this is different from the role played by money-capital in the first stage, M—C{L/Pm}. In this first stage, M circulates as money. It assumes the functions of money-capital only because it cannot serve as money unless it assumes the form of money, because it cannot transform itself in any other way into the component parts of P, L and Pm, which stand opposed to it in the form of commodities. In this circulation act it serves as money. But as this act is the first stage in the circulation of capital-value, it is also a function of money-capital, by virtue of the specific use-value of the commodities L and Pm which are bought by it. M', on the other hand, composed of M, the capital-value, and m, the surplus-value created by M, stands for materialised capital-value, expresses the purpose and the outcome, the function of the total process of circulation of capital. The fact that it expresses this outcome in the form of money, of materialised money-capital, is due to the capital-character of money-capital, not to its money-character; for capital opened the process of circulation in the form of an advance of money. Its return to the money-form, as we have seen, is a function of C', not of money-capital. As for the difference between M and M', it is simply m, the money-form of c, the increment of C. For M' is composed of M plus m only because C' was composed of C plus c. In C', this difference and the relation of capital-value to its product, surplus-value, is already present and expressed, before both of them are transformed into M'. And in this form, these two values appear independently side by side and may, therefore, be employed in separate and distinct functions.

M' is the outcome of the materialisation of C'. Both M' and C' are different forms of utilised capital-value, one of them the commodity, the other the money-form. Both of them share the quality of being utilised capital-value. Both of them are materialised capital, because capital-value here exists simultaneously with its product, surplus-value, although it is true that this relation is expressed in the undifferentiated form of the proportion of two parts of one and the same sum of money or commodity-value. But as expressions of capital, and in distinction from the surplus-value produced by it,

M' and C' are the same and express the same thing, only in different forms. In so far as they represent utilised value, capital acting in its own role, they express the result of the function of productive capital, the only function in which capital-value generates more value. What is common to both of them, is that money-capital as well as commodity-capital are different modes of existence of capital. Their distinctive and specific functions cannot, therefore, be anything else but the difference between the functions of money and of commodities. Commodity-capital, the direct product of the capitalist process of production, indicates its capitalist origin and is, therefore, to that extent more rational and less difficult to understand than money-capital, in which every trace of this process has disappeared. In general, all special use-forms of commodities disappear in money.

It is only when M' itself figures as commodity-capital, when it is the direct outcome of a productive process, instead of being a transformed product of this process, that it loses its bizarre form, that is to say, in the production of money itself. In the production of gold, for instance, the formula would be M—C{L/Pm}...P...M (M plus m), and M' would here figure as a commodity, because P furnishes more gold than had been advanced for the elements of production contained in the first money-capital M. In this case, the irrational nature of the formula M...M' (M plus m) disappears. Here a part of a certain sum of money appears as the mother of another part of the same sum of money.

Section 4. The Rotation as a Whole.

We have seen that the process of circulation is interrupted at the end of its first phase, M—C{L/Pm}, by P, which makes the commodities L and Pm parts of the substance and value of productive capital and consumes them. The result of this productive consumption is a new commodity C', which is of different composition and value than the commodities L and Pm. The interrupted process of circulation, C—M, must be completed by M—C. The basis of this second and concluding phase of circulation is C', a commodity of different composition and value than C. The process of circulation therefore appears first as M—C$_1$, then as C$_2$—M', the C$_2$ in this second phase representing a greater value and a different use-value than C$_1$, due to the interruption caused by the function of P which is the production of C' from elements of C, embodied in the productive capital P. The first form assumed by capital (Vol. 1, Chap. 4), viz., M—C—M', or extended first M—C$_1$, second C$_1$—M', shows the same commodity twice. It is the same commodity which is exchanged for money in the first phase and again exchanged for more money in the second phase.

In spite of this essential difference, these two modes of circulation share the peculiarity of transforming in their first phase money into commodities, and in the second phase commodities into money, so that the money spent in the first phase returns in the second. On the one hand, both have in common this return of money to its starting point, on the other hand the excess of the returned money over the money first advanced. To this extent, the formula M—C...C'—M' is apparently contained in the general formula M—C—M'.

It follows furthermore that equal quantities of simultaneously existing values are placed in opposition to one another and exchanged in the two metamorphoses of circulation represented by M—C and C'—M'. The change of value is due exclusively to the metamorphosis P, the process of production, which thus appears as a natural metamorphosis of capital, as compared to the merely formal metamorphosis of circulation.

Let us now consider the total movement, M—C...P...C'—M', or its more explicit form, M—C{L/Pm}...P...C' (C + c)—M' (M + m). Capital here appears as a value which goes through a series of connected metamorphoses conditioned on one another and representing so many phases of the total process. Two of these phases belong to the sphere of circulation, one of them to that of production. In each one of these phases, capital-value has a different form corresponding to a different, special, function. Within this cycle, value does not only maintain itself at the magnitude in which it was originally advanced, but it increases. Finally, in the concluding stage, it returns to the same form which it had at the beginning of the cycle. This total movement constitutes the process of rotation as a whole.

The two forms assumed by capital-value are that of money-capital and commodity-capital. In the stage of production, its form is that of productive capital. The capital which assumes these different forms in the course of its total process of rotation, discards them one after the other, and performs a special function in each one of them, is industrial capital. The term *industrial* applies to every branch of industry run on a capitalist basis.

Money-capital, commodity-capital, productive capital are not, therefore, terms indicating independent classes of capital, nor are their functions processes of independent and separate branches of industry. They are here used only to indicate special functions of industrial capital, assumed by it *seriatim*.

The circulation of capital proceeds normally only so long as its various phases flow uninterruptedly one into the other. If capital stops short in its first phase M—C, money-capital assumes the rigid form of a hoard; if it stops in the phase of production, the means of production remain lifeless on one side, while labour-power remains unemployed on the other; and if capital stops short in its last phase C'—M', masses of unsold commodities accumulate and clog the flow of rotation.

At the same time, it is a matter of course that the rotation of capital includes the stopping of capital for a certain length of time in the various sections of its cycle. In each of these sections, industrial capital is poured into a definite mould, being either money-capital, productive capital, or commodity-capital. It does not assume a form in which it may enter a new metamorphosis, until it has gone through the function corresponding to the form preceding the new metamorphosis. In order to make this plain, we have assumed in our illustration, that the capital-value of the mass of commodities created in the phase of production is equal to the total sum of values originally advanced in the form of money, or, in other words, that the entire capital-value advanced in the form of money enters undivided from one stage into the next. Now we have seen (Vol. 1, Chap. 4) that a part of the constant capital, the means of production proper, such as machinery, always serve repeatedly, for a greater or smaller number of times, in the same processes of production, so that they transfer their values piecemeal to the products. We shall see later, to what extent this circumstance modifies the process of rotation of capital. For the present, it suffices to say this: in our illustration, the value of the productive capital of 422 pounds sterling contained only the average wear and tear of buildings, machinery, etc., that is to say only that part of value which they transferred in the transformation of 10,600 pounds of cotton to 10,000 pounds of yarn, which represents the product of one week's spinning, or of 60 hours. In the means of production, into which the advanced constant capital of 372 pounds sterling is transformed, the instruments of labour, buildings, machinery, etc., figure only as would objects which were rented in the market for a weekly rate. But this does not change the problem in any way. We have but to multiply the quantity of yarn produced in one week, or 10,000 pounds of yarn, with the number of weeks contained in a certain number of years, in order to transfer the entire value of the means of production bought and consumed during this period. It is then plain that the advanced money-capital must first be transformed into these means of production, must first have gone through the phase M—C, before it can be used as productive capital, P. And it is likewise plain that, in our illustration, the capital value of 422 pounds sterling, embodied in the yarn during the process of production, cannot become a part of the value of the 10,000 pounds of yarn and enter the circulation phase C'—M', until it has been produced. The yarn cannot be sold, until it has been spun.

In the general formula, the product of P is regarded as a material thing different from the elements of the productive capital, as an object existing apart from the process of production and having a different use-value than the elements of production. And if the fruit of production assumes the form of such an object, it always corresponds to this description, even if a part of it should re-enter production as one of its elements. Grain, for instance, serves as seed for its own reproduction, but the final product is always grain and has a different composition than the elements used in its production, such as labour-power, implements, and fertiliser. But there are certain independent branches of industry, in which the result of the productive process is not a new material product, not a commodity. Among these, only the industries representing communication, such as transportation proper for commodities and human beings, and the transmission of communications, letters, telegrams, etc., are economically important.

A. Cuprov[6] says on this score: 'The manufacturer may first produce articles and then look for consumers.' (His product, having been completed in the process of production, is transferred to the process of circulation as a separate commodity.) 'Production and consumption thus appear as two acts distinct from one another in space and time. In the transportation industry, which does not create any new products, but merely transfers men and things, these two acts coincide; its services (change of place) must be consumed at the same time that they are produced. For this reason the distance, within which railroads can find customers, extends at best 50 verst (53 kilometers or about 30 miles) on either side of their tracks.'

The result in the transportation of either men or commodities is a change of place. Yarn, for instance, is thus transferred from England, where it was produced, to India.

Now transportation, as an industry, sells this change of location. This utility is inseparably connected with the process of transportation, which is the productive process of transportation. Men and commodities travel by the help of the means of transportation, and this travelling, this change of location, constitutes the production in which these means of transportation are consumed. The utility of transportation can be consumed only in this process of production. It does not exist as a use-value apart from this process, it does not, like other commodities, serve as a commodity which circulates after its process of production. The exchange value of this utility is determined, like that of any other commodity, by the value of the elements of production (labour-power and means of production) plus the surplus-value created by the surplus-labour of the labourers employed in transportation. This utility also entertains the same relations to consumption that all other commodities do. If it is consumed individually, its value is used up in consumption; if it is consumed productively by entering into the process of production of the transported commodities, its value is added to that of the commodity. The formula for the transportation industry would, therefore, be M—C {L, P}...P-M', since it is the process of production itself which is paid for and consumed, not a product distinct and separate from it. This formula has almost the same form as that of the precious metals, only with the difference, that in this case M' represents the changed form of the utility resulting during the process of production, while in the case of the precious metals it represents the natural form of the gold or silver obtained in this process and transferred from it to other stages.

Industrial capital is the only form of existence of capital, in which not only the appropriation of surplus value or surplus product, but also its creation is a function of capital. Therefore it gives to production its capitalist character. Its existence includes that of class antagonisms between capitalists and labourers. To the extent that it assumes control over social production, the technique and social organisation of the labour process are revolutionised and with them the economic and historical type of society. The other classes of capital, which appear before industrial capital amid past or declining conditions of social production, are not only subordinated to it and suffer changes in the mechanism of their functions corresponding to it, but move on it as a basis, live and die, stand and fall with this basis. Money-capital and commodity-capital, so far as they still persist as independent branches of industry along with industrial capital, are nothing but modes of existence of different functional forms either assumed or discarded by industrial capital in the sphere of circulation, made independent and developed one-sidedly by the social division of labour.

The cycle M...M' on one side intermingles with the general circulation of commodities, proceeds from it and flows back into it, is a part of it. On the other hand, it is for the individual capitalist an independent movement of his capital value, taking place partly within the general circulation of commodities, partly outside of it, but always preserving its independent character. For in the first place, its two phases taking place in the sphere of circulation, M—C and C'—M', have functionally different characters as functions of capital circulation. In M—C, the commodity C is composed of labour-power and means of production; in C'—M', capital value is realised plus surplus-value. In the second place, the process of production, P, includes productive consumption. In the third place, the return of money to its starting point makes of the cycle M...M' a process of circulation complete in itself.

Every individual capital is therefore, on the one hand, in its two phases M—C and C'—M', an active element in the general circulation of commodities, with which it is connected either as money or as a commodity. Thus it forms a link in the general chain of metamorphoses in the world of commodities. On the other hand, it goes through its own independent circulation within the general circulation. Its independent circulation passes through the sphere of production and returns to its starting point in the same form in which it left that point. Within its own circulation, which includes its natural metamorphosis in the process of production, it changes at the same time its value. It returns not only as the same money-value, but as an increased money-value.

Let us finally consider M—C...P...C'—M' as a special form of the process of circulation of capital, apart from the other forms which we shall analyse later. It is distinguished by the following points:

1. It appears as the circulation of money-capital, because industrial capital in its money form, as money-capital, forms the starting and terminal point of its total process. The formula itself expresses the fact that money is not expended as money at this stage, but advanced as the money-form of capital. It expresses furthermore that exchange-value, not use-value, is the determining aim of this movement. Just because the money-form of this value is its tangible and independent form, the compelling motive of capitalist production, the making of money, is most fittingly expressed by the circulation formula M...M'. The process of production appears merely as an indispensable and intermediate link, as a necessary evil of money-making. All nations with a capitalist mode of production are seized periodically by a feverish attempt to make money without the mediation of the process of production.

2. The stage of production, the function of P, represents an interruption of the two phases of circulation M—C...C'—M', which in their turn represent links in the simple circulation M—C—M'. The process of production appears formally and essentially in circulation as that which is typical of capitalist production, that is to say as a mere means of utilising previously advanced values. The accumulation of wealth is the purpose of production.

3. Since the series of phases is opened by M—C, the second link of the circulation is C'—M'. In other words, the starting point is M, or the money-capital to be utilised, the terminal point M', or the utilised money-capital M plus m, in which M figures together with its offspring m. This distinguishes the circulation of M from that of the two other cycles P and C', in two ways. On one side, its two extremes

are represented by the money-form. And money is the tangible form of value, the value of the product in its independent form, in which every trace of the use-value of the commodities has been extinguished. On the other side, the formula P...P is not necessarily transformed into P...P' (P plus p), and in the form C——C', no difference in value is visible between the two extremes. It is, therefore, characteristic for the formula M——M' that capital value is its starting point, and utilised capital value its terminal point, so that advanced capital value appears as the means, and utilised capital value as the end of the entire operation. And furthermore, this relation is expressed in the form of money, in the form of independent value, so that money-capital is money generating more money. The generation of surplus-value by value is not only expressed as the Alpha and Omega of the process, but more explicitly in the form of glittering money.

4. Since M', the money-capital realised as a result of C'——M', the supplementary and concluding form of M——C, has absolutely the same form in which it began its first circulation, it can immediately begin the same circulation over again as an increased (accumulated) money-capital, or as M' equal to M plus m. And it is not expressed in the formula M——M' that, in the repetition of the cycle, the circulation of m separates from that of M. Considered in its complete form, the circulation of money capital expresses simply the process of utilisation and accumulation. The consumption in it is productive consumption, as shown by the formula M——C{L/Pm}. and it is only this which is included in this circulation of individual capital. M——L means L——M, or C——M, on the part of the labourer. It is therefore the first phase of circulation which promotes his individual consumption, thus: L——M——C (means of subsistence). The second phase, M——C, no longer falls within the circulation of individual capital, but it is initiated by individual capital and an indispensable premise for it, since the labourer must above all live and maintain himself by individual consumption, in order to be always on the market for exploitation by the capitalist. But this consumption is here only assumed as the indispensable condition for the productive consumption of labour-power by capital, and it is, therefore, considered only in so far as it preserves and reproduces his labour-power by means of his individual consumption. But the means of production Pm, the commodities proper which enter into the circulation of capital, are only material feeding the productive consumption. The act L——M promotes the individual consumption of the labourer, the transformation of means of subsistence into flesh and blood. It is true, that the capitalist must also be present, must also live and consume in order to perform the function of a capitalist. To this end, he has, indeed, but to consume in

the same way as the labourer, and this is all that is assumed in this form of the circulation process. But it is not formally expressed, since the term M' concludes the formula and indicates that it may at once re-enter on its function of increased money-capital.

In the formula C'—M', the sale of C' is directly indicated; but this sale C'—M' on the part of one is M—C, or the purchase of commodities, on the part of another, and in the last analysis a commodity is bought only for its use-value, in order to enter (leaving intermediate sales out of consideration) into the process of consumption, and this may be either productive or individual consumption, according to the nature of the commodity. But this consumption does not enter into the circulation of individual capital, the product of which is C'. This product is eliminated from this circulation from the moment that it is sold. C' is explicitly produced for consumption by others. For this reason we note that certain spokesmen of the mercantile system (which is based on the formula M—C...P...C'—M') deliver lengthy sermons to the effect that the individual capitalist should consume only in his capacity as a worker, that capitalist nations should let other and less intelligent nations consume their own and other commodities, and that a capitalist nation should devote itself for life to the productive consumption of commodities. These sermons frequently remind us in form and content of analogous ascetic exhortations of the fathers of the church.

* * *

The rotation process of capital is therefore a combination of circulation and production, it includes both. In so far as the two phases M—C and C'—M' are processes of circulation, the rotation of capital is a part of the general circulation of commodities. But in so far as they are definite sections performing a peculiar function in the rotation of capital, which combines the spheres of circulation and production, capital goes through its own circulation in the general circulation of commodities. The general circulation of commodities serves capital in its first stage as a means of assuming that form in which it can perform the function of productive capital; in its second stage, it serves to eliminate the commodity function in which capital cannot renew its circulation; at the same time it enables capital to separate its own circulation from that of the surplus-value created by it.

The circulation of money-capital is therefore the most one-sided, and thus the most convincing and typical form of the circulation of industrial capital. Its aim and compelling motive, the utilisation of value, the making and accumulation of money, is thus most clearly revealed. Buying in order to sell dearer is its slogan. The first phase

M—C also indicates the origin of the elements of productive capital in the commodity market, or more generally, the dependence of the capitalist mode of production on circulation, on commerce. The circulation of money-capital is not merely the production of commodities; it is itself possible only through circulation of commodities and based on it. This is plain from the fact that the term M belongs to circulation and represents the first and most typical form of advanced capital-value. This is not the case in the other two forms of circulation.

The circulation of money-capital always remains the general expression of industrial capital, because it always implies the utilisation of the advanced value. In P...P, the money-character of capital is shown only in the price of the elements of production as a value expressed in money-terms for the purpose of calculation and book-keeping.

M...M' becomes a special form of the circulation of industrial capital when new capital is first advanced in the form of money and then returned in the same form, either in passing from one branch of industry to another, or in the case that industrial capital retires from business. This includes the capital function of the surplus-value first advanced in the form of money, and becomes most evident when surplus-value performs a function in some other business than the one in which it originated. M...M' may be the first circulation of a certain capital; it may be the last; it may be regarded as the form of the total social capital; it is that form of capital which is newly invested, either as a recently accumulated capital in the form of money, or as some old capital which is entirely transformed into money for the purpose of transfer from one branch of industry to another.

Being a form always contained in all circulations, money-capital performs this circulation precisely for that part of capital which produces surplus-value, viz. variable capital. The normal form of an advance in wages is payment in money; this process must be renewed in short intervals, because the labourer lives from hand to mouth. In his relation to the labourer, the capitalist must therefore always be a money-capitalist, and his capital must be money-capital. There can be no direct or indirect balancing of accounts in this case, such as we find in the purchase of means of production or in the sale of productive commodities, where the greater part of the money capital really exists in the form of commodities, while the money is mainly used for purposes of calculation and figures in cash only in the balancing of accounts. On the other hand, a part of the surplus-value arising out of variable capital is spent by the capitalist for his individual consumption, which is a part of the retail trade, and this surplus-value is in the last analysis always expended in the form of money. It does not matter how large or small may be this part of surplus-value. Variable capital always appears anew as money-capital invested in wages (M—L) and m as surplus-value which may be expended for the individual consumption of the capitalist. So that M, capital advanced for wages, and m, its increment, are necessarily held and spent in the form of money.

The formula M—C...P...C'—M', with its result M' equal to M plus m, is, in a certain sense, deceptive, owing to the existence of the advanced and surplus-value in the form of the general equivalent, money. The emphasis in this formula is not on the utilisation of value, but on the money-form of this process, on the fact that more money-value is finally drawn out of the circulation than had originally been advanced; in other words, the emphasis is on the multiplication of the amount of gold and silver belonging to the capitalist. The so-called monetary system is merely the expression of the abstract formula M—C—M', a movement which takes place exclusively in the circulation. And this system cannot explain the two phases M—C and C—M' in any other way than by declaring that C is sold above its value in the second phase and thus draws more money out of the circulation than was put into it in its purchase. But if M—C...P...C'—M' becomes the exclusive form of circulation, it is the basis of a more highly developed mercantile system, in which not only the circulation of commodities, but also their production, is recognised as a necessary element.

The illusive character of M—C...P...C'—M' and the resulting illusive interpretation always appear, whenever this form is considered as rigid, not as a flowing and ever renewed movement; in other words, they appear whenever this formula is considered not as one section of circulation, but as the exclusive form of circulation. But it itself points toward other forms.

In the first place, this entire circulation is conditioned on the capitalist character of the process of production, and considers it and the specific social conditions created by it as the basis. M—C is equal to M—C{L/Pm}, but M—L assumes the existence of the wage labourer, and regards the means of production as parts of productive capital. It assumes, therefore, that the process of labour and of utilisation, the process of production, is a function of capital.

In the second place, if M...M' is repeated, the return to the money-form is just as transient as the money-form in the first phase. M—C disappears and makes room for P. The recurrent advance of money-capital and its equally persistent return in the form of money appear merely as passing moments in the general circulation.

In the third place; the repeated formula has this form: M—C...P... C'—M'. M—C...P...C'—M'. M—C...P... etc.

Beginning with the second repetition of the circulation, the cycle P...C'—M'.M—C...P appears, before the second circulation of M is completed, and all other cycles may be considered under the form of P...C'—M—C...P, so that the first phase of the first circulation is merely the passing introduction for the constantly repeated circulation of the productive capital. And this is indeed the case for the first time in the investment of industrial capital in the form of money.

On the other hand, before the second circulation of P is completed, the first circulation, that of the commodity-capital, as shown in the formula C'—M'. M—C...P...C' (or abridged C'...C') has preceded. Thus the first form already contains the other two, and the money-form disappears, so far as it is a general equivalent and not merely an expression of value used for calculation.

Finally, if we consider some newly invested capital going for the first time through the circulation M—C...P...C'—M', then M—C is the introductory phase, the preparation for the first process of production undertaken by this capital. This phase M—C is not considered as existing, but is caused by the requirements of the process of production. But this applies only to this individual capital. The general form of the circulation of industrial capital is the circulation of money-capital, whenever the capitalist mode of production exists and with it the social conditions corresponding to it. It is therefore the capitalist mode of production which is the first condition for the circulation of money-capital, and if it is not assumed for the first phase of a newly invested industrial capital, it is certainly assumed for all others. The continuous movement of this process of production requires the persistent renewal of the cycle P...P. Even the first stage, M—C{L/Pm}, reveals this basic condition. For it requires on one side the existence of the wage-working class. On the other side, that which is M—C for the buyer of means of production, is C'—M' for their seller. Hence C' presupposes the existence of commodity-capital, and thus of commodities as the result of capitalist production, and this implies the function of productive capital.

Chapter 2

The Rotation of Productive Capital

The rotation of productive capital has the general formula P...C'—M'—C...P. It signifies the periodical renewal of the function of productive capital, in other words its reproduction, or its process of production as a reproductive process generating surplus-value. It is not only production, but a periodical reproduction of surplus-value; it is the function of industrial capital in its productive form, and this function is not performed merely once, but periodically so that the terminal point of one cycle is the starting point of another. A portion of C' may re-enter directly into the same labour process as means of production out of which it came in the form of commodities (for instance, in various branches of investment of industrial capital). This merely does away with the transformation of its value into money proper, or token-money, or else it finds an independent expression merely in calculation. This part of value does not enter into the circulation. Thus it is that values enter into the process of production which do not enter into circulation. The same is also true of that part of C' which is consumed by the capitalist, and which represents surplus-value in the form of means of consumption, in their natural state. But this is inconsiderable for capitalist production. It deserves consideration, if at all, only in agriculture.

Two things are at once apparent in this form.

In the first place, while in the first form, M...M', the process of production, a function of P, interrupts the circulation of money-capital and acts only as a mediator between its two phases M—C and C'—M', it is the entire circulation process of industrial capital, its entire movement within the sphere of circulation, which intervenes here and forms the connecting link between productive capitals, which begin the circulation at one extreme and close it at another, only to make this last extreme the starting point of a new cycle. Circulation proper appears but as an instrument promoting the periodic renewal, and thus the continuous reproduction, of productive capital.

In the second place, the entire circulation assumes a form which is the reverse of that which it has in the circulation of money-capital. While the circulation of money-capital proceeds after the formula M—C—M (M—C. C—M), making exception of the determination of value, it proceeds in the case of productive capital, making the same exception, after the formula C—M—C (C—M. M—C). which is the form of the simple circulation of commodities.

Section 1. Simple Reproduction.

Let us first consider the process C'—M'—C, which takes place between the two extremes P...P.

The starting point of this circulation is the commodity-capital C', equal to C plus c, or equal to P plus c. The function of commodity-capital C'—M' has been considered in the first form of the circulation. It consisted in the realisation of the capital-value P, contained in it, which now exists as a part of the commodity C, and likewise in the realisation of the surplus-value contained in it, which now exists as a part of the same mass of commodities C and has the value of c. But in the former case, this function formed the second phase of the interrupted circulation and the concluding phase of the entire cycle. In the present case, it forms the second phase of the cycle, but the first phase of the circulation. The first cycle ends with M', and since M' as well as the original M may again open the second cycle as money-capital, it was not necessary for the moment to analyse whether the parts of M', viz., M and m (surplus-value) continue in their course together, or whether each one of them pursues its own course. This would only have been necessary, if we had followed up the first cycle in its renewed course. But in studying the cycles of productive capital, this point must be decided, because the determination of its very first cycle depends on it, and because C'—M' appears in it as the first phase of circulation which has to be supplemented by M—C. It depends on the outcome of this decision, whether our formula represents the simple reproduction, or reproduction on an enlarged scale. The character of the cycle changes according to this decision.

Let us, then, take first the simple reproduction of productive capital, assuming that the conditions are the same as those taken for a basis in the first chapter, and that the commodities are bought and sold at their value. Under these conditions, the entire surplus-value enters into the individual consumption of the capitalist. As soon as the transformation of the commodity-capital C' into money has taken place, that part of the money which represents the capital-value continues in the cycle of industrial capital; the other part, which represents surplus-value in the form of gold, enters into the general circulation of commodities as a circulation of money emanating from the capitalist but taking place outside of the circulation of his individual capital.

In our illustration, we had a commodity-capital C' of 10,000 pounds of yarn, valued at 500 pounds sterling; 422 pounds sterling of this represent the value of productive capital and continue, as the money-form of 8,440 pounds of yarn, the capital circulation begun by C', while the surplus-value of 78 pounds sterling, as the money-form of 1,560 pounds of yarn, the surplus-product, leaves this circulation and describes its own separate course within the general circulation of commodities.

$$C' (C + c)...M' (M + m)...C\{L/Pm\}, c$$

The formula m—c represents a series of purchases by means of money which the capitalist spends either in commodities proper or for personal services to his cherished self or family. These purchases are made piecemeal at various times. Money, therefore, exists temporarily in the form of a supply, or hoard, of money destined for gradual consumption, for money interrupted in its circulation partakes of the nature of a hoard. Its function as a circulating medium, including that of a temporary hoard, does not share in the circulation of capital having the form of money M. This money is not advanced, but spent.

We have assumed that the advanced total capital always passed entirely from one of its phases into the other. In this case, we, therefore, assume that the mass of commodities produced by P represents the total value of the productive capital P, or 422 pounds sterling plus 78 pounds sterling of surplus-value created in the process of production. In our illustration, which deals with an easily analysed commodity, the surplus-value exists in the form of 1,560 pounds of yarn; if computed on the basis of one pound of yarn, it would exist in the form of 2.496 ounces. But if the commodity were, for instance, a machine valued at 500 pounds sterling and representing the same division of values, one part of the value of this machine would indeed be represented by 78 pounds sterling of surplus-value, but these 78 pounds sterling would exist only in the machine as a whole. This machine cannot be divided into capital-value and surplus-value without breaking it to pieces and thus destroying, with its use-value, also its exchange-value. For this reason the two parts of value can be represented only ideally as portions of a mass of commodities, not as independent elements of the commodity C', such as we are able to distinguish in each pound of yarn in the 10,000 pounds of our illustration. In the case of the machine, the total commodity representing the commodity-capital must be sold before m can enter into its independent circulation. On the other hand, when the capitalist has sold 8,440 pounds of yarn, the sale of the remaining 1,560 pounds of yarn would represent an entirely separate circulation of the surplus-value in the form of c (1,560 pounds of yarn) —m (78 pounds sterling) equal to c (articles of consumption). But the elements of value of each individual portion of yarn in the 10,000 pounds may be individually separated and valuated the same as the total quantity of yarn. Just as the entire 10,000 pounds of yarn may be divided into the value of the constant capital c (7,440 pounds of yarn worth 372 pounds sterling), variable capital v (1,000 pounds of yarn worth 50 pounds sterling, and surplus-value s (1,560 pounds of yarn worth 78 pounds sterling), so every pound of yarn may be divided into c (11.904 ounces of yarn worth 8.929d.), v (1.600 ounces of yarn worth 1.200d.), and s (2.496 ounces of yarn worth 1.872d.). The capitalist might also sell various portions of the 10,000 pounds of yarn successively and consume the different portions of surplus-value contained in them in the same way, thus realising gradually the sum of c plus v. But this operation likewise requires the final sale of the entire lot, so that the value of c plus v would be made good by the sale of 8,440 pounds of yarn (Book 1, Chap 9, 2).

However that may be, by the movement C'—M', both the capital-value and surplus-value contained in C' secure a separate existence in separate sums of money. In both cases, M and m are actually transformed values, which had originally only an ideal existence in C as prices of commodities.

The formula c—m—c represents the simple circulation of commodities, the first phase of which, c—m, is included in the circulation of the commodity-capital C'—M', in short, included in the cycle of capital; while its supplementary phase m—c falls outside of this cycle and is a separate process in the general circulation of commodities. The circulation of C and c, of capital-value and surplus-value, is differentiated after the transformation of C' into M'. Hence it follows:

First, by the realisation on the commodity-capital in the process C'—M', or C'—(M + m), the courses of capital-value and surplus-value, which are united so long as they are both embodied in the same mass of commodities in C'—M', are separated, for both of them henceforth appear in two independent sums of money.

Second, after this separation has taken place, m being spent as the income of the capitalist, while M continues its way as a functional form of capital-value in a course determined by this cycle, the movement C'—M' in connection with the subsequent movements M—C and m—c, may be represented in the form of two different circulations, viz. C—M—C and c—m—c, and both of these, so far as their general form is concerned, belong to the general circulation of commodities.

By the way, in the case of commodities which cannot be cut up into their constituent parts, it is a matter of practice to isolate their different portions of value and surplus-value ideally. In the building-business of London, for instance, which is carried on mainly on credit, the contractor receives advances in proportion to the different stages in which the construction of a house proceeds. None of these stages is a house, but only an actually existing fraction of the growing house; in spite of its actuality, each stage is but an ideal portion of the entire house, but it is real enough to serve as security for an additional advance. (See on this point Chapter 12, Book 2)

Third, if the movement of capital-value and surplus-value, which proceeds unitedly so long as they are in the form of C and M, is separated only in part (so that a portion of the surplus-value is not spent as income), or is not separated at all, a change takes place in the capital-value itself within its own cycle, before it is completed. In our illustration the value of the productive capital was equal to 422 pounds sterling. If it continues its cycle M—C, for instance as 480 pounds sterling or 500 pounds sterling, then it goes through the further stages of its cycle with an increase of 58 pounds sterling or 78 pounds sterling over its original value. This change may also go hand in hand with a change in the proportion of its component parts.

C'—M', the second stage of the circulation and the final stage of cycle I (M...M'), is the second stage in our cycle and the first in the circulation of commodities. So far as the circulation is concerned, this stage must be supplemented by M'—C. But C'—M' has not only passed the process of utilisation (in this case the function of P, the first stage), but has also realised as its result the commodity C'. The process of utilisation of capital, and the realisation on the commodities which are its product, are therefore completed in C'—M'.

We have started out with simple reproduction and assumed that m—c separates entirely from M—C. Since both circulations, c—m—c as well as C—M—C, belong to the circulation of commodities, so far as their general form is concerned (and do not show, for this reason, any difference in the value of their extremes), it is easy to conceive of the process of capitalist production, after the manner of vulgar economy, as a mere production of commodities, of use-value destined for consumption of some sort, which the capitalist produces for no other purpose than that of getting in their place commodities with different use-values, or exchanging them, as vulgar economy erroneously states.

C' appears from the very outset as commodity-capital, and the purpose of the entire process, the accumulation of wealth, does not exclude an increasing consumption on the part of the capitalist in proportion as his surplus-value (and thus his capital) increases; on the contrary, it promotes such an increasing consumption.

Indeed, in the circulation of the income of the capitalist, the produced commodity c, or the ideal fraction of the commodity C corresponding to it, serves merely for its transformation, first into money, and from money into a number of other commodities required for individual consumption. But we must not, at this point, overlook the trifling circumstance that c is that part of the commodity-value which did not cost the capitalist anything, since it is the embodiment of surplus-labour and steps originally on the stage as a part of the commodity-capital C'. This c is, by the varying nature of its existence, bound to the cycle of circulating capital-value, and if this cycle is clogged, or otherwise disturbed, not only the consumption of c is restricted or entirely arrested, but also the disposal of that series of commodities which are to take the place of c. The same is true in the case that the movement C'—M' is a failure, or that only a part of C' is sold.

We have seen that c—m—c, as representing the circulation of the revenue of the capitalist, enters into the circulation of capital only so long as c is a part of the value of C', of the commodity-capital; but that, as soon as it materialises in the form of m—c, that is to say, as soon as it completes the entire cycle c—m—c, it does not enter into the movements of the capital advanced by the capitalist, although this advance is its cause. It is connected with the movements of capital only in so far as the existence of capital presupposes the existence of the capitalist, and this is conditioned on the consumption of surplus-value by the capitalist.

Within the general circulation, C', for instance yarn, passes only as a commodity; but as an element in the circulation of capital it performs the function of commodity-capital, and capital-value alternately assumes and discards this form. After the sale of the yarn to a merchant, it has passed out of the circulation of the capital which produced it, but nevertheless, as a commodity, it moves always in the cycle of the general circulation. The circulation of one and the same mass of commodities continues, although it may have ceased to be an element in the independent cycle of the capital of the manufacturer. Hence the actual and final metamorphosis of the mass of commodities thrown into circulation by the capitalist by means of C—M, their final elimination in consumption, may be separated in space and time from that metamorphosis in which this same mass of commodities performs the function of commodity-capital. The same metamorphosis which has been completed in the circulation of capital still remains to be accomplished in the sphere of the general circulation.

This state of things is not changed by the transfer of this yarn to the cycle of some other industrial capital. The general circulation comprises as much the interrelations of the various independent fractions of social capital, in other words, the totality of the individual capitals, as the circulation of those values which are not thrown on the market as capital, but enter into individual consumption.

The different relations in the cycle of capital, according to whether it is a part of the general circulation, or forms certain links in the independent cycles of capital, may be further understood when we consider the circulation of M', or of M plus m. M as money-capital, continues the cycle of capital. On the other hand m, spent as revenue in the act m—c, enters into the general circulation, but is eliminated from the cycle of capital. Only that part enters the capital cycle which performs the function of additional money-capital. In c—m—c, money serves only as coin, and the purpose of this circulation is the individual consumption of the capitalist. It is significant for the idiocy of vulgar economy that it pretends to regard this circulation, which does not enter into the circulation of capital but is merely the circulation of that part of the surplus-product which is consumed as revenue, as the characteristic cycle of capital.

In its second phase, M—C, the capital-value M (which is equal to P, the value of the productive capital that at this point re-opens the cycle of industrial capital) is again present, delivered of its surplus-value. Therefore it has once more the same magnitude which it had in the first stage of the cycle of money-capital, M—C. In spite of the different place at which we now find it, the function of money-capital, into which form the commodity-capital has now been transformed, is the same: transformation into Pm and L, into means of production and labour-power.

Simultaneously with c—m, capital-value in the function of commodity-capital (C'—M') has also gone through the phase C—M, and enters now into the supplementary phase M—C{L/Pm}. Its complete circulation is, therefore, C—M—C Pm.

First: Money-capital M appeared in cycle I (M...M') as the original form in which capital-value is advanced; it appears at the very outset as a part of that sum of money into which commodity-capital transformed itself in the first phase of circulation, C'—M'. It is from the beginning the transformation of P by means of the sale of commodities into the money-form. Money-capital exists here as that form of capital-value which is neither its original nor its final one, since the phase M—C, which supplements the phase C—M, can only be completed by again discarding the money-form. Therefore, that part of M—C which is at the same time M—L appears now no longer as a mere advance of money in the purchase of labour-power, but also as an advance by means of which the same 1,000 pounds of yarn, valued at 50 pounds, which form a part of the commodity-value created by labour-power, are given to the labourer in the form of money. The money thus advanced to the labourer is merely a transformed equivalent of a fraction of the value of the commodities produced by himself. And for this very reason, the act M—C, so far as it means M—L is by no means simply a replacement of a commodity in the form of money by a commodity in the form of a use-value, but it includes other elements which are in a way independent of the general circulation of commodities.

M' appears as a changed form of C', which is itself a product of a previous function of P, of the process of production. The entire sum of money M is therefore a money-expression of past labour. In our illustration, 10,000 pounds of yarn (worth 500 pounds sterling), are the product of the spinning process. Of this quantity, 7,440 pounds represent the advanced constant capital c (worth 372 pounds sterling); 1,000 pounds represent the advanced variable capital v (worth 50 pounds sterling); and 1,560 pounds represent the surplus-value s (worth 78 pounds sterling). If in M', only the original capital of 422 pounds sterling is again advanced, other conditions remaining the same, then the labourer receives next week, in M—L, only a part of the 10,000 pounds of yarn produced in this week (the money-value of 1,000 pounds of yarn). As a result of C—M, money is always the expression of past labour. If the supplementary act M—C takes place at once on the commodity-market and M is given in return for commodities existing in this market, then this act is again a transformation of past labour from the money-form into the commodity-form. But M—C differs in the matter of time from C—M. True, these two acts may exceptionally take place at the same time, for instance when the capitalist who performs the act M—C and the other capitalist for whom this act signifies C—M mutually ship their commodities at the same time and M is used only to square the balance. The difference in time between the performance of C—M and M—C may be considerable or insignificant. Although M, as the result of C—M, represents past labour, it may, in the act M—C, represent the changed form of commodities which are not as yet on the market, but will be thrown upon it in the future, since M—C need not take place until C has been produced anew. M may also stand for commodities which are produced simultaneously with the C whose money-expression M is; for instance, in the movement M—C (purchase of means of production), coal may be bought before it has been mined. In so far as m represents an accumulation of money which is not spent as revenue, it may stand for cotton which will not be produced until next year. The same holds good of the revenue of the capitalist represented by m—c. It also applies to wages, in this case to L equal to 50 pounds sterling; this money is not only the money-form of the past labour of the labourers, but at the same time a draft on simultaneously performed labour or on future labour. The labourer may buy for his wages a coat which will not be made until next week. This applies especially to the vast number of necessary means of subsistence which must be consumed almost as soon as they have been produced, to prevent their being spoiled. Thus the labourer receives in the money which represents his wages the changed form of his own future labour or that of others. By means of a part of the labourer's past labour, the capitalist gives him a draft on his own future labour. It is the labourer's simultaneous or future labour which represents the not yet existing supply that will pay for his past labour. In this case, the idea of the formation of a supply disappears altogether.

Second: In the circulation C—M—C{L/Pm} the same money changes places twice; the capitalist first receives it as a seller and gives it away as a buyer; the transformation of commodities into the money-form serves only for the purpose of retransforming it from money into commodities; the money-form of capital, its existence as money-capital, is therefore only a passing factor in this movement; or, so far as the movement proceeds, money-capital appears only as a circulating medium when it serves to buy things; on the other hand, money-capital performs the function of a paying medium when capitalists buy mutually from one another and square only the balance of their accounts.

Third: The function of money-capital, whether it is a mere circulating medium or a paying medium, mediates only the renewal of C by L and Pm, that is to say, the renewal of the commodities produced by productive capital, such as yarn (after deducting the surplus-value used as revenue), out of its constituent elements, in other words, the retransformation of capital-value from its commodity-form into the elements constituting this commodity. In the last analysis, the function of money-capital mediates only the retransformation of commodity-capital into productive capital.

In order that the cycle may be completed normally, C' must be sold at its value and completely. Furthermore, C—M—C does not signify merely the replacing of one commodity by another, but also the replacing of the same relative values. We assume that this takes place here. As a matter of fact, however, the values of the means of production vary; it is precisely capitalist production which has for its characteristic a continuous change of value-relations, and this is conditioned on the ever changing productivity of labour, which is another characteristic of capitalist production. This change in the value of the factors of production will be discussed later on, and we merely refer to it here. The transformation of the elements of production into commodity-products, of P into C', takes place in the sphere of production, while their retransformation from C' into P takes place in the sphere of circulation; it is accomplished by way of the simple metamorphosis of commodities, but its content is a phase in the process of reproduction, regarded as a whole. C—M—C, considered as a form of the circulation of capital, includes a change of substance due to this function. The process C—M—C requires that C should be identical with the elements of production of the quantity of commodities C', and that these elements maintain their relative proportions toward one another. It is, therefore, understood that the commodities are not only bought at their value, but also that they do not undergo any change of value during their circulation. Otherwise this process cannot run normally.

In M...M', the factor M represents the original form of capital-value, which is discarded only to be resumed. In P...C'—M'—C...P, the factor M represents a form which is only assumed in this process and which is discarded before this process is over with. The money-form appears here only as a passing independent form of capital-value. Capital is just as anxious to assume this form in C' as it is to discard it in M' after barely assuming it, in order to again transform itself into productive capital. So long as it remains in the money-form, it does not perform the function of capital and does not, therefore, generate new values; it then lies fallow. M serves here as a circulating medium, but as a circulating medium of capital. The semblance of independence, which the money-form of capital-value possesses in the first form of the circulation of money-capital, disappears in this second form, which, therefore, is the negation of the first form and reduces it to a concrete form. If the second metamorphosis M—C meets with any obstacles – for instance, if there are no means of production in the market – the uninterrupted flow of the process of reproduction is arrested, quite as much as it is when capital in the form of commodity-capital is held fast. But there is this difference: it can remain longer in the money-form than in that of commodities. It does not cease to be money, if it does not perform the functions of money-capital; but it does cease to be a commodity, or even a use-value, if it is interrupted too long in its functions of commodity-capital. Further-more, it is capable in its money-form, of assuming another form instead of its original one of productive capital, while it does not change places at all if held in the form of C'.

C'—M'—C includes processes of circulation only for C', and they are phases in its reproduction, but the actual reproduction of C, into which C' is transformed, is necessary for the completion of C'—M'—C. This, however, is conditioned on a process of repro-duction which lies outside of the process of reproduction of the individual capital represented by C'.

In the first form, M—C Pm prepares only the first transformation of money-capital into productive capital; in the second form, it prepares the retransformation of commodity-capital into productive capital; that is to say, so far as the investment of industrial capital remains the same, the commodity-capital is retransformed into the same elements of production out of which it originated. Here as well as in the first form, the process of production is in a preparatory stage, but it is a return to it and its renewal, it is for the purpose of repeating the process of self-utilisation.

It must be noted, once more, that M—L is not merely the exchange of commodities, but the purchase of a commodity L, which is to serve for the production of surplus-value, just as M—Pm is a process which is indispensable for the same end.

When M—C{L/Pm} has been completed, M has been retransformed into productive capital P, and the cycle begins anew.

The elaborated form of P...C'—M'—C...P is

$$P...\{C + c\}...\{M + m\}...C\{L/Pm\}, c \; L...P$$

The transformation of money-capital into productive capital is the purchase of commodities for the purpose of producing commodities. Consumption falls within the cycle of capital only in so far as it is productive consumption; its premise is that surplus-value is produced by means of the commodities so consumed. And this is quite different from a production, even though it be a production of commodities, which has for its end the existence of the producer. A replacing of one commodity by another for the purpose of producing surplus-value is a different matter than the exchange of products which is perfected merely by means of money. But some economists use this sort of exchange as a proof that there can be no overproduction.

Apart from the productive consumption of M, which is transformed into L and Pm, this cycle contains the first phase M—L, which signifies, from the standpoint of the labourer L—M, or C—M. In the labourer's circulation, L—M—C, which includes his individual consumption, only the first factor falls within the cycle of capital by means of L—M. The second act, M—C, does not fall within the circulation of individual capital, although it is conditioned on it. But the continuous existence of the labouring class is necessary for the capitalist class, and this requires the individual consumption of the labourer, made possible by M—C.

The act C'—M' requires only that C' be transformed into money, that it be sold, in order that capital-value may continue its cycles and surplus-value be consumed by the capitalist. Of course, C' is bought only because the article is a use-value and serviceable for individual or productive consumption. But if C' continues to circulate, for instance, in the hand of the merchant who has bought the yarn, this does not interfere with the continuation of the cycle of individual capital which produced the yarn and sold it to the merchant. The entire process proceeds uninterruptedly and simultaneously with the individual consumption of the capitalist and the labourer. This point is important in a discussion of commercial crises.

As soon as C' has been sold for money, it may re-enter into the material elements of the labour process, and thus of the reproductive process. Whether C' is bought by the final consumer or by a merchant, does not alter the case. The quantity of commodities produced by capitalist production depends on the scale of production and on the continual necessity for expansion following from this production. It does not depend on a predestined circle of supply and demand, nor on certain wants to be supplied. Production on a large scale can have no other buyer, apart from other industrial capitalists, than the wholesale merchant. Within certain limits, the process of reproduction may take place on the same or on an increased scale, although the commodities taken out of it may not have gone into individual or productive consumption. The consumption of commodities is not included in the cycle of the capital which produced them. For instance, as soon as the yarn has been sold, the cycle of the capital-value contained in the yarn may begin anew, regardless of what may become of the sold yarn. So long as the product is sold, everything is going its regular course from the standpoint of the capitalist producer. The cycle of his capital-value is not interrupted. And if this process is expanded – including an increased productive consumption of the means of production – this reproduction of capital may be accompanied by an increased individual consumption (demand) on the part of the labourers, since this individual consumption is initiated and mediated by productive consumption. Thus the production of surplus-value, and with it the individual consumption of the capitalist, may increase, the entire process of reproduction may be in a flourishing condition, and yet a large part of the commodities may have entered into consumption only apparently, while in reality they may still remain unsold in the hands of dealers, in other words, they may still be actually in the market. Now one stream of commodities follows another, and finally it becomes obvious that the previous stream had been only apparently absorbed by consumption. The commodity-capitals compete with one another for a place on the market. The succeeding ones, in order to be able to sell, do so below price. The former streams have not yet been utilised, when the payment for them is due. Their owners must declare their insolvency, or they sell at any price in order to fulfil their obligations. This sale has nothing whatever to do with the actual condition of the demand. It is merely a question of a demand for payment, of the pressing necessity of transforming commodities into money. Then a crisis comes. It becomes noticeable, not in the direct decrease of consumptive demand, not in the demand for individual consumption, but in the decrease of exchanges of capital for capital, of the reproductive process of capital.

If the commodities Pm and L, into which M is transformed in the performance of its function of money-capital, in its capacity as capital-value destined for retransformation into productive capital, if, I say, those commodities are to be bought or paid at different dates, so that M—C represents a series of successive purchases or payments, then a part of M performs the act M—C, while another part persists in the form of money, and does not serve in the performance of simultaneous or successive acts M—C, until the conditions of this process itself demand it. This part of M is temporarily withheld from circulation, in order to perform its function at the proper moment. This storing of M for a certain time is a function conditioned on its circulation and intended for circulation. Its existence as a fund for purchase and payment, the suspension of its movement, the condition of its interrupted circulation, are conditions in which money performs one of its functions as money-capital. I say money-capital; for in this case the money remaining temporarily at rest is itself a part of money-capital M (of M'—m equal to M), of that part of commodity-capital which is equal to P, of that value of productive capital from which the cycle proceeds. On the other hand, all money withdrawn from circulation has the form of a hoard. In the form of a hoard, money is thus likewise a function of money-capital, just as the function of money in M—C as a medium of purchase or payment becomes a function of money-capital. For capital-value here exists in the form of money, the money-form is a condition of industrial capital in one of its stages, prescribed by the interrelations of processes within the cycle. At the same time it is here once more obvious, that money-capital performs no other functions than those of money within the cycle of industrial capital, and that these functions assume the significance of capital functions only by virtue of their interrelations with the other stages of this cycle.

The representation of M' as a relation of m to M, as a capital relation, is not so much a function of money-capital, as of commodity-capital C', which in its turn, as a relation of c to C, expresses but the result of the process of production, of the self-utilisation of capital which took place in it.

If the movement of the process of circulation meets with obstacles, so that M must suspend its function M—C on account of external conditions, such as the condition of the market, etc., and if it therefore remains for a shorter or longer time in its money-form, then we have once more money in the form of a hoard which it may also assume in the simple circulation of commodities, as soon as the transition from C—M to M—C is interrupted by external conditions. It is an involuntary formation of a hoard. In the present case, money has the form of fallow, latent, money-capital. But we will not discuss this point any further for the present.

In both cases, the suspension of money-capital in the form of money is the result of an interruption of its movements, no matter whether this is advantageous or harmful, voluntary or involuntary, in accord with its functions or contrary to them.

Section 2. Accumulation and Reproduction on an Enlarged Scale.

Since the proportions of the expansion of the productive process are not arbitrary, but determined by technical conditions, the produced surplus-value, though intended for capitalisation, frequently does not attain a size sufficient for its function as additional capital, for its entrance into the cycle of circulating capital-value, until several cycles have been repeated, so that it must be accumulated until that time. Surplus-value thus assures the rigid form of a hoard and is, then, latent capital. It is latent, because it cannot function as capital so long as it persists in the money-form.[1] The formation of a hoard thus appears as a phenomenon included in the process of capitalist accumulation, accompanying it, but nevertheless essentially different from it. For the process of reproduction is not expanded by latent capital. On the contrary, latent money-capital is here formed, because the capitalist producer cannot at once expand the scale of his production. If he sells his surplus-product to a producer of gold or silver, or, what amounts to the same thing, to a merchant who imports additional gold or silver from foreign countries for a part of the national surplus-product, then his latent money-capital forms an increment of the national gold or silver hoard. In all other cases, the surplus-value, for instance the 78 pounds sterling, which were a circulating medium in the hand of the purchaser, have only assumed the form of a hoard in the hands of the capitalist. In other words, a different repartition of the national gold or silver hoard has taken place, that is all.

If the money serves in the transactions of our capitalist as a means of payment, in such a way that the commodities are to be paid for by the buyer on long or short terms, then the surplus-product intended for capitalisation is not transformed into money, but into creditor's claims, into titles of ownership of a certain equivalent, which the buyer may either have in his possession, or which he may expect to possess. It does not enter into the reproductive process of the cycle any more than money which is invested in interest-bearing papers, although it may enter into the cycles of other individual industrial capitals.

The entire character of capitalist production is determined by the utilisation of the advanced capital-value, that is to say, in the first instance by the production of as much surplus-value as possible; in the second place, by the production of capital, in other words, by the transformation of surplus-value into capital (see Book 1, Chap. 24). But, as we have seen in Volume 1, the further development makes it a necessity for every individual capitalist to accumulate, or to produce on an enlarged scale, in order to produce more and more surplus-value, and this appears as a personal motive of the capitalist for his own enrichment. The preservation of his capital is conditioned on its continuous enlargement. But we do not revert any further to our previous analysis.

We considered first simple reproduction, and we assumed that the entire surplus-value was spent as revenue. But in reality and under normal conditions, only a part of the surplus-value can be spent as revenue, and another part must be capitalised. And it is quite immaterial, whether a certain surplus-value, produced within a certain period, is entirely consumed or entirely capitalised. In the average movement – and the general formula cannot represent any other – both cases occur. But in order not to complicate the formula, it is better to assume that the entire surplus-value is accumulated. The formula P...C'—M'—C'{L,Pm}...P stands for productive capital, which is reproduced on an enlarged scale and with enlarged values, and which begins its second cycle as enlarged productive capital, or, what amounts to the same, which renews its first cycle. As soon as this second cycle is begun, we have once more P as a starting point; only P is a larger productive capital than the first P was. Hence, if the second cycle begins with M' in the formula M—M', this M' functions as M, as an advanced capital of a definite size. It is a larger money-capital than the one with which the first cycle was opened; but all relations to its growth by the capitalisation of surplus-value have disappeared, as soon as it appears in the function of advanced money-capital. This origin is extinguished in its form of money-capital which begins its cycle. This also applies to P', as soon as it becomes the starting point of a new cycle.

If we compare P...P' with M...M', or with the first cycle, we find that they have not the same significance. M...M', taken by itself as an individual cycle, expresses only that M, money-capital, or industrial capital in its cycle as money-capital, is money generating more money, value generating more value, in other words, producing surplus-value. But in the cycle of P, the process of utilisation is completed as soon as the first stage, the process of production, is over with, and after going through the second stage (the first stage of the circulation), C'—M', the capital-value plus surplus-value exists already as materialised money-capital, as M', which appeared as the last extreme in the first cycle. The fact that surplus-value has been produced is registered in the first considered formula P...P by c—m—c (see expanded formula previously given). This, in its second stage, falls outside of the circulation of capital and represents the circulation of surplus-value as revenue. In this form, where the entire movement is represented by P...P and where there is no difference in value between the two extremes, the utilisation of the advanced value, or the production of surplus-value, is represented in the same way as in M...M', only the act C'—M', which appears as the last stage in M—M', and as the second stage of the cycle, appears as the first stage of the circulation P...P.

In P...P', the term P' does not express the fact that surplus-value has been produced, but that the produced surplus-value has been capit-alised, that capital has been accumulated, and that P' as distinguished from P consists of the original capital-value plus the value of capital accumulated by its movements.

M', as the closing link of M...M', and C', as it appears within all these cycles, do not express the movement, but its result, if taken by themselves: they represent the result, in the form of money or com-modities of the utilisation of capital-value, and capital-value therefore appears as M plus m, or C plus c, as a relation of capital-value to its surplus-value, its offspring. But whether this result appears in the form of M' or C', it is not a function of either money-capital or commodity-capital. As special and different forms corresponding to special functions of industrial capital, money-capital can perform only money functions, and commodity-capital only commodity functions. Their difference is merely that of money and commodity. Industrial capital, in its capacity of productive capital, can likewise consist only of the same elements as those of any other process of labour which creates products: on one side objective means of production, on the other labour-power as the productive element. Just as industrial cap-ital can exist within the process of production only in a composition which corresponds to the requirements of all production, even if it is not capitalist production, so it can exist in the sphere of circulation only in the two forms corresponding to it, viz., that of a commodity or of money. Now the sum of the elements of production reveals its character of productive capital at the outset by the fact that the labour-power belongs to another from whom the capitalist purchases it, just as he purchases his means of production from others who own them, so that the process of production itself appears as a productive function of industrial capital. In the same way money and commod-ities appear as forms of circulation of the same industrial capital, hence their functions as those of the circulation of this capital, which either introduce the function of productive capital or originate from it. The money function and the commodity function become at the same time functions of money-capital and commodity-capital for no other reason than that they enter into relationship with the functional forms through which industrial capital passes in the different stages of its process of circulation. It is, therefore, a mistake to attempt to derive the specific characters of money and commodities, and their specific functions as such, from their capital-character, and it is likewise a mistake to derive the qualities of productive capital from its existence in means of production.

As soon as M' or C' have become fixed in the relation of M plus m, or C plus c, in other words, as soon as they become parts of the relation between capital-value and its offspring surplus-value, they give expression to this relation either in the form of money or of commodities, without changing the nature of the relation itself. This relation is not due to any qualities or functions of either money or commodities as such. In both cases the characteristic quality of capital, that of being a value generating more value, is expressed only as a result. C' is always the product of the function of P, and M' is always merely a form of C' changed in the cycle of industrial capital. As soon as the realised money-capital begins its special function as money-capital anew, it ceases to express the capital-relation conveyed by the formula M' equal to M plus m. After M...M' has been completed and M' begins the cycle anew, it no longer figures as M' but as M, even if the entire capital-value contained in M' is capitalised. The second cycle begins in our case with a money-capital of 500 pounds sterling, instead of 422 pounds in the first cycle. The money-capital, which opens the cycle, is larger by 78 pounds sterling than before; this difference exists in the comparison of one cycle with another, but it does not exist within each cycle. The 500 pounds sterling advanced as money-capital, 78 pounds of which formerly existed as surplus-value, do not play any different role than some other 500 pounds sterling by which another capitalist opens his first cycle. The increased P' opens a new cycle as P, just as P did in the simple reproduction P...P.

In the stage M'—C'{L/Pm}, the increased magnitude is indicated only by C', but not by L' and Pm'. Since C is the sum of L and Pm, the term C' indicates sufficiently that the sum of the L and Pm contained in it is greater than the original P. In the second place, the terms L' and Pm' would be incorrect, because we know that the growth of capital implies a change in the relative proportions of the values composing it, and that, with the progressive changing of this proportion, the value of Pm increases, while that of L always decreases relatively, if not absolutely.

Section 3. Accumulation of Money.

Whether or not m, the surplus-value transformed into gold, is immediately combined with the circulating capital-value and is thus enabled to enter into the cycle together with the capital M in the magnitude of M', depends on circumstances which are independent of the mere existence of m. If m is to serve as money-capital in a second independent business, to be run by the side of the first, it is evident that it cannot be used for this purpose, unless it is of the minimum size required for it. And if it is intended to use it for the extension of the original business, the condition of the substances composing P and their relative values likewise demand a minimum magnitude for m. All the means of production employed in this business have not only a qualitative, but also a definite quantitative relation toward one another. These proportions of the substances and of their values entering into the productive capital determine the minimum magnitude required for m, in order to be capable of transformation into additional means of production and labour-power, or only into means of production as an addition to the productive capital. For instance, the owner of a spinning loom cannot increase the number of his spindles without at the same time purchasing a corresponding number of carders and preparatory looms, apart from the increased expense for cotton and wages, which such an extension of his business demands. In order to carry this out, the surplus-value must have reached a considerable figure (one pound sterling per spindle is generally assumed for new installations). So long as m does not reach this figure, the cycle of the original capital must be repeated several times, until the sum of the successively produced surplus-values m can take part in the functions of M, in the process M'—C'{L/Pm}. Even mere changes of detail, for instance, in the spinning machinery, made for the purpose of making it more productive, require greater expenditures for spinning material, preparatory looms, etc. In the meantime, m is accumulated, and its accumulation is not its own function, but the result of repeated cycles of P...P. Its own function consists in persisting in the form of money, until it has received sufficient additions from the outside by means of successive cycles of utilisation of capital to have acquired the minimum magnitude necessary for its active function. Only when it has reached this magnitude, can it actually serve as money-capital and eventually take part in the functions of the active money-capital M as its accumulated part. But until that time it is accumulated and exists only in the form of a hoard in a process of gradual growth. The accumulation of money, the formation of a hoard, appears here as a process which accompanies temporarily the accumulation by which industrial capital expands the scale of its productive action. This is a temporary phenomenon, for so long as the hoard remains in this condition, it does not perform the function of capital, does not take part in the process of utilisation, and remains a sum of money which grows only by virtue of the fact that other money, existing without the initiative of the hoard, is thrown into the same safe.

The form of a hoard is simply the form of money not in circulation. It is money interrupted in its circulation and stored up in the form of money. As for the process of forming a hoard, it is found in all systems of commodity-production, and it plays a role as an end in itself only in the undeveloped, pre-capitalist forms of this production. In the present case, the hoard assumes the form of money-capital, and goes through the process of forming a hoard as a temporary corollary of the accumulation of capital, merely because the money here figures as latent money-capital, and because the formation of a hoard as well as the surplus-value hoarded in the form of money represent a functionally prescribed and preliminary stage required for the transformation of surplus-value into capital actually performing its functions. It is this end which gives it the character of latent money-capital. Hence the volume, which it must have acquired before it can take part in the process of capital, is determined in each case by the values of which the productive capital is composed. But so long as it remains in the condition of a hoard, it does not perform the functions of money-capital, but is merely sterile money-capital; its functions have not been interrupted, as in a previous case, but it is as yet incapable of performing them.

We are here discussing the accumulation of money in its original and real form of an actual hoard of money. But it may also exist in the form of mere outstanding money, of credits granted by a capitalist who has sold C'. As concerns its other forms, where this latent money-capital exists in the meantime in the shape of money breeding more money, such as interest-bearing deposits in a bank, in drafts, or in bonds of some sort, these do not fall within the discussion at this point. Surplus-value realised in the form of money then performs special capital-functions outside of that cycle of industrial capital which originated it. In the first place, these functions have nothing to do with that cycle of industrial capital as such, in the second place they represent capital-functions which are to be distinguished from the functions of industrial capital and which are not yet developed at this stage.

Section 4. Reserve Funds.

In the case which we have just discussed, surplus-value in the form of a hoard represents accumulated funds, a money-form temporarily assumed by the accumulation of capital and to that extent a condition of this accumulation. However, such accumulated funds may also perform special services of a subordinate nature, that is to say they may enter into the circulation-process of capital, even if this process has not assumed the form of P—P', in other words, without an expansion of capitalist reproduction.

If the process C'—M' is prolonged beyond its normal size, so that com-modity-capital meets with abnormal obstacles during its transformation into the money-form, or if, after the completion of this transformation, the price of the means of production into which the money-capital is to be transformed has risen above the level occupied by it in the beginning of the cycle, the hoard held as accumulated funds may be used in the place of money-capital, or of a part of such capital. In that case, the accumulated funds of money serve as reserve funds for the purpose of counterbalancing disturbances of the circulation.

When in use as such a reserve fund, accumulated money differs from the fund of purchase or paying media discussed in the cycle P—P'. These media are a part of money-capital performing its functions, they are forms of existence of a part of capital-value in general going through the process of its circulation, and its different parts perform their functions successively at different times. In the continuous process of production, money-capital in reserve is always formed, obligations being incurred today which will not be paid until later, and large quantities of commodities being sold today, while other large quantities are not to be bought until some other day. In these intervals, a part of the circulating capital exists continuously in the form of money. A reserve fund, on the other hand, is not a part of money-capital in the performance of its functions. It is rather a part of capital in a preliminary stage of its accumulation, of surplus-value not yet transformed into active capital.

Of course, it requires no explanation, that the capitalist, when pressed for funds, does not concern himself about the definite functions of the money in his hands. He simply employs whatever money he has for the purpose of keeping the circulation-process of his capital in motion. For instance, in our illustration, M is equal to 422 pounds sterling, M' to 500 pounds sterling. If a part of the capital of 422 pounds sterling exists in the form of money as a fund for paying or buying, it is intended that all of it should enter into circulation, conditions remaining the same, and that it is sufficient for this purpose. The reserve fund, on the other hand, is a part of the 78 pounds sterling of surplus-value. It cannot enter the circulation process of the capital of 422 pounds sterling, unless this circulation takes place under changed conditions; for it is a part of the accumulated funds, and figures here under conditions, where the scale of the reproduction has not been enlarged.

Accumulated money-funds represent latent money-capital, or the transformation of money into money-capital.

The following is the general formula for the cycle of productive capital, combining simple reproduction and reproduction on an enlarged scale:

$$P...C'—M'. M—C\{L/Pm\}...P (P').$$

If P equals P, then M in (2) is equal to M'—m; if P equals P', then M in (2) is greater than M'—m, that is to say, m has been completely or partially transformed into money-capital.

The cycle of productive capital is that form, under which classical political economy discusses the rotation process of industrial capital.

Chapter 3
The Circulation of Commodity-Capital

The general formula for the cycle of commodity-capital is:

$$C'—M'—C...P...C'$$

C' appears not alone as the product, but also as the premise of the two previous cycles, since M—C includes for one capital that which C'—M' includes for the other, at least in so far as a part of the means of production represents the commodity-product of other individual capitals going through their circulation process. In our case, for instance, coal, machinery, etc., represent the commodity-capital of the mineowner, of the capitalist machine-manufacturer, etc. Furthermore, we have shown in Chapter 1,4, that not only the cycle P...P, but also the cycle C'...C' is assumed even in the first repetition of M...M', before this second cycle of money-capital is completed.

If reproduction takes place on an enlarged scale, then the final C' is greater than the initial C' and we shall then call the final one C".

The difference between the third form and the first two is on the one hand, that in this case the total circulation opens the cycle with its two opposite phases, while in form I the circulation is interrupted by the process of production, and in form II the total circulation with its two complementary phases appears as a connecting link for the process of reproduction, intervening as a mediating movement between P...P. In the case of M...M', the cycle has the form M—C...C'—M'=M—C—M. In the case of P...P it has the opposite form, namely, C'—M'. M—C=C—M—C. In the case of C'—C', it likewise has this last form.

On the other hand, when the cycles I and II are repeated, even if the final points M' and P' are at the same time the starting points of the renewed cycle, the form in which they were originally generated disappears. M'=M plus m, and P'=P plus p, begin the new cycle as M and P. But in form III, the starting point C must be designated as C', also in the case of the renewal of the cycle on the same scale, for the following reason. As soon as M' as such opens a new cycle in the form I, it performs the functions of money-capital M, as an advance in the form of money of the capital value to be utilised. The size of the advanced money-capital, increased by the accumulation resulting from the first cycle, is greater. But whether the size of the advanced money-capital is 422 pounds sterling or 500 pounds sterling, it nevertheless appears merely as a capital-value. M' no longer exists as a utilised capital pregnant with surplus-value, for it is still to be utilised. The same is true of P...P', for P' must always perform the functions of P, of capital-value used for the generation of surplus-value, and must renew its cycle for this purpose.

Now the circulation of commodity-capital does not open with capital-value, but with augmented capital-value in the form of commodities. It includes from the start not only the cycle of capital-value represented by commodities, but also of surplus-value. Hence, if simple reproduction takes place in this form, C' at the starting point is equal to C' at the closing point. If a part of the surplus-value enters into the circulation of capital, C'', an enlarged C', appears at the close, but the succeeding cycle is once more opened by C'. This is merely a larger C' than that of the preceding cycle, and it begins its new cycle with a proportionately increased accumulation of capital-value, which includes a proportionate increase of newly produced surplus-value. In every case, C' always opens the cycle as a commodity-capital which is equal to capital-value plus surplus-value.

C' as C does not appear in the circulation of some individual industrial capital as a form of this capital, but as a form of some other industrial capital, so far as the means of production are its products. What is M—C (or M—Pm) for the first capital, is C'—M' for this second capital.

In the circulation act M—C{L/Pm} the factors L and Pm have identical relations, in so far as they are commodities in the hands of those who sell them; on the one hand the labourers who sell their labour-power, on the other hand the owners of the means of production, who sell these. For the purchaser, whose money here performs the functions of money-capital, L and Pm represent merely commodities, so long as he has not bought them, so long as they confront his money-capital in the form of commodities owned by others. Pm and L here differ only in this respect that Pm may be C', or capital, in the hands of its owner, if Pm is the commodity-form of his capital, while L is always nothing else but a commodity for the labourer, and does not become capital, until it is made a part of P in the hand of its purchaser.

For this reason, C' can never open any cycle as a mere commodity-form of capital-value. As commodity-capital it is always the representative of two things. From the point of view of use-value it is the product of the function of P, in the present case yarn, whose elements L and Pm, coming from the circulation, have been active in creating this product. And from the point of view of exchange-value, commodity-capital is the capital-value P plus the surplus-value m produced by the function of P.

It is only in the circulation of C' itself that C equal to P, and equal to the capital-value, can and must separate from that part of C' in which surplus-value is contained, from the surplus-product representing the surplus-value. It does not matter, whether these two parts can be actually separated, as in the case of yarn, or whether they cannot be separated, as in the case of a machine. They may always be separated, as soon as C' is transformed into M'.

If the entire commodity-product is separable into independent homogeneous parts, as is the case in our 10,000 lbs. of yarn, so that the act C'—M' is performed by means of a number of successive sales, then capital-value in the form of commodities can perform the functions of C and can be separated from C', before the surplus-value, or the entire value of C', has been realised.

In the 10,000 lbs. of yarn at 500 pounds sterling, the value of 8,440 lbs., equal to 422 pounds sterling, is separated from the surplus-value. If the capitalist sells first 8,440 lbs. at 422 pounds sterling, then these 8,440 lbs. of yarn represent C, or the capital-value, in the form of commodities. The surplus-product of 1,560 lbs. of yarn, likewise contained in C', and valued at 78 pounds sterling, does not circulate until later. The capitalist may accomplish C—M—C{L/Pm} before the surplus product c—m—c circulates.

Or, if he sells 7,440 lbs. of yarn at 372 pounds sterling, and then 1,000 lbs. of yarn at 50 pounds sterling, he might replace the means of production (the constant capital c) with the first part of C and the variable capital v, the labour-power, with the second part of C, and then proceed as before.

But if such successive sales take place, and the conditions of the cycle permit it, the capitalist, instead of separating C' into c plus v plus s, may make such a separation also in the case of aliquot parts of C'.

For instance, 7,440 lbs. of yarn, valued at 372 pounds sterling, representing a constant capital as parts of C', namely of 10,000 lbs. of yarn valued at 500 pounds sterling, may be separated into 5,535 lbs. of yarn valued at 276.768 pounds sterling, which replace the constant part, the value of the means of production used up in producing 7,440 lbs. of yarn; 744 lbs. of yarn valued at 37.200 pounds sterling, which replace only the variable capital; and 1,160.640 lbs. of yarn valued at 58.032 pounds sterling, which are the surplus-product and represent surplus-value. If he sells his 7,440 lbs. of yarn, he can replace the capital-value contained in them after the sale of 6,279.360 lbs. of yarn at 313.968 pounds sterling, and he can spend as his revenue the value of the surplus-product of 1,160.640 pounds, or 58.032 pounds sterling.

In the same way, he may separate 1,000 lbs. of yarn, valued at 50 pounds sterling, or equal to the variable capital-value, into its aliquot parts and sell them successively, as follows: 744 lbs. of yarn at 37.200 pounds sterling, for the constant capital-value of 1,000 lbs. of yarn; 100 lbs. of yarn at 5 pounds sterling, for the variable capital-value; or together 844 lbs. of yarn at 42.2 pounds sterling, for replacing the capital-value contained in 1,000 lbs. of yarn; finally, 156 lbs. of yarn at 7.8 pounds sterling, representing the surplus-product contained in 1,000 lbs. of yarn, which may be spent as such.

Finally, the capitalist may divide the remaining 1,560 lbs. of yarn, valued at 78 pounds sterling, provided he succeeds in selling them, in such a way that the sale of 1,160 lbs. of yarn, valued at 58.032 pounds sterling, replaces the value of the means of production contained in those 1,560 lbs. of yarn, and 156 lbs. of yarn, valued at 7.8 pounds sterling, replaces the variable capital-value; or a total of 1,316.640 lbs. of yarn, valued at 65.832 pounds sterling, for replacing the total capital-value; finally, the surplus-product of 243.360 lbs., valued at 12.168 pounds sterling, remains, to be spent as revenue.

Just as all the elements of c, v, and s, contained in the yarn, are divisible into the same component parts, so may every individual pound of yarn, valued at 1 sh., or 12d., be divided.

$$c = 0.744 \text{ lb. of yarn} = 8.928\text{d.}$$
$$v = 0.100 \text{ lb. of yarn} = 1.200\text{d.}$$
$$s = 0.156 \text{ lb. of yarn} = 1.872\text{d.}$$
$$c + v + s = 1.000 \text{ lb. of yarn} = 12.000\text{d.}$$

If we add the results of the three above partial sales, we obtain the same result as we should when selling the entire 10,000 lbs. at one time. We have the following parts of constant capital:

In the first lot 5,535.360 lbs. of yarn at £276.768
In the second lot 744.000 lbs. of yarn at £37.200
In the third lot 1,160.640 lbs. of yarn at £58.032
Total . . . . . . 7,440.000 lbs. of yarn at £372.000

Furthermore, the following parts of variable capital:

In the first lot of 744.000 lbs. of yarn at £37.200
In the second lot 100.000 lbs. of yarn at £5.000
In the third lot 156,000 lbs. of yarn at £7.800
Total. . . . . . . 1,000.000 lbs. of yarn at £50.000

Finally, the following parts of surplus-value:

In the first lot 1,160.740 lbs. of yarn at £58.032
In the second lot 156.000 lbs. of yarn at £7.800
In the third lot 343.360 lbs. of yarn at £12.168
Total . . . . . . 1,560.000 lbs. of yarn at £78.000

Grand Total:

Constant capital . . . . . . 7,450 lbs. of yarn at £372
Variable capital . . . . 1,000 lbs. of yarn at £50
Surplus-value . . . . 1,560 lbs. of yarn at £78
Total . . . . 10,000 lbs. of yarn at £500

C'—M' stands in itself merely for the sale of 10,000 lbs. of yarn. These 10,000 lbs. of yarn are a commodity like all other yarn. The purchaser is interested in the price of 1 sh. per lb., or 500 pounds sterling for 10,000 lbs. If he analyses during the negotiations the different values of which this lot is composed, he does so simply with the malignant intention of proving that it can be sold at less than 1 sh. per pound and still leave a fair profit to the seller. But the quantity purchased by him depends on his own requirements. If he is, for instance, the owner of a cloth-factory, the amount of his purchase depends on the composition of his own capital invested in this plant, not on that of the owner of the yarn from whom he buys. The conditions, in which C' has to replace on one side the capital used up in its production (or the component parts of this capital), and on the other to serve as a surplus-product for the spending of surplus-value or for the accumulation of capital, exist only in the cycle of that capital, which exists as a commodity capital in the form of 10,000 lbs. of yarn. These conditions have nothing to do with the sale itself. In the present case we have also assumed that C' is sold at its value, so that it is only a question of its transformation from the commodity-form into that of money. Of course, it is essential for C', when performing a function in the cycle of this individual capital by which the productive capital is to be replaced, that it should be known to what extent, if at all, the price and the value vary in the sale. But this does not concern us here in the discussion of the distinctions of form.

In form 1, or M...M', the process of production intervenes midway between the two complementary and opposite phases of the circulation of capital, and is past before the concluding phase C'—M' begins. Money has been advanced as capital, transformed into means of production and labour-power, transferred from these to the commodity-product, and this in its turn changed into money. It is a complete cycle of business, which results in money, the universal medium. The renewal of the cycle is then possible, but not necessary. M...P...M' may either be the last cycle, concluding the function of some individual capital withdrawn from business, or the first cycle of some new capital beginning its active function. The general movement is here M...M', from money to more money.

In form 2, or P...C'—M'—C...P (P'), the entire circulation process follows after the first P and takes place before the second P; but it takes place in the opposite direction from that of form 1. The first P is the productive capital, and its function is the productive process, on which the succeeding circulation process is conditioned. The concluding P, on the other hand, does not stand for the productive process; it is only the return of the industrial capital to its form of productive capital. And it has that form by virtue of the last phase of circulation, in which the transformation of capital-value into L plus Pm was accomplished, those subjective and objective factors which combine to form the productive capital. The capital, whether it be P or P', is in the end once more present in a form in which it may again perform the function of productive capital, in which it must go through the productive process. The general form of the movement P...P' (P) is that of reproduction and does not indicate that capital is to be increased by new values, as does M...M'. This enables classic political economy to ignore so much easier the capitalistic form of the process of production and to pretend that production itself is the purpose of this process; just as though it were only a question of producing as much as possible, as cheaply as possible, and of exchanging the product for the greatest variety of other products, either for the renewal of the production (M—C), or for consumption (m—c). It is then quite likely that the peculiarities of money and money-capital may be overlooked, for M and m appear here merely as passing media of circulation. The entire process seems so simple and natural, but natural in the sense of a shallow rationalism. In the same way, the profit is occasionally overlooked in the commodity-capital and it is mentioned merely as a commodity when discussing the productive circulation as a whole. But as soon as the question of the values composing it comes up for discussion, it is spoken of as commodity-capital. Accumulation, of course, is seen in the same light as production.

In form 3, or C'—M'—C...P...C', the two phases of the circulation process open the cycle, in the same order which obtains in form 2, or P...P; next follows P with its function, the productive process, the same as in form 1; the cycle closes with the result of the process of production, C'. While form 2 closes with P, the return of productive capital to its mere form, so form 3 closes with C', the return of commodity-capital to its form. Just as in form 2 the capital, in its concluding form of P, must renew its cycle by beginning with the process of production, so in this case, where the industrial capital re-appears in the form of commodity-capital, the cycle is re-opened by the circulation-phase C'—M'. Both forms of the cycle are incomplete, because they do not close with M', that is to say with capital-value retransformed into money and utilised. Both cycles must, therefore, be continued and include the reproduction. The total cycle of form 3 is represented by C'...C'.

The third form is distinguished from the two first by the fact that it is the only one in which the utilised capital-value appears as the starting point of its utilisation, instead of the original value which is to be utilised. C' as a capital-relation is the starting point and has a determining influence on the entire cycle, for it includes the cycle of capital-value as well as that of surplus-value in its first phase, and the surplus-value is compelled to act partly as revenue by going through the circulation c—m—c, partly to perform the function of an element of capital accumulation, at least in the average of the cycles, if not in all of them.

In the form C'...C' the consumption of the entire commodity-product is assumed as the condition of the normal course of the cycles of capital itself. The individual consumption of the labourer and the individual consumption of the unaccumulated part of the surplus-product comprise the entire individual consumption. Hence the consumption in its totality – individual as well as productive consumption – are conditional factors in the cycle C'. Productive consumption, which includes the individual consumption of the labourer as a corollary, since labour-power is a continuous product of the labourer's individual consumption, within certain limits, is performed by every individual capital itself. Individual consumption, in so far as it is not required for the existence of the individual capitalist, is here only regarded as a social act, not as an act of the individual capitalist.

In forms 1 and 2, the aggregate movement appears as a movement of advanced capital-value. In form 3, the utilised capital, in the shape of the total commodity-product, is the starting point and has the nature of moving capital, commodity-capital. Not until the transformation into money has been accomplished, does this movement separate into movements of capital and revenue. The distribution of the total social product as well as the special distribution of the product of every individual capital for purposes of individual consumption or for reproduction, is included in the cycle of capital under this form.

In M...M', the possible expansion of the cycle is included, and depends on the volume of m entering into the renewed cycle.

In P...P, the new cycle may be started by P with the same, or even with a smaller, value, and yet may represent a reproduction on an enlarged scale, for instance in the case where certain elements of commodities become cheaper by increased productivity of labour. On the other hand, a productive capital which has increased in value may, in the opposite case, represent a reproduction on a decreased scale with less raw material, for instance, if some elements of production have become dearer. The same is true of C'...C'.

In C'...C' capital in the form of commodities is the premise of production. It re-appears as a premise within this cycle in the second C. If this C has not yet been produced or reproduced, the cycle is arrested in its course. This C must be reproduced, for the greater part as C' of some other industrial capital. In this cycle, C' is found as the point of departure, of transit, and of conclusion; it is always there. It is a permanent condition of the process of reproduction.

C'...C' is distinguished from forms 1 and 2 by still another feature. All three cycles have this in common, that capital begins its course in the same form in which it ends the cycle, and thus re-assumes the original form whenever it renews the same cycle. The initial form M,P,C', is always the one in which capital-value (in 3 together with its increment of surplus-value) is advanced, in other words always the original starting form of this cycle. The concluding form M',P,C', on the other hand, is always a changed form of a functional one, which preceded the final form in the circulation and is not the original one.

Thus M' in 1 is a changed form of C', the final P in 2 is a changed form of M, and this transformation is accomplished in 1 and 2 by a simple transaction in the circulation of commodities, by a formal change of position of commodity and money; in 3, C' is a changed form of the productive capital P. But here, in 3, the transformation does not merely concern the functional form of capital, but also its magnitude as a value; and in the second place, the transformation is not the result of a formal change of position pertaining to the circulation process, but of an actual modification experienced by the use-form and value of the commodity parts of productive capital in the process of production.

The forms m,P,C', at the starting end, always precede every one of the cycles 1, 2, 3. The return of these forms at the terminal end is conditioned on the series of metamorphoses in the cycle itself. C', as the terminal product of an individual cycle of industrial capital, presupposes only that form P of the industrial capital which does not belong to the circulation, M', since the terminal point of P representing the changed form of C' (C'—M'), presupposes the existence of M in the hand of the buyer, that is to say outside of the cycle M...M', but drawn into it and made it its terminal form by the sale of C'. In the same way, the final P in 2 presupposes the existence of L and PM (C) outside of 2, but incorporated as its final form by means of M—C. But apart from this last extreme, neither the cycle of individual money-capital presupposes the existence of money-capital in general, nor the cycle of individual productive capital that of productive capital, in these cycles. In 1, M may be the first money-capital; in 2, P may be the first productive capital appearing on the historical scene. But in 3,

$$C'\{C..., ...M', c...\} \{M...C\{L/Pm\}...P...C', m...c\}$$

C is presupposed twice outside of the cycle. The first time, it is assumed to exist in the cycle C'—M'—C{L/Pm}. The C in this formula, so far as it consists of Pm, is a commodity in the hands of the seller; it is itself a commodity-capital, in so far as it is the product of a capitalist process of production; and even if it is not, it appears as a commodity-capital in the hands of the merchant. The second time it is assumed in c, in the formula c—m—c, where it must likewise be at hand in the form of a commodity, in order to be available for purchase. At any rate, whether they are commodity-capital or not, L and Pm are commodities as well as C' and maintain towards one another the relation of commodities. The same is true of the second c in the formula c—m—c. Inasmuch as C' is equal to C (L plus Pm), it is composed of commodities and must be replaced by equal commodities in the circulation. In the same way, the second c in c—m—c must be replaced by equal commodities in the circulation.

With the capitalist mode of production for a basis, as the prevailing mode, all commodities in the hands of the seller must be commodity-capital. And they retain this character in the hand of the merchant, or assume it, if they did not have it before. Or they would have to be commodities, such as imported articles, which replace some original commodity-capital by bestowing upon it another form of existence.

The commodity-elements L and Pm, of which the productive capital is composed, do not possess the same form as modes of existence of P, which they have on the various commodity-markets where they are gathered. They are now combined, and so combined they can perform the functions of productive capital.

C appears as the premise of C within the cycle 3, because capital in commodity-form is its starting point. The cycle is opened by the transformation of C' (in so far as it performs the functions of capital-value, whether increased by surplus-value or not) into those commodities which are its elements of production. And this transformation comprises the entire process of circulation, C—M—C (equal to L plus Pm), and is its result. C here stands at both extremes, but the second extreme, which receives its form C by means of M—C from the commodity-market on the outside, is not the last extreme of the cycle, but only of its two first stages comprising the process of circulation. Its result is P, which then performs its function, the process of production. It is only as the result of this process, not as that of the circulation, that C' appears as the terminal point of the cycle and in the same form as the starting point, C'. On the other hand, in M...M' and P...P, the final extremes M' and P are the immediate results of the process of circulation. In these instances, it is only M' and P which are supposed to exist at the end in the hands of another. So far as the process of circulation takes place between the extremes, neither M in the hands of another as money, nor P as the productive process of another, are the premises of these cycles. But C'...C' requires the existence of C (equal to L plus Pm) as commodities in the hands of others who are their owners. These commodities are drawn into the cycle by the introductory process of circulation and transformed into productive capital, and as a result of the functions of this capital, C' once more appears at the end of the cycle.

But just because the cycle C'...C' presupposes for its realisation the existence of some other industrial capital in the form of C (equal to L plus Pm) – and Pm comprises various other capitals, in our case machinery, coal, oil, etc. – it demands of itself that it be considered not merely as the general form of the cycle, that is to say as a social form common to every industrial capital (except when it is first invested). It is not merely a common mobile form of all industrial capitals, but also the sum of all industrial capitals in action. It is a movement of the aggregate capital of the capitalist class, in which every individual capital appears only as a part whose movements intermingle with those of the others and are conditioned on them. For instance, if we regard the aggregate of commodities annually produced in a certain country, and analyse the movements by which a part of this aggregate product replaces the productive capital in all individual businesses, while another part enters into the individual consumption of the various classes, then we consider C'...C' as the formula indicating the movements of social capital as well as of the surplus-value, or surplus-product, generated by it. The fact that the social capital is equal to the sum of the individual capitals (including the stocks and state capital, so far as governments employ productive wage-labour in mining, railroading, etc., and perform the function of capitalists), and that the aggregate movement of social capital is equal to the algebraic sum of the movements of individual capitals, does not militate against the possibility that this movement, seen as the movement of some individual capital, may present other phenomena than the same movement studied as a part of the aggregate movement of social capital. In the latter case, when studied in connection with all its parts, the movement simultaneously solves problems, the solution of which does not follow from the study of the cycles of some individual capital, but must be taken for granted.

C'...C' is the only cycle, in which the originally advanced capital-value constitutes only a part of the value opening the movement at one extreme, and in which the movement thus reveals itself at the outset as the total movement of the industrial capital. It includes that part of the product which replaces the productive capital as well as that part which creates a surplus-product and which is on an average either spent as revenue or employed as an element of accumulation. In so far as the expenditure of surplus-value in the form of revenue is included in this cycle, the individual consumption is likewise included. The latter is furthermore included for the reason, that the starting point C, commodity, exists in the form of some article of use; but every article produced by capitalist methods is a commodity-capital, no matter whether its use-form destines it for productive or for individual consumption, or for both. M...M' indicates only the quality of value, the utilisation of the advanced capital-value for the purposes of the entire process; P...P (P') indicates the process of production of capital in the form of a process of reproduction with a productive capital of the same or of increased value (accumulation); C'...C', while it indicates at the outset that it is a part of the capitalist production of commodities, comprises productive and individual consumption from the start, and productive consumption with its implied generation of more value appears only as one branch of its movement. Finally, since C' may have a use-value which cannot enter any more into any process of production, it follows as a matter of course, that the different elements of value of C' expressed by parts of the product must occupy a different position, according to whether C'...C' is regarded as the formula for the movement of the total social capital, or for the independent movement of some individual industrial capital. All these peculiarities point to the fact that this cycle implies more than the mere cycle of some individual capital.

In the formula C'...C', the movement of the commodity-capital, that is to say of the total product created by capitalist methods, appears simultaneously as the premise of the independent cycle of individual capital and as its effect. If this formula is grasped in its peculiarities, then it is no longer sufficient to be content with the knowledge that the metamorphoses C'—M' and M—C are on the one hand functionally defined sections in the metamorphoses of capital, on the other links in the general circulation of commodities. It becomes necessary to follow the ramifications of the metamorphoses of one industrial capital among those of other individual capitals and with that part of the total product which is intended for individual consumption. In the analysis of an individual industrial capital, we therefore base our studies mainly on the two first formulas.

The cycle C'...C' appears as the movement of an individual and independent capital in the case of agriculture, where calculations are made from crop to crop. In figure 2, the sowing is the starting point, in figure 3 the harvest, or, to speak with the Physiocrats, figure 2 starts out with the *avances*, and figure 3 with the *reprises*. The movement of capital-value in 3 appears from the outset only as a part of the movement of the general mass of products, while in 1 and 2 the movement of C' is only a part of the movement of some individual capital.

In figure 3, the commodities on the market are the continuous premise of the processes of production and reproduction. If this formula is regarded as fixed, all elements of the process of production seem to originate in the circulation of commodities and to consist only of commodities. This one-sided conception overlooks those elements of the processes of production, which are independent of the commodity-elements.

Since C'...C' has for its starting point the total product (total value), it follows that (making exception of foreign trade) reproduction on an enlarged scale, productivity remaining otherwise the same, can take place only when the part of the surplus-product to be capitalised already contains the material elements of the additional productive capital; so that a surplus-product is at once produced in that form which enables it to perform the functions of additional capital, so far as the production of one year can serve as the basis of next year's production, or in so far as this can take place simultaneously with the simple process of reproduction in the same year. Increased productivity can increase only the substance of capital, but not its value; of course, it creates additional material for the generation of more value.

C'...C' is the basis of Quesnay's *Tableau Économique*, and it shows great discrimination on his part that he selected this form instead of P...P as opposed to M...M' (which is the isolated formula retained by the mercantilists).

Chapter 4
The Three Diagrams of the Process of Circulation

The three diagrams may be formulated in the following manner, using the sign Tc for 'total process of circulation':

1. M—C...P...C'—M'
2. P...Tc...P
3. Tc...P(C').

If we take all three diagrams together, all premises of the process appear as its effects, as premises produced by itself. Every element appears as a point of departure, transit, and return to the starting point. The total process appears as the unity of the processes of production and circulation. The process of production mediates the process of circulation, and vice versa.

All three cycles have the following point in common: The creation of more value as the compelling motive. Diagram 1 expresses this by its form. Diagram 2 begins with P, the process of creating surplus-values. Diagram 3 begins the cycle with the utilised value and closes with renewed utilised value, even if the movement is repeated on the same scale.

So far as C—M means M—C from the point of view of the buyer, and M—C means C—M from the point of view of the seller, the circulation of capital presents only the features of the ordinary metamorphosis of commodities, subject to the laws relative to the amount of money in circulation, as analysed in Book 1, Chap. 3, 2. But if we do not cling to this formal aspect, but rather consider the actual connection of the metamorphoses of the various individual capitals; in other words, if we study the interrelation of the cycles of individual capitals as partial movements of the process of reproduction of the total social capital, then the mere change of form between money and commodities does not explain matters.

In a continuously revolving circle, every point is simultaneously a point of departure and point of return. If we interrupt the rotation, not every point of departure is a point of return. We have seen, for instance, that not only does every individual cycle imply the existence of the others, but also that the repetition of one cycle in a certain form necessitates the rotation of this cycle through its other forms. The entire difference thus assumes a formal aspect, it appears as a mere subjective difference made for the convenience of the observer.

In so far as every one of these cycles is studied as a special form of movement through which various individual industrial capitals are passing, their differences have but an individual nature. But in reality every individual industrial capital is contained simultaneously in all three cycles. These three cycles, the forms of reproduction assumed by the three modes of capital, rotate continuously side by side. For instance, one part of capital value which now performs the function of commodity-capital, is transformed into money-capital, but at the same time another part leaves the process of production and enters the circulation as a new commodity-capital. The cycle C'...C' is thus continuously rotating, and so are the two other forms. The reproduction of capital in each one of its forms and stages is just as continuous as the metamorphoses of these forms and their successive transition through the three stages. The entire circulation is thus actually a unit with these three forms.

We assumed in our analysis that the entire volume of capital-value acts either as money-capital, productive capital, or commodity-capital. For instance, we had those 422 pounds sterling first in the role of money-capital, then we transformed them entirely into productive capital, and finally into commodity-capital, into yarn valued at 500 pounds sterling and containing 78 pounds sterling of surplus-value. Here the various stages are so many interruptions. So long as, for instance, those 422 pounds sterling retain the form of money, that is to say until the purchases M—C (L plus Pm) have been made, the entire capital exists only in the form of money-capital and performs its functions. But as soon as it is transformed into productive capital, it performs neither the functions of money-capital nor of commodity-capital. Its entire process of circulation is interrupted, just as on the other hand its entire process of production is interrupted, as soon as it performs any functions in one of its two circulation stages, either as M or as C. From this point of view, the cycle P...P would not only present a periodical renewal of the productive capital, but also the interruption of its function, the process of production, up to the time when the process of circulation is completed. Instead of proceeding continuously, production took place in jumps and was renewed only in periods of uncertain duration, according to whether the two stages of the process of circulation were completed fast or slowly. This would apply, for instance, to a Chinese artisan, who works only for private customers and whose process of production is interrupted, until he receives a new order.

This is true of every individual part of capital in process of circulation, and all parts of capital pass through this circulation in succession. For instance, the 10,000 lbs. of yarn are the weekly product of some spinner. These 10,000 lbs. of yarn leave the sphere of production in their entirety and enter the sphere of circulation. The capital-value contained in them must all be converted into money-capital, and so long as it retains the form of money-capital, it cannot return into the process of production. It must first go into circulation and be reconverted into the elements of productive capital, L plus Pm. The process of rotation of capital is a succession of interruptions, leaving one stage and entering the next, discarding one form and assuming another. Every one of these stages not only causes the next, but also excludes it.

But continuity is the characteristic mark of capitalist production, conditioned on its technical basis, although not absolutely attainable. Let us see, then, what passes in reality. While the 10,000 lbs. of yarn appear on the market as commodity-capital and are transformed into money (regardless of whether it is a paying, purchasing, or calculating medium), new cotton, coal, etc., take the place of the yarn in the process of production, having been reconverted from the form of money and commodities into that of productive capital and performing its functions. At the time when these 10,000 lbs. of yarn are converted into money, the preceding 10,000 lbs. are going through the second stage of circulation and are reconverted from money into the elements of productive capital. All parts of capital pass successively through the process of rotation and are simultaneously in its different stages. The industrial capital thus exists simultaneously in all the successive stages of its rotation and in the various forms corresponding to its functions. That part of industrial capital, which is for the first time converted from commodity-capital into money, begins the cycle C'...C', while industrial capital as a rotating body of aggregates, has passed through it. One hand advances money, the other receives it. The inauguration of the cycle M...M' at one place coincides with its return to the starting point of another. The same is true of productive capital.

The actual rotation of industrial capital in its continuity is therefore not alone the unity of the processes of production and circulation, but also the unity of its three cycles. But it can be such a unity only if every individual part of capital can go successively through the various stages of the rotation, pass from one phase and from one functional form to another, so that the industrial capital, being the aggregate of all these parts, is found simultaneously in its various phases and functions and describes all three cycles at the same time. The succession of these parts is conditioned on their simultaneous existence side by side, that is to say, on the division of capital. In a systematised manufacture, the product is as much ubiquitous in the various stages of its process of formation, as it is in the transition from one phase of production to another. As the individual industrial capital has a definite volume which does not merely depend on the means of the capitalist and which has a minimum magnitude for every branch of production, it follows that its division must proceed according to definite proportions. The magnitude of the available capital determines the volume of the process of production, and this, again, determines the size of the commodity-capital and money-capital which perform their functions simultaneously with the process of production. The simultaneous functions, which enable the production to proceed continuously, are only due to the rotation of the various parts of capital which pass successively through their different stages. The simultaneousness is merely the result of the succession. For if the rotation of one phase, for instance of C'—M', is interrupted for one of the parts of capital, if the commodity cannot be sold, then the cycle of this part is broken and the reproduction of its elements of production cannot take place; the succeeding parts, which come out of the process of production in the shape of C', find the conversion of their function blocked by their predecessors. If this is continued for some time, production is restricted and the entire process arrested. Every stop of the succession carries disorder into the simultaneousness of the cycles, every obstruction of one stage causes more or less obstruction in the entire rotation, not only of the obstructed part of capital, but of the total individual capital.

The next form, in which the process presents itself, is that of a succession of phases, so that the transition of capital into a new phase is conditioned on its departure from another. Every special cycle has therefore one of the functional forms of capital for its point of departure or return. On the other hand, the aggregate process is indeed the unity of its three cycles, which are the different forms in which the continuity of the process expresses itself: the total rotation appears as its own specific cycle to every functional form of capital, and every one of these cycles contributes to the continuity of the process. The rotation of one functional form requires that of the others. This is the inevitable requirement for the aggregate process of production, especially for the social capital, that it is at the same time a process of reproduction, and thus a rotation of each one of its elements. Different aliquot parts of capital pass successively through the various stages and functional forms. By this means, every functional form passes simultaneously with the others through its own cycles, although other parts of capital are continuously presented by each form. One part of capital, continually changing, continually reproduced, exists as a commodity-capital which is converted into money; another as money-capital converted into productive capital; and a third as productive capital converted into commodity-capital. The continuous existence of all three forms is brought about by the rotation of the aggregate cycle through these three phases.

Capital as a whole, then, exists simultaneously side by side in its different phases. But every part passes continuously and successively from one phase and functional form into the next one and performs a function in all of them. Its forms are fluid and their simultaneousness is brought about by their succession. Every form follows and precedes another, so that the return of one capital part to a certain form is conditioned on the return of another part to some other form. Every part describes continuously its own cycle, but it is always another part which assumes a certain form, and these special cycles are simultaneous and successive parts of the aggregate rotation.

The continuity of the aggregate process is realised only by the unity of the three cycles, and would be impossible with the above-mentioned interruptions. The social capital always has this continuity and its process always rests on the unity of the three cycles.

The continuity of the reproduction is more or less interrupted so far as the individual capitals are concerned. In the first place, the masses of value are frequently distributed at various periods and in unequal portions over the various stages and functional forms. In the second place, these portions may be differently distributed, according to the character of the commodity, which is to be produced. In the third place, the continuity may be more or less interrupted in those branches of production, which are dependent on the seasons, either on account of natural causes, such as agriculture, fishing, etc., or on account of conventional circumstance such as the so-called season-work. The process proceeds most regularly and uniformly in the factories and in mining. But this difference of the various branches of production does not cause any difference in the general forms of the process of rotation.

Capital, as a value creating more value, is not merely conditioned on class-relations, on a definite social system resting on the existence of labour in the form of wage-labour. It is also a movement, a rotation through various stages, comprising three different cycles. Therefore it can be understood only as a thing in motion, not as a thing at rest. Those who look upon the self-development of value as a mere abstraction forget that the movement of industrial capital is the realisation of this abstraction. Value here passes through various forms in which it maintains itself and at the same time increases its value. As we are here concerned in the form of this movement, we shall not take into consideration the revolutions, which capital-value may undergo during its rotation. But it is clear that capitalist production can only exist and endure, in spite of the revolutions of capital-value, so long as this value creates more value, that is to say, so long as it goes through its cycles as a self-developing value, or so long as the revolutions in value can be overcome and balanced in some way. The movements of capital appear as the actions of some individual industrial capitalist who performs the functions of a buyer of labour-power, a seller of commodities, and an owner of productive capital, and who brings about the process of rotation by his activity. If social capital-value experiences a revolution in value, it may happen, that the capital of the individual capitalist succumbs and fails, because it cannot adapt itself to the conditions of this conversion of values. To the extent that such revolutions in value become acute and frequent, the automatic nature of self-developing value makes itself felt with the force of elementary powers against the foresight and calculations of the individual capitalist, the course of normal production becomes subject to abnormal speculation, and the existence of individual capitals is endangered. These periodical revolutions in value, therefore, prove that which they are alleged to refute, namely, the independent nature of value in the form of capital and its increasing independence in the course of its development.

This succession of the metamorphoses of rotating capital includes the continuous comparison of the changes of value brought about by rotation with the original magnitude of capital. When the growing independence of value as compared to the power of creating value, of labour-power, has been inaugurated by the act M—L (purchase of labour-power) and is realised during the process of production as an exploitation of labour-power, this rise of independence on the part of value does not re-appear in that cycle, in which money, commodities, and elements of production are merely passing forms of rotating capital value, and in which the former magnitude of value compares itself to the present changed value of capital.

'Value', says Bailey, in opposition to the idea of the growing independence of value characteristic of capitalist production, which he regards as an illusion of certain economists, 'value is a relation between contemporary commodities, because such only admit of being exchanged with each other.' This criticism is directed against the comparison of commodity-values of different periods of time, which amounts to the comparison of the expenditure of productive labour required for the manufacture of equal commodities at different periods, once the value of money for every period has been fixed. His opposition is due to his general misunderstanding, for he thinks that exchange-value is value itself, that the form of value is identical with the volume of value; so that values of commodities cannot be compared, so long as they do not perform active service as exchange values and are not actually exchanged for each other. He has not the least inkling of the fact that value performs only the functions of capital, in so far as it remains identical with itself and is compared with itself in those different phases of its rotation, which are not at all contemporary, but succeed one another.

In order to study the formula of this rotation in its purity, it is not sufficient to assume that the commodities are sold at their value, but that this takes place under conditions which are otherwise equal. Take, for instance, the cycle P...P and make abstraction of all technical revolutions within the process of production, by which the productive capital of a certain individual capitalist might be depreciated; make abstraction furthermore of all reactions, which a change in the elements of value of productive capital might cause in the value of the existing commodity-capital, which might be increased or lowered, if a stock of it were kept on hand. Take it also, that C', or 10,000 lbs. of yarn, have been sold at their value of 500 pounds sterling; 8,440 lbs., equal to 422 pounds sterling, reproduce the capital-value contained in C'. But if the prices of cotton, coal, etc., have increased (we do not consider mere fluctuations in price), these 422 pounds sterling may not suffice for the full reproduction of the elements of productive capital; in that case, additional money-capital is required and money-value is tied up. The opposite takes place, if those prices fall, and money-capital is set free. The process takes a normal course only so long as the values remain constant; it proceeds practically normal, so long as the disturbances during the repetition of the process balance one another. But to the extent that these disturbances increase in volume, the industrial capitalist must have at his disposal a greater money-capital, in order to tide himself over the period of compensation; and as the scale of each individual process of production and thus the minimum size of the capital to be advanced increase in the process of capitalist production, we have here another circumstance to add to those others which transform the functions of the industrial capitalist more and more into a monopoly of great money-capitalists, who may be individuals or associations.

We remark incidentally that a difference in the form of M...M' on one side, and of P...P and C'...C' on the other appears, if a change in the value of the elements of production occurs.

In the cycle M...M', the formula of newly invested capital, which for the first time appears in the role of money-capital, a fall in the value of elements of production, such as raw materials, auxiliary materials, etc., will require a smaller investment of money-capital than would have been necessary before this fall for the purpose of starting a business of a definite size, because the scale of the process of production depends on the mass and volume of the means of production (provided the productivity remains unchanged), which a given quantity of labour-power can assimilate; but it does not depend on the value of these means of production nor on that of the labour-power (the latter has an influence only on the creation of more value). Take the opposite case. If the value of the elements of production of certain commodities is increased, which are required as elements of a certain productive capital, then more money-capital is required for the establishment of a business of definite proportions. In both cases it is only the quantity of the money-capital required for investment which is affected. In the former case, money-capital is set free, in the latter it is tied up, provided the advent of new industrial capitals proceeds normally in a given branch of production.

The cycles P...P and C'...C' assume the character of M...M' only to the extent that the movement of P and C' is at the same time accumulation, so that additional m, money, is converted into money-capital. Apart from this case, they are differently affected than M...M' by a change of value of the elements of production; here, too, we do not take into consideration the reaction of such changes in value on those parts of capitals which are engaged in the process of production. It is not the original investment, which is here directly affected, not a capital engaged in its first rotation, but one in a process of reproduction; in other words, C'...C{L/Pm}, the reconversion of commodity-capital into its elements of production, so far as they are composed of commodities. In a reduction of value (or price), three cases are possible: The process of reproduction is continued on the same scale; in that case a part of the available money-capital is set free and money-capital is accumulated, although no actual accumulation (production on an enlarged scale), or the transformation of m (surplus-value) into funds for accumulation initiating and accompanying it, has previously taken place. Or, the process of reproduction is renewed on a more enlarged scale than would have been ordinarily the case, provided the technical proportions admit it. Or, finally, a larger stock of raw materials, etc., is laid in.

The opposite takes place if the value of the elements of reproduction of a commodity-capital increases. In that case, reproduction does not take place on its normal scale (work is done in a shorter time, for instance); or additional money-capital must be employed in order to maintain the old scale (money-capital is tied up); or the money-fund of the accumulation, if available, is entirely or partially employed for the enlargement of the process of reproduction to its old scale. This is also tying up money-capital, only the additional money-capital does not come from the outside, from the money-market, but out of the pockets of the industrial capitalist himself.

However, there may be modifying circumstances in P...P and C'...C'. If our cotton spinner has a large stock of cotton (a large proportion of his productive capital in the form of a stock of cotton), a part of his productive capital is depreciated by a fall in the price of cotton; but if this price has risen, this part of his productive capital is enhanced in value. On the other hand, if he had tied up a large part of his capital in the form of commodity-capital, for instance in cotton yarn, a part of his commodity capital, or for that matter of any of his rotating capital, is depreciated by a fall in the price of cotton, or enhanced by a rise in that price. Finally take the process C'—M—C{L/Pm}. If C'—M, the realisation on the commodity-capital, has taken place before a change in the value of the elements of C, then capital is affected only in the way indicated in the first case, that is to say, in the second act of circulation, M—C{L/Pm}; but if such a change has occurred before the realisation of C'—M, then, other conditions remaining equal, a fall in the price of the cotton causes a corresponding fall in the price of yarn, and a rise in the price of cotton a rise in the price of yarn. The effect on the various individual capitals in the same branch of production may differ widely according to the circumstances in which they find themselves. Money-capital may also be set free or tied up by differences in the duration of the process of circulation, in other words, by the pace of the circulation. But this belongs in the discussion of the periods of turn-over. At this point, we are only interested in the real difference arising from changes of values in the elements of productive capital between M...M' and the other two cycles of the process of rotation.

In the section of circulation indicated by M—C{L/Pm}, at a period of developed and prevailing capitalist modes of production, a large portion of the commodities composing Pm, means of production, will be rotating commodity-capital of some one else. From the standpoint of the seller, therefore, the transaction is C'—M', the transformation of commodity-capital into money-capital. But this does not apply absolutely. In the opposite case, in those sections of its process of rotation, where industrial capital performs either the functions of money or of commodities, the cycle of industrial capital, whether as money-capital or as commodity-capital, crosses the circulation of commodities of the most varied social modes of production, so far as they produce commodities. No matter whether a commodity is the product of slavery, of peasants (Chinese, Indian *ryots*), of communes (Dutch East Indies), or of state enterprise (such as existed in former epochs of Russian history on the basis of serfdom), or of half-savage hunting tribes, etc., commodities and money of such modes of production, when coming in contact with commodities and money representing industrial capital, enter as much into its rotation as into that of surplus-values embodied in the commodity-capital, provided the surplus-value is spent as revenue. They enter into both of the cycles of circulation of commodity-capital. The character of the process of production from which they emanate is immaterial. They perform the function of commodities on the market, and enter into the cycles of industrial capital as well as into those of the surplus-value carried by it. It is the universal character of the commodities, the world character of the market, which distinguishes the process of rotation of the industrial capital. What is true of foreign commodities, is also true of foreign money. Just as commodity-capital has only the character of commodities in contact with foreign money, so this money has only the character of money in contact with commodity-capital. Money here performs the functions of world-money.

However, two points must be noted here.

First. As soon as the transaction M—Pm is completed, the commodities (Pm) cease to be such and become one of the modes of existence of industrial capital in its function of productive capital. Henceforth their origin is obliterated. They exist only as forms of industrial capital and are embodied in it. But it still remains necessary to reproduce them, if their places are to be filled, and to this extent the capitalist mode of production is conditioned on other modes of production outside of its own stage of development. But it is the tendency of capitalist production to transform all production as much as possible into a production of commodities. The mainspring, by which this is accomplished, is the implication of other modes of production into the circulation process of capitalist production. And developed commodity-production is capitalist production. The intervention of industrial capital promotes this transformation everywhere, and simultaneously with it also the transformation of all direct producers into wage labourers.

Second. The commodities entering into the process of circulation (including the means of existence necessary for the reproduction of the labour-power of the labourer, who receives variable capital in the form of wages), regardless of their origin and of the social form of the productive process by which they were created, entertain the relation of commodity-capital, in the form of merchandise or merchant's capital, toward industrial capital. Merchant's capital, by its very nature, includes commodities of all modes of production.

Capitalist production does not only imply production on a large scale, but also necessarily sale on a large scale, in other words, sale to the dealer, not to the individual consumer. Of course, so far as a consumer is himself a productive consumer, an industrial capitalist, whose industrial capital produces means of production for some other branch of industry, a direct sale of one industrial capitalist's product to many other capitalists takes place (orders, etc). To this extent, every industrial capitalist is a direct seller and his own dealer, also, when he sells to the merchant.

Trading in commodities as a function of merchant's capital is the premise of capitalist production and develops more and more in the course of development of this mode of production. Therefore we use it occasionally for the illustration of various aspects of the process of capitalist circulation; but in the general analysis of this process, we assume that commodities are sold directly without the intervention of the merchant, because this intervention obscures various points of the movement.

See, for instance, Sismondi, who presents the matter somewhat naively, in the following words: 'Commerce employs considerable capital, which at first sight does not seem to be a part of that capital whose movements we have just described. The value of the cloth in the stores of the cloth-merchant seems at first to be entirely foreign to that part of the annual production which the rich give to the poor as wages in order to make them work. However, this capital has simply replaced the other of which we have spoken. For the purpose of clearly understanding the progress of wealth, we have begun with its creation and followed its movements to their conclusion. We have then seen that the capital employed in manufacture, for instance in the manufacture of cloth, was always the same; and when it was exchanged for the income of the consumer, it was merely divided into two parts; one of them serving as revenue for the capitalist in the form of the product, the other serving as revenue to the labourers in the form of wages while they were manufacturing new cloth.

'But it was soon found that it would be to the advantage of all to replace the different parts of this capital one by another and, if 10,000 dollars were sufficient for the entire circulation between the manufacturer and the consumer, to divide them equally between the manufacturer, the wholesale dealer, and the retail merchant. The first then did the same work with only one-third of this capital which he had formerly done with the entire capital, because, as soon as his work of manufacturing was completed, he found that the merchant bought from him much more readily than he could have found the consumer. On the other hand, the capital of the wholesale dealer was much sooner replaced by that of the retail merchant . . . The difference between the sums advanced for wages and the purchase price paid by the last consumer was considered the profit of those capitals. It was divided between the manufacturer, the wholesale dealer, and the retail merchant, from the moment that they had divided their functions, and the work accomplished was the same, although it had required three persons and three parts of capital instead of one.' (*Nouveaux Principes*, I, pages 159, 160) 'All the merchants contributed indirectly to production; for having consumption for its object, production cannot be regarded as completed, until the product is placed into the reach of the consumer.' (*ibidem*, page 157.)

We operate in the discussion of the general forms of the rotation, in short in the entire second volume, with money as metallic money, to the exclusion of symbolic money, of mere tokens of value, which are the specialties of certain states, and of credit-money, which is not yet developed. In the first place, this is the historical order; credit-money plays only a very minor role, or none at all, during the first epoch of capitalist production. In the second place, the necessity of this order is demonstrated theoretically by the fact, that everything which Tooke and others have hitherto produced of a critical nature in regard to the circulation of credit-money was compelled to hark back to the question, what would be the aspect of the matter if nothing but metal-money were in circulation. But it must not be forgotten, that metal-money may serve as a purchase medium and as a paying medium. For the sake of simplicity, we consider it in this second volume generally only in its first functional form.

The process of circulation of industrial capital, which is only a part of its individual process of rotation, is determined by the general laws outlined in Book 1, Chapter 3, in so far as it is a series of transactions within the general circulation of commodities. The same mass of money, for instance 500 pounds sterling, starts successively so many more industrial capitals (or eventually individual capitals in the form of commodity-capitals) in circulation, the greater the velocity of rotation of money is, and the more rapidly therefore every individual capital passes through the metamorphoses of commodities or money. One and the same volume of capital-value therefore requires so much less money for its circulation, the more this money performs the functions of a paying medium; the more, for instance, in the reproduction of some commodity-capital by its corresponding means of production, nothing but balances have to be squared; and the shorter the time of the payments is, for instance in paying wages. On the other hand, assuming that the velocity of the circulation and all other conditions remain the same, the volume of money required for the circulation of money-capital is determined by the sum of the prices of commodities (price multiplied by the volume of commodities), or, if the volume and value of the commodities are given, by the value of money itself.

But the laws of the general circulation of commodities apply only to the extent that the process of circulation of capital consists of a series of simple transactions in circulation; they do not apply to the extent that such transactions are definite functional sections in the rotation of individual industrial capitals.

In order to make this plain, it is best to study the process of circulation in its uninterrupted and connected form, such as it appears in the following two formulas:

2) P...C'{C—, —M, c—} {M—C{L/Pm}...P (P'), m—c}
3) C'{C—, —M, c—} {M—C{L/Pm}...C', m—c}

As a series of transactions, in circulation, the process of circulation, whether in the form of C—M—C or of M—C—M, represents merely the two opposite lines of metamorphoses of commodities, and every individual metamorphosis in its turn includes its opposite on the part of the commodity or money in the hands of another.

C—M on the part of the owner of some commodity means M—C on the part of its buyer; the first metamorphosis of the commodity in C—M is the second metamorphosis of the commodity appearing in the form of M; the opposite applies to M—C. The statements concerning the intermingling of the metamorphosis of a certain commodity in one stage with that of another in another stage apply to the circulation of capital to the extent that the capitalist performs the functions of a buyer and seller of commodities, so that his capital in the form of money meets the commodities of another, or in the form of commodities the money of another. But this intermingling is not identical with the intermingling of the metamorphoses of capitals.

In the first place, M—C (Pm), as we have seen, may represent an intermingling of the metamorphoses of different individual capitals. For instance, the commodity-capital of the cotton-spinner, yarn, is partly replaced by coal. One part of his capital is in the form of money and is transformed into commodities, while the capital of the capitalist producer of coal exists in the form of commodities and is therefore transformed into money; the same transaction of circulation in this case represents opposite metamorphoses of two industrial capitals in different departments of production, the series of metamorphoses of these capitals intermingles in it. But we have also seen, that the Pm into which M is transformed need not be commodity-capital in the strictest sense, that is to say need not be a functional form of industrial capital, need not be produced by a capitalist. It is always a question of M—C on one side, and C—M on the other, but not always of intermingling metamorphoses of capitals. Furthermore M—L, the purchase of labour-power, never intermingles with any metamorphoses of capital, for labour-power, though a commodity from the point of view of the labourer, does not become capital until it is sold to the capitalist. On the other hand, in the process C'—M', it is not necessary that M' should represent transformed commodity-capital; it may be the money-equivalent of labour-power (wages), or of the product of some independent labourer, some slave, serf, or some commune.

In the second place, a definite functional role played by every metamorphosis of some individual capital within the process of circulation, need not represent a corresponding opposite metamorphosis in the rotation of the other capital, provided we assume that the entire production of the world-market is carried on capitalistically. For instance, in the cycle P...P, the M' which pays for C' may be merely the money-form of the surplus-value of the buyer, in case that the commodity is an article for consumption; or, in M'—C'{L/Pm} where accumulated capital is concerned, it may simply replace the advanced capital of the seller of Pm, or it may not return into the rotation of his capital at all by being side-tracked into expenditures as revenue.

This shows that the manner in which the different component parts of the aggregate social capital, of which individual capitals are merely components performing independent functions, mutually replace one another in the process of circulation (in regard to capital as well as surplus-value), is not apparent from the simple intermingling of the metamorphoses in the circulation of commodities. Such intermingling occurs in the transactions of capital circulation as it does in all other circulation of commodities, but it requires a different method of analysis. Hitherto nothing but general phrases have been employed by economists for his purpose, and if we test those phrases, they contain nothing but indefinite ideas borrowed from the intermingling of metamorphoses common to all circulations of commodities.

*   *   *

One of the most obvious peculiarities of the process of rotation of industrial capital, and therefore of capitalist production, is the fact that on the one side, the component elements of productive capital are derived from the commodity-market, are continually renewed out of it, and are sold as commodities; that, on the other side, the product of the labour-process comes forth from it as a commodity and must be continually sold over and over as a commodity. Compare, for instance, a modern tenant of Lower Scotland with an old-fashioned small farmer on the continent. The former sells his entire product and has therefore to reproduce all its elements, even his seeds, by means of the market; the latter consumes the greater part of his product directly, buys and sells as little as possible, fashions tools, clothing, etc., so far as possible himself.

Such comparisons have led to the classification of production into natural economy, the money-system, and the credit-system, as being the three characteristic stages of economy in the development of social production.

But in the first place, these three forms do not represent any equivalent phases of development. The so-called credit-system is itself merely a modification of the money-system, so far as both terms express transactions between the producers themselves. In the developed capitalist production, the money-system appears only as the basis of the credit-system. The money-system and credit-system thus correspond only to different stages in the development of capitalist production, but they are by no means independent modes of economy as compared to natural economy. With the same justification, one might place the various forms of natural economy as equivalents by the side of those two systems.

In the second place, it is not the process of production itself which is emphasised as the distinguishing mark of the two systems of that classification, the money-system, the credit-system, but rather the mode of transaction between the various producers under those systems. Then the same should apply to the natural economy, which should in that case be classified as the exchange-system. A completely rounded system of natural economy, such as the state of the Incas in Peru, would not fall under any of these classifications.

In the third place, the money-system is common to all production of commodities, and the product appears as a commodity in the most varied organisms of social production. The characteristic mark of capitalist production would then be only the extent to which the product is manufactured for purposes of trade, as a commodity, and the extent to which its own elements of formation enter as commodities into the economy which creates that product.

It is true, that capitalist production has for its general form the production of commodities. But it is so and becomes more so in its development, only because labour itself here appears as a commodity, because the labourer sells labour, that is to say the function of his labour-power, and our assumption is that he sells it at a value determined by its cost of reproduction. To the extent that labour becomes wage-labour, the producer becomes an industrial capitalist. For this reason capitalist production (and the production of commodities) does not reach its full scope, until the agricultural labourer becomes a wage-labourer. In the relation of capitalist and wage-labourer, the relation between the buyer and the seller, the money-relation, becomes an immanent relation of production. And this relation has its foundation in the social character of production, not of circulation. The character of the circulation rather depends on that of production. It is, however, quite characteristic of the bourgeois horizon, which is entirely bounded by the craze for making money, not to see in the character of the mode of production the basis of the corresponding mode of circulation, but vice versa.[1]

The capitalist throws less value in the form of money into the circulation than he draws out of it, because he throws into it more value in the form of commodities than he had withdrawn from it. To the extent that he is simply a personification of capital, an industrial capitalist, his supply of commodity-value is always larger than his demand for that value. The equality of his supply and demand in this respect would indicate that his capital had not produced any surplus-value; it would not have performed the functions of productive capital; the productive capital would have been converted into commodity-capital which would not be impregnated with surplus-value; it would not have drawn any surplus-value in commodity-form out of labour-power during the process of production, it would not have performed any capital-functions at all. The capitalist must indeed 'sell dearer than he has bought', but he succeeds only in doing so, because the capitalist process of production enables him to transform the cheaper commodity, which contains less value, into a dearer commodity with increased value. He sells dearer, not because he gets more than the value of his commodity, but because his commodity contains a greater value than that contained in the natural elements of its production.

The rate at which value is added to the capital of the capitalist increases in proportion to the difference between his supply and his demand, that is to say in proportion as the surplus of the commodities which he places on the market exceeds the value of the commodities which he has taken from it. His aim is not to equalise his supply and demand, but to make the difference between them as much as possible in favour of his supply.

What is true of the individual capital, also applies to the capitalist class.

In so far as the capitalist personifies but his industrial capital, his own demand is only for means of production and labour-power. His demand for Pm, expressed in value, is smaller than his advanced capital; he buys means of production of a value smaller than his capital, and therefore much smaller than the value of the commodity-capital which he takes back to the market.

As regards his demand for labour-power, its value is determined by the proportion of his variable capital to his total capital, as expressed by V/C. Its proportion in capitalist production decreases continually more than his demand for means of production. His purchases of Pm steadily increase over his purchases of L.

Inasmuch as the labourer generally converts his wages into means of existence, and for the overwhelmingly larger part necessities of life, the demand of the capitalist for labour-power is indirectly also a demand for the articles of consumption assimilated by the working class. But this demand is equal to v and not one atom greater. If the labourer saves a part of his wages – we do not consider any questions of credit at all – he converts a part of his wages into a hoard and does not perform the functions of a purchaser to that extent. The limit of the maximum demand of the capitalist is C, equal to c plus v, but his supply for the market is c plus v plus s. If the composition of his commodity-capital is 80c + 20v + 20s, his demand is equal to 80c + 20v, or one fifth smaller in value than his supply. His demand as compared to his supply decreases in proportion as the percentage of the mass of surplus-value produced by him (his rate of profit) increases. Although the demand of the capitalist for labour-power, and thus indirectly for necessities of life, decreases continually compared to his demand for means of production in the further development of production, it must not be forgotten that day by day his demand for Pm is always smaller than his capital. His demand for means of production must, therefore, be always smaller in value than the commodity-product of the capitalist who, working with a capital of equal value and conditions like his, furnishes him with those means of production. It does not alter the case, if many capitalists instead of one furnish him with means of production. Take it that his capital is 1,000 pounds sterling, and its constant part 800 pounds sterling; then his demand on all the capitalists supplying him is equal in value to 800 pounds sterling. Together they supply for each 1,000 pounds sterling means of production valued at 1,200 pounds sterling, assuming that the rate of profit is the same for all of them, regardless of the rate at which they share in the 1,000 and of the proportion which the share of each one may represent in his total capital. The demand of the buying capitalist covers only two-thirds of the supply of the sellers, while his total demand equals only four-fifths of the value of his own supply to the market.

It still remains to anticipate the analysis of the problem of turn-over. Let the total capital of the capitalist be 5,000 pounds sterling, of which 4,000 pounds is fixed and 1,000 pounds circulating capital; these 1,000 pounds sterling are composed of 800 c plus 200 v, as assumed before. His circulating capital must be turned over five times per year in order that his fixed capital may be turned over once. His commodity-product is then equal in value to 6,000 pounds sterling, it is valued at 1,000 pounds sterling more than his advanced capital, so that the same proportion of surplus-value is obtained as before:

$$5,000 \text{ C} / 1,000 \text{ s} = 100 \text{ (c + v)} / 20 \text{ s}.$$

This turn-over does not change anything in the proportion of the total demand of the capitalist to his total supply. The former remains one-fifth smaller than the latter.

Take it that his fixed capital must be reproduced in 10 years. Hence he sinks every year one tenth, or 400 pounds sterling, so that he has only a value of 3,600 pounds of fixed capital left plus 400 pounds in money. Inasmuch as repairs are necessary which do not exceed the average, they represent nothing but capital invested later. We may look at the matter from the standpoint that he has allowed for the expenses for repairs when calculating the value of his investment, so far as this enters into the annual commodity-product, so that they are included in that one tenth of sinking fund. If the repairs cost less than the average he is so much money in pocket, and in the reverse case he loses it. At any rate, although his demand, after his total capital has been turned over once a year, still remains at 5,000 pounds sterling which was the value of the original capital advanced, it increases so far as the circulating part of this capital is concerned, while it decreases so far as the fixed part is concerned.

We now come to the question of reproduction. Take it that the capitalist consumes the entire surplus-value composed of money m and reconverts only the original capital-value C into productive capital. Then the demand of the capitalist is equal to his supply; but this does not refer to the movements of his capital. As a capitalist, his demand is only for four-fifths of the value of his supply. He consumes one-fifth as a non-capitalist; he consumes it, not in the performance of his function as capitalist, but for his private requirements or pleasure.

His calculation, expressed in percentages, stands as follows:

Demand as capitalist . . . . 100, supply 120.
Demand as man of the world . . . 20, supply 0.
Total demand . . . . . . 120, supply 120.

This assumption amounts to a non-existence of capitalist production, and thus the non-existence of the industrial capitalist himself. For capitalism is destroyed in its very foundation, if we assume that its compelling motive is enjoyment instead of the accumulation of wealth.

But such an assumption is also technically impossible. The capitalist must not only form a reserve-capital as a protection against fluctuations of value and as a fund enabling him to wait for favourable conditions of the market for sale and purchase; he must also accumulate capital, in order to extend his production and embody the progress of technique in his productive organisation.

In order to accumulate capital, he must first withdraw a a part of the surplus-value from circulation which he obtained from that circulation in the form of money, and must hoard it until it has increased sufficiently for the extension of his old business or the opening of a side-line. So long as the formation of the hoard continues, it does not increase the demand of the capitalist. The money is then inactive. It does not withdraw from the commodity-market any equivalent in commodities for the money-equivalent which it withdrew for commodities supplied to it.

Credit is not considered here. And credit includes the depositing, on the part of the capitalist, of accumulating money in a bank on payment of interest as shown by a running account.

Chapter 5
The Time of Circulation[1]

We have seen that the movement of capital through the sphere of production and the two phases of circulation takes place in a succession of time. The duration of its sojourn in the sphere of production is its time of production, that of its stay in the sphere of circulation its time of circulation.

The time of production naturally includes the period of the labour-process, but is not comprised in it. We must first remember that a part of the constant capital exists in the form of instruments of production, such as machinery, buildings, etc., which serve for the repeated labour-processes until they are worn out. Periodical interruptions of the labour-process by night, etc., interrupt the function of these instruments of production, but not their location on the place of production. They belong to this place when they are not in function as well as when they are. On the other hand, the capitalist must have a definite supply of raw material and auxiliary substances in readiness, in order that the process of production may take place for a longer or shorter time on a previously determined scale, without being dependent on the accidents of a daily supply from the market. This supply of raw material, etc., is consumed productively by degrees. There is, therefore, a difference between its time of production[2] and its time of function. The time of production of the means of production in general comprises, therefore, first the time during which they serve as means of production by taking part in the productive process; second, the stops during which a certain process of production, and thus the function of the means of production embodied in it, is interrupted; third, the time during which the means of production are held in readiness as requirements for the process of production, during which they represent productive capital, without having entered into the process of production.

The difference so far discussed is always the difference between the time which the productive capital passes in the sphere of production and that in the process of production. But the process of production itself may require interruptions of the labour-process, and thus of the labour time, and during such pauses the object of labour is exposed to the influence of physical processes without the intervention of human labour. The process of production, and thus the function of the means of production, continue in this case, although the labour-process, and thus the function of the means of production as instruments of labour, have been interrupted. This applies, for instance, to the grain, after it has been sowed, the wine fermenting in the cellar, the labour-material of many manufacturers, such as tanneries, where the material is given over to chemical processes. The time of production is then greater than the labour-time. The difference between the two consists in an excess of the time of production over the labour-time. This excess always arises by the latent existence of productive capital in the sphere of production, without performing its function in the process of production itself, or by the performance of its function in the productive process without taking part in the labour-process.

That part of the latent productive capital, which is held in readiness as a requirement for the productive process, such as cotton, coal, etc., in a spinnery, produces neither products nor value. It is fallow capital, although its fallow condition is a requirement for the uninterrupted flow of the process of production. The buildings, apparatus, etc., necessary for the storage of the productive supply (latent capital) are requirements of the productive process and therefore component parts of the advanced productive capital. They perform their function as conservators of the elements of production in a preliminary stage. Inasmuch as labour-processes are required in this stage, they add to the cost of the raw material, etc., but they are productive labour and produce surplus-value, because a part of this labour, like all wage-labour, is not paid. The normal interruptions of the entire process of production, the pauses in which the productive capital does not perform any functions, create neither value nor surplus-value. Hence the tendency to keep the work going at night (Book 1, Chapter 10, 4). – The intervals in the labour-time, which the object of labour must endure in the process of production itself, create neither value nor surplus-value. But they advance the product, form a part of its life, a process through which it must necessarily pass. The value of the apparatus, etc., is transferred to the product in proportion to the entire time, during which they perform their function; the product is brought to this stage by labour itself, and the employment of these apparatus is as much a requirement of production as the wasting of a part of the cotton which does not enter into the product, but nevertheless transfers its value to that product. The other parts of latent capital, such as buildings, machinery, etc., that is to say those instruments of labour whose function is interrupted only by the regular pauses of the productive process (irregular interruptions caused by the restriction of production, crises, etc., are total losses) create additional values without entering into the creation of the product. The total value which this part of capital adds to the product, is determined by the average time which it lasts, for its own value, being use-value, diminishes during the time that it performs its functions as well as during that in which it does not.

Finally, the value of the constant part of capital, which continues in the productive process although the labour-process is interrupted, re-appears in the result of the productive process. Labour itself has here placed the means of production in a condition, where they pass without further assistance through certain useful processes, the result of which is a definite advantage or a change in the form of the use-values. Labour always transfers the value of the means of production to the product, to the extent that it really consumes them to good effect as means of production. And it does not change the case, whether labour has to be exerted continually on its object in order to produce this effect, or whether it merely gives the first impulse for it by placing the means of production in a condition wherein they undergo the intended transformation through the influence of natural processes, without further assistance from labour.

Whatever may be the reason for the excess of the time of pro-duction over the labour-time – whether it is that the means of production are still latent capital in a stage preliminary to the actual productive process, or that their function is interrupted within the process of production by its pauses, or that the process of production itself requires an interruption of the labour-process – in none of these cases do the means of production assimilate any labour. And if they do not assimilate any labour, they do not imbibe any surplus-labour. Hence the productive capital does not increase its value, so long as it remains in that part of its time of production which exceeds the labour-time, no matter how indispensable these pauses may be for the realisation of the process of increasing value. It is plain, that the productivity and increment of a given productive capital in a given time are so much greater, the more nearly the time of production and labour-time are equal. Hence we have the tendency of capitalist production to reduce the excess of the time of pro-duction over the labour-time as much as possible. But although the time of production of a certain capital may exceed its labour-time, it always includes the latter, and its excess is a logical condition of the process of production. The time of production, then, is always that time in which a capital produces use-values and surplus-values, and in which it performs the functions of productive capital, although it includes time in which it is either latent or produces without creating surplus-values.

Within the sphere of circulation, capital abides as commodity-capital and money-capital. Its two processes of circulation consist in its transformation from the commodity-form into that of money, and from the money-form into that of commodities. It does not alter the character of these processes as transactions in circulation, of processes in the simple metamorphosis of commodities, that this transformation of commodities into money is at the same time a realisation of the surplus-values embodied in the commodities, and that the transformation of money into commodities is at the same time a transformation or reconversion of capital-value into the forms of its elements of production.

The time of circulation and time of production mutually exclude one another. During its time of circulation, capital does not perform the functions of productive capital and therefore produces neither commodities nor surplus-value. If we study the cycle in its simplest form, so that the entire capital-value passes in one bulk from one phase into the other, we can plainly see that the process of production is interrupted and therefore also the production of surplus-value, so long as its time of circulation lasts, and that the renewal of the process of production will take place promptly or slowly, according to the length of the time of circulation. But if the various parts of capital pass through the cycle successively, so that the rotation of the entire capital-value proceeds successively by the rotation of its component parts, then it is evident that the part performing continually the function of productive capital must be so much smaller, the longer the aliquot parts of capital-value remain in the sphere of circulation. The expansion and contraction of the time of circulation are therefore a check on the contraction or expansion of the time of production or of the volume which a given capital can assume for its productive function. To the extent that the metamorphoses of circulation of a certain capital are reduced, to the extent that the time of circulation approaches zero, its productivity and increment of surplus-value will increase. For instance, if a capitalist executes an order, so that he receives payment for his goods on delivery, and if this payment is made in his own elements of production, the time of circulation of his capital approaches zero.

In short, the time of circulation of a certain capital limits its time of production and the process of creating surplus-value. And this limitation is proportional to the duration of the time of circulation. Seeing that this time may increase or decrease in different ratios, it may limit the time of production in various degrees. But political economy sees only the seeming effect, that is to say the effect of the time of circulation on the creation of surplus-values in general. It takes this negative effect for a positive one, because its results are positive. It clings so much the more to this semblance, as this seems to prove that capital has a mystic source from which surplus-value flows toward it through the circulation, independently of its process of production and the exploitation of labour. We shall see later, that even scientific political economy has been deceived by this appearance of things. Various phenomena contribute to this deception: 1. The capitalist method of calculating profit, in which the negative cause figures as a positive one, seeing that with capitals in different spheres of investment, with different times of circulation only, a longer time of circulation tends toward an increase of prices, in short serves as one of the causes which bring about an equalisation of profits. 2. The time of circulation is but a factor in the period of turn-over; and this period includes both the time of production and reproduction. What is really due to the period of turn-over, seems to be due to the time of circulation. 3. The conversion of commodities into variable capital (wages) is conditioned on their previous conversion into money. In the accumulation of capital, the conversion into additional variable capital takes place in circulation, or during the time of circulation. It thus appears as though this accumulation were due to the time of circulation.

Within the sphere of circulation, capital passes through the two opposite phases of C—M and M—C, no matter in what succession. Hence its time of circulation is likewise divided into two parts, viz. the time required for its conversion from money into commodities, and that required for its conversion from commodities into money. We have already learned from the analysis of the simple circulation of commodities (Book 1, Chap. 3), that C—M, the sale, is the most difficult part of its metamorphosis and that, therefore, under ordinary conditions, it takes up the greater part of its time of circulation. As money, value exists in its ever convertible form. But as a commodity, value must first be transformed into money in order to assume such a directly convertible form of continual readiness. However, in the process of circulation of capital, its phase C—M deals with commodities which constitute definite elements of productive capital in a certain investment. The means of production may not be on the market and must first be produced, or they must be ordered from distant markets, or their ordinary supply is interrupted, or prices change, etc., in short there are a multitude of circumstances which are not visible in the simple change of form from M to C, but which nevertheless require more or less time for this part of the phase of circulation. C—M and M—C may not only be separate in time, but also in space, the selling and the buying market may be located apart. In the case of factories, for instance, the buyer and seller are frequently different persons. In the production of commodities, circulation is as necessary as production itself, so that agents are just as much needed in circulation as in production. The process of reproduction includes both functions of capital, therefore it also includes the necessity of having representatives for both of them, either in the person of the capitalist or of wage-workers, as his agents. But this is no more a good reason for mistaking the agents in circulation for those in production, than it is to confound the functions of commodity-capital and money-capital with those of productive capital. The agents of circulation must be paid by the agents of production. And since capitalists who mutually sell and buy do not create either values or products by these transactions, this state of affairs is not changed, if they are enabled or compelled by the expansion of their business to charge others with those transactions.

In some businesses, the buyers and sellers get their wages in the form of percentages on the profits. It does not alter the matter to use the phrase that they are paid by the consumer. The consumers can pay only inasmuch as they are themselves instrumental in producing an equivalent in commodities as agents of production or appropriate it out of the product of other agents in production, whether it be by means of legal titles or of personal services.

There is a difference between C—M and M—C, which has nothing to do with the different forms of commodities and money, but arises from the capitalist character of production. Intrinsically, C—M as well as M—C is merely a conversion of a given value out of one form into another. But C'—M' is at the same time a realisation of the surplus-value contained in C'. Not so M—C. For this reason the sale is more important than the purchase. M—C is under normal conditions a necessary act for the creation of more value by means of the value contained in it, but it is not the realisation of surplus-value; it is the intimation of its production, not its after-effect.

The form in which a commodity exists, the form of its use-value, prescribes definite limits for the circulation of commodity-capital C'—M'. Use-values are naturally perishable. Hence, if they are not productively or individually consumed within a certain time, in other words, if they are not sold within a certain period, they spoil and thus lose with their use-value also the faculty of being bearers of surplus-value. The capital-value, or eventually the surplus-value, contained in them is lost. The use-values do not remain the bearers of perennial capital-value increasing by the addition of surplus-value, unless they are continually reproduced and replaced by new use-values of the same or of some other order. The sale of the use-values in the form of finished commodities, their transfer to the productive or individual consumption by means of this sale, is the ever recurring requirement for their reproduction. They must change their old use-form within a certain time, in order to continue their existence in a new form. Exchange-value maintains itself only by means of this constant renewal of its substance. The use-values of certain commodities spoil sooner or later; the time between their production and consumption may therefore be long or short; they may retain the form of commodity-capital in phase C—M of the circulation for a shorter or longer term and endure a shorter or a longer time of circulation. The limit of the time of circulation of a certain commodity-capital imposed by the spoiling of the substance of the commodity is the absolute limit of this part of the time of circulation, or of the time of circulation of commodity-capital as such. To the extent that a commodity is perishable, to the extent that it must be sold and consumed as soon as possible after its production, its capacity for removal from its place of production is restricted, the sphere of its circulation is narrowed, its selling market is localised. For this reason a commodity is so much less suited for capitalist production as it is perishable, as its physical composition limits its time of circulation. It is available for this purpose only in thickly populated districts, or to the extent that the improvement of transportation brings places closer together. But the concentration of the production of such articles into a few hands and in a populous district may create a relatively large market even for them, for instance, such as the product of large beer-breweries, dairies, etc.

Chapter 6

The Expenses of Circulation

Section 1. Genuine Expenses of Circulation.

A. The Time of Purchase and Sale.

The transformations of capital from commodities into money and from money into commodities are at the same time transactions of the capitalist, acts of purchase and sale. The time in which these transformations take place constitutes from the personal standpoint of the capitalist a purchase and selling time, it is the time during which he performs the functions of a buyer and seller on the market. Just as the time of circulation of capital is a necessary part of its time of reproduction, so the time in which the capitalist buys and sells and remains in the market is a necessary part of the time in which he performs the functions of a capitalist, in which he personifies capital. It is a part of his business time.

Since[1] we have assumed that commodities are bought and sold at their values, these transformations constitute merely a conversion of the same value from one form into another, from the form of commodities into that of money or vice versa, a change of composition in substance. If commodities are sold at their values, then the magnitude in the hands of the buyer and seller remains unchanged. Only the form of its existence is changed. If the commodities are not sold at their values, then the sum of the converted values remains the same; the plus on one side is offset by a minus on the other.

The metamorphoses C—M and M—C are transactions between buyers and sellers; they require time to perfect the trade, the more so as this represents a struggle in which each seeks to get the best of the other; for to business men applies the statement: 'When Greek meets Greek, then comes the tug of war.' The conversion of a commodity costs time and labour-power, not for the purpose of creating values, but in order to accomplish the conversion of value from one form into another. The mutual attempt to appropriate an extra share of this value, changes nothing fundamentally. This work, increased by the evil designs on either side, does not create value any more than the work done in a civil process increases the value of the object of contention. It is with this labour, which is a necessary part of the totality of the capitalist process of production, including the circulation or included by it, as it is with the labour of combustion of some element used for the generation of heat. This labour of combustion does not generate any heat, although it is a necessary part in the process of combustion. In order to employ coal as fuel, it must combine with oxygen, and for this purpose coal must be brought to the condition of carbonic acid gas; in other words, a physical change of form must take place. The separation of carbon molecules, which are united into a solid mass, and the breaking up of these molecules into their atoms, must precede the new combination, and this requires a certain effort, which is not transformed into heat, but taken from it. If the owners of commodities are not capitalists, but direct producers, the time required for buying and selling is so much loss of labour time, and for this reason such transactions were deferred in ancient and medieval times to holidays.

Of course, the dimensions acquired by the business in commodities in the hands of the capitalists cannot transform this labour, which does not create any values and promotes merely changes of form, into labour productive of surplus-value. Nor can this miracle of transsubstantiation be accomplished by unloading this work of 'combustion' from the shoulders of the industrial capitalists to those of paid employees who attend to it exclusively. These employees will not tender their services out of pure love for the capitalists. The collector of some real-estate owner or the messenger of some bank is indifferent to the fact that their labour does not add any value to the rent or to the money carried to the bank in bags.[2]

For the capitalist who has others working for him, selling and buying become primary functions. Seeing that he appropriates the products of many on a large social scale, he must sell on the same scale and then reconvert the money into elements of production. But still neither the sale nor the purchase create any values. An illusion is here created by the function of merchant's capital. But without entering at this point into a detailed discussion of this fact, we can plainly see this much: if a function, which is unproductive in itself, although a necessary link in reproduction, is transformed by a division of labour from an incidental occupation of many into an exclusive occupation of a few, the character of this function is not changed thereby. One merchant, as an agent promoting the transformation of commodities by assuming the role of a mere buyer and seller, may abbreviate by his operations the time of sale and purchase for many producers. To that extent he may be regarded as a machine which reduces a useless expenditure of energy or helps to set free some time of production.[3]

In order to simplify the matter, seeing that we shall not discuss the merchant as a capitalist and his capital as merchant's capital until later, we shall assume that this buying and selling agent is a man who sells his labour-power. He expends his labour-power and labour-time in the operations C—M and M—C. And he makes his living that way, just as another does by spinning or by making pills. He performs a necessary function, because the process of reproduction itself includes an unproductive function. He works as well as any other man, but intrinsically his labour creates neither products nor values. He belongs himself to the unproductive expenses of production. His services do not transform an unproductive function into a productive one, nor unproductive into productive labour. It would be a miracle, if such a transformation could be accomplished by a mere transfer of a function. His usefulness consists rather in the fact that a small part of the labour-power and labour-time of society is tied up in this unproductive function. We shall assume that he is a wage-worker, even though better paid than others. Whatever may be his wages, in the role of a wageworker he always works a part of his time for nothing. He may receive in wages the value of the product of eight working hours, when he performs his functions for ten hours. But his two hours of surplus-labour do not produce any surplus-values any more than his eight hours of necessary labour, although by means of these eight hours of necessary labour a part of the social product is transferred to him. In the first place, looking at it from the standpoint of society, his labour-power is used up for ten hours in a mere function of circulation. It cannot be used otherwise, for productive labour. In the second place, society does not pay for those two hours of surplus-labour, although they are expended by the man who worked during that time. Society does not appropriate any surplus-product or value through them. But the expenses of circulation, which he represents, are thereby reduced by one-fifth, from ten hours to eight. Society does not pay any equivalent for this fifth of this actual time of circulation, of which he is the agent. But if this man is employed by a capitalist, then the non-payment of these two hours reduces the expenses of circulation of his capital, which represent a deduction from his income. For the capitalist this is a positive gain, because the negative limit for the utilisation of his capital is thereby reduced. So long as small independent producers of commodities spend a part of their own time in selling and buying, this shows itself either as time spent during the intervals of their productive function, or as a reduction of their time of production.

At all events, the time required for this purpose is an expense of circulation, which does not add any increment to the converted values. It is the expense which is required in order to convert them from commodities into money. Inasmuch as the capitalist producer of commodities appears as an agent of circulation, he differs from the direct producers of commodities only by the fact that he buys and sells on a larger scale and therefore is a greater factor in circulation. And if the expansion of his business compels or enables him to hire his own wage-labourers as agents of circulation, the nature of this phenomenon is not changed in any way. A certain amount of labour-power and labour-time must be expended in the process of circulation, so far as it is merely a change of form. But this now appears as an additional expenditure of capital. A part of the variable capital must be expended in the purchase of these labour-powers active only in circulation. This advance of capital creates neither products nor values. It reduces to that extent the volume of the productive function of capital. It is as though one part of the product were transformed into a machine, which buys or sells the rest of the product. This machine deducts so much from the product. It does not participate in the productive process, although it can reduce the labour-power required for the circulation. It constitutes simply a part of the expenses of circulation.

B. Book-keeping.

Apart from the actual selling and buying, labour-time is expended in book-keeping, which assimilates more materialised labour, such as pens, ink, paper, desks, office-expenses. This function, therefore, requires labour-power and materials. It is the same condition of things which we observed in the case of the time of sale and purchase.

As a principle of unity within its cycles, as a value in process of rotation, whether it be in the sphere of production or in both phases of the sphere of circulation, capital exists ideally only in the form of accounting money, principally in the mind of the producer of commodities, more especially the capitalist producer of commodities. This movement is fixed and controlled by book-keeping, which includes also the determination of prices, or the calculation of the prices of commodities. The movement of production, especially of the production of values – in which the commodities figure as bearers of value, as mere names of things, the ideal existence of which as values is crystallised in accounting money – thus is symbolically reflected in imagination. So long as the individual producer of commodities keeps account only in his head (for instance a farmer; a book-keeping tenant is not known until capitalist production introduces him), or incidentally, outside of his time of production, makes a note of his expenses, receipts, instalment days, etc., just so long does it appear intelligible that this function, and the materials consumed by it, such as paper, etc., require an additional expenditure of labour-time and materials, which is necessary, but constitutes a deduction from the time available for productive consumption and from the materials which are used in the actual process of production and are embodied in the creation of products and values.[4] The nature of the function itself is not changed. The volume which it assumes by its concentration in the hands of the capitalist producer of commodities, who transforms it from a function of many small producers into that of one single capitalist within a process of large scale production, does not alter the case, neither is its nature affected by its separation from those productive functions, which it accompanied incidentally, nor by its modification into an independent function of agents exclusively entrusted with it.

The division of labour, the assuming of independence, does not make a function productive, if it was not so before it became independent. If a capitalist invests his capital anew, then he must invest a part of it in hiring a book-keeper, etc., and materials for book-keeping. If his capital is already in active operation, in the process of continual reproduction, then he must continually reconvert a part of his commodity-product by means of its transformation into money, into a book-keeper, salesman, etc. This part of his capital is withdrawn from production and belongs to the expenses of circulation, deductions from the total product (including the labour-power itself, which is expended wholly for this function).

But there is a certain difference between the expenses incidental to book-keeping, or the unproductive expenditure of labour-time on one side, and that of mere selling and buying time on the other. The latter arise only from the definite social form of the process of production, they are due to the fact that it is a production of commodities. Book-keeping, for the control and ideal survey of the process, becomes necessary to the extent that the process assumes a social scale and loses its purely individual character. It is, therefore, more necessary in capitalist production than in scattered handicraft and agricultural production, and still more necessary in co-operative than in capitalist production. But the expenses of book-keeping are reduced to the extent that production is concentrated and becomes social book-keeping.

We are here concerned only about the general character of the expenses of circulation, which arise out of the general metamorphoses. It is superfluous to discuss all its details. To what extent phenomena, which are mere incidents in changes of form due to the social character of the process of production, may deceive the eyes when they cease to be imperceptible and incidental accompaniments of individual production, we may observe in the case of the mere handling of money, when it is concentrated into an exclusive function of banks on a large scale, or of a cashier in individual businesses. But it must be remembered, that these expenses of circulation do not change their character by changing their form.

C. Money.

Whether a product is intended for a commodity or not, it is always a materialised form of wealth, a use-value to be productively or individually consumed. If it is a commodity, its value is ideally expressed in its price, which does not change its actual use-value. But the fact that certain commodities, such as gold and silver, may perform the function of money and as such reside exclusively in the process of circulation (even in the form of a hoard, a reserve fund, etc., they remain in the sphere of circulation, although latent), is due to the definite social form of the process of production, which is a production of commodities. Since capitalist production gives to all its products the general form of commodities, and since the overwhelming mass of products are produced for sale and must therefore assume the form of money, and since the commodity-part of the social wealth grows continually in proportion, it follows that the quantity of gold and silver employed as means of circulation, paying medium, reserve fund, etc., must likewise increase. These commodities performing the function of money do not enter either into productive or into individual consumption. They represent social labour fixed in a form in which it may serve as a mere machine in circulation. Apart from the fact that a part of the social wealth is tied up in this unproductive form, the wearing out of the money constantly requires its reproduction, or the conversion of more social labour, in the form of products, into more gold and silver. These expenses of reproduction are considerable in capitalistically developed nations, because there is a large part of the wealth tied up in the form of money. Gold and silver as money-commodities represent social expenses of circulation, due to the social form of production. They are dead expenses of commodity-production in general, and they increase with the development of this production, especially when capitalised. They represent a part of the social wealth, which must be sacrificed in the process of circulation.[5]

Section 2. Expenses of Storage.

Expenses of circulation, which are due to a mere change of form in circulation, ideally speaking, do not enter into the value of the commodities. The capital parts expended for them are deductions from the productively expended capital, so far as the capitalist is concerned. Not so the expenses of circulation which we shall consider now. They may arise from processes of production, which are continued only in circulation, the productive character of which is merely concealed by the form of the circulation. Or, on the other hand, they may represent from the standpoint of society mere unproductive expenses of subjective or materialised labour, while for this very reason they may become productive of value for the individual capitalist, by making an addition to the price of his commodities. This follows from the simple fact that these expenses are different in different spheres of production, or even for different individual capitalists in the same sphere of production. When added to the prices of commodities, they are divided in proportion as they fall upon the shoulders of the various individual capitalists. But all labour which adds value can also add surplus-value, and will always do so under capitalist production, the value created by it depending on the amount of the labour, the surplus-value added depending on the amount which the capitalist pays for it. In other words, expenses which increase the price of a commodity without adding anything to its value, which therefore are dead expenses so far as society is concerned, may be a source of profit for the individual capitalist. On the other hand, in so far as the addition to the price of commodities merely distributes these expenses of circulation equally, the unproductive character of this expenditure is not changed. For instance, insurance companies divide the losses of individual capitalists among the capitalist class. But this does not alter the fact that these equalised losses are losses so far as the aggregate social capital is concerned.

A. General Formation of Supply.

During its existence as commodity-capital, or its stay on the market, in other words, in the interval between the process of production from which it originates and the process of consumption into which it enters, the product forms a supply of commodities. As a commodity on the market, and therefore in the form of a supply, the commodity-product figures twice in each cycle: The first time as the commodity-product of that rotating capital whose cycle is being considered; the second time as the commodity-product of another capital, which must be found ready on the market, in order to be bought and converted into productive capital. It is, indeed, possible that this last-named commodity-capital is not produced until ordered. In that case, an interruption occurs until it has been produced. But the flow of the process of production and reproduction requires that a certain mass of commodities (means of production) should be always on the market, that there should be a supply of them. In the same way, productive capital comprises the purchase of labour-power, and the money-form is here only that form of the value of means of existence which the labourer must find at hand on the market, for the greater part. We shall discuss this more in detail in a short while; suffice it to make this point at present.

From the standpoint of the rotating capital-value, which has been transformed into a commodity-product and must now be sold or reconverted into money, which, therefore, has for the moment the function of commodity-capital on the market, the condition in which it forms a supply is contrary to its intentions and its stay on the market is involuntary. The sooner the sale is effected, the smoother runs the process of reproduction. The delay in the phase C'—M' prevents the actual change of substance which must take place in the rotation of capital and obstructs its further function as productive capital. On the other hand, so far as M—C is concerned, the constant presence of a supply of commodities on the market is a requirement for the flow of the process of reproduction and of the investment of new or additional capital.

The demurrage of the commodity-capital as a supply on the market requires buildings, stores, storage places, warehouses, in other words, an expenditure of constant capital; furthermore the payment of labour-power for storing the commodities. Finally, the commodities spoil and are exposed to injurious elementary influences. Additional capital is required to protect them, and this capital must be invested in material-ised labour as well as in labour-power.[6]

We see, then, that the sojourn of commodity-capital as a supply on the market causes expenses, which belong to the expenses of circul-ation, since they do not fall within the sphere of production. These expenses of circulation differ from those mentioned under I, by the fact that they enter in part into the value of the commodities, in other words, that they increase the price of commodities. Under all circumstances the capital and labour-power required for the con-servation and storage of the commodity-supply, are withdrawn from the direct process of production. On the other hand, the capitals thus employed, including their labour-power, must be reproduced by the social product. Their expenditure, therefore, reduces the product-ivity of labour-power to that extent, so that a greater amount of capital and labour is needed to obtain a certain intended effect. They are dead expenses.

Inasmuch as the expenses of circulation arising out of the formation of a supply of commodities are due merely to the time required for the transformation of existing commodity-values into money, in other words, inasmuch as they are due to the prevailing social form of production, which makes the production of commodities and their transformation into money imperative, they share the character of the expenses of circulation enumerated under I. On the other hand, the value of the commodities is here preserved or increased, because the use-value, the product itself, is placed in conditions which require an outlay of capital. The commodities are submitted to operations, which expend additional labour on the use-values. But the computation of the values of commodities, the book-keeping incidental to this process, the transactions of sale and purchase, do not influence the use-values in which the exchange-values of the commodities are embodied. These transactions concern merely the form of the values. Although, in the present case, the expenses of keeping a supply (which is done involuntarily) arise only from a delay of the metamorphosis and from its necessity, these expenses differ from those mentioned under I, in that they are not made for the purpose of effecting a change of form, but for the purpose of preserving the value embodied in the com-modity as a use-value, which cannot be preserved in any other way than by preserving the use-value, the product, itself. The use-value is neither increased nor raised in value, on the contrary, it diminishes. But its diminution is restricted and it is preserved. Neither is the advanced value contained in the commodity increased, although new materialised and subjective labour is added.

We have now to investigate furthermore, to what extent these expenses arise from the peculiar nature of the production of commodities in general and from the prevailing absolute form of this mode of production, its capitalistic form; and to what extent they are common to all social production and merely assume a peculiar form and mode of expression in capitalist production.

Adam Smith has expressed the strange opinion, that the formation of a supply is a phenomenon peculiar to capitalist production alone.[7] More recent economists, for instance Lalor, insist on the other hand, that it declines with the development of capitalist production. Sismondi even regards this as one of the drawbacks of this mode of production.

As a matter of fact, the supply exists in three forms: in the form of productive capital; in the form of a fund for individual consumption; and in the form of a commodity-supply or commodity-capital. The supply in one form decreases relatively, when it increases in another, although it may increase absolutely in all three forms simultaneously.

It is plain from the outset, that wherever production is carried on for direct consumption on the part of the producer, and only to a minor extent for exchange or sale, where the social product does not assume the character of commodities at all, or only to a small degree, there the supply in the form of commodities can be only a small and insignificant part of the social wealth. On the other hand, the supply for consumption is relatively large, especially that of the means of existence. We have but to take a look at ancient agriculture, in order to understand this. The overwhelming part of the product there constitutes directly a supply of means of production and means of existence, without becoming a supply of commodities, because it remains in the hands of its producers and owners. It does not assume the form of a supply of commodities, and for this reason Adam Smith declares that there is no supply at all in societies based on this form of production. He confounds the form of the supply with the supply itself and believes that society hitherto lived from hand to mouth or trusted to the luck of the next day.[8] This is a naive misunderstanding.

A supply in the form of productive capital exists in the shape of means of production, which are either in operation in the process of production, or at least in the hands of the producer, so that they are latent in the process of production. We have seen previously, that with the development of the productivity of labour, and therefore with the development of the capitalist mode of production, which develops the socially productive power of labour more than all previous modes of production, there is a steady increase of the mass of means of production, which are permanently embodied in the productive process as instruments of labour and perform their function in it for a longer or shorter time at repeated intervals (buildings, machinery, etc.); also, that this increase is at the same time the premise and result of the development of the productivity of social labour. It is especially capitalist production, which is characterised by relative as well as absolute growth of this sort of wealth. The material forms of existence of constant capital, the means of production, do not consist merely of such instruments of labour, but also of raw material in various stages of finish and of auxiliary substances; with the enlargement of the scale of production and the increase in the productivity of labour by co-operation, division, machinery, etc., the mass of raw materials and auxiliary substances used in the daily process of reproduction, grows likewise. These elements must be ready at hand in the shop. The volume of this form of productive capital increases absolutely. In order that the process may flow along smoothly – apart from the fact whether this supply may be renewed daily or only at fixed intervals – there must always be more raw material, etc., accumulated at the place of production than is used up, say, daily or weekly. The continuity of the process requires that the fulfilment of its conditions should neither depend on its possible interruption by daily purchases, nor on the daily or weekly sale of the product, so that the regularity of its reconversion into its elements of production may not be broken. But it is evident, that the productive capital may be latent, or form a supply, in different proportions. There is, for instance, quite a difference, whether a spinner must have on hand a supply of cotton or coal for three months or for one. Plainly this supply may decrease relatively, while it may at the same time increase absolutely.

This depends on various conditions, all of which practically amount to the requirement that there shall be a greater rapidity, regularity, and security in furnishing the necessary amount of raw material always in such a way, that there may be no interruption. To the extent that these conditions are not fulfilled, to the extent that there is no rapidity, regularity, and security of supply, the latent part of the productive capital in the hands of the producer, that is to say the supply of raw materials waiting to be used, must increase in size. These conditions are inversely proportional to the degree of development of capitalist production, and thus to the productive power of social labour. The same applies to the supply in this form.

However, that which appears as a decrease of the supply, for instance, to Lalor, is in part merely a decrease of the supply in the form of commodity-capital, or of the actual commodity-supply; it is only a change of form of the same supply. If, for instance, the mass of coal daily produced in a certain country, and therefore the scale and energy of the coal-industry, are great, the spinner does not need a large store of coal in order to ensure the continuity of his production. The security of the continuous reproduction of the coal supply makes this unnecessary. In the second place, the rapidity with which the product of one process may be transferred as means of production to another process depends on the development of the means of transportation and communication. The cheapness of transportation plays a great role in this question. The continually renewed transport, for instance, of coal from the mine to the spinnery, would be more expensive than the storing up of a large supply for a long time when the price of transportation is relatively cheap. These two circumstances are due to the process of production itself. In the third place, the development of the credit-system exerts an influence on this question. The less the spinner is dependent on the immediate sale of his yarn for the renewal of his supply of cotton, coal, etc. – and this dependence will be so much smaller, the more the credit-system is developed – the smaller can be the relative size of these supplies, in order to ensure independence from the hazards of the sale of yarn for the continuous production of yarn on a given scale. In the fourth place, many raw materials, and half-finished products, etc., require long periods of time for their production, and this applies especially to all raw materials furnished by agriculture.

If no interruption of the process of production is to take place, there must be a certain amount of raw materials on hand for the entire period, in which no new products can take the places of the old. If this supply decreases in the hands of the capitalist, it proves merely that it increases in the hands of the merchant in the form of a supply of commodities. The development of transportation, for instance, makes it possible to convey the cotton stored in the import warehouses of Liverpool rapidly to Manchester, so that the manufacturer can renew his supply in small portions according to his needs. But in that case, the cotton remains in so much larger quantities as a commodity-supply in the hands of the merchants in Liverpool. It is therefore merely a question of a change of form, and Lalor and others have overlooked this. And from the standpoint of social capital, the same quantity of products still remains in the form of a supply. The quantity of the supply required for, say, a whole nation during the period of one year decreases to the extent that the means of transportation are developed. If a large number of sailing vessels trade between America and England, the opportunities of England for the renewal of its supply of cotton are increased and the quantity of the cotton supply to be held in storage on an average decreases. The same effect is produced by the development of the world-market and thus of the multiplication of the sources of supply of the same articles. Various quantities of this supply are carried to the market from different countries and at different intervals.

B. The Commodity-Supply in Particular.

We have already seen that the product assumes the general form of commodities on the basis of capitalist production, and to the extent that the scale and scope of this production increase, this character becomes prevalent. Even if production retains the same scale, there will still be a far greater proportion of the product in the form of commodities, compared to other modes of production. And all commodities, and therefore all commodity-capital, which is but another expression for commodities in the form of capital-value, constitute an element of the commodity-supply, unless they pass immediately from the sphere of production into productive or individual consumption, instead of remaining on the market in the interval between production and consumption. If the scale of production remains the same, the commodity-supply, that is to say, the individualisation and fixation of the commodity-form of the product, grows therefore with the development of capitalist production. We have seen, furthermore, that this is merely a change of form on the part of the supply, that is to say the supply in the form of commodities increases on one side, while on the other the supply in the form of direct means of production for consumption decreases. It is merely a question of a changed form of the social supply. The fact that it is not only the relative size of the commodity-supply compared to the aggregate social product which increases, but also its absolute size, is due to the growth of the aggregate product with the advance of capitalist production.

With the development of capitalist production, the scale of production becomes less and less dependent on the immediate demand for the product and falls more and more under the determining influence of the amount of capital available in the hands of the individual capitalist, of the instinct for the creation of more value inherent in capital, of the need for the continuity and expansion of its processes of production. This necessarily increases the mass of products required in each branch of production in the shape of commodities. The amount of capital fixed for a longer or shorter period in the form of commodity-capital grows proportionately. In short, the commodity-supply increases.

Finally, the majority of the members of human society are transformed into wage workers, into people who live from hand to mouth, who receive their wages weekly and spend them daily, who therefore must find a supply of the necessities of life ready at hand. Although the individual elements of this supply may be in continuous flow, a part of them must always suffer delay in order that the supply may be ever renewed.

All these characteristics are due to the form of capitalist production and to the metamorphoses incidental to it, which the product must undergo in the process of circulation.

Whatever may be the social form of the supply of products, its preservation requires an outlay for buildings, storage facilities, etc., which protect the product; furthermore for means of production and labour, more or less of which must be expended, according to the nature of the product, in order to preserve it against injurious influences. The more the supply is socially concentrated, the smaller are the relative expenses. These expenses always consume a part of the social labour, either in a materialised or in a subjective form; they require an outlay of capital which does not enter into the productive process itself and thus diminish the product. They constitute the cost of preserving the social wealth, and are, therefore, necessary expenses, without regard to the fact whether the existence of the social product in the form of a commodity-supply is due merely to the social form of production, to the commodity-form and its metamorphoses, or whether we regard the commodity-supply merely as a special form of the supply of products, a supply common to all societies, though not always in the form of a commodity-supply, which is a form of the supply of products belonging to the process of circulation.

The question is now, to what extent these expenses enter into the value of the commodities.

If the capitalist has converted the capital advanced by him for means of production and labour-power into a product, into a mass of commodities ready for sale, and these commodities remain in stock unsold, then it is not only the creation of values by means of his capital which is interrupted. The expenses required for the conservation and storage of this supply in buildings, etc., and for additional labour, signify a positive loss for him. The final buyer would laugh in his face, if he were to say to him: 'My articles were unsaleable for six months, and their preservation during that period did not only make so and so much of my capital unproductive, but also cost me so much extra expenses.' 'So much the worse for you', would the buyer say. 'Here is another seller, whose articles were completed the day before yesterday. Your articles are old and probably more or less injured by the ravages of time. Therefore you will have to sell cheaper than your rival.'

It does not alter the life-processes of a commodity, whether its producer is a direct producer or a capitalist producer, who is merely a representative of the actual producer. The product must be converted into money. The expenses caused by the fixation of the product in the form of commodities are a part of the individual adventures of the seller, and the buyer does not concern himself about them. The buyer does not pay for the time of circulation of the commodities. Even if the capitalist holds his goods back intentionally, in times of an actual or expected revolution of values, it depends on the materialisation of this revolution of values, on the correctness or incorrectness of the seller's speculation, whether he will recover his outlay or not. Inasmuch, therefore, as the formation of a supply involves a delay in the circulation, the expenses caused thereby do not add anything to the value of the commodities. On the other hand, there cannot be any supply without a sojourn of the commodities in circulation, without the stay of capital for a longer or shorter time in the form of a commodity; hence there cannot be any supply without a delay of the circulation. It is the same with money, which cannot circulate without the formation of a money-reserve. Hence there cannot be any circulation of commodities without a supply of commodities. If this necessity does not confront the capitalist in C'—M', it will do so in M—C; not so far as his own commodity-capital is concerned, but that of other capitalists, who produce means of production for him and necessities of life for his labourers.

It appears that the nature of the case is not altered, whether the formation of a supply is voluntary or involuntary, that is to say whether the producer accumulates a supply intentionally or whether his product forms a supply in consequence of the resistance offered to its sale by the conditions of the process of circulation. But it is useful for the solution of this question to know what distinguishes the voluntary from the involuntary formation of a supply. The involuntary formation of a supply arises from, or is identical with, an interruption of the circulation, which is independent of the knowledge of the producer of commodities and thwarts his will. And what characterises the voluntary formation of a supply? The seller seeks to get rid of his commodity as much as ever. He always offers his product as a commodity. If he were to withdraw it from sale, it would be only a latent, not an effective organ of the commodity-supply. The commodity as such is still as much as ever a bearer of exchange-value and can become effective only by discarding the commodity-form and assuming the money-form.

The commodity-supply must have a certain size, in order to satisfy the demand during a given period. The continual extension of the circle of buyers is one of the factors in the calculation. For instance, in order to last to a certain day, a part of the commodities on the market must retain the form of commodities while the remainder continue in flow and are converted into money. The part which is delayed while the rest keep moving decreases continually, to the extent that the size of the entire supply decreases, until it is all sold. The delay of the commodities is thus calculated on as a necessary requirement of their sale. The size of the supply must be larger than the average sale or the average extent of the demand. Otherwise the excess over this average could not be satisfied. At the same time, the supply must be continually renewed, because it is continually dissolved. This renewal cannot come from anywhere in the last instance other than from production, from a new supply of commodities. Whether this comes from abroad or not, does not alter the case. The renewal depends on the periods required by the commodities for their reproduction. The commodity-supply must last during these periods. The fact that it does not remain in the hands of the original producer, but passes through various stores from the wholesaler to the retailer, changes merely the aspect, not the nature of the thing. From the point of view of society, a part of capital still retains the form of a commodity-supply, so long as the commodities have not been consumed productively or individually. The producer tries to keep a supply corresponding to his average demand, in order to be somewhat independent of the process of production and to ensure for himself a steady circle of customers. Corresponding to the periods of production, terms of sale are formed and the commodities form a supply for a longer or shorter time, until they can be replaced by new commodities of the same kind. The continuity and regularity of the process of circulation, and therefore of the process of reproduction, which includes the circulation, is safeguarded only by the formation of a supply.

It must be remembered that C'—M' may have been transacted for the producer of C, although C may still be on the market. If the producer were to keep his own commodities until they are sold to the last consumer, he would have to invest two capitals, one as a producer and one as a merchant. For the commodity itself, whether we look upon it as an individual commodity or as a part of social capital, it is immaterial whether the expenses of the formation of a supply fall on the shoulders of its producer or on those of a series of merchants from A to Z.

In so far as the commodity-supply is nothing but the commodity-form of the supply which would exist at a given scale of social production either as a productive supply or as a supply of means of consumption, if it did not have the form of a commodity-supply, the expenses required for its conservation and formation, that is to say the expenses for materialised and subjective labour, are merely converted expenses for maintaining either the social fund for production or the social fund for consumption. The increase of the value of commodities caused by them distributes these expenses simply *pro rata* to the different commodities, since the cost is different for different kinds of commodities. And the expenses for the formation of the supply are as much as ever deductions from the social wealth, although they are one of its requirements.

The circulation of commodities is normal only to the extent that the formation of a commodity-supply is its premise and necessarily arises by means of it, only in so far as this apparent stagnation is a part of the rotation itself, just as it is in the case of the formation of a money-reserve. But as soon as the commodities resting in the reservoirs of circulation refuse to give space to the succeeding wave of [commodities],so that the reservoirs are overstocked, the commodity-supply expands just as the hoards do, if the circulation of money is clogged. It does not make any difference, whether this stop occurs in the magazines of the industrial capitalist or in the warehouses of the merchant. The supply is in that case not the premise of the uninterrupted sale, but the result of the impossibility of selling the goods. The expenses remain the same, but since they now arise entirely out of the form, that is to say, out of the necessity of selling the commodities, and out of the obstacles to this metamorphosis into money, they do not enter into the values of the commodities, but cause deductions, losses, from the value to be realised. Since the normal and abnormal form of the supply cannot be distinguished externally, and both of them are clogging the circulation, these phenomena may be confounded and may deceive the agent in production – so much easier as the process of circulation of the capital of the producer may continue smoothly, while that of the commodities he has sold to merchants may be arrested. If the size of production and consumption increase, other conditions remaining the same, then the size of the commodity-supply increases likewise. It is renewed and absorbed just as fast, but its size is greater. Hence the growing size of the commodity-supply caused by a delay in the circulation may be mistaken for a symptom of the expansion of the process of reproduction, especially when the development of the credit-system makes it possible to mystify the real nature of the movement.

The expenses of the formation of the supply consist (1) of quantitative losses of the mass of the product (for instance, in the case of a supply of flour); (2) in a spoiling of the quality; (3) in the materialised and individual labour required for the conservation of the supply.

Section 3. Expenses of Transportation.

It is not necessary to enter at this place into all the details of the expenses of circulation, such as packing, sorting, etc. The general law is that *all expenses of circulation, which arise only from changes of form, do not add any value to the commodities.* They are merely expenses required for the realisation of value, or for its conversion from one form into another. The capital invested in those expenses (including the labour employed by it) belongs to the dead expenses of capitalist production. They must be made up out of the surplus-product and are, from the point of view of the entire capitalist class, a deduction from the surplus-value or surplus product, just as the labour required for the purchase of the necessities of life is lost time for the labourer. But the expenses of transportation play a too prominent role to pass them by without a few short remarks.

Within the rotation of capital and the metamorphoses of commodities which are a part of that rotation, the mutation-processes of social labour take place. These mutation-processes may require a change of location on the part of the products, their transportation from one place to another. Still, a circulation of commodities may take place without their change from place to place, and a transportation of products without a circulation of commodities, or even without a direct exchange of products. A house which is sold by A to B does not wander from one place to another, although it circulates as a commodity. Movable commodity-values, such as cotton or iron ore, remain in the same warehouse at a time when they are passing through dozens of circulation processes, when they are bought and resold by speculators.[9] That which really changes its place here is the title of ownership, not the thing itself. On the other hand, transportation played a prominent role in the land of the Incas, although the social product did not circulate either as a commodity or by means of exchange.

Even though the transportation industry under capitalist production appears as a cause of expenses of circulation, this special form does not alter the nature of the problem.

Quantities of products are not increased by transportation, neither is the eventual alteration of their natural qualities, with a few exceptions, the result of premeditated action, but an inevitable evil. But the use-value of things has no existence except in consumption, and this may necessitate a change of place on the part of the product, in other words, it may require the additional process of production of the transportation industry. The productive capital invested in this industry adds value to the transported products, partly by transferring value from the means of transportation, partly by adding value through the labour-power used in transportation. This last-named addition of value consists, as it does in all capitalist production, of a reproduction of wages and of surplus-value.

Within each process of production, the change of place of the object of labour and the required instruments of labour and labour-power – such as cotton which passes from the carding to the spinning room, or coal which is hoisted from the shaft to the surface – play a great role. The transition of the finished product, in the role of a finished commodity, from one independent place of production to another in a different location shows the same phenomenon on a larger scale. The transport of the products from one factory to another is finally succeeded by the passage of the finished products from the sphere of production to that of consumption. The product is not ready for consumption until it has completed these movements.

We have shown previously that a general law of the production of commodities decrees: the productivity of labour and its faculty of creating value stand in opposition to one another. This is true of the transportation industry as well as of any other. The smaller the amount of materialised and subjective labour required for the transportation of the commodities over a certain distance, the greater is the productivity of labour, and vice versa.[10]

The absolute magnitude of the value which the transportation of the commodities adds to them is smaller in proportion as the productivity of the transportation industry increases, and vice versa, and directly proportional to the distance travelled, other conditions remaining the same.

The relative magnitude of the value added to the prices of commodities by the cost of transportation, other conditions remaining the same, is directly proportional to their volume and weight. But there are many modifying circumstances. Transportation requires, for instance, more or less provision for protection against accidents, and therefore more or less expenditure of labour and instruments of labour, according to the relative fragility, perishable nature, explosiveness of the articles. In this department, the railroad magnates show a greater talent for inventing fantastic species than botanists and zoologists. The classification of the articles on English railroads fills volumes and rests in general on the tendency of transforming the many-sided natural qualities of commodities into so many difficulties of transportation and inevitable excuses for exploitation. 'Glass, which was formerly valued at the rate of 11 pounds sterling per crate, is now valued at only 2 pounds sterling in consequence of industrial improvements and the abolition of the glass-tax, but the railway rates are as high as ever and exceed the cost of transportation by water. Formerly glass and glass ware for lead work was carried for 10 shillings per ton within a radius of 50 miles of Birmingham. Now the rates have been raised to thrice that figure on the pretext of the risk involved by the fragility of the article. But if anything is broken, the railway management does not pay for it.'[11] The fact that the relative magnitude of the value added by the cost of transportation to the articles is inversely proportional to their values furnishes a special excuse for the railroads to tax the articles in direct proportion to their values. The complaints of the industrials and merchants on this score are found on every page of the testimony of witnesses given before the royal commission on railways.

The capitalist mode of production reduces the cost of transportation for the individual commodities by the development of the means of transportation and communication, by their concentration, the scale of their traffic, etc. It increases that part of the materialised and subjective social labour, which is expended in the transportation of commodities, first by converting the great majority of all products into commodities, secondly, by substituting distant for local markets.

The circulation, that is to say the actual perambulation of the commodities through space, is carried on in the form of transportation. The transportation industry forms on one hand an independent branch of production, and thus a special sphere of investment of productive capital. On the other hand, it is distinguished from other spheres of production by the fact that it represents a continuation of a process of production within the process of circulation and for its benefit.

Part 2
The Turn-Over of Capital

Chapter 7
The Period and Number of Turn-Overs

We have seen that the entire time of rotation of a given capital is equal to the sum of its time of circulation plus its time of production. It is the period of time from the moment of the advance of capital-value in a definite form to the return of the rotating capital-value in the same form.

The compelling motive of capitalist production is always the creation of value by means of the advanced value, no matter whether this value is advanced in its independent money-form, or in commodities, in which case its value is only ideally independent in the price of the advanced commodities. In both cases this capital-value passes through various forms of existence during its rotation. Its identity with itself is confirmed by the books of the capitalists, or in the ideal form of calculating money.

No matter whether we consider the formula M...M' or the formula P...P, both forms imply (1) that the advanced value performs the function of capital-value and has created more value; (2) that it has returned to the form in which it began its rotation, having completed its cycle. The creation of more value by means of the advanced value M and the return of capital to this money-form is plainly visible in M...M'. But the same takes place in the second formula. For the starting point of P is the existence of the elements of production, of commodities having a given value. The formula includes the creation of value by means of the advanced value (C' and M') and the return to the original form, for in the second P the advanced value has again the form of the elements of production in which it was originally advanced.

We have seen previously: 'If production be capitalistic in form, so, too, will be reproduction. Just as in the former the labour-process figures but as a means towards the self-expansion of capital, so in the latter it figures but as a means of reproducing as capital, i. e., as self-expanding value, the value advanced.' (Book 1, Chap. 23)

The three formulae (1) M...M', (2) P...P, and (3) C'...C', present the following distinctions: In formula 2, P...P, the renewal of the process by the process of reproduction is expressed as a reality, while it is only implied as a probability in formula 1. But both of these formulae differ from 3 by the fact that in them the advanced capital-value, either in the form of money or of material elements of production, is the starting and returning point. In M...M', the return to M' means M plus m. If the process is renewed on the same scale, M is again the starting point and m does not enter into it, but shows merely that M performed the function of capital and created surplus-value m, which it threw off. In the formula P...P, capital-value P advanced in the form of means of production is likewise the starting point. This form includes the creation of more value. If simple reproduction takes place, the same capitalist renews the same process in the same form P. If accumulation takes place, then P' (equal in magnitude of value to M' and C') reopens the cycle as an expanded capital-value. But it begins with the advanced capital-value in its original form, although it is of greater value than before. In form 3, on the other hand, capital-value does not begin the process as an advance, but as an expanded value, as the aggregate wealth existing in the form of commodities, of which the advanced value is but a part. This last form is important for the third part of this volume, in which the movement of the individual capitals is discussed in connection with the movements of the aggregate social capital. But it is not available for the discussion of the turn-over of capital, which always begins with the advance of capital-value in the forms of money or commodities, and which always requires the return of the rotating capital-value to the form in which it had been advanced. Of these cycles 1 and 2, the former is serviceable in the study of the influence of the turn-over on the formation of surplus-value, the latter in the study of its influence on the formation of the product.

Economists have not distinguished the different relations of the turn-over of capital to its cycles any more than they have distinguished between these cycles. They generally consider the formula M...M, because it dominates the individual capitalist and serves for a basis of his calculations, even if money is the starting point of this cycle only in the form of calculating money. Others start out from the outlay of capital in the form of elements of production and follow the cycle to the point of return, without alluding to the form of the returns, be they commodities or money. For instance, 'the economic cycle, . . . the whole course of production, from the time that outlays are made till returns are received. In agriculture, seed time is its commencement, and harvesting its ending.' S. P. Newman, *Elements of Political Economy*, Andover and New York, p. 81. Others begin with C', the third form. Says Th. Chalmers, in his work on *Political Economy*, 2nd Ed., London, 1832, p. 84 and following, in substance: the world of the productive traffic may be regarded as rotating in a cycle, which we will call the economic cycle. Each cycle is completed, whenever the business, after passing through its successive transactions, returns to its starting point. The beginning may be made at the point where the capitalist gets his receipts, which return his capital. From this point, the capitalist proceeds once more to hire his labourers and parcel out to them their subsistence, or rather the means to purchase it with wages. They manufacture for him the articles which are his specialty. And the capitalist then takes his articles to the market and brings the cycle of this one series of transactions to a close by selling and receiving in the price of his commodities a return for his entire investment of capital.

As soon as the entire capital-value invested by some individual capitalist in any one branch of production has completed the cycle of its movements, it finds itself once more in the form in which it started and is ready to repeat the same process. It must repeat this process, if value is to perpetuate itself as capital-value and create more value. The individual cycle is but a fragment in the life of capital, it is a period which is continually repeated. At the end of the period M...M' capital has once more the form of money-capital, which passes anew through that series of metamorphoses in which its process of reproduction, or self-expansion, is included. At the end of the period P...P, capital has resumed the form of elements of production, which are the requirement for a renewal of its cycle. The rotation of capital, considered as a periodical process, not as an individual event, constitutes its turn-over. The duration of this turn-over is determined by the sum of its time of production plus its time of circulation. This sum constitutes the time of turn-over. It measures the passing of time while the entire capital-value goes through the period of its cycle until it reaches the next one. It counts the periods in the life of capital, or, the time of the renewal, repetition, of the process of self-expansion, which is the process of production, of the same capital-value.

Apart from the individual adventures which may accelerate or retard the time of turn-over of individual capitals, this time is different according to the different spheres of investment of capitals.

Just as the working day is the natural unit for the function of labour-power, so the year is the natural unit for the periods of turn-over of rotating capital. The natural basis of this unit is found in the fact that the most important crops of the temperate zone, which is the mother country of capitalist production, are annual products.

If we designate the year as the unit of the time of turnover by T, the time of turn-over of a given capital by t, and the number of its turn-overs by n, then n = T/t. If, for instance, the time of turn-over t is 3 months, then n is equal to 12/3, or 4: in other words, capital is turned over four times per year. If t is equal to 18 months, then n = 12/18 = 2/3, capital completes only two-thirds of its turn-over in one year. If its time of turn-over is several years, it is computed in multiples of one year.

From the point of view of the capitalist, the time of turnover is the time for which he must advance his capital in order to create value with it and have it returned in its original form.

Before we can study the influence of the turn-over on the processes of production and self-expansion, we must take a look at two new forms which accrue to capital from the process of circulation and influence the form of its turnover.

Chapter 8
Fixed Capital and Circulating Capital

Section 1. Distinctions of Form.

We have seen in Book 1, Chap. 8, that a portion of the constant capital retains that form of the use-value, in which it entered into the process of production and does not share in the transfer to the products toward the creation of which it contributes. In other words, it performs for a longer or shorter period, in the ever repeated labour process, the same function. This applies, for instance, to buildings, machinery, etc., in short to all things which we comprise under the name of instruments of labour. This part of constant capital yields value to the product in proportion as it loses its own exchange-value with the dwindling of its use-value. This transfer of value from an instrument of production to the product which it helps to create is determined by a calculation of averages. It is measured by the average duration of its function, from the moment that the instrument of labour transfers its parts to the product to the moment that it is completely spent and must be reproduced, or replaced by a new specimen of the same kind.

This, then, is the peculiarity of this part of constant capital of the instruments of labour.

A certain part of capital has been advanced in the form of constant capital, of instruments of labour, which now perform their function in the labour-process so long as their own use-value lasts, which they bring with them into this process. The finished product, with the elements it absorbed from the instruments of production, is pushed out of the process of production and transferred as a commodity to the sphere of circulation. But the instruments of labour never leave the sphere of production, once they have entered it. Their function holds them there. A certain portion of the advanced capital-value is *fixed* in this form by the function of the instruments of labour in the process of production. In the performance of this function, and thus by the wear and tear incidental to it, a part of the value of the instruments of labour is transferred to the product, while another remains fixed in the instruments of labour and thus in the process of production. The value thus fixed decreases constantly, until the instrument of labour is worn out, its value having been distributed during a shorter or longer period, over a mass of products which emanated from a series of currently repeated labour processes. But so long as an instrument of labour is still effective and has not been replaced by a new specimen of the same kind, a certain amount of constant capital-value remains fixed in it, while another part of the value originally fixed in it is transferred to the product and circulates as a component part of the commodity-supply. The longer an instrument lasts, the slower it wears out, the longer will its constant capital-value remain fixed in this form of use-value. But whatever may be its durability, the proportion in which it yields its value is always inverse to its entire time of service. If of two machines of equal value, one wears out in five years and the other in ten, then the first yields twice as much value in the same time as the second.

This value fixed in the instruments of labour circulates as well as any other. We have seen that all capital-value is constantly in circulation, and that in this sense all capital is circulating capital. But the circulation of the portion of capital which we are now studying is peculiar. In the first place, it does not circulate in its use-form, but it is merely its exchange-value which circulates, and this takes place gradually and piecemeal, in proportion as it is transferred to the product which circulates as a commodity. During the entire period of its service, a portion of its value always remains fixed in it, independent of the commodities which it helps to produce. It is this peculiarity which gives to this portion of capital the character of *fixed capital*. On the other hand, all other substantial parts of the capital advanced in the process of production form the *circulating, or fluid, capital.*

Some portions of the means of production do not yield their substance to the product. Such are auxiliary substances, which are consumed by the instruments of labour themselves in the perform-ance of their function, such as coal consumed by a steam engine; or substances which merely assist in the operation, such as gas for lighting, etc. It is only their value which forms a part of the value of products. In circulating its own value, the product circulates theirs. To this extent they share the fate of the fixed capital. But they are entirely consumed in every labour-process which they enter, and must therefore be replaced by new specimens of their kind in every new labour-process. They do not preserve their own use-form while performing their function. Hence no portion of capital-value remains fixed in their natural use-value during their service. The fact that this portion of the auxiliary substances does not pass bodily into the product, but yields only its value to swell thereby the value of the product, although the function of these substances is confined to the sphere of production, has misled some economists, for instance Ramsay – who also confounded fixed capital with constant capital – to class them among the fixed capital.

That part of the means of production which yields its substance to the product, in other words, the raw materials, may eventually assume forms which enable it to pass into individual consumption. The instruments of labour, properly so called, that is to say, the material bearers of the fixed capital, can be consumed only productively and cannot pass into individual consumption, because their substance does not enter into the product, into the use-value, which they help to create, but they rather retain their independent form until they are completely worn out. The means of transportation are an exception to this rule. The useful effect which they produce by their productive function during their stay in the sphere of production, that is to say, the change of location, passes simultaneously into the individual consumption, for instance into that of a traveller. He pays for its use in the same way in which he pays for the use of other articles of consumption. We have seen that sometimes the raw material and auxiliary substances pervade one another, for instance in the manu-facture of chemicals. In the same way, instruments of labour, raw material and auxiliary substances may pervade one another. In agri-culture, for instance, the substances employed for the improvement of the soil pass into the plants and help to form the product. On the other hand, their influence is distributed over a lengthy period, say four or five years. A portion of them, therefore, passes into the product and enhances its value, while another portion remains fixed in its old use-form and retains its value. It persists as an instrument of production and retains the form of fixed capital. An ox is fixed capital, so long as it is a beast of toil. If it is eaten, it does not perform the functions of an instrument of production, and is, therefore, not fixed capital.

That which determines whether a certain portion of the capital-value invested in means of production is fixed capital or not is exclusively the peculiar manner in which this value circulates. This peculiar manner of circulation arises from the peculiar manner in which the means of production yield their value to the product, that is to say the manner in which the means of production participate in the creation of values in the process of production. This, again, arises from the special nature of the function of these means of production in the labour-process.

We know that the same use-value, which comes as a product from one labour-process, passes as a means of production into another. It is only the function of a product as a means of production in the labour-process which stamps it as fixed capital. But to the extent that it arises itself out of such a process, it is not fixed capital. For instance, a machine, as a product, as a commodity of the machine manufacturer, belongs to his commodity-capital. It does not become fixed capital, until it is employed productively in the hands of its purchaser.

All other circumstances being equal, the degree of fixity increases with the durability of the means of production. This durability determines the magnitude of the difference between the capital-value fixed in the instruments of labour and that part of its value which is yielded to the product in successive labour-processes. The slower this value is yielded – and some of it is given up in every repetition of the labour-process – the larger will be the fixed capital, and the greater will be the difference between the capital employed and the capital consumed in the process of production. As soon as this difference has disappeared, the instrument of labour has ceased to live and lost, with its use-value, also its exchange-value. It has ceased to be the bearer of value. Since an instrument of labour, the same as every other material bearer of constant capital, yields value only to the extent that its use-value is converted into exchange-value, it is evident that the period in which its constant capital-value remains fixed will be so much longer, the longer it lasts in the process of production, the more slowly its use-value is lost.

If any one means of production, which is not an instrument of labour, strictly speaking, such as auxiliary substances, raw material, partly finished articles, etc., yields and circulates its value in the same way as the instruments of production, then it is likewise the material bearer, the form of existence, of fixed capital. This is the case with the above-mentioned improvements of the soil, which add chemical substances to the soil, the influence of which is distributed over several periods of production, or years. In this case, a portion of the value continues to exist independently of the product, it persists in the form of fixed capital, while another portion has been transferred to the product and circulates with it. And in the latter case, it is not alone a portion of the value of the fixed capital which is transferred to the product, but also a portion of the use-value, the substance in which this portion of value is embodied.

Apart from the fundamental mistake – the confounding of the categories 'fixed capital and circulating capital' with the categories 'constant capital and variable capital' – the confusion of the economists in the matter of definitions is based on the following points:

They make of certain qualities, embodied in the substances of the instruments of labour, direct qualities of fixed capital, for instance, the physical immobility of a house. It is always easy in that case to prove that other instruments of labour, which are likewise fixed capital, have an opposite quality, for instance, physical mobility, such as a vessel's.

Or, they confound the definite economic form, which arises from the circulation of value, with some quality of the object itself, as though things which are not at all capital in themselves, but rather become so under given social conditions, could be of themselves and intrinsically capital in some definite forms, such as fixed or circulating capital. We have seen in Volume I that the means of production in every labour-process, regardless of the social conditions in which it takes place, are divided into instruments of labour and objects of labour. But both of them do not become capital until the capitalist mode of production is introduced, and then they become 'productive capital', as shown in the preceding part. Henceforth the distinction between instruments and objects of labour, based on the nature of the labour-process, is reflected in the new distinction between fixed and circulating capital. It is then only, that a thing which performs the function of an instrument of labour, becomes fixed capital. If it can serve also in other capacities, owing to its material composition, it may be fixed capital or not, according to the functions it performs. Cattle as beasts of toil are fixed capital; if they are fattened, they are raw material which finally enters into circulation as commodities, in other words, they are circulating, not fixed capital.

The mere fixation of some means of production for a certain length of time in repeated labour-processes, which are consecutively connected and form a period of production, that is to say, the entire period required to complete a certain product, demands advances from the capitalist for a longer or shorter term, just as fixed capital does, but this does not give to his capital the character of fixed capital. Seeds, for instance, are not fixed capital, but only raw material which is held for about a year in the process of production. All capital is held in the process of production, so long as it performs the function of productive capital, and so are, therefore, all elements of productive capital, whatever may be their substantial composition, their function and the mode of circulation of their value. Whether the period of fixation lasts a long or a short time, according to the manner of the process of production or the effect aimed at, it does not determine the distinction between fixed and circulating capital.[1]

A portion of the instruments of labour, which determine the general conditions of labour, may be located in a fixed place, as soon as it enters on its duties in the process of production or is prepared for them, for instance, machinery. Or it is produced from the outset in its locally fixed form, such as improvements of the soil, factory buildings, kilns, canals, railroads, etc. The constant fixation of the instrument of labour in the process of production is in that case also due to its mode of material existence. On the other hand, an instrument of labour may continually be shifted bodily from place to place, may move about, and nevertheless be continually in the process of production, for instance, a locomotive, a ship, beasts of burden, etc. Neither does immobility in the one case bestow the character of fixed capital on the instrument of labour, nor does mobility in the other case deprive it of this character. But the fact that some instruments of labour are attached to the soil and remain so fixed, assigns to this portion of fixed capital a peculiar role in the economy of nations. They cannot be sent abroad, cannot circulate as commodities on the market of the world. The titles to this fixed capital may be exchanged, it may be bought and sold, and to this extent it may circulate ideally. These titles of ownership may even circulate on foreign markets, for instance in the form of stocks. But the change of the persons of the owners of this class of fixed capital does not alter the relation of the immobile, substantially fixed part of national wealth to its circulating part.[2]

The peculiar circulation of fixed capital results in a peculiar turn-over. That part of value which is lost by wear and tear circulates as a part of the value of the product. The product converts itself by means of its circulation from commodities into money; hence the value of the instrument of labour circulated by the product does the same, and this value is precipitated in the form of money by the process of circulation in the same proportion in which the instrument of labour loses its value in the process of production. This value has then a double existence. One part of it remains attached to the form of its use-value in the process of production, another is detached from the instrument of labour and becomes money. In the performance of its function, that part of the value of an instrument of labour which exists in its natural form constantly decreases, while that which is transformed into money constantly increases, until at last the instrument is exhausted and its entire value, detached from its body, has assumed the form of money. Here the peculiarity in the turn-over of this element of productive capital becomes apparent. The transformation of its value into money keeps pace with the like transformation of the commodity which is its bearer. But its reconversion from the form of money into that of a use-value separates itself from the reconversion of the commodities into their other elements of production and is determined by its own period of reproduction, that is to say by the time during which the instrument of labour has worn out and must be replaced by another specimen of the same kind. If a machine lasts for, say, a period of ten years, then the period of turn-over of the value originally advanced for it amounts to ten years. It need not be replaced until this period has expired, and performs its function in this natural form until then. Its value circulates in the meantime piecemeal as a part of the value of the commodities which it turns out successively, and it is thus gradually transformed into money, until it has entirely assumed the form of money at the end of ten years and is reconverted from money into a machine, in other words, has completed its turn-over. Until this time arrives, its value is meanwhile accumulated in the form of a reserve fund of money.

The other elements of productive capital consist partly of those elements of constant capital which exist in auxiliary and raw materials, partly of variable capital which is invested in labour-power.

The analysis of the processes of labour and self-expansion (Book I, Chap. 7) showed that these different elements behave differently in their role of producers of commodities and values. The value of that part of constant capital which consists of auxiliary and raw materials – the same as of that part which consists of instruments of labour – reappears in the value of the product as transferred value, while labour-power actually adds the equivalent of its value to the product by means of the labour-process, in other words, actually reproduces its value. Furthermore, a part of the auxiliary material, fuel, gas, etc., is consumed in the process of labour without entering bodily into the product, while another part of them enters bodily into the product and forms a part of its substance. But all these differences are immaterial so far as the mode of circulation and turn-over is concerned. To the extent that auxiliary and raw materials are entirely consumed in the creation of the product, they transfer their value entirely to the product. Hence this value is entirely circulated by the product, transformed into money and from money back into the elements of production of the commodity. Its turn-over is not interrupted, as that of fixed capital is, but it rather passes uninterrupted through the entire cycle of its transformations, so that these elements of production are continually reproduced in substance.

As for the variable part of productive capital, which is invested in labour-power, it buys labour-power for a definite period of time. As soon as the capitalist has bought labour-power and embodied it in his process of production, it forms a component part of his capital, definitely speaking, the variable part of his capital. Labour-power performs its function daily during a period of time, in which it not only reproduces its own daily value, but also adds a surplus-value in excess of it to the product. We do not consider this surplus-value for the moment. After labour-power has been bought, say for a week, and performed its function, its purchase must be continually renewed within the accustomed space of time. The equivalent of its value, which labour-power embodies in its product during its function and which is transformed into money by means of the circulation of the product, must be continually reconverted from money into labour-power, must continually pass through the complete cycle of its transformations, in other words, must be turned over, lest the continuous rotation of its production be interrupted.

That part of the value of capital, then, which has been advanced for labour-power, is entirely transferred to the product – we still leave the question of surplus-value out of consideration – passes with it through the two metamorphoses belonging to the circulation, and always remains in the process of production by means of this continual reproduction. Whatever may be the differences by which labour-power is distinguished, so far as the formation of value is concerned, from those parts of constant capital which do not represent fixed capital, it nevertheless has this manner of turn-over in common with them, as compared to the fixed capital. It is these elements of productive capital – the values invested in labour-power and in means of production which are not fixed capital – that by their common characteristics of turn-over constitute the circulating capital as opposed to the fixed capital.

We have already stated that the money which the capitalist pays to the labourer for the use of his labour-power is but the form of the general equivalent for the means of subsistence required by the labourer. To this extent, the variable capital consists in substance of means of existence. But in this case, where we are discussing the turn-over, it is a question of form. The capitalist does not buy the means of the existence of the labourer, but his labour-power. And that which forms the variable part of capital is not the subsistence of the labourer, but his active labour-power. The capitalist consumes productively in the labour-process the labour-power of the labourer, not his means of existence. It is the labourer himself who converts the money received for his labour-power into means of subsistence, in order to reproduce his labour-power, to keep alive, just as the capitalist converts a part of the surplus-value realised by the sale of commodities into means of existence for himself, and yet would not thereby justify the statement, that the purchaser of his commodities pays him with means of existence. Even if the labourer receives a part of his wages in the form of means of existence, this is still a second transaction in our days. He sells his labour-power at a certain price, with the understanding that he shall receive a part of this price in means of production. This changes merely the form of the payment, but not the fact that that which he actually sells is his labour-power. It is a second transaction, which does not take place between the parties in their capacity as labourer and capitalist, but on the part of the labourer as a buyer of commodities and on that of the capitalist as a seller of commodities; while in the first transaction, the labourer is a seller of a commodity (his labour-power) and the capitalist its buyer. It is the same with the capitalist who replaces his commodity by another, for instance when he takes iron for a machine which he sells to some iron-works. It is, therefore, not the means of subsistence of the labourer which determine the character of circulating capital as opposed to fixed capital. Nor is it his labour-power. It is rather that part of the value of productive capital which is invested in labour-power that receives this character in common with some other parts of constant capital by means of the manner of its turn-over.

The value of the circulating capital – invested in labour-power and means of production – is advanced only for the time during which the product is in process of formation, in harmony with the scale of production dependent on the volume of the fixed capital. This value enters entirely into the product, is therefore fully returned by the sale of the product in the circulation, and can be advanced anew. The labour-power and means of production carrying the circulating part of capital are withdrawn from the circulation to the extent that is required for the formation and sale of the finished product, but they must be continually replaced and reproduced by purchasing them back and reconverting them from money into elements of production. They are withdrawn from the market in smaller quantities at a time than the elements of fixed capital, but they must be withdrawn so much more frequently and the advance of capital invested in them must be repeated in shorter periods. This continual reproduction is promoted by the continuous conversion of the product which circulates the entire value of these elements. And finally, they pass through the entire cycle of metamorphoses, not only so far as their value is concerned, but also their material substance. They are continually reconverted from commodities into the elements of production of the same commodities.

Together with its value, labour-power always adds surplus-value to the product, and this surplus-value represents unpaid labour. This is just as continuously circulated by the finished product and converted into money as its other elements of value. But in this instance, where we are first concerned about the turn-over of capital-value, and not of the surplus-value turned over at the same time, we dismiss the latter for the present.

From the foregoing, the following deductions are made:

1. The definite distinctions of the forms of fixed and circulating capital arise merely from the different turnovers of the capital-value employed in the process of production, the productive capital. This difference of turn-over arises in its turn from the different manner in which the various elements of productive capital transfer their value to the product; they are not due to the different participation of these elements in the production of value, nor to their characteristic role in the process of self-expansion. The difference in the transfer of value to the product — and therefore the different manner of circulating this value by means of the product and renewing it in its original material form by means of its metamorphoses — arises from the difference of the material forms in which the productive capital exists, one portion of it being entirely consumed during the creation of the individual product, and another being used up gradually. Hence it is only the productive capital, which can be divided into fixed and circulating capital. But this distinction does not apply to the other two modes of existence of industrial capital, that is to say commodity-capital and money-capital, nor does it express the difference of these two capitals as compared to productive capital. It applies only to productive capital and its internal processes. No matter how much money-capital and commodity-capital may perform the functions of capital and circulate, they cannot become circulating capital as distinguished from fixed capital, until they have been transformed into circulating elements of productive capital. But because these two forms of capital dwell in the circulation, the economists since the time of Adam Smith, as we shall presently see, have been misled into confounding them with the circulating

parts of productive capital under the head of circulating capital. Money-capital and commodity-capital are indeed circulation capital as distinguished from productive capital, but they are not circulating capital as opposed to fixed capital.

2. The turn-over of the fixed part of capital, and therefore also its time of turn-over, comprises several turn-overs of the circulating parts of capital. In the same time, in which the fixed capital turns over once, the circulating capital turns over several times. One of the component parts of the value of productive capital acquires the definite form of fixed capital only in the case that the instrument of production in which it is embodied is not worn out in the time required for the finishing of the product and its removal from the process of production as a commodity. One part of its value must remain tied up in the form of the old use-value, while another part is circulated by the finished product, and this circulation simultaneously carries with it the entire value of the circulating parts of productive capital.

3. The value invested in the fixed part of productive capital is advanced in a lump-sum for the entire period of employment of that part of the instrument of labour which constitutes the fixed capital. Hence this value is thrown into the circulation by the capitalist all at one time. But it is withdrawn from the circulation only in portions corresponding to the degree in which those values are realised which the fixed capital yields successively to the commodities. On the other hand, the means of production themselves, in which a portion of the productive capital becomes fixed, are withdrawn from the circulation in one bulk and embodied in the process of circulation for the entire period which they last. But they do not require reproduction, they need not be replaced by new specimens of the same kind, until this time is gone by. They continue for a shorter or longer period to contribute to the creation of the commodities to be thrown into circulation, without withdrawing from circulation the elements of their own reproduction. Hence they do not require from the capitalist a renewal of his advances during this period. Finally, the capital-value invested in fixed capital passes through the cycle of its transformations, not in its bodily substance, but only with its ideal value, and even this it does only in successive portions and gradually. In other words, a portion of its value is continually circulated and converted into money as a part of the value of the commodities, without reconverting itself from money into its original bodily form. This reconversion of money into the natural form of an instrument of labour does not take place until the end of its period of usefulness, when the instrument has been completely worn out.

4. The elements of circulating capital are as continually engaged in the process of production – provided it is to be uninterrupted – as the elements of fixed capital. But the elements of circulating capital held in this condition are continually reproduced in their natural form (the instruments of production by other specimens of the same kind, and labour-power by renewed purchases), while in the case of the elements of fixed capital, neither the substance has to be renewed during their employment, nor the purchases. There are always raw and auxiliary materials in the process of production, but always new specimens of the same kind, whenever the old elements have been consumed in the creation of the finished product. Labour-power is likewise always in the process of production, but only by means of ever new purchases, and frequently with changed individuals. But the same identical buildings, machinery, etc., continue their function during repeated turn-overs of the circulating capital in the same repeated processes of production.

Section 2. Composition, Reproduction, Repair, and Accumulation of Fixed Capital.

In the same investment of capital, the individual elements of fixed capital have a different life-time, and therefore different periods of turn-over. In a railroad, for instance, the rails, ties, earthworks, station-buildings, bridges, tunnels, locomotives, and carriages have different periods of wear and of reproduction, hence the capital advanced for them has different periods of turn-over. For a long term of years, the buildings, platforms, water tanks, viaducts, tunnels, excavations, dams, in short everything called 'works of art' in English railroading, do not require any reproduction. The things which wear out most are the rails, ties, and rolling stock.

Originally, in the construction of modern railways, it was the current opinion, nursed by the most prominent practical engineers, that a railroad would last a century and that the wear and tear of the rails was so imperceptible, that it could be ignored for all financial and practical purposes; from 100 to 150 years was supposed to be the life-time of good rails. But it was soon learned that the life-time of a rail, which naturally depends on the velocity of the locomotives, the weight and number of trains, the diameter of the rails themselves, and on a multitude of other minor circumstances, did not exceed an average of 20 years. In some railway-stations, which are centres of great traffic, the rails even wear out every year. About 1867, the introduction of steel rails began, which cost about twice as much as iron rails but which on the other hand last more than twice as long. The life-time of wooden ties was from 12 to 15 years. It was also found, that freight cars wear out faster than passenger cars. The life-time of a locomotive was calculated in 1867 at about 10 to 12 years.

The wear and tear is first of all a result of usage. As a rule, the rails wear out in proportion to the number of trains. (R. C. No. 17,645.)[3] If the speed was increased, the wear and tear increased faster in proportion than the square of the velocity, that is to say, if the speed of the trains increased twofold, the wear and tear increased more than fourfold. (R. C. No. 17,046.)

Wear and tear are furthermore caused by the influence of natural forces. For instance, the ties do not only suffer from actual wear, but also from mould. The cost of maintenance does not depend so much on the wear and tear incidental to the railway traffic, as on the quality of the wood, the iron, the masonry, which are exposed to the weather. One single month of hard winter will injure the track more than a whole year of traffic. (R. P. Williams, *On the Maintenance of Permanent Way*. Lecture given at the Institute of Civil Engineers, Autumn, 1867.)

Finally, here as everywhere else in great industry, the virtual wear and tear plays a role. After the lapse of ten years, one can generally buy the same quantity of cars and locomotives for 30,000 pounds sterling, which would have cost 40,000 pounds sterling at the beginning of that time. Thus one must calculate on a depreciation of 25 per cent on the market price of this material, even though no depreciation of its use-value has taken place. (Lardner, *Railway Economy*.)

Tubular bridges in their present form will not be renewed, writes W. P. Adams in his *Roads and Rails*, London, 1862. Ordinary repairs of them, removal and replacing of single parts, are not practicable. (There are now better forms for such bridges.) The instruments of labour are largely modified by the constant progress of industry. Hence they are not replaced in their original, but in their modified form. On the one hand, the quantity of the fixed capital invested in a certain natural form and endowed with a certain average vitality in that form constitutes one reason for the gradual pace of the introduction of new machinery, etc., and therefore an obstacle to the rapid general introduction of improved instruments of labour. On the other hand, competition enforces the introduction of new machinery before the old is worn out, especially in the case of important modifications. Such a premature reproduction of the instruments of labour on a large social scale is generally enforced by catastrophes or crises.

By wear and tear (excepting the so-called virtual wear) is meant that part of value which is yielded gradually by the fixed capital to the product in course of creation in proportion to the average degree in which it loses its use-value.

This wear and tear takes place partly in such a way that the fixed capital has a certain average life-time. It is advanced for this entire period in one sum. After the lapse of this period, it must be replaced. So far as living instruments of labour are concerned, for instance horses, their reproduction is timed by nature itself. Their average lifetime as means of production is determined by laws of nature. As soon as this term has expired, the worn-out specimens must be replaced by new ones. A horse cannot be replaced piecemeal, it must be replaced by another horse.

Other elements of fixed capital permit of a periodical or partial renewal. In this instance, the partial or periodical renewal must be distinguished from the gradual extension of the business.

The fixed capital consists in part of homogeneous elements, which do not, however, last the same length of time, but are renewed from time to time and piecemeal. This is true, for instance, of the rails in railway stations, which must be replaced more frequently than those of the remainder of the track. It also applies to the ties, which for instance on the Belgian railroads in the fifties had to be renewed at the rate of 8 per cent, according to Lardner, so that all the ties were renewed in the course of 12 years. Hence we have here the following proposition: a certain sum is advanced for a certain kind of fixed capital for, say, ten years. This expenditure is made at one time. But a certain part of this fixed capital, the value of which has been transferred to the value of the product and converted with it into money, is bodily renewed every year, while the remainder persists in its original natural form. It is this advance in one sum and the reproduction in natural form by small degrees, which distinguishes this capital in the role of fixed from circulating capital.

Other parts of the fixed capital consist of heterogeneous elements, which wear out in unequal periods of time and must be so replaced. This applies particularly to machines. What we have just said concerning the different life-times of different parts of fixed capital applies in this case to the life-time of different parts of the same machine, which performs a part of the function of this fixed capital.

With regard to the gradual extension of the business in the course of the partial renewal, we make the following remarks: Although we have seen that the fixed capital continues to perform its functions in the process of production in its natural state, a certain part of its value, proportionate to the average wear and tear, has circulated with the product, has been converted into money, and forms an element in the money reserve fund intended for the renewal of the capital pending its reproduction in the natural form. This part of the value of fixed capital transformed into money may serve to extend the business or to make improvements in machinery with a view to increasing the efficiency of the latter. Thus reproduction takes place in larger or smaller periods of time, and this is, from the standpoint of society, reproduction on an enlarged scale. It is extensive expansion, if the field of production is extended; it is intensive expansion, if the efficiency of the instruments of production is increased. This reproduction on an enlarged scale does not result from accumulation – not from the transformation of surplus-value into capital – but from the reconversion of the value which has detached itself in the form of money from the body of the fixed capital and has resumed the form of additional, or at least of more efficient, fixed capital of the same kind. Of course, it depends partly on the specific nature of the business, to what extent and in what proportion it is capable of such expansion, and to what amount, therefore, a reserve-fund must be collected, in order to be invested for this purpose; also, what period of time is required, before this can be done. To what extent, furthermore, improvements in the details of existing machinery can be made, depends, of course, on the nature of these improvements and the construction of the machine itself. That this is well considered from the very outset in the construction of railroads, is apparent from a statement of Adams to the effect that the entire construction should follow the principle of a beehive, that is to say, it should have a faculty for unlimited expansion. All over-solid and preconceived symmetrical structures are impracticable, because they must be torn down in the case of an extension. (page 123 of the above-named work).

This depends largely on the available space. In the case of some buildings, additional storeys may be built, in the case of others lateral extension and more land are required. Within capitalist production, there is on one side much waste of wealth, on the other much impractical lateral extension of this sort (frequently to the injury of labour-power) in the expansion of the business, because nothing is undertaken according to social plans, but everything depends on the infinitely different conditions, means, etc., with which the individual capitalist operates. This results in a great waste of the productive forces.

This piecemeal re-investment of the money-reserve fund, that is to say of that part of fixed capital which has been reconverted into money, is easiest in agriculture. A field of production of a given space is capable of the greatest possible absorption of capital. The same applies also to natural reproduction, for instance to stock raising.

The fixed capital requires special expenditures for its conservation. A part of this conservation is provided by the labour-process itself; the fixed capital spoils, if it is not employed in production. (See

Book 1, Chap. 8; and Chap. 15, on wear and tear of machinery when not in use.) The English law therefore explicitly regards it as a waste, if rented land is not used according to the custom of the country. (W. A. Holdsworth, barrister at law. *The Law of Landlord and Tenant*. London, 1857, p. 96.) The conservation due to use in the labour-process is a natural and free gift of living labour. And the conserving power of labour is of a twofold character. On the one hand, it preserves the value of the materials of labour, by transfering it to the product, on the other hand it preserves the value of the instruments of labour, provided it does not transfer this value in part to the product, by preserving their use-value by means of their activity in the process of production.

The fixed capital requires also a positive expenditure of labour for its conservation. The machinery must be cleaned from time to time. This is additional labour, without which the machinery would become useless; it is labour required to ward off the injurious influences of the elements, which are inseparable from the process of production; it is expended for the purpose of keeping the machinery in perfect working order. The normal life-time of fixed capital is, of course, so calculated that all the conditions are fulfilled under which it can perform its functions normally during that time, just as we assume in placing a man's average life at 30 years that he will wash himself. Nor is it here a question of reproducing the labour contained in the machine, but of labour which must be constantly added in order to keep it in working order. It is not a question of the labour performed by the machine itself, but of labour spent on it in its capacity of raw material, not of an instrument of production. The capital expended for this labour belongs to the circulating capital, although it does not enter into the actual labour-process to which the product owes its existence. This labour must be continually expended in production, hence its value must be continually replaced by that of the product. The capital invested in it belongs to that part of circulating capital, which has to cover the general expenses and is distributed over the produced values according to an annual average. We have seen that in industry, properly so-called, this labour of cleaning is performed gratis by the working men during pauses, and thus frequently during the process of production itself, and many accidents are due to this custom. This labour is not counted in the price of the product. The consumer receives it free of charge to this extent. On the other hand, the capitalist thus receives the conservation of his machinery for nothing. The labourer pays this expense in his own person, and this is one of the mysteries of the self-preservation of capital, which constitute in point of fact a legal claim of the labourer on the machinery, on the strength of which he is a part-owner of the machine even from the legal standpoint of the bourgeoisie. However, in various branches of production, in which the machinery must be taken out of the process of production for the purpose of cleaning, and where this labour of cleaning cannot be performed between pauses, for instance in the case of locomotives, this labour of conservation counts with the running expenses and is therefore an element of circulating capital. A locomotive must be taken to the shop after a maximum of three days' work in order to be cleaned; the boiler must cool off before it can be washed out without injury. (R. C., No. 17,823.)

The actual repairs, the small jobs, require expenditures of capital and labour, which are not contained in the originally advanced capital and cannot therefore be reproduced and covered, in the majority of cases, by the gradual replacement of the value of fixed capital. For instance, if the value of the fixed capital is 10,000 pounds sterling, and its total life-time 10 years, then these 10,000 pounds, having been entirely converted into money after the lapse of ten years, will replace only the value of the capital originally invested, but they do not replace the value of the capital, or labour, added in the meantime for repairs. This is an element of additional value which is not advanced all at one time, but rather whenever occasion arises for it, so that the terms of its various advances are accidental from the very nature of the conditions. All fixed capital demands such additional and occasional expenditures of capital for materials of labour and labour-power.

The injuries to which individual parts of the machinery are exposed are naturally accidental, and so are therefore the necessary repairs. Nevertheless two kinds of repairs are to be distinguished in the general mass, which have a more or less fixed character and fall within various periods of life of the fixed capital. These are the diseases of childhood and the far more numerous diseases in the period following the prime of life. A machine, for instance, may be placed in the process of production in ever so perfect a condition, still the actual work will always reveal shortcomings which must be remedied by additional labour. On the other hand, the more a machine passes beyond the prime of life, when, therefore, the normal wear and tear has accumulated and has rendered its material worn and weak, the more numerous and considerable will be the repairs required to keep it in order for the remainder of its average life-time; it is the same with an old man, who needs more medical care to keep from dying than a young and strong man. In spite of its accidental character, the labour of repairing is therefore unequally distributed over the various periods of life of fixed capital.

From the foregoing, and from the otherwise accidental character of the labour of repairing, we make the following deductions.

In one respect, the actual expenditure of labour-power and labour-material for repairs is as accidental as the conditions which cause these repairs; the amount of the necessary repairs is differently distributed over the various life-periods of fixed capital. In other respects, it is taken for granted in the calculation of the average life of fixed capital that it is constantly kept in good working order, partly by cleaning (including the cleaning of the rooms), partly by repairs such as the occasion may require. The transfer of value through wear and tear of fixed capital is calculated on its average life, but this average life itself is based on the assumption that the additional capital required for keeping machines in order is continually advanced.

On the other hand it is also evident that the value added by this extra expenditure of capital and labour cannot be transferred to the price of the products simultaneously as it is made. For instance, a manufacturer of yarn cannot sell his yarn dearer this week than last, merely because one of his machines broke a wheel or tore a belt this week. The general expenses of the spinning industry have not been changed by this accident in some individual factory. Here as in all determinations of value, the average decides. Experience teaches the average extent of such accidents and of the necessary labours of conservation and repair during the average life-time of the fixed capital invested in a given branch of industry. This average expense is distributed over the average life-time. It is added to the price of the product in corresponding aliquot parts and hence also reproduced by means of its sale.

The extra capital which is thus reproduced belongs to the circulating capital, although the manner of its expenditure is irregular. As it is highly important to remedy every injury to a machine immediately, every large factory employs in addition to the regular factory hands a number of other employees, such as engineers, wood-workers, mechanics, smiths, etc. The wages of these special employees are a part of the variable capital, and the value of their labour is distributed over their product. On the other hand, the expenses for means of production are calculated on the basis of the above-mentioned average, according to which they form continually a part of the value of the product, although they are actually advanced in irregular periods and therefore transferred in irregular periods to the product or the fixed capital. This capital, invested in regular repairs, is in many respects a peculiar capital, which can be classed neither with the circulating nor the fixed capital, but still belongs with more justification to the former, since it is a part of the running expenses.

The manner of book-keeping does not, of course, change in any way the actual condition of the things of which an account is kept. But it is important to note that it is the custom of many businesses to class the expenses of repairing with the actual wear and tear of the fixed capital, in the following manner: take it that the advanced fixed capital is 10,000 pounds sterling, its life-time 15 years; the annual wear and tear 666 2/3 pounds sterling. But the wear and tear is calculated at only ten years, in other words, 1,000 pounds sterling are added annually for wear and tear of the fixed capital to the prices of the produced commodities, instead of 666 2/3 pounds sterling. Thus 333 2/3 pounds sterling are reserved for repairs, etc. (The figures 10 and 15 are chosen at random.) This amount is spent on an average for repairs, in order that the fixed capital may last 15 years. This calculation does not alter the fact that the fixed capital and the additional capital invested in repairs belong to different categories. On the strength of this mode of calculation it was, for instance, assumed that the lowest estimate for the conservation and reproduction of steamships was 15 per cent, the time of reproduction therefore equal to 6 2/3 years. In the sixties, the English government indemnified the Peninsular and Oriental Co. for it at the rate of 16 per cent, making the time of reproduction equal to 6 1/2 years. On railroads, the average life-time of a locomotive is 10 years, but the wear and tear including repairs is assumed to be 12 1/2 per cent, reducing the life-time down to 8 years. In the case of passenger and freight cars, 9 per cent are estimated, or a life-time of 11 1/9 years.

Legislation has everywhere made a distinction, in the leases of houses and other things, which represent fixed capital for their owners, between the normal wear and tear which is the result of time, the influence of the elements, and normal use; and between those occasional repairs which are required for keeping up the normal life-time of the house during its normal use. As a rule, the former expenses are borne by the owner, the latter by the tenant. The repairs are further distinguished as ordinary and substantial. The last-named are partly a renewal of the fixed capital in its natural form, and they fall likewise on the shoulders of the owner, unless the lease explicitly states the contrary. For instance, the English law, according to Holdsworth (*Law of Landlord and Tenant*, pages 90 and 91), prescribes that a tenant from year to year is merely obliged to keep the buildings water-and-wind proof, so long as this is possible without substantial repairs, and to attend only to such repairs as are known as ordinary. And even in this respect the age and the general condition of the building at the time when the tenant took possession must be considered, for he is not obliged to replace either old or worn-out material by new, or to make up for the inevitable depreciation incidental to the lapse of time and normal usage.

Entirely different from the reproduction of wear and tear and from the work of preserving and repairing is the insurance, which relates to destruction caused by extraordinary phenomena of nature, fire, flood, etc. This must be made good out of the surplus-value and is a deduction from it. Or, considered from the point of view of the entire society, there must be a continuous overproduction, that is to say, a production on a larger scale than is necessary for the simple replacement and reproduction of the existing wealth, quite apart from an increase of the population, in order to be able to dispose of the means of production required for making good the extraordinary destruction caused by accidents and natural forces.

In point of fact, only the smallest part of the capital needed for making good such destruction consists of the money-reserve fund. The most important part consists in the extension of the scale of production itself, which is either actual expansion, or a part of the normal scope of the branches of production which manufacture the fixed capital. For instance, a machine factory is managed with a view to the fact that on the one side the factories of its customers are annually extended, and that on the other hand a number of them will always stand in need of total or partial reproduction.

In the determination of the wear and tear and of the cost of repairing, according to the social average, there are necessarily great discrepancies, even for investments of capital of equal size and in equal conditions, in the same branch of production. In practice, a machine lasts in the case of one capitalist longer than its average time, while in the case of another it does not last so long. The expenses of the one for repairs are above, of the other below the average, etc. But the addition to the price of the commodities resulting from wear and tear and from repairs is the same and is determined by the average. The one therefore gets more out of this additional price than he really spent, the other less. This as well as other circumstances which produce different gains for different capitalists in the same branch of industry with the same degree of the exploitation of labour-power renders an understanding of the true nature of surplus-value difficult.

The boundary between regular repairs and replacement, between expenses of repairing and expenses of renewal, is more or less shifting. Hence we see the continual dispute, for instance in railroading, whether certain expenses are for repairs or for reproduction, whether they must be paid from running expenses or from the capital itself. A transfer of expenses for repairs to capital-account instead of revenue-account is the familiar method by which railway managements artificially inflate their dividends. However, experience has already furnished the most important clues for this. According to Lardner, page 49 of the previously quoted work, the additional labour required during the first period of life of a railroad is not counted under the head of repairs, but must be regarded as an essential factor of railway construction, and is to be charged, therefore, to the account of capital, since it is not due to wear and tear or to the normal effect of the traffic, but to the original and inevitable imperfection of railway construction. On the other hand, it is the only correct method, according to Captain Fitzmaurice (Committee of Inquiry of Caledonian Railway, published in *Money Market Review*, 1867), to charge the revenue of each year with the depreciation, which is the necessary concomitant of the transactions by which this revenue has been earned, regardless of whether this sum has been spent or not.

The separation of the reproduction and conservation of fixed capital becomes practically impossible and useless in agriculture, at least in so far as it does not operate with steam. According to Kirchhoff (*Handbuch der landwirthschaftlichen Betriebslehre*, Berlin, 1862, page 137), 'it is the custom to estimate on a general average the annual wear and tear and conservation of the implements, according to the differences of existing conditions, at from 15 to 20 per cent of the purchasing capital, wherever there is a complete, though not excessive, supply of implements on the farm.'

In the case of the rolling stock of a railroad, repairs and reproduction cannot be separated. According to T. Gooch, Chairman of the Great Western Railway Co. (R. C. No. 17. 327–29), his company maintained its rolling stock numerically. Whatever number of locomotives they might have would be maintained. If one of them became worn out in the course of time, so that it was more profitable to build a new one, it was built at the expense of the revenue, in which case the value of the material remaining from the old locomotive was credited to the revenue. There always was a good deal of material left. The wheels, the axles, the boilers, in short, a good part of the old locomotive remained.

'To repair means to renew; for me there is no such word as "replacement"; . . . once a railway company has bought a car or a locomotive, they ought to keep them in such repair that they will run for all eternity (17,784). We calculate 8 1/2d. per English freight mile for locomotive expenses. Out of this 8 1/2d. we maintain the locomotives forever. We renew our machines. If you want to buy a machine new, you spend more money than is necessary . . . You can always find a few wheels, an axle, or some other part of an old machine in condition to be used, and that helps to construct cheaply a machine which is just as good as an entirely new one (17,790). I now produce every week one new locomotive, that is to say, one that is as good as new, for its boiler, cylinder, and frame are new.' (17,843.) Archibald Sturrock, locomotive superintendent of Great Northern Railway, in R. C., 1867.

Lardner says likewise about cars, on page 116 of his work, that in the course of time, the supply of locomotives and cars is continually renewed; at one time new wheels are put on, at another a new frame is constructed. Those parts on which the motion is conditioned and which are most exposed to wear and tear are gradually renewed; the machines and cars may then undergo so many repairs that not a trace of the old material remains in them . . . Even if the old cars and locomotives get so that they cannot be repaired any more, pieces of them are still worked into others, so that they never disappear wholly from the track. The rolling stock is therefore in process of continuous reproduction; that which must be done at one time for the track, takes place for the rolling stock gradually, from year to year. Its existence is perennial, it is in process of continuous rejuvenation.

This process, which Lardner here describes relative to a railroad, is not typical for an individual factory, but may serve as an illustration of continuous and partial reproduction of fixed capital intermingled with repairs, within an entire branch of production, or even within the aggregate production considered on a social scale.

Here is a proof, to what extent clever managers may manipulate the terms repairs and replacement for the purpose of making dividends. According to the above quoted lecture of R. B. Williams, various English railway companies deducted the following sums from the revenue-account, as averages of a period of years, for repairs and maintenance of the track and buildings, per English mile of track per year:

London & North Western £370
Midland £225
London & South Western £257
Great Northern £360
Lancashire & Yorkshire £377
South Eastern £263
Brighton £266
Manchester & Sheffield £200

These differences arise only to a minor degree from differences in the actual expenses; they are due almost exclusively to different modes of calculation, according to whether expenses are charged to the account of capital or revenue. Williams says in so many words that the lesser charge is made, because this is necessary for a good dividend, and a high charge is made, because there is a greater revenue which can bear it.

In certain cases, the wear and tear, and therefore its replacement, is practically infinitesimal, so that nothing but expenses for repairs have to be charged. The statements of Lardner relative to works of art, which are given in substance below, also apply in general to all solid works, docks, canals, iron and stone bridges, etc. According to him, pages 38 and 39 of his work, the wear and tear which is the result of the influence of long periods of time on solid works, is almost imperceptible in short spaces of time; after the lapse of a long period, for instance of centuries, such influences will nevertheless require the partial or total renewal of even the most solid structures. This imperceptible wear and tear, compared to the more perceptible in other parts of the railroad, may be likened to the secular and periodical inequalities in the motions of world-bodies. The influence of time on the more massive structures of a railroad, such as bridges, tunnels, viaducts, etc., furnishes illustrations of that which might be called secular wear and tear. The more rapid and perceptible depreciation, which is compensated by repairs in shorter periods, is analogous to the periodical inequalities. The compensation of the accidental damages, such as the outer surface of even the most solid structures will suffer from time to time, is likewise included in the annual expenses for repairs; but apart from these repairs, age does not pass by such structures without leaving its marks, and the time must inevitably come, when their condition will require a new structure. From a financial and economic point of view, this time may indeed be too far off to be taken into practical consideration.

These statements of Lardner apply to all similar structures of a secular duration, in the case of which the capital advanced for them need not be reproduced according to their gradual wear and tear, but only the annual average expenses of conservation and repairs are to be transferred to the prices of the products.

Although, as we have seen, a greater part of the money returning for the compensation of the wear and tear of the fixed capital is annually, or even in shorter periods, reconverted into its natural form, nevertheless every capitalist requires a sinking fund for that part of his fixed capital, which becomes mature for complete reproduction only after the lapse of years and must then be entirely replaced. A considerable part of the fixed capital precludes gradual reproduction by its composition. Besides, in cases where the reproduction takes place piecemeal in such a way that every now and then new pieces are added in compensation for worn-out ones, a previous accumulation of money is necessary to a greater or smaller degree, according to the specific character of the branch of production, before replacement can proceed. It is not any arbitrary sum of money which suffices for this purpose; a sum of a definite size is required for it.

If we study this question merely on the assumption that we have to deal with the simple circulation of commodities, without regard to the credit system, which we shall treat later, then the mechanism of this movement has the following aspect: we showed in Book 1, Chapter 3, 3a, that the proportion in which the total mass of money is distributed over a hoard and means of production varies continually, if one part of the money available in society lies fallow as a hoard, while another performs the functions of a medium of circulation or of an immediate reserve-fund of the directly circulating money. Now, in the present case, the money accumulated in the hands of a great capitalist in the form of a large-sized hoard is set free all at once in circulation for the purchase of mixed capital. It is on its part again distributed over the society as medium of circulation and hoard. By means of the sinking fund, through which the value of the fixed capital flows back to its starting point in proportion to its wear and tear, a part of the circulating money forms again a hoard, for a longer or shorter period, in the hands of the same capitalist whose hoard had been transformed into a medium of circulation and passed away from him by the purchase of fixed capital. It is a continually changing distribution of the hoard existing in society, which performs alternately the function of a medium of exchange and is again separated as a hoard from the mass of the circulating money. With the development of the credit-system, which necessarily runs parallel with the development of great industries and capitalist production, this money no longer serves as a hoard, but as capital, not in the hands of its owner, but of other capitalists who have borrowed it.

Chapter 9
The Total Turn-Over of Advanced Capital.
Cycles of Turn-Over.

We have seen that the fixed and circulating parts of productive capital turn over in different ways and at different periods, also that the different constitutents of the fixed capital of the same business have different periods of turn-over according to their different durations of life and, therefore, of their different periods of reproduction. (As concerns the actual or apparent difference in the turn-over of different constituents of circulating capital in the same business, see the close of this chapter, under No. 6.)

1. The total turn-over of advanced capital is the average turn-over of its constituent parts; the mode of its calculation is given later. Inasmuch as it is merely a question of different periods of time, nothing is easier than to compute their average. But

2. It is a question, not alone of a quantitive, but also of a qualitative difference.

The circulating capital entering into the process of production transfers its entire value to the product and must, therefore, be continually reproduced in its natural form by the sale of the product, if the process of production is to proceed without interruption. The fixed capital entering into the process of production transfers only a part of its value (the wear and tear) to the product and continues despite this wear and tear, to perform its function in the process of production. Therefore it need not be reproduced until after the lapse of intervals of various duration, at any rate not as frequently as the circulating capital. This necessity of reproduction, this term of reproduction, is not only quantitatively different for the various constituent parts of fixed capital, but, as we have seen, a part of the perennial fixed capital may be replaced annually or at shorter intervals and added in natural form to the old fixed capital. In the case of fixed capital of a different composition, the reproduction can take place only all at once at the end of its life-time.

It is, therefore, necessary to reduce the specific turn-overs of the various parts of fixed capital to a homogeneous form of turn-over, so that they remain only quantitatively different so far as the duration of their turn-over is concerned.

This quantitative homogeneity does not materialise, if we take for our starting point P...P, the form of the continuous process of production. For definite elements of P must be continually reproduced in their natural form, while others need not to be. This homogeneity of turn-over is found, however, in the form M—M'. Take, for instance, a machine valued at 10,000 pounds sterling, which lasts ten years and one tenth, or 1,000 pounds of which are annually reconverted into money. These 1,000 pounds have been converted in the course of one year from money-capital into productive capital and commodity-capital, and then reconverted into money-capital. They have returned to their original money-form, just as did the circulating capital, if we study it from this point of view; and it is immaterial whether this money-capital of 1,000 pounds sterling is once more converted, at the end of the year, into the natural form of a machine or not. In calculating the total turn-over of the advanced productive capital, we therefore fix all its elements in the mould of money, so that the return to the money-form concludes the turn-over. We assume that value has always been advanced in money, even in the continuous process of production, where this money-form of value exists only as calculating money. Then we are enabled to compute the average.

3. It follows that the capital-value turned over during one year may be larger than the total value of the advanced capital, on account of the repeated turn-overs of the circulating capital within the same year, even if by far the greater part of the advanced productive capital consists of fixed capital, whose period of reproduction, and therefore of turn-over, comprises a cycle of several years.

Take it that the fixed capital is 80,000 pounds sterling, its period of reproduction 10 years, so that 8,000 pounds of this capital annually return to their money-form, or complete one-tenth of its turn-over. Let the circulating capital be 20,000 pounds sterling, and its period of turn-over be five times per year. The total capital would then be 100,000 pounds sterling. The turned-over fixed capital is 8,000 pounds, the turned-over circulating capital five times 20,000, or 100,000 pounds sterling. Then the capital turned over during one year is 108,000 pounds sterling, or 8,000 pounds more than the advanced capital. $1 + 2/25$ of the capital have turned over.

4. The turn-over of the values of the advanced capital therefore is to be distinguished from its actual time of reproduction, or from the actual time of turn-over of its component parts. Take, for instance, a capital of 4,000 pounds sterling and let it turn over five times per year. The turned-over capital is then five times 4,000, or 20,000 pounds sterling. But that which returns at the end of its turn-over and is advanced anew is the original capital of 4,000 pounds sterling. Its magnitude is not changed by the number of its periods of turn-over, during which it performs anew its functions as capital. (We do not consider the question of surplus-value here.)

In the illustration under No. 3, then, the sums returned at the end of one year into the hands of the capitalist are (a) a sum of values in the form of 20,000 pounds sterling, which he invests again in the circulating parts of the capital, and (b) a sum of 8,000 pounds, which have been set free by wear and tear from the advanced fixed capital; at the same time, this same fixed capital remains in the process of production, but with the reduced value of 72,000 pounds, instead of 80,000 pounds sterling. The process of production, therefore, would have to be continued for nine years longer, before the advanced fixed capital would have outlived its term and ceased to perform any service as a creator of products and values, so that it would have to be replaced. The advanced capital-value, then, has to pass through a cycle of turn-overs, in the present case a cycle of ten years, and this cycle is determined by the life-time, in other words by the period of reproduction, or turn-over of the invested fixed capital.

To the same extent that the volume of the value and the duration of the fixed capital develop with the evolution of the capitalist mode of production, does the life of industry and of industrial capital develop in each particular investment into one of many years, say of ten years on an average. If the development of fixed capital extends the length of this life on one side, it is on the other side shortened by the continuous revolution of the instruments of production, which likewise increases incessantly with the development of capitalist production. This implies a change in the instruments of production and the necessity of continuous replacement on account of virtual wear and tear, long before they are worn out physically. One may assume that this life-cycle, in the essential branches of great industry, now averages ten years. However, it is not a question of any one definite number here. So much at least is evident – that this cycle comprising a number of years, through which capital is compelled to pass by its fixed part, furnishes a material basis for the periodical commercial crises in which business goes through successive periods of lassitude, average activity, overspeeding, and crisis. It is true that the periods in which capital is invested are different in time and place. But a crisis is always the starting point of a large amount of new investments. Therefore it also constitutes, from the point of view of society, more or less of a new material basis for the next cycle of turn-over.[4]

5. On the mode of calculation of the turn-overs, Scrope, an American economist, says in substance the following in his work on political economy (published by Alonzo Potter, New York, 1841, pages 141 and 142): In some lines of business the entire capital advanced is turned over, or circulated, several times inside of a year. In some others, one portion is turned over more than once a year, another portion not so often. It is the average period required by the entire capital for the purpose of passing through the hands of the capitalist, or in order to turn over once, which must furnish the basis on which the capitalist figures his profits. Take it, that a certain individual engaged in a certain business has invested half of his capital for buildings and machinery, which are replaced once in every ten years; one-quarter for tools, etc., which are replaced in two years; and the last quarter, invested in wages and raw materials, which quarter is turned over twice per year. Let his entire capital be $50,000. Then his annual expenditure will be:

50,000/2, or $25,000 in 10 years, or $2,500 in one year.
50,000/4, or $12,500 in 2 years, or $6,250 in one year.
50,000/4, or $12,500 in 1/2 year, or $25,000 in one year.
$33,750 in one year.

The average time, then, in which his capital is turned over once, is 16 months. Take another case: one quarter of the entire capital of $50,000 circulates in 10 years; another quarter in one year; the other half twice in one year. The annual expenditure will then be:

12,500/10 . . . . $1,250
12,500 . . . . $12,500
25,000/2 . . . . $50,000
Turned over in one year $63,750

6. Real and apparent differences in the turn-over of the various component parts of capital. Scrope also says in the same place that the capital invested by a manufacturer, landlord, or merchant in wages circulates most rapidly, as it is probably turned over once a week, if he pays his labourers weekly, by the weekly receipts from his sales or from paid bills. The capital invested in raw materials and finished supplies does not circulate so fast; it may be turned over two or four times per year, according to the time passing between the purchase of the one and the sale of the other, provided that the capitalist buys and sells on equal terms of credit. The capital invested in tools and machinery circulates still more slowly, as it is turned over, that is to say consumed and circulated, probably on an average of once in five or ten years; many tools, however, are used up in one single series of manipulations. The capital invested in buildings, for instance, in factories, stores, storerooms, barns, streets, irrigation works, etc., circulates almost imperceptibly. But of course these structures are likewise worn out just the same as the others, so long as they serve in production, and must be replaced, in order that the producer may be able to continue his operations. They are merely consumed and reproduced more slowly than the others. The capital invested in them is probably turned over in twenty or fifty years. So far Scrope. –

Scrope here confounds the differences in the flow of certain parts of the circulating capital, caused by terms of payment and conditions of credit so far as the individual capitalist is concerned, with the turn-overs due to the nature of capital. He says that wages are paid weekly on account of the weekly receipts from paid sales or bills. We must note in the first place, that certain differences occur relative to wages, according to the length of the term of payment, that is to say the length of time for which the labourer must give credit to the capitalist, whether it be a week, a month, three months, six months, etc. In this case, the rule stated in Book 1, Chapter 3, 3b, holds good, to the effect that 'the quantity of the means of payment required for all periodical payments (in this case the quantity of the money-capital to be advanced at one time) is in inverse proportion to the length of their periods.'

In the second place, it is not only the entire new value added to the product by means of one week's labour which enters completely into the weekly product, but also the value of the raw and auxiliary materials consumed by the weekly product. These values circulate with the product containing them. They assume the form of money by the sale of the product and must be reconverted into the same elements of production. This applies as well to the labour-power as to the raw and auxiliary materials. But we have already seen (Chapter 4,2,A) that the continuity of the production requires a supply of means of production, different for various branches of industry, and different within one and the same branch for the various component parts of the circulating capital, for instance, for coal and cotton. Hence, although these materials must be continually replaced in their natural form, they need not be bought continually. How often new purchases of them must be made, depends on the magnitude of the available supply, on the times it takes to use it up. In the case of the labour-power, there is no such storing of a supply. The reconversion into money of the capital invested in labour-power goes hand in hand with that of the capital invested in raw and auxiliary materials. But the reconversion of the money, on one side into labour-power, on the other into raw materials, proceeds separately on account of the special terms of purchase and payment of these two constituents of productive capital, one of them being bought as a productive supply for long terms, the other, labour-power, for shorter terms, for instance, for terms of one week. On the other hand, the capitalist must keep a supply of finished commodities besides a supply of materials for production. Apart from the difficulties of selling, etc., a certain quantity must be produced, say for instance, on order. While the last portion of this quantity is being produced, the finished product is waiting in storage until the order can be completely filled. Other differences in the turn-over of circulation capital arise as soon as some of its individual elements must stay in some preliminary stage of the process of production, such as the drying of wood, etc., longer than others.

The credit-system, to which Scrope here refers, and commercial capital, modify the turn-over for the individual capitalist. They modify the turn-over on a social scale only in so far as they do not accelerate merely production, but also consumption.

Chapter 10
Theories of Fixed and Circulating Capital. The Physiocrats and Adam Smith.

In Quesnay's analysis, the distinction between fixed and circulating capital assumes the form of *avances primitives* and *avances annuelles*. He correctly represents this distinction as one to be made with regard to productive capital, to capital directly engaged in the process of production. But owing to the fact that he regards the capital invested in agriculture, the capital of the capitalist farmer, as the only really productive capital, he makes these distinctions only for the capital of this farmer. This also accounts for the annual period of turn-over of one part of the capital, and the more than annual (decennial) of the other part. Incidentally it may be noted, that in the course of their development the Physiocrats applied these distinctions also to other kinds of capital, to industrial capital in general. The distinction between annual advances and others extending over a longer period retained such lasting value for social science that many economists, even after Adam Smith, returned to it.

The distinction between these two kinds of advances is not made, until money has been transformed into the elements of productive capital. It is a distinction which applies solely to the divisions of productive capital. Quesnay, therefore, never thinks of classing money either among the primitive or the annual advances. In their capacity as advances on production, these two categories confront on one side the money, on the other the commodities existing on the market. Furthermore, the distinction between these two elements of productive capital is correctly defined as resting on the different manner in which they enter into the value of the finished product, and this implies the different way in which their values are circulated together with those of the products. From this, again, follows the different method of their reproduction, the value of the one being entirely replaced annually, that of the other only partially and in longer intervals.[1]

The only progress made by Adam Smith is the generalisation of the categories. He no longer applies them to one special form of capital, the tenant's capital, but to every form of productive capital. Hence it follows as a matter of fact that the distinction between an annual period of turn-over and one of longer duration, derived from agriculture, is replaced by the general distinction of the different periods of turn-over, so that one turn-over of the fixed capital always comprises more than one turn-over of the circulating capital, regardless of the periods of turn-over of the circulating capital, whether they be annual, more than annual, or less. Thus Adam Smith transforms the annual advances into circulating capital, and the primitive advances into fixed capital. But his progress is confined to this generalisation of the categories. His analyses are far inferior to those of Quesnay.

His unclearness is manifested at the very outset by the crudely empirical manner in which he broaches the subject: 'There are two different ways in which a capital may be employed so as to yield a revenue or profit to its employer.' (*Wealth of Nations.* Book 2, Chap. 1, page 189, Aberdeen edition, 1848.)

As a matter of fact, the ways in which value may be employed so as to perform the functions of capital and yield surplus-value to its owner are as different and varied as the spheres of investment of capital. It is a question of the different spheres of production in which capital may be invested. If put in this way, the question implies still more. It includes the other question of the way in which value, even if it is not employed as productive capital, may perform the functions of capital for its owner, for instance, as interest-bearing capital, merchants' capital, etc. At this point we are already far away from the real object of the analysis, that is to say from the question: how does the division of productive capital into its various elements affect their periods of turn-over, leaving out of consideration their different spheres of investment?

Adam Smith continues immediately: 'First, it may be employed in raising, manufacturing, or purchasing goods, and selling them again with a profit.' He does not tell us anything else in this statement than that capital may be employed in agriculture, manufacture, and commerce. He speaks only of the different spheres of investment of capital, including commerce, in which capital is not directly embodied in the process of production and does not perform the functions of productive capital. In so doing he abandons the foundation on which the Physiocrats base the distinctions of the elements of productive capital and their influence on its periods of turn-over. He goes still farther and uses merchants' capital as an illustration of a problem, which concerns exclusively differences of productive capital in the process of production and the creation of value, which differences cause those of its turn-over and reproduction.

He continues: 'The capital employed in this manner yields no revenue or profit to its employer, while it either remains in his possession or continues in the same shape.' The capital employed in this manner! Smith is referring to capital invested in agriculture, in industry, and he tells us later on that a capital so employed is divided into fixed and circulating capital! But the investment of capital 'in this manner' cannot make fixed or circulating capital of it.

Or does he mean to say that capital employed in the production of commodities and their sale at a profit must again be sold after its transformation into commodities and must pass in the first place from the possession of the seller into that of the buyer, and in the second place from its commodity-form into the money-form, so that it is of no use to its owner so long as it retains the same form in his hands? In that case, the problem amounts to this: the same capital-value, which formerly performed the functions of productive capital in a form typical of the process of production, now performs those of commodity-capital and money capital in forms typical of the process of circulation, where it is no longer either fixed or circulating capital. And this applies equally to those elements of value which are added by means of raw and auxiliary material, in other words to circulating capital, and to those which are added by the consumption of instruments of production, or to fixed capital. We do not get any nearer to the distinction between fixed and circulating capital in this way.

Adam Smith says furthermore: 'The goods of the merchant yield him no revenue or profit till he sells them for money, and the money yields him as little till it is again exchanged for goods. His capital is continually going from him in one shape, and returning to him in another, and it is only by means of such circulation, or successive exchanges, that it can yield him any profit. Such capitals, therefore, may very properly be called circulating capital.'

That which Adam Smith here calls circulating capital, is a thing which I shall call capital of circulation, that is to say, capital in a form characteristic of the process of circulation, changes of form due to exchange (a change of substance and of hands); in other words, commodity-capital and money-capital, as distinguished from the form of productive capital, which is characteristic of the process of production. These are not special divisions made by the industrial capitalist of his capital, but different forms assumed and discarded by the advanced capital-value during its course of life, in ever renewed cycles. The great backward step of Adam Smith as compared with the Physiocrats is that he does not discriminate between these forms and those which arise in the circulation of capital-value through its successive metamorphoses while it exists in the form of productive capital, and which are due to different ways in which the various elements of productive capital take part in the formation of values and transfer their own value to the products. We shall see the consequences of confounding these fundamentals, productive capital and capital in the sphere of circulation (commodity-capital and money-capital) on one side, and fixed and circulating capital on the other. The capital-value advanced in fixed capital is as much circulated by the product as that which has been advanced in the circulating capital, and both are equally transformed into money-capital by the circulation of commodity-capital. The difference arises only from the fact that the value of fixed capital circulates piece-meal and is, therefore, reproduced in the same way in shorter or longer intervals in its natural form.

That Adam Smith means nothing else by this term of circulating capital in the above passage but capital of circulation, that is to say, capital in the form of commodity-capital and money-capital characteristic of the process of circulation, is shown by his singularly ill-chosen illustration. He selects for this purpose a kind of capital which does not belong to the process of production, but to the sphere of circulation. This is merchants' capital, which consists only of capital of circulation.

How absurd it is to start out with an illustration, in which capital does not perform the functions of productive capital, is immediately shown by himself. 'The capital of a merchant is altogether a circulating capital.' But later on we learn that the difference between circulating and fixed capital arises out of the essential differences within the productive capital itself. On one side, Adam Smith has the distinction of the Physiocrats in mind, on the other the different forms assumed by capital-value in its cycles. And these things are jumbled together by him without any discrimination.

But it is quite incomprehensible how profit should arise by the transformation of money and commodities, by the mere exchange of one of these forms for the other. And an explanation becomes impossible for Adam Smith, because he starts out with merchants' capital which moves only in the sphere of circulation. We shall return to this later. Let us first hear what he has to say about fixed capital.

'Secondly, it (capital) may be employed in the improvement of land, in the purchase of useful machines and instruments of trade, or in such like things as yield a revenue or profit without changing masters, or circulating any further. Such capitals, therefore, may very properly be called fixed capitals. Different occupations require very different proportions between the fixed and circulating capitals employed in them . . . Some part of the capital of every master artificer or manufacturer must be fixed in the instruments of his trade. This part, however, is very small in some, and very great in others . . . The far greater part of the capital of all such master artificers (such as tailors, shoemakers, weavers) however, is circulated, either in the wages of their workmen, or in the price of their materials, and to be repaid with a profit by the price of the work.'

Apart from the naive determination of the source of profit, the weakness and confusion of these statements becomes at once apparent, when we consider, e. g., that, for a machine manufacturer, a machine is his product, which circulates as commodity-capital, or in Adam Smith's words, 'is parted with, changes masters, circulates farther.' According to his own definition, therefore, this machine would not be fixed, but circulating capital. This confusion is due to the fact that Smith confounds the distinction between fixed and circulating capital, which arises out of the different circulation of the various elements of productive capital, with differences of form successively assumed by the same capital when performing the functions of productive capital within the sphere of production, while in the circulation it becomes capital of circulation, that is to say commodity-capital and money-capital. According to the place which the same things occupy in the life-processes of capital, they may, in the opinion of Adam Smith, perform the functions of fixed capital (means of production, elements of productive capital), or of 'circulating' commodity-capital (products transferred from the sphere of production to that of circulation).

But Adam Smith suddenly changes the entire basis of his division, and contradicts the statements with which he had opened his analysis a few lines previously. This is done especially by the statement that 'there are two different ways in which a capital may be employed so as to yield a revenue or profit to its employer,' that is to say as circulating or as fixed capital. These two categories would, therefore, be different methods of employment of different capitals independent of one another, some being employed in industries, others in agriculture. But immediately he says: 'Different occupations require very different proportions between the fixed and circulating capitals employed in them.' Here fixed and circulating capital are no longer different independent investments of different capitals, but different proportions of the same productive capital, which represent different portions of the total value of this capital in different spheres of investment. They are here differences arising from the appropriate division of the productive capital itself and valid only with respect to it. But this is contrary to the distinction of commercial capital, which according to him is circulating capital as compared to fixed capital, when he says: 'The capital of a merchant is altogether a circulating capital.' It is indeed a capital performing its functions entirely within the sphere of circulation, and is for this reason distinguished from productive capital embodied in the process of production. But for this very reason it cannot be regarded as a constituent part of the circulating portion of productive capital, as distinguished from its fixed portion.

In the illustrations given by Adam Smith, he defines the instruments of trade as fixed capital, and the portion of productive capital invested in wages and raw materials, including auxiliary materials, as circulating capital, 'repaid with a profit by the price of the work'.

He starts out, then, from the various constituents of the labour-process, from labour-power (labour) and raw materials on one side, and instruments of labour on the other. And these are constituents of capital, because a quantity of values is invested in them for the purpose of performing the functions of capital.

To this extent they are material elements, modes of existence of productive capital, that is to say, of capital serving in the process of production. But why is one of these constituents called fixed? Because 'some parts of the capital must be fixed in the instruments of trade.' But the other parts are also fixed in wages and raw materials. Machines, however, and 'instruments of trade . . . such like things . . . yield a revenue or profit without changing masters or circulating any further. Such capitals, therefore, may very properly be called fixed capitals.'

Take, for instance, the mining industry. No raw material at all is used there, because the object of labour, such as copper, is the product of nature, which must be obtained first of all by labour. The copper to be obtained, the product of the process, which circulates later on as a commodity, or commodity-capital, does not form an element of productive capital. No part of its value is thus invested. On the other hand, the other elements of the productive process, such as labour-power, and auxiliary materials such as coal, water, etc., do not enter bodily into the product. The coal is entirely consumed and only its value enters into the product, just as a part of the value of the machine is transferred to it. The labourer, finally, remains just as independent so far as the product, the copper, is concerned, as the machine. Only the value which he produces by his labour becomes a part of the value of the copper. But in this illustration, not a single constituent part of productive capital changes masters, nor do any of them circulate further, because none of them enter bodily into the product. What becomes of the circulating capital in this case? According to Adam Smith's own definition, the entire capital employed in mining would consist only of fixed capital.

On the other hand, let us look at some other industry, which utilises raw materials that form the substance of its product, and auxiliary materials that enter bodily into the product, instead of only so far as their value is concerned, as in the case of coal for fuel. Simultaneously with the product, for instance with the yarn, the raw material composing it, the cotton, likewise changes masters, and passes from the process of production to that of consumption. But so long as the cotton performs the function of an element of productive capital, its owner does not sell it, but manipulates it for the purpose of making it into yarn. He does not take his hand from it. Or, to use Smith's crudely erroneous and trivial terms, he does not make any profit by parting with it, by its changing masters, or by circulating it. He does not permit his materials to circulate any more than his machines. They are fixed in the process of production, the same as the spinning machines and the factory-buildings. Indeed, a part of the productive capital in the form of coal, cotton, etc., must be just as continually fixed as that in the form of instruments of labour. The difference is only that the cotton, coal, etc., required for the process of production, say, for one week, is always entirely consumed in the manufacture of the weekly product, so that new specimens of cotton, coal, etc., must be supplied; in other words, these elements of productive capital consist continually of new specimens of the same species, identical only so far as the species is concerned, while the same individual spinning machine, the same individual factory-building, continue their participation in a whole series of weekly productions without being replaced by new specimens of their kind. All the elements of productive capital constituting its parts must be continually fixed in the process of production, for it cannot proceed without them. And all the elements of productive capital, whether fixed or circulating, are equally distinguished as productive capital from capital of circulation, that is to say, commodity-capital and money-capital.

It is the same with labour-power. A part of the productive capital must be continually fixed in it, and the same identical labour-powers, just as in the case of the machines, are everywhere employed for a certain length of time by the same capitalist. The difference between labour-power and machines in this case is not that the machines are bought once for all (which is not even the case when they are paid for in instalments), while the labourer is not. The difference is rather that the labour expended by the labourer enters wholly into the value of the product, while the value of the machines enters piecemeal into it.

Smith confounds different definitions, when he says of circulating capital as compared to fixed: 'The capital employed in this manner yields no revenue or profit to its employer, while it either remains in his possession or continues in the same shape.' He places the merely formal metamorphosis of the commodity, which the product in the form of commodity-capital, undergoes in the sphere of circulation and which brings about the change of masters of the commodities, on the same level with the bodily metamorphosis, which the different elements of productive capital undergo during the process of production. He unceremoniously jumbles together the transformation of commodities into money, of money into commodities, or purchase and sale, with the transformation of elements of production into products. His illustration for circulating capital is merchants' capital which is transformed from commodities into money and from money into commodities – the metamorphosis C—M—C belonging to the circulation of commodities. But this metamorphosis within the circulation signifies for the industrial capital in action that the commodities into which the money is retransformed are elements of production (means of production and labour-power); in other words, that it renders the function of industrial capital continuous, that it makes of the process of production a continuous one, a process of production. This entire metamorphosis takes place in circulation. It is the process of circulation which brings about the bodily transition of the commodities from one master to another. On the other hand, the metamorphoses experienced by productive capital within the process of production take place in the labour-process and are necessary for the purpose of transforming the elements of production into the desired product. Adam Smith clings to the fact that a part of the means of production (the instruments of labour, strictly speaking) serve in the labour-process (yield a profit to their master, as he erroneously expresses it) without changing their natural form and wear out only by degrees; while another part, the materials, change their form and fulfil their duty as means of production by virtue of this very fact. This difference in the behaviour of the elements of productive capital in the labour-process, however, serves only as the point of departure for the difference between fixed capital and capital which is not fixed, but it is not this difference itself. This is evident from the mere fact that this different behaviour is common to all modes of production, whether they are capitalist or not. But on the other hand, this different behaviour of the substances is accompanied by a different yield of value to the product, and this in its turn corresponds to a different reproduction of value by the sale of the product. And this is what constitutes the difference in question. Hence capital is not fixed capital because it is fixed in the means of production, but because a part of the value invested in means of production remains fixed in them, while another part circulates as a part of the value of the product.

'If it (the stock) is employed in procuring future profit, it must procure this profit by staying with him (the employer), or by going from him. In the one case it is a fixed, in the other it is a circulating capital.' (page 189.)

In this statement, it is the crudely empirical conception of profit derived from the ideas of the ordinary capitalist, which is remarkable, being contrary to the better esoteric understanding of Adam Smith. Not only the price of the materials, but also that of the labour-power is reproduced by the price of the product, and so is that part of value which is transferred by wear and tear from the instruments of labour to the product. Under no circumstances does this reproduction yield any profits. Whether a value advanced for the production of a commodity is reproduced entirely or in part, at one time or gradually, by the sale of that commodity, cannot change anything except the manner and time of its reproduction. But it can in no way transform that which is common to both, the reproduction of value, into a production of surplus-value. We meet here once more the common idea that surplus-value arises only through sale, in the circulation, because it is not realised until the product is sold, until it circulates. As a matter of fact, the different genesis of the profit is in this case but a mistaken phrase for the truth that the different elements of productive capital are differently employed, and have a different effect in the labour-process as different productive elements. In the final analysis, the difference is not attributed to the process of production or self-expansion, not to the function of productive capital itself, but it is supposed to apply only subjectively to the individual capitalist, whom one part of capital serves a useful purpose in one way, while another does in a different way.

Quesnay, on the other hand, had derived this difference from the process of reproduction and its requirements. In order that this process may be continuous, the value of the annual advances must be annually reproduced in full by the value of the annual product, while the value of the capital stock is reproduced only by degrees, for instance, in ten years, and is not fully worn out to the point of replacement by another specimen of the same kind until then. Adam Smith here falls far below Quesnay.

Nothing remains therefore to Adam Smith for the determination of the fixed capital but the fact that it is represented by instruments of production which do not change their form in the process of production and continue to serve in production until they are worn out, as distinguished from the product, in the formation of which they co-operate. He forgets that all elements of productive capital are continually confronted in their natural form (instruments of labour, materials, and labour-power) by the product and by the circulating commodity, and that the difference between the part consisting of materials and labour-power and that consisting of instruments of labour is this: labour-power is always purchased afresh, not bought for good like the instruments of labour; the materials manipulated in the labour-process are not the same identical specimens throughout, but always new specimens of the same kind. At the same time the false impression is created that the value of the fixed capital does not participate in the circulation, although Adam Smith has previously analysed the wear and tear of fixed capital as a part of the price of the product.

In mentioning the circulating capital as distinguished from the fixed, he does not emphasise the fact, that this distinction rests on the circumstance that circulating capital is that part of productive capital which must be fully reproduced by the value of the product and must therefore fully share in its metamorphoses, while this is not so in the case of the fixed capital. On the contrary, he jumbles it together with those forms which capital assumes in its transition from the sphere of production to that of circulation, that is to say, commodity-capital and money-capital. But both forms, commodity-capital as well as money-capital, are bearers of the value of the fixed and the circulating parts of productive capital. Both of them are capitals of circulation, as distinguished from productive capital, but they do not represent circulating capital as distinguished from fixed capital.

Finally, owing to the entirely confused idea of the making of profit by the staying of the fixed capital in the process of production, and the passing from it and circulating of the circulating capital, the essential difference between the variable capital and the circulating parts of the constant capital in the process of self-expansion and the formation of surplus-value is hidden under the identity of form, so that the entire secret of capitalist production is obscured still more; by the application of the common term 'circulating capital' this essential difference is abolished; political economy subsequently went still farther by neglecting the distinction between variable and constant capital and dwelling on the difference between fixed and circulating capital as the essential and typical distinction.

After Adam Smith has defined fixed and circulating capital as two different ways of investing capital, each of which yields a profit by itself, he says: 'No fixed capital can yield any revenue but by means of a circulating capital. The most useful machines and instruments of trade will produce nothing without the circulating capital which affords the materials they are employed upon, and the maintenance of the workmen who employ them.' (page 188.)

Here it becomes apparent what the previously used phrases 'yield a revenue, make a profit, etc.', signify, viz., that both parts of capital serve in the formation of the product.

Adam Smith then gives the following illustration: 'That part of the capital of the farmer which is employed in the implements of agriculture is a fixed, that which is employed in the wages and maintenance of his labouring servants is a circulating capital.' (Here the difference of fixed and circulating capital is correctly applied as referring to the different circulation, the turn-over of different constituent parts of productive capital.) 'He makes a profit of the one by keeping it in his own possession, and of the other by parting with it. The price or value of his labouring cattle is a fixed capital,' (here he is again correct in that it is the value, not the material substance, which determines the difference) 'in the same manner as that of the instruments of husbandry; their maintenance' (meaning that of the labouring cattle) 'is a circulating capital, in the same way as that of the labouring servants. The farmer makes his profit by keeping the labouring cattle and parting with their maintenance.' (The farmer keeps the fodder of the cattle, he does not sell it. He uses it to feed the cattle, while he exploits the cattle themselves as instruments of labour. The difference is only this: the feed used for the maintenance of the cattle is wholly consumed and must be continually reproduced by new feed, either by means of the products of agriculture or by their sale; while the cattle themselves are reproduced only to the extent that each specimen becomes worn out.) 'Both the price and the maintenance of the cattle which are bought in and fattened, not for labour, but for sale, are a circulating capital. The farmer makes his profit by parting with them.' (Every producer of commodities, hence the capitalist producer likewise, sells his product, the result of his process of production, but this is not a means of constituting this product a part of either the fixed or the circulating part of his productive capital. The product has now rather that form, in which it is released from the process of production and compelled to perform the function of commodity-capital. The fattened stock serve in the process of production as raw material, not as instruments of labour like the labouring cattle. Hence the fattened cattle enter bodily into the product, and their whole value enters into it, just as that of the auxiliary material, the feed, does. The fattened cattle are, therefore, a circulating part of the productive capital, but they are not so, because the sold product, these same cattle, have the same natural form as the raw material, that is to say these cattle when not yet fattened. This is a mere coincidence. At the same time Adam Smith might have seen by this illustration that it is not the material form of the elements of production, but their function within the process of production, which determines the value contained in them as a fixed or circulating one.) 'The whole value of the seed, too, is a fixed capital . . . Though it goes backwards and forwards between the ground and the granary, it never changes masters, and therefore it does not properly circulate. The farmer makes his profit not by its sale, but by its increase.'

At this point, the utter thoughtlessness of Smith's distinction reveals itself. According to him, the seeds would be fixed capital, if there would be no change of masters, that is to say, if the seeds were directly reproduced out of the annual product by subtracting them from it. On the other hand, they would be circulating capital, if the entire product were sold and a part of its value employed for the purchase of another's seed. In the one case, there would be a change of masters, in the other there would not. Smith once more confounds circulating and commodity-capital at this point. The product is the material bearer of the commodity-capital, but of course only that part of it which actually enters into the circulation and does not re-enter directly into the process of production, from which it came as a product.

Whether the seed is directly subtracted as a part of the product, or whether the entire product is sold and a part of its value converted in the purchase of another man's seed, in either case it is mere reproduction which takes place, and no profit is produced by it. In the one case, the seed enters into circulation with the remainder of the product as a commodity, in the other it figures only in book-keeping as a part of the value of the advanced capital. But in both cases, it remains a circulating part of the productive capital. It is entirely consumed in getting the product ready, and it must be entirely reproduced by means of it, in order to make self-expansion possible.

According to Adam Smith, raw and auxiliary materials lose their independent form, which they carried as use-values into the labour-process. Not so the instruments of labour proper. An instrument, a machine, a factory-building, a vessel, etc., serve in the labour-process only so long as they preserve their original form and enter the labour-process tomorrow in the same form in which they did yesterday. Just as they preserve their independent form as compared to the product during life, in the labour-process, so they do after death. The corpses of machines, shops, factory-buildings, still exist independently of the products, which they helped to form. (Book 1, Chapter 8, page 227.)

These different ways in which means of production are used in the formation of the product, some of them preserving their independent form as compared to the product, others changing or losing it entirely – this difference pertaining to the labour-process itself, regardless of whether it is carried on for home use, without exchange, without any production of commodities, as it was, for instance, in the patriarchal family, is falsified by Adam Smith, (1) by vitiating it with the irrelevant definition of profit, saying that some of the elements of production yield a profit to their owner by preserving their form, while others do so by losing it; (2) by jumbling together the changes of a part of the elements of production in the labour-process with that metamorphosis in the circulation of commodities which consists of the exchange, the sale and purchase, of products and involves a change of masters of the circulating commodities.

The turn-over presumes the reproduction by the intervention of the circulation, by the sale of the product, by its conversion into money and its reconversion from money into elements of production. But to the extent that a part of the product of the capitalist producer serves him directly as his own means of production, he figures as its seller to himself, and this transaction is so entered in his books. This part of the reproduction is not accomplished by the intervention of the circulation, but proceeds directly. But a part of the product thus re-employed as means of production replaces circulating, not fixed, capital, to the extent, (1) that its value passes wholly into the product, and (2) that it is itself wholly reproduced in its natural form by means of the new product.

Adam Smith, however, tells us what circulating and fixed capital consist of. He enumerates the things, the material elements, which form fixed, and those which form circulating capital, just as though this character were due to the natural substance of those things, instead of to their definite function within the capitalist process of production. And yet in book 2, chapter 1, he makes the remark that although a certain thing, for instance, a residence, which is reserved for direct consumption, 'may yield a revenue to its proprietor, and thereby serve *in the function of a capital* to him, it cannot yield any to the public, nor serve in the function of a capital to it, and the revenue of the whole body of the people can never be in the smallest degree increased by it.' (page 186.) Here, then, Adam Smith clearly states that the character of capital is not inherent in the things themselves, but is a function with which they may or may not be invested, according to circumstances. But what is true of capital in general, is also true of its subdivisions.

The same things form constituent parts of the circulating or fixed capital, according to whether they perform this or that function in the labour-process. A domestic animal, for instance, as a labouring animal (instrument of labour), represents the material mode of existence of fixed capital, while as stock for fattening (raw material) it is a constituent part of the circulating capital of the farmer. On the other hand, the same things serve either as constituent parts of productive capital, or belong to the fund for direct consumption. A house, for instance, when performing the function of a workshop, is a fixed part of productive capital; when serving as a residence, it is not at all a form of productive capital. The same instruments of labour may in many cases serve now as means of reproduction, now as means of consumption.

It was one of the errors following from the conception of Smith that the capacity of fixed and circulating capital was regarded as vested in the things themselves. The mere analysis of the labour-process on his part, in Book 1, Chapter 5, shows that the capacity of instruments of labour, materials of labour, and products changes according to the different role played by one and the same thing in the process. The determination of what is fixed or circulating capital, in its turn, is based on the definite roles played by these elements in the labour-process, and therefore also in the process of the formation of value.

In the second place, in enumerating the things of which fixed and circulating capital may consist, Smith plainly discloses the fact that he jumbles together the distinction between fixed and circulating capital, applicable and justified only with reference to productive capital (capital in its productive form), with the distinction between productive capital and those of its forms which belong to the process of circulation, viz., commodity-capital and money-capital. He says in the same place (pages 187, 188): 'The circulating capital consists . . . of the provisions, materials, and finished work of all kinds that are in the hands of their respective dealers, and of the money that is necessary for circulating and distributing them, etc.' Indeed, if we look closer, we observe that he has here, contrary to previous statements, used circulating capital as being equivalent to commodity-capital and money-capital, that is to say to two forms of capital which do not belong to the process of production at all, which are not circulating capital as opposed to fixed, but capital of circulation as opposed to productive capital. It is only in co-ordination with these that those constituents of productive capital, which are advanced in materials (raw materials or partly finished products) are actually embodied in the process of production, play a role. He says:

' . . . The third and last of the three portions into which the general stock of society naturally divides itself, is the circulating capital, of which the characteristic is, that it affords a revenue only by circulating or changing masters. This is composed likewise of four parts: first, of the money . . . ' (but money is never a form of productive capital, of capital performing its function in the productive process; it is always merely one of the forms assumed by capital within its process of circulation.) . . . 'secondly, of the stock of provisions which are in the possession of the butcher, the grazier, the farmer . . . and from the sale of which they expect to derive a profit . . . fourthly and lastly, of the work which is made up and completed, but which is still in the hands of the merchant and manufacturer. And, thirdly, of the materials, whether altogether rude or more or less manufactured, of clothes, furniture, and buildings, which are not yet made up into any of those three shapes but which remain in the hands of the growers, the manufacturers, the mercers and drapers, the timber-merchants, the carpenters and joiners, the brick-makers, etc.'

His second and fourth count contain nothing but products, which have been released by the process of production and must be sold; in short, they are products which now perform the function of commodities, or commodity-capital, and which, therefore, have a form and occupy a place in the process, in which they are not elements of productive capital, no matter what may be their destination, whether they answer their final purpose as use-values in individual or productive consumption. The products mentioned under 'secondly' are foodstuffs, those under 'fourthly' all other finished products, which in their turn consist only of finished instruments of labour or finished articles of consumption not included in the foodstuffs under count two.

The fact that Smith at the same time speaks of the merchant, shows his confusion. To the extent that the producer transfers his product to the merchant, it does no longer form any part of his capital. From the social point of view, it is indeed still a commodity-capital, although in other hands than those of its producer; but for the very reason that it is a commodity-capital, it is neither a circulating nor a fixed capital.

Under every mode of production not carried on for direct home-consumption the product must circulate as a commodity, that is to say, it must be sold, not in order to make a profit out of it, but that the producer may be able to live at all. Under the capitalist mode of production we have the further fact that the surplus-value embodied in a certain commodity is realised by its sale. In its capacity as a commodity, the product leaves the process of production and is, therefore, neither a fixed nor a circulating element of this process.

By the way, Smith here testifies against himself. The finished products, whatever may be their material form, their use-value, their utility, are all commodity-capital, that is to say capital in a form typical of the process of circulation. Being in this form, they are not constituent parts of any productive capital which their owner may have. Of course, this does not argue against the fact that, after their sale, they *may* become constituent parts of productive capital in the hands of their purchaser, and then represent either fixed or circulating capital. This shows that the same things, which at a certain time appear on the market as commodity-capital distinct from productive capital, may or may not perform the function of productive capital after they have been removed from the market.

The product of the cotton spinner, yarn, is the commodity-form of his capital, is a commodity-capital from his point of view. It cannot again perform the function of some constituent part of his productive capital, neither as raw material nor as an instrument of labour. But in the hands of the weaver who buys it, it is embodied in his productive capital as one of its circulating parts. For the spinner, on the other hand, the yarn is the bearer of the value of his fixed and circulating capital (not considering the surplus-value). So is a machine, the product of a machine maker, the commodity-form of his capital, commodity-capital from his point of view. And so long as it persists in this form, it is neither fixed nor circulating capital. But if it is sold to a manufacturer for use in his production, it becomes a fixed part of his productive capital. Even if a certain product re-enters as a use-value for the purpose of production into the same process from which it emanated, for instance coal in the production of coal, even then that part of the output of coal which is intended for sale represents neither fixed nor circulating capital, but commodity-capital.

On the other hand, the utility-form of a certain product may be such that it is incapacitated for service as an element of productive capital, either as raw material or an instrument of labour. This is the case, for instance, with articles of food. Nevertheless it is a commodity-capital for its producer, in which the value of his fixed as well as his circulating capital is incorporated; and it is the representative of the value of either the one or the other of these two forms according to whether the capital employed in its production has to be reproduced in full or partially, in other words, according to whether this capital transfers its full or its partial value to the product.

With Smith, in his count No. 3, the raw material (raw material, partly finished product, auxiliary material), does not figure as a part embodied in the productive capital, but merely as a special kind of use-values of which the social product generally consists, a mass of commodities existing apart from the other material elements, food-stuffs, etc., enumerated under Nos. 2 and 4. On the other hand, these materials are indeed incorporated in the productive capital and therefore also classed as its elements in the hands of the producer. The confusion arises from the fact that they are partly regarded as performing a function in the hands of the producer (in the hands of the growers, the manufacturers, etc.), and partly in the hands of merchants (mercers, drapers, timber-merchants), where they are merely commodity-capital, not elements of productive capital.

Indeed, Adam Smith forgets here, in the enumeration of the elements of circulating capital, all about the fact that the distinction of fixed and circulating capital applies only to the productive capital. He rather places commodity-capital and money-capital, the two forms of capital typical of the process of circulation, opposite the productive capital, but quite unconsciously.

Finally, it is worthy of note that Adam Smith forgets to mention labour-power as one of the elements of productive capital. And there are two reasons for this.

We have just seen that, apart from money-capital, circulating capital is only another name for commodity-capital. But to the extent that labour-power circulates on the market, it is not capital, not a form of commodity-capital. It is not capital at all; the labourer is not a capitalist, although he brings his commodity to market, namely his own skin. Not until labour-power has been sold and incorporated in the process of production, in other words, until it has ceased to circulate as a commodity, does it become an element of productive capital, variable capital and the source of surplus-value, a circulating part of productive capital so far as the turn-over of the capital-value invested in it is concerned. Since Smith here confounds the circulating capital with commodity-capital, he cannot place labour-power under his category of circulating capital. Hence the commodity-capital here appears in the form of commodities which the labourer buys with his wages, that is to say, means of subsistence. In this form, the capital-value invested in wages is supposed to belong to the circulating capital. That which is incorporated in the process of production is labour-power, the labourer himself, not the means of subsistence by which the labourer maintains himself. True, we have seen in Volume 1, Chapter 23, that, from the point of view of society, the reproduction of the labourer himself by means of his individual consumption belongs to the process of reproduction of social capital. But this does not apply to the individual and isolated process of production which we are studying here. The 'acquired and useful abilities' which Smith mentions under the head of fixed capital, are on the contrary elements of circulating capital, when they are abilities of the wage-worker and have been sold by him with his labour.

It is a great mistake on the part of Smith to divide the entire social wealth into (1) a fund for immediate consumption, (2) fixed capital, and (3) circulating capital. According to this, wealth would have to be classified as (1) a fund for consumption, which would not represent a part of social capital engaged in the performance of its functions, although some parts of it may continually assist in this performance; and (2) as capital. In other words, a part of the wealth would be performing the functions of capital, another those of non-capital or a fund for consumption. And it seems that it is here an indispensable requirement for all capital to be either fixed or circulating, about in the same way that it is a natural necessity for a mammal to be either male or female. But we have seen that the distinction of being fixed or circulating applies solely to the elements of productive capital, that, therefore, there is also a considerable quantity of capital – commodity-capital and money-capital – existing in a form which does not permit of its being either fixed or circulating.

Seeing that the entire mass of social products, under capitalist production, circulates on the market as commodity-capital, with the exception of that part of the product which is directly consumed by the individual capitalist producers in its natural form as means of production without being sold or bought, it is evident that not only the fixed and circulating elements of productive capital, but also all the elements of the fund for consumption are derived from the commodity-capital. This is equivalent to saying that, on the basis of capitalist production, both means of production and of consumption first appear as commodity-capital, even though they are intended for later use as means of production or consumption. Labour-power itself is likewise found on the market as a commodity, if not as commodity-capital.

This accounts for the following confusion in Adam Smith: 'Of these four parts,' (meaning *circulating capital*, that is to say capital in its forms of commodity-capital and money-capital typical of the process of circulation, which Adam Smith transforms into four parts by making distinctions between the substantial parts of commodity-capital) 'three – provisions, materials, and finished work, are either annually or in a longer or shorter period, regularly withdrawn from it, and placed either in the fixed capital, or in the stock reserved for immediate consumption. Every fixed capital is both originally derived from, and requires to be continually supported by, a circulating capital. All useful machines and instruments of trade are originally derived from a circulating capital, which furnishes the materials of which they are made and the maintenance of the workmen who make them. They require, too, a capital of the same kind to keep them in constant repair.' (page 188.)

With the exception of that part of the product which is immediately consumed as means of production, the following general rule applies to capitalist production: all products are taken to market as commodities and, therefore, circulate as capital in the form of commodities, as the commodity-capital of the capitalist, regardless of whether these products must or may serve in their natural form, as use-values, in the performance of their function as elements of productive capital in the process of production, in other words, as means of production and, therefore, as fixed or circulating parts of productive capital, or whether they can serve only as means of individual, not of productive, consumption. All products are thrown upon the market as commodities; all means of production or consumption, all elements of productive and individual consumption, must therefore be released from the market by purchasing them as commodities.

Of course, this truism is correct. It applies for this reason to the fixed as well as the circulating elements of productive capital, for instruments of labour as well as raw material in all its forms. (This, moreover, is leaving aside the fact that there are certain elements of productive capital which are furnished ready by nature and are not products.) A machine is bought on the market as well as cotton. But this implies by no means that every fixed capital comes originally from some circulating capital; it is only through the confusion, on the part of Smith, of capital of circulation with circulating capital, with capital that is not fixed, that this erroneous conclusion is reached. And to cap the climax, Smith refutes himself. According to him, machines, as commodities, form a part of No. 4, the circulating capital. To say that they come from the circulating capital means that they were performing the function of commodity-capital before they performed the function of machines, but that substantially they are derived from themselves; so is cotton, as the circulating element of some spinner's capital, derived from the cotton on the market. But as for deriving fixed capital from circulating capital for the reason that labour and raw material are required for the making of machines, as Adam Smith is doing in his further arguments, we say that in the first place, fixed capital is also required for the making of machines, and in the second place, fixed capital, such as machinery, is likewise required for the making of raw materials, since the productive capital always includes instruments of labour, but not always raw materials. He says himself immediately afterwards: 'Lands, mines, and fisheries, require all both a fixed and circulating capital to cultivate them' – thus he admits that not only circulating, but also fixed capital is required for the production of raw materials – 'and' – renewed confusion at this point – 'their produce replaces with a profit, not only those capitals, but all the others in society.' (page 188.) This is entirely wrong. Their produce furnishes the raw materials, auxiliary substances, etc., for all other branches of industry. But their value does not reproduce the value of all other social capitals; it reproduces merely the value of their own capital (plus the surplus-value). Adam Smith is here stampeded by his recollection of the Physiocrats.

Socially speaking, it is true that that part of the commodity capital which consists of products available for immediate or later service as instruments of labour – unless they are produced uselessly and cannot be sold – must in fact perform this service whenever they cease to be commodities and become actual elements of the productive capital, instead of being merely its prospective ones.

But there is a distinction arising from the natural form of the product.

A spinning machine, for instance, has no use-value, unless it is consumed in spinning, so that it performs its function as an element of production and, from the point of view of the capitalist, constitutes a fixed part of his capital. But a spinning machine is movable. It may be exported from the country in which it was produced and sold in a foreign country directly or indirectly, for raw materials, etc., or even for champagne. In that case it has served only as commodity-capital in the country in which it was produced, but never as fixed capital, not even after its sale.

But products which are localised by being embedded in the soil, and therefore can be consumed only locally, such as factory buildings, railroads, bridges, tunnels, wharves, etc., improvements of the soil, etc., cannot be bodily exported. They are not movable. They are either useless, or they must serve as fixed capital, in the country that produced them, as soon as they have been sold. From the point of view of their capitalist producer, who builds factories or improves land for speculation and sale, these things are forms of his commodity-capital, or, according to Adam Smith, a form of circulating capital. But from the point of view of society, these things must finally serve in the same country as fixed capital in some process of production fixed by their own locality, unless they are to be useless. This does not imply by any means that immovable things are fixed capital of themselves. They may belong to the fund for consumption, for instance residence houses, and in that case they do not belong to the social capital at all, although they are an element of the social wealth, of which capital is only a part. The producer of these things, to use the language of Smith, makes a profit by their sale. In other words, circulating capital! Their user, their final purchaser, can use them only by utilising them in the process of production. Therefore, fixed capital!

Titles to property, for instance railroad shares, may change hands every day, and their owner may even make a profit by their sale to foreign countries, so that the title may be exported, if not the railroad. But nevertheless these things themselves must either lie fallow in the country that produced them, or serve as a fixed part of some productive capital. In the same way the manufacturer A may make a profit by the sale of his factory to the manufacturer B, but this does not prevent the factory from serving as fixed capital, the same as before.

However, it does not follow that fixed capital necessarily consists of immovable things, because the locally fixed instruments of labour, which cannot be detached from the soil, must to all intents and purposes serve at some time as fixed capital in the same country, even though they may serve as commodity-capital for their producer and do not constitute any elements of his fixed capital, which is made up of the instruments of labour required by him for the building of factories, railroads, etc. A ship and a locomotive produce their effects only by motion; yet they serve as fixed capital for the owner who uses them, although not for him who produced them. On the other hand, some things which are very decidedly fixed in the process of production, which live and die in it and never leave it any more after they have entered it, are circulating parts of the productive capital. Such are, for instance, the coal consumed by the machine in the process of production, the gas used for lighting the factory, etc. They are circulating capital not because they bodily leave the process of production together with the product and circulate as commodities, but because their entire value is transferred to that of the product in whose production they assisted, so that their value must be entirely reproduced by the sale of the product.

In the last quotation from Adam Smith, notice must furthermore be taken of the following phrase: 'a circulating capital which furnishes . . . the maintenance of the workmen who make them' (meaning machines, etc.).

In the works of the Physiocrats, that part of capital which is advanced for wages figures correctly under the *avances annuelles* as distinguished from the *avances primitives*. On the other hand it is not the labour-power used as a part of the productive capital of the farmer which figures in their accounts, but the foodstuffs given to the farm labourers (the maintenance of workmen, as Smith calls it). This corresponds exactly to their specific doctrine. For according to them the value added to the product by labour (like the value added to the product by raw material, instruments of labour, etc., in short by all the substantial parts of constant capital) is equal only to the value of the articles of consumption paid to the labourers and necessary for the maintenance of their labour functions. Their doctrine stands in the way of their discovering the distinction between constant and variable capital. If it is labour that produces surplus-value in addition to the reproduction of its own price, then it does so in industry as well as in agriculture. But since, according to their system, surplus-value arises only in one branch of production, namely, agriculture, it does not come out of labour, but out of the special activity (assistance) of nature in this branch. And only for this reason agricultural labour is for them productive labour, as distinguished from other kinds of labour.

Adam Smith classes the maintenance of labourers among the circulating capital as distinguished from fixed.

1. Because he confounds circulating capital as distinguished from fixed with forms of capital belonging to the sphere of circulation, with capital of circulation; this mistake persisted after him without being criticised. He therefore confounds the commodity-capital with the circulating part of the productive capital, and in that case it is a matter of course that, whenever the social product assumes the form of commodities, the maintenance of the labourers as well as that of the non-labourers, the materials as well as the instruments of labour, must be taken out of the commodity-capital.

2. But the physiocratic conception likewise intermingles with the analysis of Smith, although it contradicts the esoteric – really scientific – part of his own deductions.

The advanced capital is universally converted into productive capital, that is to say it assumes the form of elements of production which are themselves the products of past labour. Labour-power is included in them. Capital can serve in the process of production only in this form. Now, if instead of labour-power itself we take the labourer's necessities of life into which the variable part of capital has been converted, it is evident that these necessities of life are not essentially different, so far as the formation of values is concerned, from the other elements of productive capital, from the raw materials and the food of the labouring cattle, with whom Smith, after the manner of the Physiocrats, places the labourers on the same level, in one of the passages quoted above. The necessities of life cannot expand their own value or add any surplus-value to it. Their value, like that of the other elements, can re-appear only in that of the product. They cannot add any more to their value than they have themselves. They, like raw materials, partly finished articles, etc., differ from fixed capital composed of instruments of labour only in that they are entirely consumed in the product of the capitalist who pays for them and uses them in the manufacture of this product, so that their value must be entirely reproduced by this product, while in the case of the fixed capital this takes place gradually and piecemeal. The part of productive capital advanced for labour-power (or for the labourer's articles of consumption) differs here only in the matter of material from the other material elements of productive capital, not in the matter of the process of production or self-expansion. It differs only in so far as it falls into the same category, namely, that of circulating capital, with one part of the objective elements active in the formation of the produce (materials, Adam Smith calls them), while another part of these belongs in the category of fixed capital.

The fact that the capital invested in wages belongs to the circulating part of productive capital and shares this circulating quality, as distinguished from the fixed character of productive capital, with a part of the material objects, the raw materials, etc., instrumental in creating the product, has nothing whatever to do with the role played by this variable part of capital in the process of self-expansion, as distinguished from the constant part of capital. It refers merely to the manner in which this part of the invested capital-value is reproduced out of the value of the product by way of the circulation. The purchase and repeated purchase of labour-power belongs in the process of circulation. But it is only within the process of production that the value invested in labour-power (not for the benefit of the labourer, but that of the capitalist) is converted from a definite constant into a variable magnitude, and only thus the advanced value is converted into capital-value, into self-expanding value. But by classing the value advanced for articles of consumption among the circulating elements of productive capital, as Smith does, instead of the value invested in labour-power, the understanding of the difference between variable and constant capital, and thus the understanding of the capitalist process of production in general, is rendered impossible. The mission of this part of capital of being variable as distinguished from the constant capital invested in material objects instrumental in production, is hidden under the mission of the capital invested in labour-power of serving in the turn-over as a circulating part of productive capital. And the obscurity is made complete by enumerating the labourer's maintenance among the elements of productive capital, instead of his labour-power. It is immaterial, whether the value of labour-power is advanced in money or immediately in articles of consumption. However, under capitalist production, the last-named eventuality can be but an exception.[2]

By thus emphasising the role of the circulating capital as the determining element of the capital-value invested in labour-power, by using this physiocratic conception without the fundamental premise of the Physiocrats, Adam Smith haply rendered the understanding of the role of variable capital as a determinant of capital invested in labour-power impossible for his followers. The more profound and correct analyses given by him in other places did not survive, but this mistake of his did. Other writers after him went even farther. They were not content to make it the essential characteristic of capital invested in labour-power to be circulating as distinguished from fixed capital; they rather made it an essential mark of circulating capital to be invested in articles of consumption for labourers. This resulted naturally in the doctrine of a labour fund of definite magnitude consisting of requirements of life, which on one side established a physical limit for the share of the labourers in the social product, and on the other had to be fully expended in the purchase of labour-power.

Chapter 11
Theories of Fixed and Circulating Capital: Ricardo

Ricardo mentions the distinction between fixed and circulating capital merely for the purpose of illustrating the exceptions to the law of value, namely, in cases where the rate of wages affects the prices. The discussion of this point is reserved for Volume 3.

But the original confusion is apparent at the outset in the following indifferent parallel: 'This difference in the degree of durability of fixed capital, *and* this variety in the proportions in which the two sorts of capital may be combined.' (*Principles*, page 25.)

And if we ask him which two sorts of capital he is referring to, we are told: 'The proportions, too, in which the capital that is to support labour, and the capital that is invested in tools, machinery, and buildings, may be variously combined.' (l.c.) In other words, fixed capital consists of instruments of labour, and circulating capital is such as is invested in labour. 'Capital that is to support labour' is a senseless term culled from Adam Smith. On one hand, the circulating capital is here confounded with the variable capital, that is to say, with that part of productive capital which is invested in labour. On the other hand, twice confounded conceptions arise for the reason that the distinction is not between variable and constant capital and derived from the process of self-expansion, but from the process of circulation repeating the old confusion of Smith.

1. The difference in the degree of durability of fixed capital and the difference in the proportion in which constant and variable capital may be combined, are conceived as being of equal significance. But the last-named difference determines the difference in the production of surplus-value; the first-named, on the other hand, refers merely to the manner in which a given value is transferred from a means of production to the product, in so far as the process of self-expansion is concerned; and as for the process of circulation, this difference refers

only to the period of the reproduction of the advanced capital, or, from another point of view, the time for which it has been advanced. Of course, if one looks upon the capitalist process of production in the light of a completed phenomenon, instead of seeing through its internal machinery, then these differences coincide. In the distribution of the social surplus-value among the various capitals invested in different lines of production, the proportions of the different periods of time for which capital has been advanced (for instance, the different durability of fixed capital) and the different organic composition of capital (and therefore also the different circulation of constant and variable capital) contribute equally toward an equalisation of the general rate of profit and the conversion of values into prices of production.

2. From the point of view of the process of circulation, we have on one side the instruments of labour – fixed capital; on the other the materials of labour and wages – circulating capital. But from the point of view of the process of production and self-expansion, we have on one side means of production (instruments of labour and raw material) – constant capital; on the other, labour-power – variable capital. It is immaterial for the organic composition of capital (Book 1, Chap. 25, 2) whether the same quantity of constant capital consists of many instruments of labour and little raw material, or of much raw material and few instruments of labour, but everything depends on the proportion of the capital invested in means of production to that invested in labour-power. Vice versa, from the point of view of the process of circulation, of the difference between fixed and circulating capital, it is just as immaterial in what proportions a given amount of circulating capital is divided between raw material and wages. From one of these points of view the raw material is classed in the same category with the instruments of labour, as compared to the capital-value invested in labour-power; from the other the capital-value invested in labour-power ranks with that invested in raw material, as compared to that invested in instruments of labour.

For this reason, the capital-value invested in materials of labour (raw and auxiliary materials) does not appear on either side. It disappears entirely. For it does not agree with the side of fixed capital, because its mode of circulation coincides entirely with that of the capital-value invested in labour-power. And on the other hand, it must not be placed on the side of circulating capital, because in that case the identification of the distinction between fixed and circulating capital with that of constant and variable capital, which had been carried over from Adam Smith and tacitly perpetuated, would abolish itself. Ricardo has too much logical instinct not to feel this, and for this reason that part of capital disappears entirely for him.

It is to be noted at this point that the capitalist, to use the language of political economy, advances the capital invested in wages for different periods, according to whether he pays these wages weekly, monthly, or quarterly. But in reality, the reverse takes place. The labourer advances his labour to the capitalist for one week, one month, or three months, according to whether he is paid by the week, by the month, or every three months. If the capitalist really were to *buy* labour-power, instead of only paying for it, in other words, if he were to pay the labourer in advance for a day, a week, a month, or three months, then he would be justified in claiming that he advanced wages for those periods. But since he does not pay until labour has lasted for days, weeks, or months, instead of buying it and paying for the time which it is intended to last, we have here a confusion of terms on the part of the capitalist, who performs the trick of converting an advance of labour made to the capitalist by the labourer into an advance of money made to the labourer by the capitalist. It does not alter the case that the capitalist may not get any returns from his product by way of the circulation in the shape of a reproduction of his product or of its value (increased by the surplus value embodied in it) until after a certain length of time, according to the different periods required for its manufacture, or for its circulation. It does not concern the seller of a commodity what its buyer is going to do with it. The capitalist does not get a machine cheaper, because he must advance its entire value at one time, while this value returns to him only gradually and piecemeal by way of the circulation; nor does he pay more for cotton, because its value is assimilated fully by the product into which it is made over, and is therefore fully recovered at one time by the sale of the product.

Let us return to Ricardo.

1. The characteristic mark of variable capital is that a certain given, and to that extent constant, part of capital representing a given sum of values (supposed to be equal to the value of labour-power, although it is immaterial for this discussion whether wages are equal to the value of labour-power or higher or lower than it) is exchanged for a self-expanding power which creates value, namely, labour-power, which not only reproduces the value paid for it by the capitalist, but produces a surplus-value, a value not previously existing and not paid for by any equivalent. This characteristic mark of the capital-value advanced for wages, which distinguishes it as a variable capital from constant capital, disappears whenever the capital-value advanced for wages is considered solely from the point of view of the circulation, for then it appears as a circulating capital as distinguished from the

fixed capital invested in instruments of labour. This is apparent from the simple fact that it is then classed under one head, namely, under that of circulating capital, together with a part of the constant capital, namely, that which is invested in raw materials, and thus distinguished from another part of constant capital, namely, that invested in instruments of labour. The surplus-value, the very fact which converts the advanced sum of values into capital, is entirely ignored under these circumstances. Furthermore, the fact is ignored that the value added to the product by the capital invested in wages is newly produced (and therefore actually reproduced), while the value transferred from the raw material to the product is not newly produced, not actually reproduced, but only preserved in the value of the product and merely reappears as a part of the value of the product. The distinction, as seen from the point of view of the contrast between fixed and circulating capital, consists now simply in this: the value of the instruments of labour used for the production of a certain commodity is transferred only partially to the value of the commodity and is therefore only partially recovered by its sale, is only partially and gradually returned. On the other hand, the value of the labour-power and materials of labour (raw materials, etc.) used in the production of a certain commodity is entirely assimilated by it, and is therefore entirely recovered by its sale. From this standpoint, and with reference to the process of circulation, one part of capital appears as fixed, the other as circulating. In both cases it is a matter of a transfer of definite advanced values to the product and of their recovery by the sale of the product. The only difference which is essential at this point is whether the transfer of values, and consequently their recovery, proceeds gradually or in one bulk. By this means the really decisive difference between the variable and constant capital is blotted out, the whole secret of the production of surplus-value and of capitalist production, namely, the circumstances which transform certain values and the things in which they are contained into capital, are obliterated. All constituent parts of capital are then distinguished merely by their mode of circulation (and, of course, circulation concerns itself solely with already existing values of definite size). And the capital invested in wages then shares a peculiar mode of circulation with a part of capital invested in raw materials, partly finished articles, auxiliary substances, as distinguished from another part of capital invested in instruments of labour.

It is, therefore, easy to understand why the bourgeois political economy instinctively clung to Adam Smith's confusion of the categories of 'constant and variable capital' with the categories 'fixed and circulating capital', and repeated it parrotlike from generation to generation for a century. The capital invested in wages is not in the least distinguished by bourgeois political economy from capital invested in raw materials, and differs only formally from constant capital to the extent that it is partially or in bulk circulated by the product. In this way the first requirement for an understanding of the actual movement of capitalist production, and thus of capitalist exploitation, is buried at one stroke. It is henceforth but a question of the re-appearance of advanced values.

In Ricardo the uncritical adoption of the Smithian confusion is annoying, and not only more so than in the later apologetic writers, in whom the confusion of terms is rather otherwise than annoying, but also more than in Adam Smith himself, because Ricardo is comparatively more consistent and clear in his analysis of value and surplus-value, and indeed rescues the esoteric Adam Smith from the exoteric Adam Smith.

Among the Physiocrats this confusion is not found. The distinction between *avances annuelles* and *avances primitives* refers only to the different periods of reproduction of the various parts of capital, especially of agricultural capital; while their ideas concerning the production of surplus-value form a part of their theory, apart from these distinctions, being upheld by them as the salient point of this theory. The formation of surplus-value is not explained out of capital as such, but only attributed to one special sphere of production of capital, namely, agriculture.

2. The essential point in the determination of variable capital – and therefore for the conversion of any sum of values into capital – is that the capitalist exchanges a definite given, and to that extent constant, magnitude of values for a power which creates values, a magnitude of values for a production, a self-expansion, of values. It does not alter this essential fact that the capitalist may pay the labourer either in money or in means of subsistence. This alters merely the mode of existence of the value advanced by the capitalist, seeing that in one case it has the form of money for which the labourer himself buys his means of subsistence on the market, in the other case that of means of subsistence which he consumes directly. A developed capitalist production rests indeed on the assumption that the labourer is paid in money and more generally on the assumption that the process of production is promoted by the process of circulation, in other words, by the monetary system. But the production of surplus-value – and consequently the capitalisation of the advanced sum of values – has its source neither in the money-form, nor in the natural form, of wages, or of the capital invested in the purchase of labour-power. It arises out of the exchange of value for a power creating value, the conversion of a constant into a variable magnitude.

The greater or smaller fixity of the instruments of labour depends on the degree of their durability, on their physical properties. According to the degree of their durability, other circumstances being equal, they will wear out fast or slowly, will serve a long or a short time as fixed capital. The raw material in metal factories is just as durable as the machines used in manufacturing, and more durable than many parts of these machines, such as leather, wood, etc. Nevertheless the metal serving as raw material forms a part of the circulating capital, while the instrument of labour, although probably built of the same metal, is a part of the fixed capital, when in use. Hence it is not the substantial physical nature, not its great or small durability, to which the same metal owes its place, now in the category of the fixed, now of the circulating capital. This distinction is rather due to the role played by it in the process of production, being an object of labour in one case, and an instrument of labour in another.

The function of an instrument of labour in the process of production requires generally, that it should serve for a longer or shorter period in ever renewed labour processes. Its function, therefore, determines the greater or lesser durability of its substance. But it is not the durability of the material of which it is made that gives to it the character of fixed capital. The same material, if in the shape of raw material, becomes a circulating capital, and among those economists who confound the distinction between commodity-capital and productive-capital with that between circulating and fixed capital the same material, the same machine, are circulating capital as products and fixed capital as instruments of labour.

Although it is not the durability of the material of which it is made that gives to an instrument of labour the character of fixed capital, nevertheless its role as such an instrument requires that it should be composed of relatively durable material. The durability of its material is, therefore, a condition of its function as an instrument of labour, and consequently the material basis of the mode of circulation which renders it a fixed capital. Other circumstances being equal, the greater or lesser durability of its material endows it in a higher or lower degree with the quality of fixedness, in other words, its durability is closely interwoven with its quality of being a fixed capital.

If the capital-value advanced for labour-power is considered exclusively from the point of view of circulating capital, in distinction from fixed capital, and if consequently the distinction between constant and variable capital is confounded with that between fixed and circulating capital, then it is natural to attribute the character of circulating capital, in distinction from fixed capital, to the substantial reality of the capital invested in labour-power, just as the substantial reality of the instrument of labour constitutes an essential element of its character of fixed capital, and to determine the circulating capital by the substantial reality of the variable capital.

The real substance of the capital invested in wages is labour itself, active, value-creating, living labour, which the capitalist trades for dead, materialised labour and embodies in his capital, by which means alone the value in his hands is transformed into a self-expanding value. But this self-expanding power is not sold by the capitalist. It is always solely a constituent part of his productive capital, the same as his instruments of labour; it is never a part of his commodity-capital, as, for instance, the finished product which he sells. Within the process of production, as parts of his productive capital, the instruments of labour are not distinguished from labour-power as fixed capital any more than the raw materials and auxiliary substances are identified with it as circulating capital. Labour confronts both of them as a personal factor, while they are objective things – speaking from the point of view of the process of production. Both of them stand opposed to labour-power, to variable capital, as constant capital – speaking from the point of view of the process of self-expansion. Or, if mention is to be made here of a difference in substance, so far as it affects the process of circulation, it is only this: it follows from the nature of value which is nothing but materialised labour, and from the nature of active labour-power which is nothing but labour in process of materialisation, that labour-power continually creates value and surplus-value during the process of its function; that the thing which on the part of labour-power appears as motion and a creation of value, appears on the part of its product as rest and as a created value. If the labour-power has performed its function, then capital no longer consists of labour-power on one side, and means of production on the other. The capital value invested in labour is then value added with a surplus-value to the product. In order to repeat the process, the product must be sold, and new labour-power must be bought with the money so obtained, in order to be once more embodied in the productive capital. It is this which then gives to the capital invested in labour-power, and to that invested in raw materials, etc., the character of circulating capital as distinguished from the capital remaining fixed in instruments of labour.

But if the secondary quality of the circulating capital, which it shares with a part of the constant capital (raw and auxiliary materials), is made the essential mark of capital invested in labour-power, to wit, the transfer of the full value invested in it to the product in whose manufacture it is consumed, instead of a gradual and successive transfer such as takes place in the case of the fixed capital, and the consequent total reproduction of this value by the sale of the product, then the value invested in wages must likewise consist, not of active labour-power, but of the material elements which the labourer buys with his wages, in other words, it must consist of that part of the social commodity-capital which passes into the individual consumption of the labourer, of means of subsistence. In that case, the fixed capital would consist of the more durable instruments of labour which are reproduced more slowly, and the capital invested in labour-power would consist of the means of subsistence, which must be more rapidly reproduced.

However, the boundaries of greater or smaller durability pass imperceptibly into one another.

'The food and clothing consumed by the labourer, the buildings in which he works, the implements with which his labour is assisted, are all of a perishable nature. There is, however, a vast difference in the time for which these different capitals will endure: a steam-engine will last longer than a ship, a ship than the clothing of the labourer, and the clothing of the labourer longer than the food which he consumes.' (Ricardo, etc., page 27.)

Ricardo does not mention the house, in which the labourer lives, his tools of consumption, such as knives, forks, dishes, etc., all of which have the same quality of durability as the instruments of labour. The same things, the same classes of things, appear in one place as means of consumption, in another as instruments of labour.

The difference, as stated by Ricardo, is this: 'According as capital is rapidly perishable and requires to be frequently reproduced or is of slow consumption, it is classed under the heads of circulating or fixed capital.'

He remarks in addition thereto: 'A division not essential, and in which the line of demarcation cannot be accurately drawn.'

Thus we have once more arrived among the Physiocrats, where the distinction between *avances annuelles* and *avances primitives* was one referring to the period of consumption, and consequently also to the different time of reproduction of the invested capital. Only, that which in their case constitutes a phenomenon important for society and for this reason is assigned in the *Tableau Économique* a place of interrelation with the process of circulation, becomes here, in Ricardo's own words, a subjective and unessential division.

As soon as the capital-value invested in labour-power differs from that invested in instruments of labour only by its period of reproduction and term of circulation, as soon as one part of capital consists of means of subsistence, another of instruments of labour, so that these differ from those only by the degree of their durability, which durability is further different for the various kinds of each class, it follows as a matter of course that all specific difference between the capital invested in labour-power and that invested in means of production is obliterated.

This runs very much counter to Ricardo's theory of value, likewise to his theory of profit, which is actually a theory of surplus-value. He does not consider the difference between fixed and circulating capital any further than is required by the way in which different proportions of both of them, in equal capitals invested in different branches of production, influence the law of value, particularly the extent to which an increase or decrease of wages in consequence of these conditions affects prices. But even within this restricted analysis, he commits the gravest errors on account of the confusion in the definitions of fixed and circulating, constant and variable capital. Indeed, he starts his analysis on an entirely wrong basis. In the first place, in so far as the capital-value invested in labour-power has to be considered under the head of circulating capital, he gives a wrong definition of circulating capital and misunderstands particularly the circumstances which place the capital-value invested in labour-power under this heading. In the second place, he confounds the definition, according to which the capital-value invested in labour-power is a variable capital, with that according to which it is circulating as distinguished from fixed capital.

It is evident from the beginning that the definition of capital-value invested in labour-power as circulating capital is a secondary one, obliterating its specific difference in the process of production. For on one hand, the values invested in labour-power are identified in this definition with those invested in raw materials. A classification which identifies a part of the constant capital with the circulating capital does not appreciate the specific difference of variable from constant capital. On the other hand, while the values invested in labour-power are indeed distinguished from those invested in instruments of labour, the distinction is based only on the fact that the values incorporated in them are transferred to the product in different periods of time, not on the fact that this transfer is significant for the radically different manner in which either of them passes into the production of values.

In all of these cases, it is a question of the *manner* in which a given value, invested in the process of production of commodities, whether the investment be made in wages, in the price of raw materials, or in that of instruments of labour, is transferred to the product, then circulated by it, and returned to its starting point by the sale of the product, or reproduced. The only difference lies here in the 'how', in the particular manner of the transfer, and therefore also in the circulation of this value.

Whether the price of labour-power previously agreed upon by contract in each case is paid in money or in means of subsistence, does not alter in any way the fact that it is a fixed price. However, it is evident in the case of wages paid in money, that it is not the money which passes into the process of production in the way that the value as well as the material of the means of production do. But if the means of subsistence which the labourer buys with his wages are directly classed in the same category with raw materials, as the material form of circulating capital distinguished from instruments of labour, then the matter assumes a different aspect. While the value of *these* things, the instruments of labour, is transferred to the product in the process of production, the value of *those* things, the means of subsistence, reappears in the labour-power that consumes them and is likewise transferred to the product by the exertion of this power. In every one of these cases it is a question of the mere re-appearance of the values invested in production by means of transfer to the product. The Physiocrats for this reason took this aspect of the matter seriously and denied that industrial labour could create any values. This is shown by a previously quoted passage of Wayland, in which he says that it is immaterial in which form the capital reappears, and that the different kinds of food, clothing, and shelter which are required for the existence and well-being of man are likewise changed, being consumed in the course of time while their value reappears. (*Elements of Political Economy*, pages 31 and 32.) The capital-values invested in production in the form of means of production and means of subsistence both reappear in the value of the product. By this means the transformation of the capitalist process of production into a complete mystery is happily accomplished and the origin of the surplus-value incorporated in the product is entirely concealed.

At the same time, this perfects the fetishism typical of bourgeois political economy, which pretends that the social and economic character of things, arising from the process of social production, is a natural character due to the material substance of those things. For instance, instruments of labour are designated as fixed capital, a scholastic mode of definition which leads to contradictions and confusion. Just as we demonstrated in the case of the process of production (Book 1, Chapter 7), that it depends on the role, the function, performed by the various material substances in a certain process of production, whether they served as instruments of labour, raw materials, or products, just so we now claim that instruments of labour are fixed capital only in cases where the process of production is a capitalist process of production and the means of production are, therefore, capital and possess the economic form and social character of capital. And in the second place, they are fixed capital only when they transfer their value to the product in a certain peculiar way. Unless they do so, they remain instruments of labour without being fixed capital. In the same way, auxiliary materials, such as manure, if they transfer their value in the same peculiar manner as the greater part of the instruments of labour, become fixed capital, although they are not instruments of labour. It is not the definitions which are essential in determining the character of these things. It is their definite functions which express themselves in definite categories.

If it is considered as one of the qualities exhibited by means of subsistence under all circumstances to be capital invested in wages, then it will also be a quality of this 'circulating' capital 'to support labour'. (Ricardo, page 25.) If the means of subsistence were not 'capital', then they would not support labour, according to this; while it is precisely their character of capital which endows them with the faculty of supporting capital by means of the labour of others.

If means of subsistence are of themselves capital circulating after being converted into wages, it follows furthermore that the magnitude of wages depends on the proportion of the number of labourers to the existing quantity of circulating capital – a favourite economic law – while as a matter of fact the quantity of means of subsistence withdrawn from the market by the labourer, and the quantity of means of subsistence available for the consumption of the capitalist, depend on the proportion of the surplus-value to the price of labour.

Ricardo as well as Barton[1] everywhere confound the relation between variable and constant capital with that between circulating and fixed capital. We shall see later, to what extent this vitiates Ricardo's analyses concerning the rate of profit.

Ricardo futhermore identifies the distinctions which arise in the turn-over from other causes than the difference between fixed and circulating capital, with these same differences: 'It is also to be observed that the circulating capital may circulate, or be returned to its employer, in very unequal times. The wheat bought by a farmer to sow is comparatively a fixed capital to the wheat purchased by a baker to make into loaves. The one leaves it in the ground, and can obtain no return for a year: the other can get it ground into flour, sell it as bread to his customers, and have his capital free, to renew the same, or commence any other employment in a week.' (pages 26 and 27.)

In this passage, it is characteristic that wheat, although not serving as a means of subsistence, but as raw material when used for sowing, is supposed in the first place to be circulating capital, because it is in itself a food, and in the second place a circulating capital, because its reproduction extends over one year. However, it is not so much the slow or rapid reproduction which makes a fixed capital of a means of production, but rather the manner in which it transfers its value to the product.

The confusion caused by Adam Smith has brought about the following results:

1. The distinction between fixed and circulating capital is confounded with that between productive capital and commodity-capital. For instance, a machine is said to be circulating capital when on the market as a commodity, and fixed capital when incorporated in the process of production. Under these circumstances, it is impossible to ascertain why one kind of capital should be more fixed or circulating than another.

2. All circulating capital is identified with capital invested, or about to be invested, in wages. This is the case with John Stuart Mill, and others.

3. The difference between variable and constant capital, which had been previously mistaken by Barton, Ricardo, and others, for that between circulating and fixed capital, is finally identified with this last-named difference, for instance by Ramsay, who calls all means of production, raw materials, etc., including instruments of labour, fixed capital, and only that which is invested in wages circulating capital. But on account of the reduction of the problem to this form, the real difference between variable and constant capital is not understood.

4. The latest English, and especially Scotch, economists, who look upon all things from the inexpressibly petty point of view of a bank clerk, such as MacLeod, Patterson, and others, transform the difference between fixed and circulating capital into one of money at call and money not at call.

Chapter 12
The Working Period

Take two branches of production, with equal working days, for instance of ten hours each, one of them a cotton spinnery, the other a locomotive factory. In one of these branches, a definite quantity of finished product, cotton yarn, is completed daily, or weekly; in the other, the productive process may have to be repeated for three months in order that the finished product, a locomotive, may be ready. In one case, the product is made up of separate lots, and the same labour is repeated daily or weekly. In the other case, the labour process is continuous and extends over a prolonged number of daily labour-processes which, in their continuity, result in the finished product. Although the duration of the working day is the same in both cases, there is a marked difference in the duration of the productive act, that is to say, in the duration of the repeated labour-processes, which are required in order to complete the finished product, to get it ready for its role as a commodity on the market, in other words, to convert it from a productive into a commodity-capital. The difference between fixed and circulating capital has nothing to do with this. The difference just indicated would exist, even if the very same proportions of fixed and circulating capital were employed in both branches of production.

These differences in the duration of the productive acts are found not alone in two different spheres of production, but also within one and the same sphere of production, according to the volume of the intended product. An ordinary residence house is built in less time than a large factory and therefore requires a smaller number of consecutive labour-processes. While the building of a locomotive requires three months, that of an ironclad requires one year or more. The production of grain extends over nearly a year, that of horned cattle over several years, and the production of timber may require from twelve to one hundred years. A country road may be completed in a few months, while a railroad requires years. An ordinary carpet is made in about a week, while *Gobelins* requires years, etc. The differences in the duration of the productive act are, therefore, infinitely manifold.

It is evident that a difference in the duration of the productive act must beget a difference in the velocity of the turn-over, even if the invested capitals are equal, in other words, must make a difference in the time for which a certain capital is advanced. Take it that a cotton spinnery and a locomotive factory employ the same amount of capital, that the proportion between their constant and variable capital is the same, likewise that between fixed and circulating capital, and that finally their working day is of equal length and its division between necessary and surplus-labour the same. In order to eliminate, further-more, all the external circumstances arising out of the process of circulation, we shall assume that both the yarn and the locomotive are made to order and will be paid on delivery of the finished product. At the end of the week, the cotton spinner recovers his outlay for circulating capital (making exception of surplus-value), likewise the wear and tear of fixed capital incorporated in the value of the yarn. He can, therefore, repeat the same cycle with the same capital. It has completed its turn-over. The locomotive manufacturer, on the other hand, must advance ever new capital for wages and raw material every week for three months in succession, and it is only after three months, after the delivery of the locomotive, that the circulating capital gradually invested in one and the same productive act for the manufacture of one and the same commodity once more returns to a form in which it can renew its cycle. The wear and tear of his machinery is likewise covered only at the end of three months. The investment of the one is made for one week, that of the other is the investment of one week multiplied by twelve. All other circumstances being assumed as equal, the one must have twelve times more circulating capital at his disposal than the other.

It is, however, an immaterial condition that the capitals advanced weekly should be equal. Whatever may be the quantity of the invested capital, it is advanced for one week in one case, and for twelve weeks in the other, before the same operation can be repeated with it, or another inaugurated.

The difference in the velocity of the turn-over, or in the length of time for which the capital is advanced before the same capital-value can be employed in a new process of production or self-expansion, arises here from the following circumstances:

Take it that the manufacture of a locomotive, or of any other machine, requires 100 working days. So far as the labourers employed in the manufacture of yarn or of the locomotive are concerned, 100 working days constitute in either case a discontinuous magnitude, representing, according to our assumption, 100 consecutive, but separate labour-processes of ten hours each. But with reference to the product – the machine – these 100 working days are a continuous magnitude, a working day of 1,000 working hours, one single connected act of production. I call such a working day, which is formed by the succession of more or less numerous connected working days, a *working period*. If we speak of a working day, we mean the length of working time during which the labourer must daily spend his labour-power, must work day by day. But if we speak of a working period, then we mean a number of consecutive working days required in a certain branch of production for the completion of the finished product. In this case, the product of every working day is but a partial one, being elaborated from day to day and receiving its complete form only at the end of a longer or shorter period of labour, when it is at last a finished use-value.

Interruptions, disturbances of the process of social production, for instance by crises, therefore have very different effects on labour products of a discontinuous nature and those that require for their completion a prolonged and connected working period. In one case, today's production of a certain mass of yarn, coal, etc., is not followed by tomorrow's production of yarn, coal, etc. Not so in the case of ships, buildings, railroads, etc. It is not only the work which is interrupted, but also a connected working period. If the work is not continued, the means of production and labour so far expended in its manufacture are wasted. Even if work is resumed, a deterioration has taken place in the meantime.

For the entire duration of the working period, the value daily transferred to the product by the fixed capital accumulates successively until the product is finished. In this way, the difference between the fixed and circulating capital is revealed in its practical significance. The fixed capital is invested in the process of production for a long period, it need not be reproduced until after the expiration of, perhaps, a period of several years. Whether a steam-engine transfers its value daily to some yarn, which is the product of a discontinuous labour-process, or for three months to a locomotive, which is the product of a continuous process, is immaterial for the investment of the capital required for the purchase of the steam-engine. In the one case, its value is recovered in small doses, for instance, weekly, in the other case in larger quantities, for instance, quarterly. But in either case, the reproduction of the steam-engine may not take place until after twenty years. So long as every individual period which returns a part of the value of the steam-engine by the sale of the product, is shorter than the lifetime of this engine, the same engine continues its service in successive working periods of the process of production.

It is different with the circulating portions of the invested capital. The labour-power bought for this week is consumed in the course of the same week and transferred to the product. It must be paid for at the end of this week. And this investment of capital in labour-power is repeated every week for three months without enabling the capitalist to use the investment of this part of capital in this week's labour-power for the purchase of next week's. Every week, additional capital must be invested for the payment of labour-power, and, leaving aside the question of credit, the capitalist must be able to advance wages for three months, even if he pays them only in weekly instalments. It is the same with the other portion of circulating capital, the raw and auxiliary materials. One shift of labour after another is transferred to the product. It is not alone the value of the expended labour-power which is continually transferred to the product during the labour-process, but also surplus-value. This product, however, is unfinished, it has not yet the form of a finished commodity, it cannot yet circulate. This applies likewise to the capital-value transferred to the product by the raw and auxiliary materials.

According as the working period required by the specific nature of the product, or by the useful effect aimed at, is short or long, a continuous investment of additional circulating capital (wages, raw, and auxiliary materials) is required, none of its parts being in a form adapted for circulation and for the promotion of the repetition of the same operation. Every one of these parts is on the contrary held by the growing product as one of its parts in the sphere of production, in the form of productive capital. Now, the time of turn-over is equal to the sum of the time of production and the time of circulation. Hence a prolongation of the time of production reduces the velocity of the turn-over quite as much as the prolongation of the time of circulation. In the present case, the following must be furthermore noted:

1. The prolonged stay in the sphere of production. The capital invested, for instance, in the labour-power, raw, and auxiliary materials of the first week, the same as the portions of value transferred to the product by the fixed capital, are held in the sphere of production for the entire term of three months, and, being incorporated in a growing and as yet unfinished product, cannot pass into the circulation of commodities.

2. Since the working period required for the completion of the productive act lasts three months, and forms one connected labour-process, a new quantity of circulating capital must be continually added week after week to the preceding quantity. The amount of the successively invested additional capital grows, therefore, with the length of the working period.

We have assumed that equal capitals are invented in the spinnery and the machine factory, that these capitals contain equal proportions of constant and variable, fixed and circulating capital, that the working days are equal, in short, that all circumstances are equal with the exception of the duration of the working period. In the first week, the outlay for both is the same, but the product of the spinner can be sold and the returns from the sale employed in the purchase of new labour-power and raw materials; in short, production can be resumed on the same scale. The machine manufacturer, on the other hand, cannot reconvert the circulating capital expended in the first week into money until at the end of three months, when his product is finished and he can begin operations afresh. There is, in other words, first a difference in the return of the same quantity of capital invested. But, in the second place, the same amount of productive capital is employed during the three months in the spinnery and in the machine factory, but the magnitude of the outlay of capital in the case of the yarn manufacturer is different from that of the machine manufacturer. For in the one case, the same capital is rapidly renewed and the same operation can be repeated, while in the other case, the capital is renewed by relatively slow degrees, so that ever new quantities of capital must be added to the old up to the time of the completion of the term of its reproduction. It is, therefore, not only the time of reproduction of definite portions of capital, or the time of investment, which is different, but also the quantity of the capital to be advanced according to the duration of the productive process, although the capital employed daily or weekly is the same. This circumstance is worthy of note for the reason that the time of investment may be prolonged, as we shall see in the cases treated in the next chapter, without thereby increasing the amount of the capital to be invested in proportion to this increase in time. The capital must be advanced for a longer time, and a larger amount of capital is held in the form of productive capital.

In undeveloped stages of capitalist production, enterprises requiring a long working period, and hence a large investment of capital for a long time, such as the building of streets, canals, etc., especially when they can be carried out only on a large scale, are either not managed on a capitalist basis at all, but rather at the expense of the municipality or state (in older times generally by means of forced labour, so far as labour-power was concerned); or, such products as require a long working period are manufactured only for the smaller part by the help of the private resources of the capitalist himself. For instance, in the building of a house, the private person for whose account the house is built advances money in instalments to the contractor. The owner thus pays for his house in instalments to the extent that his productive process proceeds. But in the developed capitalist era, when on the one hand masses of capital are concentrated in the hands of single individuals, while on the other hand associations of capitalists (stock companies) appear by the side of individual capitalists and the credit system is simultaneously developed, a capitalist contractor builds only in exceptional cases for the order of private individuals. He makes it his business to build rows of houses and sections of cities for the market, just as individual capitalists make it their business to build railroads as contractors.

To what extent capitalist production has revolutionised the building of houses in London, is shown by the testimony of a contractor before the banking committee of 1857. When he was young, he said, houses were generally built to order and the payments made in instalments to the contractor when certain stages of the building were completed. Very little was built on speculation. Contractors used to consent to this mainly to give their hands regular employment and thus keep them together. In the last forty years, all this has changed. Very little is now built for order. If a man wants a house, he selects one from among those built on speculation or still in process of building. The contractor no longer works for his customers, but for the market. Like every other industrial capitalist, he is compelled to have finished articles on the market. While fomerly a contractor had perhaps three or four houses at a time building for speculation, he must now buy a large piece of real estate (which, in continental language means rent it for ninety-nine years, as a rule), build from 100 to 200 houses on it, and thus engage in an enterprise which exceeds from twenty to fifty times his resources. The funds are secured by taking up mortgages, and money is placed at the disposal of the contractor to the extent that the building of the individual houses is progressing. Then, if a crisis comes along and interrupts the payment of the advance instalments, the entire enterprise generally collapses. In the best case, the houses remain unfinished until the coming of better times, in the worst case they are sold at auction at half-price. Without building on specul-ation, and that on a large scale, no contractor can get along nowadays. The profit from building itself is extremely small. The main profit of the contractor comes from raising the ground rent, by a careful selection and utilisation of the building lots. By this method of speculation anticipating the demand for houses nearly the whole of Belgravia and Tyburnia, and the countless thousands of villas in the vicinity of London have been built. (Abbreviated from the *Report of the Select Committee on Bank Acts*. Part 1, 1857, Evidence, Questions 5413–18; 5535–36.)

The execution of enterprises with considerably long working periods and on a large scale does not fall fully within the province of capitalist production, until the concentration of capitals is very pronounced, and the development of the credit system offers, on the other hand, the comfortable expedient of advancing another's money instead of one's own capital and thus risking its loss. It goes without saying that the fact whether or not the capital advanced in production belongs to the one who uses it or to some one else has no influence on the velocity and time of turn-over.

The circumstances which augment the product of the individual working day, such as co-operation, division of labour, employment of machinery, shorten at the same time the working period of connected acts of production. Thus machinery shortens the building time of houses, bridges, etc.; a mowing and threshing machine, etc., shorten the working period required to transform the ripe grain into a finished product. Improved shipbuilding reduces by increased speed the time of turn-over of capital invested in navigation. Such improvements as shorten the working period and thereby the time for which circulating capital must be advanced are, however, generally accompanied by an increased outlay for fixed capital. On the other hand, the working period in certain branches of production may be shortened by the mere extension of co-operation. The completion of a railroad is hastened by the employment of huge armies of labourers and the carrying on of the work in many places at once. The time of turn-over is in that case hastened by an increase of the advanced capital. More means of production and more labour-power must be combined under the command of the capitalist.

While the shortening of the working period is thus mostly accompanied by an increase of the capital advanced for this shortened time, so that the amount of capital advanced increases to the extent that the time for which the advance is made decreases, it must be noted that the essential point, apart from the existing amount of social capital, is the degree in which the means of production or subsistence, or their control, is scattered or concentrated in the hands of individual capitalists, in other words, the degree of concentration of capitals. Inasmuch as credit promotes the concentration of capital in one hand, it hastens and intensifies by its contribution the shortening of the working period and thereby of the time of turn-over.

In branches of production in which the working period is continually, or occasionally, determined by definite natural conditions, no shortening of the working period can take place by the above-mentioned means. Says Walter Good, in his *Political, Agricultural, and Commercial Fallacies* (London, 1866, page 325): 'The expression, "more rapid turn-over" cannot be applied to grain crops, as only one turn-over per year is possible. As for cattle, we will simply ask: how is the turn-over of bi- or tri-ennial sheep, and of quadrennial and quinquennial oxen to be hastened?'

The necessity of securing ready money (for instance, for the payment of fixed tithes, such as taxes, ground rent, etc.) solves this question by selling or killing cattle before they have reached the normal economic age, to the great detriment of agriculture. This also causes finally a rise in the price of meat. We read on pages 12 and 13 of the above named work that the people who formerly were mainly engaged in the raising of cattle for the purpose of supplying the pastures of the midland counties in summer, and the stables of the eastern counties in winter, have been so reduced by the fluctuations and sinking of the corn prices that they are glad to avail themselves of the high prices of butter and cheese; they carry the former every week to the market, in order to cover their running expenses, while they take advance payments on the cheese from some middleman who calls for it as soon as it can be transported and who, of course, makes his own prices. As a result of this, agriculture being ruled by the laws of political economy, the calves, which were formerly taken south from the dairy districts to be raised, are now sacrificed in masses, frequently when they are only eight or ten days old, in the stock yards of Birmingham, Manchester, Liverpool, and other neighbouring cities. But if the malt were untaxed, the farmers would not only have made more profits and been able to keep their young cattle until they would have been older and heavier, but the malt would also have served instead of milk for the raising of calves by those who keep no cows: and the present appalling want of young cattle would have been avoided to a large extent. If the raising of calves is now recommended to those small farmers, they reply: 'We know very well that it would pay to raise them on milk, but in the first place we should have to lay out money, and we cannot do that, and in the second place we should have to wait long for the return of our money, while in dairying we get returns immediately.'

If the prolongation of the turn-over has such consequences for the smaller English farmers, it is easy to see what disadvantages it must produce for the small farmers of the continent.

To the extent that the working period lasts, and thus the period required for the completion of the commodity ready for circulation, the value successively yielded by the fixed capital accumulates and the reproduction of this value is retarded. But this retardation does not cause a renewed outlay of fixed capital. The machine continues its function in the process of production, no matter whether the reproduction of its wear and tear in the form of money takes place slowly or rapidly. It is different with the circulating capital. Not only must capital be tied up for a longer time in proportion as the working period extends, but new capital must also be continually advanced in the form of wages, raw and auxiliary materials. A retardation of the reproduction has therefore a different effect on either capital. No matter whether reproduction proceeds rapidly or slowly, the fixed capital continues its functions. But the circulating capital becomes unable to perform its functions, if the reproduction is retarded, if it is tied up in the form of unsold, or unfinished and as yet unsaleable, products, and if no additional capital is at hand for its reproduction in natural form.

'While the farmer is starving, his cattle thrive. There had been considerable rain and the grass pasture was luxuriant. The Indian farmer will starve alongside of a fat ox. The precepts of superstition seem cruel for the individual, but they are preserving society; the preservation of the cattle secures the continuation of agriculture and thereby the sources of future subsistence and wealth. It may sound hard and sad, but it is so: in India a man is easier replaced than an ox.' (*Return, East Indian. Madras and Orissa Famine.* No. 4, page 4.) Compare with the preceding the statement of Manara-Dharma-Sestra, chapter 10, page 862; 'The sacrifice of life without any reward, for the purpose of preserving a priest or a cow . . . can secure the salvation of these low-born tribes.'

Of course, it is impossible to deliver a quinquennial animal before the lapse of five years. But a thing that is possible is the getting ready of the animals for their destination by changed modes of treatment. This was accomplished particularly by Bakewell. Formerly, English sheep, like the French as late as 1855, were not ready for slaughtering until after four or five years. By the Bakewell system, even a one year old sheep may be fattened, and in every case it is completely grown before the end of the second year. By means of careful sexual selection, Bakewell, a farmer of Dishley Grange, reduced the skeleton of sheep to the minimum required for their existence. His sheep are called the New Leicesters. 'The breeder can now supply three sheep for the market in the same time that he formerly required for one, and at that with a broader, rounder, and larger development of the parts giving the most meat. Nearly their entire weight is pure meat.' (Lavergne, *The Rural Economy of England, etc.*, 1855, page 22.)

The methods which shorten the working periods are applicable to different branches of industry only to a very different degree and do not compensate for the differences in the length of time of the various working periods. To stick to our illustration, the working period required for the building of a locomotive may be absolutely shortened by the employment of new implement machines. But if at the same time the finished product turned out daily or weekly by a cotton spinnery is still more rapidly increased, then the length of the working period in machine building, compared with that in spinning, has nevertheless been relatively lengthened.

Chapter 13
The Time of Production

The working time is always the time of production, that is to say, the time during which capital is held in the sphere of production. But vice versa, not all time during which capital is engaged in the process of production is necessarily a working time.

It is not in this case a question of interruptions of the labour-process conditioned on natural limitations of labour-power itself, although we have seen to what extent the mere circumstance that fixed capital, factory buildings, machinery, etc., are unemployed during pauses of the labour-process, became one of the motives for an unnatural prolongation of the labour-process and for day and night work. It is rather a question of an interruption independent of the length of the labour-process and conditioned on the nature and the production of the goods themselves, during which the object of labour is for a longer or shorter time subjected to lasting natural processes, causing physical, chemical, or physiological changes and suspending the labour-process entirely or partially.

For instance, grape juice, after being pressed, must ferment for a while and then rest for some time, in order to reach a certain degree of perfection. In many branches of industry the product must pass through a drying process, for instance in pottery, or be exposed to certain conditions which change its chemical nature, for instance in bleaching. Winter grain needs about nine months to mature. Between the time of sowing and harvesting the labour-process is almost entirely suspended. In timber raising, after the sowing and the incidental preliminary work are completed, the seed may require 100 years in order to be transformed into a finished product, and during all this time it requires very insignificant contributions of labour.

In all these cases, additional labour is contributed only occasionally during a large portion of the time of production. The condition described in the previous chapter, where additional capital and labour must be contributed to the capital already tied up in the process of production, is found here only in longer or shorter intervals.

In all these cases, therefore, the time of production of the advanced capital consists of two periods: one period, during which the capital is engaged in the labour-process; a second period, during which its form of existence – being that of an unfinished product – is surrendered to the influence of natural processes, without being in the labour-process. It does not alter the case, that these two periods of time may cross and pervade one another here and there. The working period and the period of production do not coincide. The time of production is greater than the working period. But the product is not finished until the time of production is completed, only then is it mature and can be transformed from a productive into a commodity-capital. According to the length of the period of production not consisting of working time, the period of turn-over is likewise prolonged. In so far as the time of production in excess of the working time is not once and for all determined by definite natural laws, such as regulate the maturing of grain, the growth of an oak, etc., the period of turnover may be more or less shortened by an artificial reduction of the time of production. Such instances are the introduction of chemical bleaching instead of lawn bleaching, the improvement of drying apparatus in drying processes. Or, in tanning, where the penetration of the tannic acid into the skins, by the old method, required from six to eighteen months, while the new method, by means of the air-pump, does it in one and a half to two months. (J. G. Courcelle-Seneuil, *Traité theorique et pratique des Entreprises industrielles*, etc., Paris, 1857, second edition.) The most magnificent illustration of an artificial abbreviation of the time of production which is taken up with natural processes is furnished by the history of the production of iron, more especially the conversion of raw iron into steel during the last 100 years, from the puddling process discovered about 1780 to the modern Bessemer process and the latest methods introduced since then. The time of production has been enormously abbreviated, but the investment of fixed capital has increased accordingly.

A peculiar illustration of the divergence of the time of production from the working time is furnished by the American manufacture of shoe-lasts. In this case, a considerable part of the expense is due to the fact that the wood must be stored for drying for as much as 18 months, in order that the finished last may not change its form by warping. During this time, the wood does not pass through any other labour-process. The period of turn-over of the invested capital is, therefore, not determined solely by the time required for the manufacture of the lasts, but also by the time during which the wood lies unproductive in the drying process. It is for 18 months in the process of production before it can enter into the labour-process proper. This illustration shows at the same time, how it is that the periods of turn-over of different parts of the total circulating capital may differ in consequence of conditions, which do not owe their existence to the sphere of circulation, but to that of production.

The difference between the time of production and the working time becomes especially apparent in agriculture. In our moderate climates, the land bears grain once a year. The abbreviation or prolongation of the period of production (for winter grain an average of nine months) is itself dependent on the change of good or bad seasons, and for this reason it cannot be as accurately determined beforehand and controlled as in industry properly so called. Only such by-products as milk, cheese, etc., are successively producible and saleable in short periods. On the other hand, the working time meets with the following conditions: 'The number of working days in the various regions of Germany, with regard to the climatic and other determining conditions, will permit the assumption of the three following main working periods: for the spring period, from the middle of March or beginning of April to the middle of May, about 50 to 60 working days; for the summer period, from the beginning of June to the end of August, 65 to 80; and for the fall period, from the beginning of September to the end of October, or the middle or end of November, 55 to 75 working days. For the winter, only the chores customary for that time, such as the hauling of manure, wood, market goods, and building materials, are to be noted.' (F. Kirchhoff, *Handbuch der landwirthschaftlichen Betriebslehre*. Dresden, 1852, page 160.)

To the extent that the climate is unfavourable, the working period of agriculture, and thus the outlay for capital and labour, is crammed into a short space of time. Take, for instance, Russia. In some of the northern regions of that country agricultural labour is possible only during 130 to 150 days per year. It may be imagined what would be the losses of Russia, if 50 out of its 65 million of European inhabitants would remain unemployed during six or eight months of the winter, when all field work must stop. Apart from the 200,000 farmers, who work in the 10,500 factories of Russia, local house industries have everywhere developed in the villages. There are some villages in which all farmers have been for generations weavers, tanners, shoe-makers, locksmiths, knifemakers, etc. This is particularly the case in the provinces of Moscow, Vladimir, Kaluga, Kostroma, and Petersburg. By the way, this house-industry is being more and more pressed into the service of capitalist production. The weavers, for instance, are supplied with woof and web directly by merchants or middlemen. (Abbreviated from the Reports by H. M. Secretaries of Embassy and Legation, on the Manufactures, Commerce, etc., No. 8, 1865, pages 86 and 87.) We see here that the divergence of the period of production from the working period, the latter being but a part of the former, forms the natural basis for the combination of agriculture with an agricultural side-industry, and that this side-industry, on the other hand, offers points of vantage to the capitalist, who intrudes first in the person of the merchant. When capitalist production later accomplishes the separation of manufacture and agriculture, the rural labourer becomes ever more dependent on accidental side-employment and his condition is correspondingly lowered. For the capital, all the differences are compensated in the turn-over. Not so for the labourer.

While in most branches of industry proper, of mining, transportation, etc., the work proceeds uniformly, the working time being the same from year to year, and the outlay for the capital passing daily into circulation being uniformly distributed, making exception of such abnormal interruptions as fluctuations of prices, business depressions, etc.; while furthermore also the recovery of the circulating capital, or its reproduction, is uniformly distributed throughout the year, provided the conditions of the market remain the same – there is, on the other hand, the greatest inequality in the outlay of circulating capital in such investments of capital, in which the working time constitutes only a part of the time of production, while the recovery of the capital takes place in bulk at a time determined by natural conditions. If such a business is managed on the same scale as one with a continuous working period, that is to say, if the amount of the circulating capital to be advanced is the same, it must be advanced in larger doses at a time and for longer periods. The durability of the fixed capital differs here considerably from the time in which it actually performs a productive function. Together with the difference between working time and time of production, the time of investment of the employed fixed capital is, of course, likewise continually interrupted for a longer or shorter time, for instance, in agriculture in the case of labouring cattle, implements and machines. In so far as this fixed capital consists of labouring cattle, it requires continually the same, or nearly the same, amount of expenditure for feed, etc., as it does during its working time. In the case of inanimate instruments of labour, disuse also implies a certain amount of depreciation. Hence there is an appreciation of the product in general, seeing that the transfer of value is not calculated by the time in which the fixed capital performs its function, but by the time in which it depreciates in value. In such branches of production as these, the disuse of the fixed capital, whether combined with current expenses or not, forms as much a condition of its normal employment as, for instance, the waste of a certain quantity of cotton in spinning; and in the same way the labour-power unproductively consumed in any labour-process under normal conditions, and inevitably so, counts as much as its productive consumption. Every improvement which reduces the unproductive expenditure of instruments of labour, raw material, and labour-power, also reduces the value of the product.

In agriculture, both the longer duration of the working period and the great difference between working period and productive period are combined. Hodgskin truly says with regard to this circumstance that the difference in the time (although he does not here distinguish between working time and productive time) required to get the products of agriculture ready and that required for the products of other branches of production is the main cause for the great dependence of farmers. They cannot market their goods in less time than one year. During this entire period they must borrow from the shoemaker, the tailor, the smith, the wagonmaker, and various other producers, whose articles they need, and which articles are finished in a few days or weeks. In consequence of this natural circumstance, and as a result of the more rapid increase of wealth in other branches of production, the real estate owners who have monopolised the land of the entire country, although they have also appropriated the monopoly of legislation, are nevertheless unable to save themselves and their servants, the tenants, from the fate of becoming the most dependent people in the land. (Thomas Hodgskin, *Popular Political Economy*, London, 1827, page 147, note.)

All methods by which partly the expenditures for wages and instruments of labour in agriculture are distributed more equally over the entire year, partly the turn-over is shortened by the raising of various products making different harvests possible during the course of the year, require an increase of the circulating capital invested in wages, fertilisers, seeds, etc., and advanced for purposes of production. This is the case, for instance, in the transition from the three plat system with fallow land to the system of crop rotation without fallow. It applies furthermore to the *cultures dérobées* of Flanders. 'The root crops are planted in *culture dérobée;* the same field yields in succession first grain, flax, rape, for the wants of man, and after their harvest root crops are sown for the subsistence of cattle. This system, which permits the keeping of horned cattle in the stables without interruption, yields a considerable amount of manure and thus becomes the fulcrum of crop rotation. More than a third of the cultivated area in sandy districts is taken up with *cultures dérobées*; it is as though the cultivated area had been increased by one third.' Apart from root crops, clover and other leguminous crops are likewise used for this purpose. 'Agriculture, being thus carried to a point where it merges into horticulture, naturally requires a relatively considerable investment of capital. In England, a first investment of 250 francs per hectare is assumed. In Flanders, our farmers will probably consider a first investment of 500 francs far too low.' (Émile de Laveleye, *Essais sur L'Économie Rurale de la Belgique*, Paris, 1863, pages 59, 60, 63.)

Take finally timber growing. 'The production of timber differs from most of the other branches of production essentially by the fact that in it the force of nature is acting independently and does not require the power of man and capital in its natural propagation. Even in places where forests are artificially propagated the expenditure of human and capital power is inconsiderable compared to the action of natural forces. Besides, a forest will still thrive in soils and locations where grain does no longer give any yield or where its production does not pay. Forestry furthermore requires for its regular economy a larger area than grain culture, because small plats do not permit a system of felling trees in plats, prevent the utilisation of by-products, complicate the production of the trees, etc. Finally, the productive process extends over such long periods that it exceeds the aims of private management and even surpasses the age limit of human life in certain cases. The capital invested in the purchase of the real estate' (in the case of communal production there is no capital needed for this, the question being simply how much land the community can spare from its cultivated and pasturing area for forestry) 'will not yield returns until after a long period and is turned over gradually, but completely, with forests of certain kinds of wood, only after as much as 150 years. Besides, a consistent production of timber demands itself a supply of living wood which exceeds the annual requirements from ten to forty times. Unless a man has, therefore, still other sources of income and owns vast tracts of forest, he cannot engage in regular forestry.' (Kirchhof, page 58.)

The long time of production (which comprises a relatively small amount of working time), and thus the length of the periods of turn-over, makes forestry little adapted for private, and therefore, capitalist enterprise, which is essentially private even if associated capitalists take the place of the individual capitalist. The development of civilisation and of industry in general has ever shown itself so active in the destruction of forests, that everything done by it for their preservation and production, compared to its destructive effect, appears infinitesimal.

The following statement in the above quotation from Kirchhof is particularly worthy of note: 'Besides, a consistent production of timber demands itself a supply of living wood which exceeds the annual requirements from ten to forty times.' In other words, a turn-over occurs once in ten, forty, or more years.

The same applies to stock raising. A part of the herd (supply of cattle) remains in the process of production, while another part of the same is sold annually as a product. In this case, only a part of the capital is turned over every year, just as it is in the case of fixed capital, machinery, labouring cattle, etc. Although this capital is a fixed capital in the process of production for a long time, and thus prolongs the turn-over of the total capital, it is not a fixed capital in the strict definition of the term.

That which is here called a supply – a certain amount of living timber or cattle – serves in a relative sense in the process of production (being simultaneously instruments of labour and raw materials); on account of the natural conditions of its reproduction under normal circumstances of economy, a considerable part of this supply must always be available in this form.

A similar influence on the turn-over is exerted by another kind of supply, which is productive capital only potentially, but which owing to the nature of its economy, must be accumulated in a more or less considerable quantity and advanced for purposes of production for a long term, although it is consumed in the actual process of production only gradually. To this class belongs, for instance, manure before it is hauled to the field, furthermore grain, hay, etc., and such supplies of means of subsistence as are employed in the production of cattle. 'A considerable part of the productive capital is contained in the supplies of certain industries. But these may lose more or less of their value, if the precautions necessary for their preservation in good condition are not properly observed. Lack of supervision may even result in the total loss of a part of the supplies in the economy. For this reason, a careful inspection of the barns, feed and grain lofts, and cellars, becomes indispensable, the store rooms must always be well closed, kept clean, ventilated, etc. The grain, and other crops held in storage, must be thoroughly turned over from time to time, potatoes and beets must be protected against frost, rain, and fire.' (Kirchhof, page 292.) 'In calculating one's own requirements, especially for the keeping of cattle, and trying to regulate the distribution according to the nature of the product and its intended use, one must not only take into consideration the covering of one's demand, but also see to it that there is a proportionate reserve for extraordinary cases. If it is then found that the demand cannot be fully covered by one's own production, it becomes necessary to reflect first whether the missing amount cannot be covered by other products (substitutes), or by the cheaper purchase of such in place of the missing ones. For instance, if there should happen to be a lack of hay, this might be covered by root crops and straw. As a general rule, the natural value and market-price of the various crops must be kept in mind in such cases, and dispositions for the consumption must be made accordingly. If, for instance, oats are high, while pease and rye are relatively low, it will pay to substitute pease or rye for a part of the oats fed to horses and to sell the oats thus saved.' (*ibidem*, page 300.)

It has been previously stated, when discussing the question of the formation of a supply, that a definite, more or less considerable, quantity of potential productive capital is required, that is to say, of means of production intended for use in production, which must be available in proportionate quantities for the purpose of being gradually consumed in the productive process. It has been incidentally remarked, that, given a certain business or capitalist enterprise of definite proportions, the magnitude of this productive supply depends on the greater or lesser difficulties of its reproduction, the relative distance of the supplying markets, the development of means of transportation and communication, etc. All these circumstances influence the minimum of capital, which must be available in the form of a productive supply, hence they influence also the length of time for which the investment of capital must be made and the amount of capital to be advanced at one time. This amount, which affects also the turn-over, is determined by the longer or shorter time, during which a circulating capital is tied up in the form of a productive supply, of mere potential capital. On the other hand, in so far as this stagnation depends on the greater or smaller possibility of rapid reproduction, on market conditions, etc., it arises itself out of the time of circulation, out of circumstances connected with the circulation. 'Furthermore, all such parts of the equipment or auxiliary pieces, as hand tools, sieves, baskets, ropes, wagon grease, nails, etc., must be so much the more available for immediate use, the less the opportunity for their rapid purchase is at hand. Finally, the entire supply of implements must be carefully overhauled in winter, and new purchases or repairs found to be necessary must be made at once. Whether or not a man is to keep a great or small supply of articles of equipment is mainly determined by local conditions. Wherever there are no artisans and stores in the vicinity, it is necessary to keep larger supplies than in places where these are in the locality or near it. But if the necessary supplies are purchased in large quantities at a time, then, other circumstances being equal, one profits as a rule by cheap purchases, provided the right time has been chosen for them. True, the rotating productive capital is thus curtailed by a so much larger sum, which cannot always be well spared in the business.' (Kirchhof, page 301.)

The difference between the time of production and working time admits of many variations, as we have seen. The circulating capital may be in the period of production, before it enters into the working period proper (production of lasts); or, it is still in the period of production, after it has passed through the working period (wine, seed grain); or, the period of production is occasionally interrupted by the working period (agriculture, timber raising). A large portion of the product, fit for circulation, remains incorporated in the active process of production, while a much smaller part enters into the annual circulation (timber and cattle raising); the longer or shorter time for which a circulating capital must be invested in the form of potential productive capital, hence also the larger or smaller amount of this capital to be advanced at one time, depends partly on the nature of the productive process (agriculture), and partly on the proximity of markets, etc., in short on circumstances connected with the sphere of circulation.

We shall see later (Book 3) what senseless theories were advanced by MacCulloch, James Mill, etc., in the attempt of identifying the diverging time of production with the working time, an attempt which is due to a misinterpretation of the theory of value.

* * *

The cycle of turn-over, which we considered in the foregoing, is determined by the durability of the fixed capital advanced in the process of production. Since this process extends over a series of years, we have a series of annual, or less than annual, successive turn-overs of fixed capital.

In agriculture, such a cycle of turn-over arises out of the system of crop rotation. 'The duration of the lease must certainly not be figured less than the time of rotation of the adopted system of crop succession. For this reason, one always calculates with 3, 6, 9, in the three plat system. In the three plat system with complete fallow, a field is cultivated only four times in six years, being planted with both winter and summer grain in the years of cultivation, and, if the condition of the soil permits it, wheat and rye, barley and oats, are likewise introduced into the rotation. Every species of grain, however, differs in its yields from others on the same soil, every one of them has a different value and is sold at a different price. For this reason, the yield of the same field is different in every year in which it is cultivated, and different in the first half of the rotation (the first three years) from that of the second. Even the average yield of one period of rotation is not equal to that of another, for its fertility does not depend merely on the good condition of the soil, but also on the weather of the various seasons, just as prices depend on a multitude of circumstances. Now, if one calculates the income from one field on the average of the crops for the entire rotation of six years and the average prices of those years, one finds the total income of one year in either period of rotation. But this is not so, if the income is calculated only for half of the period of rotation, that is to say, for three years, for then the total yields would be unequal. It follows from the foregoing that the duration of a lease in a system of three fields must be chosen for at least six years. It would be still more desirable for tenants and owners that the duration of the lease should be a multiple of the duration of the lease (!) [a multiple of the time of rotation?], in other words, that it should be 12, 18, or more years instead of 6 years, in a system of three fields, and 14, 28 years instead of 7 in a system of seven fields.' (Kirchhof, pages 117, 118.)

(The manuscript at this place contains the note: 'The English system of crop rotation. Make a note here.')

Chapter 14
The Time of Circulation

All circumstances considered so far, which distinguish the periods of rotation of different capitals invested in different branches of industry and the periods for which capital must be advanced, have their source in the process of production itself, such as the difference between fixed and circulating capital, the difference in the working periods, etc. But the period of turn-over of capital is equal to the sum of its time of production plus its time of circulation. It is, therefore, a matter of course that a difference in the time of circulation changes the time of turn-over and to that extent the length of the period of turn-over. This becomes most plainly apparent, either in comparing the different investments of capital in which all circumstances modifying the turn-over are equal, except the time of circulation, or in selecting a given capital with a given composition of fixed and circulating parts, a given working time, etc., permitting only the time of circulation to vary hypothetically.

One of the sections of the time of circulation – relatively the most decisive – consists of the time of selling, the period during which capital has the form of commodity-capital. According to the relative length of this time, the time of circulation, and to that extent the period of turn-over, are lengthened or shortened. An additional outlay of capital may become necessary as a result of expenses of storage. It is evident from the outset that the time required for the sale of finished products may differ considerably for the individual capitalists in one and the same branch of industry; and this does not refer merely to the grand totals of capital invested in the various departments of industry, but also to the different individual capitals, which are in fact individual parts of the aggregate capital invested in the same department of production. Other circumstances remaining equal, the period of selling for the same individual capital will vary with the general fluctuations of the market conditions, or with their fluctuations in that particular business department. We do not tarry over this point any longer. We merely state the simple fact that all circumstances which produce differences in the periods of turn-over of the capitals invested in different business departments, also carry in their train differences in the turn-over of the various individual capitals existing in the same departments, provided these circumstances have any individual effects (for instance, if one capitalist has an opportunity to sell more rapidly than his competitor, if one employs more methods shortening the working periods than the other, etc.).

One cause which acts continuously in differentiating the times of selling, and thus the periods of turn-over in general, is the distance of the market, in which a commodity is finally sold from its regular place of sale. During the entire time of its trip to the market, capital finds itself fettered in the form of commodity-capital. If goods are made to order, this condition lasts up to the time of delivery; if they are not made to order, the time of the trip to the market is further increased by the time during which the goods are on the market waiting to be sold. The improvement of the means of communication and transportation abbreviates the wandering period of the commodities absolutely, but does not abolish the relative difference in the time of circulation of different commodity-capitals arising from their wanderings, nor that of different portions of the same commodity-capital which wander to different markets. The improved sailing vessels and steamships, for instance, which shorten the wanderings of commodities, do so equally for near and for distant ports. But the relative differences may be altered by the development of the means of transportation and communication in a way that does not correspond to the natural distances. For instance, a railroad, which leads from a place of production to an inland centre of population, may relatively or absolutely prolong the distance to a nearer point inland not connected with a railroad, compared to the one which is naturally more distant. In the same way, the same circumstances may alter the relative distance of places of production from the larger markets, which explains the running down of old and the rise of new places of production through changes in the means of communication and transportation. (In addition to these circumstances, there is the greater relative cheapness of transportation for long than for short distances.) Moreover, it is not alone the velocity of the movement through space, and the consequent reduction of distance in space, but also in time, which is brought about by the development of the means of transportation. It is not only the quantity of means of communication which is developed, so that, for instance, many vessels sail simultaneously for the same port, or several trains travel simultaneously on different railways between the same two points, but freight vessels may, for instance, clear on different successive days of the week from Liverpool for New York, or freight trains may start at different times of the day from Manchester to London. It is true, that the absolute velocity, or this part of the time of circulation, is not modified by this latter circumstance, a certain definite capacity of the means of transportation being given. But successive quantities of commodities can start on their passage in shorter succession of time and thus reach the market one after another without accumulating as potential commodity-capital in large quantities before shipping. Hence the return movement likewise is distributed over shorter successions of time, so that a part is continually transformed into money-capital, while another circulates as commodity-capital. By means of this distribution of the return movement over several successive periods the total time of circulation is abbreviated and thereby also the turn-over. On one hand, the greater or lesser frequency of the function of means of transportation, for instance the number of railroad trains, develops first to the extent that a place of production produces more and becomes a greater centre of production, and this development tends in the direction of the existing market, that is to say, toward the great centres of production and population, export places, etc. But on the other hand this special facilitation of traffic and the consequent acceleration of the turn-over of capital (to the extent that it is conditioned on the time of circulation) give rise to a hastened concentration of the centre of production and of its market. Along with this hastened concentration of masses of men and capital, the concentration of these masses of capital in a few hands likewise progresses. Simultaneously there is a movement, which shifts and displaces the centre of commercial gravity as a result of changes in the relative location of centres of production and markets caused by transformations in the means of communication. A place of production which once had a special advantage by its favoured location on some highway or canal then finds itself set aside on a single side-track, which runs trains only at relatively long intervals, while another place, which formerly lay removed from the main roads of traffic, then finds itself located at the crossing point of several rail-roads. This second point is built up, the former goes down. A transformation in the means of transportation thus causes a local difference in the time of circulation of commodities, the opportunity to buy, to sell, etc., or an already existing local differentiation is distributed differently. The significance of this circumstance for the turn-over of capital is shown in the disputes of the commercial and industrial representatives of the various places with the railroad managers. (See, for instance, the above quoted Blue Book of the Railway Committee.)

All branches of production which are dependent on local consumption by the nature of their product, such as breweries, are therefore developed to greatest dimensions in the main centres of population. The more rapid turn-over of capital compensates in this case for the eventual increase in the price of some elements of production, such as building lots, etc.

While on one hand, the development of the means of transportation and communication by the progress of capitalist production reduces the time of circulation for a given quantity of commodities, the same progress, on the other hand, coupled to the growing possibility of reaching more distant markets to the extent that the means of transportation and communication are improved, leads to the necessity of producing for ever more remote markets; in one word, for the world market. The mass of commodities in transit for distant places grows enormously, and with it also grows absolutely and relatively that part of social capital which remains constantly for longer periods in the stage of commodity-capital, within the time of circulation. Simultaneously that portion of social wealth increases, which, instead of serving as direct means of production, is invested in the fixed and circulating capital required for operating the means of transportation and communication.

The mere relative length of the transit of the commodities from their place of production to their market causes a difference, not only in the first part of the time of circulation, the selling time, but also in its second part, the reconversion of money into the elements of productive capital, the buying time. For instance, some commodities are shipped to India. This requires, say, four months. Let us assume that the selling time is equal to zero, that is to say, the commodities are made to order and are paid for on delivery to the agent of the producer. The return of the money (no matter what may be its form) requires again four months. Thus it takes eight months, before the same capital can again serve as productive capital and renew the same operations. The differences in the turn-over thus caused are one of the material bases of the various terms of credit. Trans-oceanic commerce in general, for instance in Venice and Genoa, is one of the sources of the credit system – strictly so called. The *London Economist* of July 16, 1866, wrote that the crisis of 1847 enabled the banking and trading business of that time to reduce the Indian and Chinese usage (for the running time of checks between those countries and Europe) from ten months after sight to six months, and the lapse of twenty years with its acceleration of the trip and the institution of telegraphs renders necessary a further reduction from six months after sight to four months after date as a preliminary step toward four months after sight. The trip of a sailing vessel from Calcutta around the cape to London lasts on an average less than 90 days. A usage of four months after sight would be equivalent to a running time of 150 days, approximately. The present usage of six months after sight is equivalent to a running time of 210 days. On the other hand, we read in the issue of June 30, 1866, of the same paper, that the Brazilian usage is still fixed at two and three months after sight, cheques of Antwerp on London are drawn for three months after date, and even Manchester and Bradford draw on London for three months and longer dates. By a tacit understanding, the merchant is thus given sufficient opportunity to realise on his goods by the time the cheques are due, if not before. For this reason, the usage of Indian cheques is not excessive. Indian products, which are sold in London generally on three months' time, cannot be realised upon in much less than five months, if some time for the sale is allowed, while another five months pass on an average between the purchase in India and the delivery to an English ware-house. Here we have a period of ten months, while the cheques drawn against the goods do not run above seven months. And again, on July 7, 1866, we read that, on July 2, 1866, five great London banks, dealing especially with India and China, and the Paris Comp-toir d'Escompte, gave notice that, beginning with January 1, 1867, their branch banks and agencies in the Orient would buy and sell only such cheques as were not drawn for more than four months after sight. However, this reduction miscarried and had to be revoked. (Since then the Suez canal has revolutionised all this.)

It is a matter of course that with the longer time of circulation the risk of a change of prices in the selling market increases, since it increases the period in which changes of price may take place.

A difference in the time of circulation, partly individually between the various individual capitals of the same branch of business, partly between different branches of business according to different usages, when payment is not made in spot cash, arises from the different dates of payment in buying and selling. We do not linger for the present over this point, which is important for the credit business.

Other differences in the period of turn-over arise from the size of contracts for the delivery of goods, and their size grows with the extent and scale of capitalist production. Such a contract, being a transaction between buyer and seller, is an operation belonging to the market, the sphere of circulation. The differences in the time of turn-over arising from it have their source for this reason in the sphere of circulation, but react immediately on the sphere of production, apart from all dates of payment and conditions of credit including cash payment. For instance, coal, cotton, yarn, etc., are discontinuous products. Every day supplies its quantity of finished product. But if the spinner or the mine owner accepts contracts for the delivery of large quantities, which require, say, a period of four or six weeks of successive working days, then this is the same, so far as the time of investment of advanced capital is concerned, as though a continuous working period of four or six weeks had been introduced in this labour-process. It is of course assumed in this case that the entire quantity ordered is to be delivered in one bulk, or at least is only paid after all of it has been delivered. Individually considered, every day had furnished its definite quantity of finished product. But this finished product is only a part of the quantity contracted for. Although the portion finished so far is no longer in the process of production, it is still in the warehouse as a potential capital.

Now let us take up the second epoch of the time of circulation, the buying time, or that epoch in which capital is converted from money back into the elements of productive capital. During this epoch, it must remain for a shorter or longer time in its condition of money-capital, so that a certain portion of the total capital advanced is all the time in the form of money-capital, although this portion consists of continually changing elements. For instance, of the total capital advanced in a certain business, n times 100 pounds sterling must be available in the form of money-capital, so that, while all the constituent parts of these n times 100 pounds sterling are continually converted into productive capital, this sum is nevertheless just as continually supplemented by new additions from the circulation, out of the realised commodity-capital. A definite part of the value of the advanced capital is, therefore, continually in the condition of money-capital, a form not belonging to its sphere of production, but to its sphere of circulation.

We have already seen that the prolongation of time caused by the distance of the market, by which capital is fettered in the form of commodity-capital, directly retards the return movement of the money and, consequently, the transformation of capital from its money into its productive form.

We have furthermore seen (Chapter 6) with reference to the purchase of commodities, that the time of buying, the greater or smaller distance from the main sources of the raw material, makes it necessary to purchase raw material for a longer period and keep it on hand in the form of a productive supply, of latent or potential productive capital; in other words, that it increases the quantity of capital to be advanced at one time, and the time for which it must be advanced, the scale of production remaining otherwise the same.

A similar effect is produced in various businesses by the longer or shorter periods, in which large quantities of raw material are thrown on the market. In London, for instance, great auction sales of wool take place every three months, and the wool market is controlled by them. The cotton market, on the other hand, is on the whole restocked continuously, if not uniformly, from harvest to harvest. Such periods determine the principal dates of buying for these raw materials and affect especially the speculative purchases requiring longer or shorter advances of these elements of production, just as the nature of the produced commodities exerts an influence on the premeditated speculative retention of the product for a longer or shorter term in the form of potential commodity-capital. 'The farmer must also be to a certain extent a speculator, and, therefore, hold back the sale of his products according to prevailing conditions . . . ' Here follow a few general rules. ' . . . However, in the sale of the products, success depends mainly on the personality, the product itself, and the locality. A man with sufficient business capital, won by ability and good luck (!), will not be blamed, if he keeps his grain crop stored for a year when prices happen to be unusually low. On the other hand, a man who lacks business capital, or enterprise in general (!), will try to get the average prices and be compelled to sell as soon and as often as opportunity presents itself. It will almost always bring losses to keep wool stored longer than a year, while grain and rape seed may be stored for several years without injury to their condition and quality. Such products as are generally subject to a large rise and fall in short intervals, for instance, rape seed, hops, teasel, etc., may be to good advantage stored during the years in which the market price is far below the price of production. It is least permissible to postpone the sale of such articles as require daily expenses for their preservation, such as fatted cattle, or which spoil easily, such as fruit, potatoes, etc. In some localities, a certain product has its lowest average price at a certain season, its highest at another. For instance, the average price of grain in some localities is lower about August than in the time between Christmas and Easter. Furthermore, some products sell well in certain localities only at certain periods, as is the case, for instance, with wool in the wool markets of those localities, where the wool trade is dull at other times, etc.' (Kirchhof, page 302.)

In the study of the second half of the time of circulation, in which money is reconverted into the elements of productive capital, it is not only this conversion itself which is important in itself, not only the time in which the money flows back according to the distance of the market on which the product is sold. It is also above all the volume of that part of the advanced capital to be held always available in the form of money, in the condition of money-capital, which must be considered.

Making exception of all speculation, the volume of the purchases of those commodities which must always be available as a productive supply depends on the time of the renewal of this supply, in other words, on circumstances which in their turn depend on market conditions and which are, therefore, different for different raw materials. In these cases, money must be advanced from time to time in larger quantities in one sum. It flows back more or less rapidly, but always in instalments, according to the turn-over of capital. One portion, namely that invested in wages, is continually re-expended in short intervals. But another part, namely that which is to be reconverted into raw material, etc., must be accumulated for long periods, as a reserve fund to be used either for buying or paying. Therefore it exists in the form of money-capital, although the volume which it has as such changes.

We shall see in the next chapter that other circumstances, whether they arise from the process of production or circulation, necessitate this existence of a certain portion of the advanced capital in the form of money. In general it must be noted that economists are very prone to forget that a part of the capital required for business not only passes alternately through the three stages of money-capital, productive capital, and commodity-capital, but that different portions of it have continuously and simultaneously these forms, although the relative size of these portions varies all the time. It is especially the portion always available as money-capital which is forgotten by economists, although this circumstance is very important for the understanding of capitalist economy and makes its importance felt in practice.

Chapter 15

Influence of the Time of Circulation on the Magnitude of an Advance of Capital

In this chapter and in the next we shall treat of the influence of the time of circulation on the utilisation of capital.

Take the commodity-capital which is the product of a certain working period, for instance, of nine weeks. Let us leave aside the question of that portion of value which is transferred to the product by the average wear and tear of the fixed capital, also that of the surplus-value added to it during the process of production. The value of this product is then equal to that of the circulating capital advanced for its production, that is to say, of the wages, raw and auxiliary materials consumed in its production. Let this value be 900 pounds sterling, so that the weekly outlay is 100 pounds sterling. The periodic time of production, which here coincides with the working time, is nine weeks. It is immaterial whether it is assumed that this working period produces a continuous product, or whether it is a continuous working period for a discontinuous product, so long as the quantity of discontinuous product, which is brought to market at one time, costs nine weeks of labour. Let the time of circulation be three weeks. Then the entire time of turn-over is twelve weeks. At the end of nine weeks, the advanced productive capital is converted into a commodity-capital, but now it exists for three weeks in the period of circulation. The new time of production, therefore, cannot commence until the beginning of the thirteenth week, and production would be at a standstill for three weeks, or for a quarter of the entire period of turn-over. It is again immaterial whether it is assumed that it takes so long on an average to sell the product, or that this term is conditioned on the distance of the market or on the terms of payment for the sold goods. Production would be at a standstill for three weeks every three months, or four times three, or twelve weeks, in a year, which means three months or one quarter of the annual period of turn-over. Hence, if production is to be continuous and to be carried along on the same scale week after week, there are only two possibilities.

Either the scale of production must be reduced, so that those 900 pounds sterling will suffice to keep the work going during the working period as well as during the time of circulation of the first turn-over. A second working period is then commenced with the tenth week, hence also a new period of turn-over, before the first period of turn-over is completed, for the period of turn-over is twelve weeks, the working period nine weeks. A sum of 900 pounds sterling distributed over twelve weeks makes 75 pounds per week. It is evident in the first place that such a reduced scale of business presupposes changed dimensions of the fixed capital, and therefore a general reduction of the entire business. In the second place, it is questionable whether such a reduction can take place at all, for the development of production in the various businesses establishes a normal minimum for the investment of capital, below which an individual business is unable to sustain competition. This normal minimum grows continually with the advance of capitalist production, hence it is not a fixed magnitude. There are numerous gradations between the existing normal minimum and the ever increasing normal maximum, and this intermediate gradation permits of many different degrees of capital investment. Within the limits of this intermediate scale, a reduction may take place, its lowest limit being the normal minimum.

In case of an obstruction of production, an overstocking of the markets, an increase in the price of raw materials, etc., there is a reduction of the normal outlay of circulating capital, compared to a given scale of fixed capital, by the reduction of the working time, work being carried on, say, for only half a day. On the other hand, in times of prosperity, the fixed capital remaining the same, there is an abnormal expansion of the circulating capital, partly by the prolongation of the working time, partly by its intensification. In businesses which are adjusted from the outset to such fluctuations, recourse is either taken to the above-named measures, or a greater number of labourers are simultaneously employed, combined with an investment of reserve capital, such as reserve locomotives of railroads, etc. However, such abnormal fluctuations are not considered here, where we assume normal conditions.

In order to make production continuous, it is necessary, in the present case, to distribute the expenditure of the same circulating capital over a longer period, over twelve weeks instead of nine. In any section of time, a reduced productive capital is therefore employed. The circulating portion of the productive capital is reduced from 100 to 75, or one quarter. The total amount by which the productive capital serving for a working period of nine weeks is reduced is 9 times 25, or 225 pounds sterling, or one quarter of 900 pounds. But the proportion of the time of circulation to that of turn-over is likewise three twelfth, or one quarter. It follows, therefore: If production is not to be interrupted during the time of circulation of the productive capital transformed into commodity-capital, if it is rather to be continued parallel with circulation and continuously week after week, and if no special circulating capital is available, it can be done only by curtailing the productive operations, reducing the circulating portions of the productive capital in service. The portion of circulating capital thus set free for production during the time of circulation is proportioned to the total circulating capital invested as the time of circulation is to the time of turn-over. We repeat, that this applies only to branches of production in which the labour-process is continued on the same scale week after week, in other words, where no different amounts of capital are invested at different working periods as is done, for instance in agriculture.

If, on the other hand, we assume that the nature of the business excludes the idea of a reduction of the scale of production and thus of the circulating capital to be invested weekly, then the continuity of production can be secured only by additional circulating capital, in the above-named case of 300 pounds sterling. During the period of turn-over of twelve weeks, 1,200 pounds sterling are successively invested in twelve weeks, and 300 is one quarter of this sum as three weeks is of twelve. At the end of the working time of nine weeks, the capital-value of 900 pounds sterling has been converted from the form of productive into that of commodity-capital. Its working period is concluded, but it cannot be re-opened with the same capital. During

the three weeks in which it exists in the sphere of circulation, performing the functions of commodity-capital, it is in a condition, so far
as the process of production is concerned, as though it did not exist
at all. We make exception, at present, of all conditions of credit, and
assume that the capitalist operates only with his own money. But while
the capital advanced for the first working period, having completed
its process of production, remains for three weeks in the process of
circulation, an additional capital of 300 pounds sterling enters into
service, so that the continuity of the production is not interrupted.

Now, the following must be noted in this connection:

First: the working period of the capital first invested, of 900 pounds
sterling, is completed at the close of nine weeks, and it does not flow
back until after three weeks, that is to say, in the beginning of the
thirteenth week. But a new working period is immediately begun
with the additional capital of 300 pounds. By this means the continuity of production is secured.

Secondly: the functions of the original capital of 900 pounds sterling, and those of the additional capital of 300 pounds sterling added
at the close of the first working period of nine weeks, inaugurating the
second working period after the conclusion of the first, without any
interruption, are clearly distinguished in the first period of turn-over,
or at least they may be, while they cross one another in the course of
the second period of turn-over.

Let us give this matter a tangible form.

First period of turn-over of 12 weeks. first working period of 9 weeks;
the turn-over of the capital advanced for this is completed at the
beginning of the 13th week. During the last 3 weeks, the additional
capital of 300 pounds sterling performs its service, opening up the
second working period of 9 weeks.

Second period of turn-over. At the beginning of the 13th week, 900
pounds sterling have flown back and are able to begin a new turn-
over. But the second working period has already been opened by the
additional 300 pounds in the 10th week. At the commencement of
the 13th week, this capital has already completed one third of its
working period and 300 pounds sterling have been converted from
a productive capital into a product. Seeing that only 6 weeks are
required for the completion of the second working period, only two-
thirds of the returned capital of 900 pounds sterling, or 600 pounds,
can take part in the productive process of the second working period.
Thus 300 pounds of the original 900 are set free and may play the same
role, which the additional capital of 300 pounds played in the first
working period. At the close of the 6th week of the second period of
turn-over, the second working period is completed. The capital of 900

pounds sterling advanced in it flows back after 3 weeks, or at the end of the 9th week of the second period of turn-over which comprises 12 weeks. During the 3 weeks of its period of circulation, the free capital of 300 pounds sterling comes into action. This begins the third working period of a capital of 900 pounds sterling in the 7th week of the second period of turn-over, which is the 19th running week.

Third period of turn-over. At the close of the 9th week of the second period of turn-over, there is a new reflux of 900 pounds sterling. But the third working period has already commenced in the 7th week of the second period of turnover, and at the beginning of the third period of turnover, 6 weeks of the third working period have already elapsed. The third working period, then, lasts only 3 weeks longer. Hence only 300 pounds of the returned 900 take part in the productive process of the second period of turnover, while the next 300 close the last three weeks of the third working period and thus open the first three weeks of the third period of turn-over. The fourth working period fills out the remaining 9 weeks of this period of turn-over, and thus the 37th running week begins simultaneously the fourth period of turn-over and the fifth working period.

In order to simplify this case for the calculation, we shall assume a working period of 5 weeks and a period of circulation of 5 weeks, making a period of turn-over of 10 weeks. Let the year be one of fifty working weeks, and the capital invested per week 100 pounds sterling. A working period then requires a circulating capital of 500 pounds sterling, and the period of turn-over an additional capital of 500 pounds sterling. The working periods and periods of turn-over then are as follows:

1. wrkg. prd.   1–5. week (£500 of goods) returned end of 10.
2. wrkg. prd.   6–10. week (£500 of goods) returned end of 15.
3. wrkg. prd. 11–15. week (£500 of goods) returned end of 20.
4. wrkg. prd. 16–20. week (£500 of goods) returned end of 25.
5. wrkg. prd. 21–25. week (£500 of goods) returned end of 30.
   etc.

If the time of circulation is zero, so that the period of turn-over is equal to the working time, then the number of turn-overs is equal to the working periods of the year. In the case of a working period of 5 weeks, this would make 10 periods of turn-over per year, and the value of the capital turned over would be 500 times 10, or 5,000. In our table, in which we have assumed a time of circulation of 5 weeks, the total value of the commodities produced per year would also be 5,000 pounds sterling, but one tenth of this, or 500 pounds, would always be in the form of commodity-capital, which would not flow back until after 5 weeks. At the end of the year, the product of the tenth working period (the 46th to the 50th working week) would have completed its period of turn-over only by half, because its time of circulation would fall within the first five weeks of the year.

Now let us take a third illustration. Working period 6 weeks, time of circulation 3 weeks, weekly advance of capital 100 pounds sterling.

1. Working period: 1–6th week. At the end of the 6th week, a commodity-capital of 600 pounds sterling, returned at the end of the 9th week.

2. Working period: 7–12th week. During the 7–9th week 300 pounds sterling of additional capital is advanced. At the end of the 9th week, return of 600 pounds sterling. Of this, 300 pounds sterling are advanced during the 10–12th week. At the end of the 12th week, therefore, 300 pounds sterling are available, and 600 pounds sterling are in the form of commodity-capital, returnable at the end of the 15th week.

3. Working period: 13–18th week. During the 13–15th week, advance of above 300 pounds sterling, then reflux of 600 pounds, 300 of which are advanced for the 16–18th week. At the end of the 18th week, 300 pounds sterling available in cash, 600 on hand as commodity-capital, which flows back at the end of the 21st week. (See the detailed illustration of this case under 2, farther along.)

In other words, during 9 working periods (54 weeks) a total of 600 times 9, or 5,400 pounds sterling is produced. At the end of the ninth working period, the capitalist has 300 pounds in cash and 600 pounds worth of commodities, which have not yet completed their time of circulation.

A comparison of these three illustrations shows first, that a successive release of Capital I of 500 pounds sterling and of additional Capital II of likewise 500 pounds sterling takes place only in the second illustration, so that these two portions of capital move independently of one another. But this is so only because we have made the exceptional assumption that the working time and the time of circulation are two equal halves of the period of turn-over. In all other cases, whatever may be the difference of the two terms of the period of turn-over, the movements of the two capitals cross one another, as they do in the first and third illustration, beginning with the second period of turn-over. The additional Capital II, with a portion of Capital I, then forms the capital serving in the second period of turn-over, while the remainder of Capital I is set free for the original function of Capital II. The capital serving during the time of circulation of the commodity-capital is not identical, in this case, with the Capital II originally advanced for this purpose, but it is of the same value and forms the same aliquot portion of the advanced total capital.

Secondly: the capital which served during the working period, lies fallow during the time of circulation. In the second illustration, the capital performs its function during 5 weeks of the working period, and lies fallow during a circulation period of 5 weeks. The entire time during which Capital I here lies fallow amounts to one-half of the year. During this time, the additional Capital II takes the place of Capital I, which in its turn lies fallow during the other half of the year. But the additional capital required for ensuring the continuity of the production during the time of circulation is not determined by the aggregate volume, or the sum, of the times of circulation during the year, but only by the proportion of the time of circulation to the time of turn-over. (We assume, of course, that all the turn-overs take place under the same conditions.) For this reason, 500 pounds sterling are required in the second illustration, not 2,500 pounds. This is simply due to the fact that the additional capital enters just as well into the turn-over as the capital originally advanced, and that it, therefore, reproduces its volume the same as the other by the number of its turn-overs.

Thirdly: it does not alter the circumstances here described, whether or not the time of production is longer than the working time. True, the aggregate of the periods of turn-over is prolonged thereby, but this prolongation does not imply any additional capital for the labour-process. The additional capital serves merely the purpose of filling up the fallow places left by the time of circulation. Its mission is simply to protect production against interruption by the time of circulation. Interruptions arising from the conditions of production itself are compensated for in another way, which we do not discuss at this point. There are, however, some businesses, in which work is carried on only in intervals and to order, so that there may be interruptions in the working periods. In such cases, the necessity of additional capital is eliminated to that extent. On the other hand, in most cases of season work, there is a limit for the time of reflux. The same work cannot be renewed next year with the same capital, if the time of circulation of this capital is not completed. Still, the time of circulation may be shorter than the intervals between two periods of production. In such an eventuality, capital lies fallow, unless it is employed otherwise in the meantime.

Fourthly: the capital advanced for a certain working period, for instance, the 600 pounds sterling in the third illustration, is invested partly in raw and auxiliary materials, in a productive supply for the working period, in constant circulating capital, partly in variable circulating capital, in the payment of labour itself. The portion invested in constant circulating capital may not exist for the same length of time in the form of a productive supply; the raw material, for instance, may not be on hand for the entire working period, coal may be purchased only every two weeks. However, credit being out of the question, according to our assumption, this portion of capital, to the extent that it is not available in the form of a productive supply, must be kept on hand in the form of money in order to be converted into a productive supply when needed. This does not alter the magnitude of the constant circulating capital-value advanced for 6 weeks. The wages, on the other hand, are generally paid weekly, making exception of the money supply for unforeseen expenses, the strict reserve fund for the compensation of disturbances. Unless the capitalist, therefore, compels the labourer to advance his labour for a longer time, the money required for the payment of wages must be on hand. During the reflux of the capital, a portion must, therefore, be reserved in the form of money for the payment of labour, while the remaining portion may be converted into a productive supply.

The additional capital is subdivided exactly like the original. But it is distinguished from Capital I by the fact that (apart from conditions of credit), in order to be available for its own period of labour, it must be advanced during the entire duration of the first working period of Capital I, in which it does not take part. During this time, it may be converted into constant circulating capital, at least in part, being advanced for the entire period of turn-over. To what extent it will assume this form, or persist in the form of additional money-capital, up to the time where this conversion becomes necessary, will depend partly on the special conditions of production of definite lines of business, partly on the fluctuations in the prices of raw material, etc. Looking at it from the point of view of the aggregate social capital, there will always be a more or less considerable part of this additional capital for a rather long time in the form of money-capital. But as for that portion of Capital II which is to be advanced for wages, it is always gradually converted into labour-power to the extent that small working periods are closed and paid for. This portion of Capital II, then, is available in the form of money-capital for the entire working period, until it is converted into labour-power and thus takes part in the function of productive capital.

The advent of the additional capital required for the transformation of the time of circulation of Capital I into a time of production increases not only the magnitude of the advanced capital and length of time for which the aggregate capital must be necessarily advanced, but it also increases specifically that portion of the advanced capital which exists in the form of a money-supply, which persists in the condition of money-capital, and has the form of potential capital.

The same also takes place, as concerns both the advance in the form of a productive supply and in that of a money supply, when the separation of capital into two parts required by the time of circulation, namely, capital for the first working period and reserve capital for the time of circulation, is not caused by the increase of the invested capital, but by a decrease of the scale of production. In proportion to the scale of production, the increase of the capital tied up in the form of money is apt to grow still more in this case.

It is the continuous succession of the working periods, the continuous function of an equal portion of the advanced capital as productive capital, which is ensured by this separation of capital into an original productive and a reserve capital.

Let us look at the second illustration. The capital continuously employed in the process of production amounts to 500 pounds sterling. The working period being 5 weeks, it works ten times during a working year of 50 weeks. Hence its product, apart from surplus-value, is 10 times 500 or 5,000 pounds sterling. From the point of view of a directly and uninterruptedly working capital in the process of production, a capital-value of 500 pounds sterling, the time of circulation seems entirely eliminated. The period of turn-over coincides with the working period, the time of circulation being assumed as equal to zero.

But if the capital of 500 pounds sterling were interrupted in its productive activity by regular times of circulation covering 5 weeks, so that it could not become productively active until after the close of the entire period of turn-over of 10 weeks, we should have 5 turn-overs of ten weeks each in 50 running weeks. These would comprise 5 periods of production of 5 weeks each, or 25 productive weeks with a total product of 5 times 500, or 2,500 pounds sterling; and 5 times of circulation of 5 weeks each, or a total period of circulation of 25 weeks. If we say in this case that the capital of 500 pounds sterling has been turned over 5 times in the year, it is evident and obvious that this capital of 500 pounds sterling did not serve at all as a productive capital during one-half of each period of turn-over, and that, taking all in all, it performed its function only during one half of the year, while it did not serve at all during the other half.

In our illustration, the reserve capital of 500 pounds sterling comes to the rescue during those five periods of circulation, and the turn-over is thus expanded from 2,500 to 5,000 pounds. But now the advanced capital is 1,000 instead of 500 pounds sterling. Hence there are only five turn-overs instead of ten. This is indeed the way in which people count. But when it is said that the capital of 1,000 pounds has been turned over five times in the year, the recollection of the time of circulation disappears in the hollow skulls of the capitalists, and a confused idea is formed that this capital has served continuously in the process of production during the successive five turn-overs. As a matter of fact, if we say that the capital of 1,000 pounds has been turned over five times in a year, we include both the time of circulation and the time of production. For, indeed, if 1,000 pounds sterling had actually been continuously active in the process of production, the product would have to be 10,000 pounds sterling instead of 5,000, according to our assumptions. But in order to have 1,000 pounds sterling continuously in the process of production, 2,000 pounds would have to be advanced. The economists, who as a general rule have nothing clear to say in reference to the mechanism of the turn-over, always overlook this main point, to wit, that only a part of the industrial capital can actually be engaged in the process of production, if production is to proceed uninterruptedly. While one part is busy in the process of production, another must always be engaged in the process of circulation. Or in other words, one part can perform the functions of productive capital only on condition that another part is withdrawn from production in the form of commodity or money-capital. In overlooking this, the significance and role of money-capital is entirely ignored.

We have now to ascertain to what extent differences in the turn-over are caused according to whether the two sections of the period of turn-over, the working period and the circulating period, are equal to one another, or the working period greater or smaller than the circulating period, and furthermore, what effect this has on the retention of capital in the form of money-capital.

We assume, that the capital advanced weekly is in all cases 100 pounds sterling, and the period of turn-over 9 weeks, so that the capital invested in each period of turn-over is 900 pounds sterling.

Section 1. The Working Period Equal to the Period of Circulation.

Although this case occurs in reality only accidentally, as an exception, it must serve as our point of departure in this analysis, because conditions here shape themselves in the simplest and most intelligible way.

The two capitals (Capital I advanced for the first working period, and reserve Capital II advanced during the time of circulation of Capital I) relieve one another in their movements without crossing. With the exception of the first period, either of the two capitals is therefore advanced only for its own period of turn-over. Let the period of turn-over be 9 weeks, as indicated in the two following illustrations, so that the working period and the time of circulation are each of them 4 1/2 weeks. Then we have the following annual diagram:

Table 1

Capital I

Periods of Turn-Over	Working Periods	Advance	Periods of Circulation
I. 1–9. week	1–4. 5. week	£450	4. 5–9 week
II. 10–18 week	10–13. 5. week	£450	13. 5–18. week
III. 19–27 week	19–22. 5. week	£450	22. 5–27. week
IV. 28–36 week	28–31. 5. week	£450	31. 5–36. week
V. 37–45 week	37–40. 5. week	£450	40. 5–45. week
VI. 46–(54) week	46–49. 5. week	£450	49. 5–(54 week)[1]

Capital II

Periods of Turn-Over	Working Periods	Advance	Periods of Circulation
I. 4. 5–13. 5. week	4. 5–9. week	£450	10–13. 5. week
II. 13. 5–22. 5. week	13. 5–18. week	£450	19–22. 5. week
III. 22. 5–31. 5. week	22. 5–27. week	£450	28–31. 5. week
IV. 31. 5–40. 5. week	31. 5–36. week	£450	37–40. 5. week
V. 40. 5–49. 5. week	40. 5–45. week	£450	46–49. 5. week
VI. 49. 5– (58. 5.) week	49. 5–(54.) week	£450	(54–58. 5. week)

Within the 50 weeks which we here assume to stand for one year, Capital I has absolved six full working periods, making 6 times 450, or 2,700 pounds sterling, and Capital II making in five full working periods 5 times 450, or 2,250 pounds sterling's worth of commodities. In addition thereto, Capital II has produced, within the last one and a half weeks of the year (middle of the 50th to the end of the 51st week) an extra 150 pounds sterling's worth, making the aggregate product 5,100 pounds sterling. So far as the direct production of surplus-value is concerned, which is produced only during the working period, the aggregate capital of 900 pounds sterling would have been turned over 5 2/3 times (5 2/3 times 900 equal to 5,100 pounds sterling). But if we consider the actual turn-over, then Capital I has been turned over 5 2/3 times, since at the close of the 51st week it still has to absolve 3 weeks of its sixth period of turn-over; 5 2/3 times 450 make 2,550 pounds sterling; and Capital II turned over 5 1/6 times, since it has completed only 1 1/2 weeks of its sixth period of turn-over, so that 7 1/2 weeks of it fall within the next year; 5 1/6 times 450 make 2,325 pounds sterling; actual aggregate turn-over 4,875 pounds sterling.

Let us regard Capital I and Capital II as two capitals independent of one another. They are independent in their movements; these movements supplement one another merely because their working and circulating periods directly relieve one another. They may be regarded as two entirely independent capitals belonging to different capitalists.

Capital I has completed five full turn-overs and two-thirds of its sixth period of turn-over. At the end of the year it has the form of commodity-capital, which lacks three weeks of its normal realisation. During this time, it cannot take part in the process of production. It performs the function of commodity-capital, it circulates. It has completed only two-thirds of its last period of turn-over. This is expressed in the words: It has been turned over only two-thirds, only two-thirds of its total value have completed their turn-over. We say that 450 pounds sterling complete their turn-over in 9 weeks, hence 300 do in 6 weeks. But in this expression, the organic conditions of the two specifically different portions of the period of turn-over are neglected. The exact meaning of the expression, that the advanced capital of 450 pounds sterling has made 5 2/3 turn-overs, is merely that it has completed five turn-overs fully and of the sixth only two-thirds. On the other hand, the expression that the turned-over capital is equal to 5 2/3 of the advanced capital, or, in the above case, 5 2/3 times 450 pounds sterling, making 2,550, is correct only in so far as it means that unless this capital of 450 pounds sterling were supplemented by another capital of 450 pounds sterling, one portion of it would have to be in the process of circulation while another is in the process of production. If the period of turn-over is to be expressed in the quantity of the turned-over capital, it can be expressed only in a quantity of existing values (embodied in the finished product). The fact that the advanced capital is not in a condition in which it may reopen the process of production is due to the circumstance that only a part of it is in a condition suitable for production, or that, in order to be in a condition suitable for continuous production, it would have to be divided into a portion which would be continually in the period of production and into another which would be continually in the period of circulation, according to the mutual relation of these periods. It is the same law which determines the quantity of the continually serving productive capital by the proportion of the time of circulation to the period of turn-over.

As for Capital II, 150 pounds sterling of it are advanced in the production of unfinished goods at the close of the 51st running week, which we regard here as the last of the year. Another part exists in the form of circulating constant capital – raw materials, etc. – that is to say, in a form in which it can serve as productive capital in the process of production. But a third part of it exists in the form of money, namely at least the amount of the wages for the remainder of the working period (3 weeks), which is not paid, however, until the end of each week. Now, although this portion of capital, in the beginning of a new year, and of a new cycle of turn-over, is not in the condition of productive capital, but in that of money-capital, in which it cannot take part in the process of production, there is, nevertheless, circulating variable capital, namely labour-power, active in the process of production at the opening of the new cycle of turn-over. This is due to the fact that labour-power is not paid until at the end of the week, although it was bought at the beginning of the working period, say, per week, and so consumed. Money serves here as a means of payment. For this reason, it is still in the hands of the capitalist, while on the other hand labour-power is already busy in the process of production. so that the same capital-value here appears twice.

If we look merely at the working periods, then there has been produced:

By Capital I, 5 2/3 times 450, or 2,550 pounds sterling,
By Capital II, 5 1/3 times 450, or 2,400 pounds sterling,
Total, 5 2/3 times 900, or 5,100 pounds sterling.

Hence the advanced capital of 900 pounds sterling has performed the function of productive capital 5 2/3 times per year. It is immaterial for the production of surplus-value, whether there are always 450 pounds sterling in the process of production and always 450 pounds sterling in the process of circulation, or whether 900 pounds sterling serve 4 1/2 weeks in the process of production and 4 1/2 weeks in the process of circulation.

On the other hand, if we consider the periods of turn-over, there has been produced:

By Capital I, 5 2/3 times 450, or 2,550 pounds sterling,
By Capital II, 5 1/6 times 450, or 2,325 pounds sterling,

Or, by the aggregate capital, 5 5/12 times 900, or 4,875 pounds sterling, in the total turn-over. For the turn-over of the total capital is equal to the sum of the quantities turned over by Capital I and II, divided by the sum of I and II.

It is to be noted, that Capital I and II, if they were independent of one another, would nevertheless be merely different independent portions of the social capital advanced for the same sphere of production. Hence, if the social capital within this sphere of production were solely composed of I and II, the same calculation would apply to the turn-over of the social capital, which here applies to the two constituent parts I and II, of the same private capital. In a wider generalisation, every portion of the entire social capital invested in any special sphere of production may be so calculated. But in the last analysis, the amount of the turn-over of the entire social capital is equal to the sum of the capitals turned over in the various spheres of production, divided by the sum of the capitals advanced in those spheres.

It must be further noted that just as the capitals I and II in the same private business have, strictly speaking, different years of turn-over (the cycle of turn-over of Capital II beginning 4 1–2 weeks later than that of Capital I, so that the year of Capital I closes 4 1–2 weeks earlier than that of Capital II), just so the various private capitals in the same sphere of production begin their activities at totally different sections of time and, therefore, conclude their years of turn-over at different times of the year. The same calculation of averages, which we employed above for capitals I and II, suffices also for the reduction of the years of turn-over of the various independent portions of the social capital to one uniform year of turn-over.

Section 2. The Working Period Greater Than the Period of Circulation.

The working and circulating periods of capitals I and II cross one another instead of relieving one another. Simultaneously some capital is set free. This was not so in the previously considered case.

But this does not alter the fact that, as before, (1) the number of working periods of the advanced total capital is equal to the sum of the values of the annual products of both advanced portions of capital divided by the advanced total capital, and (2) the amount turned over by the total capital is equal to the sum of the two amounts turned over, divided by the sum of the two advanced capitals. Here, again, we must regard both portions of capital as though they performed movements of turn-over entirely independent of one another.

* * *

We assume once more, then, that 100 pounds sterling are advanced weekly in the working process. Let the working period last 6 weeks, requiring every time an advance of 600 pounds sterling (Capital I). Let the time of circulation be 3 weeks, so that the period of turn-over is 9 weeks, as before. Let a capital of 300 pounds sterling step in as a substitute during the three weeks of the time of circulation of Capital I. Considering both capitals as independent of one another, we find the diagram of the annual turn-over to be as follows.

Table 2

Capital I. £600

Periods of Turn-Over	Working Periods	Advance	Periods of Circulation
I. 1–9. week	1–6. week	£600	7–9 week
II. 10–18. week	10–15. week	£600	16–18. week
III. 19–27. week	19–24. week	£600	25–27. week
IV. 28–36. week	28–33. week	£600	34–36. week
V. 37–45. week	37–42. week	£600	43–45. week
VI. 46–(54) week	46–51. week	£600	(52–54 week)

Additional Capital II. £300

Periods of Turn-Over	Working Periods	Advance	Periods of Circulation
I. 7–15. week	7–9. week	£300	10–15. week
II. 16–24. week	16–18. week	£300	19–24. week
III. 25–33. week	25–27. week	£300	28–33. week
IV. 34–42. week	34–36. week	£300	37–42. week
V. 43–51. week	42–45. week	£300	46–51. week

The process of production continues uninterruptedly all year on the same scale. The two capitals I and II remain entirely separate. But in order to represent them thus as separate, we had to tear apart their actual interrelations and intersections, and thus also to change the amount of turnover. For according to the above diagram, the amounts turned over would be:

Capital I, 5 2/3 times 600   or £3,400
Capital II, 5 times 300   or £1,500
Total capital, 5 4/9 times 900   or £4,900

But this is not correct, for we shall see that the actual periods of production and circulation do not absolutely coincide with the above diagrams, in which it was mainly a question of presenting capitals I and II as independent of one another.

Now, in reality, Capital II has no working and circulating periods separate and distinct from Capital I. The working period is 6 weeks, the circulation period 3 weeks. Since Capital II amounts to only 300 pounds sterling, it can fill out only a part of the working period. This is indeed the case. At the close of the 6th week, a product valued at 600 pounds sterling passes into circulation and flows back in money at the close of the 9th week. Then Capital II begins its activity at the opening of the 7th week and responds to the requirements of the next working period for the 7th to 9th week. But according to our assumption, the working period is only half completed at the end of the 9th week. Hence, in the beginning of the 10th week, Capital I of 600 pounds sterling, having just returned, comes once more into activity and advances 300 pounds sterling for the requirements of the 10th to 12th week. This completes the second working period.

Products valued at 600 pounds sterling are once again in circulation and will return in money at the close of the 15th week. Furthermore, 300 pounds sterling are set free, equal to the original amount of Capital II, and are enabled to serve in the first half of the following working period, that is to say, in the 13th to 15th week. After the lapse of these, the 600 pounds sterling flow back; 300 of them suffice for the remainder of the working period, 300 are set free for the following working period.

The course of events is, therefore, as follows:

I. Period of turn-over 1–9. week.
   1. Working period: 1–6. week. Capital I, of £600, performs its function.
   1. Period of circulation: 7–9. week. After the lapse of the 9th week, £600 flow back in money.
II. Period of turn-over: 7–15 week.
   2. Working period: 7–12. week.
     First half: 7–9. week. Capital II, of £300, performs its function. After the lapse of the 9th week, £600 (Capital I) flow back in money. Second half: 10–12. week. £300 of Capital I perform their function. The other £300 of Capital I remain free.
   2. Period of circulation: 13–15. week.
     After the close of the 15. week, £600 (one half belonging to Capital I, the other to Capital II) flow back in money.
III. Period of turn-over: 13–21. week.
   3. Working period: 13–18. week.
     First half: 13–15. week. The free £300 perform their function. After the close of the 15th week, £600 flow back in money. Second half: 16–18. week, 300 of the returned 600 perform their function, the other 300 again remain free.
   3. Period of circulation: 19–21. week. After the close of the 21st week, £600 flow back in money. In this amount of £600, Capital I and II are amalgamated and indistinguishable.

In this way, there are eight full periods of turn-over of a capital of £600 (i: 1–9. week; ii: 7–15. week; iii: 13–21; iv: 19–27; v: 25–33; vi: 31–39; vii: 37–45; viii: 43–51) to the end of the 51st week. But as the 49–51st weeks fall within the eighth period of circulation, the £300 of free capital must step in and keep production moving. Thus the turn-over at the end of the year is as follows: £600 have completed their cycle eight times, making £4,800. In addition thereto we have the product of the last 3 weeks (49–51.), which, however, has completed but one third of its cycle of 9 weeks, so that it counts in the amount turned over only with one third of its value, £100. If, then, the annual product of 51 weeks is £5,100, the capital actually turned over is only 4,800 plus 100, or £4,900. The advanced total capital of £900 has, therefore, been turned over 5 4/9 times, somewhat more than in the first case.

In the present example, we had assumed a case, in which the working time was 2/3, the circulation time 1/3, of the period of turn-over, so that the working time was a simple multiple of the circulation time. The question is now, whether capital is likewise set free, in the same way as shown before, when this assumption is not made.

Let us assume a working time of 5 weeks, a circulation time of 4 weeks, and a capital advance of £100 per week.

    I. Period of turn-over: 1–9. week.
       1. Working period: 1–5. week. Capital I, of £500, performs its
         function.
       1. Circulation period: 6–9. week. After the close of the 9th week,
         £500 flow back in money.
    II. Period of turn-over: 6–14. week.
       2. Working period: 6–10. week.
         First section: 6–9. week. Capital II, of £400, performs its
         function. After the close of the 9th week, Capital I, of £500,
         flows back in money.
         Second section: 10. week. 100 of the returned £500 perform
         their function. The remaining £400 are set free for the foll-
         owing working period.
       2. Circulation period: 11–14. week.
         After the close of the 14. week, £500 flow back in money.

Up to the end of the 14th week (11–14.), the free £400 perform their function; 400 of the £500 then returned fill the requirements of the third working period (11–15. week), so that £400 are once more set free for the fourth working period. The same phenomenon is repeated in every working period; in its beginning, £400 are ready at hand, sufficing for the requirements of the first 4 weeks. After the close of the 4th week, £500 flow back in money, only 100 of which are needed for the last week, while the remaining 400 are set free for the next working period.

Let us furthermore assume a working period of 7 weeks, with a Capital I of £700; a circulation period of 2 weeks, with a Capital II of £200.

In that case, the first period of turn-over lasts from the 1st to the 9th week; its first working period from the 1st to the 7th week, with an advance of £700, its first circulation period from the 8th to the 9th week. After the close of the 9th week, £700 flow back in money.

The second period of turn-over, from the 8th to the 16th week, contains the second working period of the 8th to 14th week. The requirements of the 8th and 9th week of this period are covered by Capital II. After the close of the 9th week, the above £700 flow back. Up to the close of this working period (10–14.), £500 of this sum are used up. £200 remain free for the next working period. The second circulation period lasts from the 15th to the 16th week. After the close of the 16th week, £700 flow back once more. From now on, the same phenomenon is repeated in every working period. The demand in capital of the first two weeks is covered by the £200 set free at the close of the preceding working period; after the close of the second week, £700 flow back in money; but the working period lasts only 5 weeks longer, so that only £500 can be consumed; therefore, £200 always remain free for the next working period.

We find, then, that in this case, where the working period has been assumed greater than the circulation period, there is under all circumstances a money-capital set free at the close of each working period, and this money-capital is of the same magnitude as Capital II, which is advanced for the circulation time. In our three illustrations, Capital II was £300, in the first, £400, in the second, £200 in the third example. Corresponding thereto, the capital set free at the close of each working period was 300, 400, and £200.

Section 3. The Working Period Smaller Than the Circulation Period.

We begin by assuming once more a period of turn-over of 9 weeks. Let the working period be 3 weeks, with an available Capital I of £300. Let the circulation period be 6 weeks. For these 6 weeks, an additional capital of £600 is required. We may divide this in turn into two portions of £300 each, so that each portion meets the requirements of one working period. We have, then, three capitals of £300 each, 300 of which are always busy in production, while 600 are circulating.

Table 3

Capital I.

Periods of Turn-Over	Working Periods	Periods of Circulation
I. 1–9. week	1–3. week	4–9. week
II. 10–18. week	10–12. week	13–18. week
III. 19–27. week	19–21. week	22–27. week
IV. 28–36. week	28–30. week	31–36. week
V. 37–45. week	37–39. week	40–45. week
VI. 46–(54) week	46–48. week	49–(54 week)

Capital II.

Periods of Turn-Over	Working Periods	Periods of Circulation
I. 4–12. week	4–6. week	7–12. week
II. 13–21. week	13–15. week	12–21. week
III. 22–30. week	22–24. week	25–30. week
IV. 31–39. week	31–33. week	34–39. week
V. 40–48. week	40–42. week	43–48. week
VI. 49–(57) week	49–51. week	(52–57 week)

Capital III.

Periods of Turn-Over	Working Periods	Periods of Circulation
I. 7–15. week	7–9. week	10–15. week
II. 16–24. week	16–18. week	19–24. week
III. 25–33. week	25–27. week	28–33. week
IV. 34–42. week	34–36. week	37–42. week
V. 43–51. week	43–45. week	46–51. week

We have, here, the exact opposite of case I, only with the difference that now three capitals relieve one another instead of two. There is no intersection or intermingling of capitals. Each one of them can be traced separately to the end of the year. Capital is no more set free in this instance than in case one, at the close of a working period. Capital I is entirely consumed at the end of the 3rd week, flows back entirely at the end of 9th, and resumes its functions in the beginning of the 10th week. Similarly in the case of Capitals II and III. The regular and complete relief excludes any release of capital.

The total turn-over is calculated as follows:

Capital I, 300 times 5 2/3,	or £1,700
Capital II, 300 times 5 1/3,	or £1,600
Capital III, 300 times 5,	or £1,500
Total capital 900 times 5 1/3,	or £4,800

Let us now choose also an illustration, in which the circulation period is not an exact multiple of the working period. For instance, let the working period be 4 weeks, the circulation period 5 weeks. The corresponding amounts of capital would then be: Capital I, £400; Capital II, £400; Capital III, £100. We present only the first three turn-overs.

Table 4

Capital I.

Periods of Turn-Over	Working Periods	Periods of Circulation
I. 1–9. week	1–4. week	5–9. week
II. 9–17. week	9. 10–12. week	13–18. week
III. 17–25. week	17. 18–20. week	21–25. week

Capital II.

Periods of Turn-Over	Working Periods	Periods of Circulation
I. 5–18. week	5–8. week	5–9. week
II. 13–21. week	13. 14–16. week	17–21. week
III. 21–29. week	21. 22–29. week	25–29. week

Capital III.

Periods of Turn-Over	Working Periods	Periods of Circulation
I. 9–17. week	9. week	10–17. week
II. 17–25. week	17. week	17–21. week
III. 25–33. week	25. week	26–33. week

There is in this case an intermingling of capitals to the extent that the working period of Capital III, which has no independent working period, because it lasts only for one week, coincides with the first working period of Capital I. On the other hand, an amount of £100, equal to Capital III, is set free by Capital I and II at the close of the working period. For when Capital III fills out the first week of the second, and of all following working periods of Capital I, and the entire Capital I of £400 flows back at the close of this first week, then only 3 weeks and a corresponding capital of £300 remain for the rest of the working period of Capital I. The £100 thus set free suffice for the first week of the immediately following working period of Capital II; at the close of this week, the entire capital of £400 then flows back (Capital II). But since the new working period can absorb only £300 more, there are once more £100 disengaged at its close. And so forth. There is, then, a setting free of capital at the close of a working period, as soon as the circulation period is not a simple multiple of the working period. And this released capital is equal to that portion of capital which has to fill out the excess of the circulating period over the working period, or over a multiple of working periods.

In all cases investigated by us it was assumed that both the working period and the circulation period remain the same throughout the year in any of the businesses selected. This assumption was necessary, if we wished to ascertain the influence of the time of circulation on the turn-over and advance of capital. It does not alter the matter, that this assumption is not borne out unconditionally in reality, and that it frequently does not apply at all.

In this entire section, we have discussed only the turn-overs of the circulating capital, not those of the fixed. The reason is that this question has nothing to do with the fixed capital. The means of production employed in the process of production form fixed capital only to the extent that their time of employment exceeds the period of turn-over of circulating capital, so long as the time during which these instruments of labour continue to serve in continually repeated labour processes, is greater than the period of turn-over of circulating capital, in other words, comprises n periods of turn-over of circulating capital. Whether the total time represented by these n periods of turn-over of circulating capital, is long or short, that portion of productive capital which was advanced for this time in fixed capital is not advanced anew during its course. It continues its functions in its old use-form. The difference is merely this: according to the different lengths of the individual working periods of each period of turn-over of circulating capital, the fixed capital yields a greater or smaller portion of its original value to the product of this working period, and according to the duration of the time of circulation of each period of turn-over, this value yielded by the fixed capital to the product flows back in money rapidly or slowly. The nature of the topic which we discuss in this section – the turn-over of the circulating portion of productive capital – is determined by the nature of this portion itself. The circulating capital employed in a working period cannot be invested in a new working period, until it has completed its turn-over, until it has been converted into commodity-capital, then into money-capital, and then back into productive capital. In order that the first working period may be immediately followed by a second, additional capital must be advanced and converted into the circulating elements of productive capital, and its quantity must be sufficient to fill out the void left by the circulation of the capital advanced for the first working period. This is the source of the influence exerted by the duration of the working period of the circulating capital over the scale of the process of production and the division of the advanced capital, or eventually the advance of new portions of capital. It is precisely this which we had to examine in this section.

Section 4. Conclusions.

From the preceding analyses, it follows that,

A. The different portions, into which capital must be divided in order that one part of it may be continually in the working period while others are in the period of circulation, relieve one another like different independent private capitals, in two cases: first, when the working period is equal to the period of circulation, so that the period of turn-over is divided into two equal sections; secondly, when the period of circulation is longer than the working period, but at the same time represents a simple multiple of the working period, so that one period of circulation is equal to n working periods, in which case n must be a whole number. In these cases, no portion of the successively advanced capital is set free.

B. On the other hand, in all cases in which, (1) the period of circulation is longer than the working period without being a simple multiple of it; and (2) in which the working period is longer than the circulation period; a portion of the circulating total capital is continually set free periodically at the close of each working period, beginning with the second turn-over. This free capital is equal to that portion of the total capital which has been advanced to fill out the time of circulation, provided the working period is longer than the period of circulation, and equal to that portion of capital which has to fill out the excess of the time of circulation over one working period, or over a multiple of one working period, provided the time of circulation is longer than the working time.

C. It follows that for the aggregate social capital, so far as its circulating capital is concerned, the setting free of capital must be the rule, while the mere relieving of portions of capital following successively in the process of production must be the exception. For the equality of the period of work and circulation, or the equality of the period of circulation with a simple multiple of the working period, in other words, a similar proportion of the two portions of the period of turn-over has nothing to do with the nature of the case, and for this reason it cannot be found in general, but only in rare instances.

A very considerable portion of the social circulating capital, which is turned over several times per year, will therefore exist periodically in the form of released capital during the annual cycle of turn-over.

It is furthermore evident that, all other circumstances being equal, the magnitude of the released capital grows with the volume of the labour-process, or with the scale of production, or with the development of capitalist production in general. In the case cited under B (2), this will be so, because the advanced total capital increases; in B (1), because the length of the period of circulation grows with the development of capitalist production, hence the period of turn-over is lengthened in cases where the working period is extended, without a regular proportion between the two periods.

In the first case, for instance, we had to invest £100 per week. This required £600 for a working period of 6 weeks, £300 for a circulation period of 3 weeks, together £900. In that case, £300 are released continually. On the other hand, if £300 are invested weekly, we have £1,800 for the working period and £900 for the circulation period. Hence £900 instead of £300 are periodically released.

D. The total capital, for instance £900, must be divided into two portions, for instance, £600 for the working period and £300 for the period of circulation. That portion which is really invested in the labour-process, is thus reduced by one third, or from £900 to £600.

The scale of production is thus reduced by one third. On the other hand, the £300 perform their function only to make the working period continuous, in order that £100 may be invested every week of the year in the labour-process.

Abstractly speaking, it is the same, whether £600 work during 6 times 8, or 48 weeks (product £4,800), or whether the total capital of £900 is expended during 6 weeks in the labour-process and then kept fallow during the period of circulation of 3 weeks. In the latter case, it would be working, in the course of the 48 weeks, 5 1/3 times 6, or 32 weeks (product 5 1/3 times 900, or £4,800), and be fallow for 16 weeks. But, apart from the greater decay of the fixed capital during the fallow of 16 weeks, and apart from the appreciation of labour, which must be rapid during the entire year, although it is employed only during a part of it, such a regular interruption of the process of production is irreconcilable with the operations of modern great industry. This continuity is itself a productive power of labour.

Now, if we take a closer look at the released, or rather suspended, capital, we find that a considerable part of it must always be in the form of money-capital. Let us adhere to our illustration: Working period 6 weeks, period of circulation 3 weeks, expenditure per week £100. In the middle of the second working period, after the close of the 9th week, £600 flow back, and 300 of them must be invested for the remainder of the working period. After the close of the second working period, £300 are then released. In what condition are these £300? We will assume that 1/3 is invested for wages, 2/3 for raw materials and auxiliary substances. Then £200 of the returned £600 exist in the form of money for wages, and £400 in the form of a productive supply, in the form of elements of the constant circulating productive capital. But since only one half of this productive supply is required for the second half of the second working period, the other half is for 3 weeks in the form of a surplus, that is to say, of a productive supply exceeding the requirements of one working period. The capitalist, on the other hand, knows that he needs only one-half (£200) of this portion (£400) of the returned capital for the current working period. It will, therefore, depend on market conditions, whether he will immediately reconvert these £200 entirely or partially into a surplus productive supply, or reserve them entirely or partially in the form of money in the expectation that the conditions of the market will improve. It goes without saying, that the portion of capital to be used for the payment of wages (£200) is reserved in the form of money. The capitalist cannot store labour-power in warehouses after he has bought it, as he may do with the raw material. He must incorporate it in the process of production and he pays for it at the end of the week. At least these £100 of the released capital of £300 will, therefore, have the form of money not required for the working period. The capital released in the form of money-capital must therefore be at least equal to the variable portion of capital invested in wages. At a maximum, it may comprise the entire released capital. In reality it fluctuates continually between this minimum and maximum.

The money-capital released by the mere mechanism of the movement of turn-over (together with the successive reflux of fixed capital and the money-capital required in every labour-process for variable capital) must play an important role, as soon as the credit system develops, and must at the same time be one of its foundations.

Let us assume that the time of circulation in our illustration is contracted from 3 weeks to 2. This is not to be a normal change, but due, say, to prosperous times, shortened terms of payment, etc. The capital of £600, which is expended during the working period, flows back one week earlier than needed, it is therefore released for this week. Furthermore, in the middle of the working period, as before, £300 are released (a portion of those £600), but in this case for 4 weeks instead of 3. There are then on the money market £600 for one week, and £300 for 4 weeks instead of 3. As this concerns not one capitalist alone, but many, and occurs at various periods in different businesses, it brings more available money-capital on the market. If this condition last for a long time, production will be expanded, wherever feasible. Capitalists working with borrowed money will bring less demand to bear on the money-market, whereby it is relieved as much as it is by an increased supply. Or, finally, the sums made superfluous by the mechanism are thrown definitely on the money-market.

In consequence of the contraction of the period of turn-over from 3 weeks to 2, and thus of the period of turn-over from 9 weeks to 8, one ninth of the advanced total capital becomes superfluous. The working period of 6 weeks can now be kept going as continuously with £800 as formerly with £900. One portion of the value of the commodity-capital, equal to £100, therefore persists in the form of money-capital without performing any more functions as a part of the capital advanced for the process of production. While production is continued on the same scale and with other conditions, such as prices, etc., remaining equal, the value of the advanced capital is reduced from £900 to £800. The remainder of the originally advanced value, to the amount of £100, is released in the form of money-capital. As such it passes over into the money-market and forms an additional portion of the capitals serving in that capacity.

This shows the way in which a plethora of money may arise – quite apart from the reason that the supply of money may be greater than the demand for it; this eventuality causes always but a relative plethora, which occurs, for instance, in the 'melancholy period' opening a new cycle after a commercial crisis. In our case we speak of a plethora in the sense that a definite portion of the capital advanced for the promotion of the entire process of social reproduction, including the process of circulation, becomes superfluous and is, therefore, released in the form of money-capital. This plethora comes about by the mere contraction of the period of turn-over, while the scale of production and prices remain the same. The amount of money in the circulation, whether great or small, did not exert the least influence on this.

Let us assume, on the other hand, that the period of circulation is prolonged from 3 weeks to 5. In that case, the reflux of the advanced capital takes place 2 weeks too late at the very next turn-over. The last part of the process of production of this working period cannot be carried on, the mechanism of the turn-over of the advanced capital itself interfering. In case of a longer duration of this condition, a contraction of the process of production, a reduction of its volume, might take place, just as an extension did in the previous case. But in order to continue the process on the same scale, the advanced capital would have to be increased by 2/9, or £200, for the entire duration of the prolongation of the circulation period. This additional capital can be obtained only from the money-market. If, then, the prolongation of the period of circulation applies to one or more great lines of business, it may cause a pressure on the money-market, unless this effect is compensated by some counter-effect from some other direction. In this case likewise it is evident and obvious that such a pressure is not in the least due to a change in the prices of the commodities nor to the quantity of the existing means of circulation.

[The preparation of this chapter for publication has given me no small amount of difficulties. Expert as Marx was in algebra, the handling of figures in arithmetic nevertheless gave him a great deal of trouble and he lacked especially the practice of commercial calculation, although he left behind a ponderous volume of computations in which he had practised by many examples the entire variety of commercial reckoning. But a knowledge of the various modes of calculation and a practice in the daily practical calculations of the merchant are by no means the same. Consequently Marx entangled himself to such an extent in his computation of turn-overs, that the result, so far as he completed his work, contained various errors and contradictions. In the diagrams given above, I have preserved only the simplest and arithmetically correct data, and my reason for so doing was mainly the following:

The indefinite results of this tedious calculation have led Marx to attribute an undeserved importance to a circumstance, which, in my opinion, has actually little significance. I refer to that which he calls the 'release' of money-capital. The actual state of affairs, based on the above premises, is this:

No matter what may be the proportion in the magnitude of the working and circulation periods, or of Capital I and II, there is returned to the capitalist, in the form of money, at the end of the first turn-over, in regular intervals of the duration of one working period, the capital required for each working period, a sum equal to Capital I.

If the working period is 5 weeks, the circulation period 4 weeks, and Capital I £500, then a sum of money equal to £500 flows back periodically at the end of the 9th, 14th, 19th, 24th, 29th, etc., week.

If the working period is 6 weeks, the circulation period 3 weeks, and Capital I £600, then £600 flow back periodically at the end of the 9th, 15th, 21st, 27th, 33rd, etc., week.

Finally, if the working period is 4 weeks, the circulation period 5 weeks, and Capital I £400, then £400 are periodically returned at the end of the 9th, 13th, 17th, 21st, 25th, etc., week.

Whether any of this returned money is superfluous, and thus released, for the current working period, and how much of it, makes no difference. It is assumed that production continues uninterruptedly on the same scale, and in order that this may be possible, money must be available and must, therefore, flow back, whether 'released' or not. If production is interrupted, release stops likewise.

In other words: there is indeed a release of money, a formation of latent, or merely potential, capital in the form of money. But it takes place under all circumstances, and not only under the conditions enumerated especially in the above analysis; and it takes place on a larger scale than that assumed there. So far as circulating Capital I is concerned, the industrial capitalist, at the end of each turn-over, is in the same situation as at the establishment of his business: he has all of it in his hands in one bulk, while he can convert it only gradually back into productive capital.

The essential point in the above analysis is the demonstration that, on one hand, a considerable portion of the industrial capital must always be available in the form of money, and, on the other hand, a still more considerable portion must temporarily assume the form of money. This proof is, if anything, still more emphasised by these additional remarks of mine. – F. E.]

Section 5. The Effect of a Change of Prices.

We had assumed that prices remained the same and the scale of production remained unaltered, while, on the other hand, the time of circulation was either contracted or expanded. Now let us assume, on the contrary, that the period of turn-over remains the same, likewise the scale of production, while prices change, that is to say, either the prices of the raw materials, auxiliaries, and labour-power rise or fall, or those of the two first-named elements alone. Take it, that the price of raw materials, auxiliaries, and labour-power falls by one half. In that case, the capital to be advanced in our above examples would be £50 instead of £100 per week, and that for the period of turn-over of 9 weeks, £450, instead of £900. A sum of £450 of the advanced capital is released in the form of money-capital, but the process of production continues on the same scale and with the same period of turn-over, and with the same sub-division as before. The quantity of the annual product likewise remains the same, but its value has fallen by one half. This change, which is at the same time accompanied by a change in the demand and supply of money-capital, is due neither to an acceleration of the turn-over, nor to a change in the quantity of money in circulation. On the contrary. A fall in the value, or price, of the elements of productive capital by one half would first have the effect of reducing by one half the capital-value to be advanced for the continuation of the business of X in the same scale, so that only one half of the money would have to be thrown on the market by the business of X, since the business of X advances this capital-value first in the form of money, of money-capital. The amount of money thrown into circulation would have decreased, because the prices of the elements of production had fallen. This would be the first effect.

In the second place, one half of the originally advanced capital of £900 or £450, which (a) passed alternately through the forms of money-capital, productive capital, and commodity-capital, and (b) existed simultaneously and continuously side by side partly in the form of money-capital, partly in the form of productive capital, partly in the form of commodity-capital, would be eliminated from the rotation of the business of X, and thus come into the money market as an additional capital, affecting it as such. These released £450 serve as money-capital, not because they have become superfluous for the operation of the business of X, but because they were a constituent portion of the original capital-value, so that they are intended for further service as capital, not as mere means of circulation. The next form in which they may serve as capital is that of money on the money-market. Or, the scale of production (apart from fixed capital) might be doubled. In that case a productive process of double the previous volume would be carried on with a capital of £900.

If, on the other hand, the prices of the circulating elements of productive capital were to increase by one half, it would require £150 per week instead of £100, or £1,350 instead of £900. An additional capital of £450 would be needed to carry on production on the same scale, and this would exert a pressure to that extent, according to the condition of the money-market, on the quotations of money. If all the capital available on this market were then engaged, there would be an increased competition for available capital. If a portion of it were unemployed, it would to that extent be called into action.

But, in the third place, given a certain scale of production, the velocity of the turn-over and the prices for the circulating elements of productive capital remaining the same, the price of the product of the business of X may rise or fall. If the price of the commodities supplied by the business of X falls, the price of his commodity-capital of £600, which it threw continually into circulation, sinks, for instance, to £500. In that case, one sixth of the value of the advanced capital does not flow back from the process of circulation, (the surplus-value contained in the commodity-capital is not considered here), and it is lost in circulation. But since the value, or price, of the elements of production remains the same, this reflux of £500 suffices only to replace 5/6 of the capital of £600 engaged in the process of production. It requires therefore an addition of £100 of money-capital to continue production on the same scale.

Vice versa, if the price of the product of the business of X were to rise, then the price of the commodity-capital of £600 would be increased, say to £700. One seventh of this price, or £100, does not come from the process of production, has not been advanced in it, but flows from the process of circulation. But only £600 are needed to replace the elements of production. Therefore £100 are set free.

It does not fall within the scope of the present analysis to ascertain why, in the first case, the period of turn-over is abbreviated or prolonged; why, in the second case, the prices of raw materials and auxiliaries; in the third case, those of the products supplied by the business, rise or fall.

But the following points fall under this analysis.

I. Case. – *A Change in the Period of Circulation, and thus of Turn-Over, while the Scale of Production, and the Prices of the Elements of Production and of Products Remain the Same.*

According to the assumptions of our example, one ninth less of the advanced total capital is needed after the contraction of the period of circulation, so that the total capital is reduced from £900 to £800 and £100 of money-capital are released.

The business of X supplies the same as ever a six weeks' product of the same value of £600, and as work continues without interruption during the entire year, the same quantity of products, valued at £5,100, is supplied in 51 weeks. There is, then, no change so far as the quantity and price of the product thrown into circulation by this business are concerned, nor in the terms of time in which it throws its product on the market. But £100 are released, because the requirements of the productive process are satisfied with £800 instead of £900, after the contraction of the period of circulation. The released £100 of capital exist in the form of money-capital. But they do not by any means represent that portion of the advanced capital, which would have to serve continually in the form of money-capital. Let us assume that 4/5, or £480 of the advanced circulating capital are continually invested in material elements of production, and 1/5, or £120, in labour-power. Then the weekly investment in materials of production would be £80, and in labour-power £20. Of course, Capital II, of £300, must also be divided into 4/5, or £240, for materials of production, and 1/5, or £60, for wages. The capital invested in wages must always be advanced in the form of money. As soon as the commodity-product to the amount of £600 has been reconverted into money, £480 of it may be transformed into materials of production (productive supply), but £120 retain their money-form, in order to serve in the payment of wages for six weeks. These £120 are the minimum of the returning capital of £600, which must always be renewed in the form of money-capital and so replaced, and therefore this minimum must always be kept on hand as that portion of the advanced capital which serves in its money-form.

Now, if £100 of the capital of £300 periodically released for three weeks, and likewise divided into £240 of a productive supply and £60 of wages, are entirely eliminated in the form of money-capital by the contraction of the circulation time, if they are completely removed from the mechanism of the turn-over, where does the money for these £100 of money-capital come from? This amount consists only one-fifth of money-capital periodically released within the turn-overs. But four-fifths, or £80, are already replaced by an additional productive supply of the same value. In what manner is this additional productive supply converted into money, and whence comes the money for this conversion?

If the contraction of the period of circulation has become a fact, then only £400 of the above £600, instead of £480, are reconverted into a productive supply. The other £80 are retained in their money-form and constitute, together with the above £20 for wages, the £100 eliminated from the process. Although these £100 come from the circulation by means of the purchase of the £600 of commodity-capital and are now withdrawn from it, because they are not re-invested in wages and materials of production, yet it must not be forgotten that, in their money-form, they are once more in that form in which they were originally thrown into circulation. In the begin-ning £900 were invested in a productive supply and wages. Now only £800 are required in order to carry along the same productive process. The £100 thus withdrawn in money now form a new money-capital seeking investment, a new constituent part of the money-market. True, they were previously periodically in the form of released money-capital and of additional productive capital, but these latent forms were the conditions for the promotion and continuity of the process of production. Now they are no longer needed for this purpose, and for this reason they form a new money-capital and a constituent part of the money-market, although they are neither an additional element of the existing social money-supply (for they existed at the beginning of the business and were thrown by it into the circulation), nor a newly accumulated hoard.

These £100 are now indeed withdrawn from circulation inasmuch as they are a portion of the advanced money-capital and are no longer employed in the same business. But this withdrawal is possible only because the conversion of the commodity-capital into money, and of this money into productive capital, in the metamorphosis C'—M—C, is accelerated by one week, so that the circulation of the money engaged in this process is likewise hastened. This sum is withdrawn from circulation, because it is no longer needed for the turn-over of the capital of X.

It has been assumed here, that the capital belongs to him who invests it. But if he had borrowed it, nothing would be altered in these conditions. With the contraction of the period of circulation, he would need only £800 of borrowed money instead of £900. This sum of £100, if returned to the lender, forms nevertheless £100 of new money-capital, only in the hands of Y instead of X. If the capitalist X receives his materials of production to the amount of £480 on credit, so that he has only to advance £120 for wages out of his own pocket, then he would now have to purchase £80's worth of goods less on credit, so that this sum would constitute an excess of commodity-capital for the capitalist giving it on credit, while the capitalist X would have released £20 of his money.

The additional supply for production is now reduced by one-third. It consisted of £240's worth of goods, constituting four-fifths of additional Capital II of £300, but now it consists only of £160's worth of goods. It is an additional productive supply for 2 instead of 3 weeks. It is now renewed every 2 weeks, instead of every 3, but only for the next 2 instead of the next 3 weeks. The purchases, for instance, on the cotton market, are repeated more frequently and in smaller portions. The same portion of cotton is withdrawn from the market, for the quantity of the product remains the same. But the withdrawal is distributed differently in time, extending over a longer period. Take it that it is a question of 3 months or 2. If the annual consumption of cotton amounts to 1,200 bales, the sales in the first case will be:

January 1, 300 bales, remaining in storage 900 bales.
April 1, 300 bales, remaining in storage 600 bales.
July 1, 300 bales, remaining in storage 300 bales.
October 1, 300 bales, remaining in storage 0 bales.

But in the second case, the situation would be:

January 1, sold 200, remaining in storage 1,000 bales.
March 1, sold 200, remaining in storage 800 bales.
May 1, sold 200, remaining in storage 600 bales.
July 1, sold 200, remaining in storage 400 bales.
September 1, sold 200, remaining in storage 200 bales.
November 1, sold 200, remaining in storage 0 bales.

In other words, the money invested in cotton flows back completely one month later, in November instead of October. If, therefore, one-ninth of the advanced capital, or £100, is eliminated in the form of money by the contraction of the period of circulation, and if these £100 are composed of £20 of periodically released money-capital for the payment of wages, and of £80 existing periodically as a released productive supply for one week, then the reduction of the productive supply in the hands of the manufacturer, so far as these £80 are concerned, corresponds to an increase of the cotton supply in the hands of the cotton dealer. The same cotton retains as much longer in his warehouse the form of a commodity as it stays a shorter time in the hands of the manufacturer under the form of a productive supply.

Hitherto we assumed that the contraction of the time of circulation was due to the fact that X sold his articles more rapidly, received his money for them in a shorter time, or, in the case of credit, that his time of payment was reduced. In that case, the contraction was attributed to the sale of the commodities, to the conversion of commodity-capital into money-capital, C'—M, the first phase of the process of circulation. But it might also be due to the second phase, M—C, and hence to a simultaneous change, either in the working period, or in the time of circulation of the capitals Y, Z, etc., which supply the capitalist X with the elements of production of his circulating capital.

For instance, if cotton, coal, etc., with the old methods of transportation, are three weeks in transit from their place of production or storage to the location of the factory of the capitalist X, then the minimum supply of X up to the arrival of new transports must last for three weeks. So long as cotton and coal are in transit, they cannot serve as means of production. They are then rather an object of labour in the transportation industry and of the capital invested in it, they represent for the producer of coal or the dealer in cotton a commodity-capital in process of circulation. Now let improvements in transportation reduce the transit to two weeks. Then the productive supply can be transformed from a three-weekly into a fortnightly supply. This releases the additional capital of £80 set aside for the purchase of the weekly supply, and likewise the £20 for wages, because the turned-over capital of £600 returns one week earlier.

On the other hand, if the working period of the capital invested in raw materials is contracted (examples of this case were given in the preceding chapter), so that the possibility of renewing the productive supply in a shorter time is given, then the productive supply may be reduced, the interval between the periods of renewal being shortened.

If, vice versa, the time of circulation and thus the period of turnover are prolonged, then advance of additional capital is necessary. This must come out of the pockets of the capitalist himself, provided he has any additional capital. If he has, it will be invested in some way, in some portion of the money-market. In order to make it available, it must be detached from its old form, for instance, stocks must be sold, deposits withdrawn, so that there is indirectly an effect on the money-market, also in this case. Or, he must borrow it. As for that portion of the additional capital which is to be invested in wages, it must under normal conditions always be advanced in the form of money, and the capitalist X exerts to that extent his share of a direct pressure on the money-market. But so far as that portion is concerned which must be invested in materials of production, money is indispensable only if he must pay for them in cash. If he can get them on credit, this does not exert any direct influence on the money-market, because the additional capital then is directly advanced in the form of a productive supply, not in the first instance in money. But if the lender throws the note received from X directly on the market and discounts it, this would to that extent influence the money-market indirectly.

II. Case. – *A Change in the Price of Materials of Production, All Other Circumstances Remaining the Same.*

We just assumed that the total capital of £900 was four-fifths invested in materials of production (£720) and one-fifth in wages (£180).

If the price of the materials of production drops by one-half, then a working period of 6 weeks requires only £240 instead of £480 for their purchase, and an additional capital of only £120 instead of £240. Capital I is then reduced from £600 to £240 plus £120, or £360, and Capital II from £300 to £120 plus £60, or £180. The total capital of £900 is therefore reduced to £360 plus £180, or £540. A sum of £360 is eliminated.

This eliminated and now unemployed capital, which seeks investment in the money-market, is nothing but a portion of the originally advanced capital of £900. This portion has become superfluous by the fall in the price of the materials of production, so long as the business is carried along on the same scale and not expanded. If this fall in prices is not due to accidental circumstances, such as a rich harvest, over-supply, etc., but to an increase of productive power in the line which supplies the raw materials, then this money-capital is an absolute addition to the money-market, or in general to the capital available in the form of money-capital, because it no longer constitutes an integral portion of the capital already invested.

III. Case. – *A Change in the Market Price of the Products Themselves.*

In this case, a fall in prices means a loss of a portion of capital, which must be made good by a new advance of additional money-capital. This loss of the seller may be recovered by the buyer. It is recovered by the buyer directly, if the market price of the product has fallen merely through an accidental fluctuation of the market and rises once more to its normal level. It is recovered indirectly, if the change of prices is caused by a change of value reacting on the product, and if this product passes as an element of production into another sphere of production and there releases capital to that extent. In either case, the capital lost by X, for the replacement of which he touches the money-market, may be introduced by his business friends as a new additional capital. Then there is a simple transfer of capital.

If, on the other hand, the price of the product rises, then a portion of the capital which was not advanced is taken away from the circulation.

This is not an organic portion of the capital advanced in this process of production and constitutes, therefore, eliminated money-capital, unless production is expanded. As we assumed that the prices of the elements of production were fixed before the product came upon the market, an actual change of value might have caused the rise of prices to the extent that it is retroactive, causing a subsequent rise in the price of raw material. In such an eventuality, the capitalist X would realise a gain on his product circulating as a commodity-capital and on his available productive supply. This gain would give him an additional capital, which would be needed for the continuation of his business with the new and higher prices of the elements of production.

Or, the rise of prices is but temporary. To the extent that additional capital is then needed on the side of the capitalist X, the same amount is released on another side, inasmuch as his product is an element of production for other lines of business. What the one has lost, the other wins.

Chapter 16

The Turn-Over of the Variable Capital

Section 1. The Annual Rate of Surplus-Value.

We start out with a circulating capital of £2,500, four-fifths of which, or £2,000, are constant capital (materials of production), and one-fifth of which, or £500, is variable capital invested in wages.

Let the period of turn-over be 5 weeks; the working period 4 weeks, the period of circulation 1 week. Then Capital I is £2,000, consisting of £1,600 of constant capital and £400 of variable capital; Capital II is £500, £400 of which are constant and £100 variable. In every working week, a capital of £500 is invested. In a year of 50 weeks an annual product of 50 times 500, or £25,000, is manufactured. The Capital I, continuously invested in one working period and amounting to £2,000, is turned over 12 1/2 times. 12 1/2 times 2000 make £25,000. Of this sum of £25,000, four-fifths, or £20,000, are constant capital invested in materials of production, and one-fifth, or £5,000, is variable capital invested in wages. The total capital of £2,500 is turned over 10 times, which is 25,000 divided by 2,500.

The variable circulating capital expended in production can serve afresh in the process of circulation only to the extent that the product in which its value is reproduced is sold, converted from a commodity-capital into a money-capital, in order to be once more expended in the payment of labour-power. But the same is true of the constant circulating capital invested in production for materials, the value of which reappears as a portion of the value of the product. That which is common to these two portions of the circulating capital, the variable and constant capital, and which distinguishes them from the fixed capital, is not that the value transferred from them to the product is circulated by the commodity-capital, circulated as a commodity through the circulation of the product. For one portion of the value of the product, and thus of the product circulating as a commodity, the commodity-capital, always consists of the wear of the fixed capital, that is to say, of that portion of the value of the fixed capital which is transferred to the product during the process of production. The difference is rather this: the fixed capital continues to serve in the process of production in its old natural form for a longer or shorter cycle of periods of turn-over of the circulating capital (which consists of constant circulating plus variable circulating capital), while every single turn-over is conditioned on the reproduction of the entire circulating capital passing from the sphere of production in the form of commodity-capital into the sphere of circulation. The constant and variable circulating capital both have in common the first phase of the circulation, C'—M'. But in the second phase they separate. The money, into which the commodity is reconverted, is in part transformed into a productive supply (constant circulating capital). According to the different terms of purchase of this material, a portion may be sooner, another later, converted from money into materials of production, but finally it is wholly consumed in that way. Another portion of the money realised by the sale of the commodity is held in the form of a money-supply, in order to be gradually expended in the payment of labour-power incorporated in the process of production. This portion constitutes the variable circulating capital. Nevertheless the entire reproduction of either portion is due to the turn-over of the capital, to their conversion into a product, from a product into a commodity, from a commodity into money. This is the reason why, in the preceding chapter, the turn-over of the circulating constant and variable capital was discussed separately and simultaneously without any regard to the fixed capital.

For the purposes of the question which we have to discuss now, we must go a step farther and proceed with the variable portion of the circulating capital as though it constituted the circulating capital by itself. In other words, we leave out of consideration the constant circulating capital which is turned over together with it.

A sum of £2,500 has been advanced, and the value of the annual product is £25,000. But the variable portion of the circulating capital is £500. The variable capital contained in £25,000 therefore amounts to 25,000 divided by 5, or £5,000. If we divide these £5,000 by £500, we find that 10 is the number of turn-overs, just as it is in the case of the total capital of £2,500.

Here, where it is only a question of the production of surplus-value, it is quite correct to make this average calculation, according to which the value of the annual product is divided by the value of the advanced capital, not by the value of that portion of this capital which is employed continually in one working period (in the present case not by 400, but by 500, not by Capital I, but by Capital I plus II). We shall see later, that, from another point of view, this is not quite exact. In other words, this calculation serves well enough for the practical purposes of the capitalist, but it does not express exactly or appropriately all the real circumstances of the turn-over.

We have hitherto ignored one portion of the commodity-capital, namely the surplus-value contained in it, which was produced during the process of production and incorporated in the product. We have now to direct our attention to this.

Take it, that the variable capital of £100 expended weekly produces a surplus-value of 100%, or £100, then the variable capital of £500, advanced for a period of turn-over of 5 weeks, produces £500 of surplus-value, in other words, one-half of the working day consists of surplus-labour.

If £500 of variable capital produce a surplus-value of £500, then £5,000 produce ten times £500, or £5,000 of surplus-value. The proportion of the total quantity of surplus-value produced during one year to the value of the advanced variable capital is what we call the annual rate of surplus-value. In the present case, this is as 5000 to 500, or 1000%. If we analyse this rate more closely, we find that it is equal to the rate of surplus-value produced by the advanced variable capital during one period of turn-over, multiplied by the number of turn-overs of the variable capital (which coincides with the number of turn-overs of the entire circulating capital).

The variable capital advanced in the present case for one period of turn-over is £500. The surplus-value produced during this period is likewise £500. The rate of surplus-value for one period of turn-over is, therefore, as 500 s to 500 v, or 100%. This 100%, multiplied by 10, the number of turn-overs in one year, makes 1000%, a rate of 5000 to 500.

This applies to the annual rate of surplus-value. As for the quantity of surplus-value obtained during a certain period of turn-over, it is equal to the value of the variable capital advanced for this period, in the present case £500, multiplied by the rate of surplus-value; in the present case, therefore, 500 times 100/100, or 500 times 1, or £500. If the advanced variable capital were £1,500, with the same rate of surplus-value, then the quantity of surplus-value would be 1500 times 100/100, or £1,500.

The variable capital of £500, which is turned over ten times per year, producing a surplus-value of £5,000, and thus having a rate of surplus-value amounting to 1000%, shall be called capital A.

Now let us assume that another variable capital, B, of £5,000, is advanced for one whole year (that is to say for 50 working weeks), so that it is turned over only once a year. We assume furthermore that, at the end of the year, the product is paid for on the same day that it is finished, so that the money-capital, into which it is converted, flows back on the same day. The circulation time is then zero, the period of turn-over equal to the working period, that is to say, one year. As in the preceding case, so there is now in the labour-process of each week a variable capital of £100, or of £5,000 in 50 weeks. Let the rate of surplus-value be likewise the same, or 100%, that is to say, one-half of the working day of the same length as before consists of surplus-labour. If we study a period of 5 weeks, then the advanced variable capital is £500, the rate of surplus-value 100%, the quantity of surplus-value produced in 5 weeks likewise £500. The quantity of labour-power, which is here exploited, and the intensity of its exploitation, are assumed to be the same as those of capital A.

In each week, the invested variable capital of £100 produces a surplus-value of £100, hence in 50 weeks the total invested capital produces a surplus-value of 50 times 100, or £5,000. The quantity of the surplus-value produced per year is the same as in the previous case, £5,000, but the annual rate of surplus-value is entirely different. It is equal to the surplus-value produced in one year, divided by the advanced variable capital, that is to say it is as 5000 s to 5000 v, or 100%, while in the case of capital A it was 1000%.

In the case of both capitals A and B, we have invested a variable capital of £100 per week. The rate of surplus-value per week, or the intensity of self-expansion, is likewise the same, 100%, so is the magnitude of the variable capital the same, £100. The same quantity of labour-power is exploited, the volume and intensity of exploitation are equal in both cases, the working days are the same and subdivided in the same way in necessary labour and surplus-labour. The quantity of variable capital employed in the course of the year is £5,000 in either case, sets the same amount of labour in motion, and extracts the same amount of surplus-value from the labour-power set in motion by these two equal capitals, namely £5,000. Nevertheless, there is a difference of 900% in the annual rate of surplus-value of the two capitals A and B.

This phenomenon makes indeed the impression as though the rate of surplus-value were not only dependent on the quantity and intensity of exploitation of the labour-power set in motion by the variable capital, but also on inexplicable influences arising from the process of circulation. It has actually been so interpreted, and has completely routed the Ricardian school since the beginning of the twenties of the 19th century, at least in its more complicated and disguised form, that of the annual rate of profit, if not in the simple and natural form indicated above.

The strangeness of this phenomenon disappears at once, when we place capital A and B in exactly the same conditions, not seemingly, but actually. These equal circumstances are present only when the variable capital B is expended in the payment of labour-power in its entire volume and in the same period of time as capital A.

In that case, the £5,000 of capital B are invested for 5 weeks. £1,000 per week makes an investment of £50,000 per year. The surplus-value is then likewise £50,000, according to our assumption. The turned-over capital of £50,000, divided by the advanced capital of £5,000, makes the number of turn-overs 10. The rate of surplus-value, 5000 to 5000, or 100%, multiplied by the number of turn-overs, 10, makes the annual rate of surplus-value as 50,000 to 5000, or 10 to 1, or 1000%. Now the annual rates of surplus-value for A and B are alike, namely 1000%, but the quantities of surplus-value are £50,000 in the case of B, and £5,000 in the case of A. The quantities of the produced surplus-values now are proportioned to one another as the advanced capital-values of B and A: to wit, as 50,000 to 5000, or 10 to 1. But at the same time, capital B has set in motion ten times as much labour-power as capital A has in the same time.

It is only the capital actually invested in the working process which produces any surplus-value and for which all laws relating to surplus-value are in force, including for instance the law according to which the quantity of surplus-value is determined by the relative magnitude of the variable capital if the rate of surplus-value is given.

The labour-process itself is determined by the time. If the length of the working period is given (as it is here, where we assume all circumstances relating to A and B to be equal, in order to elucidate the difference in the annual rate of surplus-value), the working week consists of a certain number of working days. Or, we may consider any working period, for instance this working period of 5 weeks, as one single working day of 300 hours, if the working day has 10 hours and the working week 6 days. We must further multiply this number with the number of labourers who are employed every day simultaneously in the same labour-process. If there were 10 labourers, there would be 60 times 10, or 600 working hours in one week, and a working period of 5 weeks would have 600 times 5, or 3000 working hours. Variable capitals of equal magnitude are, therefore, employed, the rate of surplus-value and the working days being the same if equal quantities of labour-power are set in motion in the same time (a labour-power of the same price multiplied with the same number).

Let us now return to our original illustrations. In both cases, A and B, equal variable capitals, of £100 per week, are invested every week during the year. The invested variable capitals actually serving in the labour-process are, therefore, equal, but the advanced variable capitals are very unequal. For A, £500 are advanced for every 5 weeks, and £100 of this are consumed every week. In the case of B, £5,000 must be advanced for the first period of 5 weeks, but only £100 per week, or £500 in 5 weeks, or one-tenth of the advanced capital is employed. In the second period of 5 weeks, £4,500 must be advanced, but only £500 of this is employed, etc. The variable capital advanced for a certain period of time is converted into employed, actually serving and active, variable capital only to the extent that it actually steps into the period of time taken up by the labour-process, to the extent that it actually takes part in it. In the intermediate time in which a certain portion of this capital is advanced, with a view to being employed at a later time, this portion is practically non-existing for the labour-process and has, therefore, no influence on the formation of either value or surplus-value. Take, for instance, capital A, of £500. It is advanced for 5 weeks, but only £100 enter successively week after week into the labour process. In the first week, one-fifth of this capital is employed; four-fifths are advanced without being employed, although they must be available, and therefore advanced, for the labour-processes of the following 4 weeks.

The circumstances which differentiate the relations of the advanced to the employed capital, influence the production of surplus-value – the rate of surplus-value being given – only to the extent that they differentiate the quantity of variable capital which can be actually employed in a certain period of time, for instance in one week, 5 weeks, etc. The advanced variable capital serves as variable capital only for the time that it is actually employed, not for the time in which it is held available without being employed. But all the circumstances which differentiate the relations between the advanced and the employed variable capital, are comprised in the difference of the periods of turn-over (determined by the difference in the working period, the circulation period or both). The law of the production of surplus-value decrees that equal quantities of employed variable capital produce equal quantities of surplus-value, if the rate of surplus-value is the same. If, then, equal quantities of variable capitals are employed by the capitals A and B in equal periods of time with an equal rate of surplus-value, they must produce equal quantities of surplus-value in equal periods of time, no matter what may be the proportion of this variable capital, employed during definite periods of time, to the variable capital advanced for the same time; and no matter, therefore, what may be the proportion of the quantities of surplus-value produced, not to the employed, but to the total advanced variable capital in general. The difference of this proportion, so far from contradicting the laws of the production of surplus-value demonstrated by us, rather corroborates them and is one of their inevitable consequences.

Let us consider the first productive section of 5 weeks of capital B. At the end of the fifth week, £500 have been employed and consumed. The value of the product is £100, hence the rate as 500 s to 500 v or 1100%, the same as in the case of capital A. The fact that, in the case of capital A, the surplus-value is realised together with the advanced capital, while in the case of B it is not, does not concern us here, where it is merely a question of the production of surplus-value and of its proportion to the variable capital advanced during its production. But if we calculate the proportion of surplus-value in B, not as compared to that portion of the advanced capital of £5,000 which has been employed and consumed in its production, but to this total advanced capital itself, we find that it is as 500 s to 5000 v, or as 1 to 10, or 10%. In other words, it is 10% for capital B and 100% for capital A, ten times more. If any one were to say that this difference in the rate of surplus-value for equal capitals, setting in motion equal quantities of labour which is equally divided into paid and unpaid labour, is contrary to the laws of the production of surplus-value, then the answer would be simple and prompted by the mere inspection of the actual conditions: in the case of A, the actual rate of surplus-value is expressed, that is to say, the proportion of a surplus-value of £500 to a variable capital of £500, which produced it in 5 weeks. In the case of B, on the other hand, we are dealing with a calculation which has nothing to do either with the production of surplus-value, or with the determination of its corresponding rate of surplus-value. For the £500 of surplus-value produced by a variable capital of £500 are not calculated with reference to the £500 of variable capital advanced in their production, but with reference to a capital of £5,000, nine-tenths of which, or £4,500, have nothing whatever to do with the production of this surplus-value of £500, but are rather intended for gradual service in the following 45 weeks, so that they do not exist at all so far as the production of the first 5 weeks is concerned, which is alone significant in this instance. Under these circumstances, the difference in the rate of surplus-value of A and B is no problem at all.

Let us now compare the annual rates of surplus-value for capitals A and B. For B it is as 5000 s to 5000 v, or 100%; for A it is as 5000 s to 500 v, or 1000%. But the proportion of the rates of surplus-value toward one another is the same as before. There we had

$$\frac{\text{Rate of Surplus-Value of Capital B}}{\text{Rate of Surplus-Value of Capital A}} = \frac{10\%}{100\%}$$

Now we have

$$\frac{\text{Annual Rate of Surplus-Value of Capital B}}{\text{Annual Rate of Surplus-Value of Capital A}} = \frac{100\%}{1000\%}$$

But 10% is to 100% as 100% is to 1000%, so that the ratio is the same.

But now the problem is reversed. The annual rate of capital B is as 5000 s to 5000 v, or 100%, offering not the slightest deviation, nor even the semblance of a deviation, from the laws of production known to us and the rate of surplus-value corresponding to this production. 5000 v have been advanced and consumed productively during the year, and they have produced 5000 s. The rate of surplus-value is, therefore the same as shown in the above proportion, 5000 s to 5000 v, or 100%. The annual rate agrees with the actual rate of surplus-value. In this case, it is not capital B, but capital A, which presents an anomaly that is to be explained.

In the case of A, we have the rate of surplus-value as 5000 s to 500 v, or 1000%. But while in the case of B, a surplus-value of £500, the product of 5 weeks, was calculated with reference to an advanced capital of £5,000, nine-tenths of which were not employed in its production, we have now a surplus-value of 5000 s calculated on a variable capital of 500 v, that is to say, on only one-tenth of the variable capital of £5,000 actually employed in the production of 5000 s. For the 5000 s are the product of a variable capital of 5000 v, productively consumed during 50 weeks, not that of a capital of £500 productively consumed in one working period of 5 weeks. In the former case, the surplus-value produced in 5 weeks had been calculated for a capital advanced for 50 weeks, a capital ten times larger than the one consumed during the 5 weeks. In the present case, the surplus-value produced in 50 weeks is calculated for a capital advanced for only 5 weeks, a capital ten times smaller than the one consumed in 50 weeks.

Capital A, of £500, is never advanced for more than 5 weeks. At the end of this time it has flown back and may repeat the same process in the course of the year ten times, by ten turn-overs. Two conclusions follow from this:

First. The Capital advanced in the case of A is only five times larger than that portion of capital which is continually employed in the productive process of one week. Capital B, on the other hand, which is turned over only once in 50 weeks, is fifty times larger than that one of its portions which can be used only in continuous successions of one week. The turn-over, therefore, modifies the relations of the capital advanced during the year for the process of production to the capital employed continuously for a certain period of production, say, for one week. And this is illustrated by the first case, in which the surplus-value of 5 weeks is not calculated for the capital employed during these 5 weeks, but for a capital ten times larger and employed for 50 weeks.

Second. The period of turn-over of 5 weeks of capital A comprises only one-tenth of the year, so that one year contains ten such periods of turn-over, in which capital A of £500 is successively reinvested. The employed capital is here equal to the capital advanced for 5 weeks, multiplied by the number of periods of turn-over per year. The capital employed during the year is 500 times 10, or £5,000. The capital advanced during the year is 5000 divided by 10, or £500. Indeed, although the £500 are always re-employed, the sum advanced for 5 weeks never exceeds these same £500. On the other hand, in the case of capital B, it is true that only £500 are employed for 5 weeks and advanced for these 5 weeks. But as the period of turn-over is in this case 50 weeks, the capital employed in one year is equal to the capital advanced for 50 weeks, not to that advanced for every 5 weeks. But the annual quantity of surplus-value depends, given the rate of surplus-value, on the capital employed during the year, not on the capital advanced for the year. Hence it is not larger for this capital of £5,000, which is turned over once a year, than it is for the capital of £500, which is turned over ten times per year. And it has this size only because the capital turned over once a year is ten times larger than the capital turned over ten times per year.

The variable capital turned over during one year – and hence that portion of the annual product, or of the annual expenditure, which is equal to that portion – is the variable capital employed and productively consumed during the year. It follows that, assuming the variable capital A turned over annually and the variable capital B turned over annually to be equal, and to be employed under equal conditions of investment, so that the rate of surplus-value is the same for both of them, the quantity of surplus-value produced annually must likewise be the same for both of them. Hence the annual rate of surplus-value must also be the same for them so far as it is expressed by the formula.

$$\frac{\text{Quantity of Surplus-Value Produced Annually}}{\text{Variable Capital Turned Over Annually}}$$

Or, generally speaking: whatever may be the relative magnitude of the turned-over variable capitals, the rate of the surplus-value produced by them in the course of the year is determined by the rate of surplus-value at which the respective capitals have been employed in average periods (for instance the average of a week or a day).

This is the only result following from the laws of the production of surplus-value and the determination of the rate of surplus-value.

Let us now consider what is expressed by the ratio of the

$$\frac{\text{Capital Turned Over Annually}}{\text{Capital Advanced}}$$

taking into account, as we have said before, only the variable capital. The division shows the number of turn-overs made by the capital advanced in one year.

In the case of capital A, we have:

$$\frac{£5,000 \text{ of Capital Turned Over Annually}}{£500 \text{ of Capital Advanced}}$$

In the case of capital B, we have:

$$\frac{£5,000 \text{ of Capital Turned Over Annually}}{£5,000 \text{ of Capital Advanced}}$$

In both ratios, the numerator expresses the capital advanced multiplied by the number of turn-overs, in the case of A, 500 times 10, in the case of B 5000 times 1. Or, it may be multiplied by the inverted time of turn-over calculated for one year. The time of turn-over for A is 1/10 year; the inverted time of turn-over is 10/1 year, hence we have 500 times 10/1, or 5000. In the case of B, 5000 times 1/1. The denominator expresses the turned-over capital multiplied by the inverted number of turn-overs; in the case of A, 5000 times 1/10, in the case of B, 5000 times 1/1.

The respective quantities of labour (the sum of the paid and unpaid labour) which is set in motion by the two variable capitals turned over annually, are equal in this case, because the turned-over capitals themselves are equal and their rate of self-expansion is likewise equal.

The ratio of the variable capital turned over annually to the variable capital advanced indicates (1) the ratio of the capital intended for investment to the variable capital employed during a definite working period. If the number of turn-overs is 10, as in the case of A, and the year is assumed to have 50 working weeks, then the period of turn-over is 5 weeks. For these 5 weeks, variable capital must be advanced, and the capital advanced for 5 weeks must be 5 times as large as the variable capital employed during one week. That is to say, only one-fifth of the advanced capital (in this case of £500) can be employed in the course of one week. On the other hand, in the case of capital B, where the number of turn-overs is 1/1, the time of turn-over is 1 year of 50 weeks. The ratio of the advanced capital to the capital employed weekly is, therefore, as 50 to 1. If matters were the same for B as they are for A, then B would have to invest £1,000 per week instead of £100. (2). It follows, that B has employed ten times as much capital (£5,000) as A, in order to set in motion the same quantity of variable capital and, the rate of surplus-value being the same, of labour (paid and unpaid), and thus to produce the same quantity of surplus-value during one year. The current rate of surplus-value expresses nothing but the ratio of the variable capital employed during a certain period to the surplus-value produced in the same time; or, the quantity of unpaid labour set in motion by the variable capital employed during this time. It has absolutely nothing to do with that portion of the variable capital which is advanced for a time in which it is not employed. Hence it has nothing to do, in the case of different capitals, with the ratio, determined and differentiated by the period of turn-over, of that portion of capital which is advanced for a definite time and that portion which is employed in the same time.

The essential result of the preceding analysis is that the annual rate of surplus-value coincides only in one single case with the current rate of surplus-value which expresses the intensity of exploitation, namely in the case that the advanced capital is turned over only once a year, so that the capital advanced is equal to the capital turned over in the course of the year, so that the ratio of the quantity of surplus-value produced during the year to the capital employed during the year in this production coincides with and is identical with the ratio of the quantity of surplus-value produced during the year to the capital advanced during the year.

(A) The annual rate of surplus-value is equal to

$$\frac{\text{the Quantity of Surplus-Value Produced during the Year}}{\text{Variable Capital Advanced}}$$

But the quantity of the surplus-value produced during the year is equal to the current rate of surplus-value multiplied by the variable capital employed in its production. The capital employed in the production of the annual quantity of surplus-value is equal to the advanced capital multiplied by the number of its turn-overs, which we shall call n in the present case. Substituting these terms in formula (A) we obtain:

(B) The annual rate of surplus-value is equal to the

$$\frac{\text{Cur. Rate of Surpl.Val. x the Var.Cap.Adv. x n}}{\text{Var. Cap. Adv.}}$$

For instance, in the case of capital B, we should have

$$\frac{100 \text{ times } 5000 \text{ times } 1}{5000} \quad \text{or } 100\%$$

Only when n is equal to 1, that is to say when the variable capital advanced is turned over once a year, so that it is equal to the capital employed or turned over, is the annual rate of surplus-value equal to the current rate of surplus-value.

Let us call the annual rate of surplus-value S', the current rate of surplus-value s', the advanced variable capital v, the number of turn-overs n. Then

$$\text{S' is equal to s'vn/v, or s'n}$$

In other words, S' is equal to s'n, and it is equal to s' only when n is 1, so that then S' is s' times 1, or s'.

It follows furthermore that the annual rate of surplus-value is always equal to s'n, that is to say, always equal to the current rate of surplus-value produced in one period of turn-over by the variable capital consumed during that period multiplied by the number of turn-overs of this variable capital during one year, or, what amounts to the same, multiplied with its inverted time of turn-over calculated for one year. (If the variable capital is turned over ten times per year, then its time of turn-over is 1/10 year, its inverted time of turn-over therefore 10/1 year, or 10 years.)

We have seen that S' is equal to s', when n is 1. S' is greater than s', when n is greater than 1, that is to say, when the advanced capital is turned over more than once a year, or the turned-over capital is greater than the capital advanced.

Finally, S' is smaller than s', when n is smaller than 1, that is to say, when the capital turned over during one year is only a part of the advanced capital, so that the period of turn-over is longer than one year.

Let us linger a moment over this last case.

We retain all the premises of our former illustration, only the period of turn-over is to be 55 weeks instead of 50 weeks. The labour-process requires a variable capital of £100 per week, so that £500 are needed for the period of turn-over, and every week 100 s is produced; s' is, therefore, smaller than 100%. Indeed, if the annual rate turn-overs, n, is then 50/55 or 10/11, because the time of turn-over is 1 plus 1/10 year (of 50 weeks), or 11/10 year.

S' is equal to

$$\frac{100\% \text{ times } 5500 \text{ times } 10/11}{5500}$$

equal to 100 times 10/11, or 1000/11, or 90 10/11%. It is, therefore, smaller than 100%. Indeed, if the annual rate of surplus-value were 100%, then 5500 v would have to produce 5500 s, while 11/10 years are required for that. The 5500 v produce-only 5000 s during one year, therefore the annual rate of surplus-value is 5000 s/5500 v, or 10/11, or 90 10/11%.

The annual rate of surplus-value, or the comparison between the surplus-value produced during one year and the variable capital advanced (as distinguished from the variable capital turned over during one year), is therefore not merely a subjective matter, but the actual movement of capital causes this juxtaposition. So far as the owner of capital A is concerned, his advanced variable capital of 500 has returned to him at the end of the year, and it has produced £5,000 of surplus-value in addition. It is not the quantity of capital employed by him during the year, but the quantity returning to him periodically, that expresses the magnitude of his advanced capital. It is immaterial for the present question, whether the capital exists at the end of the year partly in the form of a productive supply, or partly in that of money or commodity-capital, and what may be the proportions of these different parts. On the other hand, so far as the owner of capital B is concerned, his advanced capital of £5,000 has returned to him, with an additional surplus-value of £5,000. And as for the owner of capital C (the last mentioned £5,500), surplus-value to the amount of £5,000 has been produced for him (advanced £5,000, rate of surplus-value 100%), but his advanced capital has not yet returned to him, nor has he pocketed his surplus-value.

The formula S' equal to s'n indicates that the rate of surplus-value in force for the employed variable capital, to wit,

$$\frac{\text{Quantity of S-V. produced in one Period of T-O.}}{\text{Var. Cap. employed in one Period of T-O.}}$$

must be multiplied with the number of periods of turn-over, or of the periods of reproduction of the advanced variable capital, that number of periods in which it renews its cycle.

We have seen already in Book 1, Chapter 4 (The Transformation of Money into Capital), and furthermore in Book 1, Chapter 23 (Simple Reproduction), that the capital value is not all spent, but advanced, as this value, having passed through the various phases of its cycle, returns to its point of departure, enriched by surplus-value. This fact shows that it has been merely advanced. The time consumed from the moment of its departure to the moment of its return is the one for which it was advanced. The entire rotation of capital-value, measured by the time from its advance to its return, constitutes its turn-over, and the duration of this turn-over is a period of turn-over. When this period has elapsed and the cycle is completed, the same capital-value can renew the same rotation, can expand itself some more, create some more surplus-value. If the variable capital is turned over ten times in one year, as in the case of capital A, then the same advance of capital creates in the course of one year, ten times the quantity of surplus-value created in one period of turn-over.

One must come to a clear conception of the nature of this advance from the standpoint of capitalist society.

Capital A, which is turned over ten times in one year, is advanced ten times during one year. It is advanced anew for every new period of turn-over. But at the same time, A never advances more than this same capital-value of £500, and disposes never of more than these £500 for the productive process considered by us. As soon as these £500 have completed one cycle, A starts them once more on the same cycle. In short, capital by its very nature preserves its character as capital only by means of continued service in successive processes of production. In the present case, it was never advanced for more than 5 weeks. If the turn-over lasts longer, this capital is inadequate. If the turn-over is contracted, a portion of this capital is released. Not ten capitals of £500 are advanced, but one capital of £500 is advanced ten times in successive intervals. The annual rate of surplus-value is, therefore, not calculated on ten advances of a capital of £500, not on £5,000, but on one advance of a capital of £500. It is the same in the case of one dollar which circulates ten times and yet represents never more than one single dollar in circulation, although it performs the function of 10 dollars. But in the hand, which holds it after each change of hands, it remains the same value of one dollar as before.

Just so the capital A indicates at each successive return, and likewise at its return at the end of the year that its owner has operated always with the same capital-value of £500. Hence only £500 flow back into

his hand at each turn-over. His advanced capital is never more than
£500. Hence the advanced capital represents the denominator of the
fraction which expresses the annual rate of surplus-value. We had for
it the formula

S' equal to s'vn/v, or s'n

As the current rate of surplus-value, s', is equal to s/v, equal to the
quantity of surplus-value divided by the variable capital which produced it, we may substitute the value of s' in s'n, that is to say s/v, in
our formula, thus making it

S' equal to sn/v

But by its tenfold turn-over, and thus the tenfold renewal of its
advance, the capital of £500 performs the function of a ten times
larger capital, of a capital of £5,000, just as 500 dollar coins, which
circulate ten times per year, perform the same function as 5000 dollar
coins which circulate once a year.

* * *

Section 2. The Turn-Over of the Individual
Variable Capital.

'Whatever the form of the process of production in a society, it must
be a continuous process, must continue to go periodically through the
same phases . . . When viewed, therefore, as a connected whole, and as
flowing on with incessant renewal, every social process of production
is, at the same time, a process of reproduction . . . As a periodic
increment of the capital advanced, or periodic fruit of capital in
process, surplus-value acquires the form of a revenue flowing out of
capital.' (Volume 1, Chapter 23, pages 619, 620.)

In the case of capital A, we have 10 periods of turn-over of 5 weeks
each. In the first period of turn-over, £500 of variable capital are
advanced, that is to say, £100 are converted into labour-power every
week, so that £500, have been converted into labour-power at the end
of the first period of turn-over. These £500, originally a part of the
total capital advanced, have then ceased to be capital. They are paid
out in wages. The labourers in their turn pay them out in the purchase
of means of subsistence, consuming subsistence to the amount of £500.
A quantity of commodities of that value is therefore annihilated (what
the labourer may save up in money, etc., is not capital). This quantity
of commodities has been consumed unproductively from the standpoint of the labourer, except in so far as it preserves his labour-power,
an indispensable instrument of the capitalist. In the second place, these
£500 have been converted, from the standpoint of the capitalist, into
labour-power of the same value (or price). Labour-power is consumed

by him productively in the labour-process. At the end of 5 weeks, a product valued at £1,000 has been created. Half of this, or £500, is the reproduced value of the variable capital paid out for wages. The other half, or £500, is newly produced surplus-value. But 5 weeks of labour-power, by the consumption of which a portion of a capital was transformed into variable capital, is likewise expended, consumed, although productively. The labour which was active yesterday is not the one which is active today. Its value, together with that of the surplus-value created by it, exists now as the value of a thing separate from labour-power, to wit, a product. But by converting the product into money, that portion of it, which is equal to the value of the variable capital advanced, may once more be transformed into labour-power and thus perform again the functions of variable capital. It is immaterial that the same labourers, that is to say, the same bearers of the labour-power, may be employed not only with the reproduced, but also with the reconverted capital-value in the form of money. It might be possible that the capitalist might hire different labourers for the second period of turn-over.

It is, therefore, a fact that a capital of £5,000, and not of £500, is paid out for labour-power in the ten periods of turn-over of 5 weeks each. The capital of £5,000 so advanced is consumed. It does not exist any more. On the other hand, labour-power to the value of £5,000, not of £500, is incorporated successively in the productive process and reproduces not only its own value of £5,000, but also a surplus value of £5,000 over and above its value. The variable capital of £500, which is advanced for the second period of turn-over, is not the identical capital of £500, which had been advanced for the first period of turn-over. This has been consumed, expended in labour-power. But it is replaced by new variable capital of £500, which was produced in the first period of turn-over in the form of commodities and reconverted into money. This new money-capital is, therefore, the money-form of the quantity of commodities newly produced in the first period of turn-over. The fact that an identical sum of £500 is again in the hands of the capitalist, apart from the surplus-value, a sum equal to the one which he had originally advanced, disguises the circumstance that he now operates with a newly produced capital. (As for the other constituents of value of the commodity-capital, which replace the constant parts of capital, their value is not newly produced, but only the form is changed in which this value exists.) Let us take the third period of turn-over. Here it is evident that the capital of £500, advanced for a third time, is not an old, but a newly produced capital, for it is the money-form of the quantity of commodities produced in the second, not in the first, period of turn-over; that is to say, of that portion of this quantity of commodities, whose value is equal to that of the advanced variable capital. The quantity of commodities produced in the first period of turn-over is sold. Its value, to the extent that it was equal to the variable portion of the value of the advanced capital, was transformed into the new labour-power of the second period of turn-over and produced a new quantity of commodities, which were sold in their turn and a portion of whose value constitutes the capital of £500 advanced for the third period of turn-over.

And so forth during the ten periods of turn-over. In the course of these, newly produced quantities of commodities are thrown upon the market every 5 weeks, in order to incorporate ever new labour-power in the progress of production. (The value of these commodities, to the extent that it replaces variable capital, is likewise newly produced, and does not merely appear so, as in the case of the constant circulating capital.)

That which is accomplished by the tenfold turn-over of the advanced variable capital of £500, is not that this capital can be productively consumed ten times, nor that a capital lasting for 5 weeks can be employed for 50 weeks. Ten times £500 of variable capital are rather employed in those 50 weeks, and the capital of £500 lasts only for 5 weeks at a time and must be replaced at the end of the 5 weeks by a newly produced capital of £500. This applies equally to capital A and B. But at this point, the difference begins.

At the end of the first period of 5 weeks, a variable capital of £500 has been advanced and expended by both capitalists, A and B. Both B and A have transformed its value into labour-power and replaced it by that portion of the value of the new product created by this labour-power which is equal to the value of the advanced variable capital of £500. And for both B and A, the labour-power has not only reproduced the value of the expended variable capital of £500 by a new value of the same amount, but also added a surplus-value, which, according to our assumption, is of the same magnitude.

But in the case of B, the product which replaces the advanced variable capital and adds a surplus-value to it, is not in the form in which it can serve once more as a productive, or a variable, capital. On the other hand, it is in such a form in the case of A. B, however, does not possess the variable capital consumed in the first 5 and every subsequent 5 weeks up to the end of the year, although it has been reproduced by newly created value with a superadded surplus-value, in the form in which it may once more perform the function of productive, or variable, capital. Its value is indeed replaced, or reproduced, by new value, but the form of its value (in this case the absolute form of value, its money-form) is not reproduced.

For the second period of 5 weeks (and so forth for every succeeding 5 weeks of the year), £500 must again be available, the same as for the first period. Making exception of the conditions of credit, £5,000 must, therefore, be available at the beginning of the year as a latent advanced capital, although they are expended only gradually for labour-power in the course of the year.

But in the case of A, the cycle, the turn-over of the advanced capital, being completed, the reproduced value is after the lapse of 5 weeks in the precise form in which it may set new labour-power in motion for another term of 5 weeks, in its original money-form.

Both A and B consume new labour-power in the second period of 5 weeks and expend a new capital of £500 for the payment of this labour-power. The means of subsistence of the labourer paid with the first £500 are gone, their value has in every case disappeared from the hands of the capitalist. With the second £500, new labour-power is bought, new means of subsistence withdrawn from the market. In short, it is a new capital of £500 which is expended, not the old. But in the case of A, this new capital of £500 is the money-form of the newly produced substitute for the value of the formerly expended £500; while in the case of B, this substitute is in a form, in which it cannot serve as variable capital. It is there, but not in the form of variable capital. For the continuation of the process of production for the next 5 weeks, an additional capital of £500 must, therefore, be available in the form of money, which is indispensable in this case, and must be advanced. Thus both A and B expend an equal amount of variable capital, pay for and consume an equal quantity of labour-power, during 50 weeks. Only, B must pay for it with an advanced capital equal to its total value of £5,000, while A pays for it successively by the ever renewed money-form of the substitute produced in every 5 weeks for the capital of £500 advanced for every 5 weeks. In no case is more capital advanced by A than is required for 5 weeks, that is to say, £500. These £500 last for the entire year. It is, therefore, evident that, the intensity of exploitation and the current rate of surplus-value being the same for the two capitals, the annual rates of A and B must hold an inverse ratio to one another than the magnitudes of the variable money-capitals, which had to be advanced in order to set in motion the same quantity of labour-power during the year. The rate of A is as 5,000 s to 500 v, or 1,000%; that of B is as 5,000 s to 5,000 v, or 100%. But 500 v is to 5,000 v as 1 to 10, or as 100% to 1,000%.

The difference is due to the difference of the periods of turnover, that is to say, to the period in which the substitute for the value of a certain variable capital employed for a certain time can renew its function of capital, can serve as a new capital. In the case of both B and A, the same reproduction of value of the variable capital employed during the same periods take place. There is also the same increment of surplus-value during the same periods. But in the case of B, while there is every 5 weeks a reproduction of the value of £500 and a surplus-value of £500, these values do not yet make a new capital, because they are not in the form of money. In the case of A, on the other hand, the value of the old capital is not only reproduced by a new value, but it is rehabilitated in its money-form, so that it may at once assume the functions of a new capital.

So far as the mere production of surplus-value is concerned, the rapid or slow transformation of the substitute for the value advanced into money, and thus into the form in which the variable capital is advanced, is an insignificant circumstance. This production depends on the magnitude of the employed variable capital and the intensity of exploitation. But the more or less rapid transformation referred to *does* modify the magnitude of the money-capital which must be advanced in order to set a definite quantity of labour-power in motion during the year, and therefore it determines the annual rate of surplus-value.

Section 3. The Turn-Over of the Variable Capital, Considered from the Point of View of Society.

Let us look for a moment at this matter from the point of view of society. Let the wages of one labourer be £1 per week, the working day 10 hours. Both A and B employ 100 labourers per week (£100 for 100 labourers per week, or £500 for 5 weeks, or £5,000 for 50 weeks), and each one of them works 60 hours per week of 6 days. Then 100 labourers work 6,000 hours per week, and 300,000 hours in 50 weeks. This labour-power is engaged by A and B, and cannot be expended by society for anything else. To this extent, the matter is the same socially that it is in the case of A and B. Furthermore: both A and B pay their respective 100 labourers £5,000 in wages per year (or together for 200 labourers £10,000) and withdraw from society means of subsistence to that amount. So far, the matter is socially likewise the same as in the case of A and B. Since the labourers in either case are paid by the week, they weekly withdraw their means of subsistence from society and throw in either case a weekly equivalent in money into the circulation. But here the difference begins.

First. The money, which the labourer of A throws into the circulation, is not only, as it is for the labourer of B, the money-form for the value of the labour-power (an actual payment for labour already performed); it is also, beginning with the second period of turn-over since the opening of the business, the money form of the value of his own product (price of labour-power plus surplus-value) created during the first period of turn-over, by which his labour during the second period of turn-over is paid. This is not the case with the labourer of B. The money is here indeed a medium of payment for labour already performed by the labourer, but this labour is not paid for with its own product turned into money (the money-form of the value produced by itself). This cannot be done until the beginning of the second year, when the labourer of B is paid with the money-form of the value of his product of the preceding year.

The shorter the period of turn-over of capital – the shorter, therefore, the intervals in which the periods of reproduction are renewed – the quicker is the variable portion of the capital, advanced by the capitalist in the form of money, transformed into the money-form of the product (including surplus-value) created by the labourer in place of the variable capital; the shorter is the time for which the capitalist must advance money out of his own funds, the smaller is the capital advanced by him compared to the given scale of production; and the greater is the proportionate quantity of surplus-value which he realises with a given rate of surplus-value during the year, because he can buy the labourer so much more frequently with the money-form of the product created by the labour of that labourer, and set his labour into motion.

Given the scale of production, the absolute magnitude of the advanced variable capital (and of the circulating capital in general) decreases in proportion as the period of turn-over is shortened, and so does the annual rate of surplus-value increase. Given the magnitude of the advanced capital, and the rate of surplus-value, the scale of production and the absolute quantity of surplus-value created in one period of turnover increases simultaneously with the rise in the annual rate of surplus-value due to the contraction of the periods of reproduction. It follows in general from the preceding analysis that, according to the different length of the periods of turn-over, money-capital of considerably different quantity must be advanced, in order to set in motion the same quantity of productive circulating capital and the same quantity of labour-power with the same intensity of exploitation.

Second. It is due to the first difference, that the labourers of B and A pay for the means of subsistence which they buy with the variable capital that has been transformed into a medium of circulation in their hands. For instance, they do not only withdraw wheat from the market, but also leave in its place an equivalent in money. But since the money, with which the labourer of B pays for his means of subsistence and draws them from the market is not the money-form of the value of a product which he has thrown on the market during the year, as it is in the case of the labourer of A, he supplies the seller of his means of subsistence only with money, but not with products – be they materials of production or means of subsistence – which this seller might buy with the money received from the labourer, as he may in the case of the labourer of A. The market is therefore stripped of labour-power, means of subsistence for this labour-power, fixed capital, in the form of instruments of production used by B, and materials of production, and an equivalent in money is thrown on the market in their place, but no product is thrown on the market during the year by which the material elements of productive capital withdrawn from it might be replaced. If we assumed that society were not capitalistic, but communistic, then the money-capital would be entirely eliminated, and with it the disguises which it carries into the transactions. The question is then simply reduced to the problem that society must calculate beforehand how much labour, means of production, and means of subsistence it can utilise without injury for such lines of activity as, for instance, the building of railroads, which do not furnish any means of production or subsistence, or any useful thing, for a long time, a year or more, while they require labour, and means of production and subsistence out of the annual social production. But in capitalist society, where social intelligence does not act until after the fact, great disturbances will and must occur under these circumstances. On one hand there is a pressure on the money-market, while on the other an easy money-market creates just such enterprises in mass, that bring about the very circumstances by which a pressure is later on exerted on the market. A pressure is exerted on the money-market, since an advance of money-capital for long terms is always required on a large scale. And this is so quite apart from the fact that industrialists and merchants invest the money-capital needed for the carrying on of their business in railroad speculation, etc., and reimburse themselves by borrowing in the money-market. On the other hand, there is a pressure on the available productive capital of society. Since elements of productive capital are continually withdrawn from the market and only an equivalent in money is thrown on the market in their place, the demand of cash payers for products increases without supplying any elements for purchase. Hence a rise in prices, of means of production and of subsistence. To make matters worse, swindling operations are always carried on at this time, involving a transfer of great capitals. A band of speculators, contractors, engineers, lawyers, etc., enrich themselves. They create a strong demand for consumption on the market, wages rising at the same time. So far as means of subsistence are concerned, it is true that agriculture is thus stimulated. But as these means of subsistence cannot be suddenly increased within the year, their importation increases, as does the importation of exotic food stuffs, such as coffee, sugar, wine, and articles of luxury. Hence we then have a surplus importation and speculation in this line of imports. Furthermore, in those lines of business in which production may be rapidly increased, such as manufacture proper, mining, etc., the rise in prices causes a sudden expansion, which is soon followed by a collapse. The same effect is produced on the labour-market, where large numbers of the latent relative over-population, and even of the employed labourers, are attracted toward the new lines of business. In general, such enterprises on a large scale as railroad building withdraw a certain quantity of labour-power from the labour-market, which can come only from such lines of business as agriculture, etc., where strong men are needed. This still continues even after the new enterprises have become established lines of business and the wandering class of labourers needed for them has already been formed. A case in point is the temporary increase in the scale of business of railroads beyond the normal. A portion of the reserve army of labourers who kept wages down is absorbed. Wages rise everywhere, even in the hitherto engaged parts of the labour-market. This lasts until the inevitable crash throws the reserve army of labour out of work, and wages are once more depressed to their minimum or below it.[1]

To the extent that the greater or smaller length of the period of turn-over depends on the working period, strictly so called, that is to say on the period which is required to get the product ready for the market, it rests on the existing material conditions of production of the various investments of capital. In agriculture, they partake more of the character of natural conditions of production, in manufacture and the greater part of the extractive industry they vary with the social development of the process of production itself.

Furthermore, to the extent that the length of the working period is conditioned on the size of the orders (the quantitative volume in which the product is generally thrown upon the market), this point depends on conventions. But convention itself depends for its material basis on the scale of production, and it is accidental only when considered individually.

Finally, so far as the length of the period of turn-over depends on that of the period of circulation, the latter is, indeed, conditioned on the incessant change of market combinations, the greater or smaller ease of selling, and the resulting necessity to throw a part of the product to more or less remote markets. Apart from the volume of the general demand, the movement of prices plays here one of the main roles, since sales are intentionally restricted when prices are falling, while production proceeds; vice versa, production and sale keep step, when prices are rising, and sales may even be made in advance. But we must consider the actual distance of the place of production from the market as the real material basis.

For instance, English cotton goods or yarn are sold to India. The export merchant may pay the English cotton manufacturer. (The export merchant does so willingly only when the money-market stands well. If the manufacturer replaces his money-capital by operating credit on his own part, matters are already in a bad state). The exporter sells his cotton goods later in the Indian market, whence his advanced capital is returned to him. Until the time of this return the case is identical with the one in which the length of the working period necessitates the advance of new money-capital, in order to maintain the process of production on a certain scale. The money-capital with which the manufacturer pays his labourers and renews the other elements of his circulating capital, is not the money-form of the yarn produced by him. This cannot be the case until the value of this yarn has returned to England in the form of money or products. It is additional capital as before. The difference is only that it is advanced by the merchant instead of the manufacturer, and that it reaches the merchant by means of manipulations of credit. Furthermore, before this money is thrown on the market, or simultaneously with it, no additional product has been thrown on the English market, to be bought with this money and to be consumed productively or individually. If this condition occurs for a long period on a large scale, it must cause the same effects as a prolongation of the working period, previously mentioned.

Now it may be that the yarn is sold even in India on credit. With this credit, products are bought in India and sent back to England, or drafts are remitted to this amount. If this condition is prolonged, there is a pressure on the Indian money-market, and its reaction may cause a crisis in England. This crisis, even if combined with an export of precious metals to India, causes a new crisis in that country on account of the bankruptcy of English business houses and their Indian branch houses, who had received credit from the Indian banks. Thus a crisis occurs simultaneously on the market which is credited with the balance of trade and on the one which is charged with it. This phenomenon may be still more complicated. Take it, for instance that England has sent silver ingots to India, but the

English creditors of India now collect their debts in that country, and India will soon after have reshipped its silver ingots to England.

It is possible that the export trade to India and the import trade from India might approximately balance one another, although the imports (with the exception of peculiar circumstances, such as arise in the price of cotton), will be determined as to their volume and stimulated by the export trade. The balance of trade between England and India may seem to be squared, or may show but slight fluctuations on either side. But as soon as the crisis appears in England it is seen that unsold cotton goods are stored in India (and have not been transformed from commodity-capital into money-capital – an overproduction to this extent), and that, on the other hand, there are in England not only unsold supplies of Indian goods, but that a considerable portion of the sold and consumed goods is not yet paid for. Hence, that which appears as a crisis on the money-market, is in reality an expression of abnormal conditions in the process of production and reproduction.

Third. So far as the employed circulating capital (constant and variable) is concerned, the length of the period of turn-over, to the extent that it is due to the working period, makes this difference: in the case of several turn-overs during one year, an element of the variable or constant circulating capital may be supplied by its own product, for instance in the production of coal, the tailoring business, etc. Otherwise, this cannot take place, at least not within the same year.

Chapter 17
The Circulation of Surplus-Value

We have just seen that a difference in the period of turn-over causes a difference in the annual rate of surplus-value, even if the quantity of the annually produced surplus-value is the same.

But there is furthermore necessarily a difference in the capitalisation of surplus-value, the accumulation, and to that extent also in the quantity of surplus-value produced during the year, while the rate of surplus-value remains the same.

To begin with, we remark that capital A (in the illustration of the preceding chapter) has a current periodical revenue, so that with the exception of the period of turn-over beginning the business, it pays for its own consumption within the year out of its production of surplus-value, and need not cover it by advances out of its own funds.

But B has to do this. While he produces as much surplus-value in the same time as A, he does not realise on it and cannot consume it either productively or individually. So far as individual consumption is concerned, the surplus-value is discounted in advance. Funds for that purpose must be advanced.

One portion of the productive capital, which is difficult to classify, namely the additional capital required for the repair and maintenance of the fixed capital, is now likewise seen in a new light.

In the case of A, this portion of capital – in full or for the greater part – is not advanced at the beginning of production. It need not be available, or even in existence. It comes out of the business itself by a direct transformation of surplus-value into capital by its direct employment as capital. One portion of the surplus-value which is not only periodically produced but also realised may cover the expenditures required for repairs, etc. A portion of the capital needed for carrying on the business on its original scale is thus produced in the course of business by the business itself by means of capitalisation of a portion of surplus-value. This is impossible for the capitalist B. This portion of capital must in his case form a part of the capital originally advanced. In both cases this portion will figure in the books of the capitalists as an advanced capital, which it really is, since according to our assumption it is a part of the productive capital required for maintaining the business on a certain scale. But it makes a great difference out of which funds it is advanced. In the case of B, it is actually a part of the capital to be originally advanced or held available. On the other hand, in the case of A, it is a part of the surplus-value, if used as capital. This last case shows that not only the accumulated capital, but also a portion of the orginally advanced capital, may be capitalised surplus-value.

As soon as the development of credit interferes, the relation between originally advanced capital and capitalised surplus-value is still more complicated. For instance, A borrows a portion of the productive capital, with which he starts his business and continues it during the year, from banker C, not having sufficient capital of his own for this purpose. Banker C lends him the required sum, which consists only of surplus-value deposited with the banker by capitalists D, E, F, etc. From the standpoint of A, there is as yet no question of any accumulated surplus-value. But from the point of view of D, E, F, etc., A is merely their agent, capitalising surplus-value appropriated by them.

We have seen in Volume 1, Chapter 24, that accumulation, the conversion of surplus-value into capital, is substantially a process of reproduction on an enlarged scale, no matter whether this expansion is expressed extensively in the form of an addition of new factories to the old ones, or intensively by the expansion of the existing scale of production.

The expansion of the scale of production may proceed in small portions, a part of the surplus-value being used for improvements which either increase simply the productive power of the labour employed, or permit at the same time of its more intensive exploitation. Or, in places where the working day is not legally restricted, an additional expenditure of circulating capital (in materials of production and wages) suffices to expand production without an extension of the fixed capital, whose daily time of employment is thus merely lengthened, while its period of turn-over is correspondingly abbreviated. Or, capitalised surplus-value may, under favourable market combinations, permit of speculation in raw materials, an operation for which the capital originally advanced would not have been sufficient, etc.

However, it is evident that in cases where the greater number of the periods of turn-over carries with it a more frequent realisation of surplus-value within the year, there will be periods in which there can be neither a prolongation of the working day, nor an introduction of improvements in details, while, on the other hand, there is only a limited scope in which it is possible to expand the entire business on a proportional scale – partly by a reorganisation of the entire plan of business, buildings, etc., partly by an expansion of the funds for labour, as in agriculture – and a volume of additional capital is required, such as can be supplied only by several years of accumulation of surplus-value.

Along with the actual accumulation, or conversion of surplus-value into productive capital, (and a corresponding reproduction on an enlarged scale), there is, then, an accumulation of money, a hoarding of a portion of the surplus-value in the form of latent money-capital, which is not intended for service as additional productive capital until later.

This is the aspect of the matter from the point of view of the individual capitalist. But simultaneously with the development of capitalist production, the credit system also develops. The money-capital, which the capitalist cannot as yet employ in his own business, is employed by others, who pay him an interest for its use. It serves for him as money-capital in its specific meaning, that is to say as a kind of capital distinguished from productive. But it serves as capital in another's hands. It is plain, that, with the more frequent realisation of surplus-value and the rising scale on which it is produced, there must also be an increase in the proportion of new money-capital, or money in the form of capital, thrown upon the money-market and withdrawn from it for the purpose of expanding production.

The simplest form, in which the additional latent money-capital may be represented, is that of a hoard. It may be that this hoard is additional money or silver, secured directly or indirectly in exchange with countries producing precious metals. And only in this manner does the hoarded money in a country grow absolutely. On the other hand, it may be – and is so in the majority of cases – that this hoard is nothing but money withdrawn from inland circulation and has assumed the form of a hoard in the hands of individual capitalists. It is furthermore possible that this latent money-capital consists only of tokens of value – we ignore credit money at this point – or of mere claims (titles) on third persons conferred by legal documents. In all such cases, whatever may be the form of this additional money-capital, it represents, so far as it is prospective capital, nothing but additional and reserved legal titles of capitalists on future additional products of society.

'The mass of the actually accumulated wealth, considered as to magnitude, . . . is absolutely insignificant compared to the productive forces of society to which it belongs, whatever may be its stage of civilisation; or even compared to the actual consumption of this same society in the course of but a few years; so insignificant, that the attention of the legislators and political economists should be mainly directed to the forces of production and their free development in the future, not, as heretofore, to the mere accumulated wealth which strikes the eye. By far the greater part of the so-called accumulated wealth is only nominal and does not consist of actual objects, such as ships, houses, cotton goods, real estate improvements, but of mere legal titles, claims on the future annual productive forces of society, titles generated and perpetuated by the devices or institutions of insecurity . . . The use of such articles (accumulations of physical things, or actual wealth) as a mere means of appropriating for their owners a wealth which the future productive forces of society are as yet to create, this use would be gradually withdrawn from them without any force by the natural laws of distribution; with the assistance of co-operative labour, it would be withdrawn from them within a few years.' (William Thompson, *Inquiry into the Principles of the Distribution of Wealth*, London, 1850, page 453. This book appeared for the first time in 1827.)

'It is little understood, nor even suspected by most people, what an utterly insignificant portion, whether it be in quantity or effectiveness, the actual accumulations of society constitute of the human productive forces, yea, even of the ordinary consumption of a single generation of men during a few years. The reason for this is obvious, but the effect is very injurious. The wealth which is consumed annually, disappears as it is being used; it stands before the eye only for a moment, and makes an impression only while it is enjoyed or consumed. But the slowly consumable portion of wealth, furniture, machines, buildings, from our childhood to our age they are standing before our eyes, lasting monuments of human exertion. By virtue of the ownership of this fixed, lasting, slowly consumed portion of public wealth – of the soil and the raw materials on which, the instruments with which, work is done, the houses which give shelter while the work is being done – by virtue of this ownership the owners of these objects control for their own advantage the annual productive forces of all really productive labourers of society, insignificant as those objects may be in proportion to the ever recurring products of this labour. The population of Great Britain and Ireland is 20 millions; the average consumption of every man, woman, and child is about £20, making a total wealth of £400 million, the product of labour annually consumed. The total amount of the accumulated capital of those countries does not exceed, according to estimates, £1,200 million, or thrice the annual product of labour; if equally divided, £60 of capital per capita. We have here to deal more with the proportion than with the more or less inaccurate absolute amounts of these estimated sums. The interest on this total capital would suffice to maintain the total population in its present style of living for about two months of one year, and the entire accumulated capital (if buyers could be found for it) would maintain them without labour for a whole three years! At the end of which time, without houses, clothing, and food, they would have to starve, or become the slaves of those who have maintained them during these three years. As three years are to the life time of one healthy generation, say to 40 years, so the magnitude and importance of the actual wealth, the accumulated capital of even the richest country, is to its productive forces, to the productive forces of a single human generation; not to what they might really produce under intelligent institutions of equal security, and especially with co-operative labour, but to what they are actually producing under the imperfect and discouraging makeshifts of insecurity . . . And in order to maintain this apparently tremendous mass of existing capital, or rather the control and monopoly of the annual product of labour in its present condition of compulsory division this entire machinery the vices, the crimes, the sufferings of insecurity, are to be perpetuated. Nothing can be accumulated, unless the necessary wants are first satisfied, and the great current of human desires flows after enjoyment; hence the comparatively insignificant amount of actual wealth of society at any given moment. It is an eternal circulation of production and consumption. In this immense mass of annual production and consumption, the handful of actual accumulation would hardly be missed, and yet attention has been mainly directed, not to that mass of productive forces, but to this handful of accumulation. But this handful has been appropriated by a few, and transformed into an instrument for the appropriation of the ever recurring annual products of the labour of the great masses. Hence the vital importance of such an instrument for these few . . . About one-third of the annual national product is now taken from the producers under the name of public taxes, and unproductively consumed by people that do not give any equivalent for it, that is to say, none that is accepted as such by the producer . . . The eye of the crowd looks with astonishment upon the accumulated masses, especially when they are concentrated in the hands of a few. But the annually produced masses, like the eternal and innumerable waves of a mighty stream, roll by and are lost in the forgotten ocean of consumption. And yet this eternal consumption determines not alone all enjoyments, but the very existence of the human race. The quantity and distribution of this annual product should above all be made the object of study. The actual accumulation is of secondary importance, and receives even this importance almost exclusively by its influence on the distribution of the annual product . . . The actual accumulation and distribution is here (in Thompson's work) always considered in reference and subordination to the productive forces. In almost all other systems, the productive forces have been considered with reference and in subordination to accumulation and to the perpetuation of existing mode of distribution. Compared with the conservation of this existing mode of distribution, the ever recurring suffering or welfare of the entire human race is not considered worthy of a glance. To perpetuate the results of force, of fraud, and of accident, this has been called security, and for conservation of this lying security, all the forces of production of the human race have been mercilessly sacrificed.' (*ibidem*, pages, 440–443.)

*   *   *

For the reproduction, only two normal cases are possible, apart from disturbances, which interfere with reproduction even on a given scale.

There is either reproduction on a simple scale.

Or, there is a capitalisation of a surplus-value, accumulation.

Section 1. Simple Reproduction.

In the case of simple reproduction, the surplus-value produced or realised annually, or by several turn-overs during the year, is consumed individually, that is to say unproductively, by its owner, the capitalist.

The fact that the value of the product consists in part of surplus-value, in part of that portion of value which is formed by the variable capital reproduced through it plus the constant capital consumed by it, does not alter anything, either in the quantity, or in the value of the total product, which continually passes into circulation and is just as continually withdrawn from it, in order to pass into productive or individual consumption; that is to say, to serve as means of production or consumption. Making exception of the constant capital, only the distribution of the annual product between the labourers and the capitalists is thereby affected.

Even if simple reproduction is assumed, a portion of the surplus-value must, therefore, always exist in the form of money, not of products, because it could otherwise not be converted for purposes of consumption from money into products. This conversion of the surplus-value from its original commodity-form into money must be further analysed at this place. In order to simplify the matter, we assume the most elementary form of the problem, namely the exclusive circulation of metal coin, of money which is a real equivalent.

According to the laws of the simple circulation of commodities (developed in Book 1, Chapter 3), the mass of the metal coin existing in a country must not only be sufficient for the circulation of the commodities, but must also suffice for the fluctuations of the circulation of money, which arise partly from fluctuations in the velocity of the circulation, partly from a change in the prices of commodities, partly from the various and varying proportions in which the money serves as a medium of payment or as the typical medium of circulation. The proportion in which the existing quantity of money is divided into a hoard and money in circulation, varies continually, but the quantity of money is always equal to the sum of the money hoarded and the money circulating. This quantity of money (quantity of precious metal) is a gradually accumulated hoard of society. To the extent that a portion of this hoard is consumed by wear, it must be replaced annually, the same as any other product. This takes place in reality by a direct or indirect exchange of a part of the annual product of a country for the product of countries producing gold and silver. However, this international character of the transaction disguises its simple course. In order to reduce the problem to its simplest and most transparent expression, it must be assumed that the production of gold and silver takes place in the same country in which the other products are created, so that the production of gold and silver constitutes a part of the total social production within every country.

Apart from the gold and silver produced for articles of luxury, the medium of their annual production must be equal to the wear of metal coin annually occasioned by the circulation of money. Furthermore, if the value of the annually produced and circulating quantity of commodities increases, the annual production of gold and silver must likewise increase, unless the growth of the value of the circulating commodities and the quantity of money required for their circulation (and the corresponding formation of a hoard) is accompanied by a greater velocity in the circulation of money and a more extensive function of money as a medium of payment, that is to say, by a greater mutual balancing of purchases and sales without the intervention of actual money.

A portion of the social labour-power and a portion of the social means of production must, therefore, be expended annually in the production of gold and silver.

The capitalists, who are engaged in the production of gold and silver, and who, according to our assumption of simple reproduction, carry on their production only within the limits of the annual average wear and the resulting average consumption of gold and silver, throw their surplus-value, which they consume annually, according to our assumption, without capitalising any of it, directly into circulation in the form of money, which is the natural form for them, not, as in the case of the other capitalists, the converted form of their product.

Furthermore, as concerns wages, the money form in which the variable capital is advanced, it is not replaced in this case by the sale of the product, by a conversion into money, but by a product whose natural form is from the outset that of money.

Finally, the same applies also to that portion of the product in precious metals which is equal to the value of the periodically consumed constant capital, both the constant circulating and the constant fixed capital consumed during the year.

Let us study the rotation, or the turn-over, of the capital invested in the production of precious metals first in the form of M—C—P – M'. So far as the C in M—C does not only consist of labour-power and materials of production, but also of fixed capital, only a part of whose value is consumed by P, it is evident that the product, M', is a sum of money equal to the variable capital invested in wages plus the circulating constant capital invested in materials of production plus a portion of the value of the fixed constant capital plus a surplus-value. If the sum were smaller, the general value of gold remaining the same, then the mine would be unproductive, or, if this is generally the case, the value of gold, compared with the value of commodities that remains unchanged, would rise; that is to say, the prices of commodities would fall, so that henceforth the amount of money invested in M—C would be smaller.

If we consider at first only the circulating portion of capital advanced in M, the starting point of M—C...P...M', we find that it is a certain sum of money advanced and thrown into circulation for the payment of labour-power and the purchase of materials of production. But this sum is not withdrawn from circulation, by the rotation of *this* capital, in order to be thrown into it anew. The product is money even in its natural form, there is no need of transforming it into money by means of exchange, by a process of circulation. It passes from the process of production into the process of circulation, not in the form of commodity-capital which has to be converted into money-capital, but as a money-capital which is to be reconverted into productive capital, which is to be fresh labour-power and materials of production. The money-form of the circulating capital consumed in labour-power and materials of production is replaced, not by the sale of the product, but by the natural form of the product itself; not by once more withdrawing its value from circulation in the form of money, but by additional, newly produced money.

Let us assume that this circulating capital is £500, the period of turn-over is 5 weeks, the working period 4 weeks, the period of circulation only 1 week. From the outset, money must be partly advanced for a productive supply, partly available, for 5 weeks, in order to be paid out gradually for wages. At the beginning of the 6th week, £400 have flown back and £100 have been released. This is continually repeated. Here, as in previous cases, £100 will always find themselves released during a certain time of the turn-over. But they consist of additional, newly produced, money, the same as the other £400. We have in this case 10 turn-overs per year and the annual product is £5,000 in gold. (The period of circulation does not arise, in this case, from the time required for the conversion of commodities into money, but for the conversion of money into the elements of production.)

In the case of every other capital of £500, turned over under the same conditions, it is the ever renewed money-form which is exchanged for the produced commodity capital and thrown into the circulation every 4 weeks and which resumes this form in every new interval by sale, that is to say, by a periodical withdrawal of the quantity of money which entered originally into the process. But here a new additional quantity of money to the amount of £500 is thrown into circulation by the process of production itself, in order to withdraw from it continually materials of production and labour-power. This money thrown into circulation is not withdrawn from it by the rotation of this capital, but rather continually increased by newly produced quantities of gold.

Let us look at the variable portion of this circulating capital, and assume that it is, as before, £100. Then these £100 would be sufficient in the ordinary production of commodities, with 10 turnovers, to pay continually for the required labour-power. Here, in the production of money, the same amount is likewise sufficient. But the £100 of the reflux, with which the labour-power is paid every 5 weeks are not a converted form of its product, but a portion of this ever renewed product itself. The producer of gold pays his labourers directly with a portion of the gold produced by them. Thus the £1,000 invested annually in labour-power and thrown by the labourers into the circulation do not return by the way of this circulation to their starting point.

Furthermore, so far as the fixed capital is concerned, it requires the investment of a large money-capital at the opening of the business, and this capital is thus thrown into the circulation. Like all fixed capital it flows back only piece by piece in the course of years. But it flows back as an immediate portion of the product, of the gold, not by the sale of the product and its consequent monetisation. In other words, it receives gradually its money-form, not by a withdrawal of money from circulation, but by an accumulation of a corresponding portion of the product. The money-capital so replaced is not a quantity of money gradually withdrawn from circulation for a compensation of the sum originally thrown into it for fixed capital. It is an additional sum of new money.

Finally, as concerns the surplus-value, it is likewise equal to a certain portion of the new product of gold, which is thrown into circulation in every period of turn-over in order to be unproductively consumed according to our assumption, in means of subsistence and articles of luxury.

But according to our assumption, the entire annual production of gold – which continually withdraws labour-power and materials of production, but no money, from the market, while adding fresh quantities of money to it – replaces only the money worn out during the year, keeps only the quantity of social money complete which exists continually, although it consists in varying portions of the two forms, hoarded money and money in circulation.

According to the law of the circulation of commodities, the quantity of money must be equal to the amount of money required for circulation plus a certain amount held in the form of a hoard, which increases or decreases according to the contraction or expansion of circulation and serves especially for the formation of the reserve funds required as means of payment. That which must be paid in gold – to the extent that there is no balancing of accounts – is the value of the commodities. The fact that a portion of these commodities represents a surplus value, that is to say, did not cost the seller anything, does not alter the matter in any way. Take it that the producers are all independent owners of their means of production, so that circulation takes place between the immediate producers themselves. Apart from the constant portion of their capital, their annual surplus-product might then be divided into two parts, analogous with capitalist conditions: Part A, replacing the necessary means of subsistence, and Part B, consumed partly for articles of luxury, partly for an expansion of production. Part A then plays the role of the variable capital, Part B that of the surplus-value. But this division would remain without influence on the magnitude of the sum of money required for the circulation of the total product. Other circumstances remaining equal, the value of the circulating mass of commodities would be the same, and thus also the amount of money required for its circulation. The capitalists would also have to keep on hand the same money reserve, the division of the periods of turn-over remaining the same; that is to say, the same portion of their capital would have to be held in the form of money, because their production, according to our assumption, would be a production of commodities, the same as before. Hence the fact that a portion of the value of the commodities consists of surplus-value, would change absolutely nothing in the quantity of the money required for the running of the business.

An opponent of Tooke, who clings to the formula M—C—M', asks him how the capitalist manages always to withdraw more money from circulation than he threw into it. Mark well! It is not here a question of the *formation* of surplus-value. This, the only secret, is a matter of course from the capitalist standpoint. The quantity of value employed would not be capital, if it did not secure an increment of surplus-value. But as it is capital, according to our assumption, there must be surplus-value as a matter of course.

The question, then, is not – where does the surplus-value come from? It is rather: whence comes the money for which it is exchanged?

But in bourgeois political economy, the existence of surplus-value is self-understood. It is not only assumed, but also connected with the assumption that a portion of the commodities thrown into circulation is a surplus product, which was not thrown into circulation together with the capital of the capitalist. In other words, it is assumed by bourgeois political economists, that the capitalist throws a surplus over and above his capital into the circulation with his product, and that he recovers this surplus from it.

The commodity-capital, which the capitalist throws into the circulation, has a greater value than the productive capital which he withdrew from the circulation in the form of labour-power and means of production (it is neither explained nor understood by the bourgeois economists where this greater value comes from, but it is considered by them as an accomplished fact). On the basis of this assumption it is evident by what means not only the capitalist A, but also B, C, D, etc., manage always to withdraw more value from the circulation by means of the exchange of their commodities than the value of the capital originally and repeatedly advanced by them. A, B, C, D, continually throw a greater value into the circulation in the form of commodity-capital, than they withdraw from it in the form of productive capital – this operation is as many-sided as the various independent capitals in action. Hence they have continually to divide among themselves a sum of values (that is to say, every one withdaws from circulation a productive capital) equal to the sum of values of their respective productive capitals; and they furthermore divide among themselves just as continually a sum of values which they all throw into circulation in the form of commodities, representing the excess of the commodity-capital over its elements of production.

But the commodity-capital must be monetised before its conversion into productive capital, or before the surplus-value contained in it can be spent. Where does the money for this purpose come from? This question seems difficult at the first glance, and neither Tooke nor any one else has answered it so far.

The circulating capital of £500 advanced in the form of money-capital, whatever may be its period of turn-over, may now stand for the total capital of society, that is to say, of the capitalist class. Let the surplus-value be £100. How can the entire capitalist class manage to draw continually £600 out of the circulation, when they continually throw only £500 into it?

After the money-capital of £500 has been converted into productive capital, it transforms itself, within the process of production, into commodities worth £600 and throws into circulation, not only commodities valued at £500, equal to the money-capital originally advanced, but also a newly produced surplus-value of £100.

This additional surplus-value of £100 is thrown into circulation in the form of commodities. There is no doubt about that. But this same operation does not by any means supply the additional money for the circulation of this new additional value.

It should not be attempted to evade this difficulty by plausible subterfuges.

For instance: so far as the constant circulating capital is concerned, it is obvious that not all invest it simultaneously. While the capitalist A sells his commodities, so that his advanced capital assumes the form of money, there is on the other hand, the available money-capital of the buyer B which assumes the form of his means of production which A is just producing. The same transaction, which restores that of B to its productive form, transforms it from money into materials of production and labour-power; the same amount of money serves in the two-sided process as in every simple purchase C—M. On the other hand, when A reconverts his money into means of production, he buys from C, and this man pays B with it, etc., and thus the transaction would be explained.

But none of the laws referring to the quantity of the circulating money, which have been analysed in the circulation of commodities (Volume 1, Chapter 3), are in any way changed by the capitalist character of the process of production.

Hence, when we have said that the circulating capital of society, to be advanced in the form of money, amounts to £500, we have already accounted for the fact that this is on the one hand the sum simultaneously advanced, and that, on the other hand, it sets in motion more productive capital than £500, because it serves alternately as the money fund of different productive capitals. This mode of explanation, then, assumes that money as existing whose existence it is called upon to explain.

It might be furthermore said: capitalist A produces articles which capitalist B consumes unproductively, individually. The money of B therefore monetises the commodity-capital of A, and thus the same amount serves for the monetisation of the surplus-value of B and the circulating constant capital of A. But in that case, the solution of the question to be solved is still more directly assumed, the question: Whence does B get the money for the payment of his revenue? How did he himself monetise this surplus portion of his product?

It might also be answered that that portion of the circulating variable capital, which A continually advances to his labourers, flows back to him continually from the circulation, and only an alternating part stays continually tied up for the payment of wages. But a certain time elapses between the expenditure and the reflux, and meanwhile the money paid out for wages might, among other uses, serve for the monetisation of surplus-value. But we know, in the first place, that, the greater the time, the greater must be the supply of money which the capitalist A must keep continually in reserve. In the second place, the labourer spends the money, buys commodities for it, and thus monetises to that extent the surplus-value contained in them. Without penetrating any further into the question at this point, it is sufficient to say that the consumption of the entire capitalist class, and of the unproductive persons dependent upon it, keeps step with that of the labouring class; so that, simultaneously with the money thrown into circulation by the labouring class, the capitalists must throw money into it, in order to spend their surplus-value as revenue. Hence money must be withdrawn from circulation for it. This explanation would merely reduce the quantity of money required, but not do away with it.

Finally, it might be said: a large amount of money is continually thrown into circulation when fixed capital is first invested, and it is not recovered from the circulation until after the lapse of years, by him who threw it into circulation. May not this sum suffice to monetise the surplus-value? The answer to this is that the employment as fixed capital, if not by him who threw it into circulation, then by some one else, is probably implied in the sum of £500 (which includes the formation of a hoard for needed reserve funds). Besides, it is already assumed in the amount expended for the purchase of products serving as fixed capital, that the surplus-value contained in them is also paid, and the question is precisely, where the money for this purpose came from.

The general reply has already been given: when a mass of commodities valued at x times £1,000 has to circulate, it changes absolutely nothing in the quantity of the money required for this circulation, whether this mass of commodities contains any surplus-value or not, and whether this mass of commodities has been produced capitalistically or not. In other words, *the problem itself does not exist.* All other conditions being given, such as velocity of circulation of money, etc., a definite sum of money is required in order to circulate the value of commodities worth x times £1,000, quite independently of the fact how much or how little of this value falls to the share of the direct producers of these commodities. So far as any problem exists here, it coincides with the general problem: where does all the money required for the circulation of the commodities of a certain country come from?

However, from the point of view of capitalist production, the *semblance* of a special problem does indeed exist. It is in the present case the capitalist who appears as the point of departure, who throws money into circulation. The money, which the labourer expends for the payment of his means of subsistence, exists previously as the money form of the variable capital and is, therefore, thrown originally into circulation by the capitalist as a medium of buying labour-power and paying for it. The capitalist furthermore throws into circulation the money which constitutes originally the money-form of his constant, fixed and circulating, capital; he expends it as a medium of purchase, or payment, for materials of production and instruments of labour. But beyond this, the capitalist no longer appears as the starting point of the quantity of money in circulation. Now, there are only two points of departure: the capitalist and the labourer. All third classes of persons must either receive money for their services from these two classes, or, to the extent that they receive it without any equivalent services, they are joint owners of the surplus-value in the form of rent, interest, etc. The fact that the surplus-value does not all stay in the pocket of the industrial capitalist, but must be shared by him with other persons, has nothing to do with the present question. The question is: how does he monetise his surplus-value, not, how does he divide the money later after he has secured it? For the present case, the capitalist may as well be regarded as the sole owner of his surplus-value. As for the labourer, it has already been said that he is but the secondary point of departure, while the capitalist is the primary starting point of the money thrown by the labourer into circulation. The money first advanced as variable capital is going through its second circulation, when the labourer spends it for the payment of means of subsistence.

The capitalist class, then, remains the sole point of departure of the circulation of money. If they need £400 for the payment of means of production, and £100 for the payment of labour-power, they throw £500 into circulation. But the surplus-value incorporated in the product, with a rate of surplus-value of 100%, is equal to the value of £100. How can they continually draw £600 out of circulation, when they continually throw only £500 into it? From nothing comes nothing. The capitalist class as a whole cannot draw out of circulation what was not previously in it.

Exception is here made of the fact that the sum of £400 may, perhaps, suffice, when turned over ten times, to circulate means of production valued at £4,000 and labour-power valued at £1,000, and that the other £100 may likewise suffice for the circulation of £1,000 of surplus-value. The proportion of the sum of money to the value of the commodities circulated by it does not matter here. The problem remains the same. Unless the same pieces of money circulate several times, a capital of £5,000 must be thrown into circulation, and £1,000 would be required to monetise the surplus-value. The question is, where this money comes from, whether it be £1,000 or £100. There is no doubt that it is in excess of the money-capital thrown into the circulation.

Indeed, paradoxical as it may appear at first sight, it is the capitalist class itself that throws the money into circulation which serves for the realisation of the surplus-value incorporated in the commodities. But, mark well, it is not thrown into circulation as advanced money, not as capital. The capitalist class spends it for their individual consumption. The money is not advanced by them, although they are the point of departure of its circulation.

Take some individual capitalist, who opens his business, for instance, a capitalist farmer. During the first year, he advances a money-capital of, say, £5,000, paying £4,000 for means of production, and £1,000 for labour-power. Let the rate of surplus-value be 100%, the amount of surplus-value appropriated by him £1,000. The above £5,000 comprise all the money advanced by him. But the man must also live, and he does not get any receipts until the end of the year. Take it that his consumption amounts to £1,000. These he must have in his possession. He may say to himself that he has to advance these £1,000 during the first year. But this advance has only a subjective meaning, for it signifies that he must pay for his individual consumption during the first year out of his own pocket, instead of getting the money for it out of the unpaid labour of his employes. He does not advance this money as capital. He spends it, pays it out as an equivalent for means of subsistence which he consumes. This value is spent by him as money, thrown as such into circulation and withdrawn from it as commodities. He has consumed commodities of that amount. He has thus ceased to be in any way related to their value. The money with which he paid for this value is now an element of the circulating money. But he has withdrawn the value of this money from circulation in the form of products, and this value is destroyed with the commodities in which it was incorporated. It has disappeared. But at the end of the year he throws commodities worth £6,000 into circulation and sells them. By this means he recovers: (1) His advanced money-capital of £5,000; (2) the monetised surplus-value of £1,000. He had thrown £5,000 into circulation when he advanced capital, and he withdraws from it £6,000, £5,000 of which cover his capital, and £1,000, his surplus-value. The last £1,000 are monetised with the money which he had himself thrown into circulation, not as a capitalist, but as a consumer, not advanced, but spent. They now flow back to him as the money-form of the surplus-value produced by him. And henceforth this operation is repeated every year. But beginning with the second year, the £1,000 which he spends are continually the converted form, the money-form of surplus-value produced by him. He spends it annually and it flows back annually.

If his capital were turned over more frequently in one year, it would not alter this condition of things, except so far as the time is concerned, and thus the size of the amount which he would have to throw into circulation, over and above his advanced money-capital, for his individual consumption.

This money is not thrown into circulation by the capitalist as money. It is rather inherent in the character of a capitalist to be able to live on means in his possession until some surplus-value flows back to him.

In the present case we had assumed, that the sum of money, which the capitalist throws into circulation until the first surplus-value flows back to him, is exactly equal to the surplus-value which he is going to produce and monetise. This is obviously an arbitrary assumption, so far as the individual capitalist is concerned. But it must be correct when applied to the entire capitalist class, when simple reproduction is assumed. It expresses the same thing that this assumption does, namely, that the entire surplus-value is consumed unproductively, but it only, not any portion of the original capital stock.

It had been previously assumed, that the entire production of precious metals (£500) sufficed only for the wear and tear of the money.

The capitalists producing gold possess their entire product in gold, that portion which replaces constant capital as well as that which replaces variable capital and that consisting of surplus-value. A portion of the social surplus-value, therefore, consists of gold, not of a product which is monetised by means of circulation. It consists from the outset of gold and is thrown into circulation in order to draw products out of it. The same applies in this case to wages, to variable capital, and to the part replacing the advanced constant capital. Hence, while a part of the capitalist class throws into circulation commodities greater in value, (by the amount of the surplus-value) than the money-capital advanced by them, another part of the capitalist class throws into circulation money of greater value (by the amount of the surplus-value) than the commodities which they continually withdraw from circulation for the production of gold. While one part of the capitalist class pumps continually more gold out of the circulation than they throw into it, another part of them who produce gold pump continually more gold into it than they take out in means of production.

Although a part of this product of £500 in gold is surplus-value of the gold-producers, still the entire sum is intended only to replace the money worn out in the circulation of commodities. It is immaterial for this purpose, how much of this gold monetises the surplus-value incorporated in the commodities, and how much of their other constituents.

By transferring the production of gold from one country to another, nothing is changed in the fundamental condition of the matter. One part of the social labour-power and the social means of production of the country A is converted into a product, for instance, linen, valued at £500, which is exported to the country B in order to be there traded for gold. The productive capital employed for this purpose by the country A throws no more commodities, as distinguished from money, upon the market of this country than it would if it were directly engaged in the production of gold. This product of A is represented by £500 in gold, and enters into the circulation of this country only in money. That portion of the social surplus-value which is contained in this product exists directly in the form of money, and never in any other form for the country A. Although, from the point of view of the capitalist, only a part of the product represents surplus-value, and another part replaces capital, still the question as to how much of this gold replaces constant, and how much variable capital, and how much of it represents surplus-value, depends exclusively on the respective proportions which wages and surplus-value constitute of the value of the circulating commodities. That portion which represents surplus-value is distributed among the various members of the capitalist class. Although this surplus-value is continually spent by them for individual consumption and recovered by the sale of new products – it is precisely this purchase and sale which circulates the money required for the monetisation of the surplus-value among them – there is nevertheless a portion of the social surplus-value, in the form of money, in varying proportions, in the pockets of the capitalists, just as a portion of the wages stays during a certain part of the week in the pockets of the labourers in the form of money. And this portion is not limited by that portion of the money-product which forms originally the surplus-value of the capitalists producing gold, but, as we have said, by the proportion in which the above product of £500 is generally distributed between capitalists and labourers, and in which the commodity-supply to be circulated consists of surplus-value and other constituents of value.

However, that portion of surplus-value, which does not exist in other commodities, but outside of them in the form of money, consists of a portion of the annually produced gold only to the extent that a portion of the annual production of gold circulates for the realisation of surplus-value. The other portion of money, which is continually in the hands of the capitalists, in varying portions, being the money-form of their surplus-value, is not an element of the annually produced gold, but of the masses of money previously accumulated in the country.

According to our assumption, the annual production of gold just covers the annual wear of money, to the amount of £500. If we keep in mind these £500, and make abstraction of that portion of the annually produced mass of commodities which is circulated by means of previously accumulated money, then the surplus-value incorporated in the commodities will find money for its monetisation in circulation for the simple reason that surplus-value is annually produced in the form of gold on the other side. The same applies to the other parts of the gold product which replace the advanced money-capital.

Now, two things are to be noted here.

In the first place, it follows that the surplus-value spent by the capitalists as money, as well as the variable and other productive capital advanced by them in money, is actually a product of the labourers, namely of those engaged in the production of gold. They produce anew not only that portion of gold which is 'advanced' to them as wages, but also that portion of gold in which the surplus-value of the capitalist gold producers is directly embodied. As for that portion of the gold product, which replaces only the constant capital-value advanced for its production, it re-appears in the form of money (or a product in general) only through the annual labour of the working men. In the beginning of the business, it was originally expended in money by the capitalists, and this money was not newly produced, but formed a part of the circulating mass of social money. But to the extent that it is replaced by a new product, by additional money, it is the annual product of the labourer. The advance on the part of the capitalist appears here likewise merely as a form, which owes its existence to the fact that the labourer is neither the owner of his own means of production, nor able to command, during his production, the means of subsistence produced by other labourers.

In the second place, as concerns that mass of money which exists independently of this annual reproduction of £500, either in the form of a hoard, or of circulating money, things must be, or rather must have been originally just as they still are with reference to these £500 annually. We shall return to this point at the close of this section. For the present, we wish to make a few other remarks.

*   *   *

We have seen during our study of the turn-over, that, other circumstances remaining equal, a change in the length of the periods of turn-over requires different amounts of money-capital, in order to carry on production on the same scale. The elasticity of the money-circulation must, therefore be sufficient to adapt itself to this fluctuation of expansion and contraction.

If we furthermore assume other circumstances as equal – the length, intensity, and productivity of the working day also remaining unchanged — *but a different division of the value of the product*, between wages and surplus-value, so that either the former rise and the latter fall, or vice versa, the mass of the circulating money is not touched thereby. This change can take place without any expansion or contraction of the mass of money in circulation. Let us consider particularly the case in which there would be a general rise in wages, so that, under the given assumptions, there would be a general fall in the rate of surplus-value, while there would not be any change, also according to our assumption, in the mass of circulating commodities. In this case, there should be indeed an increase of the money-capital which must be advanced as variable capital in the quantity of money which serves for this purpose. But to the exact extent that the amount of money required for the function of variable capital grows, does the surplus-value decrease, and thus the amount of money required for its realisation. The amount of money required for the realisation of the values of the commodities is not affected thereby, any more than this value itself. The cost price of the commodity rises for the individual capitalist, but its social price of production remains unchanged. That which is changed is the proportion, in which, apart from the constant portion of its value, the price of production stands to wages and profits.

But, it is argued, a greater outlay of variable capital (the value of the money is, of course, considered the same) means a larger amount of money in the hands of the labourer. This causes a greater demand for commodities on the part of the labourer. This, in turn, leads to a rise in the price of commodities. Or, it is said: if wages rise, the capitalists raise the prices of their commodities. In either case, the general rise in wages causes a rise in the prices of commodities. Hence a greater amount of money is needed for the circulation of commodities, no matter whether the rise in prices is explained in this or that way.

Reply to the first argument: in consequence of a rise in wages, especially the demand of the labourers for the necessities of life will rise. In a lesser degree their demand for articles of luxury will increase, or the demand will be developed for things which did not generally belong to the scope of their consumption. The sudden and increased demand for the necessities of life will doubtless raise their prices momentarily. As a result, a greater portion of the social capital will be invested in the production of the necessities of life, and a smaller portion in the production of articles of luxury, since these fall in price on account of the decrease in surplus-value and the consequent decrease in the demand of the capitalists for these articles. And to the extent that the labourers themselves buy articles of luxury, the rise in their wages – to this degree – does not promote an increase in the prices of necessities of life, but simply fills the place of the buyers of luxuries. More luxuries than before are consumed by labourers, and relatively fewer by capitalists. That is all. After some fluctuations, the value of the circulating commodities is the same as before. As for the momentary fluctuations, they will not have any other effect than to throw unemployed money-capital into the inland circulation, capital which so far had sought employment in speculative enterprises at the stock exchange or in foreign countries.

Reply to the second argument: if it were in the power of the capitalist producers to raise the prices of their commodities at will, they could and would do so without waiting for a rise in wages. Wages would never rise while the prices of commodities were going down. The capitalist class would never resist the trades unions, since the capitalists could always and under all circumstances do what they are now doing exceptionally under definite peculiar, one might say local, circumstances, to wit, to avail themselves of every rise in wages to raise prices much higher and thus pocket greater profits.

The claim that the capitalists can raise the prices of articles of luxury, because the demand for them decreases (in consequence of the reduced demand of the capitalists whose spending money has decreased) would be a very unique application of the law of supply and demand. The prices of articles of luxury fall in consequence of reduced demand to the extent that capitalist buyers are not replaced by labouring buyers, and so far as this replacement takes effect, the demand of the labourers does not result in a rise of the prices of necessities, for the labourers cannot spend that portion of their increased wages for necessities which they spend for luxuries. Consequently capital is withdrawn from the production of luxuries, until their supply in the market is reduced to the measure which corresponds to their altered role in the process of social production. With their production thus reduced, they rise in price, provided their value is otherwise unchanged, to their normal level. So long as this contraction, or this process of compensation, takes place, there is just as constantly, with rising prices of necessities, a migration of capital into the production of these to the degree that it is withdrawn from the other line of business, until the demand is satisfied. Then the balance is restored, and the end of the whole process is that the social capital, including the money-capital, is divided in a different proportion between the production of necessary means of subsistence and that of luxuries.

The entire objection is a scarecrow set up by the capitalists and their apologists in economics.

The facts, which furnish the material for this scarecrow, are of three kinds:

(1) It is the general law of the circulation of money that the quantity of circulating money increases if the total price of the circulating commodities increases, other circumstances remaining the same, regardless of whether this increase of the totality of prices applies to the same quantity of commodities, or to a greater quantity. The effect is then taken for the cause. Wages rise (although rarely and only exceptionally in proportion) with the increasing price of the necessities of life. This rise in wages is a result, not a cause, of the rise in the prices of commodities.

(2) In the case of a partial, or local, rise of wages – that is to say, a rise only in some lines of production – a local rise in the prices of the products of this line may follow. But even this depends on many circumstances, for instance, that wages had not been abnormally depressed previously, so that the rate of profits was abnormally high, that the market is not narrowed by a rise in prices (so that a contraction of its supply previous to the raising of its prices will not be necessary), etc.

(3) In the case of a general rise of wages, the price of the produced commodities rises in lines of business where the variable capital preponderates, but falls, on the other hand, in lines where the constant, or eventually the fixed, capital preponderates.

We found in our study of the simple circulation of commodities (Book 1, Chapter 3, 2), that, even though the money-form of any definite quantity of commodities is infinitesimal within its circulation, still the money in the hand of one man disappears during the transformation of a certain commodity and takes its place in the hands of another, so that commodities are not only exchanged, or replaced by one another, but this mutual exchange of places is also promoted and accompanied by a universal precipitation of money. 'When one commodity replaces another, the money commodity sticks to the hands of some third person. Circulation sweats money from every pore.' (Book 1, Chapter 3.) The same fact is expressed, on the basis of capitalist production, of commodities, by the continual existence of a portion of capital in the form of money-capital, and by the retention of a portion of surplus-value in the hands of its owners, likewise in the form of money.

Aside from this, the *rotation* of money – that is to say, the return of money to its point of departure – so far as it is an element in the turn-over of capital, is a phenomenon entirely different from, or even the reverse of, the *circulation* of money,[1] which expresses its removal from the point of departure through a number of hands.

(Book 1, Chapter 3.) Nevertheless an accelerated turn-over implies naturally an acceleration of the circulation.

As for the variable capital, if a certain money-capital, say £500, is turned over ten times in a year, in the form of a variable capital, it is evident that this aliquot part of the quantity of money in circulation circulates ten times its value, or £5,000. It circulates ten times per year between the capitalist and the labourer. The labourer is paid, and pays, ten times per year with the same aliquot amount of money. If the same variable capital were turned over only once a year, the scale of production remaining the same, there would be only one turn-over of capital per year.

Furthermore: the constant portion of the circulating capital may be, say, £1,000. If the capital is turned over ten times, the capitalist sells his commodity, and therefore also the constant circulating portion of its value, ten times per year. The same aliquot part of the circulating quantity of money (£1,000) passes ten times from the hands of its owners into those of the capitalist. This means ten changes of place on the part of this money from one hand into another. In the second place, the capitalist buys means of production ten times per year. This again implies ten turn-overs of the money from one hand into another. With regard to the amount of £1,000, commodities valued at £10,000 have been sold by the industrial capitalist, and then commodities valued at £10,000 purchased. By means of 20 circulations of £1,000 in money a commodity supply of £20,000 has been circulated.

Finally, with an acceleration of the turn-over, that portion also of money circulates faster, which realises the surplus-value.

But, on the other hand, an acceleration in the circulation of money does not necessarily imply a more rapid turn-over of capital, and thus of money, that is to say, it does not necessarily imply a contraction and more rapid renewal of the process of reproduction.

A more rapid circulation of money takes place whenever a larger number of transactions are carried on with the same amount of money. This may take place also with the same periods of reproduction of capital, as a result of changes in the technical appliances of the circulation of money. Furthermore, there may be an increase in the number of transactions in which money circulates without expressing actual exchanges, of commodities (marginal business at the stock-exchange, etc.). On the other hand, some circulations of money may be entirely dispensed with. For instance, where the farmer is himself a real estate owner, there is no circulation of money between the capitalist farmer and the real estate owner; where the industrial capitalist is himself the owner of the capital, there is no circulation of money between him and the creditor.

As for the primitive formation of a hoard of money in a certain country, and its appropriation by a few, it is unnecessary to discuss it at this point.

The capitalist mode of production – its basis being wage-labour as well as the payment of the labourer in money and in general the transformation of services for natural products into services for money – cannot develop a larger extension and a greater systematisation, unless there is available in this country a quantity of money sufficient for the circulation and the corresponding formation of a hoard (reserve fund, etc.). This is the historical premise. However, this must not be interpreted in the sense that a sufficient hoard must first be formed, before capitalist production can begin. It rather develops simultaneously with the evolution of its foundations, and one of these foundations is a sufficient supply of precious metals. Hence the increased supply of precious metals since the 16th century is an essential factor in the history of the development of capitalist production. But so far as the necessary further supply of money-material on the basis of capitalist production is concerned, surplus-value incorporated in products is on the one hand thrown into circulation without the money required for its monetisation, and on the other hand surplus-value in the form of gold without the previous transformation of products into gold.

The additional commodities which are to be converted into money find the necessary amount of money at hand, because on the other side additional gold (and silver) intended for conversion into commodities is thrown into circulation, not by means of exchange, but by production itself.

Section 2. Accumulation and Reproduction on an Enlarged Scale.

To the extent that accumulation takes place in the form of reproduction on an enlarged scale, it is evident that it does not offer any new problem in matters of the circulation of money.

In the first place, the additional money-capital required for the function of the increasing productive capital is supplied by that portion of the realised surplus-value, which is thrown into circulation by the capitalists as money-capital, not as the money-form of their revenue. The money is already present in the hands of the capitalists. Only its employment is different.

Now, by means of the additional productive capital, its product, an additional quantity of commodities, is thrown into circulation. Together with this additional quantity of commodities, a portion of the additional money required for its circulation is thrown into circulation, so far as the value of this mass of commodities is equal to that of the productive capital consumed in their production.

This additional quantity of money has precisely been advanced as an additional money-capital, and therefore it flows back to the capitalist through the turn-over of his capital. Here the same question reappears, which we met previously. Where does the additional money come from, by which the additional surplus-value now contained in the form of commodities is to be realised?

The general reply is again the same. The sum total of the prices of the commodities has been increased, not because the prices of a given quantity of commodities have risen, but because the mass of the commodities now circulating is greater than that of the previously circulating commodities, and because this increase has not been offset by a fall in prices. The additional money required for the circulation of this greater quantity of commodities of greater value must be secured, either by greater economy in the circulating quantity of money – whether by means of balancing payments, etc., or by some measure which accelerates the circulation of the same coins – or, by the transformation of money from the form of a hoard into that of a circulating medium. This does not merely imply that barren money-capital becomes active as a means of purchase or payment, or that money-capital which is already actually circulating for the benefit of the society while representing a reserve fund for its owner is thus performing a double service (such as deposits in banks which are continually balanced). It also implies that the stagnating reserve funds of money are economised.

'In order that money should flow continuously as coin, coin must constantly coagulate as money. The continuous flow of coin depends on its constant accumulation in the form of reserve funds of coin which spring up throughout the sphere of circulation and form sources of supply; the formation, distribution, disappearance, and reformation of these reserve funds is constantly changing, their existence constantly disappears, their disappearance constantly exists. Adam Smith expressed this never-ceasing transformation of coin into money and of money into coin by saying that every owner of commodities must always keep in supply, aside from the particular commodity which he sells, a certain quantity of the universal commodity with which he buys. We saw, that in the process C—M—C the second member M—C splits up into a series of purchases which do not take place at once, but at intervals of time, so that one part of M circulates as coin while the other rests as money. Money is in that case only *suspended coin* and the separate parts of the circulating mass of coins appear now in one form, now in another, constantly changing. This first transformation of the medium of circulation into money represents, therefore, but a technical aspect of money-circulation.' (Karl Marx, *A Contribution to the Critique of*

Political Economy, 1859, page 167–168.) – ('coin' as distinguished from money is here employed to indicate the function of money as a mere medium of circulation as compared to its other functions.)

When all these measures do not suffice, an additional production of gold must take place, or, what amounts to the same, one portion of the additional product is directly or indirectly exchanged for gold – the product of countries in which precious metals are mined.

The entire amount of labour-power and social means of production expended in the annual production of gold and silver, so far as they serve as instruments of circulation, constitutes a bulky item of the dead expense of the capitalist mode of production, or of the production of commodities in general. It deprives social economy of a corresponding amount of potential additional means of production and consumption, that is to say, of actual wealth. To the extent that the cost of this expensive machinery of circulation is decreased at a given scale of circulation or a given scale of its extension, the productive power of society is increased. Hence, so far as the auxiliary means developed with the credit system have any influence in that direction, they increase the social wealth directly, either by running a large portion of the social labour-process without intervention of actual money, or by raising the capacities of the money already in circulation.

This disposes also of the absurd question, whether capitalist production in its present volume would be possible without the credit system (even if analysed only from this point of view), that is to say, if it were possible with the circulation of metallic coin alone. Evidently this is not the case. It would have found the barriers of the limited production of precious metals in its way. On the other hand, one must not entertain any myths as to the productive power of the credit system, so far as it supplies or releases money-capital. The further analysis of this question is out of place here.

* * *

We have now to study the case, in which no actual accumulation, that is to say, no immediate expansion of the scale of production, takes place, but a portion of the realised surplus-value is accumulated for a longer or shorter time as a money reserve, in order to be employed later on as productive capital.

To the extent that money so accumulating is additional money, the matter needs no explanation. It can only be a portion of the surplus-gold imported from gold producing countries. In this connection it must be remembered that the national product, in exchange for which this gold is imported, is no longer in this country. It has been exported to foreign countries in exchange for gold.

But if we assume that the same amount of money is still in the country the same as before, then the accumulated and accumulating money has accrued from the circulation. Only its function is changed. It is converted from circulating money into a gradually accruing latent money capital.

The money which is accumulated in this case is the money-form of sold commodities, and represents that portion of its value which constitutes surplus-value for its owner. (The credit system is not supposed to exist in this case.) The capitalist who accumulates this money has sold to that extent without buying.

If we look upon this transaction merely as a limited phenomenon, there is nothing to explain. A part of the capitalists keep the money realised by the sale of their products without drawing products out of the market in return for it. Another part of them, on the other hand, transform all their money into products, with the exception of the constantly recurring money-capital required for the promotion of production. One portion of the products thrown upon the market as bearers of surplus-value consists of means of production, or of the actual elements of variable capital, the necessary means of subsistence. It can serve immediately for the expansion of production. For it has not been assumed that one part of the capitalists accumulates capital, while the other consumes its surplus-value entirely, but only that one part is engaged in the accumulation of money, in the formation of latent money-capital, while the other part accumulates actually, that is to say, expands the scale of production, really adds to its productive capital. The available quantity of money remains sufficient for the requirements of circulation, even if one part of the capitalists accumulates money, while another expands production, and vice versa. Moreover, the accumulation of money on one side may proceed without cash money by the mere accumulation of outstanding claims.

But the difficulty arises when we assume, not a partial, but a general accumulation of money-capital on the part of the capitalist class. Apart from this class, there is, according to our assumption – the general and exclusive domination of capitalist production – no other class but the working class. All that the working class buys is equal to the sum total of its wages, equal to the sum total of the variable capital advanced by the entire capitalist class. This money flows back to the capitalist class by the sale of their product to the working class. The variable capital thus resumes its money-form. Let the sum total of the variable capital be x times £100, that is to say, the sum total of the variable capital actually employed, not merely advanced for the current year. It does not alter the question fundamentally, whether we know how much or how little money is actually advanced in this variable capital-value during the year, according to the velocity of the turn-over. The capitalist buys with these x times £100 a certain amount of labour-power, or pays wages to a certain number of labourers – first transaction. The labourers buy with this same amount a certain quantity of commodities from the capitalists, whereby the same x times £100 flow back into the hands of the capitalist class – second transaction. And this is continually repeated. This amount of x times £100, then, can never enable the working class to buy that portion of its product in which the constant capital is embodied, much less that in which the surplus-value of the capitalist class is incorporated. The labourers can never buy more with these x times £100 than a portion of the social product, and the value of this portion is equal to that value of the social product in which the advanced variable capital is embodied.

Apart from the case, in which this universal accumulation of money expresses nothing but the distribution of the additional incoming precious metal, in whatever proportion, among the various individual capitalists, how can the entire capitalist class accumulate money under such circumstances?

They would all have to sell a portion of their product without buying anything in return. It is not at all mysterious that they should all have a certain fund of money which they throw into circulation for their consumption, and a certain portion of which flows back to each one of them. But this fund of money, as a fund for circulation, arises precisely through the monetisation of surplus-value and is not by any means latent money-capital.

If we view the matter as it takes place in reality, we find that the latent money-capital, which is accumulated for future use, consists:

(1). Of deposits in banks; and it is a comparatively insignificant sum which is really at the disposal of the bank. Money-capital is but nominally accumulated there. What is actually accumulated are outstanding claims on money which can be monetised (so far as they are really monetised) only because there is a certain balance between the money drawn and the money deposited. It is a relatively small sum that is in the hands of the banker as money.

(2). Of public bonds. These are not capital at all, but mere claims on the annual product of the nation.

(3). Of stocks. So far as they are not bogus, they are titles of ownership of some actual capital belonging to some corporation and drafts on the surplus-value flowing from it.

There is no accumulation of money in any of these cases. What appears on the one side as an accumulation of money-capital, appears on the other as a continual and actual expenditure of money. It does not alter the case, whether the money is expended by its owner, or by others who are his debtors.

On the basis of capitalist production, the formation of a hoard is never an end in itself, but the result, either of a clogging of the circulation – larger amounts of money than is generally the case assuming the form of a hoard – or of accumulations conditioned on the turn-over; or, finally, the hoard is merely a formation of latent money-capital held temporarily and intended for future employment as productive capital.

Hence, while a portion of the money realised in surplus-value is on the one hand always withdrawn from circulation and accumulated as a hoard, another part of the surplus-value is at the same time continually converted into productive capital. With the exception of the distribution of additional precious metals among the members of the capitalist class, accumulation in the form of money never takes place simultaneously at all points.

That which is true of the other portion of the annual product, is also true of that portion of it which represents surplus-value in the form of commodities. A certain sum of money is required for its circulation. This sum of money belongs to the capitalist class quite as much as the annually produced quantity of commodities which represent surplus-value. It is originally thrown into circulation by the capitalist class itself. It is constantly redistributed among them by means of circulation itself. Just as in the case of the circulation of coin in general, so is there a clogging of a portion of this mass at ever varying points, while another portion is continually circulating. Whether a part of this accumulation is made intentionally for the purpose of forming money-capital, or not, does not alter the matter.

Exception has been made here of those adventures of circulation by which one capitalist grasps a portion of the surplus-value, or even of the capital, of another, thereby causing a one-sided accumulation and centralisation of money-capital as well as of productive capital. For instance, a portion of the appropriated surplus-value accumulated by A as money-capital may be a portion of the surplus-value of B which does not flow back to him.

Part 3

The Reproduction and Circulation of the Aggregate Social Capital

Chapter 18

Introduction [1]

Section 1. The Object of the Analysis.

The immediate process of production of capital is its labour process and self-expansion, the process whose result is the commodity-product, and whose compelling motive is the production of surplus-value.

The process of reproduction of capital comprises this immediate process of production as well as the two phases of the process of circulation, strictly so called, in other words, it comprises the entire cycle, which, as a periodic process, constantly repeated at definite intervals, constitutes the turnover of capital.

No matter whether we study the rotation in the form of $M - M'$ or that of $P—P$, the immediate process of P itself always forms but one link in the chain of this rotation. In the one form it appears as a promoter of the process of circulation, in the other the process of circulation appears as its promoter. Its continual renewal, the continual rehabilitation of capital as productive capital, is in either case conditioned on its metamorphoses in the process of circulation. On the other hand, the continually renewed process of production is the condition of the metamorphoses which the capital traverses ever anew in the sphere of circulation, its alternate incarnation as money-capital and commodity-capital.

However, every individual capital forms but an individual fraction, endowed with individual life, as it were, of the aggregate social capital, just as every individual capitalist is but an individual element of the capitalist class. The movement of the social capital consists of the totality of the movements of its individualised fractional parts, the turn-overs of the individual capitals. Just as the metamorphosis of the individual commodity is a link in the series of metamorphoses of the commodity-world – the circulation of commodities – so the meta-morphosis of the individual capital, its turn-over, is a link in the rotation of the social capital.

This total process comprises both the productive consumption (the immediate process of production) together with the metamorphoses (materially considered, exchanges) which promote it, and the indiv-idual consumption together with its corresponding metamorphoses, or exchanges. It includes on the one hand the conversion of variable capital into labour-power, and thus the incorporation of labour-power in the process of capitalist production. Here the labourer appears as the seller of his commodity, labour-power, and the capit-alist as its buyer. But on the other hand the sale of the commodities implies their purchase by the working class; in other words, their individual consumption. Here the working class appear as buyers and the capitalists as sellers of commodities to the labourers.

The circulation of the commodity-capital implies the circulation of surplus-value, hence also the purchases and sales, by which the capitalists promote their individual consumption, the consumption of surplus-value.

The rotation of individual capitals, then, in their aggregation as social capital, but in their totality, comprises not only the circulation of capital, but also the general circulation of commodities. The last named can originally consist of only two parts: (1) The rotation of the capital itself, and (2) the rotation of the commodities which pass into individual consumption, the commodities for which the labourer expends his wages and the capitalist his surplus-value (or a part of it). True, the rotation of capital comprises also the circulation of surplus-value, so far as it is a part of the commodities, and likewise the conversion of the variable capital into labour-power, the pay-ment of wages. But the expenditure of this surplus-value and wage for commodities does not form a link in the circulation of capital, although at least the expenditure of wages is a requirement for this circulation.

In Volume 1 the process of capitalist production was analysed as an individual transaction as well as a process of reproduction, the production of surplus-value as well as the production of capital. The changes of form and substance experienced by capital in the sphere of circulation were assumed without lingering over them. It was assumed that, on one hand, the capitalist sells the product at its value, and on the other, that he finds within the sphere of circulation the material means of production required for the renewal or contin-uation of the process. The only transaction within the sphere of circulation over which we had lingered in the first volume was the sale and purchase of labour-power as the fundamental condition of the capitalist mode of production.

In the first part of Volume 2, the various forms were considered which capital assumes in its rotation, and the various forms of this rotation itself.

In the second part of this volume, the rotation of capital was studied as a periodical process, as a turn-over. It was shown on one side, in what manner the various constituent parts of capital (fixed and circulating) accomplish the rotation of forms in different periods of time and different ways; and, on the other side, the circumstances were analysed on which the different duration of the working period and the period of circulation is conditioned. We observed the influence of the period of turn-over and of the different proportions of its component parts upon the volume of the process of production and upon the annual rate of surplus-value. Indeed, while it was the successive forms continually assumed and discarded by capital in its rotation which were studied in Part 1 of Book 2, it was shown in Part 2 of this volume, how a capital of a given magnitude is simultaneously divided, within this flow and succession, into the different forms of productive capital, money-capital, and commodity-capital, in varying proportions, so that they do not only relieve one another, but that different portions of the total capital-value are continually side by side and serve in these different forms. Especially money-capital was revealed in its peculiarities, which had not been shown in Book 1. Certain laws were found, according to which certain portions of different size of a given capital must be continually advanced and renewed in the form of money-capital, according to the conditions of the turn-over, in order to maintain in service a productive capital of a certain volume.

But in both the first and second parts of this volume, it was only a question of some individual capital, of the movement of some individualised part of social capital.

However, the turn-overs of individual capitals intermingle are mutually conditioned on one another, are their mutual premises, and form precisely in this interrelation the movement of social capital. Just as in the simple circulation of commodities the total metamorphosis of a certain commodity appeared as a link in the series of metamorphoses of the world of commodities, so now the metamorphosis of individual capital appears as a link in the series of metamorphoses of the aggregate social capital. But while the simple circulation of commodities did not necessarily imply the rotation of capital – since it may take place on the basis of non-capitalist production – the rotation of the aggregate social capital, as we have seen, implies also the circulation of commodities not belonging to the rotation of some individual capital, in other words, the circulation of commodities which do not represent any capital.

We have now to study the process of circulation of individual capitals in their capacity as component parts of the aggregate social capital (which circulation constitutes in its entirety the process of reproduction), that is to say, the process of rotation of this aggregate social capital.

* * *

Section 2. The Role of Money-Capital.

(Although the following belongs in a later part of this section, we shall analyse it immediately, namely, the money-capital considered as a constituent part of the aggregate social capital.)

In the study of the turn-over of the individual capital, the money-capital revealed two sides.

In the first place, it is the form in which every individual capital appears upon the scene and opens its process as capital. It therefore appears as the prime promoter, giving the first impetus to the entire process.

In the second place, according to the different durations of the periods of turn-over and the different proportion of its two parts – the working period and the period of circulation – that portion of the advanced capital-value which must be continually advanced and renewed in the form of money maintains a different proportion to the productive capital which it sets in motion, or in other words, to the continuous scale of production. But whatever may be this proportion, that portion of the active capital-value which can continually serve as productive capital is limited under any circumstances by that portion of the advanced capital-value which must exist continually beside the productive capital in the form of money. It is here merely a question of a normal turn-over, an abstract average. Exception is made of the additional money-capital required for the compensation of the interruptions of the circulation.

In regard to the first point, we have seen that the production of commodities implies the circulation of commodities, and the circulation of commodities implies the materialisation of commodities in money, the circulation of money; the duplication of commodities in commodities and money is a law of the transformation of products into commodities. The capitalist production of commodities likewise implies – whether considered socially or individually – that capital in the form of money, or money-capital, is the prime motor of every new business and its continual motor. Especially the circulating capital implies the continuous re-appearance of money-capital in short intervals as a motor. The entire advanced capital-value, that is to say, all the elements of capital composed of commodities, labour-power, instruments and materials of production, must be continually bought with money and again bought with money. What is true of the individual capital, is also true of the social capital which functions only in the form of many individual capitals. But, as we showed in Volume 1, this does not imply that the field of activity of capital, the scale of production, even on a capitalist basis, depends absolutely for its extension on the amount of the money-capital in service.

Elements of production are incorporated in the capital whose expansion within certain limits is independent of the magnitude of the advanced money-capital. The payment of labour-power remaining the same, it can yet be exploited more or less extensively or intensively. If the money-capital is increased with this greater exploitation, that is to say, if wages are raised, it is not proportionately, or, in other words, they are not actually raised.

The productively exploited materials of nature – the soil, the seas, ore, forests, etc. – which do not constitute an element in the value of capital, are intensively or extensively better exploited with an increasing exertion of the same labour-power, without requiring an additional advance of money-capital. The actual elements of productive capital are thus multiplied without requiring a greater advance of money-capital. But so far as such an advance is required for additional auxiliary materials, the money-capital, in which the capital-value is advanced, is not increased· proportionately to the augmented effectiveness of the productive capital, so that in reality it is not increased.

The same instruments of labour, and thus the same fixed capital, may be more effectively used by a prolongation of their daily use and by greater intensity of employment, without an additional investment of money for fixed capital. There is, in that case, only a more rapid turn-over of the fixed capital, but the elements of its reproduction are also supplied more rapidly.

Apart from materials of nature, it is possible to incorporate natural forces which do not cost anything as agents of the productive progress with more or less heightened effect. The degree of their effectiveness depends on the methods and scientific progress which do not cost the capitalist anything.

The same is true of the social combination of labour-power in the process of production and of the accumulated skill of the individual labourers. Carey calculates that the real estate owner never receives enough, because he is not paid for all the capital or labour which have been put into the soil since time immemorial in order to give it its present productivity. (Of course, no mention is made of the productivity of which the soil is robbed.) According to this argument, the labourer would have to be paid according to the work which had to be done by the entire human race in order to develop a savage into a modern mechanic. One should rather think: if all the unpaid labour embodied in the soil and appropriated by the real estate owner is counted, then all the capital ever invested in this soil has been paid over and over with usury, so that society has long ago bought the real estate over and over.

The increase in the productive powers of labour, so far as it does not imply an additional investment of capital-value, augments in the first analysis indeed only the quantity of the product, not its value, except the extent to which it is enabled to produce more constant capital with the same labour and thus to preserve its value. But it forms at the same time new material for capital, hence the basis for an increased accumulation of capital.

So far as the organisation of social labour itself, and thus the increase in the social productivity of labour, requires a production on a large scale and thus the advance of large quantities of money-capital on the part of individual capitalists, we have shown in Volume 1 that this is accomplished in part by the centralisation of capitals in a few hands, without necessarily implying an increase in the volume of the actively engaged capital-values, and consequently in the volume of the money-capital, in which they are advanced.

Finally, we have shown in the preceding part that a contraction of the period of turn-over permits of setting in motion the same productive capital with less money-capital, or to set in motion more productive capital with the same money-capital.

But evidently all this has nothing to do with the real question of money capital. It shows only that the advanced capital, a given sum of values consisting in its free form, in its value-form, of a certain sum of money after its conversion into productive capital, includes productive potentialities whose limits are confined within those of its values, but which may exert themselves extensively or intensively within a certain playroom. If the prices of the elements of production – the materials of production and labour-power – are given, the magnitude of the money-capital required for the purchase of a definite quantity of these elements of production in the form of commodities is determined. Or, the magnitude of the value of the capital to be advanced is determined. But the extent to which this capital acts as a creator of values and products is elastic and variable.

Now we come to the second point. It is a matter of course, that that portion of the social labour and means of production, which must be annually expended for the production or purchase of money, in order to make up for the wear and tear of coin, is to that extent a reduction of the volume of social production. But as for the money-value which functions partly as a medium of circulation, partly as a hoard, it exists, having once been acquired, it is present apart from the labour-power, the finished means of production, and the natural sources of wealth. It cannot be regarded as a barrier of production. By its transformation into elements of production, by its exchange with other nations, the scale of production might be extended. This implies, however, that the money plays its role as international money the same as ever.

According to the duration of the period of turn-over, a greater or smaller amount of money-capital is required in order to set the productive capital in motion. We have also seen that the division of the period of turn-over into a working period and a period of circulation requires an increase of the capital latent or suspended in the form of money.

So far as the period of turn-over is determined by the duration of the working period, it is determined, other conditions remaining equal, by the material nature of the process of production, not by the specific social character of this process of production. However, on the basis of capitalist production, extensive operations of a long duration require large advances of money-capital for a long time. Production in such spheres is, therefore, dependent on the limits within which the individual capitalist has money-capital at his disposal. This barrier is broken down by the credit system and associations connected with it, for instance, stock companies. Disturbances in the money-market, therefore, set such businesses out of action, while they, on the other hand cause disturbances in the money-market themselves.

On the basis of capitalist production, it must be ascertained, on what scale those operations which withdraw labour and means of production from it for a long time without furnishing in return any useful product, can be carried on without injuring those lines of production which do not only withdraw continually, or at several intervals, labour-power and means of production from it, but also supply it with means of subsistence and of production. Under social or capitalist production, the labourers in lines with short working periods will always withdraw products only for a short time without giving any products in return; while lines of business with long working periods withdraw products for a long time without any returns. This circumstance, then, is due to the material conditions of the respective labour process, not to its social form. In the case of socialised production, the money-capital is eliminated. Society distributes labour-power and means of production to the different lines of occupation. The producers may eventually receive paper cheques, by means of which they withdraw from the social supply of means of consumption a share corresponding to their labour-time. These cheques are not money. They do not circulate.

We see, then, that, so far as the need of money-capital is due to the length of the working period, it is determined by two things: first, that money is the general form in which every individual capital (apart from credit) must make its entry in order to transform itself into productive capital; this follows from the nature of capitalist production, or of commodity-production in general. Second: the magnitude of the required money advance is due to the fact that labour-power and means of production must continually be withdrawn from society for a long time without any return of products convertible into money. The first requirement, namely that capital must be advanced in the form of money, is not suspended by the form of this money itself, regardless of whether it is metal-money, credit-money, token-money, etc. The second circumstance is in no way affected by the money-medium or the form of production by means of which labour, means of subsistence, and means of production are withdrawn, without the return of some equivalent into the circulation.

Chapter 19
Former Discussions of the Subject[1]

1. The Physiocrats.

Quesnay's *Tableau Économique* shows in a few broad outlines, how the result of national production in a certain year, amounting to some definite value, is distributed by means of the circulation in such a way, that, other circumstances remaining the same, simple reproduction can take place, that is to say, reproduction on the same scale. The starting point of this period of production is fittingly last years's crop. The innumerable individual acts of circulation are at once viewed in their characteristic social mass movement – the circulation between great social classes distinguished by their economic functions. We are especially interested in the fact that a portion of the total product – which, like every other portion of it is a new result of last year's labour and intended for use – is at the same time the bearer of old capital-values re-appearing in their natural form. It does not circulate, but remains in the hands of its producers, the class of capitalist farmers, in order to begin its service as capital once more for them. In this constant portion of the capital of one year's product, Quesnay includes also some elements that do not belong to it, but he sees the main thing, thanks to the limits of his horizon, in which agriculture is the only productive sphere of investment where human labour produces surplus-value, hence the only productive one from the capitalist point of view. The economic process of reproduction, whatever may be its specific social character, intermingles in this sphere of agriculture always with a natural process of reproduction. The obvious conditions of the latter throw light on those of the former, and keep off a confusion of thought, which is due only to the witchery of circulation.

The label of a system differs from that of other articles, among other things, by the fact that it cheats not only the buyer, but often also the seller. Quesnay himself and his immediate disciples believed in their feudal shop sign. So did our school scientists to this day. But as a matter of fact, the system of the Physiocrats is the first systematic conception of capitalist production. The representative of capitalist production, the class of capitalist farmers, directs the entire economic movement. Agriculture is carried on capitalistically, that is to say, it is the enterprise of a capitalist farmer on a large scale; the immediate cultivator of the soil is the wage labourer. Production creates not only articles of use, but also their value; its compelling motive is the production of surplus-value, whose birth-place is the sphere of production, not that of circulation. Among the three classes which figure as the bearers of the process of reproduction promoted by the circulation, the immediate exploiter of 'productive' labour, the producer of surplus-value, the capitalist farmer, is distinguished from those who merely appropriate surplus-value.

The capitalist character of the system of the Physiocrats excited opposition even during its flourishing period, on one side on the part of Linguet and Mably, on the other that of the champions of the freeholders of small farms.

*   *   *

The retrogression of Adam Smith in the analysis of the process of reproduction is so much more remarkable, as he manipulates other correct analyses of Quesnay, for instance, by generalising the '*avances primitives*' and '*avances annuelles*' into 'fixed' and 'circulating' capital,[2] and even relapses entirely into physiocratic errors in some places. For instance, in order to demonstrate that the capitalist farmer produces more value than any other class of capitalists, he says: 'No other capital sets a greater quantity of productive labour in motion than that of the capitalist farmer. Not only his labouring servants, but also his labouring cattle, consist of productive labourers.' (Fine compliment for the labouring servants!) 'In agriculture, nature works as well as human beings; and although its labour does not require any expense, its product nevertheless has a value, the same as that of the most expensive labourer. The most important operations of agriculture seem to aim, not so much to increase the fertility of nature – although they do that, too – as to direct it toward the production of the plants most useful to mankind. A field grown up in thorns and weeds often enough furnishes as large a quantity of plant growth as the best tilled vineyard or corn field. Planting and cultivation serve frequently more to regulate than to stimulate the active fertility of nature; and after those have exhausted all their labours, there still remains a great deal of work to do for the latter. The labourer and the labouring cattle (!) employed in agriculture, therefore, do not only effect, like the labourers in the manufactures, the reproduction of a value which is equal to their own consumption and the capital employing them together with the profit of the capitalist, but that of a far greater value. Over and above the capital of the farmer and all his profits they effect regularly the reproduction of the rent of the land owner. The rent may be regarded as the product of the forces of nature, the use of which the land owner lends to the farmer. It is larger or smaller according to the estimated degree of these forces, in other words, according to the estimated natural or artificially ensured fertility of the soil. It is the work of nature which remains after deducting or replacing all that which may be regarded as the work of man. It is rarely less than one quarter and frequently more than one third of the total product. No other equal quantity of labour, employed in manufacture, can ever effect so large a reproduction. In manufacture nature does nothing, man everything; and reproduction must always be proportional to the strength of the agencies that carry it on. Therefore the capital invested in agriculture does not only set in motion a greater quantity of productive labour than any equal capital employed in manufacture; but it also adds, in proportion to the quantity of productive labour employed by it, a far greater value to the annual product of the soil and to the labour of a certain country, to the actual wealth and income of its inhabitants.' (Book 2, Chapter 5, page 242)

Adam Smith says in Book 1, Chapter 6, page 42: 'In value of the sowings is likewise a fixed capital in the proper meaning of the word.' Here, then, capital is the same as capital-value; it exists in a 'fixed' form. 'Although the seed passes back and forth between the soil and the barn, yet it never changes owners and therefore does not circulate in reality. The farmer does not make his profit by its sale, but by its increase.' (page 186.) The absurdity lies here in the fact that Smith does not, like Quesnay before him, notice the re-appearance of the value of constant capital in a new form, an important element of the process of reproduction, but merely another illustration, and a wrong one at that, of his distinction between circulating and fixed capital. In Smith's translation of 'avances primitives' and 'avances annuelles' into 'fixed capital' and 'circulating capital', the progress consists in the term 'capital', whose meaning is generalised and made independent of the special consideration for the 'agricultural' application of the Physiocrats; the retrogression consists in the fact that the terms 'fixed' and 'circulating' are regarded as the fundamental distinction and so maintained.

Section 2. Adam Smith.

A. The General Point of View of Adam Smith.

Adam Smith says in Book 1, Chapter 6, page 42: 'In every society the price of every commodity finally dissolves into one or the other of these three parts (wages, profit, ground rent), or into all three of them; and in every advanced society all three of them pass more or less as component parts into the price of by far the greater part of the commodities.'[3] Or, as he continues, page 63: 'Wages, profit, and ground rent are the three final sources of all income as well as of all exchange value.' We shall discuss further along this doctrine of Smith concerning the 'component parts of the prices of commodities', or of 'all exchange value'.

He says furthermore: 'As this is true of every single commodity individually, it must also be true of all commodities as a whole, constituting the entire annual product of the soil and the labour of every country. The total price or exchange-value of this annual product must dissolve into the same three parts, and be distributed among the different inhabitants of the land, either as wages of their labour, or as profit of their capital, or as rent of their real estate.' (Book 2, Chapter 2, page 190.)

After Adam Smith has thus dissolved the price of all commodities individually as well as 'the total price or exchange-value . . . of the annual product of the soil and the labour of every country' into three sources of revenue for wage-workers, capitalists, and real estate owners, he must needs smuggle a fourth element into the problem by a circuitous route, namely the element of capital. This is accomplished by the distinction between a gross and a net income. 'The gross income of all inhabitants of a large country comprises the entire annual product of their soil and their labour; the net income that portion which remains at their disposal after deducting the cost of maintenance, first of fixed, and second, of their circulating capital; or that portion which they can place in their supply for consumption, or expend for their maintenance, comfort, and pleasure, without touching their capital. Their actual wealth likewise is proportional, not to their gross, but to their net income.' (*ibidem*, page 190.)

We make the following comment:

(1). Adam Smith expressly deals here only with simple reproduction, not reproduction on an enlarged scale, or accumulation. He speaks only of expenses for maintaining the capital in process. The 'net' income is equal to that portion of the annual product, whether of society, or of the individual capitalist, which can pass into the 'fund for consumption', but the size of this fund must not encroach upon capital in process. One portion of the value of both the individual and social product, then, is dissolved neither in wages, nor in profit, nor in ground rent, but in capital.

(2). Adam Smith flees from his own theory by means of a word play, the distinction between a gross and net revenue. The individual capitalist as well as the entire capitalist class, or the so-called nation, receive in place of the consumed capital a quantity of commodities, whose value – represented by the proportional parts of this product – replaces on one hand the invested capital-value and thus forms an income, or revenue, but, mark well, a capital revenue; on the other hand, portions of value which are 'distributed among the different inhabitants of the land, either as wages of their labour, or as profits of their capital, or as rent of their real estate', a thing commonly called income. Hence the value of the entire product, whether of the individual capitalist, or of the whole country, yields an income for somebody; but it is on one hand an income of capital, on the other a 'revenue' different from it. In other words, the thing which is eliminated by the analysis of the commodity in its component parts is brought back through a side door, the ambiguity of the term 'revenue'. But only such portions of the value of a product can be taken in as previously existed in it. If the capital is to come in as revenue, capital must first have been expended.

Adam Smith says furthermore: 'The lowest ordinary rate of profits must always amount to a little more than is sufficient to make good the losses incidental to every investment of capital. It is this surplus alone which represents the clear, or net, profit.' (Which capitalist understands by profit necessary investment of capital?) 'That which people call gross profit comprises frequently not only this surplus, but also the portion retained for such extraordinary losses.' (Book 1, Chapter 9, page 72.) This means nothing else but that a portion of the surplus-value, considered as a part of the gross profit, must form an insurance fund for the production. This insurance fund is created by a portion of the surplus-labour, which to that extent produces capital directly, that is to say, the fund intended for reproduction. As regards the expense for the 'maintenance' of the fixed capital (see the above quotations), the replacement of the consumed fixed capital by a new one is not a new investment of capital, but only a renewal of the value of the old capital. And as far as the repair of the fixed capital is concerned, which Adam Smith counts likewise among the cost of maintenance, this expense belongs to the price of the capital advanced. The fact that the capitalist, instead of investing this all at one time, invests it gradually according to the requirements during the process of capital in service, and that he may invest it out of profits already pocketed, does not change the source of this profit. The portion of value of which it consists proves only that the labourer produces surplus-value, for the insurance fund as well as for the repairing fund.

Adam Smith then tells us that he excludes from the net revenue, that is to say, from the revenue in its specific meaning, the entire fixed capital, furthermore that entire portion of the circulating capital which is required for the maintenance and repair of the fixed capital, and for its renewal; as a matter of fact, all capital not in the natural form intended for the fund for consumption.

'The entire expenditure for the maintenance of the fixed capital must evidently be excluded from the net revenue of society. Neither the raw materials by means of which the machines and tools of industry must be kept in condition nor the product of the labour required for the transformation of these raw materials into their intended form can ever constitute a portion of this revenue. The price of this labour may indeed form a portion of that revenue, as the labourers so employed may invest the entire value of their wages in their immediate fund for consumption. But in other kinds of labour the price' (that is to say, the wages paid for this labour) 'as well as the product' (in which this labour is incorporated) 'enter into the fund for consumption; the price into that of the labourers, the product into that of other people, whose subsistence, comfort, and pleasure are increased by the labour of these workmen.' (Book 2, Chapter 2, page 190, 191.)

Adam Smith here comes upon a very important distinction between the labourers employed in the immediate production of means of production and those employed in the immediate production of

articles of consumption. The value of the commodities produced by
the first-named contains a part which is equal to the sum of the wages,
that is to say, equal to the value of the amount of capital invested in the
purchase of labour-power. This value exists bodily as a certain share
of the means of production produced by these labourers. The money
received by them as wages is their revenue, but their labour has not
produced any goods which are consumable, either for them or for
others. Hence these products are not an element of that portion of the
annual product which is intended for a social fund for consumption,
in which a 'net revenue' can alone be realised. Adam Smith forgets
to add here that the same thing which applies to wages is also true
for that portion of the value of the means of production, which forms
the revenue (in the first hand) of the industrial capitalist under the
categories of profit and rent. These portions of value likewise exist
in means of production, articles which cannot be consumed. They
cannot secure out of the articles of consumption produced by the
second kind of labourers a quantity corresponding to their price until
they have been sold; only then can they transfer those articles to the
individual fund for consumption of their owner. But so much more
Adam Smith should have seen that this excludes the value of the
means of production serving within the sphere of production –
the means of production which produce means of production – a
portion of value equal to the value of the constant capital employed
in this sphere and excluded from the portions of value forming a
revenue, not only by the natural form in which it exists, but also by
its function as capital.

The statements of Adam Smith regarding the second kind of labourers – who produce immediately articles of consumption – are not
quite exact. He says that in this kind of labour, both the price of
labour and the product go to the fund for immediate consumption,
'the price' (that is to say, the money received in wages) 'to the stock
for the consumption of the labourers, and the product to that of other
people, whose subsistence, comfort, and pleasure are increased by the
labour of these workmen.' But the labourer cannot consume the
'price' of his labour directly, the money in which his wages are paid;
he makes use of it by buying articles of consumption with it. These
may in part consist of classes of commodities produced by himself. On
the other hand, his own produce may be such as goes only into the
consumption of the exploiters of labour.

After Adam Smith has thus entirely excluded the fixed capital from
the 'net revenue' of a certain country, he continues:

'While the entire expense for maintaining the fixed capital is thus
necessarily excluded from the net revenue of society, the same is not

the case with the expense of maintaining the circulating capital. Of the four parts which go to make up this last-named capital – money, means of subsistence, raw materials, and finished products – the last three, as we have said, are regularly taken out of it and transferred either to the fixed capital of society, or to the fund intended for immediate consumption. That portion of the consumable articles which is not employed for the maintenance of the former' (the fixed capital) 'passes wholly into the latter' (the fund for immediate consumption) 'and forms a part of the net revenue of society. Hence the maintenance of these three parts of the circulating capital does not diminish the net revenue of society by any other portion of the annual product than that required for maintaining the fixed capital.' (Book 2, Chapter 2, page 192.)

This is but a tautology, to the effect that that portion of the circulating capital, which does not serve for the production of means of production, passes into that of means of consumption; in other words, passes into that part of the annual product, which is to serve as a fund for the social consumption. However, the immediately following passage is important:

'The circulating capital of society is different in this respect from that of an individual. That of an individual is wholly excluded from his net revenue, and can never form a part of it; it can consist only of his profit. But although the circulating capital of each individual goes to make up a portion of the circulating capital of the society to which he belongs, it is nevertheless not absolutely excluded for this reason from the net revenue of society, and may form a part of it. While all the commodities in the store of some small dealer must not by any means be placed in the supply for his own immediate consumption, still they may belong in the fund for consumption of other people, who, by means of a revenue secured by other funds, may regularly make good for him their value together with his profit, without thereby causing a reduction of either his or their capital.' (*ibidem.*)

We learn, then, the following facts from him:

(1). Just as the fixed capital, and the circulating capital required for its reproduction (he forgets the function) and maintenance, are absolutely excluded from the net revenue of the individual capitalist which can consist only of his profit, so is also the circulating capital employed in the production of means of consumption. Hence that portion of his commodity-product which reproduces his capital cannot be dissolved into portions of value which yield any revenue for him.

(2). The circulating capital of each individual capitalist constitutes a part of the circulating capital of society, the same as every individual's fixed capital.

(3). The circulating capital of society, while representing only the sum of the individual circulating capitals, has a different character than the circulating capital of every individual capitalist. The circulating capital of the individual capitalist can never be a part of his own revenue; but a portion of the circulating capital of society (namely, that consisting of means of consumption) may at the same time be a portion of the revenue of society, or, as he expressed it in the preceding quotation, it must not necessarily reduce the net revenue of society by a portion of the annual product. Indeed, that which Adam Smith here calls circulating capital, consists in the annually produced commodity-capital, which is thrown into circulation annually by the capitalists producing it. This entire annual commodity-product of theirs consists of consumable articles and, therefore, forms the fund in which the net revenue of society (including wages) is realised or expended. Instead of choosing for his illustration the commodities in the store of the small dealer, Adam Smith should have selected the masses of commodities stored away in the warehouses of the industrial capitalists.

Now if Adam Smith had summed up the snatches of thought which forced themselves upon him, first in the study of the reproduction of that which he calls fixed, then of that which he calls circulating capital, he would have arrived at the following result:

1. The annual product of society consists of two divisions: one of them comprises the means of production, the other the means of consumption. Both must be treated separately.

2. The aggregate value of the annual product consisting of means of production is divided as follows: one portion of the value represents but the value of the means of production consumed in the creation of these means of production; it is but capital-value reappearing in a renewed form; another portion is equal to the value of the capital invested in labour-power, or equal to the sum of the wages paid by the capitalists of this sphere of production. A third portion of value, finally is the source of profits, including ground rent of the industrial capitalists in this sphere.

The first portion of value, according to Adam Smith the reproduced portion of the fixed capital of all the individual capitals employed in this first section, is 'evidently excluded and can never form a part of the net revenue', either of the individual capitalist or of society. It always serves as capital, never as a revenue. To that extent the 'fixed capital' of each individual capitalist is in no way different from the fixed capital of society. But the other portions of the annual product of society consisting of means of production — portions of value which also exist in the aliquot parts of this mass of means of production — form indeed revenues for all agents engaged in this production, yielding wages for the labourers, profits and ground rent for the capitalists. But so far as society is concerned, they are capital, not revenue, although the annual product of society consists only of the sums of the products of the individual capitalists belonging to it. These things are generally fit only for service as means of production by their very nature, and even those which may eventually serve as means of consumption are intended for service as raw or auxiliary materials of new production. But they serve as such – as capital – not in the hands of their producers, but in those of their purchasers, namely,

3. The capitalists of the second category, the direct producers of means of consumption. These things reproduce for these capitalists the capital consumed in the production of means of consumption (so far as this capital is not converted into labour-power, so that it consists in the sum of the wages of the labourers of this second class), while this consumed capital, which now exists in the form of means of consumption in the hands of the capitalists producing them, constitutes in its turn – from the point of view of society – the fund intended for consumption, in which the capitalists and labourers of the first category realise their revenue.

If Adam Smith had continued his analysis to this point, then he would have lacked but little for the complete solution of the problem. He was almost on the point of solving it, for he had already observed, that certain values of one kind (means of production) of the commodity-capitals constituting the total product of society yield indeed a revenue for the labourers and capitalists engaged in production, but do not contribute anything toward the revenue of society; while another part of value of another kind (means of consumption), although it is capital for its individual owners, that is to say, for the capitalists engaged in this sphere, is only a part of the social revenue.

So much is evident from the foregoing:

First: although the social capital is but made up of the sum of the individual capitals, and for this reason the annual product in commodities (or the commodity-capital) equal to the sum of commodities produced by these individual capitals; and although the analysis of the value of commodities into its component parts, applicable to every individual commodity-capital, must also apply to the entire social commodity-capital, and actually does so result in the end, nevertheless the forms which these different component parts assume, when incorporated in the aggregate process of social production, differ.

Second: even on the basis of simple reproduction, there is not merely a production of wages (variable capital) and surplus-value, but a direct production of new constant capital, although the working day consists only of two parts, one in which the labourer reproduces the variable capital, an equivalent for the purchase price of his labour-power, and another in which he produces surplus-value (profit, rent, etc.). For the daily labour, which is expended in the reproduction of means of production – and whose value is composed of wages and surplus-value – realises itself in new means of production that take the places of the constant parts of capital consumed in the production of means of consumption.

The main difficulties, the greater part of which has been solved in the preceding analyses, are not offered by a study of accumulation, but by that of simple reproduction. For this reason, Adam Smith (Book 2) as well as Quesnay (*Tableau Économique*) take their departure from simple reproduction, whenever it is a question of the movements of the annual product of society and of its reproduction by means of circulation.

B. Smith Resolves Exchange-Value into V Plus S.

The dogma of Adam Smith, to the effect that exchangeable value, or the price of any commodity – and therefore of all commodities constituting the annual product of society (since he justly assumes everywhere the existence of capitalist production) – is made up of three component parts, or resolves itself into wages, profit, and rent, may be reduced to the fact that the value of a commodity is equal to v plus s, that is to say, equal to the value of the advanced variable capital plus the surplus-value. And we may undertake this reduction of profit and rent to a common unit called s with the expressed permission of Adam Smith, as shown by the following quotations, in which we leave aside all minor points, especially any actual or apparent deviation from his dogma that the value of the commodities resolves itself exclusively into those elements which we call v plus s.

In manufacture: 'The value which the labourers add to the material resolves itself . . . into two parts, one of which pays their wages, and the other the profit of their employer on the entire capital advanced by him in materials and wages.' (Book 1, Chapter 6, page 41) 'Although the manufacturist gets his wages advanced by his master, he does not cost the latter anything in reality, since as a rule the value of these wages is preserved together with a profit, in the increased value of the object to which the labour was applied.' (Book 2, Chapter 3, page 221). That portion of the stock which is invested 'in the maintenance of productive labour . . . after it has served him (the employer) in the function of a capital . . . forms a revenue for them' (the labourers). (Book 2, Chapter 3, page 223.)

Adam Smith says explicitly in the chapter just quoted: 'The entire annual product of the soil and the labour of each country . . . naturally resolves itself into two parts. One of them, and frequently the greater, is intended primarily to replace capital and to reproduce the means of subsistence, raw materials and finished products obtained from some capital; the other is intended to form a revenue either for the owner of this capital, as a profit on his capital, or for some one else, as a rent of his real estate.' (page 222.) Only a portion of the capital, so Adam Smith informed us just a while ago, also forms a revenue for some one, namely that which is invested in the purchase of productive labour. This portion – the variable capital – performs first 'the function of capital' for its employer and in his hands, and then it 'forms a revenue' for the productive labourer himself. The capitalist transforms a portion of the value of his capital into labour-power and thereby into variable capital; it is only due to this transformation that not alone this portion of capital, but his entire capital, serve as industrial capital. The labourer – the seller of his own labour-power – receives its value in the form of wages. In his hands, labour-power is but a saleable commodity, a commodity whose sale keeps him alive, which is the sole source of his revenue; labour-power serves as a variable capital only in the hands of its buyer, the capitalist, and the capitalist advances its purchase price only apparently, since its value has been previously supplied to him by the labourer.

After Adam Smith has thus shown that the value of a product in manufacture is equal to v plus s (s standing for the profit of the capitalist), he tells us that, in agriculture, the labourers effect, aside from 'the reproduction of a value which is equal to their own consumption and the (variable) capital employing them plus the profit of the capitalist', furthermore, 'over and above the capital of the farmer and all his profit regularly the reproduction of the rent of the owner of the real estate.' (Book 2, Chapter 5, page 243.) The fact that the rent passes into the hands of the real estate owner, is immaterial for the question under consideration. Before it can pass into his hands, it must be in those of the farmer, that is to say, of the industrial capitalist. It must form a part of the value of the product, before it can become a revenue for any one. Rent as well as profit are but component parts of surplus-value, even in the opinion of Adam Smith himself, and the productive labourer reproduces them continually together with his own wages, that is to say, with the value of the variable capital. Hence rent and profit are parts of the surplus-value s, and thus, with Adam Smith, the price of all commodities resolves itself into v plus s.

The dogma, that the price of all commodities (also of the annual product in commodities) resolves itself into wages plus profit, plus ground rent, assumes in the interspersed esoteric portion of Smith's work quite naturally the form that the value of every commodity, hence also that of the annual social product in commodities, is equal to v plus s, or equal to the value of the capital invested in labour-power and continually reproduced by the capitalist, plus the surplus-value added by the labour of the labourers.

This outcome of the analysis of Adam Smith reveals at the same time – see farther along – the source of this one-sided analysis of the component parts into which the value of a commodity resolves itself. But the determination of the magnitude of these component parts and of the limit of their value has no bearing on the circumstance that they are at the same time different sources of revenue for different classes engaged in production.

Various inconsistencies are jumbled together when Adam Smith says: 'Wages, profit, and ground rent are the three primary sources of all revenue as well as all exchange-value. Every other revenue is derived, in the last instance, from one of these.' (Book 1, Chapter 6, page 48.)

(1). All members of society not directly engaged in reproduction, with or without labour, can obtain their share of the annual product of commodities – in other words, their articles of consumption – primarily only out of the hands of those classes who are the first to handle the product, that is to say, productive labourers, industrial capitalists, and real estate owners. To that extent their revenues are substantially derived from wages (of the productive labourers), profit, and ground rent, and appear as indirect derivations when compared to these primary sources of revenue. But, on the other hand, the recipients of these revenues, thus indirectly derived, draw them by grace of their social functions, for instance that of a king, priest, professor, prostitute, soldier, etc., and they may regard these functions as the primary sources of their revenue.

(2). Here the ridiculous mistake of Adam Smith reaches its climax. After having taken his departure from a correct determination of the component parts of the value of commodities and the sum of values of the product incorporated in them, and having demonstrated that these component parts form so many different sources of revenue,[4] after having in this way deducted the revenues from the value, he proceeds in the opposite way – and this remains the ruling conception with him – and makes of the revenues 'primary sources of all exchange-value' instead of 'component parts', thereby throwing the doors wide open to vulgar economy. (See, for instance, our Roscher.)

C. The Constant Portion of Capital.

Let us now see, how Adam Smith tries to spirit away the constant portion of the value of commodities.

'In the price of corn, for instance, one portion pays the rent of the land owner.' The origin of this portion of value has no more to do with the circumstance that it is paid to the land owner and forms for him a revenue in the shape of rent than the origin of the other portions of value has to do with the fact that they constitute sources of revenue as profit and wages.

'Another portion pays the wages and subsistence of the labourers' (and of the labouring cattle, as he adds) 'employed in its production, and the third portion pays the profit of the capitalist farmer. These three portions seem' (they seem indeed) 'to constitute either directly, or in the last instance, the entire price of corn.'[5] This entire price, that is to say, the determination of its magnitude, is absolutely independent of its distribution among three kinds of people. 'A fourth portion may seem necessary in order to reproduce the capital of the farmer, or the wear of his labouring cattle and of his other implements. But it must be considered that the price of any agricultural implement, for instance of a labouring horse, is in its turn composed of the above three parts: the rent of the land on which it is bred, the labour of breeding, and the profit of the farmer who advances both the rent of this land and the wages of this labour. Hence although the price of the corn may reproduce the price as well as the cost of maintenance of the horse, the entire price still resolves itself, directly or in the last instance, into the same three parts: ground rent, labour,' (he means wages) 'and profit.' (Book 1, Chapter 6, page 42.)

This is verbatim all that Adam Smith has to say in support of his surprising doctrine. His proof consists simply in the repetition of the same contention. He admits, for instance, that the price of corn does not only consist of v plus s, but contains also the price of the means of production consumed in the production of corn, in other words, the value of a capital not invested in labour-power by the farmer. But, says he, the prices of all these means of production likewise resolve themselves into v plus s, the same as the price of corn. He forgets, however, to add in this case, that they also contain the prices of the means of production consumed in their production. He refers us from one line of production to another, and from that to a third. The contention that the entire price of commodities resolves itself 'immediately' or 'ultimately' into v plus s would not be a specious subterfuge in the sole case that he could demonstrate that the product in commodities, the price of which resolves itself immediately into c (price of consumed means of production) plus v plus s, is ultimately compensated by products which reproduce those 'consumed means of production' completely and which are themselves produced by the investment of mere variable capital, by a mere investment of capital in labour-power. The price of these last products would then be v plus s. And in that case the price of the first products, represented by c plus v plus s, where c stands for the constant portion of capital, could be ultimately resolved into v plus s. Adam Smith himself did not believe that he had furnishéd such a proof by his example of the collectors of Scotch pebbles, who, according to him, do not produce any surplus-value, but produce only their own wages, and who, in the second place, do not employ any means of production (they do, however, employ them, such as baskets, sacks, and other means of carrying the stones).

We have already seen that Adam Smith later on throws his own theory over, without, however, being conscious of his contradictions. But the source of these is found precisely in his scientific premises. The capital converted into labour produces a greater value than its own. How does it do that? It is due, says Adam Smith, to the labourers, who impregnate, during the process of production, the things on which they work with a value which forms not only an equivalent for their own purchase price, but also a surplus-value, appropriated, not by them, but by their employers (profit and rent). That is all they accomplish, and all that they can accomplish. And what is true of the industrial labour of one day, is true of the labour set in motion by the entire capitalist class during one year. Hence the aggregate mass of the annual social product in values can resolve itself only into v plus s, into an equivalent by which the labourers reproduce the value of the capital expended for the purchase of their labour-power, and into an additional value which they must deliver over and above their own value to their employers. These two elements of value form at the same time sources of revenue for the various classes engaged in reproduction: the first is the source of wages, the revenue of the labourers; the second that of surplus-value, a portion of which is retained by the industrial capitalist in the form of profit, while another is given up by him as rent, the revenue of the real estate owners. Whence, then, should come another element of value, since the value of the annual product contains no other elements but v plus s? We are working on the basis of simple reproduction. Since the entire quantity of annual labour resolves itself into labour required for the reproduction of the value of the capital invested in labour-power, and labour required for the creation of surplus-value, where would the labour required for the production of the value of a capital not invested in labour-power come from?

The situation is as follows:

(1). Adam Smith determines the value of a commodity by the quantity of labour which the wage worker adds to the object of labour. He calls it materials of labour, since he is dealing with manufacture, which is working up products of other labour. But this does not alter the matter. The value which the labourer adds to a thing (and this 'adds' is an expression of Adam Smith) is entirely independent of the fact whether or not this thing, to which value is added, had itself any value before this addition took place. The labourer creates a product of value in the form of a commodity; this, according to Adam Smith, is partly an equivalent for his wages, and this part, then, is determined by the value of his wages; according to whether his wages are high or low, he has to add more or less value in order to produce or reproduce an equivalent for his wages. On the other hand, the labourer adds more labour over and above the limit so drawn, and this constitutes the surplus value for the capitalist who employs him. Whether this surplus-value remains entirely in the hands of the capitalist or is yielded by him in portions to third persons, does not alter the qualitative fact that the additional labour of the labourer is surplus-value, not the quantity of this additional value. It is value the same as any other portion of the value of the product, but it differs from other portions by the fact that the labourer has not received any equivalent for it, nor will receive any later on, because it is appropriated by the capitalist without any equivalent. The total value of a commodity is determined by the quantity of labour expended by the labourer in its production; one portion of this total value is determined by the fact that it is equal to the value of the wages, an equivalent for them. The second portion, the surplus-value, is therefore likewise determined, for it is equal to the total value of the product minus that portion which is equivalent to the wages; it is equal to the excess of the value created in the manufacture of the product over that portion which is an equivalent for the wages.

(2). That which is true of a commodity produced in some individual industrial establishment by any individual labourer is true of the annual product of all lines of business together. That which is true of the day's work of some individual productive labourer is true of the entire year's work realised by the entire class of productive labourers. It 'fixes' (expression of Adam Smith) in the annual product a total value determined by the quantity of the annual labour expended, and this total value resolves itself into one portion determined by that part of the annual labour which reproduces the equivalent of its annual wages, or these wages themselves; and into another portion determined by the additional labour by which the labouring class creates surplus-value for the capitalist class. The value contained in the annual product then consists of but two elements, namely the equivalent of the wages received by the labouring class, and the surplus-value annually created for the capitalist class. Now, the annual wages are the revenue of the working class, and the annual quantity of surplus-value the revenue of the capitalist class; both of them represent the relative shares in the annual fund for consumption (this view is correct when simple reproduction is the premise) and are realised in it. There is, then, no room left anywhere for the value of the constant capital, for the reproduction of the capital serving in the form of means of production. And Adam Smith states explicitly in the introduction of his work that all portions of the value of commodities which serve as revenue coincide with the annual product of labour intended for a social fund for consumption: 'In what the revenue of the people consisted generally, or what was the nature of the fund, which . . . supplied their annual consumption, to explain this is the purpose of these first four books.' (page 12.) And in the very first sentence of the introduction we read: 'The annual labour of every nation is the fund, which supplies them originally with all the subsistance which they consume in the course of the year, and which always consist either of the immediate product of this labour, or in articles bought with this product from other nations.' (page 11.)

The first mistake of Adam Smith consists in identifying the value of the annual product with the annual product in values. The latter is only the product of labour of the current year, the former includes furthermore all elements of value consumed in the making of the annual product, but which have been produced in the preceding or even in earlier years, means of production whose value merely reappears, but which have been neither produced nor reproduced by the labour expended in the current year. By this mistake, Adam Smith spirits away the constant portion of the value of the annual product. His mistake rests on another error in his fundamental conception: he does not distinguish the two-fold nature of labour itself, of labour which creates exchange-value by the expenditure of labour-power, and labour which creates articles of use (use-values) as a concrete, useful, activity. The total quantity of the commodities made annually, in other words, the total annual product, is the product of the useful labour active during the the past year; all these commodities exist only because socially employed labour has been spent in a systematised network of many kinds of useful labour; it is due to this fact alone that the value of the means of production consumed in their production, re-appearing in a new natural form, is contained in their total value. The total annual product, then, is the result of the useful labour expended during the year; but only a portion of the value of the annual product has been created during the year; this portion is the annual product in values, in which the quantity of labour set in motion during the year itself is represented.

Hence, if Adam Smith says in the just cited passage: 'The annual labour of every nation is the fund, which supplies them originally with all the subsistence which they consume in the course of the year, etc.' he places himself one-sidedly upon the standpoint of mere useful labour, which has indeed given all these means of subsistence their consumable form. But he forgets that this was impossible without the assistance of instruments and materials of labour supplied by former years, and that, therefore, the 'annual labour', so far as it has created any values, did not create all the value of the products finished by it; that the product in values is smaller than the value of the products.

While we cannot reproach Adam Smith for going in this analysis no farther than all his successors (although a step toward a correct solution is already found among the Physiocrats), he loses himself, on the other hand, in a chaos further along, mainly because his 'esoteric' conception of the value of commodities in general is constantly vitiated by exoteric ideas, which on the whole prevail with him, while his scientific instinct permits his esoteric conception to reappear from time to time.

D. Capital and Revenue in Adam Smith.

That portion of the value of every commodity (and therefore also of the annual product) which is but an equivalent of the wages is equal to the capital advanced by the capitalist for labour-power, in other words, equal to the variable portion of the total capital advanced. The capitalist recovers this portion of the value of his advanced capital through a portion of the value of a commodity newly supplied by the wage labourer. Whether the variable capital is advanced in such a way that the capitalist pays the labourer his share in a product which is not yet ready for sale, or which, though ready, has not yet been sold by the capitalist, or whether he pays him with money obtained by the sale of commodities previously supplied by the labourer, or whether he has drawn this money in advance by means of credit – in all these cases the capitalist expends variable capital, which passes into the hands of the labourer in the form of money, and at the same time he possesses the equivalent of this value of his capital in that portion of the value of his commodities by which the labourer reproduces his share of its total value, in other words, by which he reproduces his own wages. Instead of giving him this portion of the value in its natural form, that of his own product, the capitalist pays him in money. The capitalist then holds the variable portion of his advanced capital in the form of commodities, while the labourer has received the equivalent for his sold labour-power in the form of money.

Now while that portion of the capital advanced by the capitalists, which has been converted by the purchase of labour-power into variable capital, serves in the process of production itself as labouring power and is produced as a new value, or reproduced, by the expenditure of this force, in the form of commodities – hence a reproduction, or new production of capital – the labourer spends the value or price of his sold labour-power in means of subsistence, in means for the reproduction of his labour-power. A quantity of money equal to the variable capital forms his revenue, which lasts only so long as he can sell his labour-power to the capitalist.

The commodity of the wage labourer – his labour-power – serves as a commodity only to the extent that it is incorporated in the capital of the capitalist and acts as capital; on the other hand, the capital expended by the capitalist as money-capital in the purchase of labour-power serves as a revenue in the hands of the seller of labour-power, the wage labourer.

Various processes of circulation and production intermingle here, which Adam Smith does not clearly distinguish.

First: Processes belonging to circulation. The labourer sells his commodity – labour-power – to the capitalist; the money with which the capitalist buys it is from his point of view money invested for gain, in other words, money-capital; it is not spent, but advanced. (This is the real meaning of 'advance' – *avance* in the language of the Physiocrats – no matter where the capitalist gets the money. Every value which the capitalist pays out for the purposes of the productive process, is advanced from his point of view, regardless of whether this takes place before or after the fact; it is advanced for the process of production.) The same takes place here as in every other sale of commodities: the seller gives away a use-value (in this case his labour-power) and receives its value (realises its price) in money; the buyer gives away his money and receives in turn the commodity itself – in this case labour-power.

Secondly: In the process of production, the purchased labour-power now forms a part of the acting capital, and the labourer himself serves here merely as one particular natural form of this capital, distinguished from the elements existing in the natural form of means of production. During the process, the labourer adds value to the means of production which he converts into products, by expending labour-power to the amount of his wages (without surplus-value); he reproduces for the capitalist that portion of his capital in the form of commodities which has been, or has to be, advanced for wages; hence he produces for the capitalist that capital which he can 'advance' once more for the purchase of labour-power.

Thirdly: In the sale of the commodities, one portion of their selling price reproduces the variable capital advanced by the capitalist, whereby he, on the one hand, is enabled to buy more labour-power, and the labourer, on the other hand, to sell more.

In all purchases and sales of commodities – so far as these transactions are merely regarded by themselves – it is quite immaterial what becomes of the money in the hands of the seller received for his commodities, and what becomes of the article of use in the hands of the buyer received in exchange for this money. Hence, so far as the mere process of circulation is concerned, it is quite immaterial that the labour-power bought by the capitalist reproduces the value of capital for him, and that, on the other hand, the money received by the labourer as a purchase-price of his labour-power serves as his revenue. The magnitude of the value of the commodity of the labourer, his labour-power, is not affected either by serving as a revenue for him or by reproducing, through its use, on the part of the buyer, the value of the capital of the buyer.

Since the value of the labour-power – that is to say, the adequate selling price of this commodity – is determined by the quantity of labour required for its reproduction, and this quantity of labour itself is here determined by that required for the necessary subsistence of the labourer, the wages become a revenue on which the labourer has to live.

It is entirely wrong, when Adam Smith says (page 223): 'That portion of capital which is invested in the maintenance of productive labour . . . after it has served him' (the capitalist) 'in the function of a capital . . . forms a revenue for them' (the labourers). The money with which the capitalist pays for the labour-power purchased by him, 'serves him in the function of a capital' to the extent that he thereby incorporates labour-power in the material elements of his capital and thus enables his capital to serve as productive capital. We make this distinction: the labour-power is a commodity, not a capital, in the hands of the labourer, and it constitutes for him a revenue, so long as he can repeat its sale; it serves as capital, after its sale, in the hands of the capitalist, during the process of production itself. That which here serves twice is labour-power; as a commodity which is sold at its value, in the hands of the labourer; as a power creating exchange-values and use-values, in the hands of the capitalist who has bought it. But the money which the labourer receives from the capitalist is not given to him until after he has given the capitalist the use of his labour-power, after it has already been realised in the value of the product of labour. The capitalist holds this value in his hands, before he pays for it. Hence it is not the money which serves twice here; first, as the money-form of the variable capital, and then as wages. It is labour-power which has served twice; first, as a commodity in the sale of labour-power (in stipulating the amount of wages to be paid, the money serves merely as an ideal measure of value and need not even be in the hands of the capitalist); secondly, in the process of production, in which it serves as capital, in other words, as an element in the hands of the capitalist creating exchange-value and use-values. Labour-power first supplies, in the form of commodities, the equivalent which is to be paid to the labourer, and then only is it paid by the capitalist to the labourer in money. In other words, the labourer himself creates the fund out of which the capitalist pays him. But this is not all.

The money, which the labourer receives, is spent by him for the maintenance of his labour-power, or – looking upon the capitalist class and working class as an aggregate mass – is spent to preserve for the capitalist an instrument by means of which alone he can remain a capitalist.

The continuous purchase and sale of labour-power, then, perpetuates on one hand labour-power as an element of capital, by the grace of which it appears as the creator of commodities, use-values having an exchange-value, by means of which, furthermore, that portion of capital which buys labour-power is continually reproduced by its own product, so that the labourer himself creates the fund of capital out of which he is paid. On the other hand, the sale of labour-power becomes the ever renewed source for the maintenance of the labourer and makes of his labour-power that faculty through which he secures his revenue, by which he lives. Revenue in this case signifies nothing else but an appropriation of values by means of ever repeated sales of a commodity (labour-power), these values serving merely for the continual reproduction of the commodity to be sold. And to this extent Smith is right when he says that that portion of the value of the labourer's product, for which the capitalist pays him an equivalent in the form of wages, becomes a source of revenue for the labourer. But this does not alter the nature or magnitude of this portion of value of the commodity any more than the value of the means of production is changed by the fact that they serve as capital-values, or the nature and magnitude of a straight line are changed by the fact that it serves as a basis for some triangle or as a diameter of some ellipse. The value of labour-power remains quite as independent as that of those means of production. This portion of the value of a commodity neither consists of a revenue as one of its independent constituent factors, nor does it resolve itself into revenue. Because this value, ever renewed by the labourer, constitutes a source of revenue for him, that is no reason why his revenue, on the other hand, should be an element of the new values produced by him. The magnitude of his share in the new value created by him determines the volume of the value of his revenue, not vice versa. The fact that this portion of the new value forms a revenue for him indicates merely what becomes of it, shows the character of its employment, and has no more to do with its formation than with that of any other value. The fact that my receipts are ten dollars a week changes nothing in the nature of the value of the ten dollars nor in the magnitude of their value. As in the case of every other commodity so in that of labour-power its value is determined by the labour necessary for its reproduction; that the quantity of this labour is determined by the value of the necessary subsistence of the labourer, in other words, that it is equal to the labour required for the reproduction of his own life's conditions, is peculiar for this commodity (labour-power), but no more peculiar than the fact that the value of labouring cattle is determined by the subsistence necessary to produce this subsistence.

But it is this category of 'revenue' which is to blame for all the confusion in Adam Smith over this question. The various kinds of revenue constitute with him the 'component parts' of the annually produced new values of commodities, while, vice versa, the two portions into which these values resolve themselves for the capitalist form sources of revenue – namely the equivalent of his variable capital advanced for the purchase of labour-power and the other portion of value, the surplus-value, which likewise belongs to him but did not cost him anything. The equivalent of the variable capital is once more advanced for labour-power and to that extent forms a revenue for the labourer in the shape of wages; the other portion, the surplus-value, which does not reproduce any advance of capital for the capitalist, may be spent by him in articles of consumption (whether necessary or luxuries), it may be consumed by him as a revenue, instead of forming capital-value of some kind. The first condition of this revenue is the value of the commodities itself, and its component parts differ from the point of view of the capitalist only to the extent that they are an equivalent for, or an excess over the variable portion of the value of the capital advanced by him. Both of them consist of nothing but labour expended and materialised during the production of commodities. They consist of an expenditure, not of an income or revenue – an expenditure of labour.

After this reversion of facts, by which a revenue becomes the source of the value of commodities instead of the value of commodities being the source of revenue, the value of commodities has the appearance of being 'composed' of various kinds of revenue; these revenues are determined independently of one another, and the total value of commodities is determined by the addition of the values of these revenues. But now the question is: how is the value of each of these revenues determined, which are supposed to be the sources of the values of commodities? In the case of wages it is done, for wages are the value of the commodity labour-power, and this is determined (the same as that of all other commodities) by the labour required for its reproduction. But surplus-value, or as Adam Smith has it, profit and ground rent, how are they determined? Here Adam Smith has but empty phrases to offer. He either represents wages and surplus-value (or wages and profit) as component parts of the value, or price, of commodities, or, sometimes in the same breath, as component parts into which the price of commodities resolves itself; but this means precisely the reverse of his contention and makes of the value of commodities the primary thing, different parts of which fall as different revenues to the share of different persons engaged in the productive process. This is by no means identical with the composition of value of these three 'component parts'. If I determine the magnitude of three different straight lines independently and then form a fourth straight line out of these three lines as 'component parts' equal to their sum, it is by no means the same process as if I have some given straight line before me and 'resolve' it, so to say, into three different parts for some purpose. In the first case, the magnitude of the line changes throughout with the magnitude of the three lines whose sum it is; in the second case, the magnitude of three parts of the line is from the outset limited by the fact that they are parts of a line of given magnitude.

However, if we keep in mind that part of the analysis of Smith which is correct, namely, that the value newly created by the annual labour and contained in the annual social product in commodities (the same as in every individual commodity, or every daily, weekly, etc., product) is equal to the value of the variable capital advanced (in other words, equal to the value intended for the purchase of new labour-power) plus the surplus-value which the capitalist can realise in means of his individual consumption – simple reproduction being assumed, and other circumstances remaining the same, if we keep furthermore in mind that Adam Smith confounds labour which creates values and is an expenditure of labour-power with labour which creates articles of use and is expended in a useful, appropriate, manner, then the entire conception amounts to this: the value of every commodity is the product of labour; hence this is also true of the value of the product of annual labour, or of the value of the annual product of society in commodities. But since all labour resolves itself, (1), into necessary labour time, in which the labourer reproduces merely an equivalent for the capital advanced in the purchase of his labour-power, and, (2), into surplus-labour, by which he supplies the capitalist with a value for which the latter does not give any equivalent, in other words, a surplus-value, it follows that all value of commodities can resolve itself only into these two component parts, so that ultimately it forms a revenue for the labouring class in the form of wages, and for the capitalist class in the form of surplus-value. As for the constant value of the capital, in other words, the value of the means of production consumed in the production of the annual product, it cannot be explained how this value gets into that of the new product (unless we accept the phrase that the capitalist charges the buyer with it in the sale of his goods), but ultimately, seeing that the means of production are themselves products of labour, this portion of value can consist only of an equivalent for variable capital and surplus-value, of a product of necessary labour and surplus-labour. The fact that the values of these means of production serve in the hands of their employers as capital-values does not prevent them from resolving themselves 'originally', even though in some other hands, if we go to the bottom of the matter, and at some previous time, into the same two portions of value, hence into two different sources of revenue.

One point is correct in this conception, namely, that the matter has a different aspect from the point of view of the movement of social capital, in other words, of the totality of individual capitals, than it has from the standpoint of the individual capital, considered by itself, or from the standpoint of each individual capitalist. For these, the value of commodities resolves itself, (1), into a constant element (a fourth one, as Adam Smith says), and (2), into the sum of wages and surplus-value, or wages, profit, and ground rent. But from the point of view of society, the fourth element of Adam Smith, the constant value of capital, disappears.

E. Recapitulation.

The absurd formula that the three revenues, wages, profit, and ground rent, form the three 'component parts' of the value of commodities, is due in the case of Adam Smith to the more plausible idea that the value of commodities resolves itself into these three parts. However, this is likewise incorrect, even granted that the value of commodities is only divisible into an equivalent of the consumed labour-power and surplus-value created by it. But the mistake rests here again on a deeper and truer basis. The capitalist mode of production is conditioned on the fact that the productive labourer sells his own labour-power, as a commodity, to the capitalist, in whose hands it then serves merely as an element of his productive capital. This trans-action, taking place in the circulation – the sale and purchase of labour-power – does not only inaugurate the process of production, but also determines implicitly its specific character. The production of a use-value, and even that of a commodity (for this can be done eventually by independent productive labourers), is here only a means of producing absolute or relative surplus-value for a capitalist. For this reason we have seen in the analysis of the process of production, that the production of absolute and relative surplus-value determines, (1) the duration of the daily labour-process, (2) the entire social and technical formation of the capitalist process of production. Within this process, there is realised the distinction between the mere con-servation of value (the value of the constant capital), the actual reproduction of advanced value (an equivalent of labour-power), and the production of surplus-value, that is to say, of value for which the capitalist has neither advanced an equivalent nor will advance one subsequently.

The appropriation of surplus-value – a value in excess of the equi-valent advanced by the capitalist – although it is inaugurated by the purchase and sale of labour-power, is a transaction taking place within the process of production itself, and forms an essential part of it.

The introductory transaction taking place in the circulation, the purchase and sale of labour-power, is itself conditioned on a distrib-ution of the elements of production, which is the premise and prelude of the distribution of the social products, and implies the separation of labour-power, as a commodity of the labourer, from the means of production, as the property of non-labourers.

However, this appropriation of surplus-value, or this separation of the production of values into a reproduction of advanced values and a production of new values (surplus-values) which do not offset any equivalent, does not alter in any way the substance of value itself nor the nature of the production of values. The substance of value is and remains nothing but expended labour-power – labour independent of the specific, useful, character of this labour – and the production of values is nothing but the process of this expenditure. A serf, for instance, expends his labour-power for six days, labours for six days, and the fact of this expenditure is not altered by the circumstances, that he may be working three days for himself, on his own field, and three days for his lord, on the field of the latter. Both his voluntary labour for himself and his compulsory labour for his lord are equally labour; so far as this labour is considered with reference to the values, or even the useful articles, created by it, there is no difference in his six days of labour. The difference refers merely to the distinct conditions by which the expenditure of his labour-power during each half of his labour-time of six days is affected. The same applies to the necessary and surplus-labour of the wage worker.

The process of production ends in a commodity. The fact that labour-power has been expended in its creation now is manifest in its attribute of value; the magnitude of this value is measured by the quantity of labour expended in it; the value of a commodity resolves itself into nothing else and is not composed of anything else. If I have drawn a straight line of definite length, I have 'produced' a straight line (true, only symbolically, as I know beforehand) by means of a certain mode of drawing which is determined by certain laws independent of myself. If I divide this line into three sections (which may correspond to a certain problem), every one of these sections remains a straight line, and the entire line, whose sections they are, does not resolve itself, by this division, into anything different from a straight line, for instance, a curve of some kind. Neither can I divide a line of a given magnitude in such a way, that the sum of its divisions is greater than the undivided line itself; hence the magnitude of the undivided line is not determined by any arbitrary division of its parts. Vice versa, the relative magnitudes of these divisions are limited from the outset by the size of the line whose parts they are.

A commodity produced by a capitalist does not differ in itself from that produced by an independent labourer, or by a labouring commune, or by slaves. But in the present case, the entire product of labour as well as its value belong to the capitalist. Like every other producer, he has to convert his commodity by sale into money, before he can manipulate it further; he must convert it into the form of the universal equivalent.

Let us look at the product in commodities before it is converted into money. It belongs wholly to the capitalist. On the other hand, as a useful product of labour, a use-value, it is entirely the product of a past labour-process. Not so its value. One portion of this value is but the value of means of production consumed in the production of the commodities and re-appearing in a new form; this value has not been produced during the process of production of this commodity; for the means of production possessed this value before this process of production, independently of it; they entered into this process as the bearers of their value; it is only the external form of this value which has been renewed and changed. This portion of the value of the commodity serves the capitalist as an equivalent of the constant value of the capital advanced by him and consumed in the production of the commodity. It existed previously in the form of means of production; it exists now as a component part of the value of the newly-produced commodity. As soon as this commodity has been turned into money, the value then existing in the form of money must be reconverted into means of production, into its original form determined by the process of production and its function in it. Nothing is altered in the character of the value of a commodity by the function of this value as capital.

A second portion of the value of a commodity is the value of the labour-power which the wage-worker sells to the capitalist. It is determined, the same as that of the means of production, independently of the process of production into which labour-power is to enter, and it is fixed in a transaction of the circulation, the purchase and sale of labour-power, before it goes to the process of production. By means of his function − the expenditure of labour-power − the wage-labourer produces a value of the commodity equal to the value which the capitalist has to pay him for the use of his labour-power. He gives this value to the capitalist in commodities, and is paid for it in money. The fact that this portion of the value of commodities is for the capitalist but an equivalent for the capital which he has to advance in wages does not alter in any way the truth that it is a value of commodities newly created during the process of production and consisting of nothing but past expenditure of labour, the same as the surplus-value. Neither is this truth affected by the fact that the value paid by the capitalist to the labourer assumes the form of a revenue for the labourer, and that not only labour-power is continually reproduced thereby, but also the class of wage-labourers itself, and thus the basis of the entire capitalist production.

However, the sum of these two portions of value does not constitute all there is to the value of commodities. There remains an excess over both of them, the surplus-value. This, like that portion of value which reproduces the variable capital advanced in wages, is a value newly created by the labourer during the process of production − materialised labour. But it does not cost the owner of the entire product, the capitalist, anything. This circumstance permits the capitalist to consume the surplus-value entirely as his revenue, unless he has to give up some portions of it to other claimants − such as ground rent to land owners, in which case such portions constitute a revenue of third persons. This same circumstance was also the compelling motive, which induced the capitalist to engage in the first place in the manufacture of commodities. But neither his original benevolent intention of securing some surplus-value, nor its subsequent expenditure as revenue, by him or others, affect the surplus-value as such. They do not impair the fact that it is coagulated, unpaid, labour, nor the magnitude of this surplus-value, things which are determined by entirely different conditions.

However, if Adam Smith wanted to occupy himself, as he did, with an analysis of the role of different constituent parts of value in the total process of reproduction, even while he was investigating the question of the value of commodities, then it was evident that, while some particular portions of value served as a revenue, others served just as continually as capital – and, according to his logic, these would likewise have to be regarded as constituent parts of the value of commodities, or parts into which this value resolves itself.

Adam Smith identifies the production of commodities in general with capitalist production; the means of production are to him from the outset 'capital', labour is wage-labour, and therefore 'the number of the useful and productive labourers is always . . . proportional to the quantity of capital stock which is employed in setting them to work.' (Introduction, page 12.) In short, the various elements of the productive process – both objective and subjective ones – appear from the first with the masks characteristic of the process of capitalist production. The analysis of the value of commodities, therefore, coincides with the reflection, to what extent this value is, on the one hand, a mere equivalent for invested capital, and, on the other, to what extent it forms 'free' value, that is to say, value not reproducing any advance of capital, or surplus-value. The proportions of value compared from this point of view transform themselves clandestinely into its independent 'component parts', and finally into the 'sources of all value'. A further consequence of this method is the alternate composition or dissolution of the value of commodities into revenues of various kinds, so that the revenues do not consist of values of commodities, but rather the value of commodities consists of revenues. But the fact that the value of a commodity may serve as a revenue for this or that man does not change the nature of value as such any more than the fact that the value of a commodity as such, or of money as such, may serve as capital changes their nature. The commodity with which Adam Smith is dealing represents from the outset a commodity-capital (which consists of the value of the capital consumed in production plus a surplus-value), it is a commodity produced by capitalist methods, a result of the capitalist process of production. It would have been necessary, then, to analyse first this process, and this would have implied an analysis of the process of self-expansion and of the formation of value, which it includes. Since this process is in its turn conditioned on the circulation of commodities, its description requires also a previous and independent analysis of a commodity. However, even where Adam Smith hits 'esoterically' upon the correct thing in a haphazard way, he refers to the formation of values only in the analysis of commodities, that is to say, in the analysis of commodity-capital.

Section 3. The Economists after Smith.[6]

Ricardo reproduces the theory of Smith almost verbatim: 'It is agreed that all products of a certain country are consumed, but it makes the greatest imaginable difference, whether they are consumed by those who reproduce another value, or by those who do not. When we say that revenue is saved up and added to the capital, we mean that the portion of revenue added to the capital is consumed by productive labourers, instead of unproductive ones.' (Principles, Page 163.)

In fact, Ricardo fully accepted the theory of Adam Smith concerning the separation of the price of commodities into wages and surplus-value (or variable capital and surplus-value). The points in which he differs from him are, 1) the composition of the surplus-value; Ricardo eliminates ground rent as one of its necessary elements; 2), Ricardo starts out from the price of commodities and dissects it into these component parts. In other words, the magnitude of value is his point of departure. The sum of its parts is assumed as given, it is the starting point, while Adam Smith frequently subverts this order and proceeds contrary to his deeper insight, by producing the quantity of value subsequently by an addition of its component parts.

Ramsay makes the following remark against Ricardo: 'Ricardo forgets that the total product is not only divided into wages and profits, but that a portion is also required for the reproduction of the fixed capital.' (An Essay on the Distribution of Wealth. Edinburgh, 1836, page 174.) Ramsay means by fixed capital the same thing which I call constant capital, for he says on page 53: 'Fixed capital exists in a form in which it contributes toward the production of the commodity in process of formation, but not toward the maintenance of labourers.'

Adam Smith refuses to accept the logical outcome of his dissolution of the value of commodities, and therefore of the value of the annual product of social labour, into wages and surplus-value, or into mere revenue. This logical outcome would be that the entire annual product might be consumed in that case. It is never the original thinkers that draw the absurd conclusions. They leave that to the Says and MacCullochs.

Say takes the matter indeed easy enough. That which is an advance of capital for one, is, or was, a revenue and net product for another. The difference between the gross and the net product is purely subjective, 'and thus the total value of all products in a society is divided as revenue.' (Say, *Traité d'Économie Politique*, 1817, ii, page 69.) 'The total value of every product is composed of the profits of the land owners, the capitalists, and the industrious people (wages figure here as *profits des industrieux*!) who have contributed toward its production. This makes the revenue of society equal to the gross value produced, not equal to the net products of the soil, as was claimed by a sect of economists.' (the Physiocrats) (page 63.)

Among others, Proudhon has appropriated this discovery of Say.

Storch, however, who likewise accepts the doctrine of Smith in principle, finds that Say's application of it does not hold water. 'If it is admitted, that the revenue of a nation is equal to its gross product, so that no capital' (that is to say, no constant capital) 'is to be deducted, then it must also be admitted that this nation may consume unproductively the entire value of its annual product, without in the least reducing its future revenue . . . The products which represent the' (constant) 'capital of a nation are not consumable.' (Storch, *Considérations sur la Nature du Revenu national.* Paris, 1824, page 150.)

However, Storch forgot to tell us how the existence of this constant portion of capital agrees with the analysis of prices by Smith, which he has accepted, and according to which the value of commodities consists only of wages and surplus-value, but not of any constant capital. He realises only through Say that this analysis of prices leads to absurd results, and his own opinion of it is 'that it is impossible to dissolve the necessary price into its simplest elements.' (*Cours d' Économie Politique*, Petersburg, 1815, ii, page 140.)

Sismondi, who occupies himself especially with the relation of capital and revenue, and makes the peculiar formulation of this relation the specific difference of his *Nouveaux Principes*, did not say one scientific word, did not contribute one atom toward a clarification of this problem.

Barton, Ramsay and Cherbuliez attempted to surpass the formulation of Smith. They failed, because they conceive the problem in a one-sided way, by not making clear the distinction of constant and variable capital-value from fixed and circulating capital.

John Stuart Mill likewise reproduces, with his usual pomposity, the doctrine handed down by Adam Smith to his followers.

As a result, the Smithian confusion of thought persists to this hour, and his dogma is one of the orthodox articles of faith of political economy.

Chapter 20
Simple Reproduction

Section 1. The Formulation of the Question.

If we study the annual function of social capital[1]— of the total capital whose fractional parts are the individual capitals, the movements of which are simultaneously their individual movements and links in the movements of the total capital — and its results; that is to say, if we study the product in commodities put forth by society during the year, then it must become apparent how the process of reproduction of the social capital proceeds, what characteristics distinguish this process of reproduction from that of an individual capital, and what characteristics are common to both. The annual product includes those portions of the social product which reproduce capital, the social reproduction, as well as those which go to the fund for consumption, which are consumed by capitalists and labourers; in other words, productive and individual consumption. It comprises the reproduction (maintenance) of the capitalist and working classes, and thus the reproduction of the capitalist character of the entire process of production.

It is evidently the circulation formula

$$C' —\{M—C...P...C', m—c\}$$

which we have to analyse, and the consumption necessarily plays a role in it. For the point of departure, C' equal to C plus c, the commodity-capital, comprises the constant and variable capital as well as the surplus-value. Its movements, therefore, include both the individual and productive consumption. In the cycles M—C...P...C'—M', and P...C'—M'—C...P, the movement of the capital is the starting and finishing point. And this implies consumption, for the commodity, the product, must be sold. When these premises are accepted, it is immaterial for the movement of the individual capitals, what becomes of these commodities subsequently. On the other hand, in the movement of C'...C' the conditions of social reproduction are precisely different in this point, since it must be shown what becomes of every portion of value of this total product of C'. In this case, the total process of reproduction includes the process of consumption by way of the circulation quite as much as the process of reproduction of the capital itself.

This process of reproduction, now, must be considered for the purposes of our study both from the point of view of the reproduction of the value and of the substance of the individual component parts of C'. We cannot rest satisfied any longer, as we did in the analysis of the value of the product of the individual capital, with the assumption that the individual capitalist must first convert the component parts of his capital into money by the sale of his commodities, before he is able to reconvert it into productive capital by renewed purchase of the elements of production in the commodity market. Those elements of production, so far as they consist of things, constitute as much a portion of the social capital as the individual finished product, which is exchanged for them and reproduced by them. On the other hand, the movement of that portion of the social product in commodities, which is consumed by the labourer in the expenditure of his labour-power, and by the capitalist in spending his surplus-value, does not only form an integral part of the movement of the total product, but also intermingles with the movements of the individual capitals, and this process cannot be explained by merely assuming it.

The question which we have to face immediately, is this: how is the value of the capital consumed in production reproduced out of the annual product, and how does the movement of this reproduction intermingle with the consumption of surplus-value by the capitalists and of wages by the labourers? We are dealing, then, first with reproduction on a simple scale. It is furthermore assumed that products are exchanged at their value, and that no revolution in the value of the elements of productive capital takes place. Should there be any divergence of prices from values, this would not exert any influence on the movements of *social* capital. On the whole, there is the same exchange of the same quantity of products, although the individual capitalists would be taking shares in it which would no longer be proportional to their respective advances and to the quantities of value produced by each one. As for revolutions of value, they do not alter anything in the proportions of the elements of value of the various component parts of the total annual product, provided they are universally and uniformly distributed. To the extent that they are limited and unevenly distributed, they are disturbances, which, in the first place, can be understood only as divergences from equal proportions of value; and, in the second place, given the law according to which one portion of the annual product reproduces constant, and another variable capital, a revolution either in the value of the constant or variable capital would not alter this law. It would change merely the relative magnitude of the portions of value which serve in the one or the other capacity, seeing that other values would have taken the places of the original ones.

So long as we looked upon the production of value and the value of products from the point of view of individual capital, it was immaterial for the analysis which was the natural form of the product in commodities, whether it was, for instance, that of a machine, of corn, or of looking glasses. It was always but a matter of illustration, and any line of production could serve that purpose. What we had to consider was the immediate process of production itself, which presented itself at every point as the process of some individual capital. So far as reproduction was concerned, it was sufficient to assume that that portion of the product in commodities, which represented capital in the sphere of circulation, found an opportunity to reconvert itself into its elements of production and thus into its form of productive capital. It likewise sufficed to assume that both the labourer and the capitalist found in the market those commodities for which they spend their wages and surplus-value. This merely formal manner of presentation does not suffice in the study of the total social capital and of the value of its products. The reconversion of one portion of the value of the product into capital, the passing of another portion into the individual consumption of the capitalist and working classes, form a movement within the value of the product itself which is created by the total capital; and this movement is not only a reproduction of value, but also of material, and is, therefore, as much conditioned on the relative proportions of the elements of value of the total social product as on its use-value, its material substance.[2]

Simple reproduction on the same scale appears as an abstraction, inasmuch as the absence of all accumulation or reproduction on an enlarged scale is an irrelevant assumption in capitalist society, and, on the other hand, conditions of production do not remain exactly the same in different years (as was assumed). The assumption is that a social capital of a given magnitude produces the same quantity of value in commodities this year as last, and supplies the same quantity of wants, although the forms of the commodities may be changed in the process of reproduction. However, while accumulation does take place, simple reproduction is always a part of it and may, therefore, be studied in itself, being an actual factor in accumulation. The value of the annual product may decrease, although the quantity of use-values may remain the same; or, the value may remain the same, although the quantity of the use-values may decrease; or, the quantity of value and of use-values may decrease simultaneously. All this amounts to saying that reproduction takes place either under more favourable conditions than before, or under more difficult ones, which may result in an imperfect reproduction. But all this can refer only to the quantitative side of the various elements of reproduction, not to the role which they are playing as a reproducing capital, or as a reproduced revenue, in the entire process.

Section 2. The Two Departments of Social Production.[3]

The total product, and therefore the total production, of society, is divided into two great sections:

I. *Means of Production*, commodities having a form in which they must, or at least may, pass over into productive consumption.

II. *Means of Consumption*, commodities having a form in which they pass into the individual consumption of the capitalist and working classes.

In each of these two departments, all the various lines of production belonging to them form one single great line of production, the one that of the means of production, the other that of articles of consumption. The aggregate capital invested in each of these two departments of production constitutes a separate section of the entire social capital.

In each department, the capital consists of two parts:

(1) *Variable Capital*. This capital, so far as its value is concerned, is equal to the value of the social labour-power employed in this line of production, in other words equal to the sum of the wages paid for this labour-power. So far as its substance is concerned, it consists of the active labour-power itself, that is to say, of the living labour set in motion by this value of capital.

(2) *Constant Capital*. This is the value of all the means of production employed in this line. These, again, are divided into *fixed* capital, such as machines, instruments of labour, buildings, labouring animals, etc., and *circulating* capital, such as materials of production, raw and auxiliary materials, half-wrought articles, etc.

The value of the total annual product created with the capital of each of the two great departments of production consists of one portion representing the constant capital c consumed in the process of production and transferred to the product, and of another portion added by the entire labour of the year. This latter portion, again, consists of one part reproducing the advanced variable capital v, and of another representing an excess over the variable capital, the surplus-value s. And just as the value of every individual commodity, so that of the entire annual product of each department consists of c plus v plus s.

The portion c of the value, representing the constant capital *consumed* in production, is not identical with the value of the constant capital *invested* in production. It is true that the materials of production are entirely consumed and their values completely transferred to the product. But of the invested *fixed* capital, only a portion is consumed and its value transferred to the product. Another portion of the fixed capital, such as machines, buildings, etc., continues to exist and serve the same as before, merely depreciating to the extent of the annual wear and tear. This persistent portion of the fixed capital does not exist for us, when we consider the value of the product. It is a portion of the value of capital existing independently beside the new value in commodities produced by this capital. This was shown previously in the analysis of the value of the product of some individual capital (Volume 1, Chapter 6). However, for the present we must leave aside the method of analysis employed there. We saw in the study of the value of the product of individual capital that the value withdrawn from the fixed capital by wear and tear was transferred to the product in commodities created during the time of wear, no matter whether any portion of this fixed capital is reproduced in its natural form out of the value thus transferred or not. At this point, however, in the study of the social product as a whole and of its value, we must for the present leave out of consideration that portion of value which is transferred from the fixed capital to the annual product by wear and tear, unless this fixed capital is reproduced *in natura* during the year. In one of the following sections of this chapter we shall return to this point.

* * *

We shall base our analysis of simple reproduction on the following diagram, in which c stands for constant capital, v for variable capital, and s for surplus-value, the rate of surplus-value between v and s being assumed at 100 per cent. The figures may indicate millions of francs, marks, pounds sterling, or dollars.

I. Production of Means of Production.
Capital   4000 c + 1000 v = 5000.
Product in Commodities   4000 c + 1000 v + 1000 s = 6000.
These exist in the form of means of production.
II. Production of Means of Consumption.
Capital   2000 c + 500 v = 2500.
Product in Commodities   2000 c + 500 v + 500 s = 3000.
These exist in articles of consumption.
Recapitulation: Total annual product in commodities:
I. 4000 c + 1000 v + 1000 s = 6000 means of production.
II. 2000 c + 500 v + 500 s = 3000 articles of consumption.

Total value 9000, exclusive of the fixed capital persisting in its natural form, according to our assumption.

Now, if we examine the transactions required on the basis of simple reproduction, where the entire surplus-value is unproductively consumed, leaving aside for the present the mediation of the money circulation, we obtain at the outset three great points of vantage.

(1) The 500 v, representing wages of the labourers, and 500 s, representing surplus-value of the capitalists, in Department II, must be spent for articles of consumption. But their value exists in the articles of consumption to the amount of 1000, held by the capitalists of Department II, which reproduce the 500 v and represent the 500 s. The wages and surplus-value of Department II, then, are exchanged within this department for products of this same department. By this means, a quantity of articles of consumption equal to 1000 (500 v plus 500 s) disappear out of the total product of Department II.

(2) The 1000 v and 1000 s of Department I must likewise be spent for articles of consumption, in other words, for some of the products of Department II. Hence they must be exchanged for the remaining 2000 c of constant value, which is equal in amount to them. Department II receives in return an equal quantity of means of production, the product of I, in which the value of 1000 v and 1000 s of I is incorporated. By this means, 2000 c of II and (1000 v + 1000 s) of I disappear out of the calculation.

(3) Nothing remains now but 4000 c of I. These consist of means of production which can be used up only in Department I. They serve for the reproduction of its consumed constant capital, and are disposed of by the mutual exchange between the individual capitalists of I, just as are the (500 v + 500 s) in II by an exchange between the capitalists and labourers, or between the individual capitalists, of II.

This may serve for the present to render easier the understanding of the following statements.

Section 3. The Transactions between the Two Departments.[4]

I (v + s) versus II c.

We begin with the great exchange between the two departments. The values of (1000 v + 1000 s), consisting of the natural form of means of production in the hands of their producers, are exchanged for 2000 c of II, for values consisting of articles of consumption in their natural form. The capitalist class of II thereby reconverts its constant capital of 2000 from the form of articles of consumption into that of means of production of articles of consumption. In this form it may serve once more as a factor in the labour-process as the value of constant capital in the process of self-expansion. On the other hand, the equivalent of the labour-power of I (1000 v) and of the surplus-value of the capitalists of I (1000 s) is realised in articles of consumption; both of them are converted from their natural form of means of production into a natural form in which they may be consumed as revenue.

Now, this mutual transaction is accomplished by means of a circulation of money, which facilitates it as much as it renders its understanding difficult, but which is of fundamental importance, because the variable portion of capital must ever resume the form of money, of money-capital converting itself from the form of money into labour-power. The variable capital must be advanced in the form of money in all lines of production carried on simultaneously, regardless of whether they belong to Department I or II. The capitalist buys the labour-power before it enters into the process of production, but does not pay for it except at stipulated terms, after it has been expended in the production of use-values. He owns, with the remainder of the value of the product, also that portion of it which is an equivalent for the money expended in the payment of labour-power, in other words, that portion of the value of the product which represents variable capital. By this portion of value the labourer has supplied the capitalist with the equivalent for his own wages. But it is the reconversion of commodities into money by their sale which restores to the capitalist his variable capital in the form of money-capital, which he may advance once more for the purchase of labour-power.

In Department I, then, the aggregate capitalist has paid 1000 pounds sterling (I use the term pounds sterling merely to indicate that it is value in the form of money), equal to 1000 v, for the v-portion of the already existing value of product I, that is to say, of the means of production created by him. The labourers buy with these 1000 pounds sterling articles of consumption of the same value from the capitalists II, thereby converting one-half of the constant Capital II into money; the capitalists II, in their turn, buy with these 1000 pounds sterling means of production, valued at 1000, from the capitalists I; the variable capital-value of 1000 v, which consisted, in the natural form of the product of capitalists I, of means of production, is thus reconverted for them into money and may serve anew in their hands as money-capital, which is transformed into labour-power, the most essential element of productive capital. In this way, their variable capital returns to them in the form of money, as a result of the realisation on some of their commodity-capital.

As for the money which is required for the exchange of the s portion of commodity-capital I for the second half of constant capital II, it may be advanced in various ways. In reality, this circulation implies innumerable small purchases and sales of the individual capitals of both departments, the money coming under all circumstances from these capitalists, since we have already disposed of the money thrown into circulation by the labourers. It may be that one of the capitalists of Department II buys, with the money-capital he has aside from his productive capital, means of production from capitalists of Department I, or that, vice versa, one of the capitalists of Department I buys, with funds reserved for individual expenses, not for capital investment, articles of consumption from capitalists of Department II. A certain supply of money, to be used either for investment as capital or for expenditure as revenue, must be assumed to exist beside the productive capital in the hands of the capitalists, under all circumstances, as we have shown in section I and II. Let us assume – it is immaterial what proportion we select for our purpose – that one-half of the money is advanced by the capitalists of Department II in the purchase of means of production intended for the reproduction of their constant capital, while the other half is spent by the capitalists of Department I for articles of consumption. For instance, let Department II advance 500 pounds sterling for the purchase of means of production from Department I, thereby reproducing (inclusive of the 1000 pounds sterling coming from the labourers of Department I) three-quarters of its constant capital in its natural form; Department I buys with the 500 pounds sterling so obtained articles of consumption from II, thus completing for one-half of the s-portion of its commodity-capital the circulation c—m—c and realising on its product in a supply of articles of consumption. By means of this second transaction, the 500 pounds sterling return to the hands of the capitalists of Department II, in the form of money-capital existing beside its productive capital. On the other hand, Department I expends money to the amount of 500 pounds sterling, in anticipation of the realisation on the other half of the s-portion of its still unsold commodity-capital, for the purchase of articles of consumption from Department II. With the same 500 pounds sterling, Department II buys from I means of production, thereby reproducing in natural form its entire constant capital (1000 + 500 + 500 = 2000), while I realises its entire surplus-value in articles of consumption. The entire transaction would represent a transfer of commodities valued at 4000 pounds sterling with a circulation of 2000 pounds sterling in money. This last amount is sufficient only because we have assumed that the entire annual product is sold in bulk in a few large transactions. The important point is here that Department II has not only reconverted its constant capital, which had been reproduced in the form of articles of consumption, into the form of means of production, but has also recovered the 500 pounds sterling which it had thrown into circulation for the purchase of means of production; and that in the same way Department I possesses once more not only its variable capital, which it had produced in the form of means of production, in the form of money-capital, readily convertible into labour-power, but also the 500 pounds sterling expended in the purchase of articles of consumption previously to the sale of the s-portion of its capital in anticipation of its realisation. It recovers these 500 pounds sterling, not by this expenditure, but by the subsequent sale of one-half of the s-portion of its commodity-capital.

In both cases, it is not merely the constant capital of Department II which is reconverted from the form of a product into the natural form of means of production, in which it can alone serve as capital; nor is it merely the variable portion of the capital of I which is reconverted into its money-form, nor the surplus-portion of the means of production of I which is transformed into its consumable form of revenue. It is also the 500 pounds sterling of money-capital, advanced by Department II in the purchase of means of production previously to the sale of the corresponding portion of the value of its constant capital, which return to II; and the 500 pounds sterling expended by I for means of consumption previously to the realisation of its surplus-value. The fact that the money advanced by II at the expense of the constant portion of its commodities, and by I at the expense of the surplus-portion of its commodities, returns to them is due to the circumstance that one class of capitalists throws 500 pounds sterling into circulation over and above the constant capital existing in the form of commodities in Department II, and another class a like amount over and above the surplus-value existing in the form of commodities in Department I. In the last analysis, the two departments have mutually paid one another in full by the exchange of equivalents in the form of their respective commodities. The money thrown into circulation by each department in excess of the value of their commodities, as a means of transacting the exchange of these commodities, returns to each one of them out of the circulation at the same rate in which they had contributed to it. Neither has grown any richer thereby. Department II possessed a constant capital of 2000 in the form of articles of consumption plus 500 pounds sterling in money; now it possesses 2000 in means of production plus 500 pounds sterling in money, the same as before; in the same way, Department I possesses, as before, a surplus-value of 1000 (consisting of commodities in the form of means of production, now converted into a supply of articles of consumption) plus 500 pounds sterling. The general conclusion is this: the money which the industrial capitalists throw into circulation for the purpose of accomplishing the mutual exchange of their commodities, either in account with the constant value of the commodities, or in account with the surplus-value existing in the commodities, to the extent that it is spent as revenue, returns into the hands of the respective capitalists in proportion to the amount advanced by them for the circulation of money.

As for the reconversion of the variable capital of Department I into the form of money, this capital exists, after the capitalists of I have invested it in wages, first in the form of the commodities produced by the labourers. The capitalists have paid this capital in the form of money to these labourers as the price of their labour-power. The capitalists have to this extent paid for that portion of the value of their commodities, which is equal to the variable capital expended in the form of money. They are, for this reason, the owners of this portion of the commodity-product. But that portion of the working class which is employed by them does not buy the means of production created by it; these labourers buy articles of consumption produced by Department II. Hence the variable capital advanced by the capitalists of I in the payment of labour-power does not return to these capitalists directly. It passes by means of the purchases of the labourers of I into the hands of the capitalist producers of the requirements of life of the labourer, or of other commodities accessible to them; in other words, it passes into the hands of capitalists of II. And not until these expend this money in the purchase of means of production does it return by this circuitous route into the hands of the capitalists of Department I.

It follows that, on the basis of simple reproduction, the sum of the values of v plus s of the commodity-capital of I (and therefore a corresponding proportional part of the total product in commodities of I) must be equal to the constant capital c of Department II, which is likewise disposed of as a proportional part of the entire product in commodities of Department II; or I (v + s) = II c.

Section 4. Transactions within Department II. Necessities of Life and Articles of Luxury.

It remains for us to analyse the portion v plus s of the value of the commodities of Department II. This analysis has nothing to do with the most important question which occupies our attention in this chapter, namely the question, to what extent the separation of the value of every individual capitalist product in commodities into c plus v plus s applies also to the value of the entire annual product in commodities, even though this separation may be based on different forms. This question is solved by the transaction between I (v + s) and II c, and, on the other hand, by the analysis of the reproduction of I c in the annual product in commodities of I, to be analysed later on.

Since II (v + s) exists in the natural form of articles of consumption; since, furthermore, the variable capital advanced in the payment of the labour-power of the labourers is mostly spent by them for articles of consumption; and since, finally, the s-portion of the value of commodities, on the basis of simple reproduction, is practically spent as revenue for articles of consumption, it is evident at the first glance that the labourers of II buy back, with the money received as wages from the capitalists of II, a portion of their own product, corresponding in value to the money-value represented by these wages. The capitalist class of II thereby reconvert the money-capital advanced by them in the payment of labour-power into the form of money. It is as though they had paid the labourers in mere cheques on commodities. As soon as the labourers realise on these cheques by the purchase of a portion of the commodities produced by them, but belonging to the capitalists, these cheques return into the hands of the capitalists. Only, these cheques do not merely represent value, but they are actually embodied in gold or silver. We shall analyse later on this sort of reflux of variable capital by means of a process in which the labourer appears as a purchaser and the capitalist as a seller. Here, however, it is a question of a different point, which must be discussed on the occasion of the return of this variable capital to its point of departure.

Department II of the annual production of commodities consists of a great variety of lines of production, which may, however, be divided into two great subdivisions according to their products.

(a) Articles of consumption required for the maintenance of the labouring class, and to the extent that they are material requirements of life, also forming a portion of the consumption of the capitalist class, although they are frequently different in quality and value. We may, for our purposes, comprise this entire subdivision under the name of *necessary articles of consumption*, regardless of whether a product of this class, such as tobacco, is really a necessary article of consumption from the physiological standpoint or not. It is sufficient that it may be habitually in demand.

(b) Articles of luxury, which are consumed only by the capitalist class, being purchased only with the surplus-value, which never falls to the share of the labourer.

It is obvious that the variable capital advanced in the production of the commodities of the class (a) must flow back directly to that portion of the capitalist class of II (in other words the capitalists of IIa) who have produced these material requirements of life. They sell them to their own labourers to the amount of the variable capital paid to them in wages. This reflux takes place in a direct way, so far as this entire subdivision (a) of the capitalist class of Department II is concerned, no matter how numerous may be the transactions between the capitalists of the various lines of industry interested in this department, by means of which the returning variable capital is distributed pro rata. These transactions are processes of circulation, whose means of circulation are supplied directly by the money expended by the labourers. It is different with subdivision IIb. The entire portion of the values produced in this subdivision, IIb (v + s), exists in the natural form of articles of luxury; that is to say, articles which the labourer can buy no more than the value of the commodities Iv existing in the form of means of production, notwithstanding the fact that both articles of luxury and means of production are the products of the working class. Hence the reflux by which the variable capital advanced in this subdivision restores to the capitalist producers its value in the form of money cannot take place directly, but must be promoted indirectly, similarly as in the case of Iv.

Let us assume, for instance, that v stands for 500 and s also for 500, as they did in the case of the entire class II; but let the division of the variable capital and of the corresponding surplus-value be as follows:

(Subdivision a) Necessities of Life: v equal to 400 and s equal to 400; hence a total quantity of necessities of life valued at 400 v plus 400 s, equal to 800; in other words, IIa (400 v + 400 s).

(Subdivision b) Articles of Luxury: valued at 100 v plus 100 s, equal to 200, or IIb (100 v + 100 s).

The labourers of IIb have received 100 in money as payment of their labour-power, or say 100 pounds sterling. They buy with this money articles of consumption from the capitalists of IIa to the same amount. This class of capitalists buys with the same money £100 worth of the commodities of IIb, thereby returning to the capitalists of IIb their variable capital in the form of money.

In IIa there are available once more 400 v in money, in the hands of the capitalists, obtained by exchange with their labourers. Furthermore, the fourth part of the product representing surplus-value has been transferred to the labourers of IIb, and IIb (100v) have been purchased in the form of articles of luxury.

Now, assuming that the capitalists of IIa and IIb divide the expenditure of their revenue in the same proportion between necessities of life and luxuries – for instance, three-fifths for necessities and two-fifths for luxuries – the capitalists of IIa will spend their revenue from surplus-value, amounting to 400 s, three-fifths, or 240, for their own product of necessities of life, and two-fifths, or 160, for articles of luxury. The capitalists of subdivision IIb will divide their surplus-value of 100 s in the same way: three-fifths, or 60, for necessities, and two-fifths, or 40, for articles of luxury, these being produced and exchanged in their own subdivision.

The 160 in articles of luxury received by IIa for its surplus-value, pass into the hands of the capitalists of IIa in the following manner: of the 400 s of IIa, we have seen that 100 were exchanged in the form of necessities of life for an equal amount of articles of luxury of IIb, and furthermore 60, consisting of necessities of life, for 60 s of IIb, consisting of luxuries. The total calculation then stands as follows:

IIa: 400 v plus 400 s; IIb: 100 v plus 100 s.

(1) 400 v of (a) are consumed by the labourers of IIa, a part of whose product is represented by that amount in necessities of life; the labourers buy these necessities from the capitalist producers of their own subdivision. These capitalists thereby recover £400, in money, which is the value of the variable capital paid by them to these same labourers. They can now buy more labour-power with it.

(2) One portion of the 400 s of (a), equal to the 100 v of (b); in other words, one-quarter of the surplus-value of (a) is exchanged for luxuries in the following way: The labourers of (b) received from the capitalists of their subdivision £100 in wages. With this amount these labourers bought one-quarter of the surplus-value of (a), in other words, commodities consisting of necessities of life. The capitalists of (a) buy with this same money articles of luxury to the same amount, which equals 100 v of (b), or one-half of the entire product in luxuries of (b). In this way the capitalists of (b) recover their variable capital in the form of money and are enabled to resume reproduction after having invested this amount once more in labour-power, since the entire constant capital of the whole Department II has been reproduced by the exchange between I (v + s) and IIc. The labour-power of the labourers of IIb, the producers of articles of luxury, is under these circumstances only saleable because the product created by them as an equivalent for their own wages is consumed by the capitalists of IIa. (The same applies to the sale of the labour-power of I, since the IIc for which I (v + s) is exchanged, consists of both articles of luxury and necessities of life, and that which is reproduced by means of I (v + s) consists of the means of production of both luxuries and necessities.)

(3) We now come to the exchange between a and b, to the extent that it is merely a transaction between the capitalists of these two subdivisions. So far we have disposed of the variable capital (400) v and of one portion of the surplus-value (100) s in (a), and of the variable capital (100) v in (b). We had furthermore assumed that the average proportion of the expenditure of the capitalist revenue was in both classes two-fifths for luxuries and three-fifths for necessities. Apart from the 100 thus expended for luxuries, the entire department therefore still has to spend 60 for luxuries in (a) and the same proportion, or 40, in (b).

(IIa) is then divided into 240 for necessities and 160 for luxuries, or 240 + 160 = 400s (IIa).

(IIb) s is divided into 60 for necessities and 40 for luxuries; 60 + 40 = 100s (IIb). The last 40 are consumed by this class out of its own product (two-fifths of its surplus-value); the 60 for necessities are obtained by this class through the exchange of 60 of its surplus-value for 60 s of a.

We have, then, for the entire capitalist class of II, the following situation (v plus s in subdivision (a) consisting of necessities, in subdivision (b) of luxuries):

IIa (400 v + 400 s) +IIb (100 v + 100 s) = 1000; by this transaction there is realised 500 v (a + b) + 500 s (a + b) = 1000; the first member in this equation being realised in 400 v of (a) and 100 s of (b), the second in 300 s of (a) plus 100 v of (b) plus 100 s of (b).

Considering a and b, each by itself, we have the transaction:

a) $\dfrac{v}{400\ v\ (a)} + \dfrac{s}{240\ s\ (a) + 100\ v\ (b) + 60\ s\ (b)} = 800$

b) $\dfrac{v}{100\ s\ (a)} + \dfrac{s}{60\ s\ (a) + 40\ s\ (b)} = \dfrac{200}{1000}$

If we retain, for the sake of simplicity, the same proportion between the variable and constant capital of each subdivision (which, by the way, is not at all necessary), we obtain for 400 v (a) a constant capital of 1600, and for 100 v (b) a constant capital of 400, and we have the following two subdivisions a and b in Department II:

(IIa) 1600 c + 400 v + 400 s = 2400
(IIb)   400 c + 100 v + 100 s = 600

making together

2000 c + 500 v + 500 s = 3000

Accordingly, 1600 of the 2000 IIc in articles of consumption, which are exchanged for 2000 I (v + s), are disposed of for means of production of necessities of life, and 400 for means of production of luxuries.

The 2000 I (v + s), then, would be divided into (800 v + 800 s) I, for the 1600 means of production of necessities of life in section a, and (200 v + 200 s) I, for the 400 means of production of luxuries in b.

A considerable part of the instruments of labour, strictly so called, as well as of the raw and auxiliary materials, etc., is homogeneous for both departments. But so far as the transaction of the exchanges of the various portions of value of the total product I (v + s) are concerned, such a division would be immaterial. Both the above named 800 v of I and 200 v of I are realised by the spending of wages for articles of consumption 1000 c of II, and the money-capital advanced for this purpose is uniformly distributed, on its return, among the capitalist producers of I, reproducing their variable capital in money at the rate advanced by them. On the other hand, so far as the realisation of the 1000 s of I is concerned, the capitalists will likewise draw uniformly, in proportion to the magnitude of their surplus-value, 600 IIa and 400 IIb out of the entire second half of IIc, equal to 1000; in other words, those who make up for the constant capital of IIa will draw 480, or three-fifths, out of 600 c of IIa, and 320, or two-fifths, out of 400 c of IIb, a total of 800; while those who make up for the constant capital of IIb will draw 120, or three-fifths, out of 600 c of IIa and 80, or two-fifths, out of 400 c of IIb, a total of 200. Grand total, 1000.

That which is arbitrary in this case is the proportion of the variable to the constant capital of both I and II, and so is the uniformity of this proportion for I and II and their subdivisions. As for this uniformity, it has been assumed merely for the sake of simplifying the matter, and it would not alter in any way the fundamental conditions of the problem and its solution, if we had assumed different proportions. However, the necessary result of all this, on the basis of simple reproduction, is the following:

(1) That the new product in values created by the labour of one year in the natural form of means of production, divisible into v plus s, must be equal to the value of the constant capital c of the product in values created by the other part of annual labour, reproduced in the form of articles of consumption. If it were smaller than IIc, it would be impossible for II to reproduce its entire constant capital; if it were greater, a surplus would remain unused. In either case, the assumption of simple reproduction would be violated.

(2) That in the case of annual product which is reproduced in the form of articles of consumption, the variable capital v advanced in the form of money can be realised by its recipients, to the extent that they are labourers producing luxuries, only in that portion of the necessities of life which embodies for its capitalist producers primarily their surplus-value; so that v, invested in the production of luxuries, is equal in value to a corresponding portion of s produced in the form of necessities, and must be smaller than the whole of this s, which is s of IIa; and that, finally, the variable capital of the capitalist producers of luxuries returns to them in the form of money only by means of the realisation of that v in this portion of s. This phenomenon is quite analogous to the realisation of I (v + s) in IIc; only that in the second case, it is the v of IIb which is realised in a portion of s of IIa of the same value. These conditions determine the proportions of the

various quantities in every distribution of the total annual product, to the extent that it actually enters into the process of the annual reproduction promoted by circulation. I (v + s) can be realised only in IIc, and IIc can renew its function as a component part of productive capital only by means of this realisation; in the same way, the v of IIb can be realised only in a portion of s of IIa, and v of IIb can only thus be reconverted into the form of money-capital. Of course, all this applies only to the extent that it is a result of the process of reproduction itself, so that the capitalists of IIb do not, for instance, take up money-capital for v by credit from others. So far as mere quantity is concerned, the transactions for the exchange of the various portions of the annual product can take place only in the way indicated above, so long as the scale and the conditions determining value remain stationary, and so long as these strict conditions are not altered by the commerce with foreign countries.

Now, if we were to say after the manner of Adam Smith that I (v + s) resolves itself in IIc, and IIc resolves itself into I (v + s), or, as he says more frequently and more absurdly, I (v + s) constitutes the component parts of the price (or value in exchange, as he has it) of IIc, and IIc constitutes the entire component part of the value of I (v + s); then we could and should say that the v of IIb resolves itself into s of IIa, or the s of IIa into the v of IIb; or the v of IIb forms a component part of the s of IIa; or, vice versa, the surplus-value thus resolves itself into wages, or into variable capital, and the variable capital forms a *component part* of the surplus-value. This absurdity is indeed found in Adam Smith, since according to him wages are determined by the value of the necessities of life, and the values of these commodities in their turn by the value of the wages (variable capital) and surplus-value contained in them. He is so absorbed in the fractional parts, into which the product in values of one working day is divided on the basis of capitalist production – namely into v plus s – that he quite forgets that it is immaterial in the simple exchange of commodities, whether the equivalents existing in various natural forms consist of paid or unpaid labour, since their production costs in either case the same amount of labour; and that it is also immaterial, whether the commodity of A is a means of production and that of B an article of consumption, and whether one commodity has to serve as a component part of capital after its sale, while another passes into the fund for consumption and is consumed, according to Adam, as revenue. The use to which the buyer puts his commodity does not fall within the scope of the exchange of commodities, does not concern the circulation, and does not affect the value of the commodity. This fact is not in the least affected by the truth that, in the analysis of the circulation of the annual social product as a whole, the definite use for which it is intended, the mode of consumption of the various component parts of that product, must be taken into consideration.

In mentioning the fact that the conversion of the v of IIb into a portion of the s of IIa of the same value, and the further transactions between the s of IIa and the s of IIb, it is by no means assumed that either the individual capitalists of IIa and IIb or their respective totalities divide their surplus-value in the same proportion between necessities of life and articles of luxury. The one may spend more in this consumption, the other more in that. On the basis of simple reproduction we have merely assumed that a sum of values equal to the entire surplus-value is realised in a fund for consumption. The limits are thus given. Within each department, the one may do more in a, the other in b. But this may compensate itself mutually, so that the capitalist classes of a and b, each taken as a whole, each participate in the same proportion in both of them. The proportions of value – the proportional share of the two classes of producers, a and b, in the total value of the product of II – and with them a definite quantitative proportion between the departments of production supplying those products, are necessarily given in any concrete case; only a proportion chosen as an illustration is a hypothetical one. It does not alter the qualitative elements of the proposition, if we select another illustration; only the quantitative determinations would be altered. But if any circumstances cause an actual change in the proportional magnitude of a and b, then the conditions of simple reproduction would likewise be changed correspondingly.

*   *   *

Since the v of IIb is realised in an equivalent portion of the s of IIa, it follows that to the extent that the portion of the annual product consisting of luxuries grows, absorbing an increasing share of the labour-power in the production of luxuries, to the same extent is the reconversion of variable capital advanced by IIb into money conditioned on the prodigality of the capitalist class, who spend a considerable portion of their surplus-value in articles of luxury. It is by this means that the reconversion of this variable capital into money is promoted, and thereby the existence and reproduction of the labourers employed in IIb, by supplying them with the articles of consumption necessary for their life.

Every crisis momentarily lessens the consumption of luxuries. It retards and checks the reconversion of the v of IIb into money-capital, permitting it only partially and thus throwing a certain number of the labourers employed in the production of luxuries out of employment, while it on the other hand clogs by this means the sale of the necessary articles of consumption and reduces it. And there are, besides, the unproductive labourers who are dismissed at the same time, labourers who receive for their services a portion of the funds spent by the capitalists for luxuries (these labourers are themselves luxuries), and who take part to a very considerable extent in the consumption of necessities of life, etc. The reverse takes place in periods of prosperity, particularly during the times of bogus prosperity, in which the relative value of money, expressed in commodities, decreases primarily for other reasons (without any other actual revolution in values), so that the price of commodities rises independently of their own value. It is not alone the consumption of necessities of life which increases at such times. The working class, actively reinforced by its entire reserve army, also enjoys momentarily articles of luxury ordinarily out of its reach, articles which at other times constitute for the greater part 'necessities' only for the capitalist class. This contributes to a rise in prices from this quarter.

It is purely a tautology to say that crises are caused by the scarcity of solvent consumers, or of a paying consumption. The capitalist system does not know any other modes of consumption but a paying one, except that of the pauper or of the 'thief'. If any commodities are unsaleable, it means that no solvent purchasers have been found for them, in other words, consumers (whether commodities are bought in the last instance for productive or individual consumption). But if one were to attempt to clothe this tautology with a semblance of a profounder justification by saying that the working class receive too small a portion of their own product, and the evil would be remedied by giving them a larger share of it, or raising their wages, we should reply that crises are precisely always preceded by a period in which wages rise generally and the working class actually get a larger share of the annual product intended for consumption. From the point of view of the advocates of 'simple' (!) common sense, such a period should rather remove a crisis. It seems, then, that capitalist production comprises certain conditions which are independent of good or bad will and permit the working class to enjoy that relative prosperity only momentarily, and at that always as a harbinger of a coming crisis.[5]

We saw a while ago that the proportion between the production of necessities of life and that of luxuries requires the division of II $(v + s)$ into IIa and IIb, and thus of IIc into (IIa) c and (IIb) c. Hence this division touches the character and the quantitative conditions of production to their very roots, and is an essential factor in its general conformation.

Simple reproduction is essentially directed toward consumption as an end, although the securing of surplus-value appears as the compelling motive of the individual capitalists; but surplus-value in this case, whatever may be its proportional magnitude, is supposed to serve merely for the individual consumption of the capitalist.

So far as simple reproduction is a part, and the most important one at that, of annual reproduction on an enlarged scale, consumption remains as a motive accompanying the accumulation of wealth as an end and distinguished from it. In reality, the matter appears more complicated, because some partners in the loot, the surplus-value of the capitalist, figure as consumers independently of him.

Section 5. The Promotion of the Transactions by the Circulation of Money.

So far as we have analysed circulation up to the present, it proceeded between the various classes of producers as indicated in the following diagrams:

(1) Between class I and class II:

$$I. \ 4000 \ c + 1000 \ v + 1000 \ s.$$
$$II. \ ......2000 \ c...... + 500 \ v + 500 \ s.$$

This disposes of the circulation of IIc (2000), which is exchanged for I (1000 v + 1000 s).

Leaving aside for the present the 4000 c of I, there still remains the circulation of v + s within class II. Now II (v + s) is subdivided between the subclasses IIa and IIb in the following manner:

(2) II. 500 v + 500 s = a (400 v + 400 s) + b (100 v + 100 s).

The 400 v of a circulate within their own subclass; the labourers paid with these wages buy with them articles of consumption, produced by themselves, from their employers, the capitalists of IIa.

Since the capitalists of both subclasses spend three-fifths of their surplus-value in products of IIa (necessities) and two-fifths in products of IIb (luxuries), the three-fifths of the surplus-value of a, or 240, are consumed within the sub-class IIa itself; likewise two-fifths of the surplus-value of b (produced in the form of articles of luxury and existing as such) within the subclass IIb.

There remains to be exchanged between IIa and IIb: on the side of IIa: 160 s; on the side of IIb: 100 v + 60 s. These compensate one another. The labourers of IIb buy with their 100 in the form of money necessities of life to that amount from IIa. The capitalists of IIb likewise buy necessities from IIa to the amount of three-fifths, or 60, of their surplus-value. The capitalists of IIa thus obtain the money required for investing, as above assumed, two-fifths of their surplus-value, or 160 s, in luxuries produced by IIb (100 v held by the capitalists of IIb as a product reimbursing them for the wages paid by them, and 60 s). The diagram for this transaction is

3) IIa.   [400 v] + [240 s] + $\underline{160\ s}$
   b. . . . . 100 v + 60 s + [40 s].

the brackets indicating the amounts circulated and consumed within their own subclass.

The direct reflux of the money-capital advanced in variable capital, which takes place only in the case of the capitalist class of IIa who produce necessities of life, is but an expression, modified by special conditions, of the previously mentioned general law, that money advanced to the circulation by producers of commodities returns to them in the normal circulation of commodities. Consequently, if a money capitalist stands behind the producer of commodities and advances to the industrial capitalist money-capital (using this term in its strictest meaning, that is to say, capital-value in the form of money), the final point of reflux for this money is the pocket of this money-capitalist. In this way the mass of the circulating money belongs to that department of money-capital which is concentrated and organised in the form of banks, etc., although the money circulates more or less through all hands. The way in which this department advances its capital necessitates continually the final reflux to it in the form of money, although this takes place by way of the reconversion of the industrial capital into money-capital.

The circulation of commodities always requires two things: commodities which are thrown into circulation, and money which is likewise thrown into it. 'The process of circulation . . . does not, like direct barter of products, become extinguished upon the use-values changing places and hands. The money does not vanish on dropping out of the circuit of the metamorphosis of a given commodity. It is constantly being precipitated into new places in the arena of circulation vacated by other commodities', etc. (Book I, Chapter 3, page 126.)

For instance, in the circulation between IIc and I (v + s) we assumed that 500 pounds sterling in gold had been advanced for it. In the innumerable processes of circulation, into which the circulation between great social groups resolves itself, now this, now that producer will first appear in one or the other group as a buyer, throwing money into circulation. Quite aside from individual circumstances, this is conditioned on the difference of the periods of production and thus of the turn-overs of the various commodity-capitals. Now II buys with these 500 pounds sterling means of production of the same value from I, and I buys from II articles of consumption valued at 500 pounds sterling. Hence the money flows back to II, but this department does not in any way increase its wealth by this reflux. It had thrown 500 pounds sterling in money into circulation and drew the same amount out of it in commodities; then it sells 500 pounds sterling worth of commodities and draws out of circulation the same amount in money; thus the 500 pounds sterling flow back to it. As a matter of fact, II has thrown into circulation 500 pounds sterling in money and 500 pounds sterling in commodities, a total of 1000 pounds sterling. It draws out of the circulation 500 pounds sterling in commodities and 500 pounds sterling in money. The circulation requires for the handling of 500 pounds sterling in commodities of I and 500 pounds sterling in commodities of II only 500 pounds sterling in money; and whoever has first advanced money in the purchase of commodities from other producers, recovers it when selling his own. Hence, if Department I had been the first to buy commodities from II for 500 pounds sterling, and to sell later on to II commodities valued at 500 pounds sterling, these 500 pounds sterling would have returned to I instead of II.

In class I, the money invested in wages, in other words, the variable capital advanced in the form of money, does not return directly in this form, but indirectly by a detour. But in II, the 500 pounds sterling return directly from the labourers to the capitalists, and this return is always direct in the case where purchase and sale take place repeatedly between the same persons in such a way that they are acting alternately as buyers and sellers of commodities. The capitalist of II pays for the labour-power in money; he thereby incorporates his labour-power in his capital and assumes the role of an industrial capitalist over his labourers as wage earners only by means of this transaction in circulation, which is for him merely a conversion of money-capital into productive capital. Thereupon the labourer, who is in the first instance a seller of his own labour-power, assumes in the second instance the role of a buyer, a possessor of money, while the capitalist acts now as a seller of commodities. In this way the capitalist recovers the money invested by him in wages. Unless this sale of his commodities implies cheating, etc., and remains but an exchange of equivalents in money and commodities, it is not a process by which the capitalist enriches himself. He does not pay the labourer twice, first in money, and then in commodities. His money returns to him as soon as the labourer exchanges it for his commodities.

Now, the money-capital converted into variable capital, the money advanced for wages, plays a prominent role in the circulation of money itself. For the labourer must live from hand to mouth and cannot give the industrial capitalists any credit for long periods. Hence variable capital in the form of money must be advanced simultaneously at innumerable localities in the social production in certain short intervals, such as weeks, etc., whatever may be the various periods of turnover of the capitals in the different lines of industry. These intervals succeed one another with relative rapidity, and the shorter they are, the smaller is relatively the total amount of money thrown into circulation through this channel. In every country with a capitalist production the money-capital so advanced constitutes a proportionately influential share of the total circulation, so much more so as the same money, before its return to its point of departure, roams through many channels and serves as a medium of circulation for innumerable other businesses.

* * *

Now let us consider the circulation between I (v + s) and IIc from a different point of view.

The capitalists of I advance 1000 pounds sterling in the payment of wages. The labourers buy with this money 1000 pounds sterling's worth of commodities from the capitalists of II. These in turn buy with the same money means of production from the capitalists of I. These capitalists of I thereby recover their variable capital in the form of money, while the capitalists of II have reconverted one-half of their constant capital from the form of commodities into that of productive capital. The capitalists of II advance 500 pounds sterling more for the purchase of means of production from the capitalists of I. The capitalists of I spend this money in articles of consumption of II. These 500 pounds sterling thus return to the capitalists of II. They advance this amount again, in order to reconvert the last quarter of their constant capital, existing in the form of commodities, into means of production of I, its natural productive form. This money flows back to I, and once more withdraws from II articles of consumption to the same amount, returning 500 pounds sterling to II. The capitalists of II are then once more in possession of 500 pounds sterling in money and 2000 pounds sterling of constant capital, the latter having been reconverted from the form of commodity-capital into that of productive capital. By means of 1500 pounds sterling, a quantity of commodities valued at 5000 pounds sterling has been circulated. (1) I paid 1000 pounds sterling to his labourers for their labour-power of the same value; (2) the labourers bought with these same 1000 pounds sterling articles of consumption from II; (3) II bought with the same money means of production from I, thereby restoring to I its variable capital of 1000 pounds sterling in the form of money; (4) II buys 500 pounds sterling's worth of means of production from I; (5) I buys with the same 500 pounds sterling articles of consumption from II; (6) II buys with the same 500 pounds sterling means of production from I; (7) I buys with the same 500 pounds sterling articles of consumption from II. Thus 500 pounds sterling have returned to II, which it had thrown into circulation aside from its 2000 pounds sterling in commodities and for which it did not withdraw any equivalent from circulation.[6]

The exchange, therefore, follows this course:

(1) I pays 1000 pounds sterling in money for labour-power, or, in short, commodities at 1000 pounds sterling.

(2) The labourers buy with their wages amounting to 1000 pounds sterling articles of consumption from II; therefore we have again commodities at 1000 pounds sterling.

(3) II buys with the 1000 pounds sterling received from the labourers means of production to the same amount; hence, once more, commodities at 1000 pounds sterling.

By this transaction the 1000 pounds sterling have returned to I in the money-form of its variable capital.

(4) II buys 500 pounds worth of means of production from I, or, commodities at 500 pounds sterling.

(5) I buys with the same 500 pounds sterling articles of consumption from II; or, commodities at 500 pounds sterling.

(6) II buys with the same 500 pounds sterling means of production from I; or, commodities at 500 pounds sterling.

(7) I buys with the same 500 pounds sterling articles of consumption from II; or, commodities at 500 pounds sterling.

Total amount of value of commodities converted: 500 pounds sterling.

The 500 pounds sterling advanced by II in its first additional purchase have returned to it.

This, then, is the result:

(1) I possesses variable capital in the form of money to the amount of 1000 pounds sterling, which it had originally advanced to the circulation. It has furthermore expended 1000 pounds sterling for its individual consumption, in the shape of its product in commodities; that is to say, has spent money which it had originally received for the sale of means of production to the amount of 1000 pounds sterling.

On the other hand, the natural form in which variable capital existing in the form of money must be incorporated in order to be preserved, in other words, labour-power, has been maintained by consumption, and having been reproduced exists once more as the sole commodity which its owners have for sale in order to make a living. The relation of wage workers and capitalists, then, has likewise been reproduced.

(2) The constant capital of II is reproduced in its natural form, and the £500 advanced by the same department to the circulation have likewise returned to its hands.

So far as the labourers of I are concerned, the circulation takes place according to the simple schedule C—M—C. Labour-power₁ C − £1,000 as the money-form of the variable capital of I; M₂ − necessities of life to the amount of £1,000; C₃ − these £1,000 monetise to the same amount the constant capital of II existing in the form of commodities, of necessities of life.

From the point of view of the capitalists of II, the process is C—M, the transformation of a portion of their product into money, from which it is reconverted into the elements of productive capital, namely into a portion of the means of production required by them.

In the case of the advance of money of £500, made by the capitalists of II in the purchase of an additional portion of means of production, the money-form of that portion of IIc which exists as yet in the form of commodities, of articles of consumption, is anticipated in the transaction M—C, in which II buys with M, and C is sold by I, the money (II) is converted into a portion of productive capital, while C (I) passes through the transaction C—M, changes itself into money, which, however, does not represent any component part of productive capital for I, but merely monetised surplus-value expended solely for articles of consumption.

In the circulation M—C . .P . .Cᴵ− Mᴵ the first act, M—C, is that of one capitalist, the last Cᴵ—Mᴵ, of another (or at least in part); whether this C, by which M is converted into productive capital, represents an element of constant capital, variable capital, or surplus-value for the seller of C (who exchanges this C for money), is immaterial for the circulation of commodities itself.

Class I, so far as concerns the portion v plus s of its product in commodities, draws more money out of circulation than it threw in. In the first place, its £1,000 of variable capital are restored to it; in the second place, it sells means of production valued at £500 (see above transaction No. 4); one-half of its surplus-value is thus monetised; then it sells once more £500's worth of means of production (transaction No. 6), the second half of its surplus-value, and thus its entire surplus-value is withdrawn from circulation in the shape of money. The successive transactions, then, have been (1) a reconversion of variable capital into money, to the amount of £1,000; (2) a monetisation of one-half of the surplus-value, to the amount of £500; (3) a monetisation of the other half of the surplus-value, to the amount of £500; altogether 1000 v plus 1000 s that have been monetised, or £2,000. Although Department I threw only £1,000 into circulation (aside from those transactions which promote the reproduction of Ic, and which we shall analyse later), it has withdrawn double that amount from it. Of course, the surplus-value passes into another hand, that of II, as soon as it has been converted into money, by being spent for articles of consumption. The capitalists of I withdrew only as much value *in money* as they threw into circulation in the form of *commodities*; the fact that this value is surplus-value, that is to say, that it does not cost the capitalists anything, does not alter the value of these commodities in any way; so far as the exchange of values in circulation is concerned, that fact is entirely irrelevant. The monetisation of surplus-value is, of course, a transient act, the same as all other phases through which the advanced capital passes in its metamorphoses. It lasts no longer than the interval between the conversion of the commodities of I into money and the subsequent conversion of the money of I into commodities of II.

If the turn-overs had been assumed to be shorter – or, from the point of view of the simple circulation of commodities, the number of turn-overs of the circulating money more rapid – even less money would be required for the circulation of the exchanged values of commodities; the amount is always determined – if the number of successive transactions is given – by the sum of the prices, or the sum of values, of the circulating commodities. It is immaterial for this question what proportion of this sum of values consists of surplus-value or of capital-value.

If the wages of I, in our illustration, were paid four times per year, we should have 4 times 250, or 1000. In other words, £250 would suffice for the circulation between Iv and 1/2 of IIc, and for that between the variable capital of I and the labour-power of the same department. Furthermore, if the circulation between Is and IIc were to take place in four turn-overs, it would require only £250 in money, or in the aggregate a sum of money, or a money-capital, or £500 for the circulation of commodities worth £5,000. In that case, the surplus-value would be converted into money by four successive transactions, monetising one-fourth each time, instead of two transactions of one-half each time.

If Department I instead of II, should assume the role of buyer in transaction No. 4 by expending £500 for articles of consumption of the same value, II would buy means of production with the same £500 in transaction No. 5; I would then buy articles of consumption with the same £500 in transaction No. 6; II would then buy means of production with the same £500 in transaction No. 7; so that the £500 would finally return to I, the same as they did in our previous illustration to II. The surplus-value is converted into money, in this second case, by means of an expenditure of money for articles of individual consumption on the part of its capitalist producer, and this expenditure of money discounts beforehand the revenue to be derived from the monetisation of the surplus-value still contained in the unsold commodities. The surplus-value is not monetised by the reflux of the £500; for aside from £1,000 in the form of commodities of Iv, Department I threw £500 in money into circulation at the close of transaction No. 4, and this was additional money, so far as we know, not money obtained by the sale of commodities. In recovering this money, Department I merely pockets once more the additional money advanced by it. It has not monetised its surplus-value by this means. The monetisation of the surplus-value of I takes place only by the sale of the commodities of Is, in which it is incorporated, and lasts only so long as the money obtained by the sale of the commodities is not expended in the purchase of new articles of consumption.

Department I buys with an additional amount of £500 in money articles of consumption from II; after spending this money, I holds its equivalent in commodities of II; the money returns for the first time by the purchase, on the part of II, of commodities to the amount of £500 from I; in other words, it returns as the equivalent of the commodities sold by I, but these commodities do not cost I anything, they constitute surplus-value for I, and *thus the money thrown into circulation by this very department monetises its own surplus-value*. On buying for the second time, in transaction No. 6, I has likewise obtained its equivalent in commodities of II. Take it, now, that II would not buy means of production from I. In that case, I would have actually paid £1,000 for articles of consumption, it would have consumed its entire surplus-value as revenue, namely 500 in its own commodities (means of production) and 500 in money; on the other hand, it would still have £500 in commodities (means of production) in stock, and would have got rid of £500 in money.

Department II, again, would have reconverted three-fourths of its constant capital from the form of commodity-capital into that of productive capital; but one-fourth, or £500, would be held by it in money, which, having interrupted its function and waiting for conversion, would be unproductive for the time being. If this condition of things should last for any length of time, II would have to cut down its scale of reproduction by one-fourth.

However, the 500 in means of production, which I has on its hands, are not surplus-value existing in the form of commodities; they occupy the place of the £500 advanced in money, which I possessed aside from its £1,000 in commodities. In the form of money, they would be always convertible, as commodities they are momentarily unsaleable. So much is evident, that simple reproduction – in which every element of productive capital must be reproduced in both II and I – remains possible in this case only, if the 500 golden birds, which I first sent flying, return to it.

If a capitalist (we have only industrial capitalists to deal with here, who are the representatives of all others) spends money for articles of consumption, it passes out of his life, it goes the way of the flesh. If it returns to him, it can do so only to the extent that he draws it out of circulation by means of his commodity-capital. The value of his entire annual product in commodities (which represents his commodity-capital) the same as that of every one of its elements, that is to say, of every individual commodity, resolves itself, from his point of view, into constant capital, variable capital, and surplus-value. The monetisation of every individual commodity (each constituting an element of the product in commodities) is at the same time a monetisation of a certain portion of the surplus-value contained in the entire product. In the cited case, then, it is literally true that the capitalist himself threw the very money into circulation by which his surplus-value is monetised, and he did so in the purchase of articles of consumption. Of course, it is not a question of the identical pieces of money, but rather of a certain amount of genuine money equal to the one (or an equal portion of the one) which he had previously thrown into circulation to satisfy his own individual wants.

In practice this is done in two ways: if the business has been opened in the current year, it will take quite a while before the capitalist will be enabled to use any portion of the receipts of his business for the satisfaction of his individual consumption. But he does not suspend his consumption for all that for a single moment. He advances to himself (immaterial whether out of his own pocket or by means of credit from others) money in anticipation of surplus-value to be realised by him. If the businesss has been running regularly for a period longer than the current year, payments and receipts are distributed over different terms of the year. But one thing continues uninterruptedly, namely the consumption of the capitalist, which anticipates a definite portion of the customary or estimated revenue and is calculated on a certain proportion of it. With every portion of commodities sold, a portion of the annually produced surplus-value is also realised. But if only as much of the produced commodities were sold during the entire year as is required to reproduce the values contained in the constant and variable capitals, or if prices were to fall to such an extent that only the value of the capital contained in it should be realised by the sale of the entire annual product in commodities, then the anticipatory character of the expenditure of money in expectation of future surplus-value would be clearly revealed. If our capitalist fails, then his creditors and the court investigate whether his anticipated private expenditures were reasonably proportionate to the volume of his business and to the receipts of surplus-value usually or normally corresponding to it.

So far as the entire capitalist class are concerned, the statement that they must themselves throw into circulation the money required for the realisation of their surplus-value (eventually for the circulation of their constant and variable capital) is not only no paradox, but is the necessary premise of the entire mechanism. For there are only two classes in this case, the working class disposing of their labour-power, and the capitalist class owning the social means of production and the money. It would rather be a paradox if the working class were to advance in the first instance out of its own pockets the money required for the realisation of the surplus-value contained in the commodities. But the individual capitalist makes this advance only by acting as a buyer, *expending* money in the purchase of articles of consumption, or *advancing* money in the purchase of elements of his productive capital. He never parts with his money unless he gets an equivalent for it. He advances money to the circulation only in the same way that he advances commodities to it. He acts in both instances as the point of departure of their circulation.

The actual transaction is obscured by two circumstances:

(1) The fact that merchant's capital (the first form of which is always money, since the merchant as such does not create any 'product' or 'commodity') and money-capital are manipulated by a special class of capitalists in the process of circulation of industrial capital.

(2) The division of surplus-value – which must always be first in the hands of the industrial capitalist – into various categories, represented, aside from industrial capitalists, by the land owner (for ground rent), the usurer (for interest), etc., furthermore by the government and its officials, by people living on their income, etc. This gentry appear as buyers as compared to the industrial capitalist, and to that extent as monetisers of his commodities; they likewise throw 'money' into circulation on their part and the industrial gets it from them. But in that case, it is always forgotten from what source they derived it originally, and continue deriving it ever anew.

Section 6. The Constant Capital of Department I.[7]

It remains for us to analyse the constant capital of Department I, amounting to 4000 c. This value is equal to that of the means of production consumed in the creation of the commodity-product of

I and incorporated in it. This re-appearing value, which was not produced in the process of production of I, but entered into it during the preceding year in the form of constant capital, representing the definite value of his means of production, exists now in the entire quantity of commodities not absorbed by Department II. And the value of this quantity of commodities thus left in the hands of the capitalists of I equals two-thirds of the value of their entire annual commodity-product. In the case of the individual capitalist producing some particular means of production, we were enabled to say: he sells his commodity-product; he converts it into money. By converting it into money, he has also reconverted into money the constant portion of the value of his product. With this portion of value, thus converted into money, he then buys his means of production once more from other sellers of commodities, or transforms the constant portion of the value of his product into its natural form, in which it can resume its function of productive constant capital. But now this supposition becomes impossible. The capitalist class of I comprises all the capitalists producing means of production. Besides, the commodity-product of 4000, which is left on their hands, is a portion of the social product which cannot be exchanged for any other portion, because no other portion of the annual product remains. With the exception of these 4000, all the remainder of the product has been disposed of. One portion has been absorbed by the social fund for consumption, and another portion has to reproduce the constant capital of Department II, which has already bargained for everything which it can exchange with I.

The difficulty is solved very easily, when we remember that the entire product of I in its natural form consists of means of production, that is to say, of material elements of the constant capital itself. We meet here the same phenomenon which we witnessed under II, only under a different aspect. In the case of II, the entire product consisted of articles of consumption. Hence one portion of it, measured by the wages plus surplus-value contained in this product, could be consumed by its own producers. Here, in the case of I, the entire product consists of means of production, such as buildings, machinery, tanks, raw and auxiliary materials, etc. One portion of them, namely that reproducing the constant capital employed in this sphere, can therefore be immediately set to work in its natural form to serve once more as an element of productive capital. So far as it goes into circulation, it circulates within Department I. While a portion of the commodity-product of II is individually consumed in its natural form by its own producers, a portion of the commodity-product of I is productively consumed in its natural form by its capitalist producers.

In these 4000c of the commodity-product of I, the constant capital-value consumed in this category re-appears in its natural form in which it can immediately resume its services as a productive constant capital. In Department II, that portion of the commodity-product of 3000 whose value is equal to the wages plus the surplus-value of 1000, passes directly into the individual consumption of the capitalists and labourers of II, while, on the other hand, the constant value of this commodity-product, equal to 2000, cannot re-enter into the productive consumption of the capitalists of II, but must be reproduced by exchange with I.

But in Department I, that portion of its commodity-product of 6000, whose value is equal to the wages plus the surplus-value, or 2000, does not pass into the individual consumption of its producers, and could not on account of its natural form. It must first be exchanged with Department II. On the other hand, the constant portion of the value of this product, or 4000, exists in a natural form, in which it can immediately resume its services as the constant capital of the capitalist class of I, taking this class as an aggregate. In other words, the entire product of Department I consists of use-values which, on account of their natural form, can serve only as elements of constant capital, in a capitalist system of production. One third of this product of 6000, then, reproduces the constant capital of Department II, or 2000, and the other two thirds the constant capital of Department I.

The constant capital of I consists of a number of different groups of capital invested in the various lines of production of means of production, so much in iron works, so much in coal mines, etc. Every one of these groups of capital, or every one of these social capital groups, is in its turn composed of a larger or smaller number of independently functioning individual capitals. In the first place, the capital of society, for instance 7500 (millions, or any other denomination) is composed of various groups of capital; the social capital of 7500 is divided into separate parts, every one of which is invested in a special line of production, each portion invested in some particular line of production consists, so far as its natural composition is concerned, partly of means of production required in that special sphere of production, partly of the labour-power employed in that business and adapted to its requirements. This labour-power is modified by division of labour, according to the specific labour to be performed in each individual sphere of production. Each portion of social capital invested in any particular line of production in its turn consists of the sum of all individual capitals invested in it. This, of course, applies equally to departments I and II.

As for the value of the constant capital re-appearing in the form of the commodity-product of I, it re-enters in part as means of production into the particular sphere whose product it is (or even into the individual business), for instance, corn into the production of corn, coal into the production of coal, iron in the form of machines into the production of iron, etc.

However, the partial products constituting the value of the constant capital of I, so far as they do not return directly to their particular or individual sphere of production, merely change their place. They pass in their natural form to some other sphere of production of Department I, while the product of other spheres of production of Department I replaces them in their natural state. It is merely a change of place of the products. All of them become once more the elements in the reproduction of constant capital of I, only in another group of I instead of the same one. To the extent that an exchange takes place between the individual capitalists of I, it is an exchange of one natural form of constant capital for another, one kind of means of production for another. It is an exchange of the different individual constant parts of capital of I among themselves. Unless the products serve directly as means of production in their own line, they are transferred to another line and thus naturally replace one another. In other words (similarly to what we saw in the case of the surplus value II), every capitalist of I draws on this constant capital of 4000, of which he is part owner, to the extent of his share, in means of production required by him. If production were socialised, instead of capitalistic, it is evident that these products of Department I would just as regularly be redistributed as means of production to the various lines of production of this department, for purposes of reproduction, one portion remaining directly in that sphere of production which created it, another passing over to other lines of production of the same department, thereby entertaining a constant mutual exchange between the various lines of production of this department.

Section 7. Variable Capital and Surplus-Value in Both Departments.

The total value of the articles of consumption annually produced is equal to the value of the variable capital of II produced during the year plus the newly created surplus-value of II (in other words, equal to the value newly produced by II during the year) plus the value of the variable capital of I reproduced during the year and the newly produced surplus-value of I (in other words, plus the value created by I during the year).

On the assumption of simple reproduction, then, the total value of the annually produced articles of consumption is equal to the annual product in values, in other words, equal to the total value produced during that year by social labour. And it must be so, for the reason that this entire value is consumed, on the basis of simple reproduction.

The total social working day is divided into two parts: (1) Necessary labour, which creates in the course of the year a value of 1500 v; (2), surplus labour, which creates an additional value, or surplus-value, of 1500 s. The sum of these values, 3000, is equal to the value of the annually produced articles of consumption of 3000. The total value of articles of consumption produced during the year is therefore equal to the total value produced by the social working day during the year, equal to the value of the variable social capital plus the social surplus-value, equal to the total new product of the year.

But we know that the total value of the commodities of II, the articles of consumption, is not produced in this department of social production, although these two classes of value are identical. They are identical, because the value of the constant capital re-appearing in Department II is equal to the value newly produced by I (value of variable capital plus surplus value); so that I (v + s) can buy that portion of the product of II which represents the value of the constant capital of the producers in Department II. This shows why the value of the product of the capitalists of II, from the point of view of society, may be resolved into v + s, although from their standpoint it is divided into c + v + s. It is because IIc is equal to I (v + s), and because these two elements of the social product are mutually exchanged in their natural forms, so that after this exchange IIc exists once more in means of production, and I (v + s) in articles of consumption.

And it is this circumstance which induced Adam Smith to claim that the value of the annual product resolves itself into v + s. But this is not true, in the first place, except for that part of the annual product which consists of articles of consumption; and in the second place, it does not apply in the sense that this total value is entirely produced by Department II, so that its value in products would be equal to the variable capital advanced by II plus the surplus-value produced by II. It is true only in the sense that II (c + v + s) is equal to II (v + s) + I (v + s), or because IIc is equal to I (v + s).

It follows, furthermore:

Although the social working day (that is to say, the labour expended by the entire working class during the whole year), like every individual working day, is divided only in two parts, namely into necessary labour and surplus-labour, and although the value produced by this working day likewise resolves itself into but two parts, namely into the value of variable capital, or that portion with which the labourer buys his own means of reproduction, and the surplus-value which the capitalist may spend for his own individual consumption, nevertheless, from the point of view of society, one portion of the social working day is exclusively devoted to the production of *new constant capital*, namely of products exclusively intended for service as means of production in the labour-process and thus as constant capital in the accompanying process of self-expansion. According to our assumption, the total social working day is represented by a money-value of 3000, only one third of which, or 1000, is produced in Department II, which manufactures articles of consumption, that is to say, commodities in which the entire value of the variable capital and the entire surplus-value of society is finally realised. According to this assumption, two thirds of the social working day are employed in the production of new constant capital. Although, from the standpoint of the individual capitalists and labourers of Department I, these two thirds of the social working day serve merely for the production of variable capital plus surplus-value, the same as the last third of the social working day in Department II, nevertheless, from the point of view of society, and of the use-value of the product, these two thirds of the social working day serve only for the reproduction of constant capital in process of productive consumption or already so consumed. From the individual point of view, these two thirds of the working day, while producing a total value equal only to the value of the variable capital plus surplus-value, so far as its producer is concerned, nevertheless do not produce any use-values of the kind on which wages or surplus-value could be expended; for their products are means of production.

It must be noted, in the first place, that no portion of the social working day, whether in I or in II, serves for the production of the value of the constant capital employed and serving in these two great spheres of production. They produce only additional value, namely 2000 I (v + s) + constant capital, represented by 4000 Ic + 2000 IIc. The 1000 II (v + s), an addition to the existing value of the new value produced in the form of means of production, is not yet constant capital. It merely is intended to be used as such in the future.

The entire product of II, the articles of consumption, viewed concretely as a use-value, in its natural form, is a creation of the one third of the social working day contributed by II. It is the product of labour in its concrete form, such as the labour of weaving, baking, etc, performed in this department as the subjective element of the labour process. But the constant portion of the value of this product of II reappears only in a new use-value, in a new natural form, namely that of articles of consumption, while it existed previously in the form of means of production. Its value has been transferred by the labour-process from its old natural form to its new natural form. But this value of these two thirds of the product, or 2000, has not been produced in this year's productive process of II.

Just as, from the point of view of the labour-process, the product of II is the result of the function of new living labour and means of production previously given to it, which are the material objects in which it incorporates itself, so, from the point of view of the process of reproduction, the value of the product of II, or 3000, is composed of the new value (500 v + 500 s = 1000) produced by the newly added one third of the social working day, and of a constant value, in which two thirds of a previous social working day are embodied, which passed away before the present process of production of II. This portion of the value of the product of II is materialised in a portion of the product itself. It exists in a quantity of articles of consumption valued at 2000, or two thirds of a social working day. This is the new use-form in which it re-appears. The exchange of a portion of the articles of consumption of 2000 IIc for means of production of I equal to I (1000 v + 1000 s) represents, therefore, indeed an exchange of two thirds of a social working day which do not constitute any portion of this year's labour, but passed away previously to this year, for two thirds of the social working day newly added this year. Two thirds of this year's social working day could not serve in the production of constant capital and yet at the same time constitute variable capital plus surplus-value for their own producers, unless they were compelled to exchange with a portion of the value of the annually consumed articles of consumption, in which two thirds of a working day spent and realised, not this year, but previously, are incorporated. It is an exchange of two thirds of this year's working day with two thirds of a preceding working day, an exchange of this year's labour with that of a previous year. This, then explains the riddle, how it is that the product in values of an entire social working day may resolve itself into variable capital plus surplus-value, although two thirds of this working day were not expended in the production of articles, in which variable capital or surplus-value can be realised, but rather in the production of means of production for the replacement of capital consumed during this year. The explanation is simply that two thirds of the value of the product of II, in which the capitalists and labourers of I realise the value of the variable capital and surplus-value produced by them (and which constitute two thirds of the value of the entire annual product), are, so far as their value is concerned, the product of two thirds of a social working day passed previously to this year.

The sum of the social product of I and II, comprising means of production and articles of consumption, so far as its concrete use-value in its natural form is concerned, is indeed the result of this year's labour, but only to the extent that this labour is regarded as useful and concrete, not as an expenditure of labour-power and creator of values. And even so, it is concrete labour only in the sense that the means of production have transformed themselves into this year's new product by dint of the living labour operating on them. On the other hand, it is also true that this year's labour could not have transformed itself into products without the help of means of production, of instruments of production and materials, which existed independently of it.

Section 8. *The Constant Capital in Both Departments.*

The analysis of the total value of the product of 9000, and of the categories into which it is divided, does not present any greater difficulties than that of the value produced by some individual capital. It is rather identical with it.

In the present instance, the entire social product of this year contains three social working days, each of one year. The value represented by each one of these working days is 3000, so that the value of the total product is 3 x 3000, or 9000.

Furthermore, the following portions of this working time belong to a period previous to that of the process of production which we now analyse: in Department I, four thirds of a working day (with a product valued at 4000), and in Department II, two thirds of a working day (with a product valued at 2000), making a total of two social working days with a product valued at 6000. For this reason, 4000 Ic + 2000 IIc = 6000 c figure as the value of the means of production, or value of the constant capital, re-appearing in the total product of society.

Furthermore, one third of the social working day of one year newly added by Department I is necessary labour, or labour reproducing the value of the variable capital of 1000 Iv and paying the price of the labour employed by I. In the same way, one sixth of the social working day of II is necessary labour valued at 500. Hence we have 1000 I v + 500 II v = 1500 v, expressing the value of one half of the social working day, the value of the first half of the working day added this year and consisting of necessary labour.

Finally, in Department I, one third of the social working day of this year, with a product valued at 1000, is surplus-labour, and one sixth of one working day in Department II, with a product valued at 500, is likewise surplus-labour. Together they constitute the other half of the newly added social working day, with a total value of surplus-labour amounting to 1000 I s + 500 II s = 1500 s.

This, then, is the situation:

Constant portion of capital in terms of the value of the social product (c): two working days expended previously to the present process of production, worth 6000 in value.

Necessary labour (v) expended during the present year: one half of one working day expended during the present year, worth 1500 in value.

Surplus-labour (s) expended during the present year: one-half of one working day expended during the present year, worth 1500 in value.

Product in values of annual labour (v + s), 3000.

Total value of product (c + v + s), 9000.

The difficulty, then, does not consist in the analysis of the social product in values. It arises in the comparison of the component parts of the *value* of the social product with its *material* elements.

The constant, merely re-appearing, portion of value is equal to the value of that part of this product which consists of means of production, and it is incorporated in that part.

The product in values of the current year, equal to v + s, is equal to the value of that part of this product, which consists of articles of consumption, and is incorporated in it.

But with the exception of cases immaterial for this analysis, means of production and articles of consumption are vastly different kinds of commodities, products of widely different natural forms and use-value, and, therefore, products of radically different classes of concrete labour. The labour which employs machinery in the production of necessities of life is vastly different from the labour which makes machinery. The entire working day of the current year, which is 3000 in terms of value, figures as an expenditure in the production of articles of consumption valued at 3000, in which no portion of any constant value re-appears, since these 3000, equal to 1500 v + 1500 s, resolve themselves only into variable capital-value and surplus-value. On the other hand, the constant capital-value of 6000 re-appears in a class of products quite different from articles of consumption, namely in means of production, while as a matter of fact no portion of the present annual working day figures as an expenditure in the production of these new products. It appears rather that this entire working day consists only of classes of labour which do not result in means of production, but in articles of consumption. We have already solved this mystery. The product in values of the labour of the present year is equal to the value of the products of Department II, the total value of the newly produced articles of consumption. But the value of these products is greater by two thirds than that portion of the annual labour which has been expended in the production of articles of consumption (Department II). Only one third of the annual labour has been expended in their production. Two thirds of this annual labour have been expended in the production of means of production, that is to say, in Department I. The value of the product created during this time in I, equal to the variable capital-value plus surplus-value produced in I, is equal to the constant capital-value of II re-appearing in articles of consumption of II. Hence they may be mutually exchanged and take one another's place in their natural form. The total value of the articles of consumption of II is, therefore, equal to the sum of the new product in values of I and II, or II (c + v + s) is equal to I (v + s) + II (v + s), in other words, equal to the sum of the new values produced by the labour of the current year in the form of v + s.

On the other hand, the total value of the means of production of I is equal to the sum of the constant capital-value re-appearing in the form of means of production of I and in that of articles of consumption of II, in other words, equal to the sum of the constant capital-values re-appearing in the total product of society. This total value is equal in terms of value to four thirds of a working day preceding the process of production of I and two thirds of a working day preceding the process of production of II, in all equal to two annual working days.

The difficulty in the analysis of the annual social product arises, therefore, from the fact that the constant portion of value is represented by a different class of products (means of production) than the new portion of value (v + s) added to this constant portion and represented by articles of consumption. Thus the appearance is created, so far as the question of values is concerned, as though two thirds of the consumed mass of products were reproduced in a new form, without any labour having been expended by society in their production. This is not so in the case of an individual capital. Every individual capitalist employs some particular concrete class of labour, which transforms the means of production peculiar to it into products. For instance, the capitalist may be a manufacturer of machines, the constant capital expended by him during the current year may be 6000 c, the variable capital 1500 v, the surplus-value 1500 s, the product 9000, represented, say, by 18 machines of 500 each. The entire product in this instance consists of the same form, of machines. If he produces various kinds, each one is calculated separately. The entire product in commodities is the result of the labour expended during the current year in machine manufacture by a combination of the same concrete labour with the same kind of means of production. The various portions of the value of the product therefore present themselves in the same natural form: 12 machines represent 6000 c, 3 machines 1500 v, and 3 machines 1500 s. It is evident that the value of the 12 machines is equal to 6000 c, not merely because there is incorporated in these machines labour performed previously to the manufacture of these machines and not expended in their making. The value of the means of production for 18 machines did not transform itself into machines of its own doing, but the value of these 12 machines (consisting itself of 4000 c + 1000 v + 1000 s) is equal to the total value of the constant capital-value contained in the 18 machines. The machine manufacturer must, therefore, sell 12 of the 18 machines, in order to recover his expended constant capital, which he requires for the reproduction of 18 new machines. On the other hand, the thing would be inexplicable, if the result of the labour expended solely in the manufacture of machines, were to be: on the one hand, 6 machines of 1500 v + 1500 s, on the other iron, copper, screws, belts, etc., to the amount of 6000 s, in other words, the natural means of production of the machines which the individual machine-building capitalist does not produce himself, but must secure by way of the process of circulation. And yet it seemed at the first glance as though the reproduction of the annual product of society took place in this absurd way.

The product of an individual capital, that is to say, of every aliquot part of the social capital endowed with a life of its own and acting independently, has some natural form. The only condition is that this product must have a certain use-value, which endows it with the character of a member of the world of commodities fit for circulation. It is immaterial and a matter of hazard, whether or not it can go back as a means of production into the same process of production from which it came as a product, in other words, whether that portion of its value as a product, in which the constant capital is incorporated, has a natural form, in which it can actually serve again as constant capital. If it has not, then this portion of the value of the product is reconverted into the form of its material elements by means of sale and purchase, and thus the constant capital is reproduced in the natural form adapted to its function.

It is different with the product of the total social capital. All the material elements of reproduction in their natural form must be a part of this product. The consumed constant portion of capital can be reproduced by the production as a whole only to the extent that the entire reappearing constant capital is represented in the product by the natural form of new means of production, which can actually serve as constant capital. Simple reproduction being assumed, the value of that portion of the product which consists of means of production must be equal to the constant portion of the value of social capital.

Furthermore: individually considered, the capitalist produces in the value of his product by means of the newly added labour only his variable capital plus surplus-value, while the constant value is transferred by the concrete form of the newly added labour to the product.

Socially considered, that portion of the social working day which produces means of production, adding new value to them and transferring to them at the same time the value of the means of production consumed in their manufacture, creates nothing but new *constant capital*, which is intended to replace that consumed in the shape of the old means of production, that is to say of the constant capital consumed in Department I and II. It creates only product intended for productive consumption. The entire value of this product, then, is a value which can serve only as a new constant capital, which can buy back only constant capital in its natural form, and which, for this reason, resolves itself neither into variable capital nor surplus-value, looking at it from the social point of view. On the other hand, if that portion of the social working day which produces articles of consumption does not create any portion of the social capital intended for reproduction, it creates only products intended, in their natural form, to realise the value of the variable capital and surplus-value of departments I and II.

Speaking of looking at things from the point of view of society as a whole, in this instance at the aggregate product of society, which comprises both the reproduction of social capital and individual consumption, we must not follow the manner copied by Proudhon from bourgeois economy, which looks upon this matter as though a society with a capitalist mode of production would lose its specific historical and economic characteristics by being taken as a unit. Not at all. We have, in that case, to deal with the aggregate capitalist. The aggregate capital appears as the capital stock of all individual capitalists combined. This stock company shares with many other stock companies the peculiarity that every one knows what he puts in, but not what he will get out of it.

Section 9. A Retrospect on Adam Smith, Storch, and Ramsay.

The total value of the social product amounts to 9000 equal to 6000 c + 1500 v + 1500 c; in other words, 6000 represent the value of the means of production, and 3000 that of the articles of consumption. The value of the social revenue (v + s), then, amounts to only one third of the value of the total product, and the totality of the consumers, labourers as well as capitalists, can draw on the total social product for commodities only to the amount of this third, for the purpose of individual consumption. On the other hand, 6000, or two thirds, of the value of the product, are the value of the constant capital which must be reproduced in its natural form. Means of production to this amount must again be incorporated in the productive fund. Storch recognizes this without being able to prove it: 'It is clear that the value of the annual product is distributed partly to capital and partly to profits, and that each one of these portions of the value of the annual product is regularly employed in buying the products which the nation needs both for the maintenance of its capital and for stocking its fund for consumption . . . The products which constitute the capital of a nation are not consumable.' (Storch, *Considérations sur la nature du revenu national*. Paris, 1824, page 150.)

Adam Smith, however, has promulgated this strange dogma, which is believed to this day, not only in the previously mentioned form, according to which the entire value of the social product resolves itself into revenue, that is to say, into wages plus surplus-value, or, as he expresses it, into wages plus profit (interest) plus ground rent, but also in the still more popular form, according to which the consumers must ultimately pay to the producers the entire value of the product. This is to this day one of the best established commonplaces, or rather of the eternal truths of the so-called science of political economy. This is illustrated in the following plausible manner: take any article, for instance linen shirts. First, the spinner of linen yarn has to pay the flax grower the entire value of the flax, in other words the value of flax seed, fertilisers, cattle feed, etc., plus the value transferred to the product from the fixed capital of the flax grower, such as buildings, agricultural implements, etc.; furthermore the wages paid in the production of the flax; the surplus-value incorporated in the flax (profit, ground rent); finally the cost of transportation of the flax from its place of production to the spinnery. Next, the weaver has not only to reimburse the spinner for linen yarn, for the price of the flax, but also for that portion of the value of machinery, buildings, etc., in short of the fixed capital, which is transferred to the yarn, furthermore all the auxiliary materials consumed in the spinning process, the wages of the spinners, the surplus-value, etc., and so forth in the case of the bleaching process, the transportation of the finished linen, and finally the shirtmaker, who has to pay the entire price of all preceding producers, who supplied him only with his raw material. There is now a further addition of value by his hands, either by means of constant capital which is consumed in the shape of materials of labour, auxiliary materials, etc., used in the making of shirts, or by means of labour expended in it, which adds the value of the wages of the shirtmakers plus the surplus-value of the shirt manufacturer. Now let this entire product in shirts cost ultimately £100, and let this be the aliquot part of the total annual value in products expended by society in shirts. The consumers of the shirts pay these £100, that is to say the value of all the means of production, and of the wages plus surplus-value of the flax grower, spinner, weaver, bleacher, shirtmaker, and all carriers. This is quite true. Indeed, every child can see that. But now they continue: the same is true of the value of all other commodities. It should rather be said that this is true of the value of all *articles of consumption*, of the value of that portion of the social product which passes into consumption, in other words, that portion of the value of the social product which may be expended as revenue. It is true that the sum of the value of all these commodities is equal to the value of all the means of production (constant portions of capital) consumed in their creation, plus the value added by the last labour expended on them (wages plus surplus-value). Hence the totality of the consumers can pay for this entire sum of values, because, although the value of each individual commodity is made up by c + v + s, nevertheless the sum of the values of all commodities passing into consumption, taken at its maximum, can be equal only to that portion of the value of the social product, which resolves itself into v + s, in other words, equal to that value which the labour expended during the current year has added to the existing means of production representing the value of the constant capital. As for the value of the constant capital, we have seen that it is reproduced out of the mass of social products in a twofold way. First, by an exchange of the capitalists of II, who produce articles of consumption, with the capitalists of I, who produce the means of production. And here is the source of the phrase that what is capital for one is revenue for the other. But this is not the actual state of affairs. The 2000 II c, existing in the shape of articles of consumption valued at 2000, constitute a constant capital-value for the capitalists of class II. They cannot consume it themselves, although the product must be consumed on account of its natural form. On the other hand, the 2000 I (v + s) are wages plus surplus-value produced by the capitalist and working classes of I. They exist in the natural form of means of production, of things in a shape in which their own value cannot be consumed. We have here, then, values to the amount of 4000, only one half of which, either before or after the change, reproduce constant capital, while the other half form revenue. In the second place, the constant capital of I is reproduced in its natural form, partly by exchange among the capitalists of I, partly by reproduction in a natural form in each individual business.

The phrase that the entire annual value in products must be ultimately paid by the consumer would be correct only in the case that we were to include in the term consumer two vastly different classes, namely individual consumers and productive consumers. But to say that one portion of the product must be consumed productively is precisely to say that it must serve as capital and cannot be consumed as revenue.

On the other hand, if we divide the total value of the entire product, equal to 9000, into 6000 c + 1500 v + 1500 s, and look upon the 3000 (v + s) in the light of a revenue, then the variable capital seems to disappear and capital, socially speaking, seems to consist only of constant capital. For that which appeared originally as 1500 v has resolved itself into a portion of the social revenue, into wages, the revenue of the working class, and has thus lost its character of capital. This conclusion is actually drawn by Ramsay. According to him, capital, socially considered, consists only of fixed capital, but he means by fixed capital the constant capital, that quantity of values which consists of means of production, whether these are instruments or materials of labour, such as raw materials, partly finished products, auxiliary materials, etc. He calls the variable capital a circulating capital: 'Circulating capital consists only of subsistence and other necessaries advanced to the workmen previously to the completion of the produce of their labour . . . Fixed capital alone, not circulating, is properly speaking a source of national wealth . . . Circulating capital is not an immediate agent in production, nor essential to it at all, but merely a convenience rendered necessary by the deplorable poverty of the mass of the people . . . Fixed capital alone constitutes an element of cost of production in a national point of view.' (Ramsay, l.c., pages 23 to 26, selected.) Ramsay defines fixed capital, by which he means constant capital, more closely in the following words: 'the length of time during which any portion of the product of that labour' (namely labour bestowed on any commodity) 'has existed as fixed capital i. e., in a form in which, though assisting to raise the future commodity, it does not maintain labourers.' (page 59.)

Here we see once more the confusion created by Adam Smith by drowning the distinction between constant and variable capital in that of fixed capital and circulating capital. The constant capital of Ramsay consists of means of production, his circulating capital of articles of consumption. Both of them are commodities of a given value. The one can no more create any surplus-value than the other.

Section 10. Capital and Revenue:
Variable Capital and Wages.[8]

The entire annual production, the entire product of a year, is the product of the useful labour of that year. But the value of this total product is greater than that portion of it in which the labour-power expended on production during the last year is incorporated. The *product in values* of this year, the new value created in its course in the form of commodities, is smaller than the *value of the product*, that is to say, THE TOTAL VALUE OF THE COMMODITIES FINISHED DURING THE ENTIRE YEAR. The difference obtained by deducting from the total value of the annual product that portion of value which was added by the labour of the last year, is not an actually reproduced value, but merely one re-appearing in a different form of existence. It is value transferred to the annual product from previously existing value, which may be of an earlier or later date, according to the wear of the constant portions of capital which have participated in that year's annual labour-process, a value which may be derived from some means of production which were first created during the year before last or in years even previous to that. It is under all circumstances a value transferred from means of production of former years to the product of the year under discussion.

Take our formula. We then have after the exchange of the elements, hitherto considered, between I and II, and within II:

(I) 4000 c + 1000 v + 1000 s (these last realised in articles of consumption of II c) = 6000.

(II) 2000 c (reproduced by exchange with I [v + s]) + 500 v + 500 s = 3000.   Sum of values 9000.

Value newly produced during the year is incorporated only in v and s. The sum of the product in values of this year is therefore equal to the sum of v + s, that is to say, 2000 I (v + s) + 1000 II (v + s) = 3000. All other portions of value in the products of this year are merely transferred values, derived from the value of means of production, previously produced and consumed in the annual production. Aside from the value of 3000, the current annual labour has not produced anything in the way of values. That 3000 represents its entire annual product in values.

Now, we have seen that the 2000 I (v + s) of Department II replace its 2000 II c in the natural form of means of production. Two thirds of the annual labour, then, expended in Department I, have newly produced the constant capital of II, both as regards its value and its natural form. Socially speaking, two thirds of the labour expended during the entire year have created a new constant capital-value, which is realised in a natural form meeting the requirements of Department II. The greater portion of the annual labour of society, then, has been spent in the production of new constant capital (means of production representing capital-value) in order to replace the value of the constant capital expended in the production of articles of consumption. That which distinguishes in this case capitalist society from a society of savages is not, as Senior thinks,[9] that it is a privilege and peculiarity of a savage to expend his labour during a certain time which does not secure for him any revenue convertible into articles of consumption, but the distinction is the following:

(a) Capitalist society employs more of its available annual labour in the production of means of production (and thus of constant capital) which are not convertible into revenue in the form of wages or surplus-value, but can serve only as capital.

(b) When a savage makes bows, arrows, stone hammers, axes, baskets, etc., he knows very well that he did not spend the time so employed in the production of articles of consumption, but that he has simply stocked his supply of means of production, and nothing else. Furthermore, a savage commits a grave economic sin by his utter indifference so far as waste of time is concerned, for Tyler[10] tells us of him that he takes sometimes a whole month to make one arrow.

The current conception, by which some political economists seek to get rid of the theoretical difficulty, in other words, of the understanding of the real state of affairs, the conception that a thing may be capital for one and revenue for another, and vice versa, is only partially true, and it becomes wholly wrong, when it is made general, since it then implies a complete misunderstanding of the entire process of transactions taking place in annual reproduction and at the same time a misunderstanding of the actual basis of the partial truth.

We now review the actual conditions, on which the partial correctness of this conception rests, and we shall at the same time expose the wrong conception of these conditions.

(1) The variable capital serves as capital in the hands of the capitalist and as revenue in the hands of the wage worker.

The variable capital exists first in the hands of the capitalist as money-capital; and it performs the function of money-capital, when he buys labour-power with it. So long as it persists in the form of money in his hands, it is nothing but a given value existing in the form of money, in other words, a constant and not a variable magnitude. It is only a potential variable capital, owing to its convertibility into labour-power. It becomes actually a variable capital only after divesting itself of its money-form and assuming the form of labour-power serving as an element of productive capital in the capitalist process.

The money which first served in the function of the money-form of the variable capital for the capitalist, now serves in the hands of the labourer as the money-form of his revenue, which he derives from the ever repeated sale of his labour-power.

We have here but the simple fact that the money in the hands of the buyer, in this case the capitalist, passes from these hands into those of the seller, in this case a seller of labour-power, the wage-worker. It is not the variable capital which serves twice, first as capital for the capitalist and then as revenue for the labourer. It is merely the same money, which exists first in the hands of the capitalist as the money-form of his variable capital representing a potential variable capital, and which serves in the hands of the labourer as an equivalent for sold labour-power, as soon as the capitalist has converted it into labour-power. But the fact that the same money serves another useful purpose in the hands of the buyer than in those of the seller is a peculiarity of the sale and purchase of all commodities.

Apologists in political economy present the matter in a wrong light, as we can see best when we keep our eye exclusively, without taking any notice of the following transactions, on the transaction in circulation indicated by M—L (a variation of M—C), the conversion of money into labour-power on the part of the capitalist buyer, which is L—M (C—M), a conversion of the commodity labour-power into money, on the part of the seller, the labourer. They say: 'The same money realises in this instance two capitals; the buyer – the capitalist – converts his money-capital into living labour-power, which he incorporates in his productive capital; on the other hand, the seller, the labourer, converts his commodity, his labour-power, into money, which he spends as his revenue, and this enables him to resell his labour-power in ever repeated turns and thereby to maintain it. His labour-power, then, represents his capital in the form of a commodity, which yields him a continuous revenue.' Labour-power is indeed his wealth (ever self-renewing and reproductive), not his capital. It is the only commodity which he must and can sell continually, in order to live, and which does not serve as capital until it reaches the hands of the capitalist. The fact that a man is continually compelled to sell his labour-power (himself) to another man proves to those apologetic economists that he is a capitalist, for lo! he is continually selling his 'commodity', himself. In that case, a slave is also a capitalist, although he is sold by another for once and all as a commodity, for the nature of this commodity, a labouring slave, has the peculiarity that its buyer does not only make it work every new day, but also provides it with the food which enables it to do ever new work – (compare on this point the remarks of Sismondi and Say in their letters to Malthus.)

(2) In the exchange of 1000 I v + 1000 I s for 2000 II c, we see that what is constant capital for one (2000 II c) is variable capital and surplus-value, or in short, revenue for others; and what is variable capital and surplus-value (2000 I (v + s), or in short, revenue for one, becomes constant capital for another.

Let us first look at the exchange of I v for II c, beginning with the point of view of the labourer.

The aggregate labourer of I has sold his labour-power to the aggregate capitalist of I for 1000; he receives this value in money as his wages. With this money, he buys from II articles of consumption of the same value. The capitalist of II meets him only in the role of a seller of commodities, nothing else, even if the labourer buys from his own capitalist, as he does in the exchange of 500 II v, as we have seen above. The form of circulation through which his commodity, labour-power, passes, is that of the simple circulation of commodities for the mere purpose of consumption in the satisfaction of needs, the form C (labour-power)—M—C (articles of consumption). The result of this transaction in circulation is that the labourer maintains himself as a labour-power for a capitalist, and in order to continue maintaining himself as such, he must continually renew the transaction L (C)—M—C. His wages are realised in articles of consumption, they are spent as revenue, and, taking the working class as a whole, are again and again spent as a revenue.

Now let us look at the same transaction, the exchange of I v for II c, from the point of view of the capitalist. The entire commodity-product of II consists of articles of consumption, of things intended for annual consumption, serving in the realisation of revenue for some one, in the present case for the aggregate labourer of I. But so far as the aggregate capitalist of II is concerned, one portion of his commodity-product, equal to 2000, is now the form of the constant portion of the value of his productive capital converted into commodities. It must be reconverted from the form of commodities into its natural form, in which it may serve again as the constant portion of a productive capital. What the capitalist of II has accomplished so far is that he has reconverted one half (1000) of the constant portion of his capital, which had been reproduced in the shape of commodities, into the form of money by means of sale to the labourers of I. Hence it is not the variable Capital I v, which has been exchanged for this first half of the value of the constant capital of II, but simply the money which served I as money-capital in the exchange for labour-power has thus been transferred to the possession of the seller of labour-power, and for him it did not represent any capital, but merely revenue in the form of money, which is to be expended in the purchase of articles of consumption. The money to the amount of 1000, on the other hand, which has come into the hands of the capitalists of II by means of the transaction with the labourers of I, cannot as yet serve as the constant element of the productive capital of II. For the present it is but the money-form of the commodity-capital of II, to be commuted into fixed or circulating portions of constant capital. Department II now buys with the money received from the labourers of I, the buyers of its commodities, means of production from I to the amount of 1000. By this means the constant value of the capital of II is renewed to the extent of one half of its total amount in its natural form, in which it can serve once more as an element of the productive capital of II. The circulation in this instance took the course C—M—C, that is to say, articles of consumption to the amount of 1000—money to the amount of 1000—means of production to the amount of 1000.

But C—M—C represents here the movement of capital. C, when sold to the labourers, is converted into M, and this M is converted into means of production. It is the reconversion of commodities into the material elements of which this commodity is made. On the other hand, just as the capitalist of II plays only the role of a buyer of commodities with regard to I, so the capitalist of I acts only as a seller of commodities with regard to II. Department I bought originally labour-power valued at 1000 with that amount of money intended for service as variable capital. It has therefore received an equivalent for the 1000 v which it expended in money. This money now belongs to the labourers, who spend it in purchases from II. Department I cannot recover this money from II unless it secures the amount by the sale of commodities of the same value to II.

Department I first had a certain sum of money amounting to 1000 and destined to serve as variable capital. The money performs this service by its exchange for labour-power to the same amount. The labourer in his turn supplied as a result of the process of production a quantity of commodities (means of production) to the amount of 6000, of which one sixth, or 1000, are equivalent in value to the variable portion of capital advanced in money. This variable portion of value no more serves as variable capital so long as it retains the form of commodities than it did while in the form of money. It serves as variable capital only after its conversion into living labour-power, and only so long as this labour-power serves in the process of production. So long as this value was incorporated in money, it represented only potential variable capital. But it had at least a form, in which it was immediately convertible into labour-power. But in the form of commodities, the same variable value is but potential money, it must first assume the form of money by means of the sale of commodities, in the present instance by the sale of 1000 in value of commodities of I to Department II. The movement of the circulation passes here through the form 1000 v (money)—1000 c (labour-power)—1000 c (commodities equivalent in value to the variable capital)—1000 v (money); in other words, M—C...C—M (identical with M—L...C—M). The process of production intervening between C...C does not belong to the sphere of circulation. It does not figure in the mutual exchange of the various elements of annual reproduction, although this exchange includes the reproduction of all the elements of productive capital, the constant as well as the variable element (labour-power). All the participants in this exchange appear either as buyers, or as sellers, or as both. The labourers appear only as buyers of commodities. The capitalists act alternately as buyers and sellers, and within certain limits only on one side, either as buyers of commodities or as sellers of commodities.

The result is that Department I possesses once more the variable part of the value of its capital in the form of money, from which alone it is immediately convertible into labour-power, in other words, Department I once more holds its variable capital value in the only form in which it can again be advanced as an actual variable element of its productive capital. On the other hand, the labourer must again act as a seller of commodities, of his labour-power, before he can act as a buyer of commodities.

So far as the variable capital of Department II (500 II v) is concerned, the circulation between the capitalists and labourers of the same department takes place without any intermediate transactions, since we look upon it as taking place between the aggregate capitalist and the aggregate labourer of II.

The aggregate capitalist of II advances 500 v for the purchase of labour-power to the same amount. In this case, the aggregate capitalist is a buyer, the aggregate labourer a seller. Thereupon the labourer acts as a buyer of a portion of the commodities produced by himself, using the money received for his labour-power. In this case, the capitalist is the seller. The labourer has reproduced for the capitalist the money paid in the purchase of labour-power by means of a portion of the newly produced commodity-capital of II, amounting to 500 v in commodities. The capitalist then holds in the form of commodities the same v, which he had in the form of money before the exchange for labour-power; while the labourer has realised the value of his labour-power in money, and uses this money by spending it as his revenue in the purchase of articles of consumption produced by himself. It is an exchange of the revenue of the labourer in money for a portion of the commodities in which he has himself reproduced 500 of the value of the variable capital of the capitalist employing him. In this way this money returns to the capitalist of II as the money-form of his variable capital. An equivalent value of revenue in the form of money thus reproduces variable value of capital in the form of commodities.

The capitalist does not increase his wealth by recovering the money paid by him to the labourer in the purchase of labour-power through the sale of an equivalent quantity of commodities to the labourer. He would really pay the labourer twice, if he were to pay him first 500 in the purchase of labour-power, and then give him in addition thereto a quantity of commodities valued at 500, after the labourer had produced them. On the other hand, if the labourer were to produce nothing but an equivalent in commodities valued at 500 for the price of his labour-power of 500, the capitalist would be no better off after the transaction than before it. But the labourer has actually reproduced a product of 3000. He has preserved the constant portion of the value of the product, that is to say, the value of the means of production incorporated in the product, to the amount of 2000, by converting it into a new product. He has furthermore added to this existing value a value of 1000 (v + s). (The idea that the capitalist grows richer by the return of 500 in money is advanced by Destutt de Tracy, as shown in detail in section 13 of this chapter.)

By the purchase of articles of consumption to the value of 500 on the part of the labourer of II, the capitalist of II recovers the value of 500 II v, which he had just held in the shape of commodities, but which he now holds in the form of money, in which he advances it originally. The immediate result of this transaction, as of any other sale of commodities, is the conversion of a given value from the form of commodities into that of money. Nor is the resulting reflux of the money to its point of departure anything specific. If the capitalist of II had bought, with 500 of money, commodities from the capitalist of I, and then sold to the capitalist of I commodities valued at 500, he would likewise have recovered 500 in money. This sum of 500 in money would merely have served for the circulation of commodities valued at 1000, and according to a law previously mentioned, the money would have returned to the one starting it into circulation.

But the 500 in money, which have returned to the capitalist of II, represent at the same time a renewed potential variable capital. Why is this so? Money, and money-capital, is a potential variable capital only to the extent that it is convertible into labour-power. The return of £500 in money to the capitalist of II is accompanied by the return of the labour-power of II to the market. The return of both of these at opposite poles – and to this extent the re-appearance of 500 in money not merely in the capacity of money, but of variable capital in the form of money – is conditioned on one and the same process. The money of 500 returns to the capitalist of II, because he sold to the labourers of II articles of consumption valued at 500, for which the labourer spent his wages, in order to maintain himself and his family and thus his labour-power. In order to be able to live on and act again as a buyer of commodities he must again sell his labour-power. The return of 500 in money to the capitalist of II is therefore at the same time a return, or a staying, of labour-power in the capacity of a commodity purchasable with 500 in money, and thereby a return of 500 in money to its capacity of potential variable capital.

As for the v of Department II b, which produces articles of luxury, this (II b) v is treated the same as I v. The money which renews the variable capital of the capitalists of II b in the form of money returns to them in a roundabout way through the hands of the capitalists of II a. But it makes nevertheless a difference, whether the labourers buy their articles of consumption by direct purchase from the same capitalist producers to whom they sell their labour-power, or whether they buy from capitalists of another department, through whose hands the money returns indirectly to the capitalists of their own department. Since the working class live from hand to mouth, they buy just as long as they have the means. It is different with the capitalists, for instance in the transaction between 1000 II c and 1000 I v. The capitalist does not live from hand to mouth. His compelling motive is the utmost self-expansion of his capital. Now, if circumstances seem to promise greater advantages to the capitalist of II by holding on to his money for a while, instead of immediately renewing his constant capital, then the return of 1000 II c in money to I is retarded. This implies a retardation in the return of 1000 I v to the form of money, and in that case the capitalist of I cannot continue his business on the same scale, unless he can draw on some reserve capital. Generally speaking, reserve capital in the form of money is always necessary, in order to be able to work without interruption, regardless of the rapid or slow reflux of the variable portion of capital-value in money.

If the transactions of the various elements of the current annual reproduction are to be investigated, the results of the labour of the preceding year, which has come to a close, must also be taken into consideration. The process of production which resulted in the product of the present year, is past and incorporated in its products, and so much more is this the case with the process of circulation preceding the process of production or running parallel with it, by which potential variable capital is transformed into actual variable capital, in other words, the sale and purchase of labour-power. The labour-market is not a part of the commodity-market which concerns us here. For the labourer has not only disposed of his labour-power before this, but also supplied an equivalent of the price of his labour-power in the shape of commodities, aside from the surplus-value created by him. He has furthermore his wages in his pocket and figures during the present transactions only as a buyer of commodities (articles of consumption). On the other hand, the annual product must contain all the elements of reproduction, must renew all the elements of productive capital, above all its most important element, the variable capital. And we have seen, indeed, that the result of the present transactions, so far as the variable capital is concerned, is this: the labourer as a buyer of commodities, by means of the expenditure of his wages, and the consumption of the purchased commodities, reproduces his labour-power, this being the only commodity which he has to sell. Just as the money advanced in the purchase of this labour-power by the capitalists returns to them, so labour-power returns to the market to be once more exchanged for this money. The result in the special case of 1000 I v is that the capitalists of I hold 1000 v in money and the labourers of I offer them 1000 in labour-power, so that the entire process of reproduction of I can be renewed. This is one result of the process of circulation.

On the other hand, the expenditure of the wages of the labourers of I drew on II for articles of consumption to the amount of 1000 II c, transforming them from commodities into money. Department II reconverted them into the natural form of its constant capital, by purchasing from I commodities valued at 1000 v and thus restoring to I the value of its variable capital in money.

The variable capital of I passes through three metamorphoses, which are only indicated in the circulation of the annual product or do not appear at all in it.

(1) The first form is 1000 I v in money, which is converted into labour-power of the same value. This transaction does not itself appear in the exchange of commodities between I and II, but its result is seen in the fact that the working class of I approach the capitalist seller of commodities of II with 1000 in money, just as the working class of II approach the capitalist of II with 500 in money in order to buy his 500 II v of commodities.

(2) The second form is the only one in which variable capital actually varies and serves as variable capital. In this form, a power which creates values takes the place of given values offered in exchange for it. It belongs exclusively to the process of production which is past.

(3) The third form, in which the variable capital as such performs its function in the process of production, is the annual product in

values, which in the case of I amounts to 1000 v plus 1000 s, or 2000 I (v + s). In the place of its original value of 1000 in money we have a value of double this amount, or 2000, in commodities. The variable capital-value of 1000 is therefore only one half of the product in values created by it as an element of productive capital. The 1000 I v in commodities are an exact equivalent of the variable part of capital originally advanced in money. But in the form of commodities they are but potential money (they do not become money until they are sold), so that they are still less directly money-capital. They finally become money-capital by the sale of the commodities of 1000 I v to II c, and by the hurried re-appearance of labour-power as a purchasable commodity, as a material for which 1000 v in money may be exchanged.

During all these transactions the capitalist of I continually holds the variable capital in his hands: (1) originally as money-capital; (2) then as an element of his productive capital; (3) still later as a portion of the value of his commodity-capital, in the form of the value of commodities; (4) finally once more in money which seeks the company of labour-power for the purpose of exchange. During the process of production, the capitalist has the variable capital in his control as a labour-power creating values, but not as a value of a given magnitude. But since he never pays the labourer until the labourer's power has been applied for a certain length of time, he always holds in his hands the value created by labour for its own reproduction and the surplus-value in excess of this, before he pays him.

Seeing that the variable capital always stays in the hands of the capitalist, it cannot be claimed in any way that it converts itself into revenue for any one. On the contrary, 1000 I v converts itself into money by its sale to II, whose constant capital it reproduces to the extent of one half in its natural form.

That which resolves itself into revenue is not the variable capital of I, represented by 1000 v in money. This money has ceased to serve as the money-form of the variable capital of I as soon as it has converted itself into labour-power, just as the money of any other seller of commodities ceases to represent any of his property as soon as he has exchanged it for commodities of some other seller. The transactions which the money paid as wages makes in the hands of the working class are not transactions of variable capital, but of the value of their labour-power converted into money. So are the transactions of the product in values (2000 I (v + s)), created by the working class, only transactions of commodities belonging to the capitalists, which do not concern the labourers. However, the capitalist, and still more his theoretical interpreter, the political economist, can rid himself only with the greatest difficulty of the idea that the money paid to the labourer is still the capitalist's money. If the capitalist is a producer of money, then the variable portion of value – in other words, the equivalent in commodities˜which reproduces for him the price of the labour-power bought by him – appears immediately in the form of money, so that it can serve again as variable money-capital without the circuitous route of a reflux. But so far as the labourer of II is concerned – aside from the labourer who produces articles of luxury – 500 v exists in the form of commodities intended for the consumption of the labourer, which he, the aggregate labourer, buys by direct purchase from the same aggregate capitalist to whom he had sold his labour-power. The variable portion of the capital of II, so far as its natural form is concerned, consists of articles of consumption, the greater portion of which are intended for the consumption of the labouring class. But it is not the variable capital which is spent in this form by the labourer. It is the wages, the money of the labourer, which by its realisation in these articles of consumption restores to the capitalist the variable capital 500 II v in its money-form. The variable capital II v is reproduced in articles of consumption, the same as the constant capital 2000 II c. The one resolves itself no more into revenue than the other does. In either case it is the wages which resolve themselves into revenue.

It is a weighty fact in the circulation of the annual production that the expenditure of wages restores both the constant and variable capital to the form of money-capital, in the one case 1000 II c, in the other 1000 I v and 500 II v. (In the case of the variable capital either by means of a direct or indirect reflux.)

Section 11. Reproduction of the Fixed Capital.

A great difficulty in the analysis of the transactions in annual reproduction is the following. Take the simplest form in which the matter may be presented, as follows:

(I.) 4000 c + 1000 v + 1000 s +
(II.) 2000 c + 500 v + 500 s = 9000.

This resolves itself finally into

4000 I c + 2000 II c + 1000 I v + 500 II v + 1000 I s
+ 500 II s = 6000 c + 1500 v + 1500 s = 9000.

One portion of the value of the constant capital, to the extent that it consists of instruments of production in the strict meaning of the term (as a distinct section of the means of production) is transferred from the instruments of labour to the product of labour (commodities); these instruments of labour continue to serve as elements of productive capital in their old natural form. It is their wear and tear, the loss in value experienced by them after a certain period of service, which re-appears as an element of value in the commodities produced by means of them, which is transferred from the instruments of labour to the product of labour. In a question of annual reproduction, therefore, only those elements of fixed capital demand consideration, which last longer than one year. If they are completely worn out within one year, then they must be completely reproduced by the annual reproduction, and the point of issue does not concern them at all. It may happen in the case of machines and other lasting forms of fixed capital – and it frequently *does* happen – that certain parts of them must be completely reproduced within one year, although the organism of the building or machine as a whole lasts a much longer time. These partial organs belong in the same category with the elements of fixed capital which must be reproduced within one year.

This element of the value of commodities must not be confounded with the cost of repairs. If a commodity is sold, this element is turned into money, the same as all others. But after it has been turned into money, its difference from all other elements becomes apparent. The raw and auxiliary materials consumed in the production of com-modities must be replaced in their natural form, in order that the reproduction of commodities may begin anew (or that the production of commodities in general may be continuous). The labour-power embodied in them must also be renewed by fresh labour-power. For this reason, the money realised on the commodities must be continually reconverted into these elements of productive capital, a conversion of money into commodities. It does not alter the matter that raw and auxiliary materials, for instance, are bought in large quantities in certain intervals, so that they constitute a productive supply, and need not be secured by new purchases during those intervals. Nor does it matter that the money coming in through the sale of commodities, to the extent that it is intended for the purchase of those means of production, may accumulate while they last, so that this portion of constant capital appears temporarily in the role of money-capital suspended from its active function. It is not a revenue-capital. It is productive capital suspended in the form of money. The renewal of the means of production must continue all the time, but the form of their renewal – with reference to the circulation – may vary. The new purchases, the transactions in the circulation by which they are renewed, may take place in more or less prolonged intervals, and a large amount may be invested at one stroke in a correspondingly large supply of means of production. Or, the intervals between purchases may be small, and in that case small amounts of money are invested in correspondingly small supplies of means of production. But this does not alter the matter itself. The same applies to labour-power. Wherever production is carried on continuously throughout the year on the same scale, there the consumed labour-power must be continuously replaced by new labour-power. Where work depends on seasons, or different portions of the work are done at different periods, as in agriculture, there the purchases of labour-power are relatively smaller. But the money received through the sale of commodities, so far as it represents the value of the wear and tear of fixed capital, is not reconverted into that component part of productive capital whose loss in value it makes good. It settles down beside the productive capital and retains the form of money. This precipitation of money is repeated, until the period of reproduction, consisting of a small or great length of time, has elapsed, during which the fixed element of constant capital continues to perform its function in the process of production in its old natural form. As soon as the fixed element, such as buildings, machinery, etc., has been worn out and can no longer serve in the process of production, its value exists fully in money, in the sum of money precipitated by the values which had been gradually transferred by the fixed capital to the commodities in whose production it assisted, and which had been converted into money by the sale of these commodities. This money then serves to replace the fixed capital (or its elements, since its various elements have a different durability) in its natural form and thus to renew this part of the productive capital in reality. This money is, therefore, the money-form of a part of the value of the productive capital, namely of its fixed part. The formation of this hoard is thus a factor in the capitalist process of reproduction, it is the reproduction and storage, in the form of money, of the value of the fixed capital, or its individual elements, until such time as the fixed capital shall be worn out, until it shall have transferred its entire value to the commodities produced and must be reproduced in its natural form. And this money does not lose the form of a hoard and resume its activity in the process of reproduction of capital promoted by the circulation, until it is re-converted into new elements of fixed capital which will replace the worn-out elements.

The transactions disposing of the annual product in commodities can no more be dissolved into a mere direct exchange of its individual elements than the simple circulation of commodities can be regarded as identical with a simple exchange of commodities. Money plays a specific role in this circulation, which is particularly marked by the manner in which the value of the fixed capital is reproduced. (It is left to a later analysis to ascertain how the matter would present itself, if production were collective and no longer a production of commodities.)

Let us now return to our fundamental diagram, which showed in Department II the formula 2000 c + 500 v + 500 s. All the articles of consumption produced in the course of the year are in that case valued at 3000. And every one of the different elements of the commodities composing the total quantity of the product consists, so far as its value is concerned, of 2/3 c + 1/6 v + 1/6 s, or in percentages, 66 2/3 c + 16 2/3 v + 16 2/3 s. The various kinds of commodities of Department II may contain different proportions of constant capital. The fixed portion of their constant capitals may be different. The duration of this fixed portion, its wear and tear and therefore that portion of value which it transfers by degrees to the commodities produced by its assistance, may also differ. But that is immaterial. So far as the process of social reproduction is concerned, it is only a question of transactions between departments II and I. These two departments are here confronted by each other only as social masses. Hence the proportional magnitude of the portion c of the value of the commodity-product of II (which is the only essential one in the settlement of the present question) gives the average proportion, if all the branches of production classed under II are taken as a whole.

Every kind of commodities (and they are largely the same kinds) classed under 2000 c + 500 v + 500 s thus shares uniformly in the value to the extent of 66 2/3 % c + 16 2/3 % v + 16 2/3 % s. This applies equally to every 100 of the commodities classed under c, or v, or s.

The commodities in which the 2000 are incorporated may be further divided into

(1) 1333 1/3 c + 333 1/3 v + 333 1/3 s = 2000 c.

Those under 500 v may be divided into

(2) 333 1/3 c + 83 1/3 v + 83 1/3 s = 500 v.

Those under 500 s may be divided into

(3) 333 1/3 c + 83 1/3 v + 83 1/3 s = 500 s.

Now, if we add these three formulas, we have 1333 1/3 c + 333 1/3 c + 333 1/3 c = 2000 c. Furthermore 333 1/3 v + 83 1/3 v + 83 1/3 v = 500 v. And the same in the case of s. The addition gives the same total value of 3000 as above.

The entire constant capital-value contained in the quantity of commodities of II represented by 3000 is therefore incorporated in 2000 c, and neither 500 v nor 500 s contain an atom of it. The same is true of v and s in the case of 500 v and 500 s.

In other words, the entire quantity of constant capital-value, embodied in the commodities of II and reconvertible either into its natural or its money-form, exists in 2000 c. Everything referring to the conversion of the constant value of the commodities of II is therefore dealing only with the movements of 2000 c of II. And these transactions can be made only with 1000 v + 1000 s of I.

In the same way, all remarks made with reference to the transactions of the constant capital-value of Department I are confined to a consideration of 4000 I c.

A. The Reproduction of the Value of the Worn-out Part in the Form of Money.

Let us first consider the diagram

$$\text{I. } 4000 \text{ c} + \underline{1000 \text{ v} + 1000 \text{ s}}$$
$$\text{II. } \ldots \ldots \ldots 2000 \text{ c} + 500 \text{ v} + 500 \text{ s}$$

The exchange of the commodities represented by 2000 II c for commodities of I of the same value (1000 v + 1000 s) is conditioned on the assumption that the entire 2000 II c are reconverted from their natural form into that of the elements of the constant capital of II, produced by I. But the value of the commodities of 2000 c, of which the constant capital of II consists, contains an element making good the loss in the value of fixed capital, which is not to be immediately reproduced in its natural form, but converted into money and accumulated until such time as shall require the natural reproduction of the fixed capital on account of its having been completely worn out. Every year registers the finish of some fixed capital which must be renewed in this or that individual business, or this or that line of industry. In the case of one and the same individual capital, this or that portion of its fixed capital must be renewed, since its elements have a different durability. In examining annual reproduction, even on a simple scale, that is to say, disregarding all accumulation, we do not begin at the very beginning of things. The year which we study is one in the flow of many, it is not the year of the first birth of capitalist production. The various capitals invested in the numerous lines of production of Department II are, therefore, of different age. Just as a great many persons die annually in the service of these lines of production, so scores of fixed capitals expire annually in the same service and must be restored in their natural form by means of the accumulated fund of money. To that extent the exchange of 2000 II c for 2000 I (v + s) implies a conversion of 2000 II c from the form of commodities (articles of consumption) into that of natural elements of constant capital, which consist not only of raw and auxiliary materials, but also of natural elements of fixed capital, such as machinery, tools, buildings, etc. The wear and tear, which must be reproduced in money in the value of 2000 II c, by no means corresponds to the volume of the actively engaged fixed capital, since a portion of this must be reproduced every year in its natural form. The necessary preparation for this reproduction is an accumulation of money in preceding years on the part of the capitalists of II. And the same condition holds good for the current year as well as for the preceding ones.

In the transaction of I (1000 v + 1000 s) it must be noted that the magnitude I (v + s) does not contain any elements of constant capital, so that none of it implies a reproduction of wear and tear, that is to say, of elements transferred from the fixed portion of some constant capital to the commodities which represent the natural form of v + s. On the other hand, such elements do exist in II c and constitute that portion of value due to fixed capital which is not immediately converted from money into its natural form, but first accumulated in the form of money. The exchange between I (1000 v + 1000 s) and 2000 II c, therefore, presents the difficulty, that the means of production of I, which are the natural form of (1000 v + 1000 s), are to be exchanged to the full value of 2000 for articles of consumption of II, while the 2000 II c of articles of consumption cannot be offered entirely in exchange for I (1000 v + 1000 s), because a portion of them, corresponding in value to the wear and tear of the fixed capital, must be accumulated in the form of money and do not serve as a medium of circulation during the current period of annual reproduction which we are examining. But the money paying for this element of wear and tear incorporated in the value of 2000 II c can come only from Department I, since II cannot pay for its own articles, but must secure payment for them by selling them, and since we have assumed that I (1000 v + 1000 s) buys the full amount of commodities of 2000 II c. Hence Department I must supply the money to cover that wear and tear of II c. Now, according to the rules previously determined, money advanced to the circulation returns to that capitalist producer who later on throws an equal amount of commodities into the circulation. It is evident that Department I, in buying II c, cannot transfer commodities worth 2000 to Department II and yield up to it every time an additional amount of money, without any equivalent returning by way of the circulation. Otherwise Department I would buy the commodities II c at a price exceeding their value. If Department II actually exchanges its 2000 c for I (1000 v + 1000 s), then it has no further claims on Department I, and the money circulating in this transaction returns either to I or to II, according to whether I or II acted first as a buyer. And in that case Department II would have reconverted the entire value of its commodity-capital into the natural form of means of production, contrary to our assumption that it would not reconvert an aliquot portion during the current period of annual reproduction into the natural form of fixed elements of its constant capital. Department II could not secure a balance of money in its favour, unless it sold a value of 2000 to Department I and bought less than that from Department I, for instance, only 1800. In that case Department I would have to make good the balance of 200 in money, which would not return to it, because it would not have recovered this amount by an equivalent surrender of commodities to the circulation. Only then could II have a fund of money which it could place to the credit of the wear and tear of its fixed capital. But then we should also have an overproduction of means of production to the amount of 200 on the part of Department I, and the basis of our diagram would be destroyed, which assumed reproduction on the same scale, in other words, a complete proportionality between the various systems of production. We should have done away with one difficulty and created another, which would be still worse.

As this problem offers peculiar difficulties and has never been mentioned by political economy, we shall consider one by one all possible solutions (at least apparent solutions), or rather all possible formulations of the problem.

In the first place, we had just assumed that Department II sells commodities valued at 2000 to Department I, but buys from it only 1800 worth. The value of the commodities of 2000 c contains 200 for wear and tear of fixed capital, which must be accumulated as money. The value of 2000 c would therefore be dissolved into 1800, which would be exchanged for means of production of I, and 200 for the reproduction of worn-out elements of fixed capital, which would be held in the form of money after the sale of 2000 II c to Department I. Expressed in terms of value, this would be 2000 II c = 1800 c + 200 w, this w standing for wear and tear.

We should then be studying the transaction

I. 1000 v + 1000 s
II.   1800 c   + 200 w.

Department I buys with £1,000, which the labourers have received as wages in payment for their labour-power, 1000 II c of articles of consumption. Department II buys with the same £1,000 means of production from Department I from the lot 1000 v. The capitalists of I thus recover their variable capital in the form of money and can employ it next year in the purchase of labour-power to the same amount, that is to say, they can reproduce the variable portion of their productive capital in its natural form. – Department II furthermore advances £400 and buys means of production from the lot I s, and Department I s buys with the same £400 articles of consumption from

II c. The £400 advanced by the capitalists of II have thus returned to them, but only as an equivalent for sold commodities. Department I now buys from II articles of consumption to the amount of £400; II buys from I 400 worth of means of production, thereby returning the £400 to Department I.

So far, then, we have the following calculation: Department I b throws into circulation 1000 v + 800 s in commodities; it also throws into circulation, in money, £1,000 of wages and £400, thus facilitating its transaction with II. After the transaction is closed, Department I has 1000 v in money, 800 s exchanged for articles of consumption from 800 II c, and £400 in money.

Department II throws into circulation 1800 c in commodities (articles of consumption) and £400 in money. At the close of the transaction it has 1800 in commodities (means of production from Department I) and £400 in money.

There still remain on the side of Department I 200 s in means of production, and on the side of II 200 c (w) in articles of consumption.

According to our assumption Department I buys with £200 the articles of consumption II w, valued at the same amount. But II holds these £200, since 200 w represents wear and tear and is not immediately reconverted into means of production. Therefore 200 I s cannot be sold. One-tenth of the surplus-value of I cannot be realised by any exchange, cannot be converted from the natural form of means of production into that of articles of consumption.

This does not only contradict our assumption of reproduction on a simple scale, but it is not even a hypothesis which would explain the payment of 200 II w in money. It is another way of saying that it cannot be explained. Since it cannot be demonstrated in what manner 200 w is converted into money, it is assumed that Department I is obliging enough to supply the money, just because it is not able to convert its own remainder of 200 s into money. This is as much a legitimate method of analysis as the assumption that £200 fall every year from the clouds in order to convert 200 II w into money.

But the absurdity of such an assumption does not become evident at once, if I s, instead of appearing, as it does in this case, in its primitive mode of existence – that is to say as an element of the value of means of production, as an element of the value of commodities which must be converted into money by their capitalist producers – appears in the hands of capitalist stockholders, for instance as ground rent in the hands of land owners, or as interest in the hands of money-lenders. Now, if that portion of the surplus-value of commodities, which the industrial capitalist yields in the form of ground rent or interest to other shareholders in the surplus-value, cannot be in the long run converted into money by the sale of the commodities, then there is an end to the payment of rent and interest, and the land owners or recipients of interest can no longer serve in the role of miraculous interlopers, who convert aliquot portions of the annual reproduction into money by spending their revenue. The same is true of the expenditures of all so-called unproductive labourers, state officials, physicians, lawyers, etc., and others who serve economists as an excuse for explaining inexplicable things, in the role of the 'general public'.

Nor does it improve the matter, if the direct transaction between departments I and II, the two great departments of capitalist producers, is circumvented and the merchant is dragged in as a mediator, in order to overcome all difficulties with his 'money'. In the present case, for instance, 200 I s must ultimately be sold to the industrial capitalists of II. It may pass through the hands of a number of merchants, but the last of them will find himself in the same predicament, in which the capitalists of I were at the outset, that is to say he cannot sell the 200 I s to the capitalists of II. And this amount, being arrested in its course, cannot renew the same process with Department I.

We see, then, that, aside from our ultimate purpose, it is quite necessary to view the process of reproduction in its fundamental simplicity, in order to get rid of all obscuring interference and dispose of the false subterfuges, which assume the semblance of scientific analysis, but which cannot be removed so long as the process of social reproduction is immediately analysed in its concrete and complicated form.

The law that under normal conditions of reproduction – whether it be on a simple or on an enlarged scale – the money advanced by the capitalist producer to the circulation must return to its point of departure (no matter whether the money is his own or borrowed) excludes decidedly the hypotheses that 200 II w can be converted into money by an advance of money on the part of Department I.

B. The Reproduction of Fixed Capital in its Natural Form.

Having disposed of the above hypothesis, only such hypotheses remain as assume the possibility of a reproduction of the worn-out fixed capital partly in money and partly in its natural form.

We had assumed in the preceding case,

(a) That £1,000 had been paid in wages by Department I and spent by the labourers for articles of consumption of II c to the same amount.

It is a simple affirmation of fact that these £1,000 are advanced by I in money. Wages must be paid in money by the various capitalist producers. This money is then spent by the labourers for articles of consumption and serves the sellers of articles of consumption in their turn as a medium of circulation in the conversion of their constant capital from a commodity-capital into a productive capital. It passes indeed through many channels (store keepers, house owners, tax collectors, unproductive labourers, such as physicians, etc., who are needed by the labourer himself) and therefore it flows only in part directly from the hands of the labourer of I into those of the capitalist of II. Its flow may be retarded more or less and the capitalist may therefore require more reserve funds of money. But all this is ruled out of the analysis of the simplest fundamental form.

(b) We had furthermore assumed that Department I advances at a certain time £400 in money for the purchase of articles from II and that this money returns to it, while at some other time Department II advances also £400 for the purchase of commodities from I and likewise recovers this money. This assumption must be granted, for it would be arbitrary to think that only the capitalist class of I, or only that of II, should advance the money required for the exchange of their commodities. Now, since we have shown (under I) that it would be absurd to think that Department I should throw money into circulation in order to promote the conversion of 200 II w into money, there would remain only the seemingly still more absurd hypothesis that Department II itself should advance this money, by which that portion of the value of its commodities which makes good the depreciation of its fixed capital through wear and tear is converted into money. For instance, that portion of value which is lost by the spinning machine of Mr X in the process of production re-appears as a portion of the value of the yarn. That which his spinning machine loses on the one hand through wear and tear, is supposed on the other hand to be accumulated by him in money. Now take it that X buys £200's worth of cotton from Y and advances £200 in money for this purpose. Y then buys from him £200's worth of yarn, and X now accumulates this money as a fund for the reproduction of the worn-out portion of his machine. This would simply amount to the statement that X, aside from his production, its product, and the sale of this product, keeps £200 in reserve, in order to make good to himself the depreciation of his machine, in other words, that he not only loses £200 by the depreciation of his machine, but must also put up £200 additional every year out of his own pocket in order to be finally able to buy a new spinning machine.

This looks only seemingly absurd. For the producers of Department II are capitalists whose fixed capital is in various stages of its reproduction. In the case of some of them it has arrived at the stage where it must be entirely renewed in its natural form. In the case of the others it is more or less removed from this stage. All the capitalists of these last named stages have this in common, that their fixed capital is not actually reproduced, that is to say, not actually renewed in its natural form by a new specimen of the same kind, but that its value is successively accumulated in money. The first class of the capitalists of II are in the same (or almost the same) position as they were at the establishment of their business, when they came on the market with their money-capital in order to convert this money partly into constant (fixed and circulating) capital, partly into labour-power (variable capital). They have once more to advance this money to the circulation, the value of fixed constant capital as well as that of circulating constant and variable capital.

Hence, if we assume that half of the £400 thrown into circulation by the capitalist class of II for the purpose of transacting business with Department I comes from those capitalists of II who have to reproduce by means of the sale of their commodities not only their means of production so far as they are circulating capital, but also to buy with money new fixed capital in its natural form, while the other half of the capitalists of II reproduce with their money only the circulating portion of their constant capital in its natural form, but not the fixed portion, then there is no contradiction in the statement that these £400, when returned by Department I in exchange for articles of consumption, are variously distributed among these two classes of Department II. They return to Department II, but they do not return into the same hands. They are distributed within this department and pass from one of its sections to another.

One section of II has secured means of production whose value is covered by their commodities, and has furthermore converted £200 of money into natural elements of new fixed capital. The money thus spent does not return to this section by way of the circulation until after a succession of years and is gradually accumulated by the sale of products created by this fixed capital and bearing the value of its worn-out portion.

But the other section of II did not purchase any commodities from I for £200. That section is rather paid with the money which the first section of II spent for elements of its fixed capital. The first section of II has its fixed capital-value once more in a natural form, while the second section is still engaged in accumulating money for the purpose of renewing its fixed capital later on.

The basis on which we now have to work, after the previous transactions have been closed, is the remainder of the commodities still to be exchanged by the two departments; 400 s on the part of I, and 400 c on the part of II.[11] We assume that II advances £400 in money for the exchange of commodities aggregating 800 in value.

One-half, or £200, must be advanced under all circumstances by that section of IIc which has accumulated 200 in money for making good the depreciation by wear and tear and which has to reconvert this fund into the natural form of its fixed capital.

Just as constant capital-value, variable capital-value, and surplus-value – being the elements of the value of the commodity-capital of II and I – may be represented by proportional quantities of the commodities of II and I, so that portion of the value of the constant capital which is not to be converted into the natural form of fixed capital for the present, but rather to be accumulated in money, may likewise be represented. A certain quantity of commodities of II (in the present case one-half of the remainder of 400, or 200) is as yet the bearer of the value of this depreciation, which has to be converted into money by sale. (The first section of the capitalists of II, who renew their fixed capital in its natural form, may have done so with a portion of its depreciation by means of a corresponding portion of the remaining commodities, but they still have to realise 200 in money.)

The second 200 of the 400 thrown into circulation by II in this remaining transaction buy circulating elements of constant capital from I. A portion of these £200 may be thrown into circulation by both sections of II, or only by the one not renewing its fixed capital in its natural form.

Department I, then, secures with these £400 in the first place commodities valued at £200, consisting only of elements of fixed capital; in the second place, commodities valued at £200, reproducing only natural elements of the circulating portion of the constant capital of II. Department I has then sold its entire annual product in commodities, so far as it is sold to Department II. And the value of one-fifth, or £400, is now held in its hands in the form of money. This money is monetised surplus-value which must be spent as revenue for articles of consumption. Department I having bought with its £400 the entire stock of Department II, valued at 400, this money flows back to II.

Now we may assume three possibilities. Let us name those capitalists of II who renew their fixed capital in its natural form, section 1, and those who accumulate the equivalent for the depreciation of fixed capital, section 2. The three possibilities are: (a) that the 400 still remaining in the shape of commodities of II may make good certain portions of the circulating part of the constant capital of both section 1 and section 2 (perhaps one-half for each); (b) that section 1 has already sold all its commodities, so that section 2 has for sale all of the 400; (c) that section 2 has sold all but the 200 which are the bearers of the value of depreciation.

Then we have the following distributions:

(a) Of the value of the commodities still in the hands of Department II, namely 400 c, section 1 holds 100, and section 2 holds 300; 200 out of the 300 represent depreciation. In that case section 1 originally advanced 300 of the 400 in money returned by Department I for commodities of II, namely 200 in money for which it secured elements of fixed capital from I, and 100 in money for the promotion of its transaction with I. Section 2, on the other hand, advanced only 100 of the 400, likewise for the promotion of its exchange with I.

Remember, then, that section 1 advanced 300, and section 2 advanced 100 of the 400.

Now these 400 return in the following manner: Section 1 recovers only one-third of the money advanced by it, or 100. But it has in place of the other 200 a renewed fixed capital. Section 1 has given money to Department I for these elements of fixed capital, but sold no more commodities. So far as this money is concerned, section 1 has met Department I for the purpose of buying, but not of selling later on. This money cannot return to section 1, otherwise it would receive the elements of fixed capital from I as a gift. So far as the last third of its advanced money is concerned, section 1 first acted as a buyer of circulating elements of its constant capital. The same money serves Department I for the purchase of the remainder of the commodities of section 1, valued at 100. This money, then, returns to section 1 of Department II, because it acts as a seller of commodities soon after having acted as a buyer. If this money did not return, then section 1 of Department II would have given to Department I a sum of 100 in money for commodities of the same value and in addition thereto 100 in commodities; in other words, it would have given away its commodities as a present.

On the other hand, section 2 receives 300 in money back, while it has advanced only 100 in money. As a buyer it first threw 100 in money into circulation, and these it receives back when acting as a seller. And it receives 200 more, because it acts only as a seller of commodities to that amount, but not in turn as a buyer. Hence the money cannot return to Department I. The value of the depreciation of the fixed capital is thus balanced by the money thrown into circulation by section 1 of Department II in the purchase of elements of fixed capital. But it reaches the hands of section 2, not as money of section 1, but as money of Department I.

(b) Under these conditions the remainder of IIc is distributed so that section 1 has 200 in money, and section 2 has 400 in commodities.

Section 1 has sold all of its commodities, but 200 in money are a changed form of the fixed elements of its constant capital which it has to renew in their natural form. It acts only as a buyer in the present case and receives in exchange for its money the same value in commodities of Department I having the natural form of elements of its fixed capital. Section 2 has to throw £200 into circulation, at a maximum (if Department I does not advance any money for the transaction between I and II), since it is to the extent of one-half of the value of its commodities only a seller to I, not a buyer from I.

It recovers from the circulation £400. It gets 200, because it has advanced them as a buyer and recovers them as a seller of commodities of the same value. It receives another 200, because it sells commodities of that value to I without buying an equivalent from I.

(c) Section 1 has 200 in money and 200 c in commodities. Section 2 has 200 c (w) in commodities.

Section 2 has not any advance of money to make under these circumstances, because it does not act any more in the role of a buyer from I, but only as a seller, so that it must wait till some one wants to buy from it.

Section 1 advances £400 in money, of which 200 serve for a mutual exchange with Department I, while 200 are used to buy from I. The last 200 serve in the purchase of the elements of fixed capital.

Department I buys from section 1 commodities to the value of 200 with £200 in money, so that section 1 thus recovers the money it had advanced for its transaction with I. And I buys with the other £200, which it has likewise received from section 1, commodities valued at 200 from section 2, which thus recovers the value of the depreciation of its fixed capital.

The matter would not be altered by the assumption that, in the case of (c), Department II instead of section 1 of this department should advance the 200 in money required for the exchange of the existing commodities. If I buys in that case first 200 in commodities from section 2 of Department II – assuming that this section has only this much left to sell – then the £200 do not return to I, since section 2 of Department II no longer acts in the role of buyer. But section 1 of Department II has in that case £200 to spend in buying and 200 in commodities to offer for sale, making a total of 400 which it has to trade with Department I. £200 in money then return to Department I from section 1 of Department II. When I spends them again in the purchase of 200 in commodities from section 1 of Department II, then they return to Department I as soon as section 1 of Department II buys the second half of the 400 in commodities from I. Section 1 of Department II has spent £200 in the purchase of elements of fixed capital, without selling anything in return. Therefore this money does not return to it, but serves to monetise the remaining 200 c of commodities of section 2 of Department II, while the £200 in money advanced by I for the promotion of the transactions return to it by way of section 1 of Department II, not section 2. In the place of its commodities of 400 it has secured an equivalent, and the £200 in money advanced by it for transacting business to the extent of 800 in commodities have likewise returned to it. Everything is therefore settled.

The difficulty encountered in the transaction between I (1000 v + 1000 s) and II 2000 c was reduced to the difficulty of balancing accounts between I 400 s and II (section 1) 200 in money plus 200 c in commodities plus (section 2) 200 c in commodities. Or, to make the matter still clearer, I (200 s + 200 s) against II (200 in money of section 1 plus 200 c in commodities of section 1 plus 200 c in commodities of section 2).

Since section I of Department II exchanges 200c for commodities of Department I representing 200s, and since all the money circulating in this exchange of 400 commodities between I and II returns to him who first advances it, be he I or II, this money promoting the exchange between I and II is not an element of the problem which troubles us here. Or, to express it differently, if we assume that the money used in the transaction between 200 I s (commodities) and 200 II c (commodities of section 1, Department II) serves only as a medium of payment, not as a medium of purchase and therefore not as a 'medium of circulation', strictly speaking, it is evident that the means of production valued at 200 are exchanged for articles of consumption valued at 200, because the commodities of 200 I s and 200 IIc (section 1) are equivalent in value, that therefore the money serves here merely ideally, and that neither side has to advance any money to the circulation for the payment of any balance. Hence the problem does not show itself in its clearest form, until we eliminate the commodities of 200 I s and their equivalent, the commodities of 200 IIc (section 1), from both sides.

After the elimination of these two amounts of commodities of equal value, which balance one another in I and II, the remainder of the transaction shows the problem clearly, namely I 200s in commodities against II (200c in money of section 1 plus 200c in commodities of section 2).

It is evident that section 1 of Department II buys with 200 in money the elements of its fixed capital from 200 I s. The fixed capital of section 1, Department II, is thereby renewed in its natural form, and the surplus-value of I, to the amount of 200, is converted from the form of commodities (means of production representing elements of fixed capital) into that of money. Department I buys with this money articles of consumption from section 2, Department II, and the result for II is that section 1 has renewed a fixed element of its constant capital in its natural form; and that section 2 has stored up another element in money which is destined to make good the depreciation of its fixed capital. And this continues every year, until this last element is also renewed in its natural form.

The first condition is here evidently that this fixed element of constant capital II, which must annually be reconverted into money to the full extent of its value and, therefore, entirely reproduced in its natural form (section 1), should be equal to the annual depreciation of the other fixed element of constant capital II, which continues its function in its old natural form and whose depreciation, represented by the value transferred by it to the commodities produced by it, is first accumulated in money. Such a balance of value would seem to be a law of reproduction on the same scale. This is equivalent to saying that the proportional division of labour in Department I, which puts out means of production, must remain unchanged, to the extent that it produces partly circulating, partly fixed portions of the constant capital of Department II.

Before we analyse this more closely, we must first see how the matter looks, if the remaining amount of II c (1) is not equal to the remainder of II c (2). It may be larger or smaller. Let us study either case.

First Case.

I. 200 s.

II. (1) 220 c in money plus (2) 200 c in commodities.

In this case II c (1) buys with £200 the commodities of 200 I s, and I buys with the same money the commodities of 200 II c (2); in other words, that portion of the fixed capital which has to be accumulated in money. This portion is thus converted into money. But 20 II c (1) cannot be reconverted into the natural form of fixed capital.

It seems that we might remedy this inconvenience by making the remainder of I s 220 instead of 200, so that only 1780 instead of 1800 of the 2000 I would be disposed of by former transactions. Then we should have:

I. 220 s.

II. (1) 220 c in money plus (2) 200 c in commodities.

Section 1 of II c buys with £220 in money the 220 I s, and I buys with £200 the 200 II c (2) of commodities. But now £20 in money remain on the side of I, a portion of surplus-value which it can hold only in money, without being able to spend it in articles of consumption. The difficulty is thus merely transferred from section 1, Department II c, to I s.

Let us now assume, on the other hand, that section 1, II c, is smaller than section 2, II c; then we have:

Second Case.

I. 200 s in commodities.

II. (1) 180 c in money plus (2) 200 c in commodities.

Section 1, Department II, buys with £180 in money the commodities of 180 I s. Department I buys with the same money commodities of the same value from section 2, Department II, that is to say, 180 II c (2). There remain 20 I s unsaleable on one side, and 20 II c of section 2 on the other. In other words, commodities valued at 40 remain unsaleable.

It would not help us any to make the remainder of I equal to 180. It is true, there would not be any surplus in I under these circumstances, but the same surplus of 20 would remain unsaleable in section 2 of Department II and could not be converted into money.

In the first case, where section 1 of Department II is greater than section 2 of Department II, there remains a surplus of money in section 1 of Department II and cannot be converted into fixed capital; or, if the remainder in I s is assumed to be equal to II c (1), the same surplus in money remains inconvertible into articles of consumption in I s.

In the second case, where II c (1) is smaller than II c (2), there remains a deficit of money on the side of 200 I s and II c (2), and an equal surplus of commodities on both sides, or, if the remainder of I s is assumed to be equal to II c (2), there remains a deficit of money and a surplus of commodities in II c (2).

If we assume the remainder of I s to be always equal to II c (1) – seeing that production is determined by demand, and reproduction is not altered by the fact that there may be a greater output of fixed elements of capital this year, and a greater output of circulating elements of constant capitals I and II next year – then I s could not be reconverted into articles of consumption in the first case, unless I brought with it a portion of the surplus-value of II and accumulated it in money instead of consuming it; in the second case there would be no other way out but an expenditure of the money on the part of I itself, an assumption which we have already rejected.

If II c (1) is greater than II c (2), then the importation of foreign commodities is required for the employment of the money-surplus in I s. If II c (1) is smaller than II c (2), then an exportation of commodities (articles of consumption) is required for the realisation of the value of the depreciation of II c in means of production. In either case, foreign trade is necessary.

Even assuming that, on the basis of simple reproduction on the same scale, the productivity of all lines of industry, and thus the proportional relation of the value of their commodities, would remain unchanged, there would nevertheless be an incentive for production on an enlarged scale whenever the two last named cases may occur, in which II c (1) is greater or smaller than II c (2).

(3) Results.

With reference to the reproduction of the fixed capital, the following general remarks may be made:

If a larger portion of the fixed element of II c expires this year than last and must be reproduced in its natural form – all other circumstances remaining the same, that is to say, not only the scale of production, but also the productivity of labour, etc. – then that portion of the fixed capital, which is as yet only declining and must be temporarily accumulated in money until its term of expiration arrives, must decline in the same proportion, since we have assumed that the sum of the fixed capital serving in II (also the sum of its values) remains unchanged. This implies the following consequences: if a greater portion of the commodity-capital of I consists of elements of the fixed capital of II c, then a correspondingly smaller portion consists of circulating elements of II c, because the total production of I for II c remains unchanged. If one of these portions increases, then the other decreases, and vice versa. On the other hand, the total production of II also retains the same volume. But how is this possible, if the production of its raw materials, half-wrought products, and auxiliary materials (the circulating elements of the constant capital of II) decreases? In the second place, a greater portion of fixed capital of II c, restored to its money-form, flows into Department I, in order to be reconverted from its money-form into its natural form. In other words, there is a greater flow of money into Department I, aside from the money circulating between I and II merely for the transaction of their business, more money which does not merely serve as a medium for the mutual exchange of their commodities, but acts one-sidedly in purchase without a corresponding sale. At the same time the quantity of commodities of II c, the bearers of the value of the depreciation of fixed capital, would have decreased proportionately. This is that quantity of commodities of II which is not exchanged for commodities of I, but must be converted into money of I. More money would have flown from II into I for one-sided purchase, and there would be fewer commodities of II which would stand only in the relation of a buyer toward I. Under these circumstances a great portion of I s – for I v has already been converted into commodities of II – would not be convertible into commodities of II, but would be held in the form of money.

The opposite case, in which the reproduction of expired fixed capitals of a certain year exceeds that of the depreciation, need not be discussed in detail after the preceding statements.

The result would be a crisis – a crisis in production – in spite of the fact that reproduction had taken place on the same scale.

In short, unless a constant proportion between expiring (and about to be renewed) fixed capital and still continuing (merely transferring the value of its depreciation to its product) fixed capital is assumed, so long as reproduction takes place on a simple scale under the same conditions, such as productivity, volume, intensity of labour, the mass of circulating elements to be reproduced in one case would remain the same while the mass of fixed elements to be reproduced would have been increased. Therefore the aggregate production of I would have to increase, or, there would be a deficit in the reproduction, even aside from money matters.

In the other case, if the proportional magnitude of the fixed capital of II, to be reproduced in its natural form, should decrease and the elements of the fixed capital of II, which must be merely accumulated in money, should increase in the same ratio, then the quantity of the circulating elements of the constant capital of II, reproduced by I, would remain unchanged, while that of the fixed elements about to be reproduced would have decreased. Hence there would be either a decrease in the aggregate production of I, or a surplus (the same as previously a deficit) which could not be converted into money.

It is true that the same labour may, in the first case, supply a greater product with an increase in its productivity, extension, or intensity, and so the deficit could be covered in the first case. But such a change could not take place without a transfer of capital and labour from one line of production of Department I to another, and every transfer would cause monetary disturbances. Furthermore, to the extent that an expansion and intensification of labour would increase, Department I would have to exchange more of its value for less value of II. In other words, there would be a depreciation of the product of I.

The reverse would take place in the second case, where I must contract its production, which implies a crisis for its labourers and capitalists, or produce a surplus, which implies another crisis. Such a surplus is not an evil in itself, but it is an evil under the capitalist system of production.

Foreign trade could relieve the pressure in either case. In the first case it would convert products of I held in the form of money into articles of consumption, in the second case it would dispose of the surplus of commodities. But foreign trade, so far as it does not merely reproduce certain elements of production, only transfers these contradictions to a wider sphere and gives them a greater latitude.

Once the capitalist mode of production is abolished, the problem resolves itself into the simple proposition that the magnitude of the expiring portion of fixed capital, which must be reproduced in its natural form every year (which served in our illustration for the production of articles of consumption), varies in successive years. If it is very large in a certain year (in excess of the average mortality, the same as among men), then it is so much smaller in the next year. The quantity of raw materials, half wrought articles, and auxiliary materials required for the annual production of the articles of consumption – other circumstances remaining the same – does not decrease in consequence. Hence the aggregate production of means of production would have to increase in the one case and decrease in the other. This can be remedied only by a continuous relative overproduction. There must be on the one hand a certain quantity of fixed capital in excess of that which is immediately required; on the other hand there must be above all a supply of raw materials, etc., in excess of the actual requirements of annual production (this applies particularly to articles of consumption). This sort of reproduction may take place when society controls the material requirements of its own reproduction. But in capitalist society it is an element of anarchy.

This illustration of fixed capital, on the basis of an unchanged scale of reproduction, is convincing. A disproportion of the production of fixed and circulating capital is one of the favourite arguments of political economists in explaining productive crises. That such a disproportion can and must arise even when the fixed capital is merely preserved by renewal is new to them. And yet, it can and must arise even on the assumption of an ideal and normal production on the basis of a simple reproduction of the already existing capital of society.

Section 12. The Reproduction of the Money Supply.

One element has so far been entirely disregarded, namely the annual reproduction of gold and silver. To the extent that these metals serve as material for articles of luxury, gilding, etc., they do not deserve any special mention, any more than any other products. But they play an important role as money-material, as potential money. For the sake of simplicity, we regard only gold as material for money.

According to older statements, the entire annual production of gold amounts to about 8–900,000 lbs., equal to about 1100 to 1250 million marks (264 to 392.5 million dollars). But according to Soetbeer[12] it amounts to only 170,675 kilograms, valued at about 476 million marks on an average of the years 1871 to 1875. Of this amount, Australia supplied about 167, the United States 166, Russia 93 million marks. The remainder is distributed over various countries in sums of less than 10 million marks each. The annual production of silver, during the same period, amounted to somewhat less than 2 million kilograms, valued at 354.5 million marks. Of this amount, Mexico supplied about 108, the United States 102, South America about 67, Germany about 26 million, etc.

Among the countries with predominating capitalist production only the United States are producers of gold and silver. The capitalist countries of Europe obtain almost all their gold and by far the greater part of their silver from Australia, the United States, Mexico, South America, and Russia.

But we transfer the gold mines into the country with capitalist production whose annual reproduction we are analysing, for the following reasons:

Capitalist production does not exist at all without foreign commerce. But when we assume annual reproduction on a given scale, we also assume that foreign commerce replaces home products only by articles of other use-value, or natural form, without affecting the relations of value, such as those of the two categories known as means of production and articles of consumption and their transactions, nor the relations of constant capital, variable capital, and surplus-value, into which the value of the products of each of these categories may be dissolved. The introduction of foreign commerce into the analysis of the annually reproduced value of products can, therefore, produce only confusion, without furnishing any new point in the aspect or solution of the problem. For this reason we leave it aside. And consequently gold as a direct element of annual reproduction is not regarded as a commodity imported from a foreign country.

The production of gold, like that of metals generally, belongs to Department I, which occupies itself with means of production. Let us assume that the annual production of gold amounts to 30 (from reasons of expediency, although it is far too high compared to the other figures of our diagrams). Let this value be resolved into 20 c + 5 v + 5 s; 20 c is to be exchanged for other elements of Department I c, and this is to be studied later; but the 5 v + 5 s are to be exchanged for elements of II c, namely, articles of consumption.

As for the 5 v, every gold-producing business begins by buying labour-power. This is done, not with money produced by this particular business, but with a portion of the money existing in the land. The labourers buy with this 5 v articles of consumption from II, and this department buys with the same money means of production from I. Let us say that II buys from I gold for elements of its commodities (elements of constant capital) to the value of 2, then 2 v flow back to the gold producers of I in money which was formerly in circulation. If II does not buy any more material from I, then I buys from II by throwing its gold into circulation, for gold can buy any commodity. The difference is only that I does not act as a seller, but as a buyer, in that case. The gold producers of I can always get rid of their product, for it is always in a form which may be directly exchanged.

Take it that some producer of yarn has paid 5 v to his labourers, who create for him in return – aside from a surplus-product – yarn to the amount of 5. The labourers buy values worth 5 from II c, and II c buys with the same 5 in money yarn from I, and this 5 in money flows back to the producer of yarn. Now we had assumed that I g (meaning the producer of gold) advanced to his labourers 5 v in money which had previously belonged to the circulation. The labourers spend it for articles of consumption, but only 2 of the 5 return from II to I g. However, I g can begin his process of reproduction anew, just as well as the producer of yarn. For his labourers have supplied him with 5 in gold, 2 of which he sold, and 3 of which he still has, so that he has but to coin it,[13] or exchange it for bank notes, in order that his entire variable capital may be immediately in his hands, without the intervention of II.

Even this very first process of annual reproduction has wrought a change in the quantity of money actually or virtually in circulation. We assumed that II c bought 2 v from I g for material, and that I g invested 3 in II as the money-form of its variable capital. In other words, 3 of the amount of money supplied by the new gold production remained within Department II and did not return to I. According to our assumption II has satisfied its needs for gold material. The 3 remain in its hands as a hoard of gold. Since they cannot constitute any elements of its constant capital, and since II had previously enough money-capital for the purchase of labour-power; since, furthermore, these additional 3 g, with the exception of the element making good the loss through depreciation, have no function to perform within II c, for a portion of which they were exchanged (they could only serve to cover a shortage in the element making good loss through depreciation, in the case that section 1 of Department II should be smaller than section 2 of Department II, which would be accidental); and since, on the other hand, the entire commodity-product of II c, with the exception of the element making up for depreciation, must be exchanged for means of production of I (v + s); therefore this money must be entirely transferred from II c to II s, no matter whether it exists in necessities of life or articles of luxury; and vice versa, a corresponding value of commodities must be transferred from IIs to II c. Result: a portion of the surplus-value is accumulated as a hoard of money.

In the second year of reproduction, when the same proportion of annually produced gold continues to be used as material, 2 will again flow back to I g, and 3 will be reproduced in its natural form, that is to say, it will be set aside in Department II as a hoard, etc.

With reference to the variable capital in general, it may be said that the capitalist of I g must continually advance money for the purchase of labour-power, the same as every other capitalist. But so far as these wages are concerned, it is not he, but his labourers who buy from II. He can never appear as a buyer, transferring gold to II, without the initiative of II. But to the extent that II buys material from him for the purpose of converting its constant Capital II c into a gold supply, a portion of the v of I g flows back to it from II in the same way that it does to other capitalist of I. And so far as this is not the case, he reproduces his v in gold direct from his product. But to the extent that the v advanced by him in money does not flow back to him from II, a portion of the existing medium of circulation (received from I and not returned to it) is converted by II into a hoard and a portion of its surplus-value is not converted into articles of consumption. Since new gold mines are continually opened or old ones re-opened, a certain proportion of the money invested by I g in v is always money existing previously to the new gold production, and passing from I g by way of its labourers into II, where it becomes an element in the formation of a hoard, or as much of it as is not returned from II to I g.

But as for (I g) s, Department I g can always act as a buyer in this case. It throws its s in the shape of gold into circulation and withdraws from it in return articles of consumption of II c. The gold is there used in part as material, and thus serves as a real element of the constant portions c of productive Capital II. And any portion of the gold not so employed becomes once more an element in the formation of a hoard in the role of that part of II s which retains the shape of money. We see, then – aside from I c which we reserve for a later analysis – that even simple reproduction, excluding accumulation strictly so called, namely reproduction on an enlarged scale, inevitably includes the accumulation, or hoarding, of money.[14] And as this is annually repeated, it explains the assumption from which we started in the analysis of capitalist production, namely that a supply of money corresponding to the exchange of commodities is in the hands of the capitalists of departments I and II at the beginning of the reproduction. Such an accumulation takes place even after deducting the amount of gold lost by the depreciation of money in circulation.

It is a matter of course, that the quantity of money accumulated on all sides increases in proportion to the advancing age of capitalist production, and that the quantity annually added to this hoard by the production of new gold decreases proportionately, although the absolute quantity thus added may be considerable. We revert once more in general terms to the objection raised against Tooke and contained in the question: how is it possible that every capitalist draws a surplus-value in money out of the circulation, in other words, draws more money out of the circulation than he throws into it, seeing that the capitalist class must be the ultimate source which throws all money into circulation?

We reply by summarising the statements made previously (in chapter 17):

(1) The only essential assumption, namely, that there is money enough available for the exchange of the various elements of annual reproduction, is not touched by the fact that a portion of the value of commodities consists of surplus-value. Take it that the entire production belonged to the labourers, so that their surplus-labour were done for themselves, not for the capitalists, then the quantity of circulating commodity-values would be the same and, other circumstances remaining equal, would require the same amount of money for circulation. The question in either case is therefore only: where does the money come from which serves as a medium of exchange for this quantity of commodity-values? It is not at all: where does the money come from which monetises the surplus-value?

It is true, to repeat it once more, that every individual commodity consists of $c + v + s$, and the circulation of the entire quantity of commodities therefore requires a certain quantity of money for the circulation of the capital $c + v$, and another for the circulation of s, the revenue of the capitalists. For the individual capitalist as well as for the entire capitalist class, the money in which they advance capital is distinct from the money in which they spend their revenue. Where does this last money come from? Simply from the entire quantity of money available in society, a portion of which circulates as the revenue of the capitalists. We have already seen in previous instances that every capitalist establishing a new business recovers the money which he spent for his maintenance in the purchase of articles of consumption, by the process of converting his surplus-value into money, once his business is fairly under way. But generally speaking the difficulty is due to two sources:

In the first place, if we analyse only the circulation and the turn-over of capital, regarding the capitalist merely as a personification of capital, not as a capitalist consumer and sport, then we see indeed that he is continually throwing surplus-value into circulation as a part of his commodity-capital, but we never see money as a form of revenue in his hands. We never see him throwing money into circulation for the consumption of his surplus-value.

In the second place, if the capitalist class throw a certain amount of money into circulation in the shape of revenue, it seems as though they were paying an equivalent for this portion of the total annual product, so that this portion is then no longer surplus-value. But the surplus product in which the surplus value is incorporated does not cost the capitalist anything. As a class, they possess and enjoy it gratuitously, and the circulation of money cannot alter this fact. The alteration due to this circulation consists merely in the fact that every capitalist, instead of consuming his surplus-product in its natural form, a thing which is generally impossible, draws commodities of all sorts up to the amount of his surplus-value out of the general stock of the annual surplus-product of society and appropriates them for his own use. But the mechanism of the circulation has shown that the capitalist class, while throwing money into the circulation for the purpose of spending their revenue, also recover this money from the circulation, so that they can continue the same process over and over; so that, as a class of capitalists, they always remain in possession of the amount of money necessary for the monetisation of their surplus-value. Hence, seeing that the capitalist does not only withdraw his surplus-value from the market in the form of commodities for his individual con-sumption, but also the money which he has paid for these com-modities, it is evident that he secures the commodities without paying an equivalent for them. They do not cost him anything, although he pays money for them. If I buy commodities for one pound sterling and recover this money from the seller by means of a surplus product which I got for nothing, it is obvious that I have received the commodities gratis. The continual repetition of this transaction does not alter the fact that I continually secure commodities and contin-ually remain in possession of my pound sterling, although I release it temporarily in the purchase of the commodities. The capitalist continually retains this money as an equivalent of surplus-value that has not cost him anything.

We have seen that with Adam Smith the entire value of the social product resolves itself into revenue, into v + s, so that the constant capital-value is set down as zero. It follows necessarily that the money required for the circulation of the yearly revenue must also suffice for the circulation of the entire annual product, so that, in our illustration, the money of 3000 required for the circulation of the articles of consumption of the same value must also suffice for the circulation of the entire annual product valued at 9000. This is indeed the opinion of Adam Smith, and it is repeated by Th. Tooke. This erroneous conception of the ratio of the quantity of money required for the realisation of the revenue to the quantity of money required for the circulation of the entire social product is a necessary result of misapprehending, thoughtlessly conceiving the manner in which the various elements of material and value of the total annual product are reproduced and annually renewed. It has already been refuted by us.

Let us listen to Smith and Tooke themselves.

Smith says in Book 2, Chapter 2: 'The circulation of every country may be divided into two parts: the circulation of the merchants among themselves and the circulation between merchants and consumers. Although the same pieces of money, paper or metal, may be used now in the one, now in the other circulation, both of them nevertheless take place continually side by side, and each one of them requires therefore a certain quantity of money of this or that kind in order to keep moving. The value of the commodities circulating among the various merchants can never exceed the value of the commodities circulating between merchants and consumers; for whatever the merchants may buy must be sold ultimately to the consumers. As the circulation between the merchants is wholesale, it generally requires a rather large sum for every exchange. The circulation between merchants and consumers, on the other hand, is mostly retail and requires often but very small sums of money: one shilling, or even half penny, suffices sometimes. But small sums circulate much more rapidly than large ones . . . Although the annual purchases of all consumers are therefore at least' – this 'at least' is rich – 'equal in value to those of the merchants, they may nevertheless be effected, as a rule, with a much smaller quantity of money', etc.

Th. Tooke remarks to this passage of Adam Smith (in *An Inquiry into the Currency Principle*, London, 1844, pages 34 to 36): 'There cannot be any doubt that the distinction here made is essentially correct . . . The exchange between merchants and consumers includes also the payment of wages, which are the principal means of the consumers . . . All transactions between merchant and merchant, that is to say, all sales from the producer or importer, through all gradations of intermediate processes of manufacture, etc., down to the retail merchant or export merchant, may be dissolved into movements transferring capital. But transfers of capital do not necessarily imply, nor indeed carry actually with them, in the great number of exchanges, a real cession of bank notes or coin – I mean a substantial, not a fictitious, cession – at the time of transfer . . . The total amount of exchanges between merchants and merchants must in the last instance be determined and limited by the amount of exchanges between merchants and consumers.'

If this last sentence stood by itself, one might think that Tooke stated simply the fact of a ratio between the exchanges of merchants and merchants and those of merchants and consumers, in other words, a ratio between the value of the total annual revenue and the value of the capital with which it is produced. But this is not the case. He explicitly endorses the view of Adam Smith. A special criticism of his theory of circulation is therefore superfluous.

(2) Every industrial capital, when beginning its career, throws at one single investment enough money into circulation to cover its entire fixed element, which it recovers but gradually in the course of years by the sale of its annual products. Thus it throws at first more money into circulation than it recovers from it. This is repeated at every renewal of its entire capital in a natural form. It is repeated every year in a certain number of enterprises whose fixed capital must be renewed in its natural form. It is repeated in fragments at every repair, every partial renewal of fixed capital. While more money is on the one hand withdrawn from circulation than is thrown into it, the opposite takes place on the other hand.

In all lines of industry whose period of production – as distinguished from the working period – extends over a long term, money is continually thrown into circulation during this period by the capitalist producers, either in payment for labour-power employed, or in the purchase of means of production to be consumed. Means of production are thus directly withdrawn from the commodity market, and articles of consumption either indirectly by the labourers spending their wages, or directly by the capitalists, who do not by any means stop consuming, although they do not immediately throw any equivalent on the market, in the shape of commodities. During this period, the money thrown by them into circulation serves for the conversion of the value of commodities, including the surplus value embodied in them, into money. This element becomes very important in an advanced stage of capitalist production in the case of lengthy enterprises, such as are undertaken by stock companies, for instance the construction of railways, canals, docks, large municipal buildings, iron ships, drainage of land on a large scale, etc.

(3) While the other capitalists, aside from the investment of fixed capital, draw more money out of the circulation than they threw into it in the purchase of labour-power and the circulating elements of

capital, the gold and silver producing capitalists, on the other hand, throw only money into the circulation, aside from the precious metals which serve as raw material, while they withdraw only commodities from it. The constant capital, with the exception of the depreciated portion, furthermore the greater portion of the variable capital and the entire surplus-value, with the exception of the hoard which is eventually accumulated in the hands of these capitalists, is thrown into the circulation as money.

(4) On one side, various things circulate as commodities which were not produced during the current year, such as real estate, houses, etc., furthermore products whose period of production extends over more than one year, such as cattle, wood, wine, etc. It is important to emphasise in this respect that aside from the quantity of money required for the immediate circulation, there is always a certain quantity in a latent state which may enter into service when so required. Furthermore, the value of such products circulates often in fractions and gradually; for instance, the value of houses in the rents of a number of years.

On the other hand, not all movements of the process of reproduction are promoted by the circulation of money. The entire process of production, once its elements have been purchased, is excluded from it. Furthermore all products, which the producer consumed directly in his own individual or productive consumption. Under this head belongs also the board of agricultural labourers.

The quantity of money, then, which circulates the annual product, exists in society, having been gradually accumulated. It does not belong to the values produced during the current year, with the exception of the gold used for making good the loss of depreciated money.

This presentation of the matter assumes the exclusive circulation of precious metals as money, and the simplest form of cash purchases and sales, although even plain metals, as a basis of circulation, may serve as money, and have actually so served in history and have been the fundament for the development of a credit system and of certain portions of its mechanism.

This assumption is not made from mere considerations of method, although these are important enough, as demonstrated by the fact that Tooke and his school as well as his adversaries were continually compelled in their controversies concerning the circulation of bank notes to revert to the hypothesis of a purely metallic circulation. They were compelled to do so subsequently, and did so very superficially, because they thus reduced to an incidental point what should have been the point of departure of their analysis.

But the simplest study of the circulation of money in its primitive form, which is the immanent factor of the process of annual reproduction, demonstrates:

(a) Assuming capitalist production to be developed to the point where the wage system predominates, money-capital evidently plays a prominent role, seeing that it is the form in which the variable capital is advanced. To the extent that the wage system develops, all products are converted into commodities and must, therefore, pass through the stage of money as one phase of their metamorphoses, with a few important exceptions. The quantity of circulating money must suffice for this conversion of commodities into money, and the greater part of this quantity is furnished in the form of wages, in that money, which is the money-form of the variable capital advanced by the industrial capitalists in payment for labour-power, and which serves in the hands of the labourers overwhelmingly as a medium of circulation (of purchase). It is quite the reverse under a system of natural economy such as was predominant under every form of vassalage (including serfdom), and still more in more or less primitive communities, whether they are infected by conditions of vassalage or slavery, or not.

In a slave system, the money-capital invested in the purchase of slaves plays the role of the fixed capital in money-form, which is but gradually replaced after the expiration of the active life period of the slaves. Among the Athenians, therefore, the gain realised by a slave owner through the industrial employment of his slaves, or indirectly by hiring them out to other industrial employers (for instance mine owners), was regarded merely as an interest (with sinking fund) on the advanced money-capital, just as the industrial capitalist under capitalist production places a portion of the surplus-value plus the depreciation of his fixed capital to the account of interest and renewal of his fixed capital. This is also the rule in the case of capitalists offering fixed capital, such as houses, machinery, etc., for rent. Mere household slaves, who perform the necessary services or are kept as luxuries, are not considered here. They correspond to the modern servant class. But the slave system – so long as it is the dominant form of productive labour in agriculture, manufacture, navigation, etc., as it was in the advanced states of Greece and Rome – preserves an element of natural economy. The slave market maintains its supply of labour-power by war, piracy, etc., and this rape is not promoted by a process of circulation, but by the natural appropriation of the labour-power of others by physical force. Even in the United States, after the conversion of the neutral territory between the wage labour states of the North and the slave labour states of the South into a slave breeding region for the South, where the slave thus raised for the market had become an element of annual reproduction, this method did not suffice for a long time, so that the African slave trade was continued as long as possible for the purpose of supplying the market.

(b) The natural flux and reflux of money by the exchange of the annual products on the basis of capitalist production; the advances of fixed capital in one bulk to the full value and the gradual and prolonged recovery of this outlay from the circulation in the course of successive years; in other words, the gradual reconstitution of fixed capital in money by the annual formation of a hoard, which is different from the simultaneous accumulation of a hoard based on the annual production of new gold; the different length of time in which money is advanced according to the duration of the periods of reproduction of commodities, and in which money must, therefore, be accumulated anew, before it can be recovered from the circulation by the sale of commodities; the different length of time for which money must be advanced, resulting even from the different distances of the places of production from their selling market; furthermore the differences in the magnitude and period of the reflux according to the relative size or condition of the productive supplies in the various lines of business and in the individual businesses of the same line, and with them the terms at which the elements of constant capital are bought – all this taking place during the year of reproduction, it was necessary that all these different factors should be noted and brought home by experience in order to give rise to a systematisation of the mechanical aids of the credit-system and to an actual discovery of whatever capital was available for lending.

This is further complicated by a difference between lines of business whose production proceeds continuously under normal conditions on the same scale, and those which are carried on at different scales at different periods of the year, such as agriculture.

Section 13. Destutt de Tracy's Theory of Reproduction.

As an illustration of the confused and at the same time boastful thoughtlessness of political economists analysing social reproduction, the great logician Destutt de Tracy may serve (compare Book 1, page 181, footnote 1), whom even Ricardo took seriously, calling him a very distinguished writer.

This distinguished writer makes the following revelations concerning the entire process of social reproduction and circulation:

'One may ask me how these industrial capitalists can make such large profits and out of whom they can draw them. I reply that they do so by selling everything which they produce for more than it has cost to produce; and that they sell

(1) to one another to the extent of the entire share of their consumption, intended for the satisfaction of their needs, which they pay with a portion of their profits;

(2) to the wage workers, both those whom they pay and those whom the idle capitalists pay; from these wage workers they recover the entire wages in this way, except what little they may save;

(3) to the idle capitalist, whom they pay with a portion of their revenue which they have not spent for the wages of the labourers employed by them directly; so that the entire rent, which they pay them annually, flows back to them in this way.' (Destutt de Tracy, *Traité de la volonté et de ses effets*. Paris, 1821, page 239.)

In other words, the capitalists enrich themselves by mutually getting the best of one another in the exchange of that portion of their surplus-value which they reserve for their individual consumption, or consume as revenue. For instance, if this portion of their surplus-value, or of their profits, is £400, this sum is supposed to be increased to, say, £500 by mutually selling their respective shares at an excess of 25% over the normal. But if all do the same, the result will be just what it would have been if they had mutually sold their shares at their normal values. They merely need in that case £500 in money for the circulation of commodities valued at £400, and this would seem to be rather a method of impoverishing than of enriching themselves, since it means that they are compelled to reserve a large portion of their total wealth unproductively in the state of a medium of circulation. The outcome is simply that the capitalist class can divide only £400's worth of commodities among themselves for their individual consumption, after nominally raising prices all around, but that they do one another the favour of circulating £400's worth of commodities by means of a quantity of money which would just as well circulate £500's worth of commodities.

And this is saying nothing about the fact that the assumption deals here only with a 'portion of their profits', or any supply of commodities representing profits. But Destutt undertook precisely to tell us where these profits come from. The quantity of money required to circulate it represents a very subordinate question. It seems that the quantity of commodities, in which the profit is incorporated, is produced by the circumstance that the capitalists do not only sell these commodities to one another (an assumption which is quite fine and profound), but also mutually sell them too dearly. Thus we are acquainted with the secret of the wealth of the capitalists. It is on a par with the secret of Reuter's funny 'Inspector Braesig' who discovered that the great poverty is due to the great '*pauvreté*'.

(2) The same capitalists, furthermore, sell 'to the wage workers, both those whom they pay and those whom the idle capitalists pay; from these wage workers they recover the entire wages in this way, except what little they may save.'

According to Destutt, then, the reflux of the money-capital advanced to the labourers as wages, is the second source of the wealth of the capitalists.

For instance, if the capitalists have paid £100 to their labourers as wages, and if these same labourers buy from the same capitalists commodities of this same value of £100, so that what the capitalists have advanced to the labourers as wages returns to the capitalists when the labourers spend it for commodities, then the capitalists get richer. A common mortal would think that the capitalists recover only their £100, which they possessed before this transaction. At the beginning of the transaction they have £100. They buy labour-power valued at £100. This labour-power, so bought, produces commodities of a certain value, which, so far as we know, amounts to £100. By selling these commodities for £100 to their labourers, the capitalists recover £100 in money. The capitalists then have once more £100, the same as before, and the labourers have £100's worth of commodities which they have themselves produced. It is hard to understand how that can make the capitalists any richer. If they did not recover the £100, then they would have to pay first £100 to the labourers in wages and then to give them their product for nothing, although it is also worth £100. The reflux of this money might therefore at best explain, why the capitalists do not get any poorer by this transaction, but not why they get richer by it.

It is another question, how the capitalists got possession of the £100, and why the labourers, instead of working for their own account, are compelled to exchange their labour-power for this money. But this is a fact which is self-explanatory for a thinker of Destutt's calibre.

However, Destutt himself is not quite satisfied with his solution. He did not simply tell us that the capitalists get richer by spending a sum of £100 in money and then recovering the same amount. He had not plainly spoken of a reflux of £100 which merely explains why this money is not lost. He had told us that the capitalists get richer 'by selling everything which they produce for more than it has cost to produce'.

Consequently the capitalists must also get richer by their transaction with the labourers by selling too dearly to them. Very well! 'They pay wages . . . and all this flows back to them by the expenditures of all these people who pay them more' (for the products) 'than they cost the capitalists in wages.' (page 240.) In other words, the capitalists pay

£100 in wages to the labourers, and then they sell to these labourers their own product at £120, so that they not only recover their £100, but also gain £20. That is impossible. The labourers can pay for the commodities only with the money which they receive in the form of wages. If they get only £100 in wages, they can buy only £100's worth, not £120's worth. This is therefore impracticable. But there is still another way. The labourers buy from the capitalists commodities for £100, but receive only £80's worth. They are cheated out of £20. Then the capitalist has certainly gained £20, because he practically pays 20% less than the actual value for labour-power. This is equivalent to cutting wages 20% by a circuitous route.

The capitalists would accomplish the same end if they paid the labourers in the first place only £80 in wages and gave them only £80's worth of commodities in exchange. This seems to be the normal way for the class of capitalists as a whole, for according to Destutt the labouring class must 'receive sufficient wages' (page 219), since their wages must be at least sufficient to maintain them alive and working, 'to gain the barest subsistence' (page 180). If the labourers do not receive such sufficient wages, then that means according to the same Destutt 'the death of industry' (page 208), which does not seem to be a way by which the capitalists can get richer. But whatever may be the scale of wages, paid by the capitalists to the labourers, they have a certain value, for instance, £80. If the capitalist class pays the labourers £80, then it has to supply them with commodities worth £80 in exchange for these wages, and the reflux of this sum does not make the capitalists any richer. If the capitalists pay the labourers £100 in wages, and supply them in exchange for £100 only with £80's worth of commodities, then they pay 20% above the normal scale in wages and supply on the other hand 20% less in commodities.

In other words, the fund from which the capitalist class would derive its profits, would be made up of deductions from the normal scale of wages of the labourers, by paying less than its value for labour-power; in other words, less than the value of the necessities of life required for the normal reproduction of the labourer. If the normal scale of wages were paid, which is supposed to be the case according to Destutt, there can be no fund for profits, neither for the industrial nor for the idle capitalists.

Hence Destutt should have reduced the entire secret of how the capitalist class get richer, to these words: a deduction from the wages of the labourers. In that case the other sources of surplus-value, which he mentions under (1) and (3), would not exist.

Under these conditions all the countries, in which the money paid to the labourers in wages is reduced to the value of the articles of consumption required for the subsistence of the working class, would not have any fund for the consumption of capitalists, nor any fund for the accumulation of capital. In other words, there would be no fund permitting a capitalist class to live, and therefore no capitalist class. And according to Destutt this would be the case in all wealthy and developed countries with an old civilisation, for in them, 'in our deep-rooted old societies, the fund from which wages are paid . . . is an almost constant magnitude.' (page 202.)

Even with a deduction from the wages, the capitalist does not enrich himself by first paying the labourer £100 in wages and then supplying him with £80's worth of commodities for £100 of wages, in other words, by circulating £80's worth of commodities by means of £100, an excess of 20%. The capitalist gets richer by appropriating, aside from the surplus-value – that portion of the product in which surplus-value is incorporated –20% of that portion of the product which the labourer should receive in exchange for his wages: the capitalist class would not gain anything by the silly method which Destutt assumes. They pay £100 for wages and give to the labourer for these £100 a part of his own product valued at £80. But in the next transaction they must again advance £100 for the same purpose. They would thus indulge in the useless sport of advancing £100 in money and giving in exchange therefor £80 in commodities, instead of paying £80 and exchanging it for £80 in commodities. That is to say, they would be continually advancing a money-capital which is 20% in excess of the normal required for the circulation of their variable capital. That is a very peculiar method to get rich.

(3) The capitalist class, finally, sells 'to the idle capitalists, whom they pay with a portion of their revenue which they have not spent for the wages of the labourers employed by them directly; so that the entire rent, which they pay them annually, flows back to them in this way.'

We have seen a while ago that the industrial capitalists pay with a portion of their profits 'the entire share of their consumption, intended for the satisfaction of their needs.' Take it, then, that their profits amount to £200. And let them consume £100 of this in their individual consumption. But the other half, or £100, does not belong to them. It belongs to the 'idle' capitalists, that is to say, to those who take ground rent and lend money on interest. In other words, they have to pay £100 to this gentry. Let us assume that this gentry use £80 for their individual consumption, and £20 for the purchase of servants, etc. They buy with those £80 articles of consumption from the industrial capitalists. These capitalists, then, give up commodities valued at £80 and receive in return £80 in money, or four fifths of the £100 paid by them to the idle capitalists under the name of rent, interest, etc. The servant class, who are the wage workers directly in attendance upon the idle capitalists, have received £20 from their masters. These servants likewise buy articles of consumption from the industrial capitalists to the amount of £20. In this way these capitalists recover also the last £20, or the last fifth, of the £100, which they have paid to the idle capitalists for rent, interest, etc., while they give up in return commodities valued at £20.

At the close of this transaction the industrial capitalists have recovered the full £100, which they paid to the idle capitalists for rent, interest, etc., in money. But one half of their surplus products, valued at £100, have passed from their hands into the fund for the individual consumption of the idle capitalists.

It is evidently immaterial for the present question, whether the division of the £100 among the idle capitalists and their dependent wage workers is drawn into this discussion or not. The matter is simple: their rent, interest, in short, their share in the surplus-value of £200, is paid to them by the industrial capitalists in money to the amount of £100. With these £100 they buy directly or indirectly articles of consumption from the industrial capitalists. They return the £100 in money to them and take from them instead articles of consumption valued at £100.

This completes the reflux of the £100 paid by the industrial capitalists to the idle capitalists. Is this transaction a means of making the industrial capitalists any richer, as Destutt imagines? Before this transaction they had values amounting to £200, 100 being money and 100 articles of consumption. After the transaction they have only one half of the original amount of values. They have once more £100 in money, but they have lost the articles of consumption valued at £100, which have passed into the possession of the idle capitalists. In other words, they have become poorer to the extent of £100, instead of being richer. If, instead of first choosing the circuitous route of paying out £100 in money, and then receiving this money back in payment for articles of consumption valued at £100, they had paid rent, interest, etc., directly in the natural form of commodities, then they would not recover any £100 in money, because they did not throw that amount of money into the circulation. In the case of a payment in commodities, the transaction would simply have been confined to keeping one-half of the surplus product of £200 for themselves and giving the other half to the idle capitalists without receiving any equivalent in return. Even Destutt would not have been able to consider this a means of getting richer.

Of course, the land and capital borrowed by the industrial capitalists from the idle capitalists and paid for by a portion of their surplus-value in the form of ground rent and interest, etc., are profitable for them, for they constitute one of the conditions for the production of any commodity, and more especially of that portion of the product, which creates surplus-value, or in which surplus-value is incorporated. This profit flows from the use of the borrowed land and capital, not out of the price paid for them. This price rather constitutes a deduction from the profit. Or one would have to contend, that the industrial capitalists do not get richer, but poorer, if they are enabled to keep the other half of their surplus-value, instead of being compelled to give it up. This is the confusion which results from the indiscriminate mixing up of such phenomena of circulation as a reflux of money with the distribution of the product, which is merely promoted by this circulation.

And yet the same Destutt is so sharp as to remark: 'Whence come the revenues of these idle people? Do they not come out of the rent paid by them out of the profits of those who put the capitals of the former to work, that is to say, who pay with the funds of the former a certain kind of labour which produces more than it costs; in other words, the profits of the industrial capitalists? It is always necessary to revert to them, in order to find the source of wealth. It is they who in reality feed the wage workers employed by the idle capitalists.' (page 246.)

In other words, in this quotation the rent, etc., of the idle capitalists is a deduction from the profit of the industrial capitalists. In former quotations it was a means of enriching them.

But at least one consolation is left for our friend Destutt. These good industrials treat the idle capitalists in the same way that they have treated one another and their labourers. They sell them all commodities too dearly, for instance, at a raise of 20%. Now there are two possibilities. The idle capitalists either have other funds of money aside from the £100 which they receive from the industrials, or they have not. In the first case, the industrials sell them commodities valued at £100 at a price of, say, £120. In other words, they recover by the sale of their commodities not only the £100 paid to the idle capitalists, but also £20 of new values. Now, how stands the account? They have given away £100 in commodities for nothing, for the £100 that paid for their commodities were their own money. Their own commodities have been paid with their own money. In other words, they have lost £100. But they have also received an additional sum of £20 in the price of their commodities. In other words, £20 of gain. Balance this against the loss of £100, and you still have a loss of £80. Never a plus, always a minus. The advantage taken by the industrials over the idle capitalists has reduced the loss of the industrials, but for all that it has not transformed a reduction of their wealth into an increase of wealth. But this method cannot go on indefinitely, for the idle capitalists cannot pay year after year £120, if they receive only £100.

There remains the other possibility. The industrials sell commodities valued at £80 in exchange for the £100 paid to the idle capitalists. In this case, they still give away £80 for nothing, in the form of rent, interest, etc. By means of cheating the industrials have reduced their tribute to the idlers, but it nevertheless is exacted from them the same as ever, and the idlers are enabled, on the same theory, assuming the prices to depend on the free will of the sellers, to demand in the future £120 instead of £100 as rent and interest on their land and capital.

This brilliant analysis is quite worthy of that depth of thought which copies on the one hand from Adam Smith that 'labour is the source of all wealth' (page 242), that the industrial capitalists 'employ their capital for the payment of labour that reproduces it with a profit' (page 246), and which concludes on the other hand that these industrial capitalists 'maintain all the other people, are the only ones who increase the public wealth, and create all the means for our enjoyment' (page 242), that it is not the capitalists who are maintained by the labourers, but the labourers who are maintained by the capitalists, for the brilliant reason that the money with which the labourers are paid, does not remain in their hands, but continually returns to the capitalists in payment of the commodities produced by the labourers. 'They receive only with one hand, and return with the other. Their consumption must therefore be regarded as being due to those who pay their wages.' (page 235).

After this exhaustive analysis of social reproduction and consumption, as promoted by the circulation of money, Destutt continues: 'This is what perfects this *perpetuum mobile* of wealth, this movement which, though ill understood' (I should say so!) 'yet has justly been named circulation. For it is indeed a circulation and always returns to its point of departure. This is the point where production is accomplished.' (pages 139, 140.)

Destutt, that very distinguished writer, *membre de l'Institut de France et de la Société Philosophique de Philadelphie*, and indeed to a certain extent a beacon light among the vulgar economists, finally requests his readers to admire the wonderful lucidity with which he has presented to them the course of the social process, the flood of light which he has poured over the matter, and he is condescending enough to communicate to his readers, where all this light comes from. This must be read in the original in order to be appreciated.

'*On remarquera, j'espère, combien cette manière de considérer la consom-mation de nos richesses est corcordante avec tout ce que nous avons dit à propos de leur production et de leur distribution, et en même temps quelle clarté elle répand sur toute la marche de la société. D'où viennent cet accord et cette lucidité! De ce que nous avons rencontré la vérité. Cela rappelle l'effet de ces miroirs où les objets se peignent nettement et dans leurs justes proportions, quand on est placé dans leur vrai point-de-vue, et où tout parait confus et désuni, quand on est trop près ou trop loin.*' (pages 242, 243). ('It will be noted, I hope, how much this manner of viewing the consummation of our wealth is in accord with all we have said concerning its production and distribution, and also *how much light it throws on the entire course of society.* Whence come this accord and this *lucidity*? It is due to the fact that we have met truth face to face. This recalls the effect of those mirrors, in which the objects are reflected clearly and in their true proportions, when we are placed in their correct focus, but in which everything appears confused and distorted, when we are too close or too far away from them').

There you have the bourgeois idiocy in all its beatitude!

Chapter 21
Accumulation and Reproduction on an Enlarged Scale [1]

It has been shown in Volume 1, how accumulation works in the case of the individual capitalist. By the conversion of the commodity-capital into money, the surplus-product, in which the surplus-value is incorporated, is also monetised. The capitalist reconverts the surplus-value thus monetised into additional natural elements of his productive capital. In the next cycle of production the increased capital furnishes an increased product. But what happens in the case of the individual capital, must also show in the annual reproduction of society as a whole, just as we have seen it done in the case of reproduction on a simple scale, where the successive precipitation of the depreciated elements of fixed capitals in the form of money, accumulated as a hoard, also makes itself felt in the annual reproduction of society.

If a certain individual capital amounts to $400 c + 100 v$, with an annual surplus-value of $100 s$, then the product in commodities amounts to 400 c + 100 v + 100 s. This amount of 600 is converted into money. Of this money, again, 400 c are converted into the natural form of constant capital, 100 v into labour-power, and – provided that the entire surplus-value is accumulated – 100 s are converted into additional constant capital by their transformation into natural elements of productive capital. The following assumptions go with this case: (1) That this amount is sufficient under the given technical conditions either to expand the existing constant capital, or to establish a new industrial business. But it may also happen that surplus-value must be converted into money and this money hoarded for a much longer time, before these steps may be taken, before actual accumulation, or expansion of production, can take place. (2) It is furthermore assumed that production on an enlarged scale has actually been in process previously. For in order that the money (the surplus-value hoarded as money) may be converted into elements of productive capital, these elements must be available on the market as commodities. It makes no difference whether they are bought as finished products, or made to order. They are not paid for until they are finished, and at any rate, until actual reproduction on an enlarged scale, an expansion of hitherto normal production, has taken place so far as they are concerned. They had to be present potentially, that is to say, in their elements, for it required only an impulse in the form of an order, that is to say, a purchase preceding their actual existence and anticipating their sale, in order to stimulate their production. The money on one side in that case calls forth expanded reproduction on the other, because the possibility for it exists without the money. For money in itself is not an element of actual reproduction.

For instance, capitalist A, who sells during one year, or during a number of successive years, certain quantities of commodities produced by him, thereby converts that portion of the commodities, which bears surplus-value, the surplus-product, or, in other words, the surplus-value produced by himself, successively into money, accumulates it gradually, and thus makes for himself a new potential money-capital. It is potential money-capital on account of its capacity and destination of being converted into the elements of productive capital. But practically he merely accumulates a simple hoard, which is not an element of actual production. His activity for the time being consists only in withdrawing circulating money out of circulation. Of course, it is not impossible that the circulating money thus laid away by him was itself, before it entered into circulation, a portion of some other hoard. This hoard of A, which is potentially a new money-capital, is not an addition to the social wealth, any more than it would be if it were spent in articles of consumption. But money, when withdrawn from circulation, having previously circulated, may have been held somewhere as a hoard, or may have been the money-form of wages, may have monetised means of production or other commodities, may have circulated portions of constant capital or of the revenue of some capitalist. It is no more new wealth than money, considered from the standpoint of the simple circulation of commodities, is the bearer, not only of its simple value, but also of its tenfold value, because it may have been turned over ten times a day and realised ten different values of commodities. The commodities exist without it, and it remains what it is (or becomes even less by depreciation) whether in one turn-over or in ten. Only in the production of gold – to the extent that the output of gold contains a surplus-product and is the bearer of surplus-value – is new value created (potential money), and the new output of gold increases the money-material of potential new money-capitals only to the extent that it enters entirely into the circulation.

Although the surplus-value hoarded in the form of money is not an addition to the social wealth, it represents an addition to the potential money-capital, on account of the function for which it is hoarded. (We shall see later that new money-capital may arise in still another way than by the gradual monetisation of surplus-value.)

Money is withdrawn from circulation and accumulated as a hoard by the sale of commodities without a subsequent purchase. If this operation is conceived as one taking place universally, then it seems inexplicable where the buyers are to come from, since in that case everybody would want to sell in order to hoard, and none would want to buy. And it must be so conceived, since every individual capital may be in process of accumulation.

If we were to conceive of the process of circulation as one taking place in a straight line between the various divisions of annual reproduction – which would be incorrect, as it consists with a few exceptions of mutually retroactive movements – then we should have to start out from the producer of gold (or silver) who buys without selling, and to assume that all others sell to them. In that case the entire social surplus-product of the current year would pass into his hands, representing the entire surplus-value of the year, and all the other capitalists would distribute among themselves their relative shares in his surplus-product, which consists naturally of money, gold being the natural form of his surplus-value. For that portion of the product of the gold producer, which has to make good his active capital, is already tied up and disposed of. The surplus-value of the gold producer, in the form of gold, would then be the only fund from which all other capitalists would have to derive the material for the conversion of their annual surplus-product into gold. The magnitude of its value would then have to be equal to the entire annual surplus-value of society, which must first assume the guise of a hoard. Absurd as this assumption would be, it would accomplish nothing more than to explain the possibility of a universal formation of a hoard at the same period. It would not further reproduction itself, except on the part of the gold producer, one single step.

Before we solve this seeming difficulty, we must distinguish between the accumulation in Department I (production of means of production) and in Department II (production of articles of consumption). We start out from I.

Section 1. Accumulation in Department I.

A. The Formation of a Hoard.

It is evident that both the investments of capital in the numerous lines of industry constituting Department I, and the different individual investments of capital within each of these lines of industry, according to their age, that is to say, the space of time during which they have served, quite aside from their volume, technical conditions, market conditions, etc., must be in different stages of the process of successive transformation from surplus-value into potential money-capital. It is immaterial whether this money-capital is to serve for the expansion of the active capital, or for the establishment of new industrial enterprises, which constitute the two forms of expansion of production. One portion of the capitalists, then, is continually converting its potential capital, when grown to a sufficient size, into productive capital, that is to say, they buy with the money hoarded by the monetisation of surplus-value means of production, additional elements of constant capital. Another portion of the capitalists is meanwhile still engaged in accumulating potential money-capital. Capitalists belonging to these two categories meet as buyers and sellers, each one of them exclusively in one of these roles.

For instance, let A sell 600, representing 400 c + 100 v + 100 s, to B, who may represent more than one buyer. A sells 600 in commodities for 600 in money, of which 100 are surplus-value which he withdraws from circulation and hoards in the form of money. But these 100 in money are but the money-form of the surplus-product in which a value of 100 was incorporated. The formation of a hoard, then, is not a production, nor is it an increment of production. The action of the capitalist consists merely in withdrawing from circulation 100 obtained by the sale of his surplus-product, in holding and hoarding this amount. This operation is carried on, not alone on the part of A, but at numerous points of the periphery of circulation by other capitalists, named A', A", A"', all of whom work busily at this sort of accumulation. These numerous points at which money is withdrawn from circulation and accumulated in numerous individual hoards appear as so many obstacles of circulation, because they stop the movement of money and deprive it of its capacity to circulate for a certain length of time. But it must be remembered that hoarding takes place in the simple circulation of commodities long before it is based on the capitalist mode of production. The quantity of money existing in society is always greater than the amount in actual circulation, although this varies according to circumstances. We meet the same hoards, and the same accumulation of hoards, at this stage, but now it is a factor immanent in the capitalist process of production.

One can understand the pleasure felt by some men when all these potential capitals, by their concentration in the hands of bankers, etc., by means of the credit system, become disposable, 'loanable capital', money-capital, which is no longer merely passive and a dream of the future, but active usury-capital, self-expanding capital.

However, A accomplishes the formation of a hoard only to the extent that he acts as a seller, so far as his surplus-product is concerned, not as a buyer. His successive production of surplus-products, the bearers of his surplus-value convertible into money, is therefore a promise for the formation of his hoard. In the present case, where we are dealing only with the circulation within Department I, the natural form of the surplus-product, and of the total product of which it is a part, is that of an element of constant capital of I, that is to say, it belongs to the category of a means of production creating means of production. We shall see presently what becomes of it, what function it performs, in the hands of the buyers such as B, B', B", etc.

It must be particularly noted at this point that A, while withdrawing money from circulation and hoarding it, on the other hand throws commodities into it without withdrawing other commodities in return. The capitalists B, B', B", etc., are thereby enabled to throw only money into it and withdraw only commodities from it. In the present case, these commodities, according to their natural form and destination, become a fixed or circulating element of the constant capital of B, B', etc. We shall hear more about this anon, when we shall deal with the buyer of the surplus-product, with B, B', etc.

*   *   *

We remark by the way: once more we find here, as we did in the case of simple reproduction, that the disposal of the various elements of annual reproduction, that is to say, their circulation which must comprise the reproduction of the capital to the point of replacing its various elements, such as constant, variable, fixed, circulating, money and commodity-capital, is not conditioned on the mere purchase of commodities followed by a corresponding sale, or a mere sale followed by a corresponding purchase, so that there would actually be a bare exchange of commodity for commodity, as the political economists assume, especially the free trade school from the time of the Physiocrats and Adam Smith. We know that the fixed capital, once its investment is made, is not replaced during the entire period of its function, but serves in its old form, until its value is gradually precipitated in the form of money. Now we have seen that the periodical renewal of the fixed capital of IIc [the entire value of the capital of IIc being converted into elements of I valued at $(v + s)$] presupposes on the one hand the mere purchase of the fixed portion of IIc, which is reconverted from the form of money into its natural form, and to which corresponds the mere sale of Is; and presupposes on the other hand the mere sale on the part of IIc, the sale of its fixed (depreciating) value, which is precipitated in money and to which corresponds the mere purchase of I s. In order that the transaction may take place normally in this case, it must be assumed that the mere purchase on the part of II c is equal in value to the mere sale on the part of II c, and that in the same way the mere sale of I s to II c, section 1, is equal in value to the mere purchase from Department II c, section 2. Otherwise simple reproduction is interrupted. The mere sale on one side must be offset by a mere purchase on the other. It must likewise be assumed that the mere sale of that portion of I s, which forms the hoards of A, A', A'' is balanced by the mere purchase of that portion of I s, which converts the hoards of B, B', B'', into elements of additional productive capital.

So far as the balance is restored by the fact that the buyer acts later on as a seller to the same amount, and vice versa, the money returns to the side that has advanced it in the first place, which sold first before it bought again. But the actual balance, so far as the exchange of commodities itself is concerned, that is to say, the disposal of the various portions of the annual product, is conditioned on the equal value of the commodities exchanged for one another.

But to the extent that only one-sided exchanges are made, a number of mere purchases on one hand, a number of mere sales on the other – and we have seen that the normal disposal of the annual product on the basis of capitalist production requires such one-sided metamorphoses – the balance can be maintained only on the assumption that the value of the one-sided purchases and one-sided sales is the same. The fact that the production of commodities is the general form of capitalist production implies the role which money is playing not only as a medium of circulation, but also as money-capital, and creates conditions peculiar for the normal transaction of exchange under this mode of production, and therefore peculiar for the normal course of reproduction, whether it be on a simple, or on an expanded scale. These conditions become so many causes of abnormal movements, implying the possibility of crises, since a balance is an accident under the crude conditions of this production.

We have also seen that there is indeed, in the exchange of I v for a corresponding value of II c, an ultimate renewal of the value of the commodities of II by an equivalent value of commodities of I, so that the sale of the commodities of the aggregate capitalist of II is balanced subsequently by the purchase of commodities from I to the same amount. This restitution takes place. But it is not an exchange which takes place between the capitalists of I and II in the disposal of their relative commodities. II c sells its commodities to the working class of I. This class meets it one-sidedly in the role of a buyer of commodities, and it meets that class one-sidedly as a seller of commodities. With the money so obtained II c meets the aggregate capitalist of I one-sidedly as a buyer of commodities, and the aggregate capitalist of I meets it one-sidedly as a seller of commodities to the extent of I v. It is only by means of this sale of commodities that Department I finally reproduces its variable capital in the form of money-capital. Just as one-sidedly as the capitalist class of I faces that of II in the role of a seller of commodities to the extent of I v, so does that class face its working class in the role of a buyer of commodities, a buyer of labour-power. And just as one-sidedly as that working class faces the capitalists of II in the role of a buyer of commodities (namely of articles of consumption), so it faces the capitalists of I as a seller of commodities, namely, a seller of its labour-power.

The continual offer of labour-power on the part of the working class of I, the reconversion of a portion of the commodity-capital of I into the money-form of variable capital, the renewal of a portion of the commodity-capital of II by natural elements of the constant capital of II c – all these are necessary premises dovetailing into one another, but they are promoted by a very complicated process including three processes of circulation which occur independently of one another, but intermingle. The complicatedness of this process presents so many opportunities for abnormal deviations.

B. The Additional Constant Capital.

The surplus-product, the bearer of surplus-value, does not cost its appropriators, the capitalists of I, anything. They are in no way obliged to advance any money or commodities in order to secure it. An advance means even in the writings of the Physiocrats the general form of value materialised in elements of productive capital. Hence what they advance is nothing but their constant and variable capital. The labourer preserves by his labour not only their constant capital; he reproduces not only the value of their variable capital by creating corresponding qualities of new values; he supplies them also by his surplus-labour with surplus-values in the form of surplus-products. By the successive sale of this surplus-product, they accumulate a hoard, additional potential money-capital. In the present case, this surplus-product consists at the outset of means of production used in the creation of means of production. It is not until it reaches the hands of B, B', B", etc. (I), that this surplus-product serves as additional constant capital. But it is virtually that even in the hands of the accumulators of hoards, the capitalists A, A', A", (I), before it is sold. If we consider merely the volume of values of the reproduction on the part of I, then we are still moving within the limits of simple reproduction, for no additional capital has been set in motion for the purpose of creating this virtual additional constant capital (the surplus-product), nor has any greater amount of surplus-labour been performed than that done on the basis of simple reproduction. The difference is here only one of the form of the surplus-labour performed, of the concrete nature of its particularly useful service. It is expended in means of production for Department I c instead of II c, in means of production of means of production instead of means of production of articles of consumption. In the case of simple reproduction it had been assumed that the entire surplus-value was spent as revenue in commodities of II. Hence it consisted only of such means of production as restore the constant capital of II c in its natural form. In order that the transition from simple to expanded reproduction may take place, the production in Department I must be enabled to create fewer elements for the constant capital of II and more for that of I. This transition, which will not always take place without difficulties, is facilitated by the fact that some of the products of I may serve as means of production in either department.

Considering the matter merely from the point of view of the volume of values, it follows, then, that the material requirements of expanded reproduction are produced within simple reproduction. It is simply a question of the expenditure of the surplus-labour of the working class of I for the production of means of production, the creation of virtual additional capital of I. The virtual additional money-capital, created on the part of A, A', A", by the successive sale of their surplus-product, which was formed without any capitalist expenditure of money, is in this case simply the money-form of the additional means of production made by I.

The production of virtual additional capital expresses in our case (we shall see that it may also be formed in a different way) merely the fact that it is a phenomenon of the process of production itself, the production of elements of productive capital in a particular form.

The production of virtual additional money-capital on a large scale, at numerous points of the periphery of circulation, is therefore but a result and expression of a multifarious production of virtual additional productive capital, whose rise does not itself require any additional expenditure of money on the part of the industrial capitalists.

The successive transformation of this virtual additional productive capital into virtual money-capital (hoard) on the part of A, A', A", etc., (I), conditioned on the successive sale of their surplus-product, which is a repeated one-sided sale without a compensating purchase, is accomplished by a repeated withdrawal of money from circulation and a corresponding formation of a hoard. This hoarding, except in the case of buyers who are gold producers, does not in any way imply an addition to the wealth in precious metals, but only a change of function on the part of money previously circulating. A while ago it served as a medium of circulation, now it serves as a hoard, as a virtual additional money-capital in process of formation. In other words, the formation of additional money-capital and the volume of the precious metals existing in a certain country are not directly connected facts.

Hence it follows furthermore: the greater the productive capital already serving in a certain country (including the labour-power incorporated in it as the producer of the surplus-product); the more developed the productive power of labour and at the same time the technical appliances for the rapid extension of the production of means of production; the greater furthermore the quantity of the surplus-product both as to value and mass; so much greater is

(1) The virtual additional productive capital in the form of a surplus-product in the hands of A, A', A", etc., and

(2) The mass of this surplus-product transformed into money; in other words, the virtual additional money-capital in the hands of A, A', A". The fact that Fullerton, for instance, will have nothing to do with any overproduction in the ordinary meaning of the term, but only with the over-production of capital, meaning money-capital, shows how pitifully little even the best bourgeois economists understand of the mechanism of their own system.

While the surplus-product, directly produced and appropriated by the capitalists A, A', A" (I), is the actual basis of the accumulation of capital, that is to say, of expanded reproduction, although it does not actually serve in this capacity until it reaches the hands of the capitalists B, B', B", etc. (I), it is quite unproductive in its chrysalis stage of money, of a hoard representing virtual money-capital in process of formation. It runs parallel with the process of production, but moves outside of it. It is a dead weight of capitalist production. The desire to utilise this surplus-value, while accumulating as virtual money-capital, for the purpose of deriving profits or revenue from it, finds in the credit system and paper securities its consummation. Money-capital thereby gains in another form an enormous influence on the course and the stupendous development of the capitalist system of production.

The surplus-product converted into virtual money-capital will grow so much more in volume, the greater the aggregate amount of capital actually engaged which produced it by its function. With the absolute increase of the volume of the annually reproduced virtual money-capital its segmentation also becomes easier, so that it is more rapidly invested in a certain business, either in the hands of the same capitalist or in those of others (for instance members of the family, in the case of a division of inheritances, etc.). By segmentation of money-capital I mean in this case that it is wholly detached from the parent capital in order to be invested as a new money capital in a new and independent business.

While the sellers of the surplus-product, A, A', A", etc., (I), have obtained it as a direct outcome of the process of production, which does not require any additional act of circulation aside from the advance of constant and variable capital made even in simple repro-duction; and while they thereby construct the real basis for a repro-duction on an expanded scale, seeing that they manufacture virtually additional capital – the attitude of B, B', B", etc., (I), is different. (1) The surplus-product of A, A', A", etc., does not actually serve as additional constant capital until it reaches the hands of B, B', B', etc. (We leave out of consideration for the present the other elements of productive capital, the additional labour-power, in other words, the additional variable capital.) (2) In order that the surplus-product may reach their hands, they must buy it.

In regard to point 1, it may be noted that a large portion of the surplus-product (virtual additional constant capital) is produced by A, A', A", (I), in the course of the current year, but may not serve as industrial capital in the hands of B, B', B", (I), until next year, or still later. With reference to point 2, the question is: whence comes the money required for the process of circulation?

To the extent that the products created by B, B', B", etc., (I), re-enter in their natural form into their own process, it goes without saying that a corresponding portion of their own surplus-product is transferred directly (without any intervention of circulation) to their productive capital and becomes an element of additional constant capital. To the same extent they do not help to convert any surplus-product of A, A', A", etc., (I), into money. Aside from this, where does the money come from? We know that they have formed their hoard in the same way as A, A', etc., by the sale of their respective surplus-products. Now they have arrived at the point where their accumulated hoard of virtual money-capital is to enter effectually upon its function as additional money-capital. But this is merely turning around in a circle. The question still remains: where does the money come from, which the various B's (1) withdrew from the circulation and accumulated?

Now we know from the analysis of simple reproduction, that the capitalists of I and II must have a certain amount of ready money in their hands, in order to be able to dispose of their surplus-products. In that case, the money which served only for the spending of revenue in articles of consumption returned to the capitalists in the same measure in which they advanced it for the purpose of disposing of their commodities. Here the same money re-appears, but in a different function. The A's and B's supply one another alternately with the money for converting their surplus-product into virtual additional capital, and throw the newly formed money-capital alternately into circulation as a medium of purchase.

The only assumption made in this case is that the amount of money existing in a certain country (the velocity of circulation, etc., being the same) suffices for both the active circulation and the reserve hoard. It is the same assumption which had to be made in the case of the simple circulation of commodities, as we have seen. Only the function of the hoards is different in the present case. Furthermore, the existing amount of money must be larger, first, because all the products (with the exception of the newly produced precious metals and the few products consumed by the producer himself) are produced as commodities under capitalist production and must, therefore, pass through the stage of money; secondly, because on a capitalist basis the quantity of the commodity-capital and the volume of its value is not only absolutely greater, but also grows with much greater rapidity; thirdly, an ever more voluminous variable capital must be converted into money-capital; fourthly, with the extension of production, the formation of new money-capital keeps step, so that the material for it must be available in the form of a hoard.

While this is a common truism for the first phase of capitalist production, in which even the credit system is accompanied by a prevalence of metallic circulation, it applies even to the most developed phase of the credit system to the extent that metallic circulation remains its basis. On the one hand, the additional production of precious metals may exert a disturbing influence on the prices of commodities according to whether it is abundant or scarce, not only in long, but also in very short intervals. On the other hand, the entire mechanism of credit is continually occupied in reducing the actual metallic circulation to a relatively more and more decreasing minimum by means of sundry operations, methods, and technical devices. To the same extent are the artificiality of the entire mechanism and the possibility of disturbing its normal flow increased.

It may be that the different B, B', B'', etc., (I), whose virtual new capital enters upon its active function, are compelled to buy from one another their product (portions of their surplus-product) or to sell it to one another. In that case the money advanced by them for the circulation of their surplus-product flows back under normal conditions to the different B's in the same proportion in which they advanced it for the circulation of their respective commodities. If the money circulates as a medium of payment, then only balances are to be paid so far as the alternate purchases and sales do not cover one another. But it is important to assume here, as everywhere, metallic circulation in its simplest form, because then the flux and reflux, the balancing of accounts, in short all elements appearing as consciously directed processes under the credit system, appear as forms independent of the credit system, show themselves in their primitive form instead of their later, reflected, one.

C. The Additional Variable Capital.

Hitherto we have been dealing only with additional constant capital. Now we must direct our attention to a consideration of the additional variable capital.

We have explained at great length in Volume I that labour-power is always held available under the capitalist system of production, and that more labour can be set in motion, if necessary, without increasing the number of labourers, or quantity of labour-power, employed. We need not detail this any further for the present, but assume without ceremony that the portion of the newly created money-capital which is to be converted into variable capital will always find as much labour-power as it cares to transform. It has also been explained in Volume I that a certain capital may expand its volume of production within certain limits without any accumulation. But now we are dealing with the accumulation of capital in the strict meaning of the term, so that the expansion of production is conditioned on the conversion of surplus-value into additional capital, and thus on an expansion of the basis of productive capital.

The gold producer can accumulate a portion of his golden surplus-value as a virtual money-capital. As soon as it reaches a sufficient volume, he can transform it directly into new variable capital, without first selling his surplus-product. In the same way he can convert it into the elements of constant capital. But in this last case, he must find the material elements of constant capital at hand. This may be accomplished by having each producer working to stock his supply, as was hitherto assumed, and then bringing his finished product on the market, or by having them work to fill orders. The actual expansion of production, that is to say, the surplus-product, is assumed in either case, in the one case as actually on hand, in the other as virtually available, because ordered.

Section 2. Accumulation in Department II.

We have hitherto assumed that the capitalists A, A', A", etc., (I), sell their surplus-product to the capitalists B, B', B", etc., who belong to the same department. But take it now that A (I) converts his surplus-product into gold by selling it to a capitalist B in Department II. This can be done only by the sale of means of production on the part of A (I) to B (II) without a subsequent purchase of articles of consumption; in other words, only by a one-sided sale on A's part. Now we have seen that II c cannot be converted into the natural form of productive constant capital unless not only I v, but also at least a portion of I s, is exchanged for a portion of II c, which II c exists in the form of articles of consumption. But now that A has converted his I s into gold by making this exchange impossible and withdrawing the money obtained from II c out of circulation, instead of spending it for articles of consumption of II c, there is indeed on the part of A (I) a formation of additional virtual money-capital, but on the other hand there is a corresponding portion of the value of the constant capital B (II) held in the form of commodity-capital, unable to transform itself into natural productive constant capital. In other words, a portion of the commodities of B (II), and at that a portion which must be sold if he wishes to reconvert his entire constant capital into its productive form, has become unsaleable. To that extent there is an overproduction, which clogs reproduction, even on the same scale.

In this case, the additional virtual money-capital on the side of A (I) is indeed a gilded form of surplus-product (surplus-value), but the surplus-product (surplus-value) as such is as yet but a phenomenon of simple reproduction, not of reproduction on an expanded scale.

In order that the reproduction of II c may take place on the same scale, I (v + s) must ultimately be exchanged for II c, and this applies at all events to a portion of I s. By the sale of his surplus-product to B (II), A (I) has supplied to B (II) a certain portion of the value of constant capital in its natural form. But at the same time he has rendered an equal portion of the value of the commodities of B (II) unsaleable by withdrawing the money from circulation and not making a compensating purchase. Hence, if we view the entire social reproduction, which comprises both the capitalists of I and II, then the conversion of the surplus-product of A (I) into a virtual money-capital implies the impossibility of reconverting an equal portion of the value of the commodity-capital of B (II) into productive (constant) capital, in other words, not a virtual production on an enlarged scale, but an obstruction of simple reproduction, a deficit in the simple reproduction. As the formation and sale of the surplus-product of A (I) are normal phenomena of simple reproduction, we have here even on the basis of simple reproduction the following mutually interdependent phenomena: the formation of virtual additional money-capital in Department I (implying underconsumption in Department II); the stagnation of commodities of Department II which cannot be reconverted into productive capital (implying a relative overproduction in Department II); a surplus of money-capital in Department I and a deficit in the reproduction of Department II.

Without pausing any longer at this point, we simply repeat that we had assumed in the analysis of simple reproduction that the entire surplus-value of I and II is spent as revenue. As a matter of fact, however, one portion of the surplus-value is spent as revenue, and another is converted into capital. Actual accumulation can take place only on this condition. That accumulation should take place at the expense of consumption, is, as a general assumption, an illusion contradicting the nature of capitalist production. For it takes for granted that the aim and compelling motive of capitalist production is consumption, instead of the gain of surplus-value and its capitalisation, in other words, accumulation.

* * *

Let us now take a closer look at the accumulation in Department II.

The first difficulty with reference to II c, that is to say the conversion of an element of the commodity-capital of II into the natural form of constant capital of II, concerns simple reproduction.

Let us take the formula previously used.

(1000 v + 1000 s) I are exchanged for 2000 II c.

Now, if one half of the surplus-product of I, or 500 s, is reincorporated in Department I as constant capital, then this portion, being detained in Department I, cannot take the place of any portion of II c. Instead of being converted into articles of consumption, it is made to serve as an additional means of production in Department I itself (and it must be noted that in this section of the circulation between I and II the exchange is actually mutual, consisting of a double change of position, different from the substitution of 1000 I v for 1000 II c by the labourers of I). It cannot perform this function simultaneously in I and II. The capitalist cannot spend the value of his surplus-product for articles of consumption, and at the same time consume the surplus-product itself productively, by incorporating it in his productive capital. Instead of 2000 I (v + s), only 1500 are exchangeable for 2000 II c, namely 1000 v + 500 s of I. But 500 I c cannot be reconverted from the form of commodities into productive constant capital of II. Hence there would be an overproduction in Department II, equal in volume to the expansion of production in Department I. This overproduction of II might react to such an extent on Department I that even the reflux of the 1000 v spent by the labourers of I for articles of consumption of II might take place but partially, so that these 1000 would not return to the hands of the capitalists of I in the form of variable money-capital. In that case, these capitalists would be hampered even in reproduction on a simple scale by the mere attempt of expanding it. And it must be remembered in this connection that Department I had actually resumed only simple reproduction, and that only the elements classified in our diagram were differently grouped with a view of expanding in the future, say, next year.

One might attempt to circumvent this difficulty in the following way: the 500 II c which are held by the capitalists, and cannot be immediately converted into productive capital, do not by any means represent any overproduction, but are, on the contrary, a necessary element of reproduction, which we have so far neglected. We have seen that a money supply must be accumulated at many points by withdrawing it from circulation, either for the purpose of facilitating the formation of new money-capital in Department I, or to the end of temporarily holding the gradually depreciating portion of the fixed capital in the form of money. But since we have placed all the available money and commodities exclusively into the hands of the capitalists of I and II, when we made up our diagram, eliminating merchants, money-changers, and bankers, and all merely consuming and not directly producing classes, it follows that the formation of supplies of commodities in the hands of their respective producers is here indispensable in order to keep the machinery of reproduction in motion. The 500 II c now held in stock by the capitalists of II therefore represent the supply of articles of consumption by which the continuity of the process of consumption included in the process of reproduction is promoted. This means in the present case the transition from this year into next. The fund for consumption, which is as yet in the hands of its sellers and producers cannot fall to the point of zero and begin with zero next year, any more than such a thing can take place in the transition from today to tomorrow. Since new supplies of commodities must be continually accumulated, even though their volume may differ, our capitalist producers of Department II must have a reserve capital, which enables them to continue their process of production, although one portion of their productive capital is temporarily tied up in the shape of commodities. Our assumption is all the time that they combine the business of a merchant with that of a producer. Hence they must also have at their disposal an additional money-capital, which would be in the hands of merchants, if the various functions in the process of reproduction were distributed among independent capitalists.

But we would reply to this argument: (1) That the forming of such supplies and the necessity for it applies to all capitalists, those of I as well as of II. Considering them in their capacity as sellers of commodities, they differ only by the fact that they sell different kinds of commodities. A supply of commodities of II implies a previous supply of commodities of I. If we neglect this supply on one side, we must also do so on the other. But if we count them in on both sides, the problem is not altered in any way. (2) Just as this year closes on the side of II with a supply of commodities for next year, so it was opened by a supply of commodities on the same side, taken over from last year. In the analysis of annual reproduction, reduced to its abstract form, we must therefore strike it out at both ends. By leaving this year in possession of its entire production, including the supply held for next year, we take from it the supply of commodities transferred from last year, and thus we have actually to deal with the aggregate product of an average year as the object of our analysis. (3) The simple circumstance that the difficulty which must be overcome did not show itself in the analysis of simple reproduction proves that it is a specific phenomenon due merely to the different arrangement of the elements of Department I with a view to reproduction, an arrangement without which reproduction on an expanded scale cannot take place at all.

Section 3. Diagrammatic Presentation of Accumulation.

We now study reproduction by means of the following diagram:

Diagram a) I. 4000 c + 1000 v + 1000 s = 6000
           II. 1500 c + 376 v + 376 s = 2252   Total, 8252

We note in the first place that the total volume of the annual product is smaller than that of the first diagram, being 8252 instead of 9000. We might just as well assume a much larger sum, for instance one ten times larger. We have chosen a smaller sum than in our first diagram, in order to demonstrate that reproduction on an enlarged scale (which is here regarded merely as a production carried on with a larger investment of capital) has nothing to do with the absolute volume of the product, and that it implies merely a different arrangement, a different distribution of functions to the various elements of a certain product, so that it is but a simple reproduction so far as the value of the product is concerned. It is not the quantity, but the destination of the given elements of simple reproduction which is changed, and this change is the material basis of a subsequent reproduction on an enlarged scale.[2]

We might vary the diagram by changing the proportions between the variable and constant capital. For instance this way:

Diagram b) I. 4000 c + 875 v + 875 s = 5750
           II. 1750 c + 376 v + 376 s = 2502   Total, 8252

In this case, the diagram would be arranged for reproduction on a simple scale, so that the surplus-value would be entirely consumed as revenue, instead of being accumulated. In either case, that of (a) as well as (b), we have an annual product of the same value. Only (b) has the functions of its elements arranged in such a way that reproduction is resumed on the same scale, while in the case of (a) the arrangement forms the material basis of reproduction on an enlarged scale. For in the case of (b), the factors (875 v + 875 s) I, equal to 1750 I (v + s), are exchanged without any remainder for 1750 II c, while in the case of (a), the exchange of (1000 v + 1000 s) I, equal to 2000 (v + s) I, for 1500 II c leaves a surplus of 500 I s for accumulation in Department I.

Now let us analyse diagram (a) closer. Let us assume that both I and II accumulate one half of their surplus-value, that is to say, convert it into an additional element of capital instead of spending it as revenue. When one half of 1000 I s, or 500, are accumulated in one form or another, that is to say, invested as additional money-capital, converted into additional productive capital, then only (1000 v + 500 s) I are spent as revenue. Hence 1500 is here inserted as the normal size of II c. We need not examine the exchange between 1500 I (v + s) and

1500 II c any more, because this has already been done under the head of simple reproduction. Nor does 4000 I c require any attention, since its re-arrangement was likewise discussed under the head of simple reproduction, although this rearrangement is now preparing for a new reproduction on an enlarged scale.

The only thing which remains for us to examine is 500 I s and (376 v + 376 s) II, both as regards the internal conditions of the two departments and the movements between them. Since we have assumed that Department II is likewise accumulating one half of its surplus-value, 188 are to be converted into capital, of which one fourth, or 47, or, to round it off, 48, are variable capital, so that 140 remain to be converted into constant capital.

Here we come across a new problem, whose very existence must appear strange to the current idea that commodities of one kind are exchanged for commodities of another kind, or commodities for money and the same money for commodities of another kind. The 140 II c can be converted into productive capital only by exchanging them for commodities of I s of the same value. It is a matter of course that that portion of I s which must be exchanged for II s must consist of means of production, which may either be fit for service in the production of both I and II, or exclusively adapted to the production of II. This change of place can be made only by means of a one-sided purchase on the part of II, as the entire remaining surplus-product of 500 I s, which we shall presently examine, is reserved for accumulation in Department I and cannot be exchanged for commodities of II; in other words, it cannot be simultaneously accumulated and consumed by I. Therefore Department II must buy 140 I s for cash without recovering this money by a subsequent sale of its commodities to I. And this is a process which is continually repeated in every new annual production, so far as it is reproduction on an enlarged scale. Where does II get the money for this?

It rather seems as though Department II were a very unprofitable field for the formation of new money-capital, by means of simple hoarding, which accompanies actual accumulation and is its basis under capitalist production.

We have first 376 II v. The money-capital of 376, advanced for labour-power, returns through the purchase of commodities of II continually as variable capital to the capitalists of II. This continually repeated departure from and return to the starting point, the pocket of the capitalist, does not add in any way to the money moving in this cycle. This, then, is not a source of the accumulation of money. Nor can this money be withdrawn from circulation in order to form a hoard, or virtual new money-capital.

But stop! Isn't there a chance to make a little profit?

We must not forget that class II has the advantage over class I that its labourers must buy back from it the commodities produced by themselves. Department II is a buyer of labour-power and at the same time a seller of the commodities to the owners of the labour-power employed by it. Department II, then, may do two things.

(1) It may depress the wages below its average level, and this privilege it shares with Department I. By this means a portion of the money serving in the function of variable capital is released, and if this process is continually repeated, it may become a normal source of hoarding, and thus of virtual additional money-capital in Department II. Of course we are not referring to a casual stolen profit here, since we are speaking of a normal formation of capital. But it must not be forgotten that the wages actually paid (which determine the magnitude of the variable capital under normal conditions) do not depend on the benevolence of the capitalists, but must be paid under certain conditions. This does away with this expedient as a source of additional money. If we assume that 376 v is the variable capital at the disposal of Department II, we cannot suddenly substitute the hypothesis that the capitalists pay only 350 v instead of 376 v, merely because we are confronted by a new problem.

(2) On the other hand, Department II, taken as a whole, has the above-mentioned advantage over I that it is at the same time a buyer of labour-power and a seller of commodities to its own labourers. Every industrial country furnishes the most tangible proofs to what extent this may be exploited, by paying nominally the normal wages, but grabbing, or in plain words, stealing back a large portion without a corresponding equivalent in wages; by accomplishing the same thing either through the truck system, or through a falsification of the medium of circulation (perhaps in a way that cannot be punished by law). England and America furnish such instances. (Illustrate this by some striking examples.) This is the same operation as under (1), only disguised and carried out by a detour. Therefore it must likewise be rejected as an explanation of the present problem. The question is here of actually paid, not of nominal wages.

We see that some extraordinary disfigurations on the face of capitalism cannot be used in an objective analysis of the mechanism of capitalism as an excuse to get over some theoretical difficulties. But strange to say, the great majority of my bourgeois critics score me as though I had wronged the capitalists by assuming in Volume I of this work that they really pay labour-power at its value, a thing which they rarely do! (Here I may exercise some of the magnanimity attributed to me by quoting Schaeffle.)

In short, we cannot accomplish anything with 376 II v for the solution of this question.

But it seems to be still more impossible to do anything with 376 II s. Here the capitalists of the same department are standing face to face, mutually buying and selling their articles of consumption. The money required for these transactions serves only as a medium of circulation and must flow back to the interested parties in the normal course of things, to the extent that they have advanced it to the circulation, in order to pass again and again over the same course.

There seem to be only two ways by which this money can be withdrawn from circulation for the purpose of forming virtual additional money-capital. Either one portion of the capitalists of II cheats the others and thus robs them of their money. We know that no preliminary expansion of the circulating medium is necessary for the formation of new money-capital. All that is necessary is that money should be withdrawn from circulation by certain parties and hoarded. It would not alter the case, if this money were stolen, so that the formation of additional money-capital on the part of a portion of the capitalists of II would be accompanied by a positive loss of money on the part of others. The cheated capitalists would have to live a little less gaily, that would be all.

Or, a certain portion of II s, represented by necessities of life, might be directly converted into new variable capital of Department II. How that is done, we shall examine at the close of this chapter (in Section D).

*   *   *

A. First Illustration.

A. Diagram of Simple Reproduction.
>   I. 4000 c + 1000 v + 1000 s = 6000
>   II. 2000 c + 500 v + 500 s = 300   Total, 9000

B. Initial Diagram for Accumulation on an Expanded Scale.
>   I. 4000 c + 1000 v + 1000 s = 6000
>   II. 1500 c + 750 v + 750 s = 3000   Total, 9000

Assuming that in diagram B one half of the surplus-value of I, amounting to 500, is accumulated, we have first to accomplish the change of place between (1000 v + 500 s) I, or 1500 I (v + s), and 1500 II c. Department I then keeps 4000 c and 500 s, the last sum being accumulated. The exchange between (1000 v + 1000 s) I and 1500 II c is a process of simple reproduction, which has been examined previously.

Let us now assume that 400 of the 500 I s are to be converted into constant capital, and 100 into variable capital. The transactions within the 400 s of I, which are to be capitalised, have already been discussed. They can be immediately annexed to I c, and in that case we get in Department I

4400 c + 1000 v + 100 s (these last to be converted into 100 v).

Department II buys from I for the purpose of accumulation the 100 I s (existing in means of production), which thus become additional constant capital in Department II, while the 100 in money, which this department pays for them, are converted into the money-form of the additional variable capital of I. We then have for I a capital of 4400 c + 1100 v (these last in money), a total of 5500.

Department II has now 1600 c for its constant capital. In order to be able to operate this, it must advance 50 v in money for the purchase of new labour-power, so that its variable capital grows from 750 to 800. This expansion of the constant and variable capital of II by a total of 150 is supplied out of its surplus-value. Hence only 600 of the 750 II s remain for the consumption of the capitalists of II, whose annual product is now distributed as follows:

II. 1600 c + 800 v + 600 s (fund for consumption), a total of 3000.

The 150 s, produced in articles of consumption, which have been converted into (100 c + 50 v) II, pass entirely into the consumption of the labourers in this form, 100 being consumed by the labourers of I (100 I v), and 50 by the labourers of II (50 II v), as explained above. Department II, where the total product is prepared in a form suitable for accumulation, must indeed reproduce surplus-value in the form of necessary articles of consumption exceeding the other portions by 100. If reproduction really starts on an expanded scale, then the 100 of variable money-capital of I flow back to II through the hands of the labourers of I, while II transfers 100 s in commodities to I and at the same time 50 in commodities to its own labourers.

The change made in the arrangement for the purpose of accumulation now presents the following aspect:

I. 4400 c + 1100 v + 500 fund for consumption = 6000
II. 1600 c + 800 v + 600 fund for consumption = 3000
Total, as before,   9000

Of these amounts, the following are capital:

I. 4400 c + 1100 v (money) = 5500
II. 1600 c + 800 v (money) = 2400   Total, 7900

while production started out with

I. 4000 c + 1000 v = 5000
II. 1500 c + 750 v = 2250   Total, 7250

Now, if actual accumulation takes place on this basis, that is to say, if reproduction is actually undertaken with this increased capital, we obtain at the end of next year:

I. 4400 c + 1100 v + 1100 s = 6600 ⎱
II. 1600 c + 800 v + 800 s = 3200 ⎰ Total, 9800

Then let Department I continue accumulation at the same ratio, so that 550 s are spent as revenue, and 550 s accumulated. In that case, 1100 I v are first replaced by 1100 I c, and 550 I s must be realised in an equal amount of commodities of II, making a total of 1650 I (v + s). But the constant capital of II, which is to be replaced, amounts only to 1600, and the remaining 50 must be made up out of 800 II s. Leaving aside the money aspect of the matter, we have as a result of this transaction:

I. 4400 c + 550 s (to be capitalised); furthermore, realised in commodities of II for the fund for consumption of the capitalists and labourers of I, 1650 (v + s).

II. 1650 c (50 added from II s as indicated above) + 800 v + 750 s (fund for the consumption of the capitalists).

But if the old proportion is maintained in II between v and c, then 25 v additional must be advanced for 50 c, and these must be taken from 750 s. Then we have

II. 1650 c + 825 v + 725 s.

In Department I, 550 s must be capitalised. If the former proportion is maintained, 440 of this amount form constant capital, and 110 variable capital. These 110 must be eventually taken out of 725 II s, that is to say, articles of consumption to the value of 110 are consumed by the labourers of I instead of the capitalists of II, so that the latter are compelled to capitalise these 110 s which they cannot consume. This leaves 615 II s of the 725 II s. But if II thus converts these 110 into additional constant capital, it requires an additional variable capital of 55. This again must be taken out of its surplus value. Subtracting this amount from 615 II s, we find that only 560 II s remain for the consumption of the capitalists of II, and we obtain the following values of capital after accomplishing all actual and potential transfers:

I. (4400c + 440c) + (1100v + 110v) = 4840c + 1210v　　　= 6050
II. (1600c + 50c + 110c) + (800v + 25v + 55v) = 1760c + 880v = 2640
　　　　　　　　　　　　　　　　　　　Total　　8690

If things are to proceed normally, accumulation in II must take place more rapidly than in I, because that portion of I (v + s) which must be converted into commodities of II c, would otherwise grow more rapidly than II c, for which it can alone be exchanged.

If reproduction is continued on this basis and with otherwise unchanged conditions, then we obtain at the end of the following year:

I. 4840 c + 1210 v + 1210 s = 7260 } Total, 10,780
II. 1760 c + 880 v + 880 s = 3520

If the rate of division of the surplus-value remains unchanged, then the capitalists of I have first to spend as revenue 1210 v and one-half of s, or 605, a total of 1815. This revenue fund is again larger than II c by 55. These 55 must be taken from 880 s, leaving 825. Furthermore, the conversion of 55 II s into II c implies another deduction from II s for a corresponding variable capital of 27.5, leaving for consumption 797.5 IIs.

Department I has now to capitalise 605 s. Of these 484 are constant, and 121 variable capital. The last named sum, deducted from 797.5 II s, leaves 676.5 II s. Department II, then, converts another 121 into constant capital and requires another variable capital of 60.5 for it, which likewise comes out of 676.5 II s, leaving for consumption 616.

Then we have the following capitals:

I. Constant capital : 4840 + 484 = 5324.
Variable capital : 1210 + 121 = 1331.
II. Constant capital : 1760 + 55 + 121 = 1936.
Variable capital: 880 + 27.5 + 60.5 = 968.

Totals: I. 5324 c + 1331 v = 6655   Grand total 9559
II. 1936 c + 968 v = 2904

And at the end of the year the product is

I. 5324 c + 1331 v + 1331 s = 7986   Total, 11,858
II. 1936 c + 968 v + 968 s = 3872

Repeating the same calculation and rounding off the fractions, we get at the end of the following year the product:

I. 5856 c + 1464 v + 1464 s = 8784   Total, 13,033
II. 2129 c + 1065 v + 1065 s = 4249

And at the end of the following year:

I. 6442 c + 1610 v + 1610 s = 9662   Total, 14,348
II. 2342 c + 1172 v + 1172 s = 4686

In the course of four years of reproduction on an expanded scale the aggregate capital of I and II has risen from 5400 c + 1750 v = 7150 to 8784 c + 2782 v = 11,566, in other words at the rate of 100: 160. The total surplus-value was originally 1750, it is now 2782. The consumed surplus-value was originally 500 for I and 535 for II, a total of 1035. In the last year it was 732 for I and 985 for II, a total of 1690 [sic]. It has therefore grown at the rate of 100:163.

* * *

B. Second Illustration.

Now take the annual product of 9000, which is altogether a commodity-capital in the hands of the industrial capitalist class, a form in which the average ratio of the variable to the constant capital is that of 1:5. This presupposes a considerable development of capitalist production and accordingly of the productivity of social labour, a previous expansion of the scale of production to a considerable extent, and finally a development of all circumstances which bring about a relative overpopulation among the working class. The annual product will then be divided as follows, after rounding off the various fractions:

$$\left. \begin{array}{l} \text{I. } 5000 \text{ c} + 1000 \text{ v} + 1000 \text{ s} = 7000 \\ \text{II. } 1430 \text{ c} + 285 \text{ v} + 285 \text{ s} = 2000 \end{array} \right\} \text{Total, } 9000$$

Now take it that the capitalist class of I consumes one-half of its surplus-value, or 500, and accumulates the other half. In that case (1000 v + 500 s) I, or 1500, must be converted into 1500 II c. Since II c amounts to only 1430, it is necessary to take 70 from the surplus-value. Subtracting this sum from 285 II s leaves 215 II s. Then we have:

I. 5000 c + 500 s (to be capitalised) + 1500 (v + s) in the fund set aside for consumption by capitalists and labourers.

II. 1430 c + 70 s (to be capitalised) + 285 v + 215 s.

As 70 II s are directly annexed by II c, a variable capital of 70/5, or 14, is required to set this additional constant capital in motion. These 14 must come out of the 215 s, so that only 201 remain, and we have:

II. (1430 c + 70 c) + (285 v + 14 v) + 201 s.

The disposal of 1500 I (v + 1/2 s) is a process of simple reproduction, and this has been dealt with. However, a few peculiarities remain to be noted here, which arise from the fact that in reproduction on an expanding scale I (v + 1/2 s) is not made up solely by way of II c, but by II c plus a portion of II s.

It goes without saying that as soon as we assume a process of accumulation, I (v + s) is greater than II c, not equal to II c, as it is in simple reproduction. For in the first place, Department I incorporates a portion of its own surplus-product in its productive capital, and converts five-sixths of it into constant capital, so that it cannot exchange these five-sixths simultaneously for articles of consumption of Department II. In the second place, Department I has to supply out of its surplus-product the material for the accumulation of the constant capital of II, just as II has to supply I with the material for the variable capital, which sets in motion a portion of the surplus-product of I used as additional constant capital. We know that the actual variable capital consists of labour-power, and therefore the additional must consist of the same thing. It is not the capitalist of I who among other things buys from II a supply of necessities of life for his labourers, or accumulates them for this purpose, as the slaveholder had to do. It is the labourers themselves who trade with II. But this does not prevent the capitalist from regarding the articles of consumption of his eventual additional labour-power as so many means of production and maintenance of that labour-power, or the natural form of his variable capital. His own immediate operation, in the present case that of Department I, consists in merely storing up the new money-capital required for the purchase of additional labour-power. As soon as he has incorporated this labour-power in his productive capital, the money becomes a medium for the purchase of commodities of II on the part of this labour-power, which must find these articles of consumption at hand.

By the way, the capitalist and his press are often dissatisfied with the way in which the labourer spends his money and with the commodities of II for which he spends it. On such occasions the capitalist philosophises, babbles of culture, and dabbles in philanthropical talk, for instance after the manner of Mr Drummond, the Secretary of the British Legation in Washington. According to him, *The Nation* (a journal) contained on the last of October, 1879, an interesting article, which contained the following passages 'The labourers have not kept step in their civilisation with the progress of inventions; a mass of objects have become accessible to them which they do not know how to make use of, and for which they do not create a market.' (Every capitalist naturally wants the labourer to buy his commodities.) 'There is no reason why the labourer should not desire as much comfort as the clergyman, the lawyer, and the physician, who earn the same amount as he.' (This class of clergymen, lawyers, and physicians have indeed to be satisfied with wishing for a good many comforts!) 'But he does not do so. The question is still, how he may be raised as a consumer by a rational and healthy method; not an easy question, since his whole ambition does not reach beyond a reduction of his hours of labour, and the demagogue incites him to this rather than to elevating his condition by an improvement of his intellectual and moral qualities.' (*Reports of H. M.'s Secretaries of Embassy and Legation on the Manufactures, Commerce, etc., of the countries in which they reside*. London, 1879, page 404.)

Long hours of labour seem to be the secret of the rational and healthy method, which is to elevate the condition of the labourer by an improvement of his intellectual and moral faculties and to make a rational consumer of him. In order to become a rational consumer of the commodities of the capitalist, he should above all begin to let the capitalist consume his labour-power irrationally and unhygienically – but the demagogue prevents him! What the capitalist means by a rational consumption, is evident wherever he is condescending enough to engage directly in the trade with his own labourers, in the truck system, which includes also among other lines the supplying of homes to the labourers, so that the capitalist is at the same time a landlord.

The same Drummond, whose beautiful soul is enamoured of the capitalist attempts to elevate the working class, tells in the same report among other things of the cotton goods manufacture in the Lowell and Lawrence Mills. The boarding and lodging houses for the factory girls belong to the company that owns the factories. The landladies of these houses are in the pay of the same company and act according to its instructions. No girl is permitted to stay out after 10 p.m. Then comes a gem: the special police of the company patrol the surrounding country, in order to prevent a violation of this rule. After 10 p.m., no girl can leave or enter any of these houses. No girl can live anywhere but on the land of the company, and every house on this land brings about 10 dollars per week in rent. And now we see the rational consumer in his full glory: 'But since the omnipresent piano is found in many of the best lodging houses of the working girls, music, singing, and dancing play a prominent role at least among those, who after ten hours of unremitting labour at the loom need a change after this monotony rather than actual rest.' (page 412) But the main secret of making a rational consumer of the labourer is yet to be told. Mr Drummond visits the cutlery factory of Turner's Falls, Connecticut River, and Mr Oakman, the treasurer of the company, after telling him that especially American table knives beat the English goods in quality, continues: 'But we shall beat England also in the matter of prices, we are ahead of it in quality even now, that is acknowledged; but we must have lower prices, and we shall get them as soon as we get our steel cheaper and bring down our labour.' (427). A reduction of wages and long hours of labour, that is the essence of the rational and healthy method which is to elevate the labourer to the dignity of a rational consumer, in order that he may create a market for the mass of objects which civilisation and the progress of invention have made accessible to him.

*　　*　　*

To repeat, then, just as Department I has to supply the additional constant capital of II out of its surplus-value, so II supplies the additional variable capital for I. Department II accumulates for itself and for I, so far as the variable capital is concerned, by reproducing a greater portion of its total product, especially of its surplus-product, in the shape of necessary articles of consumption.

I (v + s), in the case of production on the basis of increasing capital, must be equal to II c plus that portion of the surplus-product which is re-incorporated as capital, plus the additional portion of constant capital required for the expansion of the production of II; and the minimum of this expansion is that without which actual accumulation, that is to say, an actual expansion of the production of I, is impossible.

Reverting now to the case which we examined last, we find that it has the peculiarity that II c is smaller than I (v + 1/2 s), smaller than that portion of the product of I which is spent as revenue for articles of consumption, so that a portion of the surplus-product of II, equal to 70, is at once realised for the purpose of disposing of the 1500 I (v + s). As for II c, equal to 1430, it must, other circumstances remaining the same, be reproduced out of an equal amount of I (v + s), in order that simple reproduction may take place, and to that extent we need not pay any more attention to it. It is different with the additional 70 II c. That which is for I merely an exchange of revenue for articles of consumption, is for II more than a mere reconversion of its constant capital from the form of commodity-capital into its natural form, as it is in simple reproduction, for it is a process of direct accumulation, a transformation of a portion of its surplus-product from the form of articles of consumption into that of constant capital. If I buys with £70 in money (money-reserve for the conversion of surplus-value) the 70 II s, and if II does not buy in exchange 70 I s, but accumulates the £70 as money-capital, then this money is indeed always the expression of an additional product (namely the surplus-product of II, the equivalent of which it is), although this is not a product which returns into the production; but in that case this accumulation of money on the part of II would be the evidence that 70 I s in means of production are unsaleable. There would be a relative overproduction in I, corresponding to a simultaneous break in the reproduction of II.

But apart from this, the following point must be noted: during the time in which the 70 in money, which came from I, have not as yet returned to it, or have but partially done so, by the purchase of 70 I s on the part of II, this 70 in money figures entirely or in part as additional virtual money-capital in the hands of II. This is true of every transaction between I and II, before the mutual replacement of their respective commodities has accomplished the reflux of the money to its starting point. But the money, under a normal condition of things, figures here only temporarily in this role. In the credit system, however, where all momentarily released money is to be used immediately as an active additional money-capital, such a temporarily released money-capital may be engaged, for instance, in new enterprises of I, while it still would have to liquidate additional products held in other enterprises. It must also be noted that the annexation of 70 I s to the constant capital of II requires at the same time an expansion of the variable capital of II to the extent of 14. This implies, similarly as it did in the direct incorporation of the surplus-product of I s in Capital I c, that the reproduction in II is already in process with a view to further capitalisation; in other words, it implies the expansion of that portion of the surplus-product, which consists of necessary articles of consumption.

*   *   *

The product of 9000, in the second illustration, must be distributed in the following manner for the purpose of reproduction, when 500 I s is to be capitalised. We merely consider the commodities in this case and leave aside the circulation of money.

I. 5000 c + 500 s (to be capitalised) + 1500 (v + s) fund for consumption, a total of 7000 in commodities.

II. 1500 c + 299 v + 201 s, a total of 2000 in commodities. Grand total, 9000 in commodities.

Capitalisation takes place in the following manner:

In Department I, the 500 s, which are capitalised, divide themselves into five-sixths, or 417 c, plus one-sixth, or 83 v. The 83 v draw an equal amount out of II s, which buys elements of constant capital and adds them to II c. An increase of II c by 83 implies an increase of II v by one-fifth of 83, or 17. We have, then, after this transaction,

$$
\begin{aligned}
&\text{I. } (5000 \text{ c} + 417 \text{ s}) + (1000 \text{ v} + 83 \text{ s}) = 5417 \text{ c} + 1083 \text{ v} && = 6500 \\
&\text{II. } (1500 \text{ c} + 83 \text{ s}) + (299 \text{ v} + 17 \text{ s}) = 1583 \text{ c} + 316 \text{ v} && = 1899 \\
&\hphantom{\text{II. }(1500 \text{ c} + 83 \text{ s})} \text{Total} && \hphantom{=}8399
\end{aligned}
$$

The capital in I has grown from 6000 to 6500, or by 1/12. That of II has grown from 1715 to 1899, or by nearly 1/9.

The reproduction on this basis in the second year brings the capital at the end of that year up to the following figures:

$$
\begin{aligned}
&\text{I. } (5417 \text{ c} + 452 \text{ s}) + (1083 \text{ v} + 90 \text{ s}) = 5869 \text{ c} + 1173 \text{ v} && = 7042 \\
&\text{II. } (1583 \text{ c} + 42 \text{ s} + 90 \text{ s}) + (816 \text{ v} + 8 \text{ s} + 18 \text{ s}) = 1715 \text{ c} + 342 \text{ v} && = 2057
\end{aligned}
$$

And at the end of the third year, we have as a product:

I. 5869 c + 1173 v + 1173 s.
II. 1715 c + 342 v + 342 s.

If Department I then accumulates as before one-half of its surplus-value, we find that I (v + 1/2 s), 1173 v + 587 (1/2 s), amount to 1760, more than the entire 1715 II c, namely an excess of 45. This must again be balanced by annexing an equal amount of means of production to II c, which thus grows by 45. This again requires an addition of one-fifth, or 9, to II v. Furthermore, the capitalised 587 I s are divided into five-sixths and one-sixth respectively, that is to say, 489 c and 98 v. These last 98 imply a new addition of 98 to the constant capital of II, and this again an increase of the variable capital of II by one-fifth, or 20. Then we have

I. $(5889 c + 489 s) c + (1173 v + 98 s) v = 6385 c + 1271 v \quad = 7629$
II. $(1715c + 45s + 98s) c + (342v + 9s + 20s) = 1858c + 371v \quad = 2229$
$$\text{Total capital} \quad 9858$$

In three years of reproduction on an increasing scale the total capital of I has grown from 6000 to 7629, and that of II from 1715 to 2229, or the total social capital from 7715 to 9858.

C. Exchange of II c Under Accumulation.

In the exchange of I (v + s) with II c we meet with different cases.

Under simple reproduction, both of them must be equal and take one another's places, otherwise simple reproduction cannot proceed smoothly, as we have seen.

Under reproduction on an expanded scale, it is above all the rate of accumulation which is important. In the preceding cases we had assumed that the rate of accumulation in Department I was equal to one-half of I s, and also that it remained constant from year to year. We changed merely the proportion in which this accumulated capital was divided between variable and constant capital. We then had three cases.

(1) I (v + 1/2 s) equal to II c, which is therefore smaller than I (v + s). This must always be the case, otherwise I cannot accumulate.

(2) I (v + 1/2 s) greater than II c. In this case the exchange is effected by adding a corresponding portion of II s to II c, so that this becomes equal to I (v + 1/2 s). In this case, the transaction in Department II is not a simple reproduction of its constant capital, but accumulation, an augmentation of its constant capital by that portion of its surplus-product which it exchanges for means of production of I. This augmentation implies at the same time a corresponding addition to the variable capital of II out of its own surplus-product.

(3) I (v + 1/2 s) smaller than II c. In this case Department II had not fully reproduced its constant capital by means of exchange and had to make good the deficit by a purchase from I. But this did not require any further accumulation of variable capital on the part of II, since its constant capital was brought only to its full size by this operation. On the other hand, that portion of the capitalists of I who accumulate

only additional money-capital, had already accomplished a part of this accumulation by this transaction.

The premise of simple reproduction, that I (v + s) is equal to II c, is irreconcilable with capitalist production, although this does not exclude the possibility that a certain year in an industrial cycle of 10 or 11 years may not show a smaller total production than the preceding year, so that there would not have been even a simple reproduction, compared to the preceding year. Indeed, considering the natural growth of population per year, simple reproduction could take place only in so far as a correspondingly larger number of unproductive servants would partake of the 1500 representing the aggregate surplus-product. But accumulation of capital, actual capitalist production, would be impossible under such circumstances. The fact of capitalist production therefore excludes the possibility of II c being equal to I (v + s). Nevertheless it might occur even under capitalist production that in consequence of the process of accumulation during a preceding number of periods of production II c might not only be equal, but even greater than I (v + s). This would mean an overproduction in II and could not be compensated in any other way than by a great crash, in consequence of which some capital of II would be transferred to I. It does not alter the relations of I (v + s), if a portion of the constant capital of II reproduces itself, as happens, for instance, in the employment of home-raised seeds in agriculture. This portion of II c has no more reference to the exchange between I and II than has I c. Nor does it alter the matter, if a portion of the products of II are of such a nature that they may serve as means of production in I. They are covered by a portion of the means of production supplied in II by I, and this portion must be deducted on both sides at the outset, if we wish to analyse without any obscuring interference the exchange between the two great departments of social production, the producers of means of production and the producers of articles of consumption.

To repeat, then, under capitalist production I (v + s) cannot be equal to II c; in other words, the two cannot balance. On the other hand, naming I s/x that portion of I s which is spent by the capitalists as revenue, we see that I (v + s/x) may be equal to, greater or smaller than, II c. But I (v + s/x) must always be smaller than II (c + s), namely, as much smaller as that portion of II s which must be consumed under all circumstances by the capitalist class of II.

It must be noted that in this presentation of accumulation the value of the constant capital, so far as it is a portion of the value of the commodity-capital, which it helped to produce, is not exactly represented. The fixed portion of the newly accumulated constant capital is transferred to the commodity-capital only gradually and periodically according to the different nature of these fixed elements. Wherever raw materials and half-wrought articles are employed in large quantities for the production of commodities, the commodity-capital therefore consists overwhelmingly of objects replacing circulating constant elements and variable capital. (On account of the turn-over of the circulating elements this method may nevertheless be adopted. It is then assumed that the circulating portion together with that portion of value which the fixed capital has transferred to it is turned so often during the year that the aggregate sum of the commodities supplied is equal in value to all the capital invested in the annual production.) But wherever only auxiliary materials are used for machine work, and no raw material, there v, the labour element, must reappear in the commodity-capital as its largest factor. While in the calculation of the rate of profit the surplus-value is figured on the total capital, regardless of whether the fixed elements transfer periodically much or little value to the product, the fixed portion of constant capital is included in the calculation of the value of any periodically created commodity-capital only to the extent that it yields a certain average of value to the product.

Section 4. Concluding Remarks.

The original source for the money of II is v + s of the gold producers in Department I, exchanged for a portion of II c. Only to the extent that the gold producer accumulates surplus-value or converts it into means of production of I; in other words, to the extent that he expands his production, does his v + s stay out of Department II. On the other hand, to the extent that the accumulation of gold on the part of the gold producer himself leads ultimately to an expansion of production, a portion of the surplus-value of gold production not spent as revenue passes into Department II as additional variable capital of the gold producers, promotes the accumulation of new hoards in II and supplies it with means by which to buy from I without having to sell to it immediately. From this money derived from I (v + s) of gold production must be deducted that portion of gold which is employed by certain lines of II as raw material, etc., in short as an element for building up their constant capital. An element of preliminary reproduction, for the purpose of future expanded production, is created for either I or II under the following conditions: for I, only when a portion of I s is sold one-sidedly, without a balancing purchase, to II and serves there as additional constant capital; for II, when the same case occurs on the part of I with reference to the variable capital;

furthermore when a portion of the surplus-value spent by I as revenue is not covered by II c, so that a portion of II s is bought with it and thus converted into money. If I $(v + s/x)$ is greater than II c, then II c need not for its simple reproduction make up in commodities of I what I has taken out of II s. The question is, to what extent hoarding may take place within the exchange of the capitalists of II among themselves, an exchange which can consist only of a mutual crossing of II s. We know that direct accumulation takes place within II by means of direct conversion of a portion of II s into variable capital (just as Department I converts a portion of I s directly into constant capital). In the various stages of accumulation within the different lines of business of II, and for the individual capitalists of these lines, the matter explains itself, with the self-understood modifications, in the same way as in I. One side is still engaged in hoarding and sells without buying, the other is on the point of actual expansion of reproduction and buys without selling. The additional variable money-capital is first advanced for additional labour-power, but this, in its turn, buys articles of consumption from the hoarding owners of the additional articles of consumption used by the labourers. To the extent that these owners hoard the money, it does not return to its point of departure.

Notes

Notes to Volume 1

Volume 1, Editor's Preface

1 *Le Capital, par Karl Marx. Traduction de M.J. Roy, entièrement revisée par l'auteur.* Paris. Lachatre. This translation, especially in the latter part of the book, contains considerable alterations in and additions to the text of the second German edition.

[2] At the quarterly meeting of the Manchester Chamber of Commerce, held this afternoon, a warm discussion took place on the subject of Free-trade. A resolution was moved to the effect that 'having waited in vain 40 years for other nations to follow the Free-trade example of England, this Chamber thinks the time has now arrived to reconsider that position.' The resolution was rejected by a majority of one only, the figures being 21 for, and 22 against. – *Evening Standard*, Nov. 1, 1886.

Volume 1, Author's Prefaces

[1] This is the more necessary, as even the section of Ferdinand Lassalle's work against Schulze-Delitzsch, in which he professes to give 'the intellectual quintessence' of my explanations on these subjects, contains important mistakes. If Ferdinand Lassalle has borrowed almost literally from my writings, and without any acknowledgement, all the general theoretical propositions in his economic works, e.g., those on the historical character of capital, on the connection between the conditions of production and the mode of production, &c., &c., even to the terminology created by me, this may perhaps be due to purposes of propaganda. I am here, of course, not speaking of his detailed working out and application of these propositions, with which I have nothing to do.

[2] On p.395 the author explains what he comprises under this head.

[3] *Geschichtliche Darstellung des Handels, der Gewerbe und des Ackerbaus, &,* von Gustav von Gülich. 5 vols., Jena, 1830–45

[4] See my work *Zur Kritik, &c.,* p.39.

[5] The mealy-mouthed babblers of German vulgar economy fell foul of the style of my book. No one can feel the literary shortcomings in *Das Kapital* more strongly than I myself. Yet I will for the benefit and the enjoyment of these gentlemen and their public quote in this connection one English and one Russian notice. The *Saturday Review*, always hostile to my views, said in its notice of the first edition: 'The presentation of the subject invests the driest economic questions with a certain peculiar charm.' The *St Petersburg Journal (Sankt-Petersburgskie Viedomosti),* in its issue of April 20, 1872, says: 'The presenation of the subject, with the exception of one or two exceptionally special parts, is distinguished by its comprehensibility by the general reader, its clearness, and, in spite of the scientific intricacy of the subject, by an unusual liveliness. In this respect the author in no way resembles . . . the majority of Germany scholars who . . . write their books in a language so dry and obscure that the heads of ordinary mortals are cracked by it.'

Volume 1, Part 1, Chapter 1

[1] Karl Marx, *Zur Kritik der Politischen Oekonomie*. Berlin, 1859, p.3.

[2] 'Desire implies want, it is the appetite of the mind, and as natural as hunger to the body . . . The greatest number (of things) have their value from supplying the wants of the mind.' Nicholas Barbon: *A Discourse Concerning Coining the New Money Lighter. In Answer to Mr Locke's Considerations*, &c., London, 1696, pp.2,3.

[3] 'Things have an intrinsick vertue' (this is Barbon's special term for value in use) 'which in all places have the same vertue; as the loadstone to attract iron' (l.c., p.6). The property which the magnet possesses of attracting iron, became of use only after by means of that property the polarity of the magnet had been discovered.

[4] 'The natural worth of anything consists in its fitness to supply the necessities, or serve the conveniencies of human life.' (John Locke, *Some Considerations on the Consequences of the Lowering of Interest*, 1691, in *Works* Edit. Lond., 1777, vol.ii, p.28.) In English writers of the 17th century we frequently find 'worth' in the sense of value in use, and 'value' in the sense of exchange value. This is quite in accordance with the spirit of a language that likes to use a Teutonic word for the actual thing, and a Romance word for its reflection.

[5] In bourgeois societies the economic *fictio juris* prevails, that every one, as a buyer, possesses an encyclopedic knowledge of commodities.

[6] '*La valeur consiste dans le rapport d'échange qui se trouve entre telle chose et telle autre, entre telle mesure d'une production et telle mesure d'une autre.*' (Le Trosne: *De l'Intérêt Social. Physiocrates*, Ed. Daire. Paris, 1846. p.889.)

[7] 'Nothing can have an intrinsick value.' (N. Barbon, l.c., p.6); or as Butler says –

'The value of a thing
is just as much as it will bring.'

[8] N. Barbon, l.c., p.53 and 7.

[9] 'The value of them (the necessaries of life), when they are exchanged the one for another, is regulated by the quantity of labour necessarily required, and commonly taken in producing them.' (*Some Thoughts on the Interest of Money in General, and Particularly in the Publick Funds, &.* Lond., p.36) This remarkable anonymous work written in the last century, bears no date. It is clear, however, from internal evidence that it appeared in the reign of George II, about 1739 or 1740.

[10] '*Toutes les productions d'un même genre ne forment proprement qu'une masse, dont le prix se détermine en général et sans regard aux circonstances particulières.*' (Le Trosne, l.c., p.893.)

[11] K. Marx. l.c., p.6.

[12] *Tutti i fenomeni dell'universo, sieno essi prodotti della mano dell'uomo, ovvero delle universali leggi della fisica, non ci danno idea di attuale creazione, ma unicamente di una modificazione della materia. Accostare e separare sono gli unici elementi che l'ingegno umano ritrova analizzando l'idea della riproduzione: e tanto e riproduzione di valore* (value in use, although Verri in this passage of his controversy with the Physiocrats is not himself quite certain of the kind of value he is speaking of) *e di ricchezze se la terra, l'aria e l'acqua ne' campi si trasmutino in grano, come se colla mano dell'uomo il glutine di un insetto si trasmuti in velluto ovvero alcuni pezzetti di metalio si organizzino a formare una ripetizione.*' – Pietro Verri, *Meditazioni sulla Economia Politica* [first printed in 1773] in Custodi's edition of the Italian Economists, *Parte Moderna*, t.xv, p.22.

[13] Comp. Hegel, *Philosophie des Rechts*. Berlin, 1840. p.250

[14] The reader must note that we are not speaking here of the wages or value that the labourer gets for a given labour-time, but of the value of the commodity in which that labour-time is materialised. Wages is a category that, as yet, has no existence at the present stage of our investigation.

[15] In order to prove that labour alone is that all-sufficient and real measure, by which at all times the value of all commodities can be estimated and compared, Adam Smith

says, 'Equal quantities of labour must at all times and in all places have the same value for the labourer. In his normal state of health, strength, and activity, and with the average degree of skill that he may possess, he must always give up the same portion of his rest, his freedom, and his happiness.' (*Wealth of Nations*, b.i. ch.v) On the one hand Adam Smith here (but not everywhere) confuses the determination of value by means of the quantity of labour expended in the production of commodities, with the determination of the values of commodities by means of the value of labour, and seeks in consequence to prove that equal quantities of labour have always the same value. On the other hand he has a presentiment, that labour, so far as it manifests itself in the value of commodities, counts only as expenditure of labour power, but he treats this expenditure as the mere sacrifice of rest, freedom, and happiness, not as at the same time the normal activity of living beings. But then, he has the modern wage-labourer in his eye. Much more aptly, the anonymous predecessor of Adam Smith, quoted above in Note 9, says 'one man has employed himself a week in providing this necessary of life . . . and he that gives him some other in exchange cannot make a better estimate of what is a proper equivalent, than by computing what cost him just as much labour and time which in effect is no more than exchanging one man's labour in one thing for a time certain, for another man's labour in another thing for the same time.' (l.c., p.39.) [The English language has the advantage of possessing different words for the two aspects of labour here considered. The labour which creates Use-Value, and counts qualitatively, is *Work*, as distinguished from Labour; that which creates Value and counts quantitatively, is *Labour* as distinguished from Work – Engels]

[16] The few economists, amongst whom is S. Bailey, who have occupied themselves with the analysis of the form of value, have been unable to arrive at any result, first, because they confuse the form of value with value itself; and second, because, under the coarse influence of the practical bourgeois, they exclusively give their attention to the quantitative aspect of the question. 'The command of quantity . . . constitutes value.' (*Money and its Vicissitudes*. London, 1837, p.11. By S. Bailey.)

[17] The celebrated Franklin, one of the first economists, after Wm. Petty, who saw through the nature of value, says: 'Trade in general being nothing else but the exchange of labour for labour, the value of all things is . . . most justly measured by labour.' (*The works of B. Franklin, &c.*, edited by Sparks. Boston, 1836, vol.ii, p.267.) Franklin is unconscious that by estimating the value of everything in labour, he makes abstraction from any difference in the sorts of labour exchanged, and thus reduces them all to equal human labour. But although ignorant of this, yet he says it. He speaks first of 'the one labour', then of 'the other labour', and finally of 'labour', without further qualification, as the substance of the value of everything.

[18] In a sort of way, it is with man as with commodities. Since he comes into the world neither with a looking glass in his hand, nor as a Fichtian philosopher, to whom 'I am I' is sufficient, man first sees and recognises himself in other men. Peter only establishes his own identity as a man by first comparing himself with Paul as being of like kind. And thereby Paul, just as he stands in his Pauline personality, becomes to Peter the type of the genus homo.

[19] Value is here, as occasionally in the preceding pages, used in sense of value determined as to quantity, or of magnitude of value.

[20] This incongruity between the magnitude of value and its relative expression has, with customary ingenuity, been exploited by vulgar economists. For example – 'Once admit that A falls, because B, with which it is exchanged, rises, while no less labour is bestowed in the meantime on A, and your general principle of value falls to the ground . . . If he [Ricardo] allowed that when A rises in value relatively to B, B falls in value relatively to A, he cut away the ground on which he rested his grand proposition, that the value of a commodity is ever determined by the labour embodied

in it, for if a change in the cost of A alters not only its own value in relation to B, for which it is exchanged, but also the value of B relatively to that of A, though no change has taken place in the quantity of labour to produce B, then not only the doctrine falls to the ground which asserts that the quantity of labour bestowed on an article regulates its value, but also that which affirms the cost of an article to regulate its value.' (J. Broadhurst: *Political Economy*, London, 1842, pp. 11 and 14.) Mr Broadhurst might just as well say: consider the fractions 10/20, 10/50, 10/100, &c., the number 10 remains unchanged, and yet its proportional magnitude, its magnitude relatively to the numbers 20, 50, 100 &c., continually diminishes. Therefore the great principle that the magnitude of a whole number, such as 10, is 'regulated' by the number of times unity is contained in it, falls to the ground. [The author explains in section 4 of this chapter, pp.80–81, note 2, what he understands by 'Vulgar Economy'. – Engels]

[21] Such expressions of relations in general, called by Hegel reflex-categories, form a very curious class. For instance, one man is king only because other men stand in the relation of subjects to him. They, on the contrary, imagine that they are subjects because he is king.

[22] F. L. A. Ferrier, sous-inspecteur des douanes, *Du gouvernement considéré dans ses rapports avec le commerce*, Paris, 1805; and Charles Ganilh, *Des Systèmes d'Économie Politique*, – 2nd ed., Paris, 1821.

[23] In Homer, for instance, the value of an article is expressed in a series of different things. *Iliad* vii. 472–475.

[24] For this reason, we can speak of the coat-value of the linen when its value is expressed in coats, or of its corn-value when expressed in corn, and so on. Every such expression tells us, that what appears in the use-values, cost, corn, &c., is the value of the linen. 'The value of any commodity denoting its relation in exchange, we may speak of it as ... corn-value, cloth-value, according to the commodity with which it is compared; and hence there are a thousand different kinds of value, as many kinds of value as there are commodities in existence, and all are equally real and equally nominal.' (*A Critical Dissertation on the Nature, Measures and Causes of Value: chiefly in reference to the writings of Mr Ricardo and his followers. By the author of Essays on the Formation, &c., of Opinions.* London, 1825, p.39.) S. Bailey, the author of this anonymous work, a work which in its day created much stir in England, fancied that, by thus pointing out the various relative expressions of one and the same value, he had proved the impossibility of any determination of the concept of value. However narrow his own views may have been, yet, that he laid his finger on some serious defects in the Ricardian Theory, is proved by the animosity with which he was attacked by Ricardo's followers. See the *Westminster Review* for example.

[25] It is by no means self-evident that this character of direct and universal exchangeability is, so to speak, a polar one, and as intimately connected with its opposite pole, the absence of direct exchangeability, as the positive pole of the magnet is with its negative counterpart. It may therefore be imagined that all commodities can simultaneously have this character impressed upon them, just as it can be imagined that all Catholics can be popes together. It is, of course, highly desirable in the eyes of the petit bourgeois, for whom the production of commodities is the *ne plus ultra* of human freedom and individual independence, that the inconveniences resulting from this character of commodities not being directly exchangeable, should be removed. Proudhon's socialism is a working out of this Philistine Utopia, a form of socialism which, as I have elsewhere shown, does not possess even the merit of originality. Long before his time, the task was attempted with much better success by Gray, Bray, and others. But, for all that, wisdom of this kind flourishes even now in certain circles under the name of 'science'. Never has any school played more tricks with the word science, than that of Proudhon, for

wo Begriffe fehlen,
Da stellt zur rechten Zeit ein Wort sich ein.

[26] Among the ancient Germans the unit for measuring land was what could be harvested in a day, and was called *Tagwerk, Tagwanne* (*jurnale,* or *terra jurnalis,* or *diornalis*), Mannsmaad, &c. (See G. L. von Maurer, *Einleitung zur Geschichte der Mark, &c.* Verfassung, Munchen, 1854, p.129 sq.)

[27] When, therefore, Galiani says: Value is a relation between persons – *La Ricchezza e una ragione tra due persone* – he ought to have added: a relation between persons expressed as a relation between things. (Galiani: *Della Moneta,* p.221, v. iii. of Custodi's collection of *Scrittori Classici Italiani di Economia Politica.* Parte Moderna, Milano 1803.)

[28] What are we to think of a law that asserts itself only by periodical revolutions? It is just nothing but a law of Nature, founded on the want of knowledge of those whose action is the subject of it.' (Friedrich Engels: *Umrisse zu einer Kritik der National-ökonomie,* in the *Deutsch-Französische Jahrbücher,* edited by Arnold Ruge and Karl Marx. Paris. 1844.)

[29] Even Ricardo has his stories *à la* Robinson. 'He makes the primitive hunter and the primitive fisher straightway, as owners of commodities, exchange fish and game in the proportion in which labour-time is incorporated in these exchange values. On this occasion he commits the anachronism of making these men apply to the calculation, so far as their implements have to be taken into account, the annuity tables in current use on the London Exchange in the year 1817. The parallelograms of Mr Owen appear to be the only form of society, besides the bourgeois form, with which he was acquainted.' (Karl Marx: *Zur Kritik, &c.,* pp.38,39)

[30] 'A ridiculous presumption has latterly got abroad that common property in its primitive form is specifically a Slavonian, or even exclusively Russian form. It is the primitive form that we can prove to have existed amongst Romans, Teutons, and Celts, and even to this day we find numerous examples, ruins though they be, in India. A more exhaustive study of Asiatic, and especially of Indian forms of common property, would show how from the different forms of primitive common property, different forms of its dissolution have been developed. Thus, for instance, the various original types of Roman and Teutonic private property are deducible from different forms of Indian common property.' (Karl Marx, *Zur Kritik, &c.,* p.10.)

[31] The insufficiency of Ricardo's analysis of the magnitude of value, and his analysis is by far the best, will appear from the 3rd and 4th books of this work. As regards value in general, it is the weak point of the classical school of Political Economy that it nowhere expressly and with full consciousness, distinguishes between labour, as it appears in the value of a product, and the same labour, as it appears in the use-value of that product. Of course the distinction is practically made, since this school treats labour, at one time under its quantitative aspect, at another under its qualitative aspect. But it has not the least idea, that when the difference between various kinds of labour is treated as purely quantitative, their qualitative unity or equality, and therefore their reduction to abstract human labour, is implied. For instance, Ricardo declares that he agrees with Destutt de Tracy in this proposition: 'As it is certain that our physical and moral faculties are alone our original riches, the employment of those faculties, labour of some kind, is our only original treasure, and it is always from this employment that all those things are created which we call riches . . . It is certain, too, that all those things only represent the labour which has created them, and if they have a value, or even two distinct values, they can only derive them from that (the value) of the labour from which they emanate.' (Ricardo, *The Principles of Pol. Econ.,* 3 Ed. Lond. 1821, p.334.) We would here only point out, that Ricardo puts his own more profound interpretation upon the words of Destutt. What the latter really says is, that on the one hand all things which constitute wealth represent the labour that creates them, but that

on the other hand, they acquire their 'two different values' (use-value and exchange value) from 'the value of labour'. He thus falls into the commonplace error of the vulgar economists, who assume the value of one commodity (in this case labour) in order to determine the values of the rest. But Ricardo reads him as if he had said, that labour (not the value of labour) is embodied both in use-value and exchange value. Nevertheless, Ricardo himself pays so little attention to the two-fold character of the labour which has a two-fold embodiment, that he devotes the whole of his chapter on 'Value and Riches, Their Distinctive Properties', to a laborious examination of the trivialities of a J. B. Say. And at the finish he is quite astonished to find that Destutt on the one hand agrees with him as to labour being the source of value, and on the other hand with J. B. Say as to the notion of value.

[32] It is one of the chief failings of classical economy that it has never succeeded, by means of its analysis of commodities, and, in particular, of their value, in discovering that form under which value becomes exchange value. Even Adam Smith and Ricardo, the best representatives of the school, treat the form of value as a thing of no importance, as having no connection with the inherent nature of commodities. The reason for this is not solely because their attention is entirely absorbed in the analysis of the magnitude of value. It lies deeper. The value form of the product of labour is not only the most abstract, but is also the most universal form, taken by the product in bourgeois production and stamps that production as a particular species of social production, and thereby gives it its special historical character. If then we treat this mode of production as one eternally fixed by Nature for every state of society, we necessarily overlook that which is the *differentia specifica* of the value form, and consequently of the commodity-form, and of its further developments, money form, capital-form, &c. We consequently find that economists, who are thoroughly agreed as to labour-time being the measure of the magnitude of value, have the most strange and contradictory ideas of money, the perfected form of the general equivalent. This is seen in a striking manner when they treat of banking, where the commonplace definitions of money will no longer hold water. This led to the rise of a restored mercantile system (Ganilh, &c.), which sees in value nothing but a social form, or rather the unsubstantial ghost of that form. Once for all I may here state, that by classical Political Economy, I understand that economy which, since the time of W. Petty, has investigated the real relations of production in bourgeois society in contradistinction to vulgar economy, which deals with appearances only, ruminates without ceasing on the materials long since provided by scientific economy, and there seeks plausible explanations of the most obtrusive phenomena, for bourgeois daily use, but for the rest, confines itself to systematising in a pedantic way, and proclaiming for everlasting truths, the trite ideas held by the self-complacent bourgeoisie with regard to their own world, to them the best of all possible worlds.

[33] '*Les économistes ont une singulière manière de procéder. Il n'y a pour eux que deux sortes d'institutions, celles de l'art et celles de la nature. Les institutions de la feodalité sont des institutions artificielles, celles de la bourgeoisie sont des institutions naturelles. Ils ressemblent en ceci aux théologiens, qui eux aussi établissent deux sortes de réligions. Toute réligion qui n'est pas la leur, est une invention des hommes tandis que leur propre réligion est une émanation de Dieu − Ainsi il y a eu de l'histoire, mais il n'y en a plus.*' (Karl Marx. *Misère de la Philosophie. Réponse à la Philosophie de la Misère par M. Proudhon*, 1847, p.113.) Truly comical is M. Bastiat, who imagines that the ancient Greeks and Romans lived by plunder alone. But when people plunder for centuries, there must always be something at hand for them to seize; the objects of plunder must be continually reproduced. It would thus appear that even Greeks and Romans had some process of production, consequently, an economy, which just as much constituted the material basis of their world, as bourgeois economy constitutes that of our modern world. Or perhaps Bastiat

means, that a mode of production based on slavery is based on a system of plunder. In that case he treads on dangerous ground. If a giant thinker like Aristotle erred in his appreciation of slave labour, why should a dwarf economist like Bastiat be right in his appreciation of wage-labour? I seize this opportunity of shortly answering an objection taken by a German paper in America, to my work, *Zur Kritik der Pol. Oekonomie*, 1859. In the estimation of that paper, my view that each special mode of production and the social relations corresponding to it, in short, that the economic structure of society, is the real basis on which the juridical and political superstructure is raised and to which definite social forms of thought correspond; that the mode of production determines the character of the social, political, and intellectual life generally, all this is very true for our own times, in which material interests preponderate, but not for the middle ages, in which Catholicism, nor for Athens and Rome, where politics, reigned supreme. In the first place it strikes one as an odd thing for any one to suppose that these well-worn phrases about the middle ages and the ancient world are unknown to anyone else. This much, however, is clear, that the middle ages could not live on Catholicism, nor the ancient world on politics. On the contrary, it is the mode in which they gained a livelihood that explains why here politics, and there Catholicism, played the chief part. For the rest, it requires but a slight acquaintance with the history of the Roman republic, for example, to be aware that its secret history is the history of its landed property. On the other hand, Don Quixote long ago paid the penalty for wrongly imagining that knight errantry was compatible with all economic forms of society.

[34] *Observations on certain verbal disputes in Pol. Econ., particularly relating to value and to demand and supply.* Lond., 1821, p.16.

[35] S. Bailey, l.c., p.165.

[36] The author of *Observations* and S. Bailey accuse Ricardo of converting exchange value from something relative into something absolute. The opposite is the fact. He has explained the apparent relation between objects, such as diamonds and pearls, in which relation they appear as exchange values, and disclosed the true relation hidden behind the appearances, namely, their relation to each other as mere expressions of human labour. If the followers of Ricardo answer Bailey somewhat rudely, and by no means convincingly, the reason is to be sought in this, that they were unable to find in Ricardo's own works any key to the hidden relations existing between value and its form, exchange value.

Volume 1, Part 1, Chapter 2

[1] In the 12th century, so renowned for its piety, they included amongst commodities some very delicate things. Thus a French poet of the period enumerates amongst the goods to be found in the market of Landit, not only clothing shoes, leather, agricultural implements, &c., but also '*femmes folles de leur corps*'.

[2] Proudhon begins by taking his ideal of Justice, of '*justice éternelle*', from the juridical relations that correspond to the production of commodities: thereby, it may be noted, he proves, to the consolation of all good citizens, that the production of commodities is a form of production as everlasting as justice. Then he turns round and seeks to reform the actual production of commodities, and the actual legal system corresponding thereto, in accordance with this ideal. What opinion should we have of a chemist, who, instead of studying the actual laws of the molecular changes in the composition and decomposition of matter, and on that foundation solving definite problems, claimed to regulate the composition and decomposition of matter by means of the 'eternal ideas' of '*naturalité*' and '*affinité*'? Do we really know any more about 'usury', when we say it contradicts '*justice éternelle*', '*équité éternelle*', '*mutualité éternelle*', and other *vérités éternelles* than the fathers of the church did when they said it was incompatible with '*grâce éternelle*', '*foi éternelle*', and '*la volonté éternelle de Dieu*'?

[3] 'For two-fold is the use of every object . . . The one is peculiar to the object as such, the other is not, as a sandal which may be worn, and is also exchangeable. Both are uses of the sandal, for even he who exchanges the sandal for the money or food he is in want of, makes use of the sandal as a sandal. But not in its natural way. For it has not been made for the sake of being exchanged.' (Aristoteles, *De Rep.* l.i. c.9.)

[4] From this we may form an estimate of the shrewdness of the petit-bourgeois socialism, which, while perpetuating the production of commodities, aims at abolishing the 'antagonism' between money and commodities, and consequently, since money exists only by virtue of this antagonism, at abolishing money itself. We might just as well try to retain Catholicism without the Pope. For more on this point see my work, *Zur Kritik der Pol. Oekon.*, p.61, sq.

[5] So long as, instead of two distinct use-values being exchanged, a chaotic mass of articles are offered as the equivalent of a single article, which is often the case with savages, even the direct barter of products is in its first infancy.

[6] Karl Marx, l.c., p.135. '*I metalli . . . naturalmente moneta.*' (Galiani, '*Della moneta*' in Custodi's *Collection: Parte Moderna* t.iii.)

[7] For further details on this subject see, in my work cited above, the chapter on 'The precious metals'.

[8] '*Il danaro è la merce universale*' (Verri, l.c., p.16).

[9] 'Silver and gold themselves (which we may call by the general name of bullion) are . . . commodities . . . rising and falling in . . . value . . . Bullion, then, may be reckoned to be of higher value where the smaller weight will purchase the greater quantity of the product or manufacture of the countrey,' &c. (*A Discourse of the General Notions of Money, Trade, and Exchanges, as They Stand in Relation each to other. By a Merchant.* Lond., 1695, p.7.) 'Silver and gold, coined or uncoined, though they are used for a measure of all other things, are no less a commodity than wine, oil, tobacco, cloth, or stuffs.' (*A Discourse concerning Trade, and that in particular of the East Indies,* &c. London, 1689, p.2.) 'The stock and riches of the kingdom cannot properly be confined to money, nor ought gold and silver to be excluded from being merchandise.' (*The East-India Trade a Most Profitable Trade.* London, 1677, p.4.)

[10] '*L'oro e l'argento hanno valore come metalli anteriore all'esser moneta.*' (Galiani, l.c.) Locke says, 'The universal consent of mankind gave to silver, on account of its qualities which made it suitable for money, an imaginary value.' Law, on the other hand: 'How could different nations give an imaginary value to any single thing . . . or how could this imaginary value have maintained itself?' But the following shows how little he himself understood about the matter: 'Silver was exchanged in proportion to the value in use it possessed, consequently in proportion to its real value. By its adoption as money it received an additional value (*une valeur additionnelle*)'. (Jean Law: 'Considérations sur le numéraire et le commerce' in E. Daire's Edit. of *Économistes Financiers du XVIII siècle*, p.470.)

[11] '*L'Argent en (des denrées) est le signe.*' (V. de Forbonnais: '*Éléments du Commerce, Nouv. Edit.* Leyde, 1766,' t.ii, p.143.) '*Comme signe il est attiré par les denrées.*' (l.c., p.155.) '*L'argent est un signe d'une chose et la représente.*' (Montesquieu: '*Esprit des Lois,*' (*Oeuvres,* Lond. 1767, t.ii, p.2.) '*L'argent n'est pas simple signe, car il est lui-même richesse, il ne représente pas les valeurs, il les équivaut.*' (Le Trosne, l.c., p.910.) 'The notion of value contemplates the valuable article as a mere symbol – the article counts not for what it is, but for what it is worth.' (Hegel, l.c., p.100.) Lawyers started long before economists the idea that money is a mere symbol, and that the value of the precious metals is purely imaginary. This they did in the sycophantic service of the crowned heads, supporting the right of the latter to debase the coinage, during the whole of the middle ages, by the traditions of the Roman Empire and the conceptions of money to be found in the Pandects. '*Qu'aucun puisse ni doive faire doute,*' says an apt scholar of

theirs, Philip of Valois, in a decree of 1346, '*que à nous et à notre majesté royale n'appartiennent seulement . . . le mestier, le fait, l'état, la provision et toute l'ordonnance des monnaies, de donner tel cours, et pour tel prix comme il nous plait et bon nous semble.*' It was a maxim of the Roman Law that the value of money was fixed by decree of the emperor. It was expressly forbidden to treat money as a commodity. '*Pecunias vero nulli emere fas erit, nam in usu publico constitutas oportet non esse mercem.*' Some good work on this question has been done by G. F. Pagnini: *Saggio sopra il giusto pregio delle cose, 1751*; Custodi, *Parte Moderna*, t.ii. In the second part of his work Pagnini directs his polemics especially against the lawyers.

[12] 'If a man can bring to London an ounce of Silver out of the Earth in Peru, in the same time that he can produce a bushel of Corn, then the one is the natural price of the other; now, if by reason of new or more easier mines a man can procure two ounces of silver as easily as he formerly did one, the corn will be as cheap at ten shillings the bushel as it was before at five shillings, *ceteris paribus*.' William Petty. *A Treatise of Taxes and Contributions*. Lond., 1667, p.32.

[13] The learned Professor Roscher, after first informing us that 'the false definitions of money may be divided into two main groups: those which make it more, and those which make it less, than a commodity,' gives us a long and very mixed catalogue of works on the nature of money, from which it appears that he has not the remotest idea of the real history of the theory; and then he moralises thus: 'For the rest, it is not to be denied that most of the later economists do not bear sufficiently in mind the peculiarities that distinguish money from other commodities' (it is then, after all, either more or less than a commodity!) . . . 'So far, the semi–mercantilist reaction of Ganilh is not altogether without foundation.' (Wilhelm Roscher: *Die Grundlagen der Nationaloekonomie*, 3rd Edn. 1858, pp.207–210.) More! Less! Not sufficiently! So far! Not altogether! What clearness and precision of ideas and language! And such eclectic professorial twaddle is modestly baptised by Mr Roscher, 'the anatomico–physiological method' of Political Economy! One discovery however, he must have credit for, namely, that money is 'a pleasant commodity'.

Volume 1, Part 1, Chapter 3

[1] The question – Why does not money directly represent labour-time, so that a piece of paper may represent, for instance, x hours' labour, is at bottom the same as the question why, given the production of commodities, must products take the form of commodities? This is evident, since their taking the form of commodities implies their differentiation into commodities and money. Or, why cannot private labour – labour for the account of private individuals – be treated as its opposite, immediate social labour? I have elsewhere examined thoroughly the Utopian idea of 'labour-money' in a society founded on the production of commodities (l.c., p.61, seq.). On this point I will only say further, that Owen's 'labour-money', for instance, is no more 'money' than a ticket for the theatre. Owen presupposes directly associated labour, a form of production that is entirely inconsistent with the production of commodities. The certificate of labour is merely evidence of the part taken by the individual in the common labour, and of his right to a certain portion of the common produce destined for consumption. But it never enters into Owen's head to presuppose the production of commodities, and at the same time, by juggling with money, to try to evade the necessary conditions of that production.

[2] Savages and half-civilised races use the tongue differently. Captain Parry says of the inhabitants on the west coast of Baffin's Bay: 'In this case (he refers to barter) they licked it (the thing represented to them) twice to their tongues, after which they seemed to consider the bargain satisfactorily concluded.' In the same way, the Eastern Esquimaux licked the articles they received in exchange. If the tongue is thus used in

the North as the organ of appropriation, no wonder that, in the South, the stomach serves as the organ of accumulated property, and that a Kaffir estimates the wealth of a man by the size of his belly. That the Kaffirs know what they are about is shown by the following: at the same time that the official British Health Report of 1864 disclosed the deficiency of fat-forming food among a large part of the working-class, a certain Dr Harvey (not, however, the celebrated discoverer of the circulation of the blood), made a good thing by advertising recipes for reducing the superfluous fat of the bourgeoisie and aristocracy.

[3] See Karl Marx: *Zur Kritik, &c.* '*Theorien von der Masseinheit des Geldes*', p.53, seq.

[4] 'Wherever gold and silver have by law been made to perform the function of money or of a measure of value side by side, it has always been tried, but in vain, to treat them as one and the same material. To assume that there is an invariable ratio between the quantities of gold and silver in which a given quantity of labour-time is incorporated, is to assume in fact, that gold and silver are of one and the same material, and that a given mass of the less valuable metal, silver, is a constant fraction of a given mass of gold. From the reign of Edward III to the time of George II, the history of money in England consists of one long series of perturbations caused by the clashing of the legally fixed ratio between the values of gold and silver, with the fluctuations in their real values. At one time gold was too high, at another, silver. The metal that for the time being was estimated below its value, was withdrawn from circulation, melted and exported. The ratio between the two metals was then again altered by law, but the new nominal ratio soon came into conflict again with the real one. In our own times, the slight and transient fall in the value of gold compared with silver, which was a consequence of the Indo-Chinese demand for silver, produced on a far more extended scale in France the same phenomena, export of silver, and its expulsion from circulation by gold. During the years 1855, 1856 and 1857, the excess in France of gold-imports over gold-exports amounted to £41,580,000, while the excess of silver-exports over silver-imports was £14,704,000. In fact, in those countries in which both metals are legally measures of value, and therefore both legal tender so that everyone has the option of paying in either metal, the metal that rises in value is at a premium, and, like every other commodity, measures its price in the over-estimated metal which alone serves in reality as the standard of value. The result of all experience and history with regard to this equation is simply that, where two commodities perform by law the functions of a measure of value, in practice one alone maintains that position.' (Karl Marx, l.c., pp.52,53.)

[5] The peculiar circumstance, that while the ounce of gold serves in England as the unit of the standard of money, the pound sterling does not form an aliquot part of it, has been explained as follows: 'Our coinage was originally adapted to the employment of silver only, hence, an ounce of silver can always be divided into a certain adequate number of pieces of coin, but as gold was introduced at a later period into a coinage adapted only to silver, an ounce of gold cannot be coined into an aliquot number of pieces.' Maclaren, *A Sketch of the History of the Currency*. London, 1858, p.16.

[6] With English writers the confusion between measure of value and standard of price (standard of value) is indescribable. Their functions, as well as their names, are constantly interchanged.

[7] Moreover, it has not general historical validity.

[8] It is thus that the pound sterling in English denotes less than one-third of its original weight; the pound Scot, before the union, only 1/36th; the French *livre*, 1/74th; the Spanish *maravedi*, less than 1/1,000th; and the Portuguese *rei* a still smaller fraction.

[9] '*Le monete le quali oggi sono ideali sono le più antiche d'ogni nazione, e tutte furono un tempo reali, e perche erano reali con esse si contava.*' (Galiani: *Della moneta*, l.c., p.153.)

[10] David Urquhart remarks in his *Familiar Words* on the monstrosity (!) that nowadays a pound (sterling), which is the unit of the English standard of money, is equal to about a quarter of an ounce of gold. 'This is falsifying a measure, not establishing a standard.' He sees in this 'false denomination' of the weight of gold, as in everything else, the falsifying hand of civilisation.

[11] When Anacharsis was asked for what purposes the Greeks used money, he replied, 'For reckoning.' (Athen. *Deipn.* 1.iv.49 v.2. ed. Schweighauser, 1802.)

[12] 'Owing to the fact that money, when serving as the standard of price, appears under the same reckoning names as do the prices of commodities, and that therefore the sum of £3 17s. 10 1/2d. may signify on the one hand an ounce weight of gold, and on the other, the value of a ton of iron, this reckoning name of money has been called its mint-price. Hence there sprang up the extraordinary notion, that the value of gold is estimated in its own material, and that, in contradistinction to all other commodities, its price is fixed by the State. It was erroneously thought that the giving of reckoning names to definite weights of gold, is the same thing as fixing the value of those weights.' (Karl Marx, l.c., p.52.)

[13] See '*Theorien von der Masseinheit des Geldes*' in '*Zur Kritik der Poll Oekon. &c.,*' p.53, seq. The fantastic notions about raising or lowering the mint-price of money by transferring to greater or smaller weights of gold or silver, the names already legally appropriated to fixed weights of those metals; such notions, at least in those cases in which they aim, not at clumsy financial operations against creditors, both public and private, but at economic quack remedies, have been so exhaustively treated by Wm. Petty in his *Quantulumcunque concerning money: To the Lord Marquis of Halifax, 1682*, that even his immediate followers, Sir Dudley North and John Locke, not to mention later ones, could only dilute him. 'If the wealth of a nation,' he remarks, 'could be decupled by a proclamation, it were strange that such proclamations have not long since been made by our Governors.' (l.c., p.36.)

[14] '*Ou bien, il faut consentir à dire qu'une valeur d'un million en argent vaut plus qu'une valeur égale en merchandises.*' (Le Trosne, l.c., p.919), which amounts to saying '*qu'une valeur vaut plus qu'une valeur égale.*'

[15] Jerome had to wrestle hard, not only in his youth with the bodily flesh, as is shown by his fight in the desert with the handsome women of his imagination, but also in his old age with the spiritual flesh. 'I thought,' he says, 'I was in the spirit before the Judge of the Universe.' 'Who art thou?' asked a voice. 'I am a Christian.' 'Thou liest,' thundered back the great Judge, 'thou art nought but a Ciceronian.'

[16] '*ek de tou . . . puros antameibesthai panta, phesin ho Herakleitos, kai pur hapanton, hosper khrusou khremata kai khrematon khrusos.*' (F. Lassalle: *Die Philosophie Herakleitos des Dunkeln.* Berlin, 1858, vol.i, p.222.) Lassalle in his note on this passage, p.224, n.3., erroneously makes gold a mere symbol of value.

[17] '*Toute vente est achat.*' (Dr Quesnay: *Dialogues sur le Commerce et les Travaux des Artisans. Physiocrates* ed. Daire, I Partie, Paris, 1846, p.170), or as Quesnay in his *Maximes générales* puts it, '*Vendre est acheter.*'

[18] '*Le prix d'une merchandise ne pouvant être payé que par le prix d'une autre merchandise*' (Mercier de la Riviere: '*L'Ordre naturel et essentiel des sociétés politiques.*' *Physiocrates*, ed. Daire, II Partie, p.554.)

[19] '*Pour avoir cet argent, il faut avoir vendu,*' l.c., p.543.

[20] As before remarked, the actual producer of gold or silver forms an exception. He exchanges his product directly for another commodity, without having first sold it.

[21] '*Si l'argent représente, dans nos mains, les choses que nous pouvons désirer d'acheter, il y représente aussi les choses que nous avons vendues pour cet argent.*' (Mercier de la Rivière, l.c., p.586.)

[22] '*Il y a donc . . . quatre termes et trois contractants, dont l'un intervient deux fois.*' (Le Trosne, l.c., p.909.)

[23] Self-evident as this may be, it is nevertheless for the most part unobserved by political economists, and especially by the 'Free-trader Vulgaris'.

[24] See my observations on James Mill in *Zur Kritik, &c.*, pp. 74–76. With regard to this subject, we may notice two methods characteristic of apologetic economy. The first is the identification of the circulation of commodities with the direct barter of products, by simple abstraction from their points of difference; the second is, the attempt to explain away the contradictions of capitalist production, by reducing the relations between the persons engaged in that mode of production, to the simple relations arising out of the circulation of commodities. The production and circulation of commodities are however, phenomena that occur to a greater or less extent in modes of production the most diverse. If we are acquainted with nothing but the abstract categories of circulation, which are common to all these modes of production, we cannot possibly know anything of the specific points of difference of those modes, nor pronounce any judgment upon them. In no science is such a big fuss made with commonplace truisms as in Political Economy. For instance, J. B. Say sets himself up as a judge of crises, because, forsooth, he knows that a commodity is a product.

[25] *Translator's note.* – This word is here used in its original signification of the course or track pursued by money as it changes from hand to hand, a course which essentially differs from circulation.

[26] Even when the commodity is sold over and over again, a phenomenon that at present has no existence for us, it falls, when definitely sold for the last time, out of the sphere of circulation into that of consumption, where it serves either as means of subsistence or means of production.

[27] '*Il [l'argent] n'a d'autre mouvement que celui qui lui est imprimé par les productions.*' (Le Trosne, l.c., p.885.)

[28] '*Ce sont les productions qui le (l'argent) mettent en mouvement et le font circuler . . . La célérité de son mouvement (sc. de l'argent) supplée à sa quantité. Lorsqu'il en est besoin. il ne fait que glisser d'une main dans l'autre sans s'arrêter un instant.*' (Le Trosne, l.c.. pp. 915, 916.)

[29] 'Money being . . . the common measure of buying and selling, everybody who hath anything to sell, and cannot procure chapmen for it, is presently apt to think, that want of money in the. kingdom, or country, is the cause why his goods do not go off; and so, want of money is the common cry; which is a great mistake . . . What do these people want, who cry out for money? . . . The farmer complains . . . he thinks that were more money in the country, he should have a price for his goods. Then it seems money is not his want, but a price for his corn and cattel, which he would sell, but cannot . . . Why cannot he get a price? . . . (1) Either there is too much corn and cattel in the country, so that most who come to market have need of selling, as he hath, and few of buying; or (2) There wants the usual vent abroad by transportation . . . , or (3) The consumption fails, as when men, by reason of poverty, do not spend so much in their houses as formerly they did; wherefore it is not the increase of specific money, which would at all advance the farmer's goods, but the removal of any of these three causes, which do truly keep down the market . . . The merchant and shopkeeper want money in the same manner, that is, they want a vent for the goods they deal in, by reason that the markets fail' . . . [A nation] 'never thrives better, than when riches are tost from hand to hand.' (Sir Dudley North: *Discourses upon Trade*, Lond. 1691, pp. 11–15, passim.) Herrenschwand's fanciful notions amount merely to this, that the antagonism, which has its origin in the nature of commodities, and is reproduced in their circulation, can be removed by increasing the circulating medium. But if, on the one hand, it is a popular delusion to ascribe stagnation in production and circulation to insufficiency of the circulating medium, it by no means follows, on the other hand,

that an actual paucity of the medium in consequence, e.g., of bungling legislative interference with the regulation of currency, may not give rise to such stagnation.

[30] 'There is a certain measure and proportion of money requisite to drive the trade of a nation, more or less than which would prejudice the same, just as there is a certain proportion of farthings necessary in a small retail trade, to change silver money, and to even such reckonings as cannot be adjusted with the smallest silver pieces . . . Now, as the proportion of the number of farthings requisite in commerce is to be taken from the number of people, the frequency of their exchanges: as also, and principally, from the value of the smallest silver pieces of money; so in like manner, the proportion of money [gold and silver specie] requisite in our trade, is to be likewise taken from the frequency of commutations, and from the bigness of the payments.' (William Petty, *A Treatise of Taxes and Contributions*. Lond. 1667, p.17.) The Theory of Hume was defended against the attacks of J. Steuart and others, by A. Young, in his *Political Arithmetic*, Lond; 1774, in which work there is a special chapter entitled 'Prices depend on quantity of money, at p.112, sqq. I have stated in *Zur Kritik, &c.*, p.149: 'He (Adam Smith) passes over without remark the question as to the quantity of coin in circulation, and treats money quite wrongly as a mere commodity.' This statement applies only in so far as Adam Smith, *ex officio*, treats of money. Now and then, however, as in his criticism of the earlier systems of Political Economy, he takes the right view. 'The quantity of coin in every country is regulated by the value of the commodities which are to be circulated by it . . . The value of the goods annually bought and sold in any country requires a certain quantity of money to circulate and distribute them to their proper consumers, and can give employment to no more. The channel of circulation necessarily draws to itself a sum sufficient to fill it, and never admits any more.' (*Wealth of Nations*. bk.iv, ch.1) In like manner, *ex officio*, he opens his work with an apotheosis on the division of labour. Afterwards, in the last book which treats of the sources of public revenue, he occasionally repeats the denunciations of the division of labour made by his teacher, A. Ferguson.

[31] 'The prices of things will certainly rise in every nation, as the gold and silver increase amongst the people, and consequently, where the gold and silver decrease in any nation, the prices of all things must fall proportionately to such decrease of money.' (Jacob Vanderlint: *Money Answers all Things*. Lond. 1734, p.5.) A careful comparison of this book with Hume's *Essays*, proves to my mind without doubt that Hume was acquainted with and made use of Vanderlint's work, which is certainly an important one. The opinion that prices are determined by the quantity of the circulating medium, was also held by Barbon and other much earlier writers. 'No inconvenience,' says Vanderlint, 'can arise by an unrestrained trade, but very great advantage; since, if the cash of the nation be decreased by it, which prohibitions are designed to prevent, those nations that get the cash will certainly find everything advance in price, as the cash increases amongst them. And . . . our manufactures, and everything else, will soon become so moderate as to turn the balance of trade in our favour, and thereby fetch the money back again.' (l.c.. pp. 43, 44.)

[32] That the price of each single kind of commodity forms a part of the sum of the prices of all the commodities in circulation, is a self-evident proposition. But how use-values which are incommensurable with regard to each other, are to be exchanged, *en masse*, for the total sum of gold and silver in a country, is quite incomprehensible. If we start from the notion that all commodities together form one single commodity, of which each is but an aliquot part, we get the following beautiful result: The total commodity = x cwt. of gold; commodity A = an aliquot part of the total commodity = the same aliquot part of x cwt. of gold. This is stated in all seriousness by Montesquieu: '*Si l'on compare la masse de l'or et de l'argent qui est dans le monde avec la somme des merchandises qui y sont, il est cenain que chaque denrée ou merchandise, en particulier, pourra*

être comparée à une certaine portion de la masse entière. Supposons qu'il n'y ait qu'une seule denrée ou marchandise dans le monde, ou qu'il n'y ait qu'une seule qui s'achète, et qu'elle se divise comme l'argent: cette partie de cette marchandise répondra à une partie de la masse de l'argent; la moitié du total de l'une à la moitié du total de l'autre, &c . . . l'établissement du prix des choses dépend toujours fondamentalement de la raison du total des choses au total des signes.' (Montesquieu, l.c. t.iii, pp.12,13.) As to the further development of this theory by Ricardo and his disciples, James Mill, Lord Overstone, and others, see *Zur Kritik, &c.,* pp.140–146, and p.150, sqq. John Stuart Mill, with his usual eclectic logic, understands how to hold at the same time the view of his father, James Mill, and the opposite view. On a comparison of the text of his compendium, *Principles of Pol. Econ.,* with his preface to the first edition, in which preface he announces himself as the Adam Smith of his day – we do not know whether to admire more the simplicity of the man, or that of the public, who took him, in good faith, for the Adam Smith he announced himself to be, although he bears about as much resemblance to Adam Smith as say General Williams, of Kars, to the Duke of Wellington. The original researches of Mr J. S. Mill, which are neither extensive nor profound, in the domain of Political Economy, will be found mustered in rank and file in his little work, *Some Unsettled Questions of Political Economy,* which appeared in 1844. Locke asserts point blank the connection between the absence of value in gold and silver, and the determination of their values by quantity alone. 'Mankind having consented to put an imaginary value upon gold and silver . . . the intrinsic value, regarded in these metals, is nothing but the quantity.' (*Some Considerations, &c.,* 1691, *Works* Ed. 1777, vol. ii, p.15.)

[33] It lies of course, entirely beyond my purpose to take into consideration such details as the seigniorage on minting. I will, however, cite for the benefit of the romantic sycophant, Adam Müller, who admires the 'generous liberality' with which the English Government coins gratuitously, the following opinion of Sir Dudley North: 'Silver and gold, like other commodities, have their ebbings and flowings. Upon the arrival of quantities from Spain . . . it is carried into the Tower, and coined. Not long after there will come a demand for bullion to be exported again. If there is none, but all happens to be in coin, what then? Melt it down again; there's no loss in it, for the coining costs the owner nothing. Thus the nation has been abused, and made to pay for the twisting of straw for asses to eat. If the merchant were made to pay the price of the coinage, he would not have sent his silver to the Tower without consideration, and coined money would always keep a value above uncoined silver. ' (North, l.c., p.18.) North was himself one of the foremost merchants in the reign of Charles II.

[34] 'If silver never exceed what is wanted for the smaller payments it cannot be collected in sufficient quantities for the larger payments . . . the use of gold in the main payments necessarily implies also its use in the retail trade: those who have gold coin offering them for small purchases, and receiving with the commodity purchased a balance of silver in return; by which means the surplus of silver that would otherwise encumber the retail dealer, is drawn off and dispersed into general circulation. But if there is as much silver as will transact the small payments independent of gold, the retail trader must then receive silver for small purchases; and it must of necessity accumulate in his hands.' (David Buchanan; *Inquiry into the Taxation and Commercial Policy of Great Britain*. Edinburgh, 1844, pp.248,249.)

[35] The mandarin Wan-mao-in, the Chinese Chancellor of the Exchequer, took it into his head one day to lay before the Son of Heaven a proposal that secretly aimed at converting the assignats of the empire into convertible bank-notes. The assignats Committee, in its report of April, 1854, gives him a severe snubbing. Whether he also received the traditional drubbing with bamboos is not stated. The concluding part of the report is as follows: – 'The Committee has carefully examined his proposal and

finds that it is entirely in favour of the merchants, and that no advantage will result to the crown.' (*Arbeiten der Kaiserlich Russischen Gesandtschaft zu Peking über China. Aus dem Russischen von Dr K. Abel und F. A. Mecklenburg. Erster Band*. Berlin, 1858, p.47 sq.) In his evidence before the Committee of the House of Lords on the Bank Acts, a governor of the Bank of England says, with regard to the abrasion of gold coins during currency: 'Every year a fresh class of sovereigns becomes too light. The class which one year passes with full weight, loses enough by wear and tear to draw the scales next year against it.' (House of Lords' Committee, 1848, n. 429.)

[36] The following passage from Fullarton shows the want of clearness on the part of even the best writers on money, in their comprehension of its various functions: 'That, as far as concerns our domestic exchanges, all the monetary functions which are usually performed by gold and silver coins, may be performed as effectually by a circulation of inconvertible notes paying no value but that factitious and conventional value they derive from the law is a fact which admits, I conceive, of no denial. Value of this description may be made to answer all the purposes of intrinsic value, and supersede even the necessity for a standard, provided only the quantity of issues be kept under due limitation.' (Fullarton: *Regulation of Currencies*, London, 1845, p.21.) Because the commodity that serves as money is capable of being replaced in circulation by mere symbols of value, therefore its functions as a measure of value and a standard of prices are declared to be superfluous!

[37] From the fact that gold and silver, so far as they are coins, or exclusively serve as the medium of circulation, become mere tokens of themselves, Nicholas Barbon deduces the right of Governments 'to raise money', that is, to give to the weight of silver that is called a shilling the name of a greater weight, such as a crown; and so to pay creditors shillings, instead of crowns. 'Money does wear and grow lighter by often telling over . . . It is the denomination and currency of the money that men regard in bargaining, and not the quantity of silver . . . 'Tis the public authority upon the metal that makes it money.' (N. Barbon, l.c., pp.29,30,25.)

[38] '*Une richesse en argent n'est que . . . richesse en productions, converties en argent.*' (Mercier de la Rivière, l.c.) '*Une valeur en productions n'a fait que changer de forme.*' (Id., p.486.)

[39] ' 'Tis by this practice they keep all their goods and manufactures at such low rates.' (Vanderlint, l.c., pp.95,96.)

[40] 'Money . . . is a pledge.' (John Bellers: *Essays about the Poor, Manufactures, Trade, Plantations, and Immorality*, Lond., 1699, p.13.)

[41] A purchase. in a 'categorical' sense, implies that gold and silver are already the converted form of commodities, or the product of a sale.

[42] Henry III, most Christian king of France, robbed cloisters of their relics, and turned them into money. It is well known what part the despoiling of the Delphic Temple, by the Phocians, played in the history of Greece. Temples with the ancients served as the dwellings of the gods of commodities. They were 'sacred banks'. With the Phoenicians, a trading people *par excellence*, money was the transmuted shape of everything. It was, therefore, quite in order that the virgins, who, at the feast of the Goddess of Love, gave themselves up to strangers, should offer to the goddess the piece of money they received.

[43]   Gold, yellow, glittering, precious gold!
         Thus much of this, will make black white, foul, fair;
         Wrong, right; base, noble; old, young; coward, valiant.
                  . . . What this, you gods? Why, this
         Will lug your priests and servants from your sides;
         Pluck stout men's pillows from below their heads;
                  . . . This yellow slave

Will knit and break religions; bless the accurs'd;
Make the hoar leprosy ador'd; place thieves,
And give them title, knee and approbation;
With senators on the bench, this is it
That makes the wappen'd widow wed again:
. . . Come damned earth,
Though common whore of mankind.'

Shakespeare: *Timon of Athens*

[44]   *Ouden gar anthropoisin hoion arguros*
kakon nomism' eblaste. touto kai poleis
porthei, tod' andras exanistesin domon.
tod' ekdidaskei kai parallassei phrenas
khrestas pros aiskhra toisin anthropois ekhein,
kai pantos ergou dussebeian eidenai.

Sophocles, *Antigone*

[45] '*Elpizouses tes pleonexias anaxein ek ton mukhon tes ges auton ton Ploutona.*' (Athenaeus, *The Deipnosophistst*, vi,23)

[46] '*Accrescere quanto più si può il numero de'venditori d'ogni merce, diminuere quanto più si può il numero dei compratori, questi sono i cardini sui quali si raggirano tutte le operazioni di economia politica.*' (Verri, l.c., p.52.)

[47] 'There is required for carrying on the trade of the nation a determinate sum of specifick money which varies, and is sometimes more, sometimes less, as the circumstances we are in require . . . This ebbing and flowing of money supplies and accommodates itself, without any aid of Politicians . . . The buckets work alternately; when money is scarce, bullion is coined; when bullion is scarce, money is melted.' (Sir D. North, l.c., Postscript, p.3.) John Stuart Mill, who for a long time was an official of the East India Company, confirms the fact that in India silver ornaments still continue to perform directly the functions of a hoard. The silver ornaments are brought out and coined when there is a high rate of interest, and go back again when the rate of interest falls. (J. S. Mill's Evidence, *Reports on Bank Acts*, 1857, 2084.) According to a Parliamentary document of 1864 on the gold and silver import and export of India, the import of gold and silver in 1863 exceeded the export by £19,367,764. During the 8 years immediately preceding 1864, the excess of imports over exports of the precious metals amounted to £109,652,917. During this century far more than £200,000,000 has been coined in India.

[48] The following shows the debtor and creditor relations existing between English traders at the beginning of the 18th century. 'Such a spirit of crudity reigns here in England among the men of trade, that is not to be met with in any other society of men, nor in any other kingdom of the world.' (*An Essay on Credit and the Bankrupt Act*, Lond., 1707, p.2.

[49] It will be seen from the following quotation from my book which appeared in 1859, why I take no notice in the text of an opposite form: 'Contrariwise, in the process in M—C, the money can be alienated as a real means of purchase, and in that way, the price of the commodity can be realised before the use-value of the money is realised and the commodity actually delivered. This occurs constantly under the everyday form of prepayments. And it is under this form, that the English government purchases opium from the ryots of India . . . In these cases, however, the money always acts as a means of purchase . . . Of course capital also is advanced in the shape of money . . . This point of view, however, does not fall within the horizon of simple circulation.' (*Zur Kritik, &c.*, pp.119,120.)

[50] The monetary crisis referred to in the text, being a phase of every crisis, must be clearly distinguished from that particular form of crisis, which also is called a monetary

crisis, but which may be produced by itself as an independent phenomenon in such a way as to react only indirectly on industry and commerce. The pivot of these crises is to be found in moneyed capital, and their sphere of direct action is therefore the sphere of that capital, viz., banking, the stock exchange, and finance.

[51] 'The sudden reversion from a system of credit to a system of hard cash heaps theoretical fright on top of the practical panic; and the dealers by whose agency circulation is affected, shudder before the impenetrable mystery in which their own economic relations are involved.' (Karl Marx, l.c., p.126.) 'The poor stand still, because the rich have no money to employ them, though they have the same land and hands to provide victuals and clothes, as ever they had; . . . which is the true riches of a nation, and not the money.' John Bellers, *Proposals for Raising a Colledge of Industry*, London, 1696, p3.

[52] The following shows how such times are exploited by the '*amis du commerce*'. 'On one occasion (1839) an old grasping banker (in the city) in his private room raised the lid of the desk he sat over, and displayed to a friend rolls of bank-notes, saying with intense glee there were £600,000 of them, they were held to make money tight, and would all be let out after three o'clock on the same day.' (*The Theory of Exchanges. The Bank Charter Act of 1844*. Lond. 1864, p.81). *The Observer*, a semi-official government organ, contained the following paragraph on 24th April, 1864: 'Some very curious rumours are current of the means which have been resorted to in order to create a scarcity of banknotes . . . Questionable as it would seem, to suppose that any trick of the kind would be adopted, the report has been so universal that it really deserves mention.'

[53] 'The amount of purchases or contracts entered upon during the course of any given day, will not affect the quantity of money afloat on that particular day, but, in the vast majority of cases, will resolve themselves into multifarious drafts upon the quantity of money which may be afloat at subsequent dates more or less distant . . . The bills granted or credits opened, today, need have no resemblance whatever, either in quantity, amount or duration, to those granted or entered upon tomorrow or next day, nay, many of today's bills, and credits, when due, fall in with a mass of liabilities whose origins traverse a range of antecedent dates altogether indefinite, bills at 12, 6, 3 months or 1 often aggregating together to swell the common liabilities of one particular day . . .' (*The Currency Theory Reviewed; in a Letter to the Scottish People*. By a Banker in England. Edinburgh, 1845, pp.29,30 passim.)

[54] As an example of how little ready money is required in true commercial operations, I give below a statement by one of the largest London houses of its yearly receipts and payments. Its transactions during the year 1856, extending to many millions of pounds sterling, are here reduced to the scale of one million.

	Receipts		Payments
Bankers's and Merchants'		Bills payable after date	£302,674
Bills payable after date	£533,596	Cheques on London Bankers	663,672
Cheques on Bankers, &c.,		Bank of England Notes	22,743
payable on demand	357,715	Gold	9,427
Country Notes	9,627	Silver and Copper	1,484
Bank of England Notes	68,554		
Silver and Copper	1,486		
Post Office Orders	933		
Total	£1,000,000	Total	£1,000,000

[55] 'The course of trade being thus turned, from exchanging of goods for goods, or delivering and taking, to selling and paying, all the bargains . . . are now stated upon the foot of a Price in money.' (*An Essay upon Publick Credit*. 3rd Ed. Lond., 1710, p.8.)

[56] '*L'argent . . . est devenu le bourreau de toutes choses.*' Finance is the '*alambic, qui a fait évaporer une quantité effroyable de biens et de denrées pour faire ce fatal précis.*' '*L'argent déclare la guerre à tout le genre humain.*' (Boisguillebert: '*Dissertation sur la nature des richesses, de l'argent et des tributs. Edit. Daire. Économistes financiers.* Paris, 1843, t.i., pp.413,419,417.)

[57] 'On Whitsuntide, 1824,' says Mr Craig before the Commons' Committee of 1826, 'there was such an immense demand for notes upon the banks of Edinburgh, that by 11 o'clock they had not a note left in their custody. They sent round to all the different banks to borrow, but could not get them, and many of the transactions were adjusted by slips of paper only; yet by three o'clock the whole of the notes were returned into the banks from which they had issued! It was a mere transfer from hand to hand. 'Although the average effective circulation of bank-notes in Scotland is less than three millions sterling, yet on certain pay days in the year, every single note in the possession of the bankers, amounting in the whole to about £7,000,000, is called into activity. On these occasions the notes have a single and specific function to perform, and so soon as they have performed it, they flow back into the various banks from which they issued. (See John Fullarton, *Regulation of Currencies*. Lond. 1845, p.86, note.) In explanation it should be stated, that in Scotland, at the date of Fullarton's work, notes and not cheques were used to withdraw deposits.

[58] To the question, 'If there were occasion to raise 40 millions p.a., whether the same 6 millions (gold) . . . would suffice for such revolutions and circulations thereof, as trade requires,' Petty replies in his usual masterly manner, 'I answer yes: for the expense being 40 millions, if the revolutions were in such short circles, viz., weekly, as happens among poor artisans and labourers, who receive and pay every Saturday, then 40/52 parts of 1 million of money would answer these ends, but if the circles be quarterly, according to our custom of paying rent, and gathering taxes, then 10 millions were requisite. Wherefore, supposing payments in general to be of a mixed circle between one week and 13, then add 10 millions to 40/52, the half of which will be 5 1/2, so as if we have 5 1/2 millions we have enough.' (William Petty: *Political Anatomy of Ireland*. 1672, Edit.: Lond. 1691, pp.13,14.)

[59] Hence the absurdity of every law prescribing that the banks of a country shall form reserves of that precious metal alone which circulates at home. The 'pleasant difficulties' thus self-created by the Bank of England, are well known. On the subject of the great epochs in the history of the changes in the relative value of gold and silver, see Karl Marx, l.c., p.136 sq. Sir Robert Peel, by his Bank Act of 1844, sought to tide over the difficulty, by allowing the Bank of England to issue notes against silver bullion, on condition that the reserve of silver should never exceed more than one-fourth of the reserve of gold. The value of silver being for that purpose estimated at its price in the London market.

[60] The opponents, themselves, of the mercantile system, a system which considered the settlement of surplus trade balances in gold and silver as the aim of international trade, entirely misconceived the functions of money of the world. I have shown by the example of Ricardo in what way their false conception of the laws that regulate the quantity of the circulating medium, is reflected in their equally false conception of the international movement of the precious metals (l.c., pp. 150 sq.). His erroneous dogma: 'An unfavourable balance of trade never arises but from a redundant currency . . . The exportation of the coin is caused by its cheapness, and is not the effect, but the cause of an unfavourable balance,' already occurs in Barbon: 'The Balance of Trade, if there be one, is not the cause of sending away the money out of a nation; but that proceeds from the difference of the value of bullion in every country.' (N. Barbon; l.c., pp.59,60.) MacCulloch in *The Literature of Political Economy, a classified catalogue*, Lond. 1845, praises Barbon for this anticipation, but prudently passes over the naive forms, in which Barbon clothes the absurd supposition on which the 'currency principle' is

based. The absence of real criticism and even of honesty, in that catalogue culminates in the sections devoted to the history of the theory of money; the reason is that MacCulloch in this part of the work is flattering Lord Overstone whom he calls '*facile princeps argentanorum*'.

[61] For instance, in subsidies, money loans for carrying on wars or for enabling banks to resume cash payments, &c., it is the money form, and no other, of value that may be wanted.

[62] 'I would desire, indeed, no more convincing evidence of the competency of the machinery of the hoards in specie-paying countries to perform every necessary office of international adjustment, without any sensible aid from the general circulation, than the facility with which France, when but just recovering from the shock of a destructive foreign invasion, completed within the space of 27 months the payment of her forced contribution of nearly 20 millions to the allied powers, and a considerable proportion of the sum in specie, without any perceptible contraction or derangement of her domestic currency, or even any alarming fluctuation of her exchanges.' (Fullerton, l.c., p.141.)

[63] '*L'argent se partage entre les nations relativement au besoin qu'elles en ont . . . étant toujours attiré par les productions.*' (Le Trosne, l.c., p.916.) 'The mines which are continually giving gold and silver, do give sufficient to supply such a needful balance to every nation.' (J. Vanderlint, l.c., p.40.)

[64] 'Exchanges rise and fall every week, and at some particular times in the year run high against a nation, and at other times run as high on the contrary.' (N. Barbon, l.c., p.39.)

[65] These various functions are liable to come into dangerous conflict with one another whenever gold and silver have also to serve as a fund for the conversion of bank-notes.

[66] 'What money is more than of absolute necessity for a Home Trade, is dead stock . . . and brings no profit to that country it's kept in, but as it is transported in trade, as well as imported.' (John Bellers, *Essays*, p.13.) 'What if we have too much coin? We may melt down the heaviest and turn it into the splendour of plate, vessels or utensils of gold or silver, or send it out as a commodity, where the same is wanted or desired; or let it out at interest, where interest is high.' (W. Petty: *Quantulumcunque*, p.39.) 'Money is but the fat of the Body Politick, whereof too much cloth as often hinder its agility, as too little makes it sick . . . as fat lubricates the motion of the muscles, feeds in want of victuals, fills up the uneven cavities, and beautifies the body; so doth money in the state quicken its action, feeds from abroad in time of dearth at home, evens accounts . . . and beautifies the whole; altho more especially the particular persons that have it in plenty.' (W. Petty, *Political Anatomy of Ireland*, p.14.)

Volume 1, Part 2, Chapter 4

[1] The contrast between the power, based on the personal relations of dominion and servitude, that is conferred by landed property, and the impersonal power that is given by money, is well expressed by the two French proverbs, '*Nulle terre sans seigneur*,' and '*L'argent n'a pas de maître*.'

[2] '*Avec de l'argent on achète des marchandises et avec des marchandises on achète de l'argent.*' (Mercier de la Rivière: '*L'ordre naturel et essentiel des sociétés politiques*,' p.543.)

[3] 'When a thing is bought in order to be sold again, the sum employed is called money advanced; when it is bought not to be sold, it may be said to be expended.' – (James Steuart: *Works, &c.* Edited by Gen. Sir James Steuart, his son. Lond., 1805, v.i, p.274.)

[4] '*On n'échange pas de l'argent contre de l'argent,*' says Mercier de la Rivière to the Mercantilists (l.c., p.486.) In a work, which, *ex professo* treats of 'trade' and 'speculation',

occurs the following: 'All trade consists in the exchange of things of different kinds; and the advantage' (to the merchant?) 'arises out of this difference. To exchange a pound of bread against a pound of bread... would be attended with no advantage; ... Hence trade is advantageously contrasted with gambling, which consists in a mere exchange of money for money.' (Th. Corbet, *An Inquiry into the Causes and Modes of the Wealth of Individuals; or the Principles of Trade and Speculation Explained*. London, 1841, p.5.) Although Corbet does not see that M—M, the exchange of money for money, is the characteristic form of circulation, not only of merchants' capital but of all capital, yet at least he acknowledges that this form is common to gambling and to one species of trade, viz., speculation: but then comes MacCulloch and makes out, that to buy in order to sell, is to speculate, and thus the difference between Speculation and Trade vanishes. 'Every transaction in which an individual buys produce in order to sell it again, is, in fact, a speculation.' (MacCulloch: *A Dictionary Practical, &c., of Commerce.* Lond., 1847, p.1009.) With much more naiveté, Pinto, the Pindar of the Amsterdam Stock Exchange, remarks, '*Le commerce est un jeu:* (taken from Locke) *et ce n'est pas avec des gueux qu'on peut gagner. Si l'on gagnait longtemps en tout avec tous, il faudrait rendre de bon accord les plus grandes parties du profit pour recommencer le jeu.*' (Pinto: *Traité de la Circulation et du Crédit.* Amsterdam, 1771. p.231,)

[5] 'Capital is divisible . . . into the original capital and the profit, the increment to the capital . . . although in practice this profit is immediately turned into capital, and set in motion with the original.' (F. Engels, '*Umrisse zu einer Kritik der Nationalökonomie*', in: *Deutsch-Französische Jahrbücher, herausgegeben von Arnold Ruge und Karl Marx.* Paris, 1844, p.99.)

[6] Aristotle opposes Oeconomic to Chrematistic. He starts from the former. So far as it is the art of gaining a livelihood, it is limited to procuring those articles that are necessary to existence, and useful either to a household or the state. 'True wealth (*ho alethinos ploutos*) consists of such values in use; for the quantity of possessions of this kind, capable of making life pleasant, is not unlimited. There is, however, a second mode of acquiring things, to which we may by preference and with correctness give the name of Chrematistic, and in this case there appear to be no limits to riches and possessions. Trade (*he kapelike* is literally retail trade, and Aristotle takes this kind because in it values in use predominate) does not in its nature belong to Chrematistic, for here the exchange has reference only to what is necessary to themselves (the buyer or seller).' Therefore, as he goes on to show, the original form of trade was barter, but with the extension of the latter, there arose the necessity for money. On the discovery of money, barter of necessity developed into *kapelike*. into trading in commodities, and this again, in opposition to its original tendency, grew into Chrematistic, into the art of making money. Now Chrematistic is distinguishable from Oeconomic in this way, that 'in the case of Chrematistic circulation is the source of riches (*poietetike krematon . . . dia khrematon diaboles*). And it appears to revolve about money, for money is the beginning and end of this kind of exchange (*to gar nomisma stoikheion kai peras tes allages estin*). Therefore also riches, such as Chrematistic strives for, are unlimited. Just as every art that is not a means to an end, but an end in itself, has no limit to its aims, because it seeks constantly to approach nearer and nearer to that end, while those arts that pursue means to an end, are not boundless, since the goal itself imposes a limit upon them, so with Chrematistic, there are no bounds to its aims, these aims being absolute wealth. Oeconomic not Chrematistic has a limit . . . the object of the former is something different from money, of the latter the augmentation of money . . . By confounding these two forms, which overlap each other, some people have been led to look upon the preservation and increase of money ad infinitum as the end and aim of Oeconomic.' (Aristoteles, *De Rep.* edit. Bekker, lib.i .c.8,9. passim.)

[7] 'Commodities (here used in the sense of use-values) are not the terminating object of the trading capitalist, money is his terminating object.' (Th. Chalmers, *On Pol. Econ. &c.*, 2nd Ed., Glasgow, 1832, pp.165,166.)

[8] '*Il mercante non conta quasi per niente il lucro fatto, ma mira sempre al futuro.*' (A. Genovesi, *Lezioni di Economia Civile* (1765), Custodi's edit. of *Italian Economists. Parte Moderna* t.viii, p.139.)

[9] 'The inextinguishable passion for gain, the *auri sacra fames*, will always lead capitalists.' (MacCulloch: *The Principles of Polit. Econ.* London, 1830, p.179.) This view, of course, does not prevent the same MacCulloch and others of his kidney, when in theoretical difficulties, such, for example, as the question of over-production, from transforming the same capitalist into a moral citizen, whose sole concern is for use-values, and who even develops an insatiable hunger for boots, hats, eggs, calico, and other extremely familiar sorts of use-values.

[10] *sozein* is a characteristic Greek expression for hoarding. So in English to save has the same two meanings: *sauver* and *épargner*.

[11] '*Questo infinito che le cose non hanno in progresso, hanno in giro.*' (Galiani.)

[12] '*Ce n'est pas la matière qui fait le capital, mais la valeur de ces matières.*' (J. B. Say: *Traité d'Écon. Polit.* 3ème éd. Paris, 1817, t.ii, p.429.)

[13] 'Currency (!) employed in producing articles . . . is capital.' (Macleod: *The Theory and Practice of Banking.* London, 1855, v.1, ch.i, p.55.) 'Capital is commodities.' (James Mill: *Elements of Pol. Econ.* Lond., 1821, p.74.)

[14] Capital: '*portion fructifiante de la richesse accumulée . . . valeur permanents, multipliante.*' (Sismondi: *Nouveaux Principes d'Écon. Polit.*, t.i., p.88,89.)

Volume 1, Part 2, Chapter 5

[1] '*L'échange est une transaction admirable dans laquelle les deux contractants gagnent toujours.*' (!) (Destutt de Tracy: *Traité de la Volonté et de ses Effets.* Paris, 1826, p.68.) This work appeared afterwards as '*Traité d'Écon. Polit.*'

[2] Mercier de la Rivière, l.c., p.544.

[3] '*Que l'une de ces deux valeurs soit argent, ou qu'elles soient toutes deux marchandises usuelles, rien de plus indifférent en soi.*' (Mercier de la Rivière, l.c., p.543.)

[4] '*Ce ne sont pas les contractants qui prononcent sur la valeur; elle est décidée avant la convention.*' (Le Trosne, l.c., p.906.)

[5] '*Dove è egualità non è lucro.*' (Galiani, *Della Moneta in Custodi, Parte Moderna*, t.iv., p.244.)

[6] '*L'échange devient désavantageux pour l'une des parties, lorsque quelque chose étrangère vient diminuer ou exagérer le prix; alors l'égalité est blessée, mais la lésion procède de cette cause et non de l'échange.*' (Le Trosne, l.c., p.904.)

[7] '*L'échange est de sa nature un contrat d'égalité qui se fait de valeur pour valeur égale. Il n'est donc pas un moyen de s'enrichir, puisque l'on donne autant que l'on reçoit.*' (Le Trosne, l.c., p.903.)

[8] Condillac: *Le Commerce et la Gouvernement* (1776). Edit. Daire et Molinari in the *Mélanges d'Écon. Polit.* Paris, 1847, pp.267,291.

[9] Le Trosne, therefore, answers his friend Condillac with justice as follows: '*Dans une . . . société formée il n'y a pas de surabondant en aucun genre.*' At the same time, in a bantering way, he remarks: 'If both the persons who exchange receive more to an equal amount, and part with less to an equal amount, they both get the same.' It is because Condillac has not the remotest idea of the nature of exchange value that he has been chosen by Herr Professor Wilhelm Roscher as a proper person to answer for the soundness of his own childish notions. See Roscher's *Die Grundlagen der National-ökonomie, Dritte Auflage*, 1858.

[10] S. P. Newman: *Elements of Polit. Econ.* Andover and New York, 1835, p.175.

[11] 'By the augmentation of the nominal value of the produce . . . sellers not enriched . . . since what they gain as sellers, they precisely expend in the quality of buyers.' (*The Essential Principles of the Wealth of Nations, &c.*, London, 1797, p.66.)

[12] '*Si l'on est forcé de donner pour 18 livres une quantité de telle production qui en valait 24, lorsqu'on employera ce même argent à acheter, on aura également pour 18 l. ce que l'on payait 24.*' (Le Trosne, l.c., p.897.)

[13] '*Chaque vendeur ne peut donc parvenir à renchérir habituellement ses marchandises, qu'en se soumettant aussi à payer habituellement plus cher les marchandises des autres vendeurs; et par la même raison, chaque consommateur ne peut payer habituellement moins cher ce qu' il achète, qu' en se soumettant aussi à une diminution semblable sur le prix des choses qu'il vend.*' (Mercier de la Rivière, l.c., p.555.)

[14] R. Torrens. *An Essay on the Production of Wealth.* London, 1821, p.349.

[15] The idea of profits being paid by the consumers, is, assuredly, very absurd. Who are the consumers?' (G. Ramsay: *An Essay on the Distribution of Wealth.* Edinburgh, 1836, p.183.)

[16] 'When a man is in want of a demand, does Mr Malthus recommend him to pay some other person to take off his goods?' is a question put by an angry disciple of Ricardo to Malthus, who, like his disciple, Parson Chalmers, economically glorifies this class of simple buyers or consumers. (See *An Inquiry into those Principles Respecting the Nature of Demand and the Necessity of Consumption, lately advocated by Mr Malthus, &c.* Lond., 1821, p.55.)

[17] Destutt de Tracy, although, or perhaps because, he was a member of the Institute, held the opposite view. He says, industrial capitalists make profits because 'they all sell for more than it has cost to produce. And to whom do they sell? In the first instance to one another.' (l.c., p.239.)

[18] '*L'échange qui se fait de deux valeurs égales n'augmente ni ne diminue la masse des valeurs subsistantes dans la société. L'échange de deux valeurs inégales . . . ne change rien non plus à la somme des valeurs sociales, bien qu'il ajoute à la fortune de l'un ce qu'il ôte de la fortune de l'autre.*' (J. B. Say, l.c., t.ii, pp.443,444.) Say, not in the least troubled as to the consequences of this statement, borrows it, almost word for word, from the Physiocrats. The following example will show how Monsieur Say turned to account the writings of the Physiocrats, in his day quite forgotten, for the purpose of expanding the 'value' of his own. His most celebrated saying, '*On n'achète des produits qu'avec des produits*' (l.c., t.ii. p.441.) runs as follows in the original physiocratic work: '*Les productions ne se paient qu'avec des productions.*' (Le Trosne, l.c., p.899.)

[19] 'Exchange confers no value at all upon products.' (F. Wayland: *The Elements of Political Economy.* Boston, 1843, p.169.)

[20] Under the rule of invariable equivalents commerce would be impossible. (G. Opdyke: *A Treatise on Polit. Economy.* New York, 1851, pp.66–69.) 'The difference between real value and exchange value is based upon this fact, namely, that the value of a thing is different from the so-called equivalent given for it in trade, i.e., that this equivalent is no equivalent.' (F. Engels, l.c., p.96).

[21] Benjamin Franklin: *Works*, vol.ii, edit. Sparks in 'Positions to be examined concerning National Wealth', p.376.

[22] Aristotle, l.c., c.10.

[23] 'Profit, in the usual condition of the market, is not made by exchanging. Had it not existed before, neither could it after that transaction.' (Ramsay, l.c., p.184.)

[24] From the foregoing investigation, the reader will see that this statement only means that the formation of capital must be possible even though the price and value of a commodity be the same; for its formation cannot be attributed to any deviation of the one from the other. If prices actually differ from values, we must, first of all, reduce the former to the latter, in other words, treat the difference as accidental in order that

the phenomena may be observed in their purity, and our observations not interfered with by disturbing circumstances that have nothing to do with the process in question. We know, moreover, that this reduction is no mere scientific process. The continual oscillations in prices, their rising and falling, compensate each other, and reduce themselves to an average price, which is their hidden regulator. It forms the guiding star of the merchant or the manufacturer in every undertaking that requires time. He knows that when a long period of time is taken, commodities are sold neither over nor under, but at their average price. If therefore he thought about the matter at all, he would formulate the problem of the formation of capital as follows: How can we account for the origin of capital on the supposition that prices are regulated by the average price, i.e., ultimately by the value of the commodities? I say 'ultimately', because average prices do not directly coincide with the values of commodities, as Adam Smith, Ricardo, and others believe.

Volume 1, Part 2, Chapter 6

[1] 'In the form of money . . . capital is productive of no profit.' (Ricardo: *Princ. of Pol. Econ.*, p.267.)

[2] In encyclopaedias of classical antiquities we find such nonsense as this – that in the ancient world capital was fully developed, 'except that the free labourer and a system of credit was wanting.' Mommsen also, in his *History of Rome*, commits, in this respect, one blunder after another.

[3] Hence legislation in various countries fixes a maximum for labour-contracts. Wherever free labour is the rule, the laws regulate the mode of terminating this contract. In some States, particularly in Mexico (before the American Civil War, also in the territories taken from Mexico, and also, as a matter of fact, in the Danubian provinces till the revolution effected by Kusa), slavery is hidden under the form of peonage. By means of advances, repayable in labour, which are handed down from generation to generation, not only the individual labourer, but his family, become, *de facto*, the property of other persons and their families. Juarez abolished peonage. The so-called Emperor Maximilian re-established it by a decree, which, in the House of Representatives at Washington, was aptly denounced as a decree for the re-introduction of slavery into Mexico. 'I may make over to another the use, for a limited time, of my particular bodily and mental aptitudes and capabilities; because in consequence of this restriction, they are impressed with a character of alienation with regard to me as a whole. But by the alienation of all my labour-time and the whole of my work, I should be converting the substance itself, in other words, my general activity and reality, my person, into the property of another.' (Hegel, *Philosophie des Rechts.* Berlin, 1840, p.104, §67.)

[4] The capitalist epoch is therefore characterised by this, that labour power takes in the eyes of the labourer himself the form of a commodity which is his property; his labour consequently becomes wage-labour. On the other hand, it is only from this moment that the produce of labour universally becomes a commodity.

[5] 'The value or worth of a man, is as of all other things his price – that is to say, so much as would be given for the use of his power.' (Th. Hobbes: *Leviathan* in *Works*, Ed. Molesworth. Lond. 1839–44, v.iii. p.76.)

[6] Hence the Roman *villicus*, as overlooker of the agricultural slaves, received 'more meagre fare than working slaves, because his work was lighter.' (Th. Mommsen, *Röm. Geschichte*, 1856, p.810.)

[7] Compare W. H. Thornton: *Over-population and its Remedy*, Lond., 1846.

[8] Petty.

[9] 'Its (labour's) natural price . . . consists in such a quantity of necessaries and comforts of life, as, from the nature of the climate, and the habits of the country, are

necessary to support the labourer, and to enable him to rear such a family as may preserve, in the market, an undiminished supply of labour.' (R. Torrens: *An Essay on the External Corn Trade*. Lond. 1815, p.62.) The word labour is here wrongly used for labour power.

[10] Rossi: *Cours d'Écon. Polit.*, Bruxelles, 1842, p.370.

[11] Sismondi: *Nouv. Princ. etc.*, t.i, p.112.

[12] 'All labour is paid after it has ceased.' (*An Inquiry into those Principles Respecting the Nature of Demand, &c.*, p.104.) '*Le crédit commercial a dû commencer au moment où l'ouvrier, premier artisan de la production, a pu, au moyen de ses économies, attendre le salaire de son travail jusqu'à la fin de la semaine, de la quinzaine, du mois, du trimestre, &c.*' (Ch. Ganilh: *Des Systèmes d'Écon. Polit.* 2éme édit. Paris, 1821, t.ii, p.150.)

[13] '*L'ouvrier prête son industrie*,' but adds Storch slyly: he 'risks nothing' except '*de perdre son salaire . . . l'ouvrier ne transmet rien de matériel.*' (Storch: *Cours d'Écon. Polit.* Pétersbourg, 1815, t.ii, p.37.)

[14] One example. In London there are two sorts of bakers, the 'full priced', who sell bread at its full value, and the 'undersellers', who sell it under its value. The latter class comprises more than three-fourths of the total number of bakers. (p.xxxii in the Report of H. S. Tremenheere, commissioner to examine into 'the grievances complained of by the journeymen bakers', &c., Lond. 1862.) The undersellers, almost without exception, sell bread adulterated with alum, soap, pearl ashes, chalk, Derbyshire stone-dust, and such like agreeable nourishing and wholesome ingredients. (See the above cited Blue Book, as also the report of 'the committee of 1855 on the adulteration of bread', and Dr Hassall's *Adulterations Detected*, 2nd Ed. Lond. 1861.) Sir John Gordon stated before the committee of 1855, that 'in consequence of these adulterations, the poor man, who lives on two pounds of bread a day, does not now get one fourth part of nourishing matter, let alone the deleterious effects on his health.' Tremenheere states (l.c., p.xlviii), as the reason why a very large part of the workingclass, although well aware of this adulteration, nevertheless accept the alum, stonedust, &c., as part of their purchase: that it is for them 'a matter of necessity to take from their baker or from the chandler's shop, such bread as they choose to supply.' As they are not paid their wages before the end of the week, they in their turn are unable 'to pay for the bread consumed by their families, during the week, before the end of the week', and Tremenheere adds on the evidence of witnesses, 'it is notorious that bread composed of those mixtures, is made expressly for sale in this manner.' In many English and still more Scotch agricultural districts, wages are paid fortnightly and even monthly; with such long intervals between the payments, the agricultural labourer is obliged to buy on credit . . . He must pay higher prices, and is in fact tied to the shop which gives him credit. Thus at Horningham in Wilts, for example, where the wages are monthly, the same flour that he could buy elsewhere at 1s. 10d. per stone, costs him 2s. 4d. per stone. (*Sixth Report on Public Health* by 'The Medical Officer of the Privy Council, &c.', 1864, p.264.) 'The block printers of Paisley and Kilmarnock enforced, by a strike, fortnightly, instead of monthly payment of wages.' (*Reports of the Inspectors of Factories for 31st Oct., 1853*, p.34.) As a further pretty result of the credit given by the workmen to the capitalist, we may refer to the method current in many English coal mines, where the labourer is not paid till the end of the month, and in the meantime, receives sums on account from the capitalist, often in goods for which the miner is obliged to pay more than the market price (Truck-system). 'It is a common practice with the coal masters to pay once a month, and advance cash to their workmen at the end of each intermediate week. The cash is given in the shop' (i.e., the Tommy shop which belongs to the master); 'the men take it on one side and lay it out on the other.' (*Children's Employment Commission, III. Report*, Lond. 1864, p.38, n. 192.)

Volume 1, Part 3, Chapter 7

[1] 'The earth's spontaneous productions being in small quantity, and quite independent of man, appear, as it were, to be furnished by Nature, in the same way as a small sum is given to a young man, in order to put him in a way of industry, and of making his fortune.' (James Stueart: *Principles of Polit. Econ.* edit. Dublin, 1770, v.i, p.116.)

[2] 'Reason is just as cunning as she is powerful. Her cunning consists principally in her mediating activity, which, by causing objects to act and re-act on each other in accordance with their own nature, in this way, without any direct interference in the process, carries out reason's intentions.' (Hegel: *Enzyklopädie, Erster Theil, Die Logik,* Berlin, 1840, p.382.)

[3] In his otherwise miserable work (*Théorie de l'Econ. Polit.* Paris, 1815), Ganilh enumerates in a striking manner in opposition to the 'Physiocrats' the long series of previous processes necessary before agriculture properly so called can commence.

[4] Turgot in his *Réflexions sur la Formation et la Distribution des Richesses* (1766) brings well into prominence the importance of domesticated animals to early civilisation.

[5] The least important commodities of all for the technological comparison of different epochs of production are articles of luxury, in the strict meaning of the term. However little our written histories up to this time notice the development of material production, which is the basis of all social life, and therefore of all real history, yet prehistoric times have been classified in accordance with the results, not of so-called historical, but of materialistic investigations. These periods have been divided, to correspond with the materials from which their implements and weapons were made, viz., into the stone, the bronze, and the iron ages.

[6] It appears paradoxical to assert, that uncaught fish, for instance, are a means of production in the fishing industry. But hitherto no one has discovered the art of catching fish in waters that contain none.

[7] This method of determining, from the standpoint of the labour-process alone, what is productive labour, is by no means directly applicable to the case of the capitalist process of production.

[8] Storch calls true raw materials '*matières*', and accessory material '*matériaux*'. Cherbuliez describes accessories as '*matières instrumentales*'.

[9] By a wonderful feat of logical acumen, Colonel Torrens has discovered, in this stone of the savage the origin of capital. 'In the first stone which he [the savage] flings at the wild animal he pursues, in the first stick that he seizes to strike down the fruit which hangs above his reach, we see the appropriation of one article for the purpose of aiding in the acquisition of another, and thus discover the origin of capital.' (R. Torrens: *An Essay on the Production of Wealth, &c.,* pp. 70–71.)

[10] 'Products are appropriated before they are converted into capital; this conversion does not secure them from such appropriation.' (Cheibuliez: *Richesse ou Pauvreté,* edit. Paris, 1841, p.54.) 'The Proletarian, by selling his labour for a definite quantity of the necessaries of life, renounces all claim to a share in the product. The mode of appropriation of the products remains the same as before; it is in no way altered by the bargain we have mentioned. The product belongs exclusively to the capitalist, who supplied the raw material and the necessaries of life; and this is a rigorous consequence of the law of appropriation, a law whose fundamental principle was the very opposite, namely, that every labourer has an exclusive right to the ownership of what he produces.' (l.c., p.58.) 'When the labourers receive wages for their labour . . . the capitalist is then the owner not of the capital only' (he means the means of production) 'but of the labour also. If what is paid as wages is included, as it commonly is, in the term capital, it is absurd to talk of labour separately from capital. The word capital as thus employed includes labour and capital both.' (James Mill: *Elements of Pol. Econ.,* &c.,* Ed. 1821, pp.70,71.)

[11] As has been stated in a previous note, the English language has two different expressions for these two different aspects of labour: in the Simple Labour-process, the process of producing Use-Values, it is *Work*; in the process of creation of Value, it is *Labour*, taking the term in its strictly economic sense. – F. E.

[12] These figures are quite arbitrary.

[13] This is the fundamental proposition on which is based the doctrine of the Physiocrats as to the unproductiveness of all labour that is not agriculture: it is irrefutable for the orthodox economist. '*Cette façon d'imputer à une seule chose la valeur de plusieurs autres,*' (par exemple au lin la consommation du tisserand) '*d'appliquer, pour ainsi dire, couche sur couche, plusieurs valeurs sur une seule, fait que celle-ci grossit d'autant . . . Le terme d'addition peint très bien la manière dont se forme le prix des ouvrages de main d'oeuvre; ce prix n'est qu'un total de plusieurs valeurs consommées et additionnées ensemble; or, additionner n'est pas multiplier.*' (Mercier de la Rivière, l.c., p.599.)

[14] Thus from 1844–47 he withdrew part of his capital from productive employment, in order to throw it away in railway speculations; and so also, during the American Civil War, he closed his factory, and turned his work-people into the streets, in order to gamble on the Liverpool cotton exchange.

[15] 'Extol thyself, put on finery and adorn thyself . . . but whoever takes more or better than he gives, that is usury, and is not service, but wrong done to his neighbour, as when one steals and robs. All is not service and benefit to a neighbour that is called service and benefit. For an adulteress and adulterer do one another great service and pleasure. A horseman does an incendiary a great service, by helping him to rob on the highway, and pillage land and houses. The papists do ours a great service, in that they don't drown, burn, murder all of them, or let them all rot in prison; but let some live, and only drive them out, or take from them what they have. The devil himself does his servants inestimable service . . . To sum up, the world is full of great, excellent, and daily service and benefit.' (Martin Luther: '*An die Pfarherrn, wider den Wucher zu predigen*', Wittenberg, 1540.)

[16] In *Zur Kritik der Pol. Oek.*, p.14, I make the following remark on this point – 'It is not difficult to understand what "service" the category "service" must render to a class of economists like J. B. Say and F. Bastiat.'

[17] This is one of the circumstances that makes production by slave labour such a costly process. The labourer here is, to use a striking expression of the ancients, distinguishable only as *instrumentum vocale*, from an animal as *instrumentum semi-vocale*, and from an implement as *instrumentum mutum*. But he himself takes care to let both beast and implement feel that he is none of them, but is a man. He convinces himself with immense satisfaction, that he is a different being, by treating the one unmercifully and damaging the other *con amore*. Hence the principle, universally applied in this method of production, only to employ the rudest and heaviest implements and such as are difficult to damage owing to their sheer clumsiness. In the slave-states bordering on the Gulf of Mexico, down to the date of the civil war, ploughs constructed on old Chinese models, which turned up the soil like a hog or a mole, instead of making furrows, were alone to be found. cf. J. C. Cairns. *The Slave Power*, London, 1862, p.46 sqq. In his *Sea Board Slave States*, Olmsted tells us: 'I am here shown tools that no man in his senses, with us, would allow a labourer, for whom he was paying wages, to be encumbered with; and the excessive weight and clumsiness of which, I would judge, would make work at least ten per cent greater than with those ordinarily used with us. And I am assured that, in the careless and clumsy way they must be used by the slaves, anything lighter or less rude could not be furnished them with good economy, and that such tools as we constantly give our labourers and find our profit in giving them, would not last out a day in a Virginia cornfield – much lighter and more free from stones though it be than ours. So, too, when I ask why mules are so universally

substituted for horses on the farm, the first reason given, and confessedly the most conclusive one, is that horses cannot bear the treatment that they always must get from negroes; horses are always soon foundered or crippled by them, while mules will bear cudgelling, or lose a meal or two now and then, and not be materially injured, and they do not take cold or get sick, if neglected or overworked. But I do not need to go further than to the window of the room in which I am writing, to see at almost any time, treatment of cattle that would ensure the immediate discharge of the driver by almost any farmer owning them in the North.'

[18] The distinction between skilled and unskilled labour rests in part on pure illusion, or, to say the least, on distinctions that have long since ceased to be real, and that survive only by virtue of a traditional convention; in part on the helpless condition of some groups of the working-class, a condition that prevents them from exacting equally with the rest the value of their labour power. Accidental circumstances here play so great a part, that these two forms of labour sometimes change places. Where, for instance, the physique of the working-class has deteriorated, and is, relatively speaking, exhausted, which is the case in all countries with a well developed capitalist production, the lower forms of labour, which demand great expenditure of muscle, are in general considered as skilled, compared with much more delicate forms of labour; the latter sink down to the level of unskilled labour. Take as an example the labour of a bricklayer, which in England occupies a much higher level than that of a damask-weaver. Again, although the labour of a fustian cutter demands great bodily exertion, and is at the same time unhealthy, yet it counts only as unskilled labour. And then, we must not forget, that the so-called skilled labour does not occupy a large space in the field of national labour. Laing estimates that in England (and Wales) the livelihood of 11,300,000 people depends on unskilled labour. If from the total population of 18,000,000 living at the time when he wrote, we deduct 1,000,000 for the 'genteel population', and 1,500,000 for paupers, vagrants, criminals, prostitutes, &c., and 4,650,000 who compose the middle-class, there remain the above-mentioned 11,000,000. But in his middle-class he includes people that live on the interest of small investments, officials, men of letters, artists, schoolmasters and the like, and in order to swell the number he also includes in these 4,650,000 the better paid portion of the factory operatives! The bricklayers, too, figure amongst them. (S. Laing: *National Distress, &c.*, London, 1844). 'The great class who have nothing to give for food but ordinary labour, are the great bulk of the people.' (James Mill, in art.: 'Colony', *Supplement to the Encyclop. Brit.*, 1831.)

[19] 'Where reference is made to labour as a measure of value, it necessarily implies labour of one particular kind . . . the proportion which the other kinds bear to it being easily ascertained.' (*Outlines of Pol. Econ.*, Lond., 1832, pp.22 and 23.)

Volume 1, Part 3, Chapter 8

[1] 'Labour gives a new creation for one extinguished.' (*An Essay on the Polit. Econ. of Nations*, London, 1821, p.13.)

[2] The subject of repairs of the implements of labour does not concern us here. A machine that is undergoing repair, no longer plays the part of an instrument, but that of a subject of labour. Work is no longer done with it, but upon it. It is quite permissible for our purpose to assume, that the labour expended on the repairs of instruments is included in the labour necessary for their original production. But in the text we deal with that wear and tear, which no doctor can cure, and which little by little brings about death, with 'that kind of wear which cannot be repaired from time to time, and which, in the case of a knife, would ultimately reduce it to a state in which the cutler would say of it, it is not worth a new blade.' We have shown in the text, that a machine takes part in every labour-process as an integral machine, but that

into the simultaneous process of creating value it enters only bit by. bit. How great then is the confusion of ideas exhibited in the following extract! 'Mr Ricardo says a portion of the labour of the engineer in making [stocking] machines' is contained for example in the value of a pair of stockings. 'Yet the total labour, that produced each single pair of stockings . . . includes the whole labour of the engineer, not a portion; for one machine makes many pairs, and none of those pairs could have been done without any part of the machine.' (*Obs. on Certain Verbal Disputes in Pol. Econ., Particularly Relating to Value,*' p.54) The author, an uncommonly self-satisfied wiseacre, is right in his confusion and therefore in his contention, to this extent only, that neither Ricardo nor any other economist, before or since him, has accurately distinguished the two aspects of labour, and still less, therefore, the part played by it under each of these aspects in the formation of value.

[3] From this we may judge of the absurdity of J. B. Say, who pretends to account for surplus-value (Interest, Profit, Rent), by the '*services productifs*' which the means of production, soil, instruments, and raw material, render in the labour-process by means of their use-values. Mr Wm. Roscher who seldom loses an occasion of registering, in black and white, ingenious apologetic fancies, records the following specimen: 'J. B. Say (*Traité*, t.1, ch.4) very truly remarks: the value produced by an oil mill, after deduction of all costs, is something new, something quite different from the labour by which the oil mill itself was erected.' (l.c., p.82, note.) Very true, Mr Professor! the oil produced by the oil mill is indeed something very different from the labour expended in constructing the mill! By value, Mr Roscher understands such stuff as 'oil', because oil has value, notwithstanding that 'Nature' produces petroleum, though relatively 'in small quantities', a fact to which he seems to refer in his further observation: 'It (Nature) produces scarcely any exchange value.' Mr Roscher's 'Nature' and the exchange value it produces are rather like the foolish virgin who admitted indeed that she had had a child, but 'it was such a little one.' This '*savant sérieux*' in continuation remarks: 'Ricardo's school is in the habit of including capital as accumulated labour under the head of labour. This is unskilful work, because, indeed, the owner of capital, after all, does something more than the merely creating and preserving of the same: namely, the abstention from the enjoyment of it, for which he demands, e.g., interest.' (l.c.) How very 'skilful' is this 'anatomico-physiological method' of Political Economy, which, 'indeed', converts a mere desire 'after all' into a source of value.

[4] 'Of all the instruments of the farmers' trade, the labour of man . . . is that on which he is most to rely for the repayment of his capital. The other two . . . the working stock of the cattle and the . . . carts, ploughs, spades, and so forth, without a given portion of the first, are nothing at all.' (Edmund Burke: *Thoughts and Details on Scarcity, originally presented to the Right Hon. W. Pitt, in the month of November 1795*, Edit. London, 1800, p.10.)

[5] In *The Times* of 26th November, 1862, a manufacturer, whose mill employed 800 hands, and consumed, on the average, 150 bales of East Indian, or 130 bales of American cotton, complains, in doleful manner, of the standing expenses of his factory when not working. He estimates them at £6,000 a year. Among them are a number of items that do not concern us here, such as rent, rates, and taxes, insurance, salaries of the manager, book-keeper, engineer, and others. Then he reckons £150 for coal used to heat the mill occasionally, and run the engine now and then. Besides this, he includes the wages of the people employed at odd times to keep the machinery in working order. Lastly, he puts down £1,200 for depreciation of machinery, because 'the weather and the natural principle of decay do not suspend their operations because the steam-engine ceases to revolve.' He says, emphatically, he does not estimate his depreciation at more than the small sum of £1,200, because his machinery is already nearly worn out.

[6] 'Productive consumption . . . where the consumption of a commodity is a part of the process of production . . . In these instances there is no consumption of value.' (S. P. Newman, l.c., p.296.)

[7] In an American compendium that has gone through, perhaps, 20 editions, this passage occurs: 'It matters not in what form capital re-appears;' then after a lengthy enumeration of all the possible ingredients of production whose value re-appears in the product, the passage concludes thus: 'The various kinds of food, clothing, and shelter, necessary for the existence and comfort of the human being, are also changed. They are consumed from time to time, and their value re-appears in that new vigour imparted to his body and mind, forming fresh capital, to be employed again in the work of production.' (F. Wayland, l.c., pp.31,32.) Without noticing any other odd-ities, it suffices to observe, that what re-appears in the fresh vigour, is not the bread's price, but its blood-forming substances. What, on the other hand, re-appears in the value of that vigour, is not the means of subsistence, but their value. The same necessaries of life, at half the price, would form just as much muscle and bone, just as much vigour, but not vigour of the same value. This confusion of 'value' and 'vigour' coupled with our author's pharisaical indefiniteness, mark an attempt, futile for all that, to thrash out an explanation of surplus-value from a mere re-appearance of pre-existing values.

[8] *'Toutes les productions d'un même genre ne forment proprement qu'une masse, dont le prix se détermine en général et sans égard aux circonstances particulières.'* (Le Trosne, I. c., p.893.)

Volume 1, Part 3, Chapter 9

[1] 'If we reckon the value of the fixed capital employed as a part of the advances, we must reckon the remaining value of such capital at the end of the year as a part of the annual returns.' (Malthus, *Princ. of Pol. Econ.* 2nd. ed., Lond., 1836, p.269.)

[2] What Lucretius says is self-evident; *'nil posse creari de nihilo,'* out of nothing, nothing can be created. Creation of value is transformation of labour power into labour. Labour power itself is energy transferred to a human organism by means of nourishing matter.

[3] In the same way that the English use the terms 'rate of profit', 'rate of interest'. We shall see, in Book 3, that the rate of profit is no mystery, so soon as we know the laws of surplus-value. If we reverse the process, we cannot comprehend either the one or the other.

[4] Note added in the 3rd German edition. – The author resorts here to the economic language in current use. It will be remembered that . . . it was shown that in reality the labourer 'advances' to the capitalist and not the capitalist to the labourer. – F. E.

[5] In this work, we have, up to now, employed the term 'necessary labour-time', to designate the time necessary under given social conditions for the production of any commodity. Henceforward we use it to designate also the time necessary for the production of the particular commodity labour power. The use of one and the same technical term in different senses is inconvenient, but in no science can it be altogether avoided. Compare, for instance, the higher with the lower branches of mathematics.

[6] Herr Wilhelm Thucydides Roscher has found a mare's nest. He has made the important discovery that if, on the one hand, the formation of surplus-value, or surplus-produce, and the consequent accumulation of capital, is nowadays due to the thrift of the capitalist, on the other hand, in the lowest stages of civilisation it is the strong who compel the weak to economise. (l.c., p.78.) To economise what? Labour? Or superfluous wealth that does not exist? What is it that makes such men as Roscher account for the origin of surplus-value, by a mere *rechauffé* of the more or less plausible excuses by the capitalist, for his appropriation of surplus-value? It is, besides their real

ignorance, their apologetic dread of a scientific analysis of value and surplus-value, and of obtaining a result, possibly not altogether palatable to the powers that be.

[7] Although the rate of surplus-value is an exact expression for the degree of exploitation of labour power, it is, in no sense, an expression for the absolute amount of exploitation. For example, if the necessary labour = 5 hours and the surplus-labour = 5 hours, the degree of exploitation is 100%. The amount of exploitation is here measured by 5 hours. If, on the other hand, the necessary labour = 6 hours and the surplus-labour = 6 hours, the degree of exploitation remains, as before, 100%, while the actual amount of exploitation has increased 20%, namely from five hours to six.

[8] The above data, which may be relied upon, were given me by a Manchester spinner. In England the horse-power of an engine was formerly calculated from the diameter of its cylinder, now the actual horse-power shown by the indicator is taken.

[9] The calculations given in the text are intended merely as illustrations. We have in fact assumed that prices = values. We shall, however, see, in Book 3, that even in the case of average prices the assumption cannot be made in this very simple manner.

[10] Senior, l.c., pp.12,13. We let pass such extraordinary notions as are of no importance for our purpose; for instance, the assertion, that manufacturers reckon as part of their profit, gross or net, the amount required to make good wear and tear of machinery, or in other words, to replace a part of the capital. So, too, we pass over any question as to the accuracy of his figures. Leonard Horner has shown in *A Letter to Mr Senior, &c.*, London, 1837, that they are worth no more than the so-called 'Analysis'. Leonard Horner was one of the Factory Inquiry Commissioners in 1833, and Inspector, or rather Censor of Factories till 1859. He rendered undying service to the English working-class. He carried on a life-long contest, not only with the embittered manufacturers, but also with the Cabinet, to whom the number of votes given by the masters in the Lower House, was a matter of far greater importance than the number of hours worked by the 'hands' in the mills.

Apart from efforts in principle, Senior's statement is confused. What he really intended to say was this: The manufacturer employs the workman for 11 1/2 hours or for 23 half-hours daily. As the working-day, so, too, the working year, may be conceived to consist of 11 1/2 hours or 23 half-hours, but each multiplied by the number of working-days in the year. On this supposition, the 23 half-hours yield an annual product of £115,000; one half-hour yields 1/23 x £115,000; 20 half-hours yield 20/23 x £115,000 = £100,000, i.e., they replace no more than the capital advanced. There remain 3 half-hours, which yield 3/23 x £115,000 = £15,000 or the gross profit. Of these 3 half-hours, one yields 1/23 x £115,000 = £5,000; i.e., it makes up for the wear and tear of the machinery; the remaining 2 half-hours, i.e., the last hour, yield 2/23 x £115,000 = £10,000 or the net profit. In the text Senior converts the last 2/23 of the product into portions of the working-day itself.

[11] If, on the one hand, Senior proved that the net profit of the manufacturer, the existence of the English cotton industry, and England's command of the markets of the world, depend on 'the last working-hour,' on the other hand, Dr Andrew Ure showed, that if children and young persons under 18 years of age, instead of being kept the full 12 hours in the warm and pure moral atmosphere of the factory, are turned out an hour sooner into the heartless and frivolous outer world, they will be deprived, by idleness and vice, of all hope of salvation for their souls. Since 1848, the factory inspectors have never tired of twitting the masters with this 'last', this 'fatal hour'. Thus Mr Howell in his report of the 21st May, 1855: 'Had the following ingenious calculation (he quotes Senior) been correct, every cotton factory in the United Kingdom would have been working at a loss since the year 1850.' (*Reports of the Insp. of Fact. for the half-year ending 30th April, 1855*, pp.19,20.) In the year 1848, after the passing of the 10 hours' bill, the masters of some flax spinning mills, scattered, few and far

between, over the country on the borders of Dorset and Somerset, foisted a petition against the bill on to the shoulders of a few of their work-people. One of the clauses of this petition is as follows: 'Your petitioners, as parents, conceive that an additional hour of leisure will tend more to demoralise the children than otherwise, believing that idleness is the parent of vice.' On this the factory report of 31st Oct., 1848, says: 'The atmosphere of the flax mills, in which the children of these virtuous and tender parents work, is so loaded with dust and fibre from the raw material, that it is exceptionally unpleasant to stand even 10 minutes in the spinning rooms: for you are unable to do so without the most painful sensation, owing to the eyes, the ears, the nostrils, and mouth, being immediately filled by the clouds of flax dust from which there is no escape. The labour itself, owing to the feverish haste of the machinery, demands unceasing application of skill and movement, under the control of a watchfulness that never tires, and it seems somewhat hard, to let parents apply the term 'idling' to their own children, who, after allowing for meal-times, are fettered for 10 whole hours to such an occupation, in such an atmosphere . . . These children work longer than the labourers in the neighbouring villages . . . Such cruel talk about "idleness and vice" ought to be branded as the purest cant, and the most shameless hypocrisy . . . That portion of the public, who, about 12 years ago, were struck by the assurance with which, under the sanction of high authority, it was publicly and most earnestly proclaimed, that the whole net profit of the manufacturer flows from the labour of the last hour, and that, therefore, the reduction of the working-day by one hour, would destroy his net profit, that portion of the public, we say, will hardly believe its own eyes, when it now finds, that the original discovery of the virtues of "the last hour" has since been so far improved, as to include morals as well as profit; so that, if the duration of the labour of children, is reduced to a full 10 hours, their morals, together with the net profits of their employers, will vanish, both being dependent on this last, this fatal hour. (See *Repts., Insp. of Fact., for 31st Oct., 1848*, p.101.) The same report then gives some examples of the morality and virtue of these same pure-minded manufacturers, of the tricks, the artifices, the cajoling, the threats, and the falsifications, they made use of, in order, first, to compel a few defenceless workmen to sign petitions of such a kind, and then to impose them upon Parliament as the petitions of a whole branch of industry, or a whole country. It is highly characteristic of the present status of so-called economic science, that neither Senior himself, who, at a later period, to his honour be it said, energetically supported the factory legislation, nor his opponents, from first to last, have ever been able to explain the false conclusions of the 'original discovery'. They appeal to actual experience, but the why and wherefore remains a mystery.

[12] Nevertheless, the learned professor was not without some benefit from his journey to Manchester. In the *Letters on the Factory Act*, he makes the whole net gains including 'profit' and 'interests' and even 'something more', depend upon a single unpaid hour's work of the labourer. One year previously, in his *Outlines of Political Economy*, written for the instruction of Oxford students and cultivated Philistines, he had also 'discovered, in opposition to Ricardo's determination of value by labour, that profit is derived from the labour of the capitalist, and interest from his asceticism, in other words, from his abstinence.' The dodge was an old one, but the word 'abstinence' was new. Herr Roscher translates it rightly by '*Enthaltung*'. Some of his countrymen, the Browns, Jones, and Robinsons of Germany, not so well versed in Latin as he, have, monk-like, rendered it by '*Entsagung*' (renunciation).

[13] 'To an individual with a capital of £20,000, whose profits were £2,000 per annum, it would be a matter quite indifferent whether his capital would employ 100 or 1,000 men, whether the commodity produced sold for £10,000 or £20,000, provided, in all cases, his profit were not diminished below £2,000. Is not the real

interest of the nation similar? Provided its net real income, its rent and profits, be the same, it is of no importance whether the nation consists of 10 or of 12 millions of inhabitants.' (Ric. l.c., p.416.) Long before Ricardo, Arthur Young, a fanatical upholder of surplus-produce, for the rest, a rambling, uncritical writer, whose reputation is in the inverse ratio of his merit, says, 'Of what use, in a modem kingdom, would be a whole province thus divided [in the old Roman manner, by small independent peasants], however well cultivated, except for the mere purpose of breeding men, which taken singly is a most useless purpose?' (Arthur Young: *Political Arithmetic, &c.* London, 1774, p.47.)

Very curious is 'the strong inclination . . . to represent net wealth as beneficial to the labouring class . . . though it is evidently not on account of being net.' (Th . Hopkins, *On Rent of Land, &c.* London, 1828, p.126.)

Volume 1, Part 3, Chapter 10

[1] 'A day's labour is vague, it may be long or short.' (*An Essay on Trade and Commerce, Containing Observations on Taxes, &c.* London. 1770, p.73.)

[2] This question is far more important than the celebrated question of Sir Robert Peel to the Birmingham Chamber of Commerce: What is a pound? A question that could only have been proposed, because Peel was as much in the dark as to the nature of money as the 'little shilling men' of Birmingham.

[3] 'It is the aim of the capitalist to obtain with his expended capital the greatest possible quantity of labour (*d'obtenir du capital dépensé la plus forte somme de travail possible*). J. G. Courcelle-Seneuil. *Traité théorique et pratique des entreprises industrielles.* 2nd ed. Paris, 1857, p.63.

[4] 'An hour's labour lost in a day is a prodigious injury to a commercial State . . . There is a very great consumption of luxuries among the labouring poor of this kingdom: particularly among the manufacturing populace, by which they also consume their time, the most fatal of consumptions.' *An Essay on Trade and Commerce, &c.*, p.47, and 153.

[5] '*Si le manouvrier libre prend un instant de repos, l'économie sordide qui le suit des yeux avec inquiétude, prétend qu'il la volé.*' N. Linguet, *Théorie des Lois Civiles. &c.* London, 1767, t.ii, p.466.

[6] During the great strike of the London builders, 1860–61, for the reduction of the working-day to 9 hours, their Committee published a manifesto that contained, to some extent, the plea of our worker. The manifesto alludes, not without irony, to the fact, that the greatest profit-monger amongst the building masters, a certain Sir M. Peto, was in the odour of sanctity (This same Peto, after 1867, came to an end *à la* Strousberg.)

[7] 'Those who labour . . . in reality feed both the pensioners . . . [called the rich] and themselves.' (Edmund Burke, l.c., p.2.)

[8] Niebuhr in his *Roman History* says very naively: 'It is evident that works like the Etruscan, which in their ruins astound us, presuppose in little (!) states lords and vassals.' Sismondi says far more to the purpose that 'Brussels lace' presupposes wage-lords and wage-slaves.

[9] 'One cannot see these unfortunates (in the gold mines between Egypt, Ethiopia, and Arabia) who cannot even have their bodies clean, or their nakedness clothed, without pitying their miserable lot. There is no indulgence, no forbearance for the sick, the feeble, the aged, for woman's weakness. All must, forced by blows, work on until death puts an end to their sufferings and their distress.' (Diod. Sic. *Bibl. Hist.*, lib.2, c.13.)

[10] That which follows refers to the situation in the Roumanian provinces before the change effected since the Crimean war.

[11] This holds likewise for Germany, and especially for Prussia east of the Elbe. In the 15th century the German peasant was nearly everywhere a man, who, whilst subject to certain rents paid in produce and labour, was otherwise at least practically free. The German colonists in Brandenburg, Pomerania, Silesia, and Eastern Prussia, were even legally acknowledged as free men. The victory of the nobility in the peasants' war put an end to that. Not only were the conquered South German peasants again enslaved. From the middle of the 16th century the peasants of Eastern Prussia, Brandenburg, Pomerania, and Silesia, and soon after the free peasants of Schleswig-Holstein were degraded to the condition of serfs. (Maurer, *Fronhöfe* iv. vol., – *Meitzen, Der Boden des preussischen Staats* – Hanssen, *Leibeigenschaft in Schleswig-Holstein*. – F. E.)

[12] Further details are to be found in E. Regnault's *Histoire politique et sociale des Principautés Danubiennes*, Paris, 1855.

[13] 'In general and within certain limits, exceeding the medium size of their kind, is evidence of the prosperity of organic beings. As to man, his bodily height lessens if his due growth is interfered with, either by physical or local conditions. In all European countries in which the conscription holds, since its introduction, the medium height of adult men, and generally their fitness for military service, has diminished. Before the revolution (1789), the minimum for the infantry in France was 165 centimetres; in 1818 (law of March 10th), 157; by the law of March 21, 1832, 156 c.m.; on the average in France more than half are rejected on account of deficient height or bodily weakness. The military standard in Saxony was in 1780, 178 c. m. It is now 155. In Prussia it is 157. According to the statement of Dr Meyer in the *Bavarian Gazette*, May 9th, 1862, the result of an average of 9 years is, that in Prussia out of 1,000 conscripts 716 were unfit for military service, 317 because of deficiency in height, and 399 because of bodily defects . . . Berlin in 1858 could not provide its contingent of recruits, it was 156 men short.' J. von Liebig: *Die Chemie in ihrer Anwendung auf Agrikultur und Physiologie*. 1862, 7th Ed., vol.1, pp.117,118.

[14] The history of the Factory Act of 1850 will be found in the course of this chapter.

[15] I only touch here and there on the period from the beginning of modern industry in England to 1845. For this period I refer the reader to *Die Lage der arbeitenden Klasse in England*, von Friedrich Engels, Leipzig, 1845. How completely Engels understood the nature of the capitalist mode of production is shown by the Factory Reports, Reports on Mines, &c., that have appeared since 1845, and how wonderfully he painted the circumstances in detail is seen on the most superficial comparison of his work with the official reports of the Children's Employment Commission, published 18 to 20 years later (1863–1867). These deal especially with the branches of industry in which the Factory Acts had not, up to 1862, been introduced, in fact are not yet introduced. Here, then, little or no alteration had been enforced, by authority, in the conditions painted by Engels. I borrow my examples chiefly from the Free-trade period after 1848, that age of paradise, of which the commercial travellers for the great firm of Free-trade, blatant as ignorant, tell such fabulous tales. For the rest England figures here in the foreground because she is the classic representative of capitalist production, and she alone has a continuous set of official statistics of the things we are considering.

[16] *Suggestions, &c. by Mr L. Homer, Inspector of Factories, in Factories Regulation Acts. Ordered by the House of Commons to be printed, 9th August, 1859*, pp.4,5.

[17] *Reports of the Inspector of Factories for the half year. October, 1856*, p.35.

[18] *Reports, &c., 30th April, 1858*, p.9.

[19] *Reports, &c.*, l.c., p.43.

[20] *Reports &c.*, l.c., p.25.

[21] *Reports &c., for the half year ending 30th April, 1861*. See Appendix No. 2; *Reports, &c.*, 31st October, 1862, pp.7,52,53. The violations of the Acts became more numerous during the last half year 1863. cf *Reports, &c., ending 31st October, 1863*, p.7.

[22] *Reports, &c., October 31st, 1860*, p.23. With what fanaticism, according to the evidence of manufacturers given in courts of law, their hands set themselves against every interruption in factory labour, the following curious circumstance shows. In the beginning of June, 1836, information reached the magistrates of Dewsbury (Yorkshire) that the owners of 8 large mills in the neighbourhood of Batley had violated the Factory Acts. Some of these gentlemen were accused of having kept at work 5 boys between 12 and 15 years of age, from 6 a.m. on Friday to 4 p.m. on the following Saturday, not allowing them any respite except for meals and one hour for sleep at midnight. And these children had to do this ceaseless labour of 30 hours in the 'shoddyhole', as the hole is called, in which the woollen rags are pulled in pieces, and where a dense atmosphere of dust, shreds, &c., forces even the adult workman to cover his mouth continually with handkerchiefs for the protection of his lungs! The accused gentlemen affirm in lieu of taking an oath – as quakers they were too scrupulously religious to take an oath – that they had, in their great compassion for the unhappy children, allowed them four hours for sleep, but the obstinate children absolutely would not go to bed. The quaker gentlemen were mulcted in £20. Dryden anticipated these gentry:

> Fox full fraught in seeming sanctity,
> That feared an oath, but like the devil would lie,
> That look'd like Lent, and had the holy leer,
> And durst not sin! before he said his prayer!'

[23] *Rep., 31st Oct., 1856*, p.34.

[24] l.c., p.35.

[25] l.c., p.48.

[26] l.c., p.48.

[27] l.c., p.48.

[28] l.c., p.48.

[29] *Report of the Insp. &c., 30th April 1860*, p.56.

[30] This is the official expression both in the factories and in the reports.

[31] 'The cupidity of mill-owners whose cruelties in the pursuit of gain have hardly been exceeded by those perpetrated by the Spaniards on the conquest of America in the pursuit of gold.' John Wade, *History of the Middle and Working Classes*, 3rd Ed. London, 1835, p.114. The theoretical part of this book, a kind of hand-book of Political Economy is, considering the time of its publication, original in some parts, e.g., on commercial crises. The historical part is, to a great extent, a shameless plagiarism of Sir F. M. Eden's *The State of the Poor*, London, 1797.

[32] *Daily Telegraph*, 17th January, 1860.

[33] cf. F. Engels *Lage, etc.* pp.249–51.

[34] *Children's Employment Commission. First report, etc.,1863.* Evidence, p.16,19,18

[35] *Public Health, 3rd report, etc.*, pp.102,104,105.

[36] *Child. Empl. Comm. I. Report*, p.24.

[37] *Children's Employment Commission*, p.22, and xi.

[38] l.c., p.xlvii.

[39] l.c., p.liv.

[40] This is not to be taken in the same sense as our surplus-labour time. These gentlemen consider 10 1/2 hours of labour as the normal working-day, which includes of course the normal surplus-labour. After this begins 'over-time' which is paid a little better. It will be seen later that the labour expended during the so-called normal day is paid below its value, so that the over-time is simply a capitalist trick in order to extort more surplus-labour, which it would still be, even if the labour power expended during the normal working-day were properly paid.

[41] l.c., Evidence, pp.123,124,125,140, and 54.

[42] Alum finely powdered, or mixed with salt, is a normal article of commerce bearing the significant name of 'bakers' stuff'.

[43] Soot is a well-known and very energetic form of carbon, and forms a manure that capitalistic chimney-sweeps sell to English farmers. Now in 1862 the British juryman had in a law-suit to decide whether soot, with which, unknown to the buyer, 90% of dust and sand are mixed, is genuine soot in the commercial sense or adulterated soot in the legal sense. The '*amis du commerce*' decided it to be genuine commercial soot, and non-suited the plaintiff farmer, who had in addition to pay the costs of the suit.

[44] The French chemist, Chevallier, in his treatise on the 'sophistications' of commodities, enumerates for many of the 600 or more articles which he passes in review, 10, 20, 30 different methods of adulteration. He adds that he does not know all the methods and does not mention all that he knows. He gives 6 kinds of adulteration of sugar, 9 of olive oil, 10 of butter, 12 of salt, 19 of milk, 20 of bread, 23 of brandy, 24 of meal, 28 of chocolate, 30 of wine, 32 of coffee, etc. Even God Almighty does not escape this fate. See Rouard de Card, *On the Falsifications of the Materials of the Sacrament*. (*De la falsification des substances sacramentelles*, Paris, 1856.)

[45] *Report, &c., relating to the grievances complained of by the journeymen bakers, &c., London, 1862*, and *Second Report, &c., London, 1863*.

[46] l.c., *First Report, &c.*, p.vi.

[47] l.c., p.lxxi.

[48] George Read, *The History of Baking*, London, 1848, p.16.

[49] *Report (First) &c.* Evidence of the 'full-priced' baker Cheeseman, p.108.

[50] George Read, l.c. At the end of the 17th and the beginning of the 18th centuries the factors (agents) that crowded into every possible trade were still denounced as 'public nuisances.' Thus the Grand Jury at the quarter session of the Justices of the Peace for the County of Somerset, addressed a presentment to the Lower House which, among other things, states, 'that these factors of Blackwell Hall are a Public Nuisance and Prejudice to the Clothing Trade, and ought to be put down as a Nuisance.' *The Case of our English Wool., &c.*, London, 1685, pp.6,7.

[51] *First Report, &c.*

[52] *Report of Committee on the Baking Trade in Ireland for 1861*.

[53] l.c.

[54] Public meeting of agricultural labourers at Lasswade, near Edinburgh, January 5th, 1866. (See *Workman's Advocate*, January 13th, 1866.) The formation since the close of 1865 of a Trades' Union among the agricultural labourers at first in Scotland is a historic event. In one of the most oppressed agricultural districts of England, Buckinghamshire, the labourers, in March, 1867, made a great strike for the raising of their weekly wage from 9–10 shillings to 12 shillings. (It will be seen from the preceding passage that the movement of the English agricultural proletariat, entirely crushed since the suppression of its violent manifestations after 1830, and especially since the introduction of the new Poor Laws, begins again in the sixties, until it becomes finally epoch-making in 1872. I return to this in the 2nd volume, as well as to the Blue Books that have appeared since 1867 on the position of the English land labourers. Addendum to the 3rd ed.)

[55] *Reynolds' Newspaper*, January, 1866. – Every week this same paper has, under the sensational headings, 'Fearful and fatal accidents', 'Appalling tragedies', &c., a whole list of fresh railway catastrophes. On these an employé on the North Staffordshire line comments: 'Everyone knows the consequences that may occur if the driver and fireman of a locomotive engine are not continually on the look-out. How can that be expected from a man who has been at such work for 29 or 30 hours, exposed to the weather, and without rest. The following is an example which is of very frequent occurrence: – One fireman commenced work on the Monday morning at a very early

hour. When he had finished what is called a day's work, he had been on duty 14 hours 50 minutes. Before he had time to get his tea, he was again called on for duty . . . The next time he finished he had been on duty 14 hours 25 minutes, making a total of 29 hours 15 minutes without intermission. The rest of the week's work was made up as follows: – Wednesday, 15 hours: Thursday, 15 hours 35 minutes; Friday, 14 1/2 hours; Saturday, 14 hours 10 minutes, making a total for the week of 88 hours 40 minutes. Now, sir, fancy his astonishment on being paid 6 1/4 days for the whole. Thinking it was a mistake, he applied to the time-keeper, . . . and inquired what they considered a day's work, and was told 13 hours for a goods man (i.e., 78 hours) . . . He then asked for what he had made over and above the 78 hours per week, but was refused. However, he was at last told they would give him another quarter, i.e. 10d.,' l.c., 4th February. 1866.

[56] cf F. Engels, l.c., pp.253,254.

[57] Dr Letheby, Consulting Physician of the Board of Health, declared: 'The minimum of air for each adult ought to be in a sleeping room 300, and in a dwelling room 500 cubic feet.' Dr Richardson, Senior Physician to one of the London Hospitals: 'With needlewomen of all kinds, including milliners, dressmakers, and ordinary sempstresses, there are three miseries – over-work, deficient air, and either deficient food or deficient digestion . . . Needlework, in the main, . . . is infinitely better adapted to women than to men. But the mischiefs of the trade, in the metropolis especially, are that it is monopolised by some twenty-six capitalists, who, under the advantages that spring from capital, can bring in capital to force economy out of labour. This power tells throughout the whole class. If a dressmaker can get a little circle of customers, such is the competition that, in her home, she must work to the death to hold together, and this same over-work she must of necessity inflict on any who may assist her. If she fail, or do not try independently, she must join an establishment, where her labour is not less, but where her money is safe. Placed thus, she becomes a mere slave. tossed about with the variations of society. Now at home, in one room, starving, or near to it, then engaged 15, 16, aye, even 18 hours out of the 24, in an air that is scarcely tolerable, and on food which, even if it be good, cannot be digested in the absence of pure air. On these victims, consumption, which is purely a disease of bad air, feeds.' Dr Richardson: 'Work and Over-work', in Social Science Review, 18th July, 1863.

[58] Morning Star, 23rd June, 1863. – The Times made use of the circumstance to defend the American slave-owners against Bright, &c. 'Very many of us think,' says a leader of July 2nd, 1863, 'that, while we work our own young women to death, using the scourge of starvation, instead of the crack of the whip, as the instrument of compulsion, we have scarcely a right to hound on fire and slaughter against families who were born slave-owners, and who, at least, feed their slaves well, and work them lightly.' In the same manner, the Standard, a Tory organ, fell foul of the Rev. Newman Hall: 'He excommunicated the slave-owners, but prays with the fine folk who, without remorse, make the omnibus drivers and conductors of London, &c., work 16 hours a day for the wages of a dog.' Finally, spake the oracle, Thomas Carlyle, of whom I wrote, in 1850, 'Zum Teufel ist der Genius, der Kultus ist geblieben.' In a short parable, he reduces the one great event of contemporary history, the American Civil War, to this level, that the Peter of the North wants to break the head of the Paul of the South with all his might, because the Peter of the North hires his labour by the day, and the Paul of the South hires his by the life. (Macmillan's Magazine. Ilias Americana in nuce. August, 1863.) Thus, the bubble of Tory sympathy for the urban workers – by no means for the rural – has burst at last. The sum of all is – slavery!

[59] Dr Richardson, l.c.

[60] Children's Employment Commission. Third Report. London, 1864, pp.iv,v,vi.

[61] 'Both in Staffordshire and in South Wales young girls and women are employed on the pit banks and on the coke heaps, not only by day but also by night. This practice has been often noticed in Reports presented to Parliament, as being attended with great and notorious evils. These females employed with the men, hardly distinguished from them in their dress, and begrimed with dirt and smoke, are exposed to the deterioration of character, arising from the loss of self-respect, which can hardly fail to follow from their unfeminine occupation.' (l.c., 194, p.xxvi. cf. *Fourth Report (1865)*, 61, p.xiii) It is the same in glass-works.

[62] A steel manufacturer who employs children in night-labour remarked: 'It seems but natural that boys who work at night cannot sleep and get proper rest by day, but will be running about.' (l.c., *Fourth Report, 63*, p.xiii.) On the importance of sunlight for the maintenance and growth of the body, a physician writes: 'Light also acts upon the tissues of the body directly in hardening them and supporting their elasticity. Tne muscles of animals, when they are deprived of a proper amount of light, become sofl and inelastic, the nervous power loses its tone from defective stimulation, and the elaboration of all growth seems to be perverted . . . In the case of children, constant access to plenty of light during the day, and to the direct rays of the sun for a part of it, is most essential to health. Light assists in the elaboration of good plastic blood, and hardens the fibre after it has been laid down. It also acts as a stimulus upon the organs of sight, and by this means brings about more activity in the various cerebral functions.' Dr W. Strange, Senior Physician of the Worcester General Hospital, from whose work on *Health* (1864) this passage is taken, writes in a letter to Mr White, one of the commissioners: 'I have had opportunities formerly, when in Lancashire, of observing the effects of nightwork upon children, and I have no hesitation in saying, contrary to what some employers were fond of asserting, those children who were subjected to it soon suffered in their health.' (l.c., 284, p.55.) That such a question should furnish the material of serious controversy, shows plainly how capitalist production acts on the brain-functions of capitalists and their retainers.

[63] l.c., 57, p.xii.

[64] l.c.. *Fourth Report (1865)*. 58. p.xii.

[65] l.c.

[66] l.c., p.xiii. The degree of culture of these 'labour powers' must naturally be such as appears in the following dialogues with one of the commissioners: Jeremiah Haynes, age 12 – 'Four times four is 8; 4 fours are 16. A king is him that has all the money and gold. We have a king (told it is a Queen), they call her the Princess Alexandra. Told that she married the Queen's son. The Queen's son is the Princess Alexandra. A Princess is a man.' William Turner, age 12 – 'Don't live in England. Think it is a country, but didn't know before.' John Morris, age 14 – 'Have heard say that God made the world, and that all the people was drownded but one, heard say that one was a little bird.' William Smith age 15 – 'God made man, man made woman.' Edward Taylor, age 15 – 'Do not know of London.' Henry Matthewman, age 17 – 'Had been to chapel, but missed a good many times lately. One name that they preached about was Jesus Christ, but I cannot say any others, and I cannot tell anything about him. He was not killed, but died like other people. He was not the same as other people in some ways, because he was religious in some ways and others isn't.' (l.c., p.xv.) 'The devil is a good person. I don't know where he lives.' 'Christ was a wicked man.' 'This girl spelt God as dog, and did not know the name of the queen.' (*Ch. Employment Comm. V. Report, 1866* p.55, n. 278.) The same system obtains in the glass and paper works as in the metallurgical, already cited. In the paper factories, where the paper is made by machinery, night-work is the rule for all processes, except rag-sorting. In some cases night-work, by relays, is carried on incessantly through the whole week, usually from Sunday night until midnight of the following Saturday. Those who are on

day-work work 5 days of 12, and 1 day of 18 hours; those on night-work 5 nights of 12, and 1 of 6 hours in each week. In other cases each set works 24 hours consecutively on alternate days, one set working 6 hours on Monday, and 18 on Saturday to make up the 24 hours. In other cases an intermediate system prevails, by which all employed on the paper-making machinery work 15 or 16 hours every day in the week. This system, says Commissioner Lord, 'seems to combine all the evils of both the 12 hours' and the 24 hours' relays.' Children under 13, young persons under 18, and women, work under this night system. Sometimes under the 12 hours' system they are obliged, on account of the non-appearance of those that ought to relieve them, to work a double turn of 24 hours. The evidence proves that boys and girls very often work overtime, which, not unfrequently, extends to 24 or even 36 hours of uninterrupted toil. In the continuous and unvarying process of glazing are found girls of 12 who work the whole month 14 hours a day, 'without any regular relief or cessation beyond 2 or, at most, 3 breaks of half an hour each for meals'. In some mills. where regular night-work has been entirely given up, over-work goes on to a terrible extent, 'and that often in the dirtiest, and in the hottest, and in the most monotonous of the various processes.' (*Ch. Employment Comm. Report IV., 1865*, p.xxxviii, and xxxix.)

[67] *Fourth Report, &c. 1865*, 79, p.xvi.

[68] l.c., 80. p.xvi.

[69] l.c., 82. p.xvii.

[70] 'In our reflecting and reasoning age a man is not worth much who cannot give a good reason for everything, no matter how bad or how crazy. Everything in the world that has been done wrong has been done wrong for the very best of reasons.' (Hegel, l.c., p.249)

[71] l.c., 85, p.xvii. To similar tender scruples of the glass manufacturers that regular meal-times for the children are impossible because as a consequence a certain quantity of heat, radiated by the furnaces, would be 'a pure loss' or 'wasted', Commissioner White makes answer. His answer is unlike that of Ure, Senior, &c., and their puny German plagiarists *à la* Roscher who are touched by the 'abstinence', 'self-denial', 'saving', of the capitalists in the expenditure of their gold, and by their Timur-Tamerlanish prodigality of human life! 'A certain amount of heat beyond what is usual at present might also be going to waste, if meal-times were secured in these cases, but it seems likely not equal in money-value to the waste of animal power now going on in glass-houses throughout the kingdom from growing boys not having enough quiet time to eat their meals at ease, with a little rest afterwards for digestion.' (l.c., p.xiv.) And this in the year of progress 1865! Without considering the expenditure of strength in lifting and carrying, such a child, in the sheds where bottle and flint glass are made, walks during the performance of his work 15–20 miles in every 6 hours! And the work often lasts 14 or 15 hours! In many of these glass works, as in the Moscow spinning mills, the system of 6 hours' relays is in force. 'During the working part of the week six hours is the utmost unbroken period ever attained at any one time for rest, and out of this has to come the time spent in coming and going to and from work, washing, dressing, and meals, leaving a very short period indeed for rest, and none for fresh air and play, unless at the expense of the sleep necessary for young boys, especially at such hot and fatiguing work . . . Even the short sleep is obviously liable to be broken by a boy having to wake himself if it is night, or by the noise, if it is day.' Mr White gives cases where a boy worked 36 consecutive hours; others where boys of 12 drudged on until 2 in the morning, and then slept in the works till 5 a.m. (3 hours!) only to resume their work. 'The amount of work,' say Tremenheere and Tufnell, who drafted the general report, 'done by boys, youths, girls, and women, in the course of their daily or nightly spell of labour, is certainly extraordinary.' (l.c., xliii and xliv) Meanwhile, late by night, self-denying

Mr Glass-Capital, primed with port-wine, reels out of his club homeward droning out idiotically. 'Britons never, never shall be slaves!'

[72] In England even now occasionally in rural districts a labourer is condemned to imprisonment for desecrating the Sabbath, by working in his front garden. The same labourer is punished for breach of contract if he remains away from his metal, paper, or glass works on the Sunday, even if it be from a religious whim. The orthodox Parliament will hear nothing of Sabbath-breaking if it occurs in the process of expanding capital. A memorial (August 1863), in which the London day-labourers in fish and poultry shops asked for the abolition of Sunday labour, states that their work lasts for the first 6 days of the week on an average 15 hours a day, and on Sunday 8–10 hours. From this same memorial we learn also that the delicate gourmands among the aristocratic hypocrites of Exeter Hall, especially encourage this 'Sunday labour'. These 'holy ones', so zealous *in cute curanda*, show their Christianity by the humility with which they bear the overwork, the privations, and the hunger of others. *Obsequium ventris istis* (the labourers) *perniciosius est.*

[73] 'We have given in our previous reports the statements of several experienced manufacturers to the effect that over-hours . . . certainly tend prematurely to exhaust the working power of the men.' (l.c., 64. p.xiii)

[74] Cairnes, *The Slave Power*, pp.110,111.

[75] John Ward: *The Borough of Stoke-upon-Trent*, London, 1843, p.42.

[76] Ferrand's Speech in the House of Commons, 27th April, 1863.

[77] Those were the very words used by the cotton manufacturers. l.c.

[78] l.c. Mr Villiers, despite the best of intentions on his part, was 'legally' obliged to refuse the requests of the manufacturers. These gentlemen, however, attained their end through the obliging nature of the local poor law boards. Mr A. Redgrave, Inspector of Factories, asserts that this time the system under which orphans and pauper children were treated 'legally' as apprentices 'was not accompanied with the old abuses' (on these 'abuses' see Engels, l.c.), although in one case there certainly was 'abuse of this system in respect to a number of girls and young women brought from the agricultural districts of Scotland into Lancashire and Cheshire.' Under this system the manufacturer entered into a contract with the workhouse authorities for a certain period. He fed, clothed and lodged the children, and gave them a small allowance of money. A remark of Mr Redgrave to be quoted directly seems strange, especially if we consider that even among the years of prosperity of the English cotton trade, the year 1860 stands unparalleled, and that, besides, wages were exceptionally high. For this extraordinary demand for work had to contend with the depopulation of Ireland, with unexampled emigration from the English and Scotch agricultural districts to Australia and America, with an actual diminution of the population in some of the English agricultural districts, in consequence partly of an actual breakdown of the vital force of the labourers, partly of the already effected dispersion of the disposable population through the dealers in human flesh. Despite all this Mr Redgrave says: 'This kind of labour, however, would only be sought after when none other could be procured, for it is a high-priced labour. The ordinary wages of a boy of 13 would be about 4s. per week, but to lodge, to clothe, to feed, and to provide medical attendance and proper superintendence for 50 or 100 of these boys, and to set aside some remuneration for them, could not be accomplished for 4s. a-head per week.' (*Report of the Inspector of Factories for 30th April, 1860*, p.27.) Mr Redgrave forgets to tell us how the labourer himself can do all this for his children out of their 4s. a week wages, when the manufacturer cannot do it for the 50 or 100 children lodged, boarded, superintended all together. To guard against false conclusions from the text, I ought here to remark that the English cotton industry, since it was placed under the Factory Act of 1850 with its regulations of labour-time, &c., must be regarded as the model industry of

England. The English cotton operative is in every respect better off than his Continental companion in misery. 'The Prussian factory operative labours at least ten hours per week more than his English competitor, and if employed at his own loom in his own house, his labour is not restricted to even those additional hours. (*Rep. of Insp. of Fact., 31st October, 1855*, p.103.) Redgrave, the Factory Inspector mentioned above, after the Industrial Exhibition in 1851, travelled on the Continent, especially in France and Germany, for the purpose of inquiring into the conditions of the factories. Of the Prussian operative he says: 'He receives a remuneration sufficient to procure the simple fare, and to supply the slender comforts to which he has been accustomed . . . he lives upon his coarse fare, and works hard, wherein his position is subordinate to that of the English operative.' (*Rep. of Insp. of Fact. 31st Oct., 1855*, p.85.)

[79] The over-worked 'die off with strange rapidity; but the places of those who perish are instantly filled, and a frequent change of persons makes no alteration in the scene.' (*England and America*. London, 1833, vol.i, p.55. By E. G. Wakefield.)

[80] See *Public Health. Sixth Report of the Medical Officer of the Privy Council, 1863*. Published in London 1864. This report deals especially with the agricultural labourers. 'Sutherland . . . is commonly represented as a highly improved county . . . but . . . recent inquiry has discovered that even there, in districts once famous for fine men and gallant soldiers, the inhabitants have degenerated into a meagre and stunted race. In the healthiest situations, on hill sides fronting the sea, the faces of their famished children are as pale as they could be in the foul atmosphere of a London alley.' (W. Th. Thornton. *Overpopulation and its Remedy*. l.c., pp.74,75.) They resemble in fact the 30,000 'gallant Highlanders' whom Glasgow pigs together in its wynds and closes, with prostitutes and thieves.

[81] 'But though the health of a population is so important a fact of the national capital, we are afraid it must be said that the class of employers of labour have not been the most forward to guard and cherish this treasure . . . The consideration of the health of the operatives was forced upon the mill-owners.' (*Times*, November 5th, 1861.) 'The men of the West Riding became the clothiers of mankind . . . the health of the workpeople was sacnficed, and the lace in a few generations must have degenerated. But a reaction set in. Lord Shaftesbury's Bill limited the hours of children's labour,' &c. (*Report of the Registrar-General*, for October 1861.)

[82] We, therefore, find, e.g., that in the beginning of 1863, 26 firms owning extensive potteries in Staffordshire, amongst others, Josiah Wedgwood, & Sons, petition in a memorial for 'some legislative enactment'. Competition with other capitalists permits them no voluntary limitation of working-time for children, &c. 'Much as we deplore the evils before mentioned, it would not be possible to prevent them by any scheme of agreement between the manufacturers . . . Taking all these points into consideration, we have come to the conviction that some legislative enactment is wanted.' (*Children's Employment Comm. Rep. i, 1863*, p.322.) Most recently a much more striking example offers. The rise in the price of cotton during a period of feverish activity, had induced the manufacturers in Blackburn to shorten, by mutual consent, the working-time in their mills during a certain fixed period. This period terminated about the end of November, 1871. Meanwhile, the wealthier manufacturers, who combined spinning with weaving, used the diminution of production resulting from this agreement, to extend their own business and thus to make great profits at the expense of the small employers. The latter thereupon turned in their extremity to the operatives, urged them earnestly to agitate for the 9 hours' system, and promised contributions in money to this end.

[83] The Labour Statutes, the like of which were enacted at the same time in France, the Netherlands, and elsewhere, were first formally repealed in England in 1813, long after the changes in methods of production had rendered them obsolete.

[84] 'No child under 12 years of age shall be employed in any manufacturing establishment more than 10 hours in one day.' General Statutes of Massachusetts, 63, ch. 12. (The various Statutes were passed between 1836 and 1858.) 'Labour performed during a period of 10 hours on any day in all cotton, woollen, silk, paper, glass, and flax factories, or in manufactories of iron and brass, shall be considered a legal day's labour. And be it enacted, that hereafter no minor engaged in any factory shall be holden or required to work more than 10 hours in any day, or 60 hours in any week; and that hereafter no minor shall be admitted as a worker under the age of 10 years in any factory within this State.' State of New Jersey. An Act to limit the hours of labour, l.c., §1 and 2. (Law of 18th March, 1851.) 'No minor who has attained the age of 12 years, and is under the age of 15 years, shall be employed in any manufacturing atablishment more than 11 hours in any one day, nor before 5 o'clock in the morning, nor after 7.30 in the evening.' (*Revised Statutes of the State of Rhode Island, &c.*, ch.139, §23, 1st July, 1857.)

[85] *Sophisms of Free Trade.* 7th Ed. London, 1850, p.205, 9th Ed., p.253. This same Tory, moreover, admits that 'Acts of Parliament regulating wages, but against the labourer and in favour of the master, lasted for the long period of 464 years. Population grew. These laws were then found, and really became, unnecessary and burdensome.' (l.c., p.206.)

[86] In reference to this statute, J. Wade with truth remarks: 'From the statement above (i.e., with regard to the statute) it appears that in 1496 the diet was considered equivalent to one-third of the income of an artificer and one-half the income of a labourer, which indicates a greater degree of independence among the working-classes than prevails at present; for the board, both of labourers and artificers, would now be reckoned at a much higher proportion of their wages.' (J. Wade, *History of the Middle and Working Classes*, pp.24,25, and 577.) The opinion that this difference is due to the difference in the price relations between food and clothing then and now is refuted by the most cursory glance at *Chronicon Preciosum, &c.* By Bishop Fleetwood. 1st Ed., London, 1707; 2nd Ed., London, 1745.

[87] W. Petty. *Political Anatomy of Ireland, Verbum Sapienti, 1672*, Ed. 1691, p.10.

[88] *A Discourse on the necessity of encouraging Mechanick Industry*, London, 1690, p.13. Macaulay, who has falsified English history in the interests of the Whigs and the bourgeoisie, declares as follows: 'The practice of setting children prematurely to work . . . prevailed in the 17th century to an extent which, when compared with the extent of the manufacturing system, seems almost incredible. At Norwich, the chief seat of the clothing trade, a little creature of six years old was thought fit for labour. Several writers of that time, and among them some who were considered as eminently benevolent, mention with exultation the fact that in that single city, boys and girls of very tender age create wealth exceeding what was necessary for their own subsistence by twelve thousand pounds a year. The more carefully we examine the history of the past, the more reason shall we find to dissent from those who imagine that our age has been fruitful of new social evils . . . That which is new is the intelligence and the humanity which remedies them.' (*History of England*, vol. 1., p.417.) Macaulay might have reported further that 'extremely well-disposed' *amis du commerce* in the 17th century, narrate with 'exultation' how in a poorhouse in Holland a child of four was employed, and that this example of '*vertu mise en pratique*' passes muster in all the humanitarian works, *à la* Macaulay, to the time of Adam Smith. It is true that with the substitution of manufacture for handicrafts, traces of the exploitation of children begin to appear. This exploitation existed always to a certain extent among peasants, and was the more developed, the heavier the yoke pressing on the husbandman. The tendency of capital is there unmistakably; but the facts themselves are still as isolated as the phenomena of two-headed children. Hence they were noted 'with exultation' as

especially worthy of remark and as wonders by the far-seeing '*amis du commerce*', and recommended as models for their own time and for posterity. This same Scotch sycophant and fine talker, Macaulay, says: 'We hear today only of retrogression and see only progress.' What eyes, and especially what ears!

[89] Among the accusers of the workpeople, the most angry is the anonymous author quoted in the text of *An Essay on Trade and Commerce, containing Observations on Taxes, &c.*, London, 1770. He had already dealt with this subject in his earlier work: *Considerations on Taxes.* London, 1765. On the same side follows Polonius Arthur Young, the unutterable statistical prattler. Among the defenders of the working-classes the foremost are: Jacob Vanderlint, in: *Money Answers all Things.* London, 1734, the Rev. Nathaniel Forster, D. D., in *An Enquiry into the Causes of the Present High Price of Provisions*, London, 1767; Dr Price, and especially Postlethwayt, as well in the supplement to his *Universal Dictionary of Trade and Commerce*, as in his *Great Britain's Commercial Interest explained and improved.* 2nd Edition, 1755. The facts themselves are confirmed by many other writers of the time, among others by Josiah Tucker.

[90] Postlethwayt, l.c., *First Preliminary Discourse*, p.14.

[91] *An Essay, &c.* He himself relates on p.96 wherein the 'happiness' of the English agricultural labourer already in 1770 consisted. 'Their powers are always upon the stretch, they cannot live cheaper than they do, nor work harder.'

[92] Protestantism, by changing almost all the traditional holidays into workdays, plays an important part in the genesis of capital.

[93] *An Essay, &c.*, pp.15, 41, 96, 97, 55, 57, 69. – Jacob Vanderlint, as early as 1734, declared that the secret of the outcry of the capitalists as to the laziness of the working people was simply that they claimed for the same wages 6 days' labour instead of 4.

[94] l.c., p.242.

[95] l.c. 'The French,' he says, 'laugh at our enthusiastic ideas of liberty.' l.c., p.78.

[96] 'They especially objected to work beyond the 12 hours per day, because the law which fixed those hours, is the only good which remains to them of the legislation of the Republic.' (*Rep. of Insp. of Fact., 31st October, 1856*, p.80.) The French Twelve Hours' Bill of September 5th, 1850, a bourgeois edition of the decree of the Provisional Government of March 2nd, 1848, holds in all workshops without exceptions. Before this law the working-day in France was without definite limit. It lasted in the factories 14, 15, or more hours. See *Des classes ouvrières en France, pendant l'année 1848. Par M. Blanqui.* M. Blanqui the economist, not the Revolutionist, had been entrusted by the Government with an inquiry into the condition of the working-class.

[97] Belgium is the model bourgeois state in regard to the regulation of the working-day. Lord Howard of Welden, English Plenipotentiary at Brussels, reports to the Foreign Office May 12th, 1862: 'M. Rogier, the minister, informed me that children's labour is limited neither by a general law nor by any local regulations; that the Government, during the last three years, intended in every session to propose a bill on the subject, but always found an insuperable obstacle in the jealous opposition to any legislation in contradiction with the principle of perfect freedom of labour.'

[98] 'It is certainly much to be regretted that any class of persons should toil 12 hours a day, which, including the time for their meals and for going to and returning from their work, amounts, in fact, to 14 of the 24 hours . . . Without entering into the question of health, no one will hesitate, I think, to admit that, in a moral point of view, so entire an absorption of the time of the working-classes, without intermission, from the early age of 13, and in trades not subject to restriction, much younger, must be extremely prejudicial, and is an evil greatly to be deplored . . . For the sake, therefore, of public morals, of bringing up an orderly population, and of giving the great body of

the people a reasonable enjoyment of life, it is much to be desired that in all trades some portion of every working-day should be reserved for rest and leisure.' (Leonard Horner in *Reports of Insp. of Fact. for 31st Dec., 1841.*')

[99] See 'Judgment of Mr J. H. Otway, Belfast. Hilary Sessions, County Antrim, 1860.'

[100] It is very characteristic of the régime of Louis Philippe, the bourgeois king, that the one Factory Act passed during his reign, that of March 22nd, 1841, was never put in force. And this law only dealt with child-labour. It fixed 8 hours a day for children between 8 and 12, 12 hours for children between 12 and 16, &c., with many exceptions which allow night-work even for children 8 years old. The supervision and enforcement of this law are, in a country where every mouse is under police administration, left to the good-will of the *amis du commerce*. Only since 1853, in one single department – the Departement du Nord – has a paid government inspector been appointed. Not less characteristic of the development of French society, generally, is the fact, that Louis Philippe's law stood solitary among the all-embracing mass of French laws, till the Revolution of 1848.

[101] *Report of Insp. of Fact., 30th April, 1860,* p.50.

[102] *Rept. of Insp. of Fact., 31st October, 1849,* p.6.

[103] *Rept. of Insp. of Fact., 31st October, 1848,* p.98.

[104] Leonard Horner uses the expression 'nefarious practices' in his official reports. (*Report of Insp. of Fact., 31st October, 1859,* p.7.)

[105] *Rept., &c., 30th Sept., 1844,* p.15.

[106] The Act allows children to be employed for 10 hours if they do not work day after day, but only on alternate days. In the main, this clause remained inoperative.

[107] 'As a reduction in their hours of work would cause a larger number (of children) to be employed, it was thought that the additional supply of children from 8 to 9 years of age would meet the increased demand.' (l.c., p.13).

[108] *Rep. of Insp. of Fact., 31st Oct., 1848,* p.16.

[109] 'I found that men who had been getting 10s. a week, had had 1s. taken off for a reduction in the rate of 10 per cent, and 1s. 6d. off the remaining 9s. for the reduction in time, together 2s. 6d., and notwithstanding this, many of them said they would rather work 10 hours.' l.c.

[110] 'Though I signed it [the petition], I said at the time I was putting my hand to a wrong thing.' 'Then why did you put your hand to it?' 'Because I should have been turned off if I had refused.' Whence it would appear that this petitioner felt himself 'oppressed', but not exactly by the Factory Act. l.c., p.102.

[111] p.17, l.c. In Mr Horner's district 10,270 adult male labourers were thus examined in 181 factories. Their evidence is to be found in the appendix to the Factory Reports for the half-year ending October 1848. These examinations furnish valuable material in other connections also.

[112] l.c. See the evidence collected by Leonard Horner himself, Nos. 69, 70, 71, 72, 92, 93, and that collected by Sub-Inspector A., Nos. 51, 52, 58, 59, 62, 70, of the Appendix. One manufacturer, too, tells the plain truth. See No. 14, and No. 265, l.c.

[113] *Reports, &c., for 31st October, 1848,* pp.133,134.

[114] *Reports, &c., for 30th April, 1848,* p.47.

[115] *Reports, &c., for 31st October, 1848,* p.130.

[116] *Reports, &c., l.c.,* p.142.

[117] *Reports &c., for 31st October, 1850,* pp.5,6.

[118] The nature of capital remains the same in its developed as in its undeveloped form. In the code which the influence of the slave-owners, shortly before the outbreak of the American Civil War, imposed on the territory of New Mexico, it is said that the labourer, in as much as the capitalist has bought his labour power, 'is his (the capitalist's) money.' The same view was current among the Roman patricians. The money they had

advanced to the plebeian debtor had been transformed via the means of subsistence into the flesh and blood of the debtor. This 'flesh and blood' were, therefore, 'their money'. Hence, the Shylock-law of the Ten Tables. Linguet's hypothesis that the patrician creditors from time to time prepared, beyond the Tiber, banquets of debtors' flesh, may remain as undecided as that of Daumer on the Christian Eucharist.

[119] *Reports, &c.. for 30th April, 1848*, p.28.

[120] Thus, among others, Philanthropist Ashworth to Leonard Horner, in a disgusting Quaker letter. (*Reports, &c., April, 1849*, p.4.)

[121] l.c., p.140.

[122] *Reports, &c., for 30th April, 1849*, pp.21,22. cf. like examples ibid., pp.4,5.

[123] By I and II Will. IV., ch.24, s.10, known as Sir John Wobhouse's Factory Act, it was forbidden to any owner of a cotton-spinning or weaving mill, or the father, son, or brother of such owner, to act as Justice of the Peace in any inquiries that concerned the Factory Act.

[124] l.c.

[125] *Reports, &c., for 30th April, 1849*, p.5.

[126] *Reports, &c., for 31st October, 1849*, p.6.

[127] *Reports, &c., for 30th April, 1849*, p.21.

[128] *Reports, &c., for 31st October, 1848*, p.95.

[129] See *Reports, &c., for 30th April, 1849*, p.6, and the detailed explanation of the 'shifting system', by Factory Inspectors Howell and Saunders, in *Reports, &c., for 31st October, 1848*. See also the petition to the Queen from the clergy of Ashton and vicinity, in the spring of 1849, against the 'shift system'.

[130] cf. for example, *The Factory Question and the Ten Hours' Bill*, By R. H. Greg, 1837.

[131] F. Engels: *The English Ten Hours' Bill*. (In the *Neue Rheinische Zeitung. Politisch-oekonomische Revue*. Edited by K. Marx. April number, 1850, p.13.) The same 'high' Court of Justice discovered, during the American Civil War, a verbal ambiguity which exactly reversed the meaning of the law against the arming of pirate ships.

[132] *Rep., &c., for 30th April, 1850*.

[133] In winter, from 7 a.m. to 7 p.m. may be substituted.

[134] 'The present law (of 1850) was a compromise whereby the employed surrendered the benefit of the Ten Hours' Act for the advantage of one uniform period for the commencement and termination of the labour of those whose labour is restricted.' (*Reports, &c., for 30th April, 1852*, p.14.)

[135] *Reports, &c., for Sept., 1844*, p.13.

[136] l.c.

[137] l.c.

[138] l.c.

[139] *Reports, &c., for 31st Oct., 1846*, p.20.

[140] l.c., p.27. On the whole the working population, subject to the Factory Act, has greatly improved physically. All medical testimony agrees on this point, and personal observation at different times has convinced me of it. Nevertheless, and exclusive of the terrible death-rate of children in the first years of their life, the official reports of Dr Greenhow show the unfavourable health condition of the manufacturing districts as compared with 'agricultural districts of normal health'. As evidence, take the following table from his 1861 report: –

> (a) Percentage of Adult Males engaged in manufactures
> (b) Death-rate from Pulmonary Affections per 100,000 Males
> (c) Name of District
> (d) Death-rate from Pulmonary Affections per 100,000 Females
> (e) Percentage of Adult Females engaged in manufactures
> (f) Kind of Female Occupation

(a)	(b)	(c)	(d)	(e)	(f)
14.9	598	Wigan	644	18.0	Cotton
42.6	708	Blackburn	734	44.9	Do.
37.3	547	Halifax	564	20.4	Worsted
41.9	611	Bradford	603	30.0	Do.
31.0	691	Macclesfield	804	26.0	Silk
14.9	588	Leek	705	17.2	Do.
36.6	721	Stoke-upon-Trent	665	19.3	Earthenware
30.4	726	Woolstanton	727	13.9	Do.
	305	Eight healthy agricultural districts	340		

[141] It is well known with what reluctance the English 'Free-traders' gave up the protective duty on the silk manufacture. Instead of the protection against French importation, the absence of protection to English factory children now serves their turn.

[142] During 1859 and 1860, the zenith years of the English cotton industry, some manufacturer3 tried, by the decoy bait of higher wages for over-time, to reconcile the adult male operatives to an extension of the working-day. The hand-mule spinners and self-actor minders put an end to the experiment by a petition to their employers in which they say, 'Plainly speaking, our lives are to us a burthen; and, while we are confined to the mills nearly two days a week more than the other operatives of the country, we feel like helots in the land, and that we are perpetuating a system injurious to ourselves and future generations . . . This, therefore, is to give you most respectful notice that when we commence work again after the Christmas and New Year's holidays, we shall work 60 hours per week, and no more, or from six to six, with one hour and a half out.' (Reports, &c., for 30th April, 1860, p.30.)

[143] On the means that the wording of this Act afforded for its violation cf. the Parliamentary Return 'Factories Regulation Act' (6th August, 1859), and in it Leonard Horner's 'Suggestions for amending the Factory Acts to enable the Inspectors to prevent illegal working, now becoming very prevalent.'

[144] 'Children of the age of 8 years and upwards, have, indeed, been employed from 6 a.m. to 9 p.m. during the last half year in my district.' (Reports, &c., for 31st October, 1857, p.39.)

[145] 'The Printworks' Act is admitted to be a failure both with reference to its educational and protective provisions.' (Reports, &c., for 31st October, 1862, p.52.)

[146] Thus, e.g., E. Potter in a letter to The Times of March 24th, 1863. The Times reminded him of the manufacturers' revolt against the Ten Hours' Bill.

[147] Thus, among others, Mr W. Newmarch, collaborator and editor of Tooke's History of Prices. Is it a scientific advance to make cowardly concessions to public opinion?

[148] The Act passed in 1860, determined that, in regard to dye and bleachworks, the working-day should be fixed on August 1st, 1861, provisionally at 12 hours, and definitely on August 1st, 1862, at 10 hours, i.e., at 10 1/2 hours for ordinary days, and 7 1/2 for Saturday. Now, when the fatal year, 1862, came, the old farce was repeated. Besides, the manufacturers petitioned Parliament to allow the employment of young persons and women for 12 hours during one year longer. 'In the existing condition of the trade (the time of the cotton famine), it was greatly to the advantage of the operatives to work 12 hours per day, and make wages when they could.' A bill to this effect had been brought in, 'and it was mainly due to the action of the operative bleachers in Scotland that the bill was abandoned.' (Reports, &c., for 31st October, 1862, pp.14–15.) Thus defeated by the very workpeople in whose name it pretended to speak, Capital discovered, with the help of lawyer spectacles, that the Act of 1860, drawn up, like all the Acts of Parliament for the 'protection of labour', in equivocal phrases, gave them a pretext to exclude from its working the calenderers and finishers.

English jurisprudence, ever the faithful servant of capital, sanctioned in the Court of Common Pleas this piece of pettifogging. 'The operatives have been greatly disappointed . . . they have complained of over-work, and it is greatly to be regretted that the clear intention of the legislature should have failed by reason of a faulty definition.' (l.c., p.18.)

[149] The 'open-air bleachers' had evaded the law of 1860, by means of the lie that no women worked at it in the night. The lie was exposed by the Factory Inspectors, and at the same time Parliament was, by petitions from the operatives, bereft of its notions as to the cool meadow-fragrance, in which bleaching in the open-air was reported to take place. In this aerial bleaching, drying-rooms were used at temperatures of from 90° to 100° Fahrenheit, in which the work was done for the most part by girls. 'Cooling' is the technical expression for their occasional escape from the drying-rooms into the fresh air. 'Fifteen girls in stoves. Heat from 80° to 90° for linens, and 100° and upwards for cambrics. Twelve girls ironing and doing-up in a small room about 10 feet square, in the centre of which is a close stove. The girls stand round the stove, which throws out a terrific heat, and dries the cambrics rapidly for the ironers. The hours of work for these hands are unlimited. If busy, they work till 9 or 12 at night for successive nights.' (*Reports, &c., for 31st October, 1862*, p.56.) A medical man states: 'No special hours are allowed for cooling, but if the temperature gets too high, or the workers' hands get soiled from perspiration, they are allowed to go out for a few minutes . . . My experience, which is considerable, in treating the diseases of stove workers, compels me to express the opinion that their sanitary condition is by no means so high as that of the operatives in a spinning factory (and Capital, in its memorials to Parliament, had painted them as floridly healthy after the manner of Rubens). The diseases most observable amongst them are phthisis, bronchitis, irregularity of uterine functions, hysteria in its most aggravated forms, and rheumatism. All of these, I believe, are either directly or indirectly induced by the impure, overheated air of the apartments in which the hands are employed and the want of sufficient comfortable clothing to protect them from the cold, damp atmosphere, in winter, when going to their homes.' (l.c., pp.56–57.) The Factory Inspectors remarked on the supplementary law of 1860, torn from these open-air bleachers: 'The Act has not only failed to afford that protection to the workers which it appears to offer, but contains a clause . . . apparently so worded that, unless persons are detected working after 8 o'clock at night they appear to come under no protective provisions at all, and if they do so work the mode of proof is so doubtful that a conviction can scarcely follow.' (l.c., p.52.) 'To all intents and purposes, therefore, as an Act for any benevolent or educational purpose, it is a failure; since it can scarcely be called benevolent to permit, which is tantamount to compelling, women and children to work 14 hours a day with or without meals, as the case may be, and perhaps for longer hours than these, without limit as to age, without reference to sex, and without regard to the social habits of the families of the neighbourhood, in which such works (bleaching and dyeing) are situated.' (*Reports, &c., for 30th April, 1863*, p.40.)

[150] Note to the 2nd Ed. Since 1866, when I wrote the above passages, a reaction has again set in.

[151] 'The conduct of each of these classes (capitalists and workmen) has been the result of the relative situation in which they have been placed.' (*Reports, &c., for 31st October, 1848*, p.113.)

[152] 'The employments, placed under restriction, were connected with the manufacture of textile fabrics by the aid of steam or water-power. There were two conditions to which an employment must be subject to cause it to be inspected, viz., the use of steam or waterpower, and the manufacture of certain specified fibres.' (*Reports, &c., for 31st October, 1864*, p.8.)

[153] On the condition of so-called domestic industries, specially valuable materials are to be found in the latest reports of the Children's Employment Commission.

[154] 'The Acts of last Session (1864) . . . embrace a diversity of occupations, the customs in which differ greatly, and the use of mechanical power to give motion to machinery is no longer one of the elements necessary, as formerly, to constitute, in legal phrase, a "Factory".' (*Reports, &c., for 31st October, 1864*, p.8.)

[155] Belgium, the paradise of Continental Liberalism, shows no trace of this movement. Even in the coal and metal mines labourers of both sexes, and all ages, are consumed, in perfect 'freedom' at any period and through any length of time. Of every 1,000 persons employed there, 733 are men, 88 women, 135 boys, and 44 girls under 16; in the blast furnaces, &c., of every 1,000, 668 are men, 149 women, 98 boys, and 85 girls under 16. Add to this the low wages for the enormous exploitation of mature and immature labour power. The average daily pay for a man is 2s. 8d.; for a woman, 1s. 8d.; for a boy. 1s. 2 1/2 d. As a result, Belgium had in 1863, as compared with 1850, nearly doubled both the amount and the value of its exports of coal, iron, &c.

[156] Robert Owen, soon after 1810, not only maintained the necessity of a limitation of the working-day in theory, but actually introduced the 10 hours' day into his factory at New Lanark. This was laughed at as a communistic Utopia; so were his 'Combination of children's education with productive labour' and the Co-operative Societies of workingmen, first called into being by him. Today, the first Utopia is a Factory Act, the second figures as an official phrase in all Factory Acts, the third is already being used as a cloak for reactionary humbug.

[157] Ure: *French translation, Philosophie des Manufactures*. Paris, 1836, vol.ii, pp.39,40, 67,77, &c.

[158] In the *Compte Rendu* of the International Statistical Congress at Paris, 1855, it is stated: 'The French law, which limits the length of daily labour in factories and workshops to 12 hours, does not confine this work to definite fixed hours. For children's labour only the work-time is prescribed as between 5 a.m. and 9 p.m. Therefore, some of the masters use the right which this fatal silence gives them to keep their works going, without intermission, day in, day out, possibly with the exception of Sunday. For this purpose they use two different sets of workers, of whom neither is in the workshop more than 12 hours at a time, but the work of the establishment lasts day and night. The law is satisfied, but is humanity?' Besides 'the destructive influence of night-labour on the human organism,' stress is also laid upon 'the fatal influence of the association of the two sexes by night in the same badly-lighted workshops'.

[159] 'For instance, there is within my district one occupier who, within the same curtilage, is at the same time a bleacher and dyer under the Bleaching and Dyeing Works Act, a printer under the Print Works Act, and a finisher under the Factory Act.' (Report of Mr Baker, in *Reports, &c., for October 31st, 1861*, p.20.) After enumerating the different provisions of these Acts,and the complications arising from them, Mr Baker says: 'It will hence appear that it must be very difficult to secure the execution of these three Acts of Parliament where the occupier chooses to evade the law.' But what is assured to the lawyers by this is law-suits.

[160] Thus the Factory Inspectors at last venture to say: 'These objections (of capital to the legal limitation of the working-day) must succumb before the broad principle of the rights of labour . . . There is a time when the master's right in his workman's labour ceases, and his time becomes his own, even if there were no exhaustion in the question.' (*Reports, &c., for 31st Oct., 1862*, p.54.)

[161] 'We, the workers of Dunkirk, declare that the length of time of labour required under the present system is too great, and that, far from leaving the worker time for rest and education, it plunges him into a condition of servitude but little better than slavery. That is why we decide that 8 hours are enough for a working-day, and ought

to be legally recognised as enough; why we call to our help that powerful lever, the press; . . . and why we shall consider all those that refuse us this help as enemies of the reform of labour and of the rights of the labourer.' (Resolution of the Working Men of Dunkirk, New York State, 1866.)

[162] *Reports, &c., for Oct., 1848*, p.112.

[163] 'The proceedings (the manoeuvres of capital, e.g., from 1848–50) have afforded, moreover, incontrovertible proof of the fallacy of the assertion so often advanced, that operatives need no protection, but may be considered as free agents in the disposal of the only property which they possess – the labour of their hands and the sweat of their brows.' (*Reports, &c., for April 30th, 1850*, p.45.) 'Free labour (if so it may be termed) even in a free country, requires the strong arm of the law to protect it.' (*Reports, &c., for October 31st, 1864*, p.34.) 'To permit, which is tantamount to compelling . . . to work 14 hours a day with or without meals,' &c. (*Repts., &c., for April 30th, 1863*, p.40.)

[164] Friedrich Engels, l.c., p.5

[165] The 10 Hours' Act has, in the branches of industry that come under it, 'put an end to the premature decrepitude of the former long-hour workers.' (*Reports, &c., for 31st Oct., 1859*, p.47.) 'Capital (in factories) can never be employed in keeping the machinery in motion beyond a limited time, without certain injury to the health and morals of the labourers employed; and they are not in a position to protect themselves.' l.c., p.8)

[166] 'A still greater boon is the distinction at last made clear between the worker's own time and his master's. The worker knows now when that which he sells is ended, and when his own begins; and by possessing a sure foreknowledge of this, is enabled to prearrange his own minutes for his own purposes.' (l.c., p.52.) 'By making them masters of their own time (the Factory Acts) have given them a moral energy which is directing them to the eventual possession of political power' (l.c., p.47). With suppressed irony, and in very well weighed words, the Factory Inspectors hint that the actual law also frees the capitalist from some of the brutality natural to a man who is a mere embodiment of capital, and that it has given him time for a little 'culture'. 'Formerly the master had no time for anything but money; the servant had no time for anything but labour.' (l.c., p.48)

Volume 1, Part 3, Chapter 11

[1] This elementary law appears to be unknown to the vulgar economists, who, upside-down Archimedes, in the determination of the market-price of labour by supply and demand, imagine they have found the fulcrum by means of which, not to move the world, but to stop its motion.

[2] Further particulars will be given in Book 4.

[3] 'The Labour, that is the economic time, of society, is a given portion, say ten hours a day of a million of people, or ten million hours . . . Capital has its boundary of increase. This boundary may, at any given period, be attained in the actual extent of economic time employed.' (*An Essay on the Political Economy of Nations*. London, 1821, pp.47,49.)

[4] 'The farmer cannot rely on his own labour, and if he does, I will maintain that he is a loser by it. His employment should be a general attention to the whole: his thresher must be watched, or he will soon lose his wages in corn not threshed out; his mowers reapers, &c., must be looked after; he must constantly go round his fences; he must see there is no neglect; which would be the case if he was confined to any one spot.' (*An Inquiry into the Connection between the Present Price of Provisions and the Size of Farms, &c. By a Farmer.* London, 1773, p.12.) This book is very interesting. In it the genesis of the 'capitalist farmer' or 'merchant farmer', as he is explicitly called, may be studied, and his self-glorification at the expense of the small farmer who has only to do with bare

subsistence, be noted. 'The class of capitalists are from the first partially, and they become ultimately completely, discharged from the necessity of the manual labour.' (*Textbook of Lectures on the Political Economy of Nations*. By the Rev. Richard Jones. Hertford 1852. Lecture iii, p.39.)

[5] The molecular theory of modern chemistry first scientifically worked out by Laurent and Gerhardt rests on no other law. (Addition to 3rd Edition.) For the explanation of this statement, which is not very clear to non-chemists, we remark that the author speaks here of the homologous series of carbon compounds, first so named by C. Gerhardt in 1843, each series of which has its own general algebraic formula. Thus the series of paraffins: C_nH_{2n+2}, that of the normal alcohols: $C_nH_{2n+2}O$; of the normal fatty acids: $C_nH_{2n}O_2$ and many others. In the above examples, by the simply quantitative addition of CH_2 to the molecular formula, a qualitatively different body is each time formed. On the share (overestimated by Marx) of Laurent and Gerhardt in the determination of this important fact see Kopp, *Entwicklung der Chemie*. München, 1873, pp.709,716, and Schorkmmer, *The Rise and Development of Organic Chemistry*. London, 1879, p.54. – F. E.

[6] Martin Luther calls these kinds of institutions: 'The Company Monopolia'.

[7] *Reports of Insp. of Fact.*, April 30th, 1849, p.59.

[8] l.c., p.60. Factory Inspector Stuart, himself a Scotchman, and in contrast to the English Factory Inspectors, quite taken captive by the capitalistic method of thinking, remarks expressly on this letter which he incorporates in his report that it is 'the most useful of the communications which any of the factory-owners working with relays have given to those engaged in the same trade, and which is the most calculated to remove the prejudices of such of them as have scruples respecting any change of the arrangement of the hours of work.'

Volume 1, Part 4, Chapter 12

[1] The value of his average daily wages is determined by what the labourer requires 'so as to live, labour, and generate'. (Wm. Petty: *Political Anatomy of Ireland*, 1672, p.64.) 'The price of Labour is always constituted of the price of necessaries . . . whenever . . . the labouring man's wages will not, suitably to his low rank and station, as a labouring man, support such a family as is often the lot of many of them to have,' he does not receive proper wages. (J. Vanderlint, l.c., p.15.) '*Le simple ouvrier, qui n'a que ses bras et son industrie, n'a rien qu'autant qu'il parvient à vendre à d'autres sa peine . . . En tout genre de travail il doit arriver, et il arrive en effet, que le salaire de l'ouvrier se borne à ce qui lui est nécessaire pour lui procurer sa subsistance.*' (Turgot, *Réflexions, &c., Oeuvres, éd.* Daire t.i, p.10.) 'The price of the necessaries of life is, in fact, the cost of producing labour.' (Malthus, *Inquiry into, &c., Rent*, London, 1815, p.48, note.)

[2] '*Quando si perfezionano le arti, che non è altro che la scoperta di nuove vie, onde si possa compiere una manufattura con meno gente o (che è lo stesso) in minor tempo di prima.*' (Galiani, l.c., p.159.) '*L'économie sur les frais de production ne peu donc être autre chose que l'économie sur la quantité de travail employé pour produire.*' (Sismondi, *Études*, t.i. p.22.)

[3] 'Let us suppose . . . the products . . . of the manufacturer are doubled by improvement in machinery . . . he will be able to clothe his workmen by means of a smaller proportion of the entire return . . . and thus his profit will be raised. But in no other way will it be influenced.' (Ramsay, l.c., pp.168,169.)

[4] 'A man's profit does not depend upon his command of the produce of other men's labour, but upon his command of labour itself. If he can sell his goods at a higher price, while his workmen's wages remain unaltered, he is clearly benefited . . . A smaller proportion of what he produces is sufficient to put that labour into motion, and a larger proportion consequently remains for himself.' (*Outlines of Pol. Econ.* London, 1832, pp. 49,50.)

[5] 'If my neighbour by doing much with little labour, can sell cheap, I must contrive to sell as cheap as he. So that every art, trade, or engine, doing work with labour of fewer hands, and consequently cheaper, begets in others a kind of necessity and emulation, either of using the same art, trade, or engine, or of inventing something like it, that every man may be upon the square, that no man may be able to undersell his neighbour.' (*The Advantages of the East India Trade to England*, London, 1720, p.67.)

[6] 'In whatever proportion the expenses of a labourer are diminished, in the same proportion will his wages be diminished, if the restraints upon industry are at the same time taken off.' (*Considerations Concerning Taking off the Bounty on Corn Exported*, &c., London, 1753, p.7.) 'The interest of trade requires, that corn and all provisions should be as cheap as possible; for whatever makes them dear, must make labour dear also . . . in all countries, where industry is not restrained, the price of provisions must affect the price of labour. This will always be diminished when the necessaries of life grow cheaper.' (l.c., p.3.) 'Wages are decreased in the same proportion as the powers of production increase. Machinery, it is true, cheapens the necessaries of life, but it also cheapens the labourer.' (*A Prize Essay on the Comparative Merits of Competition and Co-operation*. London, 1834, p.27.)

[7] '*Ils conviennent que plus on peut, sans préjudice, épargner de frais ou de travaux dispendieux dans la fabrication des ouvrages des artisans, plus cette épargne est profitable par la diminution des prix de ces ouvrages. Cependant ils croient que la production de richesse qui résulte des travaux des artisans consiste dans l'augmentation de la valeur vénale de leurs ouvrages.*' (Quesnay: *Dialogues sur le Commerce et les Travaux des Artisans*. pp.188,189.)

[8] '*Ces spéculateurs si économes du travail des ouvriers qu'il faudrait qu'ils payassent.*' (J. N. Bidaut: *Du Monopole qui s'établit dans les arts industriels et le commerce*. Paris, 1828, p.13.) 'The employer will be always on the stretch to economise time and labour.' (Dugald Stewart: *Works* ed. by Sir W. Hamilton, Edinburgh, v, viii, 1855. *Lectures on Polit. Econ.*, p.318.) 'Their (the capitalists') interest is that the productive powers of the labourers they employ should be the greatest possible. On promoting that power their attention is fixed and almost exclusively fixed.' (R. Jones: l.c., Lecture iii)

Volume 1, Part 4, Chapter 13

[1] 'Unquestionably, there is a good deal of difference between the value of one man's labour and that of another from strength, dexterity, and honest application. But I am quite sure, from my best observation, that any given five men will, in their total, afford a proportion of labour equal to any other five within the periods of life I have stated; that is, that among such five men there will be one possessing all the qualifications of a good workman, one bad, and the other three middling, and approximating to the first, and the last. So that in so small a platoon as that of even five, you will find the full complement of all that five men can earn.' (E. Burke, l.c., pp.15,16.) Compare Quételet on the average individual.

[2] Professor Roscher claims to have discovered that one needlewoman employed by Mrs Roscher during two days, does more work than two needlewomen employed together during one day. The learned professor should not study the capitalist process of production in the nursery, nor under circumstances where the principal personage, the capitalist, is wanting.

[3] '*Concours de forces.*' (Destutt de Tracy, l.c., p.80.)

[4] There are numerous operations of so simple a kind as not to admit a division into parts, which cannot be performed without the co-operation of many pairs of hands. I would instance the lifting of a large tree on to a wain .., everything, in short, which cannot be done unless a great many pairs of hands help each other in the same undivided employment and at the same time.' (E. G. Wakefield: *A View of the Art of Colonisation*. London, 1849, p.168.)

[5] 'As one man cannot, and ten men must strain to lift a ton of weight, yet 100 men can do it only by the strength of a finger of each of them.' (John Betters: *Proposals for Raising a Colledge of Industry*. London, 1696, p.21.)

[6] 'There is also' (when the same number of men are employed by one farmer on 300 acres, instead of by ten farmers with 30 acres apiece) 'an advantage in the proportion of servants, which will not so easily be understood but by practical men; for it is natural to say, as 1 is to 4, so are 3 to 12; but this will not hold good in practice; for in harvest time and many other operations which require that kind of despatch by the throwing many hands together, the work is better and more expeditiously done: e.g. in harvest, 2 drivers, 2 loaders, 2 pitchers, 2 rakers, and the rest at the rick, or in the barn, will despatch double the work that the same number of hands would do if divided into different gangs on different farms.' (*An Inquiry into the Connection between the Present Price of Provisions and the Size of Farms. By a Farmer*. London, 1773, pp.7,8.)

[7] Strictly, Aristotle's definition is that man is by nature a town-citizen. This is quite as characteristic of ancient classical society as Franklin's definition of man, as a tool-making animal, is characteristic of Yankeedom.

[8] '*On doit encore remarquer que cette division partielle de travail peut se faire quand même les ouvriers sont occupés d'une même besogne. Des maçons par exemple, occupés à faire passer de mains en mains des briques à un échafaudage supérieur, font tous la même besogne, et pourtant il existe parmi eux une espèce de division de travail, qui consiste en ce que chacun d'eux fait passer la brique par un espace donné, et que tous ensemble la font parvenir beaucoup plus promptement à l'endroit marqué qu'ils ne le feraient si chacun d'eux portait sa brique séparément jusqu'à l'échafaudage supérieur.*' (F. Skarbek: *Théorie des richesses sociales*. Paris, 1839, t.i, pp.97,98.)

[9] '*Est-il question d'exécuter un travail compliqué, plusieurs choses doivent être faites simul-tanément. L'un en fait une pendant que l'autre en fait une autre, et tous contribuent à l'effet qu'un seul homme n'aurait pu produire. L'un rame pendant que l'autre tient le gouvernail, et qu'un troisième jette le filet ou harponne le poisson, et la pêche a un succès impossible sans ce concours.*' (Destutt de Tracy, l.c.)

[10] 'The doing of it (agricultural work) at the critical juncture is of so much the greater consequence.' (*An Inquiry into the Connection between the Present Price, &c.*, p.9.) 'In agriculture, there is no more important factor than that of time.' (Liebig: *Ueber Theorie und Praxis in der Landwirtschaft*. 1856, p.23.)

[11] 'The next evil is one which one would scarcely expect to find in a country which exports more labour than any other in the world, with the exception, perhaps, of China and England – the impossibility of procuring a sufficient number of hands to clean the cotton. The consequence of this is that large quantities of the crop are left unpicked, while another portion is gathered from the ground when it has fallen, and is of course discoloured and partially rotted, so that for want of labour at the proper season the cultivator is actually forced to submit to the loss of a large part of that crop for which England is so anxiously looking.' (*Bengal Hurkaru. Bi-Monthly Overland Summary of News*, 22nd July, 1861.)

[12] In the progress of culture 'all, and perhaps more than all, the capital and labour which once loosely occupied 500 acres, are now concentrated for the more complete tillage of 100.' Although 'relatively to the amount of capital and labour employed, space is concentrated, it is an enlarged sphere of production, as compared to the sphere of production formerly occupied or worked upon by one single independent agent of production.' (R. Jones: *An Essay on the Distribution of Wealth, Part I. On Rent*. London, 1831. p.191.)

[13] '*La forza di ciascuno uomo è minima, ma la riunione delle minime forze forma una forza totale maggiore anche della somma delle forze medesime fino a che le forze per essere riunite possono diminuere il tempo ed accrescere lo spazio della loro azione.*' (G. R. Carli, Note to P. Verri, l.c., t.xv., p.196.)

[14] 'Profits . . . is the sole end of trade.' (J. Vanderlint, l.c., p.11.)

[15] That Philistine paper, the *Spectator*, states that after the introduction of a sort of partnership between capitalist and workmen in the 'Wirework Company of Manchester', 'the first result was a sudden decrease in waste, the men not seeing why they should waste their own property any more than any other master's, and waste is, perhaps, next to bad debts, the greatest source of manufacturing loss.' The same paper finds that the main defect in the Rochdale co-operative experiments is this: 'They showed that associations of workmen could manage shops, mills, and almost all forms of industry with success, and they immediately improved the condition of the men; but then they did not leave a clear place for masters.' *Quelle horreur!*

[16] Professor Cairns, after stating that the superintendence of labour is a leading feature of production by slaves in the Southern States of North America, continues: 'The peasant proprietor (of the North), appropriating the whole produce of his toil, needs no other stimulus to exertion. Superintendence is here completely dispensed with.' (Cairns, l.c., pp.48,49.)

[17] Sir James Steuart, a writer altogether remarkable for his quick eye for the characteristic social distinctions between different modes of production, says: 'Why do large undertakings in the manufacturing way ruin private industry, but by coming nearer to the simplicity of slaves?' (*Prin. of Pol. Econ.*, London, 1767, v.i, pp.167,168.)

[18] Auguste Comte and his school might therefore have shown that feudal lords are an eternal necessity in the same way that they have done in the case of the lords of capital.

[19] R. Jones. *Textbook of Lectures, &c.*, pp.77,78. The ancient Assyrian, Egyptian, and other collections in London, and in other European capitals, make us eye-witnesses of the modes of carrying on that co-operative labour.

[20] Linguet is improbably right, when in his *Théorie des Lois Civiles*, he declares hunting to be the first form of co-operation, and man-hunting (war) one of the earliest forms of hunting.

[21] Peasant agriculture on a small scale, and the carrying on of independent handicrafts, which together form the basis of the feudal mode of production, and after the dissolution of that system, continue side by side with the capitalist mode, also form the economic foundation of the classical communities at their best, after the primitive form of ownership of land in common had disappeared, and before slavery had seized on production in earnest.

[22] 'Whether the united skill, industry, and emulation of many together on the same work be not the way to advance it? And whether it had been otherwise possible for England, to have carried on her Woollen Manufacture to so great a perfection?' (Berkeley. *The Querist*. London, 1751, p.56, par.521.)

Volume 1, Part 4, Chapter 14

[1] To give a more modern instance: the silk spinning and weaving of Lyon and Nîmes 'est toute patriarcale; elle emploie beaucoup de femmes et d'enfants, mais sans les épuiser ni les corrompre; elle les laisse dans leur belles vallées de la Drôme, du Var, de l'Isère, de Vaucluse, pour y élever des vers et dévider leurs cocons; jamais elle n'entre dans une véritable fabrique. Pour être aussi bien observé . . . le principe de la division du travail s'y revêt d'un caractère spécial. Il y a bien des dévideuses, des moulineurs, des teinturiers, des encolleurs, puis des tisserands; mais ils ne sont pas réunis dans un même établissement, ne dépendent pas d'un même maître, tous ils sont indépendants.' (A. Blanqui: 'Cours d'Écon. Industrielle. Recueilli par A. Blaise. Paris, 1838–39, p.79.) Since Blanqui wrote this, the various independent labourers have, to some extent, been united in factories. [And since Marx wrote the above, the power-loom has invaded these factories, and is now – 1886 – rapidly superseding the hand-loom.

[2] The more any manufacture of much variety shall be distributed and assigned to different artists, the same must needs be better done and with greater expedition, with

less loss of time and labour.' (*The Advantages of the East India Trade*, Lond., 1720, p.71.)

[3] 'Easy labour is transmitted skill.' (Th. Hodgskin, *Popular Political Economy*, p.48.)

[4] 'The arts also have . . . in Egypt reached the requisite degree of perfection. For it is the only country where artificers may not in any way meddle with the affairs of another class of citizens, but must follow that calling alone which by law is hereditary in their clan . . . In other countries it is found that tradesmen divide their attention between too many objects. At one time they try agriculture, at another they take to commerce, at another they busy themselves with two or three occupations at once. In free countries, they mostly frequent the assemblies of the people . . . In Egypt, on the contrary, every artificer is severely punished if he meddles with affairs of State, or carries on several trades at once. Thus there is nothing to disturb their application to their calling . . . Moreover, since they inherit from their forefathers numerous rules, they are eager to discover fresh advantages.' (Diodorus Siculus: *Bibl. Hist.* l.1. c.74.)

[5] *Historical and descriptive account of Brit. India, &c.*, by Hugh Murray and James Wilson, &c., Edinburgh 1832, v.ii, p.449. The Indian loom is upright, i.e., the warp is stretched vertically.

[6] Darwin in his epoch-making work on the origin of species, remarks, with reference to the natural organs of plants and animals: 'So long as one and the same organ has different kinds of work to perform, a ground for its changeability may possibly be found in this, that natural selection preserves or suppresses each small variation of form less carefully than if that organ were destined for one special purpose alone. Thus, knives that are adapted to cut all sorts of things, may, on the whole, be of one shape; but an implement destined to be used exclusively in one way must have a different shape for every different use.'

[7] In the year 1854 Geneva produced 80,000 watches, which is not one-fifth of the production in the Canton of Neufchâtel. La Chaux-de-Fond alone, which we may look upon as a huge watch manufactory, produces yearly twice as many as Geneva. From 1850–61 Geneva produced 720,000 watches. See 'Report from Geneva on the Watch Trade' in *Reports by H.M.'s Secretaries of Embassy and Legation on the Manufactures; Commerce, &c., No. 6, 1863.*' The want of connection alone, between the processes into which the production of articles that merely consist of parts fitted together is split up, makes it very difficult to convert such a manufacture into a branch of modern industry carried on by machinery; but in the case of a watch there are two other impediments in addition, the minuteness and delicacy of its parts, and its character as an article of luxury. Hence their variety, which is such, that in the best London houses scarcely a dozen watches are made alike in the course of a year. The watch manufactory of Messrs Vacheron & Constantin, in which machinery has been employed with success, produces at the most three or four different varieties of size and form.

[8] In watchmaking, that classical example of heterogeneous manufacture, we may study with great accuracy the above-mentioned differentiation and specialisation of the instruments of labour caused by the sub-division of handicrafts.

[9] 'In so close a cohabitation of the people, the carriage must needs be less.' (*The Advantages of the East India Trade*, p.106.)

[10] 'The isolation of the different stages of manufacture, consequent upon the employment of manual labour, adds immensely to the cost of production, the loss mainly arising from the mere removals from one process to another.' (*The Industry of Nations*. Lond., 1855, Part ii, p.200.)

[11] 'It (the division of labour) produces also an economy of time by separating the work into its different branches, all of which may be carried on into execution at the same moment . . . By carrying on all the different processes at once, which an individual must have executed separately, it becomes possible to produce a multitude

of pins completely finished in the same time as a single pin might have been either cut or pointed.' (Dugald Stewart, l.c., p.319.)

[12] 'The more variety of artists to every manufacture . . . the greater the order and regularity of every work, the same must needs be done in less time, the labour must be less.' (*The Advantages, &c.*, p.68.)

[13] Nevertheless, the manufacturing system, in many branches of industry, attains this result but very imperfectly, because it knows not how to control with certainty the general chemical and physical conditions of the process of production.

[14] 'When (from the peculiar nature of the produce of each manufactory), the number of processes into which it is most advantageous to divide it is ascertained, as well as the number of individuals to be employed, then all other manufactories which do not employ a direct multiple of this number will produce the article at a greater cost . . . Hence arises one of the causes of the great size of manufacturing establishments.' (C. Babbage. *On the Economy of Machinery*, 1st ed. London. 1832. Ch. xxi, pp.172–73.)

[15] In England, the melting-furnace is distinct from the glass-furnace in which the glass is manipulated. In Belgium, one and the same furnace serves for both processes.

[16] This can be seen from W. Petty, John Bellers, Andrew Yarranton, *The Advantages of the East India Trade*, and J. Vanderlint, not to mention others.

[17] Towards the end of the 16th century, mortars and sieves were still used in France for pounding and washing ores.

[18] The whole history of the development of machinery can be traced in the history of the corn mill. The factory in England is still a 'mill'. In German technological works of the first decade of this century, the term 'Mühle' is still found in use, not only for all machinery driven by the forces of Nature, but also for all manufactures where apparatus in the nature of machinery is applied.

[19] As will be seen more in detail in the fourth book of this work, Adam Smith has not established a single new proposition relating to division of labour. What, however, characterises him as the political economist *par excellence* of the period of Manufacture, is the stress he lays on division of labour. The subordinate part which he assigns to machinery gave occasion in the early days of modern mechanical industry to the polemic of Lauderdale, and, at a later period, to that of Ure. A. Smith also confounds differentiation of the instruments of labour, in which the detail labourers themselves took an active part, with the invention of machinery; in this latter, it is not the workmen in manufactories, but learned men, handicraftsman, and even peasants (Brindley), who play a part.

[20] 'The master manufacturer, by dividing the work to be executed into different processes, each requiring different degrees of skill or of force, can purchase exactly that precise quantity of both which is necessary for each process; whereas, if the whole work were executed by one workman, that person must possess sufficient skill to perform the most difficult, and sufficient strength to execute the most laborious of the operations into which the article is divided.' (Ch. Babbage, l.c., ch.xix.)

[21] For instance, abnormal development of some muscles, curvature of bones, &c.

[22] The question put by one of the Inquiry Commissioners, How the young persons are kept steadily to their work, is very correctly answered by Mr Wm. Marshall, the general manager of a glass manufactory: 'They cannot well neglect their work; when they once begin, they must go on; they are just the same as parts of a machine.' (*Children's Empl. Comm., 4th Rep., 1865*, p.247.)

[23] Dr Ure, in his apotheosis of Modern Mechanical Industry, brings out the peculiar character of manufacture more sharply than previous economists, who had not his polemical interest in the matter, and more sharply even than his contemporaries – Babbage, e.g., who, though much his superior as a mathematician and mechanician, treated mechanical industry from the standpoint of manufacture alone. Ure says, 'This

appropriation . . . to each, a workman of appropriate value and cost was naturally assigned, forms the very essence of division of labour.' On the other hand, he describes this division as 'adaptation of labour to the different talents of men', and lastly, characterises the whole manufacturing system as 'a system for the division or gradation of labour', as 'the division of labour into degrees of skill', &c. (Ure, l.c., pp.19–23 passim.)

[24] 'Each handicraftsman being . . . enabled to perfect himself by practice in one point, became . . . a cheaper workman.' (Ure, l.c., p.19.)

[25] 'Division of labour proceeds from the separation of professions the most widely different to that division, where several labourers divide between them the preparation of one and the same product, as in manufacture.' (Storch: *Cours d'Écon. Pol.*, Paris Edn. t.i, p.173.) '*Nous rencontrons chez les peuples parvenus à un certain degré de civilisation trois genres de divisions d'industrie: la première, que nous nommerons générale, amène la distinction des producteurs en agriculteurs, manufacturiers et commerçants, elle se rapporte aux trois principales branches d'industrie nationale; la seconde, qu'on pourrait appeler spéciale, est la division de chaque genre d'industrie en espèces . . . la troisième division d'industrie, celle enfin qu'on devrait qualifier de division de la besogne ou de travail proprement dit, est celle qui s'établit dans les arts et les métiers séparés . . . qui s'établit dans la plupart des manufactures et des ateliers.*' (Skarbek, l.c., pp.84,85.)

[26] Note to the third edition. Subsequent very searching study of the primitive condition of man, led the author to the conclusion, that it was not the family that originally developed into the tribe, but that, on the contrary, the tribe was the primitive and spontaneously developed form of human association, on the basis of blood relationship, and that out of the first incipient loosening of the tribal bonds, the many and various forms of the family were afterwards developed. F. E.

[27] Sir James Steuart is the economist who has handled this subject best. How little his book, which appeared ten years before the *Wealth of Nations*, is known, even at the present time, may be judged from the fact that the admirers of Malthus do not even know that the first edition of the latter's work on population contains, except in the purely declamatory part, very little but extracts from Steuart, and in a less degree, from Wallace and Townsend.

[28] 'There is a certain density of population which is convenient, both for social intercourse, and for that combination of powers by which the produce of labour is increased.' (James Mill, l.c., p.50.) 'As the number of labourers increases, the productive power of society augments in the compound ratio of that increase, multiplied by the effects of the division of labour.' (Th. Hodgskin, l.c., pp.125,126.)

[29] In consequence of the great demand for cotton after 1861, the production of cotton, in some thickly populated districts of India, was extended at the expense of rice cultivation. In consequence there arose local famines, the defective means of communication not permitting the failure of rice in one district to be compensated by importation from another.

[30] Thus the fabrication of shuttles formed as early as the 17th century, a special branch of industry in Holland.

[31] Whether the woollen manufacture of England is not divided into several parts or branches appropriated to particular places, where they are only or principally manufactured; fine cloths in Somersetshire, coarse in Yorkshire, long ells at Exeter, soies at Sudbury, crapes at Norwich, linseys at Kendal, blankets at Whitney, and so forth.' (Berkeley: *The Querist*, 1751, §520.)

[32] A. Ferguson: *History of Civil Society*. Edinburgh, 1767; part iv, sect.ii., p.285.

[33] In manufacture proper, he says, the division of labour appears to be greater, because 'those employed in every different branch of the work can often be collected into the same workhouse, and placed at once under the view of the spectator. In those great manufactures, (!) on the contrary, which are destined to supply the great

wants of the great body of the people, every different branch of the work employs so great a number of workmen, that it is impossible to collect them all into the same workhouse . . . the division is not near so obvious.' (A. Smith: *Wealth of Nations*, bk.i, ch.i.) The celebrated passage in the same chapter that begins with the words, 'Observe the accommodation of the most common artificer or day-labourer in a civilised and thriving country,' &c., and then proceeds to depict what an enormous number and variety of industries contribute to the satisfaction of the wants of an ordinary labourer, is copied almost word for word from B. de Mandeville's Remarks to his *Fable of the Bees, or Private Vices, Publick Benefits.* (First ed., without the remarks, 1706; with the remarks, 1714.)

[34] 'There is no longer anything which we can call the natural reward of individual labour. Each labourer produces only some part of a whole, and each part, having no value or utility in itself, there is nothing on which the labourer can seize, and say: It is my product, this I will keep to myself.' (*Labour Defended against the Claims of Capital.* Lond., 1825, p.25.) The author of this admirable work is the Th. Hodgskin I have already cited.

[35] This distinction between division of labour in society and in manufacture, was practically illustrated to the Yankees. One of the new taxes devised at Washington during the civil war, was the duty of 6% 'on all industrial products'. Question: What is an industrial product? Answer of the legislature: A thing is produced 'when it is made', and it is made when it is ready for sale. Now, for one example out of many. The New York and Philadelphia manufacturers had previously been in the habit of 'making' umbrellas with all their belongings. But since an umbrella is a *mixtum compositum* of very heterogeneous parts, by degrees these parts became the products of various separate industries, carried on independently in different places. They entered as separate commodities into the umbrella manufactory, where they were fitted together. The Yankees have given to articles thus fitted together, the name of 'assembled articles', a name they deserve, for being an assemblage of taxes. Thus the umbrella 'assembles', first, 6% on the price of each of its elements, and a further 6% on its own total price.

[36] 'On peut . . . établir en règle générale, que moins l'autorité préside à la division du travail dans l'intérieur de la société, plus la division du travail se développe dans l'intérieur de l'atelier, et plus elle y est soumise à l'autorité d'un seul. Ainsi l'autorité dans l'atelier et celle dans la société, par rapport à la division du travail, sont en raison inverse l'une de l'autre.' (Karl Marx, *Misère, &c.*, pp.130–131.)

[37] Lieut.-Col. Mark Wilks: *Historical Sketches of the South of India.* Lond., 1810–17, v.i, pp.118–20. A good description of the various forms of the Indian communities is to be found in George Campbell's *Modern India.* Lond., 1852.

[38] 'Under this simple form . . . the inhabitants of the country have lived from time immemorial. The boundaries of the villages have been but seldom altered; and though the villages themselves have been sometimes injured, and even desolated by war, famine, and disease, the same name, the same limits, the same interests, and even the same families, have continued for ages. The inhabitants give themselves no trouble about the breaking up and division of kingdoms; while the village remains entire, they care not to what power it is transferred, or to what sovereign it devolves; its internal economy remains unchanged.' (Th. Stamford Raffles, late Lieut. Gov. of Java: *The History of Java.* Lond., 1817, vol.i, p.285.)

[39] 'It is not sufficient that the capital' (the writer should have said the necessary means of subsistence and of production) 'required for the subdivision of handicrafts should be in readiness in the society: it must also be accumulated in the hands of the employers in sufficiently large quantities to enable them to conduct their operations on a large scale . . . The more the division increases, the more does the constant

employment of a given number of labourers require a greater outlay of capital in tools, raw material, &c.' (Storch: *Cours d'Écon. Polit.* Paris Ed., t.i, pp.250,251.) '*La concentration des instruments de production et la division du travail sont aussi inséparables l'une de l'autre que le sont, dans le régime politique, la concentration des pouvoirs publics et la division des intérêts privés.*' (Karl Marx, l.c., p.134.)

[40] Dugald Stewart calls manufacturing labourers 'living automatons . . . employed in the details of the work.' (l.c., p.318.)

[41] In corals, each individual is, in fact, the stomach of the whole group; but it supplies the group with nourishment, instead of, like the Roman patrician, withdrawing it.

[42] '*L'ouvrier qui porte dans ses bras tout un métier, peut aller partout exercer son industrie et trouver des moyens de subsister: l'autre (the manufacturing labourer) n'est qu'un accessoire qui, séparé de ses confrères, n'a plus ni capacité, ni indépendance, et qui se trouve forcé d'accepter la loi qu'on juge à propos de lui imposer.*' (Storch, l.c., Petersb. edit., 1815, t.i, p.204.)

[43] A. Ferguson, l.c., p.281: 'The former may have gained what the other has lost.'

[44] 'The man of knowledge and the productive labourer come to be widely divided from each other, and knowledge, instead of remaining the handmaid of labour in the hand of the labourer to increase his productive powers . . . has almost everywhere arrayed itself against labour . . . systematically deluding and leading them (the labourers) astray in order to render their muscular powers entirely mechanical and obedient.' (W. Thompson: *An Inquiry into the Principles of the Distribution of Wealth.* London, 1824, p.274.)

[45] A. Ferguson, l.c., p.280.

[46] J. D. Tuckett: *A History of the Past and Present State of the Labouring Population.* Lond., 1846.

[47] A. Smith: *Wealth of Nations*, bk.v., ch.i, art.ii. Being a pupil of A. Ferguson who showed the disadvantageous effects of division of labour, Adam Smith was perfectly clear on this point. In the introduction to his work, where he *ex professo* praises division of labour, he indicates only in a cursory manner that it is the source of social inequalities. It is not till the 5th Book, on the Revenue of the State, that he reproduces Ferguson. In my *Misère de la Philosophie*, I have sufficiently explained the historical connection between Ferguson, A. Smith, Lemontey, and Say, as regards their criticisms of Division of Labour, and have shown, for the first time, that Division of Labour as practised in manufactures, is a specific form of the capitalist mode of production.

[48] Ferguson had already said, l.c., p.281: 'And thinking itself, in this age of separations, may become a peculiar craft.'

[49] G. Garnier, vol. v. of his translation of A. Smith, pp. 4–5.

[50] Ramazzini, professor of practical medicine at Padua, published in 1713 his work *De morbis artificum*, which was translated into French 1781, reprinted 1841 in the *Encyclopédie des Sciences Médicales. 7me Dis. Auteurs Classiques.* The period of Modern Mechanical Industry has, of course, very much enlarged his catalogue of labour's diseases. See *Hygiène physique et morale de l'ouvrier dans les grandes villes en général et dans la ville de Lyon en particulier. Par le Dr A. L. Fonteret*, Paris, 1858, and *Die Krankheiten, welche verschiedenen Ständen, Altern und Geschlechtern eigenthümlich sind.* 6 Vols. Ulm, 1860, and others. In 1854 the Society of Arts appointed a Commission of Inquiry into industrial pathology. The list of documents collected by this commission is to be seen in the catalogue of the Twickenham Economic Museum. Very important are the official Reports on Public Health. See also Eduard Reich, M. D. *Ueber die Entartung des Menschen*, Erlangen, 1868.

[51] (D. Urquhart: *Familiar Words.* Lond., 1855, p.119.) Hegel held very heretical views on division of labour. In his *Rechtsphilosophie* he says: 'By well-educated men we understand in the first instance, those who can do everything that others do.'

[52] The simple belief in the inventive genius exercised *a priori* by the individual capitalist in division of labour, exists nowadays only among German professors, of the stamp of Herr Roscher, who, to recompense the capitalist from whose Jovian head division of labour sprang ready formed, dedicates to him 'various wages' (diverse *Arbeitslöhne*). The more or less extensive application of division of labour depends on length of purse, not on greatness of genius.

[53] The older writers, like Petty and the anonymous author of *Advantages of the East India Trade*, bring out the capitalist character of division of labour as applied in manufacture more than A. Smith does.

[54] Amongst the moderns may be excepted a few writers of the 18th century, like Beccaria and James Harris, who with regard to division of labour almost entirely follow the ancients. Thus, Beccaria: '*Ciascuno prova coll'esperienza, che applicando la mano e l'ingegno sempre allo stesso genere di opere e di produtte, egli più facili, più abbondanti e migliori ne traca risultati, di quello che se ciascuno isolatamente le cose tutte a se necessarie soltanto facesse . . . Dividendosi in tal maniera per la comune e privata utilità gli uomini in varie classi e condizioni.*' (Cesare Beccaria: *Elementi di Econ: Pubblica*, ed. Custodi, *Parte Moderna*, t.xi, p.29.) James Harris, afterwards Earl of Malmesbury, celebrated for the *Diaries* of his embassy at St Petersburg, says in a note to his *Dialogue Concerning Happiness*, Lond., 1741, reprinted afterwards in *Three Treatises*, 3 Ed., Lond., 1772: 'The whole argument to prove society natural (i.e., by division of employments) . . . is taken from the second book of Plato's *Republic*.'

[55] Thus, in the *Odyssey* xiv.,228, '*Allos gar t' alloisin aner epiterpetai ergois,*' and Archilochus in Sextus Empiricus, '*allos alloi ep' ergoi kardien iainetai.*'

[56] '*Poll' epistato erga, kakos d'epistato panta.*' Every Athenian considered himself superior as a producer of commodities to a Spartan; for the latter in time of war had men enough at his disposal but could not command money, as Thucydides makes Pericles say in the speech inciting the Athenians to the Peloponnesian war: '*somasi te hetoimoteroi hoi autourgoi ton anthropon h khremasi polemein.*' (Thuc.: 1.41.) Nevertheless, even with regard to material production, *autarkeia*, as opposed to division of labour, remained their ideal, '*par hon gar to eu, para touton kai to autarkes.*' It should be mentioned here that at the date of the fall of the 30 Tyrants there were still not 5,000 Athenians without landed property.

[57] With Plato, division of labour within the community is a development from the multifarious requirements, and the limited capacities of individuals. The main point with him is, that the labourer must adapt himself to the work, not the work to the labourer; which latter is unavoidable, if he carries on several trades at once, thus making one or the other of them subordinate. '*Ou gar ethelei to prattomenon ten tou prattontos scholen perimenein, all' anagke ton prattonta toi prattomenoi epakolouthein me en parergou merei. – Anagke. – Ek de touton pleio te hekasta gignetai kai kallion kai raion, hotan heis hen kata physin kai en kairoi skholen ton allon agon, prattei.*' (*Rep.* 1.2. Ed. Baiter, Orelli, &c.) So in Thucydides, l.c., c.142: 'Seafaring is an art like any other, and cannot, as circumstances require, be carried on as a subsidiary occupation; nay, other subsidiary occupations cannot be carried on alongside of this one.' If the work, says Plato, has to wait for the labourer, the critical point in the process is missed and the article spoiled, '*ergou kairon diollutai.*' The same Platonic idea is found recurring in the protest of the English bleachers against the clause in the Factory Act that provides fixed mealtimes for all operatives. Their business cannot wait the convenience of the workmen, for 'in the various operations of singeing, washing, bleaching, mangling, calendering, and dyeing, none of them can be stopped at a given moment without risk of damage . . . to enforce the same dinner hour for all the workpeople might occasionally subject valuable goods to the risk of danger by incomplete operations.' *Le platonisme où va-t-il se nicher!*

[58] Xenophon says, it is not only an honour to receive food from the table of the King of Persia, but such food is much more tasty than other food. 'And there is nothing wonderful in this, for as the other arts are brought to special perfection in the great towns, so the royal food is prepared in a special way. For in the small towns the same man makes bedsteads, doors, ploughs, and tables: often, too, he builds houses into the bargain, and is quite content if he finds custom sufficient for his sustenance. It is altogether impossible for a man who does so many things to do them all well. But in the great towns, where each can find many buyers, one trade is sufficient to maintain the man who carries it on. Nay, there is often not even need of one complete trade, but one man makes shoes for men, another for women. Here and there one man gets a living by sewing, another by cutting out shoes; one does nothing but cut out clothes, another nothing but sew the pieces together. It follows necessarily then, that he who does the simplest kind of work, undoubtedly does it better than anyone else. So it is with the art of cooking.' (Xen. *Cyrop.* i. viii., c.2.) Xenophon here lays stress exclusively upon the excellence to be attained in use-value, although he well knows that the gradations of the division of labour depend on the extent of the market.

[59] He (Busiris) divided them all into special castes . . . commanded that the same individuals should always carry on the same trade, for he knew that they who change their occupations become skilled in none; but that those who constantly stick to one occupation bring it to the highest perfection. In truth, we shall also find that in relation to the arts and handicrafts, they have outstripped their rivals more than a master does a bungler; and the contrivances for maintaining the monarchy and the other institutions of their State are so admirable that the most celebrated philosophers who treat of this subject praise the constitution of the Egyptian State above all others. (Isocrates, *Busiris*, c.8.)

[60] cf. Diodorus Siculus.

[61] Ure, l.c., p.20.

[62] This is more the case in England than in France, and more in France than in Holland.

Volume 1, Part 4, Chapter 15

[1] Mill should have said, 'of any human being not fed by other people's labour', for, without doubt, machinery has greatly increased the number of well-to-do idlers.

[2] See, for instance, Hutton: *Course of Mathematics*.

[3] 'From this point of view we may draw a sharp line of distinction between a tool and a machine: spades, hammers, chisels, &c., combinations of levers and of screws, in all of which, no matter how complicated they may be in other respects, man is the motive power, . . . all this falls under the idea of a tool; but the plough, which is drawn by animal power, and wind-mills, &c., must be classed among machines.' (Wilhelm Schulz: *Die Bewegung der Produktion*. Zürich, 1843, p.38.) In many respects a book to be recommended.

[4] Before his time, spinning machines, although very imperfect ones, had already been used, and Italy was probably the country of their first appearance. A critical history of technology would show how little any of the inventions of the 18th century are the work of a single individual. Hitherto there is no such book. Darwin has interested us in the history of Nature's Technology, i.e., in the formation of the organs of plants and animals, which organs serve as instruments of production for sustaining life. Does not the history of the productive organs of man, of organs that are the material basis of all social organisation, deserve equal attention? And would not such a history be easier to compile, since, as Vico says, human history differs from natural history in this, that we have made the former, but not the latter? Technology discloses man's mode of dealing with Nature, the process of production by which he sustains his life, and thereby also

lays bare the mode of formation of his social relations, and of the mental conceptions that flow from them. Every history of religion, even, that fails to take account of this material basis, is uncritical. It is, in reality, much easier to discover by analysis the earthly core of the misty creations of religion, than, conversely, it is, to develop from the actual relations of life the corresponding celestialised forms of those relations. The latter method is the only materialistic, and therefore the only scientific one. The weak points in the abstract materialism of natural science, a materialism that excludes history and its process, are at once evident from the abstract and ideological conceptions of its spokesmen, whenever they venture beyond the bounds of their own speciality.

[5] Especially in the original form of the power-loom, we recognise, at the first glance, the ancient loom. In its modern form, the power-loom has undergone essential alterations.

[6] It is only during the last 15 years (i.e., since about 1850), that a constantly increasing portion of these machine tools have been made in England by machinery, and that not by the same manufacturers who make the machines. Instances of machines for the fabrication of these mechanical tools are, the automatic bobbin-making engine, the card-setting engine, shuttle-making machines, and machines for forging mule and throstle spindles.

[7] Moses says: 'Thou shalt not muzzle the ox that treads the corn.' The Christian philanthropists of Germany, on the contrary, fastened a wooden board round the necks of the serfs, whom they used as a motive power for grinding, in order to prevent them from putting flour into their mouths with their hands.

[8] It was partly the want of streams with a good fall on them, and partly their battles with superabundance of water in other respects, that compelled the Dutch to resort to wind as a motive power. The wind-mill itself they got from Germany, where its invention was the origin of a pretty squabble between the nobles, the priests, and the emperor, as to which of those three the wind 'belonged'. The air makes bondage, was the cry in Germany, at the same time that the wind was making Holland free. What it reduced to bondage in this case, was not the Dutchman, but the land for the Dutchman. In 1836, 12,000 windmills of 6,000 horse-power were still employed in Holland, to prevent two-thirds of the land from being reconverted into morasses.

[9] It was, indeed, very much improved by Watt's first so-called single acting engine; but, in this form, it continued to be a mere machine for raising water, and the liquor from salt mines.

[10] 'The union of all these simple instruments, set in motion by a single motor, constitutes a machine.' (Babbage, l.c.)

[11] In January, 1861, John C. Morton read before the Society of Arts a paper on 'The forces employed in agriculture'. He there states: 'Every improvement that furthers the uniformity of the land makes the steam-engine more and more applicable to the production of pure mechanical force . . . Horse-power is requisite wherever crooked fences and other obstructions prevent uniform action. These obstructions are vanishing day by day. For operations that demand more exercise of will than actual force, the only power applicable is that controlled every instant by the human mind – in other words, man-power.' Mr Morton then reduces steam-power, horse-power, and man-power, to the unit in general use for steam-engines, namely, the force required to raise 33,000 lbs. one foot in one minute, and reckons the cost of one horse-power from a steam-engine to be 3d., and from a horse to be 5 1/2d. per hour. Further, if a horse must fully maintain its health, it can work no more than 8 hours a day. Three at the least out of every seven horses used on tillage land during the year can be dispensed with by using steam-power, at an expense not greater than that which the horses dispensed with, would cost during the 3 or 4 months in which alone they can be used effectively. Lastly, steam-power, in those agricultural operations in which it can be

employed, improves, in comparison with horse-power, the quality of the work. To do the work of a steam-engine would require 60 men, at a total cost of 15s. an hour, and to do the work of a horse, 32 men, at a total cost of 8s. an hour.

[12] Faulhaber, 1625; De Caus, 1688.

[13] The modern turbine frees the industrial exploitation of water-power from many of its former fetters.

[14] 'In the early days of textile manufactures, the locality of the factory depended upon the existence of a stream having a sufficient fall to turn a water-wheel; and, although the establishment of the water-mills was the commencement of the breaking up of the domestic system of manufacture, yet the mills necessarily situated upon streams, and frequently at considerable distances the one from the other, formed part of a rural, rather than an urban system; and it was not until the introduction of the steam-power as a substitute for the stream that factories were congregated in towns, and localities where the coal and water required for the production of steam were found in sufficient quantities. The steam-engine is the parent of manufacturing towns.' (A. Redgrave in *Reports of the Insp. of Fact., 30th April, 1860,* p.36.)

[15] From the standpoint of division of labour in Manufacture, weaving was not simple, but, on the contrary, complicated manual labour; and consequently the power-loom is a machine that does very complicated work. It is altogether erroneous to suppose that modern machinery originally appropriated those operations alone, which division of labour had simplified. Spinning and weaving were, during the manu-facturing period, split up into new species, and the implements were modified and improved; but the labour itself was in no way divided, and it retained its handicraft character. It is not the labour, but the instrument of labour, that serves as the starting-point of the machine.

[16] Before the epoch of Mechanical Industry, the wool manufacture was the predom-inating manufacture in England. Hence it was in this industry that, in the first half of the 18th century, the most experiments were made. Cotton, which required less careful preparation for its treatment by machinery, derived the benefit of the experience gained on wool, just as afterwards the manipulation of wool by machinery was developed on the lines of cotton-spinning and weaving by machinery. It was only during the 10 years immediately preceding 1866, that isolated details of the wool manufacture, such as wool-combing, were incorporated in the factory system. 'The application of power to the process of combing wool . . . extensively in operation since the introduction of the combing machine, especially Lister's . . . undoubtedly had the effect of throwing a very large number of men out of work. Wool was formerly combed by hand, most frequently in the cottage of the comber. It is now very generally combed in the factory, and hand-labour is superseded, except in some particular kinds of work, in which hand-combed wool is still preferred. Many of the hand-combers found employment in the factories, but the produce of the hand-combers bears so small a proportion to that of the machine, that the employment of a very large number of combers has passed away.' (*Rep. of Insp. of Fact. for 31st Oct., 1856,* p.16.)

[17] 'The principle of the factory system, then, is to substitute . . . the partition of a process into its essential constituents, for the division or graduation of labour among artisans.' (Andrew Ure: *The Philosophy of Manufactures,* Lond., 1835, p.20.)

[18] The power-loom was at first made chiefly of wood; in its improved modern form it is made of iron. To what an extent the old forms of the instruments of production influenced their new forms at first starting, is shown by, amongst other things, the most superficial comparison of the present power-loom with the old one, of the modern blowing apparatus of a blast-furnace with the first inefficient mechanical reproduction of the ordinary bellows, and perhaps more strikingly than in any other way, by the attempts before the invention of the present locomotive, to construct a

locomotive that actually had two feet, which after the fashion of a horse, it raised alternately from the ground. It is only after considerable development of the science of mechanics, and accumulated practical experience, that the form of a machine becomes settled entirely in accordance with mechanical principles, and emancipated from the traditional form of the tool that gave rise to it.

[19] Eli Whitney's cotton gin had until very recent times undergone less essential changes than any other machine of the 18th century. It is only during the last decade (i.e., since 1856) that another American, Mr Emery, of Albany, New York, has rendered Whitney's gin antiquated by an improvement as simple as it is effective.

[20] *The Industry of Nations*, Lond., 1855, Part ii, p.239. This work also remarks: 'Simple and outwardly unimportant as this appendage to lathes may appear, it is not, we believe, averring too much to state, that its influence in improving and extending the use of machinery has been as great as that produced by Watt's improvements of the steam-engine itself. Its introduction went at once to perfect all machinery, to cheapen it, and to stimulate invention and improvement.'

[21] One of these machines, used for forging paddle-wheel shafts in London, is called 'Thor'. It forges a shaft of 16 1/2 tons with as much ease as a blacksmith forges a horseshoe.

[22] Wood-working machines that are also capable of being employed on a small scale are mostly American inventions.

[23] Science, generally speaking, costs the capitalist nothing, a fact that by no means hinders him from exploiting it. The science of others is as much annexed by capital as the labour of others. Capitalistic appropriation and personal appropriation, whether of science or of material wealth, are, however, totally different things. Dr Ure himself deplores the gross ignorance of mechanical science existing among his dear machinery-exploiting manufacturers, and Liebig can a tale unfold about the astounding ignorance of chemistry displayed by English chemical manufacturers.

[24] Ricardo lays such stress on this effect of machinery (of which, in other connections, he takes no more notice than he does of the general distinction between the labour process and the process of creating surplus-value), that he occasionally loses sight of the value given up by machines to the product, and puts machines on the same footing as natural forces. Thus 'Adam Smith nowhere undervalues the services which the natural agents and machinery perform for us, but he very justly distinguishes the nature of the value which they add to commodities . . . as they perform their work gratuitously, the assistance which they afford us, adds nothing to value in exchange.' (Ric., l.c., pp. 336, 337.) This observation of Ricardo is of course correct in so far as it is directed against J. B. Say, who imagines that machines render the 'service' of creating value which forms a part of 'profits'.

[25] A horse-power is equal to a force of 33,000 foot-pounds per minute, i.e., to a force that raises 33,000 pounds one foot in a minute, or one pound 33,000 feet. This is the horse power meant in the text. In ordinary language, and also here and there in quotations in this work, a distinction is drawn between the 'nominal' and the 'commercial' or 'indicated' horse-power of the same engine. The old or nominal horse-power is calculated exclusively from the length of piston-stroke, and the diameter of the cylinder, and leaves pressure of steam and piston speed out of consideration. It expresses practically this: this engine would be one of 50 horse-power, if it were driven with the same low pressure of steam, and the same slow piston speed, as in the days of Boulton and Watt. But the two latter factors have increased enormously since those days. In order to measure the mechanical force exerted today by an engine, an indicator has been invented which shows the pressure of the steam in the cylinder. The piston speed is easily ascertained. Thus the 'indicated' or 'commercial' horse-power of an engine is expressed by a mathematical formula, involving diameter of cylinder,

length of stroke, piston speed, and steam pressure, simultaneously, and showing what multiple of 33,000 pounds is really raised by the engine in a minute. Hence, one 'nominal' horse-power may exert three, four, or even five 'indicated' or 'real' horse-powers. This observation is made for the purpose of explaining various citations in the subsequent pages. – F. E.

[26] The reader who is imbued with capitalist notions will naturally miss here the 'interest' that the machine, in proportion to its capital value, adds to the product. It is, however, easily seen that since a machine no more creates new value than any other part of constant capital, it cannot add any value under the name of 'interest'. It is also evident that here, where we are treating of the production of surplus-value, we cannot assume *a priori* the existence of any part of that value under the name of interest. The capitalist mode of calculating, which appears, *primâ facie*, absurd, and repugnant to the laws of the creation of value, will be explained in the third book of this work.

[27] This portion of value which is added by the machinery, decreases both absolutely and relatively, when the machinery does away with horses and other animals that are employed as mere moving forces, and not as machines for changing the form of matter. It may here be incidentally observed, that Descartes, in defining animals as mere machines, saw with eyes of the manufacturing period, while to eyes of the middle ages, animals were assistants to man, as they were later to Von Haller in his *Restauration der Staatswissenschaften*. That Descartes, like Bacon, anticipated an alteration in the form of production, and the practical subjugation of Nature by Man, as a result of the altered methods of thought, is plain from his *Discours de la Méthode*. He there says: '*Il est possible* (by the methods he introduced in philosophy) *de parvenir à des connaissances fort utiles à la vie, et qu'au lieu de cette philosophie speculative qu'on enseigne dans les écoles, on en peut trouver une pratique, par laquelle, connaissant la force et les actions du feu, de l'eau, de l'air, des astres, et de tous les autres corps qui nous environnent, aussi distinctement que nous connaissons les divers métiers de nos artisans, nous les pourrions employer en même façon à tous les usages auxquels ils sont propres, et ainsi nous rendre comme maîtres et possesseurs de la nature*' and thus '*contribuer au perfectionnement de la vie humaine*'. In the preface to Sir Dudley North's *Discourses upon Trade* (1691) it is stated, that Descartes' method had begun to free Political Economy from the old fables and superstitious notions of gold, trade, &c. On the whole, however, the early English economists sided with Bacon and Hobbes as their philosophers; while, at a later period, the philosopher [. . .] of Political Economy in England, France, and Italy, was Locke.

[28] According to the annual report (1863) of the Essen chamber of commerce, there was produced in 1862, at the cast-steel works of Krupp, with its 161 furnaces, thirty-two steam-engines (in the year 1800 this was about the number of all the steam-engines working in Manchester), and fourteen steam-hammers (representing in all 1,236 horse-power), forty-nine forges, 203 tool-machines, and about 2,400 workmen – thirteen million pounds of cast steel. Here there are not two workmen to each horse-power.

[29] Babbage estimates that in Java the spinning labour alone adds 117% to the value of the cotton. At the same period (1832) the total value added to the cotton by machinery and labour in the fine-spinning industry, amounted to about 33% of the value of the cotton. (*On the Economy of Machinery*, pp.165,166.)

[30] Machine printing also economises colour.

[31] See Paper read by Dr Watson, Reporter on Products to the Government of India, before the Society of Arts, 17th April, 1860.

[32] 'These mute agents (machines) are always the produce of much less labour than that which they displace, even when they are of the same money-value.' (Ricardo, l.c., p.40.)

[33] Hence in a communistic society there would be a very different scope for the employ of machinery than there can be in a bourgeois society.

[34] 'Employers of labour would not unnecessarily retain two sets of children under thirteen . . . In fact one class of manufacturers, the spinners of woollen yam, now rarely employ children under thirteen years of age, i.e., half-timers. They have introduced improved and new machinery of various kinds, which altogether supersedes the employment of children (i.e., under 13 years); f.i., I will mention one process as an illustration of this diminution in the number of children, wherein by the addition of an apparatus, called a piecing machine, to existing machines, the work of six or four half-timers, according to the peculiarity of each machine, can be performed by one young person (over 13 years) . . . the half-time system "stimulated" the invention of the piecing machine.' (*Reports of Insp. of Fact. for 31st Oct., 1858.*)

[35] 'Wretch' is the recognised term in English Political Economy for the agricultural labourer.

[36] 'Machinery . . . can frequently not be employed until labour (he means wages) rises.' (Ricardo, l.c., p.479.)

[37] See *Report of the Social Science Congress, at Edinburgh. Oct., 1863.*

[38] Dr Edward Smith, during the cotton crisis caused by the American Civil War, was sent by the English Government to Lancashire, Cheshire, and other places, to report on the sanitary condition of the cotton operatives. He reported, that from a hygienic point of view, and apart from the banishment of the operatives from the factory atmosphere, the crisis had several advantages. The women now had sufficient leisure to give their infants the breast, instead of poisoning them with 'Godfrey's cordial'. They had time to learn to cook. Unfortunately the acquisition of this art occurred at a time when they had nothing to cook. But from this we see how capital, for the purposes of its self-expansion, has usurped the labour necessary in the home of the family. This crisis was also utilised to teach sewing to the daughters of the workmen in sewing schools. An American revolution and a universal crisis, in order that the working girls, who spin for the whole world, might learn to sew!

[39] 'The numerical increase of labourers has been great, through the growing substitution of female for male, and above all, of childish for adult labour. Three girls of 13, at wages of from 6 shillings to 8 shillings a week, have replaced the one man of mature age, of wages varying from 18 shillings to 45 shillings.' (Th. de Quincey: *The Logic of Political Econ.*, London, 1844. Note to p.147.) Since certain family functions, such as nursing and suckling children, cannot be entirely suppressed, the mothers confiscated by capital, must try substitutes of some sort. Domestic work, such as sewing and mending, must be replaced by the purchase of ready-made articles. Hence, the diminished expenditure of labour in the house is accompanied by an increased expenditure of money. The cost of keeping the family increases, and balances the greater income. In addition to this, economy and judgment in the consumption and preparation of the means of subsistence becomes impossible. Abundant material relating to these facts, which are concealed by official Political Economy, is to be found in the Reports of the Inspectors of Factories, of the Children's Employment Commission, and more especially in the Reports on Public Health.

[40] In striking contrast with the great fact, that the shortening of the hours of labour of women and children in English factories was exacted from capital by the male operatives, we find in the latest reports of the Children's Employment Commission traits of the operative parents in relation to the traffic in children, that are truly revolting and thoroughly like slave-dealing. But the Pharisee of a capitalist, as may be seen from the same reports, denounces this brutality which he himself creates, perpetuates, and exploits, and which he moreover baptises 'freedom of labour'. 'Infant labour has been called into aid . . . even to work for their own daily bread. Without strength to endure such disproportionate toil, without instruction to guide their future life, they have been thrown into a situation physically and morally polluted. The

Jewish historian has remarked upon the overthrow of Jerusalem by Titus that it was no wonder it should have been destroyed, with such a signal destruction, when an inhuman mother sacrificed her own offspring to satisfy the cravings of absolute hunger.' (*Public Economy Concentrated*. Carlisle, 1833, p.66.)

[41] A. Redgrave in *Reports of Insp. of Fact. for 31st October, 1858*, pp.40,41.

[42] *Children's Employment Commission, Fifth Report*, London, 1866, p.81, n.31.

[43] *Children's Employment Commission, Third Report*, London, 1864, p.53, n.15.

[44] l.c., *Fifth Report*, p.22, n. 137.

[45] *Sixth Report on Public Health*, Lond., 1864, p.34.

[46] 'It (the inquiry of 1861) . . . showed, moreover, that while, with the described circumstances, infants perish under the neglect and mismanagement which their mothers' occupations imply, the mothers become to a grievous extent denaturalised towards their offspring – commonly not troubling themselves much at the death, and even sometimes . . . taking direct measures to insure it.' (l.c.)

[47] l.c., p.454.

[48] l.c., pp. 454–463. 'Report by Dr Henry Julian Hunter on the excessive mortality of infants in some rural districts of England.'

[49] l.c., p.35 and pp. 455,456.

[50] l.c., p.456.

[51] In the agricultural as well as in the factory districts the consumption of opium among the grown-up labourers, both male and female, is extending daily. 'To push the sale of opiate . . . is the great aim of some enterprising wholesale merchants. By druggists it is considered the leading article.' (l.c., p.459.) Infants that take opiates 'shrank up into little old men', or 'wizened like little monkeys'. (l.c., p.460.) We here see how India and China avenged themselves on England.

[52] l.c., p.37.

[53] *Rep. of Insp. of Fact. for 31st Oct., 1862*, p.59. Mr Baker was formerly a doctor.

[54] L. Horner in *Reports of Insp. of Fact. for 30th June, 1857*, p.17.

[55] L. Horner in *Rep. of Insp. of Fact. for 31st Oct., 1855*, pp.18,19.

[56] Sir John Kincaid in *Rep. of Insp. of Fact. for 31st Oct., 1858*, pp.31,32.

[57] L. Horner in *Reports, &c., for 31st Oct., 1857*, pp.17,18.

[58] Sir J. Kincaid in *Reports, &c., 31st Oct., 1856*, p.66.

[59] A. Redgrave in *Rep. of Insp. of Fact., 31st. Oct., 1857*, pp.41–42. In those industries where the Factory Act proper (not the Print Works Act referred to in the text) has been in force for some time, the obstacles in the way of the education clauses have, in recent years, been overcome. In industries not under the Act, the views of Mr J. Geddes, a glass manufacturer, still extensively prevail. He informed Mr White, one of the Inquiry Commissioners: 'As far as I can see, the greater amount of education which a part of the working-class has enjoyed for some years past is an evil. It is dangerous, because it makes them independent.' (*Children's Empl. Comm., Fourth Report*, Lond., 1865, p.253.)

[60] 'Mr E., a manufacturer . . . informed me that he employed females exclusively at his power-looms . . . gives a decided preference to married females, especially those who have families at home dependent on them for support; they are attentive, docile, more so than unmarried females, and are compelled to use their utmost exertions to procure the necessaries of life. Thus are the virtues, the peculiar virtues of the female character to be perverted to her injury – thus all that is most dutiful and tender in her nature is made a means of her bondage and suffering.' (Ten Hours' Factory Bill. The Speech of Lord Ashley, March 15th, Lond., 1844, p.20.)

[61] 'Since the general introduction of machinery, human nature has been forced far beyond its average strength.' (Rob. Owen: *Observations on the Effects of the Manufacturing System*, 2nd Ed., London, 1817.)

[62] The English, who have a tendency to look upon the earliest form of appearance of a thing as the cause of its existence, are in the habit of attributing the long hours of work in factories to the extensive kidnapping of children, practised by capitalists in the infancy of the factory system, on workhouses and orphanages, by means of which robbery, unresisting material for exploitation was procured. Thus, for instance, Ficiden, himself a manufacturer, says: 'It is evident that the long hours of work were brought about by the circumstance of so great a number of destitute children being supplied from different parts of the country, that the masters were independent of the hands, and that having once established the custom by means of the miserable materials they had procured in this way, they could impose it on their neighbours with the greater facility.' (J. Ficiden: *The Curse of the Factory System*, Lond., 1836, p.11.) With reference to the labour of women, Saunders, the factory inspector, says in his report of 1844: 'Amongst the female operatives there are some women who, for many weeks in succession, except for a few days, are employed from 6 a.m. till midnight, with less than 2 hours for meals, so that on 5 days of the week they have only 6 hours left out of the 24, for going to and from their homes and resting in bed.'

[63] 'Occasion . . . injury to the delicate moving parts of metallic mechanism by inaction.' (Ure, l.c., p.281.)

[64] The Manchester Spinner (*Times*, 26th Nov., 1862) before referred to says in relation to this subject: 'It (namely, the 'allowance for deterioration of machinery') is also intended to cover the loss which is constantly arising from the superseding of machines before they are worn out, by others of a new and better construction.'

[65] 'It has been estimated, roughly, that the first individual of a newly-invented machine will cost about five times as much as the construction of the second.' (Babbage, l.c., p.349.)

[66] 'The improvements which took place not long ago in frames for making patent net were so great that a machine in good repair which had cost £1,200, sold a few years after for £60 . . . improvements succeeded each other so rapidly, that machines which had never been finished were abandoned in the hands of their makers, because new improvements bad superseded their utility.' (Babbage, l.c., p.233.) In these stormy, go-ahead times, therefore, the tulle manufacturers soon extended the working-day, by means of double sets of hands, from the original 8 hours to 24.

[67] 'It is self-evident, that, amid the ebbings and flowings of the markets and the alternate expansions and contractions of demand, occasions will constantly recur, in which the manufacturer may employ additional floating capital without employing additional fixed capital . . . if additional quantities of raw material can be worked up without incurring an additional expense for buildings and machinery.' (R. Torrens: *On Wages and Combination*. London, 1834, p.64.)

[68] This circumstance is mentioned only for the sake of completeness, for I shall not consider the rate of profit, i.e., the ratio of the surplus-value to the total capital advanced, until I come to the third book.

[69] Senior, *Letters on the Factory Act*. London, 1837, pp.13,14.

[70] 'The great proportion of fixed to circulating capital . . . makes long hours of work desirable.' With the increased use of machinery, &c., 'the motives to long hours of work will become greater, as the only means by which a large proportion of fixed capital can be made profitable.' (l.c., pp.11–13.) 'There are certain expenses upon a mill which go on in the same proportion whether the mill be running short or full time, as, for instance, rent rates, and taxes, insurance against fire, wages of several permanent servants, deterioration of machinery, with various other charges upon a manufacturing establishment, the proportion of which to profits increases as the production decreases.' (*Rep. of Insp. of Fact. for 31st Oct., 1862*, p.19.)

[71] Why it is, that the capitalist, and also the political economists who are imbued with his views, are unconscious of this immanent contradiction, will appear from the first part of the third book.

[72] It is one of the greatest merits of Ricardo to have seen in machinery not only the means of producing commodities, but of creating a 'redundant population'.

[73] F. Biese. *Die Philosophie des Aristoteles*, vol. 2. Berlin, 1842, p.408.

[74] I give below the translation of this poem by Stolberg, because it brings into relief, quite in the spirit of former quotations referring to division of labour, the antithesis between the views of the ancients and the moderns. 'Spare the hand that grinds the corn, Oh, miller girls, and softly sleep. Let Chanticleer announce the morn in vain! Deo has commanded the work of the girls to be done by the Nymphs, and now they skip lightly over the wheels, so that the shaken axles revolve with their spokes and pull round the load of the revolving stones. Let us live the life of our fathers, and let us rest from work and enjoy the gifts that the Goddess sends us.'

> Schonet der mahlenden Hand, o Müllerinnen, und schlafet
> Sanft! es verkünde der Hahn euch den Morgen umsonst!
> Däo hat die Arbeit der Mädchen den Nymphen befohlen,
> Und itzt hüpfen sie leicht über die Räder dahin,
> Daß die erschütterten Achsen mit ihren Speichen sich wälzen,
> Und im Kreise die Last drehen des wälzenden Steins.
> Lasst uns leben das Leben der Väter, und laßt uns der Gaben
> Arbeitslos uns freun, welche die Göttin uns schenkt.

(*Gedichte aus dem Griechischen übersetzt von Christian Graf zu Stolberg*, Hamburg, 1782.)

[75] There are, of course, always differences, in the intensities of the labour in various industries. But these differences are, as Adam Smith has shown, compensated to a partial extent by minor circumstances, peculiar to each sort of labour. Labour-time, as a measure of value, is not, however, affected in this case, except in so far as the duration of labour, and the degree of its intensity, are two antithetical and mutually exclusive expressions for one and the same quantity of labour.

[76] Especially by piece-work, a form we shall investigate in Part 6 of this book.

[77] See *Rep. of Insp. of Fact. for 31st October, 1865*.

[78] *Rep, of Insp, of Fact. for 1844 and the quarter ending 30th April, 1845*, pp. 20–21.

[79] l.c., p.19. Since the wages for piece-work were unaltered, the weekly wages depended on the quantity produced.

[80] l.c., p.20.

[81] The moral element played an important part in the above experiments. The workpeople told the factory inspector: 'We work with more spirit, we have the reward ever before us of getting away sooner at night, and one active and cheerful spirit pervades the whole mill, from the youngest piecer to the oldest hand, and we can greatly help each other.' (l.c., p.21.)

[82] John Fielden, l.c., p.32.

[83] Lord Ashley, l.c., pp.6–9, passim.

[84] *Rep. of Insp. of Fact. for Quarter ending 30th September, 1844, and from 1st October, 1844, to 30th April, 1845*, p.20.

[85] l.c., p.22.

[86] *Rep. of Insp. of Fact. for 31st October, 1862*, p.62.

[87] This was altered in the Parliamentary Return of 1862. In it the actual horse-power of the modern steam engines and water wheels appears in place of the nominal. The doubling spindles, too, are no longer included in the spinning spindles (as was the case in the 'Returns' of 1839, 1850, and 1856); further, in the case of woollen mills, the number of 'gigs' is added, a distinction made between jute and hemp mills on the one hand and flax mills on the other, and finally stocking-weaving is for the first time inserted in the report.

[88] *Rep. of Insp. of Fact. for 31st October, 1856*, pp.13–14, 20 and *1852*, p.23.

[89] l.c., pp.14–15.

[90] l.c., p.20.

[91] *Reports, &c., for 31st October, 1858*, pp.9–10. Compare *Reports, &c., for 30th April, 1860*, p.30, sqq.

[92] *Reports of Insp. of Fact. for 31st Oct., 1862*, pp.100 and 130.

[93] On 2 modern power-looms a weaver now makes in a week of 60 hours 26 pieces of certain quality, length, and breadth; while on the old power-looms he could make no more than 4 such pieces. The cost of weaving a piece of such cloth had already soon after 1850 fallen from 2s. 9d. to 5 1/8d.

'Thirty years ago (1841) one spinner with three piecers was not required to attend to more than one pair of mules with 300–324 spindles. At the present time (1871) he has to mind with the help of 5 piecers 2,200 spindles, and produces not less than seven times as much yarn as in 1841.' (Alex. Redgrave, Factory Inspector – in the *Journal of Arts*, 5th January, 1872.)

[94] *Rep. of Insp. of Fact. for 31st Oct., 1861*, pp.25,26.

[95] The agitation for a working-day of 8 hours has now (1867) begun in Lancashire among the factory operatives.

[96] The following few figures indicate the increase in the 'factories' of the United Kingdom since 1848:

	Quantity Exported, 1860	Quantity Exported, 1851	Quantity Exported, 1848	Quantity Exported, 1865
Cotton				
Cotton yarn	lbs. 135,831,162	lbs. 143,966,106	lbs. 197,343,655	lbs. 103,751,455
Sewing thread	lbs.	lbs. 4,392,176	lbs. 6,297,554	lbs. 4,648,611
Cotton cloth	yds. 1,091,373,930	yds. 1,543,161,789	yds. 2,776,218,427	yds. 2,015,237,851
Flax & Hemp				
Yarn	lbs. 11,722,182	lbs. 18,841,326	lbs. 31,210,612	lbs. 36,777,334
Cloth	yds. 88,901,519	yds. 129,106,753	yds. 143,996,773	yds. 247,012,529
Silk				
Yarn	lbs. 466,825	lbs. 462,513	lbs. 897,402	812,580
Cloth	yds.	yds. 1,181,455	1,307,293	yds. 2,869,837
Wool				
Woollen and				
Worsted yarns	lbs.	lbs. 14,670,880	lbs. 27,533,968	lbs. 31,669,267
Cloth	yds.	yds. 241,120,973	190,381,537	yds. 278,837,438

	Value Exported, 1848 £	Value Exported, 1851 £	Value Exported, 1860 £	Value Exported, 1865 £
Cotton				
Yarn	5,927,831	6,634,026	9,870,875	10,351,040
Cloth	16,753,369	23,454,810	42,141,505	46,903,796
Flax & Hemp				
Yarn	493,449	951,426	1,801,272	2,505,497
Cloth	2,802,789	4,107,396	4,804,803	9,155,318
Silk				
Yarn	195,380	918,342	768,067	
Cloth	77,789	1,130,398	1,587,303	1,409,221
Wool				
Yarn	776,975	1,484,544	3,843,450	5,424,017
Cloth	5,733,828	8,377,183	12,156,998	20,102,259

See the Blue Books *Statistical Abstract of the United Kingdom*, Nos. 8 and 13. Lond., 1961 and 1866. In Lancashire the number of mills increased only 4 per cent. between 1839 and 1850; 19 per cent. between 1850 and 1856; and 33 per cent. between 1856 and 1862; while the persons employed in them during each of the above periods of 11 years increased absolutely, but diminished relatively. (See *Rep. of Insp. of Fact., for 31st Oct.,* *1862*, p.63.) The cotton trade preponderates in Lancashire. We may form an idea of the stupendous nature of the cotton trade in that district when we consider that, of the gross number of textile factories in the United Kingdom, it absorbs 45.2 per cent., of the spindles, 83.3 per cent.; of the power-looms, 81.4 per cent.; of the mechanical horse-power, 72.6 per cent.; and of the total number of persons employed, 58.2 per cent. (l.c., pp.62–63.)

[97] Ure, l.c., p.18.

[98] Ure, l.c., p.3 1. See Karl Marx, l.c., pp.140–141.

[99] It looks very like intentional misleading by statistics (which misleading it would be possible to prove in detail in other cases too), when the English factory legislation excludes from its operation the class of labourers last mentioned in the text, while the parliamentary returns expressly include in the category of factory operatives, not only engineers, mechanics, &c., but also managers, salesmen, messengers, warehousemen, packers, &c., in short everybody, except the owner of the factory himself.

[100] Ure grants this. He says, 'in case of need', the workmen can be moved at the will of the manager from one machine to another, and he triumphantly exclaims: 'Such a change is in flat contradiction with the old routine, that divides the labour, and to one workman assigns the task of fashioning the head of a needle, to another the sharpening of the point.' He had much better have asked himself, why this 'old routine' is departed from in the automatic factory, only 'in case of need'.

[101] When distress is very great, as, for instance, during the American Civil War, the factory operative is now and then set by the Bourgeois to do the roughest of work, such as road-making, &c.. The English '*ateliers nationaux*' of 1862 and the following years, established for the benefit of the destitute cotton operatives, differ from the French of 1848 in this, that in the latter the workmen had to do unproductive work at the expense of the state, in the former they had to do productive municipal work to the advantage of the bourgeois, and that, too, cheaper than the regular workmen, with whom they were thus thrown into competition. 'The physical appearance of the cotton operatives is unquestionably improved. This I attribute . . . as to the men, to outdoor labour on public works.' (*Rep. of Insp. of Fact., 31st Oct., 1863*, p.59.) The writer here alludes to the Preston factory operatives, who were employed on Preston Moor.

[102] An example: the various mechanical apparatus introduced since the Act of 1844 into woollen mills, for replacing the labour of children. So soon as it shall happen that the children of the manufacturers themselves have to go through a course of schooling as helpers in the mill, this almost unexplored territory of mechanics will soon make remarkable progress. 'Of machinery, perhaps self-acting mules are as dangerous as any other kind. Most of the accidents from them happen to little children, from their creeping under the mules to sweep the floor whilst the mules are in motion. Several "minders" have been fined for this offence, but without much general benefit. If machine makers would only invent a self-sweeper, by whose use the necessity for these little children to creep under the machinery might be prevented, it would be a happy addition to our protective measures.' (*Reports of Insp. of Fact. for 31st. Oct., 1866*, p.63.)

[103] So much then for Proudhon's wonderful idea: he 'construes' machinery not as a synthesis of instruments of labour, but as a synthesis of detail operations for the benefit of the labourer himself.

[104] F. Engels, l.c., p.217. Even an ordinary and optimist Free-trader, like Mr Molinari, goes so far as to say, '*Un homme s'use plus vite en surveillant, quinze heures par jour, l'évolution uniforme d'un mécanisme, qu'en exerçant, dans le même espace de temps, sa force physique. Ce travail de surveillance qui servirait peut-être d'utile gymnastique à l'intelligence, s'il n'était pas trop prolongé, détruit à la longue, par son excès, et l'intelligence, et le corps même.*' (G. de Molinari: '*Études Économiques.*' Paris, 1846.)

[105] F. Engels, l.c., p.216.

[106] *The Master Spinners' and Manufacturers' Defence Fund. Report of the Committee.* Manchester, 1854, p.17. We shall see hereafter, that the 'master' can sing quite another song, when he is threatened with the loss of his 'living' automaton.

[107] Ure, l.c., p.15. Whoever knows the life history of Arkwright, will never dub this barber-genius 'noble'. Of all the great inventors of the 18th century, he was incontestably the greatest thiever of other people's inventions and the meanest fellow.

[108] 'The slavery in which the bourgeoisie has bound the proletariat, comes nowhere more plainly into daylight than in the factory system. In it all freedom comes to an end both at law and in fact. The workman must be in the factory at half past five. If he come a few minutes late, he is punished; if he come 10 minutes late, he is not allowed to enter until after breakfast, and thus loses a quarter of a day's wage. He must eat, drink and sleep at word of command . . . The despotic bell calls him from his bed, calls him from breakfast and dinner. And how does he fare in the mill? There the master is the absolute law-giver. He makes what regulations he pleases; he alters and makes additions to his code at pleasure; and if he insert the veriest nonsense, the courts say to the workman: Since you have entered into this contract voluntarily, you must now carry it out . . . These workmen are condemned to live, from their ninth year till their death, under this mental and bodily torture.' (F. Engels, l.c., p.217, sq.) What 'the courts say' I will illustrate by two examples. One occurs at Sheffield at the end of 1866. In that town a workman had engaged himself for 2 years in a steelworks. In consequence of a quarrel with his employer he left the works, and declared that under no circumstances would he work for that master any more. He was prosecuted for breach of contract, and condemned to two months' imprisonment. (If the master break the contract, he can be proceeded against only in a civil action, and risks nothing but money damages.) After the workman has served his two months, the master invites him to return to the works, pursuant to the contract. Workman says: No, he has already been punished for the breach. The master prosecutes again, the court condemns again, although one of the judges, Mr Shee, publicly denounces this as a legal monstrosity, by which a man can periodically, as long as he lives, be punished over and over again for the same offence or crime. This judgment was given not by the 'Great Unpaid', the provincial Dogberries, but by one of the highest courts of justice in London. – The second case occurs in Wiltshire at the end of November 1863. About 30 power-loom weavers, in the employment of one Harrup, a cloth manufacturer at Leower's Mill, Westbury Leigh, struck work because master Harrup indulged in the agreeable habit of making deductions from their wages for being late in the morning; 6d. for 2 minutes; 1s. for 3 minutes, and 1s. 6d. for ten minutes. This is at the rate of 9s. per hour, and £4 10s. 0d. per diem; while the wages of the weavers on the average of a year, never exceeded 10s. to 12s. weekly. Harrup also appointed a boy to announce the starting time by a whistle, which he often did before six o'clock in the morning: and if the hands were not all there at the moment the whistle ceased, the doors were closed, and those hands who were outside were fined: and as there was no clock on the premises, the unfortunate hands were at the mercy of the young Harrup-inspired timekeeper. The hands on strike, mothers of families as well as girls, offered to resume work if the timekeeper were replaced by a clock, and a more reasonable scale of fines were introduced. Harrup summoned 19 women and girls before the magistrates for breach of contract. To the utter indignation of all present, they were each mulcted in a fine of 6d. and 2s. 6d. for costs. Harrup was followed from the court by a crowd of people who hissed him. A favourite operation with manufacturers is to punish the workpeople by deductions made from their wages on account of faults in the material worked on. This method gave rise in 1866 to a general strike in the English pottery districts. The reports of the Ch. Empl. Com. (1863–1866), give cases where the worker

not only receives no wages, but becomes, by means of his labour, and of the penal regulations, the debtor to boot, of his worthy master. The late cotton crisis also furnished edifying examples of the sagacity shown by the factory autocrats in making deductions from wages. Mr R. Baker, the Inspector of Factories, says, 'I have myself had lately to direct prosecutions against one cotton mill occupier for having in these pinching and painful times deducted 10d. a piece from some of the young workers employed by him, for the surgeon's certificate (for which he himself had only paid 6d.), when only allowed by the law to deduct 3d., and by custom nothing at all . . . And I have been informed of another, who, in order to keep without the law, but to attain the same object, charges the poor children who work for him a shilling each, as a fee for learning them the art and mystery of cotton spinning, so soon as they are declared by the surgeon fit and proper persons for that occupation. There may therefore be undercurrent causes for such extraordinary exhibitions as strikes, not only wherever they arise, but particularly at such times as the present, which without explanation, render them inexplicable to the public understanding.' He alludes here to a strike of power-loom weavers at Darwen, June, 1863. (*Reports of Insp. of Fact. for 30 April, 1863*, pp. 50–51.) The reports always go beyond their official dates.

[109] The protection afforded by the Factory Acts against dangerous machinery has had a beneficial effect. 'But . . . there are other sources of accident which did not exist twenty years since; one especially, viz., the increased speed of the machinery. Wheels, rollers, spindles and shuttles are now propelled at increased and increasing rates; fingers must be quicker and defter in their movements to take up the broken thread, for, if placed with hesitation or carelessness, they are sacrificed . . . A large number of accidents are caused by the eagerness of the workpeople to get through their work expeditiously. It must be remembered that it is of the highest importance to manufacturers that their machinery should be in motion, i.e., producing yarns and goods. Every minute's stoppage is not only a loss of power, but of production, and the workpeople are urged by the overlookers, who are interested in the quantity of work turned off, to keep the machinery in motion, and it is no less important to those of the operatives who are paid by the weight or piece, that the machines should be kept in motion. Consequently, although it is strictly forbidden in many, nay in most factories, that machinery should be cleaned while in motion, it is nevertheless the constant practice in most, if not in all, that the workpeople do, unreproved, pick out waste, wipe rollers and wheels, &c., while their frames are in motion. Thus from this cause only, 906 accidents have occurred during the six months . . . Although a great deal of cleaning is constantly going on day by day, yet Saturday is generally the day set apart for the thorough cleaning of the machinery, and a great deal of this is done while the machinery is in motion.' Since cleaning is not paid for, the workpeople seek to get done with it as speedily as possible. Hence 'the number of accidents which occur on Fridays, and especially on Saturdays, is much larger than on any other day. On the former day the excess is nearly 12 per cent. over the average number of the four first days of the week, and on the latter day the excess is 25 per cent. over the average of the preceding five days; or, if the number of working-hours on Saturday being taken into account – 7 1/2 hours on Saturday as compared with 10 1/2 on other days – there is an excess of 65 per cent. on Saturdays over the average of the other five days.' ('*Rep. of Insp. of Fact., 31st Oct., 1866*, pp.9,15,16,17.)

[110] In Part 1 of Book 3 I shall give an account of a recent campaign by the English manufacturers against the Clauses in the Factory Acts that protect the 'hands' against dangerous machinery. For the present, let this one quotation from the official report of Leonard Horner suffice: 'I have heard some mill-owners speak with inexcusable levity of some of the accidents; such, for instance, as the loss of a finger being a trifling matter. A working-man's living and prospects depend so much upon his fingers, that

any loss of them is a very serious matter to him. When I have heard such inconsiderate remarks made, I have usually put this question: Suppose you were in want of an additional workman, and two were to apply, both equally well qualified in other respects, but one had lost a thumb or a forefinger, which would you engage? There never was a hesitation as to the answer . . . ' The manufacturers have 'mistaken prejudices against what they have heard represented as a pseudo-philanthropic legis-lation.' (*Rep. of Insp. of Fact., 31st Oct., 1855.*) These manufacturers are clever folk, and not without reason were they enthusiastic for the slave-holders' rebellion.

[111] In those factories that have been longest subject to the Factory Acts, with their compulsory limitation of the hours of labour, and other regulations, many of the older abuses have vanished. The very improvement of the machinery demands to a certain extent 'improved construction of the buildings', and this is an advantage to the workpeople. (See *Rep. of Insp. of Fact. for 31st Oct., 1863*, p.109.)

[112] See amongst others, John Houghton: *Husbandry and Trade Improved*. London, 1727. *The Advantages of the East India Trade*, 1720. John Bellers, l.c. 'The masters and their workmen are, unhappily, in a perpetual war with each other. The invariable object of the former is to get their work done as cheaply as possible; and they do not fail to employ every artifice to this purpose, whilst the latter are equally attentive to every occasion of distressing their masters into a compliance with higher demands.' (*An Enquiry into the Causes of the Present High Price of Provisions*, pp.61–62. Author, the Rev. Nathaniel Forster, quite on the side of the workmen.)

[113] In old-fashioned manufactures the revolts of the workpeople against machinery, even to this day, occasionally assume a savage character, as in the case of the Sheffield file cutters in 1865.

[114] Sir James Steuart also understands machinery quite in this sense. '*Je considère donc les machines comme des moyens d'augmenter (virtuellement) le nombre des gens industrieux qu'on n'est pas obligé de nourrir . . . En quoi l'effet d'une machine diffère-t-il de celui de nouveaux habitants?*' (French trans. t.i, l.i, ch.xix.) More naïve is Petty, who says, it replaces 'Polygamy'. The above point of view is, at the most, admissible only for some parts of the United States. On the other hand, 'machinery can seldom be used with success to abridge the labour of an individual; more time would be lost in its construction than could be saved by its application. It is only really useful when it acts on great masses, when a single machine can assist the work of thousands. It is accordingly in the most populous countries, where there are most idle men, that it is most abundant . . . It is not called into use by a scarcity of men, but by the facility with which they can be brought to work in masses.' (Piercy Ravenstone: *Thoughts on the Funding System and its Effects*. London, 1824, p.45.)

[115] 'Machinery and labour are in constant competition.' Ricardo, l.c., p.479.

[116] The competition between hand-weaving and power-weaving in England, before the passing of the Poor Law of 1833, was prolonged by supplementing the wages, which had fallen considerably below the minimum, with parish relief. 'The Rev. Mr Turner was, in 1827, rector of Wilmslow in Cheshire, a manufacturing district. The questions of the Committee of Emigration, and Mr Turner's answers, show how the competition of human labour is maintained against machinery. "Question: Has not the use of the power-loom superseded the use of the hand-loom? Answer: Undoubtedly; it would have superseded them much more than it has done, if the hand-loom weavers were not enabled to submit to a reduction of wages." "Question: But in submitting he has accepted wages which are insufficient to support him, and looks to parochial contribution as the remainder of his support? Answer: Yes, and in fact the competition between the hand-loom and the power-loom is maintained out of the poor-rates." Thus degrading pauperism or expatriation, is the benefit which the industrious receive from the introduction of machinery, to be reduced from the respectable and in some

degree independent mechanic, to the cringing wretch who lives on the debasing bread of charity. This they call a temporary inconvenience.' (*A Prize Essay on the Comparative Merits of Competition and Co-operation*' Lond., 1834, p.29.)

[117] 'The same cause which may increase the revenue of the country' (i.e., as Ricardo explains in the same passage, the revenues of landlords and capitalists, whose wealth, from the economic point of view, forms the Wealth of the Nation), 'may at the same time render the population redundant and deteriorate the condition of the labourer.' (Ricardo, l.c., p.469.) 'The constant aim and the tendency of every improvement in machinery is, in fact, to do away entirely with the labour of man, or to lessen its price by substituting the labour of women and children for that of grown-up men, or of unskilled for that of skilled workmen.' (Ure, l.c., t.i, p.35.)

[118] *Rep. Insp. Fact. for 31st October, 1858*, p.43.

[119] *Rep. Insp. Fact. for 31st October, 1856*, p.15.

[120] Ure, l.c., p.19. 'The great advantage of the machinery employed in brick-making consists in this, that the employer is made entirely independent of skilled labourers.' (*Ch. Empl. Comm. V. Report*, Lond., 1866, p.130, n. 46.) Mr A. Sturrock, superintendent of the machine department of the Great Northern Railway, says, with regard to the building of locomotives, &c.: 'Expensive English workmen are being less used every day. The production of the workshops of England is being increased by the use of improved tools and these tools are again served by a low class of labour . . . Formerly their skilled labour necessarily produced all the parts of engines. Now the parts of engines are produced by labour with less skill, but with good tools. By tools, I mean engineer's machinery, lathes, planing machines, drills, and so on.' (*Royal Com. on Railways*, Lond., 1867, Minutes of Evidence, n.17, 862 and 17, 863.)

[121] Ure, l.c., p.20.

[122] Ure, l.c., p.321.

[123] Ure, l.c., p.23.

[124] *Rep. Insp. Fact., 31st Oct., 1863*, pp.108,109.

[125] l.c., p.109. The rapid improvement of machinery, during the crisis, allowed the English manufacturers, immediately after the termination of the American Civil War, and almost in no time, to glut the markets of the world again. Cloth,' during the last six months of 1866, was almost unsaleable. Thereupon began the consignment of goods to India and China, thus naturally making the glut more intense. At the beginning of 1867 the manufacturers resorted to their usual way out of the difficulty, viz., reducing wages 5 per cent. The workpeople resisted, and said that the only remedy was to work short time, 4 days a-week; and their theory was the correct one. After holding out for some time, the self-elected captains of industry had to make up their minds to short time, with reduced wages in some places, and in others without.

[126] 'The relation of master and man in the blown-flint bottle trades amounts to a chronic strike.' Hence the impetus given to the manufacture of pressed glass, in which the chief operations are done by machinery. One firm in Newcastle, who formerly produced 350,000 lbs. of blown-flint glass, now produces in its place 3,000,500 lbs. of pressed glass. (*Ch. Empl. Comm., Fourth Rep.*, 1865, pp.262–263.)

[127] Gaskell. *The Manufacturing Population of England*, London, 1833, pp.3,4.

[128] W. Fairbairn discovered several very important applications of machinery to the construction of machines, in consequence of strikes in his own workshops.

[129] Ure, l.c., pp.368–370

[130] Ure, l.c., pp.368,7,370,280,281,321,370,475.

[131] Ricardo originally was also of this opinion, but afterwards expressly disclaimed it with the scientific impartiality and love of truth characteristic of him. See l.c., ch.xxxi 'On Machinery.'

[132] *Nota bene.* My illustration is entirely on the lines of those given by the above named economists.

[133] A disciple of Ricardo, in answer to the insipidities of J. B. Say, remarks on this point: 'Where division of labour is well developed, the skill of the labourer is available only in that particular branch in which it has been acquired; he himself is a sort of machine. It does not therefore help matters one jot, to repeat in parrot fashion, that things have a tendency to find their level. On looking around us we cannot but see, that they are unable to find their level for a long time; and that when they do find it, the level is always lower than at the commencement of the process.' (*An Inquiry into those Principles Respecting the Nature of Demand, &c.*, Lond. 1821, p.72.)

[134] MacCulloch, amongst others, is a past master in this pretentious cretinism. 'If,' he says, with the affected naïveté of a child of 8 years, 'if it be advantageous, to develop the skill of the workman more and more, so that he is capable of producing, with the same or with a less quantity of labour, a constantly increasing quantity of commodities, it must also be advantageous, that he should avail himself of the help of such machinery as will assist him most effectively in the attainment of this result.' (MacCulloch: *Princ. of Pol. Econ.*, Lond. 1830, p.166.)

[135] 'The inventor of the spinning machine has ruined India, a fact, however, that touches us but little.' A. Thiers: *De la propriété.* – M. Thiers here confounds the spinning machine with the power-loom, 'a fact, however, that touches us but little.'

[136] According to the census of 1861 (Vol. ii, Lond., 1863), the number of people employed in coal mines in England and Wales, amounted to 246,613, of which 73,545 were under, and 173,067 were over 20 years. Of those under 20, 835 were between 5 and 10 years, 30,701 between 10 and 15 years, 42,010 between 15 and 19 years. The number employed in iron, copper, lead, tin, and other mines of every description, was 319, 222.

[137] In England and Wales, in 1861, there were employed in making machinery, 60,807 persons, including the masters and their clerks, &c., also all agents and business people connected with this industry, but excluding the makers of small machines, such as sewing-machines, &c., as also the makers of the operative parts of machines, such as spindles. The total number of civil engineers amounted to 3,329.

[138] Since iron is one of the most important raw materials; let me here state that, in 1861, there were in England and Wales 125,771 operative iron founders, of whom 123,430 were males, 2,341 females. Of the former 30,810 were under, and 92,620 over 20 years.

[139] 'A family of four grown-up persons, with two children as winders, earned at the end of the last, and the beginning of the present century, by ten hours' daily labour, £4 a week. If the work was very pressing, they could earn more . . . Before that, they had always suffered from a deficient supply of yarn.' (Gaskell, l.c., pp.25–27.)

[140] F. Engels, in *Lage, &c.*, points out the miserable condition of a large number of those who work on these very articles of luxury. See also numerous instances in the Reports of the Children's Employment Commission.

[141] In 1861, in England and Wales, there were 94,665 sailors in the merchant service.

[142] Of these only 177,596 are males above 13 years of age.

[143] Of these, 30,501 are females.

[144] Of these, 137,447 males. None are included in the 1,208,648 who do not serve in private houses. Between 1861 and 1870 the number of male servants nearly doubled itself. It increased to 267,671. In the year 1847 there were 2,694 game-keepers (for the landlords' preserves), in 1869 there were 4,921. The young servant girls in the houses of the London lower middle class are in common parlance called 'slaveys'.

[145] Ganilh, on the contrary, considers the final result of the factory system to be an absolutely less number of operatives, at whose expense an increased number of '*gens honnêtes*' live and develop their well-known '*perfectibilité perfectible*'. Little as he understands the movement of production, at least he feels, that machinery must needs be a very fatal institution, if its introduction converts busy workmen into paupers, and its development calls more slaves of labour into existence than it has suppressed. It is not possible to bring out the cretinism of his standpoint, except by his own words: '*Les classes condamnées à produire et à consommer diminuent, et les classes qui dirigent le travail, qui soulagent, consolent, et éclairent toute la population, se multiplient . . . et s'approprient tous les bienfaits qui résultent de la diminution des frais du travail, de l'abondance des productions, et du bon marché des consommations. Dans cette direction, l'espèce humaine s'élève aux plus hautes conceptions du génie, pénètre dans les profondeurs mystérieuses de la religion, établit les principes salutaires de la morale* (which consists in '*s'approprier tous les beinfaits*', &c.), *les lois tutélaires de la liberté* (liberty of '*les classes condamnées à produire*'?) *et du pouvoir, de l'obéissance et de la justice, du devoir et de l'humanité.*' For this twaddle, see *Des Systèmes d'Économie Politique, &c., Par M. Ch. Ganilh*, 2ème ed., Paris, 1821, t.i, p.224, and see p.212.

[146] *Reports of Insp. of Fact., 31 Oct., 1865*, p.58, sq. At the same time, however, means of employment for an increased number of hands was ready in 110 new mills with 11,625 looms, 628,576 spindles and 2,695 total horse-power of steam and water (l.c.).

[147] *Reports, &c., for 31 Oct., 1862*, p.79. At the end of 1871, Mr A. Redgrave, the factory inspector, in a lecture given at Bradford, in the New Mechanics' Institution, said: 'What has struck me for some time past is the altered appearance of the woollen factories. Formerly they were filled with women and children, now machinery seems to do all the work. At my asking for an explanation of this from a manufacturer, he gave me the following: "Under the old system I employed 63 persons; after the intro-duction of improved machinery I reduced my hands to 33, and lately, in consequence of new and extensive alterations, I have been in a position to reduce those 33 to 13." '

[148] See *Reports, &c., 31 Oct., 1856*, p.16.

[149 'The sufferings of the hand-loom weavers were the subject of an inquiry by a Royal Commission, but although their distress was acknowledged and lamented, the amelioration of their condition was left, and probably necessarily so, to the chances and changes of time, which it may now be hoped' [20 years later!] 'have nearly obliterated those miseries, and not improbably by the present great extension of the power-loom.' (*Rep. Insp. of Fact., 31 Oct., 1856*, p.15.)

[150] Other ways in which machinery affects the production of raw material will be mentioned in the third book.

[151]   *Export of Cotton From India to Great Britain*
        1846: 34,540,143 lbs.   1860: 204,141,168 lbs.   1865: 445,947,600 lbs.

[152]   *Export of Wool from India to Great Britain*
        1846: 4,570,581 lbs.   1860: 20,214,173 lbs.   1865: 20,679,111 lbs.
                Export of Wool from the Cape to Great Britain
        1846: 2,958,457 lbs.   1860: 16,574,345 lbs.   1865: 29,920,623 lbs.
                Export of Wool from Australia to Great Britain
        1846: 21,789,346 lbs.   1860: 59,166,616 lbs.   1865: 109,734,261 lbs.

[153] The economic development of the United States is itself a product of European, more especially of English modern industry. In their present form (1866) the States must still be considered a European colony.

                Export of Cotton from the United States to Great Britain
        1846: 401,949,393 lbs.   1852: 765,630,543 lbs.   1859: 961,707,264
        1860: 1,115,890,608 lbs.

Export of Corn, &c., from the United States to Great Britain

	1850	1862
Wheat, cwts.	16,202,312	41,033,503
Barley, cwts.	3,669,653	6,624,800
Oats, cwts.	3,174,801	4,426,994
Rye, cwts.	388,749	7,108
Flour, cwts.	3,819,440	7,207,113
Buckwheat, cwts.	1054	19,571
Maize, cwts.	5,473,161	11,694,818
Bere or Bigg (a sort of Barley), cwts.	2039	7675
Peas, cwts.	811,620	1,024,722
Beans, cwts.	1,822,972	2,037,137
Total exports	34,365,801	74,083,351

[154] In an appeal made in July, 1866, to the Trade Societies of England, by the shoemakers of Leicester, who had been thrown on the streets by a lock-out, it is stated: 'Twenty years ago the Leicester shoe trade was revolutionised by the introduction of riveting in the place of stitching. At that time good wages could be earned. Great competition was shown between the different firms as to which could turn out the neatest article. Shortly afterwards, however, a worse kind of competition sprang up, namely, that of underselling one another in the market. The injurious consequences soon manifested themselves in reductions of wages, and so sweepingly quick was the fall in the price of labour, that many firms now pay only one half of the original wages. And yet, though wages sink lower and lower, profits appear, with each alteration in the scale of wages, to increase.' Even bad times are utilised by the manufacturers, for making exceptional profits by excessive lowering of wages, i.e., by a direct robbery of the labourer's means of subsistence. One example (it has reference to the crisis in the Coventry silk weaving): 'From information I have received from manufacturers as well as workmen, there seems to be no doubt that wages have been reduced to a greater extent than either the competition of the foreign producers, or other circumstances have rendered necessary . . . the majority of weavers are working at a reduction of 30 to 40 per cent. in their wages. A piece of ribbon for making which the weaver got 6s. or 7s. five years back, now only brings them 3s. 3d. or 3s. 6d.; other work is now priced at 2s. and 2s. 3d. which was formerly priced at 4s. and 4s. 3d. The reduction in wage seems to have been carried to a greater extent than is necessary for increasing demand. Indeed, the reduction in the cost of weaving, in the case of many descriptions of ribbons, has net been accompanied by any corresponding reduction in the selling price of the manufactured article.' (Mr F. D. Longes, Report. *Ch. Emp. Corn., V. Rep., 1866,* p.114,1.)

[155] Cf *Reports of Insp. of Fact., 31st October, 1862,* p.30.

[156] l.c., p.19.

[157] *Rep. Insp. of Fact., 31st October, 1863,* pp.41–45.

[158] l.c., pp.41–42

[159] l.c., p.57.

[160] l.c., pp.50–51.

[161] l.c., pp.62–63.

[162] *Rep. &c., 30th April, 1864,* p.27.

[163] From a letter of Mr Harris, Chief Constable of Bolton, in *Rep. of Insp. of Fact., 31st October, 1865,* pp.61–62.

[164] In an appeal, dated 1863, of the factory operatives of Lancashire, &c., for the purpose of forming a society for organised emigration, we find the following: 'That a large emigration of factory workers is now absolutely essential to raise them from their present prostrate condition, few will deny; but to show that a continuous stream of emigration is at all times demanded, and, without which it is impossible

for them to maintain their position in ordinary times, we beg to call attention to the subjoined facts: – In 1814 the official value of cotton goods exported was £17,665,378, whilst the real marketable value was £20,070,824. In 1858 the official value of cotton goods exported, was £182,221,681; but the real or marketable value was only £43,001,322, being a ten-fold quantity sold for little more than double the former price. To produce results so disadvantageous to the country generally, and to the factory workers in particular, several causes have cooperated, which, had circumstances permitted, we should have brought more prominently under your notice; suffice it for the present to say that the most obvious one is the constant redundancy of labour, without which a trade so ruinous in its effects never could have been carried on, and which requires a constantly extending market to save it from annihilation. Our cotton mills may be brought to a stand by the periodical stagnations of trade, which, under present arrangements, are as inevitable as death itself; but the human mind is constantly at work, and although we believe we are under the mark in stating that six millions of persons have left these shores during the last 25 years, yet, from the natural increase of population, and the displacement of labour to cheapen production, a large percentage of the male adults in the most prosperous times find it impossible to obtain work in factories on any conditions whatever.' (*Reports of Insp. of Fact., 30th April 1863*, pp.51–52.) We shall, in a later chapter, see how our friends, the manufacturers, endeavoured, during the catastrophe in the cotton trade, to prevent by every means, including State interference, the emigration of the operatives.

[165] *Ch. Empt. Comm. III. Report, 1864*, p.108, n.447.

[166] In the United States the restoration, in this way, of handicrafts based on machinery is frequent; and therefore, when the inevitable transition to the factory system shall take place, the ensuing concentration will, compared with Europe and even with England, stride on in seven-league boots.

[167] See *Rep. of Insp. of Fact., 31st Oct., 1865*, p.64.

[168] Mr Gillott erected in Birmingham the first steel-pen factory on a large scale. It produced, so early as 1851, over 180,000,000 of pens yearly, and consumed 120 tons of steel. Birmingham has the monopoly of this industry in the United Kingdom, and at present produces thousands of millions of steel-pens. According to the Census of 1861, the number of persons employed was 1,428, of whom 1,268 females from 5 years of age upwards.

[169] *Ch. Empl. Comm. II. Rep. 1864*, p. lxviii., n.415.

[170] And now forsooth children are employed at file-cutting in Sheffield.

[171] *Ch. Empl. Comm., V. Rep. 1866*, p.3, n.24; p.6, n.55,56; p.7, n.59,60.

[172] l.c., pp.114,115, n.6,7. The commissioner justly remarks that though as a rule machines take the place of men, here literally young persons replace machines.

[173] See the Report on the rag trade, and numerous details in *Public Health, VIII Rep.* Lond. 1866, app., pp.196,208.

[174] *Ch. Empl. Comm. V. Rep., 1866*, pp.xvi–xviii, n.86–97, and pp.130–133, n.39–71. See also III. Rep., 1864, pp.48,56.

[175] *Public Health. Sixth Rep.*, Lond. 1864, pp.29,31.

[176] l.c., p.30. Dr Simon remarks that the mortality among the London tailors and printers between the ages of 25 and 35 is in fact much greater, because the employers in London obtain from the country a great number of young people up to 30 years of age, as 'apprentices' and 'improvers', who come for the purpose of being perfected in their trade. These figure in the census as Londoners, they swell out the number of heads on which the London death-rate is calculated, without adding proportionally to the number of deaths in that place. The greater part of them in fact return to the country, and especially in cases of severe illness. (l.c.)

[176] I allude here to hammered nails, as distinguished from nails cut out and made by machinery. See *Child. Empl. Comm., Third Rep.*, pp.x.,xix, n.125–130, p.52, n.11, p.114, n.487, p.137, n.674.

[178] *Ch. Empl. Comm., II. Rep.*, p.xxii, n.166.

[179] *Ch. Empl. Comm., II. Rep., 1864*, pp.xix,xx,xxi.

[180] l.c., pp.xxi.xxii.

[181] l.c., pp.xxix,xxx.

[182] l.c., pp.xi,xii.

[183] *Child. Empl. Comm., I. Rep. 1863*, p.185.

[184] In England millinery and dressmaking are for the most part carried on, on the premises of the employer, partly by workwomen who live there, partly by women who live off the premises.

[185] Mr White, a commissioner, visited a military clothing manufactory that employed 1,000 to 1,200 persons, almost all females, and a shoe manufactory with 1,300 persons; of these nearly one half were children and young persons.

[186] An instance. The weekly report of deaths by the Registrar-General dated 26th Feb., 1864, contains 5 cases of death from starvation. On the same day *The Times* reports another case. Six victims of starvation in one week!

[187] *Child. Empl. Comm., Second Rep., 1864*, p.lxvii, n.406–9, p.84, n.124, p.lxxiii, n.441, p.68, n.6, p.84, n.126, p.78, n.85, p.76, n.69, p.lxxii, n.483.

[188] 'The rental of premises required for workrooms seems the element which ultimately determines the point; and consequently it is in the metropolis, that the old system of giving work out to small employers and families has been longest retained, and earliest returned to.' (l.c., p.83, n.123.) The concluding statement in this quotation refers exclusively to shoemaking.

[189] In glove-making and other industries where the condition of the workpeople is hardly distinguishable from that of paupers, this does not occur.

[190] l.c., p.83, n.122.

[191] In the wholesale boot and shoe trade of Leicester alone, there were in 1864, 800 sewing-machines already in use.

[192] l.c., p.84, n.124.

[193] Instances: the Army Clothing Depot at Pimlico, London, the shirt factory of Tillie and Henderson at Londonderry, and the clothes factory of Messrs Tait at Limerick which employs about 1,200 hands.

[194] *Tendency to Factory System* (l.c., p.lxvii). 'The whole employment is at this time in a state of transition, and is undergoing the same change as that effected in the lace trade, weaving, &c.' (l.c., n.405.) 'A complete revolution' (l.c., p.xlvi, n.318). At the date of the Child. Empl. Comm. of 1840 stocking making was still done by manual labour. Since 1846 various sorts of machines have been introduced, which are now driven by steam. The total number of persons of both sexes and of all ages from 3 years upwards, employed in stocking making in England, was in 1862 about 129,000. Of these only 4,063 were, according to the Parliamentary Return of the 11th February, 1862, working under the Factory Acts.

[195] Thus, e.g., in the earthenware trade, Messrs Cochrane, of the Britain Pottery, Glasgow, report: 'To keep up our quantity we have gone extensively into machines wrought by unskilled tabour, and every day convinces us that we can produce a greater quantity than by the old method.' (*Rep. of Insp. of Fact., 31st Oct., 1865*, p.13.) 'The effect of the Fact. Acts is to force on the further introduction of machinery.' (l.c., pp.13–14).

[196] Thus, after the extension of the Factory Act to the potteries, great increase of powerjiggers in place of hand-moved jiggers.

[197] *Report of Insp. of Fact., 31st Oct., 1865*, pp.96 and 127.

[198] The introduction of this and other machinery into match-making caused in one department alone 230 young persons to be replaced by 32 boys and girls of 14 to 17 years of age. This saving in labour was carried still further in 1865, by the employment of steam power.

[199] *Ch. Empl. Comm., 11. Rep., 1864*, p. ix, n.50.

[200] *Rep. of Insp. of Fact., 31st Oct., 1865*, p.22.

[201] 'But it must be borne in mind that those improvements, though carried out fully in some establishments, are by no means general, and are not capable of being brought into use in many of the old manufactories without an expenditure of capital beyond the means of many of the present occupiers.' 'I cannot but rejoice,' writes Sub-Insp. May, 'that notwithstanding the temporary disorganisation which inevitably follows the introduction of such a measure (as the Factory Act Extension Act), and is, indeed, directly indicative of the evils which it was intended to remedy, &c.' (*Rep. of Insp. of Fact., 31st Oct., 1865*.)

[202] With blast furnaces, for instance, 'work towards the end of the week being generally much increased in duration in consequence of the habit of the men of idling on Monday and occasionally during a part or the whole of Tuesday also.' (*Child. Empl. Comm., III. Rep.*,' p.vi) 'The little masters generally have very irregular hours. They lose two or three days, and then work all night to make it up . . . They always employ their own children, if they have any.' (l.c., p.vii) 'The want of regularity in coming to work, encouraged by the possibility and practice of making up for this by working longer hours.' (l.c., p.xviii) 'In Birmingham . . . an enormous amount of time is lost . . . idling part of the time, slaving the rest.' (l.c., p.xi)

[203] *Child. Empl. Comm., IV., Rep.*, p.xxxii, 'The extension of the railway system is said to have contributed greatly to this custom of giving sudden orders, and the consequent hurry, neglect of meal-times, and late hours of the workpeople.' (l.c., p.xxxi)

[204] *Ch. Empl. Comm, IV. Rep.*, pp.xxxv, n.235,237.

[205] *Ch. Empl. Comm. IV. Rep.*, p.127, n.56.

[206] With respect to the loss of trade by non-completion of shipping orders in time, I remember that this was the pet argument of the factory masters in 1832 and 1833. Nothing that can he advanced now on this subject, could have the force that it had then, before steam had halved all distances and established new regulations for transit. It quite failed at that time of proof when put to the test, and again it will certainly fail should it have to be tried.' (*Reports of Insp. of Fact., 31 Oct., 1862*, pp.54, 55.)

[207] *Ch. Empl. Comm. IV. Rep.*, p.xviii, n.118.

[208] John Bellers remarked as far back as 1699: 'The uncertainty of fashions does increase necessitous poor. It has two great mischiefs in it. 1st, The journeymen are miserable in winter for want of work, the mercers and master-weavers not daring to lay out their stocks to keep the journeymen employed before the spring comes, and they know what the fashion will then be; 2ndly, In the spring the journeymen are not sufficient, but the master-weavers must draw in many prentices, that they may supply the trade of the kingdom in a quarter or half a year, which robs the plough of hands, drains the country of labourers, and in a great part stocks the city with beggars, and starves some in winter that are ashamed to beg.' (*Essays about the Poor, Manufactures, &c.*, p.9.)

[209] *Ch. Empl. Comm. V. Rep.*, p.171, n.34.

[210] The evidence of some Bradford export-houses is as follows: 'Under these circumstances, it seems clear that no boys need be worked longer than from 8 a.m. to 7 or 7.30 p.m., in making up. It is merely a question of extra hands and extra outlay. If some masters were not so greedy, the boys would not work late; an extra machine costs only £16 or £18; much of such over-time as does occur is to be referred to an

insufficiency of appliances, and a want of space.' *Ch. Empl, Comm. V. Rep.*, p.171, n.35,36,38.

[211] l.c. A London manufacturer, who in other respects looks upon the compulsory regulation of the hours of labour as a protection for the workpeople against the manufacturers, and for the manufacturers themselves against the wholesale trade, states: 'The pressure in our business is caused by the shippers, who want, e.g., to send the goods by sailing vessel so as to reach their destination at a given season, and at the same time want to pocket the difference in freight between a sailing vessel and a steamship, or who select the earlier of two steamships in order to be in the foreign market before their competitors.'

[212] 'This could be obviated,' says a manufacturer, 'at the expense of an enlargement of the works under the pressure of a General Act of Parliament.' l.c., p.x, n.38.

[213] l.c., p.xv, n.72. sqq.

[214] *Rep. Insp. Fact., 31st October, 1865*, p.127.

[215] It has been found out by experiment, that with each respiration of average intensity made by a healthy average individual, about 25 cubic inches of air are consumed, and that about 20 respirations are made in each minute. Hence the air inhaled in 24 hours by each individual is about 720,000 cubic inches, or 416 cubic feet. It is clear, however, that air which has been once breathed, can no longer serve for the same process until it has been purified in the great workshop of Nature. According to the experiments of Valentin and Brunner, it appears that a healthy man gives off about 1,300 cubic inches of carbonic acid per hour; this would give about 8 ounces of solid carbon thrown off from the lungs in 24 hours.' Every man should have at least 800 cubic feet.' (Huxley.)

[216] According to the English Factory Act, parents cannot send their children under 14 years of age into Factories under the control of the Act, unless at the same time they allow them to receive elementary education. The manufacturer is responsible for compliance with the Act. 'Factory education is compulsory, and it is a condition of labour.' (*Rep. Insp. Fact., 31st Oct., 1865*, p.111.)

[217] On the very advantageous results of combining gymnastics (and drilling in the case of boys) with compulsory education for factory children and pauper scholars, see the speech of N. W. Senior at the seventh annual congress of the National Association for the Promotion of Social Science, in *Report of Proceedings, &c.*, Lond. 1863, pp.63,64, also the *Rep. Insp. Fact., 31st Oct., 1865*, pp.118,119,120,126, sqq.

[218] *Rep. Insp. Fact., 31st Oct., 1865*, p.118. A silk manufacturer naively states to the Children's Employment Commissioners: 'I am quite sure that the true secret of producing efficient workpeople is to be found in uniting education and labour from a period of childhood. Of course the occupation must not be too severe, nor irksome, or unhealthy. But of the advantage of the union I have no doubt. I wish my own children could have some work as well as play to give variety to their schooling.' (*Ch. Empl. Comm. V. Rep.*, p.82, n.36.)

[219] Senior, l.c., p.66. How Modern Industry, when it has attained to a certain pitch, is capable, by the revolution it effects in the mode of production and in the social conditions of production, of also revolutionising people's minds, is strikingly shown by a comparison of Senior's speech in 1863, with his philippic against the Factory Act of 1833; or by a comparison, of the views of the congress above referred to, with the fact that in certain country districts of England poor parents are forbidden, on pain of death by starvation, to educate their children. Thus, e.g., Mr Snell reports it to be a common occurrence in Somersetshire that, when a poor person claims parish relief, he is compelled to take his children from school. Mr Wollarton, the clergyman at Feltham, also tells of cases where all relief was denied to certain families 'because they were sending their children to school!'

[220] Wherever handicraft-machines, driven by men, compete directly or indirectly with more developed machines driven by mechanical power, a great change takes place with regard to the labourer who drives the machine. At first the steam-engine replaces this labourer, afterwards he must replace the steam-engine. Consequently the tension and the amount of labour-power expended become monstrous, and especially so in the case of the children who are condemned to this torture. Thus Mr Longe, one of the commissioners, found in Coventry and the neighbourhood boys of from 10 to 15 years employed in driving the ribbon-looms, not to mention younger children who had to drive smaller machines. 'It is extraordinarily fatiguing work. The boy is a mere substitute for steam power.' (*Ch. Empl. Comm. V, Rep. 1866;* p.114, n.6.) As to the fatal consequences of 'this system of slavery', as the official report styles it, see l.c., p.114 sqq.

[221] l.c., p.3, n.24.

[222] l.c., p.7, n.60.

[223] 'in some parts of the Highlands of Scotland, not many years ago, every peasant, according to the Statistical Account, made his own shoes of leather tanned by himself. Many a shepherd and cottar too, with his wife and children, appeared at Church in clothes which had been touched by no hands but their own, since they were shorn from the sheep and sown in the flaxfield. In the preparation of these. it is added, scarcely a single article had been purchased, except the awl, needle, thimble, and a very few parts of the iron-work employed in the weaving. The dyes, too, were chiefly extracted by the women from trees, shrubs and herbs.' (Dugald Stewart's *Works;* Hamilton's Ed., vol.viii., pp.327–328.)

[224] In the celebrated *Livre des métiers* of Étienne Boileau, we find it prescribed that a journeyman on being admitted among the masters had to swear 'to love his brethren with brotherly love, to support them in their respective trades, not wilfully to betray the secrets of the trade, and besides, in the interests of all, not to recommend his own wares by calling the attention of the buyer to defects in the articles made by others.'

[225] 'The bourgeoisie cannot exist without continually revolutionising the instruments of production, and thereby the relations of production and all the social relations. Conservation, in an unaltered form, of the old modes of production was on the contrary the first condition of existence for all earlier industrial classes. Constant revolution in production, uninterrupted disturbance of all social conditions, everlasting uncertainty and agitation, distinguish the bourgeois epoch from all earlier ones. All fixed, fast-frozen relations, with their train of ancient and venerable prejudices and opinions, are swept away, all new-formed ones become antiquated before they can ossify. All that is solid melts into air, all that is holy is profaned, and man is at last compelled to face with sober senses his real conditions of life, and his relations with his kind.' (F. Engels und Karl Marx: *Manifest der Kommunistischen Partei.* Lond. 1848, p.5.)

[226]   You take my life
                    When you do take the means whereby I live.
                                                                        Shakespeare

[227] A French workman, on his return from San Francisco, writes as follows: 'I never could have believed, that I was capable of working at the various occupations I was employed on in California. I was firmly convinced that I was fit for nothing but letter-press printing . . . Once in the midst of this world of adventurers, who change their occupation as often as they do their shirt, egad, I did as the others. As mining did not turn out remunerative enough, I left it for the town, where in succession I became typographer, slater, plumber, &c. In consequence of thus finding out that I am fit to any sort of work, I feel less of a mollusk and more of a man.' (A. Corbon, *De l'enseignement professionnel,* 2ème ed., p.50.)

[228] John Bellers, a very phenomenon in the history of Political Economy, saw most clearly at the end of the 17th century, the necessity for abolishing the present system of

education and division of labour, which beget hypertrophy and atrophy at the two opposite extremities of society. Amongst other things he says this: 'An idle learning being little better than the learning of idleness . . . Bodily labour, it's a primitive institution of God . . . Labour being as proper for the bodies' health as eating is for its living; for what pains a man saves by ease, he will find in disease . . . Labour adds oil to the lamp of life, when thinking inflames it . . . A childish silly employ' (a warning this, by presentiment, against the Basedows and their modern imitators) 'leaves the children's minds silly,' (*Proposals for Raising a Colledge of Industry of all Useful Trades and Husbandry*. Lond., 1696, pp.12,14,18.)

[229] This sort of labour goes on mostly in small workshops, as we have seen in the lacemaking and straw-plaiting trades, and as could be shown more in detail from the metal trades of Sheffield, Birmingham, &c.

[230] *Ch. Empl. Comm., V. Rep.*, p.xxv, n.162, and *II. Rep.*, p.xxxviii, n.285,289, p.xxv,xxvi, n.191.

[231] 'Factory labour may be as pure and as excellent as domestic labour, and perhaps more so.' (*Rep. Insp. of Fact., 31st October, 1865*, p.129.)

[232] *Rep. Insp. of Fact., 31st October, 1865*, pp.27–32.

[233] Numerous instances will be found in *Rep. of Insp. of Fact.*

[234] *Ch. Empl. Comm., V. Rep.*, p.x, n.35.

[235] *Ch. Empl. Comm., V. Rep.*, p.ix, n.28.

[236] l.c., p.xxv, n.165–167. As to the advantages of large-scale, compared with small-scale, industries, see *Ch. Empl. Comm., III. Rep.*, p.13, n.144, p.25, n.121, p.26, n.125, p.27, n.140, &c.

[237] The trades proposed to be brought under the Act were the following: lace-making, stocking-weaving, straw-plaiting, the manufacture of wearing apparel with its numerous sub-divisions, artificial flower-making, shoemaking, hat-making, glove-making, tailoring, all metal works, from blast furnaces down to needleworks, &c., paper-mills, glassworks, tobacco factories, India-rubber works, braid-making (for weaving), hand-carpetmaking, umbrella and parasol making, the manufacture of spindles and spools, letterpress printing, book-binding, manufacture of stationery (including paper bags, cards, coloured paper, &c.), rope-making, manufacture of jet ornaments, brick-making, silk manufacture by hand, Coventry weaving, salt works, tallow chandiers, cement works, sugar refineries, biscuit-making, various industries connected with timber, and other mixed trades.

[238] l.c., p.xxv, n.169.

[240] The Factory Acts Extension Act was passed on August 12, 1867. It regulates all foundries, smithies, and metal manufactories, including machine shops; furthermore glass-works, paper mills, gutta-percha and India-rubber works, tobacco manufactories, letter-press printing and book-binding works, and, lastly, all workshops in which more than 50 persons are employed. The Hours of Labour Regulation Act, passed on August 17, 1867, regulates the smaller workshops and the so-called domestic industries.

I shall revert to these Acts and to the new Mining Act of 1872 in Volume 2.

[241] Senior, *Social Science Congress*, pp.55–58.

[242] The 'personnel' of this staff consisted of 2 inspectors, 2 assistant inspectors and 41 sub-inspectors. Eight additional sub-inspectors were appointed in 1871. The total cost of administering the Acts in England, Scotland, and Ireland amounted for the year 1871-72 to no more than £25,347, inclusive of the law expenses incurred by prosecutions of offending masters.

[243] Robert Owen, the father of Co-operative Factories and Stores, but who, as before remarked, in no way shared the illusions of his followers with regard to the bearing of these isolated elements of transformation, not only practically made the factory system the sole foundation of his experiments, but also declared that system to

be theoretically the starting-point of the social revolution. Herr Vissering, Professor of Political Economy in the University of Leyden, appears to have a suspicion of this when, in his *Handboek van Practische Staatshuishoudkunde, 1860–62*, which reproduces all the platitudes of vulgar economy, he strongly supports handicrafts against the factory system.

[244] 'You divide the people into two hostile camps of clownish boors and emasculated dwarfs. Good heavens! a nation divided into agricultural and commercial interests, calling itself sane; nay, styling itself enlightened and civilised, not only in spite of, but in consequence of this monstrous and unnatural division.' (David Urquhart, l.c., p.119.) This passage shows, at one and the same time, the strength and the weakness of that kind of criticism which knows how to judge and condemn the present, but not how to comprehend it.

[245] See Liebig: *Die Chemie in ihrer Anwendung auf Agricultur und Physiologie*, 7. Auflage, 1862, and especially the *Einleitung in die Naturgesetze des Feldbaus*, in the 1st volume. To have developed from the point of view of natural science, the negative, i.e., destructive side of modern agriculture, is one of Liebig's immortal merits. His summary, too, of the history of agriculture, although not free from gross errors, contains flashes of light. It is, however, to be regretted that he ventures on such haphazard assertions as the following: 'By greater pulverising and more frequent ploughing, the circulation of air in the interior of porous soil is aided, and the surface exposed to the action of the atmosphere is increased and renewed; but it is easily seen that the increased yield of the land cannot be proportional to the labour spent on that land, but increases in a much smaller proportion. This law,' adds Liebig, 'was first enunciated by John Stuart Mill in his *Principles of Pol. Econ.*, vol. 1, p.17, as follows: "That the produce of land increases, *ceteris paribus*, in a diminishing ratio to the increase of the labourers employed" (Mill here introduces in an erroneous form the law enunciated by Ricardo's school, for since the "decrease of the labourers employed" kept even pace in England with the advance of agriculture, the law discovered in, and applied to, England, could have no application to that country, at all events), "is the universal law of agricultural industry." This is very remarkable, since Mill was ignorant of the reason for this law.' (Liebig, l.c., Bd.1, p.143 and Note.) Apart from Liebig's wrong interpretation of the word 'labour', by which word he understands something quite different from what Political Economy does, it is, in any case, 'very remarkable' that he should make Mr John Stuart Mill the first propounder of a theory which was first published by James Anderson in A. Smith's days, and was repeated in various works down to the beginning of the 19th century; a theory which Malthus, that master in plagiarism (the whole of his population theory is a shameless plagiarism), appropriated to himself in 1815; which West developed at the same time as, and independently of, Anderson; which in the year 1817 was connected by Ricardo with the general theory of value, then made the round of the world as Ricardo's theory, and in 1820 was vulgarised by James Mill, the father of John Stuart Mill; and which, finally, was reproduced by John Stuart Mill and others, as a dogma already quite commonplace, and known to every schoolboy. It cannot be denied that John Stuart Mill owes his, at all events, 'remarkable' authority almost entirely to such *quid-pro-quos*.

Volume 1, Part 5, Chapter 16

[1] 'The very existence of the master-capitalists, as a distinct class, is dependent on the productiveness of industry.' (Ramsay, l.c., p.206.) 'If each man's labour were but enough to produce his own food, there could be no property.' (Ravenstone, l.c. p.14,15.)

[2] According to a recent calculation, there are yet at least 4,000,000 cannibals in those parts of the earth which have already been explored.

[3] 'Among the wild Indians in America, almost everything is the labourer's, 99 parts of a hundred are to be put upon the account of labour. In England, perhaps, the labourer has not 2/3.' (*The Advantages of the East India Trade, &c.*, p.73.)

[4] Diodorus, l.c., l.i, c.80.

[5] 'The first (natural wealth) as it is most noble and advantageous, so doth it make the people careless, proud, and given to all excesses; whereas the second enforceth vigilancy, literature, arts and policy.' (*England's Treasure by Foreign Trade. Or the Balance of our Foreign Trade is the Rule of our Treasure. Written by Thomas Mun of London, Merchant, and now published for the common good by his son John Mun.* London, 1669, p.181,182.) 'Nor can I conceive a greater curse upon a body of people, than to be thrown upon a spot of land, where the productions for subsistence and food were, in great measure, spontaneous, and the climate required or admitted little care for raiment and covering . . . there may be an extreme on the other side. A soil incapable of produce by labour is quite as bad as a soil that produces plentifully without any labour.' (*An Inquiry into the Present High Price of Provisions.* Lond. 1767, p.10.)

[6] The necessity for predicting the rise and fall of the Nile created Egyptian astronomy, and with it the dominion of the priests, as directors of agriculture. '*Le solstice est le moment de l'année ou commence la crue du Nil, et celui que les Egyptiens ont du observer avec le plus d'attention . . . C'était cette année tropique qu'il leur importait de marquer pour se diriger dans leurs opérations agricoles. Ils durent donc chercher dans le ciel un signe apparent de son retour.*' (Cuvier: *Discours sur les révolutions du globe*, ed. Hoefer, Paris, 1863, p.141.)

[7] One of the material bases of the power of the state over the small disconnected producing organisms in India, was the regulation of the water supply. The Mahometan rulers of India understood this better than their English successors. It is enough to recall to mind the famine of 1866, which cost the lives of more than a million Hindus in the district of Orissa, in the Bengal presidency.

[8] 'There are no two countries which furnish an equal number of the necessaries of life in equal plenty, and with the same quantity of labour. Men's wants increase or diminish with the severity or temperateness of the climate they live in; consequently, the proportion of trade which the inhabitants of different countries are obliged to carry on through necessity cannot be the same, nor is it practicable to ascertain the degree of variation farther than by the degrees of Heat and Cold; from whence one may make this general conclusion, that the quantity of labour required for a certain number of people is greatest in cold climates, and least in hot ones; for in the former men not only want more clothes, but the earth more cultivating than in the latter.' (*An Essay on the Governing Causes of the Natural Rate of Interest.* Lond. 1750. p.60.) The author of this epoch-making anonymous work is J. Massy. Hume took his theory of interest from it.

[9] '*Chaque travail doit* (this appears also to be part of the *droits et devoirs du citoyen*) *laisser un excédant.*' Proudhon.

[10] F. Schouw: *Die Erde, die Pflanze und der Mensch*, 2. Ed. Leipz. 1854, p.148.

[11] J. St. Mill. *Principles of Pol. Econ.* Lond. 1868, p.252–53 passim.

Volume 1, Part 5, Chapter 17

[1] The case considered in Chapter 12 is here of course omitted. (Note by editor of the third edition.)

[2] To this third law MacCulloch has made, amongst others, this absurd addition, that a rise in surplus-value, unaccompanied by a fall in the value of labour power, can occur through the abolition of taxes payable by the capitalist. The abolition of such taxes makes no change whatever in the quantity of surplus-value that the capitalist extorts at first-hand from the labourer. It alters only the proportion in which that surplus-value is divided between himself and third persons. It consequently makes no alteration whatever in the relation between surplus-value and value of labour power.

MacCulloch's exception therefore proves only his misapprehension of the rule, a misfortune that as often happens to him in the vulgarisation of Ricardo, as it does to J. B. Say in the vulgarisation of Adam Smith.

[3] 'When an alteration takes place in the productiveness of industry, and that either more or less is produced by a given quantity of labour and capital, the proportion of wages may obviously vary, whilst the quantity, which that proportion represents, remains the same, or the quantity may vary, whilst the proportion remains the same.' (*Outlines of Political Economy, &c.*, p.67.)

[4] 'All things being equal, the English manufacturer can turn out a considerably larger amount of work in a given time than a foreign manufacturer, so much as to counter-balance the difference of the working-days, between 60 hours a week here, and 72 or 80 elsewhere.' (*Rep. of Insp. of Fact. for 31st Oct., 1855*, p.65.) The most infallible means for reducing this qualitative difference between the English and Continental working hour would be a law shortening quantitatively the length of the working-day in Continental factories.

[5] 'There are compensating circumstances . . . which the working of the Ten Hours' Act has brought to light.' (*Rep.of Insp. of Fact. for 31st Oct. 1848*, p.7.)

[6] 'The amount of labour which a man had undergone in the course of 24 hours might be approximately arrived at by an examination of the chemical changes which had taken place in his body, changed forms in matter indicating the anterior exercise of dynamic force.' (Grove: *On the Correlation of Physical Forces*.)

[7] 'Corn and labour rarely march quite abreast; but there is an obvious limit, beyond which they cannot be separated. With regard to the unusual exertions made by the labouring classes in periods of dearness, which produce the fall of wages noticed in the evidence,' (namely, before the Parliamentary Committee of Inquiry, 1814–15) 'they are most meritorious in the individuals, and certainly favour the growth of capital. But no man of humanity could wish to see them constant and unremitted. They are most admirable as a temporary relief; but if they were constantly in action, effects of a similar kind would result from them, as from the population of a country being pushed to the very extreme limits of its food.' (Malthus: *Inquiry into the Nature and Progress of Rent*, Lond., 1815, p.48, note.) All honour to Malthus that he lays stress on the lengthening of the hours of labour, a fact to which he elsewhere in his pamphlet draws attention, while Ricardo and others, in face of the most notorious facts, make invariability in the length of the working-day the groundwork of all their investigations. But the conserv-ative interests, which Malthus served, prevented him from seeing that an unlimited prolongation of the working-day, combined with an extraordinary development of machinery, and the exploitation of women and children, must inevitably have made a great portion of the working-class 'supernumerary', particularly whenever the war should have ceased, and the monopoly of England in the markets of the world should have come to an end. It was, of course, far more convenient, and much more in conformity with the interests of the ruling classes, whom Malthus adored like a true priest, to explain this 'over-population' by the eternal laws of Nature, rather than by the historical laws of capitalist production.

[8] 'A principal cause of the increase of capital, during the war, proceeded from the greater exertions, and perhaps the greater privations of the labouring classes, the most numerous in every society. More women and children were compelled by necessitous circumstances, to enter upon laborious occupations, and former workmen were, from the same cause, obliged to devote a greater portion of their time to increase produc-tion.' (*Essays on Pol. Econ.*, in which are illustrated the principal causes of the present national distress. Lond., 1830, p.248.)

Volume 1, Part 5, Chapter 18

[1] Thus, e.g., in *Dritter Brief an v. Kirchmann von Rodbertus. Widerlegung der Ricardo'schen Theorie von der Grundrente und Begrundung einer neuen Rententheorie*. Berlin, 1851. I shall return to this letter later on; in spite of its erroneous theory of rent, it sees through the nature of capitalist production.

Note added in the 3rd German edition: It may be seen from this how favourably Marx judged his predecessors, whenever he found in them real progress, or new and sound ideas. The subsequent publications of Robertus' letters to Rud. Meyer has shown that the above acknowledgement by Marx wants restricting to some extent. In those letters this passage occurs: 'Capital must be rescued not only from labour, but from itself, and that will be best effected, by treating the acts of the industrial capitalist as economic and political functions, that have been delegated to him with his capital, and by treating his profit as a form of salary, because we still know no other social organisation. But salaries may be regulated, and may also be reduced if they take too much from wages. The irruption of Marx into Society, as I may call his book, must be warded off . . . Altogether, Marx's book is not so much an investigation into capital, as a polemic against the present form of capital, a form which he confounds with the concept itself of capital.' (*Briefe, &c., von Dr Robertus-Jagetzow, herausgg. von Dr Rud. Meyer*, Berlin, 1881, I Bd. p.111,48. *Brief von Rodbertus*.) To such ideological commonplaces did the bold attack by Robertus in his 'social letters' finally dwindle down. – F.E.

[2] That part of the product which merely replaces the constant capital advanced is of course left out in this calculation. Mr. L. de Lavergne, a blind admirer of England, is inclined to estimate the share of the capitalist too low, rather than too high.

[3] All well-developed forms of capitalist production being forms of cooperation, nothing is, of course, easier, than to make abstraction from their antagonistic character, and to transform them by a word into some form of free association, as is done by A. de Labourde in *De l'Espirit d'Association dans tout les intérêts de la communauté*. Paris 1818. H. Carey, the Yankee, occassionally performs this conjuring trick with like success, even with the relations resulting from slavery.

[4] Although the Physiocrats could not penetrate the mystery of surplus-value, yet this much was clear to them, viz., that it is *'une richesse independante et disponible qu'il* (the possessor) *n'a point achetée et qu'il vend.'* (Turgot: *Réflexions sur la Formation et la Distribution des Richesses*, p.11.)

Volume 1, Part 6, Chapter 19

[1] 'Mr Ricardo ingeniously enough avoids a difficulty which, on a first view, threatens to encumber his doctrine – that value depends on the quantity of labour employed in production. If this principle is rigidly adhered to, it follows that the value of labour depends on the quantity of labour employed in producing it – which is evidently absurd. By a dexterous turn, therefore, Mr Ricardo makes the value of labour depend on the quantity of labour required to produce wages; or, to give him the benefit of his own language, he maintains, that the value of labour is to be estimated by the quantity of labour required to produce wages; by which he means the quantity of labour required to produce the money or commodities given to the labourer. This is similar to saying, that the value of cloth is estimated, not by the quantity of labour bestowed on its production, but by the quantity of labour bestowed on the production of the silver, for which the cloth is exchanged.' – *A Critical Dissertation on the Nature, &c., of Value*, pp.50,51.

[2] 'If you call labour a commodity, it is not like a commodity which is first produced in order to exchange, and then brought to market where it must exchange with other commodities according to the respective quantities of each which there may be in the

market at the time; labour is created the moment it is brought to market; nay, it is brought to market before it is created.' – *Observations on Certain Verbal Disputes, &c.*, pp.75,76.

[3] 'Treating labour as a commodity, and capital, the produce of labour, as another, then, if the values of these two commodities were regulated by equal quantities of labour, a given amount of labour would . . . exchange for that quantity of capital which had been produced by the same amount of labour; antecedent labour would . . . exchange for the same amount as present labour. But the value of labour in relation to other commodities . . . is determined not by equal quantities of labour.' – E. G. Wakefield in his edition of Adam Smith's *Wealth of Nations*, vol.i, London, 1836, p.231, note.

[4] 'There has to be a new agreement' (a new edition of the social contract!) 'that whenever there is an exchange of work done for work to be done, the latter' (the capitalist) 'is to receive a higher value than the former' (the worker). – Simonde (i.e. Sismondi), *De la Richesse Commerciale*, Geneva, 1803, vol i, p.37.

[5] 'Labour the exclusive standard of value . . . the creator of all wealth, no commodity.' Thomas Hodgskin, *Popul. Polit. Econ.*, p.186.

[6] On the other hand, the attempt to explain such expressions as merely poetic licence only shows the impotence of the analysis. Hence, in answer to Proudhon's phrase; '*Le travail est dit valoir, non pas en tant que marchandise lui même, mais en vue des valeurs qu'on suppose renfermées puissanciellement en lui. La valeur du travail est une expression figurée,*' &c. I have remarked: '*Dans le travail-marchandise qui est d'une réalité effrayante, il (Proudhon) ne voit qu'une ellipse grammaticale. Donc, toute la société actuelle, fondée sur le travail-marchandise, est désormais fondée sur une license poétique, sur une expression figurée. La société veut-elle "éliminer tous les inconvénients", qui la travaillent, eh bien! qu'elle élimine les termes malsonnants, qu'elle change de langage, et pour cela elle n'a qu' à s'adresser à l'Académie pour lui demander une nouvelle édition de son dictionnaire.*' (Karl Marx, *Misère de la Philosophie*, pp.34,35.) It is naturally still more convenient to understand by value nothing at all. Then one can without difficulty subsume everything under this category. Thus, e.g., J. B. Say: 'What is "*valeur*"?' Answer: '*C'est ce qu'une chose vaut*'; and what is '*prix*'? Answer: '*La valeur d'une chose exprimé en monnaie.*' And why has '*le travail de la terre . . . une valeur? Parce qu'on y met un prix.*' Therefore value is what a thing is worth, and the land has its 'value', because its value is 'expressed in money'. This is, anyhow, a very simple way of explaining the why and the wherefore of things.

[7] cf. *Zur Kritik &c.*, p.40, where I state that, in the portion of that work that deals with Capital, this problem will be solved: 'How does production, on the basis of exchange-value determined simply by labour-time, lead to the result that the exchange-value of labour is less than the exchange-value of its product?'

[8] The *Morning Star*, a London Free-trade organ, naif to silliness, protested again and again during the American Civil War, with all the moral indignation of which man is capable, that the Negro in the 'Confederate States' worked absolutely for nothing. It should have compared the daily cost of such a Negro with that of the free workman in the East-end of London.

[9] I give in order that you may give; I give in order that you may produce; I produce so that you may give; I produce so that you may produce.

[10] Adam Smith only accidentally alludes to the variation of the working-day when he is referring to piece-wages.

Volume 1, Part 6, Chapter 20

[1] The value of money itself is here always supposed constant.

[2] 'The price of labour is the sum paid for a given quantity of labour.' (Sir Edward West, *Price of Corn and Wages of Labour*, London, 1836, p.67.) West is the author of the anonymous *Essay on the Application of Capital to Land*. by a Fellow of the University

College of Oxford, London, 1815. An epoch-making work in the history of Political Economy.

[3] 'The wages of labour depend upon the price of labour and the quantity of labour performed . . . An increase in the wages of labour does not necessarily imply an enhancement of the price of labour. From fuller employment, and greater exertions, the wages of labour may be considerably increased, while the price of labour may continue the same.' (West, op. cit., pp.67,68,112.) The main question: 'How is the price of labour determined?' West, however, dismisses with mere banalities.

[4] This is perceived by the fanatical representative of the industrial bourgeoisie of the 18th century, the author of the *Essay on Trade and Commerce* often quoted by us, although he puts the matter in a confused way: 'It is the quantity of labour and not the price of it' (he means by this the nominal daily or weekly wages) 'that is determined by the price of provisions and other necessaries: reduce the price of necessaries very low, and of course you reduce the quantity of labour in proportion. Master manufacturers know that there are various ways of raising and felling the price of labour, besides that of altering its nominal amount.' (op. cit., pp.48,61.) In his *Three Lectures on the Rate of Wages*, London, 1830, in which N. W. Senior uses West's work without mentioning it, he says: 'The labourer is principally interested in the amount of wages' (p.14), that is to say, the labourer is principally interested in what he receives, the nominal sum of his wages, not in that which he gives, the amount of labour!

[5] The effect of such an abnormal lessening of employment is quite different from that of a general reduction of the working-day, enforced by law. The former has nothing to do with the absolute length of the working-day, and may occur just as well in a working-day of 15, as of 6 hours. The normal price of labour is in the first case calculated on the labourer working 15 hours, in the second case on his working 6 hours a day on the average. The result is therefore the same, if he in the one case is employed only for 7 1/2, in the other only for 3 hours.

[6] 'The rate of payment for overtime (in lace-making) is so small, from 1/2d. and 3/4d. to 2d. per hour, that it stands in painful contrast to the amount of injury produced to the health and stamina of the workpeople . . . The small amount thus earned is also often obliged to be spent in extra nourishment.' (*Child Empl. Com., II. Rep.*,p.xvi, n.117.)

[7] e.g., in paper-staining before the recent introduction into this trade of the Factory Act. 'We work on with no stoppage for meals, so that the day's work of 10 1/2 hours is finished by 4:30 p.m., and all after that is over-time, and we seldom leave off working before 6 p.m., so that we are really working over-time the whole year round.' (Mr Smith's Evidence in *Child. Empl. Com., 1. Rep.*, p.125.)

[8] e.g., in the Scotch bleaching-works. 'In some parts of Scotland this trade' (before the introduction of the Factory Act in 1862) 'was carried on by a system of over-time, i.e., ten hours a day were the regular hours of work, for which a nominal wage of 1s. 2d. per day was paid to a man, there being every day over-time for three or four hours, paid at the rate of 3d. per hour. The effect of this system . . . a man could not earn more than 8s. per week when working the ordinary hours . . . without over-time they could not earn a fair day's wages.' (*Rept. of Insp. of Factories*, April 30th, 1863, p.10.) 'The higher wages, for getting adult males to work longer hours, are a temptation too strong to be resisted.' (*Rept. of Insp. of Fact.*, April 30th, 1848, p.5.) The book-binding trade in the city of London employs very many young girls from 14 to 15 years old, and that under indentures which prescribe certain definite hours of labour. Nevertheless, they work in the last week of each month until 10, 11, 12, or 1 o'clock at night, along with the older labourers, in a very mixed company. 'The masters tempt them by extra pay and supper,' which they eat in neighboring public houses. The great debauchery thus produced among these 'young immortals' (*Children's Employment*

Comm., V. Rept., p.44, n.191) is compensated by the fact that among the rest many Bibles and religious books are bound by them.

[9] See *Reports of Insp. of Fact.*, 30th April, 1863, p.10. With very accurate appreciation of the state of things, the London labourers employed in the building trades declared, during the great strike and lock-out of 1860, that they would only accept wages by the hour under two conditions: (1), that, with the price of the working-hour, a normal working day of 9 and 10 hours respectively should be fixed, and that the price of the hour for the 10 hours' working-day should be higher than that for the hour of the 9 hours' working-day; (2), that every hour beyond the normal working-day should be reckoned as over-time and proportionally more highly paid.

[10] 'It is a very notable thing, too, that where long hours are the rule, small wages are also so.' (*Report of Insp. of Fact.*, 31st. Oct., 1863, p.9.) 'The work which obtains the scanty pittance of food, is, for the most part, excessively prolonged.' (*Public Health, Sixth Report*, 1864, p.15.)

[11] *Report of Inspectors of Fact.*, 30th April, 1860, pp.31,32.

[12] The hand nail-makers in England, e.g., have, on account of the low price of labour, to work 15 hours a day in order to hammer out their miserable weekly wage. 'It's a great many hours in a day (6 a.m. to 8 p.m.), and he has to work hard all the time to get 11d. or 1s., and there is the wear of the tools, the cost of firing, and something for waste iron to go out of this, which takes off altogether 2 1/2d. or 3d.' (*Children's Employment Com., III Report*, p.136, n.671.) The women earn by the same working-time a week's wage of only 5 shillings. (l.c., p.137, n.674.)

[13] If a factory-hand, e.g., refused to work the customary long hours, 'he would very shortly be replaced by somebody who would work any length of time, and thus be thrown out of employment.' (*Reports of Inspectors of Factories*, 30th April, 1848. Evidence, p.39, n.58.) 'If one man performs the work of two . . . the rate of profits will generally be raised . . . in consequence of the additional supply of labour having diminished its price.' (Senior, l.c., p.15.)

[14] *Children's Employment Com., III Rep.*, Evidence, p.66, n.22.

[15] *Report, &c., Relative to the Grievances Complained of by the Journeymen Bakers.* London, 1862, p.411, and ib. Evidence, notes 479,359,27. Anyhow the full-priced bakers, as was mentioned above, and as their spokesman, Bennett, himself admits, make their men 'generally begin work at 11 p.m . . . up to 8 o'clock the next morning . . . They are then engaged all day long . . . as late as 7 o'clock in the evening.' (l.c., p.22.)

Volume 1, Part 6, Chapter 21

[1] 'The system of piece-work illustrates an epoch in the history of the working-man; it is halfway between the position of the mere day-labourer depending upon the will of the capitalist and the co-operative artisan, who in the not distant future promises to combine the artisan and the capitalist in his own person. Piece-workers are in fact their own masters, even whilst working upon the capital of the employer.' (John Watts: *Trade Societies and Strikes, Machinery and Co-operative Societies*. Manchester, 1865, pp.52, 53.) I quote this little work because it is a very sink of all long-ago-rotten, apologetic commonplaces. This same Mr Watts earlier traded in Owenism and published in 1842 another pamphlet: *Facts and Fictions of Political Economists*, in which among other things he declares that 'property is robbery'. That was long ago.

[2] T. J. Dunning: *Trades' Unions and Strikes*, Lond., 1860, p.22.

[3] How the existence, side by side and simultaneously, of these two forms of wage favours the masters' cheating: 'A factory employs 400 people, the half of which work by the piece, and have a direct interest in working longer hours. The other 200 are paid by the day, work equally long with the others, and get no more money for their

over-time . . . The work of these 200 people for half an hour a day is equal to one person's work for 50 hours, or 5/6ths of one person's labour in a week, and is a positive gain to the employer.' (*Reports of Insp. of Fact., 31st Oct., 1860*, p.9.) 'Over-working to a very considerable extent still prevails; and, in most instances, with that security against detection and punishment which the law itself affords. I have in many former reports shown . . . the injury to workpeople who are not employed on piece-work, but receive weekly wages.' (Leonard Horner in *Reports of Insp. of Fact.*, 30th April, 1859, pp.8,9.)

[4] 'Wages can be measured in two ways: either by the duration of the labour, or by its product.' (*Abrégé élémentaire des principes de l'économie politique*. Paris, 1796, p.32.) The author of this anonymous work: G. Garnier.

[5] 'So much weight of cotton is delivered to him' (the spinner), 'and he has to return by a certain time, in lieu of it, a given weight of twist or yarn, of a certain degree of fineness, and he is paid so much per pound for all that he so returns. If his work is defective in quality, the penalty falls on him, if less in quantity than the minimum fixed for a given time, he is dismissed and an abler operative procured.' (Ure, l.c., p.317.)

[6] 'It is when work passes through several hands, each of which is to take its share of profits, while only the last does the work, that the pay which reaches the workwoman is miserably disproportioned.' (*Child. Emp. Comm. II Report*, p.lxx., n.424.)

[7] Even Watts, the apologetic, remarks: 'It would be a great improvement to the system of piece-work, if all the men employed on a job were partners in the contract, each according to his abilities, instead of one man being interested in over-working his fellows for his own benefit.' (l.c., p.53.) On the vileness of this system, cf. *Child. Emp. Comm., Rep. III*, p.66, n.22, p.11, n.124, p.xi, n.13,53,59, &c.

[8] This spontaneous result is often artificially helped along, e.g., in the Engineering Trade of London, a customary trick is 'the selecting of a man who possesses superior physical strength and quickness, as the principal of several workmen, and paying him an additional rate, by the quarter or otherwise, with the understanding that he is to exert himself to the utmost to induce the others, who are only paid the ordinary wages, to keep up to him . . . without any comment this will go far to explain many of the complaints of stinting the action, superior skill, and working-power, made by the employers against the men' (in *Trades-Unions*. Dunning, l.c., pp.22,23). As the author is himself a labourer and secretary of a Trades' Union, this might be taken for exaggeration. But the reader may compare the 'highly respectable' *Cyclopedia of Agriculture* of J. C. Morton, Art. 'Labourer,' where this method is recommended to the farmers as an approved one.

[9] 'All those who are paid by piece-work . . . profit by the transgression of the legal limits of work. This observation as to the willingness to work over-time is especially applicable to the women employed as weavers and reelers.' (*Rept. of Insp. of Fact., 30th April, 1858*, p.9.) 'This system' (piece-work), 'so advantageous to the employer . . . tends directly to encourage the young potter greatly to over-work himself during the four or five years during which he is employed in the piece-work system, but at low wages . . . This is . . . another great cause to which the bad constitutions of the potters are to be attributed.' (*Child. Empl. Comm. 1. Rept.*, p.xiii)

[10] 'Where the work in any trade is paid for by the piece at so much per job . . . wages may very materially differ in amount . . . But in work by the day there is generally an uniform rate . . . recognised by both employer and employed as the standard of wages for the general run of workmen in the trade.' (Dunning, l.c., p.17.)

[11] '*Le travail des Compagnons-artisans sera réglé à la journée ou à la pièce . . . Ces maîtres-artisans savent à peu près combien d'ouvrage un compagnon-artisan peut faire par jour dans chaque métier, et les payent souvent à proportion de l'ouvrage qu'ils font; ainsi ces compagnons travaillent autant qu'ils peuvent, pour leur propre intérêt, sans autre inspection.*' (Cantillon,

Essai sur la Nature du Commerce en général, Amst. Ed., 1756, pp.185 and 202. The first edition appeared in 1755.) Cantillon, from whom Quesnay, Sir James Steuart & A. Smith have largely drawn, already here represents piece-wage as simply a modified form of time-wage. The French edition of Cantillon professes in its title to be a translation from the English, but the English edition: *The Analysis of Trade, Commerce, &c.*, by Philip Cantillon, late of the city of London, Merchant, is not only of later date (1759), but proves by its contents that it is a later and revised edition: e.g., in the French edition, Hume is not yet mentioned, whilst in the English, on the other hand, Petty hardly figures any longer. The English edition is theoretically less important, but it contains numerous details referring specifically to English commerce, bullion trade, &c., that are wanting in the French text. The words on the title-page of the English edition, according to which the work is 'taken chiefly from the manuscript of a very ingenious gentleman, deceased, and adapted, &c.,' seem, therefore, a pure fiction, very customary at that time.

[12] '*Combien de fois n'avons-nous pas vu, dans certains ateliers, embaucher beaucoup plus d'ouvriers que ne le demandait le travail à mettre en main? Souvent, dans la prévision d'un travail aléatoire, quelquefois même imaginaire, on admet des ouvriers: comme on les paie aux pièces, on se dit qu'on ne court aucun risque, parceque toutes les pertes de temps seront à la charge des inoccupés.*' (H. Grégoir: *Les Typographes devant le Tribunal correctionnel de Bruxelles*, Brussels, 1865, p.9.)

[13] *Remarks on the Commercial Policy of Great Britain*, London, 1815.

[14] *A Defense of the Landowners and Farmers of Great Britain*, 1814, pp.4,5.

[15] Malthus, *Inquiry into the Nature and Progress of Rent*, Lond., 1815.

[16] 'Those who are paid by piece-work . . . constitute probably four-fifths of the workers in the factories.' *Report of Insp. of Fact., 30th April, 1858.*

[17] 'The productive power of his spinning-machine is accurately measured, and the rate of pay for work done with it decreases with, though not as, the increase of its productive power.' (Ure, l.c., p.317.) This last apologetic phrase Ure himself again cancels. The lengthening of the mule causes some increase of labour, he admits. The labour does therefore not diminish in the same ratio as its productivity increases. Further: 'By this increase the productive power of the machine will be augmented one-fifth. When this event happens the spinner will not be paid at the same rate for work done as he was before, but as that rate will not be diminished in the ratio of one-fifth, the improvement will augment his money earnings for any given number of hours' work,' but 'the foregoing statement requires a certain modification . . . The spinner has to pay something additional for juvenile aid out of his additional sixpence, accompanied by displacing a portion of adults' (l.c., p.321), which has in no way a tendency to raise wages.

[18] H. Fawcett: *The Economic Position of the British Labourer*. Cambridge and London, 1865, p.178.

[19] In the *London Standard* of October 26, 1861, there is a report of proceedings of the firm of John Bright & Co., before the Rochdale magistrates 'to prosecute for intimidation the agents of the Carpet Weavers Trades' Union. Bright's partners had introduced new machinery which would turn out 240 yards of carpet in the time and with the labour (!) previously required to produce 160 yards. The workmen had no claim whatever to share in the profits made by the investment of their employer's capital in mechanical improvements. Accordingly, Messrs Bright proposed to lower the rate of pay from 1 1/2d. per yard to 1d., leaving the earnings of the men exactly the same as before for the same labour. But there was a nominal reduction, of which the operatives, it is asserted, had not fair warning beforehand.'

[20] 'Trades' Unions, in their desire to maintain wages, endeavour to share in the benefits of improved machinery.' (*Quelle horreur!*) ' . . . the demanding higher

wages, because labour is abbreviated, is in other words the endeavour to establish a duty on mechanical improvements.' (*On Combination of Trades*, new ed., London, 1834, p.42.)

Volume 1, Part 6, Chapter 22

[1] 'It is not accurate to say that wages' (he deals here with their money expression) 'are increased, because they purchase more of a cheaper article.' (David Buchanan in his edition of Adam Smith's *Wealth of Nations*, 1814, Vol.1, p.417, note.)

[2] We shall inquire, in another place, what circumstances in relation to productivity may modify this law for individual branches of industry.

[3] James Anderson remarks in his polemic against Adam Smith: 'It deserves, likewise, to be remarked, that although the apparent price of Labour is usually lower in poor countries, where the produce of the soil, and grain in general, is cheap; yet it is in fact for the most part really higher than in other countries. For it is not the wages that is given to the labourer per day that constitutes the real price of labour, although it is its apparent price. The real price is that which a certain quantity of work performed actually costs the employer; and considered in this light, labour is in almost all cases cheaper in rich countries than in those that are poorer, although the price of grain and other provisions is usually much lower in the last than in the first . . . Labour estimated by the day is much lower in Scotland than in England . . . Labour by the piece is generally cheaper in England.' (James Anderson, *Observations on the Means of Exciting a Spirit of National Industry, &c.*, Edin. 1777, pp.350,351.) On the contrary, lowness of wages produces, in its turn, dearness of labour. 'Labour being dearer in Ireland than it is in England . . . because the wages are so much lower.' (N. 2079 in *Royal Commission on Railways, Minutes*, 1867.)

[4] (Ure, op. cit., p.314.)

[5] (*Reports of Insp. of Fact.*, 31st Oct., 1866, pp.31–37, passim.)

[6] *Essay on the Rate of Wages, with an Examination of the Causes of the Differences in the Condition of the Labouring Population throughout the World*, Philadelphia, 1835.

Volume 1, Part 7, Chapter 23

[1] '*Mais ces riches, qui consomment les produits du travail des autres, ne peuvent les obtenir que par des échanges [purchases of commodities]. S'ils donnent cependant leur richesse acquise et accumulée en retour contre ces produits nouveaux qui sont l'objet de leur fantaisie, ils semblent exposés à épuiser bientôt leur fonds de réserve; ils ne travaillent point, avons-nous dit, et ils ne peuvent même travailler; on croirait donc que chaque jour doit voir diminuer leurs vieilles richesses, et que lorsqu'il ne leur en restera plus, rien ne sera offert en échange aux ouvriers qui travaillent exclusivement pour eux . . . Mais dans l'ordre social, la richesse a acquis la propriété de se reproduire par le travail d'autrui, et sans que son propriétaire y concoure. La richesse, comme le travail, et par le travail, donne un fruit annuel qui peut être détruit chaque année sans que le riche en devienne plus pauvre. Ce fruit est le revenu qui naît du capital.*' (Sismondi: *Nouv. Princ. d'Écon. Pol.* Paris, 1819, t.i, pp.81–82.)

[2] 'Wages as well as profits are to be considered, each of them, as really a portion of the finished product.' (Ramsay, l.c., p.142.) 'The share of the product which comes to the labourer in the form of wages.' (J. Mill, *Éléments, &c.* Translated by Parissot. Paris, 1823, p.34.)

[3] 'When capital is employed in advancing to the workman his wages, it adds nothing to the funds for the maintenance of labour.' (Cazenove in note to his edition of Malthus's *Definitions in Pol. Econ.* London, 1853, p.22.)

[4] 'The wages of labour are advanced by capitalists in the case of less than one fourth of the labourers of the earth.' (Rich. Jones: *Textbook of Lectures on the Pol. Econ. of Nations.* Hertford, 1852, p.36.)

[5] 'Though the manufacturer' (i.e., the labourer) 'has his wages advanced to him by his master, he in reality costs him no expense, the value of these wages being generally reserved, together with a profit, in the improved value of the subject upon which his labour is bestowed.' (A. Smith, l.c., Book 2, ch.3, p.311.)

[6] 'This is a remarkably peculiar property of productive labour. Whatever is productively consumed is capital and it becomes capital by consumption.' (James Mill, l.c., p.242.) James Mill, however, never got on the track of this 'remarkably peculiar property'.

[7] 'It is true indeed, that the first introducing a manufacture employs many poor, but they cease not to be so, and the continuance of it makes many.' (*Reasons for a Limited Exportation of Wool*. London, 1677, p.19.) 'The farmer now absurdly asserts, that he keeps the poor. They are indeed kept in misery.' (*Reasons for the Late Increase of the Poor Rates: or a Comparative View of the Prices of labour and Provisions*. London, 1777, p.31.)

[8] Rossi would not declaim so emphatically against this, had he really penetrated the secret of 'productive consumption'.

[9] 'The labourers in the mines of S. America, whose daily task (the heaviest perhaps in the world) consists in bringing to the surface on their shoulders a load of metal weighing from 180 to 200 pounds, from a depth of 450 feet, live on bread and beans only; they themselves would prefer the bread alone for food, but their masters, who have found out that the men cannot work so hard on bread, treat them like horses, and compel them to eat beans; beans, however, are relatively much richer in bone-earth (phosphate of lime) than is bread.' (Liebig, l.c., vol.i, p.194, note.)

[10] James Mill, l.c., p.238.

[11] 'If the price of labour should rise so high that, notwithstanding the increase of capital, no more could be employed, I should say that such increase of capital would be still unproductively consumed.' (Ricardo, l.c., p.163.)

[12] 'The only productive consumption, properly so called, is the consumption or destruction of wealth' (he alludes to the means of production) 'by capitalists with a view to reproduction . . . The workman . . . is a productive consumer to the person who employs him, and to the State, but not, strictly speaking, to himself.' (Malthus, *Definitions, &c.*, p.30.)

[13] 'The only thing, of which one can say, that it is stored up and prepared beforehand, is the skill of the labourer . . . The accumulation and storage of skilled labour, that most important operation, is, as regards the great mass of labourers, accomplished without any capital whatever.' (Th. Hodgskin: *Labour Defended, &c.*, p.13.)

[14] 'That letter might be looked upon as the manifesto of the manufacturers.' (Ferrand: 'Motion on the Cotton Famine.' H.o.C., 27th April, 1863.)

[15] It will not be forgotten that this same capital sings quite another song, under ordinary circumstances, when there is a question of reducing wages. Then the masters exclaim with one voice: 'The factory operatives should keep in wholesome remembrance the fact that theirs is really a low species of skilled labour, and that there is none which is more easily acquired, or of its quality more amply remunerated, or which, by a short training of the least expert, can be more quickly, as well as abundantly, acquired . . . The master's machinery' (which we now learn can be replaced with advantage in 12 months,) 'really plays a far more important part in the business of production than the labour and skill of the operative' (who cannot now be replaced under 30 years), 'which six months' education can reach, and a common labourer can learn.' (See ante, p.423.)

[16] Parliament did not vote a single farthing in aid of emigration, but simply passed some Acts empowering the municipal corporations to keep the operatives in a half-starved state, i.e., to exploit them at less than the normal wages. On the other hand, when 3 years later, the cattle disease broke out, Parliament broke wildly through its

usages and voted, straight off, millions for indemnifying the millionaire landlords, whose farmers in any event came off without loss, owing to the rise in the price of meat. The bull-like bellow of the landed proprietors at the opening of Parliament, in 1866, showed that a man can worship the cow Sabala without being a Hindu, and can change himself into an ox without being a Jupiter.

[17] '*L'ouvrier demandait de la subsistence pour vivre, le chef demandait du travail pour gagner.*' (Sismondi, l.c., p.91.)

[18] A boorishly clumsy form of this bondage exists in the county of Durham. This is one of the few counties, in which circumstances do not secure to the farmer undisputed proprietary rights over the agricultural labourer. The mining industry allows the latter some choice. In this county, the farmer, contrary to the custom elsewhere, rents only such farms as have on them labourers' cottages. The rent of the cottage is a part of the wages. These cottages are known as 'hinds' houses'. They are let to the labourers in consideration of certain feudal services, under a contract called 'bondage', which, amongst other things, binds the labourer, during the time he is employed elsewhere, to leave some one, say his daughter, &c., to supply his place. The labourer himself is called a 'bondsman'. The relationship here set up also shows how individual consumption by the labourer becomes consumption on behalf of capital – or productive consumption – from quite a new point of view: 'It is curious to observe that the very dung of the hind and bondsman is the perquisite of the calculating lord . . . and the lord will allow no privy but his own to exist in the neighbourhood, and will rather give a bit of manure here and there for a garden than bate any part of his seigneurial right.' (*Public Health, Report VII, 1864*, p.188.)

[19] It will not be forgotten, that, with respect to the labour of children, &c., even the formality of a voluntary sale disappears.

[20] 'Capital presupposes wage-labour, and wage-labour presupposes capital. One is a necessary condition to the existence of the other; they mutually call each other into existence. Does an operative in a cotton-factory produce nothing but cotton goods? No, he produces capital. He produces values that give fresh command over his labour, and that, by means of such command, create fresh values.' (Karl Marx: *Lohnarbeit und Kapital*, in the *Neue Rheinische Zeitung*: No. 266, 7th April, 1849.) The articles published under the above title in the *N. Rh. Z.* are parts of some lectures given by me on that subject, in 1847, in the German *Arbeiter-Verein* at Brussels, the publication of which was interrupted by the revolution of February.

Volume 1, Part 7, Chapter 24

[1] 'Accumulation of capital; the employment of a portion of revenue as capital.' (Malthus: *Definitions, &c.*, ed. Cazenove, p.11.) 'Conversion of revenue into capital,' (Malthus: *Princ. of Pol. Econ.*' 2nd Ed., Lond.. 1836, p.320.)

[2] We here take no account of export trade, by means of which a nation can change articles of luxury either into means of production or means of subsistence, and vice versà. In order to examine the object of our investigation in its integrity, free from all disturbing subsidiary circumstances, we must treat the whole world as one nation, and assume that capitalist production is everywhere established and has possessed itself of every branch of industry.

[3] Sismondi's analysis of accumulation suffers from the great defect, that he contents himself, to too great an extent, with the phrase 'conversion of revenue into capital', without fathoming the material conditions of this operation.

[4] '*Le travail primitif auquel son capital a dû sa naissance*'. Sismondi, l.c., ed. Paris, t.i, p.109.

[5] 'Labour creates capital before capital employs labour.' E. G. Wakefield, *England and America*, Lond., 1833, vol.ii, p.110.

[6] Just as at a given stage in its development, commodity production necessarily passes into capitalistic commodity production (in fact, it is only on the basis of capitalistic production that products take the general and predominant form of commodities), so the laws of property that are based on commodity production, necessarily turn into the laws of capitalist appropriation. We may well, therefore, feel astonished at the cleverness of Proudhon, who would abolish capitalistic property by enforcing the eternal laws of property that are based on commodity production.

[7] The property of the capitalist in the product of the labour of others 'is a strict consequence of the law of appropriation, the fundamental principle of which was, on the contrary, the exclusive title of every labourer to the product of his own labour.' (Cherbuliez, *Richesse où Pauvreté*, Paris, 1841, p.58, where, however, the dialectical reversal is not properly developed.)

[8] 'Capital, viz., accumulated wealth employed with a view to profit.' (Malthus, l.c.) 'Capital . . . consists of wealth saved from revenue, and used with a view to profit.' (R. Jones: *An Introductory Lecture on Polit. Econ.*, Lond., 1833, p.16.)

[9] 'The possessors of surplus-produce or capital.' (*The Source and Remedy of the National Difficulties. A Letter to Lord John Russell.* Lond., 1821.)

[10] 'Capital, with compound interest on every portion of capital saved, is so all-engrossing that all the wealth in the world from which income is derived, has long ago become the interest on capital.' (*London Economist*, 19th July, 1851.)

[11] 'No political economist of the present day can by saving mean mere hoarding: and beyond this contracted and insufficient proceeding, no use of the term in reference to the national wealth can well be imagined, but that which must arise from a different application of what is saved, founded upon a real distinction between the different kinds of labour maintained by it.' (Malthus, l.c., pp.38,39.)

[12] Thus for instance, Balzac, who so thoroughly studied every shade of avarice, represents the old usurer Gobseck as in his second childhood when he begins to heap up a hoard of commodities.

[13] 'Accumulation of stocks . . . upon exchange . . . over-production.' (Th. Corbet. l.c., p.104.)

[14] In this sense Necker speaks of the '*objets de faste et de somptuosité*', of which '*le temps a grossi l'accumulation*', and which '*les lois de propriété ont rassemblés dans une seule classe de la société.*' (*Oeuvres de M. Necker*, Paris and Lausanne, 1789, t.ii., p.291.)

[15] Ricardo, l.c., p.163, note.

[16] In spite of his *Logic*, John St. Mill never detects even such faulty analysis as this when made by his predecessors, an analysis which, even from the bourgeois standpoint of the science, cries out for rectification. In every case he registers with the dogmatism of a disciple, the confusion of his master's thoughts. So here: 'The capital itself in the long run becomes entirely wages, and when replaced by the sale of produce becomes wages again.'

[17] In his description of the process of reproduction, and of accumulation, Adam Smith, in many ways, not only made no advance, but even lost considerable ground, compared with his predecessors, especially the Physiocrats. Connected with the illusion mentioned in the text, is the really wonderful dogma, left by him as an inheritance to Political Economy, the dogma, that the price of commodities is made up of wages, profit (interest) and rent, i.e., of wages and surplus-value. Starting from this basis, Storch naively confesses, '*Il est impossible de résoudre le prix nécessaire dans ses élémeuts les plus simples.*' (Storch, l.c., Petersb. Edit., 1815, t.ii, p.141, note.) A fine science of economy this, which declares it impossible to resolve the price of a commodity into its simplest elements! This point will be further investigated in the seventh part of Book 3.

[18] The reader will notice, that the word revenue is used in a double sense: first, to designate surplus-value so far as it is the fruit periodically yielded by capital; secondly,

to designate the part of that fruit which is periodically consumed by the capitalist, or added to the fund that supplies his private consumption. I have retained this double meaning because it harmonises with the language of the English and French economists.

[19] Taking the usurer, that old-fashioned but ever-renewed specimen of the capitalist for his text, Luther shows very aptly that the love of power is an element in the desire to get rich. 'The heathen were able, by the light of reason, to conclude that a usurer is a double-dyed thief and murderer. We Christians, however, hold them in such honour, that we fairly worship them for the sake of their money . . . Whoever eats up, robs, and steals the nourishment of another, that man commits as great a murder (so far as in him lies) as he who starves a man or utterly undoes him. Such does a usurer, and sits the while safe on his stool, when he ought rather to be hanging on the gallows, and be eaten by as many ravens as he has stolen guilders, if only there were so much flesh on him, that so many ravens could stick their beaks in and share it. Meanwhile, we hang the small thieves . . . Little thieves are put in the stocks, great thieves go flaunting in gold and silk . . . Therefore is there, on this earth, no greater enemy of man (after the devil) than a gripe-money, and usurer, for he wants to be God over all men. Turks, soldiers, and tyrants are also bad men, yet must they let the people live, and confess that they are bad, and enemies, and do, nay, must, now and then show pity to some. But a usurer and money-glutton, such a one would have the whole world perish of hunger and thirst, misery and want, so far as in him lies, so that he may have all to himself, and every one may receive from him as from a God, and be his serf for ever. To wear fine cloaks, golden chains, rings, to wipe his mouth, to be deemed and taken for a worthy, pious man . . . Usury is a great huge monster, like a werewolf, who lays waste all, more than any Cacus, Gerion or Antus. And yet decks himself out, and would be thought pious, so that people may not see where the oxen have gone, that he drags backwards into his den. But Hercules shall hear the cry of the oxen and of his prisoners, and shall seek Cacus even in cliffs and among rocks, and shall set the oxen loose again from the villain. For Cacus means the villain that is a pious usurer, and steals, robs, eats everything. And will not own that he has done it, and thinks no one will find him out, because the oxen, drawn backwards into his den, make it seem, from their foot-prints, that they have been let out. So the usurer would deceive the world, as though he were of use and gave the world oxen, which he, however, rends, and eats all alone . . . And since we break on the wheel, and behead highwaymen, murderers and housebreakers, how much more ought we to break on the wheel and kill . . . hunt down, curse and behead all usurers.' (Martin Luther, l.c.)

[20] See Goethe's *Faust*.

[21] Dr Aikin: *Description of the Country from 30 to 40 miles round Manchester*. Lond., 1795, p.182, sq.

[22] A. Smith, l.c., bk.iii, ch iii.

[23] Even J. B. Say says: '*Les épargnes des riches se font aux dépens des pauvres*.' 'The Roman proletarian lived almost entirely at the expense of society.' . . . It can almost be said that modern society lives at the expense of the proletarians, on what it keeps out of the remuneration of labour.' (Sismondi: *Études, &c.*, t. i., p.24.)

[24] Malthus, l.c., pp.319,320.

[25] *An Inquiry into those Principles Respecting the Nature of Demand, &c.*, p.67.

[26] l.c., p.50.

[27] (Senior, *Principes fondamentaux de l'Écon. Pol.* trad. Arrivabene. Paris, 1836, p.308.) This was rather too much for the adherents of the old classical school. 'Mr Senior has substituted for it' (the expression, labour and profit) 'the expression Labour and Abstinence. He who converts his revenue abstains from the enjoyment which its expenditure would afford him. It is not the capital, but the use of the capital productively, which is the cause of profits.' (John Cazenove, l.c., p.130, note.) John St.

Mill, on the contrary, accepts on the one hand Ricardo's theory of profit, and annexes on the other hand Senior's 'remuneration of abstinence'. He is as much at home in absurd contradictions, as he feels at sea in the Hegelian contradiction, the source of all dialectic. It has never occurred to the vulgar economist to make the simple reflection, that every human action may be viewed, as 'abstinence' from its opposite. Eating is abstinence from fasting, walking, abstinence from standing still, working, abstinence from idling, idling, abstinence from working, &c. These gentlemen would do well to ponder, once in a way, over Spinoza's: *Determinatio est Negatio*.

[28] Senior, l.c., p.342.

[29] 'No one . . . will sow his wheat, for instance, and allow it to remain a twelve month in the ground, or leave his wine in a cellar for years, instead of consuming these things or their equivalent at once . . . unless he expects to acquire additional value, &c.' (Scrope, *Polit. Econ.*, edit. by A. Potter, New York, 1841, pp.133–134.)

[30] '*La privation que s'impose le capitaliste, en prêtant* (this euphemism used, for the purpose of identifying, according to the approved method of vulgar economy, the labourer who is exploited, with the industrial capitalist who exploits, and to whom other capitalists lend money) *ses instruments de production au travailleur, au lieu d'en consacrer la valeur à son propre usage, en la transforment en objets d'utilité ou d'agrément.*' (G. de Molinari, l.c., p.36.)

[31] '*La conservation d'un capital exige . . . un effort constant pour résister à la tentation de le consommer.*' (Courcelle-Seneuil, l.c., p.57.)

[32] 'The particular classes of income which yield the most abundantly to the progress of national capital, change at different stages of their progress, and are, therefore, entirely different in nations occupying different positions in that progress . . . Profits . . . unimportant source of accumulation, compared with wages and rents, in the earlier stages of society . . . When a considerable advance in the powers of national industry has actually taken place, profits rise into comparative importance as a source of accumulation.' (Richard Jones, *Textbook, &c.*, pp.16,21.)

[33] l.c., p.36, sq.

[34] Ricardo says: 'In different stages of society the accumulation of capital or of the means of employing' (i.e., exploiting) 'labour is more or less rapid, and must in all cases depend on the productive powers of labour. The productive powers of labour are generally greatest where there is an abundance of fertile land.' If, in the first sentence, the productive powers of labour mean the smallness of that aliquot part of any produce that goes to those whose manual labour produced it, the sentence is nearly identical, because the remaining aliquot part is the fund whence capital can, if the owner pleases, be accumulated. But then this does not generally happen, where there is most fertile land. (*Observations on Certain Verbal Disputes, &c.* pp.74,75.)

[35] J. Stuart Mill: *Essays on Some Unsettled Questions of Political Economy*, Lond., 1844, p.90.

[36] *An Essay on Trade and Commerce*, Lond., 1770, p.44. *The Times* of December, 1866, and January, 1867, in like manner published certain outpourings of the heart of the English mine-owner, in which the happy lot of the Belgian miners was pictured, who asked and received no more than was strictly necessary for them to live for their 'masters'. The Belgian labourers have to suffer much, but to figure in *The Times* as model labourers! In the beginning of February, 1867, came the answer: strike of the Belgian miners at Marchienne, put down by powder and lead.

[37] l.c., pp.44,46.

[38] The Northamptonshire manufacturer commits a pious fraud, pardonable in one whose heart is so full. He nominally compares the life of the English and French manufacturing labourer, but in the words just quoted he is painting, as he himself confesses in his confused way, the French agricultural labourers.

[39] l.c., pp.70,71. Note in the 3rd German edition: Today, thanks to the competition on the world-market, established since then, we have advanced much further. 'If China,' says Mr Stapleton, M.P., to his constituents, 'should become a great manufacturing country, I do not see how the manufacturing population of Europe could sustain the contest without descending to the level of their competitors.' (*Times*, Sept. 3, 1873, p.8.) The wished-for goal of English capital is no longer Continental wages but Chinese.

[40] Benjamin Thompson: *Essays, Political, Economical, and Philosophical, &c.*, 3 vols., Lond, 1796–1802, vol. i., p.294. In his *The State of the Poor, or an History of the labouring Classes in England, &c.*, Sir F. M. Eden strongly recommends the Rumfordian beggar-soup to workhouse overseers, and reproachfully warns the English labourers that 'many poor people, particularly in Scotland, live, and that very comfortably, for months together, upon oat-meal and barley-meal, mixed with only water and salt.' (l.c., vol.i, book i, ch. 2, p.503.) The same sort of hints in the 19th century. 'The most wholesome mixtures of flour having been refused (by the English agricultural labourer) . . . in Scotland, where education is better, this prejudice is, probably, unknown.' (Charles H. Parry, M. D., *The Question of the Necessity of the Existing Corn Laws Considered*. London, 1816, p.69) This same Parry, however, complains that the English labourer is now (1815) in a much worse condition than in Eden's time (1797.)

[41] From the reports of the last Parliamentary Commission on adulteration of means of subsistence, it will be seen that the adulteration even of medicines is the rule, not the exception in England. e.g., the examination of 34 specimens of opium, purchased of as many different chemists in London, showed that 31 were adulterated with poppy heads, wheat-flour, gum, clay, sand, &c. Several did not contain an atom of morphia.

[42] G. B. Newnham (barrister-at-law): *A Review of the Evidence before the Committee of the two Houses of Parliament on the Corn Laws.* Lond., 1815, p.20, note.

[43] l.c., pp.19,20.

[44] C. H. Parry, l.c., pp.77,69. The landlords, on their side, not only 'indemnified' themselves for the Anti-Jacobin War, which they waged in the name of England, but enriched themselves enormously. Their rents doubled, trebled, quadrupled, 'and in one instance, increased sixfold in eighteen years.' (l.c., pp.100,101.)

[45] Friedrich Engels, *Lage der arbeitenden Klasse in England*, p.20.

[46] Classic economy has, on account of a deficient analysis of the labour-process, and of the process of creating value, never properly grasped this weighty element of reproduction, as may be seen in Ricardo; he says, e.g., whatever the change in productive power, 'a million men always produce in manufactures the same value.' This is accurate, if the extension and degree of intensity of their labour are given. But it does not prevent (this Ricardo overlooks in certain conclusions he draws) a million men with different powers of productivity in their labour, turning into products very different masses of the means of production, and therefore preserving in their products very different masses of value; in consequence of which the values of the products yielded may vary considerably. Ricardo has, it may be noted in passing, tried in vain to make clear to J. B. Say, by that very example, the difference between use-value (which he here calls wealth or material riches) and exchange-value. Say answers: '*Quant à la difficulté qu'élève Mr Ricardo en disant que, par des procédés mieux entendus, un million de personnes peuvent produire deux fois, trois fois autant de richesses, sans produire plus de valeurs, cette difficulté n'est pas une lorsque l'on considére, ainsi qu'on le doit, la production comme un échange dans lequel on donne les services productifs de son travail, de sa terre, et de ses capitaux, pour obtenir des produits. C'est par le moyen de ces services productifs, que nous acquérons tous les produits qui sont au monde. Or . . . nous sommes d'autant plus riches, nos services productifs ont d'autant plus de valeur qu'ils obtiennent dans l'échange appelé production une plus grande quantité de choses utiles.*' (J. B. Say, *Lettres à M. Malthus*, Paris, 1820, pp.168,169.) The

'*difficulté*' – it exists for him, not for Ricardo – that Say means to clear up is this: Why does not the exchange-value of the use-values increase, when their quantity increases in consequence of increased productive power of labour? Answer: the difficulty is met by calling use-value, exchange-value, if you please. Exchange-value is a thing that is connected one way or another with exchange. If therefore production is called an exchange of labour and means of production against the product, it is clear as day that you obtain more exchange-value in proportion as the production yields more use-value. In other words, the more use-values, e.g., stockings, a working-day yields to the stocking-manufacturer, the richer is he in stockings. Suddenly, however, Say recollects that 'with a greater quantity' of stockings their 'price' (which of course has nothing to do with their exchange-value!) falls '*parce que la concurrence les (les producteurs) oblige à donner les produits pour ce qu'ils leur coûtent.*' . . . But whence does the profit come, if the capitalist sells the commodities at cost-price? Never mind! Say declares that, in consequence of increased productivity, every one now receives in return for a given equivalent two pairs of stockings instead of one as before. The result he arrives at, is precisely that proposition of Ricardo that he aimed at disproving. After this mighty effort of thought, he triumphantly apostrophises Malthus in the words: '*Telle est, monsieur, la doctrine bien liée, sans laquelle il est impossible, je le déclare, d'expliquer les plus grandes difficultés de l'économie politique, et notamment, comment il se peut qu'une nation soit plus riche lorsque ses produits diminuent de valeur, quoique la richesse soit de la valeur.*' (l.c., p.170.) An English economist remarks upon the conjuring tricks of the same nature that appear in Say's *Lettres*: 'Those affected ways of talking make up in general that which M. Say is pleased to call his doctrine and which he earnestly urges Malthus to teach at Hertford, as it is already taught "*dans plusieurs parties de l'Europe*". He says, "*Si vous trouvez une physionomie de paradoxe à toutes ces propositions, voyez les choses qu'elles expriment, et j'ose croire qu'elles vous paraîtront fort simples et fort raisonnables.*" Doubtless, and in consequence of the same process, they will appear everything else, except original.' (*An Inquiry into those Principles Respecting the Nature of Demand, &c.*,' pp.116,110.)

[47] MacCulloch took out a patent for 'wages of past labour', long before Senior did for 'wages of abstinence'.

[48] Compare among others, Jeremy Bentham: *Théorie des Peines et des Récompenses*, traduct. d'Et. Dumont, 3ème édit. Paris, 1826, t.ii, l.iv, ch.ii.

[49] Bentham is a purely English phenomenon. Not even excepting our philosopher, Christian Wolff, in no time and in no country has the most homespun commonplace ever strutted about in so self-satisfied a way. The principle of utility was no discovery of Bentham. He simply reproduced in his dull way what Helvetius and other Frenchmen had said with *esprit* in the 18th century. To know what is useful for a dog, one must study dog-nature. This nature itself is not to be deduced from the principle of utility. Applying this to man, he that would criticise all human acts, movements, relations, etc., by the principle of utility, must first deal with human nature in general, and then with human nature as modified in each historical epoch. Bentham makes short work of it. With the driest naiveté he takes the modern shopkeeper, especially the English shopkeeper, as the normal man. Whatever is useful to this queer normal man, and to his world, is absolutely useful. This yard-measure, then, he applies to past, present, and future. The Christian religion, e.g., is 'useful', 'because it forbids in the name of religion the same faults that the penal code condemns in the name of the law.' Artistic criticism is 'harmful', because it disturbs worthy people in their enjoyment of Martin Tupper, etc. With such rubbish has the brave fellow, with his motto, '*nulla dies sine linea!*' piled up mountains of books. Had I the courage of my friend, Heinrich Heine, I should call Mr Jeremy a genius in the way of bourgeois stupidity.

[50] 'Political economists are too apt to consider a certain quantity of capital and a certain number of labourers as productive instruments of uniform power, or operating with a certain uniform intensity . . . Those . . . who maintain . . . that commodities are the sole agents of production . . . prove that production could never be enlarged, for it requires as an indispensable condition to such an enlargement that food, raw materials, and tools should be previously augmented; which is in fact maintaining that no increase of production can take place without a previous increase, or, in other words, that an increase is impossible.' (S. Bailey: *Money and its Vicissitudes*, pp.58 and 70.) Bailey criticises the dogma mainly from the point of view of the process of circulation.

[51] John Stuart Mill, in his *Principles of Political Economy*, says: 'The really exhausting and the really repulsive labours instead of being better paid than others, are almost invariably paid the worst of all . . . The more revolting the occupation, the more certain it is to receive the minimum of remuneration . . . The hardships and the earnings, instead of being directly proportional, as in any just arrangements of society they would be, are generally in an inverse ratio to one another.' To avoid misunderstanding, let me say that although men like John Stuart Mill are to blame for the contradiction between their traditional economic dogmas and their modern tendencies, it would be very wrong to class them with the herd of vulgar economic apologists.

[52] H. Fawcett, Professor of Political Economy at Cambridge. *The Economic Position of the British Labourer*. London, 1865, p.120.

[53] I must here remind the reader that the categories, 'variable and constant capital', were first used by me. Political Economy since the time of Adam Smith has confusedly mixed up the essential distinctions involved in these categories, with the mere formal differences, arising out of the process of circulation, of fixed and circulating capital. For further details on this point, see Book 2, Part 2.

[54] Fawcett, l.c., pp.122,123.

[55] It might be said that not only capital, but also labourers, in the shape of emigrants, are annually exported from England. In the text, however, there is no question of the *peculium* of the emigrants, who are in great part not labourers. The sons of farmers make up a great part of them. The additional capital annually transported abroad to be put out at interest is in much greater proportion to the annual accumulation than the yearly emigration is to the yearly increase of population.

Volume 1, Part 7, Chapter 25

[1] Karl Marx, l.c., '*A égalité d'oppression des masses, plus un pays a de prolétaires et plus il est riche.*' (Colins, '*L'Economie Politique. Source des Révolutions et des Utopies prétendues Socialistes.*' Paris, 1857, t.iii, p.331.) Our '*prolétarian*' is economically none other than the wage-labourer, who produces and increases capital, and is thrown out on the streets, as soon as he is superfluous for the needs of aggrandisement of 'Monsieur capital', as Pecqueur calls this person. 'The sickly proletarian of the primitive forest', is a pretty Roscherian fancy. The primitive forester is owner of the primitive forest, and uses the primitive forest as his property with the freedom of an orang-outang. He is not, therefore, a proletarian. This would only be the case, if the primitive forest exploited him, instead of being exploited by him. As far as his health is concerned, such a man would well bear comparison, not only with the modern proletarian, but also with the syphilitic and scrofulous upper classes. But, no doubt, Herr Wilhelm Roscher, by 'primitive forest' means his native heath of Lüneburg.

[2] John Bellers, l.c., p.2.

[3] Bernard de Mandeville: *The Fable of the Bees*, 5th edition, London, 1728. Remarks, pp.212,213,328. 'Temperate living and constant employment is the direct road, for the poor, to rational happiness' [by which he most probably means long working-days and little means of subsistence], 'and to riches and strength for the state' (viz., for the

landlords, capitalists, and their political dignitaries and agents). (*An Essay on Trade and Commerce*, London, 1770, p.54.)

[4] Eden should have asked, whose creatures then are 'the civil institutions'? From his standpoint of juridical illusion, he does not regard the law as a product of the material relations of production, but conversely the relations of production as products of the law. Linguet overthrew Montesquieu's illusory *Esprit des lois* with one word: '*L'esprit des lois, c'est la propriété.*'

[5] Eden, l.c., vol. 1, book i, chapter 1, pp.1,2, and preface, p.xx.

[6] If the reader reminds me of Malthus, whose *Essay on Population* appeared in 1798, I remind him that this work in its first form is nothing more than a schoolboyish, superficial plagiary of De Foe, Sir James Steuart, Townsend, Franklin, Wallace, &c., and does not contain a single sentence thought out by himself. The great sensation this pamphlet caused, was due solely to party interest. The French Revolution had found passionate defenders in the United Kingdom; the 'principle of population', slowly worked out in the eighteenth century, and then, in the midst of a great social crisis, proclaimed with drums and trumpets as the infallible antidote to the teachings of Condorcet, &c., was greeted with jubilance by the English oligarchy as the great destroyer of all hankerings after human development. Malthus, hugely astonished at his success, gave himself to stuffing into his book materials superficially compiled, and adding to it new matter, not discovered but annexed by him. Note further: although Malthus was a parson of the English State Church, he had taken the monastic vow of celibacy — one of the conditions of holding a Fellowship in Protestant Cambridge University: '*Socios collegiorum maritos esse non permittimus, sed statim postquam quis uxorem duxerit socius collegii desinat esse.*' (*Reports of Cambridge University Commission*, p.172.) This circumstance favourably distinguishes Malthus from the other Protestant parsons, who have shuffled off the command enjoining celibacy of the priesthood and have taken, 'Be fruitful and multiply,' as their special Biblical mission in such a degree that they generally contribute to the increase of population to a really unbecoming extent, whilst they preach at the same time to the labourers the 'principle of population'. It is characteristic that the economic fall of man, the Adam's apple, the urgent appetite, 'the checks which tend to blunt the shafts of Cupid', as Parson Townsend waggishly puts it, that this delicate question was and is monopolised by the Reverends of Protestant Theology, or rather of the Protestant Church. With the exception of the Venetian monk, Ortes, an original and clever writer, most of the population-theory teachers are Protestant parsons. For instance, Bruckner, *Théorie du Système animal*, Leyde, 1767, in which the whole subject of the modern population theory is exhausted, and to which the passing quarrel between Quesnay and his pupil, the elder Mirabeau, furnished ideas on the same topic; then Parson Wallace, Parson Townsend, Parson Malthus and his pupil, the arch-Parson Thomas Chalmers, to say nothing of lesser reverend scribblers in this line. Originally, Political Economy was studied by philosophers like Hobbes, Locke, Hume; by businessmen and statesmen, like Thomas More, Temple, Sully, De Witt, North, Law, Vanderlint, Cantillon, Franklin; and especially, and with the greatest success, by medical men like Petty, Barbon, Mandeville, Quesnay. Even in the middle of the eighteenth century, the Rev. Mr Tucker, a notable economist of his time, excused himself for meddling with the things of Mammon. Later on, and in truth with this very 'principle of population', struck the hour of the Protestant parsons. Petty, who regarded the population as the basis of wealth, and was, like Adam Smith, an outspoken foe to parsons, says, as if he had a presentiment of their bungling interference, 'that Religion best flourishes when the Priests are most mortified, as was before said of the Law, which best flourisheth when lawyers have least to do.' He advises the Protestant priests, therefore, if they, once for all, will not follow the Apostle Paul and 'mortify' themselves by celibacy, 'not to breed more Churchmen than the

Benefices, as they now stand shared out, will receive, that is to say, if there be places for about twelve thousand in England and Wales, it will not be safe to breed up 24,000 ministers, for then the twelve thousand which are unprovided for, will seek ways how to get themselves a livelihood, which they cannot do more easily than by persuading the people that the twelve thousand incumbents do poison or starve their souls, and misguide them in their way to Heaven.' (Petty: *A Treatise of Taxes and Contributions*, London, 1667, p.57.) Adam Smith's position with the Protestant priesthood of his time is shown by the following. In *A Letter to A. Smith, Ll.D. On the Life, Death, and Philosophy of his Friend, David Hume. By one of the People called Christians*, 4th Edition, Oxford, 1784, Dr Horne, Bishop of Norwich, reproves Adam Smith, because in a published letter to Mr Strahan, he 'embalmed his friend David' (sc. Hume); because he told the world how 'Hume amused himself on his deathbed with Lucian and Whist,' and because he even had the impudence to write of Hume: 'I have always considered him, both in his life-time and since his death, as approaching as nearly to the idea of a perfectly wise and virtuous man, as, perhaps, the nature of human frailty will permit.' The bishop cries out, in a passion: 'Is it right in you, Sir, to hold up to our view as "perfectly wise and virtuous", the character and conduct of one, who seems to have been possessed with an incurable antipathy to all that is called Religion; and who strained every nerve to explode, suppress and extirpate the spirit of it among men, that its very name, if he could effect it, might no more be had in remembrance?' (l.c., p.8.) 'But let not the lovers of truth be discouraged. Atheism cannot be of long continuance.' (p.17.) Adam Smith, 'had the atrocious wickedness to propagate atheism through the land (viz., by his *Theory of Moral Sentiments*). Upon the whole, Doctor, your meaning is good; but I think you will not succeed this time. You would persuade us, by the example of David Hume, Esq., that atheism is the only cordial for low spirits, and the proper antidote against the fear of death . . . You may smile over Babylon in ruins and congratulate the hardened Pharaoh on his overthrow in the Red Sea.' (l.c., pp.21,22.) One orthodox individual, amongst Adam Smith's college friends, writes after his death: 'Smith's well-placed affection for Hume . . . hindered him from being a Christian . . . When he met with honest men whom he liked . . . he would believe almost anything they said. Had he been a friend of the worthy ingenious Horrox he would have believed that the moon some times disappeared in a clear sky without the interposition of a cloud . . . He approached to republicanism in his political principles.' (*The Bee*. By James Anderson, 18 vols., vol.3, pp.166,165, Edinburgh, 1791–93.) Parson Thomas Chalmers has his suspicions as to Adam Smith having invented the category of 'unproductive labourers', solely for the Protestant parsons, in spite of their blessed work in the vineyard of the Lord.

[7] 'The limit, however, to the employment of both the operative and the labourer is the same; namely, the possibility of the employer realising a profit on the produce of their industry. If the rate of wages is such as to reduce the master's gains below the average profit of capital, he will cease to employ them, or he will only employ them on condition of submission to a reduction of wages.' (John Wade, l.c., p.241.)

[8] cf. Karl Marx: *Zur Kritik der Politischen Oekonomie*, pp.166, seq.

[9] 'If we now return to our first inquiry, wherein it was shown that capital itself is only the result of human labour . . . it seems quite incomprehensible that man can have fallen under the domination of capital, his own product; can be subordinated to it; and as in reality this is beyond dispute the case, involuntarily the question arises: how has the labourer been able to pass from being master of capital – as its creator – to being its slave?' (Von Thünen, *Der isolierte Staat*, part ii., section ii., Rostock, 1863, pp.5,6.) It is Thünen's merit to have asked this question. His answer is simply childish.

[10] Note in the 3rd German edition. – In Marx's copy there is here the marginal note: 'Here note for working out later; if the extension is only quantitative, then for a greater and a smaller capital in the same branch of business the profits are as the magnitudes of the capitals advanced. If the quantitative extension induces qualitative change, then the rate of profit on the larger capital rises simultaneously.' F. E.

[11] The census of England and Wales shows: all persons employed in agriculture (landlords, farmers, gardeners, shepherds, &c., included): 1851, 2,011,447; 1861, 1,924,110. Fall, 87,337. Worsted manufacture: 1851, 102,714 persons; 1861, 79,242. Silk weaving: 1851, 111,940; 1861, 101,678. Calico-printing: 1851, 12,098; 1861, 12,556. A small rise that, in the face of the enormous extension of this industry and implying a great fall proportionally in the number of labourers employed. Hat-making: 1851, 15,957; 1861, 13,814. Straw-hat and bonnet-making: 1851, 20,393; 1861, 18,176. Malting: 1851, 10,566; 1861, 10,677. Chandlery, 1851, 4,949; 1861, 4,686. This fall is due, besides other causes, to the increase in lighting by gas. Comb-making – 1851, 2,038; 1861, 1,478. Sawyers: 1851, 30,552; 1861, 31,647 – a small rise in consequence of the increase of sawing-machines. Nail-making: 1851, 26,940; 1861, 26,130 – fall in consequence of the competition of machinery. Tin and copper-mining: 1851, 31,360; 1861, 32,041. On the other hand: Cotton-spinning and weaving: 1851, 371,777; 1861, 456,646. Coal-mining: 1851, 183,389, 1861, 246,613, 'The increase of labourers is generally greatest, since 1851, in such branches of industry in which machinery has not up to the present been employed with success.' (*Census of England and Wales for 1861*. vol.iii. London, 1863, p.36.)

[12] 'The demand for labour depends on the increase of circulating, and not of fixed capital. Were it true that the proportion between these two sorts of capital is the same at all times, and in all circumstances, then, indeed, it follows that the number of labourers employed is in proportion to the wealth of the state. But such a proposition has not the semblance of probability. As arts are cultivated, and civilisation is extended, fixed capital bears a larger and larger proportion to circulating capital. The amount of fixed capital employed in the production of a piece of British muslin is at least a hundred, probably a thousand times greater than that employed in a similar piece of Indian muslin. And the proportion of circulating capital is a hundred or thousand times less . . . the whole of the annual savings, added to the fixed capital, would have no effect in increasing the demand for labour.' (John Barton, *Observations on the Circumstances which Influence the Condition of the Labouring Classes of Society*. London, 1817, pp.16,17.) 'The same cause which may increase the net revenue of the country may at the same time render the population redundant, and deteriorate the condition of the labourer.' (Ricardo, l.c., p.469.) With increase of capital, 'the demand [for labour] will be in a diminishing ratio.' (ibid., p.480, Note.) 'The amount of capital devoted to the maintenance of labour may vary, independently of any changes in the whole amount of capital . . . Great fluctuations in the amount of employment, and great suffering may become more frequent as capital itself becomes more plentiful.' (Richard Jones, *An Introductory Lecture on Pol. Econ.*, Lond. 1833, p.13) 'Demand [for labour] will rise . . . not in proportion to the accumulation of the general capital . . . Every augmentation, therefore, in the national stock destined for reproduction, comes, in the progress of society, to have less and less influence upon the condition of the labourer.' (Ramsay, l.c., pp.90,91.)

[13] H. Merivale. *Lectures on Colonisation and Colonies*, 1841, vol.I, p.146.

[14] Malthus, *Principles of Political Economy*,' pp.215,319,320. In this work, Malthus finally discovers, with the help of Sismondi, the beautiful Trinity of capitalistic production: over-production, over-population, over-consumption – three very delicate monsters, indeed. cf. F. Engels, *Umrisse zu einer Kritik der Nationalökonomie*,' l.c., p,107, et seq.

[15] Harriet Martineau, *The Manchester Strike*, 1832, p.101.

[16] Even in the cotton famine of 1863 we find, in a pamphlet of the operative cotton-spinners of Blackburn, fierce denunciations of over-work. which, in consequence of the Factory Acts, of course only affected adult male labourers. 'The adult operatives at this mill have been asked to work from 12 to 13 hours per day, while there are hundreds who are compelled to be idle who would willingly work partial time, in order to maintain their families and save their brethren from a premature grave through being overworked . . . We,' it goes on to say, 'would ask if the practice of working over-time by a number of hands, is likely to create a good feeling between masters and servants. Those who are worked over-time feel the injustice equally with those who are condemned to forced idleness. There is in the district almost sufficient work to give to all partial employment if fairly distributed. We are only asking what is right in requesting the masters generally to pursue a system of short hours, particularly until a better state of things begins to dawn upon us, rather than to work a portion of the hands over-time, while others, for want of work, are compelled to exist upon charity.' (*Reports of Insp. of Fact.*, *Oct. 31, 1863*, p.8.) The author of the *Essay on Trade and Commerce* grasps the effect of a relative surplus-population on the employed labourers with his usual unerring bourgeois instinct. 'Another cause of idleness in this kingdom is the want of a sufficient number of labouring hands . . . Whenever from an extraordinary demand for manufactures, labour grows scarce, the labourers feel their own consequence, and will make their masters feel it likewise — it is amazing; but so depraved are the dispositions of these people, that in such cases a set of workmen have combined to distress the employer by idling a whole day together.' (*Essay, &c.*, pp.27,28.) The fellows in fact were hankering after a rise in wages.

[17] *Economist*, Jan. 21. 1860.

[18] Whilst during the last six months of 1866, 80–90,000 working people in London were thrown out of work, the Factory Report for that same half year says: 'It does not appear absolutely true to say that demand will always produce supply just at the moment when it is needed. It has not done so with labour, for much machinery has been idle last year for want of hands.' (*Rep. of Insp. of Fact., 31st Oct., 1866*, p.81.)

[19] Opening address to the Sanitary Conference, Birmingham, January 15th, 1875, by J. Chamberlain, Mayor of the town, now (1883) President of the Board of Trade.

[20] 781 towns given in the census for 1861 for England and Wales 'contained 10,960,998 inhabitants, while the villages and country parishes contained 9,105,226. In 1851, 580 towns were distinguished, and the population in them and in the surrounding country was nearly equal. But while in the subsequent ten years the population in the villages and the country increased half a million, the population in the 580 towns increased by a million and a half (1,554,067). The increase of the population of the country parishes is 6.5 per cent., and of the towns 17.3 per cent. The difference in the rates of increase is due to the migration from country to town. Three-fourths of the total increase of population has taken place in the towns.' (*Census. &c.*, pp.11 and 12.)

[21] 'Poverty seems favourable to generation.' (A. Smith.) This is even a specially wise arrangement of God, according to the gallant and witty Abbé Galiani '*Iddio af che gli uomini che esercitano mestieri di prima utilità nascono abbondantemente.*' (Galiani, l.c., p.78.) 'Misery up to the extreme point of famine and pestilence, instead of checking, tends to increase population.' (S. Laing, *National Distress*, 1844, p.69.) After Laing has illustrated this by statistics, he continues: 'If the people were all in easy circumstances, the world would soon be depopulated.'

[22] '*De jour en jour il devient donc plus clair que les rapports de production dans lesquels se meut la bourgeoisie n'ont pas un caractère un, un catactère simple, mais un caractère de duplicité;*

que dans les mêmes rapports dans lesquels se produit la richesse, la misère se produit aussi; que dans les mêmes rapports dans lesquels il y a développement des forces productives, il y a une force productive de répression; que ces rapports ne produisent la richesse bourgeoise, c'est-à-dire la richesse de la classe bourgeoise, qu'en anéantissant continuellement la richesse des membres intégrants de cette classe et en produisant un prolétariat toujours croissant.' (Karl Marx: *Misère de la Philosophie*, p.116.)

[23] G. Ortes: *Della Economia Nazionale libri sei, 1777,* in *Custodi, Parte Moderna,* t.xxi, pp.6,9,22,25, etc. Ortes says, l.c., p.32: '*In luoco di progettar sistemi inutili per la felicità de'popoli, mi limiterò a investigare la region della loro infelicità.*'

[24] *A Dissertation on the Poor Laws. By a Well-wisher of Mankind.* (The Rev. J. Townsend) 1786,' republished Lond. 1817, pp.15,39,41. This 'delicate' parson, from whose work just quoted, as well as from his *Journey through Spain,* Malthus often copies whole pages, himself borrowed the greater part of his doctrine from Sir James Steuart, whom he however alters in the borrowing. e.g., when Steuart says: 'Here, in slavery, was a forcible method of making mankind diligent,' [for the non-workers] . . . 'Men were then forced to work' [i.e., to work gratis for others], 'because they were slaves of others; men are now forced to work' [i.e., to work gratis for non-workers] 'because they are the slaves of their necessities,' he does not thence conclude, like the fat holder of benefices, that the wage-labourer must always go fasting. He wishes, on the contrary, to increase their wants and to make the increasing number of their wants a stimulus to their labour for the 'more delicate'.

[25] Storch, l.c., t.iii, p.223.

[26] Sismondi, l.c., pp.79,80,85.

[27] Destutt de Tracy, l.c., p.231: *Les nations pauvres, c'est là où le peuple est à son aise; et les nations riches, c'est là où il est ordinairement pauvre.'*

[28] *Tenth Report of the Commissioners of H. M. Inland Revenue.* Lond., 1866. p.38.

[29] Ibidem.

[30] These figures are sufficient for comparison, but, taken absolutely, are false, since, perhaps, £100,000,000 of income are annually not declared. The complaints of the Inland Revenue Commissioners of systematic fraud, especially on the part of the commercial and industrial classes, are repeated in each of their reports. So e.g., 'A Joint-stock company returns £6,000 as assessable profits, the surveyor raises the amount to £88,000, and upon that sum duty is ultimately paid. Another company which returns £190,000 is finally compelled to admit that the true return should be £250,000.' (ibid., p, 42.)

[31] *Census, &c.,* l.c., p.29. John Bright's assertion that 150 landlords own half of England, and 12 half the Scotch soil, has never been refuted.

[32] *Fourth Report, &c., of Inland Revenue.* Lond., 1860, p.17.

[33] These are the net incomes after certain legally authorised abatements.

[34] At this moment, March, 1867, the Indian and Chinese market is again overstocked by the consignments of the British cotton manufacturers. In 1866 a reduction in wages of 5 per cent. took place amongst the cotton operatives. In 1867, as consequence of a similar operation, there was a strike of 20,000 men at Preston.

[35] *Census, &c.,* l.c., p.11.

[36] Gladstone in the House of Commons, Feb. 13th, 1843. *Times,* Feb. 14th, 1843 – 'It is one of the most melancholy features in the social state of this country that we see, beyond the possibility of denial, that while there is at this moment a decrease in the consuming powers of the people, an increase of the pressure of privations and distress; there is at the same time a constant accumulation of wealth in the upper classes, an increase of the luxuriousness of their habits, and of their means of enjoyment.' (*Hansard,* 13th Feb.)

[37] Gladstone in the House of Commons, April 16th, 1863. *Morning Star,* April 17th.

[38] See the official accounts in the Blue Book: *Miscellaneous Statistics of the United Kingdom*, part vi, London, 1866, pp.260–273, passim. Instead of the statistics of orphan asylums, &c., the declamations of the ministerial journals in recommending dowries for the Royal children might also serve. The greater dearness of the means of subsistence is never forgotten there.

[39] Gladstone, House of Commons, 7th April, 1864. – 'The *Hansard* version runs: "Again, and yet more at large – what is human life, but, in the majority of cases, a struggle for existence?" The continual crying contradictions in Gladstone's Budget speeches of 1863 and 1864 were characterised by an English writer by the following quotation from Molière:

> Voilà l'homme en effet. Il va du blanc au noir,
> Il condamne au matin ses sentiments du soir.
> Importun à tout autre, à soi-même incommode,
> Il change à tout moment d'esprit comme de mode.
>
> (*The Theory of Exchanges, &c.*, London, 1864, p.135.)

[40] H. Fawcett, l.c., pp.67–82. As to the increasing dependence of labourers on the retail shopkeepers, this is the consequence of the frequent oscillations and interruptions of their employment.

[41] Wales here is always included in England.

[42] A peculiar light is thrown on the advance made since the time of Adam Smith, by the fact that by him the word 'workhouse' is still occasionally used as synonymous with 'manufactory'; e.g., the opening of his chapter on the division of labour; 'those employed in every different branch of the work can often be collected into the same workhouse.'

[43] *Public Health. Sixth Report, 1864*, p.13.

[44] l.c., p.17.

[45] l.c., p.13.

[46] l.c., Appendix, p.232.

[47] l.c., pp.232,233.

[48] l.c., pp.14,15.

[49] 'In no particular have the rights of *persons* been so avowedly and shamefully sacrificed to the rights of *property* as in regard to the lodging of the labouring class. Every large town may be looked upon as a place of human sacrifice, a shrine where thousands pass yearly through the fire as offerings to the moloch of avarice,' S. Laing, l.c., p.150.

[50] *Public Health, Eighth Report. 1866.* p.14, note.

[51] l.c., p.89. With reference to the children in these colonies, Dr Hunter says: 'People are not now alive to tell us how children were brought up before this age of dense agglomerations of poor began, and he would be a rash prophet who should tell us what future behaviour is to be expected from the present growth of children, who, under circumstances probably never before paralleled in this country, are now completing their education for future practice, as "dangerous classes" by sitting up half the night with persons of every age, half naked, drunken, obscene, and quarrelsome.' (l.c., p.56.)

[52] l.c., p.62.

[53] *Report of the Officer of Health of St Martins-in-the-Fields, 1865.*

[54] *Public Health, Eighth Report, 1866*, p.91.

[55] l.c., p.88.

[56] l.c., p.88.

[57] l.c., p.89.

[58] l.c., p.55 and 56.

[59] l.c., p.149.

[60] l.c., p.50.
[61] Collecting Agents' List (Bradford).

Houses

Vulcan Street, No. 122	1 room	16 persons
Lumley Street, No. 13	1 room	11 persons
Bower Street, No. 41	1 room	11 persons
Portland Street, No. 112	1 room	10 persons
Hardy Street, No. 17	1 room	10 persons
North Street, No. 18	1 room	16 persons
North Street, No. 17	1 room	13 persons
Wymer Street, No. 19	1 room	8 adults
Jowett Street, No. 56	1 room	12 persons
George Street, No. 150	1 room	3 families
Rifle Court Marygate, No. 11	1 room	11 persons
Marshall Street, No. 28	1 room	11 person
Marshall Street, No 49	3 rooms	10 person
George Street, No. 128	1 room	18 persons
George Street, No. 130	1 room	16 persons
Edward Street, No. 4	1 room	17 persons
George Street, No. 49	1 room	2 families
York Street, No. 34	1 room	2 families
Salt Pie Street (bottom)	2 rooms	26 persons

Cellars

Regent Square	1 cellar	8 persons
Acre Street	1 cellar	7 persons
33 Roberts Court	1 cellar	7 persons
Back Pratt Street, used as a brazier's shop	1 cellar	7 persons
27 Ebenezer Street	1 cellar	6 persons (no men above 18)

[62] l.c., p.114.

[63] l.c., p.50.

[64] *Public Health. Seventh Report. 1865*, p.18.

[65] l.c., p.165.

[66] l.c., p.18, note – The Relieving Officer of the Chapel-en-le-Frith Union reported to the Registar-General as follows: – 'At Doveholes, a number of small excavations have been made into a large hillock of lime ashes (the refuse of lime-kilns), and which are used as dwellings, and occupied by labourers and others employed in the construction of a railway now in course of construction through that neighbourhood. The excavations are small and damp, and have no drains or privies about them, and not the slightest means of ventilation except up a hole pulled through the top, and used for a chimney. In consequence of this defect, small-pox has been raging for some time, and some deaths [amongst the troglodytes] have been caused by it.' (l.c., note 2.)

[67] The details given at the end of Part 4 refer especially to the labourers in coal mines. On the still worse condition in metal mines, see the very conscientious Report of the Royal Commission of 1864.

[68] l.c., pp.180,182.

[69] l.c., pp.515,517.

[70] l.c., p.16.

[71] 'Wholesale starvation of the London Poor . . . Within the last few days the walls of London have been placarded with large posters, bearing the following remarkable announcement: – "Fat oxen! Starving men! The fat oxen from their palace of glass have gone to feed the rich in their luxurious abode, while the starving men are left to

rot and die in their wretched dens." The placards bearing these ominous words are put up at certain intervals. No sooner has one set been defaced or covered over, than a fresh set is placarded in the former, or some equally public place . . . This . . . reminds one of the secret revolutionary associations which prepared the French people for the events of 1789 . . . At this moment, while English workmen with their wives and children are dying of cold and hunger, there are millions of English gold – the produce of English labour – being invested in Russian, Spanish, Italian, and other foreign enterprises.' – *Reynolds' Newspaper*, January 20th, 1867.

[72] James E. Thorold Rogers. (Prof. of Polit. Econ. in the University of Oxford.) *A History of Agriculture and Prices in England*. Oxford, 1866, v.i, p.690. This work, the fruit of patient and diligent labour, contains in the two volumes that have so far appeared, only the period from 1259 to 1400. The second volume contains simply statistics. It is the first authentic 'History of Prices' of the time that we possess.

[73] *Reasons for the Late Increase of the Poor-Rates: or a comparative view of the prices of labour and provisions.*' Lond., 1777, pp.5,11.

[74] Dr Richard Price: *Observations on Reversionary Payments*, 6th Ed. By W. Morgan, Lond., 1803, v.ii, pp.158,159. Price remarks on p.159: 'The nominal price of day-labour is at present no more than about four times, or, at most, five times higher than it was in the year 1514. But the price of corn is seven times, and of flesh-meat and raiment about fifteen times higher. So far, therefore, has the price of labour been even from advancing in proportion to the increase in the expenses of living, that it does not appear that it bears now half the proportion to those expenses that it did bear.'

[75] Barton, l.c., p.26. For the end of the 18th century cf. Eden, l.c.

[76] Parry, l.c., p.86.

[77] id., p.213.

[78] S. Laing, l.c., p.62.

[79] *England and America*. Lond., 1833, vol.1, p.47.

[80] *London Economist*, May 29th, 1845, p.290.

[81] The landed aristocracy advanced themselves to this end, of course per Parliament, funds from the State Treasury, at a very low rate of interest, which the farmers have to make good at a much higher rate.

[82] The decrease of the middle-class farmers can be seen especially in the census category: 'Farmer's son, grandson, brother, nephew, daughter, granddaughter, sister, niece'; in a word, the members of his own family, employed by the farmer. This category numbered, in 1851, 216,851 persons; in 1861, only 176,151. From 1851 to 1871, the farms under 20 acres fell by more than 900 in number; those between 50 and 75 acres fell from 8,253 to 6,370; the same thing occurred with all other farms under 100 acres. On the other hand, during the same twenty years, the number of large farms increased; those of 300–500 acres rose from 7,771 to 8,410, those of more than 500 acres from 2,755 to 3,914, those of more than 1,000 acres from 492 to 582.

[83] The number of shepherds increased from 12,517 to 25,559.

[84] Census, l.c., p.36.

[85] Rogers, l.c., p.693, p.10. Mr Rogers belongs to the Liberal School, is a personal friend of Cobden and Bright, and therefore no *laudator temporis acti*.

[86] *Public Health. Seventh Report*, 1865, p.242. It is therefore nothing unusual either for the landlord to raise a labourer's rent as soon as he hears that he is earning a little more, or for the farmer to lower the wage of the labourer, 'because his wife has found a trade'. l.c.

[87] l.c., p.135.

[88] l.c., p.134.

[89] *Report of the Commissioners . . . relating to Transportation and Penal Servitude*, Lond., 1863, pp. 42, 50.

[90] l.c., p.77. 'Memorandum by the Lord Chief Justice'.

[91] l.c., vol.ii, Minutes of Evidence.

[92] l.c., vol.i. Appendix, p.280.

[93] l.c., pp. 274, 275.

[94] *Public Health, Sixth Report*, 1864, pp.238,249,261,262.

[95] l.c., p.262.

[96] l.c., p.17. The English agricultural labourer receives only 1/4 as much milk, and 1/2 as much bread as the Irish. Arthur Young in his *Tour in Ireland*, at the beginning of this century, already noticed the better nourishment of the latter. The reason is simply this, that the poor Irish farmer is incomparably more humane than the rich English. As regards Wales, that which is said in the text holds only for the southwest. All the doctors there agree that the increase of the death-rate through tuberculosis, scrofula, etc., increases in intensity with the deterioration of the physical condition of the population, and all ascribe this deterioration to poverty. 'His (the farm labourer's) keep is reckoned at about five pence a day, but in many districts it was said to be of much less cost to the farmer' [himself very poor] . . . 'A morsel of the salt meat or bacon, . . . salted and dried to the texture of mahogany, and hardly worth the difficult process of assimilation . . . is used to flavour a large quantity of broth or gruel, of meal and leeks, and day after day this is the labourer's dinner.' The advance of industry resulted for him, in this harsh and damp climate, in 'the abandonment of the solid homespun clothing in favour of the cheap and so-called cotton goods,' and of stronger drinks for so-called tea. 'The agriculturist, after several hours' exposure to wind and rain, gains his cottage to sit by a fire of peat or of balls of clay and small coal kneaded together, from which volumes of carbonic and sulphurous acids are poured forth. His walls are of mud and stones, his floor the bare earth which was there before the hut was built, his roof a mass of loose and sodden thatch. Every crevice is stopped to maintain warmth, and in an atmosphere of diabolic odour, with a mud floor, with his only clothes drying on his back, he often sups and sleeps with his wife and children. Obstetricians who have passed parts of the night in such cabins have described how they found their feet sinking in the mud of the floor, and they were forced (easy task) to drill a hole through the wall to effect a little private respiration. It was attested by numerous witnesses in various grades of life, that to these insanitary influences, and many more, the underfed peasant was nightly exposed, and of the result, a debilitated and scrofulous people, there was no want of evidence . . . The statements of the relieving officers of Carmarthenshire and Cardiganshire show in a striking way the same state of things. There is besides 'a plague more horrible still, the great number of idiots'. Now a word on the climatic conditions. 'A strong south-west wind blows over the whole country for 8 or 9 months in the year, bringing with it torrents of rain, which discharge principally upon the western slopes of the hills. Trees are rare, except in sheltered places, and where not protected, are blown out of all shape. The cottages generally crouch under some bank, or often in a ravine or quarry, and none but the smallest sheep and native cattle can live on the pastures . . . The young people migrate to the eastern mining districts of Glamorgan and Monmouth. Carmarthenshire is the breeding ground of the mining population and their hospital. The population can therefore barely maintain its numbers.' Thus in Cardiganshire:

	1851	1861
Males	45,155	44,446
Females	52,459	52,955
	97,614	97,401

Dr Hunter's Report in *Public Health, Seventh Report. 1865*, pp.498–502, passim.

[97] In 1865 this law was improved to some extent. It will soon be learnt from experience that tinkering of this sort is of no use.

[98] In order to understand that which follows, we must remember that 'Close Villages' are those whose owners are one or two large landlords. 'Open villages', those whose soil belongs to many smaller landlords. It is in the latter that building speculators can build cottages and lodging-houses.

[99] A show-village of this kind looks very nice, but is as unreal as the villages that Catherine II saw on her journey to the Crimea. In recent times the shepherd also has often been banished from these show-villages; e.g., near Market Harboro' is a sheep-farm of about 500 acres, which only employs the labour of one man. To reduce the long trudges over these wide plains, the beautiful pastures of Leicester and Northampton, the shepherd used to get a cottage on the farm. Now they give him a thirteenth shilling a week for lodging, that he must find far away in an open village.

[100] 'The labourers' houses (in the open villages, which, of course, are always overcrowded) are usually in rows, built with their backs against the extreme edge of the plot of land which the builder could call his, and on this account are not allowed light and air, except from the front.' (Dr Hunter's Report, l.c., p.135.) Very often the beerseller or grocer of the village is at the same time the letter of its houses. In this case the agricultural labourer finds in him a second master, besides the farmer. He must be his customer as well as his tenant. 'The hind with his 10s. a week, minus a rent of £4 a year . . . is obliged to buy at the seller's own terms, his modicum of tea, sugar, flour, soap, candles, and beer.' (l.c., p.132.) These open villages form, in fact, the 'penal settlements' of the English agricultural proletariat. Many of the cottages are simply lodging-houses, through which all the rabble of the neighbourhood passes. The country labourer and his family who had often, in a way truly wonderful, preserved, under the foulest conditions, a thoroughness and purity of character, go, in these, utterly to the devil. It is, of course, the fashion amongst the aristocratic shylocks to shrug their shoulders pharisaically at the building speculators, the small landlords, and the open villages. They know well enough that their 'close villages' and 'show-villages' are the birth-places of the open villages, and could not exist without them. 'The labourers . . . were it not for the small owners, would, for by far the most part, have to sleep under the trees of the farms on which they work.' (l.c., p.135.) The system of 'open' and 'closed' villages obtains in all the Midland counties and throughout the East of England.

[101] 'The employer . . . is . . . directly or indirectly securing to himself the profit on a man employed at 10s. a week, and receiving from this poor hind £4 or £5 annual rent for houses not worth £20 in a really free market, but maintained at their artificial value by the power of the owner to say "Use my house, or go seek a hiring elsewhere without a character from me . . . " Does a man wish to better himself, to go as a plate-layer on the railway, or to begin quarry-work, the same power is ready with "Work for me at this low rate of wages or begone at a week's notice; take your pig with you, and get what you can for the potatoes growing in your garden." Should his interest appear to be better served by it, an enhanced rent is sometimes preferred in these cases by the owner (i.e., the farmer) as the penalty for leaving his service.' (Dr Hunter, l.c., p.132.)

[102] 'New married couples are no edifying study for grown-up brothers and sisters: and though instances must not be recorded, sufficient data are remembered to warrant the remark, that great depression and sometimes death are the lot of the female participator in the offence of incest.' (Dr Hunter, l.c., p.137.) A member of the rural police who had for many years been a detective in the worst quarters of London, says of the girls of his village: 'their boldness and shamelessness I never saw equalled during some years of police life and detective duty in the worst parts of London . . . They live like pigs, great boys and girls, mothers and fathers, all sleeping in one room, in many instances.' (*Child. Empl. Com. Sixth Report, 1867*, p.77 sq. 155.)

[103] *Public Health. Seventh Report, 1865*, pp.9,14 passim.

[104] 'The heaven-born employment of the hind gives dignity even to his position. He is not a slave, but a soldier of peace, and deserves his place in married men's quarters to be provided by the landlord, who has claimed a power of enforced labour similar to that the country demands of the soldier. He no more receives market-price for his work than does the soldier. Like the soldier he is caught young, ignorant, knowing only his own trade, and his own locality. Early marriage and. the operation of the various laws of settlement affect the one as enlistment and the Mutiny Act affect the other.' (Dr Hunter, l.c., p.132.) Sometimes an exceptionally soft-hearted landlord relents at the solitude he has created. 'It is a melancholy thing to stand alone in one's country,' said Lord Leicester, when complimented on the completion of Hookham. 'I look around and not a house is to be seen but mine. I am the giant of Giant Castle, and have eat up all my neighhours.'

[105] A similar movement is seen during the last ten years in France; in proportion as capitalist production there takes possession of agriculture, it drives the 'surplus' agricultural population into the towns. Here also we find deterioration in the housing and other conditions at the source of the surplus-population. On the special '*prolétariat foncier*', to which this system of parcelling out the land has given rise, see, among others, the work of Colins, already quoted, and Karl Marx *Der Achtzehnte Brumaire des Louis Bonaparte.* 2nd edition. Hamburg, 1869, pp.56, &c. In 1846, the town population in France was represented by 24.42, the agricultural by 75.58; in 1861, the town by 28.86, the agricultural by 71.14 per cent. During the last 5 years, the diminution of the agricultural percentage of the population has been yet more marked. As early as 1846, Pierre Dupont in his *Ouvriers* sang:

> *Mal vêtus, logés dans des trous,*
> *Sous les combles, dans les décombres,*
> *Nous vivons avoc les hiboux*
> *Et les larrons, amis des ombres.*

[106] *Sixth and last Report of the Children's Employment Commission*, published at the end of March, 1867. It deals solely with the agricultural gang-system.

[107] *Child. Emp. Comm., VI. Report.* Evidence 173, p.37.

[108] Some gang-masters, however, have worked themselves up to the position of farmers of 500 acres, or proprietors of whole rows of houses.

[109] 'Half the girls of Ludford have been ruined by going out.' (in gangs) l.c., p.6, §32.

[110] 'They (gangs) have greatly increased of late years. In some places they are said to have been introduced at comparatively late dates; in others where gangs . . . have been known for many years . . . more and younger children are employed in them.' (l.c., p.79, §174).

[111] 'Small farmers never employ gangs.' 'It is not on poor land, but on land which affords rent of from 40 to 50 shillings, that women and children are employed in the greatest numbers.' (l.c., pp.17,14.)

[112] To one of these gentlemen the taste of his rent was so grateful that he indignantly declared to the Commission of Inquiry that the whole hubbub was only due to the name of the system. If instead of 'gang' it were called 'the Agricultural Juvenile Industrial Self-supporting Association', everything would be all right.

[113] 'Gang work is cheaper than other work; that is why they are employed,' says a former gang-master (l.c., p.17, §14). 'The gang-system is decidedly the cheapest for the farmer, and decidedly the worst for the children,' says a farmer (l.c., p.16, §3)

[114] 'Undoubtedly much of the work now done by children in gangs used to be done by men and women. More men are out of work now where children and women are employed than formerly.' (l.c., p.43, n. 202.) On the other hand, 'the labour question in some agricultural districts, particularly the arable, is becoming so

serious in consequence of emigration, and the facility afforded by railways for getting to large towns that I' (the 'I' is the steward of a great lord) 'think the services of children are most indispensable.' (l.c., p.80, n.180.) For the 'labour question' in , English agricultural districts, differently from the rest of the civilised world, means the landlords' and farmers' question, viz., how is it possible, despite an always increasing exodus of the agricultural folk, to keep up a sufficient relative surplus-population in the country, and by means of it keep the wages of the agricultural labourer at a minimum?

[115] The *Public Health Report*, where in dealing with the subject of children's mortality, the gang-system is treated in passing, remains unknown to the press, and, therefore, to the English public. On the other hand, the last report of the *Child. Empl. Comm.* afforded the press sensational copy – always welcome. Whilst the Liberal press asked how the fine gentlemen and ladies, and the well-paid clergy of the State Church, with whom Lincolnshire swarms, could allow such a system to arise on their estates, under their very eyes, they who send out expressly missions to the Antipodes, 'for the improvement of the morals of South Sea Islanders' – the more refined press confined itself to reflections on the coarse degradation of the agricultural population who are capable of selling their children into such slavery! Under the accursed conditions to which these 'delicate' people condemn the agricultural labourer, it would not be surprising if he ate his own children. What is really wonderful is the healthy integrity of character he has, in great part, retained. The official reports prove that the parents, even in the gang districts, loathe the gang-system. 'There is much in the evidence that shows that the parents of the children would, in many instances, be glad to be aided by the requirements of a legal obligation, to resist the pressure and the temptations to which they are often subject. They are liable to be urged, at times by the parish officers, at times by employers, under threats of being themselves discharged, to be taken to work at an age when . . . school attendance . . . would be manifestly to their greater advantage . . . All that time and strength wasted; all the suffering from extra and unprofitable fatigue produced to the labourer and to his children; every instance in which the parent may have traced the moral ruin of his child to fhe undermining of delicacy by the over-crowding of cottages, or to the contaminating influences of the public gang, must have been so many incentives to feelings in the minds of the labouring poor which can be well understood, and which it would be needless to particularise. They must be conscious that much bodily and mental pain has thus been inflicted upon them from causes for which they were in no way answerable; to which, had it been in their power, they would have in no way consented; and against which they were powerless to struggle.' (l.c., p.xx, §82, and xxii, n.96.)

[116] Population of Ireland, 1801, 5,319,867 persons; 1811, 6,084,996; 1821, 6,869,544; 1831, 7,828,347; 1841, 8,222,664.

[117] The result would be found yet more unfavourable if we went further back. Thus: Sheep in 1865, 3,688,742, but in 1856, 3,694,294. Pigs in 1865, 1,299,893, but in 1858, 1,409,883.

[118] The data of the text are put together from the materials of the *Agricultural Statistics, Ireland, General Abstracts, Dublin*, for the years 1860, et seq., and *Agricultural Statistics, Ireland. Tables showing the estimated average produce, &c., Dublin, 1866*. These statistics are official, and laid before Parliament annually.

Note to 2nd edition. The official statistics for the year 1872 show, as compared with 1871, a decrease in area under cultivation of 134,915 acres. An increase occurred in the cultivation of green crops, turnips, mangold-wurzel, and the like; a decrease in the area under cultivation for wheat of 16,000 acres; oats, 14,000; barley and rye, 4,000; potatoes, 66,632; flax, 34,667; grass, clover, vetches, rape-seed, 30,000. The soil under cultivation for wheat shows for the last 5 years the following stages of decrease: – 1868,

285,000 acres; 1869, 280,000; 1870, 259,000; 1871, 244,000; 1872, 228,000. For 1872 we find, in round numbers, an increase of 2,600 horses, 80,000 horned cattle, 68,609 sheep, and a decrease of 236,000 pigs.

[119] *Tenth Report of the Commissioners of Inland Revenue.* Lond. 1866.

[120] The total yearly income under Schedule D. is different in this table from that which appears in the preceding ones, because of certain deductions allowed by law.

[121] If the product also diminishes relatively per acre, it must not be forgotten that for a century and a half England has indirectly exported the soil of Ireland, without as much as allowing its cultivators the means for making up the constituents of the soil that had been exhausted.

[122] As Ireland is regarded as the promised land of the 'principle of population', Th. Sadler, before the publication of his work on population, issued his famous book, *Ireland, its Evils and their Remedies.* 2nd edition, London, 1829. Here, by comparison of the statistics of the individual provinces, and of the individual counties in each province, he proves that the misery there is not, as Malthus would have it, in proportion to the number of the population, but in inverse ratio to this.

[123] Between 1851 and 1874, the total number of emigrants amounted to 2,325,922.

[124] According to a table in Murphy's *Ireland Industrial, Political and Social,* 1870, 94.6 per cent. or the holdings do not reach 100 acres, 5.4 exceed 100 acres.

[125] *Reports from the Poor Law Inspectors on the Wages of Agricultural Labourers in Dublin,* 1870. See also *Agricultural labourers (Ireland). Return, etc.* 8 March, 1861, London, 1862.

[126] l.c., pp.29,1.

[127] l.c., p.12.

[128] l.c., p.12.

[129] l.c., p.25.

[130] l.c., p.27.

[131] l.c., p.25.

[132] l.c., p.1.

[133] l.c., pp.31,32.

[134] l.c., p.25.

[135] l.c., p.30.

[136] l.c., pp.21,13.

[137] *Rept. of Insp. of Fact., 31st Oct., 1866,* p.96.

[138] The total area includes also peat, bogs, and waste land.

[139] How the famine and its consequences have been deliberately made the most of, both by the individual landlords and by the English legislature, to forcibly carry out the agricultural revolution and to thin the population of Ireland down to the proportion satisfactory to the landlords, I shall show more fully in Book 3 of this work, in the section on landed property. There also I return to the condition of the small farmers and the agricultural labourers. At present, only one quotation. Nassau W. Senior says, with other things, in his posthumous work, *Journals, Conversations and Essays relating to Ireland.* 2 vols. London, 1868; vol.ii, p.282. 'Well,' said Dr G., 'we have got our Poor Law and it is a great instrument for giving the victory to the landlords. Another, and a still more powerful instrument is emigration . . . No friend to Ireland can wish the war to be prolonged [between the landlords and the small Celtic farmers] – still less, that it should end by the victory of the tenants. The sooner it is over – the sooner Ireland becomes a grazing country, with the comparatively thin population which a grazing country requires, the better for all classes.' The English Corn Laws of 1815 secured Ireland the monopoly of the free importation of corn into Great Britain. They favoured artificially, therefore, the cultivation of corn. With the abolition of the Corn Laws in 1846, this monopoly was suddenly removed. Apart from all other circumstances, this event alone was sufficient to give a great impulse to the turning of Irish

arable into pasture land, to the concentration of farms, and to the eviction of small cultivators. After the fruitfulness of the Irish soil had been praised from 1815 to 1846, and proclaimed loudly as by Nature herself destined for the cultivation of wheat, English agronomists, economists, politicians, discover suddenly that it is good for nothing but to produce forage. M. Léonce de Lavergne has hastened to repeat this on the other side of the Channel. It takes a 'serious' man, *à la* Lavergne, to be caught by such childishness.

Volume 1, Part 8, Chapter 26

[1] In Italy, where capitalistic production developed earliest, the dissolution of serfdom also took place earlier than elsewhere. The serf was emancipated in that country before he had acquired any prescriptive right to the soil. His emancipation at once transformed him into a free proletarian, who, moreover, found his master ready and waiting for him in the towns, for the most part handed down as legacies from the Roman time. When the revolution of the world-market, about the end of the 15th century, annihilated Northern Italy's commercial supremacy, a movement in the reverse direction set in. The labourers of the towns were driven *en masse* into the country, and gave an impulse, never before seen, to the *petite culture*, carried on in the form of gardening.

Volume 1, Part 8, Chapter 27

[1] 'The petty proprietors who cultivated their own fields with their own hands, and enjoyed a modest competence . . . then formed a much more important part of the nation than at present. If we may trust the best statistical writers of that age, not less than 160,000 proprietors who, with their families, must have made up more than a seventh of the whole population, derived their subsistence from little freehold estates. The average income of these small landlords . . . was estimated at between £60 and £70 a year. It was computed that the number of persons who tilled their own land was greater than the number of those who farmed the land of others.' Macaulay: *History of England*, 10th ed, 1854, I. pp.333,334. Even in the last third of the 17th century, 4/5 of the English people were agricultural. (l.c., p.413.) I quote Macaulay, because as systematic falsifier of history he minimises as much as possible facts of this kind.

[2] We must never forget that even the serf was not only the owner, if but a tribute-paying owner, of the piece of land attached to his house, but also a co-possessor of the common land. '*Le paysan* (in Silesia, under Frederick II) *est serf.*' Nevertheless, these serfs possess common lands. '*on n'a pas pu encore engager les Silésiens au partage des communes, tandis que dans la Nouvelle Marche, il n'y a guère de village où ce partage ne soit exécuté avec le plus grand succès.*' (Mirabeau: *De la Monarchic Prussienne*. Londres, 1788, t.ii, pp.125,126.)

[3] Japan, with its purely feudal organisation of landed property and its developed *petite culture*, gives a much truer picture of the European middle ages than all our history books, dictated as these are, for the most part, by bourgeois prejudices. It is very convenient to be 'liberal' at the expense of the middle ages.

[4] In his *Utopia*, Thomas More says, that in England 'your shepe that were wont to be so meke and tame, and so smal eaters, now, as I heare saye, become so great devourers and so wylde that they eate up, and swallow downe, the very men themselfes.' *Utopia*, transl. by Robinson, ed., Arber, Lond., 1869, p.41.

[5] Bacon shows the connection between a free, well-to-do peasantry and good infantry. 'This did wonderfully concern the might and mannerhood of the kingdom to have farms as it were of a standard sufficient to maintain an able body out of penury, and did in effect amortise a great part of the lands of the kingdom unto the hold and occupation of the yeomanry or middle people, of a condition between gentlemen, and

cottagers and peasants . . . For it hath been held by the general opinion of men of best judgment in the wars . . . that the principal strength of an army consisteth in the infantry or foot. And to make good infantry it requireth men bred, not in a servile or indigent fashion, but in some free and plentiful manner. Therefore, if a state run most to noblemen and gentlemen, and that the husbandman and ploughmen be but as their workfolk and labourers, or else mere cottagers (which are but hous'd beggars), you may have a good cavalry, but never good stable bands of foot . . . And this is to be seen in France, and Italy, and some other parts abroad, where in effect all is *noblesse* or peasantry . . . insomuch that they are inforced to employ mercenary bands of Switzers and the like, for their battalions of foot; whereby also it comes to pass that those nations have much people and few soldiers.' (*The Reign of Henry VII.* Verbatim reprint from Kennet's *England.* Ed. 1719. Lond., 1870, p.308.)

[6] Dr Hunter, l.c., p.134. 'The quantity of land assigned (in the old laws) would now be judged too great for labourers, and rather as likely to convert them into small farmers.' (George Roberts: *The Social History of the People of the Southern Counties of England in Past Centuries.* Lond., 1856, pp.184–185.)

[7] 'The right of the poor to share in the tithe, is established by the tenour of ancient statutes.' (Tuckett, l.c., vol.ii, pp.804–805)

[8] William Cobbett: *A History of the Protestant Reformation*, §471.

[9] The 'spirit' of Protestantism may be seen from the following, among other things. In the south of England certain landed proprietors and well-to-do farmers put their heads together and propounded ten questions as to the right interpretation of the poor-law of Elizabeth. These they laid before a celebrated jurist of that time, Sergeant Snigge (later a judge under James I) for his opinion. 'Question 9 – Some of the more wealthy farmers in the parish have devised a skilful mode by which all the trouble of executing this Act (the 43rd of Elizabeth) might be avoided. They have proposed that we shall erect a prison in the parish, and then give notice to the neighbourhood, that if any persons are disposed to farm the poor of this parish, they do give in sealed proposals, on a certain day, of the lowest price at which they will take them off our hands; and that they will be authorised to refuse to any one unless he be shut up in the aforesaid prison. The proposers of this plan conceive that there will be found in the adjoining counties, persons who, being unwilling to labour and not possessing substance or credit to take a farm or ship, so as to live without labour, may be induced to make a very advantageous offer to the parish. If any of the poor perish under the contractor's care, the sin will lie at his door, as the parish will have done its duty by them. We are, however, apprehensive that the present Act (43rd of Elizabeth) will not warrant a prudential measure of this kind; but you are to learn that the rest of the freeholders. of the county, and of the adjoining county of B, will very readily join in instructing their members to propose an Act to enable the parish to contract with a person to lock up and work the poor; and to declare that if any person shall refuse to be so locked up and worked, he shall be entitled to no relief. This, it is hoped, will prevent persons in distress from wanting relief, and be the means of keeping down parishes.' (R. Blakey: *The History of Political Literature from the Earliest Times.* Lond., 1855, vol. ii, pp.84–85.) In Scotland, the abolition of serfdom took place some centuries later than in England. Even in 1698, Fletcher of Saltoun, declared in the Scotch parliament, 'The number of beggars in Scotland is reckoned at not less than 200,000. The only remedy that I, a republican on principle, can suggest, is to restore the old state of serfdom, to make slaves of all those who are unable to provide for their own subsistence.' Eden, l.c., book 1, ch.1, pp.60–61, says, 'The decrease of villenage seems necessarily to have been the era of the origin of the poor. Manufactures and commerce are the two parents of our national poor.' Eden, like our Scotch republican on principle, errs only in this: not the abolition of villenage, but the abolition of the property of the agricultural labourer in the soil made

him a proletarian, and eventually a pauper. In France, where the expropriation was effected in another way, the *ordonnance* of Moulins, 1566, and the Edict of 1656, correspond to the English poor-laws.

[10] Professor Rogers, although formerly Professor of Political Economy in the University of Oxford, the hotbed of Protestant orthodoxy, in his preface to the *History of Agriculture* lays stress on the fact of the pauperisation of the mass of the people by the Reformation.

[11] *A Letter to Sir. T. C. Bunbury, Bart., on the High Price of Provisions. By a Suffolk Gentleman.* Ipswich, 1795, p.4. Even the fanatical advocate of the system of large farms, the author of the *Inquiry into the Connection between the Present Price of Provisions*, London, 1773, p.139, says: 'I most lament the loss of our yeomanry, that set of men who really kept up the independence of this nation; and sorry I am to see their lands now in the hands of monopolising lords, tenanted out to small farmers, who hold their leases on such conditions as to be little better than vassals ready to attend a summons on every mischievous occasion.'

[12] On the private moral character of this bourgeois hero, among other things: 'The large grant of lands in Ireland to Lady Orkney, in 1695, is a public instance of the king's affection, and the lady's influence . . . Lady Orkney's endearing offices are supposed to have been – *foeda labiorum ministeria.*' (In the Sloane Manuscript Collection, at the British Museum, No. 4224. The Manuscript is entitled: *The character and behaviour of King William, Sunderland, etc., as represented in Original Letters to the Duke of Shrewsbury from Somers Halifax, Oxford, Secretary Vernon, etc.* It is full of *curiosa.*)

[13] 'The illegal alienation of the Crown Estates, partly by sale and partly by gift, is a scandalous chapter in English history . . . a gigantic fraud on the nation.' (F. W. Newman, *Lectures on Political Economy.* London, 1851, pp. 129, 130.) [For details as to how the present large landed proprietors of England came into their possessions see *Our Old Nobility. By Noblesse Oblige.* London, 1879. – F. E.]

[14] Read, e.g., E. Burke's Pamphlet on the ducal house of Bedford, whose offshoot was Lord John Russell, the 'tomtit of Liberalism'.

[15] 'The farmers forbid cottagers to keep any living creatures besides themselves and children, under the pretence that if they keep any beasts or poultry, they will steal from the farmers' barns for their support; they also say, keep the cottagers poor and you will keep them industrious, &c., but the real fact I believe, is that the farmers may have the whole right of common to themselves.' (*A Political Inquiry into the Consequences of Enclosing Waste Lands.* London, 1785, p.75.)

[16] Eden, l.c., preface.

[17] *Capital Farms. Two letters on the Flour Trade and the Dearness of Corn. By a person in business.* London, 1767, pp. 19, 20.

[18] *Merchant Farms. An Enquiry into the Causes of the Present High Price of Provisions.* London, 1767, p.11. Note: this excellent work, that was published anonymously, is by the Rev. Nathaniel Forster.

[19] Thomas Wright: *A Short Address to the Public on the Monopoly of Large Farms*, 1779, pp. 2, 3.

[20] Rev. Addington: *Inquiry into the Reasons for or against Enclosing Open Fields*, London, 1772, pp. 37, 43 passim.

[21] Dr R. Price, l.c., v.ii, p.155, Forster, Addington, Kent, Price, and James Anderson, should be read and compared with the miserable prattle of Sycophant MacCulloch in his catalogue: *The Literature of Political Economy*, London, 1845.

[22] Price, l.c., p.147.

[23] Price, l.c., p.159. We are reminded of ancient Rome. 'The rich had got possession of the greater part of the undivided land. They trusted in the conditions of the time, that these possessions would not be again taken from them, and bought, therefore,

some of the pieces of land lying near theirs, and belonging to the poor, with the acquiescence of their owners, and took some by force, so that they now were cultivating widely extended domains, instead of isolated fields. Then they employed slaves in agriculture and cattle-breeding, because freemen would have been taken from labour for military service. The possession of slaves brought them great gain, inasmuch as these, on account of their immunity from military service, could freely multiply and have a multitude of children. Thus the powerful men drew all wealth to themselves, and all the land swarmed with slaves. The Italians, on the other hand, were always decreasing in number, destroyed as they were by poverty, taxes, and military service. Even when times of peace came, they were doomed to complete inactivity, because the rich were in possession of the soil, and used slaves instead of freemen in the tilling of it.' (Appian: *Civil Wars*, 1.7.) This passage refers to the time before the Licinian rogations. Military service, which hastened to so great an extent the ruin of the Roman plebeians, was also the chief means by which, as in a forcing-house, Charlemagne brought about the transformation of free German peasants into serfs and bondsman.

[24] *An Inquiry into the Connection between the Present Price of Provisions, &c.*, pp.124,129. To the like effect, but with an opposite tendency: 'Working-men are driven from their cottages and forced into the towns to seek for employment; but then a larger surplus is obtained, and thus capital is augmented.' (*The Perils of the Nation*, 2nd ed. London, 1843, p.14.)

[25] l.c., p.132.

[26] Steuart says: 'If you compare the rent of these lands' (he erroneously includes in this economic category the tribute of the taskmen to the clan-chief) 'with the extent, it appears very small. If you compare it with the numbers fed upon the farm, you will find that an estate in the Highlands maintains, perhaps, ten times as many people as another of the same value in good and fertile province.' (l.c., vol. i, ch. xvi, p.104.)

[27] James Anderson: *Observations on the Means of Exciting a Spirit of National Industry, &c.*, Edinburgh, 1777.

[28] In 1860 the people expropriated by force were exported to Canada under false pretences. Some fled to the mountains and neighbouring islands. They were followed by the police, came to blows with them and escaped.

[29] 'In the Highlands of Scotland,' says Buchanan, the commentator on Adam Smith, 1814, 'the ancient state of property is daily subverted . . . The landlord, without regard to the hereditary tenant (a category used in error here), now offers his land to the highest bidder, who, if he is an improver, instantly adopts a new system of cultivation. The land, formerly overspread with small tenants or labourers, was peopled in proportion to its produce, but under the new system of improved cultivation and increased rents, the largest possible produce is obtained at the least possible expense: and the useless hands being, with this view, removed, the population is reduced, not to what the land will maintain, but to what it will employ. The dispossessed tenants either seek a subsistence in the neighbouring towns,' &c. (David Buchanan – *Observations on, &c., A. Smith's Wealth of Nations.* Edinburgh, 1814, vol. iv, p.144.) 'The Scotch grandees dispossessed families as they would grub up coppice-wood, and they treated villages and their people as Indians harassed with wild beasts do, in their vengeance, a jungle with tigers . . . Man is bartered for a fleece or a carcase of mutton, nay, held cheaper . . . Why, how much worse is it than the intention of the Moguls, who, when they had broken into the northern provinces of China, proposed in council to exterminate the inhabitants, and convert the land into pasture. This proposal many Highland proprietors have effected in their own country against their own countrmen.' (George Ensor: *An Inquiry Concerning the Population of Nations.* Lond,. 1818, pp.215,216.)

[30] When the present Duchess of Sutherland entertained Mrs Beecher Stowe, authoress of *Uncle Tom's Cabin*, with great magnificence in London to show her sympathy

for the Negro slaves of the American republics – sympathy that she prudently forgot, with her fellow-aristocrats, during the civil war, in which every 'noble' English heart beat for the slave-owner – I gave in the *New York Tribune* the facts about the Sutherland slaves. (Epitomised in part by Carey in *The Slave Trade*, Philadelphia, 1853, pp.203,204.) My article was reprinted in a Scotch newspaper, and led to a pretty polemic between the latter and the sycophants of the Sutherlands.

[31] Interesting details on this fish trade will be found in Mr David Urquhart's *Portfolio*, new series. Nassau W. Senior, in his posthumous work, already quoted, terms 'the proceedings in Sutherlandshire one of the most beneficent clearings since the memory of man.' (l.c.)

[32] The deer-forests of Scotland contain not a single tree. The sheep are driven from, and then the deer driven to, the naked hills, and then it is called a deer-forest. Not even timber-planting and real forest culture.

[33] Robert Somers: *Letters from the Highlands: or the Famine of 1847*. London, 1848, pp. 12–28 passim. These letters originally appeared in *The Times*. The English economists of course explained the famine of the Gaels in 1847, by their over-population. At all events, they 'were pressing on their food-supply.' The 'clearing of estates', or as it is called in Germany, '*Bauernlegen*', occurred in Germany especially after the 30 years' war, and led to peasant-revolts as late as 1790 in Kursachsen. It obtained especially in East Germany. In most of the Prussian provinces, Frederick II for the first time secured right of property for the peasants. After the conquest of Silesia he forced the landlords to rebuild the huts, barns, etc., and to provide the peasants with cattle and implements. He wanted soldiers for his army and tax-payers for his treasury. For the rest, the pleasant life that the peasant led under Frederick's system of finance and hodgepodge rule of despotism, bureaucracy and feudalism, may be seen from the following quotation from his admirer, Mirabeau: '*Le lin fait done une des grandes richesses du cultivateur dans le Nord de l'Allemagne. Malheureusement pour l'espèce humaine, ce n'est qu'une ressource contre la misère et non un moyen de bien-être. Les impôts directs, les corvées, les servitudes de tout genre, écrasent le cultivateur allemand, qui paie encore des impôts indirects dans tout ce qu'il achète . . . et pour comble de ruine, il n'ose pas vendre ses productions où et comme il le veut; il n'ose pas acheter ce dont il a besoin aux marchands qui pourraient le lui livrer au meilleur prix. Toutes ces causes le ruinent insensiblement, et il se trouverait hors d'état de payer les impôts directs à l'échéance sans la filerie; elle lui offre une ressource, en occupant utilement sa femme, ses enfants, ses servants, ses valets, et lui-même; mais quelle pénible vie, même aidée de ce secours. En été, il travaille comme un forçat au labourage et à la récolte; il se couche à 9 heures et se lève à deux, pour suffire aux travaux; en hiver il devrait réparer ses forces par un plus grand repos; mais il manquera de grains pour le pain et les semailles, s'il se défait des denrées qu'il faudrait vendre pour payer les impôts. Il faut donc filer pour suppléer à ce vide . . . il faut y apporter la plus grande assiduité. Aussi le paysan se couche-t-il en hiver à minuit, une heure, et se lève à cinq ou six; on bien il se couche à neuf, et se lève à deux, et cela tous les jours de la vie si cc n'est le dimanche. Ces excès de veille et de travail usent la nature humaine, et de là vient qu'hommes et femmes vieillissent beaucoup plutôt dans les campagnes que dans les villes.*' (Mirabeau, l.c., t.iii. pp.212 sqq.)

Note to the second edition. In April 1866, 18 years after the publication of the work of Robert Somers quoted above, Professor Leone Levi gave a lecture before the Society of Arts on the transformation of sheep-walks into deer-forest, in which he depicts the advance in the devastation of the Scottish Highlands. He says, with other things: 'Depopulation and transformation into sheep-walks were the most convenient means for getting an income without expenditure . . . A deer-forest in place of a sheep-walk was a common change in the Highlands. The landowners turned out the sheep as they once turned out the men from their estates, and welcomed the new tenants – the wild beasts and the feathered birds . . . One can walk from the Earl of Dalhousie's estates in Forfarshire to John o'Groats, without ever leaving forest land . . . In many of these woods the fox, the wild cat, the marten, the polecat, the weasel and the Alpine hare are common; whilst the rabbit, the squirrel and the rat have lately made their way into the country. Immense tracts of land, much of which is described in the statistical account of Scotland as having a pasturage in richness and extent of very superior description, are thus shut out from all cultivation and improvement, and are solely devoted to the sport of a few persons for a very brief period of the year.' *The London Economist* of June 2, 1866, says, 'Amongst the items of news in a Scotch paper of last week, we read . . . "One of the finest sheep farms in Sutherlandshire, for which a rent of £1,200 a year was recently offered, on the expiry of the existing lease this year, is to be converted into a deer-forest." Here we see the modern instincts of feudalism . . . operating pretty much as they did when the Norman Conqueror . . . destroyed 36 villages to create the New Forest . . . Two millions of acres . . . totally laid waste, embracing within their area some of the most fertile lands of Scotland. The natural grass of Glen Tilt was among the most nutritive in the country of Perth. The deer-forest of Ben Aulder was by far the best grazing ground in the wide district of Badenoch; a part of the Black Mount forest was the best pasture for black-faced sheep in Scotland. Some idea of the ground laid waste for purely sporting purposes in Scotland may be formed from the fact that it embraced an area larger than the whole country of Perth. The resources of the forest of Ben Aulder might give some idea of the loss sustained from the forced desolations. The ground would pasture 15,000 sheep, and as it was not more than one-thirtieth part of the old forest ground in Scotland . . . it might, &c . . . All that forest land is as totally unproductive . . . It might thus as well have been submerged under the waters of the German Ocean . . . Such extemporised wildernesses or deserts ought to be put down by the decided inter-ference of the Legislature.'

Volume 1, Part 8, Chapter 28

[1] The author of the *Essay on Trade, etc.*, 1770, says, 'In the reign of Edward VI indeed the English seem to have set, in good earnest, about encouraging manufactures and employing the poor. This we learn from a remarkable statute which runs thus: "That all vagrants shall be branded, &c . . . " ' l.c., p.5.

[2] Thomas More says in his *Utopia*: 'Therfore that on covetous and unsatiable cormaraunte and very plage of his native contrey maye compasse aboute and inclose many thousand akers of grounde together within one pale or hedge, the husbandman be thrust owte of their owne, or els either by coneyne and fraude, or by violent oppression they be put besydes it, or by wrongs and iniuries they be so weried that they be compelled to sell all: by one meanes, therfore, or by other, either by hooke or crooke they muste needes departe awaye, poore, selye, wretched soules, men, women, husbands, wiues, fatherlesse children, widowes, wofull mothers with their yonge babes, and their whole households smal in substance, and muche in numbre, as husbandrye requireth many handes. Awaye thei trudge, I say, owte of their knowen accustomed houses, fyndynge no place to reste in. All their housholde stuffe, which is very little woorthe, thoughe it might well abide the sale: yet beeynge sodainely thruste owte, they be constrayned to sell it for a thing of nought. And when they haue wandered abrode tyll that be spent, what can they then els doe but steale, and then iustly pardy be hanged, or els go about beggyng. And yet then also they be caste in prison as vagaboundes, because they go aboute and worke not: whom no man wyl set a worke though thei neuer so willyngly profre themselues therto.'

Of these poor fugitives of whom Thomas More says that they were forced to thieve, '7,200 great and petty thieves were put to death', in the reign of Henry VIII

(Holinshed, *Description of England*, vol.i, p.186.) In Elizabeth's time, 'rogues were trussed up apace, and that there was not one year commonly wherein three or four hundred were not devoured and eaten up by the gallowes.' (Strype's *Annals of the Reformation and Establishment of Religion and other Various Occurrences in the Church of England during Queen Elizabeth's Happy Reign*. Second ed., 1725, vol. 2.)

According to this same Strype, in Somersetshire, in one year, 40 persons were executed, 35 robbers burnt in the hand, 37 whipped, and 183 discharged as 'incorrigible vagabonds'. Nevertheless, he is of opinion that this large number of prisoners does not comprise even a fifth of the actual criminals, thanks to the negligence of the justices and the foolish compassion of the people; and the other counties of England were not better off in this respect than Somersetshire, while some were even worse.

[3] 'Whenever the legislature attempts to regulate the differences between masters and their workmen, its counsellors are always the masters,' says A. Smith. '*L'esprit des lois, c'est la propriété*,' says Linguet.

[4] *Sophisms of Free Trade*. By a Barrister. Lond., 1850, p.206. He adds maliciously: 'We were ready enough to interfere for the employer, can nothing now be done for the employed?'

[5] From a clause of Statute 2 James I, c.6, we see that certain clothmakers took upon themselves to dictate, in their capacity of justices of the peace, the official tariff of wages in their own shops. In Germany, especially after the Thirty Years' War, statutes for keeping down wages were general. 'The want of servants and labourers was very troublesome to the landed proprietors in the depopulated districts. All villagers were forbidden to let rooms to single men and women; all the latter were to be reported to the authorities and cast into prison if they were unwilling to become servants, even if they were employed at any other work, such as sowing seeds for the peasants at a daily wage, or even buying and selling corn. (*Imperial privileges and sanctions for Silesia*, 1, 25.) For a whole century in the decrees of the small German potentates a bitter cry goes up attain and again about the wicked and impertinent rabble that will not reconcile itself to its hard lot, will not be content with the legal wage; the individual landed proprietors are forbidden to pay more than the State had fixed by a tariff. And yet the conditions of service were at times better after the war than 100 years later; the farm servants of Silesia had, in 1652, meat twice a week, whilst even in our century, districts are known where they have it only three times a year. Further, wages after the war were higher than in the following century.' (G. Freytag.)

[6] Article 1 of this law runs: '*L'anéantissement de toute espèce de corporations du même état et profession étant l'une des bases fondamentales de la constitution française, il est défendu de les rétablir de fait sous quelque prétexte et sous quelque forme que ce soit.*' Article 4 declares, that if '*des citoyens attachés aux memes professions, arts et métiers prenaient des délibérations, faisaient entre eux des conventions tendantes à refuser de concert ou à n'accorder qu'à un prix déterminé le secours de leur industrie ou de leurs travaux, les dites délibérations et conventions . . . seront déclarées inconstitutionnelles, attentatoires à la liberté et à la declaration des droits de l'homme, &c.*'; felony, therefore, as in the old labour-statutes. (*Révolutions de Paris*, Paris, 1791, t.iii, p.523.)

[7] Buchez et Roux: *Histoire Parlementaire*, t.x, p.195.

Volume 1, Part 8, Chapter 29

[1] Harrison in his *Description of England*, says 'although peradventure foure pounds of old rent be improved to fortie, toward the end of his term, if he have not six or seven yeares rent lieng by him, fiftie or a hundred pounds, yet will the farmer thinke his gaines verie small.'

[2] On the influence of the depreciation of money in the 16th century, on the different classes of society, see *A Compendious or Briefe Examination of Certayne Ordinary*

Complaints of Divers of our Countrymen in these our Days, by W. S. Gentleman (London 1581). The dialogue form of this work led people for a long time to ascribe it to Shakespeare, and even in 1751, it was published under his name. Its author is William Stafford. In one place the knight reasons as follows: Knight: You, my neighbor, the husbandman, you Maister Mercer, and you Goodman Cooper, with other artificers, may save yourselves metely well. For as much as all things are dearer than they were, so much do you arise in the pryce of your wares and occupations that ye sell agayne. But we have nothing to sell whereby we might advance ye price there of, to countervaile those things that we must buy agayne.' In another place, the knight asks the doctor: I pray you, what be those sorts that ye meane. And first, of those that ye thinke should have no losse thereby? Doctor: I mean all those that live by buying and selling, for as they buy deare, the sell thereafter. Knight: What is the next sort that ye say would win by it? Doctor: Marry, all such as have takings of fearmes in their owne manurance [cultivation] at the old rent, for where they pay after the olde rate they sell after the newe – that is, they paye for theire lande good cheape, and sell all things growing thereof deare. Knight: What sorte is that which, ye sayde should have greater losse hereby, than these men had profit? Doctor: It is all noblemen, gentlemen, and all other that live either by a stinted rent or stypend, or do not manure [cultivate] the ground, or doe occupy no buying and selling.'

[3] In France, the *régisseur*, steward, collector of dues for the feudal lords during the earlier part of the middle ages, soon became an *homme d'affaires*, who by extortion, cheating, &c., swindled himself into a capitalist. These *régisseurs* themselves were sometimes noblemen. e.g., '*C'est li compte que messire Jacques de Thoraine, chevalier chastelain sor Besancon rent és-seigneur tenant les comptes à Dijon pour monseigneur le duc et comte de Bourgoigne, des rentes appartenant à la dite chastellenie, depuis xxve jour de décembre MCCCLIX jusqu'au xxviiie jour de décembre MCCCLX.*' (Alexis Monteil: *Traité de Matériaux manuscrits etc.*, pp.234,235.) Already it is evident here how in all spheres of social life the lion's share falls to the middleman. In the economic domain, e.g., financiers, stock-exchange speculators, merchants, shopkeepers skim the cream; in civil matters, the lawyer fleeces his clients; in politics the representative is of more importance than the voters, the minister than the sovereign; in religion, God is pushed into the background by the 'Mediator', and the latter again is shoved back by the priests, the inevitable middlemen between the good shepherd and his sheep. In France, as in England, the great feudal territories were divided into innumerable small home-steads, but under conditions incomparably more favourable for the people. During the 14th century arose the farms or *terriers*. Their number grew constantly, far beyond 100,000. They paid rents varying from 1/12 to 1/5 of the product in money or in kind. These farms were fiefs, sub-fiefs, &c., according the value and extent of the domains, many of them only containing a few acres. But these farmers had rights of jurisdiction in some degree over the dwellers on the soil; there were four grades. The oppression of the agricultural population under all these petty tyrants will be understood. Monteil says that there were once in France 160,000 judges, where today, 4,000 tribunals, including justices of the peace, suffice.

Volume 1, Part 8, Chapter 30

[1] In his *Notions de Philosophie Naturelle*. Paris, 1838.

[2] A point that Sir James Steuart emphasises.

[3] '*Je permettrai,*' says the capitalist, '*que vous ayez l'honneur de me servir, à condition que vous me donnez le peu qui vous reste pour la peine que je prends de vous commander.*' (J. J. Rousseau: *Discours sur l'Économie Politique.*)

[4] Mirabeau, l.c., t.iii, pp.20–109 passim. That Mirabeau considers the separate work-shops more economical and productive than the 'combined', and sees in the latter

merely artificial exotics under government cultivation, is explained by the position at that time of a great part of the continental manufactures.

[5] 'Twenty pounds of wool converted unobtrusively into yearly clothing of a labourer's family by its own industry in the intervals of other works – this makes no show; but bring it to market, send it to the factory, thence to the broker, thence to the dealer, and you will have great commercial operations, and nominal capital engaged to the amount of twenty times its value . . . The working-class is thus emerced to support a wretched factory population, a parasitical shop-keeping class, and a fictitious commercial, monetary, and financial system.' (David Urquhart, l.c., p.120.)

[6] Tuckett is aware that the modern woollen industry has sprung, with the introduction of machinery, from manufacture proper and from the destruction of rural and domestic industries. 'The plough, the yoke, were "the invention of gods, and the occupation of heroes"; are the loom, the spindle, the distaff, of less noble parentage? You sever the distaff and the plough, the spindle and the yoke, and you get factories and poor-houses, credit and panics, two hostile nations, agriculture and commercial.' (David Urquhart, l.c., p.122.)

But now comes Carey, and cries out upon England, surely not with unreason, that it is trying to turn every other country into a mere agricultural nation, whose manufacturer is to be England. He pretends that in this way Turkey has been ruined, because 'the owners and occupants of land have never been permitted by England to strengthen themselves by the formation of that natural alliance between the plough and the loom, the hammer and the harrow.' (*The Slave Trade*, p.125.) According to him, Urquhart himself is one of the chief agents in the ruin of Turkey, where he had made Free-trade propaganda in the English interest. The best of it is that Carey, a great Russophile by the way, wants to prevent the process of separation by that very system of protection which accelerates it.

[7] Philanthropic English economists, like Mill, Rogers, Goldwin Smith, Fawcett, &c., and liberal manufacturers like John Bright & Co., ask the English landed proprietors, as God asked Cain after Abel, Where are our thousands of freeholders gone? But where do *you* come from, then? From the destruction of those freeholders. Why don't you ask further, where are the independent weavers, spinners, and artisans gone?

Volume 1, Part 8, Chapter 31

[1] Industrial here in contradistinction to agricultural. In the 'categoric' sense the farmer is an industrial capitalist as much as the manufacturer.

[2] *The Natural and Artificial Rights of Property Contrasted*. Lond., 1832, pp.98–99. Author of the anonymous work: 'Th. Hodgskin'.

[3] Even as late as 1794, the small cloth-makers of Leeds sent a deputation to Parliament, with a petition for a law to forbid any merchant from becoming a manufacturer. (Dr Aikin, l.c.)

[4] William Howitt: *Colonisation and Christianity: A Popular History of the Treatment of the Natives by the Europeans in all their Colonies*. London, 1838, p.9. On the treatment of the slaves there is a good compilation in Charles Comte, *Traité de la Législation*. 3me éd. Bruxelles, 1837. This subject one must study in detail, to see what the bourgeoisie makes of itself and of the labourer, wherever it can, without restraint, model the world after its own image.

[5] Thomas Stamford Raffles, late Lieut-Gov. of that island: *The History of Java*, Lond., 1817.

[6] In the year 1866 more than a million Hindus died of hunger in the province of Orissa alone. Nevertheless, the attempt was made to enrich the Indian treasury by the price at which the necessaries of life were sold to the starving people.

[7] William Cobbett remarks that in England all public institutions are designated 'royal'; as compensation for this, however, there is the 'national' debt.

[8] '*Si les Tartares inondaient l'Europe aujourd'hui, il faudrait bien des affaires pour leur faire entendre ce que c'est qu'un financier parmi nous.*' Montesquieu, *Esprit des lois*, t.iv, p.33, ed. Londres, 1769.

[9] Mirabeau, l.c., t.vi, p.101.

[10] Eden, l.c., vol.i, book ii, ch.1, p.42.

[11] John Fielden, l.c., pp.5,6. On the earlier infamies of the factory system, cf. Dr Aikin (1795), l.c., p.219. and Gisborne: *Enquiry into the Duties of Men*, 1795 vol. ii. When the steam-engine transplanted the factories from the country waterfalls to the middle of towns, the 'abstemious' surplus-value maker found the child-material ready to his hand, without being forced to seek slaves from the workhouses. When Sir R. Peel (father of the 'minister of plausibility'), brought in his bill for the protection of children, in 1815, Francis Horner, lumen of the Bullion Committee and intimate friend of Ricardo, said in the House of Commons: 'It is notorious, that with a bankrupt's effects, a gang, if he might use the word, of these children had been put up to sale, and were advertised publicly as part of the property. A most atrocious instance had been brought before the Court of King's Bench two years before, in which a number of these boys, apprenticed by a parish in London to one manufacturer, had been transferred to another, and had been found by some benevolent persons in a state of absolute famine. Another case more horrible had come to his knowledge while on a [Parliamentary] Committee . . . that not many years ago, an agreement had been made between a London parish and a Lancashire manufacturer, by which it was stipulated, that with every 20 sound children one idiot should be taken.'

[12] In 1790, there were in the English West Indies ten slaves for every one free man, in the French fourteen for one, in the Dutch twenty-three for one. (Henry Brougham: *An Enquiry into the Colonial Policy of the European Powers*. Edin. 1803, vol ii. p.74.)

[13] The phrase, 'labouring poor', is found in English legislation from the moment when the class of wage-labourers becomes noticeable. This term is used in opposition, on the one hand, to the 'idle poor', beggars, etc., on the other to those labourers, who, pigeons not yet plucked, are still possessors of their own means of labour. From the Statute Book it passed into Political Economy, and was handed down by Culpeper, J. Child, etc., to Adam Smith and Eden. After this, one can judge of the good faith of the 'execrable political cant-monger', Edmund Burke, when he called the expression, 'labouring poor' – 'execrable political cant'. This sycophant who, in the pay of the English oligarchy, played the romantic *laudator temporis acti* against the French Revolution, just as, in the pay of the North American Colonies, at the beginning of the American troubles, he had played the Liberal against the English oligarchy, was an out and out vulgar bourgeois. 'The laws of commerce are the laws of Nature, and therefore the laws of God.' (E. Burke, l.c., pp.31,32.) No wonder that, true to the laws of God and of Nature, he always sold himself in the best market. A very good portrait of this Edmund Burke, during his liberal time, is to be found in the writings of the Rev. Mr Tucker. Tucker was a parson and a Tory, but, for the rest, an honourable man and a competent political economist. In face of the infamous cowardice of character that reigns today, and believes most devoutly in 'the laws of commerce', it is our bounden duty again and again to brand the Burkes, who only differ from their successors in one thing – talent.

[14] Marie Angier: *Du Crédit Public*. Paris, 1842.

[15] 'Capital is said by a Quarterly Reviewer to fly turbulence and strife, and to be timid, which is very true; but this is very incompletely stating the question. Capital eschews no profit, or very small profit, just as Nature was formerly said to abhor a vacuum. With adequate profit, capital is very bold. A certain 10 per cent. will ensure

its employment anywhere; 20 per cent. certain will produce eagerness; 50 per cent., positive audacity; 100 per cent. will make it ready to trample on all human laws; 300 per cent., and there is not a crime at which it will scruple, nor a risk it will not run, even to the chance of its owner being hanged. If turbulence and strife will bring a profit, it will freely encourage both. Smuggling and the slave-trade have amply proved all that is here stated.' (T. J. Dunning, l.c., pp.35,36.)

Volume 1, Part 8, Chapter 32

[1] '*Nous sommes dans une condition tout-à-fait nouvelle de la societé . . . nous tendons a séparer toute espèce de proprieté d'avec toute espèce de travail.*' (Sismondi: *Nouveaux Principes d'Écon. Polit.* t.ii, p.434.)

[2] 'The advance of industry, whose involuntary promoter is the bourgeoisie, replaces the isolation of the labourers, due to competition, by their revolutionary combination, due to association. The development of Modern Industry, therefore, cuts from under its feet the very foundation on which the bourgeoisie produces and appropriates products. What the bourgeoisie, therefore, produces, above all, are its own grave-diggers. Its fall and the victory of the proletariat are equally inevitable . . . Of all the classes that stand face-to-face with the bourgeoisie today, the proletariat alone is a really revolutionary class. The other classes perish and disappear in the face of Modern Industry, the proletariat is its special and essential product . . . The lower middle-classes, the small manufacturers, the shopkeepers, the artisan, the peasant, all these fight against the bourgeoisie, to save from extinction their existence as fractions of the middle-class . . . they are reactionary, for they try to roll back the wheel of history.' Karl Marx and Friedrich Engels, *Manifest der Kommunistischen Partei*, London, 1848, pp.9,11.

Volume 1, Part 8, Chapter 33

[1] We treat here of real Colonies, virgin soils, colonised by free immigrants. The United States are, speaking economically, still only a Colony of Europe. Besides, to this category belong such old plantations as those in which the abolition of slavery has completely altered the earlier conditions.

[2] Wakefield's few glimpses on the subject of Modern Colonisation are fully anticipated by Mirabeau Père, the physiocrat, and even much earlier by English economists.

[3] Later, it became a temporary necessity in the international competititve struggle. But, whatever its motive, the consequences remain the same.

[4] 'A negro is a negro. In certain circumstances he becomes a slave. A mule is a machine for spinning cotton. Only under certain circumstances does it become capital. Outside these circumstances, it is no more capital than gold is intrinsically money, or sugar is the price of sugar . . . Capital is a social relation of production. It is a historical relation of production.' (Karl "Marx, '*Lohnarbeit und Kapital*', N. Rh. Z., No.266, April 7, 1849.)

[5] E. G. Wakefield: *England and America*, vol.ii. p.33.

[6] l.c., p.17.

[7] l.c., vol.i, p.18.

[8] l.c., pp.42,43,44.

[9] l.c., vol.ii, p.5.

[10] 'Land, to be an element of colonisation, must not only be waste, but it must be public property, liable to be converted into private property.' (l.c., vol.ii, p.125.)

[11] l.c., vol.i, p.247.

[12] l.c., pp.21,22.

[13] l.c., vol.ii, p.116.

[14] l.c., vol.i, p.131.

[15] l.c., vol.ii, p.5.

[16] Merivale, l.c., vol.ii, pp.235–314 passim. Even the mild, Free-trade, vulgar econ-omist, Molinari, says: '*Dans les colonies où l'esclavage a été aboli sans que le travail forcé se trouvait remplacé par une quantité équivalente de travail libre, on a vu s'opérer la contre-partie du fait qui se réalise tous les jours sous nos yeux. On a vu les simples travailleurs exploiter à leur tour les entrepreneurs d'industrie, exiger d'eux des salaires hors de toute proportion avec la part légitime qui leur revenait dans le produit. Les planteurs, ne pouvant obtenir de leurs sucres un prix suffisant pour couvrir la hausse de salaire, ont été obligés de fournir l'excédant, d'abord sur leurs profits, ensuite sur leurs capitaux mêmes. Une foule de planteurs ont été ruinés de la sorte, d'autres ont fermé leurs ateliers pour échapper à une ruine imminente . . . Sans doute, il vaut mieux voir périr des accumulations de capitaux que des générations d'hommes* [how generous Mr Molinari!]: *mais ne vaudrait-il pas mieux que ni les uns ni les autres périssent?* (Molinari, l.c., pp.51,52.) Mr Molinari, Mr Molinari! What then becomes of the ten command-ments, of Moses and the prophets, of the law of supply and demand, if in Europe the 'entrepreneur' can cut down the labourer's legitimate part, and in the West Indies, the labourer can cut down the entrepreneur's? And what, if you please, is this 'legitimate part', which on your own showing the capitalist in Europe daily neglects to pay? Over yonder, in the colonies where the labourers are so 'simple' as to 'exploit' the capitalist, Mr Molinari feels a strong itching to set the law of supply and demand, that works elsewhere automatically, on the right road by means of the police.

[17] Wakefield, l.c., vol.ii, p.52.

[18] l.c., pp.191,192.

[19] l.c., vol.i, p.47,246.

[20] '*C'est, ajoutez-vous, grâce à l'appropriation du sol et des capitaux que l'homme, qui n'a que ses bras, trouve de l'occupation et se fait un revenu . . . c'est au contraire, grâce à l'appropriation individuelle du sol qu'il se trouve des hommes n'ayant que leurs bras . . . Quand vous mettez un homme dans le vide, vous vous emparez de l'atmosphère. Ainsi faites-vous, quand vous vous emparez du sol . . . C'est le mettre dans le vide de richesses, pour ne la laisser vivre qu'à votre volonté.*' (Colins, l.c. t.iii, pp.268–71, passim.)

[21] Wakefield, l.c., vol.ii, p.192.

[22] l.c., p.45.

[23] As soon as Australia became her own law-giver, she passed, of course, laws favourable to the settlers, but the squandering of the land, already accomplished by the English Government, stands in the way. 'The first and main object at which new Land Act of 1862 aims is to give increased facilities for the settlement of the people.' (*The Land Law of Victoria*, by the Hon. C. G. Duffy, Minister of Public Lands, Lond., 1862.)

Notes to Volume 2

Volume 2, Preface

[1] In the preface to *The Poverty of Philosophy. A Reply to Proudhon's Philosophy of Poverty*, by Karl Marx. Translated into German by E. Bernstein and K. Kautsky, Stuttgart, 1885.

[2] Roscoe-Schorlemmer, *Lehrbuch der Chemie*. Braunschweig, 1877, 1, p.73, 48.

[3] 'Thus the concentration of wealth into the hands of a small number of proprietors narrows the house market more and more, and industry is more and more compelled to open up foreign markets, where still greater revolutions await it.' (namely, the crisis of 1817, which is immediately described.) *Nouveaux Principes*, edition of 1819, 1., p. 236.

Volume 2, Part 1, Chapter 1

[1] From Manuscript 2.

[2] Beginning of Manuscript 7, started July 2, 1878.

[3] End of Manuscript 7. Beginning of Manuscript 6.

[4] End of Manuscript 6. Beginning of Manuscript 5.
[5] This is true, no matter how we separate capital-value and surplus-value. 10,000 lbs. of yarn contain 1,560 lbs., or 78 pounds sterling, surplus-value; but one lb., or one shilling, likewise contains 2496 onnces, or 1,728 pence of surplus-value.
[6] A. Cuprov: *Zelexnodorosnoje chostjajstvo*, Moskva, 1875, pg. 75 and 76.

Volume 2, Part 1, Chapter 2

[1] The term 'latent' is borrowed from the idea of latent heat in physics, which has now been almost replaced by the theory of the transformation of energy. Marx therefore uses in the third part, which is of later date, another term borrowed from the idea of potential energy, viz. 'potential', or, analogous to the virtual velocities of D'Alembert, 'virtual capital'. – F. E.

Volume 2, Part 1, Chapter 4

[1] End of Manuscript 5. What follows to the end of the chapter is a note found in a Manuscript of 1877 or 1878 amid extracts from other works.

Volume 2, Part 1, Chapter 5

[1] Beginning of Manuscript 4.
[2] Time of production of the means of production does not mean, in this case, the time required for their production, but the time during which they take part in the process of production of a certain commodity. – F. E.

Volume 2, Part 1, Chapter 6

[1] From here to 10 are statements taken from a note at the end of Manuscript 8.
[2] See explanation 9a.
[3] 'The expenses of commerce, although necessary, must be regarded as a burden.' (Quesnay, *Analyse du Tableau Économique*, in Daire, *Physlocrates*, part i, Paris, 1846, page 71.) According to Quesnay, the 'profit', which the competition between merchants produces, and which he sees in the fact that competition compels them 'to figure a discount on their loss or gain . .... is really nothing but a prevention of loss for the seller at first hand or for the consuming buyer. Now, a prevention of loss on the expenses of commerce is not a real product or an increase of wealth through commerce, considering it simply as an exchange, whether with or without the cost of transportation.' (pages 145 and 146.) 'The expenses of commerce are always paid by those who sell the products and who would enjoy the full prices paid for them by the buyers, if there were no incidental expenses.' (page 163, *ibidem*) The '*propriétaires*' and '*producteurs*' are '*salariants*', the merchants are '*salariés*'. (page 164, Quesnay. *Problèmes Économiques*, in Daire, *Physiocrates*, part i, Paris, 1846.)
[4] In the middle ages, we find book-keeping for agriculture only in the convents. But we have seen in Book I, that a book-keeper was installed for agriculture as early as the primitive Indian communes. Book-keeping is then made an independent function of a communal officer. This division of labour saves time, pains, and expenses, but production and book-keeping for production remain as much two different things as a cargo of a ship and the way-bill. In the person of the book-keeper, a part of the labour-power of the commune is withdrawn from production, and the cost of his function is not reproduced by his own labour, but by a deduction from the communal product. What is true of the book-keeper of an Indian commune, is true under changed circumstances of the book-keeper of the capitalists. (From Manuscript 2)
[5] 'The money circulating in a country is a certain portion of the capital of the country, absolutely withdrawn from productive purposes, in order to facilitate or increase the productiveness of the remainder; a certain amount of wealth is, therefore,

as necessary in order to adopt gold as a circulating medium, as it is to make a machine, in order to facilitate any other production.' (*Economist*, vol. 5, page 519.)

[6] Corbet calculates, in 1841, that the cost of storing wheat for a season of nine months amounts to a loss of 1 1/2 per cent in quantity, 3 per cent for interest on the price of wheat, 2 per cent for warehouse rental, 1 per cent for sifting and drayage, 1/2 per cent for delivery, together 7 per cent, or 3s. 6d. on a price of 50 s. per quarter. (Th. Corbet, *An Inquiry Into the Causes and Modes of the Wealth of Individuals*, etc., London, 1841.) According to the testimony of Liverpool merchants before the railroad commission, the net expenses of grain storage in 1865 amounted to 2d. per month per quarter, or 9d. to 10d. per ton. (*Royal Commission on Railways, 1867.* Evidence, page 19, Nr. 831.)

[7] *Wealth of Nations*, Book 2, Introduction.

[8] Instead of a supply arising from the conversion of the product into a commodity, and of the supply of articles of consumption into commodities, as Adam Smith thinks, this transformation, on the contrary, causes violent crises in the economy of the producer during the transition from production for use to production for sale. In India, for instance, the custom of storing up large quantities of grain in years of superfluity, when little could be gotten for it, was observed until very recent times. (*Return. Bengal and Orissa Famine. H. of C., 1807,* i, page 230, Nr. 74.) The sudden increase in the demand for cotton, jute, etc., led in many parts of India to a restriction of rice culture, a rise in the price of rice, and a sale of old supplies of the producers. Then followed the unexampled export of rice to Australia, Madagascar, etc., in 1864–66. This accounts for the acute character of the famine of 1866, which cost the lives of more than a million inhabitants in the district of Orissa alone (l.c.174,175,213,214, and iii. Papers relating to the Famine in Behar, pages 32, 33, where the 'drain of the old stock' is emphasised as one of the causes of the famine). – From Manuscript 2.

[9] Storch calls this *circulation factice*.

[10] Ricardo quotes Say, who considers it one of the blessings of commerce that it increases the price, or the value, of the products by transportation. 'Commerce,' writes Say, 'enables us to obtain a commodity at its original place of production and to transport it to another place for consumption; it enables us, therefore, to increase the value of commodities by the entire difference between their price at the first and that at the second place.' Ricardo remarks with reference to this: 'True, but how is the additional value given to it? By adding to the cost of production, first, the expenses of conveyance, secondly, the profit on the advances of capital made by the merchant. The commodity is only more valuable, for the same reason that every other commodity may become more valuable, because more labour is expended on its production and conveyance before it is purchased by the consumer. This must not be mentioned as one of the advantages of commerce.' (Ricardo, *Principles of Political Economy*, 3rd ed., London, 1821, pp.309,310.)

[11] *Royal Commission of Railways*, p. 31, No. 630.

Volume 2, Part 2, Chapter 8

[1] On account of the difficulty of determining what constitutes the distinguishing mark of fixed and circulating capital, Mr Lorena Stein thinks that this distinction is suitable only for lighter study.

[2] End of Manuscript 4, beginning of Manuscript 2.

[3] The quotations marked R. C. are from the work: *Royal Commission of Railways. Minutes of Evidence taken before the commissioners. Presented to both houses of Parliament, London, 1867.* The questions and answers are numbered, as indicated above.

[4] 'Municipal production is bound to a cycle of days, agricultural production to one of years.' (Adam G. Mueller, *Die Elemente der Staatskunst*. Berlin, 1809, ii. page, 178.) This is the naive conception of industry and agriculture held by the romantic school.

Volume 2, Part 2, Chapter 10

[1] Compare with regard to Quesnay the *Analyse du Tableau Économique* in *Physiocrates*, edition of Daire, part i, Paris, 1846. There we read, for instance, that the annual advances consist of the expenses incurred annually for the work of cultivation; these advances must be distinguished from the primitive ones, which form the funds for the establishment of the farming business.' (page 59.) In the works of the later Physiocrats, these advances are sometimes termed capital, for instance by Dupont de Nemours in his *Origins et Progrès d'une Science Nouvelle*, 1767, Daire edition, i, page 291, where he speaks of 'capital or advances', furthermore by Le Trosne: 'As a result of the longer or shorter duration of the employment of manual labour, a nation possesses a considerable fund of wealth independent of its annual reproduction, and this fund is a capital accumulated in long periods and originally paid by productive acts, which are always continued and increased.' (Daire, ii, page 928.) Turgot employs the term capital more regularly for advances, and identifies the advances of the manufacturers still more with those of the tenants of land. (Turgot, *Reflexions sur la Formation et la Distribution des Richesses*, 1766.)

[2] To what extent Adam Smith has blocked his own way to an understanding of the role of labour-power in the process of self-expansion is proven by the following sentence, which places the labour of human labourers on the same level with that of labouring cattle, after the manner of the Physiocrats. 'Not only his (the farmer's) labouring servants, but his labouring cattle are productive labourers.' (Book 2, Chap. 5, p.243.)

Volume 2, Part 2, Chapter 11

[25] *Observations on the Circumstances Which Influence the Condition of the Labouring Classes of Society*, London, 1817.

Volume 2, Part 2, Chapter 15

[1] The weeks falling within the second year of turn-over are placed in parentheses.

Volume 2, Part 2, Chapter 16

[1] In the manuscript, the following note is here inserted for future elaboration: 'Contradiction in the capitalist mode of production; the labourers as buyers of commodities are important for the market. But as sellers of their own commodity – labour-power – capitalist society tends to depress them to the lowest price. Further contradiction: the epochs in which capitalist production exerts all its forces are always periods of overproduction, because the forces of production can never be utilised to such a degree that more value is not only produced but also realised; but the sale of commodities, the realisation on the commodity-capital, and thus on surplus-value, is limited, not by the consumptive demand of society in general, but by the consumptive demand of a society in which the majority are poor and must always remain poor. However, this belongs into the next part.'

Volume 2, Part 2, Chapter 17

[1] Although the Physiocrats still intermingle these two phenomena indiscriminately, they are nevertheless the first who emphasise the reflux of money to its starting point as the essential form of circulation of capital, as that form of circulation which promotes reproduction. 'Throw a glance at the *Tableau Économique*, and you will see that the productive class gives the money with which the other classes buy products from it, and that they return this money to it when they come back next year to make the same purchases . . . You see, then, that there is in this instance no other cycle but that of expenditure followed by reproduction, and of reproduction followed by expenditure.

And this cycle is described by the circulation of money, which is the measure of expenditure and reproduction.' – Quesnay, *Problèmes Économiques*, Daire edition, Physiocrats, i, pages 208, 209.) 'It is this continual advance and return of capitals which must be called the circulation of money, this useful and fertile circulation, which gives life to all the labours of society, which maintains the activity and life of the social body, and which is with good justification compared to the circulation of blood in the animal body.' (Turgot, *Réflexions*, etc., Daire edition, i, page 45.)

Volume 2, Part 3, Chapter 18

[1] From Manuscript 2.

Volume 2, Part 3, Chapter 19

[1] Beginning of Manuscript 8.

[2] Some Physiocrats had paved the way for him even here, especially Turgot. This author uses more frequently than Quesnay and the other Physiocrats the term capital instead of *avances* and identifies still more the *avances* or capital of the manufacturers with those of the capitalist farmers. For instance: 'Like these (the manufacturing *entrepreneurs*). the capitalist farmers must secure, over and above the return of their capitals, etc.' (Turgot, *Oeuvres*, Daire edition, Paris, 1844, vol. i, page 40.)

[3] In order that the reader may not be in doubt as to the meaning of the phrase 'the price of by far the greater part of the commodities', the following lines may show how Adam Smith himself explains it. For instance, no rent passes into the price of sea fish, only wages and profit; only wages pass into the price of Scotch pebbles. He says: 'In some parts of Scotland poor people make it their business to gather on the sea shore the varicolored pebbles, known as Scotch pebbles. The price which the stone cutters pay for them consists only of their wages, as neither ground rent nor profit constitute any part of it.'

[4] I reproduce this sentence verbatim from the manuscript, although it seems to contradict, in its present connection, both the preceding and the following statements. This apparent contradiction is solved farther along in (4). Capital and Revenue in Adam Smith. – F. E.

[5] We do not make anything of the fact that Adam Smith was here particularly unlucky in the choice of his example. The value of the corn resolves itself into wages, profit, and rent only, because the food consumed by the labouring cattle is regarded as wages, and the labouring cattle as labourers, so that, on the other hand, the wage labourer also appears in the role of the labouring cattle. (Note added from Manuscript 2.)

[6] From here to the end of the chapter, an extract from Manuscript 2 is presented.

Volume 2, Part 3, Chapter 20

[1] From Manuscript 2.

[2] From Manuscript 8.

[3] Mainly taken from Manuscript 2; the diagrams from Manuscript 8.

[4] Here Manuscript 8 is resumed.

[5] Advocates of the theory of crises of Rodbertus are requested to make a note of this.

[6] This presentation differs somewhat from that given in another place of this section farther along. There I throws likewise an additional amount of £500 into circulation. Here II alone supplies the additional money for the circulation. But this does not alter the final result. – F. E.

[7] Manuscript 2 resumed here.

[8] The following is from Manuscript 8.

[9] 'When a savage manufactures bows, he carries on an industry, but he does not practice any abstinence.' (Senior, *Principes foundamentaux de l'Économie Politique, traduction*

Arrivabene, Paris, 1836, page 308.) 'The more society advances, the more abstinence it requires.' (*ibidem*, page 342.) Compare *Capital*, Volume 1, Chapter 24, 3.

[10] E. B. Tyler, *Forschungen über die Urgeschichte der Menschheit*, translated by H. Müller. Leipsic, no date, page 240.

[11] These figures do not coincide with those previously assumed. But this does not alter the substance of the argument, since it is merely a question of proportions. – F. E.

[12] Ad. Soetbeer, *Edelmetall-produktion*. Gotha, 1875.

[13] 'A considerable quantity of gold bullion . . . is taken by the gold diggers directly to the Mint in San Francisco.' – Reports of H. M. Secretaries of Embassy and Legation. 1879. Part iii, p. 337.

[14] The analysis of the exchange of newly produced gold within the constant capital of Department I is not contained in the manuscript, – F. E.

Volume 2, Part 3, Chapter 21

[1] From here to the end Manuscript 8.

[2] This puts an end, once for all, to the feud over the accumulation of capital between James Mill and S. Bailey, which we have discussed from our point of view in Volume 1. Chapter 24, section 5, footnotes on pages 622 and 623, namely the feud concerning the extensibility of the effects of industrial capital without changing its magnitude. We shall revert to this later.